LAW,
BUSINESS,
AND
SOCIETY

Tony McAdams

Professor and Head, Management Department, University of Northern Iowa
B. A. (History), University of Northern Iowa
J. D., University of Iowa, M.B.A., Columbia University

Contributing Authors

Amy Gershenfeld Donnella

Staff Attorney, Federal Trade Commission
B.A. (Liberal Arts), State University of New York, Stony Brook
J.D., Harvard Law School
Ms. Gershenfeld Donnella contributed Chapter 12, Labor Law

James Freeman

Associate Professor, Department of Management, University of Kentucky
B.S. (Economics), Wharton School, University of Pennsylvania
J.D., M.A. (Economics), University of South Carolina
L.L.M., Harvard Law School
Mr. Freeman contributed Chapter 8, Business Organizations and
Securities Regulation

LAW, BUSINESS, AND SOCIETY

1986
BUSINESS PUBLICATIONS, INC.
Plano, Texas 75075

ISBN   0-256-03070-7
Library of Congress Catalog Card No. 85-73323

Printed in the United States of America

1 2 3 4 5 6 7 8 9 0 MP 3 2 1 0 9 8 7 6

To our families

Preface

Overview

This text is directed to courses at both the upper-division undergraduate and masters levels in the legal environment of business and government and business, as well as business and society. To date, authors of textbooks in these areas have rather uniformly relied on a single discipline (e.g., law, economics, management) as the foundation for their efforts. In this text we take an interdisciplinary approach utilizing elements of law, political economy, international business, ethics, social responsibility, and management. It is a large task and one that necessarily requires certain trade-offs, but the hope is that the product will more accurately embrace the fullness of the business environment.

We want to emphasize at the outset that our primary goal is to produce an interesting reading experience. Naturally, accuracy and reasonable comprehensiveness cannot be sacrificed. However, our feeling is that a law text can be both intellectually and emotionally engaging without sacrificing substantive ends. To meet our objective we have given extensive attention to readings, provocative quotes, and factual details (surveys, data, anecdotes) that add flesh to the bones of legal theory.

The book is divided into five parts as follows:

Part I—Business and Society. We do not begin with the law. Rather, in chapters on Corporate Power and Corporate Critics, Capitalism and Collectivism, and Ethics we hope to establish the influences that determine the character of our legal system.

Part I should meet these goals: *(a)* enhance student awareness of the many societal influences on business, *(b)* establish the business context from which government regulation arose, and *(c)* explore the roles of the free market, government intervention, and individual and corporate ethics in controlling business behavior.

The student must understand not merely the law, but the law in context. What forces have provoked government intervention in business? What alter-

natives to our current "mixed economy" might prove healthy? These considerations help the students respond to one of the critical questions of the day:
To what extent, if any, *should* we regulate business?

Part II—Introduction to Law.   Chapter 4 (The American Legal System) and
Chapter 5 (Constitutional Law and the Bill of Rights) survey the foundations
of our legal system. Here we set out the "nuts and bolts" of law, combining
cases, readings, and narrative.

Part III—Trade Regulation and Antitrust.   Chapter 6 (Government Regulation of Business: An Introduction) is a bit of a departure from the approach of
many texts in that significant attention is directed to state and local regulation.
Chapters 7–11 survey the heart of government regulation of business (administrative law, business organizations and securities regulation, and antitrust).

Part IV—Employer-Employee Relations.   Chapters on Labor Law and Employment Discrimination are intended not only to survey the law in those areas,
but also to introduce some of the sensitive and provocative social issues that
have led to today's extensive government intervention in the employment relationship.

Part V—Business and Selected Social Problems.   The book closes with
four chapters (The Social Responsibility of Business, Consumer Protection,
Products Liability, and Environmental Protection) that emphasize the dramatic
expansion in the past two decades of the public's demands upon the business
community.

Accreditation

Our text proposal closely conforms to current AACSB curriculum accreditation
standards. The relevant standard reads:

> . . . a background of the economic and legal environment as it pertains to profit
> and/or nonprofit organizations along with ethical considerations and social and political
> influences as they affect such organizations. . . .

An interdisciplinary thrust and emphasis on ethics is evident. At the same
time law and economics clearly must remain central ingredients in meeting our
goal of establishing the business context from which government regulation
arose.

Furthermore, as required by the rapidly changing nature of commerce and
as recommended by the AACSB, the text devotes considerable attention to
issues arising out of international business. No single chapter addresses the
area, but various topics throughout the text (e.g., comparative economic systems, the Foreign Corrupt Practices Act, and consumer protection in international markets) afford the student a sense of the worldwide implications of
American government-business regulations.

Philosophy

As noted, our primary goal is to provoke student thought. To that end, heavy
emphasis is placed on analysis. Accordingly, retention of rules of law per se is

not of paramount concern. The questions asked are considered more important than the answers. The student is acquainted with existing policy in the various areas not merely for the purposes of understanding and retention, but additionally to provoke inquiry as to the desirability of those policies. Then, where appropriate, an effort is made to explore with the student the appropriate managerial role in shaping and responding to governmental policy.

Our book represents a departure from a "pure" legal environment of business text. Part I of the text is, as explained, a necessary foundation upon which the student can build a logical understanding of the regulatory process. But the business and society themes don't stop there. In virtually every chapter we look beyond the law itself to other environmental forces. For example, in the antitrust chapter economic philosophy is of great importance. Antitrust is explored as a matter of national social policy; that is, we argue that antitrust has a good deal to do with the direction of American life generally. Law is at the heart of the fair employment practices section, but materials from management, sociology, economics, and the like are used to treat fair employment as an issue of social policy rather than as a series of narrower technical legal disputes. Those kinds of approaches characterize most chapters as we attempt to examine the various problems in the whole and, to some degree, from a managerial viewpoint. Having said all this, it should be understood that the law remains the bulky core of the book.

Key Features/Departures

Extensive use of readings (e.g., from *The Wall Street Journal* and the *Harvard Business Review*) seeks to give the book a stimulating, "real world" quality.

Ethics and social responsibility are at the heart of the text rather than an afterthought to meet accreditation standards.

International issues receive extensive attention.

Law cases are of a length sufficient to clearly express the essence of the decision while challenging the reader's intellect.

The law is studied in the economic, social, and political context from which it springs.

Attention is given to critics of business values and the American legal system.

Perhaps the key pedagogical tactic in the book is the emphasis on questions rather than on answers.

Instructor's Manual

A complete package of supplementary materials is included in the instructor's manual. Those materials include: *(a)* general advice regarding the goals and purposes of the chapters, *(b)* summaries of the law cases, *(c)* answers for the questions raised in the text, and *(d)* a test bank.

Acknowledgments

The completion of this book was dependent, in significant part, upon the hard work of others. The authors are pleased to acknowledge the contributions of those good people. Jill Minehart, secretary of the Management Department at the University of Northern Iowa, supervised the clerical production of the book and patiently corrected the authors' blunders. Becky Sanders of the University of Kentucky and the UNI School of Business Word Processing Center personnel typed major segments of the several drafts. Ann Gumz, MBA student, completed the tedious and frustrating task of securing permission to reprint the many articles and lengthy excerpts in the book. Katherine Calhoun, MBA student; Merrilee Freeburg, MBA student; and Luann McAdams, long-suffering spouse, all contributed to the lengthy and tiring proofreading process.

The authors also thank the following professors who reviewed portions of the manuscript and provided valuable guidance: David Chadwick-Brown, San Diego State University; John Collins, Syracuse University; Wayne Evenson, University of Northern Iowa; Nancy Hauserman, University of Iowa; Harold Hotelling, Oakland University; Carey Kirk, University of Northern Iowa; Eric Richards, Indiana University; and Arthur D. Wolfe, Michigan State University.

Suggestions

The authors welcome comments and critisms from all readers.

Tony McAdams

Contents

Part I   Business and Society 1

1.   Corporate Power and Corporate Critics 2

Introduction **2**   Public Opinion **3**   Concentration of Resources **3**   The
Corporate State **4**   *Public Policy. Afterword. Advocacy Advertising. Schools and
Churches. Afterword. Who Controls the Corporation?* Summary **18**   *Afterword.*
Chapter Questions **19**   Notes **22**

2.   Capitalism and Collectivism 24

Part One—Introduction **24**
Part Two—Capitalism **25**
Foundations **25**   *Capitalism in Theory—Ayn Rand. Capitalism in Practice—
Hong Kong. Capitalism in Practice—The American Experience.*
Part Three—Collectivism **35**
Communism **35**   Socialism **36**   Collectivist Goals **36**   The Command Economy **37**
The Law and the Communist State **38**   *People's Law in China.* The Middle
Ground **42**   *Note.*
Part Four—America's Economic Future—Where Are We? **50**
Selfish or Selfless? **52**   *In Opposition to Bioeconomics.* Freedom **54**
Conclusion **55**   Chapter Questions **56**   Notes **59**

3.   Ethics 61

Part One—Foundations of Ethical Theory **61**
Introduction to Ethics: McDonald's and Protesters **61**   Ethical Theory **62**
*Fletcher's Moral Continuum. Teleology or Deontology—An Overview. Teleology.
Deonotology.*
Part Two—Foundations of Business Ethics **66**
Business Values **66**   *Steiner and Steiner—The Roots of Business Ethics.*

Maccoby—Managerial Character. Corporate Ethical Conduct **68**   Why do Some Managers Cheat? **69**
Part Three—Business Ethics in Practice **70**
Pressure to Cheat **70**   Business Crime—Executive Liability **82**   Whistle Blowing **89**   Bribery Abroad **91**   A Dissent **92**   Chapter Questions **94** Notes **97**

Part II   Introduction to Law 99

4. The American Legal System 100

Part One—Legal Foundations **100**
Law Defined **100**   Objectives of the Law **101**   The Case Law: Locating and Analyzing **103**   *Briefing the Case*. Classifications of Law **106**
Part Two—Judicial Process **115**
Standing to Sue **115**   Jurisdiction **117**   Venue **121**   *State Court Systems. Federal Court System*. The Civil Trial Process **123**   *Class Actions. Due Process of Law*.
Part Three—Reform? **133**
Public Opinion **133**   Judges and Judicial Activism **133**   Lawyers **136**   Too Much Law **138**   Alternatives **141**   Chapter Questions **142**   Notes **145**

5. Constitutional Law and the Bill of Rights 146

Introduction **146**   The Regulation of Commerce **150**   Business and the Bill of Rights **150**   *I. Freedom of Religion. II. Freedom of Speech. III. Search and Seizure*. Constitutional Law Policy **166**   Chapter Questions **168** Notes **170**

Part III   Trade Regulation and Antitrust 171

6. Government Regulation of Business: An Introduction 172

Introduction **172**   Why Regulation? **173**   The History of Government Regulation of Business **174**   The Constitutional Foundation of Business Regulation **176**   State and Local Regulation of Interstate Commerce **181** *Afterword. The States in ''Combat.'' Summary of State and Local Regulation*. More Regulation? **191**   *Afterword*. Chapter Questions **194**   Notes **197**

7. Administrative Agencies and the Regulatory Process 198

Part One—Introduction to Administrative Agencies **198**
The Agencies **200**   The Agencies and the Larger Government **201**   *The Role of Congress. The Role of the President. The Role of the Courts*. Justifications for the Administrative Agency **202**

Part Two—Summary of the Administrative Process 204
Information Gathering 204   Informal Agency Action 204   Rule Making 205
Adjudication 205   Judicial Review 206
Part Three—An Example: The Food and Drug Administration 212
History of the FDA 213   Approval Process 214   The FDA Reviewed 217
Part Four—The Federal Regulatory Process Evaluated 220
Criticisms 220   *Excessive Regulation. Insufficient Regulation. Excessive Industry Influence. Excessive Legislative and Executive Influence. Underrepresentation of Public Opinion.* Regulatory Reform 224   Deregulation 227   *Introduction. The Burdens of Regulation. The Benefits of Regulations. Deregulation Decision. Afterword.*
Part Five—The Corporate Response to Government Regulation 240
Chapter Questions 241   Notes 242

8. **Business Organizations and Securities Regulation 244**

Form of the Organization 245   Partnerships 245   Corporations 247   Hybrid Organizations 248   Special Situations 249   *Piercing the Corporate Veil.* Reality of Limited Liability 250   Avoidance of Double Taxation 250   Changing the Form of a Business 251   Tax Shelters 251   Buy/Sell Agreements 252
Securities Regulation 253   *Definition of a Security. Definition of a Security— Continued. Exemptions. Exemptions—Continued. Registration Requirements. Remedies for Violations. Regulation of Publicly Held Companies.* Chapter Questions 279   Notes 279

9. **Antitrust Law—Introduction and Monopolies 280**

Preface: A New Direction in Antitrust Policy? 280
AT&T Settlement 280   IBM Suit Dismissed 281   Cereals Case Dismissed 282
Oil Industry Action Dropped 283   Implications 283
Part One—The Roots of Antitrust Law 284
Antitrust Statutes 285   *Sherman Antitrust Act, 1890. Clayton and Federal Trade Commission Acts, 1914. 1915 to the Present.* Exemptions from Federal Antitrust Law 287   Federal Antitrust Law and Other Regulatory Systems 288   *State Law. Patents, Copyrights, and Trademarks. Law of Other Nations.* Antitrust: Law for All Seasons 289
Part Two—Monopoly 289
Monopolization Analysis 291   *Product Market. Geographic Market. Market Power. Intent. Monopoly Earned.* Chapter Questions 303   Notes 304

10. **Antitrust Law—Mergers 305**

Enforcement 306   Merger Data 307   Mergers in Practice 308   Horizontal Mergers 314   Market Share and Other Considerations 320   Vertical Mergers 322   Conglomerate Mergers 324   Defenses 325   *Cases. ITT Settlement.* Joint Venture 334   Is Bigness Bad? 335   Chapter Questions 339
Notes 340

11. **Antitrust Law—Restraints of Trade 342**

Part One—Horizontal Restraints **342**
Rule of Reason **342**   Per Se Violations **342**   Horizontal Price-Fixing **343**
Price-Fixing in Practice **349**   Horizontal Division of Markets **351**
Refusals to Deal **354**   *Unilateral Refusals to Deal.* Conscious Parallelism **357**
Interlocking Directorates **359**
Part Two—Vertical Restraints **359**
Resale Price Maintenance **360**   Vertical Territorial and Customer Restraints **363**
Tying Arrangements **367**   *Fortner Enterprises, Inc. and U.S. Steel. Fortner II.*
Exclusive Dealing and Requirement Contracts **371**   *Afterword—Justice
Department Guidelines.*
Part Three—Franchises, Price Discrimination, and International Antitrust **372**
Price Discrimination **379**   American Antitrust Laws and the International Market **385**
Foreign Antitrust Laws **386**   Chapter Questions **387**   Notes **388**

Part IV   Employer-Employee Relations 391

12. **Labor Law 392**

Introduction **392**   Organizing Labor **395**   Unionization **397**   Labor Legislation
Today—The Statutory Scheme and Its Goals **400**   National Labor Relations
Board **402**   Choosing an Appropriate Bargaining Unit **403**   Choosing a
Bargaining Representative—Elections **403**   *Threats of Reprisal or Force.
Promise of Benefit. Union Persuasion. Collective Bargaining.* The Union as
Exclusive Bargaining Agent **417**   Shop Agreements and Right-to-Work
Laws **418**   Strikes **418**   *Notification of the Intent to Strike.* Secondary Boycotts,
Hot Cargo Agreements, and Common Situs Picketing **421**   Employees' Rights
within or against the Union **422**   *The Union's Duty of Fair Representation.
Afterword. The "Bill of Rights" of Labor Organization Members.* Politics and
NLRB Decisions **433**   Contemporary Issues in Labor Law **436**   *Working
Conditions. Equal Protection. Public Sector Strikes. Labor-Management
Relations.* Chapter Questions **445**   Notes **447**

13. **Employment Discrimination 449**

Part One—Introduction **449**
Discrimination Defined **449**   Employment Discrimination: The Foundation in
Law **450**   *History. Constitutional Provisions. Civil Rights Act of 1866.
Executive Orders. Civil Rights Act of 1964. Other Federal Statutes.*
Enforcement **453**   *Individual Actions. Pattern or Practice Suits. Department of
Labor.*
Part Two—Discrimination on the Basis of Race, Color, or National Origin **454**
Progress? **454**   Employment Discrimination Analysis **458**   *Disparate Treatment.*

Disparate Impact. Statutory Defenses.
Part Three—Sex Discrimination **464**
Introduction **464** *Pregnancy and Childbirth. Draft Registration. Equal Rights Amendment. Pensions. "Private" Organizations.* Equality for Women? **467**
Analysis of Sex Discrimination **468** *Bona Fide Occupational Qualification.*
Sexual Harassment **473**   Equal Pay **474**   Comparable Worth **475**
Part Four—Religious Discrimination **478**
Part Five—Affirmative Action **479**
Affirmative Action versus Seniority **481**   A Wise Policy? **486**
Part Six—Additional Discrimination Topics **487**
Age Discrimination **487**   Discrimination against the Handicapped **492**   Sexual Preference **492**   State Law **493**   The Results **494**   Chapter Questions **494**
Notes **498**

Part V   Business and Selected Social Problems 501

14. The Social Responsibility of Business 502

Introduction **502**   What is Social Responsibility? **504**   *The Social Responsibility Debate. Arguments for Social Responsibility. Arguments against Social Responsibility.* Social Responsibility Research **507**   Social Responsibility in Practice **508**   *Was Ford Liable under Civil Law? Was Ford Liable under Criminal Law?* Corporations as Criminals? **514**   A Social Responsibility for the World? **515**   On the Positive Side of Social Responsibility **520**   Beyond Social Responsibility **523**   Additional Cases for Discussion **526**   Chapter Questions **531**
Notes **534**

15. Consumer Protection 536

Introduction **536**   Consumerism: Past and Future **538**   Common Law Consumer Protection **539**   *Fraud and Innocent Misrepresentation. Fraud in Nature.*
Unconscionable Contracts **545**   Other Common Law Protections **547**   The Consumer and Government Regulation of Business **547**   *The Federal Trade Commission—Rule Making. The Federal Trade Commission—Adjudication. The Federal Trade Commission—Deceptive Practices. The Consumer Product Safety Commission.* Consumer Finance Law **554**   *Credit Regulations.* Debtor Protection **566**   *Bankruptcy.* Electronic Fund Transfers **575**   Chapter Questions **576**   Notes **578**

16. Products Liability 580

Introduction **580**   Negligence **580**   *Classes of Negligence Claims. Res Ipsa Loquitur. Defenses against Negligence.* Warranties **593**   *Express Warranties. Implied Warranties. Disclaimers.* The Limits of Warranty Law **600**   *Magnuson-Moss Warranty Act.* Strict Liability **602**   *Coverage. Defenses against Strict*

Liability. The Limits of Strict Liability **609**   Corporation Protection? **613**
Chapter Questions **621**   Notes **624**

17.   Environmental Protection 625

Introduction **625**   A Global Problem **626**   The Failure of the Invisible
Hand? **628**   The Common Law **628**   State and Local Regulation **632**   The
Federal Presence **633**   *National Environmental Policy Act. Environmental
Protection Agency*. Air Pollution **634**   *Government Policy*. Water Pollution **643**
Federal Policy. Penalties. Land Pollution **648**   *Solid Waste Disposal Act. Toxic
Substances Control Act. Resource Conservation and Recovery Act.
Comprehensive Environmental Response, Compensation, and Liability Act of
1980*. The Free Market **653**   Effectiveness of the Environmental Protection
System **655**   The Business Response **656**   Questions **659**   Notes **661**

Appendix A   The Constitution of the United States of America 1

Appendix B   The Securities Act of 1933 (excerpts) 13

Appendix C   The Securities Exchange Act of 1934 (excerpts) 15

Appendix D   The National Labor Relations Act (excerpts) 17

Appendix E   The Civil Rights Act of 1964, Title VII (excerpts) 22

Appendix F   Acknowledgments 25

Glossary 27

Table of Cases 33

Index 39

I

Business and Society

CHAPTER 1   Corporate Power and Corporate Critics
CHAPTER 2   Capitalism and Collectivism
CHAPTER 3   Ethics

1

Corporate Power and Corporate Critics

Introduction

The bulk of this text is devoted to the study of law and, more specifically, to the study of government regulation of business. However, Chapters 1 through 3 will offer only passing mention of that regulation. Before turning to the law per se it is essential to remind the reader of the context—the environment—in which the law developed. Therefore, a major purpose of this chapter is to raise some critical issues regarding the business community's relationship to the larger society. Should we "free" business from government intervention to achieve greater productivity and profit? Should business play a larger role in politics, education, and other public sector activities? Should business assume greater responsibilities in correcting societal ills? Or perhaps capitalist business values should be retarded in favor of a more cooperative, communitarian approach to life. The reader is expected to use this chapter to make some tentative assessment of the very large question: What is the proper role of business in society? Only after acquiring some preliminary grasp of that issue may one logically and fruitfully turn to various "control devices" such as law as a means of enforcing that proper role.

The second major goal of this chapter is that of alerting the reader to some of the primary criticisms raised against the corporate community. The successful businessperson and the good citizen must understand and intelligently evaluate the objections of those who criticize the role of the corporation in contemporary life. Of course, government regulation is, in part, a response to those criticisms. (A detailed investigation of the forces generating government intervention is offered in Chapter 6.)

The materials in this chapter necessarily cast some elements of business practice in an unfavorable light, but even the most ardent defender of American business should welcome the opportunity to understand and evaluate the critics' viewpoints. Having done so the student will presumably be better prepared to understand and assess—allow me to say it again—the proper role of business in society and the use of the law in regulating that role.

Public Opinion

At the outset, it must be recognized that, for some years, business has been operating in a somewhat hostile environment. That is not to say that the American people in large percentages have rejected traditional business values. Americans approve of the notion of commerce and the remarkable benefits it has afforded us, but contemporary business behavior has clearly angered many Americans.

A 1983 Gallup Poll asked this question: "How much confidence do you, yourself, have in these American institutions? Would you say a great deal, quite a lot, some, very little, or none?"[1] The response to big business: a great deal, quite a lot—28 percent; some—39 percent; very little, none—28 percent; no opinion—5 percent. That 28 percent of the adult population feels very little or no confidence in what is perhaps the key American institution is surely cause for concern, but Congress (25), labor unions (30), and television (33), fared similarly in the little or no confidence category. Fifty-one percent of the sample expressed a great deal or quite a lot of confidence in banks. Only the military (52) and church/organized religion (62) received firmer endorsements. The reasons for generally limited faith in business are, of course, many. For our purposes one line of inquiry is especially meaningful. One study of 1,000 adults in Houston, Texas, found that approximately two thirds of the sample believed large corporations have too much power and that most major industries are controlled by one or two corporations. Of special interest is the finding that those misgivings regarding corporate power are held by a significantly larger number of women than of men. (The reader might fruitfully employ a moment to reflect upon why women apparently are more concerned about corporate power than are men.) Almost 75 percent of the sample felt large corporations are necessary for growth, and less than 35 percent favored "busting up" corporate giants.[2] A nationwide survey for *U.S. News & World Report* found that 72 percent of those surveyed believed that monopoly is growing in America.[3]

Concentration of Resources

The survey data suggest and common sense demands that a good deal of the public skepticism regarding big business revolves around that very "bigness." Of course, it is hardly news that some American corporations are of Goliath proportions, but a reminder of the specifics may be useful. For example, the 1985 *Fortune* Industrial 500 shows Exxon at the top of the sales pyramid with 1984 revenues of more than $90 billion.[4] General Motors ranked second with more than $83 billion in sales. GM's assets in 1984 exceeded $52 billion, and with nearly 750,000 employees, GM was America's leading industrial employer. That employment total is roughly equal to the population of the cities of Baltimore or Indianapolis. These figures assume more meaning when compared with the gross national products of the nations of the world. Based upon World Bank and *Fortune* data, Exxon's 1982 sales of $97.2 billion ranked it 19th among the world's economic units. GM ranked 28th on that list, with sales of $60 billion. Thus Exxon placed behind Switzerland (GNP $108.5 billion) and just ahead of Indonesia (GNP $89.0 billion). GM's $60 billion in sales exceeded the gross national products of such nations as Argentina ($58.9 billion) and Norway ($58.7 billion).[5]

Size is, of course, suggestive of power, but much more frightening to business critics is the concentration of resources that characterizes the business structure. Professor Samuel Reid summarized the data in the manufacturing and mining sector:

Less than 1 percent of American manufacturers control 88 percent of the industrial assets and receive over 90 percent of the net profits of industrial firms in the American economy. About 100 firms receive a greater share of net profits than the remaining 370,000 corporations, proprietorships, and partnerships engaged in manufacturing. The sales of *Fortune's* 500 Largest Industrials are almost 10 times greater than the "second" 500 largest firms (those ranked 501–1,000). The assets of this second group are also less than one tenth of the 500 largest industrials. Combined, the 1,000 largest industrials, a fraction of a percent of American business firms, employ about 80 percent of the workers in manufacturing and mining.[6]

And the following table from the 1984 *Statistical Abstract* offers a view of industrial concentration over recent decades.

Largest Manufacturing Corporations—Percent Share of Assets Held (1955 to 1982)

Corporation Rank Group	1960	1965	1970	1975	1976	1977	1978	1979	1980	1981	1982
100 largest	46.4	46.5	48.5	45.0	45.4	45.9	45.5	46.1	46.7	46.8	47.7
200 largest	56.3	56.7	60.4	57.5	58.0	58.5	58.3	59.0	59.7	60.0	60.8

Prior to 1970, excludes newspapers. Data prior to 1974 not strictly comparable with later years.

Source: Through 1981, U.S. Federal Trade Commission; thereafter, U.S. Bureau of the Census, unpublished data. As reprinted in the *Statistical Abstract of the U.S., 1984.*

The Corporate State

While it is simply beyond credible dispute that a small number of firms control a disproportionate quantity of commercial resources, very vigorous debate rages regarding the actual concentration levels and trends in recent years. Of course, the controversy regarding corporate power would be meaningless but for the view that corporate power has resulted in harm to the public. Although scholarly opinion as to the issue varies, it is worth noting that a number of studies show a positive relationship between concentration and corporate profits.[7] Consequently, critics contend that consumers are paying the bill for "excess" profits. (Of course, others argue that higher profits merely reflect superior performance.) But the list of complaints ranges well beyond pure economics. From pollution, discrimination, white-collar crime, invasion of privacy, undue political influence, to misleading advertising, and on across the spectrum of social problems, the critics lay much of the blame on the corporate community.

Many of those issues are addressed in subsequent chapters of this book. But to make the position of the corporate critics clearer, we must now look more closely at a few of the major complaints. The critics contend that the power of the business community has become so encompassing that virtually all dimensions of American life have absorbed elements of the business ethic. Values commonly associated with businesspersons (competition, profit seeking, reliance on technology, faith in growth) have overwhelmed traditional humanist values (cooperation, individual dignity, human rights, meaningful service to society). In the name of efficiency and productivity, it is argued that the warmth, decency, and value of life have been debased. We engage in meaningless work in an artificial culture. Objects dominate our existence. We operate as replaceable cogs in a vast, bureaucratic machine. Our national environment is shredded in the gleeful pursuit of progress. Indeed, we lose ourselves, the critics argue. Charles Reich, former Yale University law professor, addressed the loss of self in his very influential book, *The Greening of America:*

> Of all of the forms of impoverishment that can be seen or felt in America, loss of self, or death in life, is surely the most devastating. It is, even more than the draft and the Vietnam War, the source of discontent and rage in the new generation. Beginning with school, if not before, an individual is systematically stripped of his imagination, his creativity, his heritage, his dreams, and his personal uniqueness, in order to style him into a productive unit for a mass, technological society. Instinct, feeling, and spontaneity are repressed by overwhelming forces. As the individual is drawn into the meritocracy, his working life is split from his home life, and both suffer from a lack of wholeness. Eventually, people virtually become their professions, roles, or occupations, and are henceforth strangers to themselves. Blacks long ago felt their deprivation of identity and potential for life. But white "soul" and blues are just beginning. Only a segment of youth is articulately aware that they too suffer an enforced loss of self—they too are losing the lives that could be theirs.[8]

Reich seems to be suggesting that the *meaning* in life, the "spiritual" tones that afford flavor and quality, are being stripped from our existence. The residue is a society of hollow men and women—long on dollars, occupiers of prestigious posts, possessors of power, but bereft of the central core of goodness and purpose that affords us worth beyond worldly achievement. In the piece that follows we are reminded of one of our losses; arguably a small one, but doubtless important if part of a much larger whole.

WHERE DID YOUR GARDEN GO?

Michael Silverman

The A train ties Rockaway to the mainland of New York City. When I was a kid, this was our main access to New York, or, to put it more precisely, to the old Madison Square Garden.

The Garden was a place where the world seemed to come alive. It is difficult for me to talk about it with an adult perspective. When we are young, we feel with a certain immediacy; things are rich; we react to life. Now, when you think about it, this is not exactly a bad way to live. So, for the moment, I won't worry about adult perspective. I'll just tell you about the old Garden back in the early 60s.

When you climbed out of the subway, Eighth Avenue was alive, people jammed under the old marquee, the bars packed three deep, and all the cigar-store phones taken by guys putting in late bets with their books. When you walked in the Eighth Avenue end of the Garden the ice was right there in front of you, not stashed away at the end of a maze of concrete tunnels. Seventy-five cents got you a seat up in the side balcony and when the players skated out on the ice you could see their faces.

Now Missing: The Human Element

You had access to the players. All it took was a good shout from up there and the inimitable Lou Fontinato would be aware of your presence in the building. The Garden and the people in it were real entities, with peeling paint and human faces. When the crowd roared on some nights, you could feel the place shake under your feet.

You could connect in that place. There were human connections. You went, you felt, and you made your own connections.

That connection is dying today. People sit in airless concrete ovals. Through the convenience of a network of escalators and tunnels, you can reach your seat in the loge and never once feel a sense of place. You are just another component in a concrete oval.

There are excellent sight lines, but of what? The players have been reduced to colorful digits. From most seats in the Garden the view is

the equivalent of what you get on an 8-inch TV screen.

Everything is hyped through the media. All aspects of sport are scrutinized, explained, magnified, and eventually mystified. The game becomes something we dissect and study at a distance. And, little by little, it loses its life; it becomes an artificial object. In the end, we become objective, but only at the expense of our humanity. The real connections wither away.

Your Life to Live

And this does not have to be. We, in the end, still have the ability to determine the course of our lives. But only if we recognize it as our responsibility and not let it be co-opted by those who have lost their vision. And this responsibility is there at every moment. It's there when you buy a ticket to a place like the Garden. It's there when you buy a rotten piece of fruit and accept it as the way things are.

Source: *New York Times*, February 1, 1976, Section 5, p. 2. Copyright © 1976/80 by The New York Times Company. Reprinted by permission.

So Michael Silverman reminds us that the progress of recent years may, in some respects, be more apparent than real. But he also argues that if some elements of the quality of life are in decline, the blame lies with us rather than the "villains" in the business community. However, we can strengthen the case of the corporate critics by directing our attention to some areas of special concern; that is, politics and the schools and churches, where it is argued that business values and the influence of the business community have been particularly destructive.

Public Policy

In recent years the corporate community has clearly taken a more direct and vigorous role in the political process. As a result, corporate critics are increasingly concerned that the financial weight of big business will prove so influential that our pluralist, democratic approach to governance may be significantly distorted. Quite obviously money today is central to the task of acquiring elective office. And following election, dollars to finance lobbying on Capitol Hill can be critical in shaping congressional opinion. A congressional study from the late 1970s has estimated that about $1 billion each year is invested in "grass roots" lobbying. It is estimated that about 85 to 90 percent of that sum is expended by corporations and trade organizations.[9]

Of course, corporate funds cannot lawfully be expended for federal campaign contributions. But corporations can and do lawfully facilitate the establishment of arrangements by which individual employees may make contributions. As explained in the following articles, campaign contributions via corporate political action committees (PACs) have proven very effective in advancing the interests of the business community, and corporations have recently become quite active in seeking to effect various referenda across the nation.

TAKING AN AX TO THE PACS

Critics of special-interest contributions fight back

"What is Representative Dan Rostenkowski going to do with half a million dollars in left-over campaign money? Take it with him?" So asked a full-page ad in Chicago's Albany Park *News*, deep in the district of the Democratic chairman of the Ways and Means Committee. "Who does Representative Mickey Edwards care more about? You and your vote? Or the auto dealers and their money?" So read another ad in the Ponca City, Okla., paper in Republican Edwards' district. Both ended with the same kicker, "Write and ask him."

The provocative ads, and eight others like them, are the first volleys in a new war against political action committees (PACs). Leading the PAC attack: Philip Stern, a Washington philanthropist and liberal Democratic activist who last September joined forces with New York Republican Whitney North Seymour Jr., a former U.S. attorney, to form the nonpartisan "citizens against PACs." The group's goal is to pressure Congress into eliminating the corporate, labor union, and special-interest PACs that make what Stern calls "ax-to-grind" con-

Jacking up the Ante (PAC Contributions to Congressional Candidates in Millions)

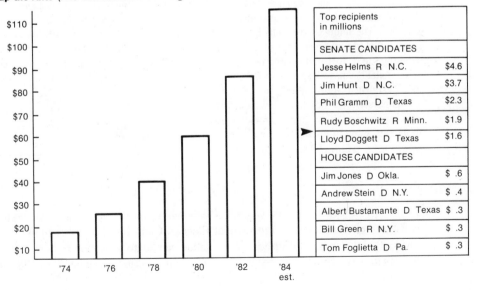

Top recipients in millions	
SENATE CANDIDATES	
Jesse Helms R N.C.	$4.6
Jim Hunt D N.C.	$3.7
Phil Gramm D Texas	$2.3
Rudy Boschwitz R Minn.	$1.9
Lloyd Doggett D Texas	$1.6
HOUSE CANDIDATES	
Jim Jones D Okla.	$ .6
Andrew Stein D N.Y.	$ .4
Albert Bustamante D Texas	$ .3
Bill Green R N.Y.	$ .3
Tom Foglietta D Pa.	$ .3

tributions to candidates. Says he: "We want to make it uncomfortable for Congress to continue accepting PAC money."

Stern has mailed copies of his ads to every Senator and Congressman to put them on notice that their campaign finances might be similarly scrutinized. When Democratic Congressman David Obey of Wisconsin received his packet, he shot back a sizzling letter decrying the tactic as "immoral." Stern counters that every ad is meticulously documented and published only after a Senator or Congressman has been offered a chance to tell his side of the story. When Democrat Jeff Bingaman of New Mexico was asked why he did not return a $10,000 gift from the American Medical Association PAC (AM–PAC), Bingaman replied forthrightly, "I can't afford to."

Indeed, elections have become so expensive that turning down funds from any legal source is difficult. Largely to blame, ironically, are the post-Watergate reforms in the law governing election spending. Amended in 1974 to reduce the influence of wealthy contributors and end payoffs by corporations and unions, the law instead legitimized PACs, enabling individuals to band together in support of candidates. It also gave such groups an outsize voice (a PAC can donate $5,000 to both a candidate's primary- and general-election campaigns, while an individual can contribute only $1,000). The unintended result: in the decade since 1974 the number of PACs has grown from 608 to 3,803; in the same period, annual PAC donations have leaped from $12.5 million to an estimated $120 million. Says Republican Congressman Jim Leach of Iowa, a virulent PAC opponent: "It's a myth to think they don't want something in return."

Democrat Steve Sovern, who lost his bid for Iowa's Second Congressional District seat in 1980, remembers his first trip to Washington to solicit campaign funds. "I found myself in line with candidates from all over," he says. Each PAC asked the money-hungry hopefuls to fill out multiple-choice questionnaires on issues important to the PAC. If a candidate's views measured up, and he looked like a good shot to win, he got the money. Says Sovern: "The process made me sick."

*   *   *   *   *

Only two members of the Senate and eight Congressmen decline to accept PAC contributions. No wonder: unless a candidate is personally wealthy or politically invulnerable, the highroad can be a short cut to defeat. Democratic Congressman Tom Harkin of Iowa, for example, takes PAC money even though he has voted repeatedly to limit PAC influence. Says a Harkin aide: "To refuse PAC money would be to lay down your sword when you know your opponent has a gun."

To make money less of a weapon, activist Stern is lobbying to include the offices of Congressman and Senator in the legislation that this year will provide $130 million in tax revenue for presidential candidates. Several bills now before Congress provide for public financing. But there is a practical roadblock on Capital Hill: incumbents, who receive 77 percent more in PAC donations than challengers, have no desire to vote away their built-in advantage. . . .

Afterword

Efforts to impose monetary limits on campaign contributions have encountered stiff constitutional hurdles. The Presidential Election Campaign Fund Act limited each PAC to $1,000 in spending to further a presidential candidate's election (where that candidate has opted to accept public financing for a general election campaign). In 1983 the Democratic Party filed suit against two PACs (the National Conservative Political Action Committee and the Fund for a Conservative Majority) that had announced their intention to expend large sums of money to support President Reagan's 1984 reelection effort.[10] The plaintiffs sought a ruling that the $1,000 limitation of the Fund Act was constitutional. In 1985 the case reached the Supreme Court, which ruled against the Democratic Party and found the $1,000 spending limitation to be a violation of the First Amendment guarantee of freedom of speech. In essence, the Court reasoned that a restriction on spending reduces the quantity of expression in a campaign. The Court noted that there is no tendency in independent expenditures by PACs (that are uncoordinated with the candidate) to corrupt, or appear to corrupt, the election process. The result, at least as to presidential campaigns, is that PAC spending cannot lawfully be limited by the provisions of the Fund Act.

BUSINESS BIG-SPENDERS HIT THE REFERENDA VOTES

Steven Lydenberg

The 1982 election reconfirmed the powerful role corporate funds can play in initiative and referenda campaigns. An examination of 18 ballot question campaigns around the country that pitted business interests against citizens or grassroots groups shows that business spending dominated 16 of the 18 campaigns—and that the side with business backing won in 13 of these 16 campaigns. In both cases where the business-backed side did not outspend its opponents, it lost.

Spending in 1982 by corporate-backed ballot question committees in these 18 campaigns totaled $29.7 million—as compared with $6.7 million by citizen sponsors. Particularly dramatic was the beverage industry's expenditure of $9.2 million fighting bottle deposit proposals in five states. (Pro-bottle-bill groups raised $2.1 million for these campaigns.) Only in Massachusetts—where the beverage industry was attempting to overturn a recently enacted bottle deposit law—did proponents of returnable beverage containers win out. In Michigan, utility companies spent an astonishing $7.3 million opposing two citizen-group-sponsored utility-reform measures and promoting a third measure of their own. . . .

Business-backed committees outspent their opponents by more than 2 to 1 in 14 of the 16 campaigns they dominated—or on an average of 18.6 to 1 for all 16 contests. The three campaigns in which citizen-backed committees won despite being outspent were in Massachusetts (the bottle bill), Michigan, and Nebraska. The Michigan Citizens Lobby overcame a spending disadvantage of 114 to one to win (but by less than one percent of the vote) on a measure to limit utilities' power in cost pass-ons and rate-setting hearings. The Nebraska Farmers Union had a solid victory in its initiative campaign to ban the corporate acquisition of farmland, in the face of a $462,000 corporate-backed opposition campaign.

* * * * *

There were also three 1982 campaigns that essentially pitted business interests against business interests (also not included on the accompanying chart). The defeat of all three of these measures confirms earlier findings that business-sponsored initiatives are generally unsuccessful. This is probably because business is hard-pressed to overcome voters' unfavorable perception that it is using the essentially

The Big Business Ballot Buyout (1982 Ballot Questions Affecting Corporate Interests)

State-Measure (Won/Lost)	Spending (Business Backed/ Other Side)	Spending Ratio	Vote Total (Percent)
Arizona			
Deposits on beverage containers (L)	$812,762/$70,085	11.6 to 1	68.1 to 31.9
California			
Deposits on beverage containers (L)	5,462,001/923,152	5.9 to 1	55.9 to 44.1
Handgun registration (L)	7,287,548/2,608,553	2.8 to 1	62.8 to 37.2
Colorado			
Deposits on beverage containers (L)	905,660/575,510	1.6 to 1	74.5 to 25.5
Maine			
Shut down Maine Yankee nuclear power plant (L)	856,514/313,535	2.7 to 1	56.0 to 44.0
Massachusetts			
Deposits on beverage containers (W)	1,090,421/269,383	4.0 to 1	40.9 to 59.1
Restrict nuclear waste disposal (W)	100,240/114,705	0.9 to 1	32.5 to 67.5
Michigan			
Elect Public Service Commissioners (L)	1,699,367/22,167	76.7 to 1	63.3 to 36.7
Regulate utilities' fuel adjustment pass-ons (W) (citizens-backed)	4,400,480/38,785	113.5 to 1	49.3 to 50.7
Michigan			
Regulate utilities' fuel adjustment pass-ons (W) (business-backed)	$1,209,481/$38,785	31.2 to 1	59.6 to 40.4
Missouri			
Establish a Citizens Utilities Board (L)	309,557/26,477	11.7 to 1	61.4 to 38.6
Nebraska			
Ban corporate purchase of farmland (W)	462,832/79,722	5.8 to 1	43.6 to 56.4
Ohio			
Elect Public Utilities Commissioners (L)	1,652,210/648,308	2.5 to 1	67.4 to 32.6
Oregon			
Abolish Land Conservation and Development Commission (L)	125,099/162,622	0.8 to 1	44.9 to 55.1
Property tax limitation (L)	424,719/282,474	1.5 to 1	50.5 to 49.5
Washington			
Deposit on beverage containers (L)	952,351/247,547	3.8 to 1	70.7 to 29.3
Limit on consumer credit interest rates (L)	1,557,987/278,203	5.6 to 1	66.0 to 34.0
Remove food sales tax (L)	398,336/24,503	16.3 to 1	66.2 to 33.8

populist initiative process for its own narrow gains. These three campaigns were: a Colorado proposal to allow grocery stores to sell wine (spending $873,000 pro, $591,000 con; lost 35 to 65 percent); a Maine proposal to deregulate milk prices ($121,300 pro, $71,600 con; lost

49 to 51 percent); an Oregon proposal to allow self-service gas stations ($163,000 pro, $22,200 con; lost 42 to 58 percent).

Source: *Business and Society Review*, no. 47 (Fall 1983), p. 53, Steven Lydenberg is a research associate with the Council on Economic Priorities.

Advocacy Advertising

As evidenced by the "Referenda" article, the corporate community is increasingly taking its political message to the public via television and print media advertising. That course of action has provoked very considerable criticism, primarily on the grounds that the resources of the business community are such that its opinion might overwhelm that of less well-financed voices. However, public opinion and legal decisions have been favorable to corporate advocacy advertising. A nationwide survey in 1978 by pollster Roger Seasonwein found 66 percent of the adults surveyed favoring corporate advertising on public issues. Responding to a closely related issue, 39 percent of those polled said such ads should be tax-deductible business expenses while 48 percent favored payment from corporate profits.[11] Of more immediate substantive value to the corporate position was a 1978 United States Supreme Court decision in the case of *First National Bank of Boston* v. *Bellotti*.[12] In that case, the Court upheld the right of the appellant national bank and some other corporations to spend company funds to advertise their opposition to a Massachusetts referendum that would have instituted a graduated personal income tax. (For the opinion, see Chapter 5.)

Apparently the corporate voice is being heard, as acknowledged in the following comments by Herbert Schmertz, director and vice president in charge of public affairs of the Mobil Oil Corporation.

At Mobil, we have seen evidence of a significant improvement in the attitudes of opinion leaders on issues we have been discussing in our messages. For example, a poll of opinion leaders in Washington, D.C., demonstrated a marked change in their attitudes toward the oil industry between 1973 and 1977. They now agree with most industry views on energy matters. One reason for the improved attitudes, says the polling organization, is "major public affairs communications efforts by oil companies," and Mobil is cited as the leader of this effort.

* * * * *

But polls are only one measure. We have also gotten our messages before the legislators, and apparently they are hearing what we say. In this area, we have seen the rejection of oil divestiture legislation, the tabling of an ill-conceived offshore drilling bill, substantial changes in the president's energy plan, and a realistic auto emissions bill. We have also finally laid to rest the myth of "obscene" oil industry profits. Of equal importance is the success we have had in making the press more responsive and responsible. We constantly see our ideas incorporated in editorials, and we know the press will be more careful before it attacks us, because we will answer back.[13]

Questions

1. The corporate community clearly possesses vast resources. Noted economist John Kenneth Galbraith, among others, has argued that consumer ''wants'' can be created by skillful persuasion. Does the application of corporate resources and skills to the shaping of public and political opinion constitute a threat to democracy? Explain.
2. Should political lobbying be curbed? If so, in what manner?
3. Should corporate political action committees be forbidden? Would such action be constitutionally permissible?
4. Are you personally aware of having been influenced by corporate advocacy advertising? If so, how?
5. Is advocacy advertising an appropriate mechanism for promoting increased understanding of the free enterprise system?

Schools and Churches

To the critic, a particularly apt example of the growth of the Corporate State is the commercial direction of not-for-profit institutions. Let us begin with our schools. It requires no distinctive perception to recognize the advance of business and technological training and the decline of the liberal arts. From kindergarten through graduate school, the ''business mentality'' is evermore pervasive. Given the competitiveness of the job market, it is argued that students and their parents willingly allow and, indeed, call for a ''quick fix'' of skills (such as accounting, management, and marketing) as a replacement for occupationally ambiguous disciplines such as history, literature, and philosophy. The bargain has been struck. The student leaves his or her formal education and proceeds into the financial security of the Corporate State, but did that person buy a good life or an empty existence? Charles Reich offers his opinion:

> The process by which man is deprived of his self begins with his institutionalized training in public school for a place in the machinery of the State. The object of the training is not merely to teach him how to perform some specific function; it is to make him become that function, to see and judge himself and others in terms of functions, and to abandon any aspect of self, thinking, questioning, feeling, loving, that has no utility for either production or consumption in the Corporate State. The training for the role of consumer is just as important as the training for a job, and at least equally significant for loss of self.

> *   *   *   *   *

> Consumer training in school consists of preventing the formation of individual consciousness, taste, aesthetic standards, self-knowledge, and the ability to create one's own satisfactions. Solitude, separateness, undirected time, and silence which are necessary for consciousness, are not permitted. Groups are encouraged to set values, inhibiting the growth of self-knowledge.[14]

How is it that our educational system is so profoundly influenced by business values? Certainly it is reasonable to argue that the schools are simply responding to the preferences of the people, but in a Corporate State can the citizens exert a free and fully knowledgeable opinion? Or have we been carefully trained to follow the lockstep demands of a thoroughly organized, bureaucratic, business society?

We find big business and its leadership directly involved in the shaping of college and university policy. A survey by the Association of Governing Boards of higher education revealed that 34.5 percent of the members of the various college and university boards of trustees are business executives.[15] While governing boards do not typically determine day-to-day institutional policy, they are ultimately responsible for the general direction of the institution, and perhaps more importantly, for hiring those who do set day-to-day policy. In that more than one third of the trustees are businesspersons, it should not be surprising that business values should assume a certain ascendancy. By contrast, 5 percent of the board members are homemakers, 4.1 percent are executives of nonprofit organizations, and 1.3 percent are farmers. Women constitute about 18 percent of the public school trustees and blacks, about 11 percent. The point is obvious. There are many voices to be heard, but some thunder while others are virtually inaudible. The consequence is an entirely predictable tilt in the direction of the more powerfully championed opinion.

Charles Reich's view of America as a Corporate State is further supported by a look at one of the nation's blossoming business giants—organized religion. The delightfully acerbic Nicholas Von Hoffman offers his interpretation of one church's marketing program.

SELLING GOD IN CALIFORNIA

Nicholas Von Hoffman

Garden Grove, Calif.—The people sit in their cars with their windows rolled up. They look out through their windshields toward the preacher who stands on an elevated, slablike platform. They can hear his words by setting their radio dials to a short-range transmitter in the church. They are safe. To express approval they need not extend the hand of Christian fellowship. They can cause their automobile horns to emit happy honks of approbation.

* * * * *

Garden Grove Church does have a more conventional edifice of worship than the automobiles on its expanse of parking lots. It has a sanctuary whose glass walls roll back to bring the people in the cars and those in the pews in somewhat closer contact. It also has a lot of other things which describe themselves simply by enumerating them.

There are 12 fountains—1 for each Apostle—whose spouts go up and down according to the mood the minister wishes to convey to his flock at various points in the service. The church also has 7,000 members. It has a 24-hour-a-day counseling service available to the atomized alcoholics of Orange County by dialing N-E-W-H-O-P-E on their Princess telephones. It has 12-story-high Tower of Hope atop of which is a 92-foot, neon-lighted cross.

Nevertheless, this garish 22-acre religious shopping center, with its dozens of groups and hundreds of activities, isn't kooky-kinky Southern California religion. The Richard Neutra–designed buildings are the angular architectural cliches of the region's branch banks and savings-and-loan associations. The people who come here to do their business with God could be spending their time in Disneyland or Anaheim Stadium where the California Angels play. Both are visible from the Tower of Hope, so that the church must offer special competition for the community's religious-entertainment dollar.

Judged by what Orange County people tell you, they are the happiest people in the world inhabiting the nicest communities ever constructed, but maybe they do hurt, and that's why they get into the steel protection of their automobiles to go find revivification in Garden Grove Church's happy, smiley, peppy, forward-thinking, adulterated Christianity which seems to promise every soul a private bungalow in the House of the Lord, Coca-Cola in the Eucharistic chalice, French fries for the bread of communion. ·

But be not deceived by the appearances of vapidity. Garden Grove does preach a subliminal doctrine of stern structure. It is that failure is death and success is life, even life everlasting.

The doctrine finds its incarnation in the person of Garden Grove's pastor, Robert Schuller, a Christian executive of rare histrionic and organizational ability. The great contribution to Christianity of this middle-aged artificer of human relations—who looks like a mildly demonic gray-haired Howdy Doody—may be the marriage of religion and the Sears, Roebuck corporate ethos.

Schuller, who is an ordained minister of the Reformed Church, founded Garden Grove 20 years ago much as Sears locates a new store. He selected a strategic place in the freeway grid, defined his market area as every unchurched person within 10 traffic lights or 20 minutes drive, pretested his product, and then began to sell like crazy. His techniques are those of mass merchandising: advertising, celebrity appearances, entertainment, multiple activities, something for everyone, and giveaways.

His approach to running the church itself is in the corporate, authoritarian mode. This is Schuller's advice to other pastors for handling ''obstacle people'' or ''impossibility thinkers'':

> If you have them in your church, and every church does have them, don't create an opportunity for them to sound off. Roberts Rules of Order is so designed that the president of the corporation and the chairman of the board can keep impossibility thinkers from disrupting the meeting. You build a stage for impossibility thinkers every time you give everyone in the congregation the chance to express their opinions on a controversial issue.

The corporate-president-minister thus becomes a Pope without the restraints of tradition and liturgy, or the humbling misgivings of philosophy. The only test of success for this kind of ministry is a booming growth curve, and there's no argument that, if they don't have the old stones and the ancient sense of man's smallness in sin here at Garden Grove, they do have many satisfied customers.

Source: King Features Syndicate. Reprinted with special permission of King Features Syndicate, Inc.

Afterword

The Von Hoffman column describes Robert Schuller's church of the 1960s and '70s. Today Mr. Schuller commands an empire of sorts. His television service, ''The Hour of Power'' reaches three million viewers. In 1982 his congregation totaled 10,000 people, and contributions reached $34 million.[16]

Who Controls the Corporation?

The critics argue that America's giant corporations possess extraordinary power. It is also argued that those corporations exert their influence across American life in a manner that threatens our lifestyle. Now we turn to what seems to be the next logical inquiry: Who controls the corporation? If corporate ownership is distributed throughout society, and if that ownership translates into effective control, even the corporate titans pose little threat. On the other hand, if corporate control is tightly concentrated in a small block of institutions and persons, we can logically feel some alarm. The article that follows contends that the real picture of corporate power is yet more threatening than is suggested by a casual perusal of the *Fortune* 500. The position is that via corporate interlocks and institutional ownership (large banks and other financial firms), a handful of companies have, if not effective control of the economy, then at the very least, a fund of influence dramatically disproportionate to their numbers. If so, the question becomes whether America operates primarily in the best interests of all citizens or whether national policy is shaped by and for the influential few.

THE INTERLOCK OF CORPORATE POWER

Markley Roberts

Superbanks and supercorporations—gigantic aggregations of private business power—are making decisions that affect the jobs and income and welfare of 220 million Americans. These decisions come from a few hundred men and women who sit on the boards of directors of these giant corporations. The boards are tied together by a vast network of interlocking directors. And the tentacles of corporate power reach out to affect the entire U.S. economy.

Far too often there's no public accountability for these big business directors' decision making—no way for workers, consumers, regulatory agencies, or even elected public officials to get information on the structure and operations of these giant corporations. . . .

The result is concentration of private decision making affecting the nation's welfare and placing private economic power in a few hands.

The danger is monopoly, destruction of competition, price-fixing and price-raising, export of jobs, big business control in politics, and undermining of basic democratic institutions and democratic processes. . . .

The Senate Subcommittee on Reports, Accounting, and Management, headed by the late Senator Lee Metcalf of Montana, in April 1978 pulled up the curtain of secrecy on one key part of concentrated corporate power, the network of interlocking directorships.

The network of big business leaders as they meet on the boards of directors was revealed by a careful, computerized staff study of the top 130 U.S. corporations—the 30 biggest industrial corporations, the 20 biggest banks, the 10 biggest insurance companies, the 10 biggest diversified financial companies, the 20 biggest utilities, the 20 biggest transportation companies, the 10 biggest retailers, the 3 major broadcasting companies, and 7 investment advisory companies.

These 130 corporations control more than $1,000 billion ($1 trillion) in assets, about 25 percent of the assets of all U.S. corporations.

"These companies at the top of corporate America were heavily concentrated through interlocking directorates," the Senate report declared, noting that such interlocking directorates "can be both good business for corporations and bad business for the public."

Although interlocking directorates among direct competitors are forbidden by federal law, congressional reports and federal agency studies have warned again and again that apparently legal direct and indirect interlocking directorates can lead to destruction of competition and to concentration of economic and political power in the hands of very few business leaders.

There is a high degree of concentration—with high potential for "you-scratch-my-back,

I'll-scratch-your-back'' collusion and antipub-lic, anticonsumer abuses. Among the 130 top corporations there was a total of 530 direct interlocks and 12,193 indirect interlocks. Direct interlocks are those where two corporations have a common director. Indirect interlocks are those where directors of two corporations meet as directors of a third corporation.

For example, the subcommittee report found the chairman of American Telephone & Telegraph sitting on the board of the giant Citicorp banking institution. This is a direct interlock between a customer of financial services (AT&T) and a financial institution (Citicorp). It is also a direct interlock between a supplier of telecommunications equipment and services and a major buyer of those same services.

But a director of International Business Machines also was sitting on the board of Citicorp. So there was an indirect interlock between two direct competitors in telecommunications—AT&T and IBM—through a third company, Citicorp. The Clayton Act of 1914 forbids direct interlocks between competitors, but they can meet legally in the boardroom of an intermediate company.

*   *   *   *   *

The boardrooms of the big banks and the big insurance companies are key meeting places for American business. Bank directors serve on insurance company boards and insurance company directors serve on bank boards. Both bank and insurance company directors interlock on the boards of the nation's biggest industrial, utility, transportation, and retailing corporation boards.

BankAmerica, [then] the biggest U.S. banking company, interlocked with the next biggest banks (Citicorp, Chase Manhattan, and J. P. Morgan) and with the two biggest insurance companies (Prudential and Metropolitan Life). BankAmerica's total 163 interlocks reached 75 of the top 130 corporations.

*   *   *   *   *

The same pattern prevailed for the other banks and insurance companies. Chase Manhattan reached 89 of the top corporations through 535 interlocking directorates. J. P.

Morgan interlocked with 99 top corporations through 533 interlocks. Prudential, the largest life insurance company, interlocked with 81 top corporations. And Metropolitan Life had 670 interlocks with 98 out of the top 130 corporations.

Obviously these financial institutions have a tremendous potential for noncompetitive coordinated action in extending credit and providing capital or refusing investment funds. They are able to control the development and direction of substantial parts of the American economy.

In addition to interlocking directorates, the big banks have tremendous power to control the nation's major corporations through the banks' stock-voting power. Often this stock-voting power comes from control over pension funds and trust funds.

The Metcalf subcommittee, in a January 1978 staff report, found that J. P. Morgan's subsidiary, Morgan Guaranty Trust Company, is the major identified stockvoter of 27 out of the top 122 corporations in the nation and is among the top five stockvoters in 56 corporations.

*   *   *   *   *

Stockvoter relations among the big banks reinforce the economic power created by interlocking directorates.

"Morgan Guaranty is Stockvoter Number 1 in four of its New York sister banks—Citicorp, Manufacturers Hanover Corp., Chemical New York Corp., and Bankers Trust New York Corp—as well as BankAmerica Corp.," the January 1978 report declared.

"In turn, Citicorp is Stockvoter No. 1 in Morgan Guaranty's parent holding company, J. P. Morgan & Co. Stockvoter No. 2 in J. P. Morgan & Co. is Chase Manhattan. Stockvoters No. 3 and 4 in J. P. Morgan & Co. are Manufacturers Hanover and Bankers Trust, in whose parent bank holding companies Morgan Guaranty Trust is Stockvoter No. 1. . . .''

*   *   *   *   *

The House Antitrust Subcommittee in 1965 also noted that corporate management interlocks present problems of conflict of interest and opportunities for ''inside dealing'' and violations of fiduciary responsibilities.

And the House Banking Committee in 1969 warned that the mixing of banking with non-banking activities within the same corporate structure "could radically change the entire economic structure of the United States by the creation of giant conglomerate cartels centered around large banking institutions. . . ."

The Metcalf subcommittee report of April 1978 likewise points to great potential for antitrust abuse as the result of interlocking directors—concentration of economic power in a few hands; elimination of competition as a result of communication and discussion (with or without agreement); blocking of expansion or diversification into competitive areas; restrictions on development of completely new business fields; preferential treatment resulting in injury to suppliers and consumers, injury to small business, and monopolistic, discriminatory allocation of credit and capital and financial services.

To deal with these threats, the Metcalf subcommittee report concluded: . . . A full-scale examination is needed of the structure of the American economy to inform Congress and the public on such economic developments as interlocking relations among the giant corporations and banks, their domination of key parts of the national economy, their effects on prices, jobs, exports of technology and their impact on America's position in the world economy and their impact on American communities and democratic institutions.

* * * * *

Source: Mark Green and Robert Massie, eds., *The Big Business Reader* (New York: The Pilgrim Press, 1980), p. 457. Reprinted with permission of the copyright holder, the AFL–CIO (*American Federationalist*).

QUESTIONS

1. Markley Roberts decries corporate interlocks.
   a. Do America's major corporations engage in meaningful competition?
   b. Discuss the argument that perhaps we should permit and even encourage a greater measure of cooperation among corporations.
2. What is a trust fund? What forces prevent Morgan Guaranty and other financial institutions from abusing the voting power afforded them via pension programs and trusts?
3. Why is it that a share holding of 5 or 10 percent might be sufficient to constitute a controlling interest in a corporation?
4. Is the ownership of the major banks so concentrated as to threaten the nation's welfare?
5. Discuss the following:
   a. Do the millions of American stockholders still maintain effective, if distant, control?
   b. Is control now sufficiently separated from ownership so that management has, via its expertise, gained dominion?
   c. Are the big financial institutions in charge?
   d. Is it the rich people who rule the corporate community?
   e. Or perhaps it is as Charles Reich suggests:

   > From all of this, there emerges the great revelation about the executive suite—the place from which power-hungry men seem to rule our society. The truth is far worse. In the executive suite, there may be a Leger or Braque on the wall, or a collection of African masks, there may be a vast glass-and-metal desk, but there is no one there. No one at all is in the executive suite. What looks like a man is only a representation of a man who does what the organization requires. He (or it) does not run the machine; he tends it.[17]

   Are the parts integrated into one self-perpetuating system with no one and no organization really in control?

Summary

To the critics, American life is increasingly and dangerously in the grip of big business values. A final excerpt from *The Greening of America* summarizes Reich's conception of America as a Corporate State. It should be noted that Reich sees the citizens as victims of a coalition of large institutions. In his view ours is a "public-private amalgamated State" wherein business, government, and large nonprofit institutions are in league. The public-private distinction becomes meaningless. Government performs primarily on behalf of private interests, and many government functions are contracted out to be performed by private interests.

The American Corporate State today can be thought of as a single vast corporation, with every person as an involuntary member and employee. It consists primarily of large industrial organizations, plus nonprofit institutions such as foundations and the educational system, all related to the whole as divisions to a business corporation. Government is only a part of the state, but government coordinates it and provides a variety of needed services. The Corporate State is a complete reversal of the original American ideal and plan. The State, and not the market or the people or any abstract economic laws, determines what shall be produced, what shall be consumed, and how it shall be allocated. It determines, for example, that railroads shall decay while highways flourish; that coal miners shall be poor and advertising executives rich. Jobs and occupations in the society are rigidly defined and controlled, and arranged in a hierarchy of rewards, status, and authority. An individual can move from one position to another, but he gains little freedom thereby, for in each position he is subject to conditions imposed upon it; individuals have no protected area of liberty, privacy, or individual sovereignty beyond the reach of the State. The State is subject neither to democratic controls, constitutional limits, or legal regulation. Instead, the organizations in the Corporate State are motivated primarily by the demands of technology and of their own internal structure. Technology has imperatives such as these: if computers have been developed, they must be put to use; if faster planes can be produced, they must be put into service; if there is a more efficient way of organizing an office staff, it must be done; if psychological tests provide added information for personnel directors, they must be used on prospective employees. A general in charge of troops at Berkeley described the use of a helicopter to attack students with chemicals as "logical." As for organizations, their imperative is to grow. They need stability, freedom from outside interference, constantly increasing profits. Everyone in the organization wants more and better personnel, more functions, increased status and prestige—in a word, growth. The medium through which these forces operate is law. The legal system is not primarily concerned with justice, equality, or individual rights; it functions as an instrument of State domination, and it acts to prevent the intervention of human values or individual choice. Although the forces driving the State are impersonal rather than evil, they are wholly indifferent to man's needs, and tend to have the same consequences as would a system expressly designed for the purpose of destroying human beings and their society.

The essence of the Corporate State is that it is relentlessly single-minded; it has only one value, the value of technology-organization-efficiency-growth-progress. The State is perfectly rational and logical. It is based upon principle. But life cannot be supported on the basis of any single principle. Yet no other value is allowed to interfere with this one, not amenity, not beauty, not community, not even the supreme value of life itself. Thus the State is essentially mindless; it has only one idea and it rolls along, never stopping to think, consider, balance, or judge. Only such single-valued mindlessness would cut the last redwoods, pollute the most beautiful beaches, invent machines to injure and destroy plant and human life. To have only one value is, in human terms, to be mad. It is to be a machine.[18]

Afterword

You have now read that life is becoming evermore arid in the Corporate State. Do you agree? If so, is the business community to blame? If we have committed ourselves too thoroughly to business values, is the fault that of all of us, or are we pawns before an over-powerful corporate community? A great American, Robert Frost, perhaps had the answer.

A Time to Talk

When a friend calls to me from the road
And slows his horse to a meaning walk,
I don't stand still and look around
On all the hills I haven't hoed
And shout from where I am, 'What is it?'
No, not as there is a time to talk.
I thrust my hoe in the mellow ground,
Blade-end up and five feet tall,
And plod: I go up the stone wall
For a friendly visit.[19]

Chapter Questions

1. The thinker and futurist Herman Kahn was asked to comment on the prospects for space colonization. Kahn speculated that colonies of significance would develop in the early 21st century. But he cited two obstacles. One was that the rate at which colonization could be achieved would be instrumental in determining the excitement it would generate. The other:

   And in the United States, we can't turn people on unless it's economic. This culture, almost alone among all cultures, will not get turned on unless it makes a profit, or is scientific or military. When NASA decided to cooperate with the Russians, the average guy said, "Down with space." He thought that the objective was to get the high ground over the Russians.[20]

   Generation of profits is a primary and necessary corporate value
   a. Was Kahn correct in believing that our culture is more committed to profit seeking than are most other cultures?
   b. If so, why?
   c. Has the supremacy of profit seeking depreciated the quality of our lives?

2. Recently *Fortune* magazine conducted a study of 82 25-year-olds who have "shown promise of becoming high-level managers or entrepreneurs." Thomas Griffith summarized the results of the study:

   They are, *Fortune* says, bright, disciplined, hardworking, motivated: "They put their jobs ahead of most other diversions and commitments—including marriage, which many are in no hurry for, and children, which some claim they'll never want. . . . Single-mindedly chasing their objectives, they ignore what doesn't blend or harmonize with their purposefully limited landscape. They view work and life as a series of 'trade-offs' rather than compromises; for each opportunity surrendered, they demand an equal benefit in return." They pride themselves on the honesty with which they proclaim their ambitions.

To Ronald Reagan, these young people may embody the self-reliant American way in its purest form, but Gwen Kinkead, the writer of the *Fortune* article, can't resist a parenthetical comment: "To a stranger from another generation, they sometimes seem a grabby bunch. . . ."

The missing note in *Fortune's* young is idealism. They are not drones; they like the good life, the ski trips, the visits to Europe or Tahiti. If they tune out on causes, if they feel no obligation to help others, the explanation is not only that they have no time for these matters, but that they have no heart for them. They are a platoon of Tin Woodmen.[21]

    a. Is the current generation of young businesspeople composed primarily of "TinWoodmen"?

    b. If so, why?

    c. Does business demand Tin Woodmen?

    d. Are you a Tin Woodman?

3. David Gil, professor of social policy at Brandeis University, has "called for the dismantling of corporations that have destroyed 'self-directed work' and for the return of resources to the people for their own direction 'in human-sized communities where people can come together and jointly determine their economic way of life'."[22]

    a. Does our economic way of life reflect the will of the people?

    b. Is the corporate form destructive of the quality of the work experience?

    c. Is Gil's proposal workable?

4. Peter McCabe, managing editor of *Harper's,* reflecting upon changes in his Manhattan neighborhood and life generally:

In place of Art's Hardware Store now stands The Sensuous Bean. Where formerly there was a reasonably priced beauty salon, now one finds Better Nature (azaleas for $8.95). Sal's Cigar Store . . . has made way for Pandemonium. . . .No matter what kind of knick-knacks they carry . . . they have one thing in common . . .—the assembling of the superfluous.

To live in America today is to be constantly impressed by the ability of the superfluous to displace the useful, and by the ease with which the gratuitous can triumph over the imperative.[23]

    a. McCabe's picture of contemporary commerce leaves us as consumers looking a bit artificial and foolish. Are his observations correct?

    b. If so, is there cause for alarm in what he says?

    c. Who is responsible for the growth of our arguably empty pop culture?

5. It has been argued that the American culture favors TV rather than opera, and pornography rather than poems because "that is what sells." If corporate directors offered quality as insistently as they push their products, we might well learn to appreciate a wholly different lifestyle. Do you find any merit in that argument? Explain your reactions.

6. Should we lament the passing of the Roxbury Russet? The Russet was an American apple that, due largely to its mottled, leathery skin, did not make the commercial grade in contemporary America. Today apple growers are further from their markets and focus on growing those varieties of apple that are most prolific and best able to withstand shipment. The surviving apples, in general, are sweet and red in color.[24] Similarly we've seen the passing of juicy, flavorful tomatoes in favor of the more easily harvested and transported "rubber" tomato.

    a. Are these examples emblematic of a trade-off of quality in favor of efficiency and productivity?

    b. If so, is that trade-off necessary?

    c. Who is responsible for the trade-off?

7. What does Reich mean by "loss of self"? Do you sense any such loss in yourself?

8. As Silverman suggests, "big-time" sports has become a big business. Has the quality of the sports experience been depreciated?

9. Has your education been designed primarily to prepare you for a utilitarian role as a producer and/or consumer in the Corporate State? Have you been encouraged to abandon "thinking, questioning, feeling, loving?"

10. According to *Business Week:*

    To their credit, most B-schools are now taking steps to prepare their graduates better for the practical demands of business. Many have introduced courses on the increased use of computers as management tools, the growing internationalization of American business, and other relatively new trends.[25]

    Journalist Ronnie Dugger says:

    American universities in recent years have gradually become more and more like big businesses and the students in them like units to be fitted into the evolving corporation-dominated civilization. This transformation . . . might be compared to a butterfly changing back into a grub. . . .

    Optimistic observers welcome the change as fine—a good and necessary extension of American values and the American way. Those of us who do not agree see the universities ceasing to be free and stimulating places of learning conducted for the students' culture and development and becoming instead new adjuncts of the corporate and governmental bureaucracies.[26]

    a. Which view do you subscribe to? Explain.
    b. Will education of the future be conducted primarily by corporations? Explain.

11. Ted Peters is associate professor of systematic theology at the Pacific Lutheran Seminary and the Graduate Theological Union:

    How will the advancing postindustrial culture influence the course of religion? It is my forecast that religion will become increasingly treated as a consumer item.

    Because our economy produces so much wealth, we are free to consume and consume beyond the point of satiation. There is a limit to what we can consume in the way of material goods—new homes, new cars, new electronic gadgets, new brands of beer, new restaurants, and so on. So we go beyond material wants to consume new personal experiences—such as broader travel, exotic vacations, continuing education, exciting conventions, psychotherapy, and sky diving.

    What will come next and is already on the horizon is the consumption of spiritual experiences—personal growth cults, drug-induced ecstasy, world-traveling gurus, training in mystical meditation to make you feel better, etc. Once aware of this trend, religious entrepreneurs and mainline denominations alike will take to pandering their wares, advertising how much spiritual realities "can do to you." It will be subtle, and it will be cloaked in the noble language of personal growth, but nevertheless the pressure will be on between now and the year 2000 to treat religious experience as a commodity for consumption.[27]

    a. Is marketing necessary to the survival and growth of religion?
    b. Is marketing a threat to the legitimacy and value of religion?

12. Barry Commoner, the distinguished environmentalist and 1980 Citizen's Party presidential candidate, said in his campaign that the biggest problem in America today is corporate control of the country.

    There's no doubt the U.S. corporations helped build the economy, he (Commoner) says, but now they've run out of steam. . . .

    Decisions by the big corporations such as General Motors are always made in the interest of maximizing their profits and do not take into account what happens to the community and the country.[28]

    Is ours a Corporate State, as Commoner, Reich, and others suggest?

13. It is argued that the media—particularly television—merely parrots upper-class values and thus fails to direct adequate attention to those who criticize corporate values.

    a. Does the television industry serve as a meaningful voice in questioning ''dominant corporate values''?

    b. Should it do so?

14. Much is made of corporate bigness, of how institutions seem to dwarf mankind. Those concerns have given rise to the *Small Is Beautiful* movement as articulated in E. F. Schumacher's book of the same name. But Samuel Florman objects:

> Perhaps what lies at the heart of the worship of smallness is an increasing revulsion against the ugliness of much of industrial America. Dams, highways, and electric transmission lines, once the symbol of a somewhat naive commercial boosterism, are now depicted as vulgar. But this association of bigness with lack of taste is not warranted. The colossal works of man are no more inherently vulgar than the small works are inherently petty. We prize robustness in life as well as delicacy.[29]

    a. Is corporate America preoccupied with growth and bigness?

    b. Is corporate America guilty of corrupting our visual landscape?

    c. If so, is that loss of significance?

    d. Is smallness an answer to problems associated with bigness?

15. Are we as individual citizens effectively helpless in the face of corporate power?

16. What forces currently operate to restrain corporate power? Do you envision any new forces developing in the future to counteract corporate power?

17. Should government go into business itself (as with oil and gas exploration) to afford competition and thus blunt corporate power?

18. Do you think allegiance to the company will become more important than allegiance to the state? Is that a desirable direction? Raise the arguments on both sides of the latter question.

19. *Business Week* stated: ''Increasingly, the corporation will take over the role of the mother, supplying day-care facilities where children can be tended around the clock.''[30] How do you feel about the corporation as mother?

20. The public opinion polls suggest very limited faith in American business. Are Americans in their frustration simply pointing their collective finger at a nearby giant, or is there a legitimate, factual foundation for their skepticism?

21. Explore the argument that a concentrated economy populated by a small number of giants in each industry is necessary to a successful American economy.

Notes

1. George Gallup, *The Gallup Report* (217), October 1983.

2. James Stafford and Robert Lehner, *Houston Community Study* (Houston: Hearne Publishing, 1976), p. 34, as reported in James Stafford and Betsy Gelb, ''Who's More Critical of Business: Men or Women?'' *Business Horizons,* vol. 21, no. 1, p. 5.

3. ''Why People Gripe about Business,'' *U.S. News & World Report,* February 20, 1978, pp. 16–17.

4. *Fortune,* April 30, 1984, p. 276.

5. Data drawn from *Fortune,* May 2, 1983, p. 228; and *The World Bank Atlas* (Washington, D.C.: International Bank for Reconstruction and Development/The World Bank, 1985), pp. 6–9.

6. Samuel R. Reid, *The New Industrial Order* (New York: McGraw-Hill, 1976), pp. 11–12.

7. Peter Asch, *Industrial Organization and Antitrust Policy.* (New York: John Wiley & Sons, 1983), p. 162.

8. Charles Reich, *The Greening of America* (New York: Bantam Books, 1970), pp. 7–8.

9. ''Business Lobbying: Threat to the Consumer Interest,'' *Consumer Reports,* September 1978, as reported in *The Big Business Reader,* ed. Mark Green and Robert Massie (New York: The Pilgrim Press, 1980), pp. 253–54.

10. *Democratic Party of the United States* v. *National Conservative Political Action Committee,* 53 *Law Week* (4293) (3/19/85).

11. *New York Times,* December 4, 1978, p. D-8.

12. 98 S. Ct. 1407 (1978).

13. "Industry Fights Back—The Debate over Advocacy Advertising," *Saturday Review,* January 21, 1978, pp. 20–21.

14. Reich, *The Greening of America,* pp. 141–42.

15. Jack Magarell, *The Chronicle of Higher Education,* September 6, 1977, p. 7.

16. Richard Stengel, "Apostle of Sunny Thoughts," *Time,* March 18, 1985, p. 70.

17. Reich, *The Greening of America,* p. 115.

18. Ibid., pp. 93–95.

19. From *The Poetry of Robert Frost,* ed. Edward Connery Lathem. Copyright 1916; © 1969 by Holt, Rinehart and Winston. Copyright 1944 by Robert Frost. Reprinted by permission of Holt, Rinehart and Winston, Publishers.

20. Herman Kahn, "Self-Indulgence, Survival, and Space," *The Futurist,* October 1980, pp. 10–11.

21. Thomas Griffith, "Me First," *The Atlantic,* July 1980, p. 20.

22. *University of Iowa Spectator,* March 1980, p. 4.

23. Peter McCabe, "Vanity Fair," *Harper's Magazine,* August 1977, p. 83.

24. Peter Wynn, *Apples, History, Folklore, Horticulture and Gastronomy,* as reported by Joanee Will for the *Chicago Tribune* and reprinted in *The Lexington (Kentucky) Leader,* October 1, 1980, p. D-1.

25. "The Swing to Practicality in the B-Schools," *Business Week,* July 23, 1979, p. 190.

26. Ronnie Dugger, "The Counting House of Academe," *Harper's Magazine,* March 1974, p. 70.

27. Ted Peters, "The Future of Religion in a Post-Industrial Society," *The Futurist,* October 1980, pp. 20, 22.

28. Tom Uhlenbock for United Press International, "Citizens' Party Attributes America's Problems to Big Corporations," *The Lexington (Kentucky) Sunday Herald-Leader,* April 6, 1980.

29. Samuel Florman, "Small Is Dubious," *Harper's,* August 1977, pp. 10, 12.

30. "More Leisure in an Increasingly Electronic Society," *Business Week,* September 3, 1979, pp. 208, 212.

2

Capitalism and Collectivism

Part One—Introduction

Chapter 1 reviewed some of the criticisms of the corporate community that have, in part, spurred intensive government intervention in a business system that had been substantially committed to free market principles. With the problem thus in mind, we turn to the mechanisms available to regulate business behavior in the manner most compatible with societal interests. In this chapter we will explore the full range of the economic spectrum, moving from a laissez faire, free market approach on the extreme right, to an absolute command economy on the far left, and concluding with a left-center, communitarian program that might be labeled social democracy or market socialism.

The free market approach assumes that we can operate our business structure and our society at large, free of all but the most basic legal mechanisms such as contract and criminal law. The wisdom of the market—that is, our individual judgments, in combination with our individual consciences—would serve to "regulate" American life. Government regulatory agencies, occupational licensure, zoning restrictions, antitrust law, and all but the most basic government services (perhaps limited to the police, the courts, and the army) would be unnecessary.

On the other hand, the collectivist alternatives (communism, socialism, and their variations) pose the notion that the business community and society at large require more expansive government intervention than now characterizes the United States system. Individual judgment would be supplemented with or largely supplanted by the collective will. Ranging from a largely equalitarian, welfare state to a completely planned economy, the collectivist alternative reflects various degrees of faith in central authority and skepticism regarding independent action.

The intention of this chapter is to offer the student a genuine intellectual adventure. Students should suspend, to the degree possible, the biases, the lessons of cultural conditioning, that so effectively shape us all. Then the student will be free to objectively evaluate the economic systems that we may call into our service. One's pride in being an American should not prevent the serious contemplation of alternative economic strategies that have proven successful elsewhere. One is not a communist, fascist, or totalitarian in spirit merely for openly exploring and even advocating political economies other than our mixture of capitalism and state intervention. On balance, the United

States may well be following the path best suited to our needs, but if so, a spirited exploration of the alternatives will only serve to illuminate that truth.

Finally, this chapter should be read as a foundation of sorts for the study of law that is to follow. Once a society settles upon some broad political and economic principles, it then typically pours a thin veneer or many heavy coats (depending on the system chosen) of social control on that foundation to implement the goals of the larger system. The law serves as a primary method of social control. So, to understand the law we need to understand its roots.

Part Two—Capitalism

Foundations

We begin with a brief reminder of the ideological foundation of American capitalism. As noted, the law develops, in part, as a response to the governing economic system. That system is a product of society's values and philosophies. We need, therefore, to assess those values and philosophies to determine which economic system is most suitable to contemporary American society.

Although many intellectual forces have played a role in shaping American capitalism, this discussion will be limited to four themes of particular historical significance.

1. John Locke's Natural Right of Property. Locke, the brilliant English philosopher, provided in his *Two Treatises of Government* (1690) much of the intellectual underpinning of the Declaration of Independence and, thus, the course of American life. Locke argued that the rights of life, liberty, and property were natural to all humans. Those rights predated any notion of an organized society. Hence society's only control over those rights was to protect them. Locke's viewpoint was a powerful intellectual and moral argument for the establishment of industrial capitalism, in which private ownership of property and freedom from government restraint were vital.

2. Adam Smith and Laissez Faire. The publication in 1776 of Smith's *An Inquiry into the Nature and Cause of the Wealth of Nations* offered profound theoretical support to free market principles. Smith argued that the invisible hand of supply and demand would determine the price of goods. Competition would ensure the greatest good for the greatest number. Thus government should not interfere in the market system. Rather government should fulfill only those public services (defense, justice, public works, and the like) in which business cannot practically engage. He believed that government interference would only disturb the natural genius of the market.

3. Herbert Spencer and Social Darwinism. Charles Darwin's explorations of the origins of the species led him to the theory that all of life evolved through a process of natural selection, so that the strongest and the most fit survived. Spencer applied Darwin's survival of the fittest to the development of society. He argued that the more capable individuals would inevitably rise to influential positions. Government interference would only inhibit the natural selection process. So to the leaders of industry, Social Darwinism provided in the late 19th century an ideal rationale for their positions of extreme wealth and power.

4. Max Weber and the Protestant Ethic.   In his book *The Protestant Ethic and the Spirit of Capitalism,* Weber argued that Protestants, and particularly Calvinists, were moved by a religious philosophy that demanded a lifetime of disciplined effort in pursuit of good work. Salvation demanded productivity. The accumulation of worldly goods was material evidence of that productivity, but one's success was not to be squandered. Rather, it was to be reinvested to enhance the value of goods placed in human hands via God's grace. Thus hard work and thrift were moral responsibilities, and in turn, the accumulation and multiplication of worldly goods to be used for the good of mankind served to judge one's success in meeting God's expectations. The Protestant ethic was a powerful spur to and justification for capitalist enterprise.

So capitalism in America arose from rather noble, if debatable, intellectual premises, but capitalism also moved to the fore on the strength of promises to the people not afforded by any previous economic system. Irving Kristol summarized the hope offered by capitalism:

What did capitalism promise? First of all, it promised continued improvement in the material conditions of all its citizens, a promise without precedent in human history. Secondly, it promised an equally unprecedented measure of individual freedom for all of these same citizens. And lastly, it held out the promise that, amidst this prosperity and liberty, the individual could satisfy his instinct for self-perfection—for leading a virtuous life that satisfied the demands of his spirit (or, as one used to say, his soul)—and that the free exercise of such individual virtue would aggregate into a just society.[1]

Capitalism in Theory—Ayn Rand

Capitalism was built on a sound intellectual footing and was stimulated by the promise of unprecedented general welfare. These forces, in combination with America's resources and an astonishingly courageous and hardy population, led to the development of a powerful economic machine. But as we know, that machine, in the view of many Americans, ran for a time out of control. The era of the Robber Barons and abuses associated with them brought widespread popular sentiment for governmental restraints on capitalism. Thus as is discussed in subsequent chapters, America's substantially free market economy was, in increasing increments, placed under government regulation. Today ours is commonly labeled a *mixed economy.*

Our purpose now is to reconsider the merits of a purer form of capitalism. Did we turn too hastily from the market? Should we gradually shed our governmental role in economic affairs and restore our faith in the Invisible Hand? Or even if the market in a substantially pure form cannot practically be achieved and be relied on, may we not profit from a reminder of the nature of that system? Are at least some strides in that direction demanded? Can we, in large measure, do without regulation by law? Will a genuinely unfettered market better serve our needs than does our current amalgam of business restrained by government? To answer these questions we need a firm understanding of capitalism in a pure form that has almost entirely slipped from view. The very controversial philosopher Ayn Rand was an uncompromising advocate of free market principles. For example, it was her position that the necessary categories of government are only three in number: the police, the armed services, and the law courts. Via her philosophy of Objectivism, Miss Rand argued that the practice of free market principles is necessary to the pursuit of a rational, moral life. Miss Rand's viewpoint has been the subject of vigorous criticism. Its merits are for the reader to assess, but it is clearly fair to say that she was among America's most ardent and articulate apostles of a genuine free market.

MAN'S RIGHTS

Ayn Rand

If one wishes to advocate a free society—that is, capitalism—one must realize that its indispensable foundation is the principle of individual rights. If one wishes to uphold individual rights, one must realize that capitalism is the only system that can uphold and protect them. And if one wishes to gauge the relationship of freedom to the goals of today's intellectuals, one may gauge it by the fact that the concept of individual rights is evaded, distorted, perverted, and seldom discussed, most conspicuously seldom by the so-called "conservatives."

"Rights" are a moral concept—the concept that provides a logical transition from the principles guiding an individual's actions to the principles guiding his relationship with others—the concept that preserves and protects individual morality in a social context—the link between the moral code of a man and the legal code of a society, between ethics and politics. *Individual rights are the means of subordinating society to moral law.*

Every political system is based on some code of ethics. The dominant ethics of mankind's history were variants of the altruist-collectivist doctrine which subordinated the individual to some higher authority, either mystical or social. Consequently, most political systems were variants of the same statist tyranny, differing only in degree, not in basic principle, limited only by the accidents of tradition, of chaos, of bloody strife and periodic collapse. Under all such systems, morality was a code applicable to the individual, but not to society. Society was placed *outside* the moral law, as its embodiment or source or exclusive interpreter—and the inculcation of self-sacrificial devotion to social duty was regarded as the main purpose of ethics in man's earthly existence.

Since there is no such entity as "society," since society is only a number of individual men, this meant, in practice, that the rulers of society were exempt from moral law; subject only to traditional rituals, they held total power and exacted blind obedience—on the implicit principle of: "The good is that which is good for society (or for the tribe, the race, the nation), and the ruler's edicts are its voice on earth."

This was true of all statist systems, under all variants of the altruist-collectivist ethics, mystical or social. "The Divine Right of Kings" summarizes the political theory of the first—"*Vox populi, vox dei*" of the second. As witness: the theocracy of Egypt, with the Pharaoh as an embodied god—the unlimited majority rule or *democracy* of Athens—the welfare state run by the Emperors of Rome—the Inquisition of the late Middle Ages—the absolute monarchy of France—the welfare state of Bismarch's Prussia—the gas chambers of Nazi Germany—the slaughterhouse of the Soviet Union.

All these political systems were expressions of the altruist-collectivist ethics—and their common characteristic is the fact that society stood above the moral law, as an omnipotent, sovereign whim worshiper. Thus, politically, all these systems were variants of an *amoral* society.

The most profoundly revolutionary achievement of the United States of America was *the subordination of society to moral law*.

The principle of man's individual rights represented the extension of morality into the social system—as a limitation on the power of the state, as man's protection against the brute force of the collective, as the subordination of *might* to *right*. The United States was the first *moral* society in history.

All previous systems had regarded man as a sacrificial means to the ends of others, and society as an end in itself. The United States regarded man as an end in himself, and society as a means to the peaceful, orderly, *voluntary* coexistence of individuals. All previous systems had held that man's life belongs to society, that society can dispose of him in any way it pleases, and that any freedom he enjoys is his only by favor, by the *permission* of society, which may be revoked at any time. The United States held that man's life is his by *right* (which means: by moral principle and by his nature), that a right is the property of an individual, that society as such has no rights, and that the only moral purpose of a government is the protection of individual rights.

A "right" is a moral principle defining and sanctioning a man's freedom of action in a social context. There is only *one* fundamental right (all the others are its consequences or corollaries): a man's right to his own life. Life is a process of self-sustaining and self-generated action; the right to life means the right to engage in self-sustaining and self-generated action—which means: the freedom to take all the actions required by the nature of a rational being for the support, the furtherance, the ful-

fillment, and the enjoyment of his own life. . . .

America's inner contradiction was the altruist-collectivist ethics. Altruism is incompatible with freedom, with capitalism, and with individual rights. One cannot combine the pursuit of happiness with the moral status of a sacrificial animal.

It was the concept of individual rights that had given birth to a free society. It was with the destruction of individual rights that the destruction of freedom had to begin.

A collectivist tyranny dare not enslave a country by an outright confiscation of its values, material or moral. It has to be done by a process of internal corruption. Just as in the material realm the plundering of a country's wealth is accomplished by inflating the currency—so today one may witness the process of inflation being applied to the realm of rights. The process entails such a growth of newly promulgated "rights" that people do not notice the fact that the meaning of the concept is being reversed. Just as bad money drives out good money, so these "printing-press rights" negate authentic rights.

Consider the curious fact that never has there been such a proliferation, all over the world, of two contradictory phenomena: of alleged new "rights" and of slave-labor camps.

The "gimmick" was the switch of the concept of rights from the political to the economic realm.

The Democratic Party platform of 1960 summarizes the switch boldly and explicitly. It declares that a Democratic Administration "will reaffirm the economic bill of rights which Franklin Roosevelt wrote into our national conscience sixteen years ago."

Bear clearly in mind the meaning of the concept of *"rights"* when you read the list which that platform offers:

"1. The right to a useful and remunerative job in the industries or shops or farms or mines of the nation.

"2. The right to earn enough to provide adequate food and clothing and recreation.

"3. The right of every farmer to raise and

sell his products at a return which will give him and his family a decent living.

"4. The right of every businessman, large and small, to trade in an atmosphere of freedom from unfair competition and domination by monopolies at home and abroad.

"5. The right of every family to a decent home.

"6. The right to adequate medical care and the opportunity to achieve and enjoy good health.

"7. The right to adequate protection from the economic fears of old age, sickness, accidents and unemployment.

"8. The right to a good education."

A single question added to each of the above eight clauses would make the issue clear: *At whose expense?*

Jobs, food, clothing, recreation (!), homes, medical care, education, etc., do not grow in nature. These are man-made values—goods and services produced by men. *Who* is to provide them?

If some men are entitled *by right* to the products of the work of others, it means that those others are deprived of rights and condemned to slave labor.

Any alleged "right" of one man, which necessitates the violation of the rights of another, is not and cannot be a right.

No man can have a right to impose an unchosen obligation, an unrewarded duty or an involuntary servitude on another man. There can be no such thing as *"the right to enslave."*

A right does not include the material implementation of that right by other men; it includes only the freedom to earn that implementation by one's own effort.

Observe, in this context, the intellectual precision of the Founding Fathers: they spoke of the right to *the pursuit* of happiness—*not* of the right to happiness. It means that a man has the right to take the actions he deems necessary to achieve his happiness; it does *not* mean that others must make him happy. . . .

Property rights and the right of free trade are man's only "economic rights" (they are, in fact, *political* rights)—and there can be no such thing as "an *economic* bill of rights." But observe that the advocates of the latter have all but destroyed the former. . . .

And while people are clamoring about "economic rights," the concept of political rights is vanishing. It is forgotten that the right of free speech means the freedom to advocate one's views and to bear the possible consequences, including disagreement with others, opposition, unpopularity, and lack of support. The political function of "the right of free speech" is to protect dissenters and unpopular minorities from forcible suppression—*not* to guarantee them the support, advantages, and rewards of a popularity they have not gained. . . .

Such is the state of one of today's most crucial issues: *political* rights versus "*economic* rights." It's either-or. One destroys the other. But there are, in fact, no "economic rights," no "collective rights," no "public-interest rights." The term "individual rights" is a redundancy: there is no other kind of rights and no one else to possess them.

Those who advocate *laissez-faire* capitalism are the only advocates of man's rights.

Source: From *The Virtue of Selfishness* by Ayn Rand. Copyright © 1961, 1964 by Ayn Rand. Copyright © 1962, 1963, 1964 by The Objectivist Newsletter, Inc. Reprinted by arrangement with New American Library, New York, New York, and with permission of the Estate of Ayn Rand.

Capitalism in Practice—Hong Kong

A free market society of the purity advocated by Miss Rand does not now exist and perhaps never did, but history does reveal many instances of successful societies much more thoroughly capitalistic than contemporary America (e.g., the Greek island of Delos, 169–166 B.C.; Gibraltar, 1704-1978; Singapore, 1819–1957; Great Britain and the

United States, the 19th century; and colonial New South Wales, Australia, 1870–1900).[2] Currently, one outpost of capitalism remains. Hong Kong, a small British Crown Colony on the southeast coast of China, has enjoyed remarkable growth and prosperity in a free market environment. Taxes are at a modest level, and government does play an important role in social services, but nonintervention is clearly at the heart of economic policy.

Hong King is unique. Its history, its geographical circumstances, and the nature of its people all contribute to Hong Kong's special affection for private enterprise. Its virtual absence of internal resources and consequent dependence on foreign trade strictly limit the government's intervention options. As the following reading suggests, Hong Kong is not without problems, but the colony represents impressive evidence that capitalism can work even in the era of the welfare state. (At this writing, Hong Kong's future as a capitalist enclave is in doubt. Great Britain and China have reached agreement on the terms for Hong Kong's passage from the British Empire to a new role as part of mainland China. The change will take effect in 1997, and China has promised to allow Hong Kong to maintain its capitalist system for 50 years thereafter.)

HONG KONG—A STUDY IN ECONOMIC FREEDOM

Alvin Rabushka

I submit that Hong Kong, among the world's more than 130 countries, most closely resembles the textbook model of a competitive market economy, encumbered only with the barest overlay of government. It is in this context that we should meet the pure form of *homo economicus*. His given name is *homo Hongkongus*.

Hong Kong man's first and most telling characteristic is his single-minded pursuit of making money. A companion characteristic is his emphasis on the material things in life. Hong Kong's free port, free trade economy offers for sale the latest in fashions, furnishings, food-stuffs, appliances, motor cars, gadgets, stereos—portable stereos, built-in stereos, automobile stereos, any and every conceivable brand and model of stereo at tax-free prices. If there is a new breakthrough in stereo goods to sell, some Hong Kong entrepreneur will be selling it that night. Tomorrow would mean foregone profits.

Material consumption and making money, or making money and worldly goods is what

life in Hong Kong is all about. The desire to acquire and accumulate as much money as possible in the shortest period of time: in Hong Kong, taxes do not discourage hard work. It so happens that I spent 29 August 1976, a pleasant enough Sunday, wandering about a very quiet London. What a sharp contrast it was to 5 December 1976, the Sunday I spent fighting the masses of Hong Kong for a space in the restaurants and stores. London was literally deserted and its citizens were clearly neither making nor spending money. Not so in Hong Kong. *Homo Hongkongus* works a 12- to 16-hour day, 7 days a week, almost 365 days a year—only Chinese New Year interrupts an otherwise single-minded obsession for making money. And Hong Kong's prosperous residents and overseas visitors have plenty of money to spend. I reckon there are more jewelry stores, good restaurants, and fasionable shops in Hong Kong's crowded streets than in any other city in the world—and why not, when the tax-free prices are taken into account. If economic man symbolizes competitive capitalism, he is alive, prosperous, and delightfully happy in Hong Kong. A quick glance across the border finds more than 800 million of his countrymen who ostensibly labor for love of ideology, not money or materialism.

Surely all is not well in Hong Kong. Would not a carefully designed survey of public opinion cast grave doubts on the soul of Hong Kong man. It would, of course, if we only interviewed the intellectuals, being absolutely careful not to talk with the ordinary working men and women. You see, apart from a few jobs in the universities and higher institutions of art and culture, the services of the literati are not in high demand. Indeed, the amount of high culture that Hong Kong's 4.5 million people demand is patently suboptimal, that is, it is less than most Western middle class intellectuals, who are used to having their cultural tastes subsidized, would like. Higher education in Hong Kong is, for the most part, a path to self-improvement; if it civilizes in the process, well, OK.

Hong Kong offers a limited cultural menu of art, music, and drama. Its critics call it a cultural desert and accuse it, correctly, of being an oversized bazaar. Hong Kong offers, in truth, exactly what the market will bear. When intellectuals complain about the lack of finer things in Hong Kong they are complaining, it seems to me, of three things: first, a limited demand for their services with corresponding low incomes; second, a failure of their fellow men (who are certainly less sophisticated and therefore need cultural tutelage) to share their tastes; and third, the government's unwillingness to subsidize their tastes at community expense, perhaps the gravest failing of the capitalist economy.

Dare I reveal my boorishness by saying that I find Hong Kong's economic hustle and bustle more interesting, entertaining, and liberating than its lack of high opera, music, and drama? East has indeed met West in the market economy. Chinese and Europeans in Hong Kong have no time for racial quarrels, which would only interfere with making money. The prospect of individual gain in the marketplace makes group activity for political gain unnecessary—the market economy is truly color-blind. Even harmony among ideological enemies lives in Hong Kong. The Hong Kong Hilton stands right across the street from the Bank of China.

There is simply no more exciting city on the face of the earth than Hong Kong—in large measure because it is the most robust bastion of free-wheeling capitalism. It may be, as is true of all human institutions, imperfect. I have previously criticized the Hong Kong government for its tendencies to increase spending on social programs, but can you name any other country which in 1976 enjoyed 18 percent real growth and only 3.4 percent inflation?

Source: *Hong Kong—A Study in Economic Freedom* (Chicago: University of Chicago Press, 1979), pp. 83–86. Reprinted with permission of the copyright holder, Alvin Rabushka.

Capitalism in Practice—the American Experience

It is often argued that capitalism forms a tight, rational argument on paper, but in practice the theory breaks down. Examples like that of Hong Kong are written off as anomalies born of special circumstances, such as Hong Kong's limited geographic dimensions. The article that follows suggests that contemporary America might profit from a rededication to capitalist principles. The point to recognize is the free market argument that virtually all services now performed by the government may be more efficiently and more equitably "managed" by the impersonal forces of the market.

WANT TO BUY A FIRE DEPT.?

Newton, Mass., is out of the ambulance business now. The prosperous Boston suburb used to spend a small fortune every year to provide the service, and its budget groaned under the load in an era of recession. Then Chaulk Ambulance Service made the town an offer it couldn't refuse: the private company would provide the service at no cost to the city. A year later service has improved—there are three rescue units instead of two, the employees are better trained, and Newton has the only 24-hour full paramedical service in the state. Chaulk is already breaking even, and Newton has saved nearly $500,000 to date. "We are very satisfied," says Police Chief William F. Quinn. "Economically, it was a real boost for the city"—such a boost, in fact, that Newton now plans to get out of the garbage business, too.

In cities across the country public services are going private. Faced with shrinking revenues and rising prices, local governments are increasingly turning to businessmen to provide fire and police protection, collect garbage, run airports, and operate libraries. "We call it creeping capitalism," says Louis Witzeman, the chairman of the Rural/Metro Fire Department, which serves half a million people in Arizona—one fifth of the state's population—and 100,000 more in Tennessee. "We're promoting free enterprise." Private companies say they do the work more cheaply than governments, which save money immediately by trimming their payrolls and save money for the future by keeping down soaring pension costs. The increasing "privatization" is sparking objections from unions and some liberal urban planners, but the trend has now gone so far that, in both San Jose, California, and Atlanta, city hall is for sale.

Cutting Payrolls

The most common form of privatization is to make contracts with private businesses to perform city functions. State and local governments spent $27.4 billion on services from the private sector in 1975, more than doubled that to $66.8 billion in 1980—and are contracting out more all the time. Watertown, Massachusetts, hired private companies to pick up garbage, clean streets, remove trees, and tend the cemeteries, helping to reduce the public-works payroll from 150 employees to just 55. Los Angeles says it has saved nearly $30 million and eliminated 1,447 public jobs in five years by contracting out. The state of Vermont lets just about everything out to contract and has a payroll of only 7,000 employees.

There is a new wrinkle in privatization, though: some cities simply stop providing some services, and allow profit-minded entrepreneurs to take their place, unencumbered by municipal unions, interest groups, and politicians. In Newton, Chaulk Ambulance Service expects to turn a profit next year. It is charging clients about $10 more per trip than the city used to, and its expenses are far lower: unlike the city, Chaulk *has* to keep its costs down and aggressively collect its debts as well.

Free Enterprise

Rural Grants Pass, Ore. (population: 15,000), takes privatization another step: in that 250-square-mile area, two private fire departments compete for business. Bertha Miller's Grants Pass Rural Fire Department, founded about 25 years ago, is battling Phil Turnbull's Valley Fire Service. "This gives people freedom of choice." says Turnbull, 26, a self-proclaimed champion of free enterprise who raised $100,000 to start the company in 1979 and grossed $400,000 last year. Both businesses rely on paid subscribers: Miller charges a flat $40 per home or business, Turnbull $2.15 per $1,000 of market value. Both companies will not only put out fires for subscribers but also rescue their cats from trees. And both will put out fires at nonsubscribers' homes, then send a bill ($150 per fire-engine hour and $10 per fire fighter hour). Miller won't talk about earnings, but Valley Fire has done well enough to be planning its fourth fire station. Most everyone in town except Miller says competition has improved service substantially—and better service means lower rates for fire insurance.

Lease-Backs
Privatization is spreading from government services to a growing number of government buildings. Many cities are selling municipal offices in complex sale-lease transactions in order to get a quick infusion of cash. The private buyers use the buildings for a number of tax advantages, such as depreciation allowances and investment tax credits. The local government then leases back its own space. Oakland, Calif., sold its museum and auditorium for $55 million. Berkeley's city council will consider this week whether to sell the civic center, a city garage, several public libraries, a refuse-disposal facility, and a senior-citizens' center.

All this private-sector fever raises serious questions. Profit-making businesses are hardly likely to be sensitive to the problems of the poor. "Government is in the business of providing service without economic motivation," says Mark Ferber, an investment banker and former budget director of the Massachusetts Legislature. If the trend continues, he says, "Who will subsidize the acutely ill patient? Who will give door-to-door mail service?" Powerful unions such as the American Federation of State, County and Municipal Employees say privatization makes employees less accountable to the public. AFSCME research director Linda Lampkin keeps a long list of unsuccessful contracting, such as New York City's discovery that it could save $575,000 a year by canceling several printing and custodial contracts and doing the jobs itself. "There is no clear-cut evidence that contracting out is cheaper," she says.

Second Thoughts
Reminderville and Twinsburg agree. Two years ago the neighboring Ohio towns hired a private security firm, Corporate Security Inc., to provide police protection. As promised, the company supplied two police cars, but they were well-worn old battleships—which may have been good for the firm's balance sheets but was bad for the towns' self-image. Now the cities are planning to fire the company, hire the guards, and set up their own force. "One guy is trying to make a profit and the village is trying to get the most amount of service," says Dayton E. Brannon, the chief of police—and a Corporate Security Inc. employee. "Quite simply, those two goals clash." As private industry creeps into more crucial areas of public protection such as firefighting and police work, the issue will be whether that's really any place for profit.

Source: *Newsweek*, April 25, 1983, pp. 55–56. Reprinted with permission of the copyright holder, Newsweek, Inc.

QUESTIONS

1. Capitalism's philosophical roots lie largely in the views of Locke, Smith, Spencer, and Weber.
   a. Do those views continue to explain our reliance on capitalism?
   b. If so, does our drift away from the free market suggest a flaw in that philosophical foundation?
   c. If not, can you suggest other doctrines or ethics that better explain our contemporary economic philosophy?
2. From the capitalist viewpoint, why is the private ownership of property necessary to the preservation of freedom?

3. Ayn Rand argued: "Altruism is incompatible with freedom, with capitalism, and with individual rights."
   a. Define altruism.
   b. Explain why Miss Rand rejected altruism.
4. In describing life in Hong Kong, Alvin Rabushka praises the "single-minded pursuit of making money" and the "emphasis on the material things in life." Rabushka admits to finding "Hong Kong's economic hustle and bustle more interesting, entertaining, and liberating than its lack of high opera, music, and drama."

a. Although it is often criticized in America, is materialism the most certain and most interesting path to personal happiness?

b. Would "sophisticated" culture (such as opera and drama) substantially disappear in America without government support?

c. If so, how may we justify that support? If not, how may we justify that support?

5. Assume the federal government removed itself from the purchase and maintenance of its parks.

a. Left to the private sector, what sorts of parks would develop under the profit incentive?

b. Would Yellowstone, for example, survive in substantially its present state?

c. How can it be argued that the federal parks are an unethical, undemocratic expropriation of private resources?

6. Assume the abolition of the federal Food and Drug Administration. How would the free market protect the citizenry from dangerous food and drug products?

7. Should education be returned to the free market? Explain. How would the poor finance a private sector education?

8. Scholar Amitai Etzioni argues that America must choose between rededication to economic growth and emphasis on a quality-of-life society (slower growth, emphasis on ecology, concern for safety, harmony with oneself and others). He argues that the monetary costs and the social-psychic strains of pursuing these two divergent courses exceed America's resources, both physical and emotional.

a. Do you agree with Etzioni?

b. Which path would you choose?

c. Will the market support the quality-of-life approach?

9. Puritan leaders felt concern over the morality of merchants selling goods for "more than their worth." That concern was particularly grave when the goods were scarce or in great demand.

a. Should our society develop an ethic wherein goods are to be sold only "for what they are worth"?

b. Can a seller make an accurate determination of worth?

c. Does a product's worth differ from the price that product will bring in the marketplace?

d. Personalize the inquiry: Assume you seek to sell your Chevette auto for $2,000. Assume you know of several identical Chevettes in a similar state of repair that can be purchased for $1,800. Assume you find a buyer at $2,000. Will you unilaterally lower your price or direct the purchaser to the other autos?

e. If not, have you acted justly?

10. Critics of our capitalist system contend that ability and effort often are less responsible for one's success than "unearned" factors such as family background, social class, luck, and willingness to cheat. Do you agree? Explain.

11. Commentator Irving Kristol asked whether it was "just" for Ray Kroc (now deceased, formerly of McDonald's) to have made so much money by merely figuring out a new way to sell hamburgers. He concluded that capitalism says it is just because he sold a good product; people want it; it is fair.

a. Do you agree with Kristol?

b. Does contemporary American capitalism offer excessive rewards to those clever enough to build near-term paper profits (lawyers, accountants, financial analysts) through mergers, tax writeoffs, and the like while diverting scarce resources from long-term productive ventures (such as new product development or more efficient production processes)?

c. If so, is capitalism fatally flawed?

12. Professor Robert E. Lane argued that the person who is motivated by needs for affiliation rather than by needs for achievement, does less well in the market. Such

a person is not rewarded so well as autonomous, achievement-oriented people.

a. Is Lane correct? Explain.

b. Is capitalism, in the long term, destructive of societal welfare in that achievement is better rewarded than is affiliation? Explain.

13. Salado, Texas (a town between Dallas and Austin), once down to a population of just 250 people and by-passed by I–35, is now enjoying a renaissance, including 1,000 to 1,500 people and seven housing developments.[3] The old native stone buildings beside the creek were converted to shops and galleries. Despite its growth Salado has declined to assume the legal status of a city. No taxes are collected. No officials are elected. Rather, an annual art festival is used to raise money for services like street sweeping. Is Salado's free market approach the key to rejuvenating America? Explain.

14. Is capitalism compatible with social justice? Irving Kristol, a firm defender of capitalism, says the answer is no. Why would an ardent defender of the free market take that position?

15. Explore the argument that the federal highway program, although well-intentioned, was merely one in a series of federal interventions that distorted the market leading, in this instance, to the long-term decline of inner cities.

16. How would the poor be cared for in a free market society?

Part Three—Collectivism

The term *collectivism* embraces various economic philosophies on the left of the political-economic spectrum; that is principally, communism and socialism. Capitalism is characterized by economic individualism. On the other hand, communism and the various styles of socialism are characterized by economic cooperation.

Communism

The Marxist-Leninist doctrine generally referred to as *communism* is, in theory, the purest form of collectivism. Like the genuine free market model discussed previously, no unadulterated collectivist economy (with the possible exception of Albania) is currently operative. Still, the Soviet Union, China, and many eastern European nations take a predominantly collectivist approach to economics and adhere to the primary tenets of communist political ideology. Karl Marx took an economic view of history. He saw the production and exchange of goods and services as the foundation for all social processes, upon which culture, law, and government are built. Thus, ownership of the means of production is the key to the entire character of the society. Marx found capitalism immoral, unjust, and humanly degrading. Workers, he argued, receive only subsistence wages and are debased in that the market converts their labor into a commodity. Marx believed that all value stems from labor, and, therefore, only labor should receive income. Thus, Marx was enraged by what he took to be capitalist oppression of the masses. To him the wealthy were literally a ruling class. In the *Communist Manifesto* Marx took the position that violent revolution is the only feasible means of changing the social order. The owners of the means of production (the bourgeoisie) will not freely give up their control over a system they sincerely believe to be best. Thus the class war is seen as the only way out of oppression.

Marx felt that capitalism was doomed by an inherent developmental imbalance. He argued that the "forces of production" (technology, science, know-how) grow more rapidly than the "relations of production" (social institutions: that is, law, monetary systems, private property arrangements). Thus, existing capitalist institutions would block the full, creative growth of the forces of production. His solution was public ownership of the means of production. Then productivity would not be limited by the faulty mechanisms of private ownership and profit.[4] This notion should be intriguing to us today, since it is evident to all that our technological capacity (such as nuclear weapons) has run substantially in advance of our facility in dealing with those innovations. Was Marx correct and yet incorrect? Or is the full picture yet to emerge?

Communism, of course, calls for a planned economy. Theoretically, private ownership of the means of production is abolished. In practice, vestiges and, in some instances, large segments of free enterprise remain in all the communist states. The state owns the land and resources, provides for the needs of all the citizens, and controls prices and supplies. The market mechanism is replaced with central decisions regarding production levels, distribution, and so on. The ultimate aim of the system is that of a classless society controlled by all of the people.

Socialism

The distinctions between communism and socialism are not entirely clear. To some socialism is the public ownership of the sources of production (such as land, minerals, and factories), while communism is the public ownership of virtually the totality of the wealth. To others socialism and communism have similar economic roots but differ as to political direction. Historically, socialism has been associated with democratic governments and peaceful change, while communism has been characterized by totalitarianism and violent revolution. The meaning of socialism has been further obscured by those who label as socialist almost every government intervention in the private sector, even though those interventions involve no element of public ownership of the means of production.[5]

Socialism in its many forms aims to retain the benefits of industrialism while abolishing the social costs often accompanying the free market. In the contemporary Western world, Norway, Denmark, Sweden, France (early in the Mitterrand era), and Great Britain (prior to Prime Minister Thatcher) are nations where socialist principles have assumed a significant presence. Nationalization is limited to only the most vital industries, such as steel, coal mining, power generation, and transportation. While nationalization may be relatively uncommon, the government is likely to be directly involved in regulating growth, inflation, and unemployment.

Collectivist Goals

A critical distinction between collectivists and capitalists is that the former believe that a society's broad directions should be carefully planned rather than being left to what some take to be the whimsy of the market. Collectivists look upon planning and government intervention as positive forces necessary to the shaping of a higher life for all.

We can identify a series of goals that characterize the general agenda of collectivism whether communist, socialist, or some variant:

1. Human Liberty.   To the capitalist, collectivism appears to harshly restrain individual freedom. To the collectivist, the freedoms of capitalism are largely an illusion, accessible only to the prosperous and powerful. Collectivists lament wage slavery and exploitation of workers by owners. Work is not an act of free will sought for fulfillment, but rather forced labor required for survival in a competitive, capitalist society designed for the welfare of the few. To the collectivist, one can hardly enjoy the meaningful, higher order freedoms of self-fulfillment, community, and love when restrained by the necessity to sustain oneself for the primary benefit of another.

2. Economic Development.   Collectivists feel that the economy must be directed toward the general interest rather than being left free to multiply the welfare of successful capitalists. The market is regarded as wasteful, unfair, and based on accidents of luck and heritage. Thus, collectivists argue for central planning or controls to achieve growth, more equitable distribution of goods, and more socially useful production.

3. General Welfare.   Collectivist states seek to ensure adequate health, education, and general human services for all citizens. Free education, free health care, generous sick pay, family planning, and alcoholism programs are illustrative of the cradle-to-grave care that characterizes most collectivist states.

Similarly, strenuous efforts are employed to modify the alienation that is said to be characteristic of capitalist economies. Marx argued that capitalist industrialism alienated (separated) workers from their work, the things produced, their employers, their coworkers, and themselves. He contended that capitalist workers were mere commodities working for the profit of others. Marx extended the analysis by contending that money converts love, friendship, and the entire course of human caring into a monetary relationship. In general, Marx took a profoundly humanist posture in pursuing self-actualization through a cooperative, loving society. Marx himself later appears to have abandoned these directions, but their preeminence in collectivist thought is clear.

4. Equality.   Class distinctions are anathema to the collectivist. Equalitarianism is elevated to the level of a moral precept. Marx expressed the economics of equalitarianism in the powerful aphorism ''from each according to his ability, to each according to his needs.'' All humans are equally meritorious, and distinctions among them are inherently unjust. This is not to say that collectivists close their eyes to the reality of differentials in natural gifts. Some obviously will contribute more than others, but so far as is possible, distinctions based on individual achievement are to be muted. Thus what are taken to be invidious divisions born of capitalism's competitive excesses are to be extinguished.

The Command Economy

Collectivism in its pure and most extreme form, a complete command economy unleavened by free market forces, does not exist. But many economies, including those of the Soviet Union, China, and some of the eastern European communist nations, already fall preponderantly in the command economy mode. Of course, in recent years the Chinese have made a rather dramatic shift toward free market practices.

In a command economy, those basic economic decisions that America leaves to the market are resolved by the government. Production targets, growth rates, distribution of income, and allocation of resources are all established by central planners. The state owns the means of production and most of the property. Salaries of all producers are established by the state. All of this is accomplished via an intricately organized, multitiered bureaucracy capable of developing the plans and ensuring their implementation.

Since its revolution in 1917, the Soviet Union has been the most successful and most durable contemporary command economy. The totalitarian nature of Soviet policies, the continuing Cold War, and our visceral disapproval of communism retards Americans' ability to objectively evaluate the strengths and weaknesses of the Soviet command economy. Scholarly evaluation suggests that the Soviet economic record, while mixed, reveals some significant strengths in the central planning approach. Consider the assessment (paraphrased) of economist Richard Gill.

1. The command system is workable. From 1913 to 1965 the total output of the USSR grew more rapidly than that of the United States. For example, U.S. GNP from 1953–65 grew at an annual average rate of 3.3 percent, while that of Russia grew at 6.1 percent. Clearly Russia was in a catch-up phase and other less developed countries have grown more rapidly. But the point is that a command economy is workable.

2. In certain respects a command economy has advantages over the free market. A planned economy can be directed to a specific target. The USSR has sought a high rate of growth. In the past, by placing perhaps one third of their output into investment, as opposed to the one-fifth ratio of the United States, the Soviets have been able, via their command mechanism, to quickly and effectively strengthen capital goods and thus their production future.

3. The command economy has some weaknesses. Problems of coordination, organization, incentives, and efficiency are clear. In recent years the USSR has increasingly accepted elements of the free market within its system. Consumer goods and agricultural production have been inadequate. And of course, the entire system relies on political coercion.[6]

We see then that the command approach is not to be dismissed out of hand.

The Law and the Communist State

The following material offers a summary view of the Chinese legal system during Chairman Mao's later years and immediately following his death. Since Mao's passing in 1976, China has altered its legal system to assume a more nearly Western mode. Clearly the rabid anticapitalist mentality of the Mao era has subsided. That state of change renders contemporary China a volatile model of collectivist thought. A look back at Chairman Mao's approach both to the law and to his principles for organizing society offers a striking and instructive contrast to the American approaches.

People's Law in China

From May 8 to 24, 1977, 18 Americans, led by Detroit Recorder's Court Judge George Crockett, toured the People's Republic of China. Most, but not all, of the participants were black judges and lawyers. None was an expert on China. . . . The main purpose of their journey was to see the Chinese justice system in action.

THE TRIAL OF RAN KAO–CHIEN

Mary Johnson Lowe

The Chinese legal system mirrors the cultural, political, and ethical imperatives of the people of China—a fusion of Maoist thought and traditional Chinese pragmatism. During our group's brief but intense observation of Chinese legal institutions in action—and especially during the criminal trial you are about to read in transcript form—we had to constantly resist the often unconscious tendency to measure the new and the strange by the old and the comfortable.

The Chinese do not believe there are two legitimate sides to every issue. They believe there is only a right and wrong side. The right side can be determined by applying Chairman Mao's Sixteen Chinese Characters for dispute resolution. They are:

1. Investigate and study.
2. Settle the dispute on the spot (the area in which it arose).
3. Rely on the masses.
4. Mediate by application of the principles of Mao.

Thus, when a crime has been committed, the Revolutionary Committee of the commune or neighborhood association—consisting only of Communist Party members—goes to the scene and investigates. When the investigation targets a suspect, he or she is subjected to a "struggle session." The suspect is confronted with the results of the investigation, and is asked to give an explanation. The accused responds by stating that he is innocent or admitting guilt. He or she may be assisted by relatives or friends. Presided over by members of the Revolutionary Committee with other community members participating, the struggle session is usually held in the community room of the commune and is informal in tone.

The evidentiary, constitutional, and procedural hurdles that we in the American system are used to are almost nonexistent. Witnesses are merely asked to come forward and "tell what you know." This telling may involve hearsay, conclusions, opinion, or direct evidence; all are equally admissible. The Chinese believe that when witnesses tell their story in their own words, the masses listening to the testimony will be able to arrive at a correct assessment of the event.

If the accused admits guilt or is found guilty by a consensus of the people attending, he or she is turned over to the masses for punishment. They "struggle with the criminal" to find out why he or she resorted to criminal conduct and how to prevent future criminal acts. The people then fashion a remedy that is in the best interests of the community.

If the accused denies guilt, or admits guilt and the crime is deemed serious, he or she is held for trial by the People's Court. This is the court of original trial jurisdiction and is held in the commune or neighborhood or factory where the accused lives or works. It was this court that our group was invited to visit last May 12.

Shortly after 8 A.M., our group and a group of Japanese lawyers assembled in a large conference room of the Printing House of the People's Fine Arts Press in Peking. Chung We-shei, vice president of the People's Higher Court of Peking, told us that the case we had come to witness would be prosecuted by the Peking Public Security Bureau. The defendant, he said, was Ran Kao-chien, a 22-year-old worker in the printing house. An aide read the indictment:

"At 9:00 P.M. on November 2, 1976, the defendant stole a car, license number 1212, from in front of a hotel. He drove the car from north to south. When he came to the traffic light, he knocked down a woman cyclist coming from work. The bike of the woman worker was broken. After he knocked down the worker, he ran the car into a telephone pole. The car was damaged. The defendant attempted to escape. At this time he was caught on the spot by people who came forth."

We were then ushered into a room about 25 by 40 feet. At one end was a platform on which stood a long table flanked by two smaller tables. The rest of the room was filled with rows of chairs. We were given seats which had earphones for simultaneous translation. After everyone was seated, two police officers in white uniforms marched in followed by two women and a man. They took seats at the center table. The judge, Comrade Wong Teng, sat in the middle; to her left was Liu Onfung, cadre in charge of political work at the Fine Arts Press, and to her right was Nien Che-hun, a worker in the printing house. The latter two were called people's assessors. The recorder (court reporter) entered, followed by two prosecutors from the Security Bureau. The prosecutors sat at the small table to the right and two advocates sat at the table to the left. The advocates were not lawyers but had been asked by the defendant to represent him. They were Cheng Ching-chin, deputy workshop director of the Fine Arts Press, and Chen Sho-bi, a worker at the factory.

At 9 A.M. sharp the recorder announced: "Today the People's Intermediate Court of Peking is open. Bring the defendant in." A third police officer dressed in white entered with the defendant, whose head was bowed as he walked the 40 feet to the platform and stood before the judge. [Testimony followed. The defendant confessed to criminal conduct.—ed.]

Prosecutor: Judge, assessors, today I prosecute according to the investigation of the court and the confession of the defendant. This criminal confessed. Now we deliver our prosecution to this court according to the eight articles of the Constitution. . . .

Advocate: Judge, assessors, we join in the trial of the defendant. After being assigned we talked to the criminal and studied the case. Now we have no suspicion of the case stated by the prosecutor. But we have other things to say to the court.

The defendant is a first offender. He is a young man. We hope the court will give leniency. He confessed and now knows the root cause of his ideological deficiency. According to the outcome, no person was seriously injured.

The defendant was influenced by the Gang of Four who preached anarchism. The defendant was born out of a worker's family. These conditions should be taken into consideration. . . .

Judge: Now we will start mass criticism and analysis. Defendant, turn around and accept criticism. (*Defendant turns and faces the audience with his head still bowed.*)

Man from audience: Your crime is great. This case has caused indignation among the masses of the people. I think we should give punishment for this crime. This city is where the party headquarters is located. It is a highly populated city. Your behavior is a manifestation of the influence of the Gang of Four. The court should fix the defendant's responsibility in accordance with law. . . . [Others from the audience criticized the defendant.—ed.]

Judge: Now for analysis and criticism. (*Addressing the defendant*) Turn around. (*Defendant turns to face the judge.*) Today the people analyzed and criticized your case. Now you must give your attitude.

Defendant: I have committed serious crimes against the people. The people gave me severe criticism and woke me up. My transformation would be helped by studying the works of Marx and Engels. My behavior has proven I was seriously corrupted by counterrevolutionaries and the Gang of Four. Serious mistakes in my ideology, which were not corrected, led me to commit a crime. I now realize I made a severe crime against the government and the people. I let the revolution down. I let down our great leader, Chairman Mao, who had great expectations of revolutionary youth.

I will accept the judgment of the people and the court and repent and try to make my way back as a revolutionary youth. That is all.

Judge: Take the defendant out. (*Defendant is led from the room.*) Now the court canvasses opinions from the people. You have heard all of the proceedings. I will hear your opinions and suggestions for the judgment.

First man: He should be severely punished. Harsh judgment must be given: three years in prison so as to guard the safety of the people.

Second man: The defendant should be punished, but he is a first offender. According to Chairman Mao's teaching, one year imprisonment outside jail, doing labor or farm work, would transform his outlook.

Third man: He should have two years in prison. He is not too young to know what he did. He committed a severe crime, he should have severe punishment.

Woman: I think one year in prison would teach him he did wrong to the people of the factory and the revolution.

Fourth man: He is sorry. I think he could be educated. He should be able to come back to the factory, and I would give him no sentence. We should put stress on education. The leadership of the proletariat should be combined with the dictatorship of the people.

Second woman: I stand for this.

Fifth man: I suggest that you put him at the convenience of the workers of the factory. But two years should be given him because of the influence of the Gang of Four. He must be transformed.

Judge: According to your opinions, you believe punishment must be given. The crime was very serious. So we bring him in for judgment. Most of you think his attitude was good. The outcome of the accident was not serious.

Do you think that two years in prison and putting him under the care of the workers in the factory is sufficient? Do you workers believe you can transform him?

Many in audience: Yes. . . . [The defendant was returned to the courtroom.—ed.]

Judge: The court holds that this defendant deliberately stole the car and violated the law. The defendant confessed and showed willingness to repent. According to our policy of leniency to those who confess and harsh treatment to those who resist, you are sentenced to two years of imprisonment and suspension of sentence while you are transformed through labor and study of the works of Chairman Mao. You are under the supervision and direction of the Revolutionary Committee of this factory.

If you are not satisfied with this judgment, you may appeal within 10 days after you receive a written copy of the judgment by filing two copies of your appeal with the People's Higher Court of Peking. Take the defendant away.

Source: *Juris Doctor*, April 1978, p. 12. Reprinted with permission of the copyright holder, Mary Johnson Lowe.

ON THE CORRECT HANDLING OF CONTRADICTIONS

Harold E. Pepinsky

The most remarkable thing about the Peking trial of Ran Kao-chien is that it took place at all. From all accounts, street crime is extremely rare in China today, even in large cities. If a Chinese were to try to commit a street crime in a strange neighborhood, he or she would be readily detected. Similarly, the life of the average Chinese would be too public for him or her to do anything untoward in a home neighborhood or in a working environment.

On its face, this method of social control may seem oppressive to Americans. But in exchange for the relative lack of privacy the Chinese seem to have, they enjoy a sense of security—the security of knowing that those they live and work with will help them through

even the most serious problems without abandoning them or sending them away.

If there is a conflict between citizens, the Chinese do not turn to a centralized legal structure as we do. Instead, they rely primarily on friends, neighbors, and co-workers of those involved to resolve the dispute. The whole Chinese legal system rests on the foundation of community.

The sense that each individual is an important part of a stable, ongoing community is emphasized to Chinese at an early age. Young people expect to work at the same job as long as they are physically able. They settle into their jobs and take time to find politically congenial spouses. Once a couple does marry, they expect to remain in one residence for a lifetime. The family is the basic social unit, and the old and infirm are cared for at home. Even in big cities, three generations commonly live together.

At work and at home, the Chinese are organized into groups and committees. Work groups meet about ten hours each week to discuss political issues and to resolve personal problems through "criticism and struggle." This is where marital problems would typically be discussed and resolved, for husbands and wives are encouraged to work together. Most neighborhood problems are handled at the basic level of the block committee, but more serious disputes including crime are taken to the lane committee or, in a few cases, to the neighborhood committee.

In the rare instances in which work or neighborhood groups cannot resolve a dispute, the leaders of a group can turn to mediation committees or ultimately take the initiative in calling in the police (public security officers) and judges to help them. These officials of state intervene only when they are invited to do so, and then instead of taking disputants out into courts, the judge comes and holds court in the meeting place of the group or committee.

Following the Soviet model, a judge will sit with a couple of "people's assessors," members of the committee or group who outnumber the judge and share her or his authority to guide the proceedings and arrive at terms of settlement. Anyone from "the masses" with whom the defendant works or lives is to be given the opportunity to "discuss and criticize" the defendant's position in the case. . . .

The distinction between civil and criminal wrongs means little to the Chinese, who figure that if any matter is serious enough to come before a court, it is of general social concern. . . .

They will . . . go to great lengths to try to arrange for group members to take responsibility for reeducating the culprit. This reeducation would take the form of regular sessions in which the defendant would have to write essays relating ideological works like those of Chairman Mao to his or her own situation, to be criticized, and to criticize his or her own thinking about life. The Chinese believe that once a person's thinking has been corrected, correct behavior will follow. Two years is an exceptionally long time for this process to take place, and reflects the seriousness of the offense in the Peking trial.

As a consequence of Chinese reluctance to take persons out of their home communities, the Chinese may well have the lowest incarceration rate in the world. . . .

The Chinese Communists not only disdain written law, but resist bureaucratization of the legal process as well. Instead of specializing functions of legal bureaucrats, the party is generalizing and simplifying the division of labor. Lawyers virtually disappeared from China by 1960. Now, as in the Peking trial, advocates for the defendant are lay members of his group. . . .

Source: *Juris Doctor*, April 1978, p. 16. Reprinted with permission of the copyright holder, Harold E. Pepinsky.

The Middle Ground

To capitalists and many collectivists the restraints and inefficiencies of central planning are so onerous and, in many instances, arbitrary that they defeat both its utility and ideological appeal. Thus, not surprisingly scholars and societal leaders have sought to develop a viable middle position that embraces the communitarian virtues of socialism and the efficiencies of the marketplace. *Social democracy,* as that approach is commonly labeled, has become a dominant political force in, for example, Great Britain, Austria, Belgium, and the Scandinavian nations. Social democrats accept multiparty politics and believe in the gradual, democratic adoption of socialist goals. They seek to reduce the hardships of capitalism rather than to reorder society in accord with a collectivist model. Sweden and Norway are probably the most notable and most controversial examples of the successful application of socialist principles on a capitalist foundation. In the main, business still resides in private hands. Thus, an attempt is made to preserve the independence and efficiency of individual initiative. However, the state plays a powerful role by erecting a complete safety net guaranteeing cradle-to-grave care to any citizen requiring assistance to meet life's necessities. The articles that follow describe both the nature of life in the Scandinavian welfare states, and the business climate in economies that seek to combine the best of both capitalism and collectivism.

NORWAY: THE COST OF SAFETY

On late summer afternoons, fleets of private boats jam the Oslofjord; in winter, thousands of Norwegians spend their weekends on the country's ski slopes or on quick trips to resorts in balmy Spain. About 75 percent of all Norwegian families own their homes and close to half also have vacation retreats—a cottage on the coast or a cabin in the mountains. The humble Volkswagen has been dethroned as king of the road, replaced as Norway's best selling car by the more luxurious Volvo.

With a per capita GNP of $7,420, Norway has one of the world's highest living standards. Whether such bounty results mostly from the drive of 4 million people inured to hard work in a cold, rugged land or primarily from the social-democratic policies pursued by the ruling Labor Party of Premier Odvar Nordli is unclear even to Norwegians. Confesses Sverre Badendyck, a retired sea captain now employed as a shipping inspector. "We *think* we live in a capitalist country. Or at least in one with a mixed economy, with a socialist government trying to make it more socialist. But we honestly don't know what we have."

Norway tolerates a considerable amount of free enterprise. All but 9 percent of industry remains in private hands, although the fledgling North Sea oil industry is state-owned. Nonetheless, one of the world's most comprehensive welfare states has been fashioned by the Labor Party, in power for 36 of the past 43 years.

The *folketrygden* (people's security) law grants everyone disability, old-age and survivors' benefits, rehabilitation assistance and unemployment payments. Other measures provide free hospitalization, surgery, and medicines. Youngsters through the ninth grade receive dental care at their schools at no cost. Every worker is guaranteed at least four weeks of paid vacation.

Taxation rather than nationalization has been Labor's method of building Norway's socialism, which the party defines as "equality among all individuals and groups." Steeply progressive personal taxes (50 percent for a couple earning $30,000) have helped to level incomes. Says Christian Erlandsen, managing director of an Oslo auto parts firm: "After taxes the difference between me and the lowest-paid guy at this company is not very great. You can't look at just income; you must look at other values. We have our cabins, our spare time. What may be most important to me is my feeling of safety. I'm not thinking of crime as much as of health and retirement benefits. If I were to die now, for example, my wife and 15-month-old son would get 80 percent of my present income for some time. That's safety."

Business earnings are also heavily taxed: 30 percent by the national government and 20 percent by municipalities. . . .

The Labor Party tries to regulate what it does not tax. Although farm land remains in private hands, most farmers have been put under legal and financial pressure to join state-dominated cooperative marketing groups.

The government's most ambitious attempt to restructure the economy while permitting private ownership has been to give workers a voice in corporate management. A 1972 scheme for "industrial democracy" requires all firms with more than 200 employees to give worker representatives one third of the votes in the new "corporate assemblies" that replaced the traditional shareholders' meeting. . . .

There are signs that Norwegians worry about too much socialism. The growing tax burden apparently prompted segments of the working class to vote conservative in the last two parliamentary elections. A more widespread form of protest is tax evasion. . . .

Although Norwegians have no intention of dismantling their social net, they are becoming increasingly irritated at its red tape. Says Ragnhild Braathen, a Telemark housewife: "The regular citizen struggles against a wall of bureaucracy." . . .

Norwegian economists fear that the state's generosity may be adversely affecting the country's economy. Norway's production costs are already the globe's highest and in large part are responsible for the country's more than $5 billion trade deficit last year.

. . . High taxes discourage overtime work, while generous sick pay spurs absenteeism, which has doubled in recent years. On the average, 10 percent of the work force now stay away from the job daily, and in some plants the figure reaches 20 percent.

Surveying the costs of the welfare state, a businessman confesses: "I'm a little bit scared of the future." Still, Norway's variant of socialism stands a good chance of thriving—if only because of potential benefits of North Sea oil.

THE EXECUTIVE IN A COMMUNITARIAN SOCIETY

Winston Oberg

To the list of the world's endangered species may soon be added the name of capitalism. The capitalist system, with its reliance on individual economic initiative and a market economy, seems increasingly anachronistic in today's socialist and socializing world. On a map coded to show the economic systems of the world's nations, fewer than one out of four—only 23 percent—are identified as capitalist states. A larger group—29 percent—consists of Marxist-style totalitarian socialist states, while the remaining 48 percent are social democratic or mixed economies in which the state plays a dominant economic part. . . . [Note that Professor Oberg is speaking of the mid-1970s.—ed.]

The Scandinavian Middle Way

Fortunately, there appears to be a middle way. The Scandinavians, among others, are said to

have found it. Nearly 40 years ago, Sweden was first called a "middle way" between capitalism and communism. More recently, Norway has emulated Sweden's socialist philosophy and practices. Both countries score a perfect 100 on the Political Freedom Index (as does the United States). It appears, therefore, that countries as communitarian as Norway and Sweden can be fully as free as is the United States, at least in the political sphere.

But what about the economic sphere? How free do the business executives who operate in these communitarian societies feel? What would it be like for business if this country were to become equally communitarian? Recently, I spent two years teaching managers in Norway. While living in Oslo, I was able to conduct extensive interviews with 45 top executives in 40 major Norwegian and Swedish companies. A great deal of information was available from my students and from visits to key government and labor officials. This article summarizes the findings, focusing primarily on the 45 executive interviews. . . .

The Communitarian Society Seen through Norwegian Executives Eyes

. . . As Table 1 shows, the most common concern of the executives interviewed was the government and its treatment of private business. The Norwegian government was increasing its scope and power, and executives were feeling threatened. Forty-one percent spoke of growing government antagonism toward business. One said: "This labor government is treating Norwegian industry like the enemy."

* * * * *

Table 1
Problems of Norwegian Top Executives

Problem	Percentage Mentioning
Government hostility to business	41
The drift to socialism	30
Taxes and their negative impact on business	30
Inflation	30
Industrial democracy	30
Restrictive government safety and environmental regulation	22

Note: N = 27.

Following the interviews with business executives, I visited key government officials to get their reactions to some of the executives' concerns. A few conceded there was substance to the belief that more socialization might be coming. One said: "What has mainly changed the situation from a gradual and stable shift to one that frightens the businessmen is the oil. There is a group in the Labor Party that thinks oil money should enable Norway to buy up all foreign investments in Norwegian companies and also to buy up shares of Norwegian-owned companies. . . ."

Interestingly, not all the executives interviewed found socialization a frightening prospect. One company president said: "Don't quote me as saying this, but I am on the board of a government-owned company and I must say I envy them. In my company, I have difficulty getting financing, but if we were socialized, I'd get the money I need. . . ."

It is probably correct to say that Norwegian executives had mixed emotions about what they saw as increasing state intervention in the private sector. Government help was welcome; government control was feared.

Taxes were another item of major concern. Thirty percent of those interviewed mentioned them. Approximately 47 percent of Norway's personal income was taken in taxes in 1974. The maximum tax on personal income was 90 percent. High individual income taxes limited money available for investment, relatively high capital gains taxes discouraged investment of money in stocks, and high individual income taxes made it difficult to motivate people with money. One executive said: "You can't use money as a motivator. It costs you too much. . . ."

Inflation was also seen as a major problem by 30 percent of those interviewed. Of course, this is neither a uniquely Norwegian nor a uniquely communitarian problem!

Another topic that was of concern to 30 percent of the executives was "industrial democracy." Norway had recently enacted legislation which required companies to put employees on their supervisory boards. Companies had fought against this so-called industrial democracy law. Some executives still expressed negative feelings about it. One said: "You can't make an instant decision any more. You have to clear it with the workers, the local community, so many groups." But others saw the industrial democracy development in a positive light. It could give companies more clout with the labor government. One president said: "I find this an excellent thing. We are closing down three sections of one of our operations. I don't think we, as management, could have gotten government approval to close them down. But the workers went to the government and convinced them it was necessary to close these units down.''

Restrictive safety or environmental legislation was the final concern mentioned by 20 percent or more of the executives. Such legislation, the executives said, had held back power plant development and raised costs needlessly. One man remarked: ''I am not against safety but to make everybody perfectly safe is very expensive. . . .''

Business . . . has had the support of virtually no Norwegian intellectuals. . . . Leftist ideals have captured the imagination of the young. The chairman of the faculty at the University of Oslo said that virtually none of the students was preparing to enter private industry. Most looked on business as an outmoded relic of a soon-to-be-discarded system, an immoral system based on selfishness and greed. Student identification, he said, was with the communists, although not with Russia. Russia, to them, was as corrupt and decadent as America. Their identification was with China or Albania. Labor won the 1977 election in Norway by a slim margin, and the movement toward greater state control probably will continue in the years ahead. . . .

To what extent is the Norwegian situation a special case? And to what extent can it be seen as a preview of what is in store for the United States?

The Communitarian Society Looks Different through Swedish Eyes

Before we can conclude that in a communitarian society government is invariably hostile to business and continually strives to enlarge its sphere of influence at the expense of the private sector, we need to ask whether Norway with its unique history, homogeneity, oil wealth, and other characteristics, can be regarded as a prototype of communitarianism. To throw light on that question, the interview study was extended to Norway's neighbor, Sweden. If Sweden were similar to Norway in its treatment of business, it would not necessarily mean that all communitarian systems follow the Norwegian pattern. But if Sweden should prove to be significantly different from Norway, strong doubt

would be cast on the proposition that all communitarian societies fall into the same mold or that being a manager in a society in which 48 percent of personal income is taken in taxes would present the same challenges and difficulties from country to country.

As in Norway, a representative group of managers was interviewed. . . .

The answers of Swedish executives to the question about their major problems and concerns differed substantially from those of the Norwegians. The most striking difference was in the attitude toward government. In an article on Sweden which appeared the month before the study, Robert Ball quoted a top Swedish businessman as saying: ''The Socialist Party is the party of business.'' That is essentially what the interviews showed. Several executives . . . said that the Social Democrats were trying to preserve and protect private capitalism against groups farther to the left.

Six problems were mentioned by more than 20 percent of the interviewees. Except for taxes, the Swedish list of problems was entirely different from the Norwegian list.

Table 2
Problems of Swedish Top Executives

Problem	Percentage Mentioning
Growing union power and control	54
Sweden's high labor and related costs	54
Decline of the will to work	31
Excessive individual taxation	23
Worsening union relations	23
Price controls and price ceilings	23

Note: N = 18.

One executive attributed the Norwegian-Swedish interview differences to the competitive situations in the two countries:

In Sweden, we have several companies with 80 percent to 90 percent of their market abroad: Volvo, SKF, L. M. Ericsson, and so on. That gives Sweden opportunity to be trained in real tough management.

Except for shipping, Norwegian companies aren't heavily engaged in world trade, they're not used to real stiff competition. . . .

A major concern of Swedish managers was a law which had recently shifted a great deal of power to unions. . . .

The second major concern mentioned by an equal number of people was Sweden's high and rising wage level. This, they said, made it difficult to compete on world markets. Swedish wage rates had reached a level 30 percent higher than U.S. wage rates. Wages and pay-roll taxes to pay for Sweden's liberal social programs had risen more than 40 percent in the previous two years alone. . . .

Another major problem, mentioned by nearly one third of the executives, was an apparent decline in the willingness of Swedish workers to work, to work hard, to work overtime, and to accept responsibility. "With the welfare system we have," said one executive, "you can't get people to work overtime or to take more responsible jobs." Another blamed the motivation problem on taxes. "We have difficulty motivating people to work overtime or on shifts. They don't get all that much take-home from their extra work because of the very high marginal taxation."

Taxes were mentioned as a serious concern by roughly one fourth of the executives. They spoke of Sweden's individual income taxes, not capital gains taxes or taxes on company profits, which were comparatively very low. For example, 60 percent of a company's inventories could be written down immediately, and 40 percent of a company's earnings could be made tax exempt if earmarked for investment. It was possible to write off in depreciation the entire cost of a new factory the year it was built. One company chief executive, quoted in *Fortune*, said: "The socialists have made good tax laws for companies."

But when it came to individual taxes, Sweden was almost as bad as Norway. The top rate was 80 percent. The president of one company, whose salary was $114,000, had a take-home share of only 15 percent, or $18,000. Overall, nearly half of personal income in Sweden (as in Norway) was taken by the government in some form of taxation. . . .

What the Two Surveys Tell Us about Communitarianism

One conclusion that can be safely drawn is that in Sweden and Norway government and labor had a good deal more power, and management less power, than in our own country. In both countries the state had assumed responsibility for guiding its people. Government officials seemed to feel they knew what was best for the country and to assume that their wisdom should be allowed to direct the nation's economic and social affairs. Capitalism and free enterprise were seen as both selfish and cruel. A key Norwegian government official said: "I think we have done pretty well in this country. . . . Differences in income are smaller than in any country I know of outside the Communist bloc. . . . Competition in the old, rough, liberal sense is not well accepted here." In short, freedom had been given a second place to equality in his value system—and not equality of opportunity but equality of outcome. . . . To be a business executive in communitarian Norway was clearly different from being a business executive in equally communitarian Sweden. In Norway, business was on the defensive; it saw the government as hostile. In Sweden, business felt that the socialist government was friendly and supportive. In Norway, pressures to equalize income and status were much greater than in Sweden. . . .

Postscript

The prospect of an American communitarian society, with its concomitant loss of freedoms, is a bit depressing. Moreover, as the Norwegian situation suggests, there is no guarantee that the middle way is a stopping point. The ideology of socialism calls for complete state ownership and control. The negative aspects of communitarianism revealed here may suggest that a rational case can be made for retaining and defending capitalism and individualism. There is growing pressure in this country for equality at the expense of freedom. If we are to choose between the two, it should be with an understanding of the trade-offs. Within this century, the United States has fought and helped win two wars on the side of democracy. If it is true that liberal democracy cannot survive in a socialist state, we may need to consider a moral equivalent to war to oppose the communitarian drift in our society. It would be

ironic and tragic to allow the paternalism of the planners and the idealism of the intellectuals to move us without resistance into the totalitarianism of the socialist society.

Source: *MSU Business Topics* 26, no. 4 (Autumn 1978), p. 5. Reprinted with permission of the copyright holder, Graduate School of Business Administration, Michigan State University.

Note

Professor Oberg closed with a rather pessimistic assessment of the Scandinavian system, at least as applied to America. However, it is revealing to reflect on the views of the Swedish citizenry. When asked if their nation had something to be proud of, 60 percent of the 18- to 24-year-old Swedes surveyed cited their social welfare system. Only 24 percent of the American young people cited our social welfare programs. As an aside, the survey results, conducted in 1977–78 by a Japanese group, disclose an interesting picture of younger citizens' preferences and goals:

The Germans and Swiss were generally most proud of their standard of living; the Americans of their science and technology; the French of their history and cultural heritage; the Indians of their religion, culture, and art. Only the Swedes and the British were proudest of their achievements in social welfare.[7]

Although recent years have seen some increase in doubts, the Swedes continue to support their present very high level of social welfare. When asked in 1978 if social welfare is too expensive and should be cut down, 39 percent replied yes, but 47 percent said no.[8] Despite concerns over a sluggish economy, Sweden's 1985 reelection of Social Democratic Prime Minister Olof Palme seems to be an affirmation of faith in cradle to grave care. Swedes clearly approve of and want to retain the welfare state, although sentiment is increasing for various strategies to reform the system.

QUESTIONS

1. As Marx argued, scientific knowledge in the capitalist community grows more rapidly than the social institutions designed to organize and cope with that knowledge. How do you account for that imbalance?
2. Marx felt that the flawed social institutions of capitalism would unduly restrain the bountiful forces of production. Has that been the case for the global economy? Explain your response.
3. Marx proposes placing the means of production in public hands. Were we to do so, would a desirable balance result so that technology and the wisdom to deal

with the effects of technology would achieve a reasonable equilibrium? Explain.
4. Socialism's historical roots may be traced to early Christianity.
   a. Are socialist values more in keeping with Christian theology than are capitalist values? Explain your response.
   b. If your response is yes, do you believe that a committed Christian must renounce capitalism?
5. The Maoist legal system described by Pepinsky relied on community involvement to resolve disputes. Is such an approach feasible in America? Why or why not?

6. Law Professor Derrick Bell commenting on China:

> . . . But if so impressive an array of social reforms can be achieved under godless communism, why with our far greater resources and long-boasted concerns for the rights of individuals are so many of our citizens clearly worse off in so many ways than they would be in China?[9]

Answer Bell's question.

7. Bell concluded his comments by challenging America:

> Most American lawyers would probably not surrender their constitutional rights for a better health care program, decent housing, effective schools, prison reform, or even a guaranteed job and income. With the benefits our government has so long provided to the upper classes, they can already provide for their own needs.
>
> But what of those large segments of our population—not all black by any means—who lack any meaningful opportunity to earn or acquire something beyond life's basic necessities? What of those who have never had a chance to know the sense of satisfaction gained from making a contribution to society through their work? It is not hard to imagine that these men and women might be willing to accept the greater measure of conformity China demands—and the loss of independence that implies—in order to obtain some of the bounty and sense of self-worth the American dream promises but, below a certain socioeconomic level, so seldom delivers.
>
> The social reforms achieved in China silently but urgently pose for us the question: if they can do it why can't we?[10]

a. Does the capitalist system deny a sense of self-worth to those who are economically unproductive? Explain your response.

b. If your answer is yes, is that denial justifiable? Explain.

c. Do you agree with Bell that many of America's disadvantaged would trade independence in favor of the security and self-worth offered by the Chinese system? Explain.

8. The Scandinavian "middle way" seems to have produced an idyllic life-style: cradle-to-grave care, very productive economies, little internal strife, material abundance, and so on.

a. Build a list of objections to the Scandinavian approach.

b. What conditions of history, culture, and resources render the Scandinavian nations more suitable to the socialist approach than is the United States?

9. In his postscript, Winston Oberg suggests that acceptance of some socialist principles is likely to produce an ever greater expansion of the role of government until the state eventually owns and controls the means of production.

a. Is he correct? Explain why or why not.

b. If you agree with Oberg, what forces compel that movement to the left?

10. Somewhat in contrast to Professor Oberg's assessment, correspondent R. W. Apple of the *New York Times* reported that Sweden has willfully pursued a policy of economic leveling:

> . . . As a result almost every family living near the sea has a boat, but almost all are small boats. A large percentage of families have summer houses, but none of them rivals the villas of the Riviera or the stately manor houses of Britain. Virtually no one has servants.
>
> Even among the handful of people who might be able to afford it, conspicuous consumption is frowned upon. There are fewer than 25 Rolls Royces in Sweden. . . .[11]

a. Is the Swedish approach preferable to the extreme conspicious consumption permitted—and even encouraged—in this country? Explain why or why not.

b. Is the opportunity to garner luxuries necessary to the successful operation of the American system? Explain.

c. Does our system generate guilt among those who enjoy its fruits in quantities well beyond the norm?

11. Should an American citizen's primary duty be to herself or himself or to all other members of society? Should all hu-

mans be regarded as being of equal value and thus equally worthy of our individual support? Can social harmony be achieved in a nation whose citizens fail to regard the state as a "superfamily"? Explain.

12. Television comes to the South Pacific:

> . . . Every evening in a small village not far from Apia, the capital of Western Samoa, a conch shell blows, announcing a communal gathering where villagers pray, read the Bible, and share the day's experiences. This gathering, called a lotu, is an ancient and much-valued part of fa'a Samoa, "the Samoan way," diligently maintained by the village elders against the inroads of modern life. But in recent years, the elders themselves—tribal chiefs marked with elaborate tatoos from waist to knee—have changed the time of the lotu on Sunday so they can watch their favorite television program All-Star Wrestling.
>
> This is just one sign of television's arrival in the isolated South Pacific. In Fiji, the largest South Pacific country without TV, government officials are tracking the approach of television across the Pacific with increasing apprehension, as they might track a hurricane. They observe the scene in American Samoa, Tahiti, New Caledonia, and parts of Micronesia, the Pacific island areas that now have TV. They ask visiting social scientists how television might affect Fiji. They talk determinedly about "controlling" TV if it comes. . . .[12]

Would the United States have preserved a more desirable life style had we, at the advent of television, been operating under a centralized economy possessing the authority to study the impact of television and more carefully regulate its influence?

13. In Sweden the spanking of children is a violation of the law.
    a. What reasoning supports that legislation?
    b. Would such legislation help reduce violence in America? Explain.

14. Collectivists believe that if the means of production reside in private hands, workers will be exploited.
    a. Does American history support that contention?
    b. Is worker exploitation necessary to the success of capitalism? Explain.

15. The Eskimos, among other cultures, regarded all natural resources as free or common goods to be used but never possessed by any individual or group. What arguments may be raised to justify our notion of private ownership of natural resources?

16. Deduce the meaning of "pension fund socialism." How is it different from "corporate socialism"?

17. Swedish legislation and the policies of many companies, such as Volvo, provide for worker participation in management decisions. American firms have begun to take that direction. Would this "socialist" goal be desirable for America?

Part Four—America's Economic Future—Where Are We?

We have inspected the entire economic continuum. Considerable attention has been devoted in this chapter to the differing roles of law and government in the various systems. The competing ideologies and the underlying value structures have been explored. Obviously, the issue that remains is which direction America should take.

Each philosophy possesses compelling features. Not surprisingly, the available empirical evidence is mixed. One study ranked the United States first among the nations of the world in a quality-of-life index based on five components—social, economic, energy and environment, health and education, and national vitality and security. Using only objective indicators capable of quantitative measurement, scholar Ben-Chieh Liu found the United States substantially ahead of second- and third-place Australia and

Canada, respectively, even though the United States led only one of the individual categories (social—fulfilling basic human needs and providing material comfort). Sweden and Norway ranked fourth and fifth according to Liu's study.[13] On the other hand, if one looks specifically at public welfare based on transfer payments (e.g., pensions and unemployment benefits), education, and infant mortality, the Netherlands, Norway, Sweden, and Denmark rank 1st through 4th in the world, while the United States ranks 15th on such a scale.[14] Indeed, the infant mortality data are particularly disquieting evidence that the U.S. system is not without its weaknesses. According to the Department of Health and Human Services, the United States ranks 15th among the nations of the world, with 10.9 infant deaths for every 1,000 live births. Sweden recorded the lowest infant death rate, with 7.0 deaths per 1,000 live births.[15] Despite recent improvement, the United States is not the world leader in economic productivity when population is taken in to account. Among industrial nations, per capita gross national product of the United States ($13,160) in 1982 ranked fourth in the world behind Switzerland ($16,960), Norway ($14,270), and Sweden ($13,840).[16]

As economist Lester Thurow explains, the conservative solution to America's economic slippage is to "liberate free enterprise" and generally reduce the role of government.

In thinking about this solution it is well to remember that none of our competitors became successful by following this route. Government absorbs slightly over 30 percent of the GNP in the United States, but over 50 percent of the GNP in West Germany. Fifteen other countries collect a larger fraction of their GNP in taxes.[17]

Thurow goes on to add more evidence to his doubts regarding the "conservative solution."

. . . Nor have our competitors unleashed work effort and savings by increasing income differentials. Indeed, they have done exactly the opposite. If you look at the earnings gap between the top and bottom 10 percent of the population, the West Germans work hard with 36 percent less inequality than we, and the Japanese work even harder with 50 percent less inequality. If income differentials encourage individual initiative, we should be full of initiative, since among industrialized countries, only the French surpass us in terms of inequality.

Moreover, our own history shows that our economic performance since the New Deal and the onset of government "interference" has been better than it was prior to the New Deal. Our best economic decades were the 1940s (real per capita GNP grew 30 percent), when we had all that growth in social welfare programs. Real per capita growth since the advent of government intervention has been more than twice as high as it was in the days when governments did not intervene or have social welfare programs. . . .[18]

Regardless of one's interpretation of the facts of America's place in the world, the American people remain firmly convinced that our system is desirable. Nationalization of major industries—even oil—is firmly rejected.[19] Indeed, 67 percent of those surveyed believe "having business and industry under private control [is] a major factor in making America great."[20] Sixty-two percent of the citizenry oppose the introduction of socialism into America,[21] and 59 percent believe the free market is essential to freedom.[22] However, the public soundly rejects a laissez-faire capitalist economy, at least concerning consumer protection. Sixty-eight percent agree that if companies were free of government regulation "the consumer would get a much worse deal."[23]

Selfish or Selfless?

From an academic point of view, the capitalist-collectivist struggle has been carried on in the highly rarefied air of philosophical inquiry in which clarifications emerge grudgingly and truths seem almost beyond reach. In recent years an interesting new theme has been injected. Borrowing from the sociobiologists who borrowed from Darwin, a group of free market economists have launched a defense of laissez-faire capitalism based on the notion that the self-interest that moves the capitalist finds its origins in human genetics.

A GENETIC DEFENSE OF THE FREE MARKET

A new and highly controversial theory of human behavior has been swirling through campuses across the country. Called sociobiology, the theory says that all human actions, even those that appear altruistic in nature, are competitive and selfish and are programmed into the human genes. Until now, sociobiology has been used by its proponents to explain social and psychological behavior. But because economics is vitally concerned with the concepts of competitiveness and self-interest, it was only a matter of time before sociobiology would move to the forefront of economic debate. Indeed, at the annual meeting of the American Economics Association last December, a session devoted to "bioeconomics" drew a standing-room crowd and was picketed by members of the Union of Radical Political Economics, who claimed that the theory is a glorified version of Hitlerism and harks back to the days when the Nazis theorized a genetically selected "master race."

Bioeconomics says that government programs that force individuals to be less competitive and selfish than they are genetically programmed to be are preordained to fail. And according to bioeconomists, a socialist society, predicated on selflessness and devotion to a collective ideal, simply will never last.

Economists are just beginning to apply the principles of sociobiology. And there is no hard evidence to support the theory. Yet, bioeconomics provides a powerful defense of Adam Smith's laissez-faire views. "Sociobiol-

ogy means that individuals cannot be molded to fit into socialist societies such as the Soviet Union without a tremendous loss of efficiency," says Jack Hirshleifer, an economist at the University of California at Los Angeles.

Genetic Fitness

Sociobiologists claim to have discovered a genetic basis for Darwin's evolutionary theory of natural selection: that organisms that adapt to the surrounding environment survive, and the rest die out. Survival of the fittest, they say, is actually built into human genes.

To be sure, sociobiologists admit that cultural factors can influence behavior, and even at times offset genetic influences. Even so, they contend, most aspects of human culture, such as law and religion, ultimately serve the drive for what they call "genetic fitness." So what appears to be altruistic behavior is really genetic selfishness. People are altruistic toward blood relatives, who share common genes. And the degree of altruism depends on how many genes are shared. Parents, for example, will be more altruistic toward their children than the offspring will be toward each other, because the parents and children have more genes in common than do brothers and sisters. In its extreme form, sociobiology paints a disturbing, even repulsive, picture of human behavior: Even the most altruistic act, such as a father diving into a raging river to save his son, is selfish. The father, sociobiologists say, is trying to save his genes, not the child.

For the past 200 years, economists by and large have agreed with Adam Smith's theory, so eloquently set forth in *The Wealth of Nations,* that self-interest and competitiveness, though seemingly un-Christian and immoral, were indeed the mechanism by which an economy became more efficient and prosperous. The individual, seeking only to increase his personal wealth, builds the better mousetrap and thereby increases the general welfare of the society. Smith, of course, did not believe that the invisible hand was in the embryo. To this 18th-century thinker the market mechanism was simply an extension of the widely accepted Newtonian laws of physics.

Where Smith Left Off

But bioeconomics goes well beyond anything Smith could envisage. For better or worse, self-interest is the driving force in the economy because it is ingrained in each individual's genes. "It provides a whole new dimension to economic theory," says University of Chicago economist Gary Becker, a pioneer in applying biology to economics. "Once we can derive the genetic basis for human desires, we can determine which policies will work and which will not," he adds. . . .

The first attempts to apply the theory deal with the behavior of the unit in which genes are passed along and which is traditionally the haven of altruism—the family. Indeed, economists have traditionally considered the family a homogeneous, all-loving, noncompetitive unit. This, says Becker, is highly oversimplified. And, because it is oversimplified, policies that seemingly benefit the entire family, but actually advance the interests of some members of the family at the expense of others, will fail.

According to Becker's analysis, a classic example of this is the apparent failure of such compensatory education programs as Head Start, which provides poor preschool children with preparatory programs. Studies have shown that Head Start children do not do any better than other pupils with a similar background. The reason, says Becker, is that parents who have a child in the Head Start program will spend less time and money on that child. Instead, they concentrate on improving the genetic fitness of their other children. While the program may benefit the family as a whole, it does not show up in the scholastic performance of the child in the program. It is this poor scholastic performance that "experts" in and out of government focus on in concluding that the program doesn't work.

"Hogwash"

Borrowing a major tenet of sociobiology—that passing on genes to future generations is the overriding consideration of all behavior, even if it means deprivation for the parent—Becker questions whether recently legislated increases in Social Security benefits will indeed raise the income of retirees down the road. Parents, he says, will eventually recognize that their children will have to pay higher taxes to finance the increased benefits. As another example of the impulse toward gene protection, parents will give their children more of their own savings while they are living, says Becker. The net effect is that on average parents will be no better off than they have been without the increased benefits.

As a member of the Chicago school of economics, Becker believes government deficit spending does not increase total demand for goods and services in the long run. And he suspects that bioeconomics may explain why. Since the higher deficits will increase the national debt, it increases interest payments needed to service that debt. This means that future generations will have to pay higher taxes. Parents know this. So, to protect their children's purchasing power, they cut down their own consumption.

Using sociobiology to evaluate economic behavior and policies has sparked a controversy within the profession reminiscent of debates that surrounded the introduction of Darwin's theories more than 100 years ago. Nobel laureate Kenneth Arrow of Harvard calls bioeconomics "hogwash." "No matter what the innermost human drives may be, they are overshadowed by culture and history," he says. "It has very little explanatory value." Other economists contend that bioeconomics will be used as a rationale for conservative economic policies. Says the Massachusetts Institute of Technology's Paul Samuelson, another Nobel Prize winner: "I call it the Chicago school of biology."

Even Milton Friedman, the dominant figure in the Chicago school of economics for the last quarter of a century and America's most recent Nobel Prize winner in economics, discounts the importance of bioeconomics. "The market is simply the most efficient way to allocate goods and services," says Friedman. "I don't need a genetic explanation for the superiority of a free market economy."

Source: *Business Week*, April 10, 1978, pp. 100–104. Reprinted from the April 10, 1978 issue of *Business Week* by special permission. © 1978 by McGraw-Hill, Inc.

In Opposition to Bioeconomics

Certainly the evidence supporting the bioeconomics position must be considered tentative. In any case, however fetching one may find the intellectual adventuresomeness of the bioeconomists, however logically compelling their argument might be, indeed however closely their view may correspond to one's own intuitive sense of human nature, it may, nevertheless, be necessary to seek out and cultivate a more cooperative, humane vision of economic life. Thus, Robert Reich argues that the compassion of social justice is necessary to a successful society, not merely because of a charitable concern for the welfare of all people, but because the only route to prosperity is not the selfishness of capitalism but rather the collaboration of all in pursuit of the well-being of all.

. . . To the question, "What conditions will generate growth and productivity?" conservatives have responded with a set of prescriptions premised upon the hypothetical power of human greed and fear. A society that simultaneously offers both the prospect of substantial wealth and the threat of severe poverty surely will inspire great feats of personal daring, dazzling entrepreneurialism, and cutthroat ambition. But just as surely it may reduce the capacity of its members to work together toward a common end. The conservative promise of prosperity is an ideology suited to a frontier economy in which risk-taking is apt to be more socially productive than cooperation, but it is hardly appropriate to an advanced industrial economy in which collaboration is critical. Liberalism must reestablish the connection between prosper·.·. and social justice. . . .[24]

Freedom

All the evidence and opinions are helpful in illuminating the proper direction for America, but the primary determinant of that direction presumably remains the issue of personal freedom. A few years ago the editors of *Commentary* asked 26 of the nation's leading intellectuals to assess the relationship between capitalism, socialism, and democracy.

The idea that there may be an inescapable connection between capitalism and democracy has recently begun to seem plausible to a number of intellectuals who would once have regarded such a view not only as wrong but even as politically dangerous. So too with the idea that there may be something intrinsic to socialism which exposes it ineluctably to the "totalitarian temptation." Thus far, the growing influence of these ideas has been especially marked in Europe—for example, among the so-called "new philosophers" in France and in the work of Paul Johnson and others in England—but they seem to be receiving more and more sympathetic attention in the United States as well.

How significant do you judge this development to be? Do you yourself share in it, either fully or even to the extent of feeling impelled to rethink your own ideas about capitalism and socialism and the relation of each to democracy?[25]

One of the respondents, Professor Eugene Genovese, concedes that the left must "solve the problem of democracy," but he argues that, in any case, it is only in the collectivist movements that the future, democratic or not, will be worth living.

A real question does exist here. Can a regime that socializes the economy avoid the total centralization of political power? How, under such political centralization, do you provide a material basis for a free press, trade unions, churches, and other institutions? And without autonomous institutions, how can the freedom of the individual be protected? For that matter, how can it even be defined? Freedom cannot be absolute: every society must define its notion of the proper balance between the claims of the individual and those of the community as a whole. Thus, a free society is one that places the burden of proof on those who would restrict the individual. It remains to be proven that a socialist society can be a free society. But then, it remains to be proven, notwithstanding the experience of the United States and precious few European countries, that democracy can sustain a meaningful freedom for more than the elite.

* * * * *

Capitalism did not need democracy to provide freedom, for it was concerned with the freedom of the few. Only lately and largely outside the United States did it come to accept democracy as a necessity, and then only under hard blows from the Left. Socialism must solve the problem of democracy or lose freedom as well. But where outside the socialist and Communist movements are these questions being fought out in a manner that promises a future worth having?[26]

Conclusion

In an insightful, and in its own way, touching evaluation of the capitalism-socialism debate, international law professor Richard Falk argues that the ultimate answer humans seek is not to be found in either ideology. Perhaps Falk's words will help inspire us all to push beyond the comfortable confines of conventional political economy to a vision of life that embraces and surpasses the limits of economics and politics.

. . . The traditional capitalism/socialism debate is a sham, quite irrelevant to our prospects as a civilization, mere words. The real challenge is whether we can summon the courage and imagination to find ways to reorganize our society around a sustainable economic, ecological, and political ethic that brings people in diverse national societies credible hope for "life, liberty, and the pursuit of happiness." A beginning, and yet no more or less than that, is to nourish feelings, thoughts, and action around the central idea of being a citizen of the planet, as well as a citizen of a country, a member of a family, race, and religion. Some sense of global identity is, I believe, the only basis on which to achieve enough detachment from the destructive forces of the modern world to form a judgment about what needs to be done within the political arena.

This may sound sentimental and apolitical; yet at this historical moment it seems critical for some of us to make the effort to stand sufficiently aside to understand what is happening. . . . Both capitalism and socialism are fundamentally methods for organizing production to maximize efficiency of output, and thereby, to assure social benefit. To go on as if the comparative merits of these two secular ideologies are what matters most ignores the dramatic, urgent reality that neither ideology has led to societies which offer much human promise for the future. We need an ideology that probes beneath the debate about productive efficiency and asks, ''What for?'' Ours is a time to dream and work for a world that our grandchildren might enjoy and feel secure in, that is, a world that is stable, equitable, and hopeful. Such a quest requires a commitment to a process of change that extends beyond our lifetimes. Hence it is more a religious than a political enterprise although it partakes of both.[27]

Chapter Questions

1. Critics accuse capitalist nations of fascism, imperialism, and slave trading.
    a. Cite a historical example of each in a capitalist state. Explain.
    b. Are those practices symptomatic of a flaw in capitalism or simply a flaw in human nature?
    c. Is socialism a more likely vehicle for avoiding the abuse of fascism, imperialism, and racial subjugation? Explain.
2. Many commentators point to capitalism's lack of a compelling philosophy, theology, or creed. Why has capitalism failed to develop the compelling ideological fervor and loyalty that has clearly been the case with collectivism?
3. It is often argued that many intellectuals (and in particular many college professors) actively criticize capitalism and support collectivism.
    a. Has that been your experience? Explain.
    b. If that assessment is accurate, how do you account for leftist inclinations among intellectuals?
4. Is altruism merely a form of selfishness? What altruistic acts have you performed? Why?
5. If we are fundamentally selfish, must we embrace capitalism as the most accurate and, therefore, most efficient expression of human nature? Explain.
6. How might sociobiology and bioeconomics be used to justify social inequity and inequality?
7. Robert Reich argues that prosperity is a necessary precondition for social justice. Explore the argument that prosperity is the best evidence of social justice.
8. Richard Falk argues for ''some sense of global identity.'' Does capitalism enhance or impede the development of a world community? Explain.
9. Is the absence of the necessity of work as a means of survival ''the kingdom of freedom'' as Marx argued? Why or why not? If it were in our power, should we seek to abolish work born of necessity? Explain.
10. Explain the nature of a life free of nonvoluntary work. What purpose would replace necessity as the motivating force in our lives?
11. Socialist Michael Harrington argues for men ''freed of the curse of money'':

    . . . [A]s long as access to goods and pleasures is rationed according to the possession of money, there is a pervasive venality, an invitation to miserliness and hostility to one's neighbor. . . .[28]

    Should we strive to make more and more goods and services ''free''? Raise the competing arguments.
12. The great intellect Adolph Berle once said: '' . . . A day may come when national glory

and prestige, perhaps even national safety, are best established by a country's being the most beautiful, the best socially organized, or culturally the most advanced in the world."[29]

a. Is collectivism necessary to achieving Berle's goal? Why or why not?

b. If faced with a choice, would most Americans opt for Berle's model or for a nation preeminent in consumer goods, sports, and general comfort? Explain.

13. The 1970s were often referred to as the "Me Decade," a period of self-absorption. Pollster Daniel Yankelovich predicted this selfishness would be replaced in the 1980s with an ethic of commitment:

> The core idea of commitment is to make people less absorbed with self and to break through the iron age of self-centeredness. The new ethic of commitment is emerging in two chief forms of expression: a hunger for deeper personal relations and a yearning to belong to a community where people share many bonds in common. At the heart of the ethic of commitment is the moral intuition that the meaning of life lies in finding a commitment outside one's self.[30]

a. Evaluate the accuracy of Yankelovich's views.

b. If Yankelovich is correct in his contention that we seek a greater sense of community and a commitment beyond self-interest, should we opt for capitalism or socialism? Explain your position.

c. Why is selfishness often considered an evil?

14. In Sweden poverty is effectively nonexistent. In America in 1983, 15.2 percent of the population had incomes below the government poverty line of $10,178 for a family of four. That is approximately 35.3 million Americans, the equivalent of, for example, the combined population of North Dakota, South Dakota, Nebraska, Minnesota, Iowa, Wisconsin, Illinois, and Michigan, led a deprived economic life.

a. Is that condition alone sufficient justification for American adoption of the Swedish approach? Why or why not?

b. It is generally assumed that giving citizens money to combat poverty reduces those citizens' incentive to work. Do you agree? Explain.

c. As you leave college, if you were given only enough money to lift you above the poverty line, would your incentive to work be significantly reduced? Explain.

d. Regardless of your personal viewpoint, make the argument that welfare does not materially reduce the incentive to work.

15. Distinguished economist Robert Lekachman, among others, has argued that a "moderate" level of unemployment is beneficial to the prosperous leaders of capitalism. He contends that a significant shift to the left is necessary if all Americans are to enjoy prosperity.

a. Build Lekachman's argument.

b. What are the strengths and weaknesses of his case?

16. It is often argued that collectivism would require a uniformity, a "sameness" that would destroy the individuality Americans prize.

a. Are Americans notably independent and individualistic? Explain.

b. Explore the argument that collectivism would actually enhance meaningful individualism.

17. A visitor to China during the Maoist period observed that the Chinese children appeared more cooperative than competitive, more altruistic than selfish. Maoist training taught children to share toys, love and help each other and, of course, venerate Mao.

a. Must we similarly curb our emphasis on competition?

b. If so, what would spur us to greater achievements?

c. Are we taught to "love and help each other"?

d. Wouldn't a tie be the optimal result in all games? Explain.

18. Hilda Scott wrote a book to which she affixed the provocative title, *Does Socialism Liberate Women?*
    a. Answer her question. Explain.
    b. Are minority oppression and oppression of women inevitable by-products of capitalism?

19. In Wisconsin, members of the Old Order Amish religion decline to formally educate their children beyond the eighth grade. The United States Supreme Court held that their First Amendment right to freedom of religion was violated by the Wisconsin compulsory education statute, which required school attendance until the age of 16. Chief Justice Burger explained:

    . . . They object to the high school, and higher education generally, because the values they teach are in marked variance with Amish values and the Amish way of life; they view secondary school education as an impermissible exposure of their children to a "worldly" influence in conflict with their beliefs. The high school tends to emphasize intellectual and scientific accomplishments, self-distinction, competitiveness, worldly success, and social life with other students. Amish society emphasizes informal learning-through-doing; a life of "goodness," rather than a life of intellect; wisdom, rather than technical knowledge; community welfare, rather than competition; and separation from, rather than integration with, contemporary worldly society. . . .[31]

    a. Have the Amish taken the course we should all follow?
    b. Could we do so? Explain.

20. Irving Kristol built the argument that American society has given rise to a "new class"—scientists, teachers, bureaucrats—who are actively opposed to business and the capitalist approach. The new class consists of:

    . . . [S]cientists, teachers and educational administrators, journalists and others in the communications industries, psychologists, social workers, those lawyers and doctors who make their careers in the expanding public sector, city planners, the staffs of the larger foundations, the upper levels of the government bureaucracy. . . . It is basically suspicious of, and hostile to the market precisely because the market is so vulgarly democratic—one dollar, one vote. . . . The "new class"—intelligent, educated, energetic—has little respect for such a commonplace civilization. It wishes to see its "ideals" more effectual than the market is likely to permit them to be. . . .[32]

    a. Is Kristol's argument sound?
    b. Have you had experience with people in this new class? Explain.

21. In 1975, *Business Week* analyzed the then robust movement for egalitarianism (equality). It focused on John Rawls, author of *Theory of Justice,* who argued that society seeks fairness, "and fairness means equality." Equality of opportunity is a delusion unless it produces equality of results. Hence, "to produce genuine equality of opportunity, society must give more attention to those with fewer native assets and to those born into less favorable social positions."[33]
    a. Complete economic equality would be a very expensive proposition and thus politically—and perhaps economically—unacceptable. What steps might be taken to increase economic equality without serious economic dislocations?
    b. Even if equality were practicable, would you support such a goal? Explain.

22. Extraordinarily successful businessman Charles Koch argues that business itself must accept some of the blame for the current crippling of capitalism.

    The majority of businessmen today are not supporters of free enterprise capitalism. Instead they prefer "political capitalism," a system in which government guarantees business profits while business itself faces both less competition and more security for itself. As [former] California Governor Jerry Brown put it, "Sometimes businessmen almost operate as though they'd feel more comfortable in a

Marxist state where they could just deal with a few commissars who would tell them what the production goals were, what quota they had. . . . I am really concerned that many businessmen are growing weary of the rigors of the free market.'' *New York Times* columnist William Safire agrees with this sobering analysis: "The secret desire of so many top-level managers for controls and regulated monopoly is never openly stated. . . . But today's managerial trend is not toward accepting risk. It is toward getting government help to avoid risk.''[34]

In the main, do you agree that American businesspeople are a threat to the continued vitality of capitalism? Explain.

23. Economist Lester Thurow believes that Americans must recognize that our economic structure has never performed as well as those of postwar Japan and Germany. He believes it is fruitless to try to return to a "golden age" that never was. Do you believe that the American solution is neither capitalism nor collectivism but the very carefully designed route of cooperation between business, labor, and government that has been successfully implemented in Japan and Germany? Explain.

24. At Memorial Junior High in San Diego, students received 25 cents for each day of perfect attendance. The money (actually paper credits) was spent only for school-related goods dispensed in the school store. Initially the absentee rate dropped dramatically (6 percent to 2.8 percent), but in 38 subsequent months the improvement was modest (7 percent to 6.2 percent).[35]

    a. Evaluate the approach.

    b. Is the profit motive the key to improving the public sector generally? Explain.

25. Brandeis University professor of social policy, David Gil, has argued that capitalism has created a population dependent on wages and that the American family is a training ground to prepare the young to be "mindless wage slaves." Families must be sexist and authoritarian to prepare children to submit to command without question.[36] On the other hand, John Hospers contends that we have all become wage slaves to the government.[37]

    a. Which view is the more accurate? Why?

    b. Which is the more ominous? Explain.

26. The Swedes, noted for their extreme tolerance of pornography, have banned the movie *The Empire Strikes Back* (a sequel to *Star Wars*) for children under 15 years of age on the grounds that the movie is too violent and too frightening.

    a. Is this a false comparison?

    b. If not, do the divergent choices Sweden and America have made about the treatment of pornography and violence bear any relation to the economic systems adopted by the two societies?

    c. If you possessed the power to ban both pornography and *The Empire Strikes Back,* what would you do? Explain.

Notes

1. Irving Kristol, "When Virtue Loses All Her Loveliness"—Some Reflections on Capitalism and "the Free Society," in *Capitalism Today*, ed. Daniel Bell and Irving Kristol (New York: New American Library, 1971), p. 15.

2. Alvin Rabushka, *Hong Kong—A Study in Economic Freedom* (Chicago: University of Chicago Press, 1979), pp. 102–3.

3. Jules Loh, "Small Town of Salado Is American Rarity," *The Lexington (Kentucky) Sunday Herald-Leader,* February 19, 1978, p. A–18.

4. The Marxist interpretation given here relies heavily on William Ebenstein and Edwin Fogelman, *Today's Isms,* 8th ed. (Englewood Cliffs, N.J.: Prentice-Hall, 1980), p. 7.

5. The materials in this paragraph are dawn from Clair Wilcox, Willis Weatherford, Holland Hunter, and Morton Baratz, *Economies of the World Today,* 3d ed. (New York: Harcourt Brace Jovanovich), p. 2.

6. Richard Gill, *Economics and the Public Interest,* 2d ed. (Santa Monica, Calif.: Goodyear Publishing, 1972), p. 46–51.

7. Hans Zetterberg, "Maturing of the Swedish Welfare State." *Public Opinion,* October–November 1979, pp. 42–43.

8. Ibid., p. 44.

9. *Juris Doctor,* April 1978, p. 11 et seq.

10. Ibid.

11. R. W. Apple, Jr., "Swedes Feel They're Lumped Together in 'National Blandness.'" reprinted from the *New York Times* in *The Lexington (Kentucky) Leader,* July 26, 1978, p. A–15.

12. Barry Siegel, "South Pacific: Some Enchanted Prime Time," *The Atlantic,* September 1980, p. 18.

13. Ben-chieh Liu, "Economic Growth and Quality of Life," *American Journal of Economics and Sociology* 39, no. 1 (January 1980), p. 1.

14. Francis G. Castles and R. D. McKinlay, "Public Welfare Provision, Scandinavia, and the Sheer Futility of the Sociological Approach to Politics," *The British Journal of Political Science,* April 1979, p. 157.

15. "Declining Death Rates Told for Heart Attacks, Strokes," *Des Moines Register,* March 23, 1985, pp. 1 and 8.

16. International Bank for Reconstruction and Development, *1985 World Bank Atlas* (Washington, D.C.: World Bank, 1985), pp. 6–9.

17. Lester Thurow, The *Zero-Sum Society* (New York: Penguin Books, 1981), p. 7. Originally published by Basic Books, 1980.

18. Ibid, pp. 7–8.

19. Cambridge Reports, 1974, and the Roper Organization, 1979, as reported in *Public Opinion,* June–July 1980, p. 35.

20. Louis Harris and Associates, 1977, as reported in *Public Opinion,* June–July 1980, p. 32.

21. Cambridge Reports, 1976, as reported in *Public Opinion,* April–May 1980, p. 22.

22. Cambridge Reports, 1979, as reported in *Public Opinion,* April–May 1980, p. 22.

23. Louis Harris and Associates, 1976, as reported in *Public Opinion,* June–July 1980, p. 33.

24. Robert Reich, "The Liberal Promise of Prosperity," *The New Republic,* February 21, 1981, pp. 20, 23.

25. "Capitalism, Socialism, and Democracy—A Symposium," *Commentary* 65, no. 4 (April 1978), p. 29.

26. Ibid., pp. 41–42.

27. Richard Falk, "A Sham Debate," in Leonard Orr, ed., "Is Capitalism on the Way Out?" *Business and Society Review* 28, Winter 1978–79, pp. 4–6.

28. Michael Harrington, "Why We Need Socialism in America," *Dissent,* May–June 1970, pp. 240, 286.

29. Adolph Berle, *Power* (New York: Harcourt Brace Jovanovich, 1969), pp. 258–59.

30. Daniel Yankelovich, "Are You Taking Risks with Your Life?" *Parade,* May 24, 1981, pp. 4, 5.

31. *Wisconsin v. Yoder,* 406 U.S. 205 (1972).

32. Irving Kristol, "Business and the 'New Class'", *The Wall Street Journal,* May 19, 1975, p. 8.

33. "Egalitarianism: Threat to a Free Market," *Business Week,* December 1, 1975, pp. 62, 64.

34. Charles Koch, "Business Can Have Free Enterprise—If It Dares," *Business and Society Review,* no. 28. (Winter 1978–79), p. 54.

35. "In California: Pay-as-You-Go Pedagogy," *Time,* May 11, 1981, p. 8.

36. "Capitalism Is Seen as Villain Turning Work into a Chore," The State University of Iowa *Spectator,* March 1980, p. 4.

37. John Hospers, "Free Enterprise as the Embodiment of Justice," in *Ethics, Free Enterprise and Public Policy,* ed. Richard DeGeorge and Joseph Pichler (New York: Oxford University Press, 1978), pp. 70, 84.

3

Ethics

Vice is a monster of so frightful mien,
As, to be hated, needs but to be seen;
Yet seen too oft, familiar with her face,
We first endure, then pity, then embrace.
                                                    Alexander Pope

Part One—Foundations of Ethical Theory

Chapter 1 set out those allegations of business misdeeds that have been a primary, but not singular, impetus for increased government regulation. Chapter 2 explored the capitalism-collectivism economic continuum to remind the reader of the fundamentals of political economy and to encourage some judgment about the degree of government intervention necessary to achieve a desirable relationship between business and the balance of society. That is, might we rely on the market alone to regulate the course of business, or must we interpose some degree of government regulation?

Chapter 3 introduces self-regulation as a technique for achieving a more desirable role for business in society. To what extent can we rely on the ethical quality, the morality, of the businessperson and the business organization to govern the path of commerce? Obviously, if we felt full faith in the free market and the ethical quality of the individuals and companies, regulation by law would be reduced at least to those minimums suggested in Chapter 2 by Ayn Rand.

No effort will be made to *teach ethics;* that is, the purpose here is not to improve the reader's "ethical quotient." Rather, the goal is to sensitize the reader to the ethical component of business life. Some sense of the ethical climate of business, some glimpse of the specific ethical problems facing the businessperson should be useful in assessing the role of ethics in the business decision-making equation and in evaluating the utility of ethics as a "regulator" of business behavior. The discussion about McDonald's that follows is an apt illustration of the complexities of ethics.

Introduction to Ethics: McDonald's and Protesters

On May 4, 1970, four students were shot to death and a number of individuals were injured when a unit of the Ohio National Guard fired into a group of demonstrators on the Kent State University campus in northeastern Ohio. The students were protesting the Nixon administration's Vietnam War policy, and particularly the so-called incursion of American troops in great numbers into Cambodia. Following the Kent State episode, college campuses around America were the scene of large, often violent, demonstrations against both the war and the student deaths. Buildings were burned on a number of campuses. At many institutions emotions were so strong that instruction was halted for the balance of the term. In that volatile climate, angry students at Southern Illinois University (SIU) in Carbondale briefly drew one of America's most successful enterprises, the McDonald's fast food chain, into the controversy. On the day following the deaths at Kent State some SIU demonstrators demanded that the American flag at the local McDonald's be lowered to half staff. The manager did so, but a passerby who happened to be acquainted with McDonald's chairman, Ray Kroc, noted the flag and phoned Mr. Kroc. Mr. Kroc immediately ordered the flag back to full mast, at which point the demonstrators returned and threatened to burn the building unless the flag was again lowered. The manager then phoned Mr. Fred Turner, president of McDonald's.[1]

Assume Mr. Turner's role. What advice would you give to the McDonald's manager? Is this decision one of ethics? What is the morally principled course of action? Or is the decision one of pragmatics? How can the building and student goodwill be preserved while meeting Mr. Kroc's express company policy? Are the ethical decision and the pragmatic decision one and the same in this instance?

Ethical Theory

Volumes of literature are devoted in general terms to the question of defining ethics. We cannot hope to advance that discussion here. Ethics, of course, involves judgments as to good and bad, right and wrong, and what ought to be. We seek to use reason in discovering how individuals ought to act. Business ethics refers to the measurement of business behavior based on standards of right and wrong, rather than relying entirely upon principles of accounting and management. (In this discussion, morals will be treated as synonymous with ethics. Distinctions certainly may be drawn between the two, but those distinctions are not vital for our purposes.)

Society has, in recent years, imposed dramatically expanded expectations on the business community. Meeting society's economic needs was once generally thought to be sufficient. Today, business is expected to contribute significantly to the solution of fundamental societal problems such as pollution, discrimination, and poverty. For the firm, those demands have a clear moral component—business is to do what is "right" and "good." Of course, the individual businessperson feels the same ethical demands. Not only must the individual comply with the law, but he or she feels increasing pressure to seek out the "good" and the "right" in order to fulfill an honorable role in life. Finding and following the "right" course is not easy for any of us, but the difficulty may be particularly acute for the businessperson. He or she may feel compelled to use rather different standards on the job than in personal life. Indeed, it is often argued that personal ethics must be laid aside in favor of the organization's values. Intense scrutiny of business ethics is a recent phenomenon that has left the businessperson a bit at sea in an era of changing expectations. Although the law provides useful guideposts for minimum comportment, no firm moral theme has emerged. Therefore, when the businessperson is faced with a difficult decision, a common tactic is simply to do what he or she takes to be correct at any given moment. Indeed, in one survey of ethical views in business, 50 percent of the respondents indicated that the word *ethical* meant "what my feelings tell me is right."[2] That view strikes at ethical absolutes and argues that all moral principles are relative depending on the environmental circumstances. However, such a philosophy, without careful consideration of the competing considerations, seems an elusive and shifting foundation on which to build an ethical perspective. Thus, a brief survey of some of the primary systems of ethical analysis may be helpful. A sense of the history of ethics should emerge, and the reader will be afforded an introductory sense of the available analytical tools that would assist in reaching a reasoned ethical posture.[3]

Fletcher's Moral Continuum

As scholar Joseph Fletcher expressed it, there are three broad routes to moral decision making.[4] They represent the two extremes and the midpoint on an "ethical continuum": (a) the legalistic—one extreme, (b) the antinomian—the opposite extreme, and (c) the situational—the middle ground.

Legalism   Here the absolute letter of the law controls. Rules abound. And those rules are not mere guidelines; rather, they are directives to be followed. All the principal Western religions have operated on a foundation of specified legalisms, including, for example, the Ten Commandments. Imposed on that foundation are layers of statutes and codes designed to specify with particularity the "right" course of conduct.

Antinomianism   This philosophy rejects all reliance on rules, laws, maxims, credos, and the like. Every situation is unique. One must call upon the elements of the situation itself to reach an ethical decision. Thus all such decisions are reached on an ad hoc, impromptu basis.

The philosophy of *existentialism,* propounded most notably by Jean-Paul Sartre, is perhaps the most powerful expression of antinomianist principles. Existentialists believe that standards of conduct cannot be rationally justified, and no actions are inherently right or wrong. Thus each person may reach his or her own choice about ethical principles. That view finds its roots in the notion that humans are only what we will ourselves to be. If God does not exist, there can be no human nature, since there is no one to conceive that nature.

In Sartre's famous interpretation, existence precedes essence. First humans exist, then we individually define what we are—our essence. Therefore, each of us is free, with no rules to turn to for guidance. Just as we all choose our own natures, so must we choose our own ethical precepts. Moral responsibility belongs to each of us individually.

Situationalism   Fletcher argues for a middle ground built on maximizing Christian love or *agape* (AH-gah-pay). An ethical decision is one that produces the greatest quantity of love. Thus, the emphasis is on leading a life of loving care as exemplified by Jesus. To the situationist, reason is the route to ethical judgment, but rules are not ignored:

. . . The situationist enters into every decision-making situation fully armed with the ethical maxims of his community and its heritage, and he treats them with respect as illuminators of his problems. Just the same he is prepared in any situation to compromise them or set them aside *in the situation* if loves seems better served by doing so. . . .[5]

Thus rules and reason play a role in discovering the decision most in keeping with Christian love.

Teleology or Deontology—An Overview

Space constraints dictate the omission of a variety of contending formulations; namely, ethical relativism, hedonism, and pragmatism. Fletcher's moral continuum operates, for our purposes, as a broad system of classification. An alternative classification is that of teleological and deontological ethics. *Teleological ethical systems* are those emphasizing the end, the product, the consequences of a decision. That is, the morality of a decision is determined by measuring the probable outcome. A morally correct decision is one that produces the greatest good. The teleological approach calls for reaching moral decisions by weighing the nonmoral consequences of an action. To repeat, for the teleologist the end is primary.

To the deontologist, principle is primary and consequence is secondary or even irrelevant. Maximizing right rather than good is the deontological standard. The deontologist might well refuse to lie even if doing so would maximize good. *Deontology,* derived from the Greek word meaning *duty,* is directed toward what ought to be, toward what is right. Relationships among people are important because they give rise to duties. A father may be morally committed to saving his son from a burning building, rather than saving another person who might well do more total good for society. Similarly, deontology considers motives. For example, why a crime was committed may be more important than the actual consequences of the crime.

The distinction here is critical. Are we to guide our behavior in terms of rational evaluations of the consequences of our acts, or are we to shape our conduct in terms of duty and principle—that which ought to be? To clarify these differences we will look briefly at three ethical philosophies that illustrate the nature of the teleological-deontological debate.

Teleology

Egoism Egoists make the universal claim that all humans act to maximize their self-interest. Every act is selfish. Concern for the self always exceeds concern for others. Even when an act (e.g., charity) appears to have been undertaken for the primary benefit of another, that act is necessarily an effort toward the maximization of self-interest. Thus, ethical conduct is measured by the degree to which the moral decision advances the self-interest of the decision maker. It is important to note that the egoist is not merely a self-indulgent hedonist, immediately embracing short-term pleasure. Rather the egoist thesis calls for the discipline to do what ought to be done; that is, to achieve the degree of self-discipline necessary to maximize one's long-term self-interest.

Utilitarianism In reaching an ethical decision, good is to be weighed against evil. A decision that maximizes the ratio of good over evil for all those concerned is the ethical course. Jeremy Bentham (1748–1832) and John Stuart Mill (1806–1873) were the chief intellectual forces in the development of utilitarianism. Their views and those of other utilitarian philosophers were not entirely consistent. As a result at least two branches of utilitarianism have developed. According to *act-utilitarianism,* one's goal is to identify the consequences of a particular act to determine whether it is right or wrong. *Rule-utilitarianism* requires that one adhere to all the rules of conduct by which society reaps the greatest value. Thus the rule-utilitarian may be forced to shun a particular act that would result in greater immediate good (punishing a guilty person whose constitutional rights have been violated) in favor of upholding a broader rule that results in the greater total good over time (maintaining constitutional principles by freeing the guilty person). In sum, the principle to be followed for the utilitarian is the greatest good for the greatest number.

Deontology

Formalism The German philosopher Immanuel Kant (1724–1804) developed perhaps the most persuasive and fully articulated vision of ethics as measured not by consequence (teleological), but by the rightness of rules. This formalistic view of ethics is one in which the rightness of an act depends little (or in Kant's view, not at all) on the results of the act. Kant believed in the key moral concept of "the good will." The moral person is a person of good will, and that person renders ethical decisions based on what is right, regardless of the consequences of the decision. Moral worth springs from one's decision to discharge one's duty. Thus, the student who refuses to cheat on exams is morally worthy if his or her decision springs from duty, but morally unworthy if the decision is merely one born of self-interest, such as fear of being caught.

How is it that the person of good will knows that which is right? Here Kant propounded the *categorical imperative;* the notion that every person should act on only those principles that he or she, as a rational person, would prescribe as universal laws to be applied to the whole of humankind. A moral rule is "categorical" rather than "hypothetical" in that its prescriptive force is independent of its consequences. The rule guides us independent of the ends we seek. Kant believed that every rational creature can act according to his or her categorical imperative, because all such persons have "autonomous, self-legislating wills" that permit them to formulate and act upon their own systems of rules. To Kant, what is right for one is right for all, and each of us can discover that "right" by exercising our rational faculties.

At this point it would not be surprising were the reader muttering a not so polite, "So what?" As always, theory must face the test of reality. The bulk of that testing will be left to the reader. Consider again the position of the president of McDonald's receiving a call for immediate advice from the Carbondale manager threatened by mob violence. Apply each philosophy articulated here to that situation. The conclusions will be strikingly dissimilar. The choice, of course, remains that of the decision maker, but a foundation in ethical theory clarifies the alternatives. For example, how would a formalist adhering to Kantian views respond to the contemporary debate (discussed later in

this chapter) regarding the morality of American businesspersons paying bribes and
kickbacks to secure contracts abroad? Remember that the test is that of the categorical
imperative: Is the moral rule one that the businessperson would prescribe as a universal
law to be applied to all humans? If one accepts Kant's views, that brief exercise substantially clarifies the ethics of bribery regardless of the customs of the host country.

Part Two—Foundations of Business Ethics

As expressed previously, ethics involves the quest, via reason, for that which is good
and right, that which ought to be. For the businessperson the quest has become, in
recent years, particularly trying. Public cynicism is substantial. One recent poll asked:[6]

How would you rate the honesty and ethical standards of people in these different fields?

	Very High or High	Average	Low or Very Low
Clergy	64%	27%	4%
Pharmacists	61	33	4
Physicians	58	35	6
College teachers	47	38	5
Journalists	28	47	17
Lawyers	24	43	27
Business executives	18	55	20
Congressmen	14	43	38
Advertising practitioners	9	42	39
Car salesmen	6	34	32

Reprinted with permission of the copyright holder, *The Gallup Report.*

Business Values

Values refer to the individual's or the collectivity's ranking of the worth, the excellence,
the utility, the desirability of life's ideas and objects. For example, one may value
leisure time in preference to securing personal profit. One's values are also instrumental
in shaping one's ethical standards. Look now at a pair of analyses of the values, the
character of the American business community, generally.

Steiner and Steiner—The Roots of Business Ethics

1st topic

Scholars George and John Steiner clarify the picture by identifying six primary sources
of the business ethics construct.[7]

Genetic Inheritance   Although the view remains theoretical, sociobiologists have in
recent years amassed persuasive evidence and arguments suggesting that the evolutionary forces of natural selection influence the development of traits such as cooperation

and altruism that lie at the core of our ethical systems. That is, those qualities of goodness often associated with ethical conduct may, in some measure, be a product of genetic traits strengthened over time by the evolutionary process.

Religion   Via a rule orientation exemplified by the Golden Rule (or its variations in many religions) and the Ten Commandments, religious morality is clearly a primary force in shaping our societal ethics. The question here concerns the applicability of religious ethics to the business community. Could the Golden Rule serve as a universal, practical, helpful standard for the businessperson's conduct?

Philosophical Systems   To the Epicureans the quantity of pleasure to be derived from an act was the essential measure of its goodness. The Stoics, like the Puritans and many contemporary Americans, advocated a disciplined, hard-working, thrifty lifestyle. These philosophies, and others like those cited earlier, have been instrumental in our society's moral development.

Cultural Experience   Here the Steiners refer to the rules, customs, and standards transmitted from generation to generation as guidelines for appropriate conduct. Individual values are shaped in large measure by the norms of the society.

The Legal System   Laws represent a rough approximation of society's ethical standards. Thus, the law serves to educate us about the ethical course in life. The law does not and, most would agree, should not be treated as a vehicle for expressing all of society's ethical preferences. Rather, the law is an ever-changing approximation of current perceptions of right and wrong.

Codes of Conduct   Steiner and Steiner identify three primary categories of such codes. Company codes, ordinarily brief and highly generalized, express broad expectations about fit conduct. Second, company operating policies often contain an ethical dimension. Express policy as to gifts, customer complaints, hiring policy, and the like serves as a guide to conduct and a shield by which the employee can avoid unethical advances from those outside the company. Third, many professional and industry associations have developed codes of ethics, such as the Affirmative Ethical Principles of the American Institute of Certified Public Accountants. In sum, codes of conduct seem to be a growing expression of the business community's sincere concern about ethics. However, the utility of such codes remains unsettled.

Maccoby—Managerial Character

In his acclaimed study, *The Gamesman*,[8] psychoanalyst Michael Maccoby identified four character types, which in his view accurately summarize the nature of those who operate America's major corporations. Maccoby secured his information via interviews, dream analysis, and Rorschach tests involving 250 managers at 12 major companies. The first character type, the *craftsman,* is committed to the intrinsic satisfaction of his or her work and to the maintenance of his or her often traditional lifestyle. Though widely admired, the craftsman is unlikely to assume a commanding managerial role.

The *jungle fighter* is a competitor whose main goal is power. He or she is aggressive and may appear to be a productive leader, but he or she shuns teamwork and foments hostility resulting in the eventual weakening of the organization.

The *company man* is the well-known stereotype of the individual beset with insecurity and relying for a sense of identity on his or her association with a powerful company.

The key figure in Maccoby's analysis is the *gamesman*. Gamesman characteristics, often in combination with others, were increasingly common as Maccoby reached higher into the corporate hierarchy. The gamesman seeks to influence change and is fascinated by risk. He or she views human relations, projects, and almost all other aspects of work as games to be mastered. He or she is fair and tough. Winning is the gamesman's primary goal.

In the jungle fighter and the company man we recognize familiar threats to the business community's ethical integrity: the one rapacious in pursuit of power, the other fearful of maintaining individual principles in the face of organizational pressure. According to Maccoby, the emergence of the gamesman as the preeminently successful managerial model may pose the most serious, but subtle, ethical threat. The problem, expressed by Maccoby in a lyrical aphorism, is that the gamesman's work "develops his head but not his heart." The gamesman does not find satisfaction in ideology or ethical practice. Qualities of the "heart"—compassion, humor, friendliness, and loyalty—are not fulfilled by the gamesman's working experience. The gamesman is of the sort who sells that which sells best, regardless of the consequences. However, the gamesman is fair, unbigoted, and without hostility.

Maccoby's investigation is difficult to interpret in other than a pessimistic light. His analysis clearly does not depict a managerial class for which ethical principle is the dominant concern. Has Maccoby revealed a representative picture of corporate America? The question is not readily answered, but a number of studies do offer some empirical insight into the ethical climate of American business.

Corporate Ethical Conduct

Perhaps the most alarming evidence emerging from the various ethical inquiries is that a very high percentage of today's businesspeople are experiencing conflict between their personal standards and organizational demands. Uniroyal and Pitney-Bowes surveyed a sample of their own managers, while Professor Archie Carroll polled a random sample of managers across America. Seventy percent of the Uniroyal sample,[9] 59 percent of those at Pitney-Bowes,[10] and nearly 65 percent of those in Carroll's sample[11] agreed with the statement that managers feel under pressure to compromise personal ethics to achieve company goals. But to add perspective, note that 60.4 percent of the public sector managers responding likewise felt pressure to compromise their ethics.[12] Professors Steven Brenner and Earl Molander in a 1977 study of *Harvard Business Review* subscribers found that 57 percent of the managers experienced a conflict between company interests and personal ethics.[13] Not surprisingly, that stress is more pronounced at the lower rungs in the corporate hierarchy. For example, Carroll found that fully 84 percent of the low-level managers felt the pressure to compromise. The percentage declined to 65 percent for middle-level managers and to 50 percent for top-level people.[14] On the other hand, the Brenner and Molander survey might be considered grounds for optimism in that the 57 percent figure is a substantial decline from the 75 percent affirmative response to a similar inquiry in a 1961 survey.[15]

Brenner and Molander found that the personal ethics–company interest conflict was most pronounced as to "honesty in communication" (22.3 percent reporting such a conflict) as well as "gifts, entertainment, and kickbacks" (12.3 percent). Interestingly, only 2.3 percent of the 1976 respondents reported conflict as to "price collusion and pricing practice," while 12.5 percent of the 1961 sample reported such conflicts.[16]

Businesspeople are clearly quite cynical about the ethical quality of the business community. The various studies consistently reveal that the managers surveyed believe themselves and their company to be more ethical than the "competition." Maccoby found that 72 percent of the 250 managers surveyed thought honesty important to their work, but only 12 percent felt that corporate work developed honesty.[17] In sum, the corporate ethics profile is confused. In the Carroll survey, 53 percent agreed and 47 percent disagreed that "business ethics today are far superior to ethics of earlier periods." On the other hand, the general public is markedly cynical about the ethical progress of our total society. Sixty-five percent of an adult sample of Americans in a 1983 Gallup poll believed that the "overall level of ethics and honesty in American society has fallen during the past 10 years."[18]

Why Do Some Managers Cheat?

We may begin by returning to an examination of the value structures of those who manage. The German philosopher Edward Spranger identified six fundamental value orientations for all humans.[19] Based on Spranger's classifications, William Guth and Renato Tagiuri surveyed a group of top-level executives and arrived at the following ranking of average value scores:[20]

Value	Score
Economic	45
Theoretical	44
Political	44
Religious	39
Aesthetic	35
Social	33

Reprinted by permission of the *Harvard Business Review*. Excerpt from "Personal Values and Corporate Strategy" by William D. Guth and Renato Tagiuri (September/October 1965). Copyright © 1983 by the President and Fellows of Harvard College; all rights reserved.

Thus, managers appear to value more strongly the features of the pragmatic person, rather than the sensitivities often associated with the lower three items. By contrast ministers, for example, ranked the values in the following order: religious, social, aesthetic, political, theoretical, and economic.[21]

As is the case with all of us, the businessperson brings to the job and develops on the job a set of values that is critical in determining his or her ethical course. Brenner and Molander asked their sample respondents what factors they believed to be influential in reaching unethical decisions. From the strongest to the weakest the primary influences cited were: (a) behavior of superiors, (b) formal policy or lack thereof, (c) industry ethical climate, (d) behavior of one's equals in the company, (e) society's moral climate, and (f) one's personal financial needs.[22] How striking it is that the first five of these factors all refer to forces external to the self. Are we so malleable and so wanting in personal conviction that we must find our moral truths in the view and behavior of others?

Brenner and Molander also inquired as to whether ethical standards had improved or declined in the previous 15 years. Then each respondent was asked to cite the one standard believed most responsible for the change. Among those who believed ethics to be in decline, the largest number (34 percent) cited declining societal standards, permissiveness, hedonism, and the like.

What are we left with? Why do some managers cheat? Why does anyone cheat? We see that many factors are at work and that in itself is an important lesson. We are often inclined to attribute cheating merely to the desire for personal advancement. But that force, important though it is, does not fully explain cheating. Most of us wish to advance, but some of us are not willing to cheat. If you have behaved unethically at some point in your life, reflect now upon the reasons. Perhaps we are all genetically predisposed to cheat in order to survive. Perhaps we are actually taught to cheat. Perhaps we simply have not fully understood the fundamental moral truths. Perhaps we all too willingly submit to the unethical example and wishes of others. Perhaps, as Karl Menninger has suggested, we have lost our sense of sin.[23]

Part Three—Business Ethics in Practice

Pressure to Cheat

Having established a general ethical foundation theoretically and practically, it is fitting now to turn to the pragmatics of dealing with specific ethical quandaries. The organization committed to ethical quality may be able to implement some structures and procedures to encourage decency. Corporate codes of conduct are probably the most commonly employed tool. Three out of four respondents to a recent survey of American corporations indicated the use of an employee code of conduct. Almost all large corporations have such a code, while the percentage declines substantially for mid-sized (75 percent) and smaller firms (40 percent).[24] Another survey ranked the "14 most frequently prohibited employee behaviors." The most commonly prohibited behaviors were extortion, gifts, and kickbacks, which were included in 67 percent of the codes. Others cited conflicts of interest (65 percent), illegal political payments (59 percent), moonlighting (25 percent), and fraud and deception (11 percent).[25] The case that follows exposes the competing, real-life forces that sometimes cloud seemingly clear-cut issues of right and wrong. As you read, consider whether a code of conduct would have effectively combatted the misdeeds recounted here.

"WHY SHOULD MY CONSCIENCE BOTHER ME?"

Kermit Vandivier

The B. F. Goodrich Co. is what business magazines like to speak of as "a major American corporation." It has operations in a dozen states and as many foreign countries, and of these far-flung facilities, the Goodrich plant at Troy, Ohio, is not the most imposing. It is a small, one-story building, once used to manufacture airplanes. Set in the grassy flatlands of west-central Ohio, it employs only about 600 people. Nevertheless, it is one of the three largest manufacturers of aircraft wheels and brakes, a leader in a most profitable industry. Goodrich wheels and brakes support such well-known planes as the F111, the C5A, the Boeing 727, the XB70 and many others. Its customers include almost every aircraft manufacturer in the world.

Contracts for aircraft wheels and brakes often run into millions of dollars, and ordinarily a contract with a total value of less than $70,000, though welcome, would not create any special stir of joy in the hearts of Goodrich sales personnel. But purchase order P-23718, issued on June 18, 1967, by the LTV Aerospace Corporation, and ordering 202 brake assemblies for a new Air Force plane at a total price of $69,417, was received by Goodrich with considerable glee. And there was good reason. Some 10 years previously, Goodrich had built a brake for LTV that was, to say the least, considerably less than a rousing success. The brake had not lived up to Goodrich's promises, and after experiencing considerable difficulty, LTV had written off Goodrich as a source of brakes. Since that time, Goodrich salesmen had been unable to sell so much as a shot of brake fluid to LTV. So in 1967, when LTV requested bids on wheels and brakes for the new A7D light attack aircraft it proposed to build for the Air Force, Goodrich submitted a bid that was absurdly low, so low that LTV could not, in all prudence, turn it down.

Goodrich had, in industry parlance, "bought into the business." Not only did the company not expect to make a profit on the deal; it was prepared, if necessary, to lose money. For aircraft brakes are not something that can be ordered off the shelf. They are designed for a particular aircraft, and once an aircraft manufacturer buys a brake, he is forced to purchase all replacement parts from the brake manufacturer. The $70,000 that Goodrich would get for making the brake would be a drop in the bucket when compared with the cost of the linings and other parts the Air Force would have to buy from Goodrich during the lifetime of the aircraft. Furthermore, the company which manufactures brakes for one particular model of an aircraft quite naturally has the inside track to supply other brakes when the planes are updated and improved.

Thus, that first contract, regardless of the money involved, is very important, and Goodrich, when it learned that it had been awarded the A7D contract, was determined that while it may have slammed the door on its own foot 10 years before, this time, the second time around, things would be different. The word was soon circulated throughout the plant: "We can't bungle it this time. We've got to give them a good brake, regardless of the cost."

There was another factor which had undoubtedly influenced LTV. All aircraft brakes made today are of the disk type, and the bid submitted by Goodrich called for a relatively small brake, one containing four disks and weighing only 106 pounds. The weight of any aircraft part is extremely important. The lighter a part is, the heavier the plane's payload can be. The four-rotor, 106-pound brake promised by Goodrich was about as light as could be expected, and this undoubtedly had helped move LTV to award the contract to Goodrich.

The brake was designed by one of Goodrich's most capable engineers, John Warren. A tall, lanky blond and a graduate of Purdue, Warren had come from the Chrysler Corporation seven years before and had become adept at aircraft brake design. The happy-go-lucky manner he usually maintained belied a temper which exploded whenever anyone ventured to offer any criticism of his work, no matter how small. On these occasions, Warren would turn red in the face, often throwing or slamming something and then stalking from the scene. As his co-workers learned the consequences of criticizing him, they did so less and less readily, and when he submitted his preliminary design for the A7D brake, it was accepted without question.

Warren was named project engineer for the A7D, and he, in turn, assigned the task of producing the final production design to a newcomer to the Goodrich engineering stable, Searle Lawson. Just turned 26, Lawson had been out of the Northrup Institute of Technology only one year when he came to Goodrich in January 1967. Like Warren, he had worked for a while in the automotive industry, but his engineering degree was in aeronautical and astronautical sciences, and when the opportunity came to enter his special field, via Goodrich, he took it. At the Troy plant, Lawson had been assigned to various "paper projects" to break him in, and after several months spent reviewing statistics and old brake designs, he was beginning to fret at the lack of challenge. When told he was being assigned to his first "real" project, he was elated and immediately plunged into his work.

The major portion of the design had already been completed by Warren, and major assemblies for the brake had already been ordered from Goodrich suppliers. Naturally, however, before Goodrich could start making the brakes on a production basis, much testing would have to be done. Lawson would have to determine the best materials to use for the linings and discover what minor adjustments in the design would have to be made.

Then, after the preliminary testing and after the brake was judged ready for production, one whole brake assembly would undergo a series of grueling, simulated braking stops and other severe trials called *qualification tests*. These tests are required by the military, which gives very detailed specifications on how they are to be conducted, the criteria for failure, and so

on. They are performed in the Goodrich plant's test laboratory, where huge machines called *dynamometers* can simulate the weight and speed of almost any aircraft. After the brakes pass the laboratory tests, they are approved for production, but before the brakes are accepted for use in military service, they must undergo further extensive flight tests.

Searle Lawson was well aware that much work had to be done before the A7D brake could go into production, and he knew that LTV had set the last two weeks in June 1968, as the starting dates for flight tests. So he decided to begin testing immediately. Goodrich's suppliers had not yet delivered the brake housing and other parts, but the brake disks had arrived, and using the housing from a brake similar in size and weight to the A7D brake, Lawson built a prototype. The prototype was installed in a test wheel and placed on one of the big dynamometers in the plant's test laboratory. The dynamometer was adjusted to simulate the weight of the A7D and Lawson began a series of tests, "landing" the wheel and brake at the A7D's landing speed, and braking it to a stop. The main purpose of these preliminary tests was to learn what temperatures would develop within the brake during the simulated stops and to evaluate the lining materials tentatively selected for use.

During a normal aircraft landing the temperatures inside the brake may reach 1,000 degrees, and occasionally a bit higher. During Lawson's first simulated landings, the temperature of his prototype brake reached 1,500 degrees. The brake glowed a bright cherry-red and threw off incandescent particles of metal and lining material as the temperature reached its peak. After a few such stops, the brake was dismantled and the linings were found to be almost completely disintegrated. Lawson chalked this first failure up to chance and, ordering new lining materials, tried again.

The second attempt was a repeat of the first. The brake became extremely hot, causing the lining materials to crumble into dust.

After the third such failure, Lawson, inexperienced though he was, knew that the fault lay not in defective parts or unsuitable lining material but in the basic design of the brake itself. Ignoring Warren's original computations, Lawson made his own, and it didn't take him long to discover where the trouble lay—the brake was too small. There simply was not enough surface area on the disks to stop the aircraft without generating the excessive heat that caused the lining to fail.

The answer to the problem was obvious but far from simple—the four-disk brake would have to be scrapped, and a new design, using five disks, would have to be developed. The implications were not lost on Lawson. Such a step would require the junking of all the four-disk-brake subassemblies, many of which had now begun to arrive from the various suppliers. It would also mean several weeks of preliminary design and testing and many more weeks of waiting while the suppliers made and delivered the new subassemblies.

Yet, several weeks had already gone by since LTV's order had arrived, and the date for delivery of the first production brakes for flight testing was only a few months away.

Although project engineer John Warren had more or less turned the A7D over to Lawson, he knew of the difficulties Lawson had been experiencing. He had assured the young engineer that the problem revolved around getting the right kind of lining material. Once that was found, he said, the difficulties would end.

Despite the evidence of the abortive tests and Lawson's careful computations, Warren rejected the suggestion that the four-disk brake was too light for the job. Warren knew that his superior had already told LTV, in rather glowing terms, that the preliminary tests on the A7D brake were very successful. Indeed, Warren's superiors weren't aware at this time of the troubles on the brake. It would have been difficult for Warren to admit not only that he had made a serious error in his calculations and original design but that his mistakes had been caught by a green kid, barely out of college.

Warren's reaction to a five-disk brake was not unexpected by Lawson, and, seeing that the four-disk brake was not to be abandoned so easily, he took his calculations and dismal test results one step up the corporate ladder.

At Goodrich, the man who supervises the engineers working on projects slated for production is called, predictably, the *projects manager*. The job was held by a short, chubby and bald man named Robert Sink. . . . Some 15 years before, Sink had begun working at Goodrich as a lowly draftsman. Slowly, he worked his way up. Despite his geniality, Sink was neither respected nor liked by the majority of the engineers, and his appointment as their supervisor did not improve their feelings about him. They thought he had only gone to high school. It quite naturally rankled those who had gone through years of college and acquired impressive specialties such as thermodynamics and astronautics to be commanded by a man whom they considered their intellectual inferior. But, though Sink had no college training, he had something even more useful: a fine working knowledge of company politics.

Puffing on a Meerschaum pipe, Sink listened gravely as young Lawson confided his fears about the four-disk brake. Then he examined Lawson's calculations and the results of the abortive tests. Despite the fact that he was not a qualified engineer in the strictest sense of the word, it must certainly have been obvious to Sink that Lawson's calculations were correct and that a four-disk brake would never have worked on the A7D.

But other things of equal importance were also obvious. First, to concede that Lawson's calculations were correct would also mean conceding that Warren's calculations were incorrect. As projects manager, he not only was responsible for Warren's activities, but, in admitting that Warren had erred, he would have to admit that he had erred in trusting Warren's judgment. It also meant that, as projects manager, it would be he who would have to explain the whole messy situation to the Goodrich hierarchy, not only at Troy but possibly on the corporate level at Goodrich's Akron offices. And, having taken Warren's judgment of the four-disk brake at face value (he was forced to do this since, not being an engineer, he was unable to exercise any engineering judgment of his own), he had assured LTV, not once but several times, that about all there was left to do on the brake was pack it in a crate and ship it out the back door.

There's really no problem at all, he told Lawson. After all, Warren was an experienced engineer, and if he said the brake would work, it would work. Just keep on testing and probably, maybe even on the very next try, it'll work out just fine.

Lawson was far from convinced, but without the support of his superiors there was little he could do except keep on testing. By now, housings for the four-disk brake had begun to arrive at the plant, and Lawson was able to build up a production model of the brake and begin the formal qualification tests demanded by the military.

The first qualification attempts went exactly as the tests on the prototype had. Terrific heat developed within the brakes and, after a few, short, simulated stops, the linings crumbled. A new type of lining material was ordered and once again an attempt to qualify the brake was made. Again, failure.

Experts were called in from lining manufacturers, and new lining "mixes" were tried, always with the same result. Failure.

It was now the last week in March 1968, and flight tests were scheduled to begin in 70 days. Twelve separate attempts had been made to formally qualify the brake, and all had failed. It was no longer possible for anyone to ignore the glaring truth that the brake was a dismal failure and that nothing short of a major design change could ever make it work.

In the engineering department, panic set in. A glum-faced Lawson prowled the test laboratory dejectedly. Occasionally, Warren would witness some simulated stop on the brake and, after it was completed, troop silently back to his desk. Sink, too, showed an unusual interest in the trials, and he and Warren would converse in low tones while poring over the results of the latest tests. Even the most inexperienced of the lab technicians and the men who operated the testing equipment knew they had a "bad" brake on their hands, and there was

some grumbling about "wasting time on a brake that won't work."

New menaces appeared. An engineering team from LTV arrived at the plant to get a good look at the brake in action. Luckily, they stayed only a few days, and Goodrich engineers managed to cover the true situation without too much difficulty.

On April 4, the 13th attempt at qualification was begun. This time no attempt was made to conduct the tests by the methods and techniques spelled out in the military specifications. Regardless of how it had to be done, the brake was to be "nursed" through the required 50 simulated stops.

Fans were set up to provide special cooling. Instead of maintaining pressure on the brake until the test wheel had come to a complete stop, the pressure was reduced when the wheel had decelerated to around 15 mph, allowing it to "coast" to a stop. After each stop, the brake was disassembled and carefully cleaned, and after some of the stops, internal brake parts were machined in order to remove warp and other disfigurations caused by the high heat.

By these and other methods, all clearly contrary to the techniques established by the military specifications, the brake was coaxed through the 50 stops. But even using these methods, the brake could not meet all the requirements. On one stop the wheel rolled for a distance of 16,000 feet, nearly three miles, before the brake could bring it to a stop. The normal distance required for such a stop was around 3,500 feet.

On April 11, the day the 13th test was completed, I became personally involved in the A7D situation.

I had worked in the Goodrich test laboratory for five years, starting first as an instrumentation engineer, then later becoming a data analyst and technical writer. As part of my duties, I analyzed the reams and reams of instrumentation data that came from the many testing machines in the laboratory, then transcribed it to a more usable form for the engineering department. And when a new-type brake had successfully completed the required qualification tests, I would issue a formal qualification report.

Qualification reports were an accumulation of all the data and test logs compiled by the test technicians during the qualification tests and were documentary proof that a brake had met all the requirements established by the military specifications and was therefore presumed safe for flight testing. Before actual flight tests were conducted on a brake, qualification reports had to be delivered to the customer and to various government officials.

On April 11, I was looking over the data from the latest A7D test, and I noticed that many irregularities in testing methods had been noted on the test logs.

Technically, of course, there was nothing wrong with conducting tests in any manner desired, so long as the test was for research purposes only. But qualification test methods are clearly delineated by the military, and I knew that this test had been a formal qualification attempt. One particular notation on the test logs caught my eye. For some of the stops, the instrument which recorded the brake pressure had been deliberately miscalibrated so that, while the brake pressure used during the stops was recorded as 1,000 psi (the maximum pressure that would be available on the A7D aircraft), the pressure had actually been 1,100 psi!

I showed the test logs to the test lab supervisor, Ralph Gretzinger, who said he had learned from the technician who had miscalibrated the instrument that he had been asked to do so by Lawson. Lawson, said Gretzinger, readily admitted asking for the miscalibration, saying he had been told to do so by Sink.

I asked Gretzinger why anyone would want to miscalibrate the data-recording instruments.

"Why? I'll tell you why," he snorted. "That brake is a failure. It's way too small for the job, and they're not ever going to get it to work. They're getting desperate, and instead of scrapping the damned thing and starting over, they figure they can horse around down here in the lab and qualify it that way."

An expert engineer, Gretzinger had been responsible for several innovations in brake design. . . . "If you want to find out what's going on," said Gretzinger, "ask Lawson, he'll tell you."

Curious, I did ask Lawson the next time he came into the lab. He seemed eager to discuss the A7D and gave me the history of his months of frustrating efforts to get Warren and Sink to change the brake design. "I just can't believe this is really happening," said Lawson, shaking his head slowly. "This isn't engineering, at least not what I thought it would be. Back in school, I thought that when you were an engineer, you tried to do your best, no matter what it cost. But this is something else."

He sat across the desk from me, his chin propped in his hand. "Just wait," he warned. "You'll get a chance to see what I'm talking about. You're going to get in the act, too, because I've already had the word that we're going to make one more attempt to qualify the brake, and that's it. Win or lose, we're going to issue a qualification report!"

I reminded him that a qualification report could only be issued after a brake had successfully met all military requirements, and therefore, unless the next qualification attempt was a success, no report would be issued.

"You'll find out," retorted Lawson. "I was already told that regardless of what the brake does on test, it's going to be qualified." He said he had been told in those exact words at a conference with Sink and Russell Van Horn.

This was the first indication that Sink had brought his boss, Van Horn, into the mess. Although Van Horn, as manager of the design engineering section, was responsible for the entire department, he was not necessarily familiar with all phases of every project, and it was not uncommon for those under him to exercise the what-he-doesn't-know-won't-hurt-him philosophy. If he was aware of the full extent of the A7D situation, it meant that matters had truly reached a desperate stage—that Sink had decided not only to call for help but was looking toward that moment when blame must be borne and, if possible, shared.

Also, if Van Horn had said, "regardless what the brake does on test, it's going to be qualified," then it could only mean that, if necessary, a false qualification report would be issued! I discussed this possibility with Gret-zinger, and he assured me that under no circumstances would such a report ever be issued.

"If they want a qualification report, we'll write them one, but we'll tell it just like it is," he declared emphatically. "No false data or false reports are going to come out of this lab."

On May 2, 1968, the 14th and final attempt to qualify the brake was begun. Although the same improper methods used to nurse the brake through the previous tests were employed, it soon became obvious that this too would end in failure.

When the tests were about half completed, Lawson asked if I would start preparing the various engineering curves and graphic displays which were normally incorporated in a qualification report. "It looks as though you'll be writing a qualification report shortly," he said.

I flatly refused to have anything to do with the matter and immediately told Gretzinger what I had been asked to do. He was furious and repeated his previous declaration that under no circumstances would any false data or other matter be issued from the lab.

"I'm going to get this settled right now, once and for all," he declared. "I'm going to see Line [Russell Line, manager of the Goodrich Technical Services Section, of which the test lab was a part] and find out just how far this thing is going to go!" He stormed out of the room.

In about an hour, he returned and called me to his desk. He sat silently for a few moments, then muttered, half to himself, "I wonder what the hell they'd do if I just quit?" I didn't answer and I didn't ask him what he meant. I knew. He had been beaten down. He had reached the point when the decision had to be made. Defy them now while there was still time—or knuckle under, sell out.

"You know," he went on uncertainly, looking down at his desk, "I've been an engineer for a long time, and I've always believed that ethics and integrity were every bit as important as theorems and formulas, and never once has anything happened to change my be-liefs. Now this . . . Hell, I've got two sons I've got to put through school and I just. . . ." His voice trailed off.

He sat for a few more minutes, then, looking over the top of his glasses, said hoarsely, "Well, it looks like we're licked. The way it stands now, we're to go ahead and prepare the data and other things for the graphic presentation in the report, and when we're finished, someone upstairs will actually write the report.

"After all," he continued, "we're just drawing some curves, and what happens to them after they leave here, well, we're not responsible for that."

He was trying to persuade himself that as long as we were concerned with only one part of the puzzle and didn't see the completed picture, we really weren't doing anything wrong. He didn't believe what he was saying, and he knew I didn't believe it either. It was an embarrassing and shameful moment for both of us.

I wasn't at all satisfied with the situation and decided that I, too, would discuss the matter with Russell Line, the senior executive in our section.

. . . Line looked and acted every inch the executive. . . . He had been transferred from the Akron offices some two years previously, and an air of mystery surrounded him. Some office gossips figured he had been sent to Troy as the result of some sort of demotion. Others speculated that since the present general manager of the Troy plant was due shortly for retirement, Line had been transferred to Troy to assume that job and was merely occupying his present position to "get the feel of things." Whatever the case, he commanded great respect and had come to be well liked by those of us who worked under him.

He listened sympathetically while I explained how I felt about the A7D situation, and when I had finished, he asked me what I wanted him to do about it. I said that as employees of the Goodrich Company we had a responsibility to protect the company and its reputation if at all possible. I said I was certain that officers on the corporate level would never knowingly allow such tactics as had been employed on the A7D.

"I agree with you," he remarked, "but I still want to know what you want me to do about it."

I suggested that in all probability the chief engineer at the Troy plant, H. C. "Bud" Sunderman, was unaware of the A7D problem and that he, Line, should tell him what was going on.

Line laughed, good-humoredly. "Sure, I could, but I'm not going to. Bud probably already knows about this thing anyway, and if he doesn't, I'm sure not going to be the one to tell him."

"But why?"

"Because it's none of my business, and it's none of yours. I learned a long time ago not to worry about things over which I had no control. I have no control over this."

I wasn't satisfied with this answer, and I asked him if his conscience wouldn't bother him if, say, during flight tests on the brake, something should happen resulting in death or injury to the test pilot.

"Look," he said, becoming somewhat exasperated, "I just told you I have no control over this thing. Why should my conscience bother me?"

His voice took on a quiet, soothing tone as he continued. "You're just getting all upset over this thing for nothing. I just do as I'm told, and I'd advise you to do the same."

He had made his decision, and now I had to make mine.

I made no attempt to rationalize what I had been asked to do. It made no difference who would falsify which part of the report or whether the actual falsification would be by misleading numbers or misleading words. Whether by acts of commission or omission, all of us who contributed to the fraud would be guilty. The only question left for me to decide was whether or not I would become a party to the fraud.

Before coming to Goodrich in 1963, I had held a variety of jobs, each a little more pleasant, a little more rewarding than the last. At 42, with seven children, I had decided that the

Goodrich Company would probably be my "home" for the rest of my working life. The job paid well, it was pleasant and challenging, and the future looked reasonably bright. My wife and I had bought a home and we were ready to settle down into a comfortable, middle-age, middle-class rut. If I refused to take part in the A7D fraud, I would have to either resign or be fired. The report would be written by someone anyway, but I would have the satisfaction of knowing I had had no part in the matter. But bills aren't paid with personal satisfaction, nor house payments with ethical principles. I made my decision. The next morning, I telephoned Lawson and told him I was ready to begin on the qualification report.

In a few minutes, he was at my desk, ready to begin. Before we started, I asked him, "Do you realize what we are going to do?"

"Yeah," he replied bitterly, "we're going to screw LTV. . . . I've sold myself. It's all I can do to look at myself in the mirror when I shave. I make me sick."

I was surprised at his vehemence. It was obvious that he too had done his share of soul-searching and didn't like what he had found. Somehow, though, the air seemed clearer after his outburst, and we began working on the report.

I had written dozens of qualification reports, and I knew what a "good" one looked like. Resorting to the actual test data only on occasion, Lawson and I proceeded to prepare page after page of elaborate, detailed engineering curves, charts, and test logs, which purported to show what had happened during the formal qualification tests. Where temperatures were too high, we deliberately chopped them down a few hundred degrees, and where they were too low, we raised them to a value that would appear reasonable to the LTV and military engineers. Brake pressure, torque values, distances, times—everything of consequence was tailored to fit the occasion.

Occasionally, we would find that some test either hadn't been performed at all or had been conducted improperly. On those occasions, we "conducted" the test—successfully, of course—on paper.

For nearly a month we worked on the graphic presentation that would be a part of the report. Meanwhile, the fourteenth and final qualification attempt had been completed, and the brake, not unexpectedly, had failed again.

During that month, Lawson and I talked of little else except the enormity of what we were doing. The more involved we became in our work, the more apparent became our own culpability. We discussed such things as the Nuremberg trials and how they related to our guilt and complicity in the A7D situation. Lawson often expressed his opinion that the brake was downright dangerous and that, once on flight tests, "anything is liable to happen."

I saw his boss, John Warren, at least twice during that month and needled him about what we were doing. He didn't take the jibes too kindly but managed to laugh the situation off as "one of those things." One day I remarked that what we were doing amounted to fraud, and he pulled out an engineering handbook and turned to a section on laws as they related to the engineering profession.

He read the definition of fraud aloud, then said, "Well, technically I don't think what we're doing can be called fraud. I'll admit it's not right, but it's just one of those things. We're just kinda caught in the middle. About all I can tell you is, Do like I'm doing. Make copies of everything and put them in your SYA file."

"What's an 'SYA' file?" I asked.

"That's a 'save your ass' file." He laughed.

Although I hadn't known it was called that, I had been keeping an SYA file since the beginning of the A7D fiasco. I had made a copy of every scrap of paper connected even remotely with the A7D and had even had copies of 16mm movies that had been made during some of the simulated stops. Lawson, too, had an SYA file, and we both maintained them for one reason: Should the true state of events on the A7D ever be questioned, we wanted to have access to a complete set of factual data. We were afraid that should the question ever come up, the test data might accidentally be "lost."

We finished our work on the graphic portion of the report around the first of June. Altogether, we had prepared nearly 200 pages of data, containing dozens of deliberate falsifications and misrepresentations. I delivered the data to Gretzinger, who said he had been instructed to deliver it personally to the chief engineer, Bud Sunderman, who in turn would assign someone in the engineering department to complete the written portion of the report. He gathered the bundle of data and left the office. Within minutes, he was back with the data, his face white with anger.

"That damned Sink's beat me to it," he said furiously. "He's already talked to Bud about this, and now Sunderman says no one in the engineering department has time to write the report. He wants us to do it, and I told him we couldn't."

The words had barely left his mouth when Russell Line burst in the door. "What the hell's all the fuss about this damned report?" he demanded loudly.

Patiently, Gretzinger explained. "There's no fuss. Sunderman just told me that we'd have to write the report down here, and I said we couldn't. Russ," he went on, "I've told you before that we weren't going to write the report. I made my position clear on that a long time ago."

Line shut him up with a wave of his hand and, turning to me, bellowed, "I'm getting sick and tired of hearing about this damned report. Now, write the goddam thing and shut up about it!" He slammed out of the office. . . .

Somehow, I wasn't at all surprised at this turn of events, and it didn't really make that much difference. As far as I was concerned, we were all up to our necks in the thing anyway, and writing the narrative portion of the report couldn't make me any more guilty than I already felt myself to be.

Still, Line's order came as something of a shock. All the time Lawson and I were working on the report, I felt, deep down, that somewhere, somehow, something would come along and the whole thing would blow over. But Russell Line had crushed that hope. The report was actually going to be issued. Intelligent, law-abiding officials of B. F. Goodrich, one of the oldest and most respected of American corporations, were actually going to deliver to a customer a product that was known to be defective and dangerous and which could very possibly cause death or serious injury.

Within two days, I had completed the narrative, or written portion of the report. As a final sop to my own self-respect, in the conclusion of the report I wrote, "The B. F. Goodrich P/N 2-1162-3 brake assembly does not meet the intent or the requirements of the applicable specification documents and therefore is not qualified."

This was a meaningless gesture, since I knew that this would certainly be changed when the report went through the final typing process. Sure enough, when the report was published, the negative conclusion had been made positive.

One final and significant incident occurred just before publication.

Qualification reports always bear the signature of the person who has prepared them. I refused to sign the report, as did Lawson. Warren was later asked to sign the report. He replied that he would "when I receive a signed statement from Bob Sink ordering me to sign it."

The engineering secretary who was delegated the responsibility of "dogging" the report through publication, told me later that after I, Lawson, and Warren had all refused to sign the report, she had asked Sink if he would sign. He replied, "On something of this nature, I don't think a signature is really needed."

On June 5, 1968, the report was officially published and copies were delivered in person to the Air Force and LTV. Within a week, flight tests were begun at Edwards Air Force Base in California. Searle Lawson was sent to California as Goodrich's representative. Within approximately two weeks, he returned because some rather unusual incidents during the tests had caused them to be canceled.

His face was grim as he related stories of several near crashes during landings—caused by brake troubles. He told me about one incident in which, upon landing, one brake was literally welded together by the intense heat developed during the test stop. The wheel locked, and the plane skidded for nearly 1,500 feet before coming to a halt. The plane was jacked up and the wheel removed. The fused parts within the brake had to be pried apart.

Lawson had returned to Troy from California that same day, and that evening, he and others of the Goodrich engineering department left for Dallas for a high-level conference with LTV.

That evening I left work early and went to see my attorney. After I told him the story, he advised that, while I was probably not actually guilty of fraud, I was certainly part of a conspiracy to defraud. He advised me to go to the Federal Bureau of Investigation and offered to arrange an appointment. The following week he took me to the Dayton office of the FBI, and after I had been warned that I would not be immune from prosecution, I disclosed the A7D matter to one of the agents. The agent told me to say nothing about the episode to anyone and to report any further incident to him. He said he would forward the story to his superiors in Washington.

A few days later, Lawson returned from the conference in Dallas and said that the Air Force, which had previously approved the qualification report, had suddenly rescinded that approval and was demanding to see some of the raw test data taken during the tests. I gathered that the FBI had passed the word.

Omitting any reference to the FBI, I told Lawson I had been to any attorney and that we were probably guilty of conspiracy.

"Can you get me an appointment with your attorney?" he asked. Within a week, he had been to the FBI and told them of his part in the mess. He too was advised to say nothing but to keep on the job reporting any new development.

Naturally, with the rescinding of Air Force approval and the demand to see raw test data, Goodrich officials were in a panic. A conference was called for July 27, a Saturday morning affair at which Lawson, Sink, Warren, and myself were present. . . .

The meeting was called, Sink began, "to see where we stand on the A7D." What we were going to do, he said, was to "level" with

LTV and tell them the "whole truth" about the A7D. "After all," he said, "they're in this thing with us, and they have the right to know how matters stand."

"In other words," I asked, "we're going to tell them the truth?"

"That's right," he replied. "We're going to level with them and let them handle the ball from there."

"There's one thing I don't quite understand," I interjected. "Isn't it going to be pretty hard for us to admit to them that we've lied?"

"Now, wait a minute," he said angrily. "Let's don't go off half-cocked on this thing. It's not a matter of lying. We've just interpreted the information the way we felt it should be."

"I don't know what you call it," I replied, "but to me it's lying, and it's going to be damned hard to confess to them that we've been lying all along."

He became very agitated at this and repeated his "We're not lying," adding, "I don't like this sort of talk."

I dropped the matter at this point, and he began discussing the various discrepancies in the report.

We broke for lunch, and afterward, I came back to the plant to find Sink sitting alone at his desk, waiting to resume the meeting. He called me over and said he wanted to apologize for his outburst that morning. "This thing has kind of gotten me down," he confessed, "and I think you've got the wrong picture. I don't think you really understand everything about this."

Perhaps so, I conceded, but it seemed to me that if we had already told LTV one thing and then had to tell them another, changing our story completely, we would have to admit we were lying.

"No," he explained patiently, "we're not really lying. All we were doing was interpreting the figures the way we knew they should be. We were just exercising engineering license."

During the afternoon session, we marked some 43 discrepant points in the report: 43

points that LTV would surely spot as occasions where we had exercised "engineering license."

After Sink listed those points on the blackboard, we discussed each one individually. As each point came up, Sink would explain that it was probably "too minor to bother about," or that perhaps it "wouldn't be wise to open that can of worms," or that maybe this was a point that "LTV just wouldn't understand." When the meeting was over, it had been decided that only three points were "worth mentioning."

Similar conferences were held during August and September, and the summer was punctuated with frequent treks between Dallas and Troy, and demands by the Air Force to see the raw test data. Tempers were short and matters seemed to grow worse.

Finally, early in October 1968, Lawson submitted his resignation, to take effect on October 25. On October 18, I submitted my own resignation, to take effect on November 1. In my resignation, addressed to Russell Line, I cited the A7D report and stated: "As you are aware, this report contained numerous deliberate and willful misrepresentations which, according to legal counsel, constitute fraud and expose both myself and others to criminal charges of conspiracy to defraud. . . . The events of the past seven months have created an atmosphere of deceit and distrust in which it is impossible to work. . . ."

On October 25, I received a sharp summons to the office of Bud Sunderman. As chief engineer at the Troy plant, Sunderman was responsible for the entire engineering division. . . .

. . . He motioned me to a chair. "I have your resignation here," he snapped, "and I must say you have made some rather shocking, I might even say irresponsible, charges. This is very serious."

Before I could reply, he was demanding an explanation. "I want to know exactly what the fraud is in connection with the A7D and how you can dare accuse this company of such a thing!"

I started to tell some of the things that had happened during the testing, but he shut me off saying, "There's nothing wrong with anything we've done here. You aren't aware of all the things that have been going on behind the scenes. If you had known the true situation, you would never have made these charges." He said that in view of my apparent "disloyalty" he had decided to accept my resignation "right now," and said it would be better for all concerned if I left the plant immediately. As I got up to leave he asked me if I intended to "carry this thing further."

I answered simply, "Yes," to which he replied, "Suit yourself." Within 20 minutes, I had cleaned out my desk and left. Forty-eight hours later, the B. F. Goodrich Company recalled the qualification report and the four-disk brake, announcing that it would replace the brake with a new, improved, five-disk brake at no cost to LTV.

Ten months later, on August 13, 1969, I was the chief government witness at a hearing conducted before Senator William Proxmire's Economy in Government Subcommittee of the Congress's Joint Economic Committee. I related the A7D story to the committee, and my testimony was supported by Searle Lawson, who followed me to the witness stand. Air Force officers also testified, as well as a four-man team from the General Accounting Office, which had conducted an investigation of the A7D brake at the request of Senator Proxmire. Both Air Force and GAO investigators declared that the brake was dangerous and had not been tested properly.

Testifying for Goodrich was R. G. Jeter, vice president and general counsel of the company, from the Akron headquarters. Representing the Troy plant was Robert Sink. These two denied any wrongdoing on the part of the Goodrich Company, despite expert testimony to the contrary by Air Force and GAO officials. Sink was quick to deny any connection with the writing of the report or of directing any falsifications, claiming to be on the West Coast at the time. John Warren was the man who supervised its writing, said Sink.

As for me, I was dismissed as a high school graduate with no technical training, while Sink

testified that Lawson was a young, inexperienced engineer. "We tried to give him guidance," Sink testified, "but he preferred to have his own convictions."

About changing the data and figures in the report, Sink said: "When you take data from several different sources, you have to rationalize among those data what is the true story. This is part of your engineering know-how." He admitted that changes had been made in the data, "but only to make them more consistent with the overall picture of the data that is available."

Jeter pooh-poohed the suggestion that anything improper occurred, saying: "We have 30-odd engineers at this plant . . . and I say to you that it is incredible that these men would stand idly by and see reports changed or falsified. . . . I mean you just do not have to do that working for anybody. . . . Just nobody does that."

The four-hour hearing adjourned with no real conclusion reached by the committee. But, the following day the Department of Defense made sweeping changes in its inspection, testing, and reporting procedures. A spokesman for the DOD said the changes were a result of the Goodrich episode.

The A7D is now in service, sporting a Goodrich-made five-disk brake, a brake that works very well, I'm told. Business at the Goodrich plant is good. Lawson is now an engineer for LTV and has been assigned to the A7D project. And I am now a newspaper reporter.

At this writing, those remaining at Goodrich are still secure in the same positions, all except Russell Line and Robert Sink. Line has been rewarded with a promotion to production superintendent, a large step upward on the corporate ladder. As for Sink, he moved up into Line's old job.

Source: "Why Should My Conscience Bother Me?" by Kermit Vandivier from *In the Name of Profit* by Robert L. Heilbroner, ed. Copyright © 1972 by Doubleday & Company, Inc. Reprinted by permission of the publisher, Warner Paperback Library Edition (1973), pp. 11–33.

QUESTIONS

1. What forces provoked the wrongdoing in the case?
2. How did the company punish the wrongdoers?
3. In essence what was the decision facing the test lab supervisor, Ralph Gretzinger?
4. What policies might be developed to protect those in Gretzinger's situation?
5. When faced with a choice between material success and honesty, as Gretzinger was, why is it that some take the honorable route and others do not?
6. Had you been Gretzinger, what course would you have taken? Explain your reasons.
7. Had someone died as a consequence of the faulty brakes, could Goodrich and the individuals responsible properly have been charged with manslaughter?
8. Is wrongdoing of this nature less likely in a smaller company?
9. Can you suggest some steps that a company might take to avoid a situation like that of Goodrich?
10. Allow your mind free rein. Assume each of the principal characters possessed the values hierarchy attributed earlier in this chapter to ministers.
    a. Would the results have been different? Why or why not?
    b. If so, should Goodrich accept as management-level personnel only those with "ministerial values"?
    c. If not, are managers essentially powerless pawns before the weight and immortality of the corporate structure?

Business Crime—Executive Liability

The relationship between law and ethics is not easily defined. Certainly the law is an approximate reflection of society's collective ethical standards, but the law could not practically embrace and codify the fullness of our ethical code. In a free society, maximum reliance on personal beliefs, customs, values, and ethics is to be prized. The law is helpful in powerfully specifying some specific codes of conduct and thus offering broad guidelines for honorable behavior. But the law must be regarded only as a minimum standard, a floor upon which the individual is expected to erect a more refined and detailed structure.

Criminal law as applied to business provides an apt illustration of the necessary tension between law and ethics. Society reaches various conclusions as to that which is wrongful (unethical or unlawful), who is responsible, and whether that wrong is of a nature and magnitude sufficient to require formal legal intervention to buttress the weight of the individual conscience. The ambiguities in the law-ethics relationship are well represented in an executive's ironic response to allegations of a price-fixing conspiracy. When asked if he realized that his meetings with his co-conspirators were illegal, he replied:

Illegal? Yes, but not criminal. I didn't find out until I read the indictment. . . . I assumed that criminal action meant damaging someone, and we did not do that.[26]

Extraordinary hurdles are arrayed against the effort to curb white-collar crime. Governmental investigations are hampered by a lack of funds. Mounds of documentary evidence, sometimes totaling hundreds of thousands of pages, are commonplace in white-collar prosecutions. Defendants are often able to hire America's best attorneys, while the government frequently must rely on bright but inexperienced counsel. Most damaging to the white-collar crime pursuit is probably public apathy. The outrage generated by street crime simply is not visited upon the clever, less violent "crimes of the suites." In recent years changing values and frustration with the legal system's success in pursuing business crime have led to an emphasis on holding executives personally liable for wrongdoing within the organization.

That trend was stunningly illustrated in 1985 by the murder convictions of three corporate managers for the death of a worker whom those officials allegedly knowingly exposed to cyanide fumes in their silver-recycling plant. Stefan Golub cleaned barrels of cyanide for Film Recovery Systems Corporation of Elk Grove Village, Illinois. He died, and the coroner ruled that the fumes were the cause of death. The firm's president, plant foreman, and plant manager were found guilty of murder for having "knowingly created a strong probability of death." They were sentenced to 25 years in prison and fined $10,000. The businessmen claim that they did not know the plant was dangerous, and they will appeal their convictions.[27] The murder conviction was apparently the first of its kind in U.S. history.

The following article (written prior to the cyanide case) summarizes the law and some complex issues involved in holding executives personally liable for company violations.

EXECUTIVE LIABILITY FOR CORPORATE LAW VIOLATIONS

S. Prakash Sethi

[S. Prakash Sethi is professor of business and social policy at Baruch College, the City University of New York. His article is based in part on testimony before the Subcommittee on Crime of the House Committee on the Judiciary.]

In the recent past, top executives and corporate officers have only rarely faced imprisonment as a penalty for criminal violation of legal statutes, even where an executive was found to have direct complicity or involvement in the corporation's illegal acts. Prison sentences most often have been levied where a corporate executive was convicted of a law violation involving a company's stockholders, that is, its legal owner. However, where law violations against other elements of society were involved, the executive seldom was imprisoned by the courts, and his fines invariably were paid by the corporation. The offender received both moral and social support from his peer group, which considered such crimes to be "technical" violations of law and a misfortune for the offender in being caught.

This situation has changed during the last few years. There has been an enormous increase in the nature and extent of business activities subjected to governmental regulation or control. Increased regulation has been accompanied by an expanded scope of personal civil and criminal liability by corporate executives for law violations by their subordinates. This seems to be happening not only in the United States but also in other industrialized countries, especially France and the United Kingdom. . . .

In developing any kind of punitive measures, we need to be extremely cautious that they do not so undermine the efficient functioning of the corporation in a way that would adversely affect productivity, incentive for risk taking, economic growth, and, thereby, society's welfare. This article is aimed at addressing these twin issues: the nature and scope of executive responsibility for compliance with various laws, and the types of penalties that may be most effective in deterring such law violations.

Expanding Scope of Executive Liability

There is growing public concern, and legitimately so, that more effective measures are needed to hold corporations, and those who guide them, responsible for corporate activities that endanger public welfare and safety through violations of safety, antipollution, and environmental protection laws. This concern is not confined to the United States. Three short cases, from the United States, France, and Great Britain, provide a vivid picture of the increasing risk and exposure of a corporate executive to criminal prosecution in the course of managing the day-to-day affairs of the company.

On June 9, 1975, the U.S. Supreme Court upheld the conviction of John R. Park, president of Acme Products, Inc., Philadelphia, for rodent infestation found by the Food and Drug Administration in the supermarket chain's Baltimore warehouse. The Court decided that the chief executive of a corporation can be found guilty of criminal charges if unsanitary conditions anywhere in his company contaminate food or otherwise endanger health or safety. The case thus greatly expanded the long-established *Dotterweich* doctrine, under which corporate officers had been held personally liable for violations of the Food, Drug, and Cosmetic Act of 1938, although they had no direct involvement or actual knowledge of the violation. However, until *Park,* all convictions involved individual executives with immediate close supervisory responsibilities over operations where law violations occurred.

The facts are not in dispute. In November and December of 1971, the company's Baltimore warehouse was investigated by an FDA investigator, who found extensive evidence of rodent infestation and other unsanitary conditions in the warehouse. In January 1972, the chief of compliance of the FDA's Baltimore

office wrote to Park, informing him of the unsanitary conditions in the Baltimore warehouse. A second investigation in March 1972, revealed some improvement but still showed evidence of rodent infestation.

In March 1973, the United States filed a suit against Acme Markets and Park, charging them with five criminal counts of violations under the Act. Acme pleaded guilty; Park moved for acquittal. The government offered no evidence that Park had participated in the violation, but contended that Park was guilty because he was aware of the sanitation problems in the Baltimore warehouse and was the corporate officer who bore general responsibility for all company activities that would subject him to criminal liability. Park testified that although he was responsible for all of Acme's employees and the general direction of the company, the size and complexity of Acme's operations demanded that he must delegate responsibility for different phases of operations to various line and staff subordinates.

The jury found Park guilty. In his appeal, Park contended, among other things, that the district court erred in its instructions to the jury in defining "responsible relationship" by stating that the statute makes individuals, as well as corporations, liable for violations when "the individual had a responsible relation to the situation, even though he may not have participated personally." A divided court of appeals reversed and remanded the case for new trial. The appeals court stated that, although the *Dotterweich* doctrine dispensed with the need to prove "awareness of wrongdoing by Park, it did not dispense with the need to prove that Park was in some way personally responsible for the act constituting the crime."

The Supreme Court reversed the appeals court decision, saying that: (1) criminal liability under the Act does not turn on awareness of some wrongdoing or conscious fraud; (2) the Act permits convictions of responsible corporate officials who have the power to prevent or correct violations; (3) viewed as a whole, the jury instruction was adequate; and (4) the evidence that Park had previously been advised of unsanitary conditions at another warehouse was admissible since it served to rebut the official's defense that he had justifiably relied upon subordinates to handle sanitation matters. The Court stated that a failure to exercise authority and supervisory responsibility was a sufficient basis for a responsible corporate executive's liability. The Act imposes not only a positive duty to seek out and remedy violations when they occur, but, also, and primarily, a duty to implement measures that will ensure that violations will not occur. Thus, a level of *absolute liability* is imposed that permits no defense when the violation occurs.

Subsequent court decisions have further clarified the defense of "powerlessness on the part of corporate executives in preventing unlawful activities," suggesting and actually limiting its scope. In each instance, the courts found that corporate officials failed to exercise the high standard of care imposed by the Act.

In France, on January 23, 1975, Roland Wuillaume was killed while trying to connect two railroad cars that were standing on an incline. One car rolled, thereby crushing him. At the time of his death, Wuillaume was employed as a temporary worker in an asphalt plant of Huttes-Goudron at Derives (HGD), a subsidiary of the state-owned Carbonnages de France-Chimie (CDF). The subsequent investigation showed that at the time of the accident the lighting in the area was defective. In addition, Wuillaume had a stiff hip and leg and was considered 67 percent incapacitated. Prior to the accident, he had been employed at the plant for 17 days, four of which were devoted to training. However, Wuillaume had been hired as a store worker from a temporary employment agency and was not qualified under the law or physically capable of performing the assigned task.

Two unions filed a lawsuit charging that "the unions are enraged by the worker's death, and after suffering many deaths and poor and unsafe working conditions, they have decided to make an example of this case—perhaps, to force the judicial branch of the French government to take a stand." On September 29, 1975, eight months after the accident, M. Jean Chapron, executive director of HGD, was charged with cumulative negligence and involuntary homicide. Following the indictment, Chapron was imprisoned for five days. Georges Tredez, the director of the temporary employment agency, was also indicted for involuntary homicide but was not arrested.

The incident aroused tremendous controversy. Organized labor and workers in general were extremely unhappy about the relative lack of concern for industrial safety on the part of plant management and even the government. The management group charged that the background and training of judges had become highly politicized, and that judges were using the laws to impose unreasonable and excessive penalties on management and to advance a particular type of political and social philosophy.

The criminal court dismissed the charges against both Chapron and Tredez. CGT and CFDT were awarded 500 francs for damages; Chapron and Tredez were fined a total of 1,000 francs. The judgment found that Chapron was not negligent and that the responsible party was the victim, Wuillaume. In addition, the suit filed by the victim's family was rejected. The grand jury stated that because a disturbance of public order must happen at the time of the violation, the detention of Chapron was not justified.

In Great Britain, the three top officials (the manager, under-manager, and deputy) of the National Coal Board's mine at Houghton Main in Yorkshire were accused of failing to enforce safety procedures when five workers were killed in an explosion in June 1976. All three officials pleaded not guilty. After lengthy hearings in July 1976, all were convicted and fined. The manager and under-manager appealed to the Crown court at Sheffield and were heard in September 1977. The conviction of the under-manager was upheld, but the conviction of the manager was dismissed.

The court's reluctance to hold the manager responsible was not in keeping with the court's own findings. First, the court held that a more stringent system of reporting and reading of safety reports would have impressed those responsible with the necessity of keeping the machinery running at all times. Second, the court held that it was satisfied that all the people to whom these duties were delegated were, in the normal usage of the word, "competent." The court contended that the fact that some of them failed to use their competence in the expected manner was not the fault of the manager. The question then arose as to whose fault it was. The pertinence of the question becomes more obvious when it is recognized that the 1976 Act imposes upon a workman a duty to exercise reasonable care, and if this duty is breached he may be prosecuted in a criminal court. The legislative mandate was clear. The court, however, was unwilling to go so far as holding top management criminally negligent.

These cases illustrate the nature of an executive's personal liability in certain specialized spheres of corporate activities, and the increasingly broad definition of this liability. However, they do not begin to show a whole new array of corporate activities where executives are to be held personally liable for corporate law violations without personal complicity. For example, in a study of 27 health-and-safety-related studies in the United States, O'-Keefe and Shapiro found that a significant number of statutes did not require prior knowledge or personal involvement on the part of the responsible executive and carried provisions for civil and criminal penalties.

The Federal Water Pollution Control Act Amendments of 1972 stipulate personal liability for executives for organizational abuse of the environment and provide both civil and criminal penalties. Another aspect of broadened personal liability for corporate officers is the Occupational Safety and Health Act of 1970 (OSHA). OSHA provides for sanctions, including fines, against individuals who are "responsible" for, though unknowledgeable about, safety infractions.

This trend is but one aspect of a demand for greater accountability by those in authority which is not limited to the field of health and personal safety. The courts also are increasingly holding corporate directors and independent auditors, lawyers, investment bankers, and brokers responsible for not exercising due care in the discharge of their duties. The trend toward greater executive accountability and

stiffer fines and prison sentences also is evident in such traditional areas as antitrust and securities fraud.

* * * * *

Why the Expanding Scope of Liability?
This trend raises questions about the changing relationship between business and other social institutions, the societal expectations of corporate executives, and the effect of expanding the personal criminal liability on top corporate decision making and performance and, by implication, on economic growth, and social welfare. Even if one accepts the desirability of the social goals these means are intended to achieve, there is a question as to whether imposition of absolute and vicarious personal criminal liability on corporate executives is the best way to achieve these goals.

At the heart of the movement toward holding managers personally responsible for corporate violations of the law lies the struggle both of individuals and entire societies to come to grips with the contemporary reality of the corporation and to subject it to effective controls. It reflects, in some cases, society's frustrations in molding the corporation in a certain direction and having to resort to successively severe measures when conventional approaches fail to work. The circumstances that have brought us to the present situation may be classified as: failure of market institutions, failure of existing enforcement structures, inadequacy of existing legal philosophy, and failure of the news media. I would like to discuss these factors briefly because they have a bearing on the type of remedies that I would like to propose.

Failure of Market Mechanism
Inherent in traditional economic dogma is the notion that corporate behavior can be effectively controlled by the mechanisms of the marketplace. Customers will withhold their patronage of a company that misbehaves, refuse to purchase its goods and services, and the company will go out of business. In order for this system to work, however, the communications channels between business and society must be clear so that the necessary adjustments can be made. In today's complex economy,

this condition rarely exists because, as firms become large and diversified and deal with a wide range of customers, they become increasingly immune to market discipline.

So, society has turned to regulation. Yet such efforts are doomed to failure. The regulators never can have the necessary expertise to anticipate future developments in technology, or to understand the organizational labyrinths through which management can work in fulfilling the legal requirements without making any substantive changes. . . .

Failure of Enforcement Structures

It is no secret that corporate executives, regardless of their culpability, have not suffered the fate of other criminals in terms of incarceration for economic crimes. While the "law in books" pertaining to corporate crimes is not dissimilar to the laws regarding other types of crimes, the "law in action"—enforcement—is characterized, in the case of corporate crimes, by slow, inefficient, and highly differential implementation.

While crimes involving physical violence against individuals are dealt with sternly, economic crimes are considered social aberrations and are dealt with quite leniently. Incarceration is deemed unnecessary since these individuals are not considered a threat to society. Fines often are quite nominal, invariably paid by the corporation employing the offenders, and carry little economic hardship. . . .

Inadequacy of Existing Legal Philosophy

The traditional model of *mens rea* in criminal law poses severe problems when applied to corporate executives within the context of corporate behavior. Large corporations, employing thousands of people and making millions of decisions, impose impossible burdens on society to isolate and identify a particular individual to be held responsible where only the last link in the long decision chain is visible. Even if the entire corporate decision process were exposed to public scrutiny, it might still be impossible to isolate and identify the guilty person because of the collectivity of the actions that resulted in law violation and the lack of specific intent or direct knowledge on the part

of the thousands of people who may have contributed in some miniscule sense to that direction.

One alternative to this problem has been the imposition of strict criminal liability. Although the Supreme Court apparently has indicated that a legislatively developed standard of strict liability is acceptable for criminal conviction, this is not a desirable course of action because of the undesirable side effects. A standard should be developed that is more relevant to the corporate context, goes beyond the restrictive scope of specific criminal intent, and provides greater incentives for corporate executives to exercise the utmost care in supervision of personnel and facilities to prevent occurrence of corporate crimes.

Failure of the News Media

Another factor in the differential treatment of corporate executives has been the inability of the mass media to explore and report complex issues relating to corporate crimes. . . .

Improving the Situation

Society has a right to use criminal penalties and imprisonment of executives to deter corporate misdeeds. There indeed may be circumstances under which corporate executives are held to higher standards of accountability than those imposed on individuals acting in their personal capacities. . . .

Potential criminal liability, will, in all likelihood, lead executives to ensure that they have knowledge of and control over any activities that could lead to their imprisonment. They may reject the option of decentralizing operations or delegating responsibility, and, in turn, the lower-echelon manager will feel a closer scrutiny by the responsible officer. This could limit initiative, stifle innovation, and sacrifice growth. Consumers may be denied the fruits of the economics of size, availability of products in closer proximity, and access to information. On the other hand, it could be argued that, by compelling the executive to maintain closer supervision and control, the company will be more responsible to society's needs; thus expansion will only come with a clear and reasoned justification for such growth. . . .

In view of these considerations, the following suggestions seem appropriate for adequate executive liability legislation:

There should be provision to cover the situation where an executive does not "discover" the existence of a dangerous situation. Such nondiscovery may occur because the executive developed a system of organization and communication which effectively insulated him from receiving information of illegal acts within his domain of authority.

In order to be applied effectively and equitably, it would be important to show that the functional area where the illegal act occurred was within the responsibility of the executive charged, and that he or she had the authority to prevent its occurrence. Every law that proscribes certain activities in health, safety, and environmental areas should require that the corporation predesignate an executive who would be responsible for ensuring corporate compliance with that law. Since this would be tantamount to prewarning, the executive so designated could not offer a "lack of knowledge" defense. More important, since compliance would be this executive's sole responsibility, any violation would become a prima facie case for reckless and negligent supervision.

In the event of a multiplicity of laws and responsibilities, a practical solution would be for corporations to develop "Social Accountability Centers." A social accountability center would be similar in purpose and goal to a profit center. The purpose of a profit center in a corporation is to group a set of complementary activities together and put them under the charge of one executive who manages this profit center as if it were an autonomous business entity. It would seem logical that the profit center concept should be made the basis of a "social accountability center" whereby all harmful and dangerous acts would be charged to the manager of that center. . . .

In order to provide maximum deterrence against corporate crimes, personal criminal penalties should be made an integral part of a prevention package. . . .

To create a societal consent toward the undesirability of corporate crimes, prison sentences could be accompanied with a public apology from the corporation and the executive, together with a description of their wrongful deeds. Such apologies are common both in Germany and Japan and seem to have been effective in bringing public attention and public condemnation to violators.

Corporations whose operations have been in violation of criminal laws should be subjected to special reporting requirements. The company and its officers could, for example, be required to make regular periodic statements to the court stating that no violations existed. . . .

Source: S. Prakash Sethi, "Executive Liability for Corporate Law Violations," *Los Angeles Business & Economics* (now titled *Business Forum*), vol. 5, no. 3 (Summer 1980), pp. 10–17.

QUESTIONS

1. What is the essence of John R. Park's defense? As a matter of law why was Park's conviction affirmed by the Supreme Court? Was the decision just?
2. Dr. Donald Cressey, a leading expert on white-collar crime, said: "restraints of trade, price fixing, and other major white-collar crimes are much more threatening to the national welfare than are burglaries, and robberies and other so-called street crimes."[28]

   a. Do you agree? Explain why or why not.
   b. Why might white collar criminals receive more gentle treatment?
   c. What punishments would be most effective against white-collar criminals?
3. What is strict criminal liability?
4. Evaluate Sethi's notion of "social accountability centers."
5. It is often argued that increased personal liability will substantially discourage qual-

ified individuals from assuming top-level executive positions. Do you agree? What are your reasons?

6. During the late 1970s and early 1980s Congress struggled to reform the U.S. criminal code. Two felony provisions caused particular consternation in the business community: (1) reckless endangerment and (2) omission to perform a duty of an organization. Reckless endangerment was intended to apply to outrageously hazardous behavior not previously reached by the code. Any company or executive who violated federal health or safety regulations so seriously that "he places another person in danger of imminent death or serious bodily injury" would have been subject to prosecution. The omission to perform a duty standard would have held executives criminally liable for failing to "exercise relatively diligent oversight and exertion." By 1985 neither provision had been enacted, nor did enactment appear imminent, given the political climate of the mid-1980s. Would you favor such legislation?

Whistle Blowing

In 1968, A. Ernest Fitzgerald was earning $31,000 annually as a civilian cost-cutting management expert for the Air Force. Under questioning before a congressional committee Fitzgerald testified that cost overruns on the C5A cargo plane might total $2 billion. Fitzgerald lost his job. After a series of court struggles he won an order compelling his reinstatement. In 1973 he was back in an office, but he was given only trivial work assignments. Then in 1981 a federal district court ordered Fitzgerald reinstated in his old job or an equivalent position. Ultimately his litigation against the Air Force was settled out of court. Fitzgerald received a promotion and $200,000 to assist in meeting his legal fees.[29]

Fitzgerald is the most famous of a burgeoning group of whistle blowers in both the public and private sectors. Today employees seem increasingly inclined to follow the dictates of conscience in speaking out—publicly if necessary—against wrongdoing on the part of their employers. Historically, complaints were to be taken to management and resolved there. "Going public" was considered an act of disloyalty. Americans continue to maintain a strong tradition against "squealing." Indeed, management has good reason to discourage irresponsible, precipitous whistle blowing that might disclose legitimate trade secrets, cause unnecessary conflict among employees, unfairly tarnish the company image, and so on. The whistle blowing conflict is illustrated in the following article.

PETER FAULKNER AND NUCLEAR SERVICES

David Clutterbuck

In the furor that has followed the near disaster at the nuclear power station at Three Mile Island in the United States [in 1979], engineer Peter Faulkner could be forgiven for saying: "I told you so." Faulkner "blew the whistle" on the nuclear industry five years before, claiming that accidents were inevitable because of mechanical and design deficiencies in nuclear power stations.

At the time Faulkner was working as a systems application engineer for a U.S. nuclear engineering firm Nuclear Services Corp. (NSC). He began to accumulate evidence which he believed showed that power station systems were being sold before serious design problems had been solved. At first, he claims, he tried to work within the company to overcome these problems. Together with several other people, he says, he designed a management information system that would detect such flaws before companies became committed to fulfilling orders. No one, he says, was interested.

Then Faulkner came across a memorandum from a top nuclear engineer detailing alleged faults in the design of a new nuclear reactor. He decided that, as he appeared unable to change attitudes from within, he would take the matter to his senator.

A paper by Faulkner detailing a series of alleged design faults in nuclear reactors was read into the proceedings of a Senate subcommittee. The president of NSC took exception to the paper and, Faulkner claims, put pressure on him not to publish his paper more widely. Faulkner was then interviewed by the company psychiatrist, apparently to determine whether his actions had their origin in any private hos-

tility towards NSC. Faulkner claims he had none. In early April 1974, the company fired him.

However, NSC maintains that Faulkner was not fired for criticizing the company. It insists that the reason was that he had made public confidential information. NSC argues that the real issue in the Faulkner case is not an employee's right to speak out about corporate behavior, but the duty of an employee to maintain client confidence.

Faulkner insists that his actions were justified. He has frequently challenged his former employers to bring charges against him if his accusations are untrue, but they have failed to do so. He is unemployed and, after innumerable unsuccessful job applications, believes he has been blacklisted.

"I am banished socially, an apostate professionally, unemployable as an engineer and regarded by conventional people as distinctly subversive," he says.

His justification for blowing the whistle is simple. "Public safety takes precedence over any consideration in this case, since nuclear plant hazards are demonstrably unacceptable," he declares.

Excerpted from David Clutterbuck, "Blowing the Whistle on Corporate Misconduct," *International Management*, January 1980, pp. 14, 16. Reprinted with special permission from *International Management*. Copyright © 1980, McGraw-Hill Publications Company. All rights reserved.

QUESTIONS

1. Why is the role of "squealer" or whistle blower so repugnant to most Americans?

2. How would you feel about a classmate who blew the whistle on you for cheating on an examination? Would you report cheating by a classmate if it came to your attention?

3. Assume an employee of an American corporation speaks out to warn the public against a danger in one of the employer's products. The employee is fired.

    a. Can the employee successfully argue that the First Amendment guarantee of

    freedom of speech protects him or her from dismissal?

    b. Would it make a difference if the firm operated a nuclear reactor for generating electricity? (You can refer to Chapter 5 for more discussion of this issue.)

4. James Roche, former chairman of the board of General Motors Corporation, said:

    Some critics are now busy eroding another support of free enterprise—the loyalty of a management team, with its unifying values of cooperative work. Some of the enemies of business now encourage an employee to be disloyal to the enterprise. They want to create suspicion and disharmony and pry into the proprietary interests of the business. However this is labelled—industrial espionage, whistle blowing, or professional responsibility—it is another tactic for spreading disunity and creating conflict.[30]

Evaluate Mr. Roche's argument.

5. Other than avoiding wrongdoing, what steps might the organization take to render whistle blowing unnecessary? (You might refer to Kenneth D. Walters, "Your Employees' Right to Blow the Whistle," *Harvard Business Review,* July–August 1975, pp. 26, 31.)

6. Carl Kaufmann, an executive assistant in public affairs at Du Pont, outlined a dilemma that arose in a giant chemicals firm:

For years, your corporation manufactures a dye intermediate called Beta-naphthylamine without any questions of risk. Then alarming evidence begins turning up—an unusual number of tumors among workers in a plant, malignant tumors. Beta is identified by company scientists as a potent carcinogen—but hundreds of your workers were already exposed.

Would you blow the whistle on yourself or try to do a cleanup quietly to prevent future injuries?[31]

Answer Kaufmann's question.

Bribery Abroad

Multinational business firms face a special and complex ethical dilemma. In many cultures the payment of bribes, *baksheesh* (Middle East), *mordita* (South America), or *dash* (Africa), is accepted as necessary and, in some cases, lawful ways of doing business. American firms and officers wishing to succeed abroad have faced great pressure to engage in practices that are, of course, illegal and unethical in the American culture. In recent years some 370 firms, including respected names such as Gulf Oil, Lockheed, Exxon, and 3M, have confessed to questionable payments abroad totaling perhaps $745 million. For example, Lockheed expended $12.6 million in Japan alone in seeking aircraft sales. Disclosure of widespread bribery by American firms, including government officials at the highest levels, led to the 1977 enactment of the Foreign Corrupt Practices Act (FCPA).

The act makes it a crime for American corporations to offer or provide bribes to foreign government officials to obtain or retain business. New accounting requirements make concealment of such payments difficult. Penalties include fines of up to $1 million for companies, while individuals may be fined $10,000 and imprisoned for as long as five years if they either participate in a violation or know of the violation. The act does not forbid "grease" payments to lower-level functionaries who require under-the-table compensation merely to carry out routine duties, such as securing permits and placing transatlantic calls. A *Business Week* survey suggests that American businesses have now become scrupulously—even excessively—careful in avoiding improprieties.[32] For example, many companies adopted policies forbidding all payments, rather than run the risk of an employee misunderstanding the distinction between forbidden payoffs and permissible "grease."

The FCPA has placed American firms at a competitive disadvantage, in that few other nations have assumed our ethical stance. For example, France has no law governing this practice, and Italy passed legislation in 1980 explicitly approving payments to foreign officials for the purpose of securing business. The FCPA has been vigorously criticized. A major problem, of course, is simply that of distinguishing between a bribe and an honest payment in return for legitimate services rendered.

In addition to causing lost contracts, the act has forced corporations to employ more lawyers and accountants and compelled them to pay close attention to trivial payments. At this writing Congress is considering legislation to relax the FCPA by, among other measures, providing that actions not considered illegal in other nations would not be prohibited by U.S. law. Despite dissatisfaction with the FCPA, few of its critics would argue that widespread bribery abroad is a credit to the American business community. The following case from Carl Kaufmann of Du Pont illustrates the ethical predicament raised by differences in host country practices and American legal-ethical standards.

As the head of a multinational corporation, you learn that one of your plant managers has been arrested in a distant republic. His alleged "crime" is that goods found in your warehouse lack the proper customs stamp and papers.

But the truth is more complicated. For years, "grease" has been a way of life in this country's bureaucracy and your plant manager has been paying gratuities to the customs officers. But he knows it is against "home office" policy and so he stops. Their "inspection" follows. The price for dropping all charges: $18,000.

Would you pay up? Or let your man be put in jail? Which alternative is more ethical?[33]

A Dissent

To this point the chapter has been directed, rather conventionally, to the notion that the cause of decency in the corporate community will be enhanced if we achieve a sufficient understanding of ethical dilemmas and the decision systems necessary to deal with them. Therefore, it is fitting to look at an aggressively cynical viewpoint that rejects ideals in favor of a pragmatism often thought to be more in keeping with today's business reality.

NOTHING SUCCEEDS LIKE AN S.O.B.

R. H. Morrison

The real key to all success is perseverance. The willingness to hang in there, take the lumps that come, and get up off the floor more than once, is the attribute that you must have.

You also have to become a dedicated, single-minded S.O.B. You have to change your thinking, your attitude toward reality, and develop what could be described as a Machiavellian outlook on the world.

1. First, you cannot be overconcerned with morality in the conventional sense. You must become convinced there is nothing essentially wrong with exploiting people and situations. The game of business is like the game of football. If the quarterback on the offensive team discovers that a defensive halfback simply cannot cover one of his pass receivers, he will use that weakness to his maximum advantage. The defender may wind up losing his job, but this is of no concern to the quarterback. The name of the game is winning, and exploiting situations and people is part of that game.

2. You have to learn to become cool and detached in dealing with other people. You

never get emotionally involved with people or situations. Essentially you view everything in terms of objects and situations. You do not suffer with intellectual analysis of the results of your actions.

3. You actually enjoy the game. You enjoy the exploitation, you derive the satisfaction from using people, things, and situations to achieve your goal. You do not do this for amusement or self-aggrandizement, but simply to get that which you are after.

4. Above all you have a rational view of society as it exists. You are neither impressed nor bothered by philosophical viewpoints that stress that the greatest goals in life are serving your fellow man.

5. In short you are not a nice guy, you are an S.O.B., dedicated to success, and having convinced yourself you need that success, it will be achieved. As for money, that's the way you keep score.

If this attitude puts some strain on your psyche, and you feel it is overly cynical or outright debasing, I would like to engage in a brief, philosophical dissertation concerning the reality of such things as truth and morals.

In point of fact, *there is no such thing as real truth in human affairs*. Let's examine the most often quoted rule of behavior, the so-called golden rule. ''Do unto others as you would have others do unto you.'' This sounds as though it is the perfect philosophical solution to human action. However, all humans are not the same, and there are aberrations in the human psyche. If, for example, a masochist were to apply the golden rule to everybody he came in contact with, there would be many unhappy people in the vicinity.

So even the most likely sounding philosophy has holes in it. The plain truth is, that truth is a point of view.

For example, let's take a common happening that affects everybody in the vicinity. Rain! Rain falls universally on everybody in an area. The farmer says the rain is good because it makes his crops grow, and this is the truth. The roadbuilder, the owner of the baseball team, and the people going on a picnic say the rain is bad because it stops them from doing what they

need to do. And that, too is the truth. So we have several people with exactly opposing opinions about an event, and all are telling the truth. So, in fact, the truth is little more than a point of view, and it depends on whose moccasins you are standing in as to whether good or bad.

The problem with things of this nature is that people tend to take extreme viewpoints. Thus, the farmer who demands that it always rains is advocating flood. The roadbuilder who advocates that it never rains is advocating drought. The truth has to be a reasonable compromise between these points of view. And so it is with all affairs of mankind—there has to be a compromise from the extremes in order to arrive at a livable situation. But those moralists who set down rules carved in stone and hand them down as the great truth from above are little more than con men attempting to force people to live in a society that advocates a single truth or a single point of view. It very seldom works.

Morals are nothing more than social customs. They change with time, generations, and societies. For example, a cannibal is moral in a cannibalistic society. He is obviously immoral in a noncannibalistic society.

In this country we have had great changes in moral attitudes over the years, and they change every day. In the Old West, horse stealing was a hanging offense. Today it is a misdemeanor. In the early days of this country, political corruption, prostitution, slavery, and other moral outrages were common coin. Yet we had a higher percentage of people going to church in those days than we do today. . . .

Such is the continuous hold of morality on a society. Therefore, the small businessman who is stepping out into the business world can be little concerned with the changing fads of human morals, or philosophical opinions about what is or is not truth.

* * * * *

When you have made it up the mountain, reached the pinnacle, you can then do what the rest of those successful entrepreneurs have done before you. You can write a code of ethics, make speeches about morality to business and civic groups, and look down with a cold smile on all the scrambling, scratching little bastards below, trying to find their path to the top. You can even do what some of the rest of them have done—roll rocks down on them just for the hell of it, and make the road a little tougher.

I like to think of the small businessman as an eagle. A high-flying loner, whose only morality is to get that which he deems is his right. He flies alone, finds what he needs himself, and lives where and as he chooses.

I think of corporations, government bureaucracies, and others as vultures. Vultures operate in groups, picking the bones of the dead and defenseless, and are simply put here to demonstrate Machiavelli's rule that only the fittest survive. Start now!

Source: *Business & Society Review* 28 (Winter 1978–79), pp. 69–70. Reprinted by permission from the *Business and Society Review*. Copyright 1978, Warren Gorham & Lamont Inc., 210 South Street, Boston, Mass. All rights reserved.

QUESTIONS

1. What is meant by a "Machiavellian outlook on the world"?
2. Is truth merely a point of view? Evaluate the author's argument.
3. Are morals merely relative or situational, changing according to time, place, and circumstance?
4. Assume a businessperson's goal is success and that issues of morality are of insignificant concern. Is Morrison's formula the best route to success?
5. In some eras and cultures, spiritual success has been preferable to material success. Is that the case in contemporary America? Explain.

Chapter Questions

1. Can the realistic businessperson expect to be both ethical and successful?

2. Resolve these ethical dilemmas posed by Carl Kaufmann of Du Pont:[34]

    a. Your corporation has developed a prescription drug that helps prevent flu or cure it. It has other potential uses too. But the Food and Drug Administration won't grant clearance. More testing, please. Your company experts think the U.S. regulators are dragging their feet beyond reason. Other governments, with high standards for judging safety and efficacy, have approved the drug for sale in their countries. Should we go ahead and market the drug overseas? Or wait for U.S. approval?

    b. Assume that Federal health investigators are pursuing a report that one of your manufacturing plants has a higher than average incidence of cancer among its employees. The plant happens to keep excellent medical records on all its employees, stretching back for decades, which might help identify the source of the problem. The government demands the files.. But if the company turns them over, it might be accused of violating the privacy of all those workers who had submitted to private medical exams. The company offers an abstract of the records, but the government insists on the complete files, with employee names. Then the company tries to obtain releases from all the workers, but some of them refuse. If you give the records to the feds, the company has broken its commitment of confidentiality. What would you do?

3. Among your classmates would you expect to find a difference in the rate of cheating between males and females? Give your reasons for your answer.

4. *a.* Kant believed all lies to be immoral. Do you agree? Why or why not?
    b. In her book *Lying,* Sissela Bok argues that lying by professionals is commonplace. For example, she takes the position that prescribing placebos for experimental purposes is a lie and immoral. Do you agree with her position? Why or why not?
    c. Is the use of an unmarked police car an immoral deception?
    d. One study estimates that Americans average 200 lies per day if one includes "white lies" and inaccurate excuses. On balance, do you believe Americans approve of lying?

5. Professor Howard Raiffa's Competitive Decision Making course at the Harvard Business School received nationwide attention when *The Wall Street Journal* ran a front-page story explaining how Raiffa's course involved, in part, "strategic misrepresentation."[35] Students were involved in negotiating sessions with one third of the course grade resting on their success. Hiding facts, bluffing, and lying were permissible and often resulted in a better deal. Raiffa argued that, rather than encouraging lying, he was merely trying to acquaint his students with the possibility that they might be lied to. (While the facts appear not to have been in dispute, Harvard Business School dean, Lawrence Fouraker, felt that the *Journal* article distorted the goals of the course.) Comment on the ethics of Professor Raiffa's approach.

6. Some excerpts from an "Ethical Aptitude Test":

    As with other goods and services, the medical care available to the rich is superior to that available to the poor. The difference is most conspicuous in the application of new and expensive lifesaving techniques.[36]

    a. Is ability to pay an acceptable way to allocate such services?
    b. If not, how should such services be apportioned?
    c. Many lifesaving drugs can be tested effectively only on human beings. But often, subjects are exposed to such dangers that only those who feel they have nothing to lose willingly participate.
        Are there any circumstances in which it would be right to conduct such tests without ensuring that the persons tested clearly understood the risks they were taking?
    d. How much in dollars is the average human life worth?

7. Aaron Burr said: "All things are moral to great men." Regardless of your personal point of view, defend Burr's position.

8. A pharmacist in Lexington, Kentucky, refused to stock over-the-counter weight reducers. His reasons were: the active ingredient is the same as that in nasal decongestants; he feared their side effects, such as high blood pressure; he felt weight reduction should be achieved via self-discipline.[37] Assume the pharmacist manages the store for a group of owners who have given him complete authority about the products stocked. Was his decision ethical?

9. When the *Business and Society Review* surveyed the presidents of 500 large U.S. companies, 51 responded with their reactions to hypothetical moral dilemmas. One question was:

    Assume that you are president of a firm which provides a substantial portion of the market of one of your suppliers. You find out that this supplier discriminates illegally against minorities, although no legal action has been taken. Assume further that this supplier gives you the best price for the material you require, but that the field is competitive.
        Do you feel that it is proper to use your economic power over this supplier to make him stop discriminating?[38]

    Give your own response to this question.

10. Paul R. Dew, executive vice president of Shamrock Foods Company, pleaded no contest in 1974 to a charge of violating antitrust laws. Mr. Dew was never sentenced or placed on

probation. Rather, sentencing was delayed on the condition that Mr. Dew contribute $35,000 to St. Mary's Food Bank and that he work 45 days for the Food Bank. Those terms completed, the judge then freed Dew at the delayed sentencing hearing.

Dew later addressed an antitrust law symposium:

I am convinced that this pattern, carefully followed with proper checks and balances, can be more effective toward serving justice, changing attitudes, and improving society than incarceration could ever accomplish in the best or poorest of prisons.[39]

Do you agree? Explain.

11. Harold Kelly rejected a corporate presidency and a six-figure income because of his belief that it is wrong to sell beer and wine in the grocery store chain he ran. "I love my job, and I love working with the people at BI-LO," he says. "They're good, loyal, dedicated people, the finest people." But Kelly said he couldn't live with the knowledge that merchandise from his stores might cause traffic accidents, destroy families, or tempt young people into alcoholism. Kelly, 50, is financially secure for the time being.[40]

   a. Would you do as Mr. Kelly did? Explain your reasons.
   b. If you would, must you then take the position that all those who sell spirits are immoral?
   c. If you would not do as Kelly did, are you implicitly arguing that you are not responsible for the welfare of others?

12. In general, does the American value system favor "cheaters" who win in life's various competitions over virtuous individuals who "lose" with regularity?

13. Why is "virtue its own reward," while tangible productivity is ordinarily accorded material compensation?

14. Louis Romberg, a Toronto behavioral scientist, hooked up devices in six of a department store chain's East Cost stores to play a subliminal, continuous message behind the stores' Muzak. Just below the threshold of conscious audibility, the devices broadcast such phrases as: "I am honest. I won't steal. Stealing is dishonest." Store employees and shoppers received the message in their subconscious. After nine months, theft losses in the six stores declined 37.5 percent ($600,000).[41]

   a. Subliminal messages may or may not be persuasive. The evidence is limited and mixed. But in any case, is the practice described here for reducing crime ethically permissible? Explain your response.
   b. How ethical is using subliminal messages to sell products?
   c. Would it be ethical to use subliminal messages to promote political candidates? How would this use differ from the others, if at all?
   d. Review your answers to *(a)* through *(c)*. Is your ethical approach teleological or deonotological?

15. *a.* Rank the following occupations as to your perception of their ethical quality: businesspersons, lawyers, doctors, teachers, farmers, engineers, carpenters, librarians, scientists, professional athletes, letter carriers, secretaries, journalists.
   b. In general, do you find educated professionals to be more ethical than skilled, but generally less-educated, laborers? Explain why or why not.
   c. Can you justify accepting an occupation that is not at or near the top of your ethical ranking? Explain how your ranking affects your career choices.

16. Can businesspeople successfully guide their conduct by the golden rule?

17. Comment on the following quotes from Albert Z. Carr:

[M]ost bluffing in business might be regarded simply as game strategy—much like bluffing in poker, which does not reflect on the morality of the bluffer.

I quoted Henry Taylor, the British statesman who pointed out that "falsehood ceases to be falsehood when it is understood on all sides that the truth is not expected to be spoken" —an exact description of bluffing in poker, diplomacy, and business.

* * * * *

. . . [T]he ethics of business are game ethics, different from the ethics of religion.

* * * * *

An executive's family life can easily be dislocated if he fails to make a sharp distinction between the ethical systems of the home and the office—or if his wife does not grasp that distinction.[42]

Notes

1. This episode was reported in J. Anthony Lucas, "As American as a McDonald's Hamburger on the Fourth of July," *The New York Times Magazine,* July 4, 1971, p. 4.
2. Raymond Baumhart, *Ethics in Business* (New York: Holt, Rinehart & Winston, 1968), p. 10.
3. The author's remarks in this paragraph owe a great debt to Vincent Barry, *Moral Issues in Business* (Belmont, Calif.: Wadsworth, 1979), pp. 7–11.
4. Joseph Fletcher, *Situation Ethics—The New Morality* (Philadelphia: Westminster Press, 1966), p. 17.
5. Ibid., p. 26.
6. *The Gallup Report* No. 214, July 1983, p. 3.
7. George Steiner and John Steiner, *Business, Government, and Society: A Managerial Perspective* (New York: Random House, 1979), pp. 370–76.
8. Michael Maccoby, *The Gamesman* (New York: Simon & Schuster, 1976, and Bantam, 1978).
9. "The Pressure to Compromise Personal Ethics," *Business Week,* January 31, 1977, p. 107.
10. Ibid.
11. Archie Carroll, "Managerial Ethics: A Post-Watergate View," *Business Horizons* 18, no. 2 (April 1975), p. 75.
12. James S. Bowman, "Managerial Ethics in Business and Government," *Business Horizons* 19, no. 5 (October 1976), p. 48.
13. Steven N. Brenner and Earl A. Molander, "Is the Ethics of Business Changing?" *Harvard Business Review* 55, no. 1 (January–February 1977), p. 57.
14. Carroll, "Managerial Ethics," p. 77.
15. Raymond C. Baumhart, "How Ethical Are Businessmen?" *Harvard Business Review* 39, no. 4 (July–August 1961), p. 6.
16. Brenner and Molander, "Ethics of Business," p. 60.
17. Maccoby, *The Gamesman* (Bantam ed.), p. 185.
18. Gallup Poll reprinted in *Public Opinion,* December–January 1984, p. 40.
19. *Types of Men,* trans. P. Pigors (Halle, Germany: Niemeyer, 1928).
20. William D. Guth and Renato Tagiuri, "Personal Values and Corporate Strategy," *Harvard Business Review* 43, no. 5 (September–October 1965), p. 123.
21. Adapted from G. W. Allport, P. E. Vernon, and G. Lindzey, *Manual for the Study of Values* (Boston: Houghton-Mifflin, 1960), p. 14, as reported in Archie B. Carroll, *Business and Society* (Boston: Little, Brown, 1981), p. 70.
22. Brenner and Molander, "Ethics of Business," p. 66.
23. Karl Menninger, *Whatever Became of Sin?* (New York: Hawthorn Books, 1973).
24. Bernard White and B. Ruth Montgomery, "Corporate Codes of Conduct," *California Management Review* 23, no. 2 (Winter 1980), p. 80.
25. Robert Chatov, "What Corporate Ethics Statements Say," *California Management Review* 22, no. 4 (Summer 1980), p. 20.
26. Cited in Gilbert Geis, "White Collar Crime: The Heavy Electrical Equipment Antitrust Cases of 1961," in *Criminal Behavior Systems: A Typology,* ed. Marshall B. Clinard and Richard Quinney (New York: Holt, Rinehart & Winston, 1967), p. 144.
27. "Murder in the Front Office," *Newsweek,* July 8, 1985; and Ernest Conine, "Prison for Corporate Crooks," *Waterloo Courier,* July 10, 1985, p. A4.
28. Alluded to in Congressional testimony, "White-Collar Crime," Subcommittee on Crime of the Committee on the Judiciary, U.S. House of Representatives, Ninety-Fifth Congress, Second session on white-collar crime, Serial No. 69 (Washington, D.C.: U.S. Government Printing Office, 1979).

29. "U.S. Agrees to Promote Employee to Settle Suit against the Air Force," *The Wall Street Journal*, June 16, 1982, p. 38.

30. James M. Roche, "The Competitive System, to Work, to Preserve, and to Protect," *Vital Speeches of the Day*, May 1, 1971, p. 445, as reported in Kenneth D. Walters, "Your Employees' Right to Blow the Whistle," *Harvard Business Review*, July–August, 1975, p. 26.

31. Carl Kaufmann, "A 5-Part Quiz on Corporate Ethics," *Washington Post*, July 1, 1979, p. C–1.

32. "Misinterpreting the Antibribery Law," *Business Week*, September 3, 1979, p. 150.

33. Kaufmann, "A 5-Part Quiz," p. C–4.

34. Ibid.

35. William Bulkeley, "To Some at Harvard, Telling Lies Becomes a Matter of Course," *The Wall Street Journal*, January 15, 1979, p. 1.

36. Leonard C. Lewin, "Ethical Aptitude Test," *Harper's*, October 1976, p. 21.

37. Reported on the WKYT TV Channel 27, Evening News, Lexington, Kentucky, May 12, 1980.

38. "Business Executives and Moral Dilemmas," *Business and Society Review*, no. 13 (Spring 1975), p. 51.

39. Paul R. Dew, "Views from a Sentenced Executive," *Antitrust Law Journal* 47, no. 2 (1978–79), p. 729.

40. David Tomlin, "Chain's President Quits Over Selling Beer," *The Lexington (Kentucky) Leader*, April 6, 1981, p. A–2.

41. Robert Runde, "Mind Benders," *Money*, September 1978, p. 24.

42. Albert Z. Carr, "Is Business Bluffing Ethical?" *Harvard Business Review* 46, no. 1 (January–February 1968), p. 143–52.

II

Introduction to Law

CHAPTER 4   The American Legal System
CHAPTER 5   Constitutional Law and the Bill of Rights

4

The American Legal System

Part One—Legal Foundations

Law Defined

Law daily intrudes upon our lives in the form of parking tickets, television detective shows, contracts, auto accidents, and so on. The rule of law is simply a given in American life. Ordinarily we are not called upon to question the meaning, purpose, and wisdom of our legal system. We will do so now. What is law?

1. Judges' interpretations: The great jurists, Oliver Wendell Holmes and Benjamin Cardozo, held similarly pragmatic visions of the meaning of law. "The prophecies of what the courts will do in fact, and nothing more pretentious, are what I mean by the law," said Holmes.[1] To Cardozo the law was "a principle or rule of conduct so established as to justify a prediction with reasonable certainty that it will be enforced by the courts if its authority is challenged."[2]

2. Sociologist's interpretation: The supremely influential thinker, Max Weber, emphasized the role of external force in explaining the meaning of law.

An order will be called law if it is externally guaranteed by the probability that coercion (physical or psychological), to bring about conformity or avenge volition, will be applied by a staff of people holding themselves specially ready for that purpose.[3]

3. Anthropologist's interpretation: The respected scholar of primitive law, Bronislaw Malinowski, seemed to regard the law as the natural product of cooperative, reciprocal human relationships.

The rules of law stand out from the rest in that they are felt and regarded as the obligations of one person and the rightful claims of another. They are sanctioned not by mere psychological motive, but by a definite social machinery of binding force, based . . . upon mutual dependence, and realized in the equivalent arrangement of reciprocal services.[4]

4. Philosophers' interpretations: To Plato, law was one method of social control, while Cicero found the heart of the law in the distinction between the just and the unjust. Perhaps the most influential legal philosopher, Roscoe Pound, built upon the social control theme to argue that the law is a mechanism for ordering private interests for the good of the whole society.

Looked at functionally, the law is an attempt to satisfy, to reconcile, to harmonize, to adjust these overlapping and often conflicting claims and demands . . . so as to give effect to the greatest total of interests or to the interests that weigh most in our civilization, with the least sacrifice of the scheme of interests as a whole.[5]

5. A dissenting opinion: To the critics of the American legal system, the foregoing explanations fail to capture the reality of the law as an instrument of repression. For example, "radical" sociologist Richard Quinney argues that we should be freed from "the dead hand of the legalistic mentality." To Quinney, our respectful, idealized view of law is a "myth" that fails to recognize the success of Oriental societies—particularly the Chinese—in rejecting the necessity for fixed laws. Quinney asks us to imagine a life without law because to him, law as practiced in America is the unjust product of the power of special interests:

While law is to protect all citizens, it starts as a tool of the dominant class and ends by maintaining the dominance of that class. Law serves the powerful over the weak. . . . Moreover, law is used by the state (and its elitist government) to promote and protect itself. . . . We are indoctrinated with the ideology that it is our law, to be obeyed because we are all citizens of a single nation. Until law is the law of the people, law can be nothing other than official oppression.[6]

Objectives of the Law

Law is shaped by social forces. The values, history, ideas, and goals of society are among the forces that determine the nature of a society's legal system. The diverse character of American society leads inevitably to differences of opinion regarding the proper direction for our legal system. However, certain broad goals can be identified.

1. Maintain order. The law is instrumental in imposing necessary structure on America's diverse and rapidly changing society. Whether with stop signs, zoning ordinances, marriage licenses, or homicide statutes, the legal system seeks to prevent harm by imposing certain established codes of conduct upon the mass of persons. Immediate self-interest is muted in favor of long-term general welfare. The problem then becomes one of how far to go in seeking to preserve a valuable but potentially oppressive commodity. Should the law require all motorcyclists to wear helmets? Or all businesses to close on Sunday? Or all motorists to limit their speed to 55 miles per hour?

2. Resolve conflict. Because society cannot and would not wish to successfully regulate all dimensions of human conduct, a system for solving differences is required. An effort is made to substitute enlightened dispute resolution for the barbarism that might otherwise attend inevitable differences of opinion. If one thinks of the law of contracts, it is evident that we have developed a sophisticated, generally accepted, and largely successful system both for imposing order and for resolving conflict. Nevertheless, enormous problems remain and new ones always arise.

One of the tests of the vitality and merit of a legal system is its ability to adapt to change. For example, some stars in the entertainment industry have recently been embroiled in "palimony" disputes. If a person functions as a spouse but never lawfully marries, is that person entitled to some form of compensation akin to alimony upon dissolution of the living arrangement? In the past, such disputes were resolved among the parties or not at all. Today the legal system is huffing mightily to understand and deal with this notion born of changing societal values.

3. Preserve dominant values. Americans have reached general accord regarding many values and beliefs, and the law has been put to work in preserving those standards. For example, in the Bill of Rights we have set out those fundamental freedoms that must be protected if we are to preserve the character of the nation. Of course, in many instances societal opinion is divided. What happens when no clear consensus emerges about an issue? What if the issue involves a conflict between two values long clutched firmly to the American breast? Freedom of speech is central to a meaningful life, but what if that speech consists of anti-Semitic parades and demonstrations organized by the Ku Klux Klan?

4. Guarantee freedom. That Americans are free and wish to remain so is surely the nation's most revered social value. It is, in a sense, a subset of the third goal in this list, but because of its preeminence, it properly stands alone. The problem, of course, is that freedom must be limited. Drawing the line often gives rise to severe societal conflict.

In general, you are free to do as you like so long as you do not violate the rights of others, but what are those rights? Do I have a right to smoke-free air, or do you have a right to smoke wherever you wish? Even if the rights of others are directly violated, personal freedom is limited. The so-called victimless crimes—vagrancy, gambling, pornography, prostitution—are examples of instances where the law retards freedom in the absence of immediate injury to the rights of others. Should each citizen be free to do as he or she likes so long as harm does not befall others? Or does pornography, for example, inevitably give rise to societal harm? In an interesting and important challenge to the notion that pornography is, indeed, victimless, a movement has emerged to declare pornography a form of discrimination based on sex and hence a violation of the civil rights of women. The heart of the argument is that pornography inspires violence against women. (See Chapter 13.)

5. Preserve justice. In sum, justice is the goal of the American legal system. In the broadest and best sense, justice is fairness. John Rawls expressed "our intuitive conviction of the primacy of justice":

Justice is the first virtue of social institutions, as truth is of systems of thought. A theory, however elegant and economical, must be rejected or revised if it is untrue; likewise laws and institutions, no matter how efficient and well-arranged, must be reformed or abolished if they are unjust. Each person possesses an inviolability founded on justice that even the welfare of society as a whole cannot override. For this reason justice denies that the loss of freedom for some is made right by a greater good shared by others. It does not allow that the sacrifices imposed on a few are outweighed by the larger sum of advantages enjoyed by many. Therefore in a just society the liberties of equal citizenship are taken as settled; the rights secured by justice are not subject to political bargaining or to the calculus of social interests. The only thing that permits us to acquiesce in an erroneous theory is the lack of a better one; analogously, an injustice is tolerable only when it is necessary to avoid an even greater injustice. Being first virtues of human activities, truth and justice are uncompromising.[7]

Is ours a just legal system? More than any other, that should be the question at the forefront of all legal studies. However, one suspects that justice as a goal sometimes slides a bit to the side in pursuit of more pragmatic goals. The *Katko* case that follows illustrates the difficulty of finding fairness in the face of persuasive competing claims.

The Case Law: Locating and Analyzing

To prepare for *Katko*, the first law case in this text, a bit of practical guidance may be useful. The study of law is founded primarily on the analysis of judicial opinion. Except for the federal level and a few states, trial courts decisions are filed locally for public inspection rather than being published. Appellate opinions, on the other hand, are generally published in volumes called *reports*. State court opinions are found in the reports of that state, as well as a regional reporter published by West Publishing Company that divides the United States into units, such as Southeastern (S.E.) and Pacific (P.).

Within the appropriate reporter the cases are arranged in a workable fashion and are *cited* by case name, volume, reporter name, and page number. For example, *Katko* v. *Briney*, 1983 N.W.2d 657 (1971) means that the opinion will be found in volume 1983 of the Northwestern Reporter, 2d series, at page 657, and that the decision was reached in 1971. Federal court decisions are found in several reporters, including the Federal Reporter and the United States Supreme Court Reports.

Briefing the Case

Most law students find the preparation of *case briefs* (outlines or digests) to be helpful in mastering the complexities of the law. A brief should evolve into the form that best suits the individual student's needs. The following approach should prove to be a useful starting point.

1. **Parties.** Identify the plaintiff and the defendant.
2. **Facts.** Summarize only those facts critical to the outcome of the case.
3. **Procedure.** Who brought the appeal? What was the outcome in the lower court(s)?
4. **Issue.** Note the central question or questions upon which the case turns.
5. **Holding.** How did the Court resolve the issues? Who won?
6. **Reasoning.** Explain the logic that supported the Court's decision.

MARVIN KATKO, APPELLEE, V. EDWARD BRINEY AND BERTHA L. BRINEY, APPELLANTS   183 N.W.2d 657 (Iowa S. Ct., 1971)

Chief Justice Moore

The primary issue presented here is whether an owner may protect personal property in an unoccupied, boarded-up farm house against trespassers and thieves by a spring gun capable of inflicting death or serious injury.

We are not here concerned with a man's right to protect his home and members of his family. Defendants' home was several miles from the scene of the incident to which we refer infra.

Plaintiff's action is for damages resulting from serious injury caused by a shot from a 20-gauge spring shotgun set by defendants in a bedroom of an old farm house which had been uninhabited for several years. Plaintiff and his companion, Marvin McDonough, had broken and entered the house to find and steal old bottles and dated fruit jars which they considered antiques.

At defendants' request plaintiff's action was tried to a jury consisting of residents of the community where defendants' property was located. The jury returned a verdict for plaintiff and against defendants for $20,000 actual and $10,000 punitive damages.

After careful consideration of defendants' motions for judgment notwithstanding the verdict and for new trial, the experienced and capable trial judge overruled them and entered judgment on the verdict. Thus we have this appeal by defendants. . . .

For about 10 years, 1957 to 1967, there occurred a series of trespassing and housebreaking events with loss of some household items, the breaking of windows and "messing up of the property in general." . . .

Defendants through the years boarded up the windows and doors in an attempt to stop the intrusions. They had posted "no trespass" signs on the land several years before 1967. The nearest one was 35 feet from the house. On June 11, 1967 defendants set "a shotgun trap" in the north bedroom. After Mr. Briney cleaned and oiled his 20-gauge shotgun, the power of which he was well aware, defendants took it to the old house where they secured it to an iron bed with the barrel pointed at the bedroom door. It was rigged with wire from the doorknob to the gun's trigger so it would fire when the door was opened. Briney first pointed the gun so an intruder would be hit in the stomach but at Mrs. Briney's suggestion it was lowered to hit the legs. He admitted he did so "because I was mad and tired of being tormented" but "he did not intend to injure anyone." He gave no explanation of why he used a loaded shell and set it to hit a person already in the house. Tin was nailed over the bedroom window. The spring gun could not be seen from the outside. No warning of its presence was posted.

Plaintiff lived with his wife and worked regularly as a gasoline station attendant in Eddyville, seven miles from the old house. He had observed it for several years while hunting in the area and considered it as being abandoned. He knew it had long been uninhabited. In 1967 the area around the house was covered with high weeds. Prior to July 16, 1967, plaintiff and McDonough had been to the premises and found several old bottles and fruit jars which they took and added to their collection of antiques. On the latter date about 9:30 P.M. they made a second trip to the Briney property. They entered the old house by removing a board from a porch window which was without glass. While McDonough was looking around the kitchen area plaintiff went to another part of the house. As he started to open the north bedroom door the shotgun went off, striking him in the right leg above the ankle bone. Much of his leg, including part of the tibia, was blown away. Only by McDonough's assistance was plaintiff able to get out of the house and after crawling some distance was put in his vehicle and rushed to a doctor and then to a hospital. He remained in the hospital 40 days.

Plaintiff's doctor testified he seriously considered amputation but eventually the healing process was successful. Some weeks after his release from the hospital plaintiff returned to work on crutches. He was required to keep the injured leg in a cast for approximately a year and wear a special brace for another year. He continued to suffer pain during this period.

There was undenied medical testimony plaintiff had a permanent deformity, a loss of tissue, and a shortening of the leg.

The record discloses plaintiff to trial time had incurred $710 medical expense, $2065.85 for hospital service, $61.80 for orthopedic service, and $750 as loss of earnings. In addition thereto the trial court submitted to the jury the question of damages for pain and suffering and for future disability.

Plaintiff testified he knew he had no right to break and enter the house with intent to steal bottles and fruit jars therefrom. He further testified he had entered a plea of guilty to larceny in the nighttime of property of less than $20 value from a private building. He stated he had been fined $50 and costs and paroled during good behavior from a 60-day jail sentence. Other than minor traffic charges this was plaintiff's first brush with the law. . . .

The main thrust of defendants' defense in the trial court and on this appeal is that "the law permits use of a spring gun in a dwelling or warehouse for the purpose of preventing the unlawful entry of a burglar or thief." . . .

In the statement of issues the trial court stated plaintiff and his companion committed a felony when they broke and entered defendants' house. In instruction 2 the court referred to the early case history of the use of spring guns and stated under the law their use was prohibited except to prevent the commission of felonies of violence and where human life is in danger. The instruction included a statement breaking and entering is not a felony of violence.

Instruction 5 stated: "You are hereby instructed that one may use reasonable force in the protection of his property, but such right is subject to the qualification that one may not use such means of force as will take human life or inflict great bodily injury. Such is the rule even though the injured party is a trespasser and is in violation of the law himself."

Instruction 6 stated: "An owner of premises is prohibited from willfully or intentionally injuring a trespasser by means of force that either takes life or inflicts great bodily injury; and therefore a person owning a premise is prohibited from setting out 'spring guns' and like dangerous devices which will likely take life or inflict great bodily injury, for the purpose of harming trespassers. The fact that the trespasser may be acting in violation of the law does not change the rule. The only time when such conduct of setting a 'spring gun' or a like dangerous device is justified would be when the trespasser was committing a felony of violence or a felony punishable by death, or where the trespasser was endangering human life by his act." . . .

The overwhelming weight of authority, both textbook and case law, supports the trial court's statement of the applicable principles of law.

Prosser on Torts, Third Edition, pages 116–18, states:

. . . the law has always placed a higher value upon human safety than upon mere rights in property, it is the accepted rule that there is no privilege to use any force calculated to cause death or serious bodily injury to repel the threat to land or chattels, unless there is also such a threat to the defendant's personal safety as to justify a self-defense. . . . spring guns and other mankilling devices are not justifiable against a mere trespasser, or even a petty thief. They are privileged only against those upon whom the landowner, if he were present in person would be free to inflict injury of the same kind.

* * * * *

In *Hooker* v. *Miller,* 37 Iowa 613, we held defendant vineyard owner liable for damages resulting from a spring gun shot although plaintiff was a trespasser and there to steal grapes. At pages 614, 615, this statement is made: "This court has held that a mere trespass against property other than a dwelling is not a sufficient justification to authorize the use of a deadly weapon by the owner in its defense; and that if death results in such a case it will be murder, though the killing be actually necessary to prevent the trespass. . . .

In Wisconsin, Oregon, and England the use of spring guns and similar devices is specifically made unlawful by statute.

* * * * *

The legal principles stated by the trial court in instructions 2, 5, and 6 are well established and supported by the authorities cited and quoted supra. There is no merit in defendants' objections and exceptions thereto.

* * * * *

Study and careful consideration of defendants' contentions on appeal reveal no reversible error. Affirmed.

All Justices concur except Larson, J., who dissents.

[Dissent omitted.]

Questions

1. Why did the Iowa Supreme Court rule in favor of Katko, the intruder?
2. Does *Katko* represent a "just" verdict?
3. According to a *Time* magazine account, a businessman in Cordele, Georgia, troubled by small thefts from a cigarette machine in front of his store, "booby-trapped" the machine after hours with dynamite. A teenager then died when tampering with the machine.[8] What legal action should be taken? Resolve.
4. In 1964 William James Rummell was convicted of fraudulent credit card use to obtain approximately $80 worth of goods and services. Rummel, who pleaded guilty, was convicted of a felony violation and served three years in the Texas state penitentiary. In 1969 Rummel was convicted of a second felony, check forgery in the amount of $28.36. Four years imprisonment followed. After his release in 1973 Mr. Rummel promised to repair an air conditioner receiving $120.75 in advance. After he failed to complete the repairs, Mr. Rummel was found guilty of his third felony offense and as provided for under the Texas recidivist statute, was sentenced to life imprisonment. Charles Alan Wright, former special counsel to President Nixon during the Watergate episode, and other very able attorneys helped Rummel appeal his sentence to the U.S. Supreme Court. They argued that Rummel's sentence was so disproportionate to his crimes that his Eighth Amendment protection against cruel and unusual punishment was violated. The Supreme Court, with four dissenting votes, upheld the constitutionality of the Texas statute. Mr. Rummel will be eligible for parole 12 years from his sentencing. See *Rummel* v. *Estelle,* 445 U.S. 263 (1980).
   a. Was justice achieved in this case?
   b. Was the Supreme Court adjudging the morality, the fairness, of the Texas statute? Should the Court do so?
   c. Do you believe Mr. Rummel's crimes, either individually or collectively, were of such a magnitude as to justify their classification as felonies with the more severe penalties that accompany that classification?

Classifications of Law

Some elementary distinctions will serve to make the role of law clearer.

1. Substantive and procedural law. *Substantive laws* create, define, and regulate legal rights and obligations. Thus, in terms of the topics of this course, the Sherman Act forbids restraints of trade. By judicial interpretation, price-fixing between competitors is a restraint of trade.

Procedural law embraces the systems and methods available to enforce the rights specified in the substantive law. So, procedural law includes the judicial system and the rules by which it operates. Questions of where to hear a case, what evidence to admit and which decisions can be appealed fall within the procedural domain.

2. Law and equity. Following the Norman conquest of England in 1066, a system of king's courts was established in which the king's representatives settled disputes. Those representatives were empowered to provide remedies of land, money, or personal property. The king's courts became known as *courts of law,* and the remedies were labeled *remedies of law*. However, some litigants sought compensation other than the three provided. They took their plea to the king.

Typically the chancellor, an aide to the king, would hear these petitions and, guided by the standard of fairness, could grant a remedy specifically appropriate to the case. The chancellors' decisions accumulated over time such that a new body of remedies— and with it a new court system, known as *courts of equity*—evolved. Thereafter, a litigant chose her or his court system according to the remedy she or he sought.

While the equitable remedies were many, two are of special significance today—the injunction and specific performance. An *injunction* is a court order commanding an individual or organization to stop the offending conduct. *Specific performance* is a remedy in which the court compels the defendant to complete the performance he or she had promised. In this situation money is deemed an inadequate remedy. For example, a Picasso painting might not be adequately replaced by a sum of money, however large. Today, actions at law and equity may normally be heard in the same court. Remaining distinctions between the two are not important for the purposes of this text.

3. Public law and private law. *Public law* deals with the relationship between government and the citizens. Constitutional, criminal, and administrative law (relating to such bodies as the Federal Trade Commission) fall in the public law category. *Private law* regulates the legal relationship between individuals. Contracts, agency, and commercial paper are traditional business law topics in the private law category.

4. Law by judicial decision and law by enactment. In general, American rules of law are promulgated, either by court decisions *(case law)* or via enactments by constitutional assemblies, legislatures, administrative agencies, chief executives, and local government authorities. Enactments include constitutions, statutes, treaties, administrative rules, executive orders, and local ordinances.

a. **Case law (judicial decisions)** Our case law has its roots in the early English king's courts where, as we have seen, rules of law gradually developed out of a series of individual dispute resolutions. That body of law was imported to America and is known as the *common law*. (There is the possibility of confusion here, because the term *common law* is sometimes used to designate not just the law imported from England of old, but all judge-made or case law.)

The development of the English common law rules and American judicial decisions into a just, ordered package is attributable in large measure to reliance on the doctrine of *stare decisis* (let the decision stand). That is, judges endeavor to follow the precedents established by previous decisions. Of course, following precedent is not mandatory.

As societal beliefs change, so does the law. For example, a Supreme Court decision approving racially separate but equal education was eventually overruled by a Supreme Court decision mandating integrated schools. However, the principle of stare decisis is generally adhered to because of its clearly beneficial effect. It offers the wisdom of the past and enhances efficiency by eliminating the need for resolving every case as though it were one of first impression. Stare decisis affords stability and predictability to the law. It promotes justice by, for example, reducing "judge-shopping" and neutralizing judges' personal prejudices.

b. **Statutes (enactments).** As to law by enactment, our primary concern is the category of legislative enactments, that is, *statutory law.* Some areas of law, such as torts, continue to be governed primarily by common law rules, but the direction of American law lies largely in the hands of legislators. A significant portion of federal and state legislation has been devoted to clarifying and modifying the common law. Of course, legislators are not free of constraints. Federal legislation may not conflict with the U.S. Constitution, and state legislation may not violate either federal law or the constitutions of that state and the nation.

Recognizing the increasing complexity of the law and an increasing general interchange among the states, an effort has been made to achieve uniform laws among the states. Law experts have compiled model statutes that are suggested for adoption by the states. Of special note is the Uniform Commercial Code, which codifies and clarifies the welter of common law rules and statutory enactments that arose over centuries of commercial practice. The Code has been adopted in whole by 49 states and in part by Louisiana.

One of the judiciary's primary tasks is the interpretation of statutory enactments. Much of this text involves an investigation of statutes—the Sherman Act, the Civil Rights Act of 1964, the Federal Trade Commission Act, and so on. Thus, a brief look at statutory interpretation is important.

The first point of examination is the words of the statute. The "plain meaning" rule suggests that jurists' interpretations should be limited to the ordinary and normal meaning commonly attributed to those words. Unfortunately, statutes are rarely drawn with a degree of precision that avoids ambiguity. Indeed, many topics require a deliberate breadth and ambiguity in statutory construction. Therefore, the court ordinarily considers other evidence, which typically includes (1) prior relevant judicial decisions, (2) consideration of the issue that provoked the enactment, and (3) examination of the legislative history of the act, such as the debates and committee hearings that preceded passage of the legislation.

5. Civil law and criminal law. *Civil law* addresses the legal rights and duties that arise between individuals. Thus, under the civil law one person can sue another for breach of contract. The *criminal law,* on the other hand, involves wrongs against the general welfare as formulated in specific criminal statutes. Murder and theft are, of course, criminal wrongs because society has forbidden those acts in specific legislative enactments. Hence, wearing one's hat backwards would be a crime if such a statute were enacted and if that statute met constitutional requirements.

Some of our stormiest societal battles have involved instances of conflict as to whether certain classes of conduct are so inimical to the general welfare as to require criminal sanction. The recurrent debate regarding criminal penalties for drug possession illustrates the difficulty in accommodating individual preferences and society's perceived needs. Some actions, such as price-fixing, can carry both civil and criminal penalties.

a. **Crimes.** Crimes are of three kinds. *Treason* is the special situation in which one levies war against the United States or gives aid and comfort to its enemies. In general, *felonies* are more serious crimes such as murder, rape, and robbery. Typically they are punishable by death or by imprisonment in a federal or state penitentiary for more than one year. In general, *misdemeanors* are less serious crimes such as petty theft, disorderly conduct, and traffic offenses. Typically they are punishable by fine or by imprisonment for no more than one year.

b. **Elements of a crime.** In a broad sense, crimes consist of two elements: (1) a wrongful act or omission *(actus reus)* and (2) evil intent *(mens rea)*. Thus, an individual who pockets a ball-point pen and leaves the store without paying for it may be charged with petty theft. However, the accused may defend by arguing that he or she merely absentmindedly and unintentionally slipped the pen in a pocket after picking it off the shelf to consider its merits. Intent is a state of mind, so the jury or judge must reach a determination from the objective facts as to what the accused's state of mind must have been.

c. **Criminal defenses.** The law recognizes certain defenses to criminal prosecution. Infancy, intoxication, insanity, and self-defense are some of the arguments available to the defendant. Precise standards for each of these and other defenses differ from state to state, depending on the relevant statutory and case law. The federal Constitution and the various state constitutions also afford protections to the accused.

As to the federal Constitution, the Fourth Amendment prevents unreasonable searches and seizures; the Fifth Amendment requires a grand jury indictment for capital crimes, forbids double jeopardy and self-incrimination, and mandates due process of law; the Sixth Amendment guarantees a speedy and public trial by jury, the right to confront and obtain witnesses, and the right to a competent lawyer; and the Eighth Amendment prohibits excessive bail or fines and cruel and unusual punishment.

d. **Criminal procedure.** In general, criminal law procedure is structured as follows: For more complex, arguably more serious, crimes the process begins with the prosecuting officials bringing their charges before a grand jury or magistrate to determine whether the charges have sufficient merit to justify a trial. If so, an *indictment* or *information* is issued, charging the accused with specific crimes. (Grand juries issue indictments; magistrates issue informations.) In those instances where action by a grand jury or magistrate is not required, cases are initiated by the issuance of a warrant by a judge, based on a showing of probable cause that the individual has committed or will commit a crime. Of course, where necessity demands, arrests may be made without a warrant, but the legality of the arrest will be tested by probable cause standards.

After indictment or arrest, the individual is brought before the court for arraignment where the charges are read and a plea is entered. If the individual pleads not guilty, he or she will go to trial, where guilt must be established *beyond a reasonable doubt.* (In a civil trial, the plaintiff must meet the lesser standard of *a preponderance of the evidence.*) In a criminal trial the burden of proof is on the State. The defendant is, of course, assumed to be innocent. He or she is entitled to a jury trial, but may choose to have the case decided by the judge alone. If found guilty the defendant can, among

other possibilities, seek a new trial or appeal errors in the prosecution. If found innocent, the defendant may, if necessary, invoke the doctrine of *double jeopardy,* under
which a person cannot be prosecuted twice in the same tribunal for the same criminal
offense.

The following readings explore the criminal law process.

ARIZONA ARREST[9]

Received the within process Arizona City, Jan. 1873 and served same by arresting defendant at
Ehrenberg, A.T., Jan. 31, 1873, but as defendant had no money and I was broke myself and the
county don't pay cash in advance, and no steamboat around and no calaboose here and defendant
wouldn't walk down to Yuma all alone by himself and I wouldn't walk down with him and as he
wouldn't stay arrested unless I boarded him which I had no money for to do, and as he gave up
the coat (value .45 cents currency—estimated) and said he never stole it but Bryson gave it to
him in presence of witnesses and that Bryson was a damned liar anyhow, and not knowing what
to do with him, I did nothing more to him up to date beyond giving him excellent moral advice
which he assured me was entirely unnecessary in his case, his life having been blameless and his
reputation spotless as he could prove by the best men in Nevada and Idaho but have allowed him
to run at large until a more favorable season when a steamboat happens to be here, and will take
scrip for his passage to Yuma and present the bill to Supervisors themselves, which is nearly all
I have done toward serving within process, though I would make return of the Balance were this
process bigger on the back.

Fees—Balance of what coat sells for after paying Justice fees.

George Tyng,
Sheriff of Yuma County,
Arizona

Source: Reprinted with permission of The Lawyers Co-operative Publishing Co.

WHY THE JUSTICE SYSTEM FAILS

Roger Rosenblatt

Anyone who claims it is impossible to get rid
of the random violence of today's mean streets
may be telling the truth, but is also missing the
point. Street crime may be normal in the
United States, but it is not inevitable at such
advanced levels, and the fact is that there are
specific reasons for the nation's incapacity to
keep its street crime down. Almost all these
reasons can be traced to the American criminal
justice system. It is not that there are no mechanisms in place to deal with American crime,

merely that the existing ones are impractical,
inefficient, anachronistic, uncooperative, and
often lead to as much civic destruction as they
are meant to curtail.

Why does the system fail? For one thing,
the majority of criminals go untouched by it.
The police learn about one quarter of the thefts
committed each year, and about less than half
the robberies, burglaries, and rapes. Either victims are afraid or ashamed to report crimes, or
they may conclude gloomily that nothing will

be done if they do. Murder is the crime the police do hear about, but only 73 percent of the nation's murders lead to arrest. The arrest rates for lesser crimes are astonishingly low—59 percent for aggravated assault in 1979, 48 percent for rape, 25 percent for robbery, 15 percent for burglary.

Even when a suspect is apprehended, the chances of his getting punished are mighty slim. In New York State each year there are some 130,000 felony arrests; approximately 8,000 people go to prison. There are 94,000 felony arrests in New York City; 5,000 to 6,000 serve time. A 1974 study of the District of Columbia came up with a similar picture. Of those arrested for armed robbery, less than one quarter went to prison. More than 6,000 aggravated assaults were reported; 116 people were put away. . . .

It is hard to pinpoint any one stage of the system that is more culpable than any other. Start with the relationship between police and prosecutors. Logic would suggest that these groups work together like the gears of a watch since, theoretically, they have the same priorities: to arrest and convict. But prosecutors have enormous caseloads, and too often they simply focus on lightening them. Or they work too fast and lose a case; or they plea-bargain and diminish justice. The police also work too fast too often, are concerned with "clearing" arrests, for which they get credit. They receive no credit for convictions. Their work gets sloppy—misinformation recorded, witnesses lost, no follow-up. That 1974 study of the District of Columbia indicated that fully one-third of the police making arrests failed to process a single conviction. A study released this week of 2,418 police in seven cities showed that 15 percent were credited with half the convictions; 31 percent had no convictions whatever.

The criminal justice system is also debased by plea bargaining. At present nine out of ten convictions occur because of a guilty plea arrived at through a deal between the state and defendant, in which the defendant forgoes his right to trial. Of course, plea bargaining keeps the courts less crowded and doubtless sends to jail, albeit for a shorter stretch, some felons

who might have got off if judged by their peers. And many feel that a bargain results in a truer level of justice, since prosecutors tend to hike up the charge in the first place in anticipation of the defendant's copping a plea. Still, there are tricks like "swallowing the gun"— reducing the charge of armed robbery to unarmed robbery—that are performed for expediency, not for justice.

"Justice delayed is justice denied," is a root principle of common law, but nowadays the right to a speedy trial is so regularly denied that the thought seems antique. Last August 1, a witness was prepared to testify that Cornelius Wright, 18, shot him five times in the chest, stomach, and legs. Because of a series of mishaps and continuances, Wright has been stewing in the Cook County jail for more than eight months. In fact, Wright's delay is the norm; eight months is the average time between arrest and trial. Continuances have so clogged Chicago's courts that the city's Crime Commission issues a monthly "Ten Most Wanted Dispositions" list in an effort to prod the system.

Detroit Deputy Police Chief James Bannon believes that trial delays work against the victim. "The judge doesn't see the hysterical, distraught victim. He sees a person who comes into court after several months or years who is totally different. He sees a defendant that bears no relationship to what he appeared to be at the time of the crime. He sits there in a nice three-piece suit and keeps his mouth shut. And the judge doesn't see the shouting, raging animal the victim saw when she was being raped, for example. Both the defendant and victim have lawyers, and that's what the court hears: law. It doesn't hear the guts of the crime."

Procedural concerns can cause delays, and in rare cases defendants' rights can be carried to absurd extremes. [Former] California Attorney General George Deumejian tells of Willie Edward Level, who was convicted of beating a Bakersfield College woman student to death with a table leg. Level was informed of his right to remain silent and/or have an attorney present (the *Miranda* ruling). He waived these rights and confessed the murder. Yet the California Court of Appeals threw out the conviction because Level had asked to speak to his mother at the time of his arrest and had not been permitted to; had he been able to do so, it was argued, he might not have made his confession.

"There's nothing in *Miranda* that says a defendant has the right to talk with his mother or a friend," says Deumejian. "It says he can talk to a lawyer or not at all. It's so much of this kind of thing that makes a mockery of the system. And every time you have one of these rulings it has the effect of dragging out the length of cases, which builds in more and more delays. We've got a murder case in Sacramento that's been in the pretrial state for four years."

Add to this the fact that witnesses are discouraged and lost by trial delays. In New York the average number of appearances a witness has to make in a given disposition is 17. Few people have the time or stamina to see a case through.

Then there is the matter of bail. In a recent speech before the American Bar Association, Chief Justice Warren Burger argued for tightening the standards for releasing defendants on bail, which seems justifiable. But the subject is complicated. Technically, judges are supposed to base their decisions about bail strictly on the likelihood of a defendant's appearing for trial. In practice, however, this is mere guesswork, and a great many serious crimes are committed by people out on bail or by bail jumpers, who are often given bail when rearrested. One sound reason for a bail system is to avoid locking up anyone before he is proved guilty. But it is simply unrealistic to disregard the criterion of likely dangerousness, even though it raises serious constitutional questions. It has probably resulted in more tragedies than a different standard would result in denials of civil liberties.

Judges blame the cops, and cops blame the judges. Patrick F. Healy, executive director of the Chicago Crime Commission, says judges are plain lazy. "Last year we did a spot check, and the judges' day on the bench totaled 3 hours 49 minutes." The judges will not concede laziness, but several of the nation's best, like Marvin Frankel, former federal judge in the District Court of Manhattan, admit to a

"remarkable lack of consistency" in the judiciary. Judge Lois Forer, a most respected criminal-court justice in Philadelphia, contends that it "simply isn't true that defendants get off on technicalities. It is just that "the system is overloaded." She also emphasizes the problem of sloppy preparations: "It's truly painful when there's someone you're pretty sure committed a crime, and they [police, prosecutors] don't bring in the evidence."

Almost every critic of the system cites the lack of prison space. Despite the enormously high operating costs ($4 billion annually for all U.S. penal institutions), more prison space is an absolute necessity. New York State has between 22,000 and 24,000 jail cells. All are filled, some beyond proper capacity. . . . This month 223 supposedly nonviolent inmates of Illinois' 13 prisons were given early release to make room for 223 newcomers. . . .

Finally, the criminal justice system fails at its most sensitive level, that of juvenile crime. Until recently few juvenile courts admitted there was such a thing as a bad boy, restricting their vision of youthful offenders to memories of Father Flanagan's Boys Town or to Judge Tom Clark's quaint view that "every boy, in his heart, would rather steal second base than an automobile." In fact, there are several boys these days who would prefer to kill the umpire, and who have done so, only to receive light sentences or none at all. A study by Marvin Wolfgang at the University of Pennsylvania traced the criminal careers of 10,000 males born in 1948. By the age of 16, 35 percent had one arrest, but then almost all stopped committing crimes. A small group, however, did not: 627 had five arrests by the time they were adults. They accounted for two thirds of all the violent crime attributed to the group and almost all the homicides. "This is the group that society is afraid of, and rightly so," says Wolfgang. He is now studying a new group, born in 1958, which is "even nastier and more violent. We should concentrate on them and capture them as soon as possible." . . .

The problem of reform in most areas is not one of principle, but one of efficiency. To be sure, there are many who believe that in order to eliminate crime, one must first eliminate the social ills of poverty, ignorance, racism, and the disintegration of the family. But the aim of improving the criminal justice system is not to eliminate crime, but to slow its rate of growth. And there are several relatively straightforward measures, such as more sensible bail procedures, more thorough police work, greater cooperation between police and prosecutors, hiring more judges and building more prisons, that can be taken if the will and money are there.

The more problematic areas of reform are juvenile justice and prison terms—areas in which crime experts go at each other with more passion than proof. Mandatory sentencing, for example, has been proposed by Massachusetts Governor Edward King, as well as many legislators throughout the country. The argument for mandatory sentencing is that it provides a definite deterrent, as the apparent success of the Massachusetts gun law has proved. It also puts judges on the line when they fail to give determinate sentences. The argument against mandatory sentencing is that there will always be exceptional circumstances in which judges must use their discretion. Most judges are naturally opposed to the reform.

The idea of extending prison terms in general has an internal logic, but again history seems to confute it. The average prison term has risen from 18 to 35 months since 1965, precisely the time when national crime began to get out of hand. As soon as former New York Governor Nelson Rockefeller won passage of a stiff drug law, narcotics-related property crime rose. A Rand Corp. report on career criminals says that a 70 percent increase in the number of robbers sent to prison would produce a 20 percent reduction in robberies. To effect that decrease in New York City, where 2,000 robbers are imprisoned each year, would mean an annual increase of 1,400 convicts.

Still, those who argue for more certain penalties are not necessarily arguing for longer ones across the board or for mandatory sentences for any but hardened and habitual offenders. The reasonableness of a recent statement by the Citizens Crime Commission of New York is compelling: "Unless we make the punishment for serious crime more certain and more appropriate, we cannot expect any respite from the violence now engulfing the city. Any criminal justice system where one murder case in ten results in a murder conviction, where one arrested robber in six and one arrested burglar in 20 receives a prison sentence of even one year, is not a system where the punishment is certain and appropriate and consequently can do little to control crime." . . .

In fact, given the limitations of prison space, money, crowded courts, procedural delays and so forth, the one relatively easy target of reform is the treatment of career criminals. Most serious crimes are committed by very few people. Baltimore Police Commissioner Donald Pomerleau cites figures showing that of 12,500 defendants appearing in district court, 80 percent have been in the dock before. . . .

In the matter of juvenile justice, career criminals are practically the whole concern. New York has recently lowered its juvenile classification from 16 years to 13 for youths who have committed serious crimes. . . . But as the Wolfgang study showed, the real trouble is with habitual young criminals, who most observers feel ought to be removed from the community as swiftly as possible. The idea, says James Q. Wilson, is not to "dump them in old hell-hole reformatories" but rather "to restrict their freedom, get them out of bad family circumstances, and keep track of them."

By far the most emotionally appealing criminal justice reform, and certainly not the most difficult, is to improve police and community relationships. Almost everyone agrees that at present the police are too distant from the communities they serve, and the communities are too disorganized to offer the police help or themselves protection. "For starters," advises Patrick Murphy, former police commissioner of New York and Detroit and current head of the Police Foundation, "police should get out of their patrol cars and onto the streets."

*   *   *   *   *

Alfred Blumstein, of Carnegie-Mellon University, offers a thoughtful connection of the community idea with the criminal justice system when he says that "one reason the courts are so overloaded is that family, church, and neighborhoods are weakened. The criminal justice system is very weak as a crime control agent. It does some good but not a lot. We've got to look and find other forms of social control than the remote, impersonal and inherently limited criminal justice system that now serves as a replacement for institutions so weakened; thus it's important that we try to find local forms of security that are more responsible and accepted."

Source: *Time*, March 23, 1981, pp. 22–29. Reported by Jeff Melvoin/Boston and Evan Thomas/Washington, with other U.S. bureaus. Copyright 1981 by Time, Inc. All rights reserved. Reprinted by permission from *Time*.

QUESTIONS

1. Several states and hundreds of communities have enacted legislation designed to ban the display and sale of drug paraphernalia (pipes, spoons, bongs, scales, roach clips, and the like).
   a. Raise the competing arguments regarding such enactments.
   b. What constitutional claim is likely to be raised by "head shop" owners?
   c. Should we rely on the free market to "regulate" commercial enterprise of this nature? That is, should we permit the government to destroy the operations of small businesses designed to meet a need expressed by the market and heretofore considered free of any illegality?

2. a. In Chicago, 48-year-old Bob Koester was arrested for cursing at a transit conductor. "Well, that motherblanker in the last train left a bunch of us stranded!"[10] Koester was convicted and sentenced to 30 days' supervision. Should vulgar language in public be subject to legal regulation?
   b. Do you believe our legal system places too much emphasis on the establishment and maintenance of order?

3. Consider the case of Phillip Becker, as drawn from a column by journalist George Will. Phillip, age 13, is retarded as a consequence of Down's Syndrome (mongolism). He also suffers from a heart defect that is easily correctable by operation and that is likely to lead to his death around age 30 unless corrected. Phillip lives in an institution. His teacher says he is working at a very high level for a retarded child. He does simple chores and can be expected, as an adult, to live in a supervised group home. The state of California sought a heart operation for Phillip. His parents refused, fearing he would not be well cared for upon their passing, that the operation was too risky, and that his life was, to quote a pediatrician's testimony, "devoid of those qualities which give it human dignity." California was willing to pay for the operation, and upon the parents' refusal the state took legal action. The Beckers prevailed and eventually the U.S. Supreme Court declined to hear the case.[11] Is Phillip's case properly a matter of exclusive parental authority?

   Afterword: A California judge granted custody of Phillip to a couple with whom Phillip had spent weekends for a five-year period. At this writing, Phillip's parents are expected to appeal.

4. Walter Polovchak, a then 12-year-old native Russian, sought to remain in America against the wishes of his Russian parents who had chosen, after living here for a time, to return to their homeland. The United States government supported Walter's desire. The case went to court. Resolve the case, raising the competing considerations.

5. Should we remove criminal penalties from the so-called victimless crimes such as vagrancy, prostitution, pornography, and gambling? Should we regulate those practices in any way?

6. In *Hemby* v. *State*, 589 S.W.2d 922

(Tenn., 1978), the record indicated that the defendant, while intoxicated, fell asleep in a bed in which his infant son was sleeping. The defendant apparently rolled over on the baby, suffocating him. Is the defendant guilty of criminal conduct? Explain.

7. In your judgment are criminals simply "bad people" or are they victims of poverty, ignorance, racism, and the disintegration of the family?
8. What steps would you advocate to reduce crime in America?

Part Two—Judicial Process

Of course, most disputes are settled without resort to litigation, but when agreement cannot be reached, the citizenry can turn to the highly sophisticated dispute resolution mechanisms of the American judicial system.

Standing to Sue

Resorting to the courts is an undesirable method of problem solving. Therefore, all who wish to bring a claim before a court may not be permitted to do so. To receive the court's attention, the litigant must demonstrate that she or he has *standing to sue*. That is, that person must show that her or his interest in the outcome of the controversy is sufficiently direct and substantial as to justify the court's consideration. The litigant must show that she or he personally is suffering, or will be suffering, injury. Mere interest in the problem at hand is insufficient to grant standing to sue. Thus, in *Sierra Club* v. *Morton*, the U.S. Supreme Court held that the Sierra Club did not have standing to challenge federal approval of a private skiing development in the Mineral King Valley of the Sequoia National Forest. The membership had a general interest in the issue, but they failed to show a direct, personal stake.

Should trees and other inanimate objects be accorded standing in environmental litigations? Dissenting in *Sierra Club,* Justice Douglas articulated that imaginative argument.

SIERRA CLUB V. MORTON   405 U.S. 727, 741 (1972)

Justice Douglas, dissenting

*   *   *   *   *

The critical question of "standing" would be simplified and also put neatly in focus if we fashioned a federal rule that allowed environmental issues to be litigated before federal agencies or federal courts in the name of the inanimate object about to be despoiled, defaced, or invaded by roads and bulldozers and where injury is the subject of public outrage. Contemporary public concern for protecting nature's ecological equilibrium should lead to the conferral of standing upon environmental objects to sue for their own preservation. . . . .

Inanimate objects are sometimes parties in litigation. A ship has a legal personality, a fiction found useful for maritime purposes. The corporation sole—a creature of ecclesiastical law—is an acceptable adversary and large fortunes ride on its cases. The ordinary corporation is a "person" for purposes of the adjudicatory processes, whether it represents proprietary, spiritual, aesthetic, or charitable causes.

So it should be as respects valleys, alpine meadows, rivers, lakes, estuaries, beaches, ridges, groves of trees, swampland, or even air that feels the destructive pressures of modern technology and modern life. The river, for example, is the living symbol of all the life it sustains or nourishes—fish, aquatic insects, water ouzels, otter, fisher, deer, elk, bear, and all other animals, including man, who are dependent on it or who enjoy it for its sight, its sound, or its life. The river as plaintiff speaks for the ecological unit of life that is part of it. Those people who have a meaningful relation to that body of water—whether it be a fisherman, a canoeist, a zoologist, or a logger—must be able to speak for the values which the river represents and which are threatened with destruction. . . .

Mineral King is doubtless like other wonders of the Sierra Nevada such as Tuolumne Meadows and the John Muir Trail. Those who hike it, fish it, hunt it, camp in it, frequent it, or visit it merely to sit in solitude and wonderment are legitimate spokesmen for it, whether they may be few or many. Those who have that intimate relation with the inanimate object about to be injured, polluted, or otherwise despoiled are its legitimate spokesmen.

The Solicitor General . . . takes a wholly different approach. He considers the problem in terms of "government by the Judiciary." With all respect, the problem is to make certain that the inanimate objects, which are the very core of America's beauty, have spokesmen before they are destroyed. It is, of course, true that most of them are under the control of a federal or state agency. The standards given those agencies are usually expressed in terms of the "public interest." Yet "public interest" has so many differing shades of meaning as to be quite meaningless on the environmental front. . . .

[T]he pressures on agencies for favorable action one way or the other are enormous. The suggestion that Congress can stop action which is undesirable is true in theory; yet even Congress is too remote to give meaningful direction and its machinery is too ponderous to use very often. The federal agencies of which I speak are not venal or corrupt. But they are notoriously under the control of powerful interests who manipulate them through advisory committees, or friendly working relations, or who have that natural affinity with the agency which in time develops between the regulator and the regulated. As early as 1894, Attorney General Olney predicted that regulatory agencies might become "industry-minded," as illustrated by his forecast concerning the Interstate Commerce Commission:

The Commission . . . is, or can be made, of great use to the railroads. It satisfies the popular clamor for a government supervision of railroads, at the same time that supervision is almost entirely nominal. Further, the older such a commission gets to be, the more inclined it will be found to take the business and railroad view of things. [M. Josephson, The Politicos 526 (1938).] . . .

The Forest Service—one of the federal agencies behind the scheme to despoil Mineral King—has been notorious for its alignment with lumber companies, although its mandate from Congress directs it to consider the various aspects of multiple use in its supervision of the national forests.

The voice of the inanimate object, therefore, should not be stilled. That does not mean that the judiciary takes over the managerial functions from the federal agency. It merely means that before these priceless bits of Americana (such as a valley, an alpine meadow, a river, or a lake) are forever lost or are so transformed as to be reduced to the eventual rubble of our urban environment, the voice of the existing beneficiaries of these environmental wonders should be heard.

Perhaps they will not win. Perhaps the bulldozers of ''progress'' will plow under all the aesthetic wonders of this beautiful land. That is not the present question. The sole question is, who has standing to be heard?

Those who hike the Appalachian Trail into Sunfish Pond, New Jersey, and camp or sleep there, or run the Allagash in Maine, or climb the Guadalupes in West Texas, or who canoe and portage the Quetico Superior in Minnesota, certainly should have standing to defend those natural wonders before courts or agencies, though they live 3,000 miles away. Those who merely are caught up in environmental news or propaganda and flock to defend these waters or areas may be treated differently. That is why these environmental issues should be tendered by the inanimate object itself. Then there will be assurances that all of the forms of life which it represents will stand before the court—the pileated woodpecker as well as the coyote and bear, the lemmings as well as the trout in the streams. Those inarticulate members of the ecological group cannot speak. But those people who have so frequented the place as to know its values and wonders will be able to speak for the entire ecological community. . . .

Questions

1. Explain the requirements for securing standing in the courts.
2. Write an opinion either supporting or rejecting Justice Douglas's position.
3. Why should the law treat corporations as persons while declining to accord standing to trees and other valued inanimate objects?
4. An urban renewal project threatened to result in the destruction of 14 historic buildings in Lexington, Kentucky. A nonprofit corporation, designed to preserve such buildings, filed suit to stop the demolition. The plaintiffs did not own any of the buildings. The defendant government agency argued that the plaintiffs did not have standing to sue. Decide. See *South Hill Neighborhood Association* v. *Romney,* 421 F.2d 454 (1969).

Jurisdiction

A plaintiff may not simply take his or her case to the court of his or her preference. The plaintiff must go to a court with *jurisdiction;* that is, with the necessary power and authority to hear the dispute. The court must have jurisdiction over both the subject matter and the persons (or in some instances, the property) involved in the case. Subject matter jurisdiction imposes bounds on the classes of cases a court may hear. The legislation or constitution creating the court will normally specify that court's jurisdictional authority. For example, state courts of general jurisdiction may hear most types of cases, but a criminal court or probate court is clearly limited as to the subject matter it may hear.

The outer bounds of federal jurisdiction are specified in the Constitution, while Congress has further particularized that issue by statute. Essentially, the federal district courts may hear two types of cases: (1) those involving a federal question and (2) those involving diversity of citizenship and more than $10,000.

Federal question jurisdiction exists in any suit where the plaintiff's claim is based on the U.S. Constitution, a U.S. treaty, or a federal statute. Thus, litigants may bring to the federal courts cases involving, for example, the federal antitrust statutes, federal criminal laws, constitutional issues such as freedom of the press, and federal tax questions. Federal question jurisdiction does not require an amount in controversy exceeding $10,000. It should be understood that federal and state courts have *concurrent jurisdiction* for some federal questions. Thus, some federal question cases are decided in state courts applying federal law. Congress has accorded the federal courts exclusive jurisdiction over certain subjects including federal criminal laws, bankruptcy, and copyrights.

Under *diversity of citizenship,* federal district courts may hear cases involving more than $10,000 where the plaintiff(s) and the defendant(s) are citizens of different states. (Corporations are treated as citizens both of their state of incorporation and the state in which their principal place of business is located.) Diversity cases may also be heard in state courts, but plaintiffs frequently prefer to bring their actions in federal courts. The quality of the federal judiciary is generally believed to be superior to that of the states. The federal courts are less likely to be influenced by local bias, and federal court action may have procedural advantages such as greater capacity to secure witnesses' testimony.

Judicial authority over the person is known as *in personam jurisdiction.* In general, a state court's powers are limited to the bounds of the state. While the matter is fraught with potential complexities, it is fair to say that state court jurisdiction may be established in three ways: (1) When the defendant is a resident of the state, a summons may be served at that residence. (2) When the defendant is not a resident, a summons may be personally served should he or she be physically present in the state. (3) All states have legislated "long-arm" statutes that allow a court to secure jurisdiction against an out-of-state party where that defendant has committed a tort in the state or where the defendant is conducting business in the state. Hence, in an auto accident in Iowa involving both an Iowa resident and an Illinois resident the Iowan may sue in Iowa and achieve service of process over the Illinois defendant as a consequence of the jurisdictional authority afforded by the "long-arm" statute.

A state court may also acquire jurisdiction via an *in rem action.* In that instance the defendant may be a nonresident, but his or her property, which must be the subject of the suit, must be located within the state.

The case that follows illustrates the due process limitations of a state's power to assert in personam jurisdiction.

HELICOPTEROS NACIONALES DE COLOMBIA, S. A., PETITIONER, V. ELIZABETH HALL ET AL.   80 L. Ed.2d 404, 104 S. Ct. _____ (1984)

Justice Blackmun

We granted certiorari in this case. . . . to decide whether the Supreme Court of Texas correctly ruled that the contacts of a foreign corporation with the State of Texas were sufficient to allow a Texas state court to assert jurisdiction over the corporation in a cause of action not arising out of or related to the corporation's activities within the State.

I

Petitioner Helicopteros Nacionales de Colombia, S.A., (Helicol) is a Colombian corporation with its principal place of business in the city of Bogota in that country. It is engaged in the business of providing helicopter transportation for oil and construction companies in South America. On January 26, 1976, a helicopter owned by Helicol crashed in Peru. Four United States citizens were among those who lost their lives in the accident. Respondents are the survivors and representatives of the four decedents.

At the time of the crash, respondents' decedents were employed by Consorcio, a Peruvian consortium, and were working on a pipeline in Peru. Consorcio is the alter-ego of a joint venture named Williams-Sedco-Horn (WSH). The venture had its headquarters in Houston, Texas. Consorcio had been formed to enable the venturers to enter into a contract with Petro Peru, the Peruvian state owned oil company. Consorcio was to construct a pipeline for Petro Peru running from the interior of Peru westward to the Pacific Ocean. Peruvian law forbade construction of the pipeline by any non-Peruvian entity.

Consorcio/WSH needed helicopters to move personnel, materials, and equipment into and out of the construction area. In 1974, upon request of Consorcio/WSH, the chief executive officer of Helicol, Francisco Restrepo, flew to the United States and conferred in Houston with representatives of the three joint venturers. At that meeting, there was a discussion of prices, availability, working conditions, fuel, supplies, and housing. Restrepo represented that Helicol could have the first helicopter on the job in 15 days. The Consorcio/WSH representatives decided to accept the contract proposed by Restrepo. Helicol began performing before the agreement was formally signed in Peru on November 11, 1974. The contract was written in Spanish on official government stationery and provided that the residence of all the parties would be Lima, Peru. It further stated that controversies arising out of the contract would be submitted to the jurisdiction of Peruvian courts. In addition, it provided that Consorcio/WSH would make payments to Helicol's account with the Bank of America in New York City.

Aside from the negotiation session in Houston between Restrepo and the representatives of Consorcio/WSH, Helicol had other contacts with Texas. During the years 1970–1977, it purchased helicopters (approximately 80 percent of its fleet), spare parts, and accessories for more than $4 million from Bell Helicopter Company in Fort Worth. In that period, Helicol sent prospective pilots to Fort Worth for training and to ferry the aircraft to South America. It also sent management and maintenance personnel to visit Bell Helicopter in Fort Worth during the same period in order to receive "plant familiarization" and for technical consultation. Helicol received into its New York City and Panama City, Florida, bank accounts over $5 million in payments from Consorcio/WSH drawn upon First City National Bank of Houston.

Beyond the foregoing, there have been no other business contacts between Helicol and the State of Texas. Helicol never has been authorized to do business in Texas and never has had an agent for the service of process within the State. It never has performed helicopter operations in Texas or sold any product that reached Texas, never solicited business in Texas, never signed any contract in Texas, never had any employee based there, and never recruited an employee in Texas. In addition, Helicol never has owned real or personal property in Texas and never has maintained an office or establishment there. Helicol has maintained no records in Texas and has no shareholders in that State. None of the respondents or their decedents were domiciled in Texas, but all of the decedents were hired in Houston by Consorcio/WSH to work on the Petro Peru pipeline project.

Respondents instituted wrongful death actions in the District Court of Harris County, Texas, against Consorcio/WSH, Bell Helicopter Company, and Helicol. Helicol filed special appearances and moved to dismiss the actions for lack of *in personam* jurisdiction over it. The motion was denied. After a consolidated jury trial, judgment was entered against Helicol on a jury verdict of $1,141,200 in favor of respondents.

The Texas Court of Civil Appeals . . . reversed the judgment of the District Court, holding that *in personam* jurisdiction over Helicol was lacking. . . . The Supreme Court of Texas . . . reversed the judgment of the intermediate court. In ruling that the Texas courts had *in personam* the Due Process Clause of the Fourteenth Amendment permits. . . . Thus, the only question remaining for the court to decide was whether it was consistent with the Due Process Clause for Texas courts to assert *in personam* jurisdiction over Helicol.

II

The Due Process Clause of the Fourteenth Amendment operates to limit the power of a State to assert *in personam* jurisdiction over a nonresident defendant. . . . Due process requirements are satisfied when *in personam* jurisdiction is asserted over a nonresident corporate defendant that has "certain minimum contacts with [the forum] such that the maintenance of the suit does not offend 'traditional notions of fair play and substantial justice.' ". . . When a controversy is related to or "arises out of" a defendant's contacts with the forum, the Court has said that a "relationship among the defendant, the forum, and the litigation" is the essential foundation of *in personam* jurisdiction. . . .

Even when the cause of action does not arise out of or relate to the foreign corporation's activities in the forum State, due process is not offended by a State's subjecting the corporation to its *in personam* jurisdiction when there are sufficient contacts between the state and the foreign corporation. . . .

All parties to the present case concede that respondents' claims against Helicol did not "arise out of," and are not related to, Helicol's activities within Texas. We thus must explore the nature of Helicol's contacts with the State of Texas to determine whether they constitute the kind of continuous and systematic general business contacts the Court found to exist in *Perkins*. We hold that they do not.

It is undisputed that Helicol does not have a place of business in Texas and never has been licensed to do business in the State. Basically, Helicol's contacts with Texas consisted of sending its chief executive officer to Houston for a contract-negotiation session; accepting into its New York bank account checks drawn on a Houston bank; purchasing helicopters, equipment, and training services from Bell Helicopter for substantial sums; and sending personnel to Bell's facilities in Fort Worth for training.

The one trip to Houston by Helicol's chief executive officer for the purpose of negotiating the transportation-services contract with Consorcio/WSH cannot be described or regarded as a contact of a "continuous and systematic" nature, . . . and thus cannot support an assertion of *in personam* jurisdiction over Helicol by a Texas court. Similarly, Helicol's acceptance from Consorcio/WSH of checks drawn on a Texas bank is of negligible significance for purposes of determining whether Helicol had sufficient contacts in Texas. There is no indication that Helicol ever requested that the checks be drawn on a Texas bank or that there was any negotiation between Helicol and Consorcio/WSH with respect to the location or identity of the bank on which checks would be drawn. Common sense and everyday experience suggest that, absent unusual circumstances, the bank on which a check is drawn is generally of little consequence to the payee and is a matter left to the discretion of the drawer. Such unilateral activity of another party or a third person is not an appropriate consideration when determining whether a defendant has sufficient contacts with a forum State to justify an assertion of jurisdiction.

The Texas Supreme Court focused on the purchases and the related training trips in finding contacts sufficient to support an assertion of jurisdiction. We do not agree with that assessment. . . . [P]urchases and related trips, standing alone, are not a sufficient basis for a State's assertion of jurisdiction.

. . . [W]e hold that mere purchases, even if occurring at regular intervals, are not enough to warrant a State's assertion of *in personam* jurisdiction over a nonresident corporation in a cause of action not related to those purchase transactions. Nor can we conclude that the fact that Helicol sent personnel into Texas for training in connection with the purchase of helicopters and equipment in that State in any way enhanced the nature of Helicol's contacts with Texas. . . . The brief presence of Helicol employees in Texas for the purpose of attending the training sessions is [not] a significant contact. . . .

III

We hold that Helicol's contacts with the State of Texas were insufficient to satisfy the requirements of the Due Process Clause of the Fourteenth Amendment. Accordingly, we reverse the judgment of the Supreme Court of Texas.

Questions

1. Summarize the Supreme Court's standards for meeting due process requirements in achieving *in personam* jurisdiction.
2. Outline the contacts between Helicol and Texas. Why were those contacts insufficient?
3. Why are the states prevented from reaching throughout America to assert jurisdictional authority regardless of "minimal contacts"?
4. The Robinsons filed a product liability suit in an Oklahoma state court to recover for injuries sustained in an automobile accident in Oklahoma. The auto had been purchased in New York from the defendant, World-Wide Volkswagen Corp. Oklahoma's long-arm statute was used in an attempt to secure jurisdiction over the defendant. World-Wide conducted no business in Oklahoma. Nor did it solicit business there.
   a. Build an argument to support the claim of jurisdiction for the Oklahoma court.
   b. Decide the outcome. See *World-Wide Volkswagen Corp.* v. *Woodson*, 100 S.Ct. 559 (1980).

Venue

Venue refers to the geographical locale where a court action is held. Proper venue is specified by statute. In general, the aim is to provide for trials in the most convenient and logical location. Thus a trial ordinarily will be held where, for example, the defendants reside or where the incident in question occurred. In some instances, one of the parties may request a change of venue, which may be granted by the court where required by the demands of fairness.

State Court Systems

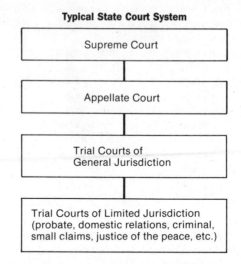

Typical State Court System

While state court systems vary substantially, a general pattern can be summarized. At the heart of the court pyramid in most states is a *trial court of general jurisdiction,* commonly labeled a *district court* or a *superior court*. It is here that most trials—both civil and criminal—arising out of state law would be heard, but certain classes of cases are reserved to courts of limited subject matter jurisdiction. Family, small claims, juvenile, and traffic courts are exemplary of this class of inferior trial level courts. At the top of the judicial pyramid in all states is a court of appeals, ordinarily labeled the *supreme court*. Some states also provide for an intermediate court of appeals located in the hierarchy between the trial courts and the highest appeals court.

Federal Court System

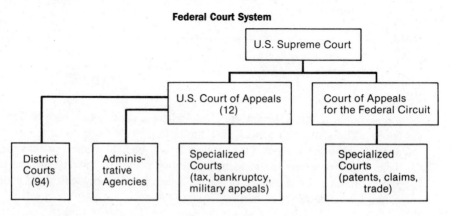

Federal Court System

District Courts   The district courts provide the foundation of the federal judicial system. The Constitution provides for a Supreme Court and such inferior courts as Congress shall authorize. Pursuant to that authority, Congress has established at least one district court for each state and territory. These are trial courts where witnesses are heard and questions of law and fact are resolved. More populous areas with heavier case loads have additional district courts. As circumstances demand, Congress adds courts at the district level. Most federal cases begin in the district courts. Congress has also provided for several courts of limited jurisdiction, including a tax court, a U.S. Claims Court, a Court of Military Appeals, and a bankruptcy court.

Court of Appeals   Congress has divided the United States into 11 judicial circuits and the District of Columbia with a court of appeals for each. Those courts hear appeals from the district courts within their circuit as well as reviewing decisions and enforcing orders of the various federal administrative agencies (such as the Interstate Commerce Commission and Federal Communications Commission).

In 1982 Congress created the U.S. Court of Appeals for the Federal Circuit. That court hears all patent appeals and all appeals from the U.S. Claims Court (monetary claims against the United States). Certain district court cases may be appealed directly to the U.S. Supreme Court.

Supreme Court   The Supreme Court consists of nine justices appointed for life by the president and confirmed by the Senate. In limited instances, the Supreme Court serves as an original or trial court, but by far the bulk of its cases rests in appeals and petitions.

Cases may reach the Supreme Court under two procedures: by appeal and petition. Congress has provided that certain classes of cases, if appealed, must be reviewed by the Supreme Court. One example is a decision of a federal court of appeals holding a state statute invalid because it violates the U.S. Constitution or a U.S. statute. The Court decides whether these appeals are granted a full hearing or are simply affirmed or dismissed after preliminary scrutiny, without filing written briefs or hearing oral arguments. Upon dismissal, the lower court order remains in effect.

Parties whose cases do not fall into one of the appeals categories can petition the Supreme Court to hear their cases by issuing *writs of certiorari* commanding the lower courts to forward the trial records to the Supreme Court. Decisions as to those petitions are, once again, entirely discretionary with the Court. Typically it will hear those cases that will assist in resolving conflicting court of appeals decisions, as well as those that raise questions of special significance about the Constitution or the national welfare. The Court annually receives more than 5,000 cases, but agrees typically to a full hearing for only about 150 to 200 of those.

The Civil Trial Process

Civil procedure varies by jurisdiction. The following generalization merely typifies the process.

Pleadings   *Pleadings* are the documents by which each party sets his or her case before the court. A civil action begins when the plaintiff files his or her first pleading, which is labeled a *complaint*. The complaint specifies (1) the parties to the suit, (2) evidence as to the court's jurisdiction in the case, (3) a statement of the facts, and (4) a prayer for relief (a remedy).

The complaint is filed with the clerk of court, and a *summons* is issued directing the defendant to appear in court to answer the claims alleged against him or her. A sheriff or some other official attempts to personally deliver the summons to the defendant. If personal delivery cannot be achieved, the summons may be left with a responsible party at the defendant's residence. Failing that, other modes of delivery are permissible, including a mailing. Publication of a notice in a newspaper will, in some instances, constitute good service of process. Ordinarily a copy of the complaint accompanies the summons so that the defendant is apprised of the nature of the claim.

The defendant has several options. He or she may do nothing, but failure to respond may result in a default judgment in favor of the plaintiff. The defendant may choose to respond by filing a *demurrer* or a *motion to dismiss,* the essence of which is to argue that even if the plaintiff's recitation of the facts is accurate, he or she has not stated a claim on which relief can be granted. For example, a student may be offended by a teacher's ''bizarre'' manner of dress, but barring unusual circumstances, the student could not, as a matter of law, successfully challenge the teacher's costume.

Alternatively, the defendant may file with the court his or her initial pleading, called an *answer,* wherein the defendant enters a denial by setting out his or her version of the facts and law, or in which the defendant simply concedes the validity of the plaintiff's position. The answer may contain an *affirmative defense,* which is an allegation of facts that would bar the plaintiff's claim. For example, the defendant might assert the statute of limitations or the statute of frauds. The defendant's answer might include a counterclaim or cross-claim. A *counterclaim* is the defendant's assertion of a claim of action against the plaintiff. A *cross-claim* is the defendant's assertion of a claim of action against a codefendant. In some states these would be labeled *cross-complaints*. In the event of a counterclaim or the assertion of new facts in the answer, the plaintiff will respond with a *reply*. The complaint, answer, reply, and their components are the pleadings that serve to give notice, to clarify the issues, and to limit the dimensions of the litigation.

Motions   As necessary during and after the filing of the pleadings, either party may file motions with the court. For example, a party may move to clarify a pleading or to strike a portion deemed unnecessary. Of special importance is a motion for a judgment on the pleadings or a motion for summary judgment. In a *motion for a judgment on the pleadings,* either party simply asks the judge to reach a decision based on the information in the pleadings. However, the judge will do so only if the defendant's answer constitutes an admission of the accuracy of the plaintiff's claim, or if the plaintiff's claim clearly has no foundation in law.

In a *motion for a summary judgment,* the party filing the motion is claiming that no facts are in dispute. Therefore, the judge may make a ruling about the law without taking the case to trial. In a summary judgment hearing, the court can look beyond the pleadings to hear evidence from affidavits, depositions, and so on. These motions serve to avoid the time and expense of trial.

Discovery   Justice is the goal of the legal system. Information is central to reaching a just result. *Discovery* is the primary information-gathering stage in the trial process. Discovery principally serves these purposes: (1) it preserves the testimony of witnesses who may not be available for trial, (2) it reduces the likelihood of perjury, (3) it aids in defining and narrowing the facts and issues, (4) it promotes pretrial settlements, (5) it increases the likelihood of concluding the case with a summary judgment, and (6) it helps prevent surprises at the trial.

In general, five discovery techniques are provided.

1. *Depositions.* A party or a witness may be required to appear before a court officer to give recorded, sworn testimony in response to questions raised by the attorneys for both sides of the controversy. Testimony is much like that at trial, except that it is not limited by the technical rules of evidence. *Depositions* help in trial preparation, in impeaching a witness whose trial testimony differs from her or his deposition, and in securing testimony from witnesses not available at trial due to death or absence from the court's jurisdiction.

2. *Interrogatories.* Written questions calling for written answers signed under oath may be required. Unlike depositions, *interrogatories* may be directed to parties, and they can call for information outside the party's personal knowledge, requiring the party to peruse her or his records.

3. *Discovery of documents and property.* Either party may request access to documents, as well as real and personal property, for the purposes of inspections relevant to the trial. Where appropriate, copies and photographs may be secured. If cooperation is not forthcoming, a court order may be requested.

4. *Physical and mental examinations.* When the physical and/or mental state of a party is at issue, the court may be asked to enter an order calling for an examination. Good cause must be shown, and the court must be satisfied that the need for information outweighs the party's constitutional right to privacy.

5. *Admissions.* Either party may make written request of the other, seeking an *admission* as to the truth of a specified issue of fact or law. If the receiving party agrees to or fails to deny the truth of the admission, that issue of fact or law is conclusively established for trial purposes. The use of such admissions resolves issues before they reach court, thus enhancing order and reducing trial time. For example, in a suit alleging a defective transmission in a recently purchased automobile, the auto dealer might be asked to agree that the auto was sold under a warranty and that the warranty included the transmission.

Pretrial Conference   Either party may request, and many courts require, a pretrial meeting involving the attorneys, the judge, and occasionally the parties. Usually following discovery, the conference is designed to plan the course of the trial in the interests of efficiency and justice. The discussion is informal as the participants seek to define and narrow the issues. The parties also attempt to settle the dispute in advance of trial. If no settlement is reached, a trial date is set.

The Judge and Jury The federal Constitution and most state constitutions provide for the right to a jury trial in a civil case (excepting equity actions). Some states place dollar minimums on that guarantee. At the federal level and in most states, unless one of the parties requests a jury, the judge alone will hear the case and decide all questions of law and fact. If the case is tried before a jury, that body will resolve questions of fact.

Jurors are selected from a jury pool composed of a cross section of the community. A panel is drawn from that pool. The individuals in that panel are questioned by the judge, by the attorneys, or by both to determine if any individual is prejudiced about the case such that he or she could not reach an objective decision on the merits. The questioning process is called *voir dire*.

From an attorney's point of view, jury selection is often not so much a matter of finding jurors without bias as it is a matter of identifying those jurors who are most likely to reach a decision favorable to one's client. To that end, elaborate mechanisms and strategies have been employed—particularly in criminal trials—to identify desirable jurors. For example, sophisticated, computer-assisted surveys of the trial community have been conducted to develop objective evidence by which to identify jurors who would not admit to racial prejudice, but whose "profile" suggests the likelihood of such prejudice. A few attorneys have taken the rather exotic tactic of employing body language experts to watch potential jurors during *voir dire* for those mannerisms that are said to reveal their inner views.

After questioning, the attorneys may *challenge for cause,* arguing to the judge that the individual cannot exercise the necessary objectivity of judgment. Additionally, attorneys are afforded a limited number of *peremptory challenges,* by which the attorney can have a potential juror dismissed without the judge's concurrence and without offering a reason.

Jury selection and the jury system are the subject of considerable debate in the legal community. Are juries necessary to a just system? How small can a jury be and still fulfill its duty? Is the jury process too slow and expensive? Should very long and complex cases, such as those in the antitrust area, be heard only by judges?

The case that follows illustrates the central role of jury selection in the outcome of a case.

ROSALES–LOPEZ V. UNITED STATES   451 U.S. 182 (1981)

Justice White

I

Petitioner is of Mexican descent. In February 1979, he was tried before a jury in the United States District Court for the Southern District of California for his alleged participation in a plan by which three Mexican aliens were illegally brought into the country.

The Government's evidence at trial described the following events. On the night of December 10, 1978, three aliens were led across the Mexican-American border and taken to a car, previously left for them on the American side. They drove to Imperial Beach, California, a town about eight miles inside the border. Early in the morning of December 11, they reached the home of Virginia Hendricks Bowling, where they were admitted into the garage of the house by petitioner. Bowling was an American citizen, apparently Caucasian, living in Imperial Beach with her 19-year-old daughter. Petitioner had been living with Bowling's daughter in her mother's house since July 1978.

Later in the morning, petitioner hid the three aliens and their guide in the trunk of a green Oldsmobile. Bowling drove the Oldsmobile north, through the San Clemente checkpoint, while petitioner followed in a grey Ford. After passing through the checkpoint, Bowling and petitioner exchanged cars. Petitioner proceeded to Los Angeles in the Oldsmobile and Bowling returned to Imperial Beach in the Ford. In Los Angeles, petitioner went to an apartment, which agents of the Immigration and Naturalization Service had had under surveillance for several weeks because they suspected that it was a drop site for illegal aliens. Upon arrival, the aliens were let out of the trunk and told to go into the apartment by petitioner. Shortly thereafter, petitioner was arrested when he left the apartment with one of the aliens.

At trial, the INS agents, Bowling, the three illegal aliens, and David Falcon-Zavala, another named principal in the smuggling arrangement who was arrested with petitioner, testified for the Government. Petitioner did not testify; his defense was principally to challenge the credibility of the Government witnesses. The jury convicted him of all the charges, and the Court of Appeals for the Ninth Circuit affirmed. . . .

Prior to trial, petitioner's counsel formally requested that he be allowed personally to *voir dire* the prospective members of the jury. At the same time, he filed a list of 26 questions that he requested the trial judge to ask, if the court denied his first motion. Among the questions submitted was one directed toward possible prejudice toward Mexicans:

Would you consider the race or Mexican descent of Humberto Rosales-Lopez in your evaluation of this case? How would it affect you?

. . . [T]he trial judge conducted the *voir dire* himself. He asked about half of the questions submitted by petitioner. Although he did not ask any question directed specifically to possible racial or ethnic prejudice, he did ask a question directed to attitudes toward the substantive charges involved: . . . "Do any of you have any particular feelings one way or the other about aliens or could you sit as a fair and impartial juror if you are called upon to do so?" . . .

Following the *voir dire*, defense counsel restated his request with respect to six of the submitted questions, including the one directed toward racial or ethnic prejudice. . . . The judge declined to ask any further questions of the jury panel. . . .

II

Voir dire plays a critical function in assuring the criminal defendant that his Sixth Amendment right to an impartial jury will be honored. Without an adequate *voir dire*, the trial judge's responsibility to remove prospective jurors who will not be able impartially to follow the court's instructions and evaluate the evidence cannot be fulfilled. . . .

Because the obligation to impanel an impartial jury lies in the first instance with the trial judge, and because he must rely largely on his immediate perceptions, federal judges have been accorded ample discretion in determining how best to conduct the *voir dire*. . . .

Rule 24 (a), Federal Rules of Criminal Procedure, provides that the trial court may decide to conduct the *voir dire* itself or may allow the parties to conduct it. If the court conducts it, the parties may "supplement the examination by such further inquiry as [the court] deems proper"; alternatively, the court may limit participation to the submission of additional questions, which the court must ask only "as it deems proper." . . .

There is no constitutional presumption of juror bias for or against members of any particular racial or ethnic groups. . . . [T]here is no per se constitutional rule in such circumstances requiring inquiry as to racial prejudice. . . . Only when there are more substantial indications of the likelihood of racial or ethnic prejudice affecting the jurors in a particular case does the trial court's denial of a defendant's request to examine the jurors' ability to deal impartially with this subject amount to an unconstitutional abuse of discretion.

Absent such circumstances, the Constitution leaves it to the trial court, and the judicial system within which that court operates, to determine the need for such questions. In the federal court system, we have indicated that under our supervisory authority over the federal courts, we would require that questions directed to the discovery of racial prejudice be asked in certain circumstances in which such an inquiry is not constitutionally mandated. . . .

Determination of an appropriate nonconstitutional standard for the federal courts does not depend upon a comparison of the concrete costs and benefits that its application is likely to entail. These are likely to be slight: some delay in the trial versus the occasional discovery of an unqualified juror who would not otherwise be discovered. There is, however, a more significant conflict at issue here—one involving the appearance of justice in the federal courts. On the one hand, requiring an inquiry in every case is likely to create the impression "that justice in a court of law may turn upon the pigmentation of skin [or] the accident of birth." . . . Balanced against this, however, is the criminal defendant's perception that avoiding the inquiry does not eliminate the problem, and that his trial is not the place in which to elevate appearance over reality. . . .

In our judgment, it is usually best to allow the defendant to resolve this conflict by making the determination of whether or not he would prefer to have the inquiry into racial or ethnic prejudice pursued. Failure to honor his request, however, will be reversible error only where the circumstances of the case indicate that there is a reasonable possibility that racial or ethnic prejudice might have influenced the jury. . . .

III

Evaluated against these standards, there was no reversible error in the *voir dire* afforded petitioner. At no point has petitioner argued that the matters at issue in his trial involved allegations of racial or ethnic prejudice: neither the Government's case nor his defense involved any such allegations. There were, then, no "special circumstances" of constitutional dimension in this case. Neither did the circumstances of the case reveal a violent criminal act with a victim of a different racial or ethnic group. In fact, petitioner was accused of a victimless crime: aiding members of his own ethnic group to gain illegal entry into the United States. Petitioner, therefore, falls within that category of cases in which the trial court must determine if the external circumstances of the case indicate a reasonable possibility that racial or ethnic prejudice will influence the jury's evaluation of the evidence. For two reasons, we do not believe that such a reasonable possibility has been demonstrated in this case.

First, the trial court reasonably determined that a juror's prejudice toward aliens might affect his or her ability to serve impartially in this case. The court, therefore, questioned the prospective jurors as to their attitudes toward aliens. There can be no doubt that the jurors would have understood a question about aliens to at least include Mexican aliens. The trial court excused two jurors for cause, based on their responses to this question. Removing these jurors eliminated, we believe, any reasonable possibility that the remaining jurors would be influenced by an undisclosed racial prejudice toward Mexicans that would have been disclosed by further questioning.

Second, petitioner contends that "any latent racial antagonism" of the jurors toward Mexicans was likely to be exacerbated by Bowling's testimony concerning the relationship between petitioner and her daughter. Petitioner, however, failed to make this argument to the trial court in support of his requested question. Even if he had, however, it would not create a reasonable possibility that the jury's determination would be influenced by racial prejudice. Bowling's testimony as to petitioner's role in the particular smuggling operation involved in this trial was substantially corroborated by the other witnesses presented by the Government, including Falcon-Zavala and the three illegal aliens. Under the circumstances of this case, the racial or ethnic differences between the defendant and a key Government witness did not create a situation meeting the standard set out above. The judge was not, therefore, required to inquire further than he did.

Under these circumstances, we cannot hold that there was a reasonable possibility that racial or ethnic prejudice would affect the jury. . . .

Affirmed.

Questions

1. State the issue in this case. How did the Court resolve that issue?
2. What reasoning supported the Court's position?
3. Write a brief dissenting opinion.
4. According to the Supreme Court, when must a trial court inquire into the issue of a juror's possible prejudice?
5. A petitioner, who was a young, bearded, black male, was convicted in a South Carolina trial court of unlawful possession of marijuana. At trial, the petitioner's attorney had asked the judge to question the prospective jurors regarding their bias due to (1) race, (2) beards, and (3) pretrial publicity relating to the drug problem. The judge asked general questions regarding bias, but the petitioner's specific questions were not raised. The petitioner ultimately appealed his case to the U.S. Supreme Court.
   a. What constitutional law violation would you allege on behalf of the petitioner?
   b. Decide. See *Ham* v. *South Carolina*, 409 U.S. 524 (1973).

The Trial   The trial begins with the opening statement by the attorney having the burden of proof. Then the opposing attorney offers his or her statement. Each is expected to outline what he or she intends to prove. The plaintiff then presents evidence, which may include both testimony and physical evidence, such as documents and photos, which are called *exhibits*.

The attorney secures testimony from his or her own witness via questioning labeled *direct examination*. After the plaintiff's attorney completes direct examination of the plaintiff's own witness, the defense attorney may question that witness in a process labeled *cross examination*. *Re-direct* and *re-cross* may then follow. The plaintiff's attorney then summarizes the testimony and the exhibits, and then "rests" his or her case.

At this stage the defense may make a motion for a *directed verdict*, arguing, in essence, that the plaintiff has offered insufficient evidence to justify relief, so time and expense may be saved by terminating the trial. Understandably, the judge considers the motion in the light most favorable to the plaintiff. Such motions ordinarily fail. In that case, the trial goes forward with the defendant's presentation of evidence.

At the completion of the defendant's case, both parties may be permitted to offer *rebuttal* evidence, and either party may move for a directed verdict. Barring a directed verdict, the case goes forward with each party making a *closing argument*. When the trial is by jury, the judge must instruct the jurors as to the law to be applied to the case. The attorneys often submit to the judge their view of the proper instructions. Because the law lacks the clarity that lay persons often attribute to it, framing the instructions is a difficult task, one frequently resulting in an appeal to a higher court. Finally, the verdict is rendered and a judgment is entered.

Post-Trial Motions   The losing party may seek a *judgment notwithstanding the verdict (judgment n.o.v)* on the grounds that in light of the controlling law, insufficient evidence was offered to permit the jury to decide as it did. The judge is also empowered to enter a judgment n.o.v. on his or her own initiative. However, such motions are rarely granted.

Either party may also move for a new trial. The winning party might do so on the grounds that the remedy provided was inferior to that warranted by the evidence. The losing party commonly claims an error of law to support a motion for a new trial. Other possible grounds for a new trial include jury misconduct or new evidence. If the motion is granted, a new trial will be conducted before a different judge and jury.

Appeals   After the judgment is rendered, either party may appeal the decision to a higher court. The winner may do so if he or she feels the remedy is inadequate. Ordinarily, of course, the losing party brings the appeal. The appealing party is the *appellant* or the *petitioner,* while the other party is the *appellee* or *respondent*. The appeals court does not try the case again. In theory at least, its consideration is limited to mistakes of law at the trial level. For example, the appellant will argue that a jury instruction was erroneous or that the judge erred in failing to grant a motion to strike certain testimony, alleged to have been prejudicial. The appeals court does not hear new evidence. It bases its decision on the trial record, materials filed by the opposing attorneys, and oral arguments.

The appellate court announces its judgment and ordinarily explains that decision in an accompanying document labeled an *opinion*. (Most of the cases in this text are appellate court opinions.) If no error is found, the lower court decision is *affirmed*. In finding prejudicial error, the appellate court may simply *reverse* (overrule) the lower court. Or, the judgment may be to *reverse and remand*, wherein the lower court is overruled and the trial court must try the case again in accordance with the law as articulated in the appeals court opinion. After the decision of the intermediate appellate court, a further appeal may be directed to the highest court of the jurisdiction. Most of those petitions are declined.

Class Actions

A specialized form of civil proceeding, the class action suit, is worthy of attention. A *class action* allows a group of individuals to sue or be sued in one judicial proceeding, provided their claim or the claim against them arises out of similar or closely related grievances. For example, if hundreds of people were injured in a hotel fire, a subset of that group might file an action against the hotel on behalf of all the injured parties. The class action thus permits lawsuits that might otherwise be impractical due to the number of people involved or the small amount of each claim. (For example, all purchasers of an elixir guaranteed to stimulate hair growth and sold at $5 a unit join in an action when the potion does not achieve the advertised success.) The class action is also expedient; many potential causes of action can be disposed of in one suit.

Nevertheless, the concept of the class action has received mixed reviews. Some suits are so large and unwieldy that they impose an extreme burden on the judicial process. Others, it is argued, line attorneys' pockets but achieve few substantive legal benefits. Class actions also give rise to considerable problems of procedural fairness. For example, under a recent U.S. Supreme Court decision, all identifiable class members in federal court cases must receive individual notice of the impending action. In some instances, that requirement will prove to be very weighty, but other statutes and rules remain under which class actions may be brought more easily.[12] Despite its complexities, the class action can be a very effective tool in securing justice, particularly in those instances where the "little guy" must challenge one of America's giant institutions.

Due Process of Law

Guiding and, in a sense, governing our very complex judicial procedure is the constitutional principle of *due process of law*. The Fifth and Fourteenth Amendments to the federal Constitution prohibit the federal and state governments, respectively, from depriving individuals of life, liberty, and property without due process of law. Hence, it follows that the judicial process, to meet constitutional standards, must be conducted in accordance with fundamental fairness. The process must not be unreasonable, arbitrary, or capricious. The standard is necessarily broad and not readily clarified by definition, but it is our indispensable measure of judicial equity.

Questions

1. What are the purposes and uses of the concept of jurisdiction? Why do we limit the courts to which a claim can be taken?
2. In 1980 a state judge ruled that a black man charged with shooting a Ku Klux Klansman during a civil rights march in Decatur, Alabama, could receive a fair trial in that venue. The Poverty Law Center, representing the defendant, had commissioned a survey of the attitudes of the Decatur community. A majority of the whites surveyed opposed protests of any kind and, in general, blamed the black demonstrators for provoking the violence. Poverty Law Center attorneys also offered evidence of the "tense racial climate" that had existed, they contended, since the 1978 arrest of a retarded black man for the alleged rape of a white woman.[13]
    a. Did the judge rule correctly?
    b. Are black citizens and white citizens treated equally before the law?
3. The Fifth and Fourteenth Amendments to the U.S. Constitution guarantee that the citizenry will not be deprived of life, liberty, and property without due process of law, while the

Seventh Amendment guarantees the right to trial by jury. In an unusually complex antitrust case it was argued that the due process clause prohibits trial by jury in instances where the complexity of the case exceeds a jury's ability to reach a reasoned judgment.

    a.   Should unusually complex cases be heard by a judge alone? See *In Re U.S. Financial Securities Litigation,* 609 F.2d 411 (9th Cir. 1979) cert. denied, 446 U.S. 929 (1979). But see *In Re Japanese Electronic Products Antitrust Litigation* (U.S. Court of Appeals for the 3rd Circuit, No. 79-2540) *Antitrust and Trade Regulation Report,* No. 973, July 17, 1980, p. F–1.

    b.   Are juries usually successful in reaching fair, impartial verdicts, or do the personal deficiencies and prejudices of the ordinary citizen result in unfair, irrational decisions?

    c.   Should the jury system be abolished?

4.   Scholar Amitai Etzioni has suggested that the advance of science may constitute a threat to the jury system.

> Man has taken a new bite from the apple of knowledge, and it is doubtful whether we will be better for it. This time it is not religion or the family that are being disturbed by the new knowledge but that venerable institution of being judged by a jury of one's peers. The jury's impartiality is threatened because defense attorneys have discovered that by using social science techniques, they can manipulate the composition of juries to significantly increase the likelihood that their clients will be acquitted.[14]

How can the use of the computer, advanced survey techniques, and the like threaten the validity of the trial process?

5.   [I]n an out-of-court settlement, $218 million in damages was awarded to 30,000 customers of a group of folding-box manufacturers accused of fixing prices. The settlement came after several years of litigation. For the customers, the average award was $6,790, hardly a large sum to them since more than a few were multimillion-dollar businesses. But for the lawyers representing the customers it was a different matter. The 50 law firms involved split $13 million in legal fees, with the most active firms in the case reeling in a cool million each.[15]

On balance, does the class action serve a useful public purpose, or does it merely afford consumer activists the opportunity to harass corporate "villians" while lawyers line their pockets?

6.   The Incompatibility Clause of the constitution provides that "no person holding any office under the United States, shall be a member of either House during his continuance in the office." An association of Armed Forces Reservists, including several U.S. citizens and taxpayers, was opposed to the Vietnam War. The association brought a class action on behalf of all U.S. citizens and taxpayers against the secretary of defense and others. The association argued that several members of Congress violated the Incompatibility Clause by virtue of their Armed Forces Reserve membership.

    Do the plaintiffs have standing to sue? Explain. See *Schlesinger* v. *Reservists Committee to Stop the War,* 418 U.S. 208 (1974).

7.   Law cases often read like soap operas while they reveal important truths. A woman and man, each married to others, had engaged in a long-term love affair. The woman's husband died, and she pleaded with her paramour to leave his New York home to visit her in Florida. She affirmed her love for the man. They made arrangements to meet in Miami, but upon his arrival at the airport he was served a summons informing him that he was being sued. His Florida "lover" sought $500,000 for money allegedly loaned to him, and for seduction inspired by a promise of marriage.

    a.   Does the Florida court have proper jurisdiction over him?

       b.   What if he had voluntarily come to Florida on vacation? See *Wyman* v. *Newhouse,* 93 F.2d 313 (2d Cir. 1937).

  8. Rossville Crushed Stone Co. was incorporated in Tennessee and conducted business in a number of states. One of Rossville's stone quarries was located in Georgia near the home of Mr. and Mrs. Still. One day blasting was underway in Rossville's Georgia quarry and tremors severely damaged the Stills' home. Still brought suit in the federal District Court for the Eastern District of Tennessee. Damages exceeded $10,000. *Should* the case be heard in Tennessee? See *Still* v. *Rossville Crushed Stone Co.,* 370 F.2d 324 (6th Cir. 1966).

Part Three—Reform?

Public Opinion

To many Americans our system of justice is neither systematic nor just. We have gone to elegant and expensive extremes to provide justice for all, but popular sentiment is not particularly approving of the results. A 1978 survey of 1,931 adults for the National Center for State Courts found that the more laypersons knew of the law, the more they favored reform. Of those claiming extensive knowledge of the justice system, 17 percent felt confidence in the courts. Of those with average knowledge 23 percent felt confidence, as against 29 percent of those with limited knowledge.[16]

    Twenty-six percent of those surveyed thought that political influence on court decisions was a "serious problem," 25 percent thought the poor were not treated as well as the rich, and 19 percent thought blacks were not treated as equitably as whites. On the other hand, of 194 judges interviewed, 98 percent felt the courts were generally unaffacted by politics, and 97 percent found blacks and the poor receiving treatment equal to all others. Only 6 percent of the 278 community leaders surveyed found political influence a serious problem. How do you account for the considerable divergence of opinion between the leaders and those being led? (As an aside, it is interesting to note that those surveyed knew little of the law. For example, 37 percent of the laypersons surveyed believed that one accused of a crime is responsible for proving one's own innocence.)

Judges and Judicial Activism

The U.S. Supreme Court is routinely accused of upsetting the constitutional balance of power by exercising authority historically vested in the executive and legislative branches. The Court has been accused of "legislating" sweeping changes in American life in such areas as the rights of the criminally accused, discrimination, and abortion. In general, the Court has, according to its critics, failed to maintain the self-discipline and restraint deemed necessary for a carefully deliberative body. The article that follows reveals some of the dangers and virtues in an activist judicial stance.

FEDERAL JUDGE PREACHES GOSPEL OF "THE LITTLE GUY"

Larry Fruhling

Minneapolis, Minn. The man who delivered the sermon looked like nothing as much as the preacher for the Lutheran flock of a small, Minnesota town. And his message seemed suitable for the pulpit.

Balding, graying, his austere features set off by wire-rim glasses, District Judge Miles Lord—the Lord of Federal Court, as he is known—told the three officials of A. H. Robins Co., maker of a contraceptive device called the Dalkon Shield, to "confess to your Maker and beg forgiveness and mend your ways."

The judge said A. H. Robins had sinned grievously by refusing to recall the Dalkon Shield and to make prompt restitution to the women who were injured by it. Rather, Lord said, the company and its lawyers had dragged their feet for 12 years, using every means available to discourage women from gaining compensation for their illnesses.

"You have taken the bottom line as your guiding beacon and the low road as your route," he declared. "Under your direction your company has in fact continued to allow women, tens of thousands of them, to wear this device, a deadly depth charge in their wombs, ready to explode at any time."

Lord said Robins was guilty of corporate greed and irresponsibility. He begged the company to settle its accounts with women who had been made ill and infertile by the device and to appeal to women still using the shields to have them removed at once.

Then the chief federal judge for Minnesota closed his lengthy tirade against the Robins officials on this note: "I just want to say I love you. I am not mad at you."

It was vintage Miles Welton Lord, at either his best as the self-anointed conscience of corporate America and champion of "the little guy," or at his worst as a cannon rumbling loose on the deck of the federal judiciary.

Both views have found many supporters during Lord's 18 turbulent years as one of

America's most controversial federal judges, a man whose blunt and frequent rulings and speeches focused attention sharply on the environment, discrimination against women, the abuses by government bureaucracy, corporate misdeeds and, most recently, the arms race.

In November, the 8th Circuit Court of Appeals, acting on a petition from A. H. Robins, erased Lord's "deadly depth charge" speech from the official record of the proceeding, saying Lord had jumped off the deep end before hearing Robins' side of the case.

* * * * *

Lord has been condemned by *The American Lawyer* magazine as the worst federal judge in the seven Midwestern states that answer to the 8th Circuit Court of Appeals.

"Impartiality is a quality that Lord rarely seemed to view as a virtue," the magazine declared in 1980, quoting an unnamed Minnesota lawyer as saying, "Lord loves a good fight, and that's exactly what makes him such a bad judge. He'd rather do the fighting himself than decide the case."

He was praised the following year as the best federal trial judge in the United States by the American Association of Trial Lawyers, which cited his determination to find his way to the heart of a matter by chopping through the labyrinth of delay and obfuscation that corporate lawyers are paid to construct.

A veteran Minnesota lawyer who is no particular fan says Lord probably is no more arbitrary in running his courtroom than some other federal judges secure in their lifetime appointments. What sets Lord apart, the lawyer said, is that "the other judges are on the side of the corporations—they're establishment arbitrary. Miles is little-guy arbitrary." . . .

Last November, just as the appeals court was clearing the last of the smoke from Lord's "deadly depth charge" speech, the judge again was busy delivering a full measure.

This time the case concerned two young antiwar demonstrators convicted by a jury of sneaking into a Sperry Corp. plant in the Twin-Cities area and smashing $36,000 worth of computer parts Sperry was building for the Defense Department.

Lord could have sent John LaForge and Barbara Ann Katt to jail for 10 years, a sentence, he said, that some judges might have been inclined toward and that the public likely would have applauded.

Instead, Lord put LaForge and Katt on probation for six months, gave Sperry a public lashing for allegedly ripping off the federal government for $3.6 million in military contract overcharges by "wrongfully and feloniously juggling the books" and sounded a call for an end to the arms race.

"As I ponder over the punishment to be meted out to these two people who were attempting to unbuild weapons of mass destruction," Lord said, "we must ask ourselves: Can it be that those of us who build weapons to kill are engaged in a more sanctified endeavor than those who would by their acts attempt to counsel moderation and mediation as an alternative method of settling international disputes?

"Why are we so fascinated by a power so great that we cannot comprehend its magnitude? What is so sacred about a bomb, so romantic about a missile?

"Why do we condemn and hang individual killers, while extolling the virtues of war-mongers?"

Another Corporation Lectured
As for Sperry, Lord said the government required the corporation to pay back only 10 percent of the $3.6 million it had allegedly "embezzled," and no corporate officer or employee had been punished.

"Could it be," Lord asked, "that these men—who are working to build weapons of mass destruction—receive special treatment because of the nature of their work?

"I would here in this instance attempt in my own small way to take the sting out of the bomb, attempt in some way to force the government—though I know it will be futile—to

remove the halo which it seems to hold over any device which can kill, and, instead, to place thereon a shroud, the shroud of death, destruction, mutilation, disease and debilitation."

Lord, who is 65, says he is a devoted fan of the American corporation. Never mind the scalding speeches he has delivered from the bench against Sperry, A. H. Robins, and, in one remarkable case from which he was removed by an appeals court for his biases, Reserve Mining Co. . . .

"If we didn't have corporations I would try to invent them," Lord says. "They're the greatest mechanisms for collecting capital and for production that there is. We have the most powerful, wealthy, productive country in the world, and 85 percent of our gross national product is produced by corporations. There is no way you can help but admire that."

Down Primrose Paths
It's just that corporations occasionally are lured away from the paths of righteousness by pressure to produce profits for their stockholders and by organizational mazes that defy the pinpointing of responsibility for the actions of a big company, he says. . . .

He complains that corporations hire "boosters" to give one-day seminars, at a price of $5,000 or more, on efficiency, productivity, the glories of capitalism. Lord says he is just trying to balance the equation. "These guys don't want to hear that it's a sin to poison a river, to make people sick downstream." . . .

Lord has judged hundreds of cases, ranging from big antitrust suits against drug companies to supermarket mergers, kidnappings, bank robberies, the question of permitting motorboats in the Boundary Waters Canoe Area and the free-expression rights of naked dancers.

The decision he is proudest of was his ruling in 1972 that two Minnesota high schools had to give girls access to boys' athletic teams or provide equal athletic programs.

"That thing revolutionized the whole country," he says, adding that his daughter's bristling reaction when he wisecracked about girl wrestlers "changed my whole aspect of thinking about the feminist movement."

But the cases that always intrigued him most, he says, are "the ones where you see the avarice of the human being, individually or collectively."

*   *   *   *   *

"Maybe I should have been a preacher and pounded the pulpit every day," Lord says.

[Judge Lord retired from the federal bench in 1985.—ed.]

Source: *Des Moines Sunday Register*, February 3, 1985, Section A, pp. 1, 9. Reprinted with permission of the copyright holder, *The Des Moines Register*.

QUESTIONS

1. Should judges use the bench as a pulpit of sorts to remind corporate officials of lessons they "don't want to hear"? If judges do not do so, where will those lessons be expressed?

2. What dangers might result from following the activist posture of Judge Lord?

Lawyers

Not surprisingly, lawyers themselves are the subject of particularly acute public disapproval. In 1978 the American Bar Association released the results of a survey of 2,046 adults regarding their views of the legal profession and the quality of law practice.

The public generally thought quite poorly of lawyers. Of those surveyed 59 percent perceived lawyers as not being prompt about getting things done, 30 percent felt lawyers needlessly complicated clients' problems, 50 percent thought lawyers were generally not very good at keeping their clients informed of progress in their cases and 68 percent thought most lawyers charged more for their services than they were worth.

Asked if "most lawyers would engage in unethical or illegal activities to help a client in an important case" 38 percent of those interviewed said yes. Fifty-nine percent agreed with the statement that "the legal system favors the rich and powerful over everyone else."[17]

In fairness, the survey also revealed that most of those people whose cases had been completed felt their attorneys had done a competent job.

Evidently many Americans hold a distaste for lawyers. With the unfolding of the Watergate scandal, even the extreme image of lawyers as criminals was seen by many to have some foundation in fact. America is awash in lawyers. Our ratio of lawyers to population—1 for every 500 citizens—is 3 times greater than that of Great Britain and 21 times greater than that of Japan. Yet it is argued that most Americans receive inadequate legal assistance.

So when the American Bar Association makes the remarkable admission that it "has long been aware that the middle 70 percent of the population is not being reached or served adequately by the [legal] profession," it is acknowledging that nearly three quarters of the American people lack full access to the system of justice.[18]

In 1501, Shakespeare said in *Henry VI:* "The first thing we do, let's kill all the lawyers." In 1978 former President Jimmy Carter said, "We are over-lawyered and under-represented." President Carter went on to say that lawyers are often guilty of thwarting justice by producing "interminable delay." U.S. Supreme Court Chief Justice

Warren Burger caused convulsions in the legal community by asserting that one half of all U.S. trial lawyers are incompetent to satisfactorily represent their clients.

The legal profession as an institution is also under attack for inhibiting competition and thus inflating legal fees. Such tasks as probate, simple divorces, and the preparation of incorporation documents could often be done at greatly reduced costs, either by the parties or by skilled laypersons. Depending on state law, however, such action is often either forbidden as the unauthorized practice of law or rendered difficult by state bar association policy. Of course, such laws and policies are, from the bar's point of view, designed to protect the public.

Lawyers have recently been under attack on antitrust grounds. Court decisions have forced the bar to permit its members to advertise their services and fees. Other decisions have directly forbidden price-fixing by lawyers. Those decisions were based broadly on restraint of trade grounds in that price competition presumably will result in reduced fees for legal services. Even the notion of the practice of law—particularly trial law—as an adversarial process is the subject of increasingly strident complaint. Despite reforms in the process, critics feel that trials amounting to civilized combat are not the ultimate means of resolving disputes. It is argued that the pursuit of victory sometimes is not consistent with the pursuit of justice. For example, counsel in some instances knows a client to be guilty but is required to withhold that information and pursue the client's needs to the fullest. The article that follows questions the foundations of the adversarial process.

INCIVILITY IN COURT AS LAWYERS STRIVE TO WIN

Elliott M. Abramson

According to Chief Justice Warren Burger, American lawyers are sorely lacking in civility. In a recent talk in London, he stated that "the current generation of lawyers . . . seem[s] to act more like warriors eager to do battle than healers seeking peace."

I believe that the chief justice has definitely put his finger on something—but it may be more than he realizes. Many people who have dealt with attorneys will readily agree that lawyers are hard-driving to (perhaps well beyond) the point of incivility. "Ruthlessness" may be the right word.

Not often remarked on is that such attitudes are bred by, integral to and entirely consistent with the very core and sinews of our legal system and its training grounds—a system in which, first of all, winning and losing are very sharply demarcated and with very little middle ground.

Take a simple example: X has a piece of jewelry she believes to be an imitation diamond. Y wishes to buy it, and they agree on $25. Later, it develops that the object is a real diamond worth perhaps $5,000. X offers Y his $25 back in return for the diamond.

If Y does not comply, and X sues, one party will basically win everything. For, under the fundamental rules of the American legal system, it will be found either that the diamond belongs to Y, with X having no further rights, or Y must return it to X and relinquish all of his rights in it.

The hard rules of the game do not recognize the possibility of coming together in the following way: Neither X nor Y realized the worth of the gem. Since they have now both been rather strongly connected with it, and it suddenly turns out to be worth $5,000, each might be accorded $2,500. Both would thereby gain from a stroke of good fortune for which neither can take credit.

But the contemporary American legal structure mandates that one be a total winner, the other a total loser. Such a state of affairs can induce only frenzy and desperation in its practitioners, certainly not graciousness and civility.

Another contributor to the brusqueness and callousness in the professional conduct of American lawyers is the powerful endorsement of competition, generated by legal education. American law is an enthusiastic helpmate of the American economic system, which assumes that social welfare is best promoted when people and institutions strive, sometimes viciously, against each other in seeking to maximize their own gain and leave very little for others.

*   *   *   *   *

Another factor that may generate an urgent need to succeed, at the cost of insensitivity and incivility, is lawyers' observation of how the losers are treated. Their experience is with a legal system that administers the complex daily affairs of the wealthiest, most resource-laden nation in history, yet has never satisfactorily solved the problems of malnutrition, poverty, or hopelessly despairing mental illness.

*   *   *   *   *

The true and just way to repair that incivility of lawyers, which the chief justice noted, is not by cosmetic adjustment to the tones of voices, but by thoroughgoing, authentic transformation of the American legal system.

Source: *Des Moines Register*, April 4, 1984, p. 8A. Reprinted with permission of the copyright holder, The Associated Press. (Elliott M. Abramson is a professor in the College of Law at DePaul University.)

Too Much Law

The final lament is undoubtedly that most in vogue currently; that is, we are simply the victims of too many laws and too much litigation. In an honorable effort to improve the general welfare, government's legislative and regulatory reach has been dramatically expanded. (Much of Chapters 6 and 7 are devoted to the regulatory debate.)

The citizenry certainly has not been reluctant to call upon the legal system when the need, however trivial, was felt. What of the child who sued his parents for emotional distress because they made him cut the lawn after he was suspended from school for selling drugs? Or the professional football fans who sued the official whose critical call turned the outcome of a game against their team? Almost as a reflex, citizens turn to the law to resolve their grievances. To a dangerous degree the law has supplanted, rather than supplemented, noncoercive regulatory forces such as custom, conscience, and the free market. However, the leading scholarly inquiry in the area concludes that the litigation mania does not exist. According to a study funded by the Justice Department, for every 1,000 grievances where more than $1,000 was at stake only 50 resulted in the filing of a lawsuit.[19]

The article that follows evaluates the current litany of complaints.

HAS U.S. TOO MANY LAWS, LAWSUITS AND LAWYERS?

Stuart Taylor, Jr.

Prominent lawyers, judges, and scholars warn that the justice system is choking on its own complexity and cost as swollen case loads place ever greater demands on it.

Experts as diverse as Chief Justice Warren Burger, Attorney General William French Smith, former Attorney General Griffin Bell, and Derek Bok, president of Harvard University, argue that the country suffers from too many laws, too many lawsuits, too many legal entanglements and—at least in Bok's view too many lawyers.

* * * * *

In his most recent of many complaints about the Supreme Court's swollen case load, Burger declared that the nation is plagued "with an almost irrational focus—virtually a mania—on litigation as a way to solve all problems."

* * * * *

Warnings about increased litigiousness alternate with expressions of concern that most citizens cannot afford to hire lawyers to press legitimate claims.

Lloyd Cutler, one of Washington's most prominent corporate lawyers, has written of large law firms like his own: "The rich who pay our fees are less than 1 percent of our fellow citizens, but they get at least 95 percent of our time. The disadvantaged we serve for nothing are perhaps 20 to 25 percent of the population and get at most 5 percent of our time. The remaining 75 percent cannot afford to consult us and get virtually none of our time."

But Bok stresses that "the wealthy and the powerful also chafe under the burden" of regulations, delays, legal uncertainties, and manipulations. Some landlords, for example, complain that federally subsidized legal-aid lawyers use technicalities to help poor tenants avoid eviction while they refuse to pay rent.

Even if the legal system is not too overloaded with lawsuits, examples of the increase in suing abound:

● The number of civil suits filed in the federal courts grew by 14 percent to 206,193 in 1982 from 1981. The 1982 figure was double the number filed in 1974 and three and one-half times the number filed in 1960.

* * * * *

● Many lawsuits nowadays would have been unheard of only a few years ago: high school football coaches sued by injured players, psychiatrists sued by victims of their patients' crimes, young people sued by sex partners over herpes infections, universities sued by students, bishops sued by nuns, parents sued by children.

● Complex cases in which opposing lawyers bury one another under thousands of documents and marshal legions of experts and other witnesses have become more common.

Trials are only the top of a pyramid. Most lawyers rarely set foot in court, spending their time drafting memorandums, letters of opinion, interrogatories, motions, and briefs, as well as counseling, lobbying, taking depositions, negotiating deals. The vast majority of lawsuits are settled out of court.

* * * * *

Each year more than 35,000 new law-school graduates spill into the market. Big New York corporate law firms offer starting salaries as high as $50,000 to top graduates of elite law schools, but thousands of less fortunate graduates can find no jobs in their chosen profession.

With a glut of law graduates competing for jobs and a bevy of law firms competing for clients, a profession that once prohibited most overt forms of competition has become engaged in a competitive scramble for business. Advertising and soliciting of clients have increased dramatically, and rules that once barred such activities have been held unconstitutional.

Bok says too many of the nation's most talented students are going to law school and then "into legal pursuits that often add little to the growth of the economy or the pursuit of culture or the enhancement of the human spirit."

While Japan trains more engineers to design better products, he said, America trains lawyers whose activities contribute to "a stifling burden of regulations, delays and legal uncertainties that can inhibit progress and allow unscrupulous parties to misuse the law to harass and manipulate their victims."

Potentially far-reaching changes in the law and the way it is practiced have begun to emerge in the past decade in response to the perceived overlawyering of America.

They include no-fault auto insurance and divorce legislation and new approaches to resolving disputes out of court, such as "minitrials" before mediators in business cases and "neighborhood justice centers" to mediate minor personal disputes.

* * * * *

At the same time, the growth of prepaid group legal plans and of low-cost, no-frills legal clinics has brought legal services within the reach of some middle-income people.

* * * * *

A central obstacle to developing any consensus for reforming the civil-justice system is that steps to solve one set of problems tend to aggravate others.

The cures for litigiousness proposed by conservatives, business and medical groups, and insurance companies would also raise new barriers to individuals seeking justice at an affordable price.

But proposals from some liberals, consumer groups, and the American Bar Association to subsidize lawyers' fees for the middle class and to increase federal financing of legal aid for the poor would surely spur more lawsuits.

The American tendency to settle issues through formal legal combat that other nations settle by governmental fiat or other means has been remarked on since the birth of the United States.

A Growing Profession

Lawyers in the civilian labor force (000)

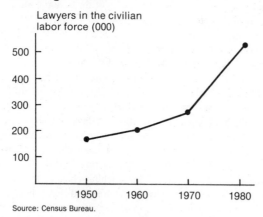

Source: Census Bureau.

In 1782, St. John de Crevecoeur, in "Letters from an American Farmer," compared lawyers to weeds and said they "promote litigiousness and amass more wealth than the most opulent farmer with all his toil." In 1835, Alexis de Tocqueville wrote, "There is hardly a political question in the United States which does not sooner or later turn into a judicial one."

The current swollen case loads and other problems of the civil-justice system are symptoms of pervasive social problems and reflect the efforts of legislatures and courts in recent decades to adapt to rapid social changes and in some cases to accelerate them.

As the United States became increasingly urbanized, affluent, crowded, socially fragmented, and economically specialized, more dependent on complex machines and chemicals and more expert at detecting the causes of injuries, disputes that used to be resolved within families, schools, community groups, and churches have spilled over into the courts.

A more direct cause of increased legal activity, especially in federal courts, is an outpouring of new laws, regulations, and judicial decisions expanding the regulation of business, the legal rights of individuals, and access to the courts.

These include the Supreme Court's rulings striking down racial segregation, new civil-rights laws and statutes that created new agencies to regulate environmental and consumer protection, workplace safety, and other activities.

The number of civil-rights suits filed annually in the federal courts (excluding suits by prisoners) grew to 17,038 in 1982 from 3,985 in 1970 and 296 in 1961.

* * * * *

Meanwhile, state courts, led by California's, have developed new doctrines that make it easier for people to win lawsuits, especially those seeking compensation for medical malpractice and injuries caused by machines and other products. Many courts have held manufacturers liable for injuries caused by defective products without requiring proof that they were at fault.

Juries, which tend to sympathize with individual plaintiffs injured by corporate or governmental defendants, are increasingly willing to award staggering amounts of damages, including millions of dollars for "pain and suffering" and "punitive damages" on top of measurable losses such as medical expenses.

Million-Dollar Verdicts*

1962	1	1976	47
1970	8	1977	70
1971	14	1978	74
1972	22	1979	106
1973	19	1980	130
1974	24	1981	235
1975	26		

*Number of jury verdicts each year awarding $1 million or more to individual plaintiffs in personal injury suits, including libel and slander suits.

Source: Jury Verdict Research Inc. Reprinted by permission of the copyright holder, Jury Verdict Research Inc.

---

*   *   *   *   *

Most people injured in such accidents could not bring lawsuits or obtain redress if they had to pay their legal fees in advance, as in England. But under the American "contingent fee" approach, lawyer-entrepreneurs agree to represent injured plaintiffs in exchange for a share, typically one third, of any damages they win. The lawyers get nothing if they lose.

According to insurance-industry statistics, more of the money that changes hands in product-liability suits goes to the opposing lawyers and for other legal costs than to compensate plaintiffs.

*   *   *   *   *

Since 1965, the federal government has subsidized local programs around the country providing free legal assistance to poor people, at a rate of $241 million this year. This pays for around 4,800 full-time lawyers in legal-aid offices.

Although dwarfed by the $10 billion to $20 billion in federal subsidies for the legal fees of corporations, which deduct them from their taxes, this subsidy has been under attack from President Reagan.

Economic and social change also has made for more complicated disputes, especially in big antitrust and other business lawsuits and cases involving injuries allegedly caused by toxic chemicals and drugs.

*   *   *   *   *

Source: *Des Moines Register*, June 5, 1983, p. 1. Reprinted with permission of the copyright holder, The Associated Press. (Stuart Taylor, Jr., writes for the *New York Times*.)

Alternatives

The frustrations just explored account for imaginative efforts, particularly of late, to seek cheaper, less time-consuming, more equitable means of dispute resolution. *Small claims courts* now are commonplace, but initially they met with great resistance from some parts of the community. In these courts claims typically are limited to $1,000 or $2,000, and legal formalities are retarded to the point that lawyers are unnecessary. Minimal forms and fees are involved. In essence, the judge hears the parties' statements as well as those of witnesses and renders a decision. Small claims courts permit the resolution of complaints that would otherwise be of insufficient value to justify a full-blown legal proceeding. Wronged consumers and tenants have been particularly benefited by this sensible process.

Frustrated by the time and expense of the trial process, some litigants have developed creative variations of their own. For example, two resourceful Los Angeles lawyers, representing NBC and Johnny Carson in a contract dispute, relied on an 1872 California statute to implement what is sometimes labeled a "rent-a-judge" system. For approximately $100 per hour, retired judges can be hired to quickly and privately reach binding decisions in civil cases. Both sides simply agree on the judge and on rules for presenting the case.

In a variant on the private trial approach, a number of corporations have agreed upon minitrials to resolve some conflicts. Typically the minitrial follows a format of this nature:

1. The formal court proceedings, if underway, are held in abeyance.
2. The parties develop their own procedural rules and establish deadlines demanding quick resolution.
3. A neutral expert is hired, and the parties submit short statements of their positions.
4. The trial itself is limited to a very brief period, perhaps two days. A critical ingredient is the presence at the trial of top management.
5. After the trial the managers seek to reach an accord. Failing that, the neutral expert issues a nonbinding opinion.[20]
6. Should the minitrial fail, the parties may then turn to the formal judicial process.

One remedy for the flaws in our judicial system is to look for alternatives outside the courthouse. Various methods of conciliation, mediation, and arbitration are sometimes employed in the United States. Conciliation and mediation are dispute-resolution techniques wherein third parties seek, via negotiation, to assist the disputants to voluntarily reach a solution to their conflict. Arbitration typically involves the use of one or more skilled third parties to render a binding decision regarding the conflict. In 1980, Congress endorsed alternative dispute resolution systems by allocating federal funds to local governments to support arbitrators and mediators for small claims and other appropriate civil suits. A state-funded community dispute resolution system using conciliation, mediation, and arbitration resolved more than 25,000 controversies during its 21 initial months of operation in New York.

Maine has established a Court Mediation Service in which impartial third parties (professors, businesspeople, retired citizens, and others) devote several hours per week to helping settle arguments out of court. About two thirds of the small claims and contested divorce cases are settled during mediation. State law now requires mediation for all contested divorce cases involving minor children. Mediators now handle about 1,000 such cases annually. Overall about 20 percent of the mediated cases cannot be settled and must be referred to a judge.[21]

Chapter Questions

1. Are the flaws in our legal system of such magnitude that respect for the law is threatened?
2. According to Warren Avis, founder of Avis Rent-a-Car:

We've reached a point in this country where, in many instances power has become more important than justice—not a matter of who is right, but of who has the most money, time, and the largest battery of lawyers to drag a case through the courts.[22]

    a.   Should the rich be entitled to better legal representation, just as they have access to better food, better medical care, better education, and so on?

    b.   Should we employ a nationwide legal services program sufficient to guarantee able legal aid to all?

3. In your opinion, are lawyers as a group any more or less ethical than other Americans?

4. Most jurisdictions have been unwilling to permit television, radio, and still cameras in courtrooms, but in 1981 the U.S. Supreme Court ruled that, despite defense objections, trial coverage of that nature does not, in and of itself, violate the Constitution. Of course, the defendant still may show that the media coverage did, in fact, deprive him of due process.

    a.   What are the arguments for and against televised court proceedings?

    b.   How would you rule on the issue? See *Chandler* v. *Florida,* 449 U.S. 560 (1981).

5. French correspondent Alain Clement, commenting on the role of lawyers in America:

Truly, American lawyers come as close to being a "ruling class" as is possible in a country too vast and varied to produce one. Since Franklin D. Roosevelt, each president has had around him lawyer-confidants, so that Congress and state legislatures are dominated—even if less so than before— by a majority who come from the bar.[23]

    a.   Do you agree with Clement?

    b.   If so, have lawyers earned their influence?

6. Clement also offered a partial explanation for Americans' increasing reliance on law suits to resolve their conflicts:

Diverse causes explain the growth of the contentious mood in America. One could be called the devaluing of the future. In 1911, the Russian political scientist Moise Ostrgorski wrote: "Confident of the future, Americans manifest a remarkable endurance to an unhappy present, a submissive patience that is willing to bargain about not only civic rights, but even the rights of man."[24]

    a.   What does Clement mean?

    b.   How do you explain our increased reliance on litigation?

7. Maintenance of our adversary system of justice sometimes compels lawyers to engage in practices that some consider unethical. Anne Strick relates one such situation.

Once upon a time, Williston, called by a colleague "One of the most distinguished and conscientious lawyers I or any man have ever known," was defending a client in a civil suit. In the course of trial, Williston discovered in his client's letter file material potentially damaging to the man's case. The opposition failed to demand the file; nor did Williston offer it. His client won. But, recounts Williston in his autobiography, the judge in announcing his decision made clear that his ruling was based in part on his belief in one critical fact: a fact Williston, through a letter from the file in his possession, knew to be unfounded.

Did Williston, that "most conscientious lawyer," speak up? Did he correct the Court's unfounded belief, the better to serve both truth and justice? He did not.

"Though," he wrote, "I had in front of me a letter which showed his [Honor's] error," Williston kept silent. Nor did he question the propriety of his behavior. For, said he, the lawyer "is not only not obliged to disclose unfavorable evidence, but it is a violation of his duty to his client if he does so."[25]

    a.   Did Williston act properly?

    b.   Should we turn to a more cooperative, less combative, approach to dispute resolution?

8. Terence Cannon, a Marxist "radical activist" and a member of the "Oakland Seven":

If you didn't know anything about how the law works in America, if all you did was read the papers, you would know that American courts and American law are the enemies of the people. If you're too poor to pay the rent, who puts you out on the street? The law. If workers go out on a wildcat strike, who lays the injunction down on them? The law. . . . Law is the tool that politicians and businessmen use to keep down the people they oppress.

Did you ever hear of a cop busting in the head of a supermarket owner because he charged too much for food? . . . No. Law is the billyclub of the oppressor. He isn't about to use it on himself.[26]

Comment.

9. On July 5, 1884, four sailors were cast away from their ship in a storm 1,600 miles from the Cape of Good Hope. Their lifeboat contained neither water nor much food. On the 20th day of their ordeal Dudley and Stevens, without the assistance or agreement of Brooks, cut the throat of the fourth sailor, a 17- or 18-year-old boy. They had not eaten since day 12. Water had been only occasionally available. At the time of the death, the men were probably about 1,000 miles from land. Prior to his death, the boy was lying helplessly in the bottom of the boat. The three surviving sailors ate the boy's remains for four days, at which point they were rescued by a passing boat. They were in a seriously weakened condition.

   a.   Were Dudley and Stevens guilty of murder? Explain.

   b.   Should Brooks have been charged with a crime for eating the boy's flesh? Explain.
            See *The Queen* v. *Dudley and Stephens,* 14 Queen's Bench Division 273 (1884).

10. Tompkins is a citizen of Pennsylvania. While walking on a railroad footpath in that state, he was struck by an object protruding from a passing freight train owned by the Erie Railroad Company, a New York Corporation. Tompkins, by virtue of diversity of citizenship, filed a negligence suit against Erie in a New York federal court. Erie argued for the application of Pennsylvania common law, in which case Tompkins would have been treated as a trespasser. Tompkins argued that the absence of a Pennsylvania statute addressing the topic meant that federal common law had to be applied to the case. Should the court apply the relevant Pennsylvania state law, or should the federal court be free to exercise its independent judgment about what the common law of the state is or should be? See *Erie Railroad* v. *Tompkins,* 304 U.S. 64 (1938).

11. Burger King conducts a franchise, fast food operation from its Miami, Florida headquarters. John Rudzewicz and a partner, both residents of Michigan, secured a Burger King franchise in Michigan. Subsequently, the franchisees allegedly fell behind in payments, and after negotiations failed, Burger King ordered the franchisees to vacate the premises. They declined to do so, and continued to operate the franchise. Burger King brought suit in a federal district court in Florida. The defendant franchisees argued that the Florida court did not have personal jurisdiction over them because they were Michigan residents and because the claim did not arise in Florida. However, the district court found the defendants to be subject to the Florida long-arm statute which extends jurisdiction to "[a]ny person, whether or not a citizen or resident of this state" who, "[b]reach[es] a contract in this state by failing to perform acts required by the contract to be performed in this state." The franchise contract provided for governance of the relationship by Florida law. Policy was set in Miami although day-to-day supervision was managed through various district offices. The case ultimately reached the U.S. Supreme Court. (a) What constitutional argument would you raise on behalf of the defendent franchisees? (b) Decide. See *Burger King Corp.* v. *Rudzewicz,* 53 *Law Week* 4541 (US S.Ct., 1985).

Notes

1. Oliver Wendell Holmes, *Collected Legal Papers* (New York: Harcourt Brace Jovanovich, 1920), p. 173.

2. Benjamin Cardozo, *The Growth of Law* (New Haven, Conn.: Yale University Press, 1924), p. 52.

3. Max Weber, *Law in Economy and Society,* ed. Max Rheinstein (Cambridge, Mass.: Harvard Univ. Press, 1954), p. 5.

4. Bronislaw Malinowski, *Crime and Custom in Savage Society* (Patterson, N.J.: Littlefield, 1959), p. 55. Originally published in 1926.

5. Roscoe Pound, "A Survey of Social Interest," *Harvard Law Review* 57 (1943), pp. 1, 39.

6. Richard Quinney, "The Ideology of Law: Notes for a Radical Alternative to Legal Oppression," *Issues in Criminology* 7 (1972), p. 1, as reported in Charles E. Reasons and Robert M. Rich, *The Sociology of Law: A Conflict Perspective* (Toronto: Butterworth & Co., 1978), p. 42.

7. John Rawls, *A Theory of Justice* (Boston: Belknap Press, 1971), pp. 3–4.

8. "Burglars and Booby Traps," *Time,* June 12, 1978, p. 61.

9. "Arizona Arrest," reprinted in *The Judicial Humorist,* ed. William Prosser (Boston: Little, Brown, 1952), p. 222.

10. Roger Simon, "Don't Say !?*!* in Chicago," *Washington Post,* October 12, 1980, p. F–12.

11. George Will, "The Case of Phillip Becker," *Newsweek,* April 14, 1980, p. 112.

12. The remarks to this point in this section owe much to Mary Kay Kane, *Civil Procedure in a Nutshell* (St. Paul, Minn.: West Publishing, 1979), p. 226–37.

13. "Venue Change Refused," *Poverty Law Report,* April–May 1980, p. 1.

14. Amitai Etzioni, "Science: Threatening the Jury," *Washington Post,* May 26, 1974, p. C–3.

15. Howard Rudnitsky with Jeff Blyskal, "Getting into Those Deep Pockets," *Forbes,* August 4, 1980, p. 59.

16. Jerrold Footlick, "Vox Populi," *Newsweek,* March 27, 1978, p. 87; and Tom Goldstein, "Survey Finds Most People Uninformed on Courts," *New York Times,* March 19, 1978, p. 20.

17. Tom Goldstein, "Survey Finds Public Critical of Lawyers," *New York Times,* February 11, 1978, p. 26.

18. Philip Stern, "How to Bribe Judges, Fix Prices, and Delay the Inevitable," *The Washington Monthly,* June 1980, p. 34.

19. "Challenging the 'Hired Guns,' " *Time,* February 27, 1984, p. 103, reporting study by David Trubek et al., *U.C.L.A. Law Review,* 1984.

20. "Business Saves Big Money with the 'Minitrial,' " *Business Week,* October 13, 1980, p. 168.

21. Beverly Watkins, "Unusual Sideline for Maine Academics: Helping People Settle Their Arguments," *The Chronicle of Higher Education* 29, no. 22 (February 13, 1985), p. 41.

22. Warren Avis, "Court before Justice," *New York Times,* July 21, 1978, p. 25.

23. Alain Clement, "Judges, Lawyers Are the Ruling Class in U.S. Society," *Washington Post,* August 22, 1980, p. A–25.

24. Ibid.

25. Anne Strick, *Injustice for All* (New York: Penguin Books, 1978), p. 123.

26. Terence M. Cannon, "Law and Order in America," in *Up Against the American Myth* ed. Tom Christoffel, David Finkelhor, and Dan Gilbarg (New York: Holt, Rinehart & Winston, 1970), pp. 348–49, as quoted in Frederick Sturdivant, *Business and Society—A Managerial Approach,* rev. ed. (Homewood, Ill.: Richard D. Irwin, 1981), p. 52.

5

Constitutional Law and the Bill of Rights

We the people of the United States, in order to form a more perfect union, establish justice, insure domestic tranquility, provide for the common defense, promote the general welfare, and secure the blessings of liberty to ourselves and our posterity, do ordain and establish this Constitution for the United States of America.

Introduction

Those words, the Preamble to our Constitution, summarize the lofty goals of America's most central and superior law. It is both inspiring and touching to reflect upon the idealism that is embodied in those words, and one must marvel a bit at the strength that causes us all, nearly 200 years later, to continue to be guided by the vision of the creators of the Constitution. It is a remarkable document. Hence we will do well to dwell upon its subtleties for a time.

The reader may recall that the Constitution grew out of the Articles of Confederation as enacted by Congress in 1778. The Articles contemplated a ''firm league of friendship,'' but each state was to maintain its ''sovereignty, freedom and independence.'' The Articles soon proved faulty in that, for example, no general taxing provision had been enacted, and the Congress had failed to develop the general principles necessary to resolve problems arising from trade among the states. The Constitutional Convention met in Philadelphia in 1787. The new Constitution and the Bill of Rights (the first 10 amendments) were ratified by the states and put into effect in 1789 and 1791, respectively.

A good deal of the success and longevity of our Constitution must be ascribed to its clever balancing of central, federal authority with dispersed, state power. The federal government holds only those powers granted to it by the states. The people via the states hold all of those powers not expressly denied them by the Constitution.

The Constitution serves four broad roles:

1. ''It establishes a national government.''
2. ''It controls the relationship between the national government and the government of the states.''
3. ''It defines and preserves personal liberty.''
4. ''It contains provisions to enable the government to perpetuate itself.''[1]

The Constitution defines and organizes the government. It is an essential guidepost for the maintenance of order, but the Constitution is much more than the whole of its enormous mechanical functions. It is an expression of the values of the nation. The Constitution embodies our need for strength and certainty in a confused existence, but we recognize the need for change, and we acknowledge the power of the Supreme Court to interpret the Constitution in a manner that fairly accommodates the needs of a constantly changing America. Our constitutional law is under stress from the demands of a complex society, but the system continues to display a remarkable adaptability and fortitude that stand as a tribute to our legal system, and by extension, to us.

In the case that follows, the Supreme Court struck down the use of the legislative veto, a device for conveniently imposing congressional restraint upon executive action. For example, Congress might delegate to the executive branch broad authority to regulate occupational safety while retaining the right to veto any specific strategy that it does not favor. Justice White referred to this decision as "probably the most important case that the court has handed down in many years." Justice White was not applauding the seven to two decision. He was unhappy with what he took to be a reshaping of the delicate balance between the legislative and executive branches. The decision is an enormous boost for presidential authority. Executive-legislative-judicial balance is, of course, central to our theory of government, so the case is a helpful lesson in basic civics. For the student of business the case is specifically important because of its impact on government regulation. The legislative veto was a favorite strategy in forcing the various federal regulatory agencies—such as the Environmental Protection Agency and the Occupational Safety and Health Administration—to comply with the will of Congress. Prior to the decision Congress kept a convenient thumb over the work of the agencies by having the power simply to veto agency decisions without actually passing a law and presenting it to the president. Now Congress will need to employ other strategies.

IMMIGRATION AND NATURALIZATION SERVICE V. CHADHA   103 S. Ct. 2764 (1983)

Chief Justice Burger

[Section 244(c) (2) of the Immigration and Nationality Act authorizes either House of Congress, by resolution, to invalidate the decision of the Executive Branch, pursuant to authority delegated by Congress to the attorney general, to allow a particular deportable alien to remain in the United States.]

Chadha is an East Indian who was born in Kenya and holds a British passport. He was lawfully admitted to the United States in 1966 on a nonimmigrant student visa. His visa expired on June 30, 1972. On October 11, 1973, the District Director of the Immigration and Naturalization Service ordered Chadha to show cause why he should not be deported for having "remained in the United States for a longer time than permitted. . . ."

[A] deportation hearing was held before an immigration judge on January 11, 1974. Chadha conceded that he was deportable for overstaying his visa, and the hearing was adjourned to enable him to file an application for suspension of deportation. . . .

[T]he immigration judge suspended Chadha's deportation and a report of the suspension was transmitted to Congress. . . .

Once the Attorney General's recommendation for suspension of Chadha's deportation was conveyed to Congress, Congress had the power . . . to veto the Attorney General's determination that Chadha should not be deported. . . .

On December 12, 1975, Representative Eilberg, Chairman of the Judiciary Subcommittee on Immigration, Citizenship, and International Law, introduced a resolution opposing "the granting of permanent residence in the United States to [six] aliens," including Chadha. . . .

The resolution was passed without debate or recorded vote. . . .

Chadha filed a petition for review of the deportation order in the United States Court of Appeals for the Ninth Circuit. . . . [T]he Court of Appeals held that the House was without constitutional authority to order Chadha's deportation. . . . The essence of its holding was that § 244(c) (2) violates the constitutional doctrine of separation of powers.

We granted certiorari. . . .

We turn . . . to the question whether action of one House of Congress under § 244(c) (2) violates strictures of the Constitution. . . .

Explicit and unambiguous provisions of the Constitution prescribe and define the respective functions of the Congress and of the Executive in the legislative process. Since the precise terms of those familiar provisions are critical to the resolution of this case, we set them out verbatim. Art. I provides:

All legislative Powers herein granted shall be vested in a Congress of the United States, which shall consist of a Senate *and* a House of Representatives. [Art. I, § 1. Emphasis added].

Every Bill which shall have passed the House of Representatives *and* the Senate, *shall,* before it becomes a law, be presented to the President of the United States; . . . [Art. I, § 7, cl. 2. [Emphasis added].

Every Order, Resolution, or Vote to which the Concurrence of the Senate and House of Representatives may be necessary (except on a question of Adjournment) *shall be* presented to the President of the United States; and before the Same shall take Effect, *shall be* approved by him, or being disapproved by him, *shall be* repassed by two thirds of the Senate and House of Represenatives, according to the Rules and Limitations prescribed in the Case of a Bill. [Art. I, § 7, cl. 3. [Emphasis added].

These provisions of Art. I are integral parts of the constitutional design for the separation of powers. . . .

The Presentment Clauses

The records of the Consitutional Convention reveal that the requirement that all legislation be presented to the President before becoming law was uniformly accepted by the framers. Presentment to the President and the presidential veto were considered so imperative that the draftsmen took special pains to assure that these requirements could not be circumvented. . . .

Bicameralism

The bicameral requirement of Art. I, § § 1, 7 was of scarcely less concern to the framers than was the presidential veto and indeed the two concepts are interdependent. By providing that no law could take effect without the concurrence of the prescribed majority of the members of both

Houses, the framers reemphasized their belief . . . that legislation should not be enacted unless it has been carefully and fully considered by the nation's elected officials. . . .

Not every action taken by either House is subject to the bicameralism and presentment requirements of Art. I. . . . Whether actions taken by either House are, in law and fact, an exercise of legislative power depends not on their form but upon "whether they contain matter which is properly to be regarded as legislative in its character and effect."

Examination of the action taken here by one House . . . reveals that it was essentially legislative in purpose and effect. . . .

Finally, we see that when the framers intended to authorize either House of Congress to act alone and outside of its prescribed bicameral legislative role, they narrowly and precisely defined the procedure for such action. There are but four provisions in the Constitution, explicit and unambiguous, by which one House may act alone with the unreviewable force of law, not subject to the President's veto:

a. The House of Representatives alone was given the power to initiate impeachments.

b. The Senate alone was given the power to conduct trials following impeachment on charges initiated by the House and to convict following trial.

c. The Senate alone was given final unreviewable power to approve or to disapprove presidential appointments.

d. The Senate alone was given final unreviewable power to ratify treaties negotiated by the President. . . .

Since it is clear that the action by the House . . . was not within any of the express constitutional exceptions authorizing one House to act alone, and equally clear that it was an exercise of legislative power, that action was subject to the standards prescribed in Article I. The bicameral requirement, the Presentment Clauses, the President's veto, and Congress' power to override a veto were intended to erect enduring checks on each Branch and to protect the people from the improvident exercise of power by mandating certain prescribed steps. To preserve those checks and maintain the separation of powers, the carefully defined limits on the power of each branch must not be eroded. To accomplish what has been attempted by one House of Congress in this case requires action in conformity with the express procedures of the Constitution's prescription for legislative action: passage by a majority of both Houses and presentment to the President.

The veto . . . doubtless has been in many respects a convenient shortcut; the "sharing" with the executive by Congress of its authority over aliens in this manner is, on its face, an appealing compromise. In purely practical terms, it is obviously easier for action to be taken by one House without submission to the President; but it is crystal clear from the records of the Convention, contemporaneous writings and debates, that the framers ranked other values higher than efficiency. . . .

We hold that the congressional veto provision in § 244(c) (2) is serverable from the Act and that it is unconstitutional. Accordingly, the judgment of the Court of Appeals is *affirmed.*

Questions

1. Why did the Supreme Court strike down the legislative veto?
2. What legislative procedure is required by the Presentment Clauses of the Constitution?
3. Supporters of the *Chadha* decision have argued that the legislative veto was a direct contravention of three fundamental constitutional principles—separation of powers, checks and balances, and bicameralism. Explain how the decision affirms those principles.
4. Deprived of the legislative veto, how can Congress maintain firm control over the federal regulatory agencies? See Chapter 7.

The Regulation of Commerce

Of course, the Constitution profoundly shapes the practice of American business. The Constitution embodies and supports America's belief in capitalism. Indeed, it has been argued that the economic self-interest of the framers had a persuasive impact on the principles embodied in the Constitution. Article I, Section 8 of the Constitution (the Commerce Clause) affords Congress enormous authority in regulating business. Discussion of the Commerce Clause will be deferred to Chapter 6. This chapter is devoted to a brief exploration of the Bill of Rights. It is hoped that the reader will acquire an appreciation for the complex tensions that arise as the government attempts to identify and ensure individual rights while simultaneously seeking to defend and promote both U.S. commerce and the rights of American business.

As the reader proceeds through the chapter, it is essential to recall that the Constitution was enacted to protect the citizenry from the government. The Constitution does not protect the citizenry from purely private concentrations of power such as large corporations. Furthermore, corporations, as we shall see, are themselves entitled to the protections of the Constitution.

Business and the Bill of Rights

We begin, logically enough, with the First Amendment:

Congress shall make no law respecting an establishment of religion, or prohibiting the free exercise thereof; or abridging the freedom of speech, or the press; or the right of the people peaceably to assemble, and to petition the Government for a redress of grievances.

These few words constitute one of the most powerful and noble utterances in recorded history. The freedoms guaranteed in the First Amendment reflect the basic beliefs of American life. Much of the magnificence that we often associate with America is embodied in the protections of the First Amendment. After nearly 200 years it remains a source of wonder that our vast bureaucratic system and our 230 million independent citizens continue to rely on that sentence as a cornerstone of our way of life.

Originally, the Constitution applied only to the federal government. However, by Supreme Court interpretation, the Constitution now prohibits encroachments on personal freedom by state governments as well. As noted, the First Amendment forbids federal intrusions on the freedoms of religion, speech, press, and association. The Supreme Court has held that those freedoms are among those fundamental liberties that are protected by the Due Process Clause of the Fourteenth Amendment. The Fourteenth (and the Fifth Amendment as well) provide that no person shall be "deprived of life, liberty, or property, without due process of law." Under a process that has come to be known as the *incorporation doctrine* or *absorption doctrine,* the Supreme Court has incorporated most of the Bill of Rights into the Fourteenth Amendment generally, thereby making the first ten amendments generally applicable to the states.

When we think of the Bill of Rights, corporations ordinarily do not come to mind. However, extensive litigation in recent years serves ample notice that the relationship between the corporate "person" and the fundamental freedoms is both important and murky. We will look at some of the key intersections between the business community and the Bill of Rights.

I. Freedom of Religion

Prayer. The First Amendment clearly forbids the establishment of an official state religion. Government may not give preference to one religion over another. The religion clause is designed to separate church and state. However, the precise boundary of that separation has become one of the more contentious social issues in contemporary life. President Reagan made the voluntary school prayer question a centerpiece of his social agenda. Of course, students may pray at their own discretion so long as they avoid disturbing the academic setting. The issue is one of whether government-sponsored, yet voluntary, prayer would be permissible.

In 1962 the Supreme Court struck down as unconstitutional the following non-denominational school prayer: "Almighty God, we acknowledge our dependence upon Thee, and we beg Thy blessings upon us, our parents, our teachers, and our Country."[2] The State Board of Regents of New York had recommended that the prayer be offered aloud at the beginning of each school day. Similarly unconstitutional is the reading of verses from the Bible.[3] The most recent decisions appear to have been significant setbacks for those supporting prayer in the schools. In 1985 the Supreme Court by a 6–3 margin struck down an Alabama statute authorizing a one-minute period of silence in the public schools "for meditation or voluntary prayer." The Court held that the statute violated the Establishment Clause of the First Amendment in that the legislature's motive was the endorsement of religion.[4]

Fundamentalist religious groups, such as the followers of the Reverend Jerry Falwell, and political conservatives led by President Reagan and other influential figures such as Senator Jesse Helms of North Carolina have struggled to return organized, voluntary prayer to the schools. As of this writing, in 1985, the United States Senate has considered but failed to approve a constitutional amendment that would have permitted organized prayer in the public schools.

Blue Laws. Freedom of religion as a business issue is less common and ordinarily less volatile than the school prayer question, but some provocative and important questions have arisen. Statistically most notable are the many and continuing conflicts over the so-called *blue laws,* those statutes and ordinances limiting or prohibiting the conduct of business on Sundays. Blue laws are rather common about the nation. While those laws are often clearly inspired by religious considerations, the courts have rather consistently affirmed their constitutionality. The blue laws cause inconvenience and economic loss to those of religious sects not practicing their Sabbath on Sunday and to those who do not recognize a Sabbath. In the leading case of *McGowan* v. *Maryland*[5] the Supreme Court upheld the constitutionality of a blue law on the grounds that the primary purpose of the law was the furtherance of a legitimate social goal, in this case, provision of a uniform day of rest, rather than a furtherance of religious goals. The Court felt that the practice of treating Sunday as a religious holiday had fallen into disuse.

The Amish. Minority religious sects often must struggle to maintain their principles in the face of the general will of the masses. Struggles between "Christian schools" and states seeking to apply minimum educational standards regarding such things as teachers' educational credentials and curricular content have been commonplace in recent years. In an important Supreme Court decision, an Amish sect was able to establish the principle that religious belief can, under some circumstances, justify refusal to meet state compulsory education requirements.[6] However, as described in the following article, one Amish citizen has been less successful in his struggle to maintain his business, honor his religious principles, and comply with the law of the land.

IN PENNSYLVANIA: THE AMISH AND THE LAW

Dean Brelis

There are only two kinds of people in northwestern Pennsylvania's Lawrence County—the "English" and the "Dutch." The first category includes nearly everybody—Wasps, Italians, Jews, Irish, blacks. The second category covers only the Amish. To say that the Amish are different is merely to state the obvious. They are followers of a sect that originated in Switzerland back in the 17th century and, in search of religious freedom, fled to England and Holland in the 18th century and moved to America in the 19th. In this day of home computers and space travel, the Amish eschew zippers as decadent, electricity as unnecessary, and flush toilets as wasteful. They forgo the automobile in favor of sleek trotters and canvas-topped carriages of hickory wood. They use fine, sturdy workhorses to spread manure and plow their fields, which is what they are doing these days as spring spreads over their green country.

Ed Lee is one of 5,000 Amish in Lawrence County. He differs from his neighbors for reasons other than the fact that he is not a Byler or a Swatzentrooper or a Hofstader or the bearer of some other traditionally Amish name. Lee is different because he has done something that the Amish rarely do. He has ended up in court. His offense: refusing to pay Social Security taxes for 30 Amish men who worked for him over an eight-year period as carpenters, building houses. The Internal Revenue Service claimed that he owed the Government $27,000. Lee challenged the IRS ruling in federal district court in Pittsburgh. To prove his good intentions, he offered his farm as security in the event he lost. As it turned out, he won, but the IRS then appealed to the Supreme Court.

Lee's refusal to pay Social Security taxes did not stem from any disrespect for the law. He personally has no quarrel with the Social Security system, and believes it is fine—for those who need it. But it is a tenet of their religious belief that the Amish people should take care of their own. They do not collect unemployment or welfare benefits. They do not buy insurance of any kind. By an act of Congress in 1965, self-employed Amish men are exempt from paying Social Security taxes on religious grounds. But the act does not cover Amish men who work for Amish employers. It is this apparent inconsistency that has propelled Lee into the courts.

The Supreme Court, which ruled on Lee's case in February, upheld the IRS. "A comprehensive national Social Security system providing for voluntary participation would be almost a contradiction in terms and difficult, if not impossible, to administer," wrote Chief Justice Warren Burger in the unanimous opinion.

Faced with the loss of his farm, Lee might have bowed to federal *force majeure* at this point. Instead, aided by two non-Amish friends, he is quietly carrying on his fight. Francis X. Caiazza, 46, a local lawyer who had represented Lee before the Supreme Court, was elected a judge the day after arguing the case and is now prevented by law from providing more than moral support. "Amish do not break laws; they are not seen in the courts," Caiazza says. "The Amish care about reason, law and order, and they are a God-fearing people. This wasn't just another case. It involves a sincere belief in religious freedom and religious rights. We lost the case in the Supreme Court, but I still feel the religious argument should have been the bottom line."

Lee's other friend, Robert Gardner, 43, a high school teacher, is urging another tactic. Aided by hundreds of "English" volunteers, he has collected upwards of 10,000 signatures and hopes to get 10,000 more on petitions urging Congress to enact a law exempting all Amish from paying for Social Security. "The Amish," he says, "are not a fly-by-night religion, just formed to avoid taxes. Legislation already exists which exempts an Amish individual from paying Social Security taxes when he is self-employed. It should be extended to cover Amish workers on the job for an Amish employer."

Amish customs, Gardner argues, constitute a "built-in form of Social Security." Forcing the Amish to pay Social Security cuts at the heart of their religion, he maintains . . .

The predicament is something that Lee ponders as he sits by the coal stove in the kitchen of his neat, sturdy farmhouse. His feet are covered with thick blue socks; the Amish remove their shoes before entering the home. His blue eyes are gentle behind sensible, old-fashioned glasses, his beard is appropriately patriarchal, his voice surprisingly soft. "I'm a man who wakes every morning and thanks God for what is," Lee says. "I believe that the Government of the United States is fair and just. It is not the Amish habit to be in confrontation; we avoid it. So it was with great difficulty and much prayer that I took this on." . . .

QUESTIONS

1. Should all Amish be exempt from paying Social Security taxes?
2. Should all conscientious objectors be exempt from paying that portion of their taxes which is used for national defense?
3. A Seventh Day Adventist was discharged by her employer when she refused to work on Saturday. Those of her faith celebrate the Sabbath on Saturday. She sought unemployment compensation, but the South Carolina Employment Security Commission denied her petition. The Commission ruled that she had failed, without good cause, "to accept available work when offered." She carried an appeal to the Supreme Court. How would you rule? Explain. See *Sherbert* v. *Verner*, 374 U.S. 398 (1963).

II. Freedom of Speech

None of the remarkable freedoms guaranteed by the Constitution receives greater respect from the judiciary than the right to free expression. And so it should be. Freedom of speech is the primary guarantor of the American approach to life. Americans believe not merely that we should be able to say what we think because it feels good to do so, but also that the free expression of ideas is the most likely path to finding the best of ideas. We believe in a marketplace of ideas just as we believe in a marketplace of goods. So freedom of speech is central to self-respect, to political freedom, and to the maximization of wisdom. Freedom of speech is not an absolute. We cannot, for example, utter obscenities at will or yell "fire" in a crowded theatre. Interpretation of the very broad bounds of freedom of speech has led to some of the more interesting decisions in judicial history. For example, the wearing of black armbands at school as a protest against the Vietnam War was constitutionally protected where no evidence of disruption was offered.[7] Similarly, the Court accorded First Amendment protection to a display of the American flag flying upside down from an apartment on private property with peace symbols attached to the flag.[8]

Speech and Private Property.   In recent years the application of the First Amendment to business issues has been the subject of increased litigation. Often the complexity of First Amendment interpretation has been further clouded by competing constitutional issues. Guaranteed freedoms and protections sometimes appear to be in direct conflict, and the courts must sort through the resulting intellectual rubble. The case that follows illustrates just such a quandary. The appellee relied for protection on the freedom of expression guarantee of the California state constitution while the appellant claimed that its federal First Amendment, Fifth Amendment, and Fourteenth Amendment rights should prevail. It is well-established that our governments have the right of *eminent domain*, that is, the right to take private property for public use. The Fifth Amendment, however, provides that the owner of that property must receive fair compensation, and the Fourteenth Amendment forbids the deprivation of property without due process of law.

PRUNEYARD SHOPPING CENTER V. ROBINS   447 U.S. 74 (1980)

Justice Rehnquist

. . . Appellant PruneYard is a privately owned shopping center in the city of Campbell, Cal. It covers approximately 21 acres—5 devoted to parking and 16 occupied by walkways, plazas, sidewalks, and buildings that contain more than 65 specialty shops, 10 restaurants, and a movie theater. The PruneYard is open to the public for the purpose of encouraging the patronizing of its commercial establishments. It has a policy not to permit any visitor or tenant to engage in any publicly expressive activity, including the circulation of petitions, that is not directly related to its commercial purposes. This policy has been strictly enforced in a nondiscriminatory fashion. The PruneYard is owned by appellant Fred Sahadi.

Appellees are high school students who sought to solicit support for their opposition to a United Nations resolution against "Zionism." On a Saturday afternoon they set up a card table in a corner of PruneYard's central courtyard. They distributed pamphlets and asked passersby to sign petitions, which were to be sent to the President and Members of Congress. Their activity was peaceful and orderly and so far as the record indicates was not objected to by PruneYard's patrons.

Soon after appellees had begun soliciting signatures, a security guard informed them that they would have to leave because their activity violated PruneYard regulations. The guard suggested that they move to the public sidewalk at the PruneYard's perimeter. Appellees immediately left the premises and later filed this lawsuit in the California Superior Court of Santa Clara County. They sought to enjoin appellants from denying them access to the PruneYard for the purpose of circulating their petitions.

The Superior Court held that appellees were not entitled under either the Federal or California Constitution to exercise their asserted rights on the shopping center property. It concluded that there were "adequate, effective channels of communication for [appellees] other than soliciting on the private property of the [PruneYard]." The California Court of Appeal affirmed.

The California Supreme Court reversed, holding that the California Constitution protects "speech and petitioning, reasonably exercised, in shopping centers even when the centers are privately owned." . . .

Appellants first contend that *Lloyd Corp.* v. *Tanner,* prevents the State from requiring a private shopping center owner to provide access to persons exercising their state constitutional rights of free speech and petition when adequate alternative avenues of communication are available. *Lloyd* dealt with the question whether under the Federal Constitution a privately owned shopping center may prohibit the distribution of handbills on its property when the handbilling is unrelated to the shopping center's operations. . . .

We stated that property does not "lose its private character merely because the public is generally invited to use it for designated purposes," and that "[t]he essentially private character of a store and its privately owned abutting property does not change by virtue of being large or clustered with other stores in a modern shopping center."

Our reasoning in *Lloyd,* however, does not limit the authority of the State to exercise its police power or its sovereign right to adopt in its own Constitution individual liberties more expansive than those conferred by the Federal Constitution. In *Lloyd,* supra, there was no state constitutional or statutory provision that had been construed to create rights to the use of private property by strangers, comparable to those found to exist by the California Supreme Court here. It is, of course, well established that a State in the exercise of its police power may adopt reasonable restrictions on private property so long as the restrictions do not amount to a taking without just compensation or contravene any other federal constitutional provision.

Appellants next contend that a right to exclude others underlies the Fifth Amendment guarantee against the taking of property without just compensation and the Fourteenth Amendment guarantee against the deprivation of property without due process of law.

It is true that one of the essential sticks in the bundle of property rights is the right to exclude others. And here there has literally been a "taking" of that right to the extent that the California Supreme Court has interpreted the State Constitution to entitle its citizens to exercise free expression and petition rights on shopping center property. But it is well established that "not every destruction or injury to property by governmental action has been held to be a 'taking' in the constitutional sense." Rather, the determination whether a state law unlawfully infringes a landowner's property in violation of the Taking Clause requires an examination of whether the restriction on private property "forc[es] some people alone to bear public burdens which, in all fairness and justice, should be borne by the public as a whole." This examination entails inquiry into such factors as the character of the governmental action, its economic impact, and its interference with reasonable investment-backed expectations.

Here the requirement that appellants permit appellees to exercise state-protected rights of free expression and petition on shopping center property clearly does not amount to an unconstitutional infringement of appellants' property rights under the Taking Clause. There is nothing to suggest that preventing appellants from prohibiting this sort of activity will unreasonably impair the value or use of their property as a shopping center. The PruneYard is a large commercial complex that covers several city blocks, contains numerous separate business establishments, and is open to the public at large. The decision of the California Supreme Court makes it clear that the PruneYard may restrict expressive activity by adopting time, place, and manner regulations that will minimize any interference with its commercial functions. Appellees were orderly, and they limited their activity to the common areas of the shopping center. In these circumstances, the fact that they may have "physically invaded" appellants' property cannot be viewed as determinative. . . . A State is, of course, bound by the Just Compensation Clause of the Fifth Amendment, but here appellants have failed to demonstrate that the "right to exclude others" is so essential to the use or economic value of their property that the state-authorized limitation of it amounted to a "taking."

There is also little merit to appellants' argument that they have been denied their property without due process of law. . . .

"[N]either property rights nor contract rights are absolute. . . . Equally fundamental with the private right is that of the public to regulate it in the common interest. . . .

". . . [T]he guaranty of due process, as has often been held, demands only that the law shall not be unreasonable, arbitrary or capricious, and that the means selected shall have a real and substantial relation to the objective sought to be attained."

. . . Appellants have failed to provide sufficient justification for concluding that this test is not satisfied by the State's asserted interest in promoting more expansive rights of free speech and petition than conferred by the Federal Constitution.

Appellants finally contend that a private property owner has a First Amendment right not to be forced by the State to use his property as a forum for the speech of others. They state that in *Wooley* v. *Maynard,* this Court concluded that a State may not constitutionally require an individual to participate in the dissemination of an ideological message by displaying it on his private property in a manner and for the express purpose that it be observed and read by the public. This rationale applies here, they argue, because the message of *Wooley* is that the State may not force an individual to display any message at all.

Wooley, however, was a case in which the government itself prescribed the message, required it to be displayed openly on appellee's personal property that was used "as part of his daily life," and refused to permit him to take any measures to cover up the motto even though the Court found that the display of the motto served no important state interest. Here, by contrast, there are a number of distinguishing factors. Most important, the shopping center by choice of its owner is not limited to the personal use of appellants. It is instead a business establishment that is open to the public to come and go as they please. The views expressed by members of the public in passing out pamphlets or seeking signatures for a petition thus will not likely be identified with those of the owner. Second, no specific message is dictated by the State to be displayed on appellants' property. There consequently is no danger of governmental discrimination for or against a particular message. Finally, as far as appears here appellants can expressly disavow any connection with the message by simply posting signs in the area where the speakers or handbillers stand. Such signs, for example, could disclaim any sponsorship of the message and could explain that the persons are communicating their own messages by virtue of state law. . . .

We conclude that neither appellants' federally recognized property rights nor their First Amendment rights have been infringed by the California Supreme Court's decision recognizing a right of appellees to exercise state protected rights of expression and petition on appellants' property. The judgment of the Supreme Court of California is therefore affirmed.

Questions

1. Why is the power of eminent domain arguably necessary to the effective operation of government?
2. Explain PruneYard's position that allowing free speech on its property would constitute an infringement of its property rights.
3. Develop the argument in support of the position that free speech (appropriately regulated) in a shopping center is constitutionally required.
4. Might the result in this case have been different had the case arisen in a state other than California?

Corporate Political Speech.   Corporations, of course, are not natural persons. However, as expressed so eloquently by Chief Justice Marshall in the *Dartmouth College* case of 1819, the corporation is an "artificial being, invisible, intangible, and existing only in contemplation of law." Are the expressions of artificial beings accorded constitutional protection equivalent to that of a person? The question has become increasingly important in recent years as corporations have taken a very much more active role in public affairs.

Corporations have rapidly established themselves in a critical place in the political process. To some that development is as it should be. It is argued that corporations should be able to defend their stake in American life, and presumably the marketplace of ideas profits from a fuller dialogue. To others, corporations, with their enormous resources, are a threat to the democratic process. The fear is that the corporate view, supported by extraordinary wealth and power, may drown out other opinions. (See Chapter 1 for a more complete discussion.) Paid corporate expressions on public issues are often labeled *advocacy advertising*. The Mobil ad on the preceding page and the *Bellotti* case that follows illustrate and analyze the difficult question of the corporation's First Amendment rights.

FIRST NATIONAL BANK OF BOSTON V. BELLOTTI   435 U.S. 765
(1978)

Justice Powell

In sustaining a state criminal statute that forbids certain expenditures by banks and business corporations for the purpose of influencing the vote on referendum proposals, the Massachusetts Supreme Judicial Court held that the First Amendment rights of a corporation are limited to issues that materially affect its business, property, or assets. The court rejected appellants' claim that the statute abridges freedom of speech in violation of the First and Fourteenth Amendments. . . .

[Section 8 of a Massachusetts criminal statute] prohibits appellants, two national banking associations and three business corporations, from making contributions or expenditures "for the purpose of . . . influencing or affecting the vote on any question submitted to the voters, other than one materially affecting any of the property, business or assets of the corporation." The statute further specifies that "[n]o question submitted to the voters solely concerning the taxation of the income, property or transactions of individuals shall be deemed materially to affect the property, business or assets of the corporation." A corporation that violates § 8 may receive a maximum fine of $50,000; a corporate officer, director, or agent who violates the section may receive a maximum fine of $10,000 or imprisonment for up to one year, or both.

Appellants wanted to spend money to publicize their views on a proposed constitutional amendment that was to be submitted to the voters as a ballot question. . . . The amendment would have permitted the legislature to impose a graduated tax on the income of individuals. After appellee, the Attorney General of Massachusetts, informed appellants that he intended to enforce § 8 against them, they brought this action seeking to have the statute declared unconstitutional. . . .

The court below framed the principal question in this case as whether and to what extent corporations have First Amendment rights. We believe that the court posed the wrong question. The Constitution often protects interests broader than those of the party seeking their vindication. The First Amendment, in particular, serves significant societal interests. The proper question therefore is not whether corporations "have" First Amendment rights and, if so, whether they are coextensive with those of natural persons. Instead, the question must be whether § 8 abridges expression that the First Amendment was meant to protect. We hold that it does.

The speech proposed by appellants is at the heart of the First Amendment's protection.

The freedom of speech and of the press guaranteed by the Constitution embraces at the least the liberty to discuss publicly and truthfully all matters of public concern without previous restraint or fear of subsequent punishment . . . . Freedom of discussion, if it would fulfill its historic function in this nation, must embrace all issues about which information is needed or appropriate to enable the members of society to cope with the exigencies of their period. . . .

The referendum issue that appellants wish to address falls squarely within this description. In appellants' view, the enactment of a graduated personal income tax, as proposed to be authorized by constitutional amendment, would have a seriously adverse effect on the economy of the State. The importance of the referendum issue to the people and government of Massachusetts is not disputed. Its merits, however, are the subject of sharp disagreement.

As the Court said in *Mills* v. *Alabama,* "there is practically universal agreement that a major purpose of [the First] Amendment was to protect the free discussion of governmental affairs." If the speakers here were not corporations, no one would suggest that the State could silence their proposed speech. It is the type of speech indispensable to decision making in a democracy, and this is no less true because the speech comes from a corporation rather than an individual. The inherent worth of the speech in terms of its capacity for informing the public does not depend upon the identity of its source, whether corporation, association, union, or individual.

The court below nevertheless held that corporate speech is protected by the First Amendment only when it pertains directly to the corporation's business interests. In deciding whether this novel and restrictive gloss on the First Amendment comports with the Constitution and the precedents of this Court, we need not survey the outer boundaries of the Amendment's protection of corporate speech, or address the abstract question whether corporations have the full measure of rights that individuals enjoy under the First Amendment. The question in this case, simply put, is whether the corporate identity of the speaker deprives this proposed speech of what otherwise would be its clear entitlement to protection. We turn now to that question. . . .

We find no support in the First or Fourteenth Amendment, or in the decisions of this Court, for the proposition that speech that otherwise would be within the protection of the First Amendment loses that protection simply because its source is a corporation that cannot prove, to the satisfaction of a court, a material effect on its business or property. The "materially affecting" requirement is not an identification of the boundaries of corporate speech etched by the Constitution itself. Rather, it amounts to an impermissible legislative prohibition of speech based on the identity of the interests that spokesmen may represent in public debate over controversial issues and a requirement that the speaker have a sufficiently great interest in the subject to justify communication.

Section 8 permits a corporation to communicate to the public its views on certain referendum subjects—those materially affecting its business—but not others. It also singles out one kind of ballot question—individual taxation—as a subject about which corporations may never make their ideas public. The legislature has drawn the line between permissible and impermissible speech according to whether there is a sufficient nexus, as defined by the legislature, between the issue presented to the voters and the business interests of the speaker.

In the realm of protected speech, the legislature is constitutionally disqualified from dictating the subjects about which persons may speak and the speakers who may address a public issue. If a legislature may direct business corporations to "stick to business," it also may limit other corporations—religious, charitable, or civic—to their respective "business" when addressing the public. Such power in government to channel the expression of views is unacceptable under the First Amendment. Especially where, as here, the legislature's suppression of speech suggests an attempt to give one side of a debatable public question an advantage in expressing its views to the people, the First Amendment is plainly offended. . . .

Appellee advances two principal justifications for the prohibition of corporate speech. The first is the State's interest in sustaining the active role of the individual citizen in the electoral process and thereby preventing diminution of the citizen's confidence in government. The second is the interest in protecting the rights of shareholders whose views differ from those expressed by management on behalf of the corporation. However weighty these interests may be in the context of partisan candidate elections, they either are not implicated in this case or are not served at all, or in other than a random manner, by the prohibition in § 8.

Because that portion of § 8 challenged by appellants prohibits protected speech in a manner unjustified by a compelling state interest, it must be invalidated. The judgment of the Supreme Judicial Court is reversed.

Questions

1. In your opinion, is the Mobil ad an effective, useful message? How would you respond to a Mobil ad supporting the passage of the Equal Rights Amendment?
2. Should Mobil be allowed to take a federal income tax deduction for the expenses associated with its ad, ''Capitalism: moving target''? Explain.
3. Does the *Bellotti* decision establish the principle that corporations hold First Amendment rights equivalent to those of natural citizens? Explain.
4. Critics express the fear that the corporate community's vast resources could permit it to dominate political dialogue. Based on the *Bellotti* opinion, do we have reason to believe that the Constitution might not afford complete protection for all corporate advocacy?

Commercial Speech. On occasion governments seek to regulate communications of a profit-seeking nature (e.g., paid political advertisements or ads for abortion services). In 1942 the Supreme Court held that commercial speech was not entitled to the protection of the First Amendment.[9] In that instance Chrestensen delivered an advertisement in the streets promoting the submarine he was operating as a commercial amusement enterprise. A city ordinance forbade commercial distributions in the public way. Chrestensen challenged the ordinance and ultimately took his appeal to the Supreme Court, which upheld the constitutionality of the ordinance. However, a series of decisions since *Chrestensen* have accorded constitutional protection to commercial speech. The law has experienced a profound about face in the 40 years since *Chrestensen*. However, it is clear that governments may yet impose reasonable restrictions upon commercial speech where those restrictions are necessary for the public welfare. The case that follows illustrates the current judicial treatment of commercial speech.

CENTRAL HUDSON GAS V. PUBLIC SERVICE COMMISSION   447 U.S. 557 (1980)

Justice Powell

This case presents the question whether a regulation of the Public Service Commission of the State of New York violates the First and Fourteenth Amendments because it completely bans promotional advertising by an electrical utility.

In December 1973, the Commission, appellee here, ordered electric utilities in New York State to cease all advertising that ''promot[es] the use of electricity.''

The order was based on the Commission's finding that ''the interconnected utility system in

New York State does not have sufficient fuel stocks or sources of supply to continue furnishing all customer demands for the 1973–1974 winter.'' . . .

Appellant challenged the order in state court, arguing that the Commission had restrained commercial speech in violation of the First and Fourteenth Amendments. The Commission's order was upheld by the trial court and at the intermediate appellate level. The New York Court of Appeals affirmed. It found little value to advertising in ''the non-competitive market in which electric corporations operate.'' . . .

The Commission's order restricts only commercial speech, that is, expression related solely to the economic interests of the speaker and its audience. . . . The First Amendment, as applied to the States through the Fourteenth Amendment, protects commercial speech from unwarranted governmental regulation. . . . Commercial expression not only serves the economic interest of the speaker, but also assists consumers and furthers the societal interest in the fullest possible dissemination of information. In applying the First Amendment to this area, we have rejected the ''highly paternalistic'' view that government has complete power to suppress or regulate commercial speech. . . .

Nevertheless, our decisions have recognized ''the 'commonsense' distinction between speech proposing a commercial transaction, which occurs in an area traditionally subject to government regulation and other varieties of speech.'' . . . The Constitution, therefore, accords a lesser protection to commercial speech than to other constitutionally guaranteed expression. . . .

The First Amendment's concern for commercial speech is based on the informational function of advertising. . . . Consequently, there can be no constitutional objection to the suppression of commercial messages that do not accurately inform the public about lawful activity. The government may ban forms of communication more likely to deceive the public than to inform it, . . . or commercial speech related to illegal activity. . . .

If the communication is neither misleading nor related to unlawful activity, the government's power is more circumscribed. The State must assert a substantial interest to be achieved by restrictions on commercial speech. Moreover, the regulatory technique must be in proportion to that interest. The limitation on expression must be designed carefully to achieve the State's goal. Compliance with this requirement may be measured by two criteria. First, the restriction must directly advance the state interest involved; the regulation may not be sustained if it provides only ineffective or remote support for the government's purpose. Second, if the governmental interest could be served as well by a more limited restriction on commercial speech, the excessive restrictions cannot survive. . . .

In commercial speech cases, then, a four-part analysis has developed. At the outset, we must determine whether the expression is protected by the First Amendment. For commercial speech to come within that provision, it at least must concern lawful activity and not be misleading. Next, we ask whether the asserted governmental interest is substantial. If both inquiries yield positive answers, we must determine whether the regulation directly advances the governmental interest asserted, and whether it is not more extensive than is necessary to serve that interest. . . .

The Commission does not claim that the expression at issue either is inaccurate or relates to unlawful activity. . . .

The Commission offers two state interests as justifications for the ban on promotional advertising. The first concerns energy conservation. Any increase in demand for electricity—during peak or off-peak periods—means greater consumption of energy. The Commission argues . . . that the State's interest in conserving energy is sufficient to support suppression of advertising designed to increase consumption of electricity. In view of our country's dependence on energy resources beyond our control, no one can doubt the importance of energy conservation. Plainly, therefore, the state interest asserted is substantial. [Second ''interest'' omitted.]

Next, we focus on the relationship between the State's interests and the advertising ban. . . .

[T]he State's interest in energy conservation is directly advanced by the Commission order at issue here. There is an immediate connection between advertising and demand for electricity. Central Hudson would not contest the advertising ban unless it believed that promotion would increase its sales. Thus, we find a direct link between the state interest in conservation and the Commission's order.

We come finally to the critical inquiry in this case: whether the Commission's complete suppression of speech ordinarily protected by the First Amendment is no more extensive than necessary to further the State's interest in energy conservation. The Commission's order reaches all promotional advertising, regardless of the impact of the touted service on overall energy use. But the energy conservation rationale, as important as it is, cannot justify suppressing information about electric devices or services that would cause no net increase in total energy use. In addition, no showing has been made that a more limited restriction on the content of promotional advertising would not serve adequately the State's interests.

Appellant insists that but for the ban, it would advertise products and services that use energy efficiently. These include the "heat pump," which both parties acknowledge to be a major improvement in electric heating, and the use of electric heat as a "backup" to solar and other heat sources. . . .

The Commission's order prevents appellant from promoting electric services that would reduce energy use by diverting demand from less efficient sources, or that would consume roughly the same amount of energy as do alternative sources. In neither situation would the utility's advertising endanger conservation or mislead the public. To the extent that the Commission's order suppresses speech that in no way impairs the State's interest in energy conservation, the Commission's order violates the First and Fourteenth Amendments and must be invalidated. See *First National Bank of Boston* v. *Bellotti*.

The Commission also has not demonstrated that its interest in conservation cannot be protected adequately by more limited regulation of appellant's commercial expression. To further its policy of conservation, the Commission could attempt to restrict the format and content of Central Hudson's advertising. It might, for example, require that the advertisements include information about the relative efficiency and expense of the offered service, both under current conditions and for the foreseeable future. In the absence of a showing that more limited speech regulation would be ineffective, we cannot approve the complete suppression of Central Hudson's advertising. . . .

Accordingly, the judgment of the New York Court of Appeals is reversed.

Questions

1. Distinguish commercial speech from political speech.
2. Why is commercial speech accorded less protection than other categories of expression?
3. The Township of Willingboro prohibited the posting of real estate "For Sale" or "Sold" signs. The town's purposes were to promote racial integration and to retard the flight of white homeowners. Is the Willingboro action constitutionally permissible? See *Linmark Associates, Inc.* v. *Willingboro*, 431 U.S. 85 (1977).
4. Presumably the primary justification for according First Amendment protection to commercial speech is our interest in maximizing the efficiency of the marketplace. On the other hand, it is evident that we have accorded legislatures broad power to regulate the economy. The traditional rationales for protecting free speech generally are those of personal self-fulfillment and the improvement of the political decision-making process.[10] Given these considerations, should commercial speech be accorded First Amendment protection?

III. Search and Seizure

In an increasingly complex and interdependent society, the right of the individual to be free of unjustified governmental intrusions has arguably become more important. The Fourth Amendment provides that: "[T]he right of the people to be secure in their persons, houses, papers, and effects, against unreasonable searches and seizures, shall not be violated, and no Warrants shall issue, but upon probable cause." It is generally conceded that some constitutional limitations on the police powers of government officials are a necessity. However, the boundaries of freedom from unreasonable search and seizure are the subject of great controversy. For example, the *general* rule is that the scope of a search incident to an arrest is limited to the person being arrested and the physical area within the arrested party's immediate control, but that standard is the target of many challenges.

Certainly the most controversial dimension of Fourth Amendment interpretation is the *exclusionary rule,* which provides that no evidence secured as the product of an illegal search may be admitted as evidence in a court of law. As ultimately applied to all courts by the 1961 U.S. Supreme Court decision in *Mapp* v. *Ohio,*[11] the reader will readily recognize that the exclusionary rule is a very effective device for discouraging illegal searches. In the *Mapp* case, police officers without a search warrant, without permission to search, and without probable cause for arrest broke into a private home. A person was hiding in the home who was wanted for questioning in connection with a bombing. Ms. Mapp was arrested, and during the search of her home, police discovered certain lewd and lascivious books and pictures. Ms. Mapp was subsequently convicted of a criminal offense of possession of obscene materials, but the U.S. Supreme Court reversed the Ohio Supreme Court's decision upholding the validity of Ms. Mapp's conviction.

The *Mapp* case clearly reveals the competing considerations in typical search and seizure cases. On one hand, the police sometimes abuse the rights of individuals. On the other hand, Chief Justice Burger has lamented the impact of the exclusionary rule: "[Some] clear demonstration of the benefits and effectiveness of [the rule] is required to justify it in view of the high price it extracts from society—the release of countless guilty criminals."[12] However, a 1984 Supreme Court decision has created a good faith exception to the exclusionary rule. When judges issue search warrants that are later ruled defective, any illegally gathered evidence, nevertheless, may ordinarily be used at trial. Justice White noted that the principal justification for the exclusionary rule was to deter police misconduct. Therefore, where police have conducted a search in the good-faith belief that their conduct was lawful, "there is no police illegality and thus nothing to deter." However, evidence would be suppressed in instances where the judge granting the warrant was not impartial or where police lied to secure the warrant.[13]

So we know that the Fourth Amendment has been the subject of dispute in criminal cases, but it may come as a surprise to learn that the contentious issues surrounding search and seizure have also been of importance in civil actions involving the government's efforts to regulate the conduct of business. The case that follows illustrates one of the constitutional limitations on the government's ability to secure whatever information it may desire without benefit of a proper search warrant.

MARSHALL V. BARLOW'S INC.   436 U.S. 307 (1978)

Justice White

Section 8(a) of the Occupational Safety and Health Act of 1970 (OSHA or Act) empowers agents of the secretary of labor (secretary) to search the work area of any employment facility within the Act's jurisdiction. The purpose of the search is to inspect for safety hazards and violations of OSHA regulations. No search warrant or other process is expressly required under the Act.

On the morning of September 11, 1975, an OSHA inspector entered the customer service area of Barlow's, Inc., an electrical and plumbing installation business located in Pocatello, Idaho. The president and general manager, Ferrol G. "Bill" Barlow, was on hand; and the OSHA inspector, after showing his credentials, informed Mr. Barlow that he wished to conduct a search of the working areas of the business. Mr. Barlow inquired whether any complaint had been received about his company. The inspector answered no, but that Barlow's, Inc., had simply turned up in the agency's selection process. The inspector again asked to enter the nonpublic area of the business; Mr. Barlow's response was to inquire whether the inspector had a search warrant. The inspector had none. Thereupon, Mr. Barlow refused the inspector admission to the employee area of his business. He said he was relying on his rights as guaranteed by the Fourth Amendment of the United States Constitution.

Three months later, the Secretary petitioned the United States District Court for the District of Idaho to issue an order compelling Mr. Barlow to admit the inspector. The requested order was issued on December 30, 1975, and was presented to Mr. Barlow on January 5, 1976. Mr. Barlow again refused admission, and he sought his own injunctive relief against the warrantless searches assertedly permitted by OSHA. A three-judge court was convened. On December 30, 1976, it ruled in Mr. Barlow's favor . . . . [T]he court held that the Fourth Amendment required a warrant for the type of search involved here and that the statutory authorization for warrantless inspections was unconstitutional. An injunction against searches or inspections pursuant to § 8(a) was entered. The Secretary appealed. . . .

The Secretary urges that warrantless inspections to enforce OSHA are reasonable within the meaning of the Fourth Amendment. Among other things, he relies on § 8(a) of the Act, which authorizes inspection of business premises without a warrant and which the Secretary urges represents a congressional construction of the Fourth Amendment that the courts should not reject. Regrettably, we are unable to agree.

The Warrant Clause of the Fourth Amendment protects commercial buildings as well as private homes. To hold otherwise would belie the origin of that Amendment, and the American colonial experience. . . . "[T]he Fourth Amendment's commands grew in large measure out of the colonists' experience with the writs of assistance . . . [that] granted sweeping power to customs officials and other agents of the King to search at large for smuggled goods." . . . Against this background, it is untenable that the ban on warrantless searches was not intended to shield places of business as well as of residence.

*   *   *   *   *

The Secretary urges that an exception from the search warrant requirement has been recognized for "pervasively regulated business[es]," and for "closely regulated" industries "long subject to close supervision and inspection." These cases are indeed exceptions, but they represent responses to relatively unique circumstances. Certain industries have such a history of government oversight that no reasonable expectation of privacy could exist for a proprietor over the stock of such an enterprise. Liquor (*Colonnade*) and firearms (*Biswell*) are industries of this type; when an entrepreneur embarks upon such a business, he has voluntarily chosen to subject himself to a full arsenal of governmental regulation.

* * * * *

The Secretary submits that warrantless inspections are essential to the proper enforcement of OSHA because they afford the opportunity to inspect without prior notice and hence to preserve the advantages of surprise. While the dangerous conditions outlawed by the Act include structural defects that cannot be quickly hidden or remedied, the Act also regulates a myriad of safety details that may be amenable to speedy alteration or disguise. The risk is that during the interval between an inspector's initial request to search a plant and his procuring a warrant following the owner's refusal of permission, violations of this latter type could be corrected and thus escape the inspec-tor's notice. To the suggestion that warrants may be issued ex parte and executed without delay and without prior notice, thereby preserving the element of surprise, the Secretary expresses concern for the administrative strain that would be experienced by the inspection system, and by the courts, should ex parte warrants issued in advance become standard practice.

We are unconvinced, however, that requiring warrants to inspect will impose serious burdens on the inspection system or the courts, will prevent inspections necessary to enforce the statute, or will make them less effective. In the first place, the great majority of businessmen can be expected in normal course to consent to inspection without warrant; the Secretary has not brought to this Court's attention any widespread pattern of refusal.

* * * *

Nor is it immediately apparent why the advantages of surprise would be lost if, after being refused entry, procedures were available for the Secretary to seek an ex parte warrant and to reappear at the premises without further notice to the establishment being inspected.

* * * * *

Nor do we agree that the incremental protections afforded the employer's privacy by a warrant are so marginal that they fail to justify the administrative burdens that may be entailed. The authority to make warrantless searches devolves almost unbridled discretion upon executive and administrative officers, particularly those in the field, as to when to search and whom to search. A warrant, by contrast, would provide assurances from a neutral officer that the inspection is reasonable under the Constitution, is authorized by statute, and is pursuant to an administrative plan containing specific neutral criteria. Also, a warrant would then and there advise the owner of the scope and objects of the search, beyond which limits the inspector is not expected to proceed. . . .

The judgment of the District Court is therefore affirmed.

Questions

1. How does the Supreme Court support its view that the Fourth Amendment extends to commercial buildings as well as to private homes?
2. Why are certain classes of businesses open to government inspection in the absence of a search warrant?
3. In light of the *Barlow's* case can the government conduct searches on a systematic basis in the absence of evidence establishing probable cause of a violation? Explain.
4. The Court cites a series of virtues that arise from the warrant requirement. List those virtues.

5. The EPA conducted a warrantless, aerial surveillance of a Dow Chemical Company plant. The EPA was investigating the possibility of Clean Air Act violations. Dow had built a security fence around its 2,000 acre site and had otherwise taken "great pains" to prevent intrusions at ground level. However, it had taken no steps to prevent aerial incursions. Was the EPA action a search requiring a warrant? See *Dow Chemical Co.* v. *U.S.*, 749 F.2d 307 (1984). Appealed to the U.S. Supreme Court, 1985.

Constitutional Law Policy

We have taken a brief look at the impact of selected elements of the Constitution, and more particularly the Bill of Rights, on the business community. Many important Constitutional components are discussed elsewhere in the text.

The article that follows captures some of the flavor of the formulation of constitutional policy by the Supreme Court. The reader should achieve both a sense of the profound impact of the Court and the Constitution and the constrained (by precedent) but necessarily evolutionary nature of Supreme Court decision making.

YOU CAN'T GO HOME AGAIN

Anthony Lewis

When Warren E. Burger succeeded Earl Warren as chief justice of the United States in 1969, many expected to see the more striking constitutional doctrines of the Warren years pulled back or even abandoned. The reapportionment cases, *Brown* v. *Board of Education* and other decisions against racial discrimination, the criminal-law decisions imposing what amounted to a code of fair procedure on the states, the cases enlarging the freedom of speech and the press: in these, it was often said, the Warren Court had launched a constitutional revolution. Now a counterrevolution was seemingly at hand.

It is 14 years later as I write. Six members of the Warren Court are gone, replaced by nominees of Republican presidents: Nixon, four; Ford, one; Reagan, one. And what has happened to those controversial Warren Court doctrines? They are more securely rooted now than they were in 1969, accepted by the Burger Court as the premises of constitutional decision making. Of course particular results have swung away from the trend apparent before 1969; of course this decision or that has disappointed those who welcomed the changes of the Warren years. But there has been nothing like a counterrevolution. It is fair to say, in fact, that the reach of earlier decisions on racial equality and the First Amendment has been enlarged. Even the most hotly debated criminal-law decision, *Miranda,* establishing the right of a suspect to consult counsel before being questioned by police, stands essentially unmodified.

The Burger Court approved busing as a judicial remedy for school segregation. The Burger Court made the press virtually immune to "gag orders," forbidding publication of stories about pending criminal cases, and said that newspapers could not be made to balance critical stories by publishing replies; it held unconstitutional a state tax imposed on newspapers alone and held for the first time that the press and the public have a right to observe certain public proceedings, in particular trials.

* * * * *

How has it happened, this extraordinary continuity of doctrine? Why have judges appointed by conservative presidents clung to the libertarian principles of the previous judicial generation and even enlarged upon them? These questions are evoked again and again in *The Burger Court*, a fascinating collection of analyses of the Court's work since 1969.*

An irony must be part of the answer. Conservative judges—meaning by that term those who are more cautious in lawmaking—are naturally committed to the doctrine of *stare decisis*. It follows logically that they should respect a precedent once established, even though they opposed that result during the process of decision. For such a true conservative as Justice John Marshall Harlan, this consideration was certainly a factor; he might warn in dissent against what he foresaw as the baleful effects of a decision, but he would hesitate thereafter to subject it to repeated litigation. He valued stability over perfection.

A psychological truism supports *stare decisis*. Yesterday's surprise becomes today's commonplace. That is true of life generally in a changing world and of judicial life in particular, for it is the nature of the judicial process in our legal system to use yesterday's innovation as the accepted premise, the platform for further decision. Not only most judges but virtually all lawyers reason that way: they incrementally consolidate the past into the future. It is the lawyer's way of thinking, taught in law schools.

Moreover, the public believes it is entitled to a certain reliance on constitutional decisions of the Supreme Court—and judges sense that. Reconsideration of doctrine in the light of changed circumstances is one thing; our view

of race was different after Hitler from what it had been in 1896, when *Plessy* v. *Ferguson* was decided. But reconsideration after a few years because of the changing cast of judges is something quite different.

It is also true that doctrines seen as radical when they first appear in Supreme Court opinions have a way of turning out to feel familiar and right. The decision that state legislators and members of the federal House of Representatives must be elected from districts of roughly equal population did force a lot of change—but it was change quite acceptable to the public. The United States still has much racial injustice, and much hypocrisy on the subject, but few Americans would want to go back to the *Plessy* v. *Ferguson* rule and have the Supreme Court say that segregation in public facilities meets the Constitution's demand for "the equal protection of the laws." Probably the most bitterly disputed decision of the Burger Court is *Roe* v. *Wade*, the abortion case, which a majority reaffirmed during the last term. But if it were overruled by the Court itself or by constitutional amendment, would the American public easily accept now the criminal prosecution of women or doctors involved in abortions?

* * * * *

The Burger Court is doing what comes naturally to judges in the post-Warren era: trimming here and there, notably where egalitarianism looks to have costly consequences, but also building on the cases of the 1950s and 1960s when the spirit moves it—and doing so without any great concern for "self-restraint." . . .

One thing to be learned from the essays in *The Burger Court* is that the great conflict of the 1930s and 1940s between judicial "restraint" and "activism" has become a matter of history. . . .

We are all activists now. So *The Burger Court* tells us. Vincent Blasi, in his powerful summing up, suggests that this period in Supreme Court history will be seen as one in which judicial intervention came to be ac-

---

The Burger Court: The Counterrevolution That Wasn't, edited by Vincent Blasi. (New Haven, Conn.: Yale University Press, 1983). This essay appeared in different form as an introduction.

cepted—by judges and the rest of us—as a matter of course. . . .

Activists for what is a different question. Professor Blasi concludes, convincingly, that the Burger Court's interventionism has not been programmatic, deriving from some ideological theme. It has lacked what he calls the energizing moral vision of the Warren years, with their emphasis on egalitarian ideals. The

present Court acts strongly but pragmatically—one could use the less polite adverb "opportunistically"—reacting to events with moves in this direction or that, avoiding fundamental choices of values. Professor Blasi's phrase for it is "rootless activism." . . .

Source: *The New York Review of Books*, September 29, 1983, pp. 16–17. Reprinted with permission from *The New York Review of Books*. Copyright © 1983 Nyrev, Inc.

QUESTIONS

1. According to the article, why has the more "conservative" Burger court failed to overturn the "revolutionary" decisions of the more "liberal" Warren court?
2. Blasi suggests that Supreme Court intervention across much of life has come to be accepted as a matter of course. In your view, are any of the Supreme Court decisions in this chapter evidence of ill-advised Supreme Court intrusion?
3. Blasi argues that the Burger Court has acted pragmatically without the benefit of an evident ideological theme. On the other hand, he notes the "energizing moral vision" of the Warren Court with its concern for "egalitarian ideals." Blasi apparently disdains the "rootless activism" of the Burger Court. In your view, should a Supreme Court develop its own ideological theme with its decisions springing in a reasonably coherent pattern from that shared philosophical platform?

Chapter Questions

1. The Labor Department conducts regular investigations of business records in order to ensure compliance with the wages and hours provisions (e.g., higher pay for overtime) of the Fair Labor Standards Act. When a compliance officer sought to inspect certain financial records at the Lone Steer restaurant/motel in Steele, North Dakota, the restaurant declined his admittance until the government detailed the scope of the investigation. Not receiving a satisfactory response, the Lone Steer demanded a search warrant prior to inspection. As provided for under the FLSA, the government secured an administrative subpoena which, unlike a search warrant, does not require judicial approval. Once again, Lone Steer denied admission. The government then filed suit. Decide. See *Donovan* v. *Lone Steer*, 52 *Law Week* 4087 (U.S. S. Ct., 1984).

2. A Texas statute forbade the practice of optometry under a trade name. The Texas legislature feared possible deception in optometric practice, such as changes in the staff of optometrists while the trade name remained unchanged or the use of different trade names at shops under common ownership, which practices might create a false impression of competition between the shops. Was the Texas statute a violation of the freedom of speech safeguards of the First Amendment? See *Friedman* v. *Rogers*, 440 U.S. 1 (1979).

3. This chapter noted a number of decisions affording expanded protection to commercial speech. Why is it unlikely that corporations will begin to use their vast resources to speak out on the wide range of public issues from abortion to organized prayer in schools to the death penalty?

4. A New York State Public Service Commission regulation prohibited the inclusion of information about "controversial" public policy issues with utility companies' monthly bills to customers. Consolidated Edison had previously mailed an insert saying, "Independence is still a goal, and nuclear power is needed to win the battle." The Natural Resources Defense Council then sought a commission order requiring the utility to include opposing views with the bills. Rather than issue a "fairness" order, the commission settled on a ban against all such inserts. Is the ban constitutionally permissible? See *Consolidated Edison* v. *Public Service Commission,* 447 U.S. 530 (1980).

5. Dissenting in the *Consolidated Edison* decision (discussed in question 4), Justice Blackmun argued that the utility inserts "amounted to forced aid for the utility's speech." Explain what he meant.

6. Restaurant-owner Smith reads of studies suggesting that women typically work more diligently than men. He decides therefore to hire only women for his new restaurant. He runs an employment ad in the local newspaper and includes the language, "Only women need apply." Smith is challenged in court on the grounds that the ad violates Title VII of the Civil Rights Act of 1964, which forbids discrimination in employment on the basis of race, religion, color, sex, or national origin. Smith loses the lawsuit, but he appeals the decision on constitutional grounds.
   a. What constitutional law argument might be raised in Smith's behalf?
   b. Decide. See *Pittsburgh Press* v. *Human Relations Commission,* 413 U.S. 376 (1973) for a relevant decision.

7. Members of Local 590 were picketing a grocery store located in Logan Valley's shopping center. The grocery store had hired only nonunion personnel. An injunction was served barring the picketing on the grounds of trespass. The decision was appealed to the United States Supreme Court.
   a. What constitutional law argument would you raise on behalf of Local 590?
   b. What argument would you raise on behalf of Logan Valley?
   c. Decide. See *Amalgamated Food Employees Union Local 590 et al.* v. *Logan Valley Plaza, Inc. et al.,* 391 U.S. 308 (1968).

8. Tanner and others sought to distribute handbills in the interior mall of the Lloyd Corporation shopping center. The literature concerned an anti-Vietnam War meeting. Lloyd Corporation had a strict rule forbidding handbilling. When security guards terminated distributions within the Center, Tanner et al. claimed a violation of their First Amendment rights. Both the district court and the Court of Appeals relied on *Amalgamated Food* (see question 7) in finding a violation of constitutional rights. The decision was appealed to the U.S. Supreme Court. Decide. Explain. See *Lloyd Corporation* v. *Tanner,* 407 U.S. 551 (1972).

9. Philip Zauderer, an Ohio attorney, ran a newspaper ad promising a full refund of legal fees if clients accused of drunk driving were convicted. He later ran an ad soliciting clients who believed themselves to have been harmed by the Dalkon Shield intrauterine contraceptive. That ad included a line drawing of the device as well as a promise that "[i]f there is no recovery, no legal fees are owed by our clients." The office of Disciplinary Counsel of the Supreme Court of Ohio charged that Zauderer violated several provisions of the Disciplinary Rules of the Ohio Code of Professional Responsibility, including:
   i. The drunk driving ad was deceptive because it purported to allow a contingent fee arrangement in a criminal case when that payment method was explicitly forbidden by Ohio rules.
   ii. The Dalkon Shield ad failed to disclose the fact that clients might be liable for *litigation costs* (rather than *legal fees*), and, therefore, was deceptive.

iii. The Dalkon Shield ad violated rules forbidding the use of illustrations in ads.

iv. The Dalkon Shield ad violated rules forbidding "soliciting or accepting legal employment through advertisements containing information or advice regarding a specific legal problem."

Zauderer was found to have violated the Ohio Disciplinary Rules and a public reprimand was issued. He took his case to the U.S. Supreme Court.

a. What constitutional claim should be raised on behalf of Zauderer?

b. Decide. See *Zauderer* v. *Office of Disciplinary Counsel of the Supreme Court of Ohio,* 53 *Law Week* 4587 (U.S. S. Ct., 1985).

Notes

1. Jerre Williams, *Constitutional Analysis in a Nutshell* (St. Paul, Minn.: West Publishing, 1979), p. 33.
2. *Engel* v. *Vitale,* 370 U.S. 421.
3. *Abington School District* v. *Schempp,* 374 U.S. 203 (1963).
4. *Wallace* v. *Jaffree,* 53 *Law Week* 4665 (U.S. S. Ct., 1985).
5. 366 U.S. 420 (1961).
6. *Wisconsin* v. *Yoder,* 406 U.S. 205 (1972).
7. *Tinker* v. *Des Moines School District,* 393 U.S. 503 (1969).
8. *Spence* v. *Washington,* 418 U.S. 405 (1974).
9. *Valentine* v. *Chrestensen,* 316 U.S. 52 (1942).
10. Jackson and Jeffries, "Commercial Free Speech: Economic Due Process and the First Amendment," 65 *Virginia Law Review* 1 (1979).
11. 367 U.S. 643.
12. Dissenting in *Bivens* v. *Six Unknown Agents,* 403 U.S. 388 (1971), as reported in Lockhart, Kamisar, and Choper, *The American Constitution* (St. Paul, Minn.: West Publishing, 1981), p. 312.
13. *Nix* v. *Williams,* 81 L. Ed. 2d 377, 104 S. Ct. _____ (1984).

III

Trade Regulation
and Antitrust

CHAPTER 6   Government Regulation of Business: An Introduction
CHAPTER 7   Administrative Agencies and the Regulatory Process
CHAPTER 8   Business Organizations and Securities Regulation
CHAPTER 9   Antitrust Law—Introduction and Monopolies
CHAPTER 10 Antitrust Law—Mergers
CHAPTER 11 Antitrust Law—Restraints of Trade

6

Government Regulation of Business: An Introduction

Introduction

In Chapter 1 attention was directed to those criticisms commonly leveled at the business community. Chapter 2 investigated the use of the free market on the one end of the economic continuum and government dominance on the other end, as systems by which the role of business in society may be controlled. Chapter 3 addressed the utility of individual and corporate ethics as self-regulatory mechanisms for governing the behavior of the corporate community. Chapters 4 and 5 offered a brief overview of the justice system.

The balance of the text is largely devoted to the government regulation of business. Throughout that investigation the reader is urged to keep in mind the issues of the introductory chapters. What is the proper role of business in society? Has business abused the public trust? If so, is the government the answer to the problem? Or might we rely on self-regulation (ethics and social responsibility) and market regulation? What is the proper blend of these "control" devices as well as others left unexplored (e.g., custom)?

The phrase *mixed economy* is commonly applied to the contemporary American system. In an honorable pursuit of the greatest good for the greatest number, America has turned to the government to ameliorate the injustices and discomforts of contemporary life. Market regulation and self-regulation have been supplemented by government intervention.

Government regulation pervades our existence. The government directly controls certain dimensions of the economy, such as the public utilities. Indirectly the government intervenes across the spectrum of the economy in matters as diverse as child labor and zoning restrictions, and in the larger sense of national economic policy, the government engages in antitrust activity designed to preserve our conception of a free, efficient marketplace. To the proponents of government intervention, the successes are evident: cleaner air, safer cars, fewer useless drugs, more jobs for minorities, safer workplaces, and so on. To the critics, many government regulatory efforts either did not achieve their purpose or did so at a cost exceeding the benefits. The late 70s and early 80s have been marked by increasingly insistent calls from virtually all segments of society to retard the reach of government. Indeed, significant deregulation has been effected. More specifically, freeing business from a portion of its regulatory burden has been a key ingredient in President Reagan's plans to reorder the nation. His intentions for deregulation have been broadly applauded, but it stretches credulity to think that the American government will ever play less than a prepossessing role in American business.

It is important, therefore, to explore the regulatory structure and process both to understand them and seek to improve them. With the budding businessperson in mind, this inquiry will pursue those strategies that might be employed to operate successfully within the regulatory framework and to favorably influence that framework.

Why Regulation?

I.   Market Failure   In theory, government intervention in a free enterprise economy would be justified only when it becomes clear that the market is unable to maximize the public interest; that is, in instances of market failure.

Market failure is attributed to certain inherent imperfections in the market itself.

1. Inadequate information. Can the consumer choose the best pain reliever in the absence of complete information about the virtues of the competing products? An efficient free market presumes reasoned decisions about production and consumption. Reasoned decisions require adequate information. Because we cannot have perfect information and often will not have adequate information, the government, it is argued, may impose regulations either to improve the available information or to diminish the unfavorable effect of inadequate information. Hence we have, for example, labeling mandates for consumer goods, licensure requirements for many occupations, and health standards for the processing and sale of goods.

2. Monopoly. Of course, the government intervenes to thwart anticompetitive monopolies and oligopolies throughout the marketplace. (That process is addressed in Chapter 9.) Of immediate interest here is the so-called natural monopoly. Telephone and electrical services are classic examples of a decline in per-unit production costs as the firm becomes larger. Thus, a single large firm is more efficient than several small ones, and a natural monopoly results. In such situations the government has commonly intervened (in the form of public service commissions) to preserve the efficiencies of the large firm while preventing that firm from taking unfair advantage of the consumer.

3. Externalities. When all the costs and/or benefits of a good or service are not fully internalized or absorbed, those costs or benefits fall elsewhere as what economists have labeled *externalities* or *neighborhood effects* or *spillovers*. Pollution is a characteristic example of a negative externality. The environment is used without charge as an ingredient in the production process (commonly as a receptical for waste). Consequently, the product is underpriced. The consumer does not pay the full social cost of the product, so those remaining costs are thrust upon parties external to the transaction. Government regulation is sometimes considered necessary to place the full cost burden on those who generated it, which in turn is expected to result in less wasteful use of resources. Positive externalities are those in which a producer confers benefits not required by the market. An example of such a positive externality is a business firm that through no

direct market compulsion, landscapes its grounds and develops a sculpture garden to contribute to the aesthetic quality of its neighborhood. Positive externalities ordinarily are not the subject of regulation.

4. *Public Goods.* Some goods and services cannot be provided through the pricing system because we have no method for excluding those who choose not to pay. In such situations, the added cost of benefiting one person is zero or nearly so and, in any case, no one can effectively be denied the benefits of the activity. National defense, insect eradication, and pollution control are exemplary of this phenomenon. Presumably most individuals would refuse to voluntarily pay for what others would receive free. Thus, absent government regulations, public goods would not be produced in adequate quantities.

II. Philosophy and Politics   The correction of market failure arguably explains the full range of government regulation of business, but an alternative or perhaps supplemental explanation lies in the political process. Three general arguments have emerged.

One view is that regulation is considered necessary for the protection and general welfare of the public. We find the government engaging in regulatory efforts designed to achieve a more equitable distribution of income and wealth. Many believe government intervention in the market to be necessary to stabilize the economy, thus curbing the problems of recession, inflation, and unemployment. Affirmative action programs seek to reverse and correct the racism and sexism of the past. We even find the government protecting us from ourselves, both for our benefit and for the well-being of the larger society. For example, cigarette advertising is banned on television, and in some states motorcyclists must wear helmets.

Another view is that regulation is developed at the behest of industry and is operated primarily for the benefit of industry. Here the various subsidies and tax advantages afforded to business might be cited. In numerous instances government regulation has been effective in reducing or entirely eliminating the entry of competitors. Antitrust law has been instrumental in sheltering small businesses. Government regulation has also permitted legalized price-fixing in some industries. Of course, it may be that regulation is often initiated primarily for the public welfare, but that industry eventually "captures" the regulatory process and ensures its continuation for the benefit of the industry. As we see in the historical overview that follows, both the public interest and business interests have been very influential in generating government intervention in the marketplace.

Finally, it seems clear that bureaucrats who perform government regulation are themselves a powerful force in maintaining and expanding that regulation.

The History of Government Regulation of Business

Government has always played some role in American commerce. In the early years of the republic, tariffs were imposed to protect manufacturers, subsidies were provided to stimulate commerce, and a few agencies were established (e.g., Army Corps of Engineers in 1824 and the Patent and Trademark Office in 1836).

Prior to the Civil War the major, if weak, link between government and business was the national bank, which possessed very limited authority. Banking remained a fundamentally private enterprise restrained only by weak state statutes. A meaningful federal banking system simply did not exist. Indeed, it is estimated that by 1860 "some 1,500 banks were issuing about 10,000 different types of bank notes."[1] Then the need for a centralized approach to the Civil War forced Congress to pass the National Banking Act of 1864, which laid the foundation for the dual system of extensive federal and state banking regulation that we know today. However, Americans continued to stoutly resist government intrusion in business affairs. The years following the Civil War were perhaps the zenith of the capitalist era. The "Robber Barons" (Carnegie, Rockefeller, and their colleagues) came to the fore. Philosopher Herbert Spencer adapted Darwin's "survival of the fittest" theory to the world of commerce, thereby giving the business community an intellectual foundation for asserting its leadership. Extraordinary industrial growth followed.

But the public in the late 1880s began to feel the impact of big business, and the feeling often was not pleasant. Anger over the conduct of the rail and industrial trusts manifested itself in the Populist movement, which embodied the struggle of the "common people" against the predatory acts of the monied interests. The railroads, then the nation's most powerful private economic force, were bent on growth and seemingly unconcerned with the general welfare.

By discriminating in freight charges between localities, articles, and individuals, the railroads were terrorizing farmers, merchants, and even whole communities until, as a government agency said in 1887, matters "had reached such a pass, that no man dared engage in any business in which transportation largely entered without first obtaining permission of a railway manager."[2]

Rural discontent led to the Grange movement, which became an important lobbying force for agrarian interests. Several states enacted railroad regulatory legislation. By then the confusion and abuse in the rail industry prompted Congress to pass the Interstate Commerce Commission Act of 1887 and ban, among other practices, rate discrimination against short hauls and the practice of keeping rates secret until the day of shipment. In addition to the farmers, small merchants and shippers and the railroads themselves ultimately supported federal intervention. Apparently the railroad owners felt regulation would be meaningless or even advantageous to them. Subsequently the Hepburn Act of 1906 greatly strengthened ICC effectiveness. Then the Mann-Elkins Act of 1910 extended ICC jurisdiction to interstate telegraph, telephone, cable, and wireless enterprises.

As explained in greater detail in Chapter 9, the development of giant trusts and holding companies (e.g., Standard Oil) led to extraordinary commercial advances but also to widespread abuse in the form of price-fixing, price-slashing to drive out competitors, market-sharing, and the like. Blacklists and other anti-labor tactics were common. At the same time, small merchants and wholesalers were being squeezed by the weight of big manufacturing interests. Around the turn of the century, commercial giants such as American Tobacco, Quaker Oats, Heinz, Swift, and Anheuser-Busch made purchases directly from farmers and other suppliers and sold directly to retailers. The result was that wholesalers, who had previously occupied a key economic role in most communities, were increasingly unnecessary. Similarly, retail giants such as Sears and Woolworth were applying extreme competitive pressure on smaller businesses. The passage of the Sherman Antitrust Act in 1890 had relatively little immediate impact, but Presidents Roosevelt, Taft, and Wilson all took up the regulatory cause, and with the passage in 1914 of the Clayton and Federal Trade Commission Acts antitrust law became an important ingredient in American business life. The fever for regulation subsided somewhat during the prosperous 1920s, but the Depression prompted detailed government regulation.

The Depression compelled many arch-conservatives to surrender to the need for government intervention. President Roosevelt took office in 1933, and the first 100 days of his term saw the passage of 15 major pieces of legislation. In all, Roosevelt secured approval of 93 major bills during his first two terms in office. The federal government became the biggest voice in America as the administration sought to correct the tragedy of the Depression. The legislation literally changed the character of American life. Congress established the Civilian Conservation Corps to place the unemployed in public works projects. The Federal Emergency Relief Act funded state-operated welfare programs. The Tennessee Valley Authority established the government as a major participant in producing electrical energy. The Glass-Steagall Act divided investment and commercial banking and provided for insurance on bank deposits. The list went on and on, and the result was a new view of the business-government relationship. Effectively, the government and the citizenry conceded that the old view of an automatically self-correcting economy was invalid. The Depression revealed a fundamental instability in the unregulated market.[3]

Distrust of the market provoked further government regulation in the decades subsequent to the Depression, and that regulation has followed a much broader path. Rather than regulating single industries (transportation, banking, communication) the government interventions of recent years have swept across the entire economy to address issues such as discrimination, pollution, and worker safety. In the 1960s and 1970s, no social problem seemed too daunting for the government's regulatory efforts.[4]

The Constitutional Foundation of Business Regulation

The Commerce Clause of the United States Constitution broadly specifies the power accorded to the federal government to regulate business activity. Article I, Section 8 of the Constitution provides that: ''The Congress shall have the Power . . . To regulate Commerce with foreign Nations, and among the several States, and with the Indian Tribes. . . .'' State authority to regulate commerce resides in the police power reserved to the states by the Constitution. Police power refers to the right of the state governments to promote the public health, safety, morals, and general welfare by regulating persons and property within each state's jurisdiction. The states have, in turn, delegated portions of the police power to local government units.

The Commerce Clause, as interpreted by the judiciary, affords Congress exclusive jurisdiction over foreign commerce. States and localities, nevertheless, sometimes seek in various ways to regulate foreign commerce. For example, a state may seek, directly or indirectly, to impose a tax on foreign goods that compete with those locally grown or manufactured. Such efforts violate both the Commerce Clause and the Supremacy Clause (holding federal law supreme over state law where the two are in conflict) of the U.S. Constitution.

Federal control over interstate commerce was designed to create a free market throughout the United States, wherein goods would move among the states, unencumbered by state and local tariffs and duties. Not surprisingly, that profoundly sensible policy has been the source of extensive conflict and litigation. As with foreign commerce, the states and localities have endeavored in ways subtle and sometimes not so subtle to influence the course of interstate commerce. The judiciary has not been sympathetic with those efforts. Indeed, to the great chagrin of states' rights advocates, judicial decisions have very dramatically expanded the reach of the federal government. Even intrastate activities, having an effect on interstate commerce, are now subject to federal regulation. In *Wickard* v. *Filburn*,[5] the Supreme Court, in interpreting a federal statute regulating the production and sale of wheat, found that 23 acres of home-grown and largely home-consumed wheat affected interstate commerce, and that it was subject to federal regulation. (As a small test of the mind, the student may wish to deduce the economic reasoning that supported the Court's position.) Clearly, the federal lawmakers with the approval of the judiciary have expanded the power of the central government at the expense of states and localities. The argument goes that expansion has been necessary to maximize the general good, which might otherwise be thwarted by narrow self-interest or prejudice in specific states and localities. The case that follows illustrates both the technical difficulties in determining the constitutional bounds of federal regulation and the conflict between individual rights and the government's view of the general welfare.

HEART OF ATLANTA MOTEL V. UNITED STATES
379 U.S. 241 (1964)

Justice Clark

This is a declaratory judgment action, attacking the constitutionality of Title II of the Civil Rights Act of 1964. . . . [The lower court found for the United States.]

1. The Factual Background and Contentions of the Parties

. . . Appellant owns and operates the Heart of Atlanta Motel, which has 216 rooms available to transient guests. The motel is located on Courtland Street, two blocks from downtown Peachtree Street. It is readily accessible to interstate highways 75 and 85 and state highways 23 and 41. Appellant solicits patronage from outside the State of Georgia through various national advertising media, including magazines of national circulation; it maintains over 50 billboards and highway signs within the State, soliciting patronage for the motel; it accepts convention trade from outside Georgia and approximately 75 percent of its registered guests are from out of State. Prior to passage of the act the motel had followed a practice of refusing to rent rooms to Negroes, and it alleged that it intended to continue to do so. In an effort to perpetuate that policy this suit was filed.

The appellant contends that Congress in passing this act exceeded its power to regulate commerce under [Article I] of the Constitution of the United States; that the act violates the Fifth Amendment because appellant is deprived of the right to choose its customers and operate its business as it wishes, resulting in a taking of its liberty and property without due process of law and a taking of its property without just compensation; and, finally, that by requiring appellant to rent available rooms to Negroes against its will, Congress is subjecting it to involuntary servitude in contravention of the Thirteenth Amendment.

The appellees counter that the unavailability to Negroes of adequate accommodations interferes significantly with interstate travel, and that Congress, under the Commerce Clause, has power to remove such obstructions and restraints; that the Fifth Amendment does not forbid reasonable regulation and that consequential damage does not constitute a "taking" within the meaning of that amendment; that the Thirteenth Amendment claim fails because it is entirely frivolous to say that an amendment directed to the abolition of human bondage and the removal of widespread disabilities associated with slavery places discrimination in public accommodations beyond the reach of both federal and state law. . . .

[A]ppellees proved the refusal of the motel to accept Negro transients after the passage of the act. The district court sustained the constitutionality of the sections of the act under attack and issued a permanent injunction. . . . It restrained the appellant from "[r]efusing to accept Negroes as guests in the motel by reason of their race or color" and from "[m]aking any distinction whatever upon the basis of race or color in the availability of the goods, services, facilities, privileges, advantages, or accommodations offered or made available to the guests of the motel, or to the general public, within or upon any of the premises of the Heart of Atlanta Motel, Inc."

2. The History of the Act

. . . The act as finally adopted was most comprehensive, undertaking to prevent through peaceful and voluntary settlement discrimination in voting, as well as in places of accommodation and public facilities, federally secured programs and in employment. Since Title II is the only portion under attack here, we confine our consideration to those public accommodation provisions.

3. Title II of the Act

This Title is divided into seven sections beginning with §201 (a), which provides that:

"All persons shall be entitled to the full and equal enjoyment of the goods, services, facilities, privileges, advantages, and accommodations of any place of public accommodation, as defined in this section, without discrimination or segregation on the ground of race, color, religion, or national origin."

4. Application of Title II to Heart of Atlanta Motel

It is admitted that the operation of the motel brings it within the provisions of §201 (a) of the act and that appellant refused to provide lodging for transient Negroes because of their race or color and that it intends to continue that policy unless restrained.

The sole question posed is, therefore, the constitutionality of the Civil Rights Act of 1964 as applied to these facts. The legislative history of the act indicates that Congress based the act on §5 and the Equal Protection Clause of the Fourteenth Amendment as well as its power to regulate interstate commerce. . . .

[Part 5 deleted.]

6. The Basis of Congressional Action

While the act as adopted carried no congressional findings the record of its passage through each house is replete with evidence of the burdens that discrimination by race or color places upon interstate commerce. . . . This testimony included the fact that our people have become increasingly mobile with millions of people of all races traveling from state to state; that Negroes in particular have been the subject of discrimination in transient accommodations, having to travel great distances to secure the same; that often they have been unable to obtain accommodations and have had to call upon friends to put them up overnight, and that these conditions have become so acute as to require the listing of available lodging for Negroes in a special guidebook which was itself "dramatic testimony to the difficulties" Negroes encounter in travel. These exclusionary practices were found to be nationwide, the Under Secretary of Commerce testifying that there is "no question that this discrimination in the North still exists to a large degree" and in the West and Midwest as well. This testimony indicated a qualitative as well as quantitative effect on interstate travel by Negroes. The former was the obvious impairment of the Negro traveler's pleasure and convenience that resulted when he continually was uncertain of finding lodging. As for the latter, there was evidence that this uncertainty stemming from racial discrimination had the effect of discouraging travel on the part of a substantial portion of the Negro community. This was the conclusion not only of the Under Secretary of Commerce but also of the Administrator of the Federal Aviation Agency who wrote the Chairman of the Senate Commerce Committee that it was his "belief that air commerce is adversely affected by the denial to a substantial segment of the traveling public of adequate and desegregated public accommodations." We shall not burden this opinion with further details since the voluminous testimony presents overwhelming evidence that discrimination by hotels and motels impedes interstate travel.

7. The Power of Congress over Interstate Travel

The power of Congress to deal with these obstructions depends on the meaning of the Commerce Clause.

* * * * *

In short, the determinative test of the exercise of power by the Congress under the Commerce Clause is simply whether the activity sought to be regulated is "commerce which concerns more States than one" and has a real and substantial relation to the national interest. Let us now turn to this facet of the problem.

* * * * *

The same interest in protecting interstate commerce which led Congress to deal with segregation in interstate carriers and the white-slave traffic has prompted it to extend the exercise of its power to gambling, to criminal enterprises, to deceptive practices in the sale of products, to fraudulent security transactions, and to racial discrimination by owners and managers of terminal restaurants. . . .

That Congress was legislating against moral wrongs in many of these areas rendered its enactments no less valid. In framing Title II of this act Congress was also dealing with what it considered a moral problem. But that fact does not detract from the overwhelming evidence of the disruptive effect that racial discrimination has had on commercial intercourse. It was this burden which empowered Congress to enact appropriate legislation, and, given this basis for the exercise of its power, Congress was not restricted by the fact that the particular obstruction to interstate commerce with which it was dealing was also deemed a moral and social wrong.

It is said that the operation of the motel here is of a purely local character. But, assuming this to be true, "[i]f it is interstate commerce that feels the pinch, it does not matter how local the operation which applies the squeeze."

*   *   *   *   *

Thus the power of Congress to promote interstate commerce also includes the power to regulate the local incidents thereof, including local activities in both the States of origin and destination, which might have a substantial and harmful effect upon that commerce. One need only examine the evidence which we have discussed above to see that Congress may—as it has—prohibit racial discrimination by motels serving travelers, however "local" their operations may appear.

Nor does the act deprive appellant of liberty or property under the Fifth Amendment. The commerce power invoked here by the Congress is a specific and plenary one authorized by the Constitution itself. The only questions are: (1) whether Congress had a rational basis for finding that racial discrimination by motels affected commerce, and (2) if it had such a basis, whether the means it selected to eliminate that evil are reasonable and appropriate. If they are, appellant has no "right" to select its guests as it sees fit, free from governmental regulation.

There is nothing novel about such legislation. Thirty-two states now have it on their books either by statute or executive order and many cities provide such regulation. Some of these acts go back four-score years. It has been repeatedly held by this Court that such laws do not violate the Due Process Clause of the Fourteenth Amendment.

*   *   *   *   *

It is doubtful if in the long run appellant will suffer economic loss as a result of the act. Experience is to the contrary where discrimination is completely obliterated as to all public accommodations. But whether this be true or not is of no consequence since this Court has specifically held that the fact that a "member of the class which is regulated may suffer economic losses not shared by others . . . has never been a barrier" to such legislation. . . . Likewise in a long line of cases this Court has rejected the claim that the prohibition of racial discrimination in public accommodations interferes with personal liberty. . . . Neither do we find any merit in the claim that the act is a taking of property without just compensation. The cases are to the contrary. . . .

We find no merit in the remainder of appellant's contentions including that of "involuntary servitude." . . . We could not say that the requirements of the act in this regard are in any way "akin to African slavery." . . .

We, therefore, conclude that the action of the Congress in the adoption of the act as applied here to a motel which concededly serves interstate travelers is within the power granted it by the Commerce Clause of the Constitution, as interpreted by this Court for 140 years. . . .

Affirmed.

Questions

1. In your judgment does the Commerce Clause afford the federal government the authority to regulate a local business such as the Heart of Atlanta motel? Explain.
2. Should the federal government regulate local business in order to further the cause of racial equity? Explain.
3. What arguments were offered by the government to establish that the Heart of Atlanta racial policy affected interstate commerce? Are you persuaded by those arguments? Explain.
4. Explain the Fifth and Thirteenth Amendment arguments raised in *Heart of Atlanta*.
5. What test did the Court articulate to determine when Congress has the power to pass legislation based on the Commerce Clause?

6. Ollie's Barbecue, a neighborhood restaurant in Birmingham, Alabama, discriminated against black customers. McClung brought suit to test the application of the public accommodations section of the Civil Rights Act of 1964 to his restaurant. In the suit the government offered no evidence to show that the restaurant ever had served interstate customers or that it was likely to do so. Decide the case. See *Katzenbach* v. *McClung,* 379 U.S. 294 (1964).
7. May a private club lawfully decline to serve liquor to a black person who is accompanying a white person to the club bar? Build the argument that the club is not "private" as a matter of law. See *Moose Lodge No. 107* v. *Irvis,* 407 U.S. 163 (1972).
8. What economic consequences would you project from a judicial decision permitting Congress to regulate public accommodations clearly interstate in character, while leaving more preponderantly local public accommodations to the regulation of state and local governments?

State and Local Regulation of Interstate Commerce

As noted, the states via their constitutional police power have the authority to regulate commerce within their jurisdictions for the purpose of maintaining the general welfare. That is, in order to assist in maintaining the public health, safety, and morals, states must be able to control persons and property within their jurisdictional authority. However, we have seen that the Commerce Clause, as interpreted, accords the federal government broad authority over commerce. As explained, the federal government has exclusive authority over foreign commerce. Purely intrastate commerce, having no significant effect on interstate commerce, is within the exclusive regulatory jurisdiction of the states. Of course, commerce purely intrastate in nature is quite rare. The confusion arises in the category of interstate commerce. While federal government regulation of interstate commerce is pervasive, it is not exclusive. In broad terms, states may regulate interstate commerce where:

1. The commerce being regulated does not require uniform, consistent treatment throughout the nation,
2. Congress has not preempted the area by its own complete regulation,
3. The state regulation is not an undue burden on commerce, and
4. The state regulation is not in conflict with federal law.

In the *Commonwealth Edison* case that follows, we see how the Supreme Court recently grappled with the problem of a state's use of its taxing power to regulate interstate commerce. Interstate commerce is not exempt from state and local taxes. However, the Constitution does impose limits on that taxation. Before turning to the case, a warning is in order. This introductory treatment of the Commerce Clause has been quite brief. Many subtleties and complexities have not been addressed. Furthermore, it should be understood that several other elements of the Constitution, directly related to government regulation of business, have not been addressed or are treated elsewhere in the text.

COMMONWEALTH EDISON CO. V. MONTANA   453 U.S. 609 (1981)

Justice Marshall

Montana, like many other states, imposes a severance tax on mineral production in the state. In this appeal, we consider whether the tax Montana levies on each ton of coal mined in the state . . . violates the Commerce and Supremacy Clauses of the United States Constitution.

Buried beneath Montana are large deposits of low-sulphur coal, most of it on federal land. Since 1921, Montana has imposed a severance tax on the output of Montana coal mines, including coal mined on federal land. After commissioning a study of coal production taxes in 1974. . . . the Montana Legislature enacted the tax schedule at issue in this case. . . . The tax is levied at varying rates depending on the value, energy content, and method of extraction of the coal, and may equal, at a maximum, 30 percent of the "contract sales price." Under the terms of a 1976 amendment to the Montana Constitution, after December 31, 1979, at least 50 percent of the revenues generated by the tax must be paid into a permanent trust fund, the principal of which may be appropriated only by a vote of three fourths of the members of each house of the legislature. . . .

Appellants, 4 Montana coal producers and 11 of their out-of-state utility company customers, filed these suits in Montana state court in 1978. They sought refunds of over $5.4 million in severance taxes paid under protest, a declaration that the tax is invalid under the Supremacy and Commerce Clauses, and an injunction against further collection of the tax. Without receiving any evidence, the court upheld the tax and dismissed the complaints.

On appeal, the Montana Supreme Court affirmed the judgment of the trial court. . . . [T]he Montana court held, as a matter of law, that the tax survives scrutiny under the four-part test articulated by this Court in *Complete Auto Transit, Inc.* v. *Brady,* 430 U.S. 274 (1977). The Montana court also rejected appellants' Supremacy Clause challenge, concluding that appellants had failed to show that the Montana tax conflicts with any federal statute.

*   *   *   *   *

We agree with appellants that the Montana tax must be evaluated under Complete Auto Transit's four-part test. Under that test, a state tax does not offend the Commerce Clause if it "is applied to an activity with a substantial nexus with the taxing state, is fairly apportioned, does not discriminate against interstate commerce, and is fairly related to services provided by the state." . . .

Appellants do not dispute that the Montana tax satisfies the first two prongs of the Complete Auto Transit test. . . . Appellants do contend, however, that the Montana tax is invalid under the third and fourth prongs of the Complete Auto Transit test.

Appellants assert that the Montana tax "discriminate[s] against interstate commerce" because 90 percent of Montana coal is shipped to other states under contracts that shift the tax burden primarily to non-Montana utility companies and thus to citizens of other states. But the Montana tax is computed at the same rate regardless of the final destination of the coal, and there is no suggestion here that the tax is administered in a manner that departs from this even-handed formula. We are not, therefore, confronted here with the type of differential tax treatment of interstate and intrastate commerce that the Court has found in other "discrimination" cases. . . .

Instead, the gravamen of appellants' claim is that a state tax must be considered discriminatory for purposes of the Commerce Clause if the tax burden is borne primarily by out-of-state consumers. . . .

The premise of our discrimination cases is that "[t]he very purpose of the Commerce Clause was to create an area of free trade among the several states." . . . Consequently, to accept appellants' theory and invalidate the Montana tax solely because most of Montana's coal is shipped across the very state borders that ordinarily are to be considered irrelevant would require a significant and, in our view, unwarranted departure from the rationale of our prior discrimination cases.

Furthermore, appellants' assertion that Montana may not "exploit" its "monopoly" position by exporting tax burdens to other states, cannot rest on a claim that there is need to protect the out-of-state consumers of Montana coal from discriminatory tax treatment. As previously noted, there is no real discrimination in this case; the tax burden is borne according to the amount of coal consumed and not according to any distinction between in-state and out-of-state consumers. Rather, appellants assume that the Commerce Clause gives residents of one state a right of access at "reasonable" prices to resources located in another state that is richly endowed with such resources, without regard to whether and on what terms residents of the resource-rich state have access to the resources. We are not convinced that the Commerce Clause, of its own force, gives the residents of one state the right to control in this fashion the terms of resource development and depletion in a sister state. . . .

In any event, appellants' discrimination theory ultimately collapses into their claim that the Montana tax is invalid under the fourth prong of the Complete Auto Transit test: that the tax is not "fairly related to the services provided by the state." . . . Because appellants concede that Montana may impose *some* severance tax on coal mined in the state, the only remaining foundation for their discrimination theory is a claim that the tax burden borne by the out-of-state consumers of Montana coal is excessive. This is, of course, merely a variant of appellants' assertion that the Montana tax does not satisfy the "fairly related" prong of the Complete Auto Transit test, and it is to this contention that we now turn.

Appellants argue that they are entitled to an opportunity to prove that the amount collected under the Montana tax is not fairly related to the additional costs the state incurs because of coal mining. Thus, appellants' objection is to the *rate* of the Montana tax, and even then, their only complaint is that the *amount* the state receives in taxes far exceeds the *value* of the services provided to the coal mining industry. In objecting to the tax on this ground, appellants may be assuming that the Montana tax is, in fact, intended to reimburse the state for the cost of specific services furnished to the coal mining industry. Alternatively, appellants could be arguing that a state's power to tax an activity connected to interstate commerce cannot exceed the value of the services specifically provided to the activity. Either way, the premise of appellants' argument is invalid. Furthermore, appellants have completely misunderstood the nature of the inquiry under the fourth prong of the Complete Auto Transit test.

The Montana Supreme Court held that the coal severance tax is "imposed for the general support of the government" and we have no reason to question this characterization of the Montana tax as a general revenue tax. . . .

This court has indicated that states have considerable latitude in imposing general revenue taxes. The Court has, for example, consistently rejected that the Due Process Clause of the Fourteenth Amendment stands as a barrier against taxes that are "unreasonable" or "unduly burdensome." . . . Moreover, there is no requirement under the Due Process Clause that the amount of general revenue taxes collected from a particular activity must be reasonably related to the value of the services provided to the activity. Instead, our consistent rule has been:

Nothing is more familiar in taxation than the imposition of a tax upon a class or upon individuals who enjoy no direct benefit from its expenditure, and who are not responsible for the condition to be remedied.

A tax is not an assessment of benefits. It is, as we have said, a means of distributing the burden of the cost of government. The only benefit to which the taxpayer is constitutionally entitled is that derived from his enjoyment of the privileges of living in an organized society, established and safeguarded by the devotion of taxes to public purposes. Any other view would preclude the levying of taxes except as they are used to compensate for the burden on those who pay them, and would involve abandonment of the most fundamental principle of government—that it exists primarily to provide for the common good.

*   *   *   *   *

Furthermore, there can be no question that Montana may constitutionally raise general revenue by imposing a severance tax on coal mined in the state. The entire value of the coal, before transportation, originates in the state, and mining of the coal depletes the resource base and wealth of the state, thereby diminishing a future source of taxes and economic activity. . . . In many respects, a severance tax is like a real property tax, which has never been doubted as a legitimate means of raising revenue by the situs state (quite apart from the right of that or any other state to tax income derived from the use of the property). . . . When, as here, a general revenue tax does not discriminate against interstate commerce and is apportioned to activities occurring within the state, the state

is free to pursue its own fiscal policies, unembarassed by the Constitution, if by the practical operation of a tax the state has exerted its power in relation to opportunities which it has given, to protection which it has afforded, to benefits which it has conferred by the fact of being an orderly, civilized society.

The relevant inquiry under the fourth prong of the Complete Auto Transit test is not, as appellants suggest, the *amount* of the tax or the *value* of the benefits allegedly bestowed as measured by the costs the state incurs on account of the taxpayer's activities. Rather, the test is closely connected to the first prong of the Complete Auto Transit test. Under this threshold test, the interstate business must have a substantial nexus with the state before any tax may be levied on it. . . . Beyond that threshold requirement, the fourth prong of the Complete Auto Transit test imposes the additional limitation that the *measure* of the tax must be reasonably related to the extent of the contact, since it is the activities or presence of the taxpayer in the state that may properly be made to bear a "just share of state tax burden." . . .

Against this background, we have little difficulty concluding that the Montana tax satisfies the fourth prong of the Complete Auto Transit test. The "operating incidence" of the tax is on the mining of coal within Montana. Because it is measured as a percentage of the value of the coal taken, the Montana tax is in "proper proportion" to appellants' activities within the state and, therefore, to their "consequent enjoyment of the opportunities and protections which the state has afforded" in connection with those activities. . . .

When a tax is assessed in proportion to a taxpayer's activities or presence in a state, the taxpayer is shouldering its fair share of supporting the state's provision of "police and fire protection, the benefit of a trained work force, and "the advantages of a civilized society." . . .

We are satisfied that the Montana tax, assessed under a formula that relates the tax liability to the value of appellant coal producers' activities within the state, comports with the requirements of the Complete Auto Transit test. . . .

[The Supreme Court rejected the appellants' Supremacy Clause argument, and the judgment of the Supreme Court of Montana was affirmed.]

Afterword

The *Commonwealth Edison* decision is consistent with the Reagan administration's efforts to shift decision making back to the state and local government levels. The new emphasis on federalism is defended as being both more efficient and more philosophically in keeping with democratic values than is the concentration of authority in Washington, D.C. However, critics fear the rebirth of regional conflicts between the "haves" and the "have-nots." Montana and Wyoming hold about 60 percent of the low-sulfur coal heavily used by middle western utility companies. Given high coal severance taxes in the western states, Detroit Edison Company, for example, expects to pay about $1 billion extra for contracted coal in the 1980s and 90s. Consequently, Congress has been lobbied to place a cap of perhaps 12.5 percent on states' taxes on coal mined from federal lands. However, as is usually the case, the power of the market appears to be asserting itself in the Montana coal industry. At this writing in 1985, a weakened coal market has caused the Montana legislature to consider proposals to provide credits against the severance tax for some new coal contracts. In any event, the coal tax dispute highlights the continuing philosophical and legal dispute between states' rights advocates and those who find a greater probability of justice in enhanced centralized authority.

Questions

1. The majority in *Commonwealth Edison* took the position that the level of taxation is a legislative matter and, therefore, not to be subjected to judicial review. If so, what test is to be employed in determining whether the tax in question unduly burdens interstate commerce?

2. Do the *Commonwealth Edison* decision and the Reagan administration's pressure for increased state and local authority present a threat to the welfare of the nation as a unified, cooperative body?

3. During the 1973 gasoline shortage, Maryland gasoline stations operated by producers or refiners had received, according to a state government survey, preferential treatment over "independent" dealers in obtaining supplies of gasoline. Thereafter, a statute was enacted providing " . . . a producer or refiner of petroleum products (1) may not operate any retail service station within the state, and (2) must extend all 'voluntary allowances' uniformly to all service stations it supplies." Exxon challenged the statute.

   a. What is the essence of Exxon's claim?

   b. Decide the case. See *Exxon Corp.* v. *Governor of Maryland,* 98 S.Ct. 2207 (1978).

4. In the interest of safety an Illinois statute required rear fender mudguards of a special contoured design on trucks using Illinois roadways. The required design was not typical of that in use in the industry and possessed no clearly established safety advantage. Was the statute constitutional? See *Bibb* v. *Navajo Freight Lines, Inc.,* 359 U.S. 520 (1959).

5. In the interest of safety an Iowa statute prohibited the use of 65-foot double-trailer trucks within its borders. Scientific studies revealed that 65-foot doubles were as safe as 55-foot singles (permissible under Iowa law). The State of Iowa argued that the statute promoted safety and reduced road wear by diverting much truck traffic to other states. Consolidated Freightways challenged the statute. Decide. See *Raymond Kassel et al.* v. *Consolidated Freightways Corporation of Delaware,* 101 S.Ct. 1309 (1981).

6.   A New York state statute prohibited the export of milk produced in the state to other states. New York argued that the statute was necessary to avoid milk shortages. Is the statute constitutional? See *H. P. Hood & Sons* v. *DuMond*, 336 U.S. 525 (1949).

The States in "Combat"

The article that follows illustrates many of the issues in the continuing debate over federal versus state regulation of commerce.

A WAR BETWEEN THE STATES: HOME—GROWN U.S. TRADE BARRIERS COSTLY

David R. Francis

The shooting war between the Union and the Confederacy ended in 1865. But something of an "invisible" trade war between states continues today.

According to two University of Houston-University Park economists, the United States of America is not as united a market as many believe. In fact, they calculate that "fantastic numbers" of interstate trade barriers could cost consumers as much as $150 billion a year in higher prices for goods and services.

For instance, one study found more than 1,500 agriculture restrictions on interstate trade in 11 western states alone. Steven G. Craig and Joel Sailors note in a paper done for their school's Center for Public Policy.

Craig admitted that his $150 billion figure is a "rough guesstimate." Since interstate trade is some 15 times as large as international trade, however, the impediments to a unified American trading market are important. Here are some examples:

● State and local governments often give preference to products or services from their own state or town. The usual restriction says local contractors or manufacturers win the bid if their price comes within 5 percent of an out-of-state offer. Since state and local governments purchase around $400 billion of goods and services each year, the preference is costly to taxpayers.

● In the agricultural area, some of the restrictions on interstate trade may be legitimate.

Other restrictions are purely protectionist. For example, since 1967 Texas has not allowed its consumers to eat Florida grapefruit, since Texas maturity standards require that grapefruit must test out at nine parts of sugar to one part acid. Since Florida grapefruit tests out at 7.5 to 1, it is banned from sale in Texas.

Eight states tax imported wine more heavily than wine produced in-state. Or they impose arbitrary licensing, storage, and marketing regulations on imported wine.

● The mobility of professional labor services is sharply restricted through the use of local licensing and certification. One study cited by the two Houston economists found 2,800 state laws affecting more than 7 million workers, including doctors, lawyers, dentists, others in medical professions, and teachers.

Another study calculated that a dentist's income is 12 percent higher than it would be in a free market where professionals could move about without restriction.

● Texas severely restricts insurance sales by out-of-state firms through complicated sets of reserve requirements on firms.

● States have various laws aimed at discouraging competition from out-of-state or foreign banks.

The Supreme Court has stopped some protective measures, invoking the commerce clause of the United States Constitution. For example, it prevented North Carolina from restricting the import of soft drinks bottled out of state with tax and administrative burdens. It blocked Louisiana from attempting to tax oilfield equipment made out of state.

. . . Craig says the Supreme Court set federal interstate trade policy on a case-by-case basis without a clear legislative mandate from Congress.

State barriers have been upheld by the Supreme Court about 50 percent of the time, Craig notes.

* * * * *

But, Craig concludes, "What may be good for one state industry may be bad for the economy as a whole. Congress needs to look at the problem seriously. If we did not have so many of these trade restrictions, the gross national product would expand, and the nation would be better off."

Source: *The Christian Science Monitor*, September 20, 1984, p. 23. © 1984, *The Christian Science Monitor*. Reprinted with permission.

Summary of State and Local Regulation

The visibility and magnitude of federal regulation of business has obscured our bountiful web of state and local regulations. Indeed, state, rather than federal, government is one of America's true growth industries. From 1960 through 1983, federal civilian employment increased slightly more than five fold, while state employment during the same period multiplied more than ten times.[6] Abundant state and local legislation is designed to regulate business behavior. Those regulations fall into three broad categories: (1) controlling entry into business, (2) regulating competition, and (3) preventing consumer fraud.

The states are primarily responsible for regulating the insurance industry and are heavily involved in regulating banking, securities, and liquor sales. Many businesses and professions—from funeral preparations, to barbering, to the practice of medicine—require a license from the state. Public utilities (e.g., gas, electricity, and sewage disposal) are the subject of extensive regulation governing entry, rates, customer service, and virtually the fullness of the companies' activities. All states have some form of public service commission charged with regulating utilities in the public interest. Many states seek to directly enhance competition via antitrust legislation. In the interest of consumer protection many states have passed laws forbidding usury, false advertising, stock fraud, and other practices calculated to harm the consumer.

Local regulation is much less economically significant than state regulation. Local government intervention in business typically involves various licensure requirements. For example, businesses such as bars and theatres often require a local permit to operate. Certain tradespeople such as plumbers, electricians, and builders may be required to gain local (and/or state) occupational licensure to legally engage in their craft. Licensure, it is argued, serves to protect the public from unsafe, unhealthy, and substandard goods and services, but critics contend that the presumed benefits of licensure are exceeded by its costs in increased prices, decreased services, and administrative overhead. It is useful to remember that government planning is frequently unable to anticipate the convoluted repercussions of its policies. For example, it is argued that government licensure policies may paradoxically retard progress toward another laudable government goal—that of racial equity. Temple University economist Walter Williams criticized the impact of some government regulation and licensing:

> The classic case is the taxicab business. . . . In New York City, to own and operate one taxi, you have to buy a license [which costs up to $68,000] that black people can't afford. In Washington [with no such expense], 80 percent of the taxis are owned and operated by blacks.[7]

Can you think of other reasons to help explain the disparity in black ownership of taxis in New York City and Washington? (Many cities are now deregulating their cab industries. In 1984 the Federal Trade Commission charged that taxi regulation in Minneapolis and New Orleans violated federal antitrust laws.)

In 1985, the Supreme Court handed down an important banking industry decision which clearly reaffirms the vitality of state regulation, while perhaps temporarily impeding the advance of the nation's banking giants. In *Northeast Bancorp, Inc.* v. *Board of Governors of the Federal Reserve System*[8] a unanimous Court ruled that states may lawfully join together in regional compacts to regulate banking. A 1982 Massachusetts statute permitted the acquisition of an in-state bank by another New England-based bank so long as the state law in the acquiring bank's principal place of business accorded the same purchasing privileges to Massachusetts banks. Rhode Island and Connecticut passed similar legislation. Those laws were designed to limit bank expansion in the region to New England banks, while closing the door to acquisition by the enormous banks located in New York, California, and the other major commercial centers. Several banks, including Citicorp, challenged certain acquisitions by New England banks arguing, in part, that the regional banking laws were discriminatory in permitting purchases by some banks but not by others. They argued that the state regional banking laws restrained federal power over interstate commerce in violation of the Commerce, Compact (no state may enter an agreement with another state in the absence of congressional approval where that agreement may encroach upon federal supremacy), and Equal Protection clauses of the Constitution. The Court found no constitutional violation. In particular, the Court found a rational basis for the regional banking approach. Justice Rehnquist noted, " . . . the historical fact that our country traditionally has favored widely dispersed control of banking. While many other Western nations are dominated by a handful of centralized banks, we have some 15,000 commercial banks attached to a greater or lesser degree to the communities in which they are located."[9]

Federal law has banned full interstate banking for decades, but many argue that giant aggregations of capital are necessary to remain competitive in today's technologically advanced, international market. Others believe that banking control must remain at the local level in order to protect local interests. The *Northeast Bancorp* decision was, in an immediate sense, a setback for interstate banking interests, but in the next few years the decision may well be seen as a major step forward in consolidating American banking.

In the article that follows, the governor of Arizona offers a glimpse of the regulatory maze in his state and explores some of the options for reform. (The reader should understand that Governor Babbitt's article was published in 1980. Some reforms have been effected since that time, but the general condition of state regulation remains very much as described.)

THE "STATE" OF REGULATORY REFORM

Bruce E. Babbitt

The job of regulatory reform is fairly begun at the federal level—but that is only half the job. We must also intensify parallel efforts at the state and local levels. All around the compass, moreover, the goal is the same: to place increasing reliance on the competitive marketplace as our principal and "natural" regulator.

My own initiation to regulatory reform came when I was elected attorney general of Arizona in 1974. I was confronted at once with the bittersweet task of defending the state regulatory agencies against a tidal wave of complaints, grievances, and litigation brought by members of the public. And more often than not, the aggrieved consumer was right: regulation had itself become the biggest part of the problem. Even more disquieting, these new clients of mine often wanted to solve the problems of regulation by engaging in more of the same—urged on by the regulated occupations or industries. My only recourse was a crash self-education program to learn what it is these agencies do, and why.

What I discovered, of course, was that most of them had been spawned by the New Deal and steeped in post-depression attitudes of pessimism about the free market system. State legislatures, following the example of Congress, assumed that the best response to almost any problem was to set up a government agency to solve it. . . .

Our experience with regulatory reform in Arizona—and I suspect it is typical—suggests that economic regulation tends mostly to benefit those being regulated and that it passes the costs, both needless and substantial, along to the public. . . .

Rate and Entry Regulation

In Arizona, as in many other states, bus and trucking companies are required to have public service certificates granting them monopolies on particular intrastate routes. The regulatory agency then maintains a rate-setting bureaucracy in order to prevent abuse of the monopoly power that the agency created in the first place. This regulatory framework replicates to some extent those found in federal regulation of air transport, trucking, railroads, and buses—where, happily, the controls are now being relaxed.

These monopoly operating certificates are bought and sold for enormous sums at both the state and federal levels—one good measure of the added costs that this type of regulatory scheme imposes on the public. It is governmental regulation pure and simple that creates "value" for an otherwise worthless piece of paper and, in turn, artificially inflates the cost of transportation. For example, several years ago a Tucson firm acquired from the Arizona Corporation Commission a common-carrier certificate allowing it to operate heavy trucks and machinery. But the company never purchased so much as a single truck. It simply leased its certificate to another operator. At the end of the lease period, the certificate holder—still with absolutely no tangible holdings, goodwill, or operating history—sold its "assets" to yet another company for $150,000. All it really had to sell, of course, was that original state-granted monopoly, whose purchase price will be amortized (as was the lease) by higher rates to consumers.

* * * * *

Moreover, monopoly privileges can lead to utterly absurd results. For example, riders who board one major company's buses in Phoenix can be carried *through* but not *to* Flagstaff. The buses stop there to pick up passengers headed out of state, but passengers boarding in Phoenix cannot be allowed to disembark because the company does not have service rights between Phoenix and Flagstaff. For a similar crazy reason, passengers cannot travel from Phoenix to Tuscon on the buses of another major carrier, even though the buses stop in Tucson to discharge travelers from out of state. . . .

So it is more than time for the state legislatures to follow the lead of the U.S. Congress—emulating its actions in air and surface transportation—and move to deregulate intrastate transportation. While estimates differ, it is reasonable to conclude that federal and state deregulation of trucking, buses, and taxis would probably save consumers a cool $6 to $7 billion a year. . . .

Some of the opponents complain that small towns will be the losers—that they will be denied service now required as a condition of certification. They argue that inflated profits on monopoly routes—between Phoenix and Tucson, for example—are necessary in order to subsidize service to the less profitable outlying areas of the state. Yet, all of the available evidence suggests that there is in fact no such cross-subsidization of trucking service and that, for a host of reasons, trucking deregulation is more likely to benefit than harm small communities. . . .

Our efforts in Arizona to deregulate motor carriers have engendered some unlikely alliances. Most of the regulated bus, truck, and taxi companies—the certificate holders, that is—are fighting hard to preserve monopoly regulation, notwithstanding their usual complaints about government interference with private enterprise. . . .

Occupational Licensing
The granting of occupational permits to lawyers, doctors, geologists, surveyors, landscape architects, and myriad other callings is a traditional state function, long justified as a way of guaranteeing quality service and protecting consumers from fraud. A number of recent studies strongly suggest, however, that occupational licensing more generally protects those in the regulated occupation than it does the consumer of the service. Too often, licensing boards use their statutory powers primarily to restrict entry and prevent competition. The economic effect is not to make the market work better but rather to transfer income from the consumer to the service provider. In some instances, occupational licensing boards have simply become the captives of the very professions they are supposed to regulate. . . .

In Arizona . . . the course of instruction for barbers requires a minimum of 1,250 hours of study, more class time than is generally needed to obtain a law degree in most American universities. The 1,250-hour requirement includes no less than 250 hours devoted to such esoteric subjects as bacteriology; the structure of the head, face, and neck; and the various diseases of the skin, hair, and glands. With refreshing candor, the chairman of the state Board of Barber Examiners recently admitted that such regulation was necessary "to protect the barbers." Without such stringent requirements, he added, "anyone can come into the state and become a barber." Barbering, however, is for beginners. Cosmetology—a more sophisticated art—requires 1,800 hours of instruction!

*   *   *   *   *

Some of the most interesting examples that we found involve the Registrar of Contractors, whose regulations embody an elaborate market division scheme. In the first place, specialty contractors are protected from encroachment by general contractors. Because a general contractor's work must involve "more than two unrelated trades," he or she can build a sidewalk or patio wall if it is part of a larger job—like building a house—but not if that is all that is wanted. Moreover, any one type of specialty contractor is protected from competition from other types—and the list is endless. . . .

Even in Arizona, a free market state—or so we are proud to claim—more and more occupational groups are demanding regulatory agencies of their own as shelters from the vicissitudes of competition. My office has recently been flooded with demands that palm tree trimmers be regulated. Now, the trimming of palm trees is a venerable trade in Arizona, usually plied by college students, itinerants, and others who like occasional piecework and are unafraid of heights. In this particular case, the demand for regulation is coming not from those itinerant trimmers but from licensed landscape architects who claim that palm-tree trimming is part of *their* regulatory turf. Landscape architects frequently voice similar complaints—and demand prosecution—against un-licensed entrepreneurs caught planting lawns and trees and doing similar work suitable only for landscape architects. . . . At this point I am happy to report that a Board of Palm Frond Cutters does not appear to be imminent.

Obviously we cannot do away with all occupational licensing. Nor should we. Doctors and lawyers ought to be licensed, and probably security salesmen as well—even if landscape architects should not. Some rules are needed to protect consumer health and safety from the incompetent, but we should be careful not to extend license laws beyond this narrow justification—stringently applied. . . .

Statutory Prohibitions on Competition
Along with rate regulation and occupational licensing, a third major area of needed reform is that of statutory bans on competition. . . .

"Unfair" sales laws—which are . . . a product of the depression—prohibit retailers from selling below some prescribed markup. The minimum markup in Arizona was 12 percent. Their purpose is to protect retailers from competition, "unfair" or otherwise. Whatever validity this idea may have had 40 or 50 years

ago, its time has certainly passed. Government has no business insulating the inefficient from competition by mandating that the consumer pay a higher price. "Unfair" cuts both ways.

In the same vein is the assortment of state laws that prohibit certain businesses and professions from advertising. The landmark case of *Bates* v. *State Bar of Arizona* began while I was attorney general; the U.S. Supreme Court's decision in this case guarantees the right of lawyers to advertise and of consumers to shop for the lowest price. Since *Bates,* we have been able to prevent professional trade organizations from prohibiting advertisements by their members. For example, the State Bar has adopted a new conduct code that prohibits only "unprofessional" advertising.

. . . Until all such laws are rooted out, competition will still be foreclosed and consumers denied the benefits of the lower prices and the greater availability and quality of services that come with increased competitive marketing.

Source: *Regulation* (September/October 1980) pp. 38–41. Reprinted by permission of the American Enterprise Institute. (The author is governor of Arizona.)

More Regulation?

Of course, it is easy and intellectually tidy to call for a reduced state and local regulatory presence in the business community and, indeed, throughout life. Certainly that direction is widely applauded currently and perhaps properly so, but the competing considerations must be carefully weighed. In the article that follows we have a brief history of some states' efforts to deal with the very difficult issue of the proper age at which individuals may buy alcoholic beverages. Here we find that the glow of this particular easing of regulatory strictures dimmed for some states, after a few years of experience with drinking by youths. For example, after raising the drinking age from 18 to 21, accidents resulting in death or injury in Michigan involving young people fell 28 percent, thus sparing an estimated 1,600 youthful drivers in 1979 alone.[10]

At this writing, the federal government has approved legislation designed to impose pressure on all of the states to raise the lawful drinking age to 21. Those states failing to do so would lose a portion of their federal highway funds. The issue provides a vivid example of the conflict between local preferences and the perceived need for nationwide uniformity.

TEENS DENIED BOOZE BY NEW STATE LAWS RESPOND WITH BOOS

William M. Bulkeley

Boston—On Saturday, April 14, the King's Row bar and discotheque, near Kenmore Square in the midst of half a dozen college campuses, was hopping. By 9 P.M. teenagers were lined up outside, huddled against the wall for shelter from the steady drizzle, waiting to get in. Four bouncers were minding the door and five bartenders were hustling drink orders while dancers jammed the floor under a rotating, mirrored ball.

A week later the King's Row was about as lively as a morgue. A bartender, a waitress, and two doormen had been laid off. Seats were easy to find at the circular bar, and waitresses had plenty of time to be solicitous of the few occupied tables. Nobody was dancing.

The King's Row and countless bars like it are suffering from the effects of a new Massachusetts law that went into effect at 2 A.M. on Monday April 16, raising the minimum drinking age to 20 from 18.

Because of the concentration of colleges around Kenmore Square, the bars in the area had been dependent on a youthful crowd, and the change in the law could be disastrous for business. "Business is down more than 50 percent" says Paul Salvi, manager of the King's Row, glumly. . . .

Too Many for Road
The National Highway Traffic Safety Administration notes that auto accidents are the leading cause of death among those under 35, and alcohol is involved in more than half of those fatalities. Studies have shown that road accidents among teenagers increased in Maine and Michigan after the drinking age was lowered. No one yet knows if raising the drinking age will slow the accident rate.

John Moulden, a research psychologist with the highway safety agency, says that teenagers don't seem to drink greater amounts of alcohol than adults, but they have a harder time with it. "They are both learning to drive and learning about drinking," he says.

Schoolteachers and administrators say it's becoming increasingly common to find high school and even junior high school students drunk in class. In fact, one objective of raising the drinking age is to prevent 18-year-olds from buying alcohol for younger students.

* * * * *

Few students in Massachusetts believe the higher drinking age will really prevent them from buying alcohol. "As soon as we get a good pipeline for fake ID's, we'll be back here," says a Massachusetts Institute of Technology freshman. But the ID's—identification cards issued by the state to young people—aren't easy to forge. And the state says the only other proof of age acceptable by a bar or liquor store is a Massachusetts driver's license.

Other students voice the hope that liquor will still flow freely in school dormitories. But colleges around Boston say they are cracking down on underage drinking in dormitories and at school functions. Nor will teenagers be able to head north to New Hampshire to buy liquor much longer: New Hampshire's law raising the drinking age to 20 goes into effect on May 24.

But some observers . . . wonder if raising the drinking age is the right approach. Massachusetts State Senator John Olver, whose Amherst district includes thousands of college students, fears the new law will have negative effects by pushing teenagers into breaking the law and leading to increased drinking in cars. "Social changes have created the increase in drinking. This law won't change that," he says.

To operators of bars, the higher age seems particularly unfair. "People drinking in bars weren't sneaking drinks out to people of a very tender age," says Ronald A. Wysocki, a lobbyist for an association of bar owners. His members, he says, want to raise the age for buying liquor by the bottle while allowing teenagers to continue drinking in bars. The bar owners say that liquor stores will profit at their expense under the new law because teenagers will simply ask older friends to buy bottles for them.

But the angriest objections to the law come from the 250,000 college students in the Boston area and the hundreds of thousands of other 18, and 19-year-olds in the Bay State. "I think it stinks. I've been given the privilege and now

its taken away," complains Dorothy Horner, an 18-year-old freshman at Northeastern University. "How do you think a guy feels if he's old enough to die for his country but isn't old enough to drink in it?" asks Dana Higgins, a 19-year-old Navy machinist's mate. . . .

Source: *The Wall Street Journal*, May 17, 1979, pp. 1 and 40. Reprinted by permission of *The Wall Street Journal*. © Dow Jones & Company, Inc., 1979. All rights reserved.

Afterword

The moment is appropriate to remind ourselves of our central inquiries. Should government regulate business? If so, to what extent, and in what manner? Can we safely rely on the market and ethics to ensure the honorable and effective conduct of business? The article that follows offers an opinion and sets the foundation for the balance of the book where we will review government's very extensive regulatory role.

GOVERNMENT OVERSIGHT NEEDED TO KEEP BUSINESS HONEST, RETIRED MANAGERS SAY

Washington, D.C. (AP)—Nearly three out of four recently retired mid-level managers of large corporations say government regulation is necessary because industry cannot police itself entirely, according to a survey released Sunday.

*   *   *   *   *

The 117-page study, entitled "Corporate Ethics, Illegal Behavior, and Government Regulation: Views of Middle Management," was conducted by Marshall Clinard, sociology professor emeritus at the University of Wisconsin, for the Justice Department's National Institute of Justice.

Clinard based his findings on lengthy interviews with 64 managers who had retired within the past five years from 51 companies on Fortune magazine's listing of the 500 largest companies. The companies included Bendix, Dow Chemical, Firestone Tire & Rubber, General Motors Corp., Lockheed Aircraft Corp., Mobil

Oil Corp., RCA Corp. and Westinghouse. The executives had jobs like manager of assembly operations, regional sales manager or plant manager.

Clinard defined corporate crime as any company action punishable under criminal, civil or administrative law.

*   *   *   *   *

The retired executives were asked, "What do you see as an alternative to government regulations: Can industry police itself?" A majority, 57.2 percent, answered that government is needed and industry cannot police itself. Another 14.1 percent said that, even with industry help, some government regulation is necessary.

When asked whether top management sets the tone for compliance with laws, 92.2 percent said "very much" and 6.3 percent said "some."

The retired managers were asked whether top management knew about legal violations either in advance or afterwards, but before it was detected by the government. Some 71.9 percent said top executives generally did know, 21.9 percent said their superiors knew about some violations, and 6.3 percent said the top executives knew little about them.

Some 69.8 percent said they would report serious unsafe working conditions to the government if the company did nothing about them. But only 23.4 percent said they would report price fixing, 31.7 percent said they would report illegal rebates and kickbacks, and 35.5 percent said they would report illegal foreign payments.

On the reasons for not reporting price-fixing, Clinard quoted the former manager of a steel company's international division as saying, "Price-fixing is none of middle manage-

ment's damn business. If there is a general in charge you do not blow the whistle on him."

The former director of business development for a toiletries company was quoted as saying, "Price-fixing involves money, not people's safety or the national interest."

On kickbacks and rebates, a former auto industry general purchasing agent was quoted as saying, "It is not the government's business. I usually got enough gifts from suppliers to fill the bedroom. I gave them away."

A former division manager in the machinery industry said, "We might lose business if we did not give illegal rebates and kickbacks."

Source: *The Des Moines Register*, May 16, 1983, p. 3T. Reprinted with permission of the copyright holder, The Associated Press.

Chapter Questions

1. This chapter addressed the issue of increased government involvement in regulating business. How do you explain that trend?

2. What are the definitions given in this chapter for positive and negative externalities? For public goods?

3. If we had not experienced the Depression, would government regulation of business be substantially less pervasive than is now the case?

4. As a safety measure, Arizona enacted a statute that limited the length of passenger trains to 14 cars and freight trains to 70 cars. Trains of those lengths and greater were common throughout the United States. The Southern Pacific Railroad challenged the Arizona statute.
   a. What was the legal foundation of the Southern Pacific Claim?
   b. Decide the case. See *Southern Pacific Railroad* v. *Arizona*, 325 U.S. 761 (1945).

5. Oregon enacted a "bottle bill" for the purpose of reducing the problems of litter and solid waste. Under the terms of the statute, retailers of beer and carbonated beverages were required to pay consumers a specified refund on all containers. In turn, distributors were required to accept the containers from the retailers and pay the refund value. Pull-top cans were declared unlawful. American Can challenged the constitutionality of the statute arguing, among other positions, that the impact on interstate commerce outweighed the benefits to the state and that the bill seriously impeded the flow of interstate commerce. Decide. See *American Can Co.* v. *Oregon Liquor Control Commission*, 517 P.2d 691 (Ore. 1973).

6. Governor Babbitt, in his article, "The 'State' of Regulatory Reform," argues that Arizona operating certificates for intrastate bus and truck routes is a regulatory requirement that

"creates 'value' for an otherwise worthless piece of paper and, in turn, artificially inflates the cost of transportation."

    a. Explain Babbitt's position.

    b. Build an argument justifying the licensing of public transportation routes.

7. Many state dental boards decline to recognize licenses granted in other states. Professor Lawrence Shepard studied the effects of that policy on the price of dental services. He concluded:

> Empowered by the state legislatures and aligned with the profession they oversee dental licensing boards inhibit competition through restrictive licensing practices. In the manner of a cartel, most boards have used licensing exams to limit the entry of nonresident practitioners while the number of new dentists trained in their states has also been constrained. This study provides evidence that where regulatory authorities have constructed competitive barriers, dentists systematically raise fees augmenting their earnings. It is estimated that the price of dental services and mean dentist income are between 12 and 15 percent higher in nonreciprocity jurisdictions when other factors are accounted for. Overall, the annual cost of this form of professional control is approximately $700 million. Pending proposals for licensure reform could eliminate these costs while effecting a more efficient geographical distribution of dentists. These conclusions may have broader applicability, given the large number of occupational groups that control the competitive environment in which they operate through state licensing boards.[11]

    a. Why do many states not adopt a policy of reciprocity as to dental licensure?

    b. Should the dental profession be entirely free of licensure requirements? Accountants?

    c. Outline the considerations you believe should be used in deciding which occupations should be licensed.

8. Outline the opposing factors involved in the Massachusetts decision to raise the legal drinking age from age 18 to 20. Do you approve of that decision? Explain.

9. Although the following article is not addressed directly to government regulation of business, it does have clear business implications and it is a topic of special interest to many.

> Raising the legal age for drivers to 18 would save at least 2,000 lives a year, a public health researcher has concluded. If 16- and 17-year-olds were allowed to drive only during the day, the accident death toll would be cut by more than 1,000 annually, said Dr. Leon S. Robertson, of Yale University.
>
> Robertson studied 236,205 fatal automobile crashes in the United States from 1975 to 1977, paying particular attention to the 19,470 crashes involving drivers under 18 years of age.
>
> He said that nearly half of all fatal crashes involving young drivers occurred after 8 P.M. and before 4 A.M. with the peak concentrated in the wee hours of weekends.
>
> "The evidence indicates that if these youngsters weren't driving, at least half of these fatalities, and probably three fourths of them, wouldn't occur," said Robertson, whose study was financed by the Insurance Institute for Highway Safety.
>
> "At least one third of these fatalities involved a single vehicle—a car hitting a tree or a lamp post," Robertson said.
>
> "Studies have found that some measures intended to reduce teen driving accidents actually have produced more accidents," Robertson said.
>
> "The growth in publicly financed high school driver education greatly increased the number of 16- and 17-year-olds licensed without reducing the crashes per licensed driver," he said. "The net result was more crashes.
>
> "In Connecticut, when high school driver education was eliminated from nine school districts in 1976, 75 percent of 16- and 17-year-olds who would have been expected to be licensed if driver education had been continued waited until they were 18 or older to obtain a license.
>
> "As a consequence of there being fewer drivers, there was a commensurate reduction in numbers of crashes involving 16- and 17-year-olds," Robertson said. "If young people didn't have driver's

licenses or had licenses that permit daytime driving only, it is likely that few would drive illegally," Robertson said.

In the fatal accidents he studied, very few involved drivers without licenses or with suspended licenses, especially among younger drivers.

"Young people have difficulty obtaining automobiles," he said. "Their parents won't let them have the family car if they were not licensed or if they wanted to drive during hours when it was illegal.

"I suspect many parents would welcome such restrictions."[12]

Should the states tighten their driving regulations for the young in the interests of increased safety? Explain.

10. The following excerpt is from a recent article criticizing local and state regulations designed to stem growth.

The growth control and environmental movements have had a very favorable press, stressing the widespread benefits they can achieve by protecting the quality of our common environment against the onslaught of the bulldozer.

A closer look at how the growth control and environmental coalition operates in local controversies shows that its effects are far less benign. It has made a clear and substantial contribution to the escalation of new home prices, yet its success in discouraging home building has failed to produce important environmental benefits for the public at large. Instead, it has protected the environmental, social, and economic advantages of *established* suburban residents who live near land that could be used for new housing.[13]

   a. What are the opposing factors in weighing a no-growth policy?
   b. Should a state or locality be permitted to enact such a policy? Explain.

11. The preponderant government regulatory thrust is currently at the federal level. Should we shift that emphasis to the state and local levels? Explain.

12. In the "Government Oversight" article, a majority of the retired executives surveyed felt that "industry cannot police itself entirely."

   a. In your judgment, which conditions or forces, if any, prevent effective industry self-regulation?
   b. The executives were much less willing to report price-fixing violations than unsafe working conditions. Do you agree that, in general, a manager should not report price-fixing to the government? Explain.

13. A San Francisco law bans smoking in many public places and requires employers to establish smoking and nonsmoking areas satisfactory to employees.

   a. Do you favor the San Francisco law? Explain.
   b. Should the federal government enact similar legislation? Explain.
   c. Why might such laws be to the advantage of much of the business community?

14. The public mass transit authority (SAMTA) in San Antonio, Texas, had been receiving substantial federal aid. In 1979, the Wage and Hour Administration of the Department of Labor took the position that SAMTA, although a local agency, was subject to the federal minimum-wage and overtime requirements of the Fair Labor Standards Act (FLSA). In *National League of Cities* v. *Usery,* 426 U.S. 833 (1976), the Supreme Court had held that the Commerce Clause does not accord Congress the power to enforce those requirements against the states "in areas of traditional government functions." The district court in Texas held that municipal ownership and operation of a mass transit system is a "traditional government function," and, therefore, SAMTA was exempt from the FLSA minimum-wage and overtime requirements. The case was appealed to the U.S. Supreme Court. Decide. See *Garcia* v. *San Antonio Metropolitan Transit Authority,* 53 *Law Week* 4135 (1985).

15. Alabama's legislature imposed a higher tax on out-of-state insurance companies than on in-state firms. Out-of-state companies could reduce, but not eliminate, the differential by investing in Alabama.
    a. What constitutional objection was raised by the out-of-state firms?
    b. What defense was raised by the state?
    c. Decide. See *Metropolitan Life Ins. Co.* v. *Ward*, 53 *Law Week* 4399 (U.S. S. Ct. 1985).

Notes

1. Karl Schriftgiesser, *Business and the American Government* (Washington, D.C.: Robert B. Luce, 1964), p. 14.

2. Ibid., p. 27.

3. The remarks in this paragraph are drawn, in part, from "Interventionist Government Came to Stay," *Business Week,* September 3, 1979, p. 39.

4. Ibid.

5. 317 U.S. 111 (1942).

6. Table No. 472, "Governmental Employment and Payrolls: 1960 to 1983," *Statistical Abstract of the United States* (Washington, D.C.: U.S. Department of Commerce, 1985), p. 292.

7. "The Black Conservatives," *Newsweek,* March 9, 1981, pp. 23, 30.

8. *Northeast Bancorp., Inc.* v. *Board of Governors of the Federal Reserve System,* 53 *Law Week* 4699 (U.S. S. Ct. 1985).

9. Ibid., p. 4704.

10. "Researcher Finds Accidents Fewer If Drinking Age Reduced," *The Lexington (Kentucky) Leader,* November 4, 1981, p. A–18.

11. Lawrence Shepard, "Licensing Restrictions and the Cost of Dental Care," *The Journal of Law and Economics* XXI, no. 1 (April 1978), pp. 187, 200.

12. Jon Van, "Raise Driving Age to 18, Researcher Says," for the *Chicago Tribune* as reprinted in *The Lexington (Kentucky) Sunday Herald-Leader,* February 1, 1981, p. A-11.

13. Bernard Frieden, "Regulating the American Dream," *Across the Board,* August 1979, p. 67.

7

Administrative Agencies and the Regulatory Process

This chapter is divided into five parts. Parts One through Three discuss the nature and duties of the many federal regulatory agencies. Part Four evaluates the strengths and weaknesses of the federal regulatory process. Part Five explores the business community's methods of dealing with government regulation.

Part One—Introduction to Administrative Agencies

The following reading reflects, in a puckish manner, the concerns of Murray Weidenbaum, former chair of President Reagan's Council of Economic Advisers, regarding the growth of the federal government's regulation of private enterprise. The federal regulatory agencies that Professor Weidenbaum cites are the government's primary vehicles in implementing the regulatory process.

THE PROBLEM OF GOVERNMENT ENCROACHMENT ON U.S. BUSINESS

Murray Weidenbaum

The United States has discovered a new disease called "regulation." It is as prevalent as athlete's foot in a locker room.

The morning alarm rings. John and Mary start another day in what will turn out to be a highly regulated existence.

The alarm clock that awakens them is run by electricity provided by a utility regulated by the Federal Energy Regulatory Commission and by state utility agencies. John then goes to the bathroom, where he uses a mouthwash and other products made by companies regulated by the Food and Drug Administration (FDA). He only mildly loses his temper while trying to open a bottle of aspirin, which has the child-proof cap required by the Consumer Product Safety Commission (CPSC). In the kitchen Mary reaches for a box of cereal containing food processed by a firm subject to the regulations of the United States Department of Agriculture (USDA) and required to label its product under the regulations of the Federal Trade Commission (FTC). John, who is under doctor's orders to limit his calorie intake, uses an artificial sweetener in his coffee. Since the banning of cyclamates by the FDA, he has switched to saccharin, but he is worried because that too is on the FDA's proposed ban list. All that is doing his ulcer no good.

As John and Mary are pulling their car out of the garage, the seat belt buzzer is sounding (courtesy of the National Highway Safety Administration). The car they are driving to work has cost them more than they would like to have paid because it contains a catalytic converter and other expensive devices stipulated by the Environmental Protection Agency (EPA). The car can use only unleaded gasoline (another government requirement). They drive at speeds regulated by state and municipal ordinances and subject to the federally mandated 55-mile-an-hour speed limit.

Mary enters the business office where she works, which is located in a building whose construction was repeatedly delayed before it met the Environmental Protection Agency's regulations and state and local building codes. She was hired after a suit was filed by the Equal Employment Opportunity Commission (EEOC), which had accused the firm of discrimination against women. During the course of the day, Mary provides information about the financial activities of her company to an investigator from the Securities and Exchange Commission (SEC), and she also fills out a variety of statistical forms for the Bureau of Census. In the personnel office she finds that she lost her retirement benefits; the small company in which she is employed recently terminated its pension plan because of the onerous requirements imposed by the Internal Revenue Service and the Department of Labor under the Employee Retirement Income Security Act (ERISA).

John goes to the factory where he works under conditions negotiated by his union (chosen, after a prolonged strike, in an election supervised by the National Labor Relations Board,

or NLRB). The equipment he currently uses in his job is more cumbersome than it used to be, but it was selected in order to meet the requirements of the Occupational Safety and Health Administration (OSHA)—a government agency which could be returning any day for another surprise inspection. He works on materials shipped to his firm by companies under authority granted by government—the Interstate Commerce Commission (ICC, for rail and truck) . . . and the Federal Maritime Commission (for sea).

During their lunch hour, John and Mary negotiated for a mortgage on the house they are buying with financing from a savings and loan association (regulated by the Federal Home Loan Bank Board), with a guarantee (subject to numerous, detailed regulations) by the Federal Housing Administration of the Department of Housing and Urban Development. If they had the time, they would also have liked to visit their commercial bank (regulated by the Federal Reserve System) to obtain a loan for the furniture they will need. But the paperwork requirements—involving truth in lending, equal credit opportunity, and several related credit rulings of the government—will force them to come back the next day.

At home in the evening, John, Mary, and their children watch commercial television, the programming and advertising of which are regulated by the Federal Communications Commission (FCC). Simultaneously, John is cleaning his shotgun (regulated by the Alcohol, Tobacco, and Firearms Bureau of the Treasury Department), and Mary is lighting up a cigarette, whose package label is mandated by the Surgeon General in the Department of Health, Education, and Welfare.

Watching, they are barely aware that they, in turn, are being watched over almost continuously by an imposing number and variety of regulatory agencies.

Source: Murray Weidenbaum, *The Future of Business Regulation*, (New York: AMACOM, 1979), p. 1. Reprinted, by permission of the publisher, from *The Future of Business Regulation*, by Murray L. Weidenbaum, pp. 1–3. © 1979 by AMACOM, a division of American Management Associations, New York. All rights reserved.

The Agencies

That branch of the law that governs the administrative operations of government is *administrative law*. The federal Administrative Procedure Act defines an *agency* as any government unit other than the legislature and the courts. Thus administrative law technically addresses the entire executive branch of government. However, our attention will be directed to the prominent regulatory agencies (Interstate Commerce Commission, Federal Communications Commission, Securities and Exchange Commission, etc.) rather than the various executive departments (Agriculture, Defense, etc.) and nonregulatory, welfare agencies (Social Security Administration, Veterans Administration, and the Public Health Service). While our fundamental concern lies at the federal level, it should be understood that administrative law principles are fully applicable to the conduct of state and local governments. At the local level, planning and zoning boards and property tax assessment appeals boards are examples of administrative agencies. At the state level one might cite public utility commissions and the various state licensure boards for law, medicine, architecture, and the like.

The authority of the federal regulatory agencies falls broadly into three categories.

1. Control of Supply   Several agencies control entry into various economic activities. Historically, the Civil Aeronautics Board (now defunct) reached decisions about the airlines that would be granted operating licenses and the routes they could serve. The Interstate Commerce Commission possessed similar authority as to rail, motor, and water carriers and pipelines. The Federal Communications Commission regulates entry to and use of television and radio broadcasting. As will be discussed later in this chapter, the government is in the midst of various deregulation initiatives that have substantially depreciated the agencies' licensing powers. However, much of that authority, such as the Securities and Exchange Commission's regulation of the investment business, will doubtless persist.

2. Control of Rates   Those federal agencies charged with regulating utilities and carriers (Federal Power Commission, ICC, and CAB) have historically set the prices to be charged for the services offered within their jurisdictions. For example, the consumer facing an interstate change of address found little value in comparison shopping for the least expensive furniture mover because the rates, regulated by the Interstate Commerce Commission, were virtually identical. Government regulation of rates remains common, but the deregulation movement has significantly increased the role of the free market in rate setting.

3. Control of conduct   (*a*) *Information*. A major element of government regulation is simply requiring information. Agencies commonly compel companies to disclose consumer information that would otherwise remain private. For example, warning labels may be mandated. (*b*) *Standards*. Where simply requiring information is deemed inadequate to the public need, the government may establish minimum standards that the private sector must meet. For example, a ladder might be required to safely hold at least a specified weight or workers might lawfully be exposed only to a specified maximum level of radiation. (*c*) *Product banishments*. In those unusual instances where information alone is deemed inadequate to protect the public, products can be banned from the market. The Consumer Product Safety Commission banned the flame retardant Tris (used in children's sleepwear) from the market because of evidence of the product's cancer-causing properties.

The Environmental Protection Agency has extensive authority to alter business behavior in accord with society's interest in minimizing pollution. The Equal Employment Opportunity Commission, in attacking employment discrimination, has been instrumental in altering personnel policies in American business. These agencies and others like them (e.g., the National Labor Relations Board, the Federal Trade Commission, and the Occupational Safety and Health Administration) were specifically established to regulate particular dimensions of business behavior. Other agencies (e.g., ICC, FCC) were established to regulate entire industries, and in doing so they necessarily influence the course of virtually every dimension of those industries' business practices.

In sum, via regulation of supply, rates, and conduct, the grand maze of local, state, and federal regulatory agencies is a significant determinant of the course of American business. The administrative agencies have in some instances largely replaced free market decision making and, in many instances, have acted as supplements to a market taken to be inadequate to the task of fully governing American commerce.

The Agencies and the Larger Government

The various agencies do not fit altogether comfortably into the larger scheme of the federal government. Some agencies are independent regulatory bodies acting as mini-governments with rather broad executive, legislative, and judicial powers. Other agencies are departments of the executive branch (the Food and Drug Administration and the Social Security Administration are elements of the Department of Health and Human Services) and, as such, are inevitably more nearly subject to pressure from the executive authority. For example, the FTC is fully involved in the traditional executive duties of investigation and prosecution, while at the same time it both enacts rules in the legislative manner and conducts trials (hearings) in the judicial mode. On the other hand, the SEC's duties are largely confined to the executive role of supervising the investment securities industry.

The breadth of duties performed by the agencies has provoked a pair of important policy disputes. It is argued that the agencies are undemocratic centers of extraordinary power, in that they perform all the traditional duties of government but are not subject to public review via elections. And many legal challenges to agency conduct have argued that the agencies are in violation of the constitutional requirement of separation of powers. However, the well-settled judicial view is that the various checks and balances on the administrative agencies are sufficient to meet the constitution framers' goals in providing for the separation of government powers. The formal checks and balances will become apparent in this section. (Perhaps the reader can identify certain informal, but nevertheless persuasive, external influences on agency action?)

The Role of Congress

The agencies are the product of congressional legislation. In creating an agency Congress is, in effect, delegating a portion of its authority to that body. Congress may not simply give away the power vested in it by the people. Constitutional safeguards must be met by providing standards to guide the agency in its rule making. However, numerous judicial decisions have established the position that those standards need not be drawn with great precision. Thus the agencies have rather broad mandates within which to operate. Congressional dissatisfaction can, of course, result in retarding or dissolving agency authority. Indeed, the Federal Trade Commission has recently been the subject of just such a pruning.

As a consequence of the *Chadha* decision (see Chapter 5), Congress can no longer use the legislative veto to govern agency conduct. New strategies will doubtless be employed to ensure that the agencies remain accountable to Congress.

The Role of the President

The president, with the advice and consent of the Senate, appoints the administrator or the several commissioners who direct each agency's affairs. Commissioners are appointed in staggered terms, typically of seven years duration. The appointment of commissioners for most of the agencies must reflect an approximate political balance between the two major parties. Commissioners can be removed from office only for dereliction of duty. Despite these procedural buffers between the agencies and the executive branch, the president can inevitably exert considerable political pressure on the agencies' affairs.

The Role of the Courts

Most agency actions are subject to judicial review. Agencies must operate within the bounds of the Constitution and the legislation creating the agency. In general, courts do not inquire into the wisdom of agency decisions. After all, the agencies are created as specialized centers of expertise. The courts, therefore, defer to that expertise, assuming constitutional and legislative standards have been met.

Justifications for the Administrative Agency

Administrative agencies are the day-to-day, operating arm of a vast array of government programs. The government has sought to attack a range of social problems, including that of misconduct in the business community. We have looked at the historical roots of business regulation. That some elements of business subjected society to serious abuse is generally acknowledged. That business itself sought certain regulatory measures is likewise widely accepted. So we can fairly conclude that business was instrumental in the growth of government regulation and, hence, the growth of administrative agencies. Perhaps the point here is to recognize that the agencies that clearly intrude dramatically in all our lives were not born of government's malevolent distaste for business. Rather, with the best of intentions the legislative and executive branches sought to improve the quality of life, and one might powerfully argue that government has been quite successful in that regard.

Clearly, Congress might have taken more direct control of the various regulatory and administrative programs. Wisely it has instead chosen to create what is, in effect, a fourth branch of government. Why did Congress decide to delegate its authority by creating a welter of administrative agencies?

1. As the government gradually assumed a larger regulatory role, it became apparent that Congress could not manage the responsibility on its own. Congress is not in session on the daily basis necessary to attend to regulatory details. Since members of Congress are burdened with heavy work loads, the pragmatics of time dictated the delegation of authority.
2. Similarly, Congress cannot write legislation with the flexibility and breadth necessary to embrace the myriad circumstances altered by changing times. Congress, therefore, delegated to the agencies the task of writing and enforcing the specific rules necessary to fill in and render operative the broad policy guidelines embodied in congressional legislation.
3. Congress also displayed rare wisdom in acknowledging its own deficiencies as to technical expertise. Life has grown increasingly complex. The duties of agencies such as the Nuclear Regulatory Commission, the Environmental Protection Agency, and the Federal Reserve Board require detailed, specialized knowledge. Congress, as a policymaking body, is not well suited to technical fine tuning.
4. The dual constraints of time and expertise likewise prevent the court system from assuming a greater proportion of the regulatory burden. Therefore, many agencies conduct their own ''trial-level'' hearings.

Questions

1. The phrase *government regulation* embraces many functions. Define it.
2. For a number of years, the Federal Trade Commission has sought to establish rules regulating ''children's advertising.'' Regardless of your personal point of view, make the argument that the issue is more appropriately one for Congress than for the FTC.
3. Is the federal regulatory process limited in its goals to the correction of market failures? Should it be so limited?
4. Scholar Neil Jacoby commenting on business' alleged ability to control government:

    There is also abundant evidence that during the 1960s and early 1970s, corporate businesses were generally unable to bend federal administrative agencies to their will—contrary to the popular notion that they have ''captured'' those agencies.

    Today it (business) is relatively less influential than ever. Far from being excessive, it may be too weak to maintain a vibrant market economy over the long run.[1]

    a. Has business ''captured'' the regulatory process?
    b. Is business relatively less powerful in relation to the government than was the case during the 19th century?
    c. Is government regulation a force of such magnitude as to threaten the viability of our market system?

5. Scholar James Q. Wilson has said: "All democratic regimes tend to shift resources from the private to the public sector and to enlarge the size of the administrative component of government." . . .[2]
    a. Is this so?
    b. Explain.
6. Scholar George Stigler asked: What benefits can a state provide to an industry?[3] Answer Stigler's inquiry.
7. Does the real origin of government regulation of business lie in the citizen's fear? That is, do the people consider the market too risky and, therefore, opt for a system that affords them some protection from economic loss?
8. Have we reason for concern because the federal agencies have become a fourth branch of government not directly accountable to the public via the electoral process?
9. Do federal agencies perform executive, legislative, and judicial functions to such an extent that they conflict with the constitutional dictate of separation of powers between the three branches? Explain.

Part Two—Summary of The Administrative Process

Law students should acquire some understanding of the variety of tasks undertaken by the administrative agencies and the procedures by which those tasks are accomplished. The administrative process is, not surprisingly, quite detailed. Administrative law seeks to govern that process in a manner in keeping with the general welfare and constitutional safeguards. The tasks undertaken and the procedures followed differ from agency to agency. Administrative law itself has become a complex, specialized discipline with a vast reservoir of rules and court decisions. What follows is a brief outline of the administrative process and administrative law.[4] It is important to remember that agency duties include the full spectrum of government activities, embracing quasi-legislative (rule-making), quasi-judicial (adjudicatory) and executive functions.

Information Gathering

The success of setting rates, managing government property, preventing fraud, protecting the environment, and so on is substantially dependent on the quality of information the agency is able to acquire. For example, in seeking to maintain safe workplaces, the Occupational Safety and Health Administration (OSHA) conducts on-site inspections, along with other information-gathering procedures. Congress has conferred broad investigatory powers on the agencies, but constitutional and statutory safeguards prevent agencies from abusing their authority. In tasks such as developing rules, supervising regulated industries, and prosecuting wrongdoers, information is required for appropriate agency action.

Informal Agency Action

Procedural flexibility is central to the success of administrative agency conduct. While formal proceedings such as rulemaking and adjudication achieve greater visibility, a large portion of agency business is conducted on an informal basis of negotiation and day-to-day bureaucratic decision making. For example, each year the Internal Revenue Service engages more than 100 million taxpayers in the process of settling accounts with the government. For most of those taxpayers the procedure remains entirely informal. In a like manner various government agencies process millions of applications and claims each year (e.g., applications for citizen band radio licenses). Another critical, informal role played by many agencies is that of protecting the public with testing and inspection procedures. (The Food and Drug Administration prefers to keep unhealthy products off the market rather than being compelled to take formal, adjudicatory action after the fact). Likewise most agencies offer informal advice, both in response to requests and on their own initiative, to explain agency policy and positions. For example, each year the FTC receives several hundred inquiries regarding the legal sufficiency of warning labels on various potentially dangerous products. Supervisory duties, including most notably the very active and close attention given to the banking industry, are a further illustration of informal agency duties. Finally, the agencies, as required by the Administrative Procedure Act, seek to reach informal, negotiated settlements of cases otherwise bound for administrative adjudication.

Rule Making

A major portion of the typical agency's activities are legislative in nature. That is, the agencies adopt rules that often touch the lives of millions and are, in their effect, the equivalent of laws. Acting thus in a quasi-legislative manner, agencies enact three types of rules: (1) *Procedural rules* delineate the agency's internal operating structure and methods. (2) *Interpretive rules* offer the agency's view of the meaning of statutes governing the agency's action. Via both informal policy statements and formal guidelines based on open hearings, the agency seeks to clarify for interested parties the meaning of statutory language that is often very broadly drawn. Interpretive rules do not have the force of law, but they are important expressions of opinion as to what the governing legislation requires. The Internal Revenue Service regulations are an example of interpretive rules. (3) *Legislative rules* are policy expressions having the effect of law. The agency is exercising the lawmaking function delegated to it by the legislature. Rate setting is a particularly important agency legislative function. The Federal Trade Commission rules providing for a cooling-off period of three business days within which the buyer may cancel door-to-door sales contracts is an example of agency lawmaking that significantly affects business behavior.[5]

A rule can be generated at the agency's own initiative or as a response to public petition. Commonly, as it draws a rule, the agency informally seeks advice from appropriate sources (although it need not do so). After preparing the rule, the agency is typically required by statute to offer a reasonable opportunity for public comment. A formal hearing is not necessary. The final rule is then published in the *Federal Register* (a daily publication of all federal rules, regulations, and orders) and later codified in the Code of Federal Regulations.

Adjudication

Although informal procedures such as settlements are preferred, agencies commonly must turn to judicial proceedings to enforce agency duties. Administrative hearings touch the breadth of American life in the form of thousands of judicial-like hearings annually. Indeed, administrative hearings are equal in significance and much superior in numbers to all federal court trials each year. Many issues facing agencies could properly be resolved either in the rule making or in the adjudicatory format. The decision lies within the agency's discretion (subject to judicial review) and is based on the nature of the task involved, as well as fairness to the affected parties. In general, adjudication involves either a trial, in which a firm or individual is charged with a violation, or a proceeding to set rates or confer benefits (e.g., a license). For example, when it was the policy of the Federal Power Commission to set the natural gas rates of individual companies, the decisions had to be made on the basis of individual hearings (quasi-judicial). However, when the commission turned to fixing rates on a geographic basis—the Rocky Mountain area—it was able to proceed on a rule making basis (quasi-legislative).[6]

Should an administrative hearing prove necessary, the process is, in general terms, as described in the next paragraphs.

Typically an investigation is conducted and, if the facts merit, a complaint may be filed. Or the agency may instead submit the proposed complaint to the respondent first in an effort to reach a settlement via a *consent order,* in which the party being investigated agrees to steps suitable to the agency but under which the respondent makes no admission of guilt (thus retarding the likelihood of subsequent civil liability). If a formal complaint is filed, the respondent may file an answer, and the parties would engage in prehearing discovery proceedings.

After the complaint is filed the agency will, as required by the Administrative Procedure Act, seek to settle the dispute. If evidence of a violation exists, the case may be disposed of via a consent order. If a settlement is not forthcoming, the case goes forward much in the manner of a civil trial. Of course, a settlement is welcomed throughout the proceeding. The case is heard by an administrative law judge. The respondent may be represented by counsel. Parties have the right to present their cases, cross examine, file motions, raise objections, and so on. However, they do not have the right to a jury trial.

The hearing examiner (judge) decides all questions of law and fact, and then issues a decision. In general, that decision is final unless appealed to the agency. Internal agency review may be conducted by intermediate reviewing boards or by the full commission, or both. After exhausting opportunities for review within the agency, appeal may be taken to the appropriate federal court of appeals.

Judicial Review

An individual aggrieved by an act or decision of an agency may bring a challenge in court. Perhaps the major constraint on agency power is the threat of judicial review. However, the sheer bulk of agency activities means that only a very small portion of those activities will receive judicial scrutiny. Indeed, on technical grounds (as when the appealing party does not have standing to sue) many appeals of agency actions may be denied. However, assuming those procedural hurdles are scaled and review is granted, the question becomes that of the scope of judicial review. Into which issues will the court inquire? Historically the courts have taken a rather narrow approach to judicial review. Two common sense considerations supported that restrained judicial stance. The first is that of deference to the presumed expertise of the administrative agencies. The jurists, being generalists in the field of law, have been reluctant to overrule the judgment of specialists specifically chosen to regulate within their area of expertise. Second, very crowded judicial calendars act as a natural brake on activist judicial review. For those reasons, judges have traditionally disposed of administrative law cases in an expeditious manner, by readily sustaining the judgment of the agency. Of course, the courts have overruled the agencies when appropriate. Indeed, of late one sees evidence of a firmer judicial role.

Not surprisingly, judicial review of agency decisions raises a variety of technical, esoteric issues of law. Those issues differ in part depending on whether the court is reviewing an agency's rule-making function or its adjudicatory function. Cases turn upon questions such as these:

1. Does the legislature's delegation of authority meet constitutional requirements?
2. Has the agency exceeded the authority granted by the enabling legislation?
3. Has the appealing party exhausted all the available administrative remedies?
4. Are the agency's findings of fact supported by substantial evidence in the record as a whole?

These issues are close to the heart of the administrative law practitioner, but their exploration is not necessary to the layperson's understanding of the larger regulatory process. The case that follows will be our only consideration of the formalities of judicial review. This appeal from a Federal Communications Commission adjudication sheds some light on the agency regulatory process and judicial review, but much more importantly the case raises fundamental questions regarding freedom of speech in a technologically advanced society.

F. C. C. V. PACIFICA FOUNDATION   98 S.Ct. 3026 (1978)

Justice Stevens

This case requires that we decide whether the Federal Communications Commission has any power to regulate a radio broadcast that is indecent but not obscene.

A satiric humorist named George Carlin recorded a 12-minute monologue entitled "Filthy Words" before a live audience in a California theater. He began by referring to his thoughts about "the words you can't say on the public, ah, airwaves, um, the ones you definitely wouldn't say, ever." He proceeded to list those words and repeat them over and over again in a variety of colloquialisms. The transcript of the recording . . . indicates frequent laughter from the audience.

At about 2 o'clock in the afternoon on Tuesday, October 30, 1973, a New York radio station, owned by respondent Pacifica Foundation, broadcast the "Filthy Words" monologue. A few weeks later a man, who stated that he had heard the broadcast while driving with his young son, wrote a letter complaining to the commission. He stated that, although he could perhaps understand the "record's being sold for private use, I certainly cannot understand the broadcast of same over the air that, supposedly, you control."

The complaint was forwarded to the station for comment. In its response, Pacifica explained that the monologue had been played during a program about contemporary society's attitude toward language and that, immediately before its broadcast, listeners had been advised that it included "sensitive language which might be regarded as offensive to some." Pacifica characterized George Carlin as a "significant social satirist" who "like Twain and Sahl before him, examines the language of ordinary people. . . . Carlin is not mouthing obscenities, he is merely using words to satirize as harmless and essentially silly our attitudes toward those words." Pacifica stated that it was not aware of any other complaints about the broadcast.

On February 21, 1975, the commission issued a declaratory order granting the complaint and holding that Pacifica "could have been the subject of administrative sanctions." . . . The Commission did not impose formal sanctions, but it did state that the order would be "associated with the station's license file, and in the event that subsequent complaints are received, the commission will then decide whether it should utilize any of the available sanctions it has been granted by Congress."

* * * * *

[T]he Commission concluded that certain words depicted sexual and excretory activities in a patently offensive manner, noted that they "were broadcast at a time when children were undoubtedly in the audiences (i.e., in the early afternoon)" and that the prerecorded language, with these offensive words "repeated over and over," was "deliberately broadcast." . . .

In summary, the commission stated: "We therefore hold that the language as broadcast was indecent and prohibited." . . .

The United States Court of Appeals for the District of Columbia Circuit reversed, with each of the three judges on the panel writing separately. . . .

Judge Tamm concluded that the order represented censorship and was expressly prohibited by ¶ 326 of the Communications Act. Alternatively, Judge Tamm read the commission opinion as the functional equivalent of a rule and concluded that it was "overbroad." . . .

Chief Judge Bazelon's concurrence rested on the Constitution. He was persuaded that ¶ 326's prohibition against censorship is inapplicable to broadcasts forbidden by ¶ 1464 (prohibiting "obscene, indecent, or profane language by means of radio communications"). However, he concluded that ¶ 1464 must be narrowly construed to cover only language that is obscene or otherwise unprotected by the First Amendment. . . .

Judge Leventhal, in dissent, stated that the only issue was whether the commission could regulate the language "as broadcast." . . .

Emphasizing the interest in protecting children, not only from exposure to indecent language, but also from exposure to the idea that such language has official approval, . . . he concluded that the commission had correctly condemned the daytime broadcast as indecent.

Having granted the commission's petition for certiorari, . . . we must decide: (1) whether the scope of judicial review encompasses more than the Commission's determination that the monologue was indecent "as broadcast"; (2) whether the Commission's order was a form of censorship forbidden by ¶ 326; (3) whether the broadcast was indecent within the meaning of ¶ 1464; and (4) whether the order violates the First Amendment of the United States Constitution.

(I)

The general statements in the Commission's memorandum opinion do not change the character of its order. Its action was an adjudication. . . . It did not purport to engage in formal rule making or in the promulgation of any regulations. The order "was issued in a specific factual context"; questions concerning possible action in other contexts were expressly reserved for the future. The specific holding was carefully confined to the monologue "as broadcast." . . .

(II)

The relevant statutory questions are whether the commission's action is forbidden "censorship" within the meaning of ¶ 326 and whether speech that concededly is not obscene may be restricted as "indecent" under the authority of ¶ 1464. . . .

* * * * *

The prohibition against censorship unequivocally denies the commission any power to edit proposed broadcasts in advance and to excise material considered inappropriate for the airwaves. The prohibition, however, has never been construed to deny the commission the power to review the content of completed broadcasts in the performance of its regulatory duties.

* * * * *

Entirely apart from the fact that the subsequent review of program content is not the sort of censorship at which the statue was directed, its history makes it perfectly clear that it was not intended to limit the commission's power to regulate the broadcast of obscene, indecent, or profane language. A single section of the (Radio Act of 1927) is the source of both the anticensorship provision and the commission's authority to impose sanctions for the broadcast of indecent or obscene language. Quite plainly, Congress intended to give meaning to both provisions. Respect for that intent requires that the censorship language be read as inapplicable to the prohibition on broadcasting obscene, indecent, or profane language.

We conclude, therefore, that ¶ 326 does not limit the Commission's authority to impose sanctions on licensees who engage in obscene, indecent, or profane broadcasting.

(III)

The only other statutory question presented by this case is whether the afternoon broadcast of the "Filthy Words" monologue was indecent within the meaning of ¶ 1464. . . .

The commission identified several words that referred to excretory or sexual activities or organs, stated that the repetitive, deliberate use of those words in an afternoon broadcast when children are in the audience was patently offensive and held that the broadcast was indecent. Pacifica takes issue with the commission's definition of indecency, but does not dispute the commission's preliminary determination that each of the components of its definition was present. Specifically, Pacifica does not quarrel with the conclusion that this afternoon broadcast was patently offensive. Pacifica's claim that the broadcast was not indecent within the meaning of the statute rests entirely on the absence of prurient appeal.

The plain language of the statute does not support Pacifica's argument. The words "obscene, indecent, or profane" are written in the disjunctive, implying that each has a separate meaning. Prurient appeal is an element of the obscene, but the normal definition of "indecent" merely refers to nonconformance with accepted standards of morality.

* * * * *

Because neither our prior decisions nor the language or history of ¶ 1464 supports the conclusion that prurient appeal is an essential component of indecent language, we reject Pacifica's construction of the statute. When that construction is put to one side, there is no basis for disagreeing with the commission's conclusion that indecent language was used in this broadcast.

(IV)

Pacifica makes two constitutional attacks on the Commission's order. First, it argues that the commission's construction of the statutory language broadly encompasses so much constitutionally protected speech that reversal is required even if Pacifica's broadcast of the "Filthy Words" monologue is not itself protected by the First Amendment. Second, Pacifica argues that inasmuch as the recording is not obscene, the Constitution forbids any abridgment of the right to broadcast it on the radio.

A

The first argument fails because our review is limited to the question whether the commission has the authority to proscribe this particular broadcast. As the commission itself emphasized, its order was "issued in a specific factual context.". . .

That approach is appropriate for courts as well as the commission when regulation of indecency is at stake, for indecency is largely a function of context—it cannot be adequately judged in the abstract.

*   *   *   *   *

It is true that the commission's order may lead some broadcasters to censor themselves. At most, however, the commission's definition of indecency will deter only the broadcasting of patently offensive references to excretory and sexual organs and activities. While some of these references may be protected, they surely lie at the periphery of First Amendment concern. . . .

B

When the issue is narrowed to the facts of this case, the question is whether the First Amendment denies government any power to restrict the public broadcast of indecent language in any circumstances. For if the government has any such power, this was an appropriate occasion for its exercise.

The words of the Carlin monologue are unquestionably "speech" within the meaning of the First Amendment. It is equally clear that the commission's objections to the broadcast were based in part on its content. The order must therefore fall if, as Pacifica argues, the First Amendment prohibits all governmental regulation that depends on the content of speech. Our past cases demonstrate, however, that no such absolute rule is mandated by the Constitution.

The classic exposition of the proposition that both the content and the context of speech are critical elements of First Amendment analysis is Mr. Justice Holmes's statement. . . .

We admit that in many places and in ordinary times the defendants in saying all that was said in the circular would have been within their constitutional rights. But the character of every act depends upon the circumstances in which it is done. . . . The most stringent protection of free speech would not protect a man in falsely shouting fire in a theatre and causing a panic. It does not even protect a man from an injunction against uttering words that may have all the effect of force. . . . The question in every case is whether the words used are used in such circumstances and are of such a nature as to create a clear and present danger that they will bring about the substantive evils that Congress has a right to prevent.

Other distinctions based on content have been approved. . . . The government may forbid speech calculated to provoke a fight. . . . It may pay heed to the "common sense differences between commercial speech and other varieties." . . . It may treat libels against private citizens more severely than libels against public officials. . . . Obscenity may be wholly prohibited. . . .

The question in this case is whether a broadcast of patently offensive words dealing with sex and excretion may be regulated because of its content. Obscene materials have been denied the protection of the First Amendment because their content is so offensive to contemporary moral standards. . . . But the fact that society may find speech offensive is not a sufficient reason for suppressing it. Indeed, if it is the speaker's opinion that gives offense, that consequence is a reason for according it constitutional protection. For it is a central tenet of the First Amendment that the government must remain neutral in the marketplace of ideas. If there were any reason to believe that the commission's characterization of the Carlin monologue as offensive could be traced to its political content—or even to the fact that it satirized contemporary attitudes about four-letter words—First Amendment protection might be required. But that is simply not this case. These words offend for the same reasons that obscenity offends. . . .

* * * * *

In this case it is undisputed that the content of Pacifica's broadcast was "vulgar," "offensive," and "shocking." Because content of that character is not entitled to absolute constitutional protection under all circumstances, we must consider its context in order to determine whether the commission's action was constitutionally permissible.

C

We have long recognized that each medium of expression presents special First Amendment problems. . . . And of all forms of communication, it is broadcasting that has received the most limited First Amendment protection. . . . The reasons for (that distinction) are complex, but two have relevance to the present case. First, the broadcast media have established a uniquely pervasive presence in the lives of all Americans. Patently offensive, indecent material presented over the airwaves confronts the citizen, not only in public, but also in the privacy of the home, where the individual's right to be left alone plainly outweighs the First Amendment rights of an intruder. . . . Because the broadcast audience is constantly tuning in and out, prior warnings cannot completely protect the listener or viewer from unexpected program content . . . .

Second, broadcasting is uniquely accessible to children, even those too young to read. . . .

It is appropriate, in conclusion, to emphasize the narrowness of our holding. This case does not involve a two-way radio conversation between a cab driver and a dispatcher, or a telecast of an Elizabethan comedy. We have not decided that an occasional expletive in either setting would justify any sanction or, indeed, that this broadcast would justify a criminal prosecution. The commission's decision rested entirely on a nuisance rationale under which context is all-important. The concept requires consideration of a host of variables. The time of day was emphasized by the commission. The content of the program in which the language is used will also affect the composition of the audience, and differences between radio, television, and perhaps closed-circuit transmissions, may also be relevent. . . .

The judgment of the court of appeals is reversed.

(Omitted are the Appendix containing a transcript of the "Filthy Words" monologue as well as the concurring opinions of Justices Powell and Blackmun and the dissenting opinions of Justices Brennan, Marshall, Stewart, and White.)

Questions

1. Why was the question of whether the Federal Communication Commission's decision constituted adjudication or rule making significant to the subsequent judicial appeals? Explain the Supreme Court's resolution of that issue.
2. What is "prurient appeal"?
3. Are you persuaded by the Court's distinction between "obscene" language and "indecent" language? Explain.
4. Why was the commission's action not considered censorship?
5. Do children of all ages require the same degree of FCC protection?
6. At what hour, if any, might a broadcaster legitimately conclude that the percentage of children in the audience is sufficiently small as to no longer require freedom from indecent language? Explain.
7. The *Pacifica* decision is explicitly limited to the facts of the case. But the Court conceded that the decision might lead to some self-censorship. "At most, however, the commission's definition of indecency will deter only the broadcasting of patently offensive references to excretory and sexual organs and activities." Do you agree that the commission's position will cast only a very limited chill over broadcasting? Explain.
8. What is the significance of the distinction the Court draws between the content and the context of the speech in question?
9. Should the Court adopt the Pacifica view that the First Amendment prohibits all government regulation that depends on the content of the speech? Explain.
10. Would a rock tune making occasional reference to sexual and excretory expletives and aired at five P.M. on an FM radio station fall within the doctrine suggested in *Pacifica?* Explain.
11. Does this decision constitute a threat to your conception of freedom of speech? Explain.
12. Is any group, however well qualified, capable of specifying national standards of broadcasting decency? Explain.
13. Develop the argument that rule making is preferable to litigation as a means of settling public policy issues.

Part Three—An Example: The Food and Drug Administration

Having achieved an overview of the administrative process generally, it should now be helpful to take a closer look at a single agency.

The Food and Drug Administration, a division of the Department of Health and Human Services, is responsible for protecting the public from dangerous food, drugs, and cosmetics and for ensuring the effectiveness of drugs. Our inquiry will be limited largely to those situations in which the FDA governs the entry of new products into the market and in which the agency recalls products from the market that fail to meet government standards (on grounds of mislabeling, subpotency, etc.).

Food and Drug Administration

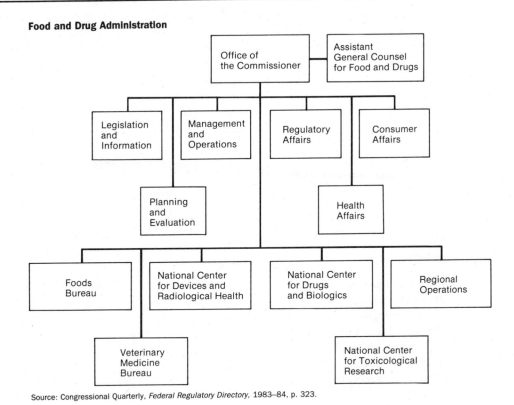

Source: Congressional Quarterly, *Federal Regulatory Directory,* 1983–84, p. 323.

History of the FDA

Today's FDA had its roots in the Bureau of Chemistry in the Department of Agriculture beginning in the 1880s. Consumer abuse of a magnitude that would today generate outrage was commonplace around the turn of the century. For example, adulterated, dangerous, worthless, sometimes habit-forming patent medicines, sold as miracle cures, constituted a significant health hazard. The muckraking literature of the day (e.g., Upton Sinclair's *The Jungle,* an expose of unsanitary conditions in the meatpacking industry) and the increasing support of the American Medical Association and various industry trade associations led Congress in 1906 to enact the Food and Drug Act. In essence the act prohibited the adulteration and misbranding of foods and drugs under federal jurisdiction. The legislation had been encouraged by the colorful tactics of Dr. Harvey Wiley, head of the Bureau of Chemistry, who formed what he called a "poison squad"—a group of 12 volunteers who ate meals laced with common preservatives of the era (borax, boric acid, formaldehyde, sulfurous acids, and others) and then Wiley submitted the results to Congress.[7]

Weaknesses in the 1906 law generated appeals for further legislation. In 1937 a drug manufacturer released a new sulfa drug without benefit of toxicity tests. The first 40 gallons of "Elixir Sulfanilamide-Massengill" caused more than 100 deaths before its removal from the market.[8] Soon thereafter Congress approved the Food, Drug, and Cosmetics Act of 1938 which, among other requirements, prevented the marketing of new drugs until their safety was established and authorized the new FDA to remove from the market drugs found to be hazardous.

The final major piece of legislation investing the FDA with its current authority was the 1962 Kefauver Drug Amendments Act which, among other provisions, required that the effectiveness of a drug be established by "substantial evidence" before it could lawfully be marketed. Interestingly, passage of the Kefauver Act was likewise secured by a major scandal. Many pregnant women in Europe and Canada who had used the sedative thalidomide gave birth to children with deformed or missing limbs. The drug had been limited to experimental use in the United States. Although the Kefauver Amendment would have had no impact on the thalidomide product, the publicity surrounding that horror was instrumental in passage of the act.

Approval Process

The administrative process by which drugs are evaluated illustrates the general nature of FDA decision making. (The lengthy, expensive nature of that process provoked a thorough regulatory review in keeping with the Reagan Administration's deregulation thrust. At this writing in 1985, major rule changes are in place, and others are being studied.) After a drug or other sponsor has completed the initial screening and animal testing of a new drug, the FDA is petitioned for permission to initiate testing on humans. Thereafter, having secured what it takes to be sufficient evidence as to the safety and efficacy of the drug, the sponsor applies for marketing approval by filing a "New Drug Application." The FDA must respond to the NDA within 180 days. The FDA may issue either an "approval" letter (a safe and effective drug), an "approvable" letter (basically sound but with certain issues to be resolved), or a "not approvable" letter (serious deficiencies). Prior to final approval the FDA and the sponsor negotiate an agreement about the language of the official label directed to doctors and pharmacists and describing the uses of the drug, instructions for use, side effects, and so on. In an interesting departure from the old standards, new drugs may now be admitted to the American market based solely on foreign testing data (when the testing meets FDA standards). The FDA believes that the new standard ensures quality while eliminating the need for testing here on products already tested abroad. Following marketing approval, the marketing company must notify the FDA of any problems associated with the drug. The FDA can also receive information from the public, doctors, medical journals, and any other avenues. If warranted, the FDA may take the necessary steps to remove a drug from the market or make adjustments (e.g., a change in labeling) necessary to protect the public interest.

The FDA continues to suffer from serious deficiencies. Because of funding limitations, the agency is arguably understaffed. Original research must be left to sponsoring companies, with the FDA limiting itself to reviewing those findings. That rather unappealing role has limited recruitment of particularly skilled professionals. The work load can be extreme, since some new drug applications may total 200 volumes in length.

The agency is regularly plagued by allegations that it is either too submissive to the drug industry or that it has taken an unnecessarily adversarial stance toward those being regulated.[9]

The 1985 case of *Heckler* v. *Chaney*[10] offers a novel glimpse both of the drug approval process and of plaintiffs' often strikingly imaginative use of the law. In that case a group of prison inmates had been sentenced to death by lethal injection. They petitioned the Food and Drug Administration alleging that the use of those drugs for that purpose violated the federal Food, Drug, and Cosmetics Act. Their claim, among others, was that the drugs had not been approved for use in human executions. The FDA declined to intervene. The inmates filed suit and after a Court of Appeals decision in their favor, the case reached the Supreme Court. The Court held for the government in finding that agency enforcement decisions are presumed to be immune to judicial review under the Administrative Procedure Act in those instances where agency actions are "committed to agency discretion by law." Here the FDCA, as drafted by Congress, revealed no meaningful standard by which to judge the exercise of discretion. Therefore, it may be assumed that Congress intended the decision making to be left exclusively in the hands of the agency. Not without irony, Justice Rehnquist, speaking for the Court, remarked: "We granted certiorari to review the implausible result that the FDA is required to exercise its enforcement power to ensure that States use only drugs that are 'safe and effective' for human execution."[11]

The article that follows illustrates a more conventional FDA regulatory problem.

FDA INQUIRY INTO CARTER–GLOGAU IS LATEST OF MANY CONFRONTATIONS

Gregory Stricharchuk

In January 1976, the Food and Drug Administration sent a letter to Carter–Glogau Laboratories, a small Arizona drug manufacturer, rebuking the company for marketing an unapproved drug.

In that instance, the company quickly pulled the drug off the market. But since that time, Carter–Glogau and the FDA have clashed repeatedly.

Now, the agency is investigating E-Ferol, a Carter–Glogau product that grabbed headlines two months ago when it was suspected by the FDA of being linked to the deaths of 39 infants across the country.

The FDA has said that E-Ferol, an injectable vitamin E supplement, was introduced without its approval. Carter–Glogau's parent,

Ohio-based Revco D.S. Inc., has replied that the product didn't require such approval because vitamin E is a long-established substance.

But FDA records show that the E–Ferol case is not unique. The disagreements between the agency and Carter–Glogau have focused on the company's marketing of unapproved new drugs and the quality of its products. The records also allege a string of manufacturing abuses at Carter–Glogau that continued almost until the November 1983 introduction of E-Ferol.

The FDA's records, obtained under the Freedom of Information act, say that:

● The agency sent 14 warnings concerning 36 unapproved new drugs to the company between 1976 and 1982. In that time, the FDA made several seizures of drugs produced by the company.

- A routine FDA inspection of Carter–Glogau in 1981 found "severe adverse conditions which impact on the quality of finished drug products."

- In June 1983, the agency considered seeking an injunction to stop the company from making any drugs until it corrected manufacturing deficiencies. But the FDA eventually decided that the violations weren't serious enough to support such an action.

Both Carter–Glogau and Revco refused repeated requests to discuss the FDA's findings and the E-Ferol investigation.

Carter–Glogau was founded in 1953 by its president, Ronald Carter, and a partner. The company makes injectable vitamin preparations, hormones, and other drugs under its own label and private labels. Revco bought the concern in 1979.

Still, Mr. Carter runs "virtually all aspects of the firm's operations, in spite of considerable growth" at the company, an FDA inspection report states. The records also appear to show a chief executive at odds with regulators in Washington.

Mr. Carter has repeatedly taken a firm stand against FDA policies on approving new drugs. In May 1981, for example, he wrote the agency: "We don't interpret the (regulations) as requiring premarket approval of generic copies of drugs which have been marketed for dozens of years. (Mr. Carter did not return numerous calls to his office seeking comment on the FDA records).

In 1979, Carter–Glogau began marketing—without FDA approval—an injectable drug called phenylpropanolamine as an appetite suppressant. The drug had been on the market since the late 1940s to treat nasal congestion. But the FDA said the company hadn't done any scientific studies to show that the drug was safe and effective as a diet aid.

The company, which had marketed the drug with a label that said it could be used for appetite control, discontinued selling the product in May 1980.

At times, the agency has seized new Carter–Glogau drugs that weren't submitted for approval. In June 1981, FDA officials received a federal court's permission to seize 2,379 vials of Carter–Glogau's dalalone, a steroid used to treat swelling, that was distributed by O'Neal Jones & Feldman of St. Louis, the company that later distributed E-Ferol. In the same year, the government made four separate seizures of steroids and female sex hormones produced by Carter–Glogau because the company hadn't received FDA approval to market the products.

The recurring issue of quality control has presented more serious problems, according to FDA records. In 1981, for example, the FDA said the company made a practice of using data from reference books to show that a drug with a similar formula remains stable, rather than conducting its own tests to back the claim.

A January 1983 inspection report says the company's "sterility testing logbook was discontinued" nine months earlier. According to the report, two Carter–Glogau managers apparently thought the other was keeping the log, which lists results of sterility tests by product name, lot number, and the room where a specific drug was packaged.

Maintaining sterile conditions in drug manufacturing is crucial, says Richard C. Nelson, an FDA compliance officer in Los Angeles. Contaminated drugs may have limited effectiveness and pose a danger to patients. "Injectable drugs are easy to formulate," he says, "but lots of companies don't make them because sterilization has to be perfect."

Mr. Carter did respond to some of the agency's rebukes. In February 1983, the agency's records show, he sent the head of the company's quality-validation department to an FDA-sponsored seminar on proper manufacturing practices.

Still, on August 12, 1983, Mr. Carter was sent a "notice of adverse findings" by Thomas L. Sawyer, head of the FDA's compliance branch in Los Angeles. While noting that the company had corrected some earlier problems, the report stated: "We are concerned that subsequent inspections repeatedly have revealed (manufacturing) deficiencies not previously encountered. . . .''

Inspectors wrote that the company didn't have formalized standards for making water for injectable drugs and for washing vials. They also wrote that Carter–Glogau didn't have adequate environmental controls in sterile rooms, including records on the type of organisms and the amount of particles found in the air during drug-filling operations.

Three months later, Carter–Glogau introduced E-Ferol.

The company scored an apparent coup when it became the first drug maker to introduce the intravenous vitamin E solution. Researchers had found that the vitamin helped prevent blindness and other problems that sometimes afflict premature babies as side effects of the extra oxygen they get. Such infants, however, usually don't have enough muscle tissue to withstand repeated injections.

But by January, 11 babies at hospitals in Ohio, Tennessee, and Washington died after treatment with E-Ferol. By April, more deaths suggested a link with the drug, and a recall was started.

FDA officials refuse to answer questions about their investigation of Carter–Glogau, although Mr. Nelson, the FDA compliance officer in Los Angeles, says the company's problems ''weren't commonplace.'' The FDA refuses to compare the frequency of the company's problems with other drug firms.

Meanwhile, four lawsuits totaling almost $100 million have been filed against Carter–Glogau and Revco, claiming that E-Ferol caused the death or illness of four babies. Martin Zeiger, secretary and counsel for Revco, says the company is ''vigorously defending'' all lawsuits over E-Ferol.

Some physicians now suggest that the drug may have provided infants with too much vitamin E. Dr. Frank Bowen, a director of neonatology at Pennsylvania Hospital in Philadelphia who has studied vitamin E since 1978, says his research shows that babies develop infections at dosage levels one fifth that of E-Ferol's. ''There's no question,'' he says, ''that babies could overdose at levels provided by E-Ferol.''

The FDA Reviewed

Both the FDA and the pharmaceutical industry are the subject of ongoing criticism. Former FDA Commissioner Alexander Schmidt admitted that some research laboratories have deliberately falsified test data as to safety.[12] In more general terms, the FDA's own data suggest some deficiencies in protection of the public. In 1982, an FDA examination of 6,410 samples revealed violations of quality or labeling in 1,061 of the drugs.[13] In response to these problems Congress has appropriated additional funds, and the FDA has instituted closer surveillance of drug company testing and reporting. Some drugs have been approved for marketing only on the condition that the drug company agrees to post-approval testing and monitoring.

Even as the FDA has been criticized for lax drug regulation, the agency has been the subject of complaints for imposing regulatory standards so demanding that they can harm consumers and industry. The time and resources necessary to meet FDA standards necessarily restrict the availability of some valuable new drugs. The average new drug is admitted to the British market approximately nine months more rapidly than to the United States market.[14] For example, the cardiovascular drug, practolol, was proved effective in Britain in reducing deaths from heart attacks, but marketing approval in the United States was delayed. William Wardell has estimated that the introduction of the drug in America could have saved 10,000 lives per year with minimal side effects.[15] Similarly persuasive (although disputed) evidence has been offered that regulatory demands have sharply retarded drug innovation in this country. Some estimates suggest that the cost of discovering and introducing new drugs has increased eighteenfold since 1960, with about one half of the increase being attributed to FDA regulation.[16] The impact of these conditions is illustrated by the finding that the number of new drugs approved since the 1962 Kefauver Amendments has averaged 17 per year while the annual average for the five years prior to the amendments was more than three times higher.[17] On the other hand, a 1981 General Accounting Office study found that for "breakthrough" drugs average FDA approval time fell from about 17 months in 1977 to about 11 months in 1980.[18] Noted economist Frederic Scherer argues for an injection of free market principles in drug regulation. He would prefer a two-tier system wherein the doctor and patient could exercise their choice from among FDA-approved drugs and those not yet accorded government sanction.

While the Reagan administration has not adopted Scherer's bold approach, it has been aggressive in streamlining the drug approval process. The FDA regulations are expected to reduce drug approval time by up to six months, while reducing new drug documentation (formerly averaging 100,000 pages) by as much as 30,000 pages. Industry representatives have applauded the new standards and promised to seek further streamlining, while critics fear the new efficiency efforts may cripple safety procedures.[19] Interestingly, a large and increasing share of the public favors strict drug regulation. A 1983 Roper poll found 73 percent of the respondents favoring tight controls and fewer new drugs, while 15 percent preferred less strict regulation with more new drugs on the market.[20]

The question that remains is intriguing—admittedly not so compelling as where to spend one's Spring Break—but interesting, nevertheless. It involves the kind of cost-benefit analysis that goes to the heart of most government regulation. Clearly, drug approval deprives us, at least for a time, of drugs that ultimately prove to be beneficial. On the other hand, regulation protects us from inferior or even dangerous and useless medicines.

Questions

1. On May 25, 1979, an American Airlines DC-10 crashed in Chicago, Illinois, with 273 persons aboard:

   The Federal Aviation Administration [FAA] certified the DC-10 wide-bodied jet without having its own employees check all preproduction tests and design plans, an FAA official says.

   Douglas Sharman, an FAA aerospace engineer, told a National Transportation Safety Board hearing that only a fraction of the work approved by aircraft manufacturing engineers designated as agents of the FAA actually is checked by the government agency. Thus McDonnell Douglas Corp., which made the DC-10, "approved" its own work for the government.[21]

   a. Can American corporations be trusted to do their own testing prior to product approval? Explain.

    b. Does the presence of the various regulatory agencies afford the public a false sense of security? Explain.

2. In 1977 a Du Pont official estimated the average cost of bringing a new drug from the laboratory to the pharmacy at $10 million.[22]

    Even if the FDA meets new goals for reduced processing time, average drug approval cases will still require 15 to 17 months, and the total testing process will consume many years.

    a. Would the public be willing to absorb a greater percentage of the cost of drug testing in the interest of greater safety? Explain.

    b. Would a shift of drug testing responsibility to the government be likely to result in greater safety? Explain.

    c. Have the costs of drug regulation outweighed the benefits? Explain.

    d. Could we rely to a greater degree on the free market for protection against dangerous products? Explain.

3. In recent years the federal government has been the subject of vigorous criticism for its various decisions regarding the protection of the public from alleged carcinogens (cancer-causing agents) such as tobacco, asbestos, nitrites, and Red Dye No. 2. Should the government (*a*) ban proven carcinogens where practical, (*b*) warn the public of the dangers involved, but leave the substance in the marketplace, or (*c*) remove itself from the business of protecting the public from carcinogens? Explain.

4. Laetrile, an apricot-pit derivative, is thought by some to be useful in the treatment of cancer while the weight of medical and scientific opinion considers it therapeutically valueless. The Supreme Court has upheld a federal ban on the interstate shipment of laetrile and has let stand an appeals court decision that terminal cancer victims do not have a constitutional right to laetrile. At least 23 states have legalized the use of laetrile, and Americans may seek its use in other nations (commonly, Mexico).

    Should the U.S. government remove existing barriers to the marketing and consumption of laetrile? Explain.

5. The director of the FDA's Bureau of Drugs, in speaking of his agency's regulation of prescription medicines, stated that "We do not pay any attention to the economic consequences of our decisions."[23]

    a. Defend that seemingly arrogant and wasteful attitude.

    b. Should economic considerations be irrelevant to regulations regarding human health and safety? Explain.

6. Oraflex, an arthritis drug manufactured by Eli Lilly & Co., was rejected for the American market in 1980. It was subsequently admitted to the British market. Later the FDA reversed its position and permitted the sale of Oraflex in the United States. After reports of many illnesses and a number of deaths apparently linked to the drug, it was removed from the market by Lilly. In a subsequent congressional investigation, the acting director of the FDA testified that Lilly had submitted data revealing various side effects from Oraflex, but the FDA did not look at the data, and Lilly failed to bring the data directly to the attention of the FDA.[24]

    a. Should all new drug applicants be required to explicitly identify all hazards known to be associated with their products? Explain.

    b. Should cigarette manufacturers be required to reveal all the evidence in their possession regarding the health hazards associated with their products? Explain.

    c. In either of the cases explored in (*a*) and (*b*), should producers be required not merely to reveal known hazards, but to advertise that information broadly? Explain.

Part Four—The Federal Regulatory Process Evaluated

In recent years a variety of forces, including a sometimes sluggish economy, have provoked a zealous inspection of government intervention. In this portion of the chapter we will begin by simply building a list of those criticisms most commonly visited upon the federal regulatory process generally and the administrative agencies specifically. That evaluation will be followed by a series of proposed reforms. One of those reforms, deregulation, is so sweeping in its implications and so much at the forefront of contemporary business and government thinking that it will be accorded separate, detailed attention.

It should be understood that the following criticisms, while applying directly to the federal administrative agencies, constitute an evaluation of the total program of federal regulation of business.

Criticisms

Excessive Regulation

The complaint is familiar. The government has intruded unnecessarily into the economic life of the nation. The businessperson's freedom of action has been significantly circumscribed. Table 7–1 depicts the dramatic growth of government regulation in recent years. A major component of the issue is that of expense. The federal budget for the regulatory agencies in 1974 was $2.2 billion. The sum expanded by 115 percent to $4.8 billion by 1979. Of course, the more serious financial burden lies in the cost of complying with government regulations. The bill for filling out the required forms, meeting pollution requirements, installing safety devices, declining productivity, and so on is estimated at a cost of over $100 billion annually to businesses. These direct and second-order costs provoke third-order expenses such as declining innovation and impaired ability to finance growth, which may be severely handicapping the economy.[25]

Table 7–1
Percent of GNP In the Regulated Sector of the Economy

Category	Percent of GNP under Regulation in 1965	Percent of GNP under Regulation in 1975
Price regulation	5.5%	8.8%
Financial markets regulation	2.7	3.0
Health and safety regulation	—	11.9
Total	8.2%	23.7%

Source: U.S. Department of Commerce. *Workfile 1205–02–02.* 1976 revision. Reprinted from Paul MacAvoy, *The Regulated Industries and the Economy* (New York: W. W. Norton, 1979), p. 25. Reprinted by permission of the publisher, W. W. Norton & Company, Inc.

The results of a survey of 300 business executives reveal a general feeling of excessive and costly regulation. Some of the primary complaints:

1. Overlap and conflict among agencies.
2. Overextension of agency authority, not merely in setting goals but in dictating how those goals are to be met.
3. Adversary attitudes toward business.
4. Agency delay in issuing required permits, rules, and standards.
5. Escalating reporting requirements.

A more extended discussion of these concerns is offered in the deregulation section that follows.

Insufficient Regulation

Although it is not currently fashionable, consumer advocates and big business critics believe that *more,* rather than *less,* regulation is necessary to protect citizen interests. They acknowledge the inefficiencies and excesses of some agency efforts, but they favor correcting those problems and strengthening the regulatory structure. Therefore, they argue that the problem is, in part, one of inadequate funds in those areas where sensible regulation is needed. Would not consumer protection be enhanced if the FDA were able to complete its own testing? And would not antitrust violations be retarded if the FTC were funded such that its lawyers and economists could compete on an equal footing with the resources of the business community? Advocates of increased regulation point to the successes of government intervention: legal equality for blacks; prevention of the sale of dangerous drugs such as thalidomide; and the Auto Safety Act which, by some estimates, saves 12,000 lives per year; et al. The 1978 defeat of a bill to create a federal Consumer Protection Agency (CPA) is an apt illustration of the consumer advocates' position. Led by Ralph Nader, the pro-CPA forces had argued that an umbrella agency charged with a general duty to protect consumer interests was necessary to counteract abuses in the business community. From 1969 to 1978 the CPA had on several occasions been approved by either the House or the Senate, but a complete victory was not secured. Then a combination of allegedly poor tactics by Nader, a changing national mood, and vigorous business lobbying defeated the bill. Mark Green commented on the lobbying effort:

Big Business interests—such as the U.S. Chamber of Commerce, the Business Roundtable, the National Association of Manufacturers, Armstrong Cork, Procter & Gamble, Sears—made the bill a litmus-test issue of a representative's fidelity to their creed.

House Speaker Tip O'Neill said that he had "never seen such extensive lobbying" in his quarter-century in Congress. A campaign of stimulated mail inundated the desks of undecided members. The Business Roundtable hired Leon Jaworski to lobby against the bill in early 1977, and later hired the North American Precis Syndicate (NAPC) to send around canned editorials and cartoons against the consumer agency to 3,800 newspapers and weeklies. These prepared statements—statements that never acknowledged as their source a business lobby opposed to this bill—appeared approximately 2,000 times, according to NAPC. Identical hostile editorials appeared in 10 newspapers around the country, newspapers not of the same chain.

The Chamber of Commerce conducted a national opinion poll in 1975, which it then reproduced several times over the next three years. The poll concluded that "81 percent of Americans are opposed to a new consumer agency." The Library of Congress, however, discredited this survey as biased and unfair because the key question was phrased as follows (underline added): "Those in favor of setting up an <u>additional</u> consumer protection agency on top of all the other agencies," etc. An outraged Sen. Charles Percy denounced the poll from the floor, saying, "The dissemination of useless poll information does nothing to help the image of American business, which is at an all-time low."[26]

Current public mistrust of big government rivals or exceeds that of big business. Thus, the advocates of more regulation are currently in some disarray.

Excessive Industry Influence

As we have noted, the industries to be regulated were often instrumental in spawning the various federal agencies. Noted economist George Stigler summarizes the argument: "[R]egulation is acquired by the industry and is designed and operated primarily for its benefit."[27] Stigler further contends that, where possible, firms will encourage government regulations restricting entry (licensing) thus limiting competition: "Every industry or occupation that has enough political power to utilize the state will seek to control entry."[28]

Agency commissioners and staff members are often drawn from the industry being regulated. For example, the primary voice of the oil industry, the American Petroleum Institute, is widely considered more knowledgeable in oil affairs than the government's own energy authorities. Not surprisingly, API's influence in setting regulatory policy is profound:

One of the clearest indications of the API's power came during the 1975–76 Senate battle over a proposed break-up of the large oil companies on grounds that they were anticompetitive.

While the issue was being debated toward its eventual death on the Senate floor, an API lobbyist turned to a reporter in the gallery and said with proud disdain: "We wrote about half the speeches and they don't even have enough pride to change a word."[29]

As further evidence of industry influence in agency affairs, critics argue that upon leaving federal service agency employees frequently turn to jobs in the industry they were formerly charged with regulating. Similarly, agency recruits often are drawn from the industry being regulated. Certainly industry influence in government generally, and in the agencies specifically, is considerable. However, the public interest is arguably best served by drawing from the private sector's plentiful repository of information and expertise. The many scholarly studies of this topic offer mixed results. For example, one House subcommittee study of top officials in federal regulatory agencies found that about 35 percent of the employees "had prior direct or indirect employment in the regulated industry."[30] But other studies show that a background in law and/or prior government service were common avenues to upper level agency roles.[31] The House subcommittee study found that one third of the top officials "became directly or indirectly employed in the regulated industry within five years of leaving office."[32] Though specific findings differ, movement from agencies to the regulated industry does appear to be common and arguably a source of concern.

Perhaps more alarming are the findings from a study of 25 years of appointments to the Federal Communications Commission and the Federal Trade Commission:

> Partisan political considerations dominate the selection of regulators to an alarming extent. Alarming, in that other factors—such as competence, experience, and even, on occasion, regulatory philosophy—are only secondary considerations. Most commission appointments are the result of well-stoked campaigns conducted at the right time with the right sponsors, and many selections can be explained in terms of powerful political connections and little else: Commission seats are good consolation prizes for defeated Congressmen; useful runner-up awards for persons who ricochet into the appointment as a result of a strong yet unsuccessful campaign for another position; appropriate resting berths for those who have labored long and hard in the party vineyards; and a convenient dumping ground for people who have performed unsatisfactorily in other, more important Government posts.[33]

To summarize, industry influence over the regulatory process is considerable. The industry voice should be heard. The question is one of the "volume" of the voice. The allegations of an industry-agency-industry revolving door clearly have some merit and may constitute a threat to the integrity of the regulatory process, but the demands of expertise presumably require some industry-agency ties. In closing, it should be understood that the argument of industry "capture" of an agency is much more persuasive as to the older, "industrial regulation" agencies such as the ICC and the FCC than as to the newer "social regulation" agencies such as OSHA, EPA, and EEOC. The former are directed primarily at one industry. The latter reach across the face of American commerce. It is difficult to envision an industry capturing the conduct of one of the social regulation agencies.

Excessive Legislative and Executive Influence

Objectivity and a substantial degree of independence are essential to the role agencies have been assigned to play, but the charge is regularly offered that personal and political pressure from the legislative and executive branches colors agency decision making. Overt abuse, such as the attempts by members of the Nixon Administration to use the Internal Revenue Service for political purposes, is uncommon. However, more subtle pressure to influence day-to-day decisions is a well-documented and probably inevitable ingredient in the administrative process.

Of course, Congress in particular has a duty of oversight in ensuring that agency power serves the public interest. Although the line between legitimate political persuasion and abusive influence peddling is elusive, clearly agency action is subject to substantial legislative and executive influence.

Underrepresentation of Public Opinion

Another criticism of agencies charges that the diffuse voice of public opinion does not receive the attention accorded to the pleas of special interests. For example, a Common Cause (national government reform organization) survey found that commissioners heading federal regulatory agencies meet with industry representatives 10 times more frequently than with spokespersons for consumer or public interest groups.[34] A former

commissioner of the Federal Communications Commission has said that "citizen participation in the decision-making process 'is virtually nonexistent,' with the 'necessary
but unhappy result . . . that the FCC is a "captive" of the very industry it is purportedly attempting to regulate.' "[35] According to one account, the American Petroleum Institute's budget of $32 million in 1979 was 30 times greater than the combined budgets of
all Washington energy-related public interest organizations.[36] Of course, public opinion
is received by many routes, and the final word in the voting booth is preeminently
persuasive. Nevertheless, it is generally acknowledged that public sentiment, being
largely unorganized, is greatly underrepresented in regulatory matters, while well-financed, skillfully organized special interests carry political weight far beyond the numbers they represent.

These complaints are not meant to represent the full range of criticisms of the federal
regulatory process. In particular, the mechanics of agency conduct are frequently assailed. Allegations of inefficiency, incompetence, and arbitrariness are commonplace.
The pace of work is said to be slow, and enforcement of policy often appears to be
weak and ineffectual. That such problems exist in many bureaucratic structures is evident. Those problems are real and important, but here the weight of attention seems
more appropriately accorded to broader, policy issues.

Regulatory Reform

Dissatisfaction with the federal regulatory process is widespread and reaches across the
political spectrum. For example, liberal Senator Edward Kennedy played a leading role
in deregulating the airline industry. Proposals for reform and deregulation have blos-
somed in staggering abundance. (Indeed, as an aside, it is interesting to speculate about
the confluence of events that lifts a simmering issue to that critical mass necessary for
widespread exposure and publicity. Obviously, regulatory reform and deregulation are
not new issues, but it is clear that the late 1970s and early 80s have witnessed an
unprecedented antiregulatory fervor.)

Regulatory reform deals with efforts to improve the efficiency and equity of the
existing regulatory process. The deregulation movement seeks to reduce the quantity of
federal regulatory interventions in favor of increased reliance on the free market. Certainly some reform strategies may ultimately lead to deregulation. Therefore, the reader
should recognize that the line between reform and deregulation is a bit fuzzy.

The Carter administration initiated several reforms, the success of which remains
unclear. New legislation required that all rules and regulations be written in plain English. Other legislation eased formidable hurdles against dismissing incompetent federal
employees and rewarding those who performed with special distinction. As noted earlier, Congress has taken specific steps under its oversight authority to retard the regulatory authority of the Federal Trade Commission.

Proposed reforms are plentiful. The following list captures their flavor.

1. Under sunset legislation, agencies and programs would automatically cease to
exist if not periodically (usually every 5 or 10 years) renewed after appropriate review
by Congress. Common Cause introduced sunset legislation in Colorado for the purpose
of rendering agencies more accountable to the legislature. In 1976 Colorado adopted a

sunset provision. Other states have followed suit. Whether the desired improvements in efficiency and accountability will come to pass is as yet uncertain. Many states apparently seized upon sunset provisions as a deregulation method. However, the sunset notion seems ill-suited to the goal of deregulation. Careful legislative review is a very time-consuming process, and virtually all agencies have considerable lobbying support. Congress has moved slowly on sunset legislation.[37]

2. Various mechanisms have been proposed for reducing unnecessary paperwork. For example, regulators might be expected to accept the information they seek, where feasible, in the form it was developed for the company's own purposes.

3. Regulatory burdens might be adjusted according to the size and nature of the firms involved.

4. More of the regulatory burden is thought to be the proper concern of the states.

5. Various suggestions have been offered to afford Congress and the executive branch greater control over the administrative agencies. One proposal is to give either house of Congress the power to review and veto agency rules before they become effective. Another is that personnel appointments to the agencies would be at the pleasure of the president. Thus the agency would presumably be more responsive to the president and hence to the citizenry.

6. Regulatory overlap could be attacked by creating a coordinating board to eliminate conflicting and redundant regulations.

7. Intervenor funding might be provided. That is, government funds could be appropriated to permit public interest group witnesses and perhaps small-business witnesses to testify before appropriate agencies.

8. Many, perhaps most, economists support the use of market incentives to achieve regulatory goals. Thus, rather than forbidding undesirable conduct such as pollution and industrial accidents, the government might impose a tax on those behaviors that society wants to discourage. In effect, a business would purchase the right to engage in conduct that society considers injurious or inefficient. Similarly, rather than rationing portions of the radio spectrum or the right to land at airports at peak times, the government might auction those rights to the highest bidder. Market incentives would (*a*) encourage companies to use cost-effective compliance means and (*b*) raise the price of dangerous products, thus discouraging their use. However, monitoring difficulties, particularly in the case of pollution, render the taxing or auction methods inexact at best. Some object to the idea of allowing businesses to engage in undesirable conduct or highly prized conduct merely because they have the resources to pay for those privileges.

9. Cost/benefit analysis would be applied to all regulations. Regulations would be imposed only if added benefits equaled or exceeded the added costs. A cost effectiveness system might be developed for those cases where a dollar value could not be fairly and accurately assigned (e.g., the value of a human life). A goal would be identified, and a cost effectiveness study would be employed to determine the least expensive way of reaching that goal. The point here is perhaps best illustrated by reference to mandated auto safety standards. For example, seat belts in autos are thought to save approximately 5,000 lives per year at a cost to society of approximately $80,000 per life.[38] On the other hand, the air bag safety device is expected to save as many as 9,000 lives per year but the cost may reach $2 billion for the first year and an additional $2 billion for

each year of their use.[39] (It should be understood that these cost and benefit figures vary substantially depending on the study cited). President Reagan has sought to firmly inject cost/benefit analysis in federal regulation. In 1981 the president signed an executive order providing, in part, that: "Regulatory action shall not be undertaken unless the potential benefits to society from the regulation outweigh the potential costs to society."[40] Soon thereafter the Supreme Court ruled in the "cotton dust" case[41] that a cost/benefit analysis is not required under Occupational Safety and Health Act provisions designed to insure workers' protection from "toxic materials or harmful physical agents." So the degree to which government will rely on cost/benefit principles remains to be seen. The article that follows offers an interesting example of cost/benefit analysis.

EPA PLAN WOULD CUT GAS LEAD, RAISE PRICE

Courier News Wires

Washington—The Environmental Protection Agency Monday proposed regulations reducing the amount of lead in gasoline 91 percent by January 1, 1986, and said it may ban the fuel additive entirely by 1995 as a health danger, particularly for pregnant women and children.

The move could cost refiners more than half a billion dollars, an expense that presumably would be passed on to motorists.

Lead is by far the cheapest way to raise the octane rating of gasoline to permit its use in efficient high-compression engines. Refiners have been using it since 1925.

"The evidence is overwhelming that lead, from all sources, is a threat to human health," EPA Administrator William D. Ruckelshaus said in announcing the proposal.

* * * * *

He estimated the standard would reduce the number of children with potentially damaging levels of lead in their blood from 97,000 to 47,000 by 1988. . . .

Beginning in 1986, refiners would have to limit the concentration of lead in gasoline to 1/10th (0.1) of a gram per gallon. That is 11 times more stringent than the current standard.

The Ethyl Corp., which produces about 40 percent of the lead additive blended into gasoline to prevent engine knocking, said it would oppose the new regulations but stopped short

of saying it would try to block them in court.

* * * * *

Surveys have shown that up to 17 percent of American motorists whose cars are equipped with catalytic converters use leaded gasoline in violation of air pollution laws.

* * * * *

"Leaded gasoline is responsible for about 80 percent of all lead emissions to the air," he said, "and we know that there is a direct relationship between lead in gasoline and the amount of lead in human blood."

Ruckelshaus said that the agency intends to allow a small amount of lead to remain in gasoline because the owners of cars made before 1971 need leaded gas to protect their engines. But he said there will be little need for lead as a fuel additive by the mid-1990s.

* * * * *

He estimated it would cost refiners about $575 million to meet the new standards.

"But, from a social point of view," Ruckelshaus said, "this expense is more than offset by the $1.8 billion that will be saved during 1986 alone from lower costs for medical treatment and rehabilitation, reduced vehicle maintenance bills and improved fuel efficiency, not to mention a higher quality environment."

Lead is a poison, and tests in recent years have shown that concentrations in the blood of inner-city children closely track the amount of leaded gasoline sold in the area. Though those children get most of their blood lead from eating lead-based paint, EPA scientists believe a sizable fraction comes from compounds put into the air by automobile exhaust.

In sufficient concentrations in children, lead causes mental retardation. An EPA analysis estimated that the IQs of anywhere from 14,000 to 4 million children could be raised by an average of 2.2 points if lead were removed from gasoline.

Source: *Waterloo (Iowa) Courier*, July 30, 1984, p. 1. Reprinted with permission of the copyright holders, *Waterloo Courier* and The Associated Press.

Deregulation

Introduction

Deregulation moves beyond mere reform of the regulatory process toward efforts at actually reducing the amount of regulation to which business is subjected. The free market, rather than the market supplemented or supplanted by rules and regulations, becomes the "umpire" of American commerce.

Let us immediately dispose of one dimension of the deregulation debate that provides amusement to all—a particularly easy target for James Kilpatrick, Paul Harvey, and other critics of government intervention—but little in the way of grist for useful analysis. That is, we can all agree that some, perhaps many, government regulations are silly. Regrettably bureaucrats, like the rest of us, are imperfect. Pointing to absurd government rules is useful in acquiring publicity, but the practice helps little in reaching a judgment as to the proper balance between freedom and regulation. Noted economist Lester Thurow explains:

Gleefully finding silly government regulations has almost reached the status of a national parlor game. And nowhere is it easier to play the game than in the domain of OSHA—the Occupational Safety and Health Administration. Whenever silliness arises, it is well to ask why. It could arise because we are chasing after silly ends, or it could arise because we are using inappropriate means to achieve perfectly respectable ends. In the case of OSHA, the latter is clearly true. No one questions the virtues or the seriousness of reducing industrial deaths and injuries. The question is one of means.

Basically the problem is not one of stupid bureaucrats, but one of trying to write universal regulations in an area where it is impossible. A regulation that makes sense in one context, may not in another. Take the problem of providing toilet facilities for farm workers. A regulation that may be eminently sensible in a densely populated truck-farming area (a toilet every 40 acres) with hundreds of farm laborers, may not make sense on a Montana ranch where it is miles to the nearest person, and where there are hundreds of thousands of empty acres that seldom, if ever, see an agricultural worker. Yet for a set of regulations to be sensible in every section of a country as large as the United States, it would have to be so lengthy that it would be equally silly. Suppose that someone were to report that it took the government 10,000 pages of regulations to spell out the appropriate toilet facilities for every conceivable condition. Each of those regulations could be sensible, yet the aggregate effect is nonsense. The problem is using an inappropriate means to achieve a respectable objective.

It is also well to remind ourselves that silliness is not limited to public actions or to other individuals. Every example of stupid government action could be matched by a private example. The Edsel, for example, has entered our language as the paradigm example of a stupid action that wasted millions of dollars worth of resources. Boston's John Hancock building, with its falling panes of glass, was a fiasco from the day it was built. What would have happened if some government bureaucrat had built it? The U.S. steel industry misinvested millions on openhearth furnaces, when it should have been building oxygen furnaces. Most of us would have to admit, at least to ourselves, that we have made stupid mistakes in our own budgets.[42]

So we are beset with some foolish regulations. It is generally agreed that some areas are burdened with excessive regulation. Indeed, substantial deregulation in transportation, communications, and some other industries is already underway. But the issue of excessive regulation should be kept in perspective. The United States remains the least regulated of all the industrialized nations. Central planning, direct government investment, and social welfare regulation greatly exceeding our own are represented in varying proportions among all other advanced economies. It is well to note that some of those nations, such as Japan and Germany, currently enjoy economic health in many respects exceeding our own. Thurow reminds us that America's economic performance has improved since the onset of the intensive government intervention of the New Deal.[43] Government regulation does not arise from ideology, but from actual problems.[44] America is not committed to government regulation as a matter of political policy—as is the case in many nations. Rather, regulation in this country has, in many instances, resulted from an honorable effort to correct evident wrongs. Much maligned agencies such as the EPA, OSHA, and FDA were not born of a desire for big government and central planning. Industrial pollution, industrial accidents, and dangerous food and drugs were clearly the impetus for the creation of those agencies.

As a final measure of perspective, note the following excerpts from a recent *Fortune* magazine interview of prominent management consultant, Jewell Westerman.

LOOK WHO'S COVERED IN RED TAPE

Ask a businessman if the bureaucracy is getting him down, and he becomes a fountain of indignation about the vexations of dealing with government red tape. Ask him about the bureaucracy in his own company, and you'll likely find he hasn't given the matter much thought. Jewell G. Westerman, 46, a vice president of Hendrick & Co., a management-consulting firm in Waltham, Massachusetts, has given the matter quite a bit of thought. At Hendrick and at the Travelers Insurance Companies before that, Westerman developed some provocative views on the productivity of managers, which he set out in an interview with *Fortune* associate editor Jeremy Main.

Q. How would you compare the penalties imposed on business by government bureaucracy and the penalties imposed by the bureaucracy of business management itself?

A. The latter are far larger. It is very difficult to estimate the cost of the extra requirements imposed by the government, but in a study of a large insurance company we were able to pin it down to something on the order of about $8 million to $10 million a year. Compared with the total salary costs of about $600 million, that was a very small percentage and you're talking mostly about things like filing W-2 forms, making payments to social security, and filing income-tax reports. These are standard activities and you probably couldn't eliminate them. I read recently that Goodyear reported it spent 34 employee-years filling out reports required by government regulation. Do you know how many employees Goodyear has? 154,000. So 34 out of 154,000 is not even a measurable percentage.

Q. In the studies done here at Hendrick, how do you go about costing out such activities?

A. When we study a company we create an index of activities, by subfunction and function. We measure the amount of time it takes to perform between 225 and 300 different activities. Several of them result from government regulations. We don't enter any data for an activity that takes less than 5 percent of an employee's time. In many of our studies no labor costs at all show up for complying with government regulations. We have done over 200 such studies at Hendrick & Co., and we cannot recall a single company in which coping with government regulations raised a significant opportunity for lowering labor costs.

Q. And what did you find out about business bureaucracy?

A. The costs are phenomenal. Manager costs are usually No. 1 and secretarial costs No. 2—or vice versa.

Q. Do you mean among white-collar workers?

A. No. Out of all workers.

Q. Even in manufacturing companies?

A. Even in manufacturing companies secretarial costs are higher than the costs of line workers. When you have one manager for every four or five employees and one secretary for every two managers, you're starting to build up a lot of secretaries in an organization. Management, secretaries, data processing, and sometimes budgeting are usually the most costly activities. You usually get down to about the 10th or 12th category of labor expense before you get to line workers. So you have to ask, why are we in business: to manage it and administer it, or to make products? . . .

Source: "A Difference of Opinion," *Fortune*, May 4, 1981, p. 357. Reprinted with permission of the publisher, *Fortune*. Written by Jeremy Main from an interview with Jewell G. Westerman. © 1981 Time Inc. All rights reserved.

The Burdens of Regulation

We turn now to the encompassing inquiry: In what measure and manner, if any, should the American economy be deregulated? Some argue for more regulation. Others would favor exlusive reliance on the free market. Most fall somewhere between. Many of the arguments and data supporting deregulation were offered earlier in this chapter and in the preceding chapter. Perhaps the arguments favoring deregulation may be best understood in light of the direct, day-to-day impact upon a single business. In a colorful, rather "down-home" fashion, the piece that follows immerses us in some of the frustrations that often accompany the government's well-meaning and arguably necessary efforts to regulate some business practices.

KENTUCKY ENTREPRENEUR FINDS AN OBSCURE PEN PAL IN UNCLE SAM

Ward Sinclair

Jimmy Carter promised to streamline the government, put the literature of Federalspeak in plain English. Ronald Reagan's pledge to get government off our backs is graven on the tablets.

Now it's time to meet Eli Simpson, a fairly ordinary sort of fellow who in a special way symbolizes the people Carter and Reagan were talking to over these last few months.

He lives in rural central Kentucky. He got an eighth grade education. Worked as a meat cutter. Served in Vietnam. Disabled. Wants to get off the monthly pension, make a mark, help his country.

Somehow, he and an uncle who farms in Michigan got the idea they could do their part by building stills and encouraging farmers to make their own alcohol fuel by cooking their corn.

They got the required permits and built a 300-gallon still up in Michigan. It worked, as any good Kentuckian knew it would have to work, and they were all set to go. They wanted farmers to run their tractors on pure alcohol.

About a year ago Simpson wrote to the Department of Energy, asking for some federal assistance to get the little scheme going. What he got in return was a big packet of materials from DOE with forms to fill out and with—let's be honest—very confusing explanations.

DOE's packet indicated he could conduct a feasibility study for alternative fuels production. Or he could respond to program solicitation No. DE–PAO1–80RA50204 and propose a cooperative agreement to make alternative fuel.

A month later, DOE invited him to attend a Washington seminar, at his own expense, on submitting a proposal. DOE included a nice map of the city.

That began an unusual back-and-forth between Eli Simpson and his government in Washington, an exasperating exercise that led

to an amassing of papers that might loosely be called The Simpson Chronicle.

He wrote to Washington, to people in high places, and remarkably enough, he got answers. But he still got no grant.

The Simpson Chronicle includes letters from President Carter on White House notepaper and a signature that purports to be Carter's, thanking him for his views.

Hamilton Jordan, the presidential assistant, wrote to say, "I appreciate your thoughtful concern in writing to comment about the world energy crisis."

Agriculture Secretary Bob Bergland wrote a couple times, the most recent being this week, responding to an earlier Simpson complaint about USDA's distrust of the farmer, and the interest it charges on loans.

Through it all, Eli Simpson was taking it personally, feeling that perhaps it was he, rather than the government, that wasn't being coherent.

He took the DOE booklets from his home near Cynthiana over to Lexington, where a researcher at the University of Kentucky looked them over and agreed with Simpson.

"She said they contained a lot of technical language, etc., for the common person to understand." Simpson wrote to a reporter. "At least I gave it one heck of a good try before giving up on it. I was more screwed up the sixth time I read it than the first time. Oh, well. The strain on my brain is too much pain and not worth the drain of the nervous system. Good luck and thank you."

Later on, between his jottings to officialdom, he penned another item into the Chronicle. "We lack the language that it takes to communicate with our very own government. We find this disheartening and disappointing," he wrote.

"We are the first to admit that none of us obtained more than a grade school education but it appears as if a person has to be a college graduate in order to understand how to fill out a request for a grant or loan from the Energy Department and the other government agencies like Farmers Home, Agriculture Department, etc.,'' he continued.

Still later, he wrote more. ''We feel so alienated because of the lack of communication on the part of our government and the lack of understanding on our part. We are beginning to feel as if we are victims instead of citizens,'' Simpson said.

That was not entirely fair, for the White House was trying. Somebody sent him a copy of a Carter statement on gasohol policy. And he got a copy of a gasohol fact sheet, the same thing reporters had been handed in January.

Up at the top, the sheet said, ''Embargoed for release until after the briefing.'' Simpson circled that, put 13 question marks next to it and wrote, ''What the heck does that word mean?,'' with a little arrow aimed at ''embargoed.''

No grant ever turned up. Part of it was because Simpson could not really grasp what the forms were about and what his obligations would be if DOE gave him the $17,000 he wanted to set up his farm-still operation.

A newsman in Louisville got wind of Simpson's plight and interviewed him. The resulting story produced a phone call from an official at the Bluegrass Area Development District, who wondered if he could help.

Technically speaking, development districts aren't supposed to be soliciting that kind of business. But give someone credit.

In September they filled out a DOE application form for Simpson, with his proposal to set up a cooperative, hook up with 4-H Clubs, build a still, put it on a truck and take it from farm to farm to show farmers how they can make their own fuel from corn and other organic matter.

As a side angle, they are proposing to take the leftover mash and use it for feed for catfish that would be bred in a little pond. Maybe start a whole new business and keep the tractors running, too.

''I'm crazier than hell, but I'm hanging in there,'' Simpson said the other day. ''It's partly my fault because I only made it to the eighth grade, but you know, I sometimes think they've got these programs only for big business and the rest of us don't count.''

The Simpson Chronicle is missing a final reply from DOE.

Source: *The Washington Post*, November 15, 1980, p. A3. © *The Washington Post*, 1980. Reprinted with permission. (Ward Sinclair is a staff writer for the newspaper.)

The Benefits of Regulation

Now we can properly review the benefits of regulation. Measurement is difficult, but some responsible calculations have emerged, as summarized in Nicholas Ashford's article and Frederick Thayer's subsequent letter.

IN MANY CASES, REGULATION PAYS

Nicholas A. Ashford

Critics of government intervention in the private sector often bemoan the costs of complying with environmental, health, and safety regulation and allege that new product development is encumbered by regulation.

While grudgingly conceding that some benefits do result, these critics would have us believe that we must choose between our health and our jobs, between environmental quality and a higher standard of living, and between product safety and competition in international markets. And they issue a call for cost/benefit analysis of regulation to ensure that the benefits are worth the cost.

Most such studies, however, until recently have focused only on the cost.

* * * * *

The Massachusetts Institute of Technology's Center for Policy Alternatives has reviewed and classified over 350 such studies and has identified substantial benefits that have resulted from regulation.

* * * * *

Among the center's findings are the following:

● Regulation of air pollution from major sources has produced estimated benefits ranging widely from $5 billion to $58 billion a year, with automotive pollution controls alone worth $2.5 billion to $10 billion a year.

● Water pollution control, in a breakdown, produces a reduction in water-borne disease valued at $100 million to $1 billion a year, provides recreational potential valued at up to $9.4 billion a year and substantially increases property values. And these evaluations do not take into account programs directed at such long-term or large-scale problems as carcinogens in water supplies, stratospheric ozone depletion, atmospheric sulfate transport, or acid rain.

● Inspections by the Occupational Safety and Health Administration are estimated to have prevented between 40,000 and 60,000 accidents in which workdays would have been lost and up to 350 deaths in both 1974 and 1975. Regulations limiting worker exposure to asbestos, the data indicate, may result in a reduction of 630 to 2,500 deaths a year from lung cancer and asbestosis. OSHA regulation of such hazards as vinyl chloride, cotton dust, lead, and noise are expected to provide significant additional benefits in the form of reduced incidence of disease.

● Motor vehicle occupant protection standards promulgated between 1966 and 1970

saved an estimated 28,000 lives from 1966 to 1974, equivalent to a 15 to 30 percent reduction in deaths and serious injuries from those occurring with older cars. The seatbelt requirement has reduced deaths an estimated 20 percent and lowered auto accident injuries 34 percent, despite relatively low use rates.

● As a result of consumer product safety regulations, child-resistant drug packaging has prevented an estimated 34,000 injuries from accidental drug ingestion between 1973 and 1976. Crib safety standards have reduced crib-related injuries to infants by 44 percent since 1974. Fully implemented fabric flammability standards could have reduced by about 20 percent the frequencies of deaths and serious burns experienced by children in 1975.

More broadly, the benefits of Federal inspection of meats, poultry, and processed food are manifest in the overall quality and purity of America's food supply. They have become deeply ingrained in the quality control efforts of the food processing and distribution industry since regulation began in 1890. Recent studies have found considerable benefits in the form of reduced consumer exposure to potentially carcinogenic food preservatives and of more efficient utilization of meat carcasses.

In a final category, food, drug and cosmetic regulations, the benefits have been quantified in only a few instances. It has been estimated that the benefits of the drug efficacy requirements under the 1962 Kefauver-Harris Amendments have been a reduction of $100 million to $300 million a year in consumer purchases of ineffective drugs.

* * * * *

The benefits derived from direct regulation of a particular hazard are only a part of the gains that the regulatory process can provide. Indirect, or *leveraged,* benefits accrue from the very presence of a particular regulation.

It induces industry to control unregulated hazards in anticipation of regulation, to innovate and to find ways to meet the public's need for a cleaner, healthier environment while maintaining industrial capacity. These long-term, positive side effects accompanying a regulation need to be included in a complete assessment of the benefits of a regulatory strategy.

One example of leveraging is the fact that chemical companies are now routinely conducting short-term tests on new chemicals for possible carcinogenic activity, even though specific regulatory requirements under the Toxic Substances Control Act have not been promulgated. These long-term benefits are substantial, though difficult to quantify. Their exclusion omits from estimates of benefits what may be the largest contribution of regulation—a restructuring of the nature of industrial pro-duction and earlier anticipation of avoidable problems, such as the hazardous waste disposal at Love Canal.

In sum, scattered evidence not organized or generated for lobbying purposes does indicate substantial benefits from environmental, health and safety regulation.

REGULATION [Response to preceding article]

To the Business Editor:

It is all to the good that a strong case for certain types of public regulation (environment, health, safety) has now appeared in your pages ("In Many Cases, Regulation Pays," June 15). I wish only to add a footnote about a type of regulation Nicholas A. Ashford chose to overlook.

While many insist that safety and economic (price) regulation are not, and should not be, related to each other, the history of transportation regulation (airlines and trucking companies) indicates they cannot be separated. A large part of the trucking industry has been unregulated for years, and its safety record is much worse than that of the regulated companies.

Historically, the less regulated the airline industry, the greater the safety problems. All-out competition on prices requires companies to cut corners and costs; in transportation systems, training and maintenance are the only ways to do this.

Frederick C. Thayer
Associate Professor, Graduate School
of Public and International Affairs
University of Pittsburgh
Pittsburgh, Pa., June 16, 1980

In some instances the benefits of government regulation defy meaningful computation. Perhaps we should resist the contemporary tendency to deprecate what cannot be subjected to meaningful quantitative analysis. The article that follows illustrates just such an occasion.

FORESTS OVERGROWN WITH RED TAPE

Brooks Jackson

Basswood Lake, Ontario—As our canoes slice through the sparkling black water, I have the feeling I am being watched.

The four of us—a doctor, a lawyer, a computer specialist and myself, a reporter—have come to this birch-and-pine wilderness to escape comfortably civilized routines.

But up ahead, in a log cabin on a remote island, I will soon encounter a stout little man in a square cap with a shiny black bill. On his desk will be a small metal stand holding a half-dozen or so rubber stamps, the tools of his profession.

He is a bureaucrat, the very sort I left Washington, D.C., to elude. I know he may cause us trouble; we are going to ask him for the permits needed to camp and fish in this protected wilderness area on the United States–Canadian border. I have the same feeling I get when I renew my driver's license.

As we paddle along, our soft city muscles are already beginning to complain. We are on a route used 250 years ago by French and later by British and American fur traders. Indian wigwams and wooden forts are long gone. In their places one occasionally sees tents made of red or yellow synthetic fabric. Otherwise, the dense forest and stony shores look as they must have for centuries.

To the left is the Boundary Waters Canoe Area of northern Minnesota, and to the right is the Quetico Provincial Park of Ontario. It seems an odd place to have trouble with a government official. We had in mind an encounter of a different sort: man against nature, survival in the wilderness. But we are discovering that the wilderness survives only by pitting government officials against campers.

Motor boats, for instance, are allowed only along a few routes. Cans and bottles are banned. Trash and garbage must be burned or carried out. Heavy fines await the litterbug.

*   *   *   *   *

The ultimate hassle may still be ahead. As we shoved off early this morning, we got word that authorities might decide to close the entire park as a precaution against fires. Our trip would be over.

Apprehensively we glide up to the forest ranger's pier after nearly 2½ hours of paddling. He smiles. We will be allowed in.

We pay customs duty on our freeze-dried

foods, fees for camping and fees for fishing licenses. The ranger issues us a sheaf of permits and papers—white, pink and green. I notice that one of his rubber stamps reads "Cancelled," and give silent thanks that he isn't using it today.

Days later we are catching trout on a lake deep in the park. A small forest fire, perhaps an acre or two in size, has started burning on a hillside a couple of miles downwind. A white single-engine airplane circles to investigate the fire, then glides down to set its pontoons on the lake, about 200 yards from my canoe.

The government ranger tells us that lightning has started more fires, that the park has been closed and that campers are being asked to move out. We comply and break camp a day earlier than planned.

On the canoe trip back the thought strikes me that this isn't a real wilderness at all. It is a museum. And it survives in a "natural" state only by unnaturally vigorous human effort.

In a truly wild area, that small fire would have spread by now, whipped by the high wind. But a large orange airplane appeared here and doused the flames by dumping water from aloft.

Moreover, this "wild" area is surprisingly delicate. At our campsite, we wore paths into the forest floor in only a few days. The clear, cold lake water purges itself of waste matter far more slowly than warmer bodies. Without the entry-permit system, this increasingly popular area could be overrun. Before the quota system took effect in the mid-1970s, U.S. rangers counted 180 canoe parties going up popular Moose Lake in a single day. The limit now is 40.

The red tape can be maddening. But as our canoes slide past beaver lodges and over lakes filled with fish, it somehow seems a small price to preserve such a treasure.

Source: *The Wall Street Journal*, June 27, 1980, p. 25. Reprinted by permission of *The Wall Street Journal*. © Dow Jones & Company, Inc., 1980. All rights reserved.

Deregulation Decision

The Carter Administration was successful in achieving significant deregulation in the airline, trucking, and rail industries. In general, the affected industries have been accorded pricing and operating flexibility previously forbidden. Fares and rates more nearly reflect market conditions. New entry has been eased, and levels of service may now respond to demand. Among the effects is that large markets may receive greater service and small markets less or none at all. Of course, where dictated by demand small firms have replaced loss of service occasioned by the departure of large firms to mass market.

Under the terms of the Airline Deregulation Act of 1978, existing firms were allowed to automatically enter one new route in 1979 and 1980. Finally, in January 1985, the CAB was dissolved with the bulk of its duties shifted to the Department of Transportation.

In a similar vein the Federal Communications Commission voted in 1980 to remove most restraints on the radio and cable television industry. In 1984, the FCC repealed guidelines requiring commercial television stations to offer news and local affairs programs. At the same time, limitations on the number of commercials that could be telecast were lifted. The guidelines had provided for devoting a minimum of 10 percent of air time to non-entertainment features, while commercials had been limited to not more than 16 minutes per hour.

The Garn-St. Germain Act of 1982 is one of several legislative initiatives in recent years that have opened the financial institutions market to much greater competition. For example, the law now permits bank interest rates to be competitive with those offered at savings and loan institutions. Recent Interstate Commerce Commission action has implemented Congressional legislation calling for deregulation of household goods' shippers, an area which has been characterized by tight regulations resulting in little variation in rates and service.

Deregulation has mainly transpired in the older, "industry" regulation areas (ICC—transportation, FCC—communications, CAB—airlines) where economic concerns predominate. Deregulation in the new agencies (EPA, EEOC, OSHA) designed to protect health, safety, civil rights, and such seem unlikely. However, regulatory reform in those areas is well underway. For example, the EPA is adopting more flexible standards that set a goal but allow managers to find the best way of meeting that goal. Illustrative of that flexibility about air pollution is the EPA adoption of the "bubble concept," which treats an industrial plant as though it were a bubble and measures the sum of the pollution rather than that from each pollution source. Thus, the business can reduce pollution from whichever sources best serve its needs and costs, so long as the total reduction meets EPA standards.

Is deregulation desirable? The importance of the issue cannot be discounted. The question is at the heart of this text and of American commerce, and its resolution will significantly shape the nature of American life. Public opinion is a critical ingredient in the deregulation debate. The results are mixed. It is not news that Americans are frustrated with big government. In 1984, 43 percent of those surveyed favored a "cutback in government regulation of business," while 31 percent opposed that direction, and 26 percent had mixed feelings or could not decide.[45] A 1979 survey found 58 percent of those surveyed favoring airline deregulation and 44 percent favoring trucking/railroad deregulation (with 25 percent opposed, and 31 percent unable to reach a decision).[46] The evidence shows that attitudes toward regulation are closely tied to general cynicism regarding big government. Virtually everyone favors reducing paperwork, eliminating red tape, getting bureaucrats off our backs, and the like. However, when applied to specifics, we continue to find support for regulation. On being questioned in a 1980 poll regarding the desirability of government regulation in specific areas, public support for intervention was quite strong.[47]

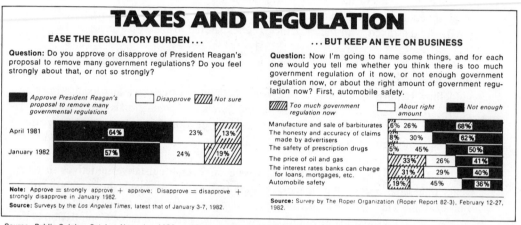

TAXES AND REGULATION

EASE THE REGULATORY BURDEN...

Question: Do you approve or disapprove of President Reagan's proposal to remove many government regulations? Do you feel strongly about that, or not so strongly?

■ Approve President Reagan's proposal to remove many governmental regulations   □ Disapprove   ▨ Not sure

April 1981	64%	23%	13%
January 1982	57%	24%	19%

Note: Approve = strongly approve + approve; Disapprove = disapprove + strongly disapprove in January 1982.
Source: Surveys by the *Los Angeles Times*, latest that of January 3–7, 1982.

...BUT KEEP AN EYE ON BUSINESS

Question: Now I'm going to name some things, and for each one would you tell me whether you think there is too much government regulation of it now, or not enough government regulation now, or about the right amount of government regulation now? First, automobile safety.

▨ Too much government regulation now   □ About right amount   ■ Not enough

	Too much	About right	Not enough
Manufacture and sale of barbiturates	6%	26%	68%
The honesty and accuracy of claims made by advertisers	8%	30%	62%
The safety of prescription drugs	5%	45%	50%
The price of oil and gas	33%	26%	41%
The interest rates banks can charge for loans, mortgages, etc.	31%	29%	40%
Automobile safety	19%	45%	36%

Source: Survey by The Roper Organization (Roper Report 82-3), February 12–27, 1982.

Source: *Public Opinion,* October–November 1982, p. 23. Reprinted from *Public Opinion* by permission of The American Enterprise Institute.

Interestingly, the business community itself is not wholly committed to deregulation. Indeed, the loudest opposition to, for example, trucking deregulation came from the industry and the Teamsters Union. For some businesspeople, restraints on competition provide a safe harbor. Many simply see some regulation as necessary for the well-being of society and, in turn, for their firms. A Conference Board survey of 300 executives revealed a general acceptance of the need for some regulation, but the executives were also firmly committed to regulatory reform. The comment of a personnel vice president was representative of the survey findings:

As a company, we cannot argue against sensible safety and health regulations, nor reasonable legislation covering equal opportunity in its broadest aspect. But we are critical of the application and enforcement of these laws by the respective agencies involved. It has been estimated that 40 percent of a personnel department's time currently is spent in dealing with the handling of laws enforced by OSHA, EEOC, and ERISA. This is absolutely ludicrous.[48]

As time passes, ample evidence regarding the effects of deregulation will be available. Of course, the issues involved are matters of public policy choice that cannot be fully resolved via scholarly analysis. However, some preliminary observations can be offered.

Some costs are inevitable. As of 1983, deregulation was a factor in the bankruptcy of several hundred trucking firms, along with Braniff Airlines. Some communities had lost airline and/or bus services. Rates on low-use routes had often increased dramatically. Even if service was retained, the quality of that service often declined. Local telephone rates appear to be poised for large increases, barring further government intervention.

However, one finds much support for the view that deregulation was long overdue. The efficiency of the free market is generally conceded. Transportation rates in competitive markets have fallen (when prices are adjusted for inflation). Labor costs are down, and productivity is up in deregulated transportation markets. Paperwork has been reduced, and entrepreneurial freedom has increased. The financial markets have witnessed an explosion of new services and investment opportunities.

The following account summarizes the results of a study of truck and bus deregulation in Florida. While this study reports generally favorable results, other observers, both of the Florida situation[49] and of deregulation generally,[50] reach less sanguine conclusions.

FLORIDA BUS, TRUCK INDUSTRY SURVIVES DEREGULATION

George Thurston

Tallahassee, Florida—When Florida became the first state in the country totally to deregulate intrastate trucking and buses, industry executives predicted anarchy. They feared an excess of free enterprise would paralyze the state's transportation system. At least, that's what lobbyists told the legislature.

But regulation lapsed at the end of June under a "sunset" provision of the law, and predictions involving the death of trucking proved to be greatly exaggerated.

A recent survey of the transportation industry in Florida showed that the immediate effects were:

● Price adjustments, both up and down in both trucking and busing.

● Some routes added, others dropped.

● A surge of small new trucking companies filling gaps left by bigger ones.

● A surge of new ridership on some bus lines where fares were cut and routes added.

A vice president of Greyhound Bus Lines told a recent Interstate Commerce Commission seminar in Washington that his company had opposed deregulation in Florida but was now pleased because it found that Greyhound could

better allocate resources without having to deal with state government regulations. But he cautioned against moving "too fast" on deregulation nationwide.

* * * * *

The Florida survey, conducted by a Miami consulting firm (Industrial Traffic Consultants, Inc.), found that bus lines responded to deregulation by cutting fares and dropping service to some towns and some routes. Florida Trailways cut fares 10 percent between intrastate points and offered discounts for children and elderly riders. A company spokesman said the reduced rates produced as much as 20 percent more ridership on some runs.

Trailways dropped some of its less lucrative runs, especially in small towns, but state representative George Sheldon (D-Tampa) said most of the points dropped by Trailways have been picked up by other carriers. . . .

By dropping some routes and some stops, Trailways cut its trip time on the 250-mile Tallahassee-to-Tampa run by more than two hours, and shortened other trip times by similar amounts. It also added 1,620 miles a day of routes connecting 16 towns that previously had not had bus service. . . .

* * * * *

Greyhound dropped service to 34 towns, mostly in rural north and central Florida, producing some complaints, but Sheldon said most residents didn't realize they had bus service and didn't notice losing it.

On the other hand, according to Sheldon, charter bus rates in Florida have dropped by between 30 percent and 50 percent and the industry has almost doubled in size.

Truckers also dropped many small communities from their regular routes, but almost overnight small independent truckers stepped in to pick up the slack. Bus lines, no longer restricted in the kinds of package express they can handle, have taken over some of the small-town shipping. In some cases, the added package revenue kept bus lines from dropping pas-senger service.

A major problem for Florida truckers is that out-of-state truckers bringing cargoes into Florida now can haul new loads out instead of deadheading back. Previously, regulations against "backhauling" required the trucks to return empty.

* * * * *

It was mostly the larger companies that lost business with deregulation. Independent truckers have found the market much looser. The Miami survey found that the total number of trucking firms in the state jumped about 25 percent after deregulation. Most of the firms are going after the "gravy accounts" in large urban areas, according to the survey. . . .

Source: *Washington Post*, December 26, 1980, pp. C6–C7. © *The Washington Post*, 1980. Reprinted with permission.

Afterword

The urge for regulations may be unquenchable. Even as the federal government has been about the business of deregulation, the states seem to be swelling their own complex of regulatory measures. New Jersey recently approved a very strict chemical labeling law and New York is enforcing its own "lemon law" to protect car buyers. As a consequence, some business spokespeople are in the paradoxical position of *seeking* federal regulation in some areas to achieve uniformity across the nation.[51]

Questions

1. From the reading materials we saw that a major complaint about the federal regulatory process is that the regulators share an excessively "cozy" relationship with those being regulated. In Japan, cooperation between government, business, workers, and the public seems to have been instrumental in their remarkable economic success. Indeed, it is commonplace for retiring high-level bureaucrats to be hired as top executives of the companies they once regulated. The practice is labeled *amakudari* (descent from heaven).

   Should the United States emulate the Japanese *amakudari* policy as a step toward a more unified, cooperative industrial policy? Explain.

2. The "Kentucky Entrepreneur" Eli Simpson faced aggravating bureaucratic hurdles in his efforts to build stills for producing alcohol to be used as fuel.

   a. Does the production of alcohol for fuel require regulation? Explain.

   b. Should government regulations be written at an eighth grade or lower reading level when possible? Explain.

3. Would the free market succeed in preserving areas such as the Boundary Waters described in "Forests Overgrown with Red Tape"? Explain.

4. As mentioned, transportation deregulation has resulted in an immediate loss of service to some smaller communities. Some of that loss will be compensated for with the entry of smaller, independent firms.

   a. Will deregulation endanger small town America? Explain.

   b. Should we apply free market principles to postal service, thus, among other consequences, compelling those in small and remote communities to pay the full cost of service rather than the "subsidized" cost now paid? Explain.

   c. Should the government eliminate the U.S. Postal Service monopoly on the delivery of first-class mail? Explain.

5. Would an unregulated market produce the benefits cited by Ashford in the article, "In Many Cases Regulation Pays"? Explain. Are those benefits worth the costs as expressed in this chapter? Explain.

6. The expense of government regulation is not limited to the direct cost of administering the various agencies. Explain and offer examples of the other expenses that are produced by regulation.

7. To the extent the federal government achieves deregulation, what substitutes will citizens find for protection?

8. Motor carriers have argued that by allowing open entry to new carriers the government has confiscated their property. Explain that argument.

9. From 1976 to 1980, 27 states repealed or weakened laws requiring the use of motorcycle helmets. During that time, new motorcycle registrations increased by less than 1 percent, but fatalities increased by more than 40 percent.[52] Congress has considered reimposing on states the sanctions (e.g., withholding highway safety funds) deemed necessary to encourage states to approve helmet laws.

   a. Build the arguments for and against such federal sanctions.

   b. How would you vote on such legislation? Explain.

10. Many states, particularly western ones, favor repealing or raising the 55 mile per hour speed limit in effect at this writing. Those in the West argue that higher speeds are necessary there given the greater distances to be covered. They argue that their less congested roads permit safe, high-speed travel. They object to federal regulation of what they take to be a state issue. On the other hand, studies indicate that savings of 3 to 4 billion gallons of fuel per year and 45,000 lives (1974–1981) have resulted from the 55 mile per hour limit.[53]

    a. Should the states be allowed to set their own limits? Explain.

    b. Assume a pattern emerges of primarily 55 mph limits in the East and 70 mph in the West. Would such a pattern constitute an unfair economic burden on the eastern states? Explain.

11. Physicians Lawrence Berger and Frederick Rivara have argued that minibikes (with engines up to three horsepower, reaching speeds up to 50 miles per hour) should be regulated by the federal Consumer Product Safety Commission.[54] The doctors sought speed and structural requirements and the application of warning labels. About 20,000 children per year are injured in minibike accidents. There are about 3.5 million unlicensed, two-wheeled, motorized vehicles in the United States.

    a. How would you rule on the doctors' petition? Explain.

    b. What of skateboards? Fireworks? Explain.

    c. Should the entire regulatory burden in these areas rest with parents? Explain.

Part Five—The Corporate Response to Government Regulation

The weight of government intervention has provoked, in many businesses, an activist stance toward the regulatory process. Traditionally, most companies relied on occasional monitoring, a bit of lobbying, and support of their trade association to achieve their government relations goals. That may well continue to be the dominant mode, but increasingly we find businesspeople seeking to shape government-business relations by anticipating critical issues and endeavoring to cast the outcome in a manner advantageous to the business community. Government relations offices are achieving higher visibility within companies today. The Washington governmental relations office is now less likely to be a place to which soon-to-be retired executives are shipped.

In a recent Conference Board survey of government relations executives, 29 percent of respondents indicated that their companies have made a "very aggressive commitment" to improved government relations.[55] Trade associations have been strengthened. The Business Roundtable (a group of chief executive officers from America's major corporations) has emerged as perhaps the leading voice of business views in Washington. High-level interaction between business and government is increasing. Business is actively seeking allies among stockholders, competitors, special-interest groups, and so on. Political action committees appear to be a significant new force in the electoral process. As discussed in Chapter 1 some view this new political vigor with alarm. The fear is that business resources will come to dominate political decision making, but the business community takes the position that it is merely exercising its democratic rights in an honorable effort to maximize its interests and the interests of the nation. In any case, it is clear that dealing with the government is and will remain an important ingredient in corporate success.

So businesspeople are gradually, probably reluctantly, adopting the view that government must be dealt with in an affirmative, even activist, manner. If business must give more attention to that domain, the question then becomes one of tactics. How best may business implement such an effort? Of course, the possibilities are many. The reading that follows sketches one particularly interesting system.

CHASE MANHATTAN'S CORPORATE ISSUES DEPARTMENT

Phyllis S. McGrath

Government relations sometimes can take the form of an issues management program, as is the case at The Chase Manhattan Bank. The government relations unit at the bank actually is called "Corporate Issues."

Utilizing a series of early warning systems, the corporate issues unit identifies legislative matters of potential concern to the bank and its customers. Analyses and summaries of emerging issues are prepared, and as many of Chase's issues contact officers (ICOs) as might be affected are alerted.

Each line department has an ICO, a senior officer named by the department executive, who is responsible for issues interface. Each ICO, and Chase presently has about 20 of them, is charged with bringing departmentwide resources to bear on legislative issues. When corporate issues apprises an ICO, or group of ICOs, of an emerging issue, each of them is asked, in effect, to develop an "impact statement"—setting forth the cost effects and operational constraints implicit in the issue for the department.

It is the responsibility of corporate issues to receive this information from the ICOs, synthesize it, and to develop a corporationwide position on the issue—with the approval of Chase's top management.

Then a strategy to deal with the issue is developed. Chase's Washington office identifies legislators involved in the matter at hand and, with the corporate issues unit, also identifies officers within the bank appropriate to communicate the Chase position to these legislators, or present testimony. Allies in trade associations and other outside groups are involved, and continuing efforts are made to coordinate activities relative to the issue. Chase's public relations department sometimes is brought in to develop speeches, articles, and other pertinent communications, and some issues have been utilized in advertising campaigns directed to the public.

From time to time, Chase's issues contact officers have a general meeting. At one such recent session, presentations were made on developing societal and legislative trends, as well as on issues expected to emerge in a shorter time frame—which would have specific impact on the business of banking.

Source: *Redefining Corporate-Federal Relations* (New York: The Conference Board, 1979), p. 25. Reprinted with permission of the copyright holder, The Conference Board.

CHAPTER QUESTIONS

1. General Motors executive R. F. Magill argued that business lobbying must be "identified with the public interest."
   a. Has the business community shown itself able to look beyond its self-interest to the larger concerns of society? Explain.
   b. Should the business community seek to do so? Explain.
2. Explain "issue management" in the corporate context.
3. Assume Chase Manhattan learns that a congressional committee staff is preparing a position paper advocating an embargo of all commerce (including loans) with a Middle Eastern nation, Rabatan, on the grounds that Rabatan is fomenting rebellion in Central America. Chase Manhattan would suffer a serious (but not fatal) financial reversal if the policy were effected. Rabatan's Central American involvement has been fully verified. Should Chase Manhattan seek to influence the government's foreign policy decision? Explain.
4. List what you believe are the critical ingredients in effectively linking the identification of public affairs issues and the development of corporate plans for dealing with those issues.
5. California Republican Representative Robert F. Dorman: "Corporate managers are whores. They don't care who's in office, what party or what they stand for, they're just out to buy you."[56]
   a. Do you agree? Explain.
   b. If you look forward to a business career, can you envision yourself assuming the apolitical, self-serving, corrupt stance Mr. Dorman attributes to business people? Explain.
6. Charles Koch, highly successful chairman of Koch Industries: "The majority of businessmen today are not supporters of free enterprise capitalism."[57] Does the bulk of the business community favor government intervention? Explain.
7. The passing of the Civil Aeronautics Board means that the Department of Transportation's Federal Aviation Administration presumably will be left to address some unresolved problems. Such issues include congestion in the airways caused by too many planes seeking

to take off or land at peak times at high-demand airports. How might we solve that problem while maintaining reasonable service?

8. Historically, American cities have regulated the taxicab industry by, among other strategies, specifying fares and limiting the number of cab operator permits available to the market. Since 1979, many cities have begun to deregulate the taxi markets by removing controls on fares and by issuing many more medallions.

   a. Build the arguments for and against deregulation of the taxi industry.

   b. What legal challenges are likely to be raised by current permit holders if a city increases the number of available permits?

Notes

1. Neil H. Jacoby, ''The Corporate State: Pure Myth,'' *Wharton Magazine,* Summer 1977, as quoted in Murray Weidenbaum, *The Future of Business Regulation* (New York: AMACOM, 1979), pp. 168–69.

2. J. Wilson, ''The Rise of the Bureaucratic State,'' *The Public Interest,* No. 41 (Fall 1975), as quoted in Robert L. Rabin, *Perspectives on the Administrative Process* (Boston: Little, Brown, 1979), pp. 16 and 33.

3. George Stigler, ''The Theory of Economic Regulation,'' *Bell Journal of Economics and Management Science* 2 (Spring 1971), p. 3.

4. For a more detailed discussion of the materials in this section, see Ernest Gellhorn, *Administrative Law and Process in a Nutshell* (St. Paul, Minn.: West Publishing, 1972), pp. 76–237.

5. Federal Trade Commission Rule § 429.1, 38 Stat. 717, as amended; 15 U.S.C. 41–58 (37 FR 22934, Oct. 26, 1972; 38 FR 30105, November 1, 1973; 38 FR 31828, November 19, 1973).

6. See Bernard Schwartz, *Administrative Law* (Boston: Little, Brown, 1976), p. 205.

7. Jerry Mashaw, ''Regulation, Logic, and Ideology,'' *Regulation,* November–December 1979, p. 48.

8. Ibid.

9. For a more detailed discussion of the FDA, see Paul J. Quirk, ''Food and Drug Administration,'' in *The Politics of Regulation,* James Q. Wilson (New York: Basic Books, 1980), p. 191.

10. 53 *Law Week* 4385 (U.S. S. Ct., 1985).

11. Ibid., p. 4386.

12. ''FDA Chief Says Reports Falsified,'' *Lexington (Kentucky) Leader,* November 16, 1976, p. A–6.

13. Judy Grande, ''Rules Approving New Drugs Eased by Administration,'' *Waterloo (Iowa) Courier,* August 7, 1983, p. D–1.

14. William M. Wardell, ''A Close Inspection of the 'Calm Look,' '' *Journal of the American Medical Association,* as cited in Paul J. Quirk, ''Food and Drug Administration'' in *The Politics of Regulation,* ed. James Q. Wilson (New York: Basic Books, 1980), p. 226.

15. Ibid., p. 227.

16. ''The Hidden Cost of Drug Safety,'' *Business Week,* February 21, 1977, p. 80.

17. Ibid.

18. Judy Grande (Newhouse News Service), ''Rules for Approving New Drugs Eased by Administration,'' *Waterloo (Iowa) Courier,* August 7, 1983, p. D–1.

19. ''Data Needed for FDA to Approve Drugs Reduced under Rules Signed by Heckler,'' *The Wall Street Journal,* December 12, 1984, p. 14.

20. ''Drug Controls Preferred,'' *FDA Consumer* 18, no. 4 (May 1984), p. 2.

21. ''DC-10 Jet Was 'Certified' but Never Seen by FAA,'' *Lexington (Kentucky) Leader,* August 7, 1979, p. A-4.

22. Mitchell Lynch, ''Backing Off Basics,'' *The Wall Street Journal,* October 18, 1977, pp. 1, 36.

23. J. Richard Crout, in *Drug Development and Marketing,* ed. Robert Helms, (Washington, D.C.: American Enterprise Institute, 1975), p. 197, as quoted in Murray Weidenbaum, *The Future of Business Regulation* (New York: AMACOM, 1979), p. 116.

24. ''Congress Wondering How Oraflex Was Approved,'' *Waterloo (Iowa) Courier,* August 4, 1982, p. B-1.

25. See Murray L. Weidenbaum, *The Future of Business Regulation* (New York: AMACOM, 1979), p. 23.

26. Mark Green, ''Why the House Voted Down the Consumer Bill,'' *Washington Post,* February 26, 1978, p. D-3.

27. George Stigler, ''The Theory of Economic Regulation,'' *Bell Journal of Economics and Management Science* 2, (Spring 1971), p. 3, as cited in *The Politics of Regulation,* ed. James Q. Wilson (New York: Basic Books, 1980), p. 358.

28. Stigler, p. 5, cited in Wilson, *The Politics of Regulation,* p. 358.

29. Frank Greve, ''American Petroleum Institute: Gospel According to Big Oil,'' *Lexington (Kentucky) Sunday Herald Leader,* August 5, 1979, p. A-19.

30. Barry M. Mitnick, *The Political Economy of Regulation* (New York: Columbia University Press, 1980), p. 219, citing U.S. House of Representatives, Subcommittee on Oversight and Investigations, Committee on Interstate and Foreign Commerce, *Federal Regulation and Regulatory Reform*, 94th Congress, 2d Session (Washington, D.C.: U.S. Government Printing Office, October 1976), pp. 451–52.

31. Mitnick, *Political Economy of Regulation*, pp. 215–24.

32. Mitnick, *Political Economy of Regulation*, p. 225, citing U.S. House of Representatives, Subcommittee on Oversight and Investigations, *Federal Regulation and Regulatory Reform*.

33. Mitnick, *Political Economy of Regulation*, p. 218, citing James M. Graham and Victor H. Kramer, *Appointments to the Regulatory Agencies: The Federal Communications Commission and The Federal Trade Commission* (1949–1974). Committee print, Committee on Commerce, U.S. Senate, 94th Congress, 2d session (Washington, D.C.: U.S. Government Printing Office, April 1976).

34. "Regulators Too 'Cozy'—Cause," *Lexington (Kentucky) Leader,* August 24, 1977, p. A-8.

35. Morton Mintz and Jerry Cohen, *America, Inc.* (New York: Dell Publishing Co., 1971), p. 296.

36. Greve, "Gospel According to Big Oil," p. A-19.

37. For a more detailed discussion, see e.g., "Sunset Laws: One More Brave Idea That's Gone Awry?," *U.S. News and World Report,* May 29, 1978, p. 45.

38. See, e.g., James Affleck, "Toward Realistic Risk/Benefit Decisions," *New York Times,* April 29, 1979, Section III, p. 16.

39. See, e.g., John Tomerlin, "Billion Dollar Trial Balloon: The Facts Behind the Air Bag Mandate," *Road and Track,* May 1979, as reviewed in "Bagfuls of Air?" *Regulation,* January–February 1980, p. 45.

40. *Weekly Compilation of Presidential Documents* 17, no. 8 (February 23, 1981), pp. 124–25.

41. *American Textile Manufacturers Institute* v. *Donovan,* 452 U.S. 490 (1981).

42. Lester Thurow, *The Zero-Sum Society* (New York: Basic Books, 1980), Penguin Books edition, pp. 131–32.

43. Ibid., p. 140.

44. Ibid., p. 136.

45. Roper Report 84–2, January 7–21, 1984, as reported in *Public Opinion,* April–May 1984, p. 24.

46. Cambridge Reports, May 12–June 13, 1979, as reported in *Public Opinion,* June–July 1980, p. 39.

47. Roper Report 80–3, February 9–23, 1980, as reported in *Public Opinion,* June–July, 1980, p. 38.

48. James Greene, *Regulatory Problems and Regulatory Reform: The Perceptions of Business* (New York: The Conference Board, 1980), p. 6.

49. "Florida's Test of Truck Deregulation," *Business Week,* September 22, 1980, p. 125.

50. L. L. Waters, "Deregulation—For Better or for Worse," *Business Horizons* 24, no. 1 (January–February 1981), p. 88.

51. "State Regulators Rush in Where Washington No Longer Treads," *Business Week,* September 19, 1983, p. 124.

52. "Keep Kentucky's Helmet Law," *Lexington (Kentucky) Leader,* November 5, 1980, p. A-20. Also see "Motorcycles, Safety, and Freedom," *Regulation,* July–August 1980, p. 11.

53. "Keep the Speed Limit," *Washington Post* editorial, reprinted in *Lexington (Kentucky) Leader,* March 6, 1981, p. A-10.

54. "Mini-Bikes: A Case Study in Under-Regulation," *Business and Society Review* 34, Summer 1980, p. 41.

55. Phyllis S. McGrath, *Redefining Corporate-Federal Relations* (New York: The Conference Board, 1979), p. 3.

56. Quoted in Charles Koch, "Business Can Have Free Enterprise—If It Dares," *Business and Society Review,* no. 28 (Winter 1978–79), p. 58.

57. Charles Koch, Ibid., p. 54.

8

Business Organizations and Securities Regulation

When starting a business, one of the first decisions that must be made by its promoters is which legal format to use to establish the firm. This decision can be crucial for it will determine many of the rules and requirements governing the operations of the fledgling business. Most large-scale concerns opt for the corporate form, while many smaller ones choose to begin as partnerships or sole proprietorships. Size alone, however, does not determine which form the promoters of a business should prefer. All of the available options—sole proprietorships, partnerships, corporations, Sub S Corporations, and so on—offer various advantages and disadvantages, each of which must be considered, given the circumstances of the particular investment opportunity.

After deciding how the business will be set up, its promoters must determine how and from whom to raise the money needed to establish the business and commence operations. Many small businesses rely solely on their owners for capital, perhaps supplementing their available money with loans from friends or relatives, loans guaranteed by a federal agency such as the Small Business Administration, or loans collateralized by the owner's house or other assets. Other promoters choose to raise money from banks, insurance companies, or other financial institutions by using the assets of the business or the attractiveness of the investment opportunity to convince the bank to lend the money. Others rely on risk-taking venture capitalists who are willing to back new companies with impressive expertise, product lines, or ideas in return for a share of ownership in the business, while still other firms opt for issuing stock or securities to small segments of the public, such as friends or acquaintances, or even to the public at large.

Naturally, the decision of how to raise capital is dictated by market forces. If no bank is willing to extend credit, or no broker is willing to attempt to sell shares in the company, those avenues of money-raising activity must be eliminated from consideration. Of those possibilities that are economically viable, however, the promoters must choose wisely if they are to raise the needed capital at the lowest possible cost to the business and their ownership of the business. As will be seen in the second section of this chapter, major expenses can be avoided if the firm can raise capital without subjecting itself to the requirements of federal securities laws. Many deals are structured in a particular manner solely for the purpose of assuring that the capital raised will not cause the business to fall under the scrutiny of the Securities and Exchange Commission and its mandates.

Form of the Organization

When determining which legal form a business will adopt, most thoughtful promoters focus on five factors: cost, continuity, control, liability, and taxes. The order of importance of these considerations will vary from business to business, but all five certainly merit serious analysis before a final decision is made. Cost reflects the initial and subsequent expenses (direct and indirect) associated with a particular form of organization. Continuity refers to the consequences of an owner dying or otherwise withdrawing from participation in the firm, or a new owner joining the business. Control focuses on who will have the ability to set firm policy and run the business. Liability concerns what assets of the owners may be used to pay firm debts, while tax considerations are based on maximizing the share of corporate resources available to the owner and minimizing those due the government.

Partnerships

Many small businesses start out as sole proprietorships or partnerships. A partnership is defined as two or more people carrying on as co-owners of a business for profit. A sole proprietorship exists when there is but a single owner of the business. Under either of these arrangements, costs are minimal. There are no legal requirements. A group of people who agree to form a partnership and who act like partners have done just that— created a partnership. No written agreement, filings at the courthouse, or other legal notice must be given. While a written partnership agreement is advisable to set forth rights and responsibilities and to limit confusion, it is not necessary. Furthermore, the partners' agreement, whether written or oral, can be changed at any time with their consent.

In the situation where a partnership is created without any thought, either written or oral, being given to how it will operate, the state laws supply the operating conditions for the partnership. Most jurisdictions have basically adopted the Uniform Partnership Act, which provides, for instance, that in the absence of agreements to the contrary:

1. All partners share equally in partnership profits and losses.
2. All partners are expected to devote their full time and energies to partnership business, without compensation.
3. Unanimous consent is necessary to admit a new partner.
4. The partnership can be terminated at any time for any reason by any partner.

A partnership is free to tailor the provisions of its agreement to the particular needs of the partners. Many times, profits and losses are not shared equally, or one partner receives a salary in addition to his or her share of profits, but such variances from the UPA must be spelled out and agreed to. Failure to do so automatically triggers the

UPA's provisions and may have costly and perhaps fatal consequences when disputes arise.

Continuity is a problem for partnerships. Every time a partner leaves the firm for any reason (e.g., death, insanity, voluntary or involuntary withdrawal, or personal bankruptcy) or a new partner joins the firm, the partnership must be dissolved and a new one created. Dissolution requires that all firm creditors be notified and appropriate arrangements made. The value of the partnership must be determined, and the withdrawing partner must be given his appropriate share or monetary equivalent of the partnership assets. This process can provoke many disputes and is often time-consuming and expensive. Furthermore, from a business point of view, it can be disastrous if partnership assets must be sold quickly to pay off a withdrawing partner. A good partnership agreement can limit the potential problems caused by a partner withdrawal, but can never totally eliminate them.

Control in a partnership is relatively simple. Either each partner has an equal say-so in partnership policy, or the partnership agreement sets forth an alternative scheme under which some partners have a greater voice than others. On most issues, unless otherwise agreed to by the partners, a majority vote is necessary to approve a course of action. Thus, if the initial partners are willing, it is easy to set up a system in which one or more partners own less than half the interest of the partnership but have more than half—or effective control—for voting purposes. Other than to benefit or protect individual partners, the most critical issue that must be addressed concerning control is making certain that the votes among the partners do not occur continually. Many small partnerships have failed because the partners were not able to muster 50 percent or more votes to approve a policy (typically 1–1 or 2–2 votes on a major issue) and had not established procedures to prevent the deadlock from becoming a permanent pitfall capable of stifling any partnership action.

Liability is often the issue that forces promoters to choose the corporate form over a partnership. All members of a partnership are personally liable to the full extent of their assets for all partnership debts. If, for instance, the partnership were to lose money and be unable to pay a bank loan on time, or if a partnership truck were to cause the deaths of 10 children in a school bus, the partners might be forced to sell their houses, stock, bonds, and other possessions to meet the demands of various creditors. Because of this uncertainty, many people with substantial assets refuse to invest or participate in partnerships. Clearly, if the business is likely to be sued regularly or could face catastrophic losses from accidents or other tort liability, a partnership probably would not be appropriate. On the other hand, if the partners are relatively poor or judgment proof (i.e., have no unencumbered assets), the penalty associated with the unlimited personal liability for partnership debts is largely illusory and may not be dispositive of the issue.

Taxation is the reason many small businesses choose to be partnerships. Not taxable entities for income tax purposes, partnerships merely serve as conduits for profits flowing from the business directly to the partners. The partners then report partnership profits or losses on their tax returns and pay the appropriate taxes at the ordinary income tax rate. The partnership itself merely reports the amount of income to appropriate taxing agencies, not actually paying any income tax. Additionally, many states levy a yearly tax against the authorized shares of corporations chartered in their states. Partnerships typically escape taxes such as this.

Corporations

Partnerships and sole proprietorships made economic sense for people who were essentially selling their own and their partners' labor, expertise, or experience (three doctors, eight attorneys, or five radio repairmen). Larger businesses, which utilize many different factors in production, need large amounts of capital, and expect to continue unabated after the founding owners have departed, often find partnerships unwieldy and economically unfeasible. For these businesses, a corporate entity is more appropriate. Corporations do business under a charter provided by a state and are an economic entity totally separate and distinct from their owners. Typically, but not always, corporations are chartered in the state where their headquarters are located. Many corporations, however, choose to incorporate in Delaware or Texas regardless of where they plan on doing business because the corporate laws and low taxation policies of these jurisdictions give management more leeway in how they run the corporation, control its policies, and benefit themselves and the shareholders. Quite often, such state regulations and laws are decisive tools in corporate mergers or takeover attempts.

The cost of setting up a corporation is often substantially higher than that associated with a partnership. Obtaining a charter typically requires an attorney and the completion of numerous forms and procedures dictated by the state. Taxes and license fees often have to be paid. The corporation must also undertake similar obligations in other states in which it plans to do business. After the corporation is chartered, it must file regular reports with the state, pay appropriate taxes and fees, maintain an agent for service of process, and generally comply with the state's corporate law. This might require election of a board of directors, regular audits, shareholder meetings, and any number of other items thought by the state to be necessary to ensure that the corporation is run fairly for the benefit of all shareholders.

As long as all state requirements are met, a corporation may enjoy a perpetual existence, thus eliminating continuity problems such as those which occur in a partnership when an important partner decides to withdraw at an inopportune time. Ownership of stock in a corporation does not connote a personal, fiduciary duty such as that which exists between partners. Shares may be transferred freely to anyone without corporate approval, and the corporation is under no obligation to buy back the shares of a disgruntled or departing shareholder. Likewise, upon the death of a shareholder, the shares simply transfer to his or her heirs, and corporate structure remains unchanged.

Control is usually much easier to maintain in a corporation than in a partnership. Shares of stock often are sold to widely diverse groups of people who have no connection with each other, little in common, and no interest in being involved in corporate dealings. Often, large blocks of shares are controlled by banks or insurance companies, which tend to vote for the continuation of current management except in the most unusual situations. The groups that control major corporations often own or control very small percentages of the company's stock, but are able to maintain their positions as board members or top corporate officers. Corporations sometimes issue nonvoting as well as voting stock. This nonvoting stock shares in firm profits and dividends, but does not vote at shareholder meetings. Through this technique, existing owners can raise additional capital for the firm without risking loss of control.

Shareholder liability is much more limited than partner liability. Since a corporation is a separate entity, it can sue and be sued. Corporate debts are sole obligations of the corporation and must be paid from corporate assets. In other words, a party that is aggrieved by an action of a corporation (an unpaid debt or an accident caused by a corporate-owned automobile) but that is unable to recoup adequate damages from the corporation may not expect to recover its losses from the personal assets of the individual shareholders. Except in the most egregious or unusual circumstances, shareholders' losses are limited to their original investment in the corporation. Their personal assets may not be seized to satisfy judgments against a corporation that has gone bankrupt or is unable to raise the funds to pay its debts or judgments.

This inability of creditors to use personal shareholder assets to satisfy corporate debts or obligations is referred to as the "corporate veil," the existence of which is often powerful incentive to incorporate. By incorporating, a person starting a small business can rest at night with the assurance that a business reverse will not cause the owner's house, automobiles, jewelry, and so on to be sold to pay corporate debts.

The issue of taxation presents the major drawback for choosing a corporate existence. Since a corporation is a separate economic entity, it is also a separate taxable entity. As such, corporations must pay a corporate income tax to the federal government as well as to most states in which they conduct business. Joint state and federal income taxes can approach 40 percent of profits, although many corporations can substantially lower this figure by means of the many provisions of the income tax code. An individual receiving dividends from a corporation must pay income tax on the dividend to state and federal authorities. Thus, corporate profits are said to be subject to "double taxation"—first when the corporation reports a profit, and later when those profits are distributed to owners in the form of dividends. For each dollar of corporate profits, it would not be inconceivable to suggest that less than 35 cents would eventually find its way into the shareholders' pockets.

Hybrid Organizations

For some investments, a limited partnership may be appropriate. A limited partnership is like a partnership in many respects: it is not a taxable entity, and all losses or gains are passed through to the partners. The principal difference is that there are two classes of partners. One class, typically investors, is referred to as limited partners. They are not allowed to participate in management decision making, but they are also granted limited liability so that their maximum potential exposure to loss is their original investment in the project. The other class of partner, typically the promoters, is referred to as general partners. They manage the business and are personally liable for all losses. A corporation can be the general partner in many instances, thus offering the general partners (the owners of the corporation) the equivalent of limited liability. Limited partnerships are particularly suitable for raising capital for single-project alliances among diverse groups of investors (e.g., developing an office building or shopping mall), and when one of the primary motivations for investing in the project is to shelter other income from taxation.

In a limited partnership, the shares or interests of the limited partners may be sold or transferred freely. Death, bankruptcy, insanity, and so on have no effect on the partnership. The general partners, on the other hand, are subject to roughly the same restrictions as in a regular partnership. However, provision is usually made in the limited partnership agreement for an alternate general partner so that the project can continue unabated should a general partner be forced to withdraw. Limited partnerships are at least as complicated as corporations to form. Failure to comply with all the requirements may subject the limited partners to unlimited liability just as if they were general partners.

Some business projects call for the formation of a Sub S Corporation. This is a creation of tax law which, in certain situations, allows an incorporated business to escape most corporate income tax. The owners of the business then have the best of both worlds—limited liability without double taxation. In order to qualify, a corporation must have fewer than 17 shareholders, over 80 percent of its income must be "earned" income (i.e., not derived from dividends, interest, royalties, and other passive sources), and almost all of its income or losses must be distributed to the owners each year. The shareholders then pay the appropriate personal income tax on their earnings. Because of these restrictions, Sub S Corporations are suitable only for smaller projects that do not need to retain capital for growth purposes. A suitable situation might be eight individuals who decide to develop 100 acres of land into 200 lots, which will then be sold over a period of years. The early losses generated from building roads, sewers, parks, and so on will be passed through to the individual shareholders to reduce their current income tax. Furthermore, no additional capital will be needed by the business. When all the lots have been sold, the deal will end and the corporation will simply cease operations.

Special Situations

Piercing the Corporate Veil

Although shareholders in corporations are said to have limited liability for the debts of the corporation, there are certain instances in which they can be held personally liable when the corporation is unable to pay its obligations. For instance, the corporate veil of limited liability can be pierced if a business is started with so little capital that it is obvious to the courts that the sole purpose of the corporation was for the shareholders to escape liability for their actions.

Suppose that a corporation was established with little or no capital to supply propane gas to civic arenas, theaters, and so on. This business kept no insurance, had no assets, and would have nothing to lose should a tank explode killing or injuring numerous people. Although its owners might think themselves to be insulated from liability and the corporation to be judgment-proof, a court might pierce the corporate veil and hold the owners personally liable on the theory that the gross undercapitalization of their business so abused the corporate privileges granted them in their charter that they should be denied limited liability. In other situations, limited liability is denied the owners of a corporation that received a charter but does not comply with all the state requirements that directors be elected, board meetings be held, and so on. Typically, this occurs when one corporation sets up another corporation to perform some activity but the larger corporation does not allow the new one to be run as an independent entity, treating it instead like it was simply another division of the original corporation. If the new corporation suffers large losses, the courts might hold the founding corporation liable for its debts on the grounds that the two were run like a single corporation even though they were issued two charters. One is said to be the alter ego of the other and thus liable.

Reality of Limited Liability

Many businesspeople automatically assume they want to form a corporation because of their concerns about personal liability for business debts. These debts could come from two main sources: tort liability resulting from an accident involving business activities (such as an accident caused by a firm truck) or contract liability occurring because the firm is unable to pay its obligation to a supplier of goods or a lender of money. Concerning tort liability, only the most irresponsible business would fail to have insurance adequate to pay foreseeable losses resulting from accident or death due to negligence. Thus, personal tort liability can be as easily avoided in a partnership as in a corporation. Insurance is not available to pay contract liabilities resulting from a firm's inability to meet its debts and other obligations, so the corporate form might appear to be advantageous as many more businesses fail due to contractual indebtedness than due to negligence actions. Banks and other lenders, however, recognize this economic fact of life and want to protect themselves from the limited liability afforded corporate shareholders. The principal way they do this is by refusing to lend money to small or new corporations unless the owners personally guarantee the loans. This usually means that the owners must pledge their houses, stocks, bonds, and other assets to the bank. If the business fails, their personal fortunes are just as likely to be lost in a corporation as in a partnership. For a small corporation, limited liability is not always what it seems.

Avoidance of Double Taxation

One of the principal problems for small businesses that choose the corporate form is double taxation. Many corporations that are owned and managed by the same people can take various steps to minimize the bite of corporate taxation. In all instances, the strategy involved revolves around the same simple principle: maximize the benefits received by the owners and minimize the profitability of the corporation. The proper procedure is to use corporate assets in a way that is advantageous to the owners and deductible to the corporation. For instance, the owners can pay themselves large salaries and substantial fringe benefits for running the business. They receive those salaries and benefits directly, and if they can arrange it so that the corporation earns no profit each year, no corporate income tax will be paid and double taxation avoided. The IRS recognizes this game, however, and will allow only the deduction of reasonable salaries and benefits. Still, salaries and benefits can be stretched to minimize corporate profitability.

Equally, the owner can choose to lend the firm money and receive interest rather than purchasing stocks in the corporation and receiving dividends in return. As interest is deductible to the corporation while dividends are not, and both are taxable to the recipients at ordinary income tax rates, this strategy also eliminates double taxation. Again, the IRS is not blind to the possibilities of abuse and has the power to disallow interest payments it believes are excessive. Clearly, a business funded 100 percent with debt provided by its owner would not pass IRS muster, but a 50 percent debt/50 percent equity ratio would probably appear reasonable in most circumstances.

Some businesses choose to minimize double taxation by not paying dividends and accumulating earnings. If, at some future time, the business is sold, the earnings will be taxed at lower capital gains rates rather than ordinary income tax rates, and in the meantime the money can be profitably invested in other stocks or bonds. The IRS can minimize this ploy by taxing excess accumulated earnings, which it defines as earnings accumulated not for business-related reasons but for tax avoidance purposes. Before the IRS can consider levying the tax, several million dollars of earnings must be accumulated and there must be no valid reason, such as future plans for expansion, for retaining the earnings.

Changing the Form of a Business

Within certain IRS-imposed limitations, businesses are free to change their legal form as they deem advantageous. One simple strategy might be to start out as a partnership, because it is cheaper and easier and because any business losses can be deducted from the partners' personal income tax. If the corporate form were chosen, business losses could not be deducted until such time as the corporation itself earned money, an event which might not occur for years. Later, after profitability is attained and as the needs for continuity and increased capital become more pressing, a transfer to corporate status might be appropriate.

Tax Shelters

The theory of tax shelters is based on taking advantage of provisions in the tax code that allow certain bookkeeping entries (such as depreciation and depletion) to be deducted from the profits of specific investments. If economically viable and properly set up, these projects may have a negative taxable income plus a positive cash flow for a period of years, thus offering shelter from taxation to some part of a wealthy person's income. Suppose, for instance, that a real estate salesperson wants to buy a building but has no money. Doctors have money and tax problems, but do not have real estate management skills. This marriage made in heaven results in a limited partnership. Typically, the doctors (limited partners) would invest money to make the down payment on the building, and the real estate salesperson (general partner) would borrow the remaining money using the building as collateral. The general partner would receive a small percentage of ownership in the building and a fee for managing it, while the limited partner would receive all the benefits. In sketchy form, the benefits might flow as follows:

Building purchase price	$20,000,000
Down payment (10 Doctors @ $100,000 each)	1,000,000
Amount borrowed	$19,000,000
Annual interest	$ 2,500,000
Depreciation (first year)	2,000,000
Other expenses	500,000
Total expenses	$ 5,000,000
Total income (Building is being renovated)	—0—
Total loss	($ 5,000,000)
Loss per doctor	(500,000)
Tax savings per doctor (Assuming 50% personal income tax rate)	250,000
Return on investment	250%

In other words, the building has not even been rented, and the investors have already received their investment back plus a substantial return. Should the project fail, the investors will not lose; should it succeed, their return will only increase. This example is an extreme one, and is based on the ability to borrow substantial amounts of money with the building as collateral, but similar leads are offered to investors daily. The IRS has recently begun cracking down on fraudulent tax shelters, and many which appear to offer the greatest tax savings will not pass IRS audit. Additionally, the rules on tax shelters are continually being tightened. For instance, in the past, many types of tax shelters could be based on the nonrecourse, borrowed money leverage principle utilized in the previous example. Currently, nonrecourse financing (in which the partners are not personally liable to pay back the loan should the enterprise fail) is allowable only in real estate tax shelters. Bulls, movie scripts, and myriad other shelter offerings can no longer use borrowed, nonrecourse money to leverage their expected returns to extremely high levels.

Buy/Sell Agreements

Many small businesses fail because one of the principal owner/managers dies. The death causes numerous hardships for the firm. First of all, the deceased's expertise is unexpectedly lost. Second, he or she will have to be replaced, often with more than one person, and the new people must be trained. The time and expense can be substantial. Also, from the deceased's point of view, the spouse and children need to be provided for. Most small businesses are totally illiquid in that there is no ready purchaser available to buy the deceased's shares. The remaining owners will probably be unable to purchase the shares due to the increased costs to the business associated with the death and the precarious financial position that the firm is likely to find itself in at this time.

One very attractive solution to this dilemma is a buy/sell agreement. This consists of an agreement *negotiated at the formation of the business* concerning the terms under which the business will be valued should an owner die. Once the valuation formula is agreed to, the firm purchases a joint life insurance policy which pays a specified amount upon the first death of an owner. The firm then uses the proceeds of the policy to purchase the shares, and all remaining parties benefit. The spouse and children receive cash to pay estate taxes and living expenses, and the firm receives a cash infusion just when it is needed most. The premiums on the policy typically are not deductible, however the proceeds normally escape taxation. The only caveat that needs to be expressed is that these agreements must be negotiated before an owner's health fails. When all parties are healthy, buy/sell agreements are easy to negotiate because all sides want the purchase price to be relatively low. They all expect to be purchasing the stock (i.e., alive), not selling it for the benefit of their heirs. Once it becomes apparent who is likely to survive, the issue of valuation becomes much more difficult.

Once the form of organization has been established and the business has started operation and begun to progress, the need for additional funds beyond the financial capacity of the founders and promoters becomes acute. At this time, many firms choose to "go public" or to attempt to raise capital from the general public in a variety of ways in order to finance their business or personal plans for expansion and growth. In order to attract this new money, a business not only must offer an attractive investment opportunity, but also must comply with numerous state and federal requirements concerning the sale and resale of securities. The following section discusses some of the applicable statutes and regulations.

Securities Regulation

Condominiums	Stocks
Gold	Annuities
Bonds	Warehouse receipts
Orange groves	Limited partnerships
Bourbon	

Any of the above can be securities and thus subject to many state and federal laws. As these examples suggest, the definition of a security is a broad one, and care has to be taken so that inadvertent violations of these laws do not occur. State laws, referred to as "blue sky" laws, must be complied with in all states in which the securities are to be sold. Furthermore, one or more federal statutes may be applicable. For instance, the Securities Act of 1933 regulates the public offering of new, nonexempt securities and prohibits their sale until they have been properly registered with the Securities and Exchange Commission (SEC). Fraudulent and deceptive practices are barred by this act. The Securities Exchange Act of 1934 controls the resale of securities and sets up the

SEC for the purpose of exercising that responsibility. This act prohibits manipulative or deceptive practices, requires the registration of brokers and dealers, and limits their activities in many respects. Stock exchanges, clearinghouses, and other participants involved in transferring securities also come under its broad umbrella of coverage. The Investment Advisors Act of 1940 is roughly analogous to the 1934 act in the requirements it places on investment counselors.

The Public Utilities Holding Company Act of 1935 corrected problems that had arisen in the financing of gas and electric holding companies. Very few problems now confront the SEC concerning this area of regulation. The Trust Indenture Act of 1939 sets forth standards of independence for trustees involved in large debt issues. Thus, a bond issue might be subject to the provisions of both this act and the 1933 act.

The Investment Company Act of 1940 regulates any publicly owned entities that primarily invest in or buy and sell securities. Insider dealings, capital requirements, sales charges, and so on are covered by this statute. Finally, the Securities Investor Protection Act of 1970 set up the Securities Investor Protection Corporation, which aids customers of bankrupt or illiquid securities companies.

While the SEC is the primary federal agency established to regulate the securities industry, it cannot do the entire job itself. Thus, all regulatory schemes involve a good deal of "self regulation," in which the regulated entities become participants in their own regulation. The New York Stock Exchange, with SEC approval and oversight, continues to establish many regulations for its members and is active in investigating insider abuses and manipulations by its members. The National Association of Securities Dealers plays a similar role for dealers in over-the-counter securities.

Definition of a Security

The Securities Act of 1933 defines a security as

any note, stock, treasury stock, bond, debenture, evidence of indebtedness, certificate of interest or participation in any profit-sharing agreement, collateral-trust certificate, preorganizational certificate or subscription, transferable share, investment contract, voting-trust certificate, certificate of deposit for a security, fractional undivided interest in oil, gas, or other mineral rights, or, in general, any interest or instrument commonly known as a "security," or any certificate of interest or participation in, temporary or interim certificate for, receipt for, guarantee of, or warrant or right to subscribe to or purchase, any of the foregoing.

Any instrument called a bond, stock, debenture, share, and so on will almost certainly be considered a security. Most of the disputes involving the applicability of securities laws involve investment contracts or certificates of participation in any profit-sharing agreement. Typically, these involve attempts by promoters to raise money for various schemes in which investors pool their money with the expectation of future returns, but no pieces of paper that look like securities are involved. In the *SEC* v. *W. J. Howey Co.*, case, cited here, orange groves were held to be securities and the following test was put forward: "the person invests his money in a common enterprise and is led to expect profits solely from the efforts of the promoter or a third party."

SECURITIES & EXCHANGE COMMISSION V. W. J. HOWEY CO.
328 U.S. 293 (1946)

Justice Murphy

This case involves the application of § 2(1) of the Securities Act of 1933 to an offering of units of a citrus grove development coupled with a contract for cultivating, marketing and remitting the net proceeds to the investor.

* * * * *

Most of the facts are stipulated. The respondents, W. J. Howey Company and Howey-in-the-Hills Service, Inc., are Florida corporations under direct common control and management. The Howey Company owns large tracts of citrus acreage in Lake County, Florida. During the past several years it has planted about 500 acres annually, keeping half of the groves itself and offering the other half to the public "to help us finance additional development." Howey-in-the-Hills Service, Inc., is a service company engaged in cultivating and developing many of these groves, including the harvesting and marketing of the crops.

Each prospective customer is offered both a land sales contract and a service contract, after having been told that it is not feasible to invest in a grove unless service arrangements are made. While the purchaser is free to make arrangements with other service companies, the superiority of Howey-in-the-Hills Service, Inc., is stressed. Indeed, 85 percent of the acreage sold during the three-year period ending May 31, 1943, was covered by service contracts with Howey-in-the-Hills Service, Inc.

The land sales contract with the Howey Company provides for a uniform purchase price per acre or fraction thereof, varying in amount only in accordance with the number of years the particular plot has been planted with citrus trees. Upon full payment of the purchase price the land is conveyed to the purchaser by warranty deed. Purchases are usually made in narrow strips of land arranged so that an acre consists of a row of 48 trees. During the period between February 1, 1941, and May 31, 1943, 31 of the 42 persons making purchases bought less than five acres each. The average holding of these 31 persons was 1.33 acres and sales of as little as 0.65, 0.7, and 0.73 of an acre were made. These tracts are not separately fenced and the sole indication of several ownership is found in small land marks intelligible only through a plat book record.

The service contract, generally of a 10-year duration without option of cancellation, gives Howey-in-the-Hills Service, Inc., a leasehold interest and "full and complete" possession of the acreage. For a specified fee plus the cost of labor and materials, the company is given full discretion and authority over the cultivation of the groves and the harvest and marketing of the crops. The company is well established in the citrus business and maintains a large force of skilled personnel and a great deal of equipment, including 75 tractors, sprayer wagons, fertilizer trucks and the like. Without the consent of the company, the land owner or purchaser has no right of entry to market the crop; thus there is ordinarily no right to specific fruit. The company is accountable only for an allocation of the net profits based upon a check made at the time of picking. All the produce is pooled by the respondent companies, which do business under their own names.

The purchasers for the most part are nonresidents of Florida. They are predominantly business and professional people who lack the knowledge, skill, and equipment necessary for the care and cultivation of citrus trees. They are attracted by the expectation of substantial profits. It was represented, for example, that profits during the 1943–1944 season amounted to 20 percent and that even greater profits might be expected during the 1944–1945 season, although only a 10 percent annual return was to be expected over a 10-year period. Many of these purchasers are patrons of a resort hotel owned and operated by the Howey Company in a scenic section adjacent to the groves. The hotel's advertising mentions the fine groves in the vicinity and the attention of the patrons is drawn to the groves as they are being escorted about the surrounding countryside. They are told that the groves are for sale; if they indicate an interest in the matter they are then given a sales talk.

It is admitted that the mails and instrumentalities of interstate commerce are used in the sale of the land and service contracts and that no registration statement or letter of notification has ever been filed with the commission in accordance with the Securities Act of 1933 and the rules and regulations thereunder.

Section 2(1) of the act defines the term "security" to include the commonly known documents traded for speculation or investment. This definition also includes "securities" of a more variable character, designated by such descriptive terms as "certificate of interest or participation in any profit-sharing agreement," "investment contract" and "in general, any interest or instrument commonly known as a 'security.'" The legal issue in this case turns upon a determination of whether, under the circumstances, the land sales contract, the warranty deed and the service contract together constitute an "investment contract" within the meaning of § 2(1). An affirmative answer brings into operation the registration requirements of § 5(a), unless the security is granted an exemption under § 3(b). The lower courts, in reaching a negative answer to this problem, treated the contracts and deeds as separate transactions involving no more than an ordinary real estate sale and an agreement by the seller to manage the property for the buyer.

. . . [A]n investment contract for purposes of the Securities Act means a contract, transaction or scheme whereby a person invests his money in a common enterprise and is led to expect profits solely from the efforts of the promoter or a third party, it being immaterial whether the shares in the enterprise are evidenced by formal certificates or by nominal interests in the physical assets employed in the enterprise. Such a definition necessarily underlies this Court's decision in *S.E.C. v. Joiner Corp.* and has been enunciated and applied many times by lower federal courts. It permits the fulfillment of the statutory purpose of compelling full and fair disclosure relative to the issuance of "the many types of instruments that in our commercial world fall within the ordinary concept of a security." H. Rep: No. 85, 73d Cong., 1st Sess., p. 11. It embodies a flexible rather than a static principle, one that is capable of adaptation to meet the countless and variable schemes devised by those who seek the use of the money of others on the promise of profits.

The transactions in this case clearly involve investment contracts as so defined. The respondent companies are offering something more than fee simple interests in land, something different from a farm or orchard coupled with management services. They are offering an opportunity to contribute money and to share in the profits of a large citrus fruit enterprise managed and partly owned by respondents. They are offering this opportunity to persons who reside in distant localities and who lack the equipment and experience requisite to the cultivation, harvesting, and marketing of the citrus products. Such persons have no desire to occupy the land or to develop it themselves; they are attracted solely by the prospects of a return on their investment. Indeed, individual development of the plots of land that are offered and sold would seldom be economically feasible due to their small size. Such tracts gain utility as citrus groves only when cultivated and developed as component parts of a larger area. A common enterprise managed by respondents or third parties with adequate personnel and equipment is therefore essential if the investors are to achieve their paramount aim of a return on their investments. Their respective shares in this enterprise are evidenced by land sales contracts and warranty deeds, which serve as a convenient method of determining the investors' allocable shares of the profits. The resulting transfer of rights in land is purely incidental.

Thus all the elements of a profit-seeking business venture are present here. The investors provide the capital and share in the earnings and profits; the promoters manage, control and operate the enterprise. It follows that the arrangements whereby the investors' interests are made manifest involve investment contracts, regardless of the legal terminology in which such contracts are clothed. The investment contracts in this instance take the form of land sales contracts, warranty deeds and service contracts which respondents offer to prospective investors. And respondents' failure to abide by the statutory and administrative rules in making such offerings, even though the failure result from a bona fide mistake as to the law, cannot be sanctioned under the act.

This conclusion is unaffected by the fact that some purchasers choose not to accept the full offer of an investment contract by declining to enter into a service contract with the respondents. The Securities Act prohibits the offer as well as the sale of unregistered, nonexempt securities. Hence it is enough that the respondents merely offer the essential ingredients of an investment contract.

We reject the suggestion of the Circuit Court of Appeals, that an investment contract is necessarily missing where the enterprise is not speculative or promotional in character and where the tangible interest which is sold has intrinsic value independent of the success of the enterprise as a whole. The test is whether the scheme involves an investment of money in a common enterprise with profits to come solely from the efforts of others. If that test be satisfied, it is immaterial whether the enterprise is speculative or nonspeculative or whether there is a sale of property with or without intrinsic value. The statutory policy of affording broad protection to investors is not to be thwarted by unrealistic and irrelevant formulae.

Reversed.

Definition of a Security—Continued

In subsequent cases, various courts have expanded on the *Howey* doctrine of whether the scheme involves an investment of money in a common enterprise with profits to come solely from the efforts of others. For instance, it would be quite easy to avoid this definition and ensuing SEC regulation by structuring the investment so that some effort on the part of investors was required. As the Circuit Court in *SEC* v. *Koscot Interplanetary, Inc.*[1] and other cases pointed out, however, the critical question is "whether the efforts by those other than the investor are the undeniably significant ones, those essential managerial efforts which affect the failure or success of the enterprise." In *Koscot Interplanetary*, the court discussed a pyramid scheme in which people gave the company money in return for the right to wholesale cosmetics to "beauty advisers" who then sold the cosmetics to the public. For a larger sum, the person could obtain the right to distribute cosmetics to wholesalers and the beauty advisers, and to recruit new participants. Additionally, these "supervisors" and "distributors" were allowed to keep a substantial portion of the money that any new prospects they recruited paid to Koscot for the right to participate in the cosmetics scheme. The court held that the involvement of the "supervisors," "distributors," and "beauty advisers" in selling cosmetics was merely incidental to the pyramid scheme of attracting more money from new prospects, and that such payments to Koscot for the right to introduce other prospects to the company, thus receiving a share of *their* initiation payments, was properly an investment subject to SEC jurisdiction.

Given that the courts appear to take an expansive view of what constitutes a security, several other cases yield somewhat surprising results. For instance, in *United Housing Foundation* v. *Forman,*[2] subsidized cooperative nonprofit housing communities were held not to be securities. In a co-op, one buys shares in a corporation that owns or builds an apartment building. Ownership of the shares gives these purchasers the right to occupy certain rooms (an apartment) in the building as long as all fees, rents, expenses, and so on are paid. Typically, there are restrictions on the occupancy of the apartment and the transferability of shares. In this instance, prospective dwellers bought the shares with the expectation that the rent would be around $23 per room. Ten years later, the estimate had escalated to almost $40 per room. Claims by purchasers that this was a securities offering that should have been registered with the SEC were rejected by the Supreme Court on the grounds that the primary motive of the participants was to obtain decent housing. In other words, this "investment" was for personal consumption, not an attempt to receive profits from the efforts of others. The mere inclusion of the word *stock* or *shares* in the deal did not automatically make it a "security" pursuant to federal securities law.

In *International Brotherhood of Teamsters* v. *Daniel*[3] nonparticipatory retirement plans were held excluded from securities law. Daniel worked as a driver from 1950 to 1973, with the exception of a six month layoff in 1961. During this period, his employer contributed money on a weekly basis to the Teamsters Union, who invested it for the purpose of paying Daniel and others a pension upon retirement. Daniel directly contributed no money himself to the fund. When Daniel retired, he expected a pension of about $500 monthly, but was totally denied it because the pension fund rules required 20 years continuous service to qualify for any pension. Despite the compelling facts of this case and the obvious unfairness to Daniel, the court held that a compulsory, noncontributory pension fund was not the type of investment Congress had in mind when it passed the securities acts and that no relief for this unfairness could be had. While securities laws have a broad scope, they do not encompass all investments.

Exemptions

Any securities issued or guaranteed by federal, state, or local governments are exempt from all securities laws, as are those of banks and savings and loans, charitable and religious institutions, and common carriers. The issuance of most insurance and annuity contracts and commercial paper are also exempt from federal laws. Reselling these securities may be subject to one or more provisions of the various laws; however, constitutional concerns play a key role in the exemptions of government, religion, and charitable securities. Most of the others are removed from SEC jurisdiction because they are regulated by other state or federal agencies, such as the Federal Reserve System, Interstate Commerce Commission, and so on.

In recent years, major cities such as New York and Cleveland have defaulted on some bond issues, and numerous industrial development bonds issued under the auspices of local governments have gone bad. Furthermore, speculations in these securities have proliferated because of their unregulated status. From a stodgy, low pressure backwater of the securities industry, trading in municipal securities has now become, for many, a very speculative and aggressive arena. By 1985, trades of government securities exceed by many times (in dollar volume) trades on The New York Stock Exchange and are in excess of $60 billion daily.

TREASURYS ON TRIAL

Daniel Hertzberg and Alan Murray

James Kasch has been rushing around New York City lately, seeing banks and credit-rating agencies and trying to save the financial standing of Toledo, Ohio. He is a man with problems.

Officially, Mr. Kash is suspended from his job as Toledo's finance director, but he is still at his desk. Toledo faces a possible loss of $19.2 million from its dealings with E.S.M. Government Securities Inc., of Fort Lauderdale, Fla. E.S.M. owes its customers, including many municipalities, $315 million.

Mr. Kasch's hand shakes as he lights a cigarette and describes "the tragedy." He laments, "There isn't any protection when you deal with government-securities dealers." And he insists on the need for a "watchdog" to prevent further disasters.

He is talking about the huge, largely unregulated government-securities market, where major dealers trade more than $60 billion daily. For the bold and the skilled, there are rich rewards, but for the unwary or the unlucky, the losses can be swift—and enormous.

Latest Crisis

Right now, the risks, rather than the rewards, are focusing the spotlight on the government-securities market. In the latest in a series of scandals to strike the market, the collapse of E.S.M. has sent shock waves through the banking system. E.S.M.'s failure triggered the run by depositors that forced the temporary closing of 71 Ohio thrift institutions.

Pressure for more regulation of this huge market thus is mounting. "If you have a free market, accidents are bound to happen," says Federal Reserve Board Governor Henry Wallich. "But if the accidents get too big and too frequent, the response cannot be the same." Voices are also being raised in Congress supporting increased regulation.

*   *   *   *   *

Role of Federal Debt

The ballooning federal deficits play a big role. They are forcing the Treasury to pump out unprecedented amounts of new government securities. And that is straining major dealers who bid for and then market this new supply of government debt.

Dealings In Treasurys (average daily transactions by primary dealers)

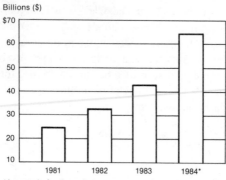

Billions ($)

*Average in fourth quarter.
Source: Federal Reserve.

The government debt tripled during the 1970s and hit $1 trillion in 1981, the first year of the Reagan administration. Next year, it will surpass $2 trillion. With federal deficits still running at $200 billion a year, the day-to-day operation of government depends on finding ever more buyers in the U.S. and abroad for that mountain of debt. Indeed, the federal government is like a hospital patient, sustained by intravenous infusions from the credit markets.

Soon, dealers say, the Treasury may be selling as much as $23 billion in securities at a time during its quarterly refunding operations, when the government rolls over some of its old debt and sells new issues. The most recent one, in February, totaled $19 billion. As the amounts keep growing, "who is going to underwrite those securities?" Kim Schappert, a managing director of J. P. Morgan Investment Management, asks rhetorically.

With the large volumes, any kinks in the market can raise the cost of servicing the federal debt by billions of dollars. As Edward Geng, senior vice president of the New York Fed, told Congress last year, "the U.S. Treasury cannot wait for favorable markets to sell its debt."

To the federal government, the market is a

lifeline. But to investors, the government-securities market sometimes can be a casino. A look at how the market works is in order.

The market operates largely without regulation. With no centralized marketplace or exchange, the market consists of hundreds of dealers and tens of thousands of customers—mainly portfolio managers at banks, savings and loans, pension funds and bond funds—watching video-display screens and trading over the telephone.

On the stock exchanges, customers buying securities on credit must put up at least 50 percent in cash, but the government securities market hasn't any such hard-and-fast rules. Dealers are left to decide how much credit to extend to customers. It isn't unusual for a customer to put up only $1 to $3 in cash for every $100 in securities he buys, especially when a dealer believes the customer is credit-worthy.

With this huge leverage, both dealers and investors can make huge bets on the direction of interest rates by assembling big securities holdings with borrowed funds. "As a dealer, you can leverage yourself so much, you can take a huge position," says S. Waite Rawls of New York's Chemical Bank. It isn't uncommon for a dealer to take a $1 billion position, he says, "so your losses can be tremendous." He adds, "Your margin of error is much less" than in other markets.

Even for investors who don't use large amounts of credit, losses can be huge. "Believe me, going home at night, having a beer and realizing you've lost $100 million is a rude awakening," says William H. Gross, a managing director of Pacific Investment Management Co., which runs an $8.25 billion portfolio of bonds.

The government-securities market has been increasingly entwined with the market for Treasury bond futures and futures options. Dealers now routinely use futures to hedge their securities positions and to speculate on the direction of interest rates.

Although the government-securities market outwardly appears unstructured, it has its own hierarchy.

The big, privileged players are 36 government securities dealers known as primary dealers. They are the only ones who can trade with the Fed, which buys and sells huge quantities of government securities in its efforts to control the nation's supply of money. In return for that privilege–which dealers use to boost their reputation among customers—they submit to Fed oversight, and report to the Fed daily on trading activity and regularly on capital.

The main obligation of a primary dealer is to bid in government auctions of new securities and help sell the national debt. The leading primary dealers include such financial heavyweights as Salomon Brothers Inc., First Boston Corp., Merrill Lynch & Co., Goldman, Sachs & Co., Citibank, Bank of America and Chase Manhattan Bank.

The relationship between the Fed and the 36 is so cozy that the Justice Department has been investigating whether it violates antitrust laws. Justice Department officials say the investigation has been going on for more than a year, but they won't say when it will be completed.

The vast majority of trading in the government market involves those primary dealers. There aren't any good estimates of trading in the secondary market, which includes hundreds of small dealers like E.S.M. But that trading is tiny compared with that of the primary traders, according to Francis Cavanaugh, director of the Treasury's office of government finance.

Although no primary dealer ever has failed, there has been a string of disasters among smaller dealers in recent years: Winters Government Securities in 1977, Drysdale Government Securities Inc. in 1982, Lombard-Wall Inc. the same year, Lion Capital Group last year, and now E.S.M.

The Typical Losers

Typically, it isn't the biggest investors who get caught in these collapses. The victims usually have been smaller investors with cash but little experience in judging a dealer's financial soundness. They include thrift institutions, school districts, and city governments.

Frequently, victims have had their money tied up in repurchase agreements, a common type of short-term cash investment. In simple terms, a "repo" is a loan backed by government securities as collateral. A borrower, say a securities dealer, sells government securities to an investor. The dealer agrees to buy back the securities later at a higher price. Meantime, the dealer uses the cash to trade government securities, and he hopes to reap enough of a profit to offset his "repo" costs.

Repos make the market work. Primary dealers routinely use them to finance their huge securities holdings, including securities bought at government auctions. The procedure "allows a large pool of liquid money to slosh back and forth in the market," says Mr. Rawls of Chemical Bank.

Changes in federal law have eliminated one pitfall for investors. If a borrower, such as a dealer, goes into bankruptcy proceedings, the lender can sell the collateral securities and get all his money quickly. Most other creditors in a bankruptcy have to wait months or years before getting paid and don't have any guarantee that they will get anything back.

Toledo's Trap

But sometimes there's a catch. Toledo, like many losers in the E.S.M. failure, thought it had sole right to the government securities that collateralized its loans. It didn't. Investigators allege that E.S.M. pledged the same securities as collateral for transactions with several customers.

Every time interest rates change, the value of the securities underlying the repo agreement changes. If rates soar, and the bond market nosedives, the value of the collateral can shrink appreciably. The risk increases the longer the repo agreement lasts, especially for long-term bonds. For example, with a 20-year government bond, a one-percentage-point rise in rates, say to 11 percent from 10 percent slashes the value of the bond by $7 to $8 for every $100 of its face amount, says Ian Giddy, associate professor of finance at the New York University Graduate School of Business.

As each successive scandal has hit the government securities market, the circle of victims has widened. When Drysdale went bust in 1982, it cost Chase Manhattan Bank more than

$135 million and threatened to hobble securities firms.

After Drysdale's collapse, the Fed tentatively tried to expand its influence beyond the primary dealers. It now receives monthly reports on the activities of about 40 secondary dealers, and it will soon publish guidelines on the amount of capital dealers should have in case they suffer large trading losses. But those guidelines will be entirely voluntary, and critics say none of this would have saved E.S.M.

Source: *The Wall Street Journal*, April 1, 1985, p. 1. Reprinted by permission of *The Wall Street Journal*, © Dow Jones & Company, Inc., 1985. All rights reserved.

Exemptions—Continued

While some securities are totally exempt from federal securities laws, others are only exempt from certain provisions of the laws. Primarily, Congress has chosen to exempt certain types of securities from registration and disclosure under the 1933 Act, although they may still be subject to the antifraud provisions of the law. A security attempting to qualify for an exemption has an affirmative duty to demonstrate that it fits under the explicit terms of the particular exemption. In other words, if challenged, the company issuing the security must prove the exemption requirements were satisfied—the SEC does not have to prove they were not complied with. Record-keeping, then, becomes paramount for a company attempting to qualify for an exemption.

Despite the problems of claiming an exemption, the alternatives can be much worse from the point of view of the company promoting the investment. The legal, accounting, and professional fees involved in registering a nonexempt security can be substantial, as are the printing and underwriting costs. Delays in getting approval from regulatory bodies or other costly mistakes can also make prohibitive the expense of obtaining regulatory approval. The costs of floating a $10 million initial public offering could easily exceed $1 million. Thus, for financial reasons, there is quite an incentive to structure a proposed offering so that it is exempt from federal registration requirements.

The three main types of exemptions from compliance with SEC requirements are private placements, intrastate offerings, and simplified registrations. *Private placements* are securities that are sold to a limited number of investors or to "accredited" investors—banks; insurance companies; and financially sophisticated, wealthy individuals and businesses. Up to $500,000 of unregistered securities may be sold to anyone pursuant to this exemption. Up to $5 million in securities may be sold during a 12-month period to accredited investors and to no more than 35 unaccredited ones. Unlimited amounts can be sold solely to accredited investors. All nonaccredited investors must be provided with information similar to that required by the SEC for the sale of new securities, and there are stringent limitations on the resale of these securities for a period of time. This last prohibition is necessary to keep private placements from becoming a tool by which SEC registration requirements could be avoided and the securities immediately marketed to the general public.

Intrastate offerings are those sold only in a single state to residents of that state. Even if this requirement is met, the issuers must demonstrate that 80 percent of its business (sales, assets, and so on) and 80 percent of the proceeds from the issue are to be used in that state. This exemption is designed to aid purely local business people in obtaining funds without meeting costly SEC registration requirements. Finally, a company desiring to issue less than about $1.5 million within 12 months to persons other than those involved with the company may file a much-simplified offering circular with the SEC. While not a complete exemption, this *simplified registration* procedure for small placements can lower offering costs substantially and encourage small businesses that need to raise capital to seek it from the public.

Although an issue may qualify for a total or partial exemption from SEC rules, state blue sky laws in those jurisdictions in which the security is to be sold may not offer the same exemptions. In that case, state laws would still have to be complied with.

Registration Requirements

If no total or partial exemption is available to the issuers, both state and federal laws will have to be considered. State blue sky laws are based on the theory that the state has the duty to protect its citizens from unwise, fraudulent, or excessively speculative investments. Before a security can be sold, most states require that the state securities commission be convinced that the issue has some investment merit and is not a fraudulent scheme. Normally, securities which qualify under federal laws have no difficulty (just expense) in meeting state blue sky requirements, but as recently as the 1970s, Massachusetts denied its residents the opportunity to buy Apple Computer stock when it was initially offered because the state felt the risk was too great and the price too high. The clamor was so great and so many residents simply decided to have brokers in other states purchase the stock for them that Massachusetts finally was forced to relent.

The Securities Act of 1933, on the other hand, is not concerned with the value and speculative nature of an issue; rather it focuses on full disclosure of all the material facts. Before an offering can be sold, a detailed registration statement must be submitted to the SEC, which can then scrutinize it to make sure that it contains all the data investors need to evaluate the desirability of a security for their investment purposes. A major part of the registration statement is the prospectus, which must be given to every potential investor before they are allowed to purchase the security. The prospectus contains all relevant data, such as the nature of the business and the background of the principals, the uses of the funds, the risks inherent in the enterprise, possible benefits, and various financial statements.

The SEC reviews the prospectus and other data it requires before the security can be sold. It can require that additional data or information be added and risks or other unusual factors highlighted. While the SEC cannot reject an offering based on its perception of the likelihood of success, the SEC can lengthen the approval process (and increase the expense) so that offerings it deems undesirable become practically impossible to market.

Furthermore, the prospectus and any other data on file with the SEC have to be updated if necessary due to changed conditions since the prospectus was originally created. The company issuing the security may not take any unusual actions, such as advertising on television, exceptional press conferences, and so on, which gain favorable publicity for the company. The only advertising that it may undertake relating to the sale of new securities is a tombstone ad, which simply sets forth what is being offered, when it is available, and from whom a prospectus may be obtained. The purchaser is to make decisions based on the data in the prospectus, not some flattering facts put together by the company and contained in a glossy brochure that has not met SEC scrutiny. This is not to imply that all investors read the prospectus and develop informed opinions based on it. Many rely on brokers and other professionals, independent newspaper columns, their own experiences with the product, and so on; but before they buy the stock, they must have received a prospectus. The SEC is not supposed to protect foolish investors from folly, but rather is to ensure that all investors have access to information adequate to reach a reasonable conclusion about the merits of the offering. Whether the potential investor properly evaluates the available data or chooses to ignore the proffered prospectus entirely is totally the investor's business.

Remedies for Violations

If one has been sold a share of the Brooklyn Bridge, a Ponzi scheme, or a nonexistent South African gold mine, the purchaser may be able to use common law fraud theory to recover money from the promoter or the company, assuming that either can be found. In order to recover for fraud, the investor must show all of the following:

1. A material fact was misstated or omitted from the data given the purchaser.
2. The promoter/seller had knowledge of the error—scienter.
3. Reliance on the misstatement by the purchaser.
4. Intent to defraud the purchaser by the seller.
5. Privity of contract between seller and purchaser.
6. The misstatement was the cause of the investor's losses—proximate cause.
7. Damages.

Failure to prove properly any one of these elements of fraud prohibited recovery by the seller. Thus, only in the most egregious cases could an investor recover any money. Typically, the person committing the fraud—the promoter—was unavailable, bankrupt, or in jail and therefore judgment-proof, while the other persons the investor had dealt with, such as his broker and financial adviser, the firm's accountants, and attorneys for the firm, had not actively participated in the fraud and could not be liable for the fraud of the promoter.

The 1933 act, however, gave investors much greater potential for recovery when they felt they were defrauded. First of all, criminal liability may be imposed for willful violations of the act. Additionally, the 1933 act imposes civil liability for all misstatements, misleading data, or omissions in the prospectus and other registration material filed with the SEC. Quite simply, anyone who purchases a new security that is subject to registration requirements which contains errors, omissions, or misleading statements or for which no registration material is filed may recover damages up to the price originally paid for the security for all money lost as a result of the investment. No proof of reliance and causation is necessary. The mere fact that the error was made and that the investor lost money (the price of the security fell) is enough to entitle the investor to a recovery. This means that an investor can be perfectly satisfied with a purchase for a long period of time, but if the investment goes bad at a later date, the purchaser can then scan the prospectus for the error, misstatement, or omission. Finding such a problem with the prospectus can lead to the recovery of the total damages resulting from the decline in price of the original purchase.

Furthermore, another section of the act has been used to hold promoters and others liable for material misstatements or omissions regarding the offer or sale of securities that are not subject to the filing of a registration statement. Under either of these provisions, the company; any officer or director of the company; its accountants, attorneys, real estate appraisers and other experts who helped develop the offering and registration; the underwriters; and anyone who signed the registration statement are personally liable for all damages suffered by all purchasers of the security. Thus, an aggrieved purchaser can have a veritable field day in finding the "deepest pockets" from the available, solvent parties and forcing a recovery from them. Once the error or omission has been found, the only defense these persons have to a suit by an investor is that they exercised due diligence and the mistake was made by someone else. In other words, the CPA firm cannot be held liable for a mistake by the law firm. However, the issuer of the security is absolutely liable for the mistake regardless of who was at fault.

It should now be readily apparent why the underwriting and registration process is so expensive. Each time an underwriter, accountant, attorney, appraiser, or financial printer becomes involved in a new offer, that person is potentially liable for the total amount of the offering to its purchasers—not only for intentional omissions and misstatements but also for the most mundane typographical error, skipped line, or misplaced modifier. It is not surprising that Wall Street lawyers often become the world's most expensive proofreaders for many hours before a prospectus is released. An error could translate into hundreds of millions of dollars of liability for their firm and the other involved parties.

WOLFSON LAWYERS TO APPEAL HIS CONVICTION; LANDMARK SECURITIES LAW RULING POSSIBLE

Stanford N. Sesser

New York—His attorneys said they will appeal the conviction of Louis Elwood Wolfson, the financier and builder of a corporate empire, on criminal charges of illegally selling stock in a company he controlled.

Mr. Wolfson and a close associate, Elkin B. Gerbert, were found guilty in federal court on all 19 counts of conspiracy and sales of unregistered securities. The jury deliberated 6 hours 20 minutes before returning its verdict late Friday night.

Sentencing will come later. The two men could each be given a maximum of 95 years in prison and $95,000 in fines.

Mr. Wolfson once battled unsuccessfully for control of Montgomery Ward & Co., became a major stockholder in American Motors Corp., and built Merritt-Chapman & Scott Corp. into an industrial giant with sales of more than $300 million a year. He was convicted of selling stock in what his lawyer described as "a little nothing company," Continental Enterprises Inc. Continental, a Florida concern that owns movie theaters and real estate, had revenue of only $1 million a year when Mr. Wolfson's activities took place.

The jury found that Mr. Wolfson and Mr. Gerbert willfully violated the Securities Act of 1933 when they sold 690,000 shares of Continental on the open market between 1960 and 1962. The company then had 2.5 million shares outstanding.

The case is believed likely to reach the Supreme Court and result in a landmark interpretation of the Securities Act. Mr. Wolfson's lawyers say a controlling stockholder has never before been prosecuted on criminal charges of selling unregistered shares.

* * * * *

There were two major issues in the case: Whether the law required that the Continental stock be registered, and whether the defendants deliberately conspired to violate the registration requirements. Registration involves the filing of detailed information about the company with the Securities and Exchange Commission before the stock is sold by the controlling interests.

Mr. Wolfson and Mr. Gerbert both testified that they weren't familiar with the securities laws. Mr. Wolfson said that he "knew nothing" about the Securities Act, that he had no clear idea of what a registration statement was, and that he customarily left such matters to subordinates.

The government countered with two key pieces of evidence. They brought a Jacksonville stockbroker to the stand who produced a memorandum signed by Mr. Gerbert in January 1961 that said no Continental stock had been sold in the past year. The broker, John Morley, testified he had insisted on the memorandum as evidence of compliance with the Securities Act before he would place an order for Mr. Gerbert's selling of Continental shares.

Conference on Laws

U.S. Attorney Michael F. Armstrong, the forceful, 34-year-old prosecutor, also concentrated heavily on last-minute testimony by a former assistant regional administrator for the SEC, James Duncan. Mr. Duncan said he had a two-hour conference with Mr. Wolfson in 1950 concerning registration provisions of the securities laws.

Mr. Armstrong showed the jury an SEC memorandum recounting the meeting and called it "the most dramatic evidence in the case." The memorandum told of efforts to persuade Mr. Wolfson to register an offering of Capital Transit Co., which was later reorganized into Universal Marion Corp. Continental Enterprises was created in 1954 as a spinoff from Capital Transit.

* * * * *

The other major question at the trial—whether the sales of Continental legally had to be registered—is one that will likely reach the Supreme Court on appeal, Mr. Wolfson's lawyers contend that the transactions were exempt from the registration provision of the Securities Act.

The registration requirement is Rule 154, which governs the sale of stock in a company by those who control it. The controlling interests are allowed to sell only 1 percent of the outstanding stock of their company in a six-month period, unless the sale is registered with the SEC.

The Wolfson lawyers, however, point to Section 4(1) of the Securities Act, which exempts "transactions by any person other than issuer, underwriter, or dealer." They claim that Mr. Wolfson doesn't fall into any of the three categories.

In his charge to the jury Friday morning, Judge Edmund L. Palmieri disagreed. He said that "a broker is an underwriter for our purposes when he assists a controlling person in the sale of large blocks of the stock to the public."

* * * * *

Mr. Wolfson, the son of an immigrant junk dealer, founded his fortune on $10,000 of borrowed money and his own daring. From buying and selling Government surplus during World War II, he expanded to operating a shipyard in Jacksonville, Florida. In 1949, he moved north, buying control of Capital Transit, the bus and streetcar system of the District of Columbia, which he later sold at a substantial profit.

Mr. Wolfson moved into national prominence after becoming chairman of Merritt-Chapman in 1951, an office he still holds. He started that venerable construction company on a diversification program that expanded operating revenue more than five-fold in seven years, moving into paint-making, steel production, chemicals and shipbuilding. Merritt-Chapman currently is in the process of liquidation.

In 1955, Mr. Wolfson confronted the late Sewell Avery, then chairman of Montgomery Ward, with demands that he resign and turn over control of the company, which then had more than $300 million in cash and liquid assets. This assault brought him widespread characterization as a corporate "raider," but the attempt was unsuccessful. Though Mr. Avery later resigned, Mr. Wolfson wasn't able to muster enough proxy votes to control the board, and he eventually sold his shares in the company at a sizable profit.

His most controversial move came in the summer of 1958 with American Motors. Mr. Wolfson, with his family, held 400,000 of the auto maker's shares. On June 20, a spokesman for Mr. Wolfson in a newspaper interview stated that Mr. Wolfson was in the process of selling his shares.

Later, it was established that at the time of the interview Mr. Wolfson had sold all his shares and was in a substantial short position, hoping for the stock to go down. Mr. Wolfson signed a consent decree with the SEC agreeing to a permanent injunction against his making "false and misleading" statements about his holdings of American Motors Corp. or engaging in transactions that might "operate a fraud or deceit" on traders of the shares. However, he denied all allegations of wrongdoing.

In the Continental Enterprises indictment, the Government contended that Mr. Wolfson made a profit of $3.5 million from his sale of the Continental shares. Mr. Gerbert, who relayed to brokers most of the stock transactions for the Wolfson interests, was a director of Continental, Merritt-Chapman, and other Wolfson-controlled companies.

LOUIS WOLFSON KEEPS UP FIGHT TO CLEAR NAME

Stanley Penn

New York—Thirteen years ago, Louis Wolfson, who headed the big, diversified Merritt-Chapman & Scott Corp., was sentenced to a year in federal prison and fined $100,000 for the illegal sale of securities. Mr. Wolfson's life since then has pursued a theme right out of literature, the obsession of a convicted man to prove his innocence.

As in any novel on the subject, there's another protagonist—in this case, federal Judge Edmund Palmieri, of New York. Mr. Wolfson has spent more than $2 million in legal and other fees to prove his innocence, some 25 percent of it on what he calls "Investigative work and research" partly intended to discredit the judge.

Judge Palmieri said in court in 1978: "His continuous and baseless petitions constitute a wanton abuse of process for which he and his attorneys may well deserve appropriate penalties."

Roy Cohn, Mr. Wolfson's current lawyer, praises Mr. Wolfson as a "man with courage and heart" for his persistence. Four times Mr. Wolfson has petitioned the federal appeals court in New York for a new trial on grounds that official misconduct caused his conviction, or that new evidence shows he shouldn't have been jailed. All his motions have been denied, most recently last July. . . .

Mr. Wolfson's long and costly effort has disturbed his family and friends. "They say you can't buck the power structure, so enjoy your life," Mr. Wolfson says. Mr. Wolfson manages his own investments, but he has pleasurable outside pursuits. He breeds and raises thoroughbreds, for example, and in 1978 one of his horses, Affirmed, won racing's Triple Crown—the Kentucky Derby, the Preakness and the Belmont Stakes.

Mr. Wolfson still works as a consultant for Merritt-Chapman & Scott and for Universal Marion Corp. . . .

Regulation of Publicly Held Companies

The Securities Exchange Act of 1934 regulates many aspects of the financial dealings of publicly held companies. Because of its emphasis on publicly held companies, thousands of smaller businesses that are subject to the 1933 act when they issue securities are not subject to the dictates of the 1934 act. Basically, any company with more than $1 million in assets and 500 shareholders may be subject to some provisions of the act, as are any businesses which have issued a class of securities traded on a national securities exchange. All companies required to register with the SEC must file annual and quarterly reports with the SEC, as well as monthly reports if certain specified occurrences take place. Investment companies, banks, insurance companies, and various other industries are exempt from these disclosure requirements, but something over 10,000 firms are required to disclose the specified data to the SEC and the public on a regular basis.

In addition, the 1934 act sets up the SEC and gives markets such as the New York Stock Exchange some power of self-regulation, to be exercised with SEC oversight. Furthermore, the SEC is authorized to regulate the extension of credit to buy securities, trading by members of the exchanges, and manipulative practices by members. It may also suspend trading of securities if it becomes necessary. The SEC also requires the regulation of brokers and dealers, municipal securities dealers, clearing and transfer agencies, and entities dealing in securities information.

Besides registration and submission of various reports, publicly held companies are regulated concerning their record-keeping, repurchases of securities, proxy solicitations, director changes, corrupt foreign practices, and many other areas of day-to-day activities. Stockholders who are officers or directors of a company or who own large blocks of the stock are required to report their transactions involving the company's securities to the SEC and are prohibited from engaging in certain stock transactions in which their position could give them an unfair advantage over the uninformed public. Additionally, it is a violation for anyone to trade shares on the basis of inside information—information that is not available to the investing public at the time. An officer of the company might be able to do this, but on occasion so could a low-level employee such as a field engineer who learns of an oil strike before it is announced to the public. Restrictions also are placed on tender offers (explained below), purchases of substantial blocks of stock, and institutional investment managers. Misleading statements in proxy solicitations or about the purchase or sale of a security, along with other unfair or deceptive practices, can result in criminal or civil liability under the 1934 act.

Short-Swing Profits   In an attempt to limit the ability of major participants in corporate affairs to gain a short-term economic advantage due to their early access to earnings reports and other inside, nonpublic information that might cause a temporary rise in stock prices when made public, the 1934 act prohibits officers, directors, and 10 percent beneficial owners of a corporation from receiving *short-swing profits*. These are defined as any profits made on company stock held for less than six months. Any such profits must be returned to the company, and applicable attorneys' fees may also have to be paid by the person violating the rule. As mentioned previously, the SEC interprets short-swing profits as occurring if any sale price is greater than any purchase price during any six-month period. This interpretation can have some surprising results for someone unaware of how it works, as the following example indicates.

> Director
> Buys 500 shares at $35 on June 4.
> Sells 300 shares at $30 on September 15.
> Buys 1,000 shares at $25 on November 20.
> Sells 800 shares at $20 on December 19.

Pursuant to this provision, the director has short-swing profits of $1,500 (300 shares × $5) because he sold on September 15 at $30 and bought on November 20 at $25. From the example given, it is obvious that he was not trading on nonpublic information or that the information was erroneous, because the stock fell continually during the period. Adding insult to his trading losses is this extra SEC penalty for violating the short-swing profit rule.

Tender Offers   When one company attempts to take over another, SEC rules can often be crucial. All such *tender offers* must be registered with the SEC. Furthermore, certain disclosure rules are triggered when groups purchase more than 5 percent of a company's outstanding stock. In recent years, as hostile takeover attempts have become more frequent, many strategies have been developed to limit their success. The raiders, however, are sometimes able to use the rules to their advantage. In many such takeovers, both state laws and SEC requirements play a part. Typically, management uses state requirements to slow down or eliminate the possibility of a hostile takeover, while the raiders usually enlist the aid of SEC rules. This is not a hard-and-fast rule, and in this fast-paced, tricky area, the positions can flip-flop regularly.

Bidders for a company can rely on recent amendments to the 1934 act to get more information about the target company and to shorten the period of time during which shareholders can decide whether to accept the offer. These amendments also appear to have placed additional restrictions on a company's ability to use state law to fend off a takeover. For instance, in the Mobil-Marathon takeover battle, the "lockout" defense was rejected by the courts. In this maneuver, the target's board opposed a "totally inadequate" offer by giving another friendly corporation ("white knight") the right to purchase 10 million authorized but unissued shares and a contingent option to purchase a major oil field in the event of a hostile takeover. The court held this practice to be "manipulative" in that it set an artificial ceiling on what the shareholders could expect to receive should the company or its assets be sold.

On the other hand, such other defenses as questioning whether a takeover violates antitrust law and claiming access to insider information by the bidder or violations of SEC disclosure rules remain important in stopping hostile bids. Another effective technique is to buy a business, such as a radio or television station, railroad, bank, insurance company, or airline, for which state or federal regulatory approval is necessary prior to a change in ownership. Getting necessary regulatory approval may add to the time and expense involved in a takeover and may force a bidder to reconsider. For instance, several attractive takeover candidates have bought Florida-based insurance companies because of that state's rules concerning sales of insurance companies. Other options involve selling large blocks of stock to employees, issuing much new debt, attempting to take over the hostile bidder, requiring that the same sale or exchange terms be offered to all shareholders, mandating that the board or a super-majority of all shareholders must approve takeover bids, selling off the most attractive corporate assets, finding another purchaser, or buying out the bidder at a profit to his group ("greenmail"). Clearly, some of these techniques are more desirable than others from the standpoint of the corporation, and many such as taking on substantial new debt or selling off attractive corporate assets ("scorched earth" defense) can seriously damage the long-run prospects of the business. One last defense, which has been used frequently but is likely to be curtailed, is "golden parachutes," in which officers are paid large bonuses in the event of a hostile takeover. The shareholder ill will engendered by these is often substantial and their legality may be subject to question.

The best way to avoid a takeover remains unchanged, however—run a well-managed company with attractive share prices. Only companies whose assets are thought to be undervalued or whose parts can be spun off at prices greater than current share prices become takeover targets.

HOW T. BOONE PICKENS FINALLY MET HIS MATCH: UNOCAL'S FRED HARTLEY

Frederick Rose, Laurie P. Cohen, and James B. Stewart

Fred Hartley vividly remembers his reaction when he first confirmed that T. Boone Pickens, Jr., was going after Unocal Corp.

The Unocal chairman went home that evening and broke the news to his wife. "I told her that I was born in World War I, survived World War II and now my management and I were going to have to gird for World War III," the 68-year-old Mr. Hartley recalls.

And a war it was. Immediately at stake was the fate of one of the nation's largest oil companies, with sales of $11 billion a year and some 20,000 employees. For the longer run, it seems likely to be remembered as a landmark in the frenzied takeover struggles of recent years, both for some innovative defensive tactics dreamed up by Unocal and its advisers and for a Delaware Supreme Court decision upholding one of the most crucial maneuvers. Some observers see far-reaching consequences for future takeover battles.

In Messrs. Hartley and Pickens, the fight matched two of the toughest, most determined leaders in American business. Even one of Mr. Hartley's advisers calls him "a pain"—but also someone who clearly called the shots for his side, someone whom "Boone wasn't going to walk around like a chimpanzee." Mr. Pickens, the chairman of Mesa Petroleum Co., had walked around and over several top oil executives in recent years on his way to becoming America's best-known corporate raider.

Each antagonist had his own legion of high-powered, high-priced lawyers, investment bankers, and public-relations specialists as well as a war chest running into billions of dollars. The struggle raged in courtrooms from Delaware to California and in executive suites around the country. At times, it took bizarre, even amusing twists.

At one point, during the talks that eventually produced a settlement, the Pickens forces chose to huddle in a hallway of a Los Angeles hotel rather than in a room offered by Unocal, fearing that the room was bugged. At another point Mr. Hartley lectured Mr. Pickens for taking a limousine to one of their secret meetings, saying it was too conspicuous a way to travel; Mr. Pickens replied that he was paying for the transportation and would travel any way he pleased.

Now, Mr. Pickens undoubtedly isn't happy about where his travels ended. He is generally perceived to have sustained his first defeat after a long string of victories in takeover battles against such oil giants as Gulf Corp., Phillips Petroleum Co. and Cities Service Co. In each of those battles the target company ended up either being acquired by another concern or buying off the Pickens group, which came out ahead in either event and raked in profits totaling several hundred million dollars.

In the Unocal battle, the Pickens group may face losses that some observers estimate could exceed $100 million. Mr. Pickens himself contends that the group will break even or perhaps turn a profit if Unocal's management enhances the value of its remaining shares over the next year. If it does, he says, "we can make $200 million or $300 million here."

In any event, Unocal will remain an independent company. The Pickens group has agreed to sell its 13.6 percent Unocal stake over an extended period and not to make another bid for the company for 25 years.

But although Mr. Hartley "won," Unocal hardly came out of the war unscathed. To buy back stock from the Pickens group and other Unocal shareholders, it will more than quadruple its long-term debt to some $5.3 billion—a move that could pinch its cash flow and its operations for years. "I don't think there is anything to brag about," Mr. Hartley says.

Mr. Hartley had been preparing for such a battle for some time. Besides worrying about his own company, Mr. Hartley sees the wave of takeovers as an attack on the crucial ability of corporations to manage their businesses for long-term goals. "Change can come along, but we don't have to do it in a barbaric manner," he says.

In 1983, Unocal enacted a number of takeover defenses, including staggered terms for directors—so the board couldn't be taken over all at once—and elimination of cumulative voting—so dissidents couldn't concentrate their votes and easily elect their own people to the board. The company also became an active supporter of so-far-unsuccessful efforts in Washington to enact legislation that would curtail takeovers by corporate raiders.

And though Mr. Hartley has almost-legendary disdain for investment bankers, who, he believes, have helped fuel takeover campaigns, Unocal picked two such firms—Dillon, Read & Co. and Goldman, Sachs & Co.—to serve as advisers if needed. Though Mr. Hartley won't say he ruled out investment bankers active in helping raiders in the past, he does say he insisted on firms "spiritually committed to what I consider to be the American economic way." Goldman Sachs, for example, refuses, as a matter of policy, to advise companies making hostile bids.

*   *   *   *   *

Purchases Begun

In February, a Pickens-led partnership announced the purchase of 7.9 percent of Unocal's stock but said it was only an investment and not a takeover effort—an assertion that met with widespread skepticism. Unocal played along, at least publicly. Mr. Hartley complimented the Pickens group for choosing a "good investment."

Privately, though, Unocal went on a war footing. "Quite simply," Mr. Hartley says, "we quit working on what we were working on and started working on the immediate problem." Unocal set up a five-executive "strategy" committee headed by Mr. Hartley. Though the professional advisers were frequently called on, all parties on the Unocal side agree that this group, and Mr. Hartley in particular, had the final say on all major decisions. This approach, some observers note, contrasts sharply with the tack taken by some previous managements fighting Mr. Pickens; they tended to give much more power to their investment bankers and lawyers.

As the Pickens group continued to accumulate shares, Unocal started taking more openly hostile steps. It further tightened its rules concerning director nominations and shareholder votes. In March, it also filed suit against its own principal bank, Security Pacific, because the Los Angeles institution was a lender to the Pickens group, too. The Pickens group retaliated with a suit against Unocal, contending that the company was conducting an "intimidation campaign" against the partnership's banks. These suits were only the first of a seemingly endless—and eventually crucial—string of litigation.

Changed Tune

Mr. Pickens still insists that, in February, his group began acquiring Unocal shares for "investment purposes only." He adds that by late March, however, the group had changed its plans because of the company's defensive actions and several remarks by Mr. Hartley.

Unocal amended its bylaws, Mr. Pickens says, "so that management could further entrench itself." In addition, he cites the company's suit against Security Pacific, which later withdrew from the Mesa credit pool. And finally, Mr. Hartley "started calling me an idiot and attacking me verbally," Mr. Pickens says, adding, "He also said he was unwilling to restructure [the company] in any way."

By late March, the Pickens group had accumulated about 23.7 million Unocal shares, some 13.6 percent of those outstanding, and it announced that it was contemplating a takeover or major restructuring of the oil company.

The Pickens group then unveiled a takeover plan similar to ones it has used previously: a $54-a-share cash tender offer that would lift the group's holding to just over 50 percent of Unocal. The bid was several dollars a share over the market price of the stock at the time. The rest of the shares, under the plan, would be bought later for notes valued at $54 a share. The Pickens group put the total value of the offer at $8.1 billion.

Financing Arranged

To show it meant business, the Pickens group, within a week, announced that Drexel Burnham had lined up $3 billion in financing commitments from more than 130 investors. Moreover, Mesa also arranged an additional credit line of $925 million from commercial banks.

"All of us were just shocked," one Unocal adviser says, "when Boone came up with that money. . . . Think of it! That's green for half the company."

However, Unocal unleashed a few maneuvers of its own. It apparently beat back an effort by the Pickens group to postpone Unocal's annual meeting. By delaying the meeting, the Pickens group would have a chance to put together its own slate of directors to run against Unocal's. For a while, the Pickens group—backed by major institutional stockholders, whom Mr. Hartley derides as "absentee landlords"—seemed likely to win that vote.

However, Unocal launched a huge proxy-gathering effort. It was aided by the firm of D. F. King and some 900 Unocal employees, including Mr. Hartley, who boasted on the morning the voting ended of having won over a holder of 600,000 shares. Though an official vote count on the question hasn't been announced, the Pickens camp has already said it believes that it lost.

Probably Unocal's most important move was its offer to repurchase 29 percent of its stock at $72 a share in notes. The company included the crucial and extremely controversial condition that it wouldn't accept any shares from the Pickens group.

The genesis of this idea is murky. Mr. Hartley will say only that it was "the outgrowth of a lot of discussion. I don't think you can pick out any individual genius."

But the amount of talking that went into the plan was nothing compared with the amount it produced. Observers ranging from Wall Street analysts to federal securities regulators said the move seemed to violate the principle of equal treatment of all shareholders.

No one cried foul more loudly than the Pickens group, of course. It stood to make a quick gain in the range of $175 million if it could sell some of its shares back to Unocal. But if it couldn't tender, the group faced the unpleasant prospect that Unocal might simply outbid it for the remaining shares while piling up a mountain of debt. The Pickens group might eventually inherit a company hardly worth having.

The Battle Shifts

So, the main battle shifted to the group's challenge of the exclusion provision in state courts in Delaware, where Unocal is incorporated. And the changing shifting tides of this legal struggle opened the way for settlement talks.

* * * * *

[The first day of talks brought some progress.]

A Setback

On the following day, the atmosphere quickly turned sour when Mr. Pickens and his colleagues read the four-page draft settlement. "It went backwards from where we were the day before. It was the most ridiculous deal you ever saw," a member of the Pickens group says. Mr. Pickens became so incensed he told Uno-

cal, "I've decided to set my watch back to Central Time," and he abruptly left to fly back home to Amarillo, Texas.

Sources say Mr. Hartley and his advisers quickly decided that there wasn't any reason to make major concessions immediately. For one thing, they still hoped the Delaware Supreme Court would overturn a lower-court decision ordering Unocal to include the Pickens group in its repurchase offer. And if not, Unocal planned to abandon its exchange offer rather than include the Pickens group—no matter how angry that made its shareholders.

On the court decision, "everybody I knew was praying for me, including the minister of my church," Mr. Hartley says.

Earlier this month, Unocal's prayers were answered when the Delaware Supreme Court, reversing the lower court, upheld the company's exclusion of the Pickens group as a legitimate exercise of business judgment. As a practical matter, Mesa had nowhere to appeal the decision, because "business judgment" is deemed a matter of state law and not appealable to the federal courts. The decision rocked the takeover community and set the stage for the final negotiations on a settlement.

Attorney's Call

About 10 minutes after the court decision was announced on Friday, May 17, Andrew Bogan, an attorney for Unocal, received a call from Robert Stillwell, a partner in the Houston law firm of Baker & Botts and Mesa's general counsel. Mr. Stillwell suggested that the talks resume. "They came running to us like wounded ducks," Mr. Hartley gloats.

Representatives of the two sides talked frequently by telephone over that weekend, trying to whittle down the major hurdles blocking a settlement. Unocal wanted up to $65 million from the Pickens group to cover its costs. Mesa was demanding that Unocal increase its repurchase offer to 75 million shares from 50 million.

Gradually, progress was made. Despite having gained enormous momentum from the Delaware court, Unocal was anxious to end the battle. For one thing, Mr. Hartley admits that he was concerned about what the Pickens group might do next. "He (Mr. Pickens) had 23.7 million shares. Let your imagination run wild," Mr. Hartley says.

Indeed, Mr. Pickens was lining up additional funds to make a cash tender offer for all the shares, though he and his advisers worried that Unocal could continue to outbid them while saddling the company with more debt.

The two sides got down to serious negotiating Sunday and worked through the night at Gibson Dunn's offices without breaking for meals. Breakfast for the Pickens side Monday morning consisted of four cans of warm Coca-Cola.

By 9 A.M. that morning, an agreement had been hammered out. Neither side would pay the other's expenses. Unocal would increase its repurchase offer only enough to include 7.7 million shares from the Pickens group, with the rest to be sold over time under conditions con-

trolled partly by Unocal.

Unocal also agreed to distribute to shareholders over time units in a limited partnership the company is setting up for much of its domestic oil and gas reserves. Pickens sources call this distribution a major victory in the negotiations; Unocal sources contend the company had been thinking about doing something like it for some time.

Though their direct confrontation is over, neither Mr. Hartley nor Mr. Pickens seems to think that the broader struggle over corporate takeovers is finished. Mr. Hartley says the nation still needs "intelligent legislation" to stop the wave of hostile takeovers. And Mr. Pickens says that although "it would be unlikely for us to do another deal for a while," he is still very much interested in future takeover efforts.

Securities Fraud   The 1934 Act and SEC Rule 10b–5 prohibit securities fraud with respect to the sale of registered or unregistered securities. While the requirements under the SEC are greater than those under state common law fraud rules, they are not as burdensome as those of the 1933 act. Reckless behavior, knowledge, or participation in the fraud imposes civil and perhaps criminal liability on all involved persons, but recent cases have established that negligence alone (as is the case with the 1933 act) is not enough to establish an entity as responsible for the losses suffered by investors. These findings have had important implications for professionals such as attorneys and accountants. An additional limitation is that under the 1934 act the aggrieved party must demonstrate that it bought or sold the securities and that there is a relationship between the fraud, the transactions, and the losses suffered. Still, the 1934 act can be, and often is, used to hold CPAs and others liable to investors when a company fails.

INVESTORS CALL CPAs TO ACCOUNT

Lee Berton

The accounting profession, which more than a half century ago volunteered to protect the public against financial chicanery, is wondering whether it has put its own head in the lion's mouth.

A recent explosive expansion of liability suits against major accounting firms after their clients reveal financial problems or go bankrupt is beginning to chip away at the financial viability of the biggest CPA firms. Indeed, some partners privately concede that big out-of-court settlements are starting to put reins on their stake in their firm and what they can take out as income each year.

"Our liability insurance is getting expensive enough so that we are seriously considering going bare and covering our own court exposure," says Carl D. Liggio, general counsel for Arthur Young & Co., one of the Big Eight accounting firms.

"Public interest" lawyers filing increasing numbers of class actions against big accounting firms aren't very sympathetic. "When an accountant signs his name to an annual report, a lot of investors, widows, and retirees place trust in that name," says Stuart Savett, a senior partner at a Philadelphia law firm involved in suits against such big CPA firms as Peat, Marwick, Mitchell & Co., and Coopers & Lybrand.

"Professional Standards"

Accounting firms contend that they can only stick to their professional standards but aren't policemen who can unearth fraud. But James E. Treadway Jr., a Securities and Exchange Commission member who will soon leave the SEC to return to private law practice, recently told an accounting group that it has a way to go before it can claim public confidence. "Public perceptions as to whether a professional is living up to expectations are fragile at best and constantly open to question," he said.

What Mr. Treadway says makes sense. Instead of trying to dodge its responsibilities, the accounting profession should take a harder line with some of its clients; not sticking to the narrow confines of "professional standards," but trying to perceive its job in terms of what the public needs and will take court action to pursue. It should recognize that an intense battle for clients that now includes widespread fee discounts may be eroding its professionalism in the eyes of the public and its critics.

Indeed, Donald Kirk, chairman of the Financial Accounting Standards Board, the rule-making body for accountants, recently told a group of students that "this competitive environment gives rise to a situation in which the

[CPA] firms' positions on accounting principles may sometimes be construed as a way of developing new business. This comes about through the giving of accounting opinions on possible financial transactions to investment bankers for their marketing use and the giving of opinions to nonclient corporations for their use in argument with their auditors. . . ."

Critics say this erosion of professionalism is hurting accounting firms in the courts. A decade ago, major accounting firms would carry liability insurance of up to only $50 million total, with deductibles ranging up to $250,000. But with settlements now reaching $50 million for major CPA firms and deductibles ranging as high as $1 million to $5 million per case, accounting firms and their lawyers are beginning to wonder how wide their liability exposure can become. Some insurance rates are due to double this year, and while major CPA firms probably will be able to shoulder this burden, it could lead to more mergers among weaker CPA firms and even stiffer competition for new business.

In the wake of many recent well-publicized examples of "audit failures," the accounting profession feels the public really doesn't understand the limitations of an audit. "The audit may be entirely competent, even though the business later fails," asserts Newton N. Minow, a Chicago lawyer who was a member of the internal quality review board of Arthur Andersen & Co., one of the biggest of the Big Eight, from 1974 through 1983.

* * * * *

For his part, Mr. Savett, the class-action lawyer, believes it's more equitable for big CPA firms with millions of dollars in insurance to shoulder or share in the losses of depositors in failed banks or of unsophisticated shareholders in companies that have concealed their problems. "Someone has to pay when a person living on meager retirement income invests in a company that goes sour," he says.

Some critics of the accounting profession wonder whether the big insurance umbrella that major CPA firms carry hasn't made them careless about their duties to the public. Abraham

Briloff, an accounting professor at Baruch College in New York and a well-known fault-finder of major accounting firms, says accountants shouldn't carry any insurance: "They only duck behind it after they make mistakes."

State and federal courts increasingly have acted to widen the accountant's responsibilities for protecting the public. But this was a duty the profession sought out when officials began looking for ways to prevent another depression-triggering bank collapse.

Congress in 1933 was told by Arthur H. Carter, president of the New York Society of CPAs, that accountants wouldn't leave their practices to go into government employ and that government expenses for the needed army of 500 to 600 auditors would be prohibitive. Congress bought this argument and gave the job to the private sector.

Toward the end of the 1930s, individuals began suing CPA firms whose clients had business problems or went bankrupt. But until fairly recently, the courts had held that accountants were liable for damages only if they displayed negligence or failed to adhere to their professional standards in certifying their clients' financial reports.

Today, lawyers for accounting firms maintain, the courts are holding accountants more responsible for the business health of their clients and how it may hurt their company's stock performance. In recent years, for example, federal courts have upheld a controversial "fraud-on-the-market" theory that says if financial reports are faulty, even if they aren't relied upon by an investor, third parties such as auditors who helped prepare those reports are liable for damages.

"If a stock goes sour or a business fails, everyone is now looking beyond the distressed or bankrupt company to the outside accountant," frets Harris Amhowitz, the general counsel for Coopers & Lybrand, another large U.S. CPA firm. The accountants, he contends, have become "the deepest of deep pockets" into which claimants want to reach.

Over the past three years, for example, Arthur Andersen has paid out more than $100 million in cases where companies have gone bankrupt or experienced unexpected or questionable losses. In 1982, a jury ordered Arthur Andersen to pay $80.7 million to the Fund of Funds for not properly auditing the mutual fund's books in the late 1960s. A judge subsequently reduced the award, but it's believed to be substantial.

While there's no exact tally of CPA firms' out-of-court settlements with plaintiffs, their increase in recent years has been spectacular. More lawsuits have been filed against accountants in the past 15 years "than in the entire previous history of the profession," says Mr. Minow, the Chicago lawyer. "All that seems necessary to prove now is that the CPA firm has insurance."

A recent decision by the New Jersey Supreme Court, for example, "seems to say that the existence of such insurance justifies pursuing a claim against an accounting firm for false information in financial reports the CPA firms audit," states Mr. Amhowitz.

In a March 1984 decision by the U.S. Supreme Court that forced Arthur Young to give the Internal Revenue Service internal work papers the firm used in auditing a client's tax strategy, Chief Justice Warren Burger broadly extended the outside auditor's role as a "public watchdog."

"By certifying the public reports that collectively depict a corporation's financial status, the independent auditor assumes a *public* responsibility transcending any employment relationship with the client," Justice Burger declared.

Hidden under Gobbledygook

Accounting firms maintain that they battle clients over the information to be included in annual financial statements, often to the point of getting fired, but that these relationships must be kept private or their clients would never reveal all their warts to the outside auditor.

* * * * *

In truth, too many outside auditors would like to enjoy big fees under the guise of protecting the public but plead ignorance when it comes to client fraud or manipulation of accounting principles.

Accounting firms acting as auditors may not want to don the policeman's hat, but they did ask for the job of certifying annual reports in the 1930s. And they have to agree that there isn't anyone more qualified to keep public companies honest in their disclosure of financial information. The courts obviously aren't going to let them forget that.

Insider Trading   The rule on insider trading appears to be very simple—anyone who has access to nonpublic information of a material nature (such as a recent oil strike, results of a major lawsuit, huge earnings increases, an impending takeover bid) (1) must refrain from trading in the stock and telling friends, relatives, and so on to trade in the stock or (2) must release the information to the public, wait a reasonable period of time, and then trade as desired. In recent years, the question of who is an *insider* under Rule 10b–5 and the conditions under which someone can be held liable for dealing in insider information have been in a state of flux. Clearly, corporate officers, directors, and attorneys may have access to inside information; in particular instances, engineers in an oil field also could—but so could brokers, analysts, printers, and eavesdroppers.

SEC PROBE OF SEARLE OPTIONS RAISES QUESTIONS ON ETHICS, INSIDE TRADES

Bruce Ingersoll

Washington—Viewers of CBS Evening News last month saw Arizona scientist Woodrow Monte challenge the safety of NutraSweet, the low-calorie sweetener made by G. D. Searle & Co., as part of a three-part report that raised questions about the product.

What the viewers didn't know was that Mr. Monte had bought "put" options on Searle stock just a few weeks before the report was aired. So did his Phoenix lawyer, Richard Faerber. They concede that they bought the options because they expected Searle stock to fall as a result of the adverse publicity.

As it turned out, they lost money because Searle's stock didn't fall as much as they had expected. But the trading raises difficult ethical questions about what constitutes illegal insider trading.

Messrs. Monte and Faerber defend their actions. "I honestly believe I had a right to do it," Mr. Monte says. "Gosh, I'm an American citizen. I don't feel it's unethical. It's the American way."

As for his trading, Mr. Faerber says, "I am not ashamed or sorry about what I did. I don't think it was illegal."

The Securities and Exchange Commission may disagree. It is investigating a highly unusual series of upsurges in Searle options trading from November 22 until the network presented the NutraSweet series on January 16, 17, and 18. SEC investigators are focusing on a group of people—including Messrs. Monte and Faerber, other Arizona investors, and CBS employees, who were in a position to know the series was in the works and could have reprofited from buying put options on Searle's stock.

A put is an option contract that gives the buyer the right to sell 100 shares of a given stock at a certain price within a specified period of time. If the stock drops in price, a put buyer makes money.

The SEC could have trouble making an insider-trading case against Messrs. Monte and Faerber, according to Bevis Longstreth, a former SEC commissioner. The reason: The information on which they traded didn't come from inside any company to whose shareholders they had a fiduciary responsibility.

Mr. Monte, director of Arizona State University's Food Sciences and Research Laboratory, and Mr. Faerber insist that they were relying on the same kind of public information that Wall Street analysts and institutional investors use.

At CBS News, the legal question could turn on whether any employees "misappropriated" private information entrusted to them—specifically, plans to televise a series that could alarm consumers and batter Searle's stock. But Mr. Longstreth believes the SEC would face an "uphill fight" trying to prove insider-trading violations on that basis.

* * * * *

Mr. Faerber says the passion of Mr. Monte's scientific convictions prompted him to join the anti-NutraSweet camp as a pro bono lawyer. "The guy couldn't sleep at night," he says. One of Mr. Monte's main concerns is that aspartame, the generic name for Nutra-Sweet, breaks down into potentially toxic methyl alcohol, particularly when diet soft drinks are stored at high temperatures. Neither Searle nor the Food and Drug Administration sees this as a health threat.

"We don't know what a small amount of methyl alcohol will do over a long time," Mr. Monte said on the CBS Evening News program. He and the Arizona Dietetic Association made the same argument in petitioning the Arizona Department of Health Services to ban the sale of aspartame-sweetened beverages and in asking the FDA to hold hearings. Mr. Faerber is also the lawyer for the dietetic association.

Taking on a corporate giant like Searle, however, takes money. Mr. Monte and Mr. Faerber say they were investing neophytes, but decided to try trading in Searle put contracts. "I felt the CBS report, if they went with it, would have an impact," Mr. Monte says.

That feeling was reinforced by what Mr. Faerber was hearing from securities analysts who follow Searle. "I did tell some of them a network had interviewed Dr. Monte," he says. "One guy's response was 'Boy, this will kill the stock.' What's so weird, it didn't. The stock went up every day the program was aired."

Searle's stock peaked at $54.625 on November 25 and then began a gradual slide to the low $40s by early January, but it didn't fall far enough for the investors to profit. The company's stock closed Friday on the New York Stock Exchange at $46.25 a share.

Mr. Monte says he invested $1,994 in Searle puts and lost $1,224. Mr. Faerber says he and two friends invested $2,000 to $5,000 each during December and early January, and also incurred losses.

"On the bottom line what we were doing is betting we would succeed with our (FDA and Arizona) petitions," Mr. Faerber says, "It certainly was a wrong bet, because we haven't succeeded yet."

What they did is "sleazy," says Michael F. Jacobson, executive director of the Center for Science in the Public Interest. "Outrageous," says Dr. Sidney Wolfe, director of Public Citizens' Health Research Group. "That kind of behavior is unethical.

"If I get a phone call from Wall Street analysts asking about something we're working on before it's public, I refuse to give them any information," Dr. Wolfe says.

Mr. Monte insists his actions weren't unethical. "If any money was made, it was to go toward fighting the (NutraSweet) battle," he says. Mr. Faerber says he only regrets handling Searle "on a silver platter" a chance to impugn the motives of its scientific adversaries.

Source: *The Wall Street Journal*, February 27, 1984, p. 23. Reprinted by permission of *The Wall Street Journal*, © Dow Jones & Company, Inc., 1984. All rights reserved.

Chapter Questions

1. Recent crises in the government securities market have provoked calls for increased government regulation. Do you favor that direction? Explain.

2. Define: *(a)* security, *(b)* private placements, *(c)* blue sky laws, *(d)* fraud, *(e)* short-swing profits, *(f)* tender offers, *(g)* buy/sell agreement, *(h)* partnerships, *(i)* Sub S Corporation, *(j)* registration, *(k)* prospectus.

3. Should accountants be expected to discover and reveal fraud perpetrated by their clients?

4. Why is insider trading unlawful?

5. X, Y, and Z desire to start a business. X is concerned about liability because he is rich. Y wants to have the right to control all decisions made in running the firm. X and Z do not plan to participate in managing the firm, but will contribute money to start it. They expect to lose money for at least three years. How should they structure their organization?

6. Should additional restraints be placed on the limited liability afforded shareholders of corporations? What would be the consequences of doing this?

7. Should tax shelters be eliminated? How?

8. Discuss the advantages and disadvantages of partnerships and corporations.

9. Discuss the exemptions available for certain types of securities.

10. Explain how federal securities laws attempt to make provisions for small businesses.

11. Ivan Landreth and his sons owned all of the stock in a lumber business they operated in Tonasket, Washington. The owners offered the stock for sale. During that time a fire severely damaged the business, but the owners made assurances of rebuilding and modernization. The stock was sold to Dennis and Bolten and a new organization, Landreth Timber Company, was formed with the senior Landreth remaining as a consultant on the side. The new firm was unsuccessful and was sold at a loss. The Landreth Timber Company then filed suit against Ivan Landreth and his sons seeking recession of the first sale alleging, among other arguments, that Landreth and sons had widely offered and then sold their stock without registering it as required by the Securities Act of 1933. The district court acknowledged that *stocks* fit within the definition of a *security,* and that the stock in question "possessed all of the characteristics of conventional stock." However, it held that the federal securities laws do not apply to the sale of 100 percent of the stock of a closely held corporation. Here the district court found that the purchasers had not entered into the sale with the expectation of earnings secured via the labor of others. Managerial control resided with the purchasers. Thus the sale was a commercial venture rather than a typical investment. The Court of Appeals affirmed, and the case reached the Supreme Court. Decide. See *Landreth Timber Co.* v. *Landreth.* 53 *Law Week* 4602 (U.S. S.Ct., 1985).

Notes

1. 497 F.2d 473 (5th Cir. 1974).
2. 421 U.S. 837 (1975).
3. 439 U.S. 551 (1979).

9

Antitrust Law— Introduction and Monopolies

Preface: A New Direction in Antitrust Policy?

Perhaps the most important lesson to be derived from contemporary antitrust law is that the entire field is in a state of flux. Spurred by the scholarly insights of the "Chicago School" of free market economics and the ideological preferences and political resources of the Reagan administration, federal antitrust policy is undergoing a searching evaluation.

In a striking implementation of its policy, the Reagan administration in a space of six months dropped or settled four of the lengthiest and most complex cases in American history.

AT&T Settlement

On January 8, 1982, the Justice Department announced an out-of-court settlement of its seven-year-pursuit of the phone company. The settlement, labeled "one of the most significant events in modern economic history,"[1] required AT&T to divest itself of nearly two thirds of its assets by spinning off its 22 local operating companies (which had a combined value of approximately $80 billion). AT&T retained its long distance service, the Bell Labs, and Western Electric—its manufacturing division. AT&T had been charged with restraint of trade, attempted monopolization, and monopolization. In sum, AT&T was alleged to have used its dominance over local telephone exchanges to impede competitors' progress in developing telecommunications technology that might have reduced AT&T's market share. In the 1960s, after the Federal Communications Commission and the courts authorized new entrants in the intercity telecommunications market (particularly via microwave radio and satellites), AT&T allegedly sought to use its control of local exchanges to thwart potential intercity competitors by, in various ways, making it costly and difficult for the competition to "hook up" with the AT&T local lines monopoly. In a similar vein, AT&T allegedly placed unnecessary impediments in the path of Bell Telephone service subscribers who sought to connect equipment produced by a Bell competitor to the lines or equipment of the telephone company.

And the government alleged that, in diverse ways, AT&T gave preference in its equipment purchasing decisions to Western Electric, thus retarding competition in the telephone equipment market.

The settlement might be viewed as a victory for the government, since the divestiture corresponds, in general terms, to the Justice Department's goals for the lawsuit. At the same time, the evidence against AT&T was so persuasive that some would have preferred a full litigation as a clearer condemnation of corporate abuse. The impact of the settlement will not be fully understood for many years. However, since the divestiture local phone bills have risen substantially because local service is no longer subsidized with long distance revenues. The slimmed-down AT&T may become both more profitable and more aggressive. In addition to keeping its very healthy long distance, manufacturing, and research elements, Bell is in the midst of building a subsidiary to compete in the new technology domains of communications such as data transmission, information processing, and cable television. Thus, on the one hand, AT&T lost a great deal of its bulk—and perhaps as a consequence some of its business and political leverage. Competitors are now guaranteed nondiscriminatory access to local phone networks. On the other hand, AT&T is now free to direct its vast research resources away from the regulated telephone market into various unregulated fields. The settlement revises a 1956 consent decree prohibiting AT&T's expansion into the "knowledge business." Thus, we can expect such advances as electronic Yellow Pages, linkage of home televisions with data banks, and expanded linkage of telephones with computers.

IBM Suit Dismissed

Four and one half hours after the AT&T settlement announcement, the administration's emerging antitrust policy assumed added clarity when the government decided to end its 13-year action against IBM. Filed by then Attorney General Ramsey Clark on the last business day (January 17, 1969) of the Johnson administration, the suit accused IBM of monopolizing the computer market (with an alleged 70 percent share) and of maintaining that monopoly by predatory practices including:

1. Discriminatory pricing that permitted a "cornering" of the educational market.
2. "Bundling" the price of hardware, software, and support services.
3. Pricing new models at unusually low profit levels.

The government sought to break up IBM into smaller units. IBM officials viewed the decision as a "complete vindication" and noted that 16 federal judges in various antitrust actions had ruled in favor of IBM. While the suit may have had merit initially, it became clear over the course of the affair that IBM was facing increasingly firm competition and experiencing a declining market share.

According to International Data Corporation, IBM's share of the various computer markets was estimated as follows: Mainframes, 68 percent; smaller business computers, 34 percent; personal computers, 11 percent, and minicomputers, 3 percent. With the very aggressive Japanese competition in recent years, the growth of newer firms in the top end of the market, and IBM's tardy entry into manufacturing small computers, the market appeared to then government antitrust chief, William Baxter, to be bristling with competition. Baxter concluded that the government simply had a "very, very weak" case. Additionally, the Justice Department decision doubtless reflected concern over the stunning costs of the suit. The direct government expense was estimated at $13.4 million. While IBM has not revealed its expenditures, it is assumed that the defendant likewise expended many millions (a portion of which was assumed by the taxpayers, since the legal bills were tax deductible). The case had generated 2,500 depositions, 66 million pages of documents and work for 300 lawyers. IBM arguably suffered even more serious losses in business revenues due to the distraction, uncertainty, and at least temporary marketing timidity provoked by the lingering litigation.

On the other hand, the federal judge hearing the case and many of the government lawyers trying the case clearly disapproved of the decision to withdraw. The government contended that IBM engaged in "bad practices," but Baxter was unconvinced that those practices, if any, materially contributed to IBM's very strong market share.

An interesting consequence of the nearly simultaneous AT&T and IBM decisions is that those two firms are now free to wage what promises to be a titanic struggle for dominance in information processing and communications.

Cereals Case Dismissed

In early 1982, the Federal Trade Commission, by a three-to-one vote, dropped its decade-long antitrust suit against Kellogg, General Mills, and General Foods. Earlier an administrative law judge had dismissed the case after concluding that the government had failed to prove its claim. In summary, the government alleged both a conspiracy to monopolize and a "shared monopoly." The former claim was built upon the notion that an implied conspiracy could be inferred from the defendants' generally parallel behavior in a variety of areas—instituting price changes, eliminating inpack premiums, and refusing to sell to private label brands. While conspiracy can, in some instances, be inferred from parallel behavior, the administrative law judge dismissed the claim on the grounds that the pleadings had not properly raised the conspiracy theory.

The most notable element of the cereals case was the shared monopoly theory, a novel approach alleging that the competitors may respond to each other's behavior much in the manner of a cartel. They learn that independent action (such as price cuts) will be observed and matched by the competition, thereby resulting only in lower profits for the entire industry. Thus, among other "anticompetitive" practices, the government alleged that by benignly following a price leader (Kellogg), by avoiding competition for retail shelf space allocations, and by brand proliferation to discourage entry by new competitors, the cereal companies violated section 5 of the Federal Trade Commission Act (forbidding unfair methods of competition). As a consequence the FTC argued that cereal was 29 percent more expensive than it would have been in a competitive market. According to the government, consumers were overcharged by $100 million per year. A remedy under consideration was the division of the big three into eight smaller firms.

The FTC based its shared monopoly argument on a series of studies and investigations, the results of which suggested that the cereal companies behaved differently than would have been expected in a competitive market. The shelf allocation issue provides a particularly intriguing example. Cereal shelf locations were found to be surprisingly uniform nationwide. The FTC alleged that Kellogg with its forty percent market share had effectively guaranteed itself the desirable mid-aisle shelf spaces. Kellogg encouraged store managers to submit cereals' sales figures to computer analysis, with Kellogg using the results to produce a display system reflecting the cereals' sales mix. The result, of course, was that Kellogg got the center space and was flanked on one side by General Mills with 21 percent of the market and on the other by General Foods with 17 percent. The FTC alleged that the large companies decided to go along with Kellogg's plan because it guaranteed desirable shelf space for all the industry leaders.

In declining to hear an appeal from the decision of the administrative law judge, three of the four FTC commissioners did not explicitly reject the shared monopoly notion. The Commission's concerns focused on the remedy. The proposed divestiture, along with a requirement that the Big Three license their trademarks amounted to the restructuring of an entire industry. The majority commissioners thought the remedy too extreme and doubted that it would achieve the desired result. Additionally, they were unwilling to find a violation in the absence of evidence of actual predatory conduct. Reagan appointee James Miller III maintained that too much money had been spent on a case built, in his view, on insufficient evidence and on inadequate legal theory. Thus the shared monopoly theory itself seems yet to have some life, but it seems unlikely that the government will soon immerse itself in a similar litigation.

Oil Industry Action Dropped

In June 1981 the Federal Trade Commission voted to dismiss its eight-year claim against the nation's eight largest oil companies (Exxon, Texaco, Gulf, Standard Oil of California, Standard Oil of Indiana, Shell, Atlantic Richfield, and Mobil). With a trial at least three years off, the commission found the litigation "not in the public interest." Clearly the length of the proceeding and its uncertain progress influenced the commissioners, who noted that they were not ruling on the merits of the case. Originally FTC lawyers had sought to break up the vertically integrated oil giants, but that strategy was revised to one of partial divestitures and remedies for various impermissible forms of conduct. The commission left open the possibility of a "more focused proceeding" in the future. Then in 1983 the Justice Department ended its six-year antitrust investigation of the Aramco consortium (Arab-American Oil Co.—Exxon, Mobil, Texaco, and Standard Oil of California). The Justice Department took the position that the suit held little likelihood of successful litigation in that the firms involved no longer held the power to control the world price of oil.

Implications

These decisions bespeak a significant reshaping of government antitrust policy born of a shift in favor of free market principles and away from the "bigness is bad" notion that has proved quite persuasive in recent decades. The political and social considerations (such as fear of concentrated power) that so vigorously influenced antitrust law over the years appear to be in descent. Noted economist Lester Thurow has referred to the AT&T and IBM cases as "the last dinosaurs" of the antitrust era:

Never again are we apt to witness massive cases that stretch on for decades and grind up hundreds of millions of dollars in corporate and Federal resources.[2]

Thurow holds the broadly shared view that a rapidly changing environment has required a departure from antitrust philosophies that found their roots in the business and social conditions of the 1890s. Dramatic technological advances and intensified international competition—particularly from giant, government-supported combines—has, in Thurow's view, rendered obsolete the traditional American views of bigness.

To former Assistant Attorney General Baxter the purpose of antitrust law is to make the economy as technically efficient as possible. In consequence, he thinks the government should be much less disturbed about a variety of behaviors that have traditionally been considered potentially anticompetitive. Among those is the area of vertical mergers (a combination between a firm and any other firm in its vertical chain of supply, production, or distribution). Baxter argues that those combinations often result in lower costs, since a customer linked to a supplier will often receive lower prices. Similarly, Baxter finds little to fear from conglomerate mergers (those betwen firms in unrelated markets) because such alliances rarely result in collusion, price-fixing, or a general reduction in competition. On the other hand, Baxter favors a very hard line including jail sentences for those involved in price-fixing or other collusion between competitors. Horizontal mergers (between competitors) will continue to receive close government scrutiny.

These and other changes in philosophy and practice certainly suggest a "pro-business" climate for the near future, but it is clear that the Reagan administration has not abandoned antitrust. Indeed, government action in 1981–82 effectively foreclosed mergers involving Mobil-Conoco, Schlitz-Heileman, and LTV-Grumman. However, the view that technical economic efficiency is the goal of antitrust law is certain to be challenged. American antitrust law was founded on political and social concerns that transcended economics. The fears that provoked antitrust legislation will not be entirely quieted by the view that the free market continues to offer the best protection from abuse of power.

Having outlined the current rather dramatic shift in antitrust policy, it is now appropriate to turn to a detailed exploration of antitrust law as it has evolved over the decades. The student is urged to contrast the most recent initiatives with the developed case law.

Part One—The Roots of Antitrust Law

More than any other, the promise of America is that of personal freedom. The constitutions of the United States and the 50 states are designed to preserve our individual freedom against encroachment by government. As we saw in Chapter 1, Americans likewise fear excessive concentrations of power in private hands. Since the federal and state constitutions afford us no protection from abuse of private power, it has been thought necessary to turn to legislation to curb private concentrations of authority. A primary component of that legislation is the various federal antitrust statutes to which this chapter is addressed.

Anger directed at corporate power came to the fore following the Civil War. Farmers and small businesspersons were particularly incensed by high railroad freight charges and high prices for commodities. Interest groups such as ''The National Anti-Monopoly Cheap Freight Railway League'' called for action to abate the power of the railroads and the so-called trusts in sugar, whiskey, fuel oil, and others.[3] By the 1880s, Standard Oil was producing perhaps 80 percent of America's domestic oil, and by the turn of the century U.S. Steel was responsible for as much as 65 percent of the nation's steel production. Indeed, by 1914, the upper 2.2 percent of all manufacturing firms employed 35.3 percent of the manufacturing workers and produced 48.7 percent of the manufactured products.[4] A new America was emerging, and many citizens were angry and frightened by what they witnessed.

Public outrage and a growing congressional recognition of free market inadequacies (in company with some elements of the business lobby seeking protection from competition) led in 1887 to the creation of the Interstate Commerce Commission and in 1890 to the passage of the Sherman Antitrust Act as the federal government's first major business regulation measures. The view that market forces must be tempered by government intervention has, of course, resulted in a profound alteration of American life. The merits of big government, income redistribution, welfare, environmental protection, and so on are at the heart of contemporary public policy debate, and all those issues find at least a portion of their genesis in the critical turn of the century decision to place those rather modest restraints on the free market. To the contemporary student of the law, a primary inquiry must be that of whether those restraints have been carried too far or, contrariwise, whether U.S. economic policy should embrace a more expansive government role.

Antitrust Statutes

A brief look at the various antitrust statutes will serve to place them in historical context. A further examination will accompany the case materials.

Sherman Antitrust Act, 1890

Section 1 of the act forbids restraints of trade and Section 2 forbids monopolization, attempts to monopolize, and conspiracies to monopolize. Several enforcement options are available to the federal government:

1. Violation of the Sherman Act subjects participants to criminal penalties. As amended in 1974, the maximum corporate fine is $1 million, while individuals may be fined $100,000 and imprisoned for three years. Sherman Act violations are classified as felonies.
2. Injunctive relief is provided under the civil law. That is, the government or a private party may secure a court order preventing continuing violations of the act and affording appropriate relief (such as dissolution or divestiture).

Perhaps the most important remedy is that available to private parties. An individual or organization harmed by a violation of the act may bring a civil action seeking three times the damages (treble damages) actually sustained. Thus, the victim is compensated, and the wrongdoer is punished. However, the treble-damages remedy is currently being questioned as an excessive penalty.

Clayton and Federal Trade Commission Acts, 1914

After nearly 25 years of experience with the Sherman Act, many members of Congress, along with President Woodrow Wilson, held the view that the federal antitrust law required strengthening. Sherman forbade the continued practice of specified anticompetitive conduct, but it did not forbid conduct that was *likely to lead to* anticompetitive behavior. Furthermore, many felt that judicial interpretations of Sherman had seriously weakened that legislation. The Clayton Act forbids price discrimination, exclusive dealing, tying arrangements, requirements contracts, mergers restraining commerce or tending to create a monopoly, and interlocking directorates.

Civil enforcement of the Clayton Act is similar to the Sherman Act in that the government may sue for injunctive relief, and private parties may seek treble damages. Injunctive relief was also extended to private parties under both the Clayton and Sherman Acts. In general, no criminal law remedies are available under the Clayton Act.

The Federal Trade Commission Act created a powerful, independent agency designed to devote its full attention to the elimination of anticompetitive practices in American commerce. The commission is composed of five members, no more than three of whom may belong to a single political party. The commissioners are appointed by the president and confirmed by the Senate to staggered seven-year terms. As a consequence of the legislation itself and judicial interpretation of that legislation, the FTC is now empowered to proceed under both the Sherman Act (via section 5 of the FTC Act) and Clayton Act. Section 5 of the FTC Act declares unlawful "unfair methods of competition" and "unfair or deceptive acts or practices in or affecting commerce." The commission's primary enforcement device is the cease and desist order. The agency's action is subject to judicial review under the principles articulated in the preceding chapter. Should the commission's order not be appealed, or if the order is upheld on appeal, the offending party may be fined up to $5,000 per day for each violation until the cease and desist order is obeyed.

In recent years the FTC has instituted actions against many of America's major industries and firms, including soft drink bottlers, the American Medical Association, General Motors, and as mentioned, the major cereal manufacturers and oil companies. Several of these suits represent rather bold efforts on the part of the commission to strike out at practices not explicitly forbidden by statute but which are believed to be "unfair methods of competition." However, it is apparent that the current FTC is taking a less interventionist stance. Some commissioners consider the "unfair and deceptive" language overly broad, but the FTC holds in Congress a powerful ally in that the agency affords Congress its "own antitrust arm" corresponding to the executive branch's Justice Department.

It should be noted that FTC authority extends well beyond antitrust matters to touch the fullness of unfair trade practices. That dimension of FTC activity is addressed in Chapter 15.

1915 to the Present

The antitrust zeal that produced the Clayton and FTC Acts was muted by World War I and largely extinguished by a strong free enterprise spirit following the war. The Harding, Coolidge, and Hoover administrations of 1920 to 1932 constituted perhaps the zenith of faith in capitalist principles in America. In time, the suffering of the Depression era brought a search for solutions in the form of renewed government intervention. Among President Roosevelt's many legislative programs to achieve economic recovery, the Robinson-Patman Act of 1936 and the Miller-Tydings Act of 1937 were the only antitrust measures. Robinson-Patman amended the Clayton Act in an effort to achieve firmer controls against price discrimination. Miller-Tydings legalized "fair-trade" pricing where state law allowed such pricing. "Fair-trade" pricing is a policy of resale price maintenance wherein the seller specifies the minimum price at which its product may be resold. The McGuire Act of 1952 sought to strengthen Miller Tydings, but in 1975 the Consumer Goods Pricing Act repealed both. However, many states still retain fair trade pricing, and as will be discussed, resale price maintenance agreements remain a relatively common merchandising strategy.

Since World War II antitrust legislative activity has been relatively sparse. Of particular note, however, was the 1950 passage of the Celler-Kefauver Act, which strengthened the Clayton Act, and the 1976 Hart-Scott-Rodino Antitrust Improvement Act, which requires notice to the Federal Trade Commission and the Justice Department in advance of major mergers.

Exemptions from Federal Antitrust Law

Congress has accorded labor unions partial exemption from antitrust law. One result of the exemption is that unions are able to restrict the supply of labor, thus "artificially" raising prices. The labor exemption has provoked complaints. Robert Tollison observes:

For a variety of reasons, the most serious cases of monopoly have traditionally been those monopolies sanctioned by the government. . . . . It seems clear that without legal sanction, the monopoly power of unions would be quickly eroded by competition in labor markets.[5]

Why have unions been partially shielded from federal antitrust laws? Should unions be fully subject to free market forces? If so, how would all our lives be altered?

Regulated industries (e.g., insurance, utilities, shipping, banking, and securities) have been, in the main, free of the impact of the antitrust laws. Congress and the courts have recognized the government's direct supervisory authority in critical areas such as entry, exit, and pricing and thus have generally declined to apply the antitrust laws. Recent cases, however, suggest an increasing judicial willingness to intervene, particularly in industries where regulation is less intense. State action (laws and regulations) is generally exempt from the Sherman Act when the state has clearly developed a policy of regulating the commerce in question rather than allowing the free market to work its will. A state monopoly over the sale of liquor is an example of state action that inhibits competition, but is exempt from the Sherman Act. Two 1985 Supreme Court decisions affirmed the validity of the state action exemption.[6]

Perhaps recalling the innocence of their own sandlot days, the judiciary has seen fit to view baseball as a sport rather than a business, thus removing it from antitrust proscriptions. Curiously, other professional sports are subject to antitrust, and football, in particular, has lately been the subject of extensive litigation. That baseball is considered a sport while football is labeled a business is a reminder that forces other than logic sometimes shape the course of law. The cooperative marketing of agricultural and fish products has been specifically excluded from the sweep of the antitrust laws. Associations organized for the purpose of engaging in cooperative export trade are also partially exempt under the terms of the Export Trading Company Act of 1982. Some difficult questions remain about how much professional services (law, medicine, real estate) should be subject to antitrust. In 1975, the Supreme Court in the *Goldfarb* case[7] held that the Sherman Act applies to at least some anticompetitive conduct for lawyers. Mr. and Mrs. Goldfarb successfully argued that the minimum fee schedule published by the Virginia State Bar constituted a price-fixing scheme in violation of Sherman I. The Goldfarbs' victory has led to a continuing series of challenges to the professions, making it evident that professional services do constitute commerce and that anticompetitive practices may be challenged. However, the judiciary clearly believes that regulation of the professions is a matter not best administered at the federal level. In *Goldfarb*, the Supreme Court affirmed the limited role of antitrust:

In holding that certain anticompetitive conduct by lawyers is within the reach of the Sherman Act we intend no diminution of the authority of the State to regulate its professions.[8]

Federal Antitrust Law and Other Regulatory Systems

State Law

Most states, through legislation and judicial decisions, have developed their own antitrust laws. However, enforcement at the state level ordinarily receives only passing attention. Indeed, due to the interstate nature of most antitrust problems, states could not effectively pursue the bulk of the cases.

Patents, Copyrights, and Trademarks

Each of these devices constitutes a limited, government granted monopoly. As such they are in direct conflict with the general thrust of antitrust law. However, each of those devices serves to protect—and thus encourage—commercial creativity and development. The resulting antitrust problem is essentially that of limiting the patent, copyright, or trademark holder to the narrow terms of its privilege.

Law of Other Nations

Refer to the "International Issues" section at the end of Chapter 11.

Antitrust: Law For All Seasons

What is it that antitrust law seeks to accomplish? To the reader unacquainted with the national goals embodied in the antitrust laws, the case decisions that follow would seem, at best, confusing, and at worst, irrational. Indeed, even given an understanding of "antitrust philosophy," some of the decisions may agitate the lucid mind.

Many businesses in competition means that none of them may corner economic, political, or social power. It follows that the character and course of American life will reflect the varied inputs of the many rather than the vested interests of the powerful few. Hence, antitrust law seeks to preserve democracy.

Of course, the major, express goal of antitrust legislation has been the preservation of the merits of capitalism. We continue to believe that free and open markets will result in the best product at the lowest price. More specifically, we seek the benefits of competition—efficient allocation of resources, technological innovations, high productivity, price stability, and so on. The development of the law has demonstrated the impossibility of achieving *perfect competition*. Hence, the goal of current antitrust policy is that of *workable competition*, wherein market forces are sufficiently effective to prevent the development of monopolies and other anticompetitive practices.

Furthermore, a charming, but arguably anachronistic, clinging to the American Dream seems to continue to shape our attitude toward "trust-busting." As we will see, most notably in the case of the Robinson-Patman Act, the small business lobby has been most effective in structuring the law to preserve the opportunity for the "little guys" to compete with the giants. However, it has been argued that our protectionist efforts regarding small business have actually resulted in reduced market efficiency. It may be that the national spirit requires the preservation of at least a long-shot opportunity for each of us to start our own business and build our way to the top. Indeed, it could be persuasively argued that the destruction of that key ingredient in the American Dream would ultimately destroy the fabric of the nation. So antitrust legislation is very much more than rules to regulate specific dimensions of business conduct. It is designed to do nothing less than preserve the American way of life.

Finally, it should be noted that the antitrust laws have been, for a segment of society, an expression of a strain of political radicalism. Sentiments against big business are not uncommon in America. For those who feel that business power lies at the heart of American ills, the antitrust laws are taken to be useful tools in reshaping America so that business more nearly meets the needs of the people.

Part Two—Monopoly

Principal legislation: Sherman Act, section 2.

Every person who shall monopolize, or attempt to monopolize, or combine or conspire with any other person or persons, to monopolize any part of the trade or commerce among the several States, or with foreign nations, shall be deemed guilty of a felony punishable by a fine not exceeding $1,000,000 if a corporation, or if any other person, $100,000 or by imprisonment not exceeding three years or both.

(Throughout the three antitrust chapters, the "principal legislation" is identified. But it should be understood that most, if not all, antitrust violations are subject to more than one piece of legislation. In particular, Section 5 of the Federal Trade Commission Act is arguably applicable to all antitrust violations.)

From an economic viewpoint, a *monopoly* is a situation in which one firm holds the power to control prices and/or exclude competition in a particular market.

By contrast, an *oligopoly* is the situation in which a few firms share monopoly power. (See the earlier discussion of the alleged shared monopoly in the cereals industry.)

In practice, the courts' analyses of monopoly problems have not adhered particularly rigorously to established economic theory. Jurists have focused their attention on both the structure of the industry in question and on the intent of the alleged monopolist as measured by its conduct. Thus, the critical inquiries are the percentage of the market held by the alleged monopolist and the behavior that produced that market share.

It is important to note that a considerable debate rages in the legal community about whether conduct or structure (or, indeed, several other possibilities) constitutes the best test of anticompetitive conditions. Should we concern ourselves with a firm's behavior, or should we focus on those industries in which a few firms control a large percentage of the market? Is a concentrated market undesirable in and of itself, or should we challenge market concentration only when it has been acquired and/or maintained via abusive conduct? Since current legal and economic reasoning affords us no definitive answer, the student can only be advised to consider the implications of each policy.

The Sherman Act does not, as interpreted, punish the efficient companies who legitimately earn and maintain a large market share. Hence, it is as the Supreme Court stated in the 1966 *Grinnell* decision:

> The offense of monopoly under § 2 of the Sherman Act has two elements: (1) the possession of monopoly power in the relevant market and (2) the willful acquisition or maintenance of that power as distinguished from growth or development as a consequence of a superior product, business acumen, or historic accident.[9]

Thus we see that the Sherman Act forbids monopolization (market power *plus* purposefulness or general intent) rather than mere monopoly. The issue of intent has provoked considerable confusion. Monopolization requires no more than a *general* intent to do the act that results in monopoly power. *Specific* intent to achieve a monopoly is not required. General intent can then be established if we show that a monopoly has resulted as a natural and probable consequence of the defendant's acts, even though we cannot show any specific intent to establish a monopoly.

The prohibitions in Section 2 against combinations and conspiracies and attempts to monopolize are subjected to standards different than those for monopolization. A combination or conspiracy requires two or more persons deliberately joining together with the specific intent to achieve an unlawful monopoly. Those persons must commit at least one overt act in aid of their monopolization goal, but they need not achieve that goal in order to violate the statute. An unlawful attempt to monopolize embraces three components: (1) a specific intent to monopolize, (2) improper conduct, and (3) a dangerous probability of success. Because of the problems of proof associated with combinations, conspiracies, and specific intent, these provisions of Section 2 are not particularly useful.

Finally, it should be understood that "pure" free market advocates hold a markedly different view of monopoly than those just articulated. Alan Greenspan, noted economist and chairman of the Council of Economic Advisers during the Ford administration, explains:

A "coercive monopoly" is a business concern that can set its prices and production policies independent of the market, with immunity from competition, from the law of supply and demand. An economy dominated by such monopolies would be rigid and stagnant.

The necessary precondition of a coercive monopoly is closed entry—the barring of all competing producers from a given field. This can be accomplished only by an act of government intervention, in the form of special regulations, subsidies, or franchises. Without government assistance, it is impossible for a would-be monopolist to set and maintain his prices and production policies independent of the rest of the economy. For if he attempted to set his prices and production at a level that would yield profits to new entrants significantly above those available in other fields, competitors would be sure to invade his industry.[10]

To some laissez-faire advocates the alleged monopolies that, in part, provoked the creation of the Interstate Commerce Commission and the Sherman Act were really the product of government intervention. For example, the railroads that engendered the farmers' rage over their rate policies in the latter half of the 1800s were able to secure market dominance in the West only after unusually favorable government treatment including grants of tens of millions of acres.

Monopolization Analysis

While the case law is not a model of clarity, a rather straightforward framework for monopoly analysis has emerged:

1. Define the relevant *product market.*
2. Define the relevant *geographic market.*
3. Compute the defendant's *share of the market* and determine if that share is sufficient to constitute a monopoly. If the share is clearly beneath that necessary for market dominance, the case may be dismissed. As explained later, factors other than market share often strongly influence the court's decision about market power.
4. Assuming the market share is of threatening proportions, the next inquiry is that of *intent.* Do the defendant's acts evidence the necessary deliberateness or purposefulness? If not, the case should be dismissed. If yes, the defendant is, in the absence of further evidence, in violation of the law.
5. The defendant may yet prevail if the evidence demonstrates that the monopoly was *"thrust upon"* the firm, rather than that the firm affirmatively sought its monopoly posture. The thrust upon defense had its genesis in Judge Learned Hand's opinion in the *Alcoa* case[11] where that most aptly named jurist suggested that the Sherman Act would not be violated if monopoly power were innocently acquired via superior skill, foresight, or industry or by failure of the competition as a consequence of changes in costs or consumer preference. Depending on the circumstances, other

defenses such as possession of a patent, for example, may be persuasive. Recent cases suggest that federal judges increasingly accept the argument that the alleged monopolist earned its market position legitimately and thus should not be punished.

Product Market

Here the court seeks, effectively, to draw a circle that encompasses categories of goods in which the defendant's products or services compete and excludes those that are not in the same competitive arena. The fundamental test is that of interchangeability as determined primarily by the price, use, and quality of the product in question. An analysis of cross elasticity of demand is a key ingredient in defining the product market.

Geographic Market

Once the product market has been defined, we still must determine where the product can be purchased. The cases offer no definitive explanation of the geographic market concept. A working definition might be "any section of the country where the product is sold in commercially significant quantities." From an economic perspective, the geographic market is defined by elasticity. If prices rise or supplies are reduced within the geographic area in question (e.g., New England) and demand remains steady, will products from other areas enter the market in quantity sufficient to affect price and/or supply? If so, the geographic market must be broadened to embrace those new sources of supply. If not, the geographic market is not larger than the area in question (New England). Perhaps the better approach is to read the cases and recognize that each geographic market must simply be identified in terms of its unique economic properties.

UNITED STATES V. GRINNELL CORP.   384 U.S. 563 (1966)

Justice Douglas

[The United States charged Grinnell with monopolization of the central station protection business in violation of Section 2 of the Sherman Act.]

Grinnell manufactures plumbing supplies and fire sprinkler systems. It also owns 76 percent of the stock of ADT, 89 percent of the stock of AFA, and 100 percent of the stock of Holmes. ADT provides both burglary and fire protection services; Holmes provides burglary services alone; AFA supplies only fire protection service. Each offers a central station service under which hazard-detecting devices installed on the protected premises automatically transmit an electric signal to a central station. The central station is manned 24 hours a day. Upon receipt of a signal, the central station, where appropriate, dispatches guards to the protected premises and notifies the police or fire department direct. There are other forms of protective services. But the record shows that subscribers to accredited central station service (i.e., that approved by the insurance underwriters) receive reductions in their insurance premiums that are substantially greater than the reduction received by the users of other kinds of protection service. . . . ADT, Holmes, and

AFA are the three largest companies in the business in terms of revenue: ADT (with 121 central stations in 115 cities) has 73 percent of the business; Holmes (with 12 central stations in three large cities) has 12.5 percent; AFA (with three central stations in three large cities) has 2 percent. Thus the three companies that Grinnell controls have over 87 percent of the business. . . .

ADT over the years reduced its minimum basic rates to meet competition and renewed contracts at substantially increased rates in cities where it had a monopoly of accredited central station service. ADT threatened retaliation against firms that contemplated inaugurating central station service. And the record indicates that, in contemplating opening a new central station, ADT officials frequently stressed that such action would deter their competitors from opening a new station in that area.

The district court found that the defendant companies had committed per se violations of [Sherman I and II] . . . .

I

The offense of monopoly under § 2 of the Sherman Act has two elements: (1) the possession of monopoly power in the relevant market and (2) the willful acquisition or maintenance of that power as distinguished from growth or development as a consequence of a superior product, business acumen, or historic accident. We shall see that this second ingredient presents no major problem here, as what was done in building the empire was done plainly and explicitly for a single purpose. . . . In the present case, 87 percent of the accredited central station service business leaves no doubt that the congeries of these defendants have monopoly power—power which, as our discussion of the record indicates, they did not hesitate to wield—if that business is the relevant market. The only remaining question therefore is, what is the relevant market?

[A] product . . . may be of such a character that substitute products must also be considered, as customers may turn to them if there is a slight increase in the price of the main product. That is the teaching of the *Du Pont* case . . . *viz.,* that commodities reasonably interchangeable make up that "part" of trade or commerce which §2 protects against monopoly power.

The district court treated the entire accredited central station service business as a single market and we think it was justified in so doing. Defendants argue that the different central station services offered are so diverse that they cannot under *Du Pont* be lumped together to make up the relevant market. For example, burglar alarm services are not interchangeable with fire alarm services. They further urge that *Du Pont* requires that protective services other than those of the central station variety be included in the market definition.

But there is here a single use, i.e., the protection of property, through a central station that receives signals. It is that service, accredited, that is unique and that competes with all the other forms of property protection. We see no barrier to combining in a single market a number of different products or services where that combination reflects commercial realities. . . .

. . . First, we deal with services, not with products; and second, we conclude that the accredited central station is a type of service that makes up a relevant market and that domination or control of it makes out a monopoly. . . .

Burglar alarm service is in a sense different from fire alarm service; from waterflow alarms; and so on. But it would be unrealistic on this record to break down the market into the various kinds of central station protective services that are available. Central station companies recognize that to compete effectively, they must offer all or nearly all types of service. . . .

There are, to be sure, substitutes for the accredited central station service. But none of them appears to operate on the same level as the central station service so as to meet the interchangeability test of the *Du Pont* case. Nonautomatic and automatic local alarm systems appear on this record to have marked differences, not the low degree of differentiation required of substitute services as well as substitute articles.

Watchman service is far more costly and less reliable. Systems that set off an audible alarm at the site of a fire or buglary are cheaper but often less reliable. They may be inoperable without anyone's knowing it. Moreover, there is a risk that the local ringing of an alarm will not attract the needed attention and help. Proprietary systems that a customer purchases and operates are available; but they can be used only by a very large business or by government and are not realistic alternatives for most concerns. There are also protective services connected directly to a municipal police or fire department. But most cities with an accredited central station do not permit direct, connected service for private businesses. These alternate services and devices differ, we are told, in utility, efficiency, reliability, responsiveness, and continuity, and the record sustains that position. And, as noted, insurance companies generally allow a greater reduction in premiums for accredited central station service than for other types of protection.

* * * * *

The accredited, as distinguished from nonaccredited, service is a relevant part of commerce. Virtually the only central station companies in the status of the nonaccredited are those that have not yet been able to meet the standards of the rating bureau. The accredited ones are indeed those that have achieved, in the eyes of underwriters, superiorities that other central stations do not have. . . .

We also agree with the district court that the geographic market for the accredited central station service is national. The activities of an individual station are in a sense local as it serves, ordinarily, only that area which is within a radius of 25 miles. But the record amply supports the conclusion that the business of providing such a service is operated on a national level. There is national planning. The agreements we have discussed covered activities in many states. The inspection, certification and rate-making is largely by national insurers. The appellant ADT has a national schedule of prices, rates, and terms, though the rates may be varied to meet local conditions. It deals with multistate businesses on the basis of nationwide contracts. The manufacturing business of ADT is interstate.

* * * * *

We largely agree with the government's views on the relief aspect of the case. We start with ADT, which presently does 73 percent of the business done by accredited central stations throughout the country. It is indeed the keystone of the defendants' monopoly power. The mere dissolution of the combination through the divestiture by Grinnell of its interests in the other companies does not reach the root of the evil. In 92 of the 115 cities in which ADT operates there are no other accredited central stations. Perhaps some cities could not support more than one. Defendants recognized prior to trial that at least 13 cities can; the government urged divestiture in 48 cities. That there should be some divestiture on the part of ADT seems clear; but the details of such divestiture must be determined by the district court as the matter cannot be resolved on this record.

* * * * *

The defendants object to the requirements that Grinnell divest itself of its holdings in the three alarm company defendants, but we think that provision is wholly justified. The defendants object to that portion of the decree that bars them from acquiring interests in firms in the accredited central station business. But since acquisition was one of the methods by which the defendants acquired their market power and was the method by which Grinnell put the combination together, an injunction against the repetition of the practice seems fully warranted. . . .

The judgment below is affirmed except as to the decree. We remand for further hearings on the nature of the relief consistent with the views expressed herein.

* * * * *

Mr. Justice Fortas, with whom Mr. Justice Steward joins, dissenting.

I agree that the judgment below should be remanded, but I do not agree that the remand should be limited to reshaping the decree. Because I believe that the definition of the relevant market here cannot be sustained, I would reverse and remand for a new determination of this basic issue, subject to proper standards.

* * * * *

In this case, the relevant geographical and product markets have not been defined on the basis of the economic facts of the industry concerned. They have been tailored precisely to fit defendants' business. The government proposed and the trial court concluded that the relevant market is not the business of fire protection, or burglary protection, or protection against waterflow, etc., or all of these together. It is not even the business of furnishing these from a central location. It is the business, viewed nationally, of supplying "insurance accredited central station protection services" . . . that is, fire, burglary and other kinds of protection furnished from a central station which is accredited by insurance companies. The business of defendants fits neatly into the product and geographic market so defined. In fact, it comes close to filling the market so defined.
. . .

The geographical market is defined as nationwide. But the need and the service are intensely local. . . .

But because these defendants, the trial court found, are connected by stock ownership, interlocking management and some degree of national corporate direction, and because there is some national participation in selling as well as national financing, advertising, purchasing of equipment, and the like, the court concluded that the competitive area to be considered is national. This Court now affirms that conclusion.

This is a non sequitur. It is not permissible to seize upon the nationwide scope of defendants' operation and to bootstrap a geographical definition of the market from this. The purpose of the search for the relevant geographical market is to find the area or areas to which a potential buyer may rationally look for the goods or services that he seeks. . . .

The central issue is where does a potential buyer look for potential suppliers of the service—what is the geographical area in which the buyer has, or, in the absence of monopoly, would have, a real choice as to price and alternative facilities? This depends upon the facts of the market place, taking into account such economic factors as the distance over which supplies and services may be feasibly furnished, consistently with cost and functional efficiency.

The incidental aspects of defendants' business which the court uses cannot control the outcome of this inquiry. They do not measure the market area in which buyer and sellers meet. . . .

Questions

1. Why was the word *accredited* critical in defining the product market in the *Grinnell* case?
2. Explain how the Court could logically place fire and burglary protection in the same market, when the two are clearly not interchangeable.
3. Explain Justice Fortas' objection to the majority's "bootstrapped" geographic market definition. Now build the argument that the majority's geographic market is correct, but not for the reasons Justice Douglas offers.
4. Assume we have historical data showing that when the price of rolled steel has increased

the sales volume of rolled aluminum has remained constant. What, if anything, does that fact tell us about the product market for rolled steel?

5. Define the product market for championship boxing matches. *See United States* v. *International Boxing Club of New York, Inc.,* 358 U.S. 242 (1959).

Market Power

We have no firm guidelines as to what percentage of the market must be controlled to give rise to a monopoly. In the *Alcoa* case, Judge Hand found a monopoly where Alcoa had 90 percent of the virgin ingot aluminum market.[12] In *U.S.* v. *United Shoe Machinery Corporation*[13] a 75 percent share of the shoe machinery market was a monopoly share, but a 50 percent share in some supply markets was not large enough to constitute a monopoly. The Fifth Circuit Court of Appeals has indicated that "something more than 50 percent of the market is a prerequisite to a finding of monopoly."[14] In any case, it is well understood that market share is not the only factor of importance in determining the existence of monopoly power. In *ILC Peripherals* v. *IBM,*[15] the judge cited a number of factors that were influential in concluding that IBM, regardless of the size of its market share, lacked the power to control prices or exclude competition:

1. The fact that IBM's market share had declined over time.
2. The testimony of both competitors and customers of IBM to the effect that the computer business was "extremely competitive."
3. The fact that IBM was forced to lower its prices on numerous occasions to prevent competitors from "squeezing it out of these markets entirely."
4. The fact that a substantial number of new competitors had entered the market.
5. The fact that the degree of product innovation in the computer industry is high.[16]

Intent

Regrettably, the evidentiary burden necessary to prove purposefulness or deliberateness or general intent is probably even less clear than the market share issue. Certainly overt predatory acts (e.g., deliberately slashing prices below cost to drive a competitor from the market) would be persuasive evidence of intent to monopolize. General intent may be inferred from normal business behavior, depending on the circumstances. In practice, what probably happens in most monopoly cases is a weighing of evils. If the market share is large, the necessary measure of intent is likely to be smaller. Contrariwise, if the market share in question is a borderline threat as to size, the court may well expect a higher standard of proof as to intent.

Monopoly Earned

A reading of the *Aspen* decision that follows addresses the issues of intent and the lawful acquisition of monopoly power. Judge Hand, in the *Alcoa* case, appeared to condemn a monopolist unless it was a "passive beneficiary of a monopoly"; that is, unless the monopoly was "thrust upon" the monopolist. Recent decisions reflect a judicial unease with that view. But the *Aspen* case demonstrates at least a measure of vitality in contemporary monopoly law.

ASPEN SKIING COMPANY, PETITIONER V. ASPEN HIGHLANDS SKIING CORPORATION   53 *Law Week* 4818 (U.S. S.Ct., 1985)

Justice Stevens

In a private treble damages action, the jury found that petitioner Aspen Skiing Company (Ski Co.) had monopolized the market for downhill skiing services in Aspen, Colorado. The question presented is whether that finding is erroneous as a matter of law because it rests on an assumption that a firm with monopoly power has a duty to cooperate with its smaller rivals in a marketing arrangement in order to avoid violating § 2 of the Sherman Act.

I

Aspen is a destination ski resort with a reputation for ''super powder,'' ''a wide range of runs,'' and an ''active night life,'' including ''some of the best restaurants in North America.'' Between 1945 and 1960, private investors independently developed three major facilities for downhill skiing: Aspen Mountain (Ajax), Aspen Highlands (Highlands), and Buttermilk. A fourth mountain, Snowmass, opened in 1967.

The development of any major additional facilities is hindered by practical considerations and regulatory obstacles. The identification of appropriate topographical conditions for a new site and substantial financing are both essential. Most of the terrain in the vicinity of Aspen that is suitable for downhill skiing cannot be used for that purpose without the approval of the United States Forest Service. That approval is contingent, in part, on environmental concerns. Moreover, the county government must also approve the project, and in recent years it has followed a policy of limiting growth.

Between 1958 and 1964, three independent companies operated Ajax, Highlands, and Buttermilk. In the early years, each company offered its own day or half-day tickets for use of its mountain. In 1962, however, the three competitors also introduced an interchangeable ticket. The six-day, all-Aspen ticket provided convenience to the vast majority of skiers who visited the resort for weekly periods, but preferred to remain flexible about what mountain they might ski each day during the visit. It also emphasized the unusual variety in ski mountains available in Aspen.

As initially designed, the all-Aspen ticket program consisted of booklets containing six coupons, each redeemable for a daily lift ticket at Ajax, Highlands, or Buttermilk. The price of the booklet was often discounted from the price of six daily tickets, but all six coupons had to be used within a limited period of time—seven days, for example. The revenues from the sale of the three-area coupon books were distributed in accordance with the number of coupons collected at each mountain.

In 1964, Buttermilk was purchased by Ski Co., but the interchangeable ticket program continued. . . .

In the 1971–1972 season, the coupon booklets were discontinued and an ''around the neck'' all-Aspen ticket was developed. This refinement on the interchangeable ticket was advantageous to the skier, who no longer found it necessary to visit the ticket window every morning before gaining access to the slopes. Lift operators at Highlands monitored usage of the ticket in the 1971–1972 season by recording the ticket numbers of persons going onto the slopes of that mountain. Highlands officials periodically met with Ski Co. officials to review the figures recorded at Highlands, and to distribute revenues based on that count.

There was some concern that usage of the all-Aspen ticket should be monitored by a more scientific method than the one used in the 1971–1972 season. After a one-season absence, the four-area ticket returned in the 1973–1974 season with a new method of allocating revenues based on usage. Like the 1971–1972 ticket, the 1973–1974 four-area ticket consisted of a badge worn around the skier's neck. Lift operators punched the ticket when the skier first sought access to the mountain each day. A random-sample survey was commissioned to determine how many skiers with the four-area ticket used each mountain, and the parties allocated revenues from the ticket sales in accordance with the survey's results.

*   *   *   *   *

In the 1970s the management of Ski Co. increasingly expressed their dislike for the all-Aspen ticket. They complained that a coupon method of monitoring usage was administratively cumbersome. They doubted the accuracy of the survey and decried the "appearance, deportment, [and] attitude" of the college students who were conducting it. In addition, Ski Co.'s president had expressed the view that the four-area ticket was siphoning off revenues that could be recaptured by Ski Co. if the ticket was discontinued. In fact, Ski Co. had reinstated its three-area, six-day ticket during the 1977–1978 season, but that ticket had been outsold by the four-area, six-day ticket nearly two to one.

In March 1978, the Ski Co. management recommended to the board of directors that the four-area ticket be discontinued for the 1978–1979 season. The board decided to offer Highlands a four-area ticket provided that Highlands would agree to receive a 12.5% fixed percentage of the revenue—considerably below Highland's historical average based on usage. Later in the 1978–1979 season, a member of Ski Co.'s board of directors candidly informed a Highland's official that he had advocated making Highlands "an offer that [it] could not accept."

Finding the proposal unacceptable, Highlands suggested a distribution of the revenues based on usage to be monitored by coupons, electronic counting, or random sample surveys. If Ski Co. was concerned about who was to conduct the survey, Highlands proposed to hire disinterested ticket counters at its own expense—"somebody like Price Waterhouse"—to count or survey usage of the four-area ticket at Highlands. Ski Co. refused to consider any counterproposals, and Highlands finally rejected the offer of the fixed percentage.

As far as Ski Co. was concerned, the all-Aspen ticket was dead. In its place Ski Co. offered the three-area, six-day ticket featuring only its mountains. In an effort to promote this ticket, Ski Co. embarked on a national advertising campaign that strongly implied to people who were unfamiliar with Aspen that Ajax, Buttermilk, and Snowmass were the only ski mountains in the area. For example, Ski Co. had a sign changed in the Aspen Airways waiting room at Stapleton Airport in Denver. The old sign had a picture of the four mountains in Aspen touting "Four Big Mountains" whereas the new sign retained the picture but referred only to three.

Ski Co. took additional actions that made it extremely difficult for Highlands to market its own multi-area package to replace the joint offering. Ski Co. discontinued the three-day, three-area pass for the 1978–1979 season, and also refused to sell Highlands any lift tickets, either at the tour operator's discount or at retail. Highlands finally developed an alternative product, the "Adventure Pack," which consisted of a three-day pass at Highlands and three vouchers, each equal to the price of a daily lift ticket at a Ski Co. mountain. The vouchers were guaranteed by funds on deposit in an Aspen bank, and were redeemed by Aspen merchants at full value. Ski Co., however, refused to accept them.

Later, Highlands redesigned the Adventure Pack to contain American Express Traveler's

Checks or money orders instead of vouchers. Ski Co. eventually accepted these negotiable instruments in exchange for daily lift tickets. Despite some strengths of the product, the Adventure Pack met considerable resistance from tour operators and consumers who had grown accustomed to the convenience and flexibility provided by the all-Aspen ticket.

Without a convenient all-Aspen ticket, Highlands basically "becomes a day ski area in a destination resort." Highlands' share of the market for downhill skiing services in Aspen declined steadily after the four-area ticket based on usage was abolished in 1977: from 20.5 percent in 1976–1977, to 15.7 percent in 1977–1978, to 13.1 percent in 1978–1979, to 12.5 percent in 1979–1980, to 11 percent in 1980–1981. Highlands' revenues from associated skiing services like the ski school, ski rentals, amateur racing events, and restaurant facilities declined sharply as well.

II

In 1979, Highlands filed a complaint in the United States District Court for the District of Colorado naming Ski Co. as a defendant. Among various claims, the complaint alleged that Ski Co. had monopolized the market for downhill skiing services at Aspen in violation of §2 of the Sherman act, and prayed for treble damages. The case was tried to a jury which rendered a verdict finding Ski Co. guilty of the §2 violation and calculating Highlands' actual damages at $2.5 million.

In her instructions to the jury, the District Judge explained that the offense of monopolization under §2 of the Sherman Act has two elements: (1) the possession of monopoly power in a relevant market, and (2) the willful acquisition, maintenance, or use of that power by anticompetitive or exclusionary means or for anticompetitive or exclusionary purposes. Although the first element was vigorously disputed at the trial and in the Court of Appeals in this Court Ski Co. does not challenge the jury's special verdict finding that it possessed monopoly power. Nor does Ski Co. criticize the trial court's instructions to the jury concerning the second element of the §2 offense.

On this element, the jury was instructed that it had to consider whether "Aspen Skiing Corporation willfully acquired, maintained, or used that power by anticompetitive or exclusionary means or for anticompetitive or exclusionary purposes." The instructions elaborated:

"In considering whether the means or purposes were anti-competitive or exclusionary, you must draw a distinction here between practices which tend to exclude or restrict competition on the one hand and the success of a business which reflects only a superior product, a well-run business, or luck, on the other. The line between legitimately gained monopoly, its proper use and maintenance, and improper conduct has been described in various ways. It has been said that obtaining or maintaining monopoly power cannot represent monopolization if the power was gained and maintained by conduct that was honestly industrial. Or it is said that monopoly power which is thrust upon a firm due to its superior business ability and efficiency does not constitute monopolization."

* * * * *

III

* * * * *

"The central message of the Sherman Act is that a business entity must find new customers and higher profits through internal expansion—that is, by competing successfully rather than by arranging treaties with its competitors." *United States* v. *Citizens & Southern National Bank*, 422 U.S. 86, 116 (1975). Ski Co., therefore, is surely correct in submitting that even a firm with monopoly power has no general duty to engage in a joint marketing program with a competitor. Ski Co. is quite wrong, however, in suggesting that the judgment in this case rests on any such proposition of law. For the trial court unambiguously instructed the jury that a firm possessing monopoly power has no duty to cooperate with its business rivals.

The absence of an unqualified duty to cooperate does not mean that every time a firm declines to participate in a particular cooperative venture, that decision may not have evidentiary significance, or that it may not give rise to liability in certain circumstances. The absence of a duty to transact business with another firm is, in some respects, merely the counterpart of the independent businessman's cherished right to select his customers and his associates. The high value that we have placed on the right to refuse to deal with other firms does not mean that the right is unqualified.

In *Lorain Journal* v. *United States,* 342 U.S. 143 (1951), we squarely held that this right was not unqualified.

*   *   *   *   *

In *Lorain Journal,* the violation of §2 was an "attempt to monopolize," rather than monopolization, but the question of intent is relevant to both offenses. In the former case it is necessary to prove a "specific intent" to accomplish the forbidden objective—as Judge Hand explained, "an intent which goes beyond the mere intent to do the act." *United States* v. *Aluminum Co. of America,* 148 F.2d 416, 432 (CA2 1945). In the latter case evidence of intent is merely relevant to the question whether the challenged conduct is fairly characterized as "exclusionary" or "anticompetitive"—to use the words in the trial court's instructions—or "predatory," to use a word that scholars seem to favor. Whichever label is used, there is agreement on the proposition that "no monopolist monopolizes unconscious of what he is doing." As Judge Bork stated more recently: "Improper exclusion (exclusion not the result of superior efficiency) is always deliberately intended."

. . . In the actual case that we must decide, the monopolist did not merely reject a novel offer to participate in a cooperative venture that had been proposed by a competitor. Rather, the monopolist elected to make an important change in a pattern of distribution that had originated in a competitive market and had persisted for several years. The all-Aspen, six-day ticket with revenues allocated on the basis of usage was first developed when three independent companies operated three different ski mountains in the Aspen area. It continued to provide a desirable option for skiers when the market was enlarged to include four mountains, and when the character of the market was changed by Ski Co.'s acquisition of monopoly power. Moreover, since the record discloses that interchangeable tickets are used in other multimountain areas which apparently are competitive, it seems appropriate to infer that such tickets satisfy consumer demand in free competitive markets.

Ski Co.'s decision to terminate the all-Aspen ticket was thus a decision by a monopolist to make an important change in the character of the market. Such a decision is not necessarily anticompetitive, and Ski Co. contends that neither its decision, nor the conduct in which it engaged to implement that decision, can fairly be characterized as exclusionary in this case. . . .

*   *   *   *   *

IV

The question whether Ski Co.'s conduct may properly be characterized as exclusionary cannot be answered by simply considering its effect on Highlands. In addition, it is relevant to consider its impact on consumers and whether it has impaired competition in an unnecessarily restrictive way. If a firm has been "attempting to exclude rivals on some basis other than efficiency," it is fair to characterize its behavior as predatory. It is, accordingly, appropriate to examine the effect of the challenged pattern of conduct on consumers, on Ski Co.'s smaller rival, and on Ski Co. itself.

Superior Quality of the All-Aspen Ticket

The average Aspen visitor "is a well-educated, relatively affluent, experienced skier who has skied a number of times in the past. . . ." Over 80 percent of the skiers visiting the resort each year have been there before—40 percent of these repeat visitors have skied Aspen at least five times. Over the years, they developed a strong demand for the six-day, all-Aspen ticket in its various refinements. Most experienced skiers quite logically prefer to purchase their tickets at once for the whole period that they will spend at the resort; they can then spend more time on the slopes and enjoying apres-ski amenities and less time standing in ticket lines. The four-area attribute of the ticket allowed the skier to purchase his six-day ticket in advance while reserving the right to decide in his own time and for his own reasons which mountain he would ski on each day. It provided convenience and flexibility, and expanded the vistas and the number of challenging runs available to him during the week's vacation.

While the three-area, six-day ticket offered by Ski Co. possessed some of these attributes, the evidence supports a conclusion that consumers were adversely affected by the elimination of the four-area ticket. In the first place, the actual record of competition between a three-area ticket and the all-Aspen ticket in the years after 1967 indicated that skiers demonstrably preferred four mountains to three. . . .

Highlands' Ability to Compete

The adverse impact of Ski Co.'s pattern of conduct on Highlands is not disputed in this Court. Expert testimony described the extent of its pecuniary injury. The evidence concerning its attempt to develop a substitute product either by buying Ski Co.'s daily tickets in bulk, or by marketing its own Adventure Pack, demonstrates that it tried to protect itself from the loss of its share of the patrons of the all-Aspen ticket. . . .

Ski Co.'s Business Justification

Perhaps most significant, however, is the evidence relating to Ski Co. itself, for Ski Co. did not persuade the jury that its conduct was justified by any normal business purpose. Ski Co. was apparently willing to forgo daily ticket sales both to skiers who sought to exchange the coupons contained in Highlands' Adventure Pack, and to those who would have purchased Ski Co. daily lift tickets from Highlands if Highlands had been permitted to purchase them in bulk. The jury may well have concluded that Ski Co. elected to forgo these short-run benefits because it was more interested in reducing competition in the Aspen market over the long run by harming its smaller competitor.

That conclusion is strongly supported by Ski Co.'s failure to offer any efficiency justification whatever for its pattern of conduct. In defending the decision to terminate the jointly offered ticket, Ski Co. claimed that usage could not be properly monitored. The evidence, however, established that Ski Co. itself monitored the use of the three-area passes based on a count taken by lift operators, and distributed the revenues among its mountains on that basis. Ski Co. contended that coupons were administratively cumbersome, and that the survey takers had been disruptive and their work inaccurate. Coupons, however, were no more burdensome than the credit cards accepted at Ski Co. ticket windows. Moreover, in other markets Ski Co. itself participated in interchangeable lift tickets using coupons. As for the survey, its own manager testified that the problems were much overemphasized by Ski Co. officials, and were mostly resolved as they arose. Ski Co.'s explanation for the rejection of Highlands' offer to hire—at its own expense—a reputable national accounting firm to audit usage of the four-area tickets at Highlands' mountain, was that there was no way to "control" the audit.

In the end, Ski Co. was pressed to justify its pattern of conduct on a desire to disassociate itself from—what it considered—the inferior skiing services offered at Highlands. The all-Aspen ticket based on usage, however, allowed consumers to make their own choice on these matters of quality. Ski Co.'s purported concern for the relative quality of Highlands' product was supported in the record by little more than vague insinuations, and was sharply contested by numerous witnesses. Moreover, Ski Co. admitted that it was willing to associate with what it considered to be inferior products in other markets.

. . . [T]he record in this case comfortably supports an inference that the monopolist made a deliberate effort to discourage its customers from doing business with its smaller rival. The sale of its three-area, six-day ticket, particularly when it was discounted below the daily ticket price, deterred the ticket holders from skiing at Highlands. The refusal to accept the Adventure Pack coupons in exchange for daily tickets was apparently motivated entirely by a decision to avoid providing any benefit to Highlands even though accepting the coupons would have entailed no cost to Ski Co. itself, would have provided it with immediate benefits, and would have satisfied its potential customers. Thus the evidence supports an inference that Ski Co. was not motivated by efficiency concerns and that it was willing to sacrifice short-run benefits and consumer goodwill in exchange for a perceived long-run impact on its smaller rival. . . .

Affirmed.

Questions

1. Summarize the fundamental lessons of *Aspen*.
2. Write a brief dissenting opinion for the *Aspen* case.
3. As the *Aspen* Court says, "Aspen Skiing Company (Ski Co.) had monopolized the market for downhill skiing services in Aspen, Colorado." That being the case, why doesn't the government challenge Aspen Skiing Company's market dominance?
4. Kodak dominated the American market for provision of amateur photographic films, cameras, and film-processing services. Berkey was a much smaller, but still significant, competitor in that market. In some markets Kodak served as Berkey's supplier. In the "amateur conventional still camera" market (consisting primarily of 110 and 126 instant-loading cameras), Kodak's share of the sales volume between 1954 and 1973 ranged from 64 to 90 percent. Kodak invented both the "126" and "110" cameras. The introduction of the 110 "Pocket Instamatic" and the companion Kodacolor II film in 1972 resulted in a dramatic Kodak camera sales increase of from 6.2 million units in 1971 to 8.2 million in 1972. Rivals were unable to bring competitive units into the market until nearly one year later. Even then, Kodak retained a strong lead. Thereafter, Berkey filed suit claiming that the introduction of the 110 system was an illegal monopolization of the camera market. The essence of the Berkey argument was as follows:

> Kodak, a film and camera monopolist, was in a position to set industry standards. Rivals could not compete effectively without offering products similar to Kodak's. Moreover, Kodak persistently refused to make film available for most formats other than those in which it made cameras. Since cameras are worthless without film, the policy effectively prevented other manufacturers from introducing cameras in new formats. Because of its dominant position astride two markets, and by use of its film monopoly to distort the camera market, Kodak forfeited its own right to reap profits from such innovations without providing its rivals with sufficient advance

information to enable them to enter the market with copies of the new product on the day of Kodak's introduction.

On appeal, the Court noted "little doubt that . . . Kodak had monopoly power in cameras," and the Court observed that Kodak had sometimes "predisclosed" its innovations to its rivals, and sometimes it had not done so.

Was Kodak under a legal duty to predisclose innovations to rivals? What defense would you offer to counter Berkey's monopolization claim? Decide the case, and explain the reasons for your decision. See *Berkey Photo, Inc.* v. *Eastman Kodak Company*, 603 F. 2d 263 (2 Cir. 1979). Cert. denied, 444 U.S. 1093 (1980).

Chapter Questions

1. A federal district court found IBM guilty of unlawful monopolization in a portion of the computer industry. IBM manufactured and distributed both central processing units (CPUs) and various peripheral devices (PDs), including magnetic tape drives and printers. Telex manufactured PDs compatible with IBM's CPUs, but not with the CPUs of other manufacturers. It was established at trial that relatively inexpensive interfaces could be used to make Telex PDs compatible with the CPUs of manufacturers other than IBM, and at a relatively modest cost Telex could produce PDs compatible with CPUs other than those of IBM. The district court concluded that the relevant product market was PDs compatible with IBM CPUs and that IBM controlled at least 80 percent of that market. Given IBM's monopoly power, the district court also found IBM guilty of predatory behavior. For example, in response to competition from Telex and others, IBM lowered its leasing fees for PDs and offered more desirable leasing terms. Similarly, IBM reduced the sales prices of its PDs. In setting those prices, IBM considered the ability or inability of its competitors to respond to those prices. At the reduced prices, IBM achieved a 20 percent profit margin and increased its market share.

    Was the district court correct? Explain. See *Telex Corporation* v. *IBM Corporation* (10th Cir. 1975) 510 F.2d 894, cert. denied, 423 U.S. 802 (1975).

2. It is frequently argued that monopolies must be opposed because a lack of competition discourages efficiency and innovation. Argue that monopolies may actually *encourage* innovation.

3. Even if monopolies do not discourage invention, we have firm economic grounds for opposing monopolies. Explain.

4. Historically, perhaps the most important interpretation of the Sherman Act's proscription of monopolization was Judge Learned Hand's opinion in the aforementioned *Alcoa* case. After finding that Alcoa controlled 90 percent of the aluminum ingot market, Hand had to determine whether Alcoa possessed a general intent to monopolize. Hand concluded that Alcoa's market dominance could have resulted only from a "persistent determination" to maintain control [148 F.2d 416, 431 (1945)].

    It was not inevitable that it should always anticipate increases in the demand for ingot and be prepared to supply them. Nothing compelled it to keep doubling and redoubling its capacity before others entered the field. It insists that it never excluded competitors; but we can think of no more effective exclusion than progressively to embrace each new opportunity as it opened, and to face every newcomer with new capacity already geared into a great organization.

Comment on Judge Hand's remarks.

5. Is a monopolist who makes only a "fair" profit in violation of the law? Explain.

6. May a monopolist lawfully increase its market share assuming it does so without recourse to predatory or exclusionary tactics? Should it be able to do so?

7. The U.S. government sued Du Pont claiming a monopolization of the cellophane market. Du Pont produced almost 75 percent of the cellophane sold in the United States. Cellophane constituted less than 20 percent of the "flexible packaging materials" market. The lower court found "[g]reat sensitivity of customers in the flexible packaging markets to price or quality changes."

What is the relevant product market? Who wins the case? Explain. See *United States* v. *E.I. du Pont de Nemours & Co.,* 351 U.S. 377 (1956).

8. The National Football League was organized in 1920. During the 1960 season it had 14 teams located in 13 cities [Chicago (two teams), Cleveland, New York, Philadelphia, Pittsburgh, Washington, Baltimore, Detroit, Los Angeles, San Francisco, Green Bay, Dallas, and Minneapolis]. The rival American Football League commenced play in 1960 with eight teams in eight cities (Boston, Buffalo, Houston, New York, Dallas, Denver, Los Angeles, and Oakland).

In its first season, the AFL was successful in competing for outstanding players and in acquiring a desirable television contract. "[R]epresentatives of the American League declared that the League's success was unprecedented." Nevertheless, the AFL sued the NFL claiming monopolization. A central issue in the case was that of the geographic market. The AFL characterized the market as those 17 cities either having an NFL franchise or seriously considered for a franchise. The NFL saw the market as nationwide.

Define the geographic market in this case. Explain. See *American Football League* v. *National Football League,* 323 F.2d 124 (4th Cir. 1963).

Notes

1. Ben Enis and E. Thomas Sullivan, "The AT&T Settlement," *Journal of Marketing,* 49 (Winter 1985), p. 127.
2. Lester Thurow, "A New Era of Competition," *Newsweek,* January 18, 1982, p. 63.
3. See A. D. Neale, *The Antitrust Laws of the U.S.A.,* 2d ed., (Cambridge: Cambridge University Press, 1970), p. 190.
4. Solomon Fabricant, *The Output of Manufacturing Industries, 1899–1937,* (New York: National Bureau of Economic Research, 1940), pp. 84–85, as reported in Martin C. Schnitzer, *Contemporary Government and Business Relations* (Skokie, Ill.: Rand McNally, 1978), p. 114.
5. Robert Tollison, "Labor Monopoly and Antitrust Policy," *Policy Report,* April 1979.
6. *Town of Hallie* v. *City of Eau Claire,* 53 Law Week 4418 (7th Cir. 1985); and *Southern Carriers Rate Conference, Inc.* v. *U.S.,* 53 Law Week 4422 (11th Cir. 1985).
7. *Goldfarb* v. *Virginia State Bar et al.,* 95 S.Ct. 2004 (1975).
8. Ibid, p. 2016.
9. *United States* v. *Grinnell Corp.,* 384 U.S. 563 (1966).
10. Alan Greenspan, "Antitrust" in Ayn Rand, *Capitalism: The Unknown Ideal* (New York: Signet, 1967), p. 68.
11. *U.S.* v. *Aluminum Company of America* (2d Cir. 1945), 148 F.2d 416.
12. Ibid.
13. 110 F. Supp. 295 (Mass. 1953), aff'd per curium (1954) 347 U.S. 521.
14. *Cliff Food Stores, Inc.* v. *Kroger Co.,* 417 F.2d 203, 207 N.2 (5th Cir. 1969).
15. 458 F. Supp. 423 (Cal. 1978).
16. Wesley J. Liebeler, 1980 Cumulative Supplement, *Antitrust Adviser,* 2d ed. (Colorado Springs: Shepard's/McGraw-Hill, 1978), pp. 26–27, citing *ILC Peripherals* v. *IBM* (Cal. 1978), 458 F. Supp. 423.

10

Antitrust Law—Mergers

Principal legislation: Sherman Act, section 1 (see Chapter 9), and Clayton Act, section 7:

That no person engaged in commerce or in any activity affecting commerce, shall acquire, directly or indirectly, the whole or any part of the stock or other share capital and no person subject to the jurisdiction of the Federal Trade Commission shall acquire the whole or any part of the assets of another person engaged also in commerce or in any activity affecting commerce, where in any line of commerce or in any activity affecting commerce in any section of the country, the effect of such acquisition may be substantially to lessen competition, or to tend to create a monopoly.

No person shall acquire, directly or indirectly, the whole or any part of the stock or other share capital and no person subject to the jurisdiction of the Federal Trade Commission shall acquire the whole or any part of the assets of one or more persons engaged in commerce or in any activity affecting commerce, where in any line of commerce or in any activity affecting commerce in any section of the country, the effect of such acquisition, of such stocks or assets, or of the use of such stock by the voting or granting of proxies or otherwise, may be substantially to lessen competition, or to tend to create a monopoly.

Technically, a merger involves the union of two or more enterprises wherein the property of all is transferred to the one remaining firm. However, antitrust law embraces all those situations wherein previously independent business entities are united—whether by acquisition of stock, purchase of physical assets, creation of holding companies, consolidation, or merger. Mergers fall, somewhat awkwardly, into three categories. Horizontal mergers are those where the firms were in direct competition and occupied the same product and geographic markets. A merger of two vodka producers in the same geographic market would clearly fall in the horizontal category. Would the merger of a vodka producer and a gin producer constitute a horizontal merger? Vertical mergers are those involving two or more firms at different levels of the same channel of distribution, such as a furniture manufacturer and a fabric supplier. Conglomerate mergers involve firms dealing in unrelated products. Thus the conglomerate category embraces all those mergers that are neither horizontal nor vertical. Exemplary of such a merger would be the acquisition of a pet food manufacturer by a book publisher. Identification of the type of merger being dealt with is essential because, as will be seen, the analysis differs for each.

Enforcement

Because a merger to be challenged would allegedly involve either an unlawful monopoly or another restraint of trade, the Sherman Act can and sometimes is used as the necessary legislative vehicle. However, it will be recalled that Sherman requires a showing of the *existence* of anticompetitive conditions, while Clayton requires only a showing of a *reasonable probability* of lessening competition or a *tendency* toward monopoly. However, since Clayton has no criminal provision, the government must rely on Sherman in those cases where a criminal suit is warranted.

Clayton 7 is enforced by the government via the Justice Department and the FTC, as well as by companies and individuals. Those challenging mergers often seek injunctions either to stop the merger or to secure relief after the consummation of a merger. Under the FTC's premerger notification rules, mergers must be reported to the FTC and the Justice Department if the mergers involve purchases of $15 million or more and meet several other criteria. Either agency may then choose to challenge the merger. In order to afford warning about likely challenges, both the FTC and the Justice Department have issued merger guidelines. The Justice Department guidelines, first issued in 1965, were revised in 1982 and 1984 to improve the technical evaluation of mergers and, presumably, to reflect the Reagan administration's rather sanguine view of the dangers of mergers. Justice Department policy in the mid-1980s has not normally regarded most vertical and conglomerate mergers as threatening to competition. Therefore, the guidelines focus upon horizontal mergers.

The heart of the guidelines lies in determining market share and in identifying any increase in market concentration arising from a horizontal merger. The degree of market concentration is measured by use of the Herfindahl-Hirschman Index (HHI). Notwithstanding the forbidding title, the index is computed quite easily. The market share of each firm in a market is squared and the results are summed. Thus, if five companies each had 20 percent of a market, the index for that market would be 2000. The HHI is useful because it measures both concentration and dispersion of market share between big and small firms. If 10 firms each have 10 percent of the market, the resulting HHI is 1000. The larger the HHI, the more concentrated the market. A merger is unlikely to be challenged if the HHI is 1,000 or less because that market is not considered to be concentrated. If the HHI is greater than 1,800, the market is considered highly concentrated. If the merger within that market produces an HHI increase of 50 points or more the government will probably challenge the merger. In the 1,000–1,800 range the government will "more likely than not" challenge a merger if it increases the HHI by 100 points or more. To illustrate, consider again a market composed of five companies, each with 20 percent of the market. If two of them merge, the HHI would rise from 2,000 to 2,800, and the merger presumably would be challenged.

It should be understood that while the HHI is perhaps the central component of the guidelines, many other factors will be influential. Among others, ease of entry, foreign competition, the presence of a failing firm, the premerger conduct of the firms, and efficiencies produced by the merger may all be considered.

Merger Data

Before turning to the more technical dimensions of merger analysis, it is important to acquire some understanding of the business conditions within which merger law operates. As discussed in Chapter 1, the law, to be interesting and understood, must be placed in the context in which it was conceived. The United States has recently been in the midst of what has been labeled, not so charitably, a merger mania. Mergers seem to build in waves of sorts, the most pronounced of which embraced the 1955 to 1969 period. From 1955 to 1959 mergers averaged 1,162 per year, and by the period 1967–69 that annual average reached 3,605. The early and mid-70s witnessed moderated—but still high—merger totals: 1972 (2,839 acquisitions), 1973 (2,359), 1974 (1,474), 1975 (1,047), 1976 (1,171). According to W. T. Grimm & Co. reports, 1981 saw 2,395 mergers with a dollar value of $82.6 billion, which was nearly double the 1980 record total of $44.3 billion (1,889 acquisitions).[1] But those dollar figures pale beside the 1984 total of at least $123 billion (2,930 deals).[2] A general restructuring of the economy appears to be underway. That condition—in conjunction with deregulation, a perceived federal reluctance to interfere, and a combination of some undervalued companies and other cash-rich companies—appears to be producing a merger boom that was expected to continue through at least the mid-1980s. Acquisition, once the province of "wheeler-dealers," has fast become a central ingredient in strategic planning.[3] Just three of the more active companies—Textron, Georgia-Pacific, and Ashland Oil—acquired more than 350 other companies between 1955 and 1980.[4]

At this point the skeptical reader may be politely muttering: "So what?" The fact that we are experiencing another merger boom is not in and of itself threatening, but the further industrial concentration that appears to be accompanying those mergers may, indeed, be cause for concern. For example, of the 500 firms appearing in the 1955 *Fortune* 500 industrial listing, 185 had been absorbed by merger as of the close of 1979.

The concern is that further concentration will lead to an expansion of the problems outlined in Chapter 1. Political and economic power will reside in fewer hands. Small firms will fail in greater numbers, and barriers to market entry by small firms will increase. Lives will be disrupted by plant closings, changes in management, and relocations. Absentee owners, ignorant of local needs, will alter community lifestyles. Nevertheless, even the most ardent advocate of firmer merger controls will concede the desirability of some mergers. Some of the potential virtues of mergers are:

1. Mergers permit the replacement of inefficient management. Similarly, the threat of replacement disciplines managers to achieve greater efficiency.
2. Mergers may permit stronger competition with formerly larger rivals.
3. Mergers may improve credit access.
4. Mergers may produce efficiencies and economies of scale.
5. Mergers frequently offer a pool of liquid assets for use in expansion.
6. Very often mergers offer tax advantages to at least one of the participants.
7. Growth by merger is often less expensive than internal growth.
8. Mergers help to satisfy the personal ambitions and needs of management.

Mergers in Practice

Most of us have great difficulty in relating to the machinations of mammoth enterprises and their billion dollar deals. Several particularly robust mergers in recent years have brought the merger "game" closer to the public eye. In 1984 the federal government approved the largest mergers in U.S. history. Standard Oil of California purchased Gulf Oil for $13.2 billion, and Texaco acquired Getty Oil for $10.1 billion. Between 1981 and 1984, five of America's largest oil firms (Gulf, Getty, Conoco, Marathon, and Cities Service) were gobbled up by mergers. In 1981 the then-biggest takeover struggle in corporate history ended as Du Pont (15th in the 1980 *Fortune* 500, according to sales) acquired Conoco (ranked 14th) in a deal valued at $7.4 billion.

The articles that follow put a bit of flesh on the sometimes arid terrain of merger law. The first one reveals some of the complexities of engineering a multibillion dollar transaction, while the second article reminds us of the human dimension of corporate high finance.

THE MAKING OF THE MEGAMERGER

Lee Smith

At a crucial meeting two chief executives misunderstood one another. It was not so much that the two—Ralph E. Bailey, chairman of Conoco, and John P. Gallagher, chairman of Dome Petroleum—misinterpreted one another's words, as that one misinterpreted the other's silence. That turned out to be a multibillion-dollar misunderstanding. Without it the biggest takeover in corporate history—the acquisition of Conoco by Du Pont for $7.6 billion—might never have come about, and Conoco might not have been taken over by anybody.

That is one of the dramatic stories, one of the intriguing "what ifs" now emerging in the aftermath of a war that fascinated the entire country for weeks. Companies with household names—Du Point, Mobil, and Seagram—were waging combat with sums of money that would make convincing defense budgets in many countries. . . .

A Problem Called HBOG

Most chronologies mark the beginning as the announcement by Dome on May 5 that it was making a tender offer for 20 percent of Conoco's stock. But the story actually began much

earlier—in the middle of 1980. Pierre Trudeau had returned to power in Canada with his plan to impose heavy tax burdens on energy resources under foreign control. Conoco, the ninth-largest oil company in the U.S., was just the sort of outsider that the Trudeau government wanted to send south. Conoco owned 53 percent of Hudson's Bay Oil & Gas Co., holder of proved reserves of 265 million barrels of oil and 3.4 trillion cubic feet of natural gas.

And so Conoco started to think about selling the company Wall Street knows as HBOG—pronounced "H-bog," appropriately perhaps because the subsidiary is in effect the swamp in which Conoco sank. Morgan Stanley drew up a list of 18 or so possible Canadian buyers, including Dome and Seagram, but Petro-Canada, the huge government-owned energy company, seemed the likeliest candidate. Greenhill talked with Petro-Can Chairman Wilbert H. Hopper, who thought Conoco's half-interest in HBOG was worth about $1.7 billion. That was close to Morgan Stanley's own estimate, but Conoco thought its share could be worth as much as $900 million more.

The first of two fateful encounters between

Bailey of Conoco and Gallagher of Dome took place on March 12. Gallagher is a director of Texasgulf, which happens to be only a rolling lawn away from Conoco in a verdant corporate headquarters park on the outskirts of Stamford, Connecticut. Gallagher had telephoned Bailey, whom he knew slightly. Could they get together? Bailey said he would be happy to have Gallagher drop by.

* * * * *

At the end of the first meeting Gallagher mentioned that he would like to visit again sometime and talk about HBOG. Bailey was noncommittal. In late April Gallagher did come by again. This time he brought along Dome's president, William Richards, and the outlines of a plan. Gallagher pointed out that if Dome were to buy HBOG for cash, Conoco would have to pay a capital-gains tax.

Gallagher had an alternative in mind that would benefit both companies. Dome could make a tender offer for Conoco stock and then swap that stock for HBOG. Conoco would not have to pay taxes on a deal like that. Or so Dome's tax advisers had told him. Gallagher figured that if there were no government to pay, Dome could acquire HBOG more cheaply and Conoco, on an after-tax basis, would also come out better.

The Golden Silence

Bailey replied cryptically that he could listen to what Gallagher had to say but couldn't comment. Just why Bailey remained silent is still a mystery. All he will say is that it had nothing to do with either Dome or HBOG. "There were other reasons important to the company why I did not want to enter into those negotiations," he says.

Yet what Bailey apparently intended as a neutral or even negative silence, Gallagher interpreted as a signal to go ahead with the tender offer. Gallagher's understanding of the law was that a deal like the one he had mentioned would have a much better chance of getting the favorable tax treatment if there were no negotiations between Dome and Conoco prior to the tender offer. "At no time did he say, 'I like

the deal,' but at no time did he say that he didn't like the deal," recalls Gallagher. "I said, 'I understand, Ralph,' "

And with a wink, so to speak, Gallagher departed, thinking they had a deal. Bailey left the meeting thinking nothing important had happened.

When Dome made its tender offer on May 5, Conoco and Morgan Stanley were stunned. "I called Jack Gallagher and told him it was crazy," says Greenhill. "We were amenable to doing a deal, but only if he called off the tender offer." Gallagher went ahead anyway.

As Greenhill sees it, if Dome had simply purchased HBOG for cash, the undoing of Conoco would have stopped right there. Instead, the tender offer demonstrated to the world just how vulnerable to a takeover Conoco was. Dome offered $65 a share for Conoco when Conoco was trading on the New York Stock Exchange for about $50. Oil stocks in general were depressed, largely because of the oil glut, and Conoco's immediate prospects were especially gloomy. It has large reserves in Libya, a worrisome exposure at a time when relations between the United States and Libya appear to be getting ever worse. Moreover, the United Mine Workers were striking Conoco's coal fields.

The banks, pension funds, and other institutions that held a majority of Conoco's shares saw an opportunity to trim their portfolios of some burdensome oil stocks. They were willing to sell Dome not just 20 percent of Conoco's outstanding shares, but 51 percent. The message was obvious and is familiar by now: indisputable control of Conoco could be bought cheaply, at only a moderate premium above the market price. Despite its immediate problems, Conoco's prospects are bright. It was one of the few U.S. energy companies that added to its proved oil and gas reserves last year, and it has 14 billion tons of coal, enough to keep it shoveling for centuries. Moreover, Conoco could be had at an irresistible discount from the company's asset value, estimated at $150 a share or more. . . .

One of the first people who found the discount irresistible was Edgar Bronfman, chairman of Seagram, which had been disappointed earlier in the year because of its unsuccessful attempt to buy St. Joe Minerals. On Friday, May 29—much as Gallagher had done earlier—Bronfman called Bailey cold and said he wanted to drop by and discuss the possibility that Seagram might become an investor in Conoco. Bailey, burned before, on this occasion passed the request along to Greenhill. Greenhill says he told Bronfman that he could come out to Stamford and talk to Conoco, but only with the understanding that any deal reached would be friendly. "He told me 'absolutely,' " says Greenhill. "Furthermore, he told me that he was employing Goldman Sachs as his representative, and that, as I knew, they never do unfriendly deals." The Morgan Stanley negotiators knew that their counterparts and respected archrivals at Goldman Sachs cast themselves as conscientious objectors when it comes to helping raiders. But they also knew that if the guns began to roar, Goldman Sachs would excuse itself from the battle and let its client secure the services of more bellicose advisers. And so the name Goldman Sachs did not set Morgan Stanley entirely at ease.

The Seagram entourage—including Bronfman and some lawyers and bankers—arrived from Manhattan on Saturday for a weekend in the country. . . . Bronfman explained that he wanted an investment for the future, something that would provide for his grandchildren. In short, he wasn't interested in control. That afternoon, a helicopter whisked Bronfman off to attend his son's graduation from Taft School 40 miles away. And Bailey, who had some acquisitive notions of his own, jetted off to Oklahoma for some deep discussions with the chairman of Cities Service.

Separate Negotiating Tables

On Sunday the two teams met again in Bailey's office. Meanwhile, the Conoco directors assembled—as they would 16 times in all during Conoco's three-month siege—not just to listen to Bronfman but to receive another very important guest, President Richards of Dome. He was arriving with the Conoco shares in his pocket, figuratively, to negotiate a swap for Conoco's chunk of HBOG.

. . . Conoco thought it might be risky mixing Dome and Seagram. Richards might decide that he would just as soon sell Dome's 22 million shares to Seagram as trade for HBOG.

While they listened to the Bronfmans on the third floor, the Conoco negotiators kept Richards in a small, austere conference room on the first floor with security people posted outside to prevent chance encounters between stray lawyers or investment bankers. Then the negotiators trooped downstairs to bargain with Richards for a while. The shuttling went on all afternoon, until the Conoco negotiating team reached an agreement with Richards and presented it to the Conoco directors waiting in the boardroom. The agreement was accepted: Dome could have HBOG in return for its 22 million Conoco shares and $245 million in cash, a total price of $1.68 billion. (It still isn't clear whether Conoco will have to pay taxes on the stock portion.)

At about 7 o'clock the same evening, Bronfman made his presentation to the Conoco board. The climate wasn't ideal: the air conditioning had broken down hours before and the windows in the glass building don't open. Bronfman and other participants had tossed aside their jackets and neckties in the sweltering heat. But the handsome, polished, 52-year-old Bronfman made an imposing presentation nonetheless. He would like 35 percent of the stock. Part of it he would acquire from the Conoco treasury, which would soon be receiving Dome's shares. The arrangement had some appeal for Conoco. The company could use the cash for exploration and perhaps for expansion. Moreover, ownership of a third of the company by an investor with a long-term interest could provide stability, a counterweight against the fickle institutions.

But the board was worried about whether the Bronfmans would really remain passive. The Bronfmans agreed to sign a "standstill agreement," a pact in which the group acquiring shares promises to vote with management for a stated period, in this case 15 years. The question was what would happen when the pact expired. Conoco wanted Seagram to agree it would either renew the standstill agreement or sell the shares widely. Seagram held out for the right to dispose of its shares as it chose after the expiration date, or keep them.

The Conoco directors rejected the Seagram proposal on June 17. They maintain that with the limited standstill agreement the Bronfmans insisted upon, Seagram would have had effective control of the company. The price suggested, $70 to $75 a share, struck them as too low for a controlling interest, as distinct from a passive one.

Critics have questioned whether the board, in this matter as in others surrounding the sale of the company, was acting dispassionately and in the interests of the shareholders—as opposed to voting their own interests or those of Conoco management. But on the surface at least, Conoco's board had little to lose in a takeover by Seagram or anybody else.

The Conoco board is a model of the sort of independent board that reformers have been demanding in recent years. Of the 14 directors only two are corporate officers, who might have lost their jobs—Bailey and Michael B. Morris, president of petroleum operations. A third, Howard W. Blauvelt, is a former Conoco chairman, who arguably might have an especially strong loyalty to management. But the other 11 are outsiders with not much more directly at stake than the prestige of their positions and director's fees ($12,000 a year plus $500 for each board meeting attended). Many are strong personalities not likely to be cowed by management. . . .

When the Bronfmans left the boardroom, Conoco and Morgan Stanley believed the original understanding—friendly deal or no deal at all—was still in force. But they took the precaution of making up some preliminary lists of companies that could afford to come to Conoco's rescue should Seagram turn hostile. . . . At least one newspaper speculated that Conoco had been in touch with several prospective "white knights"—among them Du Pont, Dow Chemical, and AMAX. In truth things hadn't progressed that far, but the rumor that Conoco might be wooing Dow traveled to Colorado, where Edward Jefferson, chairman of Du Pont for only two months, was vacationing.

Few words get the competitive juices flowing at Du Pont faster than "Dow." The two

companies don't compete directly in many markets; Dow is primarily a producer of basic chemicals, Du Pont of fibers and plastics closer to consumer use. But they compete for the leadership of the chemical industry. . . .

Jefferson recently described how he first contacted Conoco: "I don't remember what I read in which paper but I do remember when I got back from vacation I came back with this question in my mind, 'What's going on?' That was what led me to call Bailey. He told me then that he was not negotiating with another chemical company." By making the call, Jefferson encouraged hopes that Du Pont might be a white knight. . . .

On the very next day, June 25, Seagram made a tender offer for 41 percent of Conoco's stock at $73 a share. . . . With that, Seagram became the enemy. Virtually every action Conoco and Morgan Stanley took from then on was to prevent Seagram from gaining control. The tender was unwelcome for a couple of reasons. First, it killed a Conoco merger with Cities Service, structured as an exchange of stock, even as press releases on the linkup were being written. (The tender would send Conoco's stock so high that relative values of the two oil companies would be disrupted.) Conoco and Morgan Stanley felt that Bronfman had double-crossed them. Bronfman declines to be interviewed, but a spokesman says that commitments made by a chief executive at an earlier time in different circumstances are not necessarily binding on the company and that by the day of the tender offer, the friendly times were past. True to form, Goldman Sachs had departed; Shearson Loeb Rhoades and Lazard Frères were now on the Seagram team.

Conoco and Morgan Stanley also maintain that all through the bidding Seagram offered the shareholders a poor deal. In its final and best offer Seagram promised to pay $92 a share, but the offer was good for just slightly more than half the stock. The 49 percent Seagram did not need for control would be worth only whatever price the market put on it after the Seagram takeover. That price might not be much different from the $50 or so at which Conoco was trading before anyone took much of an interest in it.

Bailey reacted to the tender by telephoning Jefferson to say that he was interested in Du Pont's services as a white knight. The truth was that Conoco did not have many choices: most companies with the financial strength to buy Conoco simply aren't interested in plunging into the oil business. The most eager suitors, in fact, were other oil companies. Both Mobil and Texaco contacted Bailey after the Seagram tender. Bailey spurned Mobil's overtures. Says Greenhill: "I don't know why. Maybe there's a lack of chemistry." The Conoco board seriously considered Texaco, which Greenhill says was talking about paying $85 in cash for Conoco stock. But that was not high enough to provide an adequate "antitrust premium"—something extra to offset the risk that a union between two big oil companies would be delayed and perhaps destroyed by the Justice Department.

What's in It for Du Pont

Du Pont Chairman Edward G. Jefferson, 60, discussed the Conoco acquisition last week with *Fortune* associate editor Susie Nazem. Excerpts:

On why Conoco attracted Du Pont: The first obvious reason is it's an opportunity to obtain a strong natural-resource asset position at a substantial discount. If you look at, say, Herold's [John S. Herold Inc., oil analysts] valuation of the Conoco assets, they showed around $160 a share. [We paid] roughly $88 a share. Secondly, Conoco was available. Conoco was ready and willing to merge.

On how Conoco could stabilize Du Pont's earnings when oil prices rise: If prices are rising at the crude-oil level then it becomes difficult to raise the prices of [Du Pont's] downstream products [which use oil as a raw material]. As soon as you have a crude-oil position you're insulated from that. The fact that you lost a little downstream is protected by what you have upstream. It's the economic result that is crucial.

On using Conoco's coal as a raw material: A consultant approached me about four years ago with a proposal to study chemicals from coal. Much of what was in this proposal was chemistry we had employed. If you ask what is the future, I don't see this being a major thing until into the Nineties.

On petrochemical competition from oil-producing countries and U.S. oil companies: By 1985 Saudi Arabia will have a capability for first-tier petrochemicals—things like ethylene that are roughly 4 percent of the worldwide industry. What Conoco does is put us in a position to be competitive . . . I would be the last to say that having [Conoco] can narrow all gaps, but it sure puts you in a much stronger position vis-à-vis another integrated company.

On what he'll do about Edgar Bronfman of Seagram, which now owns 20 percent of Du Pont: What do I need to do? The comments by Seagram so far are cordial. It's a constructive relationship. . . . What do you want me to say?

Du Pont was picked as dragon slayer. But Du Pont insisted on a weapon—an option from the Conoco board to buy 16 million shares from the Conoco treasury for $87.50 a share, the price it offered Conoco shareholders on July 6. So Du Pont started the rescue knowing it had at least 18.5 percent of the stock sewed up. Du Pont also stipulated that if it did not acquire a majority of Conoco shares, it could return those it did collect.

Mobil entered the struggle uninvited, less than two weeks after Du Pont. And its offer, with revisions, became the most generous of all; at the end Mobil was offering $120 a share in cash for half the stock, securities for the rest. Somewhat surprisingly, it was an offer that most shareholders could refuse. The "antitrust premium" was there, but it just wasn't big enough. Du Pont had the deal in the bag by August 4. At the end of the day some 55 percent of Conoco's stock was in the chemical company's hands.

Conoco management and Morgan Stanley

believe they did the best they could for Conoco shareholders. They also did well for themselves. Jefferson says that Du Pont never would have made an attempt to acquire Conoco without an invitation. He adds that he wants Conoco intact, complete with its top managers. Conoco guaranteed Morgan Stanley a minimum fee of $1 million to remain at its side from the Dome tender offer onward, and a maximum of two-tenths of 1 percent of the total value of the final deal—that is, of the $7.6

billion Du Pont has paid. The fee has not yet been nailed down, but Morgan Stanley could collect, in other words, as much as $15 million, a record merger fee. It will probably have to share the record, however. First Boston Corp. is likely to get $15 million for representing Du Pont.

THE TRAUMA IN A TAKEOVER

Robert E. Tomasson

Stamford, Conn., January 8—As the United States Steel Corporation went about completing its acquisition of the Marathon Oil Company, Marathon's 16,000 employees today began receiving assurances that they need not fear any changes that the new order might bring.

"Marathon will continue to operate and manage the corporate assets utilizing all of the personnel and facilities now in place around the world" was the message sent out from Marathon's headquarters in Findlay, Ohio.

It is in the nature of corporate takeovers, however, that all such guarantees of the status quo tend to be short-lived. Indeed, the recent experiences of three other major corporate acquisitions—Conoco, Kennecott, and Texasgulf—show how profoundly the changes that follow takeovers can affect the lives of thousands of employees, from board chairmen to receptionists and laborers.

Some may be dismissed, others transferred; some careers will be cut short while others will climb. Some will find excitement in being taken over by a stronger corporate entity. For others, there will be despair as their business world is turned upside down.

The acquisitions of Conoco, Kennecott and Texasgulf, all with headquarters in Stamford, offer some striking contrasts in the nature of takeovers of large giant natural resource corporations.

At all three companies, the first reaction was apprehension if not dread, employees said. . . .

"I know that this situation is difficult for employees and their families," said Thomas D. Barrow, the chairman of Kennecott who has since been named a vice chairman of the parent Sohio.

"They walk out that door without even saying goodbye," said a receptionist outside the 15th-floor executive offices, referring to the exodus of headquarters staff over the past several weeks. . . .

Major Staff Changes
Of the 50 employees of the 200-member headquarters staff who have left thus far, 46 have been dismissed, have quit or have retired. Four others have been taken by Sohio.

About 100 of the remaining staff personnel will be dismissed, will retire or will resign, according to Eric Nielsen, vice president in charge of personnel. If Kennecott had not been purchased, Mr. Barrow said, "we'd be in very serious financial shape today."

"Yes, it's hard on the headquarters staff, but there are the 38,000 other Kennecott workers out there and for them it has been a very sound move," he added.

What Mr. Barrow called the "fairly toughminded" position affecting the Kennecott headquarters staff was in distinct contrast to the corporate paternalism at Texasgulf, which was taken over by by the French Government-controlled oil giant, Société Nationale Elf Aquitaine last June.

For Texasgulf's chairman, Richard D. Mollison, the takeover was the second stunning event within months of what was to have been the last year of his career.

Expecting to retire as vice chairman of the company he had been with since 1947, Mr. Mollison was named to replace Charles F. Fogerty, the company's chairman, who was killed with five other top Texasgulf officers in a Westchester County plane crash in February 1981.

Agreeing to stay on until his 65th birthday last June, Mr. Mollison was presented with the fait accompli of the French takeover. He said he had neither participated in nor been informed about the takeover.

For Texasgulf officials, however, initial apprehension gave way to reassurances as the French company moved to maintain the existing corporate leadership. Mr. Mollison and 22 other top executives were all offered five-year contracts and not one of the more than 200 persons on the office staff has been shifted because of the takeover.

Other Employees Shifted

But while the Texasgulf headquarters staff remained intact, the number of workers in company mines and plants throughout North America has dropped to 3,850 from the pre-takeover force of 6,480. Most were shifted to the Canada Development Corporation, which had been Texasgulf's largest shareholder and which had engineered the sale of the company in secret to Elf Aquitaine.

One jarring element that confronted employees at Texasgulf was the requirement to cash in their stock in the company as it could not be exchanged for stock of the new parent.

Since Elf Aquitaine is not traded in this country, many executives of Texasgulf found they were at a noticeable tax disadvantage as the stock was cashed in all at once.

A hundred yards or so from the fortress-like Texasgulf building, complete with moat, stands the corporate headquarters of Conoco, object of the largest corporate takeover ever in this country, where the 200-member headquarters staff oversees 41,000 employees worldwide.

"Business as Usual"

While there have been distinct changes at Kennecott, which sought merger, and at Texasgulf, which did not, the atmosphere at Conoco, after an initial wave of anxiety following its acquisition by Du Pont last August, has returned to what some employees call "business as usual."

"For a corporation with combined 1980 sales of over $30 billion, there is little overlap in either operations or business lines" with the new parent, said C. S. Nicandros, a Conoco group executive vice president.

To Ralph E. Bailey, Conoco's chairman and chief executive officer, "the merger creates a synergistic partnership, a company that is even stronger than the sum of its parts."
. . .

Horizontal Mergers

The government's concern with horizontal mergers rests on the presumed decline in competition and increase in market concentration that accompanies the acquisition by one firm of another firm in the same market. The resulting firm raises concerns similar to those in a monopoly situation, and, indeed, the market analysis to be applied to horizontal mergers is very similar to that previously discussed in the monopoly section. (See Chapter 9.) Essentially, we must define the product and geographic markets and then apply the Clayton Act, section 7 test; that is, some unspecified probability of substantially lessening competition or tending to create a monopoly. The *Brown Shoe* case illustrates the Court's early efforts to interpret Congress' intent in passing the amended Clayton Act. Note that *Brown* embraces both horizontal and vertical dimensions. Vertical analysis will be treated in some detail later in the chapter.

BROWN SHOE CO. V. UNITED STATES   370 U.S. 294 (1961)

Chief Justice Warren

This suit was initiated in November 1955 when the Government filed a civil action in the United States District Court for the Eastern District of Missouri alleging that a contemplated merger between the G. R. Kinney Company, Inc. (Kinney), and the Brown Shoe Company, Inc. (Brown), through an exchange of Kinney for Brown stock, would violate Sec. 7 of the Clayton Act. . . .

* * * * *

In the District Court, the Government contended that the effect of the merger of Brown—the third largest seller of shoes by dollar volume in the United States, a leading manufacturer of men's, women's, and children's shoes, and a retailer with over 1,230 owned, operated or controlled retail outlets—and Kinney—the eighth largest company, by dollar volume, among those primarily engaged in selling shoes, itself a large manufacturer of shoes, and a retailer with over 350 retail outlets—"may be substantially to lessen competition or to tend to create a monopoly."

* * * * *

The Industry

The District Court found that although domestic shoe production was scattered among a large number of manufacturers, a small number of large companies occupied a commanding position. Thus, while the 24 largest manufacturers produced about 35 percent of the Nation's shoes, the top 4—International, Endicott-Johnson, Brown (including Kinney), and General Shoe—alone produced approximately 23 percent of the Nation's shoes or 65 percent of the production of the top 24.

In 1955, domestic production of nonrubber shoes was 509.2 million pairs, of which about 103.6 million pairs were men's shoes, about 271 million pairs were women's shoes, and about 134.6 million pairs were children's shoes. The District Court found that men's, women's, and children's shoes are normally produced in separate factories.

The public buys these shoes through about 70,000 retail outlets, only 22,000 of which, however, derive 50 percent or more of their gross receipts from the sale of shoes and are classified as "shoe stores" by the Census Bureau. These 22,000 shoe stores were found generally to sell (1) men's shoes only, (2) women's shoes only, (3) women's and children's shoes, or (4) men's, women's, and children's shoes.

The District Court found a "definite trend" among shoe manufacturers to acquire retail outlets. For example, International Shoe Company had no retail outlets in 1945, but by 1956 had acquired 130; General Shoe Company had only 80 retail outlets in 1945 but had 526 by 1956. . . . Brown, itself, with no retail outlets of its own prior to 1951, had acquired 845 such outlets by 1956. Moreover, between 1950 and 1956 nine independent shoe store chains, operating 1,114 retail shoe stores, were found to have become subsidiaries of these large firms and to have ceased their independent operations.

And once the manufacturers acquired retail outlets, the district court found there was a "definite trend" for the parent-manufacturers to supply an ever increasing percentage of the retail outlets' needs, thereby foreclosing other manufacturers from effectively competing for the retail accounts. Manufacturer-dominated stores were found to be "drying up" the available outlets for independent producers.

Another "definite trend" found to exist in the shoe industry was a decrease in the number of plants manufacturing shoes. And there appears to have been a concomitant decrease in the number of firms manufacturing shoes. In 1947, there were 1,077 independent manufacturers of shoes, but by 1954 their number had decreased about 10 percent to 970.

Brown Shoe

Brown Shoe was found not only to have been a participant, but also a moving factor, in these industry trends. Although Brown had experimented several times with operating its own retail outlets, by 1945 it had disposed of them all. However, in 1951, Brown again began to seek retail outlets by acquiring the Nation's largest operator of leased shoe departments, Wohl Shoe Company (Wohl), which operated 250 shoe departments in department stores throughout the United States. Between 1952 and 1955 Brown made a number of smaller acquisitions. . . .

The acquisition of these corporations was found to lead to increased sales by Brown to the acquired companies. . . .

During the same period of time, Brown also acquired the stock or assets of seven companies engaged solely in shoe manufacturing. As a result, in 1955, Brown was the fourth largest shoe manufacturer in the country, producing about 25.6 million pairs of shoes or about 4 percent of the Nation's total footwear production.

Kinney

Kinney is principally engaged in operating the largest family-style shoe store chain in the United States. At the time of trial, Kinney was found to be operating over 400 such stores in more than 270 cities. These stores were found to make about 1.2 percent of all national retail shoe sales by dollar volume. . . .

In addition to this extensive retail activity, Kinney owned and operated four plants which manufactured men's, women's, and children's shoes and whose combined output was 0.5 percent of the national shoe production in 1955, making Kinney the 12th largest shoe manufacturer in the United States.

Kinney stores were found to obtain about 20 percent of their shoes from Kinney's own manufacturing plants. At the time of the merger, Kinney bought no shoes from Brown; however, in line with Brown's conceded reasons for acquiring Kinney, Brown had, by 1957, become the largest outside supplier of Kinney's shoes, supplying 7.9 percent of all Kinney's needs.

It is in this setting that the merger was considered and held to violate § 7 of the Clayton Act. The District Court ordered Brown to divest itself completely of all stock, share capital, assets or other interests it held in Kinney. . . .

Legislative History

The dominant theme pervading congressional consideration of the 1950 amendments [to ton Act, section 7] was a fear of what was considered to be a rising tide of economic concen... tion in the American economy. . . .

Other considerations cited in support of the bill were the desirability of retaining "local control" over industry and the protection of small businesses. Throughout the recorded discussion may be found examples of Congress' fear not only of accelerated concentration of economic power on economic grounds, but also of the threat to other values a trend toward concentration was thought to pose.

The Vertical Aspects of the Merger

. . . The primary vice of a vertical merger or other arrangement tying a customer to a supplier is that, by foreclosing the competitors of either party from a segment of the market otherwise open to them, the arrangement may act as a "clog on competition." . . .

The Product Market

The outer boundaries of a product market are determined by the reasonable interchangeability of use or the cross-elasticity of demand between the product itself and substitutes for it. However, within this broad market, well-defined submarkets may exist which, in themselves, constitute product markets for antitrust purposes. . . . The boundaries of such a submarket may be determined by examining such practical indicia as industry or public recognition of the submarket as a separate economic entity, the product's peculiar characteristics and uses, unique production facilities, distinct customers, distinct prices, sensitivity to price changes, and specialized vendors. . . .

Applying these considerations to the present case, we conclude that the record supports the District Court's finding that the relevant lines of commerce are men's, women's, and children's shoes. These product lines are recognized by the public; each line is manufactured in separate plants; each has characteristics peculiar to itself rendering it generally noncompetitive with the others; and each is, of course, directed toward a distinct class of customers. . . .

The Geographic Market

We agree with the parties and the District Court that insofar as the vertical aspect of this merger is concerned, the relevant geographic market is the entire Nation. The relationships of product value, bulk, weight and consumer demand enable manufacturers to distribute their shoes on a nationwide basis, as Brown and Kinney, in fact, do. . . .

The Probable Effect of the Merger

Once the area of effective competition affected by a vertical arrangement has been defined, an analysis must be made to determine if the effect of the arrangement "may be substantially to lessen competition, or to tend to create a monopoly" in this market.

Since the diminution of the vigor of competition which may stem from a vertical arrangement results primarily from a foreclosure of a share of the market otherwise open to competitors, an important consideration in determining whether the effect of a vertical arrangement "may be substantially to lessen competition, or to tend to create a monopoly" is the size of the share of the market foreclosed. However, this factor will seldom be determinative.

* * * * *

[I]t is apparent both from past behavior of Brown and from the testimony of Brown's President, that Brown would use its ownership of Kinney to force Brown shoes into Kinney stores. . . .

Another important factor to consider is the trend toward concentration in the industry. . . .

The existence of a trend toward vertical integration, which the District Court found, is well substantiated by the record. Moreover, the court found a tendency of the acquiring manufacturers to become increasingly important sources of supply for their acquired outlets. The necessary corollary of these trends is the foreclosure of independent manufacturers from markets otherwise open to them. . . .

Brown argues, however, that the shoe industry is at present composed of a large number of manufacturers and retailers, and that the industry is dynamically competitive. But remaining vigor cannot immunize a merger if the trend in that industry is toward oligopoly. It is the probable effect of the merger upon the future as well as the present which the Clayton Act commands the courts and the commission to examine.

Moreover, as we have remarked above, not only must we consider the probable effects of the merger upon the economics of the particular markets affected but also we must consider its probable effects upon the economic way of life sought to be preserved by Congress. Congress was desirous of preventing the formation of further oligopolies with their attendant adverse effects upon local control of industry and upon small business. Where an industry was composed of numerous independent units, Congress appeared anxious to preserve this structure. . . .

The Horizontal Aspects of the Merger

. . . The acquisition of Kinney by Brown resulted in a horizontal combination at both the manufacturing and retailing levels of their businesses. Although the District Court found that the merger of Brown's and Kinney's *manufacturing* facilities was economically too insignificant to come within the prohibitions of the Clayton Act, the Government has not appealed from this portion of the lower court's decision. Therefore, we have no occasion to express our views with respect to that finding. On the other hand, appellant does contest the District Court's finding that the merger of the companies' *retail* outlets may tend substantially to lessen competition.

The Product Market

. . . In . . . this opinion we hold that the District Court correctly defined men's, women's, and children's shoes as the relevant lines of commerce in which to analyze the vertical aspects of the merger. For the reasons there stated we also hold that the same lines of commerce are appropriate for considering the horizontal aspects of the merger.

The Geographic Market

The criteria to be used in determining the appropriate geographic market are essentially similar to those used to determine the relevant product market. Moreover, just as a product submarket may have § 7 significance as the proper "line of commerce," so may a geographic submarket be considered the appropriate "section of the country." Congress prescribed a pragmatic, factual approach to the definition of the relevant market and not a formal, legalistic one. The geographic market selected must, therefore, both "correspond to the commercial realities" of the industry and be economically significant. Thus, although the geographic market in some instances may encompass the entire nation, under other circumstances it may be as small as a single metropolitan area. The fact that two merging firms have competed directly on the horizontal level in but a fraction of the geographic markets in which either has operated, does not, in itself, place their merger outside the scope of § 7. That section speaks of "any . . . section of the country" if anticompetitive effects of a merger are probable in "any" significant market, the merger—least to that extent—is proscribed.

The parties do not dispute the findings of the District Court that the nation as a whole is the relevant geographic market for measuring the anticompetitive effects of the merger viewed vertically or of the horizontal merger of Brown's and Kinney's manufacturing facilities. As to the retail level, however, they disagree.

* * * * *

We agree that the District Court properly defined the relevant geographic markets in which to analyze this merger as those cities with a population exceeding 10,000 and their environs in which both Brown and Kinney retailed shoes through their own outlets. Such markets are large enough to include the downtown shops and suburban shopping centers in areas contiguous to the city, which are the important competitive factors, and yet are small enough to exclude stores beyond the immediate environs of the city, which are of little competitive significance.

The Probable Effect of the Merger

. . . The market share which companies may control by merging is one of the most important factors to be considered when determining the probable effects of the combination on effective competition in the relevant market. In an industry as fragmented as shoe retailing, the control of substantial shares of the trade in a city may have important effects on competition. If a merger achieving 5 percent control were now approved, we might be required to approve future merger efforts by Brown's competitors seeking similar market shares.

* * * * *

At the same time appellant has presented no mitigating factors, such as the business failure or the inadequate resources of one of the parties that may have prevented it from maintaining its competitive position, nor a demonstrated need for combination to enable small companies to enter into a more meaningful competition with those dominating the relevant markets. . . .

The judgment is affirmed.

Questions

1. As to the vertical element of *Brown Shoe,* what potential harm did the Court identify?
2. In *Brown Shoe* why did the Supreme Court settle on different geographic markets for the horizontal and vertical elements of the merger?
3. In *Brown Shoe* the Court followed the mandate of Congress that tendencies toward concentration are to be curbed in their incipiency. Why must the Court bow to the will of Congress in this matter?
4. How did the Supreme Court justify its prohibition of the merger in light of the rather small market shares involved (e.g., Brown produced 4 percent of the nation's shoes, while Kinney sold about 1.2 percent of the nation's total)?
5. In 1958 Pabst Brewing Company acquired Blatz Brewing Company. Pabst was America's 10th largest brewer, while Blatz was the 18th largest. After the merger Pabst had 4.49 percent of the beer market and was the fifth largest brewer. In the regional market of Wisconsin, Michigan, and Illinois the merger gave Pabst 11.32 percent of the sales after the merger. The beer market was becoming increasingly concentrated, with the total number of brewers declining from 206 to 162 during the years 1957 to 1961. In *United States* v. *Pabst Brewing Co.,* 384 U.S. 546 (1966), the Supreme Court found the merger violative of the

Clayton Act, section 7. The Court did not choose among the three geographic market configurations, saying that the crucial inquiry is whether a merger may substantially lessen competition *anywhere* in the United States. Thus the Court held that, under these facts, a 4.49 percent share of the market was too large.

Respected scholar and jurist Richard Posner labeled the *Pabst* decision an "atrocity" and the product of a "fit of nonsense" on the part of the Supreme Court.[5] What economic arguments would support Posner's colorful complaint?

Market Share and Other Considerations

Of course, determination of market share and what those shares signal as to market concentration is at the heart of horizontal merger analysis. A footnote in the 1963 *Philadelphia National Bank* case summarized the Supreme Court's determination, at that time, to fulfill Congress' expressed intent to curb market concentration. "[I]f concentration is already great, the importance of preventing even slight increases in concentration and so preserving the possibility of eventual deconcentration is correspondingly great."[6] However, a 1974 Supreme Court horizontal merger decision seems to have signaled a departure from virtually exclusive concern with market shares and increased market concentration.

UNITED STATES V. GENERAL DYNAMICS CORPORATION
415 U.S. 486 (1974)

Justice Stewart

On September 22, 1967, the government commenced this suit in the United States District Court for the Northern District of Illinois, challenging as violative of § 7 of the Clayton Act, . . . the acquisition of the stock of United Electric Coal Companies by Material Service Corp. and its successor, General Dynamics Corporation. . . . The District Court issued an opinion and judgment finding no violation of the Clayton Act. . . .

The government appealed directly to this court.

At the time of the acquisition involved here, Material Service Corporation was a large midwest producer and supplier of building materials, concrete, limestone, and coal. All of its coal production was from deepshaft mines operated by it or its affiliate, appellee Freeman Coal Mining Corporation, and production from these operations amounted to 6.9 million tons of coal in 1959 and 8.4 million tons in 1967. In 1954, Material Service began to acquire the stock of United Electric Coal Companies. . . .

Some months after this takeover, Material Service was itself acquired by the appellee General Dynamics Corporation. General Dynamics is a large diversified corporation, much of its revenues coming from sales of aircraft, communications, and marine products to government agencies. . . .

As a result of the purchase of Material Service, and through it, of Freeman and United Electric, General Dynamics became the nation's fifth largest commercial coal producer. . . .

The thrust of the government's complaint was that the acquisition of United Electric by Material Service in 1959 violated § 7 of the Clayton Act because the takeover substantially lessened competition in the production and sale of coal in either or both of two geographic markets. It contended that a relevant "section of the country" within the meaning of § 7 was, alternatively, the State of Illinois or the Eastern Interior Coal Province Sales Area, the latter being one of four major coal distribution areas recognized by the coal industry and comprising Illinois and Indiana, and parts of Kentucky, Tennessee, Iowa, Minnesota, Wisconsin, and Missouri. . . .

The government sought to prove a violation of § 7 of the Clayton Act principally through statistics showing that within certain geographic markets the coal industry was concentrated among a small number of large producers, that this concentration was increasing, and that the acquisition of United Electric would materially enlarge the market share of the acquiring company and thereby contribute to the trend toward concentration.

*   *   *   *   *

Much of the District Court's opinion was devoted to a description of the changes that have affected the coal industry since World War II. . . . First, it found that coal had become increasingly less able to compete with other sources of energy in many segments of the energy market. Following the War the industry entirely lost its largest single purchaser of coal—the railroads—and faced increasingly stiffer competition from oil and natural gas as sources of energy for industrial and residential uses. Because of these changes in consumption patterns, coal's share of the energy resources consumed in this country fell from 78.4 percent in 1920 to 21.4 percent in 1968.

. . .

Second, the court found that to a growing extent since 1954, the electric utility industry has become the mainstay of coal consumption. While electric utilities consumed only 15.76 percent of the coal produced nationally in 1947, their share of total consumption increased every year thereafter, and in 1968 amounted to more than 59 percent of all the coal consumed throughout the nation.

Third, and most significantly, the court found that to an increasing degree, nearly all coal sold to utilities is transferred under long-term requirements contracts, under which coal producers promise to meet utilities' coal consumption requirements for a fixed period of time, and at predetermined prices. . . .

Because of these fundamental changes in the structure of the market for coal, the District Court was justified in viewing the statistics relied on by the government as insufficient to sustain its case. Evidence of past production does not, as a matter of logic, necessarily give a proper picture of a company's future ability to compete. . . .

The bulk of the coal produced is delivered under long-term requirements contracts, and such sales thus do not represent the exercise of competitive power but rather the obligation to fulfill previously negotiated contracts at a previously fixed price. The focus of competition in a given time frame is not on the disposition of coal already produced but on the procurement of new long-term supply contracts. In this situation, a company's past ability to produce is of limited significance, since it is in a position to offer for sale neither its past production nor the bulk of the coal it is presently capable of producing, which is typically already committed under a long-term supply contract. A more significant indicator of a company's power effectively to compete with other companies lies in the state of a company's uncommitted reserves of recoverable coal. A company with relatively large supplies of coal which are not already under contract to a consumer will have a more important influence upon competition in the contemporaneous negotiation of supply contracts than a firm with small reserves, even though the latter may presently produce a greater tonnage of coal. In a market where the availability and price of coal are set by long-term contracts rather than immediate or short-term purchases and sales, reserves rather than past production are the best measure of a company's ability to compete.

The testimony and exhibits in the District Court revealed that United Electric's coal reserve prospects were "unpromising." United's relative position of strength in reserves was considerably weaker than its past and current ability to produce. While United ranked 5th among Illinois coal producers in terms of annual production, it was 10th in reserve holdings, and controlled less than 1 percent of the reserves held by coal producers in Illinois, Indiana, and western Kentucky. Many of the reserves held by United had already been depleted at the time of trial, forcing the closing of some of United's midwest mines. Even more significantly, the District Court found that of the 52,033,304 tons of currently mineable reserves in Illinois, Indiana, and Kentucky controlled by United, only 4 million tons had not already been committed under long-term contracts. United was found to be facing the future with relatively depleted resources at its disposal, and with the vast majority of those resources already committed under contracts allowing no further adjustment in price. In addition, the District Court found that "United Electric has neither the possibility of acquiring more [reserves] nor the ability to develop deep coal reserves," and thus was not in a position to increase its reserves to replace those already depleted or committed.

Viewed in terms of present and future reserve prospects—and thus in terms of probable future ability to compete—rather than in terms of past production, the District Court held that United Electric was a far less significant factor in the coal market than the government contended or the production statistics seemed to indicate. While the company had been and remained a "highly profitable" and efficient producer of relatively large amounts of coal, its current and future power to compete for subsequent long-term contracts was severely limited by its scarce uncommitted resources. Irrespective of the company's size when viewed as a producer, its weakness as a competitor was properly analyzed by the District Court and fully substantiated that court's conclusion that its acquisition by Material Service would not "substantially . . . lessen competition. . . ."

Affirmed.

Questions

1. As noted previously, the *General Dynamics* case has been labeled a change in direction in horizontal merger analysis. How does the Court's reasoning in *General Dynamics* differ from that in *Brown Shoe?*
2. The Court in *General Dynamics* acknowledged that the market shares established by the government were sufficient by themselves to support a finding of "undue concentration." How then was the Court able to find in favor of General Dynamics?
3. The Supreme Court asserted that the failing-company defense was "simply inapposite" to the *General Dynamics* case.
   a. What is the failing company defense? (Think about it, then refer to the "Defenses" section later in this chapter.)
   b. Is that defense applicable to the *General Dynamics* case?

Vertical Mergers

In the period 1917–1919 Du Pont acquired 23 percent of the stock in the then fledgling General Motors Corporation. By 1947 Du Pont supplied 68 percent of GM's automotive finish needs and 38 percent of its fabric needs. In 1955 General Motors ranked first in sales and second in assets among all United States industrial corporations, while accounting for approximately two fifths of the nation's annual automobile sales. In 1949 the Justice Department challenged Du Pont's 1917–1919 acquisitions of GM stock. See

United States v. *E. I. Du Pont de Nemours & Co. (General Motors)*, 353 U.S. 586 (1957).

> Why did the government challenge Du Pont's acquisition?
> May an acquisition be properly challenged 30 years after the fact, as in *Du Pont?*
> Given your general understanding of finishes and fabrics, how would you defend
>   Du Pont?

A *vertical merger* involves an alliance between a supplier and a purchaser. The primary threat thus arising is that of market foreclosure. As illustrated in the accompanying diagram, a vertical merger may deny a source of supply to a purchaser or an outlet for sale to a seller, which might then threaten competition so as to violate the Clayton Act.

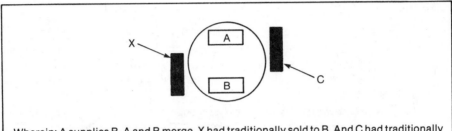

Wherein: A supplies B. A and B merge. X had traditionally sold to B. And C had traditionally purchased from A. How then do we decide the legality of such a merger?

Some other economic considerations may influence the legality of a vertical merger.

1. *Deep pockets.* That is, the merger may provide the merged firm with financial advantages that smaller rivals could not match.
2. *Price squeeze.* In the diagram, the newly merged AB may be able to arbitrarily raise prices of raw materials to C while temporarily depressing the price of its finished goods. The result may, of course, severely pinch C.
3. *Barriers to entry.* A market composed of integrated—and thus often larger—firms would pose a more formidable hurdle in terms of capital requirements and psychic courage than one of many small suppliers and purchasers.

In 1961 Ford Motor Company acquired the trade name and other assets of the Electric Autolite Company, a producer and distributor of spark plugs and other automotive parts. At the time of the acquisition three firms controlled 95 percent of the spark plug market: Champion (50 percent), General Motors-AC (30 percent), and Autolite (15 percent). Spark plug producers traditionally sold them to automakers at a price below cost. The profit came in the replacement market where mechanics ordinarily replaced the original plug with the same brand of aftermarket plug. Ford, in seeking entry to the profitable aftermarket, concluded that it would require five to eight years to successfully create its own spark plug division, and the cost involved would be greater than that of buying Autolite. Ford accounted for approximately 9.6 percent of all the spark plugs sold in America. After the acquisition Autolite began a new spark plug business, which garnered 1.6 percent of the market by 1964.

Questions

1. What category—or categories—of merger are we dealing with here?
2. What harm did the government fear with the acquisition of Electric Autolite?
3. Argue that the Ford–Electric Autolite merger strengthened competition.
4. Decide the *Ford* case. (See *Ford Motor Company* v. *United States*, 405 U.S. 562 (1972).

Conglomerate Mergers

In essence conglomerate mergers fall into four categories of analysis:

1. **Potential Entrant.** When a firm might have entered a market on its own but chose instead to acquire an existing firm, the government may raise a challenge under Clayton § 7. Potential entrant mergers are of two types: product extension and market extension.

Product extension involves two products that are not competitors but are closely related in their production or distribution. The merger of Procter & Gamble, a soap manufacturer, and Clorox, a bleach manufacturer, exemplifies the product extension conglomerate merger.

Market extension involves two companies that produce the same product but sell it in different geographic markets. The merger of Narragansett Brewing, marketing its products in New England, and Falstaff Brewing, marketing in 32 states but not in New England, is exemplary of the market extension conglomerate.[7]

2. **Market Power Entrenchment.** The government may challenge those conglomerate mergers involving a large firm acquiring a leading firm in a concentrated market, in cases when the acquisition may solidify or entrench the acquired firm's already strong market posture. For example, where the acquiring and acquired firms deal in related products, the size of the acquiring firm may convince distributors of the advisability of according the acquired firm favored treatment. (See the *Heublein* case at the end of the chapter.) The government is concerned that some conglomerate mergers will enhance the ability of the merged firm to increase product differentiation. That is, the acquiring firm can use its superior resources in the acquired firm's market, via advertising and the like, with the result that competition is reduced and barriers to entry are increased. The general area of market entrenchment is sometimes referred to by the term *deep pockets* or *rich parent*. Consideration of the merger guidelines and the *Procter & Gamble* case that follow will clarify this line of analysis.

3. **Reciprocity.** Essentially, reciprocity involves a "you scratch my back, and I'll scratch yours" sales arrangement wherein purchases are made on the strength of mutual benefit rather than the merits of the products. Conglomerate mergers often exacerbate reciprocity. The accompanying diagram illustrates the problem.

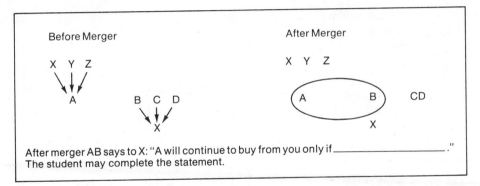

After merger AB says to X: "A will continue to buy from you only if_____."
The student may complete the statement.

Just as a significant potential for reciprocal buying may render a merger unlawful, so may reciprocity itself be illegal. Reciprocal buying may violate both sections 1 and 2 of the Sherman Act, as well as section 5 of the Federal Trade Commission Act. In the next diagram firms A and Z agree, either by mutual consent or as a result of coercion by one of the parties, to sell to and buy from each other. The impact on the market then depends on the market shares involved.

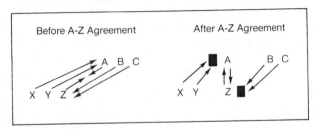

   4. **Aggregate Concentration.** In several cases the Justice Department has secured consent decrees on the grounds that the mergers in question would have resulted in unacceptable increases in overall commercial concentration. The argument is that commerce is already substantially concentrated, therefore, further significant concentration should be challenged on that ground alone. Despite the Justice Department's occasional success with this line of analysis, no recorded judicial opinion has explicitly supported it.

Defenses

At least in theory, certain conditions would seem to justify otherwise illegal mergers. However, of the defenses that follow only the fourth has received judicial approval. The defenses are:

1. Economies born of efficiencies unrelated to advertising or promotion.
2. The market in question retains substantial ease of entry.
3. The merger may enhance competition. How might a merger improve competition in, for example, the steel or telephone industries?
4. A company or division is failing.

The government in its 1984 merger guidelines has explicitly approved the failing company defense.

Cases

A careful reading of the *Procter & Gamble* and *ITT* cases should provide a reasonably clear picture of the main lines of conglomerate analysis.

FTC V. PROCTER & GAMBLE CO.   386 U.S. 568 (1967)

Justice Douglas

This is a proceeding initiated by the Federal Trade Commission charging that respondent, Procter & Gamble Co., had acquired the assets of Clorox Chemical Co. in violation of § 7 of the Clayton Act, . . . The charge was that Procter's acquisition of Clorox might substantially lessen competition or tend to create a monopoly in the production and sale of household liquid bleaches.

[The FTC found the merger unlawful and ordered divestiture.] The Court of Appeals for the Sixth Circuit reversed and directed that the Commission's complaint be dismissed. . . . We find that the Commission's findings were amply supported by the evidence, and that the Court of Appeals erred.

. . . This merger may most appropriately be described as a "product-extension merger," as the commission stated. . . .

At the time of the merger, in 1957, Clorox was the leading manufacturer in the heavily concentrated household liquid bleach industry. It is agreed that household liquid bleach is the relevant line of commerce. . . . It is a distinctive product with no close substitutes. . . . The relevant geographical market is the nation and a series of regional markets. Because of high shipping costs and low sales price, it is not feasible to ship the product more than 300 miles from its point of manufacture. Most manufacturers are limited to competition within a single region since they have but one plant. Clorox is the only firm selling nationally; it has 13 plants distributed throughout the nation. Purex, Clorox's closest competitor in size, does not distribute its bleach in the northeast or mid-Atlantic States; in 1957, Purex's bleach was available in less than 50 percent of the national market.

At the time of the acquisition, Clorox was the leading manufacturer of household liquid bleach, with 48.8 percent of the national sales—annual sales of slightly less than $40 million. Its market share had been steadily increasing for the five years prior to the merger. Its nearest rival was Purex, which accounted for 15.7 percent of the household liquid bleach market. The industry is highly concentrated; in 1957, Clorox and Purex accounted for almost 65 percent of the nation's household liquid bleach sales, and, together with four other firms, for almost 80 percent. The remaining 20 percent was divided among over 200 small producers. Clorox had total assets of $12 million; only eight producers had assets in excess of $1 million, and very few had assets of more than $75,000.

* * * * *

Since all liquid bleach is chemically identical, advertising and sales promotion are vital. In 1957 Clorox spent almost $3.7 million on advertising, imprinting the value of its bleach in the mind of the consumer. In addition, it spent $1.7 million for other promotional activities. The Commission found that these heavy expenditures went far to explain why Clorox maintained so high a market share despite the fact that its brand, though chemically indistinguishable from rival brands, retailed for a price equal to or, in many instances, higher than its competitors.

Procter is a large, diversified manufacturer of low-price, high-turnover household products sold through grocery, drug, and department stores. Prior to its acquisition of Clorox, it did not produce household liquid bleach. Its 1957 sales were in excess of $1.1 billion, from which it realized profits of more than $67 million; its assets were over $500 million. Procter has been marked by rapid growth and diversification. . . .

In the marketing of soaps, detergents, and cleansers, as in the marketing of household liquid bleach, advertising and sales promotion are vital. In 1957, Procter was the nation's largest advertiser, spending more than $80 million on advertising and an additional $47 million on sales promotion. Due to its tremendous volume, Procter receives substantial discounts from the media. As a multiproduct producer Procter enjoys substantial advantages in advertising and sales promotion. Thus, it can and does feature several products in its promotions, reducing the printing, mailing, and other costs for each product. It also purchases network programs on behalf of several products, enabling it to give each product network exposure at a fraction of the cost per product that a firm with only one product to advertise would incur.

Prior to the acquisition, Procter was in the course of diversifying into product lines related to its basic detergent-soap-cleanser business. Liquid bleach was a distinct possibility since packaged detergents—Procter's primary product line—and liquid bleach are used complementarily in washing clothes and fabrics, and in general household cleaning.

* * * * *

The anticompetitive effects with which this product-extension merger is fraught can easily be seen: (1) the substitution of the powerful acquiring firm for the smaller, but already dominant, firm may substantially reduce the competitive structure of the industry by raising entry barriers and by dissuading the smaller firms from aggressively competing; (2) the acquisition eliminates the potential competition of the acquiring firm.

The liquid bleach industry was already oligopolistic before the acquisition, and price competition was certainly not as vigorous as it would have been if the industry were competitive. Clorox enjoyed a dominant position nationally, and its position approached monopoly proportions in certain areas. The existence of some 200 fringe firms certainly does not belie that fact. Nor does the fact, relied upon by the court below, that, after the merger, producers other than Clorox "were selling more bleach for more money than ever before."

. . . In the same period, Clorox increased its share from 48.8 percent to 52 percent. The interjection of Procter into the market considerably changed the situation. There is every reason to assume that the smaller firms would become more cautious in competing due to their fear of retaliation by Procter. It is probable that Procter would become the price leader and that oligopoly would become more rigid.

The acquisition may also have the tendency of raising the barriers to new entry. The major competitive weapon in the successful marketing of bleach is advertising. Clorox was limited in this area by its relatively small budget and its inability to obtain substantial discounts. By contrast, Procter's budget was much larger; and, although it would not devote its entire budget to advertising Clorox, it could divert a large portion to meet the short-term threat of a new entrant. Procter would be able to use its volume discounts to advantage in advertising Clorox. Thus, a new entrant would be much more reluctant to face the giant Procter than it would have been to face the smaller Clorox.

Possible economies cannot be used as a defense to illegality. Congress was aware that some mergers which lessen competition may also result in economies but it struck the balance in favor of protecting competition. . . .

The Commission also found that the acquisition of Clorox by Procter eliminated Procter as a potential competitor. . . . The evidence . . . clearly shows that Procter was the most likely entrant. . . . Procter was engaged in a vigorous program of diversifying into product lines closely related to its basic products. Liquid bleach was a natural avenue of diversification since it is complementary to Procter's products, is sold to the same customers through the same channels, and is advertised and merchandised in the same manner. . . .

It is clear that the existence of Procter at the edge of the industry exerted considerable influence on the market. First, the market behavior of the liquid bleach industry was influenced by each firm's predictions of the market behavior of its competitors, actual and potential. Second, the barriers to entry by a firm of Procter's size and with its advantages were not significant. There is no indication that the barriers were so high that the price Procter would have to charge would be above the price that would maximize the profits of the existing firms. Third, the number of potential entrants was not so large that the elimination of one would be insignificant. Few firms would have the temerity to challenge a firm as solidly entrenched as Clorox. Fourth, Procter was found by the Commission to be the most likely entrant. . . .

The judgment of the Court of Appeals is reversed and remanded with instructions to affirm and enforce the commission's order.

Questions

1. Make the argument that Procter & Gamble beneficially influenced and disciplined the bleach market, even though it had not actually entered that market.
2. Argue that Procter & Gamble was not a likely potential entrant into the bleach market.
3. Could American Motors lawfully acquire Clorox?
4. Could Procter & Gamble lawfully acquire Purex, at that time the number two liquid bleach producer with 15.7 percent of the market?
5. Would the outcome of the *Procter & Gamble* case be altered if bleaches were of differing chemical composition and quality?

UNITED STATES V. INTERNATIONAL TELEPHONE AND TELEGRAPH CORPORATION   324 F. Supp. 19 (1970)

Chief Judge Timbers

Question Presented

In this action brought by the United States . . . to enjoin the acquisition by International Telephone and Telegraph Corporation (ITT) of the stock of Grinnell Corporation as an alleged violation of Section 7 of the Clayton Act, the essential question for determination by the Court . . . [is whether] the government has sustained its burden of establishing that "in any line of commerce in any section of the country, the effect of such acquisition may be substantially to lessen competition."

For the reasons stated below the Court holds that the government has not sustained its burden.

* * * * *

. . . [ITT] employs approximately 353,000 persons; during 1969, it had consolidated sales and revenues of slightly less than $5.5 billion, consolidated net income of $234 million and consolidated assets of approximately $5.2 billion, at the end of that year; it is the ninth largest industrial corporation in the United States according to Fortune Magazine; approximately 40 per-cent–45 percent of its consolidated sales and revenues and income are from operations outside the United States and Canada; during the period 1955 through 1969, its total consolidated sales and revenues increased from $448 million to almost $5.5 billion; during the decade 1960–1969, it acquired 85 domestic corporations; and at the end of 1969, it had in excess of 200 subsidiaries worldwide engaged in a wide variety of enterprises.

* * * * *

Claim That Grinnell Is the Dominant Competitor in Certain Lines of Commerce and in Certain Sections of the Country

The law is well settled that when a company which is the dominant competitor in a relatively oligopolistic market is acquired by a much larger company, such acquisition violates Section 7 of the Clayton Act if the acquired company gains marketing and promotional competitive advantages from the merger which will further entrench its position of dominance by raising barriers to entry to the relevant markets and by discouraging smaller competitors from aggressively competing. The effect of such a merger will be substantially to lessen competition. . . .

. . . [T]he Court holds that the evidence establishes that Grinnell is not the dominant com-petitor in any relevant product or geographic market.

[The Court's reasoning as to this claim is omitted.]

Access to ITT's Financial Resources and Advertising

The government further claims that Grinnell will gain a competitive marketing advantage through access to ITT's financial resources and comprehensive advertising program; more particularly, it is claimed that through ITT's finance companies Grinnell will be able to finance the purchase and leasing of sprinkler systems on a larger scale than it now does, and that through access to ITT's advertising expertise and experience Grinnell will be able to expand its advertising and sales promotion programs.

The question naturally arises, in light of this claim, whether Grinnell *needs* such financing and advertising help. The answer provided by the trial record in this case is unequivocally in the negative.

The evidence is uncontroverted that Grinnell already is in a position to offer credit and leasing arrangements to sprinkler customers without financing assistance from ITT and is capable itself of expanding such financing as broadly as is desirable commercially.

* * * * *

With respect to advertising, the Court finds that it simply is not a significant factor in the sprinkler industry. Witnesses from various sprinkler companies, including Grinnell, testified that advertising is unimportant in the award of sprinkler work; that it is not worthwhile; and, even if they were in a position to invest more in advertising, that they would not do so.

Grinnell has had an advertising budget of less than $100,000 for automatic sprinkler systems—far less than it could provide itself if in its business judgment it considered more advertising prudent. . . .

Reciprocal Dealing

The major marketing and promotional competitive advantage which the government claims Grin-nell will gain from the ITT-Grinnell merger is an enhancement of Grinnell's market position through reciprocal dealing caused by ITT's large purchasing power. More particularly, the government asserts that the merger will give rise to "reciprocity," referring to a seller's practice of utilizing the volume or potential volume of its purchases to induce others to buy its goods or services; and to "reciprocity effect," referring to the tendency of a company selling or desiring to sell to another company to channel its purchases to that company.

There are two essential factual requisites of the government's reciprocal dealing claim. First, whether the merger will create an opportunity for reciprocal dealing through a market structure conducive to such dealing. Second, whether such reciprocal dealing in fact is likely to occur, even if the merger were to create an opportunity for it. . . .

Indeed, the Court is persuaded by a preponderance of the evidence that reciprocity and reciprocity effect are not significant factors in the sprinkler installation industry. The government's witnesses, representing substantial experience in the sprinkler business, with few exceptions testified to no instances of actual or suspected reciprocity involving their companies or any other companies.

Most sprinkler work, for all classes of customers, is awarded on a competitive bidding basis, thus minimizing reciprocity and reciprocity effect potential. . . .

Turning from the sprinkler industry and from Grinnell, the Court now directs its attention to the other party to the merger, ITT, to ascertain whether the evidence demonstrates that reciprocal dealing in fact is likely to occur. There are several aspects of ITT's organization and practices which are directly relevant. First, ITT is organized into a series of "profit centers," each managed and staffed by personnel whose business careers, advancement, financial rewards and reputations depend upon the success of the specific profit center with which the men are identified, rather than upon the performance of ITT as a whole. These profit centers on occasion cooperate with one another, as unrelated companies would cooperate; but they do so only when it is in their mutual interest to do so. The management of one profit center has no motivation to tailor its purchasing decisions to facilitate the sales of another profit center.

*   *   *   *   *

Witnesses with extensive ITT experience testified that they never have encountered any instance of reciprocity or reciprocity effect. And the government has adduced no evidence that any ITT unit has ever obtained business as a result of reciprocity or reciprocity effect.

[T]he Court holds that the government has not sustained its burden of establishing that the merger will create an opportunity for reciprocal dealing. . . .

Claim of Economic Concentration

The new twist to the government's economic concentration claim is that in the wake of a "trend among large diversified industrial firms to acquire other large corporations", it can be established that "anticompetitive consequences will appear in numerous though *undesignated individual 'lines of commerce'*." (Emphasis added)

The Court's short answer to this claim . . . is that the legislative history, the statute itself and the controlling decisional law all make it clear beyond a peradventure of a doubt that in a Section 7 case the alleged anticompetitive effects of a merger must be examined in the context of *specific product and geographic markets;* and the determination of such markets is a necessary predicate to a determination of whether there has been a substantial lessening of competition within an area of effective competition. To ask the Court to rule with respect to alleged anticompetitive consequences in *undesignated lines of commerce* is tantamount to asking the Court to engage in judicial legislation. This the Court most emphatically refuses to do. . . .

Recognition of the trend toward economic concentration in American industry, including extensive conglomerate merger activity in recent years, is not exactly new. The government points out that the trend during the last two decades toward concentration of assets in the hands of fewer and larger corporate entities, together with an increasing diversification of those firms which primarily control the assets, has resulted in certain anticompetitive effects.

* * * * *

The legislative history of the 1950 amendments to Section 7 of the Clayton Act . . . reflects a concern on the part of Congress about the rising tide of economic concentration in American industry caused by all types of mergers, including conglomerate mergers. . . . But the legislative history also indicates that Section 7 as amended was not intended to proscribe all mergers which result in economic concentration.

* * * * *

Whatever may be the merits of the arguments as a matter of social and economic policy in favor of, or opposed to, a standard for measuring the legality of a merger under the antitrust laws by the degree to which it may increase economic concentration rather than by the degree to which it may lessen competition, that is beyond the competence of the Court to adjudicate. As the Court attempted to make clear in its preliminary injunction opinion if that standard is to be changed, it is fundamental under our system of government that any decision to change the standard be made by the Congress and not by the courts.

[Complaint dismissed.]

ITT Settlement

The government appealed the *ITT* district court decision directly to the Supreme Court, but before the case was heard, an agreement was reached. The story of that settlement is certainly one of the most detailed pictures we have of the formulation of government antitrust policy. Whether the somewhat dubious manipulations leading to the ITT settlement are typical of this domain seems doubtful, but certainly the ITT story is useful, even critical, in acquainting the student with the many influences that ultimately determine the outcome of a case. Under the terms of the settlement announced July 31, 1971, ITT was required:

1. To divest itself of the Canteen Corporation and the Fire Protection Division of Grinnell.
2. To divest itself of either Hartford Fire or Avis Rent-a-Car and three other ITT holdings.
3. To refrain for 10 years from acquisitions, without governmental approval, of certain specified categories of firms.
4. To refrain from the practice of reciprocity.

The settlement proved to be a disappointment to many. It provoked a rather surprising objection from the editorial voice of *Business Week:*

The sudden settlement last weekend of the government's package of antitrust cases against International Telephone & Telegraph Corp. is a singularly unsatisfying end to an important episode in government-business relations.

The ITT cases were promoted by the Nixon administration as an attempt to establish a clear judicial definition of the limits on corporate growth in a modern society. By suddenly agreeing to accept the settlement, the government antitrusters have thrown away the chance to do that. They have added another scalp to the Justice Department's belt, but they have not done anything to clarify the vague legal rules under which merger-minded corporations must operate.

Clarification not only of the law but of the economics of mergers is badly needed. Very little serious investigation of the implications of corporate bigness has been undertaken in this country either by the government or by students of business. It will take a major series of legal tests, ending in the Supreme Court, to prompt the rigorous analysis necessary to determine how big and how fast a company can grow without endangering the public interest.[8]

Jack Anderson Investigation   It was the manner of the settlement, rather than its merits, that generated government investigations and a considerable public outcry. The following column by journalist Jack Anderson raised the claim that political considerations determined the outcome of the *ITT* case:

We now have evidence that the settlement of the Nixon Administration's biggest antitrust case was privately arranged between Attorney General John Mitchell and the top lobbyist for the company involved.

We have this on the word of the lobbyist herself, crusty, capable Dita Beard of the International Telephone and Telegraph Co. She acknowledged the secret deal after we obtained a highly incriminating memo, written by her, from ITT's files.

The memo, which was intended to be destroyed after it was read, not only indicates that the antitrust case had been fixed but that the fix was a payoff for ITT's pledge of up to $400,000 for the upcoming Republican convention in San Diego.

Confronted with the memo, Mrs. Beard acknowledged its authenticity. . . .

The memo detailed a meeting between Mrs. Beard, Attorney General John Mitchell, and Republican Governor Louis Nunn at the governor's Kentucky mansion. Mrs. Beard indicated that Mitchell confided to her that he was sympathetic to ITT but had been prevented until then from helping the company because of the zeal of the Justice Department's antitrust chief, Richard McLaren.

After his harangue, Mrs. Beard said, Mitchell agreed to discuss the antitrust matters and asked bluntly, ''What do you want?'' meaning what companies did ITT most want to keep if the antitrust case were settled.

''We have to have Hartford Fire because of the economy,'' Mrs. Beard recalled saying. . . .

And, she said, when the Justice Department announced its settlement with ITT on July 31, more than two months later, it conformed to the agreement she had made with Mitchell. . . .

It [the memo] is addressed to W. R. (Bill) Merriam, head of ITT's Washington office. It is marked ''Personal and Confidential'' and its last line asks, ''Please destroy this, huh?''

The memo warns Merriam to keep quiet about the ITT cash pledge for the Republican convention. ''John Mitchell has certainly kept it on the higher level only,'' the memo says, ''we should be able to do the same. . . .

''I am convinced, because of several conversations with Louie (Governor Nunn) re Mitchell that our noble commitment has gone a long way toward our negotiations on the mergers coming out as Hal (ITT President Harold Geneen) wants them.

''Certainly the President has told Mitchell to see that things are worked out fairly. It is still only McLaren's mickey-mouse that we are suffering. . . .

''If (the convention commitment) gets too much publicity, you can believe our negotiations with Justice will wind up shot down. Mitchell is definitely helping us, but cannot let it be known.''[9]

ITT immediately denied that its convention contribution was in any way related to the case settlement. Additionally Ms. Beard later denied the accuracy of the Anderson column. However, the scandal continued to grow and eventually came under investigation by Watergate prosecutors Archibald Cox and Leon Jaworski. Jaworski found no evidence of criminal conduct on the part of ITT officials, but evidence of inaccurate testimony (Deputy Attorney General Richard Kleindienst pleaded guilty to a federal misdemeanor charge for making false or misleading sworn statements), unusually lazy memories, contradictory statements, and the like on the part of both public and ITT officials left a suspicion of impropriety, it is fair to say, in the minds of many. Regardless of the reasons for the settlement, it is important to note that the weight of opinion among many lawyers in a position to understand the case and its many implications seems to be that the government achieved an equitable result.

Undue Influence Beyond the convention contribution itself, the *ITT* case brought to light, probably more emphatically than ever before, the problem of undue special interest influence in the processes of government. Does the personal familiarity of business and government leaders and their ease of access to each other inevitably and perhaps innocently result in favored treatment for vested interests? The following letter from Edward Gerrity, ITT vice president for public relations, to his long-time friend, Vice President Spiro Agnew, reveals ITT's lobbying approach and offers a sense of the Nixon administration's view of the bigness is bad issue. (John refers to Attorney General John Mitchell. Hal refers to ITT president Harold Geneen.)

You will recall at our meeting on Tuesday, I told you of our efforts to try and settle the three antitrust suits that Mr. McLaren has brought. Before we met, Hal had a very friendly session with John, whom, as you know, he admires greatly and in whom he has the greatest confidence. John made plain to him that the President was not opposed to mergers per se, that he believed some mergers were good, and that in no case had we been sued because "bigness is bad." Hal discussed this in detail because McLaren had said and in his complaints indicated strongly that bigness is bad. John made plain that was not the case. Hal said on that basis he was certain we could work out something. John said he would talk with McLaren and get back to Hal.[10]

Taming the Bureaucracy Political payoffs and corporate influence have doubtless played some role in antitrust practice and policy, but a White House conversation between President Nixon, John Ehrlichman, and then director of the Office of Management and Budget, George Shultz, reveals yet another villain. Nixon felt that he did not have firm, direct control over the federal bureaucracy. In studying the law, we may profit from occasional reminders that greater reliance on the law is inevitably accompanied by an expanded bureaucracy with all its well-documented problems. Nixon speaks of imposing discipline upon the government.

President: You've got to do it. That is the trouble with McLaren. McLaren thinks he's going to do everything. To hell with him. I mean, we, we're willing to go along with it but he cannot deliberately just thumb his nose at everything that comes from this office, John. He is not that big, and of course, if John Mitchell won't stand up to him, I will. I don't want to, but I'll have to. We are not going to have it. All that they have to do in this case—I know what the procedure is—is that the Justice Department decides whether or not it's going to continue to fight the case. Isn't that what it is?

Ehrlichman: Right.

President: Then—well, God damn it, they lost the case before. Lose it. Lose it for once. They fought the good fight, and they lost. And, let the little bastards work on something else. Work on the study that you've asked them to send us. That would be very good.

Ehrlichman: That would be done here.

President: I'll say. You've got to get us some discipline, George. You've got to get it, and the only way you get it, is when a bureaucrat deliberately thumbs his nose, we're going to get him.[11]

Questions

1. Why is the government opposed to reciprocal dealing?
2. Make the argument that reciprocal buying arrangements do not harm competition.
3. Are you persuaded by the evidence and reasoning the Court offered to support the conclusion that the ITT merger is not threatening in terms of reciprocity? Explain.
4. Was the government wise in settling the *ITT* case out of court? Explain.
5. *Should* the government attack conglomerate mergers on the grounds that there is a "trend among large diversified industrial firms to acquire other large corporations" and that "anticompetitive consequences will appear in numerous though undesignated individual 'lines of commerce'". . .?

Joint Venture

Principal legislation: Clayton Act, section 7; Sherman Act, section 1.

A *joint venture* is a business organization established by two or more firms which pool their assets and skills for their mutual benefit. The Alaskan Pipeline was built under such an arrangement because of the enormous funds involved. A joint venture may be created by competitors, by those in a supplier-purchaser relationship, or by unrelated firms. The Supreme Court has held that section 7 of the Clayton Act applies to such arrangements even though they do not constitute mergers. Therefore, joint ventures should be analyzed in much the same manner as mergers. However, in November 1984 the Justice Department announced a new policy encouraging joint ventures as an alternative to mergers. Government antitrust chief J. Paul McGrath took the position that joint ventures will be vital to the growth and competitiveness of America in international markets. McGrath indicated that while joint ventures would be subject to much less stringent antitrust evaluation than mergers, the government would continue to challenge agreements restricting competition. Striking evidence of the new direction was the government's 1984 decision to permit General Motors and Toyota to build small cars jointly in Fremont, California. The approval by the Federal Trade Commission limits the information that the two firms may exchange and thus attempts to guard against unfair collusion.

Question

1. Sodium chlorate is used in the pulp and paper industry as a bleaching ingredient. The sodium chlorate market in the southeastern United States in the early 1960s was:

	Prior to 1961	1962
	(percent of sales)	(percent of sales)
Hooker	49.5	33.3
American P&C	41.6	23.4
Pennsalt	8.9	
Penn-Olin		27.6
PPG		15.6

Penn-Olin organized in 1960 as a joint venture of Olin and Pennsalt and built a production plant in Kentucky. Pennsalt was producing sodium chlorate in Portland, Oregon, and had sold in the Southeast only through its agent, Olin (Mathewson). Prior to the joint venture, Olin had manufactured other chemicals but had not produced sodium chlorate. Between 1950 and 1958, both Pennsalt and Olin had contemplated independent entry into the southeastern market. In 1958 the companies agreed that neither "should move in the chlorate or perchlorate field without keeping the other party informed." The joint venture arose from those negotiations. Pennsalt took care of production responsibilities, and Olin handled sales.

Is this an unlawful joint venture under Sherman § 1 or Clayton § 7? See *United States* v. *Penn-Olin Chemical Co*. 378 U.S. 158 (1964), on remand, 246 F. Supp. 917 (D. Del. 1965), aff'd per curium, 389 U.S. 308 (1967).

Is Bigness Bad?

The *ITT* case fails to answer the question that is, at least emotionally, at the heart of much antitrust analysis. Is bigness bad? The question calls for an assessment of one's economic and political philosophies. Can the free market operate effectively? Even if it can, are we satisfied with the resulting distribution of benefits? Is some government intervention necessary? If so, how do we know when enough is enough? Is market concentration a threat to political freedom? The article that follows raises and seeks to refute the various elements of the bigness is bad argument.[12] Regardless of one's personal sentiments, a defense of big business against further antitrust intervention seems a fair conclusion to these many pages of "trustbusting." Please note that the realignment of congressional power following the 1980 election saw Senator Kennedy remove himself from the Senate Judiciary Committee chaired by Senator Strom Thurmond (R.S.C.). Presumably, the legislation discussed here will languish at least until the next shift in congressional power.

"BIGNESS" BECOMES THE TARGET OF THE TRUSTBUSTERS

A. F. Ehrbar

A radical revision of the antitrust laws is taking shape. Traditionally, antitrust has been concerned with protecting competition; the trustbusters have sought to prevent restraints of trade and to bar mergers that would give rise to monopoly power. Now Senator Edward M. Kennedy is leading a movement to prohibit mergers on the basis of size alone. Bigness itself should be added to the roster of antitrust offenses, Kennedy says, because large corporations cause social problems even when they do not impair competition.

Kennedy, who is widely perceived as the most powerful individual in Congress, certainly has the strongest voice on antitrust matters: since January, he has been chairman of the Senate Judiciary Committee. He began his assault on bigness last year with a series of "fact-finding" hearings, and stepped it up this year with a bill that would put a halt to virtually all large acquisitions. . . .

Assaults on bigness in business are a constant feature of the Washington scene, of course. Yet there is something wonderfully ironic about the timing of this major new assault. It has been launched at a time when the intellectual case *for* bigness is stronger than ever. Over the last 10 years or so, a group of economists—most of them at the University of Chicago and the University of California at Los Angeles—has compiled evidence suggesting powerfully that big companies are vigorous competitors and play a major role in the dynamism and growth of the economy.

Seemingly oblivious to this evidence, the people leading the assault on bigness argue that economic concentration has had disastrous results. [Justice Department Antitrust chief, John] Shenefield notes with alarm that the share of manufacturing assets owned by the 200 largest companies rose from 46 percent in 1947 to 61 percent in 1972. He argues that the trend is bothersome because it means that fewer and fewer companies are making the decisions about what goods are produced and where factories are located.

Kennedy believes, furthermore, that large corporations make poor decisions about these matters. "Our experience as a people," says the senator, "is that independent businessmen are more likely to be responsive to needs of their employees, community, customers, and suppliers than hired managers of an absentee conglomerate."

Kennedy and the trustbusters are also concerned that the managers of giant companies are gaining an unhealthy measure of power over society. FTC Chairman Michael Pertschuk, explaining his worries during one of Kennedy's hearings last summer, warned: "Unrestrained conglomeration could conceivably result in . . . an enormous aggregation of economic, social, and political power in the hands of a small number of corporate leaders, responsible . . . only to themselves." . . .

Pertschuk has also fretted publicly about the "insensitivity" of conglomerates, whose absentee managers are oblivious to the needs of the communities in which their companies operate. He worries that "the increasing trend of conglomeration can limit individuals' opportunities to obtain self-fulfillment through their economic roles."

The proposed merger restrictions clearly would curb the rapacity of the conglomerates. Under Kennedy's plan, companies with $2.5 billion of sales or $2 billion of assets would be prohibited from merging with one another. Companies with $350 million of sales or $200 million of assets would have to prove that a merger would be pro-competitive or yield economies of scale or other efficiencies. Those restrictions would also apply to mergers between companies with more than $100 million of assets if their combined assets amounted to more than $1 billion.

Kennedy, who is not constrained by the FTC's truth-in-advertising rules, describes his plan as a modest one. According to his staff people, the merger limitations—except for the $1-billion-combination rule—would affect only *Fortune* 500 companies, and the absolute prohibition of mergers would apply only to the 100 or so largest. In fact, however, there are more than 200 corporations (excluding commercial banks and insurance companies) with $2.5 billion of revenues or $2 billion of assets. . . .

In practice, the rules would stifle nearly all large mergers or takeovers. The efficiency that most commonly results from takeovers is the replacement of inadequate managers. Given the prospect of libel suits if a takeover attempt failed, few businessmen eyeing a takeover would be eager to make the case that the target company was run by dunderheads. It could also be dangerous to argue that a merger would create efficiencies through vertical integration, or that a takeover would increase a target's competitive strength. These are the very arguments that the Antitrust Division and the FTC use to challenge conglomerate acquisitions now.

* * * * *

Both the hand wringing over concentration and the proffered remedies are strikingly reminiscent of numerous past efforts to curtail mergers and attack bigness. This time around, however, it appears that Congress might actually enact some form of size limits. For one thing, antitrust is one of the few "liberal" causes around that can be pushed without adding to federal spending. For another, the antimerger bill actually has some support from business. The major business lobbies oppose it, of course, but some zealous business critics of hostile takeovers think merger restrictions are a good idea.

* * * * *

The assertion that business is too big and powerful is nothing new, of course, and it is a case that has sometimes been made by conservatives. George Stigler, an uncommonly eloquent opponent of government intervention in the marketplace, argued in an article he wrote for *Fortune* in 1952 that the big companies in concentrated industries ought to be broken up.

Stigler then subscribed to the so-called structural theory, which holds that such companies behave monopolistically because they have more to gain from cooperation than from competition. Recently, however, most economists have rejected the structural theory. Stigler, along with Yale Brozen at Chicago, Harold Demsetz and J. Fred Weston at U.C.L.A., and others, reexamined the evidence and found that companies in concentrated industries do compete. Says Stigler: "I have great faith in the willingness of executives to double-cross one another."

Unfortunately, the antitrust authorities have chosen to reject the new evidence and cling instead to the belief that most large companies collude to fix prices. Most antitrust enforcers, as well as a lot of judges, have seen their mission as one of fostering the Jeffersonian ideal of a society composed of many small competitors. This mind-set has had a perverse effect on antitrust: laws that were intended to preserve competition and benefit the consumer have frequently been interpreted, in painful twists of economic logic, in ways to protect small businessmen from larger, more efficient rivals, to the clear *detriment* of the consumer.

There is no doubt that the Jeffersonian ideal is politically popular nowadays—certainly more popular than conglomerates are. Shenefield was surely right when he observed recently: "The indications I've seen—Gallup polls, polls in *U.S. News*—suggest there is a disquiet with expansions of government, large business, large labor." . . .

Though the crusade against mergers has a lot of political appeal, it does not stand up under close analysis. It is ignoring some important recent studies suggesting that conglomerate mergers—the principal target of the new assault on bigness—make economic sense.

Those who are leading the assault see an emerging American zaibatsu in those alarming concentration statistics. But the statistics are, to put it mildly, misleading. It is true, as Shenefield says, that the assets of the 200 largest manufacturers increased from 46 percent of total manufacturing assets in 1947 to 61 percent in 1972. However, those percentages have little to do with either the level or the trend of concentration.

The assets used in the numerator of that calculation are the total assets of the top 200 manufacturing companies, including their nonmanufacturing and foreign assets. RCA, for instance, owns Hertz, and all of its rental cars are included. ITT and Teledyne own insurance companies, Anheuser-Busch owns amusement parks, and the automakers have substantial overseas operations; all are counted. The denominator, however, includes only U.S. manufacturing assets. That increase in the percentage share of the 200 largest manufacturers since 1947 may reflect only the fact that manufacturers (of all sizes) have been increasing their foreign investments and nonmanufacturing diversification.

Other measures suggest a much lower level of concentration and little if any increase over the last thirty or forty years. These measures are more reliable because they include only domestic assets and output. Consider, for example, the share of nonfinancial assets held by the 50 or 200 largest nonfinancial companies. The shares have remained constant for the last twenty years, at 24 percent and 40 percent, respectively.

*   *   *   *   *

In the end, the case against mergers turns out to be a brief against big business in general. . . .

To many Americans, the control of several billion dollars of assets certainly looks like a form of power. But if managers are in fact constrained by the rigors of the marketplace, they are forced to exercise their power in precisely the ways that best serve society: to produce the goods that consumers want at the lowest cost possible. Moreover, they cannot afford to be insensitive—or overly sensitive—to the demands of their employees, suppliers, or communities. With the market mechanism operating smoothly, managers simply do not have the latitude to indulge their personal whims to any meaningful extent.

The critics of bigness believe, of course, that giant corporations are not constrained—

that their size insulates them from the marketplace. If any companies possess such power, it should be the ones that dominate large, concentrated industries. The structural theory holds that those companies do, in fact, have market power because their small numbers make it easy to collude. The result is that prices are higher and output lower than they would be if the companies competed aggressively. The structural theory used to draw strong support from studies showing that returns on investment are higher in concentrated industries. However, the work by Brozen, Demsetz, and others casts serious doubts on the old studies and leads to the conclusion that big companies are fierce, innovative competitors.

*   *   *   *   *

Studies have also been made of the hoary charge that big companies are engines of inflation because they have so much market power that they can "administer" their prices. Administered prices are said to feed inflation because managers accede to exorbitant wage demands, secure in the knowledge that they can pass the higher costs on to consumers. . . .

The notion that big companies stimulate inflation is surely false. It's true that these companies pay higher wages. Indeed, the top 50 companies pay their production workers a whopping 54 percent more than other manufacturers (a fact that suggests their workers might quibble with Pertschuk's views on self-fulfillment). But the higher wages apparently reflect the greater capital intensity, and higher levels of worker skill, at large companies.

*   *   *   *   *

It would appear that whatever power the managers of giant corporations possess is severely circumscribed by their need to match the efficiency of competitors. Brozen, summing up the new evidence on concentrated industries, comments: "The only real power that large firms have lies in their ability to produce goods at a price that attracts buyers, and at a low enough cost to offer wage rates and profits that are attractive to workers and investors. In essence, any member of the top 200 is there because it uses resources more productively.''

The brief against mergers concludes with the assumption that conglomerate acquisitions usually amount to nothing more than empire building. Hence, they can be prohibited at little or no cost to society. Says Pertschuk: "The strength of this proposal is that there is very little evidence that these acquisitions serve any economic purpose." Kennedy suggests that barring acquisitions might even help the economy because money that could pay for capital investment is merely being used to transfer ownership of existing assets. Kennedy's analysis relies on what might be called the mattress theory—that the owner of acquired companies stuff the proceeds under their mattresses instead of reinvesting them. By the same logic, it would make sense to proscribe dividends.

[T]here is impressive evidence that conglomerate acquisitions serve an important economic purpose: rescuing assets from inept managers. The evidence is contained in some studies that focus on the stock prices of acquirers and takeover targets. Peter Dodd and Richard Ruback, two University of Rochester graduate students, looked at the stock-market performance of companies making tender offers for five years before and after the offers. They found that the acquirers' stocks move up about 3 percent during the month of a successful offer; for the following five years, the stocks do as well as the market as a whole, adjusted for the companies' risk levels. Since acquirers pay large premiums over market value for the companies they buy, *something* must be going on other than empire building.

Otherwise, acquirers' stocks would drop when their managers paid out all that extra money.

* * * * *

It seems abundantly clear that the anti-merger forces have the facts backward. Restraining mergers would involve some very high costs without yielding any perceptible benefits. As Brozen puts it: "What the people who want to stop mergers are saying is that workers shouldn't have the chance to earn higher wages, and stockholders shouldn't be able to bail out of bad situations." What's more, the possibility of a takeover is an important reason for managers to refrain from indulging their whims. Insulating them from that threat would give rise to the power that the anti-merger forces say they fear.

Instead of pushing for a radical departure into costly and ill-conceived social engineering, Kennedy and the antitrust authorities ought to refocus on the task of protecting competition. Some businessmen do get together and fix prices, and the large companies in some concentrated industries probably do collude; those conspiracies need to be rooted out. In addition, new antitrust legislation is needed to dismantle the cartels that government regulation has created and nurtured in such industries as trucking and ocean shipping. Kennedy himself has been leading the deregulation movement in Congress. He would do well to concentrate on that effort and forget about mergers.

Source: *Fortune* March 26, 1979, pp. 34–40. Reprinted with permission of the copyright holder, *Fortune*. Written by A. F. Ehrbar. © 1979, Time, Inc. All rights reserved.

Chapter Questions

1. Is the influence of big business so persuasive that it nullifies the effective enforcement of the antitrust laws?

2. On the average, would firms pursuing expansion via an active merger policy be more or less profitable than those firms not involved in frequent acquisitions? See Linda Hayes, "Twenty-Five Years of Change in the Fortune 500," *Fortune,* May 5, 1980, p. 88.

3. Consolidated, a large food processor and distributor, acquired Gentry, a producer of dehy-

drated onion and garlic. Consolidated made substantial purchases from various food processors who, in turn, used dehydrated onion and garlic in preparing and packaging their foods. Prior to the merger, Gentry had 32 percent of its market while its chief competitor, Basic, held about 58 percent, with two other firms splitting the balance. Eight years after the merger, Gentry's share rose to 35 percent, while Basic's fell to 5 percent. Basic's products were considered, even by Gentry's president, to be superior to Gentry's products. The Federal Trade Commission challenged the merger as a violation of section 7 of the Clayton Act. See *Federal Trade Commission* v. *Consolidated Foods Corp.*, 380 U.S. 592 (1965).

    a.   What anticompetitive practice did the FTC allege?

    b.   Decide the case.

4.   The Justice Department has traditionally been reluctant to accept economies of scale as a defense to an otherwise unlawful merger. Why?

5.   How can a merger be beneficial to society?

6.   Which economic considerations support the view that unilateral growth is preferable to growth by merger?

7.   In 1968 Heublein, Inc. was America's 5th largest producer and 16th largest seller of wine. In 1969 Heublein acquired United Vintners, Inc., which as the producer of Italian Swiss Colony, Petri, and Inglenook, was the nation's second ranking wine seller. In 1979 an administrative law judge found the acquisition in violation of the Clayton Act, section 7, and the Federal Trade Commission Act, section 5. Heublein appealed to the full commission.

    Horizontal Theory. The commission concluded that the appropriate market was all wines, with Heublein having .79 percent of that market and United, 17.9 percent. The commission further found that the market was not highly concentrated nor was it moving in that direction. The four-firm concentration ratio was 47.9 percent, with the top two firms holding 41.9 percent of the wine market.

    Potential Competition. The commission found that Heublein had the capacity, interest, and economic incentive to expand and thus strengthen competition, but the commission also found 21 other firms similarly prepared to enter or expand. In addition, the commission noted that the wine market was rapidly expanding.

    Entrenchment. The administrative law judge found that the acquisition conferred three significant competitive benefits on United: (1) the ability to obtain desirable financing, (2) the ability to share in a large advertising budget, and (3) possible leverage from Heublein's Smirnoff vodka and other liquor products, but commission studies suggested that those advantages were unlikely to have a significant competitive effect.

    Decide the case. In re *Heublein, Inc.,* Dkt. No. 8904, FTC, October 7, 1980 [rel. October 15, 1980].

Notes

1. Reported in *Antitrust and Trade Regulation Report,* 42, no. 1048 (January 21, 1982), p. 154.
2. Reported in "Merger Deals Worth $123 billion in 1984," *Des Moines Register,* February 7, 1985, p. 7S.
3. Ibid.
4. Linda Snyder Hayes, "Twenty-Five Years of Change in the *Fortune* 500," *Fortune,* May 5, 1980, pp. 88, 94.
5. Richard Posner, *Antitrust Law* (Chicago: The University of Chicago Press, 1976), p. 130.
6. *United States* v. *Philadelphia Nat'l Bank,* 374 U.S. at 365 (1963) n. 42.
7. *U.S.* v. *Falstaff Brewing Corp.,* 410 U.S. 526 (1973).

8. *Business Week,* August 7, 1971, p. 84, quoted in S. Prakash Sethi, *Up Against the Corporate Wall,* 2d ed. (Englewood Cliffs, N.J.: Prentice-Hall, 1974), p. 61.

9. S. Prakash Sethi, *Up Against the Corporate Wall,* 3d ed. (Englewood Cliffs, N.J.: Prentice-Hall, 1977), pp. 86–87, citing Jack Anderson's nationally syndicated column "Washington Merry-Go-Round."

10. Robert M. Goolrich, *Public Policy toward Corporate Growth* (Port Washington, New York: Kennikat Press, 1978), p. 88, citing Gerrity's letter to Agnew.

11. Ibid., p. 124, citing a tape of a conversation in President Nixon's office.

12. For an argument in support of the "Bigness Is Bad" position, see Mark Green, "The Unmet Promises of Antitrust" *Antitrust Law Journal* 46 (1977), p. 752, as reprinted in *Industrial Concentration and the Market System,* ed., Eleanor Fox and James Halverson (1979 Section of Antitrust Law, American Bar Association), p. 5.

11

Antitrust Law—Restraints of Trade

Part One—Horizontal Restraints

Rule of Reason

It should not be surprising that the law casts a particularly unyielding eye upon horizontal restraints of trade. After all, cooperation among putative competitors nullifies much of the virtue of the market system. The various horizontal restraints are governed by section 1 of the Sherman Act, which, it will be recalled, forbids contracts, combinations, or conspiracies in restraint of trade. The statute was, of course, broadly drawn to embrace the many possibilities that arise in American commerce. Therefore, the courts were left to determine what Congress meant by the phrase *restraint of trade*. In the *Standard Oil*[1] decision of 1911, the United States Supreme Court articulated what has come to be known as the Rule of Reason. In essence the Court said that the Sherman Act forbids only *unreasonable* restraints of trade. Standard Oil was charged with controlling in 1904 approximately 90 percent of all the refined oil produced in the United States. It was accused of intentionally seeking that monopoly posture through the use of espionage, bribery, secret rebates, and other predatory practices. In ordering the dissolution of the company, the Court found that Standard Oil had abused its power and subverted commerce, thus *unreasonably* restraining trade. The Rule of Reason has remained a source of considerable controversy because it recognized the possibility of lawful restraints of trade and "good" as well as "bad" trusts. However, that 1911 interpretation, as applied to both sections 1 and 2, remains the law today.

Per Se Violations

Some antitrust violations are perceived to be so injurious to competition that their mere existence constitutes unlawful conduct. That is, the plaintiff must prove that the violation in question occurred, but he or she need not prove that the violation caused, or is likely to cause, harm. Such violations are simply unreasonable on their face. The per se rule has been applied by the courts to a number of offenses including, for example, horizontal price-fixing.

Horizontal Price-Fixing

Principal legislation: Sherman Act, section 1.

> Every contract, combination in the form of trust or otherwise, or conspiracy, in restraint of trade or commerce among the several States, or with foreign nations, is hereby declared to be illegal: . . .

A contract, combination, or conspiracy among competitors that dampens price competition is an unreasonable restraint of trade and is per se unlawful. We need not inquire into the reasonableness of the price, nor need we offer proof of its harmful effect. It is simply illegal. We must give attention to perhaps the major dilemma in price-fixing and all other Sherman 1 violations; that is, what measure of proof satisfies the requirement of a contract, combination, or conspiracy. We need not worry over the precise meaning of the three critical words. Rather a general showing of cooperative action must be offered. That action in concert may, of course, be proved by evidence of an explicit accord, but it may also be inferred from a collection of circumstantial evidence. Law professor Lawrence Sullivan offers this very useful summary:

> All considered, there is a wide range of possible ways to show conspiracy; anything logically indicative will likely be admissible and will warrant a jury making the damning inference. Thus, evidence of meetings or correspondence of memoranda or opportunities for communication may be admissible as foundation evidence of concerted agreement and, given such a foundation, acts of one or more conspirators consistent with the alleged conspiracy may be admitted against all. For example, evidence that a series of meetings among competitors occurred shortly before each change of price in the industry is enough to warrant the inference that price changes were agreed upon. Alternatively, evidence of the entire course of dealings by major firms in an industry, including various acts that seem explicable only on the assumption of concerted goals, may be used to establish a conspiracy.[2]

In an interesting variation on the general conspiracy theme, the Supreme Court in 1984 firmly rejected the "intra-enterprise conspiracy" doctrine in holding that a parent corporation and its wholly-owned subsidiary are incapable, as a matter of law, of conspiracy in violation of Sherman 1.[3]

The *NCAA* case that follows illustrates the Court's reasoning in a price-fixing situation. This case is unusual in that it represents one of those rare instances where horizontal price-fixing was analyzed under the rule of reason rather than the per se standard.

NATIONAL COLLEGIATE ATHLETIC ASSOCIATION PETITIONER V. BOARD OF REGENTS OF THE UNIVERSITY OF OKLAHOMA AND UNIVERSITY OF GEORGIA ATHLETIC ASSOCIATION
82 L.Ed. 2d 70, 104 S.Ct. _____ (1984)

Justice Stevens

The University of Oklahoma and the University of Georgia contend that the National Collegiate Athletic Association has unreasonably restrained trade in the televising of college football games.

After an extended trial, the District Court found that the NCAA had violated § 1 of the Sherman Act. . . . The Court of Appeals agreed that the statute had been violated but modified the remedy in some respects. . . . We granted certiorari . . . and now affirm.

I   The NCAA

Since its inception in 1905, the NCAA has played an important role in the regulation of amateur collegiate sports. It has adopted and promulgated playing rules, standards of amateurism, standards for academic eligibility, regulations concerning recruitment of athletes, and rules governing the size of athletic squads and coaching staffs. In some sports, such as baseball, swimming, basketball, wrestling and track, it has sponsored and conducted national tournaments. It has not done so in the sport of football, however. With the exception of football, the NCAA has not undertaken any regulation of the televising of athletic events.

The NCAA has approximately 850 voting members. The regular members are classified into separate divisions to reflect differences in size and scope of their athletic programs. Division I includes 276 colleges with major athletic programs; in this group only 187 play intercollegiate football. Divisions II and III include approximately 500 colleges with less extensive athletic programs. Division I has been subdivided into Divisions I–A and I–AA for football.

Some years ago, five major conferences together with major football-playing independent institutions organized the College Football Association (CFA). The original purpose of the CFA was to promote the interests of major football-playing schools within the NCAA structure. The Universities of Oklahoma and Georgia, respondents in this Court, are members of the CFA. . . .

The Current [Television] Plan

The plan adopted in 1981 for the 1982–1985 seasons is at issue in this case. This plan, like each of its predecessors, recites that it is intended to reduce, insofar as possible, the adverse effects of live television upon football game attendance. It provides that ''all forms of television of the football games of NCAA member institutions during the Plan control periods shall be in accordance with this Plan.'' . . .

The plan recites that the television committee has awarded rights to negotiate and contract for the telecasting of college football games of members of the NCAA to two ''carrying networks.''

* * * * *

The plan also contains ''appearance requirements'' and ''appearance limitations'' which pertain to each of the two-year periods that the plan is in effect. The basic requirement imposed on each of the two networks is that it must schedule appearances for at least 82 different member institutions during each two-year period. Under the appearance limitations no member institution is eligible to appear on television more than a total of six times and more than four times nationally, with the appearances to be divided equally between the two carrying networks. . . .

Thus, although the current plan is more elaborate than any of its predecessors, it retains the essential features of each of them. It limits the total amount of televised intercollegiate football and the number of games that any one team may televise. No member is permitted to make any sale of television rights except in accordance with the basic plan.

Background of this Controversy

Beginning in 1979 CFA members began to advocate that colleges with major football programs should have a greater voice in the formulation of football television policy than they had in the NCAA. CFA therefore investigated the possibility of negotiating a television agreement of its own, developed an independent plan, and obtained a contract offer from the National Broadcasting Co. (NBC). This contract, which it signed in August 1981, would have allowed a more liberal number of appearances for each institution, and would have increased the overall revenues realized by CFA members. . . .

In response the NCAA publicly announced that it would take disciplinary action against any CFA member that complied with the CFA-NBC contract. . . .

Decision of the District Court

After a full trial, the District Court held that the controls exercised by the NCAA over the televising of college football games violated the Sherman Act. The District Court defined the relevant market as "live college football television" because it found that alternative programming has a significantly different and lesser audience appeal. . . .The District Court then concluded that the NCAA controls over college football are those of a "classic cartel" with an

almost absolute control over the supply of college football which is made available to the networks, to television advertisers, and ultimately to the viewing public. Like all other cartels, NCAA members have sought and achieved a price for their product which is, in most instances, artificially high. The NCAA cartel imposes production limits on its members and maintains mechanisms for punishing cartel members who seek to stray from these production quotas. The cartel has established a uniform price for the products of each of the member producers, with no regard for the differing quality of these products or the consumer demand for these various products.

The District Court found that competition in the relevant market had been restrained in three ways: (1) NCAA fixed the price for particular telecasts; (2) its exclusive network contracts were tantamount to a group boycott of all other potential broadcasters and its threat of sanctions against its own members constituted a threatened boycott of potential competitors; and (3) its plan placed an artificial limit on the production of televised college football. . . .

In the District Court the NCAA offered two principal justifications for its television policies: that they protected the gate attendance of its members and that they tended to preserve a competitive balance among the football programs of the various schools. The District Court rejected the first justification because the evidence did not support the claim that college football television adversely affected gate attendance. With respect to the "competitive balance" argument, the District Court found that the evidence failed to show that the NCAA regulations on matters such as recruitment and the standards for preserving amateurism were not sufficient to maintain an appropriate balance. . . .

Decision of the Court of Appeals

The Court of Appeals held that the NCAA television plan constituted illegal per se price-fixing.

* * * * *

II

There can be no doubt that the challenged practices of the NCAA constitute a "restraint of trade" in the sense that they limit members' freedom to negotiate and enter into their own television contracts. In that sense, however, every contract is a restraint of trade, and as we have repeatedly recognized, the Sherman Act was intended to prohibit only unreasonable restraints of trade.

It is also undeniable that these practices share characteristics of restraints we have previously held unreasonable. The NCAA is an association of schools which compete against each other to attract television revenues, not to mention fans and athletes. As the District Court found, the policies of the NCAA with respect to television rights are ultimately controlled by the vote of member institutions. By participating in an association which prevents member institutions from competing against each other on the basis of price or kind of television rights that can be offered to broadcasters, the NCAA member institutions have created a horizontal restraint—an agreement among competitors on the way in which they will compete with one another. A restraint of this type has often been held to be unreasonable as a matter of law. Because it places a ceiling on the number of games member institutions may televise, the horizontal agreement places an artificial limit on the quantity of televised football that is available to broadcasters and consumers. By restraining the quantity of television rights available for sale, the challenged practices create a limitation on output; our cases have held that such limitations are unreasonable restraints of trade. Moreover, the District Court found that the minimum aggregate price in fact operates to preclude any price negotiation between broadcasters and institutions, thereby constituting horizontal price-fixing, perhaps the paradigm of an unreasonable restraint of trade.

Horizontal price-fixing and output limitation are ordinarily condemned as a matter of law under an "illegal per se" approach because the probability that these practices are anticompetitive is so high; a per se rule is applied when "the practice facially appears to be one that would always or almost always tend to restrict competition and decrease output." *Broadcast Music, Inc.* v. *CBS*, 441 U.S. 1, 19–20 (1979). In such circumstances a restraint is presumed unreasonable without inquiry into the particular market context in which it is found. Nevertheless, we have decided that it would be inappropriate to apply a per se rule to this case. This decision is not based on a lack of judicial experience with this type of arrangement, on the fact that the NCAA is organized as a nonprofit entity, or on our respect for the NCAA's historic role in the preservation and encouragement of intercollegiate amateur athletics. Rather, what is critical is that this case involves an industry in which horizontal restraints on competition are essential if the product is to be available at all.

As Judge Bork has noted: "[S]ome activities can only be carried out jointly. Perhaps the leading example is league sports. When a league of professional lacrosse teams is formed, it would be pointless to declare their cooperation illegal on the ground that there are no other professional lacrosse teams." . . . What the NCAA and its member institutions market in this case is competition itself—contests between competing institutions. Of course, this would be completely ineffective if there were no rules on which the competitors agreed to create and define the competition to be marketed. A myriad of rules affecting such matters as the size of the field, the number of players on a team, and the extent to which physical violence is to be encouraged or proscribed, all must be agreed upon, and all restrain the manner in which institutions compete. . . . Thus, the NCAA plays a vital role in enabling college football to preserve its character, and as a result enables a product to be marketed which might otherwise be unavailable. In performing this role, its actions widen consumer choice—not only the choices available to sports fans but also those available to athletes—and hence can be viewed as procompetitive.

III

Because it restrains price and output, the NCAA's television plan has a significant potential for anticompetitive effects. The findings of the District Court indicate that this potential has been realized. The District Court found that if member institutions were free to sell television rights, many more games would be shown on television, and that the NCAA's output restriction has the effect of raising the price the networks pay for television rights. Moreover, the court found that by fixing a price for television rights to all games, the NCAA creates a price structure that is unresponsive to viewer demand and unrelated to the prices that would prevail in a competitive market. And, of course, since as a practical matter all member institutions need NCAA approval, members have no real choice but to adhere to the NCAA's television controls.

* * * * *

Petitioner argues, however, that its television plan can have no significant anticompetitive effect since the record indicates that it has no market power—no ability to alter the interaction of supply and demand in the market. We must reject this argument for two reasons, one legal, one factual.

As a matter of law, the absence of proof of market power does not justify a naked restriction on price or output. To the contrary, when there is an agreement not to compete in terms of price or output, ''no elaborate industry analysis is required to demonstrate the anticompetitive character of such an agreement.'' . . .

As a factual matter, it is evident that petitioner does possess market power. The District Court employed the correct test for determining whether college football broadcasts constitute a separate market—whether there are other products that are reasonably substitutable for televised NCAA football games. . . . It found that intercollegiate football telecasts generate an audience uniquely attractive to advertisers and that competitors are unable to offer programming that can attract a similar audience. These findings amply support its conclusion that the NCAA possesses market power. . . .

IV

Relying on *Broadcast Music,* petitioner argues that its television plan constitutes a cooperative ''joint venture'' which assists in the marketing of broadcast rights and hence is procompetitive.
. . .

The District Court did not find that the NCAA's television plan produced any procompetitive efficiencies which enhanced the competitiveness of college football television rights; to the contrary it concluded that NCAA football could be marketed just as effectively without the television plan. There is therefore no predicate in the findings for petitioner's efficiency justification. Indeed, petitioner's argument is refuted by the District Court's finding concerning price and output. If the NCAA's television plan produced procompetitive efficiencies, the plan would increase output and reduce the price of televised games. The District Court's contrary findings accordingly undermine petitioner's position. . . .

V

Throughout the history of its regulation of intercollegiate football telecasts, the NCAA has indicated its concern with protecting live attendance.

* * * * *

There is, however, a . . . fundamental reason for rejecting this defense. The NCAA's argument that its television plan is necessary to protect live attendance is not based on a desire to maintain the integrity of college football as a distinct and attractive product, but rather on a fear that the product will not prove sufficiently attractive to draw live attendance when faced with competition from televised games. At bottom the NCAA's position is that ticket sales for most college games are unable to compete in a free market. The television plan protects ticket sales by limiting output—just as any monopolist increases revenues by reducing output.

VI

Petitioner argues that the interest in maintaining a competitive balance among amateur athletic teams is legitimate and important and that it justifies the regulations challenged in this case. We agree with the first part of the argument but not the second.

* * * * *

The NCAA does not claim that its television plan has equalized or is intended to equalize competition within any one league. The plan is nationwide in scope and there is no single league or tournament in which all college football teams compete. . . .

The television plan is not even arguably tailored to serve such an interest. It does not regulate the amount of money that any college may spend on its football program, nor the way in which the colleges may use the revenues that are generated by their football programs, whether derived from the sale of television rights, the sale of tickets, or the sale of concessions or program advertising. The plan simply imposes a restriction on one source of revenue that is more important to some colleges than to others. There is no evidence that this restriction produces any greater measure of equality throughout the NCAA than would a restriction on alumni donations, tuition rates, or any other revenue producing activity. At the same time, as the District Court found, the NCAA imposes a variety of other restrictions designed to preserve amateurism which are much better tailored to the goal of competitive balance than is the television plan, and which are "clearly sufficient" to preserve competitive balance to the extent it is within the NCAA's power to do so.

Affirmed.

Questions

1. Why was the NCAA's challenged television arrangement analyzed under the Rule of Reason rather than the per se rule?
2. What defenses were offered by the NCAA?
3. Does the *NCAA* ruling mean that colleges and universities may not lawfully join together in groups to arrange mutually agreeable television football packages? Explain.
4. Describe some of the likely effects of the *NCAA* decision on the television football market and upon the schools involved.
5. Assume two drugstores, located across the street from each other and each involved in interstate commerce, agree to exchange, on a monthly basis, a list of prices charged for all nonprescription medications. Is that arrangement lawful in the absence of any further cooperation?
6. As common sense and the cases reveal, sharing of price information among competitors can facilitate anticompetitive collusion, but how may that sharing facilitate competition?
7. Justify the use of per se rulings.
8. The gasoline dealers association in a community reaches an agreement providing: (1) both major brands and independents will not give trading stamps or other premiums; (2) majors agree not to advertise their prices except on the pumps.
   a. What is the purpose of the arrangement?
   b. What violation of law might be alleged? Decide the case. See *U.S.* v. *Gasoline Retailers Association,* 285 F.2d 688 (1961).
9. Assume 10 real estate firms operate in the city of Gotham. Further assume that each charges a 7 percent commission on all residential sales.
   a. Does that uniformity of prices in and of itself constitute price-fixing? Explain.
   b. Assume we have evidence that the firms agreed to set the 7 percent level. What defense would be raised against a price-fixing charge?
   c. Would that defense succeed? See *McLain* v. *Real Estate Board of New Orleans, Inc.,* 444 U.S. 232 (1980).
10. Assume the bar owners in a college community are concerned about serving liquor to patrons younger than the legal drinking age (18 in this case). The owners reach an agreement to reject admission to anyone under 19 years of age. Is that agreement lawful?

Price-Fixing in Practice

Regrettably, the evidence suggests that price-fixing remains a not unusual commercial practice. For example, in recent years the Justice Department has vigorously pursued the problem of bid-rigging in the highway construction business. From 1979 to 1982, the Justice Department initiated 230 criminal prosecutions involving 208 corporations and 221 individuals in 15 states. The conviction rate was about 90 percent, with 154 companies and 167 individuals actually pleading guilty. The result is savings of at least $750 million annually based on a General Accounting Office estimate that bid-rigging inflates contract prices by about 10 percent. The following article provides a detailed picture of an alleged price-fixing conspiracy of vast dimensions in the oil industry.[4]

GETTING TOGETHER

Brooks Jackson and Andy Pasztor

Los Angeles—Regular exchanges of price information and sensitive marketing data were a way of life in the oil business from the late 1950s into the early 1970s, according to a mass of once-secret industry documents.

The federal court records from antitrust cases, made public after a 2½-year legal fight for access by this newspaper, depict major oil companies working in concert to prop up retail prices of gasoline in several states at the expense of consumers and cut-rate independent marketers; the records also show the companies cooperating to preserve the bargain prices they were paying for supplies of heavy crude oil in California.

While the defendant companies deny violating any laws, the documents portray an industry so clubby and inbred that executives considered it bad manners to compete too aggressively with each other on price. The court record is filled with instances of major oil concerns working together to crack down on "bad actors" or "maverick" service-station operators who tried to underprice them.

"The industry operated . . . as a single fraternal organization," California's attorney general asserted in one legal brief. He said "the exchange of information within the petroleum industry was so pervasive, regular and commonplace" that it resembled "a single company. . . ."

Barter System

The records show, for example:

● Representatives of major oil companies met repeatedly during 1961 and 1962 to work out a system for swapping California crude oil among themselves without assigning cash prices. According to the plaintiffs, the system was central to the ability of the oil companies to maintain artificially low prices they paid for California crude. A federal judge now says he sees troubling evidence that this barter system was part of a price-fixing conspiracy.

● Major oil companies regularly made "courtesy calls" to their competitors when changing the prices they were willing to pay for crude-oil supplies. One official of Chevron Corp., then known as Standard Oil Co. of California, testified that he felt "ambushed" when Mobil Corp. failed to give the customary notice of a price change.

● High-level company managers routinely used a legal loophole to hold private meetings and swap internal pricing information and strategies to try to "stabilize" the volatile gasoline market in California and elsewhere until the U.S. Supreme Court outlawed such direct communication in 1969.

● A series of confidential memos among Chevron marketing officials in 1970 discussed ways to get an independent Florida retailer to raise prices. "Unless something is done to get this particular outlet to go up with their prices," one of the memos asserted, "we are never going to be able to maintain a normal price."

It may be years before a federal judge rules whether the oil companies broke any laws. But the plaintiffs say it is clear that these industry-wide practices cost consumers and independent California oil producers, including the state and the city of Long Beach, hundreds of millions of dollars over a period of many years.

It isn't clear from the just-released records in the 10-year-old antitrust cases whether the practices still occur in today's oil industry. Few of the documents deal specifically with events after the 1973 Arab oil embargo. That event brought radical changes to the oil industry and spawned a bevy of state and local government lawsuits that have been consolidated in the U.S. district court here for pretrial proceedings.

Theodore Wellman, a Chevron marketing official and head of its "industry contact group" in the late 1950s and much of the 1960s, testified he met regularly with his counterparts from the other major oil concerns. Meeting in restaurants and hotel rooms, they discussed future pricing moves and arranged an approach to gasoline pricing that would "contribute something toward a steadier market," he said. At one such meeting in 1959, Mr. Wellman held a special briefing for his major competitors at the California Club in Los Angeles—complete with graphs and charts—to make sure they were aware of overall industry trends showing increased demand for jet fuel and reduced sales of heating oil.

Contacting Competitors

Members of Mr. Wellman's group at Chevron didn't keep written records of their contacts with competitors, according to depositions. They eventually set up a system that allowed officials of other companies to contact them by telephone without having to directly dial their offices and leave a printed record of the encounter.

Plaintiffs quote in their briefs an Exxon official describing a call from Agnar Nerheim, one of Chevron's top pricing strategists on the West Coast in the late 1960s. Mr. Nerheim "asked me whether I was familiar with the system of getting in touch with him on pricing problems," the executive is quoted as saying. Mr. Nerheim then "outlined a system where any time I had a problem or he had a problem . . . I could get in touch with him and nobody would ever know about it." The executive insisted he never used the system.

*   *   *   *   *

One Southern California independent gasoline retailer testified under oath that periodic, industrywide price increases continued to be carefully orchestrated in the early 1970s. Every few weeks he received telephone calls from his supplier indicating that "the boys are going to be at" a specific price within a few hours—a message he understood to refer to competing independents and retailers for major oil concerns. Independents who refused to go along faced the cutoff of gasoline supplies, he testified.

*   *   *   *   *

And the old chumminess died slowly. When Mr. Nerheim retired in January 1973, he introduced his successor, Art Feiler, to some of the pricing officials of Chevron's competitors. When attorneys for the plaintiffs asked in a deposition why that was necessary, he replied: "So that after I'm gone they would know that somebody else was there." Mr. Feiler testified he invited competitors to find out where he could look at publicly posted prices.

*   *   *   *   *

Price Swings

One result of such intense intelligence gathering was a pattern of sharp, upward swings of gasoline prices in Florida, California and other states a handful of times each year, the plaintiffs contend in their suits. In some cases, more than a dozen major companies made nearly identical pricing moves that prompted retail prices to go up by as much as 40 percent at most branded and independent stations across entire regions of the United States, the suits allege. And the entire cycle could be completed in less than a week.

But the defendant oil companies in the gas-oline-overcharge cases note that despite the enormous amount of material turned over in the litigation, the plaintiffs haven't been able to document "any direct proof of conspiratorial agreements or understandings." . . .

Source: *The Wall Street Journal,* December 17, 1984, p. 1. Reprinted by permission of *The Wall Street Journal.* © Dow Jones & Company, Inc., 1984.

Horizontal Division of Markets

Principal legislation: Sherman Act, section 1.

The issue here is whether competitors can lawfully agree (1) to divide their market geographically and/or (2) to allocate customers among themselves. In simplest terms, could Company X lawfully agree to sell only on the east side of the Mississippi River if Company Y (X's competitor) agrees to sell only on the west side? Why would they wish to do so? Under what conditions might such an arrangement enhance competition? Similarly could Manufacturers X and Y lawfully agree to sell only to retailers rather than to wholesalers? The *Topco* case that follows answers these questions.

UNITED STATES V. TOPCO ASSOCIATES, INC.   405 U.S. 596 (1972)

Justice Marshall

I

Topco is a cooperative association of approximately 25 small and medium-sized regional super-market chains that operate stores in some 33 states. Each of the member chains operates independently; there is no pooling of earnings, profits, capital, management, or advertising resources. No grocery business is conducted under the Topco name. Its basic function is to serve as a purchasing agent for its members. In this capacity, it procures and distributes to the members more than 1,000 different food and related nonfood items, most of which are distributed under brand names owned by Topco. The association does not itself own any manufacturing, processing, or ware-housing facilities, and the items that it procures for members are usually shipped directly from the packer or manufacturer to the members. Payment is made either to Topco or directly to the manufacturer at a cost that is virtually the same for the members as for Topco itself. . . .

Topco was founded in the 1940s by a group of small, local grocery chains, independently owned and operated, that desired to cooperate to obtain high quality merchandise under private labels in order to compete more effectively with larger national and regional chains. . . . By 1964, Topco's members had combined retail sales of more than $2 billion; by 1967, their sales totaled more than $2.3 billion, a figure exceeded by only three national grocery chains.

Members of the association vary in the degree of market share that they possess in their respective areas. The range is from 1.5 percent to 16 percent, with the average being approxi-mately 6 percent. While it is difficult to compare these figures with the market shares of larger regional and national chains because of the absence in the record of accurate statistics for these chains, there is much evidence in the record that Topco members are frequently in as strong a competitive position in their respective areas as any other chain. The strength of this competitive position is due, in some measure, to the success of Topco-brand products. Although only 10 percent of the total goods sold by Topco members bear the association's brand names, the profit on these goods is substantial and their very existence has improved the competitive potential of Topco members with respect to other large and powerful chains.

II

. . . The United States charged that, beginning at least as early as 1960 and continuing up to the time that the complaint was filed, Topco had combined and conspired with its members to violate § 1 . . . in two respects. First, the government alleged that there existed:

a continuing agreement, understanding and concert of action among the co-conspirator member firms acting through Topco, the substantial terms of which have been and are that each co-conspirator member firm will sell Topco-controlled brands only within the marketing territory allocated to it, and will refrain from selling Topco-controlled brands outside such marketing territory.

Following approval, each new member signs an agreement with Topco designating the territory in which that member may sell Topco-brand products. No member may sell these products outside the territory in which it is licensed. Most licenses are exclusive, and even those denominated "coextensive" or "non-exclusive" prove to be *de facto* exclusive. . . . When combined with each member's veto power over new members, provisions for exclusivity work effectively to insulate members from competition in Topco-brand goods. Should a member violate its license agreement and sell in areas other than those in which it is licensed, its membership can be terminated. . . .

From the inception of this lawsuit, Topco accepted as true most of the government's allegations regarding territorial divisions and restrictions on wholesaling, although it differed greatly with the government on the conclusions, both factual and legal, to be drawn from these facts. . . .

Topco essentially maintains that it needs territorial divisions to compete with larger chains; that the association could not exist if the territorial divisions were anything but exclusive; and that by restricting competition in the sale of Topco-brand goods, the association actually increases competition by enabling its members to compete successfully with larger regional and national chains.

*   *   *   *   *

While the Court has utilized the "rule of reason" in evaluating the legality of most restraints alleged to be violative of the Sherman Act, it has also developed the doctrine that certain business relationships are per se violations of the act without regard to a consideration of their reasonableness. . . .

. . . One of the classic examples of a per se violation of § 1 is an agreement between competitors at the same level of the market structure to allocate territories in order to minimize competition. Such concerted action is usually termed a "horizontal" restraint, in contradistinction to combinations of persons at different levels of the market structure, e.g., manufacturers and distributors, which are termed "vertical" restraints. This Court has reiterated time and time again that "[h]orizontal territorial limitations . . . are naked restraints of trade with no purpose except stifling of competition." . . .

Such limitations are per se violations of the Sherman Act. . . .

*   *   *   *   *

In applying these rigid rules, the Court has consistently rejected the notion that naked restraints of trade are to be tolerated because they are well intended or because they are allegedly developed to increase competition.

* * * * *

The District Court determined that by limiting the freedom of its individual members to compete with each other, Topco was doing a greater good by fostering competition between members and other large supermarket chains. But, the fallacy in this is that Topco has no authority under the Sherman Act to determine the respective values of competition in various sectors of the economy. On the contrary, the Sherman Act gives to each Topco member and to each prospective member the right to ascertain for itself whether or not competition with other supermarket chains is more desirable than competition in the sale of Topco-brand products. . . .

There have been tremendous departures from the notion of a free-enterprise system as it was originally conceived in this country. These departures have been the product of congressional action and the will of the people. If a decision is to be made to sacrifice competition in one portion of the economy for greater competition in another portion, this too is a decision that must be made by Congress and not by private forces or by the courts. Private forces are too keenly aware of their own interests in making such decisions and courts are ill-equipped and ill-situated for such decision-making. To analyze, interpret, and evaluate the myriad of competing interests and the endless data that would surely be brought to bear on such decisions, and to make the delicate judgment on the relative values to society of competitive areas of the economy, the judgment of the elected representatives of the people is required.

* * * * *

We reverse the judgment of the District Court and remand the case. . . .

Chief Justice Burger, dissenting.

This case does not involve restraints on interbrand competition or an allocation of markets by an association with monopoly or near-monopoly control of the sources of supply of one or more varieties of staple goods. Rather, we have here an agreement among several small grocery chains to join in a cooperative endeavor that, in my view, has an unquestionably lawful principal purpose; in pursuit of that purpose they have mutually agreed to certain minimal ancillary restraints that are fully reasonable in view of the principal purpose and that have never before today been held by this Court to be per se violations of the Sherman Act.

In joining in this cooperative endeavor, these small chains did not agree to the restraints here at issue in order to make it possible for them to exploit an already established line of products through noncompetitive pricing. There was no such thing as a Topco line of products until this cooperative was formed. The restraints to which the cooperative's members have agreed deal only with the marketing of the products in the Topco line, and the only function of those restraints is to permit each member chain to establish, within its own geographical area and through its own local advertising and marketing efforts, a local consumer awareness of the trademarked family of products as that member's ''private-label'' line. The goal sought was the enhancement of the individual members' abilities to compete, albeit to a modest degree, with the large national chains which had been successfully marketing private-label lines for several years. The sole reason for a cooperative endeavor was to make economically feasible such things as quality control, large quantity purchases at bulk prices, the development of attractively printed labels, and the ability to offer a number of different lines of trademarked products. All these things, of course, are feasible for the large national chains operating individually, but they are beyond the reach of the small operators proceeding alone.

After a careful review of the economic considerations bearing upon this case, the District Court determined that "the relief which the government here seeks would not increase competition in Topco private label brands"; on the contrary, such relief "would substantially diminish competition in the supermarket field." . . . This Court has not today determined, on the basis of an examination of the underlying economic realities, that the District Court's conclusions are incorrect. . . .

Questions

1. In *Topco* how does the defendant association seek to justify its division of the market? How do you evaluate that defense?

2. In exchange for royalties, Sealy allocated mutually exclusive sales territories among the various firms that it licensed to construct and sell mattresses bearing the Sealy label. Sealy's agreement with each licensee provided that Sealy would not license others to manufacture or sell in the designated area, and the licensee agreed not to manufacture or sell Sealy products outside its designated area. Sealy's licensees numbered approximately 30. Those licensees owned substantially all of Sealy's stock. Sealy's business was managed by its board of directors. Each director had to be a stockholder or his nominee. Sealy contended that its primary purpose in its licensing arrangement was to exploit the Sealy name and trademark. The government filed suit against Sealy alleging price-fixing and horizontal territorial limitations. At the trial level, Sealy was found guilty of price-fixing but innocent as to territorial restraint. The government appealed the latter while Sealy chose not to contest the former.

   Defend Sealy. Decide the case. See *United States* v. *Sealy, Incorporated,* 388 U.S. 350 (1967).

3. In analyzing horizontal territorial restraints, Professor Wesley Liebeler argues:

   > But it does not appear that collusion between dealers who handle the product of only one manufacturer—White truck dealers, Chevrolet dealers, or Sylvania television dealers, for example—will result in higher prices and restricted output.[5]

   What economic logic supports his position?

Refusals to Deal

Principal legislation: Sherman Act, section 1.

A *group boycott* is yet another instance of concerted action in which a collectivity of traders jointly refuses to deal with another trader or traders. Typically, the purpose of such an arrangement is to remove or "police" a competitor, but whatever the purpose, group boycotts are ordinarily treated as per se violations. What boycott might logically arise from the facts diagrammed here?

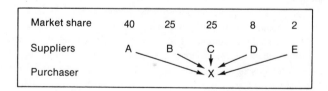

The case that follows reveals both the utility of a boycott to a group of traders and its potential harm to the market.

KLOR'S, INC. V. BROADWAY–HALE STORES, INC.   359 U.S. 207 (1959)

Justice Black

Klor's Inc. operates a retail store on Mission Street, San Francisco, California; Broadway-Hale Stores, Inc., a chain of department stores, operates one of its stores next door. The two stores compete in the sale of radios, television sets, refrigerators, and other household appliances. Claiming that Broadway-Hale and 10 national manufacturers and their distributors have conspired to restrain and monopolize commerce in violation of § § 1 and 2 of the Sherman Act, Klor's brought this action for treble damages and injunction in the United States District Court.

In support of its claim Klor's made the following allegations: George Klor started an appliance store some years before 1952 and has operated it ever since either individually or as Klor's, Inc. Klor's is as well equipped as Broadway-Hale to handle all brands of appliances. Nevertheless, manufacturers and distributors of such well-known brands as General Electric, RCA, Admiral, Zenith, Emerson, and others have conspired among themselves and with Broadway-Hale either not to sell to Klor's or to sell to it only at discriminatory prices and highly unfavorable terms. Broadway-Hale has used its "monopolistic" buying power to bring about this situation. . . .

The defendants did not dispute these allegations, but sought summary judgment and dismissal of the complaint for failure to state a cause of action. They submitted unchallenged affidavits which showed that there were hundreds of other household appliance retailers, some within a few blocks of Klor's, who sold many competing brands of appliances, including those the defendants refused to sell to Klor's. From the allegations of the complaint, and from the affidavits supporting the motion for summary judgment, the District Court concluded that the controversy was a "purely private quarrel" between Klor's and Broadway-Hale, which did not amount to a "public wrong proscribed by the [Sherman] Act." On this ground the complaint was dismissed and summary judgment was entered for the defendants. The Court of Appeals for the Ninth Circuit affirmed the summary judgment. . . . It stated that "a violation of the Sherman Act requires conduct of defendants by which the public is or conceivably may be ultimately injured." . . . It held that here the required public injury was missing since "there was no charge or proof that by any act of defendants the price, quantity, or quality offered the public was affected, nor that there was any intent or purpose to effect a change in, or an influence on, prices, quantity, or quality." . . . The holding, if correct, means that unless the opportunities for customers to buy in a competitive market are reduced, a group of powerful businessmen may act in concert to deprive a single merchant, like Klor, of the goods he needs to compete effectively. We granted certiorari to consider this important question in the administration of the Sherman Act.

*   *   *   *   *

Group boycotts, or concerted refusals by traders to deal with other traders, have long been held to be in the forbidden category. They have not been saved by allegations that they were reasonable in the specific circumstances, nor by a failure to show that they "fixed or regulated prices, parcelled out or limited production, or brought about a deterioration in quality." Even when they operated to lower prices or temporarily to stimulate competition they were banned.

For, as this Court said, "Such agreements, no less than those to fix minimum prices, cripple the freedom of traders and thereby restrain their ability to sell in accordance with their own judgment."

Plainly the allegations of this complaint disclose such a boycott. This is not a case of a single trader refusing to deal with another, nor even of a manufacturer and a dealer agreeing to an exclusive distributorship. Alleged in this complaint is a wide combination consisting of manufacturers, distributors and a retailer. This combination takes from Klor's its freedom to buy appliances in an open competitive market and drives it out of business as a dealer in the defendants' products. It deprives the manufacturers and distributors of their freedom to sell to Klor's at the same prices and conditions made available to Broadway-Hale and in some instances forbids them from selling to it on any terms whatsoever. It interferes with the natural flow of interstate commerce. It clearly has, by its "nature" and "character," a "monopolistic tendency." As such it is not to be tolerated merely because the victim is just one merchant whose business is so small that his destruction makes little difference to the economy. Monopoly can as surely thrive by the elimination of such small businessmen, one at a time, as it can by driving them out in large groups. In recognition of this fact the Sherman Act has consistently been read to forbid all contracts and combinations "which 'tend to create a monopoly,' " whether "the tendency is a creeping one" or "one that proceeds at full gallop." . . .

The judgment of the Court of Appeals is reversed and the cause is remanded to the District Court for trial.

Unilateral Refusals to Deal

While *Klor's* clearly involved group action, it should be understood that completely unilateral refusals to deal have been found unlawful where the refusal to deal serves to further an unlawful arrangement such as tying, price-fixing, or market allocation. Further, any refusal to deal, which is entered for predatory purposes (e.g., to drive a party out of business) rather than as a normal business judgment, would be suspect.

Questions

1. Why was the government concerned about harm to Klor's when hundreds of competitors remained to amply serve the public's need?
2. Boycotts often serve what might generally be regarded as "good" purposes. Give some examples of those boycotts. As a matter of law, are "good" boycotts treated differently than anticompetitive boycotts? Explain.
3. In 1977 the board of directors of the National Organization for Women (NOW) approved the use of economic boycotts, where appropriate, as a means of securing passage of the Equal Rights Amendment to the Constitution. NOW was successful in discouraging other organizations (e.g., the American Association of University Women), from holding meetings or conventions in states where the ERA had not been adopted. Was NOW's boycott program unlawful? Explain. See *Missouri* v. *National Organization for Women*, 620 F.2d 1301 (8th Cir. 1980), Cert. den. No. 79–2037, October 6, 1980.

4. Each year the member teams of the National Football League conduct a draft of college seniors. The draft is conducted in inverse order of the teams' records in the previous season. By giving the weaker teams the earlier choices the hope is that the competitive balance of the League will be enhanced. Yazoo Smith was drafted by the Washington Redskins, and under the League rules he was compelled to sign with them if he wanted to play in the NFL that season. He did so, but he was injured in preseason play. The injury ended his career. He brought an antitrust action to recover his economic losses.
   a. What violation did he allege?
   b. Is it a per se violation? Explain.
   c. Decide the case. *Smith* v. *Pro Football, Inc.,* 593 F.2d 1173 (D.C. Cir. 1978).

5. Jane Blalock, a member of the Ladies Professional Golf Association, was accused of cheating by moving her ball without permission and without recording an additional stroke. The LPGA Executive Committee voted to suspend Ms. Blalock from play for one year. Ms. Blalock filed suit to contest the suspension. Decision? *Blalock* v. *Ladies Professional Golf Ass'n,* 359 F. Supp. 1260 (N.D. Ga. 1973).

Conscious Parallelism

Principal legislation: Sherman Act, section 1.

The foregoing cases make clear the general impermissibility of concerted action among competitors, but can we infer a conspiracy from evidence that competitors have operated in the same manner? That is, will the consciously parallel behavior of competitors suffice, in and of itself, to establish a claim of unlawful concerted action? Or must the evidence show that the competitors were, in fact, a group acting together rather than individual enterprises that happened to be conducting themselves in a very similar manner? *Theatre Enterprises* helps in answering these difficult questions.

THEATRE ENTERPRISES V. PARAMOUNT   346 U.S. 537 (1954)

Justice Clark

Petitioner brought this suit for treble damages and an injunction under §§ 4 and 16 of the Clayton Act, alleging that respondent motion picture producers and distributors had violated the antitrust laws by conspiring to restrict "first-run" pictures to downtown Baltimore theatres, thus confining its suburban theatre to subsequent runs and unreasonable "clearances." After hearing the evidence a jury returned a general verdict for respondents. The Court of Appeals for the Fourth Circuit affirmed the judgment based on the verdict. We granted certiorari.

. . . [P]etitioner owns and operates the Crest Theatre, located in a neighborhood shopping district some six miles from the downtown shopping center in Baltimore, Maryland. The Crest, possessing the most modern improvements and appointments, opened on February 26, 1949. Before and after the opening, petitioner, through its president, repeatedly sought to obtain first-run features for the theatre. Petitioner approached each respondent separately, initially requesting exclusive first-runs, later asking for first-runs on a "day and date" basis. But respondents uniformly rebuffed petitioner's efforts and adhered to an established policy of restricting first-runs in Baltimore to the eight downtown theatres. Admittedly there is no direct evidence of illegal agreement between the respondents and no conspiracy is charged as to the independent exhibitors in Baltimore, who account for 63 percent of first-run exhibitions. The various respondents advanced much the same reasons for denying petitioner's offers. Among other reasons they asserted that day and date first-runs are normally granted only to noncompeting theatres. Since the Crest is in "substantial competition" with the downtown theatres, a day and date arrangement would be economically unfeasible. And even if respondents wished to grant petitioner such a license, no downtown exhibitor would waive his clearance rights over the Crest and agree to a simultaneous showing. As a result, if petitioner were to receive first-runs, the license would have to be an exclusive one. However, an exclusive license would be economically unsound because the Crest is a suburban theatre, located in a small shopping center, and served by limited public transportation facilities; and, with a drawing area of less than one 10th that of a downtown theatre, it cannot compare with those easily accessible theatres in the power to draw patrons. Hence the downtown theatres offer far greater opportunities for the widespread advertisement and exploitation of newly released features, which is thought necessary to maximize the overall return from subsequent runs as well as first-runs. . . .

The crucial question is whether respondents' conduct toward petitioner stemmed from independent decision or from an agreement, tacit or express. To be sure, business behavior is admissible circumstantial evidence from which the fact finder may infer agreement. But this Court has never held that proof of parallel business behavior conclusively establishes agreement or, phrased differently, that such behavior itself constitutes a Sherman Act offense. Circumstantial evidence of consciously parallel behavior may have made heavy inroads into the traditional judicial attitude toward conspiracy; but "conscious parallelism" has not yet read conspiracy out of the Sherman Act entirely. . . . Here each of the respondents had denied the existence of any collaboration and in addition had introduced evidence of the local conditions surrounding the Crest operation which, they contended, precluded it from being a successful first-run house. They also attacked the good faith of the guaranteed offers of the petitioner for first-run pictures and attributed uniform action to individual business judgment motivated by the desire for maximum revenue. . . .

Affirmed.

Questions

1. Assume that two fertilizer dealerships, Grow Quick and Fertile Fields, respectively hold 70 percent and 30 percent of the fertilizer business in the farm community of What Cheer, Iowa. Assume that the owner of Fertile Fields learns via inquiry, hearsay, and the like of Grow Quick's price quotes. Then each growing season the Fertile Fields owner sets his prices exactly equal to those of his competitor. Is that practice unlawful? Explain.

2. Given identical competing products, why is identical pricing virtually inevitable—at least over the long run?

3. The FTC found the Boise Cascade Corporation in violation of Section 5 of the Federal Trade Commission Act (forbidding unfair methods of competition) for using a delivered pricing system for southern plywood, the price for which was based in part on a rail freight charge computed as though the shipping point of origin was the Pacific Northwest. Historically, plywood had originated largely in the Northwest, but technological developments spurred southeastern production. However, southeastern producers continued to quote plywood prices as though the material had been shipped from the West Coast. The commission contended that the practice inhibited price competition. Boise Cascade argued

that the freight factor eased price comparisons between southeastern and northwestern plywood. No agreement among southern plywood producers as to West Coast delivered pricing was proved. In the absence of an agreement, is this practice unlawful? Explain. *Boise Cascade Corp.* v. *FTC,* 637 F.2d 573 (9th Cir. 1980).

Interlocking Directorates

Principal Legislation: Clayton Act, section 8:

[N]o person at the same time shall be a director in any two or more corporations, any one of which has capital, surplus, and undivided profits aggregating more than $1,000,000 engaged in whole or in part in commerce, other than banks, banking associations, trust companies, and common carriers subject to the Act to regulate commerce, . . . if such corporations are or shall have been . . . competitors, so that the elimination of competition by agreement between them would constitute a violation of any of the provisions of any of the antitrust laws . . .

Federal Trade Commission Act, section 5:

Unfair methods of competition in or affecting commerce, and unfair or deceptive acts or practices in or affecting commerce are hereby declared unlawful.

Congress was concerned that companies that appeared to be competitors might actually behave cooperatively by the simple expedient of having the same set of persons control each company through their roles as directors. Obviously the possibilities for information sharing and other potentially anticompetitive conduct are considerable. The government has successfully broken certain important interlocks, but section 8 is replete with loopholes. As a consequence the government has of late turned more frequently to Section 5 of the Federal Trade Commission Act to intercede against interlocks. Interlocks remain somewhat common, the government having given them only modest attention.

A 1983 Supreme Court decision did clarify a continuing dispute in interpreting section 8. We have known that interlocks involving two or more banks are, with exceptions, forbidden by the Clayton Act. However, the *BankAmerica* decision makes it clear that interlocks involving banks and competing nonbank institutions are exempt from the Act. Therefore, individuals can continue to lawfully serve as directors of both banks and competing nonbank financial institutions (e.g., insurance companies).[6]

Part Two—Vertical Restraints

(Note: Under Justice Department guidelines issued in January 1985, the law of vertical restraints as explained in this section may undergo significant adjustments. At this writing we can only speculate as to the effect of the guidelines. Read the law as set out in this section. Then for a summary of the Justice Department position, read the Afterword that closes Part Two.)

Resale Price Maintenance

Principal legislation: Sherman Act, section 1; Federal Trade Commission Act, section 5.

Manufacturers and distributors often seek to specify the price at which their customers may resell their products. Having sold its product, why should a manufacturer or distributor seek to influence the price at which the product is resold? The primary reasons are twofold: (1) By establishing a minimum price, the product's reputation for quality may be enhanced. (2) Resale price maintenance policy seeks to prevent discount stores from undercutting regular retail outlets. (Why does the manufacturer or distributor prefer that its products are sold in traditional retail stores rather than in discount enterprises?)

An *agreement* between a seller and its buyer, fixing the price at which the buyer may resell the product, is a per se violation. However, sellers may lawfully engage in resale price maintenance if they do nothing more than specify a price at which their product is to be sold and unilaterally refuse to deal with anyone who does not adhere to that price.

The Justice Department filed a brief in the 1984 *Monsanto*[7] case asking the Supreme Court to reevaluate the per se standard. The Court declined to do so noting that such actions "have been per se illegal since the early years of antitrust enforcement."[8]

The *Parke, Davis* case makes clearer the very limited conditions under which resale price maintenance is permissible. This case is perhaps more important as an example of the judicial juggling act that accompanies the common dilemma wherein the opposing parties are both arguing from sound positions. Here the court seeks to preserve the seller's freedom to refuse to deal with whomever he or she wishes (except for limited exceptions, such as racial or sexual discrimination), while protecting the interests of the buyer and the public in purchasing the best products at the lowest possible prices. A moment's reflection on the complexity of the judiciary's duties would not be wasted.

UNITED STATES V. PARKE, DAVIS & CO.   362 U.S. 29 (1960)

Justice Brennan

The government sought an injunction under § 4 of the Sherman Act against the appellee, Parke, Davis & Company on a complaint alleging that Parke, Davis conspired and combined, in violation of §§ 1 and 3 of the act, with retail and wholesale druggists in Washington, D.C., and Richmond, Virginia, to maintain the wholesale and retail prices of Parke, Davis pharmaceutical products. . . .

Parke, Davis makes some 600 pharmaceutical products which it markets nationally through drug wholesalers and drug retailers. The retailers buy these products from the drug wholesalers or may make large quantity purchases directly from Parke, Davis. Some time before 1956 Parke, Davis announced a resale price maintenance policy in its wholesalers' and retailers' catalogues. The wholesalers' catalogue contained a Net Price Selling Schedule listing suggested minimum resale prices on Parke, Davis products sold by wholesalers to retailers. The catalogue stated that it was Parke, Davis' continuing policy to deal only with drug wholesalers who observed that schedule and who sold only to drug retailers authorized by law to fill prescriptions. Parke, Davis, when selling directly to retailers, quoted the same prices listed in the wholesalers' Net Price Selling Schedule but granted retailers discounts for volume purchases. Wholesalers were not authorized to grant similar discounts. . . .

There are some 260 drugstores in Washington, D.C., and some 100 in Richmond, Virginia. . . . There are five drug wholesalers handling Parke, Davis products in the locality who do business with the drug retailers. The wholesalers observed the resale prices suggested by Parke, Davis. However, during the spring and early summer of 1956 drug retailers in the two cities advertised and sold several Parke, Davis vitamin products at prices substantially below the suggested minimum retail prices. . . .

. . . The Baltimore office manager of Parke, Davis in charge of the sales district which included the two cities sought advice from his head office how to handle this situation. The Parke, Davis attorney advised that the company could legally "enforce an adopted policy arrived at unilaterally" to sell only to customers who observed the suggested minimum resale prices. He further advised that this meant that "we can lawfully say 'we will sell you only so long as you observe such minimum retail prices' but cannot say 'we will sell you only if you agree to observe such minimum retail prices,' since . . . agreements as to resale price maintenance are invalid." Thereafter in July the branch manager put into effect a program for promoting observance of the suggested minimum retail prices by the retailers involved. The program contemplated the participation of the five drug wholesalers. In order to ensure that retailers who did not comply would be cut off from sources of supply, representatives of Parke, Davis visited the wholesalers and told them, in effect, that not only would Parke, Davis refuse to sell to wholesalers who did not adhere to the policy announced in their catalogue, but also that it would refuse to sell to wholesalers who sold Parke, Davis products to retailers who did not observe the suggested minimum retail prices. Each wholesaler was interviewed individually but each was informed that his competitors were also being apprised of this. The wholesalers without exception indicated a willingness to go along.

Representatives called contemporaneously upon the retailers involved, individually, and told each that if he did not observe the suggested minimum retail prices, Parke, Davis would refuse to deal with him, and that furthermore he would be unable to purchase any Parke, Davis products from the wholesalers. Each of the retailers was also told that his competitors were being similarly informed.

Several retailers refused to give any assurances of compliance and continued after these July interviews to advertise and sell Parke, Davis products at prices below the suggested minimum retail prices. Their names were furnished by Parke, Davis to the wholesalers. Thereafter Parke, Davis refused to fill direct orders from such retailers and the wholesalers likewise refused to fill their orders. This ban was not limited to the Parke, Davis products being sold below the suggested minimum prices but included all the company's products, even those necessary to fill prescriptions.

The District Court held that the government's proofs did not establish a violation of the Sherman Act because "the actions of [Parke, Davis] were properly unilateral and sanctioned by law under the doctrine laid down in the case of *United States* v. *Colgate & Co.* . . .

. . . The government concedes for the purposes of this case that under the *Colgate* doctrine a manufacturer, having announced a price maintenance policy, may bring about adherence to it by refusing to deal with customers who do not observe that policy. The government contends, however, that subsequent decisions of this Court compel the holding that what Parke, Davis did here by entwining the wholesalers and retailers in a program to promote general compliance with its price maintenance policy went beyond mere customer selection and created combinations or conspiracies to enforce resale price maintenance in violation of §§ 1 and 3 of the Sherman Act.

. . . Parke, Davis did not content itself with announcing its policy regarding retail prices and following this with a simple refusal to have business relations with any retailers who disregarded that policy. Instead Parke, Davis used the refusal to deal with the wholesalers in order to elicit their willingness to deny Parke, Davis products to retailers and thereby help gain the retailers' adherence to its suggested minimum retail prices. The retailers who disregarded the price policy were promptly cut off when Parke, Davis supplied the wholesalers with their names.

The large retailer who said he would "abide" by the price policy, the multi-unit Peoples' Drug chain, was not cut off. In thus involving the wholesalers to stop the flow of Parke, Davis products to the retailers, thereby inducing retailers' adherence to its suggested retail prices, Parke, Davis created a combination with the retailers and the wholesalers to maintain retail prices and violated the Sherman Act. Although Parke, Davis' originally announced wholesalers' policy would not under *Colgate* have violated the Sherman Act if its action thereunder was the simple refusal without more to deal with wholesalers who did not observe the wholesalers' Net Price Selling Schedule, that entire policy was tainted with the "vice of . . . illegality." . . . when Parke, Davis used it as the vehicle to gain the wholesalers' participation in the program to effectuate the retailers' adherence to the suggested retail prices.

* * * * *

. . . It must be admitted that a seller's announcement that he will not deal with customers who do not observe his policy may tend to engender confidence in each customer that if he complies his competitors will also. But if a manufacturer is unwilling to rely on individual self-interest to bring about general voluntary acquiescence which has the collateral effect of eliminating price competition, and takes affirmative action to achieve uniform adherence by inducing each customer to adhere to [the suggested retail prices to] avoid such price competition, the customers' acquiescence is not then a matter of individual free choice prompted alone by the desirability of the product. The product then comes packaged in a competition-free wrapping—a valuable feature in itself—by virtue of concerted action induced by the manufacturer. The manufacturer is thus the organizer of a price-maintenance combination or conspiracy in violation of the Sherman Act. Under that act "competition, not combination, should be the law of trade," . . . and "a combination formed for the purpose and with the effect of raising, depressing, fixing, pegging, or stabilizing the price of a commodity in interstate or foreign commerce is illegal per se."

Judgment reversed and case remanded with directions.

Questions

1. *a.* What is the *Colgate* doctrine?
    b. How did Parke, Davis violate the *Colgate* doctrine?
    c. Is the *Colgate* doctrine, as interpreted in *Parke, Davis,* a practical, workable standard of conduct? Explain.
2. Assume a manufacturer communicates to her or his distributors a "suggested retail price" for her or his product. Further assume that the distributors individually decide to follow that suggestion.
    a. Does that conduct violate the law? Explain.
    b. Would it matter whether the product is heavily advertised? Explain.
3. *a.* What is fair trade pricing?
    b. What is its current status?
4. In *Albrecht* v. *Herald Co.* [390 U.S. 145 (1968)] a newspaper distributor, Albrecht, lost his distributorship because he charged a retail price in excess of that specified by the *Herald.*

a. Is the setting of a maximum resale price illegal? Explain.

b. Argue the case both for and against Albrecht.

c. What if the newspaper company had delivered the papers itself?

Vertical Territorial and Customer Restraints

Principal Legislation: Sherman Act, section 1; Federal Trade Commission Act, section 5.

Manufacturers commonly wish to impose restrictions upon where and to whom their products may be resold. Typically those restrictions afford an exclusive sales territory to a distributor. Similarly manufacturers may prevent distributors from selling to some classes of customers (e.g., a distributor might be forbidden to sell to an unfranchised retailer). Of course, such arrangements necessarily retard or eliminate intrabrand competition. Because competition among dealers in the same brand is clearly of benefit to the consumer, particularly for price and service, the courts have frequently struck down such arrangements. Indeed, until the *GTE* case, set out in this section, the leading Supreme Court case of *United States* v. *Arnold, Schwinn & Co.*[9] held that such restraints were per se unlawful. Still, it is generally agreed that territorial and customer allocations also have merits. The *GTE* case enunciates those virtues and establishes the position that vertical restrictions are to be judged on a case by case basis, balancing interbrand and intrabrand competitive effects. Thus the Rule of Reason is now to be applied to vertical territorial and customer restraints.

At this point, the student will want to understand the critical distinction between horizontal and vertical territorial and customer allocations. The former is per se unlawful. The latter is to be resolved under the Rule of Reason. *Horizontal* restrictions are those arising from an agreement among the *competitors* themselves, while *vertical* restrictions are those imposed upon buyers by their *suppliers*.

CONTINENTAL T.V., INC., ET AL. V. GTE SYLVANIA INC.
433 U.S. 36 (1977)

Justice Powell

I

Respondent GTE Sylvania Inc. (Sylvania) manufactures and sells television sets through its Home Entertainment Products Division. Prior to 1962, like most other television manufacturers, Sylvania sold its televisions to independent or company-owned distributors who in turn resold to a large and diverse group of retailers. Prompted by a decline in its market share to a relatively insignificant 1 percent to 2 percent of national television sales, Sylvania conducted an intensive reassessment of its marketing strategy, and in 1962 adopted the franchise plan challenged here. Sylvania phased out its wholesale distributors and began to sell its televisions directly to a smaller and more select group of franchised retailers. An acknowledged purpose of the change was to decrease the number of competing Sylvania retailers in the hope of attracting the more aggressive and competent retailers thought necessary to the improvement of the company's market position. . . . To this end, Sylvania limited the number of franchises granted for any given area and required each franchisee to sell his Sylvania products only from the location or locations at which he was franchised. A franchise did not constitute an exclusive territory, and Sylvania retained sole discretion to increase the number of retailers in an area in light of the success or failure of existing retailers in developing their market. The revised marketing strategy appears to have been successful during the period at issue here, for by 1965 Sylvania's share of national television sales had increased to approximately 5 percent, and the company ranked as the nation's eighth largest manufacturer of color television sets.

This suit is the result of the rupture of a franchiser-franchisee relationship that had previously prospered under the revised Sylvania plan. Dissatisfied with its sales in the city of San Francisco, Sylvania decided in the spring of 1965 to franchise Young Brothers, an established San Francisco retailer of televisions, as an additional San Francisco retailer. The proposed location of the new franchise was approximately a mile from a retail outlet operated by petitioner Continental T.V., Inc. (Continental), one of the most successful Sylvania franchisees. . . .

During this same period, Continental expressed a desire to open a store in Sacramento, California, a desire Sylvania attributed at least in part to Continental's displeasure over the Young Brothers decision. Sylvania believed that the Sacramento market was adequately served by the existing Sylvania retailers and denied the request. In the face of this denial, Continental advised Sylvania in early September 1965, that it was in the process of moving Sylvania merchandise from its San Jose, California warehouse to a new retail location that it had leased in Sacramento. . . . Shortly thereafter, Sylvania terminated Continental's franchises. . . .

* * * * *

The antitrust issues before us originated in cross-claims brought by Continental against Sylvania. . . . Most important for our purposes was the claim that Sylvania had violated [Sherman 1] by entering into and enforcing franchise agreements that prohibited the sale of Sylvania products other than from specified locations. . . .

[The trial jury found that Sylvania had engaged in restraint of trade with respect to location restrictions. The Court of Appeals for the Ninth Circuit reversed. The Supreme Court granted certiorari.]

II

A

We turn first to Continental's contention that Sylvania's restriction on retail locations is a per se violation of § 1 of the Sherman Act as interpreted in *Schwinn*. The restrictions at issue in *Schwinn* were part of a three-tier distribution system comprising, in addition to Arnold, Schwinn & Co. (Schwinn), 22 intermediate distributors and a network of franchised retailers. Each distributor had a defined geographic area in which it had the exclusive right to supply franchised retailers. Sales to the public were made only through franchised retailers, who were authorized to sell Schwinn bicycles only from specified locations. In support of this limitation, Schwinn prohibited both distributors and retailers from selling Schwinn bicycles to nonfranchised retailers. At the retail level, therefore, Schwinn was able to control the number of retailers of its bicycles in any given area according to its view of the needs of that market.

The Court . . . proceeded to articulate the following "bright line" per se rule of illegality for vertical restrictions: "Under the Sherman Act, it is unreasonable without more for a manufacturer to seek to restrict and confine areas or persons with whom an article may be traded after the manufacturer has parted with dominion over it." . . . But the Court expressly stated that the rule of reason governs when "the manufacturer retains title, dominion, and risk with respect to the product and the position and function of the dealer in question are, in fact, indistinguishable from those of an agent or salesman of the manufacturer." . . .

B

In the present case, it is undisputed that title to the televisions passed from Sylvania to Continental. Thus, the *Schwinn* per se rule applies unless Sylvania's restriction on locations falls outside *Schwinn's* prohibition against a manufacturer's attempting to restrict a "retailer's freedom as to where and to whom it will resell the products." . . . As the Court of Appeals conceded, the language of *Schwinn* is clearly broad enough to apply to the present case. Unlike the Court of Appeals, however, we are unable to find a principled basis for distinguishing *Schwinn* from the case now before us. . . .

III

Sylvania argues that if *Schwinn* cannot be distinguished, it should be reconsidered. Although *Schwinn* is supported by the principle of *stare decisis*, . . . we are convinced that the need for clarification of the law in this area justifies reconsideration. . . . The great weight of scholarly opinion has been critical of the decision, and a number of the federal courts confronted with analogous vertical restrictions have sought to limit its reach.

* * * * *

The market impact of vertical restrictions is complex because of their potential for a simultaneous reduction of intrabrand competition and stimulation of interbrand competition.

* * * * *

Vertical restrictions reduce intrabrand competition by limiting the number of sellers of a particular product competing for the business of a given group of buyers. Location restrictions have this effect because of practical constraints on the effective marketing area of retail outlets. Although intrabrand competition may be reduced, the ability of retailers to exploit the resulting market may be limited both by the ability of consumers to travel to other franchised locations and perhaps more importantly, to purchase the competing products of other manufacturers. None of these key variables, however, is affected by the form of the transaction by which a manufacturer conveys his products to the retailers.

Vertical restrictions promote interbrand competition by allowing the manufacturer to achieve certain efficiencies in the distribution of his products. These "redeeming virtues" are implicit in every decision sustaining vertical restrictions under the rule of reason. Economists have identified a number of ways in which manufacturers can use such restrictions to compete more effectively against other manufacturers. . . . For example, new manufacturers and manufacturers entering new markets can use the restrictions in order to induce competent and aggressive retailers to make the kind of investment of capital and labor that is often required in the distribution of products unknown to the consumer. Established manufacturers can use them to induce retailers to engage in promotional activities or to provide service and repair facilities necessary to the efficient marketing of their products. Service and repair are vital for many products, such as automobiles and major household appliances. The availability and quality of such services affect a manufacturer's good will and competitiveness of his product. Because of market imperfections such as the so-called free-rider effect, these services might not be provided by retailers in a purely competitive situation, despite the fact that each retailer's benefit would be greater if all provided the services than if none did.

*   *   *   *

Accordingly, we conclude that the per se rule stated in *Schwinn* must be overruled. . . . In so holding we do not foreclose the possibility that particular applications of vertical restrictions might justify per se prohibition. . . . But we do make clear that departure from the rule-of-reason standard must be based upon demonstrable economic effect rather than—as in *Schwinn*—upon formalistic line drawing.

In sum, we conclude that the appropriate decision is to return to the rule of reason that governed vertical restrictions prior to *Schwinn.* . . .

Accordingly, the decision of the Court of Appeals is *affirmed*.

Questions

1. In the *GTE* case, the Supreme Court takes the position that interbrand, rather than intrabrand, agreements must be the primary concern of antitrust law.
   a. Why does the Court take that view?
   b. Is the Court correct? Explain.
2. The *GTE* decision distinguishes vertical "nonprice" restrictions (such as location clauses) from vertical price restrictions (resale price maintenance). Make the argument that the Court's distinction is not meaningful.
3. Could a manufacturer lawfully erect vertical territorial restraints and customer allocations by engaging his or her distributor in a consignment sales arrangement or an agency arrangement? Explain.
4. What is the "free-rider" problem that frequently concerns the courts in cases involving vertical territorial restraints?
5. Assume a manufacturer assigns an "area of primary responsibility" to a distributor. The distributor's sales are not confined to that area, but he/she must devote his/her best efforts to that area and failure to do so may result in termination of the distributorship. Is that arrangement lawful? Explain.
6. In 1977 Michelin failed to renew its dealership agreement with the Donald B. Rice Tire Company of Frederick, Maryland. After seven years with Michelin, approximately 80 percent of Rice's business was derived from wholesaling the tires to smaller authorized and unauthorized dealers. Other authorized dealers complained to Michelin of Rice's wholesale business. In an effort to assume primary wholesaling responsibility, Michelin chose not to renew its relationship with Rice. Rice contended that the nonrenewal was a consequence of its refusal to comply with Michelin's customer and territorial restraints, and Rice filed an antitrust action on that basis. Michelin argued that it was a new entrant into a concentrated market, and as such, restraints on intrabrand competition were necessary to induce retailers to carry Michelin tires. However, the court found frequent shortages of Michelin tires. Michelin also argued that nonrenewal was "necessary to prevent free riding by retailers on the services provided by other dealers."

   Rice had not advertised in a quantity commensurate with his sales volume. He sold to unauthorized dealers who were not bound to do any advertising and could thus reap the benefits of advertising by authorized dealers. Michelin wanted to encourage point of sales services and the offering of specialized services, but feared that authorized dealers would not invest the necessary expenditures because of their fear of being underpriced by unauthorized dealers. Decide the case. See *Donald B. Rice Tire Company, Inc.* v. *Michelin Corporation*, 483 F. Supp. 750 (D. Md., 1980), 638 F.2d 15 (1981), cert. den. 454 U.S. 864 (1981).

Tying Arrangements

Principal Legislation: Clayton Act, section 3; Sherman Act, sections 1 and 2; Federal Trade Commission Act, section 5.

Clayton Act, section 3. That it shall be unlawful for any person engaged in commerce, in the course of such commerce, to lease or make a sale or contract for sale of goods . . . or other commodities . . . or fix a price charged therefor, or discount from or rebate upon, such price, on the condition, agreement or understanding that the lessee or purchaser thereof shall not use or deal in the goods . . . or other commodities of a competitor or competitors of the lessor or seller, where the effect of such lease, sale, or contract for sale or such condition, agreement, or understanding may be to substantially lessen competition or tend to create a monopoly in any line of commerce.

The typical tying arrangement permits a customer to lease or buy a desired product only if she or he also leases or buys another product. Of course, such an arrangement harms the consumer, but the primary antitrust concerns are twofold: (1) A party who already enjoys market power over the tying product is able to extend that power into the tied product market. (2) Competitors in the tied product market are foreclosed from equal access to that market.

In brief, a violation requires:

1. Proof of a tying arrangement (that is, two products bound together, not merely one product consisting of two or more components bound together, or two entirely separate products that happen to be a part of a single transaction).
2. Market power in the tying product.
3. That a substantial amount of commerce in the tied product is adversely affected. Where those conditions are established, the arrangement constitutes a per se violation.

Under guidelines announced in 1985, the Justice Department has refined its view of the tying standards. Justice will challenge a tying arrangement only if the party imposing the tie (the seller) controls more than 30 percent of the market for the tying product. If so, if the seller has "dominant" market power, and if the other elements of the aforementioned tying test are satisfied, the tying arrangement will be considered per se unlawful. Whether the courts will adopt the Justice Department's stance remains to be seen.

While the courts have clearly looked with disfavor on tying agreements, certain conditions do justify such arrangements. For example, a tying agreement is more likely to be acceptable when employed by a new competitor seeking entry against established sellers. What argument would the reader offer in defense of a computer lessor who required his lessee to use only the tabulating cards supplied by the lessor? [See *IBM* v. *U.S.* 298 U.S. 131 (1936)].

Fortner Enterprises, Inc. and U.S. Steel

The *Principe* case that follows in the Franchises, Price Discrimination, and International Antitrust section of this chapter is an excellent illustration of the judiciary's treatment of tying cases. But perhaps the most interesting such case is one involving a Louisville, Kentucky, home builder and United States Steel [See *Fortner* v. *United States Steel Corp.*, 394 U.S. 495 (1969)]. Fortner sought to obtain loans totaling over $2 million for the purchase and development of land in Louisville, Kentucky. Fortner claimed that he was able to secure the loan from a wholly owned U.S. Steel subsidiary, U.S. Steel Homes Credit Corporation, only by agreeing to erect a U.S. Steel prefabricated house on each lot purchased with the proceeds of the loan. Rather than looking at the Supreme Court's *Fortner* opinion, it may be more helpful to read a journalistic account of the tying arrangement analysis while glimpsing the frustrating path of a complex antitrust litigation. The full *Fortner* story reveals both the judicial confusion and the practical demands in time, money, and spirit that often attend such cases. In the end, the *Fortner* story is also an encouraging recital of a laborious but honorable search for justice.

SETTLE OR FIGHT? U.S. STEEL'S 14–YEAR CASE

When the 1976 term of the U.S. Supreme Court opens next week, the justices will find, among the 99 cases they have agreed to hear, one of numbing familiarity. *U.S. Steel Corp.* vs. *Fortner Enterprises Inc.*, a controversy that has been in the federal courts for 14 years, is now on its third trip to the highest court.

* * * * *

At stake is somewhat less than $300,000 in damage payments and an antitrust principle that is important but of limited applicability. In fact, Harvard Law School Professor Philip Areeda, a leading antitrust authority, thinks "the case was silly to start with." Nonetheless, its long and tortuous history is far from unique, and it shows just what tangling with the American legal system can mean to corporate managements that are considering whether to settle a conflict or fight it out in the courts.

"As a layman, it's unblievable," says A.B. Fortner Jr., the Louisville (Ky.) real estate operator who is fighting Big Steel in the case.

"You think you're right, and the court says you're right, and you keep on fighting."

* * * * *

Lawyers' Fees
The litigation has been a drain on Fortner. "It's taken quite a bit of time," he complains. "Whatever time it's taken I wasn't in my business." He has paid out direct expenses of around $10,000. But the biggest cost of suing—attorneys' fees—is being handled on a contingency basis. Fortner's lawyers will be paid only if they eventually win. Two years ago, before the most recent two appeals, U.S. District Judge James F. Gordon pegged the total value of Fortner's lawyers' work at $172,500. U.S. Steel will not talk about its legal cost but it cannot have been less.

No one connected with the case when it began had an inkling that it would consume the money and executive effort that it has. In retrospect, two key characteristics are responsible for the time-consuming process. First, the central legal issue of tie-in sales was, in Hamilton's words, "an area of the law that had not been fully adjudicated." And second, U.S. Steel has large enough ongoing legal expenses to absorb the cost of fighting for a principle rather than settling the case—as a smaller company almost surely would have done.

* * * * *

Fortner's Project

The controversy involves prefabricated houses that Fortner bought from a U.S. Steel operation just across the Ohio River from Louisville (a business that U.S. Steel has since dropped). U.S. Steel Homes Credit Corp. gave Fortner generous financing. . . . The lots are in the Golden Meadows subdivision at Valley Station, Kentucky, south of Louisville . . .

Fortner says he went into the deal for the U.S. Steel Homes financing because no other source in the area was offering 100 percent for both land and materials. But he quickly became dissatisfied. "We had trouble from the first model," he testified in the 1970 trial. "So we called over the factory men, and when they got over there, it took them seven days just to put the roof on." And then they ended up putting on a conventional roof, not a prefab one, Fortner said. "And when they got the roof up," he continued, "why, the trusses all fell—or not fell, but they sagged quite a bit."

Fortner built 70 of the houses, most of them for specific buyers. Sales went well when the houses were first offered in the spring of 1961—the cheapest models sold for some $4,000 less than the $15,000 going price for other houses in Golden Meadows. But by summer sales slowed to a trickle. Fortner claims that business dried up because word got around about basic defects in the houses. . . . U.S. Steel points instead to the general real estate slump at the time. But both sides agree that Fortner Enterprises ran out of money.

Fortner decided that the terms of the original deal had violated antitrust laws, and he brought suit against U.S. Steel in mid-1962. He charged that by tying its favorable financing to a demand that the money be spent on houses made by U.S. Steel, the company was trying to monopolize the market for prefabs.

U.S. Steel Forecloses

The next four years were spent arguing over attempts to collect evidence. U.S. Steel meanwhile foreclosed on Fortner's outstanding loans, sold off the remaining Golden Meadows homes, and won a deficiency judgment for the difference still owed. Fortner Enterprises was by then dormant, although A. B. Fortner continues to run other substantial real estate businesses that he owns.

The trial was set to begin on July 7, 1966, but it never took place. Asserting that there was nothing even arguably unlawful about the financing arrangement, U.S. Steel won a summary judgment. . . .

[I]n 1969 . . . by a narrow majority of 5 to 4, the U.S. Supreme Court overturned U.S. Steel's victory, which the U.S. Court of Appeals in Cincinnati had previously upheld. For the five-member majority, Justice Hugo Black wrote that the general suspicion of tying sales of one item to another applied to credit just as much as to any other service or product, and that the combination is unlawful when the company that does the tying has sufficient economic power to have an impact on competition. A clue to whether such power exists, Black said, is "the ability of a single seller to raise price and restrict output." But none of those questions was yet answered in the Fortner fight.

The Jury's Decision

That opinion has become the bible on the law of tie-ins, and it was cited in more than 200 other cases while the Louisville homes dispute wended its way up and down the court system. After a 1970 trial that lasted the entire month of June, Judge Gordon of the U.S. District Court ruled, that as a matter of law U.S. Steel was liable for damages. He restricted the jury to figuring out how much money to award. The jury decided on $93,200, which is automatically trebled in private antitrust litigation.

U.S. Steel appealed. The circuit court agreed that Fortner had made out the basic case but that the issue of whether U.S. Steel had "sufficient economic power" to be liable for any losses that Fortner suffered should have been decided by the jury, not the trial judge.

The verdict: a new trial.

U.S. Steel asked the Supreme Court to review that ruling. The justices declined. It took them until May 1972, six months after the Sixth Circuit Court had ruled, to reach that decision. That paved the way for the second trial. After months of haggling over just what the jury should be told in the new trial, both sides finally decided to let Gordon himself settle the matter. Based on the earlier trial record, plus three more days of testimony, Gordon held that on the facts U.S. Steel was liable for the damages to Fortner Enterprises.

Up for Review

U.S. Steel again took the case to the appeals court. The company argued that even though no other Louisville lenders were making housing loans as generous as the company's credit subsidiary, nothing prevented other institutions from meeting the terms. So the "uniqueness" was no proof of economic power. The circuit judges agreed, but said that when all the factors were weighed, including Gordon's finding that U.S. Steel's homes each cost $455 more than

competing prefabs, the decision for Fortner was not "clearly erroneous"—the only basis the appeals court had for overturning it. The Supreme Court has now agreed to review this ruling.

The legal community has a variety of explanations for the court's decision to review. A key one is that five of the members of the high court in 1969, including three of the five-man majority, are no longer on the bench.

To James T. Halverson, former antitrust chief at the Federal Trade Commission, the case provides the Burger court with a chance to apply to tie-in sales arrangements an approach that it has been taking on other antitrust matters. They look at "economic realities" to see if the requisite market power exists, instead of relying on "rather far-fetched analyses, which really grasp for some indicators of power," he says.

Few expect the court to repudiate the 1969 ruling outright . . .

Source: *Business Week*, October 11, 1976, pp. 81–86. Reprinted by special permission, © 1976 by McGraw-Hill, Inc.

Fortner II

In 1977, the Supreme Court reversed itself and found for U.S. Steel on the grounds that it did not possess sufficient economic power in the tying product. *United States Steel Corporation* v. *Fortner Enterprises, Inc.*, 429 U.S. 610 (1977). Fortner had, of course, contended that the Credit Corporation loan was unique, thus compelling him to accept U.S. Steel houses in order to secure Credit's financing. Justice Stevens said the "question is whether the seller has some advantage not shared by his competitors in the market for the tying product." The Court found no such advantage for Credit Corporation. Hence the finding of insufficient economic power in the tying product.

Questions

1. Argue that the tying arrangement in *Fortner* actually enhanced efficiency.
2. The cases suggest that one who holds market power in the tying product would naturally wish to achieve market power in the tied product. That is precisely the evil the government seeks to prevent.

    a. However, at least as to complementary products (computers and disks, mimeograph machines and ink, or stereos and records), make the argument that possession of market power in the tying product would not, of itself, permit that producer to seek monopoly power and charge monopoly prices for the tied product.

    b. Put another way, how can a seller force a buyer to accept an undesired tied product?

3. Is a tying arrangement the economic equivalent of predatory pricing? If so, is the law regarding tying arrangements essentially the same as the law regarding predatory pricing? Explain.

4. Audio manufacturers a stereo receiver that is technically superior to all others on the market. Audio will sell its receiver only in conjuction with its own turntable and speakers. Is Audio in violation of the law? Explain.

5. Assume Shoes Unlimited has market power in the retail sale of cowboy boots. James buys a pair of boots at Shoes Unlimited and inadvertently loses one in a peculiar affair of the night. James now seeks to replace the lost boot by purchasing one identical to it, but the store policy requires the purchase of both boots or none at all. Could James successfully challenge Shoes Unlimited on tying grounds?

6. In *Belliston* v. *Texaco, Inc.,* 455 F2d 175 (1972), cert. den. 408 U.S. 928 (1972), certain Texaco dealers claimed damages because of Texaco's policy of requesting that they buy only those brands of tires, batteries, and accessories specified by Texaco. Texaco received a 10 percent commission from the manufacturers of those items. Texaco did nothing to coerce its dealers into compliance with that request.

    a. What phrase describes this rather commonplace marketing tactic?

    b. What violation of law was alleged?

    c. Decide the case. Explain.

Exclusive Dealing and Requirements Contracts

Principal Legislation: Clayton Act, section 3; Sherman Act, section 1.

An *exclusive dealing* contract is an agreement in which a buyer commits itself to deal only with a specific seller, thus cutting competing sellers out of that share of the market. *A requirements* contract is one in which a seller agrees to supply all of a buyer's needs, or a buyer agrees to purchase all of a seller's output, or both. These arrangements have the disadvantage of closing markets to potential competitors. After defining the relevant product and geographic markets, the test to be employed is essentially that applied to vertical mergers; that is, what percentage of the relevant market is foreclosed by the agreement? Does the agreement foreclose a source of supply of sufficient magnitude as to substantially lessen competition? Does the agreement foreclose a market for sales of sufficient magnitude to substantially lessen competition?

Exclusive dealing and requirements contracts do not constitute per se violations of the law. Indeed, it is important to recognize some of the merits of such arrangements, as once articulated by Justice Frankfurter of the U.S. Supreme Court.[10] For the buyer, these merits are:

1. Assure supply.

2. Protect against price rises.

3. Enable long-term planning on the basis of known costs.
4. Reduce the risk and expense of storing products with fluctuating demand.

For the seller, the merits are:

1. Reduce selling expenses.
2. Protect against price fluctuation.
3. Offer a predictable market.

Afterword—Justice Department Guidelines

As noted at the outset of Part Two, the Justice Department's recently released guidelines addressing vertical restraints call into question the bulk of the materials in this section. Of course, the guidelines only express the opinion of the Justice Department. However, they are accorded great respect by the courts, and they do clearly confirm the federal government's reluctance to challenge most vertical marketing restrictions. The Justice Department believes that most *nonprice* marketing arrangements between manufacturers and wholesalers or distributors (e.g., territorial restrictions and exclusive dealing arrangements) should not be unlawful. For example, the guidelines declare that the Justice Department will not challenge vertical marketing arrangements when the manufacturer controls less than 10 percent of the market in question or when the distributors or dealers involved control 60 percent or less of the relevant market.

Vertical *price-fixing* arrangements will not be challenged merely because they raise consumer prices. Rather, the Justice Department will insist upon ''direct or circumstantial evidence'' showing a conspiracy about ''specific prices at which goods or services would be sold.''

The Justice Department has not been aggressively pursuing nonprice vertical restraint cases since at least the inception of the Reagan administration. However, several hundred private suits are currently awaiting hearings in courts around the country.[11] Presumably the guidelines will influence the outcome of some of those cases. Whether the Justice Department position remains persuasive over the years depends on analyses of the actual effects in the marketplace of the new leniency, as well as the outcome of future presidential and congressional elections. For now, the law of vertical restraints remains as expressed in this section.

Part Three—Franchises, Price Discrimination, and International Antitrust

A *franchise* is a contractual arrangement wherein a parent firm grants a person or group of persons the right to conduct business in a specified manner and place and for a specified time. The rights accompanying the franchise may include selling the parent's products, using its name, using its business techniques, or copying its symbols, trademark, or architecture.[12] Franchises, exemplified perhaps most visibly by McDonald's and Kentucky Fried Chicken, are a powerful force in the American economy, accounting for more than one quarter of all retail sales and employing some five million persons.

The economic significance of franchising and evidence of abuse in franchising arrangements led the Federal Trade Commission to establish a rule regulating the offering of franchises. In sum, the rule requires franchise sellers to provide purchasers with a document embodying a series of disclosures. (A number of franchises, including those for oil, gas, and autos and those not requiring a payment of $500 or more to the franchisor within the first six months, are exempt from the rule.)

The required document must disclose, among other details:

1. The franchisor's name and address and the names of its officers and directors.
2. The business experience, relevant felony convictions, relevant civil or administrative agency litigation, and bankruptcy proceedings of the officers and directors.
3. A description of the franchise (e.g., trademarks, expected competition, expected market), and the requirements imposed on the franchisee (e.g., payments; training program; territorial, site, or customer restrictions).
4. Rules for franchise termination or nonrenewal, data regarding the frequency of terminations, as well as balance sheets and income statements for the three previous years.
5. The reasonable basis for any projections regarding sales, income, or profit for the franchisee. The existing franchisees' success in meeting those projections must also be recorded.
6. Finally, a series of caveats warning the potential franchisee of the hazards of income projection and advising the potential franchisee to proceed cautiously.

Violators of the FTC rule may be fined in a civil suit up to a maximum of $10,000. The FTC may bring actions on behalf of individual franchisees to secure damages or appropriate injunctive relief.

Given the nature of the franchise relationship, it is not surprising that lawsuits alleging tying arrangements, exclusive dealing, vertical territorial restrictions, and the like are not uncommon. Resolution of these allegations is significantly complicated by some rather well-balanced competing considerations. The franchisor's interest in maintaining its product image may cause it to impose restrictions that may impinge on the franchisee's independence and efforts at profit maximization. In holding a government-approved trademark, under the terms of the Lanham Act (the federal trademark act) as interpreted by the judiciary, the franchisor must maintain control over the use of the mark so that the source of the goods is not misrepresented. The act is designed, in part, to prevent the passing or "palming off" of one party's goods as those of a competitor.

On the other hand, the government's antitrust policy is designed to curb some of the very practices that are most useful in protecting the trademark. The *Principe* case that follows addresses the trademark issue and goes on to explore the franchise as an entire business method reaching well beyond the limits of the mark itself. The case is also of value as an indication of the arrangements, financial and otherwise, involved in franchise ownership. The reader is cautioned that the law in this area remains unsettled, although the *GTE Sylvania* decision certainly suggests a greater willingness to consider the merits, if any, of vertical trade restraints imposed by a franchisor.

PRINCIPE V. McDONALD'S CORP.   631 F.2d 303 (4th Cir., 1980)

Senior Circuit Judge Phillips

This appeal presents the question of whether a fast food franchisor that requires its licensees to operate their franchises in premises leased from the franchisor is guilty of an illegal tying arrangement in violation of § 1 of the Sherman Act. . . . On the facts of this case we hold it does not and affirm the directed verdict for the defendants.

I

The appellants, Frank A. Principe, Ann Principe, and Frankie, Inc., a family owned corporation, are franchisees of McDonald's System, Inc. The Principes acquired their first franchise, a McDonald's hamburger restaurant in Hopewell, Virginia, in 1970. At that time, they executed a 20-year franchise license agreement and a store lease of like duration. In consideration for their rights under these agreements, the Principes paid a $10,000 license fee and a $15,000 security deposit, and agreed to remit 2.2 percent of their gross receipts as royalties under the franchise agreement and 8.0 percent as rent under the lease. In 1974, Frank Principe and his son, Raymond, acquired a second franchise in Colonial Heights, Virginia, on similar terms. The Colonial Heights franchise subsequently was transferred to Frankie, Inc., a corporation owned jointly by Frank and Raymond Principe.

The Principes sought to purchase a third franchise in 1976 in Petersburg, Virginia. Robert Beavers, McDonald's regional manager, concluded the plaintiffs lacked sufficient management depth and capabilities to take on a third store without impairing the quality of their existing operations. During the next 20 months, the Principes obtained corporate review and reconsideration of the decision to deny them the franchise. They were notified in May 1978 that the Petersburg franchise was being offered to a new franchisee.

They filed this action a few days later alleging violations of federal and state antitrust and securities laws and state franchising laws. Counts I and II alleged McDonald's violated federal antitrust laws by tying store leases and $15,000 security deposit notes to the franchise rights at the Hopewell and Colonial Heights stores. Count XII alleged McDonald's denied the Principes a third franchise in retaliation for their refusal to follow McDonald's pricing guidelines. . . .

Following discovery the district court granted summary judgment for McDonald's on the security deposit note tie in claims. District Judge D. Dortch Warriner found the notes represented deposits against loss and do not constitute a product separate from the store leases to which they pertain.

The court directed a verdict for McDonald's on the store lease tie in counts at the close of all the evidence. . . . Judge Warriner held the Principes had failed to introduce any evidence of McDonald's power in the tying product market, which he held is the food retailing market. The court held, however, McDonald's sells only one product: the license contract and store lease are component parts of the overall package McDonald's offers its prospective franchisees. Accordingly, Judge Warriner held as a matter of law there was no illegal tie in.

The remaining issue, whether McDonald's denied the Principes a third franchise in retaliation for their pricing independence, went to the jury which held for the defendants. The jury returned an unsolicited note stating they felt the Principes had been wronged, although price fixing was not the reason, and should be awarded the Petersburg franchise. The court disregarded the jury's note and entered judgment on the verdict for McDonald's.

The Principes appeal. . . . We affirm.

II

. . . McDonald's is not primarily a fast food retailer. While it does operate over a thousand stores itself, the vast majority of the stores in its system are operated by franchisees. Nor does McDonald's sell equipment or supplies to its licensees. Instead its primary business is developing and collecting royalties from limited menu fast food restaurants operated by independent business people.

McDonald's uses demographic data generated by the most recent census and its own research in evaluating potential sites. McDonald's attempts to analyze and predict demographic trends in the geographic area. This process serves a twofold purpose: (1) by analyzing the demographic profile of a given market area, McDonald's hopes to determine whether the residents are likely to buy fast food in sufficient quantities to justify locating a restaurant there; (2) by anticipating future growth, McDonald's seeks to plan its expansion to maximize the number of viable McDonald's restaurants within a given geographic area. Based on a comparison of data for various available sites, the regional staffs select what they believe is the best site in each geographic area.

* * * * *

After the specifics of each proposed new restaurant are approved, McDonald's decides whether the store will be company operated or franchised. If the decision is to franchise the store McDonald's begins the process of locating a franchisee. This involves offering the store either to an existing franchisee or to an applicant on the franchise waiting list. Applicants need not live near the store in order to be offered the franchise, and they need not accept the first franchise they are offered. The Principes lived in Kenosha, Wisconsin, and rejected eleven separate McDonald's restaurants before accepting their first franchise in Hopewell, Virginia. McDonald's often does not know who will operate a franchised store until it is nearly completed because a new restaurant may be offered to and rejected by several different applicants.

Meanwhile, Franchise Realty acquires the land, either by purchase or long term lease and constructs the store. Acquisition and development costs averaged over $450,000 per store in 1978. . . .

As constructed, McDonald's restaurants are finished shells; they contain no kitchen or dining room equipment. Furnishing store equipment is the responsibility of the operator, whether a franchisee or McOpCo. McDonald's does provide specifications such equipment must meet, but does not sell the equipment itself.

Having acquired the land, begun construction of the store and selected an operator, McDonald's enters into two contracts with the franchisee. Under the first, the franchise agreement, McDonald's grants the franchisee the rights to use McDonald's food preparation system and to sell food products under the McDonald's name. The franchise pays a $12,500 franchise fee and agrees to remit three percent of his gross sales as a royalty in return. Under the second contract, the lease, McDonald's grants the franchisee the right to use the particular store premises to which his franchise pertains. In return, the franchisee pays a $15,000 refundable security deposit (as evidence of which he receives a 20-year nonnegotiable noninterest-bearing note) and agrees to pay eight and one-half percent of his gross sales as rent. These payments under the franchise and lease agreements are McDonald's only sources of income from its franchised restaurants. The franchisee also assumes responsibility under the lease for building maintenance, improvements, property taxes and other costs associated with the premises. Both the franchise agreement and the lease generally have 20-year durations, both provide that termination of one terminates the other, and neither is available separately.

III

The Principes argue McDonald's is selling not one but three distinct products, the franchise, the lease, and the security deposit note. The alleged antitrust violation stems from the fact that a prospective franchisee must buy all three in order to obtain the franchise.

As evidence that this is an illegal tying arrangement, the Principes point to the unfavorable terms on which franchisees are required to lease their stores. Not only are franchisees denied the opportunity to build equity and depreciate their property, but they must maintain the building, pay for improvements and taxes, and remit 8.5 percent of their gross sales as rents. In 1978 the gross sales of the Hopewell store generated about $52,000 in rent. That figure nearly equalled Franchise Realty's original cost for the site and corresponds to more than a fourth of the original cost of the entire Hopewell restaurant complex. At that rate of return, the Principes argue, Franchise Realty will have recouped its entire investment in four years and the remainder of the lease payments will be pure profit. The Principes contend that the fact the store rents are so high proves that McDonald's cannot sell the leaseholds on their own merits.

Nor has McDonald'a shown any need to forbid its licensees to own their own stores, the Principes say. . . . Before 1959 McDonald's itself permitted franchisees to own their own stores. McDonald's could maintain its desired level of uniformity by requiring franchisees to locate and construct stores according to company specifications. The company could even provide planning and design assistance as it apparently does in connection with food purchasing and restaurant management. The Principes argue McDonald's has not shown that the success of its business or the integrity of its trademarks depends on company ownership of all store premises.

A separate tied product is the note that evidences the lessee's $15,000 security deposit, according to the appellants. The Principes argue the security deposit really is a mandatory contribution to McDonald's working capital, not security against damage to the store or breach of the lease contract. By tying the purchase of these $15,000 20-year nonnegotiable noninterest-bearing notes to that of the franchise, McDonald's allegedly has generated a capital fund that totalled over $45 million in 1978. It is argued that no one would purchase such notes on their own merits. The Principes assert that only by requiring franchisees to purchase the notes as a condition of obtaining a franchise has McDonald's been able to sell them at all.

McDonald's responds that it is not in the business of licensing use of its name, improving real estate for lease, or selling long-term notes. Its only business is developing a system of hamburger restaurants and collecting royalties from their sales. The allegedly tied products are but parts of the overall bundle of franchise benefits and obligations. . . .

IV

"There is, at the outset of every tie-in case, including the familiar cases involving physical goods, the problem of determining whether two separate products are in fact involved." . . . Because we agree with McDonald's that the lease, note, and license are not separate products but component parts of the overall franchise package, we hold on the facts of this case there was no illegal tie in. . . .

As support for their position, the Principes rely primarily on the decision of the Ninth Circuit in *Siegel* v. *Chicken Delight, Inc.* 448 F.2d 43 (9th Cir. 1971), cert. denied, 405 U.S. 955 (1972), one of the first cases to address the problem of franchise tie-ins. Chicken Delight was what McDonald's characterizes as a "rent a name" franchisor: it licensed franchisees to sell chicken under the Chicken Delight name but did not own store premises or fixtures. The company did not even charge franchise fees or royalties. Instead, it required its franchisees to purchase a specified number of cookers and fryers and to purchase certain packaging supplies and mixes exclusively from Chicken Delight. These supplies were priced higher than comparable goods of competing sellers. . . .

. . . Viewing the essence of a Chicken Delight franchise as the franchisor's trademark, the court sought to determine whether requiring franchisees to purchase common supplies from Chicken Delight was necessary to ensure that their operations lived up to the quality standards the trademark represented. Judged by this standard, the aggregation was found to consist of separate products:

This being so, it is apparent that the goodwill of the Chicken Delight trademark does not attach to the multitude of separate articles used in the operation of the licensed system or in the production of its end product. It is not what is used, but how it is used and what results that have given the system and its end product their entitlement to trademark protection. It is to the system and the end product that the public looks with the confidence that established goodwill has created.

* * * * *

The Principes urge this court to apply the *Chicken Delight* reasoning to invalidate the McDonald's franchise lease note aggregation. They urge that McDonald's can protect the integrity of its trademarks by specifying how its franchisees shall operate, where they may locate their restaurants and what types of buildings they may erect. Customers do not and have no reason to connect the building's owner with the McDonald's operation conducted therein. Since company ownership of store premises is not an essential element of the trademark's goodwill, the Principes argue, the franchise, lease, and note are separable products tied together in violation of the antitrust laws.

* * * * *

Without disagreeing with the result in *Chicken Delight,* we conclude that the court's emphasis in that case upon the trademark as the essence of a franchise is too restrictive. Far from merely licensing franchisees to sell products under its trade name, a modern franchisor such as McDonald's offers its franchisees a complete method of doing business. It takes people from all walks of life, sends them to its management school, and teaches them a variety of skills ranging from hamburger grilling to financial planning. It installs them in stores whose market has been researched and whose location has been selected by experts to maximize sales potential. It inspects every facet of every store several times a year and consults with each franchisee about his operations's strengths and weaknesses. Its regime pervades all facets of the business. . . .

Given the realities of modern franchising, we think the proper inquiry is not whether the allegedly tied products are associated in the public mind with the franchisor's trademark, but whether they are integral components of the business method being franchised. Where the challenged aggregation is an essential ingredient of the franchised system's formula for success, there is but a single product and no tie in exists as a matter of law.

Applying this standard to the present case, we hold the lease is not separable from the McDonald's franchise to which it pertains. McDonald's practice of developing a system of company owned restaurants operated by franchisees has substantial advantages, both for the company and for franchisees. It is part of what makes a McDonald's franchise uniquely attractive to franchisees.

First, because it approaches the problem of restaurant site selection systematically, McDonald's is able to obtain better sites than franchisees could select. Armed with its demographic information, guided by its staff of experts and unencumbered by preferences of individual franchisees, McDonald's can wield its economic might to acquire sites where new restaurants will prosper without undercutting existing franchisees' business or limiting future expansion. . . .

Second, McDonald's policy of owning all of its own restaurants assures that the stores remain part of the McDonald's system. McDonald's franchise arrangements are not static: franchisees retire or die; occasionally they do not live up to their franchise obligations and must be replaced; even if no such contingency intervenes, the agreements normally expire by their own terms after 20 years. If franchisees owned their own stores, any of these events could disrupt McDonald's business and have a negative effect on the system's goodwill. . . .

Third, because McDonald's acquires the sites and builds the stores itself, it can select franchisees based on their management potential rather than their real estate expertise or wealth. Ability to emphasize management skills is important to McDonald's because it has built its reputation largely on the consistent quality of its operations rather than on the merits of its hamburgers. A store's quality is largely a function of its management. McDonald's policy of owning its own stores reduces a franchisee's initial investment, thereby broadening the applicant base and opening the door to persons who otherwise could not afford a McDonald's franchise. . . . Their ability to begin operating a McDonald's restaurant without having to search for a site, negotiate for the land, borrow hundreds of thousands of dollars and construct a store building is of substantial value to franchisees.

Finally, because both McDonald's and the franchisee have a substantial financial stake in the success of the restaurant, their relationship becomes a sort of partnership that might be impossible under other circumstances. McDonald's spends close to half a million dollars on each new store it establishes. Each franchisee invests over $100,000 to make the store operational. Neither can afford to ignore the other's problems, complaints, or ideas. . . .

All of these factors contribute significantly to the overall success of the McDonald's system. The formula that produced systemwide success, the formula that promises to make each new McDonald's store successful, that formula is what McDonald's sells its franchisees. To characterize the franchise as an unnecessary aggregation of separate products tied to the McDonald's name is to miss the point entirely. Among would be franchisees, the McDonald's name has come to stand for the formula, including all that it entails. We decline to find that it is an illegal tie in. . . .

We have examined the Principes' other contentions and do not believe they warrant extended discussion. The security deposit note was just that: evidence of a security deposit on a lease which we have held was a legitimate part of the franchise package. . . . The jury's unsolicited comment that the Principes had been wronged was expressly qualified by their statement that price fixing was not the reason. The district court correctly determined that the note did not affect the integrity of the jury verdict.

Affirmed.

Questions

1. *a.* Do you agree with the court's view that McDonald's franchises an entire business system rather than an aggregation of separate products? Explain.
    b. Does the court's decision benefit or harm the consumer? Explain.
2. Can Fotomat lawfully require its franchisees to lease kiosks (small, drive-in, photo sevice buildings) from the franchisor? See *Photovest Corporation* v *Fotomat Corporation* 606 F.2d 704 (7th Cir. 1979) cert. den. 100 S. Ct. 1278 (1980).
3. For approximately a decade, Alpha Distributing Company of California had held the exclusive distribution rights for Jack Daniel's liquor in northern California. Alpha had built the distributorship to some 3,500 customers when Jack Daniel's turned the distributorship over to Rathjen Bros. and encouraged Rathjen to assume Alpha's customers.
    a. What violation of antitrust law should Alpha allege?
    b. Decide the case. See *Alpha Distrib. Co. of Cal., Inc.* v. *Jack Daniel Distillery* 454 F2d 442 (9th Cir. 1972) cert. den. 419 U.S. 842 (1974).

Price Discrimination

Principal Legislation: Clayton Act, section 2, as amended by the Robinson-Patman Act:

That it shall be unlawful for any person engaged in commerce . . . to discriminate in price between different purchasers of commodities of like grade and quality, where either or any of the purchases involved in such discrimination are in commerce . . . and where the effect of such discrimination may be substantially to lessen competition or tend to create a monopoly in any line of commerce, or to injure, destroy, or prevent competition with any person who either grants or knowingly receives the benefit of such discrimination, or with customers of either of them. . . . Provided that nothing herein contained shall prevent differentials which make only due allowance for differences in the cost of manufacture, sale, or delivery resulting from the differing methods or quantities in which such commodities are to such purchasers sold or delivered. . . . And, provided further, that nothing herein contained shall prevent price changes from time to time where in response to changing conditions affecting the market for or the marketability of the goods concerned, such as but not limited to actual or imminent deterioration of perishable goods, obsolescence of seasonal goods, distress sales under court process, or sales in good faith in discontinuance of business in the goods concerned. . . . Provided, however, that nothing herein contained shall prevent a seller rebutting the prima facie case thus made by showing that his lower price or the furnishing of services or facilities to any purchaser or purchasers was made in good faith to meet an equally low price of a competitor, or the services or facilities furnished by a competitor.

Having persevered to this point in exploring antitrust law, the reader cannot be unacquainted with at lease a measure of intellectual frustration. If so, what follows may produce a paroxysm of despair. Price discrimination may be the most confused and confusing dimension of antitrust law.

In brief, *price discrimination* involves selling substantially identical goods (not services) at reasonably contemporaneous times to different purchasers at different prices, where the effect may be to substantially lessen competition or to tend to create a monopoly. A seller may prevail against such a charge by establishing one of the following defenses: (1) The price differential is attributable to cost savings associated with the least expensive sale. However, in practice the difficulties in proving cost savings have made successful defenses on that ground quite uncommon. (2) The price differential is attributable to a good faith effort to meet the equally low price of a competitor. (3) Certain transactions are exempt from the act. Of special note is a price change made in response to a changing market. Thus, prices might lawfully be altered for seasonal goods or perishables. Price discrimination is perhaps best understood by reference to a series of diagrams.[13]

Primary Line

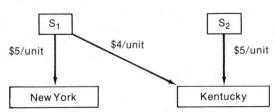

The harm here falls at the seller's level, the primary line, in that S_1's pricing policy may harm S_2. The specific fear is that S_1 will use its income from sales in New York to subsidize its lower price in Kentucky. S_1 may then be able to drive S_2 from the market. That is precisely the harm that Congress feared would be generated by the advance of chain stores across the nation. Of course, S_1 may be able to offer a defense to explain the pricing differential. For example, the price differential might be permissible if designed to allow S_1 to get a foothold in a new market. It must be recalled that a price discrimination violation requires a showing of competitive injury. At the risk of oversimplification, competitive harm will probably be found where this is proof of (*a*) predatory intent or (*b*) a general decline in the strength of the seller's competitors. The *Utah Pie* case both explores the competitive injury issue and reveals much of the philosophical confusion surrounding Robinson-Patman. The case offers the reader a particularly useful vehicle for assessing the relative merits of government regulation versus a free market approach. This case and Robinson-Patman generally have been criticized for promoting inefficiency and actually harming competition. However, the economic history of the 1920s and 30s reveals the increasing power of the chain stores and the decline of the smaller businesses prior to the enactment of Robinson-Patman. Specifically, volume buyers were able to extract various price concessions from suppliers. It does not seem exaggerated to say that an understanding of America requires an understanding of the competing economic ideologies, so usefully illustrated by the facts of *Utah Pie*.

UTAH PIE CO. V. CONTINENTAL BAKING CO.   386 U.S. 685 (1967)

Justice White

[This suit for treble damages was brought by Petitioner, Utah Pie Company, against respondents, Continental Baking Company, Carnation Company, and Pet Milk Company. The complaint charged violations by each respondent of 2(a) of the Clayton Act as amended by the Robinson-Patman Act. The jury found for petitioner on the price discrimination charge.]

The Court of Appeals reversed, addressing itself to the single issue of whether the evidence against each of the respondents was sufficient to support a finding of probable injury to competition within the meaning of § 2(a) and holding that it was not. . . .

We granted certiorari. . . . . We reverse.

The product involved is frozen dessert pies. . . . Petitioner is a Utah corporation which for 30 years has been baking pies in its plant in Salt Lake City and selling them in Utah and surrounding states. It entered the frozen pie business in late 1957. It was immediately successful with its new line and built a new plant in Salt Lake City in 1958. The frozen pie market was a rapidly expanding one: 57,060 dozen frozen pies were sold in the Salt Lake City market in 1958, 111,729 dozen in 1959, 184,569 dozen in 1960, and 266,908 dozen in 1961. Utah Pie's share of this market in those years was 66.5 percent, 34.3 percent, 45.5 percent, and 45.3 percent, respectively, its sales volume steadily increasing over the four years. Its financial position also improved. Petitioner is not, however, a large company. At the time of the trial, petitioner operated with only 18 employees, 9 of whom were members of the Rigby family, which controlled the business. . . .

Each of the respondents is a large company and each of them is a major factor in the frozen pie market in one or more regions of the country. Each entered the Salt Lake City frozen pie market before petitioner began freezing dessert pies. None of them had a plant in Utah. . . .

The major competitive weapon in the Utah market was price. . . . For most of the period involved here [petitioner's] prices were the lowest in the Salt Lake City market. It was, however, challenged by each of the respondents at one time or another and for varying periods. There was ample evidence to show that each of the respondents contributed to what proved to be a deteriorating price structure over the period covered by this suit, and each of the respondents in the course of the ongoing price competition sold frozen pies in the Salt Lake market at prices lower than it sold pies of like grade and quality in other markets considerably closer to its plants. Utah Pie, which entered the market at a price of $4.15 per dozen at the beginning of the relevant period, was selling "Utah" and "Frost 'N' Flame" pies for $2.75 per dozen when the instant suit was filed some 44 months later. Pet, which was offering pies at $4.92 per dozen in February 1958, was offering "Pet-Ritz" and "Bel-air" pies at $3.56 and $3.46 per dozen, respectively, in March and April 1961. Carnation's price in early 1958 was $4.82 per dozen but it was selling at $3.46 per dozen at the conclusion of the period, meanwhile having been down as low as $3.30 per dozen. The price range experienced by Continental during the period covered by this suit ran from a 1958 high of over $5 per dozen to a 1961 low of $2.85 per dozen.

I

We deal first with petitioner's case against the Pet Milk Company.

First, Pet successfully concluded an arrangement with Safeway, which is one of the three largest customers for frozen pies in the Salt Lake market, whereby it would sell frozen pies to Safeway under the latter's own "Bel-air" label at a price significantly lower than it was selling its comparable "Pet-Ritz" brand in the same Salt Lake market and elsewhere. . . .

Second, it introduced a 20-ounce economy pie under the "Swiss Miss" label and began selling the new pie in the Salt Lake market in August 1960 at prices ranging from $3.25 to $3.30 for the remainder of the period. This pie was at times sold at a lower price in the Salt Lake City market than it was sold in other markets.

Third, Pet became more competitive with respect to the prices for its "Pet-Ritz" proprietary label. . . . According to the Court of Appeals, in seven of the 44 months Pet's prices in Salt Lake were lower than prices charged in the California markets. This was true although selling in Salt Lake involved a 30- to 35-cent freight cost.

* * * * *

[T]he Court of Appeals almost entirely ignored . . . evidence which provides material support for the jury's conclusion that Pet's behavior satisfied the statutory test regarding competitive injury. This evidence bore on the issue of Pet's predatory intent to injure Utah Pie. . . . [T]he jury could have concluded that Pet's discriminatory pricing was aimed at Utah Pie. . . . Moreover, Pet candidly admitted that during the period when it was establishing its relationship with Safeway, it sent into Utah Pie's plant an industrial spy to seek information that would be of use to Pet in convincing Safeway that Utah Pie was not worthy of its custom. Pet denied that it ever in fact used what it had learned against Utah Pie in competing for Safeway's business. The parties, however, are not the ultimate judges of credibility. . . .

Finally, Pet does not deny that the evidence showed it suffered substantial losses on its frozen pie sales during the greater part of the time involved in this suit. . . .

It seems clear to us that the jury heard adequate evidence from which it could have concluded that Pet had engaged in predatory tactics in waging competitive warfare in the Salt Lake City market. Coupled with the incidence of price discrimination attributable to Pet, the evidence as a whole established, rather than negated, the reasonable possibility that Pet's behavior produced a lessening of competition proscribed by the act.

II

Petitioner's case against Continental is not complicated. . . . Effective for the last two weeks of June it offered its 22-ounce frozen apple pies in the Utah area at $2.85 per dozen. It was then selling the same pies at substantially higher prices in other markets. The Salt Lake City price was less than its direct cost plus an allocation for overhead . . . The Court of Appeals concluded that Continental's conduct had had only minimal effect, that it had not injured or weakened Utah Pie as a competitor, that it had not substantially lessened competition and that there was no reasonable possibility that it would do so in the future.

* * * * *

We again differ with the Court of Appeals. Its opinion that Utah was not damaged as a competitive force apparently rested on the fact that Utah's sales volume continued to climb in 1961 and on the court's own factual conclusion that Utah was not deprived of any pie business which it otherwise might have had. But this retrospective assessment fails to note that Continental's discriminatory below-cost price caused Utah Pie to reduce its price to $2.75. . . .

. . .[The jury] could have reasonably concluded that a competitor who is forced to reduce his price to a new all-time low in a market of declining prices will in time feel the financial pinch and will be a less effective competitive force. . . .

III

We need not dwell long upon the case against Carnation, which in some respects is similar to that against Continental and in others more nearly resembles the case against Pet. After Carnation's temporary setback in 1959 it instituted a new pricing policy to regain business in the Salt Lake City market. The new policy involved a slash in price of 60 cents per dozen pies, which brought Carnation's price to a level admittedly well below its costs, and well below the other prices prevailing in the market. The impact of the move was felt immediately, and the two other major sellers in the market reduced their prices. Carnation's banner year, 1960, in the end involved eight months during which the prices in Salt Lake City were lower than prices charged in other markets. The trend continued during the eight months in 1961 that preceded the filing of the complaint in this case. In each of those months the Salt Lake City prices charged by Carnation were well below prices charged in other markets, and in all but August 1961 the Salt Lake City delivered price was 20 cents to 50 cents lower than the prices charged in distant San Francisco. . . .

IV

Section 2(a) does not forbid price competition which will probably injure or lessen competition by eliminating competitors, discouraging entry into the market or enhancing the market shares of the dominant sellers. But Congress has established some ground rules for the game. Sellers may not sell like goods to different purchasers at different prices if the result may be to injure competition in either the sellers' or the buyers' market unless such discriminations are justified as permitted by the act. In this context, the Court of Appeals placed heavy emphasis on the fact that

Utah Pie constantly increased its sales volume and continued to make a profit. But we disagree with its apparent view that there is no reasonably possible injury to competition as long as the volume of sales in a particular market is expanding and at least some of the competitors in the market continue to operate at a profit. Nor do we think that the act only comes into play to regulate the conduct of price discriminators when their discriminatory prices consistently undercut other competitors. . . . Courts and commentators alike have noted that the existence of predatory intent might bear on the likelihood of injury to competition. In this case there was some evidence of predatory intent with respect to each of these respondents. . . . We believe that the act reaches price discrimination that erodes competition as much as it does price discrimination that is intended to have immediate destructive impact. In this case, the evidence shows a drastically declining price structure which the jury could rationally attribute to continued or sporadic price discrimination. . . .

[Reversed and remanded.]

Questions

1. Why is *Utah Pie* a case of primary line price discrimination?
2. What is predatory intent?
3. Make the argument that the *Utah Pie* decision is unsound as a matter of economic reasoning.
4. Is it always unlawful to sell one's products below cost (as Continental did)? Explain.

Secondary Line

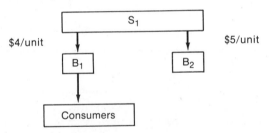

B$_1$ and B$_2$ are direct competitors. Absent a defense, S$_1$ is clearly engaging in price discrimination. Here the harm falls at the buyers' level (secondary line). Again these facts illustrate the concerns that caused Congress to approve Robinson-Patman. That is, the fear was that the economic power of the large chain stores would permit them to extract price concessions from sellers. Small stores would then be unable to compete, and the American Dream would be threatened. Additional facts will alter the situation and remind the student of the importance of doing the proper product and geographic market analysis. Assume the product involved is plywood. If S$_1$ is a lumber mill, B$_1$ is a lumberyard, and B$_2$ is a building contractor, no violation is likely to result because B$_1$ and B$_2$ are not competitors. They operate in different product markets and, therefore, could not harm competition. Similarly if B$_1$ is located in Oregon and B$_2$ in Florida, no competitive harm is likely to result because they would ordinarily be in separate geographic markets.

Third Line

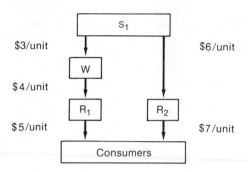

Here the injury falls at the third line; that is, customers of customers. Assume this lumber mill S_1 sells plywood to a favored purchaser W (a wholesaler) at $3 beneath the price charged to R_2. W and R_2 are not competitors and one might, therefore, argue that the price differential could not cause harm. However, if as in the case here, the lower price to W leads to a lower price to R_1—who does compete with R_2—thus permitting R_1 to undersell R_2, a court might well find a violation of Robinson-Patman (absent a sound defense). This reasoning may appear a bit awkward and at odds with normal marketing practices. However, a decision to the contrary would seriously limit the effectiveness of Robinson-Patman. If S_1 wished to sell to R_1 at a lesser price than to R_2 or perhaps was forced to do so by pressure from R_2, how might a skeptic explain the presence of W in the chain of distribution?

Questions

1. Assume firms A, B, C, D, E are charged with price-fixing under Sherman 1 because they have a program of exchanging pricing information among themselves.
   a. What element of Robinson-Patman might be used as a defense in that Sherman 1 action?
   b. Would the court find that defense persuasive? Explain.

2. The A. E. Staley Manufacturing Company, located in Decatur, Illinois, sold its glucose products at a delivered price computed as though Chicago was the shipping point, when in fact shipments originated some distance from Chicago in Decatur. The Federal Trade Commission challenged this policy.
   a. What was the basis of that challenge?
   b. What name is applied to such pricing systems? What predatory purposes might be achieved by those pricing systems?
   c. Decide the case. Explain. *Federal Trade Commission* v. *A. E. Staley Manufacturing Co.*, 324 U.S. 746 (1945).

3. In *Bruce's Juices, Inc.* v. *American Can Co.*, 87 F. Supp. 985 (S.D. Fla. 1949) aff'd, 187 F.2d 919 (5th Cir.), modified, 190 F.2d 73 (5th Cir.), cert. dismissed, 342 U.S. 875 (1951), American Can defended itself against a price discrimination charge by arguing that the cans in question were not of "like grade and quality." The cans sold to Bruce's Juices

were 3.14 inches in height, while those sold at a reduced price to Bruce's competitiors, but refused to Bruce's were 3.12 inches in height. Otherwise the cans were functionally identical.

a. Is American Can's defense persuasive? Explain.

b. Why is the presence of price discrimination good evidence of the presence of a monopoly?

c. In what sense does the Robinson-Patman Act conflict with the Sherman Act?

American Antitrust Laws and the International Market

America's commercial market now very clearly embraces the entire globe. Multinational corporations dominate international business. Antitrust questions can become extremely complex in transactions involving multiple companies, in multiple nations, where those transactions are potentially governed by U.S. and foreign antitrust laws. U.S. antitrust laws are, of course, applicable to foreign firms doing business here. The Sherman, Clayton, and FTC Acts, among others, are all potentially applicable to American business abroad.

Sherman Act   The Sherman Act applies to the conduct of American business abroad when that business has a direct effect on domestic commerce. That the business was conducted entirely abroad or that the agreement was entered in another nation does not excuse an American firm from the reach of the Sherman Act (assuming American courts can achieve the necessary jurisdiction).

Clayton Act   Section 7 of the Clayton Act is clearly applicable to acquisitions combining domestic and foreign firms and is potentially applicable to acquisitions not involving American firms if the effect would be harmful to competition in the American market. For example, in 1975, Gillette was prevented from acquiring Braun, a leading European manufacturer of electric razors. Braun had not entered the American market, but it did have the potential to do so. Thus under the potential entrant reasoning illustrated in the *Procter & Gamble* case, the merger was disallowed. Braun, as a potential entrant, could "police" the conduct of Gillette and the others in the oligopolistic American razor market.

FTC Act   As noted earlier, the Federal Trade Commission shares antitrust enforcement authority with the Justice Department, and section 5 of the act strengthens Clayton 7.

The complexity and uncertainty of the antitrust laws can be particularly daunting in the international arena. However, the Justice Department has provided a mechanism for achieving greater clarity. Under its Business Review Procedure, the Justice Department will prepare a statement of its likely response to a proposed "transaction so that the parties will have advance notice of the government's antitrust stance."

Foreign Antitrust Laws

It is generally conceded that the United States historically has taken a much more aggressive attitude toward antitrust policy and enforcement than have the nations of western Europe and Japan. Indeed, those nations generally regard cooperative economic arrangements and concentrations of industrial power as necessary and desirable components in economic success. Of course, the Japanese and western Europeans also practice an economic policy of involving government quite directly in regulating and "managing" commercial practice for the general good.

Japanese antitrust laws are very similar to those in the United States, but enforcement has been quite mild. However, we have recent evidence that the European Community intends to take a more aggressive antitrust stance. In 1983 Ford was compelled to lift export restrictions on dealer-distributors in the expectation that greater intrabrand competition would follow in the European market. The European Community has called for higher fines for antitrust violations, and private antitrust litigations are actively encouraged. Fines may total as much as 10 percent of the defendant's worldwide revenues. Further complicating the lot of the American businessperson is the fact that conduct which may be lawful in the United States is not necessarily permissible in Europe. For example, a dominant firm may run afoul of European rules simply by pricing its products "too high" or "too low."[14] The following article depicts the new European antitrust zeal.

IBM SETTLES EUROPEAN COMPUTER ANTITRUST SUIT

Bonn, West Germany—In a major settlement that could boost the fortunes of European computer makers, the European Community's executive Commission announced Thursday that it was dropping a four-year antitrust suit against International Business Machines, Inc. after the giant firm agreed to change disputed business practices.

Following months of negotiations, IBM has consented to provide its competitors with more prompt and detailed information about its new computers sold in Europe, thus allowing rival firms to design and market compatible equipment more quickly.

European computer manufacturers have complained for years that IBM's reluctance to release technical data about its computers prevented them from gaining a larger share of their home markets. IBM controls more than 60 percent of the European market in computer hardware.

"No Victors or Vanquished"

Frans Andriessen, the EC Commissioner in charge of competition policy, told a news conference in Brussels Thursday that the compromise worked out with IBM will open up the microelectronics industry in Europe and permit the European firms to compete more effectively.

*   *   *   *   *

Andriessen said that IBM agreed to furnish interface data within four months of the unveiling of new products. Typical delays in the past lasted seven months, but in some cases went on for two years.

*   *   *   *   *

Andriessen claimed that IBM now would have to make substantial changes in the way it conducts business in Europe.

IBM Responds

But his words were sharply disputed by IBM chairman John Opel, who issued a statement saying that the compromise successfully "puts the matter behind us without requiring us to make significant changes in the way we do business."

* * * * *

Under European antitrust law, IBM's sheer dominance coupled with the political necessity of rescuing the future prospects of Europe's own microelectronics industry left the company vulnerable to the charge of "abuse of a dominant position" under Article 86 of the EC's founding Treaty of Rome.

The commission's demand that IBM share information relating to its new computers more promptly was considered the most plausible way to rectify a monopolistic situation.

If the settlement had not been reached, the commission might have taken more draconian measures, such as imposing quotas or sanctions that would directly curtail IBM's share of the market and provide European firms a better chance to grow.

The revolution in computers and microelectronics has been dominated in recent years by U.S. and Japanese companies, while European firms lagged far behind for reasons variously ascribed to weak entrepreneurial spirit, a lack of venture capital and a pervasive social welfare ethic that inhibits private initiative.

Source: *Des Moines (Iowa) Register*, August 3, 1984, p. 6S. © 1984 *Washington Post*. Reprinted with permission.

Chapter Questions

1. After reading this entire chapter, what is your judgment about the antitrust system?
    a. Does it work? Explain.
    b. How might it be altered?
    c. Could we place more reliance on the market? Explain.
    d. Do the statutes and case law, as a body, seem to form a rational package? Explain.

2. Scholar and jurist Richard Posner argues:

    [T]he protection of small business whatever its intrinsic merit cannot be attained within the framework of antitrust principles and procedures. The small businessman is, in general, helped rather than hurt by monopoly, so unless the antitrust laws are stood completely on their head they are an inapt vehicle (compared, say, to tax preferences) for assisting small business.[15]

    a. Is antitrust law an inappropriate vehicle for protecting small business? Explain.
    b. Should we protect small business? Explain.
    c. How does the presence of monopolies benefit small business?
    d. If it is not the proper vehicle for protecting small business, what role should antitrust law properly serve? For example, should "social considerations" such as the maintenance of full employment and the dispersal of political power assume greater importance? Or should antitrust policy hew as closely as possible to economic goals? Explain.

3. Falls City, formerly a brewer in Evansville, Indiana, raised prices to its wholesale distributor in Kentucky, just across the state line from Evansville. At the same time, Falls City raised its prices to its distributor in Indiana, Vanco Beverages, by a greater margin than that to the Kentucky distributor. The resulting price differential caused higher retail beer prices in the Indiana market than in Kentucky. (Indiana law prohibits wholesalers from selling out of state and prohibits retailers from going out of state to make purchases. Further, brewers must

maintain a uniform price throughout Indiana.) The higher Indiana price was, at least in part, a product of Falls City's policy of following the pricing patterns of other Indiana brewers. Vanco sued claiming a violation of the Robinson-Patman Act.

a. Are the facts sufficient to support a *prima facie* case of price discrimination? Explain.

b. What defense would you raise on behalf of Falls City?

c. Decide the case. Explain. See *Falls City Industries, Inc.* v. *Vanco Beverage, Inc.*, 103 S.Ct. 1282 (1983).

4. A California statute requires wine producers and wholesalers to file a fair-trade pricing schedule or fair-trade contracts with the state. If a producer has not established prices via a fair-trade contract, wholesalers must post a price schedule and adhere to it in sales to retailers. A California wine wholesaler challenged the state statute.

a. What violation do you think was alleged?

b. Decide the case. See *California Retail Liquor Dealers Ass'n* v. *Midcal Alum.*, 100 S.Ct. 937 (1980).

5. A utility charged home building contractors up to $200 as the fee for completing underground connections, but no charge for connection was assessed where the builder agreed to make the home "all electric." In *Washington Gas Light Co.* v. *Virginia Elec. and Power Co.*, 438 F.2d 248 (4th Cir. 1971), the plaintiff alleged a violation of the antitrust laws.

a. What do you think was the alleged violation?

b. Decide the case. Explain.

6. Could Amana, the appliance manufacturer, lawfully refuse to deal with any purchaser who sells the products of a competitor, such as Maytag? Explain

7. Assume you seek to build and operate a clothing store. You hire a contractor who purchases cement blocks from a manufacturer. After the building is complete you discover evidence suggesting that your contractor was overcharged for the blocks because of a price-fixing scheme to which the block manufacturer was a party. Does the law permit you as an indirect purchaser to file an antitrust suit to recover the damages you sustained as a consequence of the conspiracy? Explain. See *Illinois Brick Co.*, v. *Illinois*, 431 U.S. 720 (1977) for a similar situation.

8. Northwest Wholesale Stationers is a purchasing cooperative composed of approximately 200 office supply retailers. Northwest is the primary wholesale source of supply for the member retailers. Non-member retailers may purchase from Northwest, but they may not take advantage of the profit-sharing and warehousing privileges that are accorded to members. Effectively, therefore, members are able to purchase at lower prices than non-members. Pacific Stationery, a long-time member, was expelled from the cooperative in 1978. Pacific was not accorded notice, hearing, or explanation. Pacific then filed suit claiming that the expulsion in the absence of procedural protections was a group boycott and a per se violation of the Sherman Act. The factual reasons for the expulsion were in dispute. Should the cooperative's decision be treated as a per se violation? See *Northwest Wholesale Stationers, Inc.* v *Pacific Stationery and Printing Co.*, 53 *Law Week* 4733 (U.S. S.Ct., 1985).

Notes

1. *Standard Oil Co. of New Jersey* v. *United States*, 221 U.S. 1 (1911).
2. See L. Sullivan, *Handbook of the Law of Antitrust* (St. Paul, Minn.: West Publishing, 1977), p. 315.
3. *Copperweld Corporation* v. *Independence Tube Corp.*, 52 *Law Week* 4821 (U.S. S.Ct., 1984).

4. The materials in this paragraph are drawn from "How the Justice Dept. is Bagging Highway Bid-Riggers," *Business Week*, July 4, 1983, p. 89; and Albert Karr and Robert Taylor, "Building Costs on Highways Are Declining," *The Wall Street Journal*, March 25, 1983, p. 17.

5. Wesley J. Liebeler, 1980 Cumulative Supplement to *Antitrust Advisor, 2d ed.* (Colorado Springs: Shepard's/McGraw-Hill, 1978).

6. *BankAmerica Corporation, et al.* v. *United States*, 462 U.S. 122 (1983).

7. *Monsanto Co.* v. *Spray-Rite Service Corp.*, 104 S.Ct. 1464 (1984).

8. Ibid., p. 1469.

9. 388 U.S. 365 (1967).

10. *Standard Oil of Cal.* v. *United States*, 337 U.S. 293 (1949).

11. The remarks in this section are based on Andy Pasztor, "Justice Department Guidelines Support Most Marketing Restrictions by Makers," *The Wall Street Journal*, January 24, 1985, p. 10.

12. See Charles L. Vaughn, *Franchising* (Lexington, Mass.: Lexington Books, 1979), p. 2, for a detailed discussion.

13. See Earl Kintner, *A Robinson-Patman Primer* (New York: MacMillan, 1970), p. 93.

14. The remarks in this paragraph draw heavily upon Jill Andresky, "Yankee Go Home," *Forbes*, July 2, 1984, p. 92.

15. Richard Posner, *Antitrust Law* (Chicago: University of Chicago Press, 1976), p. 4.

IV

Employer-Employee Relations

CHAPTER 12   Labor Law
CHAPTER 13   Employment Discrimination

12

Labor Law

Introduction

In order to understand contemporary labor relations and labor law, one must first know something about the history of labor conflict in this country and the causes of that conflict. The Industrial Revolution brought about vast changes—not only in terms of means and methods of production in the United States and throughout the world, but also in terms of the effects those changes had on the social order and the distribution of wealth.[1]

During a relatively short period of time, the United States moved from an agrarian to an industrial society. Goods formerly produced in the home or in small shops by a craftsman and a few apprentices, suddenly became the products of factories employing hundreds of people. Then because of the large number of workers, intermediaries were necessary to supervise and manage the operation of the workplace. The personal relationship that had once existed between workers and their employer disappeared.[2]

Competition among these developing firms in the late 1800s was fierce. Increases in demand often caused firms throughout an industry to expand their operations to keep pace with the growing market. However, since the firms within a given industry all increased output at the same time, production often exceeded the demand for goods.[3] In order to stay in business, companies had to cut production costs, both so that they could sell their goods at lower prices than their competitors and so that they could reap a greater profit from their sales. Faced with fixed costs for raw materials and overhead expenses, companies found that one production cost that could be reduced was the cost of labor. By paying workers as little as possible and making them work 14- or 18-hour days, employers could lower their total production costs. Thus, employers had an economic incentive for ignoring the human needs of the workers. The presence of an economic incentive to abuse workers, combined with the absence of the personal relationship between employer and worker, led to a severe deterioration of working conditions.[4]

At the same time, two other situations arose that had a significant influence on the development of labor conflict. The first was that workers often left the farms and moved to cities in order to be near their jobs. Unfortunately, that movement destroyed an important safety net. That is, if wages did not provide the full measure of living expenses, farm families still had their gardens and chickens and cows to use for food. Once these families moved to the cities, all expenses had to be covered by whatever wages were paid, no matter how meager an amount that might be.[5]

A second major factor generating labor conflict was the influx into northern and midwestern industrial centers of foreign immigrants. The availability of people anxious to work meant that competition for jobs was fierce, and employers could fill jobs easily, regardless of low wages and deplorable working conditions.[6] In addition, some highly educated immigrants were escaping political and religious persecution in their homelands. These people brought to the United States ideas, philosophies, and experiences in class struggle and labor conflict that presumably exacerbated a struggle that was coming to a head in any case.[7]

> The immigrant is usually accustomed to some form of social organization. He is not as individualistic as is the typical American. He can be organized with others into labor unions; and when the unskilled immigrants from a variety of birthplaces are thus associated, the resulting union is usually strong, coherent, and easily directed by capable and enthusiastic leaders.[8]

To say that working conditions for many people at this time were unpleasant or even dismal would be a vast understatement. The term *desperate* might better describe the problem. Children were impressed into service as soon as they were big enough to do a job and then made to work 12- and 14-hour days.[9] Textile companies would send men called "slavers" to New England and southern farm communities to gather young women to work in the mills.[10] Factory and mining towns were built by employers where workers would be forced to rent company-owned tenements and buy provisions from company stores at exorbitant rates.[11] Reports such as the following about labor and living conditions in the forepart of the 20th century reveal the grim picture:

> When I moved from the North to the South in my search for work, I entered a mill village to work in a cotton mill as a spinner. There I worked eleven hours a day, five and a half days a week, for $7 a week. In a northern mill I had done the same kind of work for $22 a week, and less hours. I worked terribly hard. My boss was a farmer who knew nothing about regulating the machines. I had not been there long when he was fired and an overseer from the North with his speed-up and efficiency system was hired in his place. I do not know which was worse: to work under a man who did not know how to make the work run well but who was pleasant to work with, or to have well-regulated machines which ran better but a driving boss.
> The sanitary conditions were ghastly. When I desired a drink of water, I had to dip my cup into a pail of water that had been brought into the mill from a spring in the fields. It tasted horrible to me. Often I saw lint from the cotton in the room floating on top of the lukewarm water. All of the men chewed tobacco, and most of the women used snuff. Little imagination is needed to judge the condition of the water which I had to drink, for working in that close, hot spinning room made me thirsty. Toilet facilities were provided three stories down in the basement of the mill in a room without any ventilation. Nowhere was there any running water; even in the houses provided by the company there was no running water.
> The married women of the South work extremely hard. The majority of them work in the mill besides having large families to care for. They arise about five to take the cow out to the pasture, to do some weeding in the garden, and to have hot cakes ready for their husbands' breakfasts when they arise. Then they prepare their children for school and finally start their work in the

mills at 6:30, where they work for 11 hours. Upon their return to their homes, they have housework to do. They have no conveniences. Instead of a sink they have a board stretched across one corner of a room. When the washing on the dishes is done, the refuse is thrown out of the back door. When a woman desires meat for her family, she orders it at the company store. When the manager has enough orders of meat he kills a cow.

Everything in the village is company owned. The houses look like barns on stilts, and appear to have been thrown together. When I would go inside one of them, I could see outside through the cracks in the walls. The workers do all of their trading at the company store and bank, and use the company school and library for they have no means of leaving the village. The money is kept circulating from the employer to the employees, employees to company store, store to company bank, and from the bank to the company again. The result is old torn bills in the pay envelope each week.

I worked in the South for nine months, and during that time I could not reconcile myself to the conditions of the mills and village. Therefore, I left the South and returned to the North—back to the clock punching, speed-up and efficiency system of the northern mills.

Five years have passed since then, and I have learned through experience that I may go North, South, East, or West in my search for work, and find miserable working conditions for miserable wages. I know that the workers in any industry are in a most deplorable condition, but the workers of the South are in virtual slavery.[12]

Consider this account of the tenements found in the small factory town of Danvers, Massachusetts:

Take them as a whole, they are horrid; those belonging to the factory especially. There are tenement houses there that ought not to be occupied. Four families have complained to me, that if they go to bed at night and there comes a shower, they have to rise up and put dishes in different places to catch the water, and that they can't sleep in their beds; and to prove it I went and examined and saw it was actually worse than they had said; one house, especially, where a person came to me, and I saw he didn't look right, and I said, "Are you going to work?" "No," he says, "had no sleep last night." It had been raining and his mother had been baking and preparing things for the house, and, in the morning almost everything had swum off and gone away—in all directions. . . . Another house, I was almost afraid to go into. I could see right through into the cellar; the plastering was entirely off the ceiling and they told me it leaked in just about the same way. There is another house, where there is a yard square without a shingle on it; and then another has an addition to it, and you can put your whole arm right in betwixt the two. It is more like a pig-pen than a decent house . . . when people are in the water-closet, the people on the road can see them. There is not a good tenement in the village.[13]

And of a company town settled primarily by German immigrants:

The attic rooms are used to deposit the filthy rags and bones as they are taken from the gutters and slaughterhouses. The yards are filled with dirty rags hung up to dry, sending forth their stench to all the neighborhood. . . . The tenants are all Germans. . . . They are exceedingly filthy in person and their bedclothes are as dirty as the floors they walk on. Their food is of the poorest quality, and their feet and hands, doubtless their whole bodies are suffering from what they call rheumatism, but which in reality is a prostrate nervous system, the result of foul air and inadequate supply of nutritious food. . . . The yards are all small and the sinks running over with filth. . . . Not one decent sleeping apartment can be found on the entire premises and not one stove properly arranged. The carbonic-acid gas, in conjunction with the other emanations from bones, rags, and human filth, defies description. The rooms are 6 by 10 feet; bedrooms 5 by 6 feet. The inhabitants lead a miserable existence, and their children wilt and die in their infancy.[14]

Compare these working-class conditions with those of the more famous American entrepreneurs of the same era:

[Frederick Allen] describes the homes of the wealthy.

Frederick W. Vanderbilt's great house at Hyde Park, in which the dining room was approximately 50 feet long; . . . William K. Vanderbilt's Idle Hour at Oakdale—with 110 rooms, 45 bathrooms, and a garage ready to hold 100 automobiles. But the champion of all the turn-of-the-century chateaux was George W. Vanderbilt's ducal palace at Asheville, North Carolina, which he called Biltmore. . . .

It had 40 master bedrooms, a Court of Palms, an Oak Drawing Room, a Banqueting Hall, a Print Room, a Tapestry Gallery, and a Library with 250,000 volumes. It was surrounded by an estate which . . . covered 203 square miles.

The secretary of agriculture noted that George W. employed more men and spent more money on his hobby of landscape gardening and wildlife management at Biltmore than did the entire Department of Agriculture on the needs of all the farmers in the United States.

Historians have depicted John D. Rockefeller as a man of notoriously frugal habits—his standard tip for any service was a dime. Allen describes his estate at Pocantico Hills as containing

more than 75 buildings. . . . Within his estate were 75 miles of private roads on which he could take his afternoon drive; a private golf links on which he could play his morning game; and anywhere from 1,000 to 1,500 employees, depending on the season.

. . . Rockefeller also owned an estate at Lakewood, which he occupied in the spring; an estate at Ormond Beach in Florida for his winter use; a townhouse . . . in New York; an estate at Forest Hill, Cleveland, which he did not visit; and a house on Euclid Avenue in Cleveland, likewise unused by him.

Concludes Allen, "Never, perhaps, did any man live a more frugal life on a more colossal scale."[15]

Contrasting these conditions with those of the workers, one is better able to understand the sense of injustice felt by many workers, and the belief of many that a redistribution of the wealth might provide the only solution to the class conflict. Because these fortunes were built in part through the exploitation of workers, it is not surprising that the characterization of these men and women of the leisure class as American heroes is distasteful to many.

Organizing Labor

The Knights of Labor, initially a secret society, was the first major labor organization in the United States. The Knights of Labor, led first by Uriah Stephens and then by Terence V. Powderly, had a large following during the 1870s and 1880s.[16] The order admitted any workers to its ranks, regardless of occupation, race, sex, or nationality; in fact, the only people excluded from the group were gamblers, bankers, stockbrokers, and liquor dealers.[17] The Knights of Labor dedicated itself to principles of social reform. For example, the group sought the protection of wage and hour laws, improved health care systems, and mandatory education.[18] The goals of the Knights of Labor were perhaps too broad and far-reaching to bring workers any relief from their immediate problems. Thus, despite Powderly's insistence that workers should strike only as a last resort, dissidents within the organization instigated strikes under the name of the order.[19] Great philosophical divisions within the Knights brought about its rapid decline.[20]

Samuel Gompers, who came along to build and develop the American Federation of Labor (AFL), had more practical, attainable goals in mind for his organization.

Gompers, a worker in the cigar industry, saw the need to organize workers along craft lines so that each craft group could seek gains for its own workers, all of whom had the same type of skills and, presumably, all of whom shared the same occupational goals.[21] The efforts of the craft groups were directed toward getting higher wages and better working conditions for laborers.[22] This approach proved to be much more effective than had that of the Knights of Labor.

The Congress of Industrial Organizations (CIO) was organized in response to the need of an entire segment of the working population to which the AFL was virtually unresponsive.[23] The AFL consisted of unions of craft labor. By the 1930s, however, millions of workers were employed in jobs highly compartmentalized, requiring very little skill. Assembly-line production fostered jobs that required repetitive tasks capable of being performed by untrained workers.[24] The interests of these unskilled workers differed greatly from those of skilled workers, and ordinarily the unskilled workers did not qualify for membership in most craft unions. Therefore, funneling these workers into the craft unions was not a particularly practical solution to their need for organization. Further, the members of the AFL were not willing to accept the idea of unions set up along industry, rather than craft, lines. John L. Lewis, Sidney Hillman, David Dubinsky, and a number of others saw the need for industry-wide unionization in mass production industries. When their suggestions were rejected out of hand at the 1935 international meeting of the AFL, these people started the CIO.[25]

A great deal of competition existed between the AFL and CIO through the 1930s and 40s. Each organization had its own approach to improving the lot of workers. The AFL remained attached to traditional notions of labor-management struggle, that is, trying to achieve gains through intrafirm improvements. The CIO was less conventional (in its day) in its approach. It strove for industry-wide improvements coupled with political solutions such as price control, public health, low-cost housing, better educational opportunities, and foreign trade policies that would minimize competition from low-cost foreign labor.[26]

Eventually, the two labor federations decided to combine forces against their common "foe"—management. In 1952, the organizations agreed to stop raiding one another for members. Three years later the two groups united forces, and they function together today as the AFL–CIO.[27]

It should be noted that the AFL and the CIO were not the only organizations that sought to unite workers in the 1800s and 1900s. These included, for example, the National Labor Union and the National Colored Labor Union (created in response to the exclusionary policies of the white labor organizations.)[28] Groups representing the political left enjoyed a large measure of success, as well. Perhaps the most notable of these was the Industrial Workers of the World, known popularly as the IWW or the Wobblies, and led by Eugene V. Debs, Daniel DeLeon, and Mother Mary Jones.[29] The IWW believed that an inherent conflict would always exist between the "capitalist class and the workers it employed." Thus, the Wobblies sought ultimately to achieve a socialist society.[30] In addition, the IWW recognized the special needs and problems of black people and women. This approach should be contrasted with the highly exclusionary and racist attitudes adopted by large segments of the AFL and CIO.

Do you agree with the IWW that an inherent conflict exists between the interests of the capitalist and working classes? Why or why not? If such an inherent conflict exists, do you believe there is any way to resolve that conflict? How would you approach the problem? If you do not believe such a conflict exists, is there any reason you would prefer being a member of one class rather than the other? Why?

Unionization

Attempts to unionize have traditionally met with a great deal of resistance from employers. Not only did companies have economic power to wield over the workers but, until the passage of protective legislation in 1935, employers had the backing of the legal system, as well.

Two devices used by employers to block or discourage unionization were ''yellow dog'' contracts and blacklists. A *yellow dog contract* was an employment agreement under which the employee was bound by the contract's terms not to become a member of a union. *Blacklists* were simply lists of union organizers or sometimes even participants in labor activities circulated among all the companies in an industry or geographic locale, telling employers not to hire the people named on the lists because they were union instigators.[31]

The legal means used most effectively to halt unionization in its incipiency was the court injunction. If a group of workers began picketing a factory, for example, an employer could easily obtain from the state or federal court an order forbidding the workers to continue such activities. Although picketing itself was not actually considered illegal, judicial doctrine developed that tied the act of picketing inextricably to violence. Thus, striking employees could be stopped for taking part in criminal conspiracies. Eventually, the idea that union activities constituted criminal actions was rejected and replaced by the notion that such actions involved civil tort liability. In either event, once an injunction had been issued, any workers who continued picketing were in contempt of court, subject to imprisonment and dismissal by their employer.[32]

The passage of the Sherman Antitrust Act in 1890 added a new legal weapon to the employers' arsenal against employees. In 1908, the U.S. Supreme Court used the Sherman Act prohibition on activities that were in ''restraint of trade'' to find workers involved in a boycott liable for treble damages under the provisions of that act. The Court's opinion indicated that virtually any concerted activity that employees engaged in could be construed as a restraint of trade and that federal courts could issue injunctions to prevent such activities under the authority vested in them by the Sherman Act.[33]

By 1932, public pressure had mounted so that Congress, in passing the Norris-LaGuardia Act (legislation designed primarily to prevent antitrust problems), withdrew from the federal courts the right to issue injunctions against labor activities and clarified its legislative intent that the terminology ''restraint of trade'' was not meant to include the organization or activities of labor. The Norris-LaGuardia Act also specifically outlawed the use of yellow dog contracts. Even the passage of the Norris-LaGuardia Act proved ineffectual, however, because employers were still able to go into state courts to obtain injunctive relief.[34]

From 1932 to 1935, labor tensions continued to mount. The nation was still caught in the Great Depression. Believing that one element essential to economic recovery was stability in the work force, Congress addressed the labor "question" with comprehensive legislation.[35] Congress had tried its hand at drafting labor legislation once before when it enacted the Railway Labor Act of 1926, an act designed to protect workers in the railroad industry who chose to organize. Although the Railway Labor Act affected workers *only* in the railroad industry, the 1926 legislation laid a good foundation from which Congress could work in developing a statutory scheme to apply to workers in other segments of industry and the work force.[36]

Congress passed the Wagner Act in 1935. This legislation, patterned after the Railway Labor Act, gave workers for the first time the unequivocal right to organize and to engage in concerted activities for their mutual aid and benefit. In order to protect this right, Congress identified a number of "unfair labor practices" and made them illegal. These unfair labor practices were all activities that Congress feared employers might use to thwart workers' attempts to unionize and to undermine the economic power that would come from workers' newfound rights.[37] Through the Wagner Act, Congress also established the National Labor Relations Board (NLRB or "the Board"), an administrative agency charged with the responsibility of overseeing and ensuring fair union representation elections, and investigating, prosecuting and trying employers accused of committing unfair labor practices.[38]

Armed with these legislative protections and a governmental bias in favor of unionization, labor organized rapidly. In 1935, only 3 million workers were members of labor organizations; 12 years later, the ranks had swelled to 15 million.[39] By 1947, Congress decided that labor no longer needed such a protective watchdog and, in fact, thought that management might need a little help in coping with ever-growing labor organizations.[40] Thus, Congress decided to "neutralize" its position vis-à-vis labor organizations by imposing some responsibilities on these organizations where before there had been none. Congress did so by enacting the Taft-Hartley Act, a series of amendments to the Wagner Act that identified as unfair labor practices certain activities unions used to hamper, rather than help, the collective bargaining process. The Taft-Hartley Act also added a provision to the existing labor legislation that ensured employers' right to speak out in opposition to unionization, in effect, protecting their First Amendment right to freedom of speech. Thus, the Taft-Hartley Act signaled a move by the government away from unconditional support for labor, toward a balance of rights between labor and management.[41]

Congressional hearings in the 1950s uncovered a new source of concern in the area of labor relations. This time the problems were not between labor and management, although certainly friction between the two continued to exist. Attention now was focused on union leaders who were abusing their power. Once in power, some union leaders had prevented others from challenging their power by not holding meetings of the union's rank and file, not scheduling elections, and using union funds to promote their own election campaigns. Stories came to light accusing some union officials of accepting collective bargaining agreements with terms that were against the interest of their constituencies, in exchange for bribes paid to them by corporate management. These agreements were aptly called "sweetheart" deals. Evidence indicated that certain union officials had looted their unions' treasuries.[42]

In response to the growing evidence that union leaders were benefiting at the expense of the membership, Congress in 1959 enacted the Landrum-Griffin Act, also known as the Labor-Management Reporting and Disclosure Act (LMRDA). This act contains provisions that require unions to keep records of their funds, including statements of their assets, liabilities, salaries paid, and all other expenditures. It also prohibits unions from loaning money except under specified circumstances and in conformity with certain procedural rules. These financial statements and transactions must all be reported annually to the government.

The Landrum-Griffin Act also contains a set of provisions often referred to as the "Bill of Rights" for the individual laborer. These provisions are designed to protect union members by requiring that union meetings be held, that members be permitted to speak and vote at these meetings, that every employee covered by a collective bargaining agreement have the right to see a copy of that agreement, and that a union member be informed of the reasons and given a chance for a hearing if the union wishes to suspend or take disciplinary action against that member, unless he or she is being suspended for nonpayment of dues.[43] Although these provisions had the potential for eliminating the internal union problems, recent court decisions have done much to emasculate the protections provided in Landrum-Griffin. These court decisions will be discussed later in this chapter.

This historical progression, from labor's helplessness to active unionization following passage of the Wagner Act in 1935, to restoration of balance between labor and management in 1947 and, finally, to a recognition of the powerlessness of the individual within the union, sounds very smooth and logical. The entire process has been likened by many to the swinging of a pendulum. One should not forget, however, that labor conflicts in the United States have often been attended by severe violence; have driven apart towns, factories, even families; and have raised emotions to higher pitches than perhaps any other social or political issue. Labor disputes have the potential, as with nationwide strikes, for bringing industry and production to a grinding halt. Any exposition of the law on this subject must be understood within this context as illustrated in the following report of the U.S. Commission on Industrial Relations appointed by Congress in 1915:

Mr. Chairman, my name is George P. West, staff investigator for the Senate Committee. We have found that the mine owners cooperated in organizing a new troop of cavalry called Troop A of the National Guard. This troop consisted of not more than 30 mine guards employed by the company. The others were pit bosses, mine superintendents, clerks and the like.

On April 20, 1914, these sworn militia men in the paid employment of the company destroyed a tent colony of strikers in Ludlow, Colorado. Commanding Officer Linderfeldt believed the strikers to be unarmed.

Notwithstanding, the militia opened rifle and machine gun fire killing five men and one boy and firing the tents with a torch. Eleven children and two women of the colony were burnt to death.

Hundreds of women and children were driven terror-stricken into the hills while others huddled for 12 hours in pits underneath their tents while bullets from machine guns whistled overhead and kept them in constant terror.[44]

Labor Legislation Today—The Statutory Scheme and Its Goals

Today labor-management relations are governed by the National Labor Relations Act (NLRA).[45] This act includes the Wagner Act, the Taft-Hartley Act, and portions of the Landrum-Griffin Act. The remaining provisions of the Landrum-Griffin Act make up the aforementioned Labor-Management Reporting and Disclosure Act and the "Bill of Rights of Members of Labor Organizations." These provisions deal with the internal operations of labor organizations and the relationship between the individual union member and the union itself rather than with the relationship between the union and the employer.

The National Labor Relations Act sets out the following policy statement:

Findings and Declaration of Policy

The denial by some employers of the right of employees to organize and the refusal by some employers to accept the procedure of collective bargaining lead to strikes and other forms of industrial strife or unrest, which have the intent or the necessary effect of burdening or obstructing commerce by (a) impairing the efficiency, safety, or operation of the instrumentalities of commerce; (b) occurring in the current of commerce; (c) materially affecting, restraining, or controlling the flow of raw materials or manufactured or processed goods from or into the channels of commerce, or the prices of such materials or goods in commerce; or (d) causing diminution of employment and wages in such volume as substantially to impair or disrupt the market for goods flowing from or into the channels of commerce.

The inequality of bargaining power between employees who do not possess full freedom of association or actual liberty of contract, and employers who are organized in the corporate or other forms of ownership association substantially burdens and affects the flow of commerce, and tends to aggravate recurrent business depressions, by depressing wage rates and the purchasing power of wage earners in industry and by preventing the stabilization of competitive wage rates and working conditions within and between industries.

Experience has proved that protection by law of the right of employees to organize and bargain collectively safeguards commerce from injury, impairment, or interruption, and promotes the flow of commerce by removing certain recognized sources of industrial strife and unrest, by encouraging practices fundamental to the friendly adjustment of industrial disputes arising out of differences as to wages, hours, or other working conditions, and by restoring equality of bargaining power between employers and employees.

Experience has further demonstrated that certain practices by some labor organizations, their officers, and members have the intent or the necessary effect of burdening or obstructing commerce by preventing the free flow of goods in such commerce through strikes and other forms of industrial unrest or through concerted activities which impair the interest of the public in the free flow of such commerce. The elimination of such practices is a necessary condition to the assurance of the rights herein guaranteed.

It is declared to be the policy of the United States to eliminate the causes of certain substantial obstructions to the free flow of commerce and to mitigate and eliminate these obstructions when they have occurred by encouraging the practice and procedure of collective bargaining and by protecting the exercise by workers of full freedom of association, self-organization, and designation of representatives of their own choosing, for the purpose of negotiating the terms and conditions of their employment or other mutual aid or protection.

Note that Congress couches its findings and declarations of policy in terms of maintaining the free flow of commerce or, conversely, eliminating the obstructions to freely flowing commerce caused by labor conflicts. Note, too, that Congress identifies labor conflict to be due, in large part, to lack of bargaining power on the part of individual employees and, thus, sets out to correct the problem by promoting concerted activity by employees and collective bargaining between labor organizations and management.

It is important to keep these ideas in mind as one examines the choices made by Congress in regulating labor-management relations and the decisions made by the NLRB and the courts in interpreting and applying these statutory mandates. First, the NLRA gives employees the right to engage in concerted activity. Section 7 of the NLRA states:

Employees shall have the right to self-organization, to form, join or assist labor organizations, to bargain collectively through representatives of their own choosing, and to engage in other concerted activities for the purpose of collective bargaining or other mutual aid or protection, and shall also have the right to refrain from any or all of such activities except to the extent that such right may be affected by an agreement requiring membership in a labor organization as a condition of employment.

Second, as was mentioned previously, the act describes and outlaws certain activities by employers that would hamper or discourage employees from exercising the rights granted to them in section 7. Thus, section 8(a) of the act makes it an unfair labor practice for an employer:

1. To interfere with employees in the exercise of the rights given to them by section 7.
2. To dominate, interfere or assist with the formation of any labor organization (including contributing financial support to it).
3. To encourage or discourage membership in any labor organization by discrimination in regard to hire, tenure of employment promotion, salary, or any other term of employment.
4. To discharge or take any other action against an employee because he or she has filed charges or given testimony under this Act.
5. To refuse to bargain collectively with a duly certified representative of the employees.

These five provisions are designed to allow employees to organize in an atmosphere free from intimidation by the employer, with minds clear of the fear that the employer might be able to affect their jobs adversely because of their choice to participate in a labor organization. The provisions also ensure that the employer, through his or her position of authority, will not be able to interfere with union activities either by seizing control of the union or by rendering it impotent by refusing to bargain collectively.

Section 8(b) lists those activities that constitute unfair labor practices by a labor organization. Some of these provisions mirror some of the activities prohibited to employers. That is, at least since the enactment of the Taft-Hartley Act, the law is not sympathetic to labor organizations that try to use coercive tactics, threats of the loss of livelihood, or any other "strong-arm" methods, to recruit members. Reasoned persuasion is the order of the day. Thus, a labor organization is not permitted:

1. To restrain or coerce any employee in the exercise of his or her rights as granted by section 7.
2. To cause or attempt to cause an employer to discriminate against an employee who has chosen not to join a particular labor organization or has been denied membership in such an organization.
3. To refuse to bargain collectively with an employer on behalf of the bargaining unit it is certified to represent.
4. To induce or attempt to induce an employer to engage in secondary boycott activities.
5. To require employees to become union members and then charge them excessive or discriminatory dues.
6. To try to make an employer compensate workers for services that are not performed.
7. To picket or threaten to picket an employer where the object of the picketing would be to try and force the employer to recognize or bargain with a labor organization that is not the duly certified representative of a bargaining unit.

The remaining subparts of section 8 cover a variety of problems: Section 8(c) protects the First Amendment rights of people involved in labor disputes while spelling out limitations on those rights. Section 8(d) describes and defines the duties of employers and labor organizations to bargain collectively over certain mandatory subjects. This section also sets up a "cooling-off" process under which a party who wishes to renegotiate a collective bargaining agreement must serve notice of its desire to do so 60 days in advance of the agreement's expiration date. Sections 8(e) and (f) describe situations in which it is impermissible for both employers and labor organizations to pursue their disputes in ways that extend those disputes beyond the confines of their own internal conflict. This type of conduct, referred to generally as "secondary" activity, includes secondary boycotts, hot cargo agreements, and common situs picketing, all of which will be described in greater detail later in the chapter.

National Labor Relations Board

The National Labor Relations Board is an administrative agency that is instrumental in regulating labor-management relations. Its primary tasks are: designating appropriate bargaining units of workers (that is, deciding which workers have a sufficient "community of interest" to afford them unity when bargaining); conducting elections for union representation within the chosen bargaining unit; certifying the results of such elections; and investigating, prosecuting, and adjudicating charges of unfair labor practices.[46]

Although the congressional mandate by which the NLRB was formed gives the agency jurisdiction theoretically to the full extent of the interstate commerce powers vested in Congress, in fact, the agency has neither funding nor the staff to administer its duties to all of American industry. Thus, some limitations have been placed on the board both by statute and by the agency's own decisions.

These restrictions on jurisdiction take two basic forms. First, the board itself requires that the portion of an employer's business involved in interstate commerce must exceed certain dollar amounts. These amounts differ depending on the nature of the industry. Second, entire groups of employees are excluded from coverage. For example, public employees, agricultural workers, and supervisors and other managerial employees are not protected by the board.[47]

Why do you think these groups have been excluded from coverage? Do these groups share any common characteristics? Do you agree that they ought to be excluded?

Choosing an Appropriate Bargaining Unit

A *bargaining unit* is a group of employees that is entitled to have a bargaining representative with whom management must negotiate. The employee group seeking representation typically suggests those employees it wants to include in the unit. The board will then decide whether the unit so described constitutes an "appropriate" bargaining unit by deciding whether a "community of interest" exists among the workers. Rarely will one choice of employees to be included in a bargaining unit constitute the *only* suitable group that has the necessary community of interest. For example, a bargaining unit might consist of all of the employees at a plant, all of the nonskilled workers, or perhaps all of the pipe-fitters.[48]

What are the implications of the choice of members for the bargaining unit? What factors do you think the board should consider in determining whether a bargaining unit has a "community of interest"? Do the varying needs of the employees make a difference? Would it be appropriate under the community of interest concept to set up separate bargaining units on the basis of skill levels? Gender distinctions? Disability versus nondisability? Pro-union sentiment?

Question

1. Assume a union seeks a bargaining unit that would include all full-time and regular part-time employees at a supermarket, including head cashiers, produce managers, stock managers, and baggers. The unit would exclude meat department employees, salespeople, security guards, store managers, and assistant managers.
   a. Do you think the board should approve this unit?
   b. If not, how should the group be changed?
   c. Are there any additional facts you need before making your decision? See *Daylight Grocery Co., Inc.* v. *NLRB,* 678 F.2d 905 (11th Cir. 1982).

Choosing a Bargaining Representative— Elections

A bargaining representative is chosen by an election held within the bargaining unit that has been certified appropriate by the National Labor Relations Board. The NLRB oversees the election to make sure that the process is carried on under "laboratory conditions."[49] In other words, the elections must be held under circumstances that, to the extent possible, are free from undue or unfair influence by either the employer or by unions vying for the position of representative of the bargaining unit.

Unfair labor practices are frequently committed at this juncture by employers anxious to prevent their plants from becoming unionized. This is not meant to suggest that overzealous unions never commit unfair labor practices or that employers always do. However, employers who are resistant to unionization have a great many natural advantages in the struggle against unionization. For example, employers have at their disposal lists of names and addresses for all their employees; the union does not. The employer could distribute written arguments and objections to unionization along with paychecks and thereby ensure that every employee sees the document. (Such an action, by itself, is *not* an unfair labor practice.)[50] The employer effectively has a captive audience. The employer generally is in better financial shape to stage a battle than the union is. Finally, and perhaps most importantly, the employer is the one who, in the final analysis, doles out or withholds benefits to the employees and the one who provides them with jobs in the first place. It is not always terribly difficult for an employer to cross the line from using this position of natural authority to abusing the position and committing an unfair labor practice.

Certain actions taken by employers prior to union elections are clearly unfair labor practices. Under section 8(a)(3) employers are prohibited from discriminating against employees so as to discourage them from voting for the union. Thus, discharging union activists or sympathizers as an example to others who might follow suit is a violation of the NLRA.

Before Congress passed the Taft-Hartley Act, board decisions reflected its belief that any attempts (including, for example, the distribution of antiunion pamphlets, speeches, or circulars) by an employer to influence the voting of his or her employees was an unfair labor practice. These decisions, however, raised First Amendment questions in the minds of many who thought that the employers' constitutional right to free speech was being abridged by these rulings.[51]

Congress determined to remedy this problem with a provision of the Taft-Hartley Act by adding section 8(c) to the NLRA. Section 8(c) was designed to ensure employers' and labor organizations' traditional First Amendment rights so long as they do not overstep certain bounds. The section states the following:

The expressing of any views, argument or opinion, or the dissemination thereof, whether in written, printed, graphic, or visual form, shall not constitute or be evidence of an unfair labor practice . . . if such expression contains no threat of reprisal or force or promise of benefit.

Even with the inclusion of section 8(c) in the NLRA, the board and the courts have continued in a struggle to define the parameters of protected and unprotected speech. The following decision of the NLRB provides an example of an employer's pre-election tactics that contained no threats of force or reprisal, but for which the board was nonetheless willing to set aside an election.

SEWELL MFG. CO. and AMALGAMATED CLOTHING WORKERS OF AMERICA, AFL–CIO   138 NLRB No. 12, Case No. 10-RC-5016, August 9, 1962

Before McCulloch, Leedom, Fanning, and Brown

[A]n election by secret ballot was conducted . . . to determine whether the employees therein desired to be represented by the petitioner for purposes of collective bargaining. Upon the conclusion of the balloting the parties were furnished with a tally of ballots which showed that of approximately 1,339 eligible voters, 1,322 cast ballots of which 331 were for, and 985 against, the petitioner, 5 ballots were challenged, and 1 ballot was void. The number of challenged ballots was insufficient to affect the election results. Thereafter the petitioner filed timely objections to conduct affecting the results of the election.

* * * * *

The petitioner objected to the election upon the ground . . . that the employer, by various propaganda means, had resorted to appeals to racial prejudice to prevent a free election.

The elections were held on July 21, 1961, at Bremen and Temple, Georgia, where the employer's plants are located. Bremen has a population of less than 3,000; Temple a population of under 1,000. Both are located in Haralson County, on the Alabama border, in northwest Georgia, approximately 50 miles west of Atlanta.

On July 7, 1961, two weeks before the scheduled election, the employer mailed to its employees a large picture showing a close-up of an unidentified Negro man dancing with an unidentified white lady. Underneath was a caption in large, bold letters reading: "The CIO Strongly Pushes and Endorses the FEPC." On the same day the employer also sent the employees a reproduction of the June 4, 1957, front page of the *Jackson Daily News,* a newspaper published in Jackson, Mississippi, which contains a picture, four columns wide, of a white man dancing with a Negro lady. The caption beneath the picture reads:

UNION LEADER JAMES B. CAREY
DANCES WITH A LADY FRIEND
He is president of the IUE
Which Seeks to Unionize
Vickers Plant here.

Underneath the picture is a story headed: "Race Mixing Is An Issue As Vickers Workers Ballot."

On July 19, 1961, the president of the employer sent a letter to employees setting forth reasons why the president would vote against the petitioner if he were permitted to vote. Among these reasons is the following: "I would object to paying assessments so the union can promote its political objectives such as the National Association for the Advancement of Colored People, and the Congress of Racial Equality."

On July 13, 1961, the *Haralson County Tribune,* under a headline describing the election to be held at the employer's plants, carried the following news story:

The following reprint of a letter sent out by this union shows how some of the dues paid to this union by union members is being spent: Following is a letter from and [sic] James B. Carey, secretary-treasurer to James Farmer, national director, Congress of Racial Equality, covering transmittal of a check for $5,000 for expenses incurred by CORE in connection with the "Freedom Riders."

Appended to the article was a letter from the Industrial Union Department, AFL–CIO, signed by Walter Reuther and James B. Carey, to the national director of the Congress of Racial Equality. The letter stated that the Industrial Union Department was enclosing a check for $5,000 "as an expression of our solidarity with CORE and our support of its work in the field of civil rights. We are requesting that this money be used in connection with expenses arising from CORE's 'Freedom Ride' project." The letter went on to praise the "Freedom Riders" and to criticize actions of state officials in Alabama and Mississippi as allegedly violative of federal law. According to the Regional Director, the wife of the publisher of the *Haralson County Tribune* was responsible for the article.

During the four months preceding the election, the employer distributed to employees copies of *Militant Truth,* a four-page monthly paper published in Greenville, South Carolina. In its columns are a number of statements dealing with racial matters. In a two-page article entitled "Militant Truth and the Labor Unions," there is this statement:

It isn't in the interest of our wage earners to tie themselves to organizations that demand racial integration, socialistic legislation, and free range of communist conspirators.

In a two-column article listing plants in which unions had lost elections, there is the statement:

Another factor that merits consideration is the large percentage of union victories in plants that employ all, or nearly all, Negro labor. Because the communists always operate under the guise of being "the great uplifters" of "the underprivileged," and promise social equality to the Negro, it is easy to understand why many Negroes are more easily influenced and misled by the radical labor union organizers.

In an article on integration (not on labor matters), there is a reference to the Garland Fund as having made a contribution to the NAACP, and reference to "Sidney Hillman, the Russian-born Founder of the Amalgamated Clothing Workers," as one of its directors. The same issue contains a reprint of an article from "The Worker," dealing with "freedom riders." According to *Militant Truth,* the "Worker" article takes time out "to praise the various AFL–CIO unions for their part in demanding total integration and promoting both class and race warfare." Another article dealing with the Negro's progress in America refers to "The Communist Party, the NAACP, the labor unions, the National Council of Churches, the Kennedy Administration and their ilk . . ." as those who "would have us believe that the Negro race in America is a poor, starving, downtrodden people."

The Regional Director ruled that the foregoing literature did not justify setting aside the election upon the ground that, "while the Board has consistently held that appeals to religious and racial prejudices are not condoned, such literature does not exceed the permissible bounds of preelection propaganda." For this conclusion, the Regional Director cited the Sharnay case, in which a union objected to an election because the employer, in a letter to employees, had discussed the union's position on the issue of racial integration. The letter had stated that the union was strongly prointegration, had submitted a prointegration brief to the Supreme Court, was striving to eliminate segregation from every walk of life, and was a member of the AFL–CIO which had made a monetary contribution to the NAACP. In refusing to set aside the election because of this letter, the Board said:

. . . The petitioner concedes that there were no threats or promises, and it is not suggested that the employer misrepresented the petitioner's position. We are asked, rather, to hold that the mere mention of the racial issue, in an election campaign, is per se improper and grounds for setting aside any and all elections where such might occur. . . . We note that there is no misrepresentation, fraud, violence, or coercion and that the statements here were temperate and factually correct. They therefore afford no basis for setting aside the results of the election.

We do not agree with the Regional Director that the rationale of the Sharnay case requires overruling of the objections in the present case.

A Board election is not identical with a political election. In the latter, public officials conducting the election have no responsibility beyond the mechanics of the election. Aside from such things as libel restrictions and legal requirements to identify the source of campaign literature and advertising, the law permits wide latitude in the way of propaganda—truth and untruth, promises, threats, appeals to prejudice. It is only the sense of decency of the candidates and their supporters and the maturity of the electorate which places a restraint upon the kind of propaganda used.

By way of contrast, the Board not only conducts elections, but it also oversees the propaganda activities of the participants in the election to insure that the voters have the opportunity of exercising a reasoned, untrammeled choice for or against labor organizations seeking representation rights. The Board has said that in election proceedings it seeks "to provide a laboratory in which an experiment may be conducted, under conditions as nearly ideal as possible, to determine the uninhibited desires of the employees." Where for any reason the standard falls too low the Board will set aside the election and direct a new one. Unsatisfactory conditions for holding elections may be created by promises of benefits, threats of economic reprisals, deliberate misrepresentations of material facts by an employer or a union, deceptive campaign tactics by a union, or by a general atmosphere of fear and confusion caused by a participant or by members of the general public. Standards, particularly those of permissive propaganda, are not fixed and immutable. They have been changed and refined, generally in the direction of higher standards.

Our function, as we see it, is to conduct elections in which the employees have the opportunity to cast their ballots for or against a labor organization in an atmosphere conducive to the sober and informed exercise of the franchise, free not only from interference, restraint, or coercion violative of the act, but also from other elements which prevent or impede a reasoned choice.

We are faced in this case with a claim that by a deliberate sustained appeal to racial prejudice the employer created conditions which made impossible a reasoned choice of a bargaining representative and therefore that the election should be set aside.

Some appeal to prejudice of one kind or another is an inevitable part of electoral campaigning, whether in the political or labor field. Standards must be high, but they cannot be so high that for practical purposes elections could not effectively be conducted. There are propaganda appeals used in elections which we do not approve or condone, but which we tolerate, leaving the proper weighing of such appeals to the good sense and judgment of the electorate. Such tolerated propaganda has been characterized as "prattle rather than precision." The Board has stated its practice as follows:

The Board normally will not censor or police preelection propaganda by parties to elections, absent threats or acts of violence . . . Exaggerations, inaccuracies, partial truths, name-calling, and falsehoods, while not condoned, may be excused as legitimate propaganda, provided they are not so misleading as to prevent the exercise of a free choice by employees in the election of their bargaining representative. The ultimate consideration is whether the challenged propaganda has lowered the standards of campaigning to the point where it may be said that the uninhibited desires of the employees cannot be determined in an election.

The Board has considered as propaganda a single sentence reference to the religious background of the employer. But the appeals made to racial prejudice in this case are different both in kind and intensity from the single, casual religious reference made in the *Paula Shoe* case.

We take it as datum that prejudice based on color is a powerful emotional force. We think it also indisputable that a deliberate appeal to such prejudice is not intended or calculated to encourage the reasoning faculty.

What we have said indicates our belief that appeals to racial prejudice on matters unrelated to the election issues or to the union's activities are not mere "prattle" or puffing. They have no place in Board electoral campaigns. They inject an element which is destructive of the very purpose of an election. They create conditions which make impossible a sober, informed exercise of the franchise. The Board does not intend to tolerate as "electoral propaganda" appeals or arguments which can have no purpose except to inflame the racial feelings of voters in the election.

This is not to say that a relevant campaign statement is to be condemned because it may have racial overtones. In *Sharnay,* supra, the employer in a letter to employees made a temperate, factually correct statement of the petitioning union's position on integration. In the *Allen-Morrison Sign* case. . . . the employer also informed the employees about the petitioning union's position on segregation as well as on union monetary contributions towards eliminating segregation. In the view of Chairman McCulloch, and Members Leedom and Fanning again the statement was temperate in tone, germane and correct factually.

We would be less than realistic if we did not recognize that such statements, even when moderate and truthful, do in fact cater to racial prejudice. Yet we believe that they must be tolerated because they are true and because they pertain to a subject concerning which employees are entitled to have knowledge—the union's position on racial matters. As Professor Sovern has pointed out: no one would suggest that Negro employees were not entitled to know that the union which seeks to represent them practices racial discrimination.

So long, therefore, as a party limits itself to *truthfully* setting forth another party's position on matters of racial interest and does not deliberately seek to overstress and exacerbate racial feelings by irrelevant, inflammatory appeals, we shall not set aside an election on this ground. However, the burden will be on the party making use of a racial message to establish that it was truthful and germane, and where there is doubt as to whether the total conduct of such party is within the described bounds, the doubt will be resolved against him.

Viewed against the test set forth above, we find that the employer's propaganda directed to race exceeded permissible limits and so inflamed and tainted the atmosphere in which the election was held that a reasoned basis for choosing or rejecting a bargaining representative was an impossibility. It seems obvious from the kind and extent of propaganda material distributed that the employer calculatedly embarked on a campaign so to inflame racial prejudice of its employees that they would reject the petitioner out of hand on racial grounds alone. This is most readily apparent from the distribution of photographs showing a Negro man dancing with a white woman, and a white man, identified in the photograph as James B. Carey, president of the IUE, (which is not the petitioner in this case), dancing with a Negro woman, to the latter of which was appended a news story headed: "Race Mixing Is An Issue As Vickers Workers Ballot." These photographs and the news articles were not germane to any legitimate issue involved in the election and reinforce our conclusion that their purpose was to exacerbate racial prejudice and to create an emotional atmosphere of hostility to the petitioner.

Accordingly, we shall set aside the election and direct that a second election be held.

Questions

1. Does it surprise you to learn that a company would use tactics such as those described above to try and discredit unions and their leadership?
2. If you were called upon, as a manager or officer in a company, to participate in such tactics, what would you do?
3. If you were instructed by your superiors at the company to develop a program designed to discourage unionization, what would be your plan of action?
4. Suppose the employees of Steno Office Supply, Inc., a large manufacturing firm, have petitioned the NLRB for an election. Company management personnel begin inviting

workers to lunch to discuss the upcoming election and the likely "consequences" of unionization. These lunches are held at the local country club. During these discussions, at which employee comments are encouraged, although not forced, managers make allusions to the union organizers' sexual orientation. The comments, made in the form of jokes, suggest that homosexual favors may be required in lieu of dues.

a. If the union loses the election, should the NLRB set the election aside because of the tactics used?
b. Which, if any, of these tactics seem problematic?
c. Would any one of the tactics by itself be enough to set aside the election?
d. What standard should the Board use in making its determination?
e. What additional information might you want to have before making a decision in this particular case? See *General Knit of California,* 239 NLRB 619 (1978) 99 LRRM 1687, for a discussion of the general standard.

Threats of Reprisal or Force

Even within the confines of section 8(c)'s language, problems often arise in determining whether "antiunion" arguments put forth by an employer are legitimate or whether they contain veiled threats. Suppose, for instance, that a company owner warns her employees that if she has to pay higher wages (a demand that a union would be likely to make), she will be forced to go out of business and the employees will all lose their jobs. Such statements of economic "forecast" by employers have been the subject of a great deal of litigation. The following case explains the issues involved.

NLRB V. GISSEL PACKING CO.   395 U.S. 575 (1969)

[The president of Sinclair Company, one of four companies whose actions were being examined in this case, tried to dissuade his employees from joining a union. To that end, he informed them that, if the union won the election, it was bound to call a strike because the Teamsters were a "strike-happy" outfit. He told the employees on more than one occasion that the company's financial position was precarious and that a strike would likely force the plant to close. He suggested that the out-of-work employees would have a difficult time finding new jobs because of their age and lack of education. The union lost the election by a vote of 7 to 6 and filed objections to the election with the NLRB.

Both the NLRB and later the Court of Appeals agreed that the election should be set aside, despite the company's claim that it had merely been exercising its First Amendment rights to express its views to employees. The Supreme Court affirmed the Court of Appeals decision.]

Chief Justice Warren

We note that an employer's free speech right to communicate his views to his employees is firmly established and cannot be infringed by a union or the Board. Thus, § 8(c) [29 U.S.C. § 158(c)] merely implements the First Amendment by requiring that the expression of "any views, argument, or opinion" shall not be "evidence of an unfair labor practice," so long as such expression contains "no threat of reprisal or force or promise of benefit" in violation of § 8(a)(1). Section 8(a)(1), in turn, prohibits interference, restraint, or coercion of employees in the exercise of their right to self-organization.

Any assessment of the precise scope of employer expression, of course, must be made in the context of its labor relations setting. Thus, an employer's rights cannot outweigh the equal rights of the employees to associate freely, as those rights are embodied in § 7 and protected by § 8(a)(1) and the proviso to § 8(c). And any balancing of those rights must take into account the economic dependence of the employees on their employers, and the necessary tendency of the former, because of that relationship, to pick up intended implications of the latter that might be more readily dismissed by a more disinterested ear. Stating these obvious principles is but another way of recognizing that what is basically at stake is the establishment of a nonpermanent, limited relationship between the employer, his economically dependent employee, and his union agent, not the election of legislators or the enactment of legislation whereby that relationship is ultimately defined and where the independent voter may be freer to listen more objectively and employers as a class freer to talk.

Within this framework, we must reject the company's challenge to the decision below and the findings of the Board on which it was based. The standards used below for evaluating the impact of an employer's statements are not seriously questioned by petitioner and we see no need to tamper with them here. Thus, an employer is free to communicate to his employees any of his general views about unionism or any of his specific views about a particular union, so long as the communications do not contain a "threat of reprisal or force or promise of benefit." He may even make a prediction as to the precise effects he believes unionization will have on his company. In such a case, however, the prediction must be carefully phrased on the basis of objective fact to convey an employer's belief as to demonstrably probable consequences beyond his control or to convey a management decision already arrived at to close the plant in case of unionization. If there is any implication that an employer may or may not take action solely on his own initiative for reasons unrelated to economic necessities and known only to him, the statement is no longer a reasonable prediction based on available facts but a threat of retaliation based on misrepresentation and coercion, and as such without the protection of the First Amendment. We therefore agree with the court below that "[c]onveyance of the employer's belief, even though sincere, that unionization will or may result in the closing of the plant is not a statement of fact unless, which is most improbable, the eventuality of closing is capable of proof." As stated elsewhere, an employer is free only to tell "what he reasonably believes will be the likely economic consequences of unionization that are outside his control," and not "threats of economic reprisal to be taken solely on his own volition."

Equally valid was the finding by the court and the Board that petitioner's statements and communications were not cast as a prediction of "demonstrable 'economic consequences,' " but rather as a threat of retaliatory action. The Board found that petitioner's speeches, pamphlets, leaflets, and letters conveyed the following message: that the company was in a precarious financial condition; that the "strike-happy" union would in all likelihood have to obtain its potentially unreasonable demands by striking, the probable result of which would be a plant shutdown, as the past history of labor relations in the area indicated; and that the employees in such a case would have great difficulty finding employment elsewhere. In carrying out its duty to focus on the question: "[W]hat did the speaker intend and the listener understand?" the Board could reasonably conclude that the intended and understood import of that message was not to predict that unionization would inevitably cause the plant to close but to threaten to throw employees out of work regardless of the economic realities. In this connection, we need go no further than to point out (1) that petitioner had no support for its basic assumption that the union, which had not yet even presented any demands, would have to strike to be heard, and that it admitted at the hearing that it had no basis for attributing other plant closings in the area to unionism; and (2) that the Board has often found that employees, who are particularly sensitive to rumors of plant closings, take such hints as coercive threats rather than honest forecasts.

Affirmed.

Questions

1. Why does the Court suggest that the NLRB has a duty to determine what the speaker intended and what the listener understood?
2. How does that differ from merely looking at what the employer actually said?
3. Why is that difference important?

Promise of Benefit

While threats of force or reprisal are considered objectionable elements in union campaigns, the rationale behind the prohibition against promises of benefit is not as intuitively obvious. In the case of *NLRB* v. *Exchange Parts Co.* 375 U.S. 409 (1964), Exchange Parts sent its employees a letter shortly before a representation election, which spoke of "the *Empty Promises* of the Union" and "the *fact* that *it is the Company that puts things in your envelope . . .*" After mentioning a number of benefits, the letter said: "The Union can't put any of those things in your envelope—*only the Company can do that.*" Further on, the letter stated: ". . . [I]t didn't take a Union to get any of those things and . . . it won't take a Union to get additional improvements in the future." Accompanying the letter was a detailed statement of the benefits granted by the company since 1949 and an estimate of the monetary value of such benefits to the employees.

In addition, the letter outlined further benefits, such as additional vacation days and overtime pay, that the company had recently decided to institute. In the representation election held two weeks later, the union lost. The Court of Appeals did not think the employer's action constituted an unfair labor practice. The Supreme Court disagreed. Justice Harlan stated:

We think the Court of Appeals was mistaken in concluding that the conferral of employee benefits while a representation election is pending, for the purpose of inducing employees to vote against the union, does not "interfere with" the protected right to organize.

The broad purpose of § 8(a)(1) is to establish "the right of employees to organize for mutual aid without employer interference." We have no doubt that it prohibits not only intrusive threats and promises but also conduct immediately favorable to employees which is undertaken with the express purpose of impinging upon their freedom of choice for or against unionization and is reasonably calculated to have that effect. In *Medo Photo Supply Corp.* v. *N.L.R.B.,* this Court said: "The action of employees with respect to the choice of their bargaining agents may be induced by favors bestowed by the employer as well as by his threats or domination." Although in that case there was already a designated bargaining agent and the offer of "favors" was in response to a suggestion of the employees that they would leave the union if favors were bestowed, the principles which dictated the result there are fully applicable here. The danger inherent in well-timed increases in benefits is the suggestion of a *fist inside the velvet glove.* [Emphasis added.] Employees are not likely to miss the inference that the source of benefits now conferred is also the source from which future benefits must flow and which may dry up if it is not obliged. The danger may be diminished if, as in this case, the benefits are conferred permanently and unconditionally. But the absence of conditions or threats pertaining to the particular benefits conferred would be of controlling significance only if it could be presumed that no question of additional benefits or renegotiation of existing benefits would arise in the future; and, of course, no such presumption is tenable.

Other Courts of Appeals have found a violation of § 8(a)(1) in the kind of conduct involved here. It is true, as the court below pointed out, that in most cases of this kind the increase in benefits could be regarded as "one part of an overall program of interference and restraint by the employer," and that in this case the questioned conduct stood in isolation. Other unlawful conduct may often be an indication of the motive behind a grant of benefits while an election is pending, and to that extent it is relevant to the legality of the grant; but when as here the motive is otherwise established, an employer is not free to violate § 8(a)(1) by conferring benefits simply because it refrains from other, more obvious violations. We cannot agree with the Court of Appeals that enforcement of the Board's order will have the "ironic" result of "discouraging benefits for labor." The beneficence of an employer is likely to be ephemeral if prompted by a threat of unionization which is subsequently removed. Insulating the right of collective organization from calculated good will of this sort deprives employees of little that has lasting value.

Reversed.

Questions

1. What is the Court talking about when it refers to the "fist inside the velvet glove"?
2. Do you think the Court is justified in thinking that workers would be fooled or cowed by a sudden move by management to grant benefits?
3. Do you think the efforts to unionize or negotiate would be undermined?

Union Persuasion

Employers, of course, are not the only parties affected by section 8(c). Unions are also restricted in the type of pre-election persuasion they employ. In cases involving promises of benefits made by the union, the board has been more reluctant to set aside elections than it has when such promises have been made by management. The board's reasoning is that employees realize that union pre-election promises are merely expressions of a union platform, so to speak. Employees recognize that these are benefits for which the union intends to fight. Employers, on the other hand, really do hold within their power the ability to confer or withdraw benefits—the so-called "fist inside the velvet glove." Nonetheless, occasionally a situation does arise where a union does promise a benefit in a manner that violates section 8(c).

For example, suppose a union seeking to organize employees tells those employees that any employee who voices support for the union before the election will not have to pay union dues for a full year if the union is voted in. Do you see any difference between this and the *Gissel* case? Who do you think workers feel more threatened by—

their employers or their peers? Should the Court's reasoning in this case be the same as it was in *Gissel?* Why or why not? See *NLRB* v. *Savair Manufacturing Co.,* 414 U.S. 274 (1973).

Collective Bargaining

NLRA Section 8(a)(5) requires an employer to engage in collective bargaining with a representative of the employees. Section 8(b)(3) imposes the same duty on labor organizations; that is, if the organization is the representative of the employees, that organization has an obligation to bargain collectively with the employer. Failure to bargain by either an employer or representative of the employees constitutes an unfair labor practice.

What is collective bargaining? What must one do to discharge the duty imposed? According to section 8(d) of the National Labor Relations Act:

[T]o bargain collectively is the performance of the mutual obligation of the employer and the representatives of the employees to meet at reasonable times and confer in good faith with respect to wages, hours, and other terms and conditions of employment . . . but such obligation does not compel either party to agree to a proposal or require the making of a concession.

Three distinct questions are raised by sections 8(a)(5), 8(b)(3), and 8(d). First, what duties are imposed on employers and employees' representatives by the requirement that they confer "in good faith"? Second, what are the subjects about which the parties must bargain? Finally, what are the implications of the union's recognition as the *exclusive* bargaining agent for a bargaining unit?

Bargaining in Good Faith   The concept that collective bargaining requires the parties to bargain in good faith is one of the controversial legal issues arising from the NLRA. Attempts to define the term *good faith* generally result in some notion that good faith is related to the intent of the parties. Trying to determine the state of mind of the participants in a negotiation session is a tricky proposition at best, especially if the determination has to be made on the basis of evidence presented by the parties to that negotiation.[52]

Because of the difficulties involved in trying to determine whether an employer or bargaining agent has the appropriate frame of mind, the board and the courts tend to apply tests that look at objective rather than subjective factors. The act itself specifies that a mere inability to reach an agreement or the failure to make a concession does not mean that the parties have abrogated their duties to bargain collectively. Would that duty be abrogated, though, by an unwillingness on the part of one party to agree to *anything?*

Although cases of this sort continue to be decided on the basis of the peculiar facts of each incident, the Circuit Courts of Appeal diverge greatly on the issue of whether they should consider the final terms of the agreement or the bargaining posture of one of the parties to be relevant in demonstrating lack of good faith.[53]

The board and the courts have struggled with the question of whether or not there are any actions that, if taken by one of the bargaining parties, would constitute a per se breach of the duty to bargain in good faith; that is, are there actions that are so detrimental to the bargaining process that use of them is enough to justify a finding of bad faith?

Suppose a union was in the midst of bargaining with management over terms of a new collective bargaining agreement and began using economic weapons against the employer while negotiations were proceeding. Do you think such actions would constitute evidence of bad faith on the part of the union?

In the case of *NLRB* v. *Insurance Agents' International Union*,[54] Insurance Agents' International Union was negotiating a collective bargaining agreement with Prudential Insurance Company of America. The union decided to use its economic power to harass the company during these negotiations. The Union's tactics included:

[R]efusal for a time to solicit new business, and refusal (after the writing of new business was resumed) to comply with the company's reporting procedures; refusal to participate in the company's "May Policyholders' Month Campaign"; reporting late at district offices the days the agents were scheduled to attend them, and refusing to perform customary duties at the offices, instead engaging there in "sit-in-mornings," "doing what comes naturally," and leaving at noon as a group; absenting themselves from special business conferences arranged by the company; picketing and distributing leaflets outside the various offices of the company on specified days and hours as directed by the union; distributing leaflets each day to policyholders and others and soliciting policyholders' signatures on petitions directed to the company; and presenting the signed policyholders' petitions to the company at its home office while simultaneously engaging in mass demonstrations there.[55]

What do you think motivated the union to use this strategy? Do you think it was fair for the union to use this strategy? Do you think the union demonstrated lack of good faith to bargain collectively by using this strategy?

The NLRB thought the union's use of economic weapons against the company during a time when negotiations were not at an impasse showed bad faith on the part of the union, even though no evidence had been presented that indicated the union had refused to cooperate at the bargaining table. The Board's reasoning was that:

[T]he respondent's [Union's] reliance upon harassing tactics during the course of negotiations for the avowed purpose of compelling the company to capitulate to its terms is the antithesis of reasoned discussion it was duty-bound to follow. Indeed, it clearly revealed an unwillingness to submit its demands to the consideration of the bargaining table where argument, persuasion, and the free interchange of views could take place. In such circumstances, the fact that the respondent continued to confer with the company and was desirous of concluding an agreement does not *alone* establish that it fulfilled its obligation to bargain in good faith.[56]

Justice Brennan, writing the opinion for the Supreme Court, disagreed with the Board, saying that:

It is apparent from the legislative history of the whole Act that the policy of Congress is to impose a mutual duty upon the parties to confer in good faith with a desire to reach agreement, in the belief that such an approach from both sides of the table promotes the over-all design of achieving industrial peace. Discussion conducted under that standard of good faith may narrow the issues, making the real demands of the parties clearer to each other, and perhaps to themselves, and may encourage an attitude of settlement through give and take. The mainstream of cases before the Board and in the courts reviewing its orders, under the provisions fixing the duty to bargain collectively, is concerned with insuring that the parties approach the bargaining table with this attitude. But apart from this essential standard of conduct, Congress intended that the parties should have wide latitude in their negotiations, unrestricted by any governmental power to regulate the substantive solution of their differences.

We believe that the Board's approach in this case—unless it can be defended, in terms of § 8(b)(3), as resting on some unique character of the union tactics involved here—must be taken as proceeding from an erroneous view of collective bargaining. It must be realized that collective bargaining, under a system where the government does not attempt to control the results of negotiations, cannot be equated with an academic collective search for truth—or even with what might be thought to be the ideal of one. The parties—even granting the modification of views that may come from a realization of economic interdependence—still proceed from contrary and to an extent antagonistic viewpoints and concepts of self-interest. The system has not reached the ideal of the philosophic notion that perfect understanding among people would lead to perfect agreement among them on values. The presence of economic weapons in reserve, and their actual exercise on occasion by the parties, is part and parcel of the system that the Wagner and Taft-Hartley Acts have recognized. Abstract logical analysis might find inconsistency between the command of the statute to negotiate toward an agreement in good faith and the legitimacy of the use of economic weapons, frequently having the most serious effect upon individual workers and productive enterprises, to induce one party to come to the terms desired by the other. But the truth of the matter is that at the present statutory stage of our national labor relations policy, the two factors—necessity for good-faith bargaining between parties, and the availability of economic pressure devices to each to make the other party incline to agree on one's terms—exist side by side. One writer recognizes this by describing economic force as "a prime motive power for agreements in free collective bargaining." Doubtless one factor influences the other; there may be less need to apply economic pressure if the areas of controversy have been defined through discussion; and at the same time, negotiation positions are apt to be weak or strong in accordance with the degree of economic power the parties possess. A close student of our national labor relations laws writes: "Collective bargaining is curiously ambivalent even today. In one aspect collective bargaining is a brute contest of economic power somewhat masked by polite manners and voluminous statistics. As the relation matures, Lilliputian bonds control the opposing concentrations of economic power; they lack legal sanctions but are nonetheless effective to contain the use of power. Initially it may be only fear of the economic consequences of disagreement that turns the parties to facts, reason, a sense of responsibility, a responsiveness to government and public opinion, and moral principle; but in time these forces generate their own compulsions, and negotiating a contract approaches the ideal of informed persuasion." Cox, The Duty to Bargain in Good Faith, 71 *Harv. L. Rev.* 1401, 1409.

For similar reasons, we think the Board's approach involves an intrusion into the substantive aspects of the bargaining process—again, unless there is some specific warrant for its condemnation of the precise tactics involved here. The scope of § 8(b)(3) and the limitations on Board power which were the design of § 8(d) are exceeded, we hold, by inferring a lack of good faith not from any deficiencies of the union's performance at the bargaining table by reason of its attempted use of economic pressure, but solely and simply because tactics designed to exert economic pressure were employed during the course of the good-faith negotiations. Thus the Board in the guise of determining good or bad faith in negotiations could regulate what economic weapons a party might summon to its aid. And if the Board could regulate the choice of economic weapons that may be used as part of collective bargaining, it would be in a position to exercise considerable influence upon the substantive terms on which the parties contract. As the parties' own devices became more limited, the government might have to enter even more directly into the negotiation of collective agreements. Our labor policy is not presently erected on a foundation of government control of the results of negotiations. Nor does it contain a charter for the National Labor Relations Board to act at large in equalizing disparities of bargaining power between employer and union.

The use of economic pressure, as we have indicated, is of itself not at all inconsistent with the duty of bargaining in good faith.[57]

Bargaining in Good Faith—Continued   If using economic weapons during the negotiating process is not an exercise of bad faith and if the NLRB must close the door of the bargaining room, so to speak, and not judge what goes on behind it, can you think of any activities short of a complete refusal to bargain that would constitute lack of good faith?

Two practices have provided the major source of "bad-faith" findings by the Supreme Court. The first arises when a company, during negotiations, announces that it cannot accede to higher wage demands, for example, without sending the company into bankruptcy. The union is willing to accept that limitation since, after all, it will do the employees no good to have high wages if they then lose their jobs as a result. The union, however, asks to see the company's books to verify that the company is, indeed, in the financial straits that it claims. If the company refuses to disclose such information to the union, this is a refusal to bargain in good faith.[58]

The second set of circumstances involves a situation in which the company institutes a change unilaterally during the bargaining period that affects one of the subjects of collective bargaining or offers better terms directly to the employees than the company has ever proposed to the union. For example, at the bargaining table, the company has only been willing to offer one week's paid vacation to employees of two years or less. Company officials then announce (not at the bargaining table but directly to the employees themselves) that effective immediately, all employees who have worked for six months or more are entitled to two weeks' paid vacation. According to the Supreme Court, such an action taken by the company would be strong evidence of bad faith.[59]

Do you understand why the activities described above would demonstrate bad faith? Do you think the Court's decisions are consistent with each other? Do you think the Court's decisions make sense? Do you think there may be a difference between "bad faith" and "lack of good faith"? If so, which standard should the courts use?

Subjects of Bargaining   While employers and labor representatives are free to discuss whatever they mutually choose to discuss, section 8(d) of the NLRA clearly sets out some mandatory subjects over which the parties must bargain. These are wages, hours, and "other terms and conditions of employment." Although these topics for mandatory bargaining seem simple enough, questions still arise frequently. For example, suppose the union and employer bargain over wages and agree to instituting merit increases for employees. Must the employer also bargain over which employees are entitled to receive these increases or who will make the decision at the time the increases are to be given? Does the question of bringing in subcontractors to perform certain jobs fall within the scope of "wages, hours, and terms and conditions of employment," since the use of subcontractors may reduce the amount of work available to regular employees? Or is that a subject that belongs more directly to the management of the firm? What about a decision to close a plant?

Generally, the board and the courts will balance three factors. First, they look to the effect of a particular decision on the workers; how direct is it and to what extent is the effect felt? Second, they consider the degree to which bargaining would constitute an intrusion into entrepreneurial interests, or, from the opposite side, the degree of intrusion into union affairs. Third, they examine the practice historically in the industry or the company itself.[60]

Another question that sometimes arises is whether it is unfair for one of the negotiating parties to refuse to consider any of the mandatory bargaining subjects until the other party agrees to a demand that does not fall within the range of mandatory bargaining subjects.

In the case of *NLRB* v. *Wooster Division of Borg-Warner*,[61] the Supreme Court was called upon to answer that question. There, Borg-Warner insisted that the union agree to a "ballot" clause calling for a prestrike secret vote of all employees regarding the company's most recent offer. Borg-Warner also insisted that the collective bargaining agreement was to be signed by the uncertified local affiliate of the certified international union rather than by the international union itself. Borg-Warner took the position that it would offer the employees an economic package only if the union agreed to these two "noneconomic" clauses. The Supreme Court found this to be an unfair labor practice.

Do you think that insistence upon a demand that is not a mandatory subject of bargaining should be construed as a failure to bargain in good faith? Might such a demand effectively constitute a refusal to bargain altogether? Is there anything about the two particular demands made by Borg-Warner that made the Court's decision easier to reach than it otherwise might have been? Can you think of a nonmandatory bargaining point about which the Court might have had greater sympathy?

The Union as Exclusive Bargaining Agent

Once a union has been elected and certified as the representative of a bargaining unit, it becomes the exclusive agent for employees within that bargaining unit, whether they voted for the union or not. The exclusivity of the union's authority has a number of implications, but one is particularly relevant in determining whether an employer has failed to demonstrate good faith at the bargaining table.

Specifically, the employer must deal with the certified representative. The employer commits an unfair labor practice if he or she attempts to deal directly with the employees or recognizes someone other than the workers' chosen representative. In both instances, the issue is fairly straightforward. The employer is undermining the position of the representative by ignoring him or her.

Somewhat less obvious than this direct violation, but based on the same reasoning, is the problem of an employer who, during the course of negotiations, institutes a unilateral change in employee benefits. For example, in the 1962 Supreme Court case of *NLRB* v. *Katz*,[62] an employer made three unilateral changes. He granted merit increases, he changed the sick leave policy, and he instituted a new system of automatic wage increases. This strategy was considered a failure to bargain in good faith because it effectively denied the union the right to joint participation in the decision making, and because the employer's actions tended to obstruct the process and make the negotiations more difficult. If negotiations had come to a complete impasse before the employer instituted these changes, the Court might have decided differently. However, the employer clearly demonstrated a lack of good faith when it unilaterally granted better benefits than any that were offered at the bargaining table.

Can you imagine any instance in which the unilateral granting of benefits might be permissible? If raises are always given in December and labor negotiations are in progress during December in a given year, should the employer be permitted to grant pay increases without negotiating them? Is your answer conditional in any way?

Shop Agreements and Right-to-Work Laws

Unions must keep their forces strong if they wish to wield economic power. Thus, in order to maintain their membership, unions typically seek a collective bargaining clause requiring all employees to become union members after they have been employed for some period of time—generally, 30 days—or, at the least, requiring them to pay union dues and fees. These clauses are called "union shop agreements." At one time, unions with a great deal of bargaining leverage would insist upon clauses in collective bargaining agreements that restricted employers from hiring anyone not already a union member. These were called "closed shop agreements" and are now prohibited by the NLRA.

Most states do allow collective bargaining agreements to have "open shop" or union security clauses in them. The former require workers to join the union after being employed for some period of time. The latter require all workers to pay union dues and fees, even if they choose not to join the union. The courts have upheld these practices. What grounds do you think the courts have used in allowing union security clauses? (Consider the fact that the union is the exclusive bargaining representative for an employee whether or not he or she wishes to be represented.) See *NLRB* v. *General Motors Corp.,* 374 U.S. 734 (1963).

Although the NLRA preempts state law with regard to labor legislation in almost all respects, the act does give states the right to enact so-called "right-to-work" laws. These laws prohibit union security arrangements in collective bargaining agreements. In other words, in these states, collective bargaining agreements may not require either membership in a union or payment by nonmembers of union dues, despite the fact that these employees receive all the benefits of having union representation in collective bargaining. Needless to say, unionized plants are far less common in right-to-work states than in states that do not have those laws.

Strikes

For many, the initial image of labor conflict is one of employees on strike, picketing a store or factory. Striking is, however, an extremely drastic measure under which employees must bear an immediate loss of wages while, in many instances, risking job loss.

Strikes fall in two basic categories: (1) those that are used purely as economic weapons to persuade an employer to provide more favorable employee benefits or better working conditions, and (2) those that workers institute in response to the commission by the employer of an unfair labor practice. Both types of strikes are considered "concerted activities" for the mutual aid or benefit of the workers. Thus, as long as workers are not striking in violation of a collective bargaining agreement provision, their actions are protected under section 7 of the National Labor Relations Act.[63]

A strike that begins as an economic strike may be converted into a strike in protest of an unfair labor practice if an employer, during the course of the strike, violates one of the provisions of NLRA section 8(a). The permissibility of replacing striking workers depends upon the type of strike that is being waged. The following case states the rules that the courts have applied and illustrates the problems involved in classifying a strike as economic or as an unfair labor practice protest.

NATIONAL LABOR RELATIONS BOARD V. INTERNATIONAL VAN LINES   409 U.S. 48 (1972)

[Four employees of International Van Lines refused to cross a picket line in front of the company's premises. The following day each received a telegram informing him that he was being permanently replaced for having failed to report to work. At the time of the discharge, the company (respondent) had not yet hired any permanent replacements. The employees brought an action against the company, claiming that they had been engaging in protected activity when they refused to cross the picket line and that the company had, therefore, committed an unfair labor practice in discharging them. The NLRB agreed with the employees. The Court of Appeals reversed in part, deciding that the employees were economic strikers, rather than unfair labor practice strikers. The latter, according to the Court of Appeals, were entitled to unconditional reinstatement, while the former could be discharged if the employer had substantial business justification for letting them go. The Supreme Court granted certiorari to examine the question.]

Justice Stewart

It is settled that an employer may refuse to reinstate economic strikers if in the interim he has taken on permanent replacements. . . . It is equally settled that employees striking in protest of an employer's unfair labor practices are entitled, absent some contractual or statutory provision to the contrary, to unconditional reinstatement with back pay, "even if replacements for them have been made." . . . Since the strike in the instant case continued after the unfair labor practices had been committed by the employer, the Board reasoned that the original economic strike became an unfair labor practice strike on October 5, when the telegrams were sent.

*   *   *   *   *

Both the Board and the Court of Appeals have agreed that the labor picketing was a lawful economic strike, and the validity of that conclusion is not before us. Given that hypothesis, the Board and the Court of Appeals were clearly correct in concluding that the respondent committed unfair labor practices when it fired its striking employees. "[T]he discharge of economic strikers prior . . . to the time their places are filled constitutes an unfair labor practice." . . .

We need not decide, however, whether the Board was correct in determining that the discharged employees assumed the status of unfair labor practice strikers on October 5, 1967, to reach the conclusion that the Court of Appeals erred in refusing to enforce the Board's order of reinstatement with back pay.

Unconditional reinstatement of the discharged employees was proper for the simple reason that they were the victims of a plain unfair labor practice by their employer. Quite apart from any characterization of the strike that continued after the wrongful discharges occurred, the discharges *themselves* were a sufficient ground for the Board's reinstatement order. "Reinstatement is the conventional correction for discriminatory discharges," . . . and was clearly within the Board's authority.

It would undercut the remedial powers of the Board with respect to § 8 violations, and subvert the protection of § 7 of the Act, to hold that the employees' rights to reinstatement arising from the discriminatory discharges were somehow forfeited merely because they continued for a time to engage in their lawful strike after the unfair labor practices had been committed.

The judgment of the Court of Appeals is reversed insofar as it refused to enforce the Board's order that the discharged employees be reinstated with back pay.

Questions

1. Can you envision any problems that are likely to arise as a result of the distinction drawn between economic strikers and unfair labor practice strikers?
2. What do you think the policy justifications are for distinguishing between these two types of strikers?
3. Assume Mary Wills, a bottle inspector for Pop Soda Inc., and a member of a certified bargaining unit, struck along with other bottle inspectors to protest an allegedly unfair labor practice committed by the employer. The bottle inspectors offered to return to work after a one-week strike, and, although their positions were not filled, Pop Soda offered them entirely different positions as bottle sorters, telling the employees that they would shortly thereafter be returned to their regular inspector jobs. Wills was the only one who accepted this offer; the other employees insisted that they were legally entitled to their former jobs. Wills made subsequent inquiries, attempting to get her inspecting job back, but the company at no time made a proper offer for that position. After three and a half months of working as a bottle sorter, Wills resigned because of physical problems with her hand. She then made a claim to the NLRB that Pop Soda had committed an unfair labor practice by not reinstating her to her inspecting position. She asked for reinstatement and back pay.

   Do you think she is entitled to either or both of these remedies? See *The Coca-Cola Bottling Company of Memphis and International Brotherhood of Teamsters, et. al.*, 269 NLRB No. 160 (1983–84 CCH NLRB ¶ 16,259), decided April 23, 1984.

Notification of the Intent to Strike

Congressional desire to maintain industrial peace is mainifested, in part, through the conditions imposed by section 8(d) of the NLRA. These provisions are designed to prevent ill-conceived strikes by requiring that any party desiring to terminate or renegotiate a collective bargaining agreement must serve written notice on the other party at least 60 days prior to the expiration of the agreement then in force. Within 30 days of notifying the other party of its desires, the moving party must also notify the Federal

Mediation and Conciliation Service and any state or local conciliation boards set up for the purpose of resolving that type of dispute. Failure to give this notice is considered a refusal to bargain in good faith. Moreover, any worker who goes on strike during this "cooling-off" period loses his or her status as an employee for purposes of being protected by the NLRA. Such an employee may be discharged by the employer without any repercussions from the act. The strike itself is called a "wildcat" strike.

The 60-day notification period allows both parties some leeway during which they can discuss and hopefully resolve their contract disputes before the old contract terminates. The notification provision ensures that neither employers nor employees are left in the lurch, unprepared for or unaware of the other party's dissatisfaction with the present bargaining agreement. Perhaps more importantly, the public is protected to a great extent. A strike in any sector of industry tends to have a ripple effect, creating disturbances throughout the economy.

Secondary Boycotts, Hot Cargo Agreements, and Common Situs Picketing

The National Labor Relations Act is designed to protect workers who are involved in a primary dispute, that is, a dispute with their own employer. Because the act, in addition to providing rights for workers, has as its goal maintaining industrial peace and a smooth-flowing economy, the act does not permit workers to extend their dispute by involving other businesses in it, except in very limited respects.

For example, suppose the workers at Company A ask for higher wages and are refused. The workers can bring to bear as much economic pressure as they can muster against their employer, because that is all part of a primary dispute. The workers may even try to persuade other companies not to cross picket lines and to stop dealing with Company A until Company A responds to the demands. All of this is permissible under the NLRA.

Suppose, however, that Company B, a supplier of parts for Company A, continues to carry on business with Company A, despite the request made by Company A employees that Company B cease making deliveries. Company A employees are *not* permitted to use economic weapons against Company B in order to get Company B to stop trading with Company A. Such unlawful activity is referred to as a *secondary boycott* and is prohibited by the NLRA.

Unions have, on occasion, tried to persuade employers to put clauses in their collective bargaining agreements, stating that the employers will refuse to handle any product that comes from a company involved in a labor dispute. Such a clause is usually called a *hot cargo agreement*. Judicial interpretations and statutory amendments have made it an unfair labor practice for a union to insist on such a clause and for an employer to agree to be bound by such a term. A secondary company is, of course, permitted to voluntarily avoid handling the goods of another company that is having labor difficulties.

The problem of a labor dispute affecting secondary companies becomes more pronounced when a workplace or marketplace is shared by a number of companies. A supermarket, for example, carries many different types and brands of food. If workers at Terrific Bread Company want to exert economic pressure on their employer, they may decide to picket local supermarkets in an attempt to convince customers not to buy Terrific Bread. If the Terrific Bread employees· decide to use this approach, they must make sure that their picket signs clearly identify that the dispute the picketers have is with Terrific Bread Company and not with the supermarket owner. The picketers may not try in any way to keep customers from patronizing the supermarket, even though doing so might force the supermarket owner to stop selling Terrific Bread.

A similar problem arises frequently in the construction industry. Construction work is often doled out to subcontractors, each of whom may be responsible for the completion of a certain type of craftwork, such as electrical wiring, plumbing, pipefitting, masonry, and carpentry. The craftworkers within each of these specialty groups may or may not be unionized. All of the craftworkers, though, regardless of who their employer is, work side by side on the same job site.

What then happens if one set of workers has a grievance it wants to air against its employer? Those workers are very likely to picket the job site because construction contractors typically do not have a physical plant around which the workers could parade.

The problem presented by this *common situs picket* is that the people working for employers other than the one involved in the primary dispute are likely to sympathize with the plight of their fellow workers and honor the picket lines. Again, not only is the primary employer subjected to economic pressure, but so are all the other companies involved in the construction.

The National Labor Relations Act does not provide a clear solution to this problem, nor have the courts developed a standard that answers all the questions that can arise with common situs picketing.

What factors do you think the NLRB ought to consider in examining common situs picketing? What competing interests need to be balanced? Is there any sort of activity or behavior that you would clearly deem to be permissible? Impermissible? Do you think the NLRB should look at the acts themselves or the intent of the workers?

Employees' Rights within or against the Union

The Union's Duty of Fair Representation

As you have seen in previous sections of this chapter, the union is given statutory authority to be the *exclusive* bargaining agent for the employees in the designated bargaining unit. This means that even if an individual employee in the bargaining unit does not agree with union policies or is not a member of the union, he or she cannot bargain individually with the employer. Such an employee will still be bound by the terms of the collective bargaining agreement.

Can you see any need for limits on the union's authority to negotiate a collective bargaining agreement? How could a union use its exclusive right to the disadvantage of an individual or groups of employees? What reasons might discourage a union from fully representing all the needs of all the employees in the bargaining unit? Might management suffer in any way if the union does not adequately represent the interests of all the employees in the bargaining unit?

There is no express statutory provision in the federal labor laws that requires a union to represent employees fairly, be they union members or not. The Supreme Court, however, was asked to address the question of whether an implicit duty of fair representation by the union exists. Consider, for example, the following case.

STEELE V. LOUISVILLE AND NASHVILLE RAILROAD
323 U.S. 192 (1944)

[The Louisville and Nashville Railroad (''Railroad'') employed a class of workers known as ''firemen.'' The majority of the firemen were white, although a substantial minority were black. The union designated to be the exclusive bargaining agent for all firemen was called the Brotherhood. The constitution and the practice of the Brotherhood excluded all blacks from membership in that union.

During 1940 and 1941, the Brotherhood amended its collective bargaining agreement with the Louisville and Nashville Railroad and 20 other railroads located primarily in the southeastern United States, ''in such manner as ultimately to exclude all Negro firemen from service.'' This arrangement was accomplished through a series of agreements entered into between the Brotherhood and the railroads, which limited the percentage of blacks who could be employed, restricted the number of vacancies and new jobs that could be filled by blacks, and put complete control of seniority rights of black employees in the hands of the Brotherhood. All of these changes were made without informing the black firemen and without giving them a chance to voice their opinions.]

[The Supreme Court of Alabama, which had heard this case earlier, held that the petitioner had no legal basis on which to bring a claim. That court interpreted the Railway Labor Act as conferring on the Brotherhood the exclusive right to bargain with no parallel duty to represent all employees fairly, no matter how grave the injustices imposed on a segment of the employee unit might be. The United States Supreme Court took issue with the Alabama court's decision.]

Chief Justice Stone

The question is whether the Railway Labor Act . . . imposes on a labor organization, acting by authority of the statute as the exclusive bargaining representative of a craft or class of railway employees, the duty to represent all the employees in the craft without discrimination because of their race, and, if so, whether the courts have jurisdiction to protect the minority of the craft or class from the violation of such obligation.

. . . The Brotherhood has acted and asserts the right to act as exclusive bargaining representative of the firemen's craft. It is alleged that in that capacity it is under an obligation and duty imposed by the Act to represent the Negro firemen impartially and in good faith; but instead, in its notice to and contracts with the railroads, it has been hostile and disloyal to the Negro firemen, has deliberately discriminated against them, and has sought to deprive them of their seniority rights and to drive them out of employment in their craft, all in order to create a monopoly of employment for Brotherhood members.

*   *   *   *   *

The Supreme Court of Alabama took jurisdiction of the cause but held on the merits that petitioner's complaint stated no cause of action. It pointed out that the Act places a mandatory duty on the Railroad to treat with the Brotherhood as the exclusive representative of the employees in a craft, imposes heavy criminal penalties for willful failure to comply with its command, and provides that the majority of any craft shall have the right to determine who shall be the representative of the class for collective bargaining with the employer. . . . It thought that the Brotherhood was empowered by the statute to enter into the agreement of February 18, 1941, and that by virtue of the statute the Brotherhood has power by agreement with the Railroad both to create the seniority rights of petitioner and his fellow Negro employees and to destroy them. It construed the statute, not as creating the relationship of principal and agent between the members of the craft and the Brotherhood, but as conferring on the Brotherhood plenary authority to treat with the Railroad and enter into contracts fixing rates of pay and working conditions for the craft as a whole without any legal obligation or duty to protect the rights of minorities from discrimination or unfair treatment, however gross. Consequently it held that neither the Brotherhood nor the Railroad violated any rights of petitioner or his fellow Negro employees by negotiating the contracts discriminating against them.

If, as the state court has held, the Act confers this power on the bargaining representative of a craft or class of employees without any commensurate statutory duty toward its members, constitutional questions arise. For the representative is clothed with power not unlike that of a legislature which is subject to constitutional limitations on its power to deny, restrict, destroy, or discriminate against the rights of those for whom it legislates and which is also under an affirmative constitutional duty equally to protect those rights.

*   *   *   *   *

But we think that Congress, in enacting the Railway Labor Act and authorizing a labor union, chosen by a majority of a craft, to represent the craft, did not intend to confer plenary power upon the union to sacrifice, for the benefit of its members, rights of the minority of the craft, without imposing on it any duty to protect the minority. Since petitioner and the other Negro members of the craft are not members of the Brotherhood or eligible for membership, the authority to act for them is derived not from their action or consent but wholly from the command of the Act. Section 2, Fourth, provides: "Employees shall have the right to organize and bargain collectively through representatives of their own choosing. The majority of any craft or class of employees shall have the right to determine who shall be the representative of the craft or class for the purposes of this Act . . . ." Under § 2, Sixth and Seventh, when the representative bargains for a change of working conditions, the latter section specifies that they are the working conditions of employees "as a class." Section 1, Sixth, of the Act defines "representative" as meaning "Any person or . . . labor union . . . designated either by a carrier or a group of carriers or by its or their employees, to act for it or them." The use of the word "representative," as thus defined and in all the contexts in which it is found, plainly implies that the representative is to act on behalf of all the employees which, by virtue of the statute, it undertakes to represent.

*   *   *   *   *

Section 2, Second, requiring carriers to bargain with the representative so chosen, operates to exclude any other from representing a craft. . . . The minority members of a craft are thus deprived by the statute of the right, which they would otherwise possess, to choose a representative of their own, and its members cannot bargain individually on behalf of themselves as to matters which are properly the subject of collective bargaining. . . .

The labor organization chosen to be the representative of the craft or class of employees is thus chosen to represent all of its members, regardless of their union affiliations or want of them. As we have pointed out with respect to the like provision of the National Labor Relations Act, . . . "The very purpose of providing by statute for the collective agreement is to supersede the terms of separate agreements of employees with terms which reflect the strength and bargaining power and serve the welfare of the group. Its benefits and advantages are open to every employee of the represented unit. . . .'' The purpose of providing for a representative is to secure those benefits for those who are represented and not to deprive them or any of them of the benefits of collective bargaining for the advantage of the representative or those members of the craft who selected it.

As the National Mediation Board said in In The Matter of Representation of Employees of the St. Paul Union Depot Company, Case No. R-635: ''Once a craft or class has designated its representative, such representative is responsible under the law to act for all employees within the craft or class, those who are not members of the represented organization, as well as those who are members.''

Unless the labor union representing a craft owes some duty to represent non-union members of the craft, at least to the extent of not discriminating against them as such in the contracts which it makes as their representative, the minority would be left with no means of protecting their interests, or indeed, their right to earn a livelihood by pursuing the occupation in which they are employed.

While the majority of the craft chooses the bargaining representative, when chosen it represents, as the Act by its terms makes plain, the craft or class, and not the majority. The fair interpretation of the statutory language is that the organization chosen to represent a craft is to represent all its members, the majority as well as the minority, and it is to act for and not against those whom it represents. It is a principle of general application that the exercise of a granted power to act in behalf of others involves the assumption toward them of a duty to exercise the power in their interest and behalf, and that such a grant of power will not be deemed to dispense with all duty toward those for whom it is exercised unless so expressed.

We think that the Railway Labor Act imposes upon the statutory representative of a craft at least as exacting a duty to protect equally the interests of the members of the craft as the Constitution imposes upon a legislature to give equal protection to the interests of those for whom it legislates. Congress has seen fit to clothe the bargaining representative with powers comparable to those possessed by a legislative body both to create and restrict the rights of those whom it represents . . . but it has also imposed on the representative a corresponding duty. We hold that the language of the Act to which we have referred, read in the light of the purposes of the Act, expresses the aim of Congress to impose on the bargaining representative of a craft or class of employees the duty to exercise fairly the power conferred upon it in behalf of all those for whom it acts, without hostile discrimination against them.

This does not mean that the statutory representative of a craft is barred from making contracts which may have unfavorable effects on some of the members of the craft represented. Variations in the terms of the contract based on differences relevant to the authorized purposes of the contract in conditions to which they are to be applied, such as differences in seniority, the type of work performed, the competence and skill with which it is performed, are within the scope of the bargaining representation of a craft, all of whose members are not identical in their interest or merit.

Without attempting to mark the allowable limits of differences in the terms of contracts based on differences of conditions to which they apply, it is enough for present purposes to say that the statutory power to represent a craft and to make contracts as to wages, hours and working conditions does not include the authority to make among members of the craft discriminations not based on such relevant differences. Here the discriminations based on race alone are obviously irrelevant and invidious. Congress plainly did not undertake to authorize the bargaining representative to make such discriminations.

The representative which thus discriminates may be enjoined from so doing, and its members may be enjoined from taking the benefit of such discriminatory action. No more is the Railroad bound by or entitled to take the benefit of a contract which the bargaining representative is prohibited by the statute from making. In both cases the right asserted, which is derived from the duty imposed by the statute on the bargaining representative, is a federal right implied from the statute and the policy which it has adopted. It is the federal statute which condemns as unlawful the Brotherhood's conduct. "The extent and nature of the legal consequences of this condemnation, though left by the statute to judicial determination, are nevertheless to be derived from it and the federal policy which it has adopted." *Deitrick* v. *Greaney*, 309 U.S. 190, 200, 201.

So long as a labor union assumes to act as the statutory representative of a craft, it cannot rightly refuse to perform the duty, which is inseparable from the power of representation conferred upon it, to represent the entire membership of the craft. While the statute does not deny to such a bargaining labor organization the right to determine eligibility to its membership, it does require the union, in collective bargaining and in making contracts with the carrier, to represent nonunion or minority union members of the craft without hostile discrimination, fairly, impartially, and in good faith. Wherever necessary to that end, the union is required to consider requests of nonunion members of the craft and expressions of their views with respect to collective bargaining with the employer and to give to them notice of and opportunity for hearing upon its proposed action.

* * * * *

The judgment is accordingly reversed and remanded for further proceedings not inconsistent with this opinion.

Afterword

Although the *Steele* case involved the Railway Labor Act, the Supreme Court has announced that the same duty is implicit in section 9(a) of the National Labor Relations Act.

Questions

1. Looking back at the questions posed at the beginning of this section, would any of your answers be different now that you have read the *Steele* case?
2. What is your opinion of the analogy drawn by the Court between a legislator's duty to represent his or her constituents and a union's duty to represent all employees within the craft?
3. In what way(s) does the Court here leave the door open to narrow its holding in the future?
4. The Court says that the Brotherhood's "statutory power to represent a craft and to make contracts as to wages, hours, and working conditions does not include the authority to make among members of the craft discriminations not based on such relevant differences." What might be some relevant differences that would authorize a bargaining representative to draw distinctions? Seniority? Age? Gender? Previous military service?
5. Assume an aerospace company is negotiating a collective bargaining agreement with its unionized employees' certified bargaining representative. The union asks for a 40-cent-per-hour raise for all employees to be covered by the collective bargaining agreement. The company negotiators say they cannot agree to such a demand because it would seriously hurt the company's competitive position in the marketplace. The union asks the company to substantiate its claim by showing the union the company's books. The company refuses to do so. Has the company committed an unfair labor practice? See *Goodyear Aerospace Corp.*, 204 NLRB 831 (1973).

More about Duty of Fair Representation   A union, despite its duty to fairly represent all members of a bargaining unit, may have serious difficulty doing so because of divergent interests within that unit. (That is one reason that the choice of an appropriate bargaining unit is such an important part of unionization.) For example, if a company is in difficult financial straits, it may tell union negotiators that the company must do one of two things to stay viable: lay off workers or give all employees a cut in salary. The workers who have seniority and would not lose their jobs in a layoff are likely to push for the former; workers with less seniority, who would normally be let go during a layoff, will prefer in most instances to retain their jobs even if they are forced to take a cut in wages. In such a situation, the union could not possibly represent both groups' interests to the fullest.

This type of situation, however, is a far cry from those in which a union has arbitrarily or with purposeful intent discriminated against some segment of its rank and file membership. In addition to the racial discrimination found in many unions, sex discrimination was also rampant. Unions were notorious for negotiating contracts in which women were excluded from certain jobs and paid lower wages for performing work identical to their male counterparts. In recognition of the discrimination being practiced by many unions, Congress built special provisions into the Equal Pay Act of 1963 and the Civil Rights Act of 1964, making it illegal for unions to discriminate on the basis of race, color, creed, national origin, or sex.

The "Bill of Rights" of Labor Organization Members

The "Bill of Rights" for members of labor organizations is contained in Title I, Section 101 of the Labor-Management Reporting and Disclosure Act (LMRDA or Landrum-Griffin Act). The Bill of Rights was designed to ensure equal voting rights, the right to sue the union, and the rights of free speech and assembly, as embodied in the United States Bill of Rights. These rights of union members are tempered, as the following case will demonstrate, by the union's right to enact and enforce "reasonable rules governing the responsibilities of its members."[64] Both the majority and dissenting opinions are presented in the case so that the student can see the very great difference that exists in the amount of faith that the Justices place in the machinery of union democracy.

STEELWORKERS V. SADLOWSKI   457 U.S. 102 (1982)

[United Steelworkers of America, petitioner in this case, amended its union constitution to include an "outsider rule." This rule prohibited candidates for union office from accepting campaign contributions from anyone not then a member of the union. The amendment also set up a committee to oversee the enforcement of this rule. The committee's decisions were to be final and binding.

The respondent had challenged the "outsider rule" in the lower courts and had been successful there, arguing that the rule violated the "freedom of speech and assembly provisions" of Section 101(a)(2) of the LMRDA.

The Court's majority first rejected the notion expressed by the Court of Appeals that the rights of free speech provided by the LMRDA are as broad as the First Amendment guarantees of free speech. In doing so, the Supreme Court noted that Congress specifically added a proviso to Section 101(a)(2) making it subject to reasonable rules of the union "governing the responsibilities of its members." The Court then analyzed the "outsider rule" itself to determine whether it did, in fact, provide a reasonable restriction.]

Justice Marshall

. . To determine whether a union rule is valid under the statute, we first consider whether the rule interferes with an interest protected by the first part of § 101(a)(2). If it does, we then determine whether the rule is "reasonable" and thus sheltered by the proviso to § 101(a)(2). In conducting these inquiries, we find guidance in the policies that underlie the LMRDA in general and Title I in particular. First Amendment principles may be helpful, although they are not controlling. We must look to the objectives Congress sought to achieve, and avoid "'placing great emphasis upon close construction of the words.'" . . .

The critical question is whether a rule that partially interferes with a protected interest is nevertheless reasonably related to the protection of the organization as an institution.

Applying this form of analysis here, we conclude that the outsider rule is valid. Although it may limit somewhat the ability of insurgent union members to wage an effective campaign, an interest deserving some protection under the statute, it is rationally related to the union's legitimate interest in reducing outsider interference with union affairs.

I

An examination of the policies underlying the LMRDA indicates that the outsider rule may have some impact on interests that Congress intended to protect under § 101(a)(2). Congress adopted the freedom of speech and assembly provision in order to promote union democracy. . . . It recognized that democracy would be assured only if union members are free to discuss union policies and criticize the leadership without fear of reprisal. Congress also recognized that this freedom is particularly critical, and deserves vigorous protection, in the context of election campaigns. For it is in elections that members can wield their power, and directly express their approval or disapproval of the union leadership.

* * * * *

The interest in fostering vigorous debate during election campaigns may be affected by the outsider rule. If candidates are not permitted to accept contributions from persons outside the union, their ability to criticize union policies and to mount effective challenges to union leadership may be weakened. Restrictions that limit access to funds may reduce the number of issues discussed, the attention that is devoted to each issue, and the size of the audience reached. . . .

Although the outsider rule does affect rights protected by the statute, as a practical matter the impact may not be substantial. Respondents, as well as the Court of Appeals, suggest that incumbents have a large advantage because they can rely on their union staff during election campaigns. Challengers cannot counter this power simply by seeking funds from union members; the rank and file cannot provide sufficient support. Thus, they must be permitted to seek funds from outsiders. In fact, however, the rank and file probably can provide support. The USWA is a very large union whose members earn sufficient income to make campaign contributions. . . . Requiring candidates to rely solely on contributions from members will not unduly limit their ability to raise campaign funds. Uncontradicted record evidence discloses that challengers have been able to defeat incumbents or administration-backed candidates, despite the absence of financial support from nonmembers. . . .

In addition, although there are undoubtedly advantages to incumbency, . . . respondents and the Court of Appeals may overstate those advantages. Staff employees are forbidden by § 401(g) of the LMRDA, and by internal USWA rules, to campaign on union time or to use union funds, facilities, or equipment for campaign purposes. Staff officers have a contractual right to choose whether or not to participate in any USWA campaign without being subjected to discipline or reprisal for their decision.

The impact of the outsider rule on rights protected under § 101(a)(2) is limited in another important respect. The union has stated that the rule would not prohibit union members who are not involved in a campaign from using outside funds to address particular issues. That is, members could elicit funds from outsiders in order to focus the attention of the rank and file on a specific problem. The fact that union members remain free to seek funds for this purpose will serve as a counter to the power of entrenched leadership, and ensures that debate on issues that are important to the membership will never be stifled.

II

Although the outsider rule may implicate rights protected by § 101(a)(2), it serves a legitimate purpose that is clearly protected under the statute. The union adopted the rule because it wanted to ensure that nonmembers do not unduly influence union affairs. USWA feared that officers who received campaign contributions from nonmembers might be beholden to those individuals and might allow their decisions to be influenced by considerations other than the best interests of the union. The union wanted to ensure that the union leadership remained responsive to the membership. . . . An examination of the policies underlying the LMRDA reveals that this is a legitimate purpose that Congress meant to protect.

Evidence that Congress regarded the desire to minimize outsider influence as a legitimate purpose is provided by the history to Title I. On the Senate floor, Senator McClellan argued that a bill of rights for union members was necessary because some unions had been ''invaded'' or ''infiltrated'' by outsiders who had no interest in the members but rather had seized control for their own purposes. . . . He stated that the strongest support for the bill of rights provisions ''should come from traditional union leaders. It will protect them from the assaults of those who would capture their unions.''

*   *   *   *   *

It is true that Senator McClellan was particularly concerned about infiltration of unions by racketeers: he described situations in which ''thugs and hoodlums'' had taken over unions so that they could exploit the members for pecuniary gain. . . . However his statements also indicate a more general desire to ensure that union members, and not outsiders control the affairs of their union.

Indeed, specific provisions contained in Title IV provide support for our conclusion that the outsider rule serves a legitimate and protected purpose.

*   *   *   *   *

Respondents argue that even if the desire to reduce outside influence is a legitimate purpose, the rule is not rationally related to that purpose. They contend, first, that the union could simply have established contribution ceilings, rather than placing an absolute ban on nonmember contributions. However, USWA feared not only that a few individual nonmembers would make large contributions, but also that outsiders would solicit many like-minded persons for small contributions which, when pooled, would have a substantial impact on the election. This fear appears to have been reasonable. In the 1977 election, Sadlowski received a significant percentage of his campaign funds from individuals who made contributions after receiving mail solicitations signed by prominent nonmembers. . . .

Respondents also contend that even if the union was justified in limiting contributions by true outsiders, it need not have limited contributions by relatives and friends. Again, however, the USWA had a reasonable basis for its decision to impose a broad ban. An exception for family members and friends might have created a loophole that would have made the rule unenforceable: true outsiders could simply funnel their contributions through relatives and friends. . . .

Finally, respondents contend that USWA could simply have required that candidates for union office reveal the sources of their funds. But a disclosure rule, by itself, would not have solved the problem. Candidates who received such funds might still be beholden to outsiders.

The member's right to run for office and to speak and assemble was to be subject to reasonable union rules, but the reasonableness of a particular rule must surely be judged with reference to the paradigmatic situation that Congress intended to address by guaranteeing free elections: a large union with entrenched, autocratic leadership bent on maintaining itself by fair means or foul.

Those leaders have normally appointed the union staff, the bureaucracy that makes the union run. The staff is dependent upon and totally loyal to the leadership. It amounts to a built-in campaign organization that can be relied upon to make substantial contributions and to solicit others for more. Such a management is in control of the union's communication system and has immediate access to membership lists and to the members themselves. Obviously, even if the incumbents eschew violence, threats, or intimidation, mounting an effective challenge would be a large and difficult endeavor. And if those in office are as unscrupulous as Congress often found them to be, the dimensions of the task facing the insurgent are exceedingly large. But Congress intended to help the members help solve these very difficulties by guaranteeing them the right to run for office and to have free and open elections in the American tradition.

It is incredible to me that the union rule at issue in this case can be found to be a reasonable restriction on the right of Edward Sadlowski, Jr., to speak, assemble, and run for union office in a free and democratic election. The scope and stringency of the rule cannot be doubted. It forbids any candidate for union office and his supporters to solicit or accept financial support from any nonmember. The candidate cannot accept contributions from members of his family, relatives, friends, or well-wishers unless they are members of the union. Retired members such as Edward Sadlowski, Sr., may not contribute; neither may members not in good standing. Even a fully secured loan from a nonmember with a standard rate of interest is forbidden under the rule. The rule goes even further. It forbids the acceptance of "any other direct or indirect support of any kind from any nonmember," except an individual's volunteered personal time. The regulations issued under the rule clearly show that the union intends to prohibit, as far as it is within its power to do so, all nonmember contributions on behalf of a member running for union office.

. . . A candidate unable to rebut this presumption (when prohibited support is contributed, it has been purposefully accepted) may be disqualified, fined, suspended, or expelled. This is a Draconian rule. How could any candidate "correct the effects of the prohibited support"?

We hold that USWA's rule prohibiting candidates for union office from accepting campaign contributions from nonmembers does not violate § 101(a)(2). Although it may interfere with rights Congress intended to protect, it is rationally related to a legitimate and protected purpose, and thus is sheltered by the proviso to § 101(a)(2). We reverse the decision below and remand for further proceedings consistent with this opinion.

Justice White, with whom the Chief Justice, Justice Brennan, and Justice Blackmun join, dissenting.

The question before us is what Congress intended when in 1959 it passed § 101(a)(2), the Bill of Rights provision of the LMRDA. That question is best answered by identifying the problem that Congress intended to solve by adopting the provision. The answer, in turn, is not at all difficult to discover.

After long and careful examination and hearings dealing with the labor union movement, Congress found that too often unions were run by entrenched, corrupt leaders who maintained themselves and discouraged challenge by any means available, including violence and threats. As Senator McClellan explained: "[T]he records of our committee's investigations show over and over again that a rank-and-file member dare not risk any opposition to a corrupt or autocratic leadership. If he does so, he may be beaten, his family threatened, his property destroyed or damaged, and he may be forced out of his job—all of these things can happen and have happened." . . . And again: "Members had better not offer any competition. They had better not seek election. They had better not aspire to the presidency or the secretaryship, or they will be expelled or disciplined." . . .

What Congress then did was to guarantee the union member's right to run for election, § 401(e), and to guarantee him freedom of speech and assembly. § 101(a)(2). There is no question, and the Court concedes as much, that the Act created statutory protection for the union member's right effectively to run for union office. Without doubt, § 101(a)(2) was not only aimed at protecting the member who speaks his mind on union affairs, even if critical of the leadership, but was also "specifically designed to protect the union member's right to seek higher office within the union." *Hall* v. *Cole,* 412 U.S. 1, 14 (1973). The LMRDA was a major effort by Congress "to insure union democracy." S.Rep. No. 187, 86th Cong., 1st Sess., 2 (1959). The chosen instrument for curbing the abuses of entrenched union leadership was "free and democratic union elections." *Steelworkers* v. *Usery,* 429 U.S. 305, 309 (1977). The abuses of "entrenched union leadership" were to be curbed, among other means, by the "check of democratic elections." *Wirtz* v. *Hotel Employees,* 391 U. S. 492, 499 (1968). These elections were to be modeled on the "political elections in this country." *Wirtz* v. *Hotel Employees, supra,* at 504; *Steelworkers* v. *Usery, supra,* at 309.

$$* \quad * \quad * \quad * \quad *$$

The impact of the rule with respect to Edward Sadlowski, Sr., illustrates the rigor of the rule. It prohibits him from contributing to the campaign of Edward Sadlowski, Jr., even though the elder Sadlowski is the father of the candidate, was a charter member of the USWA, remained a member for 32 years prior to his retirement, and receives a USWA pension, the terms of which are negotiated by USWA's officers.

Restrictions such as this are a far cry from the free and open elections that Congress anticipated and are wholly inconsistent with the way elections have been run in this country. The Court has long recognized the close relationship between the ability to solicit funds and the ability to express views. "[W]ithout solicitation, the flow of . . . information and advocacy would likely cease." It goes without saying that running for office in a union with 1.3 million members spread throughout the United States and Canada requires a substantial war chest if the campaign is to be effective and to have any reasonable chance of succeeding. Attempting to unseat the incumbents of union office is a substantial undertaking.

$$* \quad * \quad * \quad * \quad *$$

Thus, in the best of circumstances, the role of the challenger is very difficult. And if one keeps in mind that Congress intended to give the challenger a fair chance even in a union controlled by unscrupulous leaders with an iron grip on the staff and a willingness to employ means both within and without the law, it is wholly unrealistic to confine the challenger to financial support garnered within the union.

. . . [T]he majority somehow finds the absolute, unbending, no-contribution rule to be a reasonable regulation of a member's right to seek office and of the free and open elections that Congress anticipated. This, in spite of the availability of other means to satisfy the union's legitimate concerns about outsiders controlling their affairs through those whose campaigns they have financed. A requirement of disclosure of all contributions, together with a ceiling on contributions, would avoid outside corruption without trampling on the rights of members to raise reasonable sums for election campaigns. Such rules would honor both purposes of the legislation: protecting against outside influence and empowering members to express their views and to challenge established leadership. As I see it, the rule at issue contradicts the values the statute was designed to protect and thwarts its purpose.

I respectfully dissent.

Questions

1. Whose argument do you find more persuasive—the majority's or the dissent's? Why?
2. Are there any groups of people who might have a legitimate stake in the outcome of such an election (not a corrupt interest) that you think ought to be allowed to make contributions, even if all other outsiders are restricted?
3. How would you address the issue (not specifically raised by the Court here) of whether contributions by members of a bargaining unit represented by the union but not members of the union ought to be able to contribute funds to an election campaign?
4. In which opinion did you think the Justices were taking a more realistic view of the world?

More about the "Bill of Rights"   As the *Sadlowski* case vividly illustrates, people hold widely divergent views of the honesty and trustworthiness of union officials. Many people are extremely skeptical about the union leaders' ability and/or desire to be responsive to the interests of the membership rather than to their own needs for power or money. This skepticism is due, at least in part, to the information brought to light in congressional hearings in the late 1950s. The Court of Appeals summarized some of these congressional findings in its decision in the *Sadlowski* case:

Prior to the enactment of the LMRDA in 1959, the Select Senate Committee discovered widespread corruption, dictatorship, and racketeering in a number of large international unions. The committee found that the president of the Bakery and Confectionary Workers' International Union of America had "railroaded through changes in the union constitution which destroyed any vestigial pretenses of union democracy . . ." it reported that Dave Beck, general president of the International Brotherhood of Teamsters, "shamefully enriched himself at [the] expense [of the union members] and that in the final instance he capitulated to the forces within the union who promoted the interests of racketeers and hoodlums . . ." The committee likewise found Teamster officials joining with others to take over illegal gambling operations with an "underworld combine," . . . and the top officers of the United Textile Workers of America avariciously misappropriating union funds . . . "Democracy [was] virtually nonexistent" in the International Union of Operating Engineers because the union was ruthlessly dominated through "violence, intimidation, and other dictatorial practices." . . . Practices in the Teamsters "advanced the cause of union dictatorship." The committee cited other similar instances of widespread abuses in its 462-page report.[65]

Even though union members are guaranteed the rights of free speech and assembly, federal court cases at both the district and circuit court levels have made clear that unions are not obligated to provide space in union newspapers for articles containing viewpoints opposed to those of union leadership, nor is the union obligated to hold meetings at the behest of their membership even when the union constitution provides a procedural means for calling such a meeting. Moreover, the union meeting agenda can be set by the union leadership in such a way as to preclude discussion of particular issues. Again, the union is permitted to establish "reasonable" rules to govern such situations. In the 1967 circuit court case of *Yanity* v. *Benware*,[66] the Court of Appeals found that the protections for freedom of speech and assembly included in the employee Bill of Rights were only designed to safeguard union members who met with each other outside of regular union meetings. Supposedly the reason for Congress adopting the clause was to enable workers to meet with other workers without union approval and without fear that the union would, in some way, retaliate against the union members.

Other federal court decisions have come down equally firmly in interpreting other "rights" guaranteed by the workers' Bill of Rights. Thus, although union members are entitled to vote in union elections, they do not have the right to demand a vote on a decision of whether to strike. Likewise, the union is not required to submit a proposed collective bargaining agreement to the membership for ratification or approval, although the Bill of Rights gives members the right to see a copy of the agreement under which they are working.[67]

As a result of these court rulings, one could make a tenable argument that employees are now caught in a double-bind. Not only is the employer a potential source of trouble for the employee, but so may be the very union that was supposed to be his or her vehicle for relief. These conditions should raise concerns for the psychological well-being of those workers who are made to feel alienated because they cannot effectuate any meaningful change in the work environment to which they are captive 40 hours a week. The consequences of a labor force experiencing widespread despair and power-lessness might be worth considering.

Politics and NLRB Decisions

One problem that has plagued the student of labor law is the inconsistency in NLRB decisions over time. While you may have the impression, after reading the bulk of this chapter, that the development of labor law has progressed along a straight and rational line, that in fact has not been the case at all. The NLRB has been (and continues to be) affected by political winds. Consider, for example, the following article.

NLRB RULINGS THAT ARE INFLAMING LABOR RELATIONS

The National Labor Relations Board . . . has been churning out bitterly controversial rulings, igniting a firestorm in Washington and inflaming labor relations across the nation.

Since late last year, NLRB Chairman Donald L. Dotson has led a drive to overturn precedents that conservatives consider pro-union. . . .

Reason to Worry

Predictably, the NLRB's actions have prompted an explosion of criticism from organized labor. . . . AFL–CIO President Lane Kirkland: "The board now is a deterrent, a weapon of the most retrograde, antiunion employers and forces in this country."

Unions have ample reason to worry about the drift of NLRB decisions since December, when Reagan appointees gained a majority on the five-member board. In only 150 days the new majority has reversed at least eight major precedents (table). By some estimates, it has already recast nearly 40 percent of the decisions made since the mid-1970s that conserva- tives found objectionable. The AFL–CIO says that the current board is ruling in favor of unions only about one third as often as the boards that preceded it since 1970. . . .

Already the board is making sweeping changes that favor employers. In April, for example, it held that companies do not have to bargain over the relocation of jobs to nonunion sites, unless the primary goal is to reduce labor costs. This makes it easier to shut plants unilaterally. "There always have been periods of more liberal and more conservative interpretations of the law," says Elliot Bredhoff, a veteran union attorney. "But this board is gutting statutes."

How Reagan's NLRB Is Changing U.S. Labor Law

Date 1984	Case	Decision	Effect
Jan. 6	Meyers Industries	At least two workers must be involved for an activity to be "concerted" and thus covered by the National Labor Relations Act (reversed a 1975 decision)	Reduces protection for workers under the NLRA
Jan. 19	United Technologies, Olin	Unions must exhaust grievance procedures before filing complaints with NLRB (overturned 1977 and 1980 precedents)	Narrows the scope of union complaints and delays NLRB action on disputes covered by grievance procedures
Jan. 23	Milwaukee Spring	A company need not bargain over the transfer of work unless a labor contract requires it to, and there is no requirement to bargain at all if the move hinges on factors other than cutting labor costs (reversed a 1979 decision)	Makes it easier for employers to move union jobs to nonunion locations
Apr. 6	Otis Elevator		
May 14	Gourmet Foods	Under no circumstances can the NLRB order a company to bargain with a union unless the union proves it represents a majority of employees (reversed a 1969 precedent)	Weakens NLRB authority to penalize companies that egregiously violate labor laws

Data: *BusinessWeek.*

Flip-Flopping

Dotson insists that the board is not on an ideological, antiunion campaign. He says: "The pendulum had swung too far to the left; now it is moving back toward the middle, where it should remain." Still, the pendulum is swinging so rapidly that it is creating chaos, some experts contend. "We already have turmoil in labor-management relations, and the flip-flopping will only lead to even more instability," argues William N. Cooke, associate professor of industrial relations at the University of Michigan. Adds a prominent Washington management attorney: "The politicization of the board is very disturbing. Dramatic swings in the law leave labor and management confused about the rules of the game and only escalate the existing level of tension."

Indeed, unions claim they are already taking a more militant approach toward disputes that might have been settled quietly by the board, because, says one labor lawyer, "our respect for the agency is gone, and our confidence in it is going." Labor law gives unions the option of petitioning the NLRB to hold an election to determine if workers want representation. But unions also can shun the NLRB and threaten boycotts and strikes to force recognition—which is starting to happen. Says William H. Wynn, president of the United Food & Commercial Workers, the largest AFL–CIO affiliate: "If we cannot get fairness from the board, why fool with it?"

Created in 1935 by the National Labor Relations Act, the board always has been subject to political influence because its members and general counsel are White House appointees. But some labor law experts believe that the swings in political philosophy at the board have become more pronounced since the mid-1970s.

Extremely Liberal

Conservatives point to several decisions they say destroyed the neutrality of the board. In a 1975 case, a Republican-appointed board ruled that a single worker trying to enforce occupational safety law provisions could be considered to be acting on behalf of other employees and thus was protected from firing under the "concerted activity" provisions of the law. Decisions in 1979 and 1982 further angered conservatives by interpreting federal labor law as requiring employers in many cases to bargain over decisions to relocate jobs. In 1980 the board stunned business when it threw out a 30-year-old precedent by deciding that asking workers about their union sympathies is inherently coercive, thus an unfair labor practice.

"The board was on an extremely liberal, pro-union jag," argues John S. Irving, the NLRB general counsel from 1975 to 1979 and now a management attorney. "But unions did not complain about the NLRB being monolithic then because its holdings were to their liking."

When Ronald Reagan won election in 1980, his supporters pressed for a more pro-business NLRB. The Administration's first candidate for NLRB chairman, management consultant John Van de Water, withdrew after labor blocked his confirmation. But having used up a lot of chits in that fight, labor was forced to acquiesce on the subsequent appointment of . . . Dotson. . . .

Had the unions looked closely at Dotson then, they might have noted that he was easily as conservative as Van de Water. In a letter to the *American Bar Association Journal* in the late 1970s, Dotson contended that collective bargaining "frequently means labor monopoly, the destruction of individual freedom, and the destruction of the marketplace as the mechanism for determining the value of labor." Asked about this view recently, Dotson said: "Taken out of context, it could be construed as being antiunion, but was not meant to be. Instead, the statement was antimonopoly, antiviolence, and anticoercion."

Last December the Dotson board began reversing earlier precedents. It decided that a single worker cannot be considered to be engaging in protected "concerted activity," overturning the 1975 decision. In other decisions, the board ruled that it would defer more often to grievance procedures at companies, discouraging workers from taking a complaint directly to an NLRB regional office.

In April the board declared that employers

could ask workers who are avowed union supporters about their union sympathies as long as questions were not coercive—a standard that union attorneys complain is unrealistic. Most recently, in a case called *Gourmet Foods,* the Dotson board reversed a precedent, set in the wake of a 1969 U.S. Supreme Court decision, whereby the NLRB had certified bargaining units at companies that flagrantly violated labor law even though the union could not prove support of a majority of workers. This eliminates one of the board's few punitive tools. By law most of its powers are remedial, such as ordering back pay for an illegally fired worker.

As this pattern has emerged, says a lawyer for one major union, "strikes have occurred over issues that in other days would have resulted in the filing of an unfair labor practice. In most cases, they are wildcat strikes." Adds the general counsel for another major union: "It's not doing anybody any good, particularly employers, to have unions resorting to strikes and other devices."

Wildcat Strikes

Another factor in union determination to skirt the NLRB is the board's huge backlog of routine cases. A big backlog stymies union organizing, because long delays between the filing of a charge and a ruling make it harder for union organizers to convince union members that they will be protected by the law if illegally fired for union activity.

*   *   *   *   *

Should Democrats win control of the Senate . . . organized labor may . . . press for sweeping changes in the law—including revisions that would alter the structure and authority of the NLRB. . . .[O]ne idea being discussed would eliminate the NLRB altogether and pass responsibility for interpreting labor law to the federal courts. This, say some experts, would make the system less political.

*   *   *   *   *

Source: *BusinessWeek,* June 11, 1984, pp. 122, 127 and 130. Reprinted by special permission, © 1984 by McGraw-Hill, Inc.

QUESTIONS

1. Why is the inconsistency in the board's decisions a problem?
2. Do you think such inconsistency creates problems equally for labor and management? Explain.
3. Do you think that the board's "political" nature is a positive force in any way? Explain.

Contemporary Issues in Labor Law

Working Conditions

In recent years many observors have voiced the opinion that labor concerns have become a dead letter. While there may be an element of truth in that position, it would probably be more accurate to say that some of the problems afflicting the American worker have been so well handled by labor legislation that a shift in emphasis has occurred. It is argued that working conditions have improved so that we are no longer faced with extremes wherein workers are not paid subsistence wages or are required to work intolerable hours. However, the belief that those extremes have disappeared is not completely justified. Consider the following article.

LOUISIANA LABOR CAMPS SUPPLY "WARM BODIES" THE OIL BUSINESS NEEDS

George Getschow

Morgan City, La.—In the early 1800s, when labor shortages threatened to stop the expansion of sugar-cane cultivation in this swampy part of southern Louisiana, some European settlers seized the opportunity to strike it rich by selling slaves to the landowners. Soon the slave trade flourished throughout St. Mary Parish. Traders became wealthy plantation owners, and their descendants are still among the socially prominent here.

In the 1970s, a labor shortage again imperiled the expansion of a local industry: the building and servicing of offshore oil-drilling rigs. Again local residents responded. Newspaper ads brought jobless out-of-towners streaming into the area, and to house them entrepreneurs turned old buildings into spartan bunkhouses for transients. Thus developed an institution known hereabouts as the labor camp.

In some cases, alas, their origins are not the camps' only resemblance to the 19th century system.

A job seeker acquires a debt for lodging and other items as soon as he joins one of the 100 or so labor camps in what is called Louisiana's oil patch. When he is sent on a job, generally of a few days' or weeks' duration, he must begin to pay the debt out of his wages. Sometimes, this system enables a transient to keep a roof over his head and get a few dollars ahead of the game. But in other cases, he is ensnared by the constantly accumulating charges combined with only sporadic job assignments.

No Exit

"So many of these people that come down from the North to better themselves get caught in a web and find it hard to get out." says Bruce Stansbury, a state police investigator. Alfred Ramsey, a wage-and-hour official of the U.S. Labor Department whose agency has sued

several labor camps, says that all too frequently "the camps take all the money and the workers wind up with nothing."

Despite the hazards of generalizing, it can be said that both men's impressions were confirmed in a four-month investigation by this newspaper.

Twenty-four hours a day, seven days a week, the offshore oil industry needs a supply of roustabouts, dishwashers, and other largely unskilled laborers. "Warm bodies" is the universal term for them here in Morgan City, the mainland headquarters for offshore drilling. Shell Oil, Mobil, Texaco, Kerr-McGee and nearly all the major oil companies, as well as big suppliers and caterers, are clients of the labor camps.

Pillars of Community

Many of the owners are prominent local people. They include businessmen, elected officials, deputy sheriffs, physicians and a churchman or two. C. R. Brownell, who was Morgan City's mayor until this week and used labor-camp residents as garbage collectors and for other work, explains the town's thinking this way: "The camps serve a legitimate need; it's just that some undesirables have given them a bad name."

The operators do not call their places labor camps. One, for instance, is known as the St. Mary Council on Alcoholism & Drug Abuse. It was started 12 years ago as a nonprofit rehabilitation center and now includes a halfway house. Directors include a state senator, a physician and ex-mayor, an optometrist, a deputy sheriff and a former police chief.

But the boss at the halfway house is John Carli, a 6 foot 5, 250-pound ex-convict who many former camp residents say carries a derringer in his hip pocket. (He denies it.) A former tavern keeper from Hurley, Wis., Mr.

Carli has been convicted of operating illegal gambling tables, possession of dangerous drugs, simple assault and assault with intent to do great bodily harm.

"Everybody's afraid of him," says Robert Morgan, who until recently lived at the halfway house. "I've stood there and watched him beat people up and been too scared to do anything." ("That's not true," Mr. Carli replies, "We're the ones who get beat up.")

Sheriff's Commission
Despite his criminal record, Mr. Carli holds a St. Mary Parish sheriff's commission. And the sheriff's department has been helpful to him and the labor camp. Every week, sheriff's deputies deliver men to the halfway house. "We do it to give these people who are transient a place to stay," says Deputy Sheriff Duval Arthur. "We don't have a drunk-tank facility."

But Thor Holm, who sought refuge at the halfway house two years ago, says drunkenness sometimes has nothing to do with being in the camp. "I was unemployed, flat broke and had no place else to go," he says.

Mr. Holm says that at the halfway house he was given a steady stream of alcoholic drinks and sedative drugs that kept him in a "hypnotic state." After 11 days, he continues, Mr. Carli took him off this regimen and sent him to work at a large offshore catering company called Oceanic Butler.

At the time, according to Mr. Holm and several other former workers, Mr. Carli had an arrangement with five of Oceanic Butler's personnel people: In exchange for cash payments, they would use laborers from the St. Mary Council halfway house—but deliver the men's paychecks not to the men but to Mr. Carli. He then was able to cash the checks because each laborer, upon entering the camp, must sign a form giving Mr. Carli power of attorney.

Thus, Mr. Holm says, he never saw a paycheck for the four months he washed dishes offshore. Mr. Carli, he states, was cashing his checks, giving him a few dollars in spending money and occasionally sending Mr. Holm's ex-wife alimony payments. He says Mr. Carli kept the bulk of the more than $3,200 he

earned to cover lodging, transportation, alcohol, drugs, doctors' visits (Mr. Holm says they actually were visits to Mr. Carli's office) and other "detoxification" costs.

The camp's itemized statement lists the sedative drugs Elavil, Atarax, and Vistaril, plus $155 for whisky and wine. "He charged me for five drinks a day, whether I drank anything or not," Mr. Holm states.

Oceanic Butler says it cut its ties with the halfway house about a year and a half ago and fired the personnel people involved. Mr. Carli denies paying them to "work" his men but says the power-of-attorney arrangement was no secret. "Every man that worked (in payroll) at Oceanic Butler got a copy of the power-of-attorney form. . . . For every 10 (laborers), at least half of them never paid us back."

As for Mr. Holm, Mr. Carli says that "anything he got was approved by one of our doctors. He's a bad alcoholic and schizophrenic." Mr. Carli and the halfway house's medical adviser, Dr. Julius Fernandez, say Mr. Carli doesn't give out prescription drugs on his own.

However, the St. Mary Parish coroner, Dr. Evariste Trahan, says he resigned some years ago as a medical adviser to the halfway house because "Carli always had a generous supply of drugs that he administered to people without my supervision and without a legal license." They included the barbiturates Seconal and Nembutal, he says. Mr. Carli contends he fired Dr. Trahan.

* * * * *

Not far from the St. Mary Council on Alcoholism & Drug Abuse stands a camp called Roustabouts Inc., owned by a city councilman of Morgan City, Gregory Hamer. A former salesman for the camp, Ray Beadle, says it has lured droves of jobless Northerners with ads in Northern newspapers telling of "top pay" and "nice accommodations" at its "roustabout company on the Gulf Coast." But at the camp, he adds, these people "get stuck in there and are treated like dogs."

The camp is a windowless metal warehouse behind a towering chain-link fence hidden behind railroad tracks on the outskirts of town. It resembles a cellblock, with row on row of steel doors. The rooms, four-man cubicles with bunkbeds and a single ceiling lightbulb, can be opened or locked only by one of the dispatchers. Despite the cramped conditions, the laborers must stay in their rooms anytime they aren't working, former residents say.

Economics of the Camp

The camp's economic system makes it difficult to do more than survive. With a $98 weekly tab for room and board, residents have to work 27 hours a week just to cover this basic charge—and 27 hours is frequently all the work they get. But residents also face assessments for such things as sheets ($7), towels ($5), boots ($29), hardhats ($9), a glass ($2.25), a fork (80 cents) and soap (90 cents). The charges are deducted from their wages.

Because the residents are nearly always in the hole, the bunkhouse manager, Cecil Jones lends them money for incidentals at a 50 percent markup for a loan of a few weeks (an effective annual interest rate of several hundred percent). The camp itself cashes the residents' paychecks each Friday.

Mr. Hamer, the principal owner, who also is the president of the Sacred Heart Catholic School board, says he makes "a good profit" renting out his hired hands to local oil facilities for $7.50 to $18.00 an hour, depending on the job. (They earn $3.55). He figures that he runs "a dignified camp." Mr. Hamer concedes that "abuses surely go on sometimes" but adds, "You'd have to be there to find out they're happening, and I'm seldom there because I'm busy doing other things."

Abuses or no—the labor camps commonly are filthy and are referred to as "slave camps"—many local citizens express support for the camp system. The state employment office in Morgan City and local churches, all flooded with job-hungry Northerners, refer people to the camps. "The camps provide a humanitarian service, in a sense," says the Rev. John Gallen, the pastor of the Sacred Heart Catholic Church here. "If it weren't for them, hundreds of transients would be stranded here without even a roof over their head."

Source: *The Wall Street Journal*, June 23, 1983, p. 1. Reprinted by permission of *The Wall Street Journal*, © Dow Jones & Company, Inc., 1983. All rights reserved.

QUESTION

1. Recall the conditions of workers described in the opening sections of this chapter. Does it surprise you that this article describes conditions that existed in 1983 rather than in 1883?

Working Conditions—OSHA Worker health and safety has received increased attention in recent years. Under the NLRA, employees can demand that employers negotiate over wages, hours, and terms and conditions of employment. Nonetheless, Congress recognized that some standards had to be set to ensure relatively danger-free workplaces. Congress chose to accomplish that end, not through the NLRB, but rather through a separate agency called the Occupational Safety and Health Administration (OSHA). (Note that the enabling legislation for the agency is called the Occupational Safety and Health Act and is also referred to as OSHA or "the Act.")

OSHA contains some very broad grants of power to the agency, allowing it to regulate virtually any aspect of the workplace that could have an effect on worker health and safety. During its first years in existence, the agency was sharply criticized for promulgating volumes of regulations, most of which addressed comparatively insignificant matters in a very detailed manner while ignoring wide-ranging and serious threats to worker health. For example, OSHA developed very exacting standards to regulate the size of "exit" signs and the height of toilet seats but failed to address problems such as exposure of workers to toxic chemical fumes.

OSHA has subsequently taken steps to correct its past "sins." The agency has eliminated some of the many rules it had originally adopted and has simplified many of those that it kept. In addition, OSHA has begun tackling some of the serious problems of worker safety.

Perhaps the most far-reaching of OSHA's regulations to date is the Hazard Communication Rule,[68] which took effect in 1985. This rule requires all employers who are classified as manufacturers to develop rather elaborate programs to inform workers about the hazards of chemicals used in the workplace. All hazardous substances must be identified and labeled, and the employer must keep on hand, in readily accessible form, detailed information sheets about each of the chemicals. In addition, employees must each be given a written manual and an in-person training session in the proper and safe use of each of the chemicals they might encounter in the workplace, both in normal use and due to an accident, spill, or leak.

Thus, OSHA can have a tremendous impact on worker safety. At the same time, its effects on the cost of doing business could be profound. Do you think the Hazard Communication Rule goes far enough, or do you think it is overly intrusive? What are some of the societal costs of work-related injury and disease? Do you think a cost-benefit analysis of regulations proposed by OSHA would be an appropriate factor for the agency to consider when deciding whether to adopt certain rules? Or should worker safety transcend all questions of cost? What ethical dilemmas could arise when trying to balance worker safety and health against other societal costs?

OSHA has instituted a voluntary protection program. This program, described in the following article, is designed to provide incentives to industry for adopting health and safety measures before having its arm twisted by OSHA inspectors.

OSHA'S VOLUNTARY PROTECTION PROGRAM

James Chelius and Harry F. Stark

The Occupational Safety and Health Administration has surely been one of the most controversial of government agencies. This tradition of controversy is currently being upheld by the agency's role as the Reagan Administration's vanguard of regulatory voluntarism. While the secretary of labor has already pointed to voluntarism as having produced lower injury rates, many representatives of organized labor have decried it as an important impediment to worker safety and health. A key feature of OSHA's new nonadversarial strategy is the voluntary protection program. Since the program was recently initiated and is now underway at several worksites, it is useful to review voluntary protection and its implications.

* * * * *

The basic idea of the voluntary protection program is that government's usual regulatory techniques of promulgating and enforcing rules have inherently limited potential for improving safety and health. Even if rules and enforcement were complete, it is estimated that only about 10 to 30 percent of all injuries would be affected. In addition, because many violations are transitory and, therefore, difficult to detect by periodic government inspections, the potential impact of the traditional methods is lowered to about 5 to 10 percent of all injuries.

In its search for supplementary regulatory methods, OSHA is attempting to identify those firms considered successful at providing a safe work environment. It is felt that "certifying" these successful operations and exempting them from inspections will release regulatory resources to be used with more dangerous worksites and provide an example for others to follow.

While as early as 1909 the Wisconsin Industrial Commission used "voluntary compliance" as one of its operating principles, the immediate prototype of the program was the Bechtel Corporation's San Onofre, California, nuclear power plant construction project. Union and management representatives developed a program that involved reliance on government-established safety standards. Compliance with these rules, however, was monitored by a joint labor-management committee rather than government inspectors. Reports of a 39 percent reduction in injury rates encouraged OSHA to broaden participation so as to include other worksites and industries.

* * * * *

In July of 1982, OSHA announced the final version of its voluntary compliance program . . . To be eligible for any of the three subprograms, a firm is required to meet six basic conditions. There must be: an ongoing safety program: an internal employee complaint mechanism; assurances that workers who file complaints will not be subject to discrimination; a cooperative atmosphere between workers and the employer; no diminution of employee rights under the OSH Act; and a good injury rate record.

If a worksite is unionized but the union chooses not to participate, the employer must have the union's approval. The rewards offered are removal from routine inspections and expedited consideration of requests for variances from existing OSHA standards.

The most straightforward of the three subprograms is PRAISE, which deals only with safety and is limited to low-hazard industries. It is explicitly designed simply as "recognition for past achievement" and encouragement for "continued improvements where possible."

There are two programs for more hazardous environments—the STAR program for proven well-established safety and or health plans and the TRY program for more experimental arrangements. Each program may be a "management initiative" or based on "employee participation" via labor-management committees. The key requirements of the STAR program are that for the previous three years the worksite have *both* injury frequency and severity rates below the national average for the industry and no willful violations of OSHA standards. The TRY program requires *either* a frequency or severity rate below the national average for that industry or specific goals and methods for reducing injury rates. A good inspection record as indicated by no willful violations is also required for TRY. There are also requirements as to the structure of the "employee participation" and "management initiative" arrangements.

As of October 1983, 19 companies are participating in the program. Outside of the construction industry where joint labor-management programs are the only option, all of the programs are unilateral management initiatives.

Participation Incentives

As mentioned above, there are only two explicit incentives for participation—exemption from routine OSHA inspections and expedited consideration of requests for variances from standards. However, OSHA's policy of targeting the more hazardous situations for inspection virtually guarantees that any worksite with a record close to being good enough to qualify for voluntary protection would not be inspected anyway. Similarly, priority for variances is at best a modest reward. If there are any substantial incentives for participation, one must look beyond the *Federal Register* to the process of safety and health management.

A key theme throughout the literature on safety management is the importance of employee involvement in the prevention process. It is possible that the recognition and attention accorded by participation in the voluntary protection program can be useful in capturing employees' attention to the prevention process. Similarly, a frequent complaint of safety and health managers is the lack of attention paid to their function by line managers. The recognition of quality performance implied by acceptance into the program may also serve to direct line management attention to this area. Recognition for a good safety and health program is, of course, also helpful for a firm's public image. The positive results derived from employee and line management involvement as well as general goodwill may be important. However, it is uncomfortably like the classic Hawthorne situation in which virtually any form of attention yields desirable results in the short run, but after the initial positive results the situation regresses to the prior steady state.

A more subtle incentive for participating is that it preserves one's informal authority to influence future OSHA policy. Many in the corporate safety and health community have complained for years about the rigid, often adversarial methods used by OSHA. While no one advocates that the voluntary protection program should be the only method for administering safety and health regulation, it may be a symbolically important movement away from past practices.

Because the corporate community has advocated changing these past practices, many may go along with the first changes, however slight, simply to preserve their role as spokespersons for further movement. If the slightest movement away from past practices was to be met with disinterest or even disdain, it could lessen the impetus toward more substantial later change. Unfortunately, such motivations will probably limit the impact of the voluntary protection program to those already performing

satisfactorily with no influence on the problem situations.

* * * * *

Public Policy Strategy
American regulation using the voluntary actions of private parties generally has several faces. Frequently a private group captures regulatory authority as a device to use the powers of government to their own advantage. Prime examples of such regulation are the occupational licensure boards controlled by the licensed groups. Among their many purposes, such bodies frequently restrict the supply of labor and hence raise compensation for the "regulated" group. Another type of regulatory voluntarism is a substitute for government action when there is a weak political consensus for strong regulation. Examples of such efforts are the wage-price guidelines (as opposed to controls) of the early 1960s and the voluntary import restrictions used periodically.

A third type of what might be categorized as voluntary regulation occurs when the government attempts to change the workplace by enhancing the power of private groups. The most significant example is the National Labor Relations Act. Other countries now use such empowerment of private groups as a strategy for dealing with occupational safety and health. While there is no solid evidence on how these foreign efforts at occupational health and safety regulation have worked, there does appear to be a broad consensus in these countries that it is a useful public policy. Whether the voluntary protection program is simply another weak version of government action or the portent of a new kind of decentralized regulation through empowerment is uncertain.

U.S. Secretary of Labor Raymond Donovan has stated that greater cooperation between labor and management "is critically important" to increasing productivity and improving the quality of life for workers. In urging "labor-management cooperation rather than their historic confrontation," the Secretary attempted to reassure management and labor leaders that cooperation would not result in a loss of management control or union power. The Secretary related that: "[t]he working man no longer sees himself as a working unit. He wants to be involved in the decisionmaking. Rather than be an assembly line robot, he wants to be involved in the planning."

It appears that joint union-management implementation of the voluntary OSHA strategy is likely to require some increase of governmental encouragement, contradictory as that may seem. The future of voluntarism not only requires positive government support but also requires management willingness to enlarge the scope of decision-sharing and organized labor's ability (as well as willingness) to respond in increasingly technical areas.

The voluntary protection program, however, seems likely to find acceptance with those employers who need regulation least and are quite anxious to involve employees directly without the intervention of bargaining representatives; that is, among large, well-managed firms without unions.

Many employers have indicated that it is in their own interest to educate and prepare workers for increased participation. However, for technical and competitive reasons as well as for the preservation of prerogative, American employers generally oppose mandatory informa-

tion-sharing for bilateral decision processes both in the United States legislatures and the European Economic Community. Although pressing for more and earlier access to critical information, unions have often been incapable of or unwilling to share responsibility for an enlarged scope of decision making.

In a highly dynamic situation and with the obvious stimulus of both economic expansion and international competition, management and labor may be surprisingly inventive, provided that mutual fears of diminution of rights can be allayed. It is unlikely that voluntarism as a public policy will succeed unless it is part of a broader range of regulatory tactics. Perhaps the "right to know" laws recently passed in several states and the subject of a recent OSHA standard will give us insight into whether a decentralized regulatory mechanism based on widely available information and private action can be combined into a viable public policy mechanism.

Source: *Labor Law Journal* 35 (March 1984), pp. 167–74. Reproduced from the March 1984 issue of the *Labor Law Journal,* published and copyrighted 1984 by Commerce Clearing House, Inc., 4025 W. Peterson Avenue, Chicago, IL 60646. (The authors are associate professor and professor, respectively, at the Institute of Management and Labor Relations, Rutgers University.)

Equal Protection

A great deal of interest is now directed to ensuring that all workers receive fair and equal treatment without consideration being given to their race, color, gender, religion, age, or physical infirmities. Laws addressing these issues are discussed in Chapter 13. Those laws prohibit discrimination by labor organizations as well as by employers. Furthermore, workers who have traditionally been discriminated against are exerting pressure on employers via the collective bargaining process to erase any of the remaining vestiges of that past discrimination. Thus, we now find some labor organizations taking a firm and aggressive stand on the issue of *comparable worth,* that is, determining the compensation to be paid for a position based on the job's intrinsic value in comparison to wages being paid in the workplace for other jobs requiring comparable skills, effort, and responsibility, and having comparable worth to the organization.

Public Sector Strikes

Yet another area of immediate concern is that of the rights of public sector employees to engage in strikes. As the law now stands, in most states public employees are not permitted to strike and, in fact, air traffic controllers who did strike in 1981 were fired by President Reagan. Yet in cities across the country, teachers, police, and fire fighters have begun voicing strong opposition to the prohibitions placed on them. This will likely be an area of hot debate for some period of time. List the arguments for and against public employees being allowed to strike. Why should public employees be treated differently than employees in the private sector?

Labor-Management Relations

The economic turmoil of the late 1970s and early 1980s, the growing sophistication of the workforce, changing demographics, and an increased awareness of labor practices in foreign countries have led many people to question the general health of the labor-management relationship in the United States. The following article identifies a few of the issues that are of present concern to labor leaders.

AMERICAN WORKERS NEED UNIONS MORE THAN EVER

Jeffrey Cox

Having just spent several evenings as a phone-bank volunteer for a union organizing drive, I have fresh in my mind almost every possible objection to unions.

Most of the serious objections, those which are not simple bigotry, can be summed up in the word *obsolete*.

There was a time when we needed unions I was told, a time when employers were mean and nasty. Now employers are good people, and we no longer need unions. Unions, it is said, used to stand up for downtrodden working people, but now they are just another special interest, like the Tobacco Wholesalers Trade Association, or the horse-racing lobby.

Is it true? Are American working people now in such a strong position that they no longer need the protection of a union contract? Do they [employers] no longer make arbitrary or biased or politically based hiring and firing decisions? How do American workers fare compared to workers in the other industrial democracies?

The answer to that last question is not very

encouraging for people who believe in human rights and democracy. In many ways America is the freest and most democratic of all the industrial democracies; but when Americans go to work, they have to leave their freedoms at home. American workers suffer from a degree of employer tyranny, especially regarding dismissal, that would be regarded as outrageous in any other major industrial democracy.

Japanese workers in many industries have life-time employment, a practice virtually unknown in this country outside of our universities. In Britain, employees in a wide range of industries can challenge what they regard as an unjust dismissal in "industrial tribunals," and employers must show that dismissal was justified. Workers in most other European nations have some equivalent form of statutory protection. Finally, in virtually every other industrial nation, many more employees have the protections of a union contract.

In America, however, the land of the free, employers can dismiss their workers, and do, for virtually any reason other than racial or sexual discrimination. The notions that workers should have, not only rights, but a positive say in how their business or industry or bureaucracy is run is unheard of and positively discouraged in law.

Employers would have to be superhuman not to abuse the wide-ranging power to order workers around, dismiss them and otherwise violate their rights. The only right American workers have is the right to quit, a precious and valuable right, but it hardly adds up to democracy at work.

Other nations are not only ahead of us giving working people civil liberties on the job, they are ahead of us giving workers some positive say in how their business is run. This is especially the case in Sweden where 70 percent of the work force is unionized, and where unions and the government cooperate in encouraging contracts which provide workers with a say in how industries are run.

Almost all European nations encourage experiments in worker-owned and run cooperative industries, especially when socialist governments are in power. The Japanese habit of consulting their workers is widely known. The few American experiments in worker democracy and power sharing have been subverted by big corporations who see them primarily as a means of undercutting the unions, increasing managerial prerogatives, and dumping unprofitable industries into the laps of workers.

Even in the unionized sectors of our economy, the valuable protections extended to workers by a union contract rarely go beyond a negative concept of rights. The National Labor Relations Act in effect prohibits unions from negotiating about anything other than wages, hours and working conditions.

Many unions would be delighted to bargain about an investment policy which would protect American jobs in the future, only to find that employers will only bargain about wages. The public then blames the unions for negotiating large wage increases when the law prohibits them from negotiating about anything else. Public employees suffer under even more repressive legislation, as the Polish-style treatment of the air-traffic controllers and now the postal workers by the federal government demonstrates. . . .

Unions do promote specific legislation to benefit their members which may or may not be in the public interest, as do thousands of other organizations which are not singled out for special criticism; but unions also represent the frontiers of democracy in America—of democracy at work.

America will be a better country to live in when we begin to treat the right to bargain collectively about everything as a fundamental right like freedom of speech, freedom of the press, and freedom of religion.

*   *   *   *   *

Source: *Des Moines (Iowa) Register*, September 1, 1984, p. 7A. Reprinted with permission of the author, Jeffrey Cox. Copyright 1984, *Des Moines Register* and Tribune Company. (The author is an associate professor of history at the University of Iowa.)

Chapter Questions

1. In your opinion, what are the average blue-collar worker's biggest sources of dissatisfaction? Can these sources of dissatisfaction be eliminated through collective bargaining? Explain why or why not.

2. In your opinion, what are the average white-collar worker's biggest sources of job dissatisfaction? What means do such workers have for eliminating those sources of dissatisfaction?

3. If chimpanzees could be trained to perform unskilled, repetitious jobs, should they be allowed to do so? If chimpanzees could be trained to perform hazardous jobs like mining coal, should they be allowed to do so? Explain your answer.

4. Many workers in the United States are very disturbed by the practices of some American companies which set up factories in other countries.

   a. What is the basis for the U.S. workers' hostility to such practices?

   b. Why do American companies choose to move their operations to other countries?

   c. Do you think there should be some attempt by the federal government to regulate these practices?

   d. If so, what form should the legislation take?

5. Imagine what the world will be like 100 years from now. In what ways do you picture the work life of the average American to have changed?

6. Imagine the ideal work world. How close does that picture come to the one you conjured up in response to question 5? What types, if any, of labor or other legislation would bring society closer to that ideal?

7. What societal changes over the past 30 years have affected the workplace the most, in your estimation? Has labor law kept pace with workplace changes? If not, what new legislation is necessary?

8. A union representing a bargaining unit comprised of both men and women, and different racial and ethnic groups, demands to see detailed information that the employer keeps on wages paid to women and minorities, as well as hiring statistics about these members of the work force.

   a. Should the employer be required to let the union see this data?

   b. What circumstances might affect your decision? See *Westinghouse Electric Corp.*, 239 NLRB No. 18 (1978).

   c. Suppose that, instead of asking for wage information, the union asked to see the questions, answers, and individual scores achieved by employees on psychological aptitude tests that the employer requires employees to take. If the employer refuses to turn these scores over, has it committed an unfair labor practice?

   d. Does this situation differ significantly from the previous situation? See *Detroit Edison Co.* v. *NLRB*, 440 U.S. 301 (1979).

9. Aavco Hardware Co. learns that union organizers (not Aavco employees) have been passing out literature to Aavco employees in the Aavco parking lot, which is surrounded by a chain link fence but does not have a closed gate or guardhouse. Aavco officials want to throw these ''union instigators'' off the property.

   a. Will the officials be committing an unfair labor practice if they do?

   b. Would it matter if Aavco had a general ''no-solicitation'' rule?

   c. What if Aavco adopted a no-solicitation rule only after the first union organizers started handing out literature? See *Central Hardware Co.* v. *NLRB*, 407 U.S. 539 (1972).

10. United Plant Guard Workers of America (UPGWA) sought union certification at Arbitron Security Services, Inc. The union and the company stipulated certain election procedures to be followed including, among other things, the hours, date, and location at which balloting would be held, and the posting of notices of the election. Several days before the election, the company posted notices of the election in several conspicuous locations. Two days before the election, the union mailed notices to employees listed on sheets supplied to the union by the company. The election was held on a regular payday. Out of 314 employees eligible to vote, a total of only 64 valid votes (26 of them for the union) were cast. The UPGWA petitioned the NLRB following the union's defeat, claiming that the low voter turnout led to the inference that notice of the election to the employees had been inadequate and that the election results should be set aside. What do you think the NLRB's response is likely to be? See *Iowa Security Services, Inc. and National Union, United Plant Guard Workers of America*, 269 NLRB No. 53 (1983–84 CCH NLRB ¶16,145), March 21, 1984.

11. A bargaining unit, consisting of 56 employees at the time of a union representation election, voted in favor of unionization by a vote of 29 to 23. The employer sought to have the election results nullified, alleging that six days prior to the election, a union official meeting with 20 employees had referred repeatedly to a company vice president as a "stingy Jew." The company had witnesses to substantiate this claim, and the union did not deny it.

    a. Do you think the election results should be set aside? See *NLRB* v. *Silverman's Men's Wear, Inc.,* 656 F.2d 53 (3d Cir. 1981).

    b. Suppose, instead, union officers came to campaign meetings for a Japanese-owned company wearing T-shirts that said, "Remember Pearl Harbor" and "Japs speak with forked tongue and slant eyes." Do you think the result would be any different? See *YKK (U.S.A.) Inc. and Sandra M. Collins et al.,* 296 NLRB No. 8 (1983–84 CCH NLRB ¶16,158), decided March 8, 1984.

12. A major advertising agency is housed on the 87th floor of a skyscraper located on Madison Avenue in New York City. Unionized clerical workers, protesting an allegedly unfair labor practice committed by the agency, picket in front of the entrance to the agency, in the hallway of the building. (The entire 87th floor, including the hallway space, is leased by the agency.) Does the employer have the right to order the striking employees off the premises? See *Seattle First National Bank,* 258 NLRB 164 (1981).

13. On January 9, 1980, the president of the International Longshoremen's Association (ILA) ordered members to stop handling cargo going to or coming from the Soviet Union. This action was taken as a protest against the Soviet Union's invasion of Afghanistan and was strongly supported by union members. A U.S. company that imported Russian dry goods to resell had its business totally disrupted by the ILA strike. The company filed an unfair labor practice proceeding with the NLRB, claiming that the Longshoremen were engaged in an illegal secondary boycott. Do you think the company will prevail? See *International Longshoremen's Association* v. *Allied International, Inc.,* 102 S.Ct. 1656 (1982).

Notes

1. The historical and political background information used in this chapter was drawn from a number of sources and amalgamated in such a way that precise footnoting was difficult. Many of the sociological trends described, for example, are discussed in three or four sources. The author would, therefore, like to acknowledge the works of the following people, whose research and insights proved to be invaluable resources upon which to draw: Richard S. Belous, Hyman Berman, Angela Y. Davis, Richard Edwards, John J. Flagler, Eli Ginzberg, J. David Greenstone, Isaac A. Hourwich, and Sar A. Levitan.

The author of this chapter would like specially to acknowledge and thank Professor Archibald Cox, from whom she took a course in labor law in 1978, and whose textbook and class lectures provided the cornerstone of her understanding of the subject. The author hopes that her own good fortune at having had the opportunity to study labor law under Professor Cox will translate into a richer educational experience for students using this textbook.

2. Archibald Cox, with Derek Bok and Robert A. Gorman, *Cases and Materials on Labor Law,* 8th ed. (Mineola, N.Y.: Foundation Press, 1977), pp. 7–8.

3. Richard Edwards, *Contested Terrain: The Transformation of the Workplace in the Twentieth Century* (New York: Basic Books, 1979), pp. 40–41.

4. John J. Flagler, *The Labor Movement in the United States* (Minneapolis: Lerner Publications, 1972), pp. 26–33.

5. Cox, *Labor Law,* p. 8.

6. Isaac A. Hourwich, *Immigration and Labor* (New York: Arno Press, 1969), pp. 125–45.

7. Cox, *Labor Law,* p. 9.

8. Hourwich, *Immigration and Labor* p. 349, quoting Frank Tracy Carlton, *The History and Problems of Organized Labor,* pp. 346–47.

9. Flagler, *The Labor Movement,* pp. 26–28.

10. Ibid.

11. Hourwich, *Immigration and Labor,* pp. 232–49.

12. Eli Ginzberg and Hyman Berman, *The American Worker in the Twentieth Century: A History Through Autobiogra-*

phies (New York: Free Press, 1963), pp. 193–95, taken from Andria Taylor Hourwich and Gladys L. Palmer, eds., *I Am a Woman Worker,* Affiliated Schools for Workers, 1936, pp. 17 ff.

13. Hourwich, *Immigration and Labor,* p. 243, quoting *Reports of the Massachusetts Bureau of Labor Statistics,* 1871, pp. 442–43.

14. Ibid., pp. 232–33, quoting *Report of the Industrial Commission,* 15, p. 461.

15. Flagler, *The Labor Movement,* pp. 33 and 36, quoting Frederick Lewis Allen, *The Big Change . . . 1900–1950.*

16. Ibid., p. 47.

17. J. David Greenstone, *Labor in American Politics* (New York: Alfred A. Knopf, 1969), p. 21.

18. Cox, *Labor Law,* p. 11.

19. Flagler, *The Labor Movement,* p. 47.

20. Greenstone, *Labor in American Politics,* p. 22.

21. Ibid., p. 23.

22. Cox, *Labor Laws,* pp. 11–12.

23. Flagler, *The Labor Movement,* pp. 81–83.

24. Greenstone, *Labor in American Politics,* pp. 41–42.

25. Cox, *Labor Law,* pp. 86–87.

26. Ibid., pp. 87–88.

27. Ibid., p. 88.

28. Angela Y. Davis, *Women, Race and Class* (New York: Random House, 1981), p. 138.

29. Flagler, *The Labor Movement,* p. 60.

30. Davis, *Women, Race and Class,* p. 150.

31. Flagler, *The Labor Movement,* pp. 54–56.

32. Cox, *Labor Law,* pp. 18–35.

33. Ibid., pp. 35–40; see *Loewe* v. *Lawlor,* 208 U.S. 274 (1908).

34. Cox, *Labor Law,* pp. 60–66.

35. Greenstone, *Labor in American Politics,* p. 47.

36. Cox, *Labor Law,* p. 75.

37. Ibid., p. 83.

38. Greenstone, *Labor in American Politics,* p. 47.

39. Cox, *Labor Law,* p. 89.

40. Ibid., p. 91.

41. Ibid., p. 94.

42. Ibid., pp. 1107–08.

43. Ibid., p. 1108.

44. Flagler, *The Labor Movement,* p. 64.

45. The National Labor Relations Act is found in Title 29 U.S.C. § 151 et seq.

46. Cox, *Labor Law,* pp. 113–22.

47. Ibid., pp. 99–101.

48. See, e.g., *Daylight Grocery Co., Inc.* v. *NLRB,* 678 F.2d 905 (11th Cir. 1982).

49. See, e.g., *Dal-Tex Optical Co.,* 137 NLRB 1782, in which repeated references are made to the departure in the election process from ''laboratory conditions.''

50. Section 8(c) of the NLRA specifically states that ''[t]he expressing of any views, arguments, or opinion, or the dissemination thereof . . . shall not constitute or be evidence of an unfair labor practice . . . if such expression contains no threat of reprisal or force or promise of benefit.''

51. See discussion, e.g., in *NLRB* v. *Golub Corp.,* 388 F.2d 921 (2d Cir. 1967).

52. See, e.g., *NLRB* v. *General Electric Co.,* 418 F.2d 736 (2d Cir. 1970). See also Section 8(c) of the NLRA, which indicates that the mere expression of a viewpoint cannot constitute, in and of itself, an unfair labor practice. This is true at the bargaining table as it is elsewhere.

53. See, e.g., *NLRB* v. *Fitzgerald Mills Corp.,* 313 F.2d 260 (2d Cir.), cert. denied 375 U.S. 834 (1963); *NLRB* v. *Herman Sausage Co.,* 275 F.2d 229 (5th Cir. 1960). Contra *NLRB* v. *Reed & Prince Mfg. Co.,* 205 F.2d 131 (1st Cir.), cert. denied 346 U.S. 887 (1953).

54. *NLRB* v. *Insurance Agents' International Union,* 361 U.S. 477 (1960).

55. 361 U.S. at 480–481.

56. 361 U.S. at 482, citing 119 NLRB 769–771.

57. 361 U.S. at 488.

58. *NLRB* v. *Truitt Mfg. Co.,* 351 U.S. 149 (1956).

59. *NLRB* v. *Katz,* 369 U.S. 736 (1962).

60. See, e.g., *First National Maintenance Corporation* v. *NLRB,* 101 S.Ct. 2573 (1981).

61. *NLRB* v. *Wooster Division of Borg-Warner,* 356 U.S. 342 (1958).

62. *NLRB* v. *Katz,* 369 U.S. 736 (1962).

63. See, e.g., *NLRB* v. *Mackay Radio and Telegraph Co.,* 304 U.S. 333 (1938), and *NLRB* v. *Erie Resistor Co.,* 373 U.S. 221 (1963).

64. *United Steelworkers of America* v. *Sadlowski,* 457 U.S. 102 (1982).

65. 645 F.2d 1114, 1124 (D.C. Cir. 1981).

66. 376 F.2d 197 (2d Cir.), cert. denied 389 U.S. 874 (1967).

67. Zech and Kuhn, ''National Labor Policy: Is It Truly Designed to Protect the Worker?'' Selected Papers of the American Business Law Association: *National Proceedings,* 1982, 433, at 442–43.

68. 29 C.F.R. 1910. 1200 (Revised July 1, 1984.)

13

Employment Discrimination

Part One—Introduction

The study of discrimination, perhaps more than any other topic in this text, reflects both the base spirit and the grandeur of American values. We have affirmed our belief that all men and women are created equal. We have undertaken what has been, in retrospect, a profoundly complex and burdensome effort to eliminate and even make up for the wrongs of the past. The abolition of slavery, voting rights, school integration, open accommodations, equal pay, protection of the handicapped, broadened religious safeguards—we have sought and achieved a remarkable reformation in human conduct, and we have achieved those results in a comparatively short time. However, the problem of discrimination remains far from resolution.

At this writing the law of employment discrimination appears to be at a critical juncture. In July 1984 the Supreme Court handed down one of the most significant discrimination decisions in the two decades following the passage of the Civil Rights Act of 1964. In *Firefighters Local Union No. 1784* v. *Stotts*,[1] the Court held that lower courts were wrong in ordering the City of Memphis, Tennessee, to ignore a seniority system and lay off white employees rather than more recently hired black fire fighters when the city faced a budget crisis. The decision is clearly a serious blow to affirmative action in the context of seniority, and in the eyes of many, to the policy of affirmative action generally. The full effect of the decision may not be clear for years. However, the policies of the Reagan administration, the *Firefighters* decision, and the tone of the times suggest that the civil rights movement may have been slowed significantly. Therefore, the reader is cautioned to keep abreast of new decisions in this volatile area of law. (The *Firefighters* opinion is set out later in the chapter.)

Discrimination Defined

University students sometimes think themselves the victims of discrimination. May landlord lawfully decline to rent to students? May a publicly supported university fund, for example, a men's swim team while declining to do the same for women? May an insurance company lawfully impose higher premiums upon younger drivers? May a bar owner offer free admission to women while imposing a cover charge for men? May a state university lawfully impose higher tuition charges for out-of-state students? Each of these issues involves a distinction in treatment among identifiable classes of citizens. Of course, life is replete with such distinctions. How are we to identify those that constitute unlawful discrimination? In the broadest sense, such distinctions become unlawful when not grounded in reason. That is, the distinction must be based upon objective criteria such that the difference in treatment is rational rather than the product of whim, caprice, or bias. In practice, the measure of discrimination lies in the constitutional provisions, laws, regulations, executive orders, and judicial opinions that address discrimination. For example, one court elegantly identified discrimination in these words:

> In constitutional law, the effect of a statute which confers particular privileges on a class arbitrarily selected from a large number of persons, all of whom stand in the same relation to the privileges granted and between whom and those not favored no reasonable distinction can be found.[2]

More directly pertinent to this chapter is one scholar's view of discrimination in job selection:

> Unfair discrimination or bias is said to exist when members of a minority group have lower probabilities of being selected for a job when, in fact, if they had been selected, their probabilities of performing successfully in a job would have been equal to those of nonminority group members.[3]

Employment Discrimination: The Foundation in Law

History

In 1941 A. Philip Randolph, president of the predominantly black Brotherhood of Sleeping Car Porters, organized black leaders who threatened a massive protest march in Washington, D.C. In response, President Roosevelt issued Executive Order 8802 (such orders have the force and effect of law) creating a Fair Employment Practice Committee. Congress was hostile to the order and limited the committee's budget, but Roosevelt's action was a striking first step for the federal government in addressing racial discrimination.

Likewise, during the 1940s several states enacted their own fair employment laws. While civil rights lawyers actively pursued litigation during the 1930s and 1940s and several significant decisions were handed down, the next firm impetus for racial equality was the landmark *Brown* v. *Board of Education*[4] decision in 1954 in which the Supreme Court forbade "separate but equal" schools. *Brown* repudiated the doctrine enunciated in an 1896 Supreme Court case, *Plessy* v. *Ferguson*,[5] in which the court held that a Louisiana statute requiring equal but separate accommodations for whites and blacks on trains was not unconstitutional. (The history of *Plessy* and *Brown* is a particularly apt illustration of the living, changing character of the law. While stability and hence predictability in the law are important, they must not stand in the way of achieving justice in a changing society.) A period of intense activism followed *Brown* as citizens engaged in sit-ins, freedom rides, boycotts, and the like to press claims for racial equality in housing, public transportation, employment, et al. It was a turbulent, sometimes violent era, but it can scarcely be doubted that those activities were critical ingredients in subsequent advances for the black population. Then, in 1964, the National Labor Relations Board asserted its jurisdiction over racial discrimination where it constitutes an unfair labor practice. With the passage of the 1964 Civil Rights Act the campaign against discrimination solidified as one of the most energetic and successful social movements in American history.[6]

Constitutional Provisions

The Fourteenth Amendment to the federal Constitution provides that no state shall deny to any person life, liberty, or property without *due process of law* or deny him or her the *equal protection of the laws*. Thus, citizens are protected from discrimination at the instigation of a state government. Then by Supreme Court decision in 1954 the due process clause of the Fifth Amendment (''nor shall any person . . . be deprived of life, liberty, or property, without due process of law'') was interpreted to forbid invidious discrimination by the federal government. Thus the Fifth and Fourteenth Amendments have been useful tools against government discrimination. Problems arise when a government body passes a law or takes some other action that results in treating one class of people differently than another. For example, an Oklahoma statute provided that females could lawfully purchase 3.2 percent beer at age 18 but males could not do so until age 21. The equal protection clause does not require that all persons be treated equally. Rather, the test is that of whether the classification (women may drink at 18, but men must wait until 21) is substantially related to the achievement of an important government goal. In general the courts have deferred to the lawmakers unless the classification is clearly arbitrary. How would you rule in the Oklahoma case [*Craig* v. *Boren,* 97 S.Ct. 451 (1976)]?

Civil Rights Act of 1866

Of course, the constitutional provisions are broadly drawn and thus open to variation in interpretation. The Constitution protects the citizenry from the government but not from private sector abuse. Therefore, statutes and executive orders were necessary to attack discrimination more explicitly and to reach private sector problems. Two civil rights provisions dating from the Reconstruction period (subsequently codified as sections 1981 and 1983 of Title 42 of the United States Code) have become important in discrimination cases involving questions of race or lineage. Section 1981 provides that all persons within the jurisdiction of the United States shall have the same right in every state or territory to make and enforce contracts as is enjoyed by white citizens. Employment relationships are, of course, founded in contract. Thus, when a black person is discriminated against by a private employer or by a labor union, section 1981 has been violated. In 1982, the Supreme Court held that a violation of section 1981 requires proof of *intentional* racial discrimination.[7]

The Supreme Court found a violation of section 1983 when a private school denied admission to black applicants.[8] Section 1983 provides that any person whose constitutional or legal rights are impaired by another person acting ''under color'' of state or territorial law or custom is entitled to redress. The key inquiry is that of the closeness of the relationship between the government and the wrongdoer. For example, if a state government grants a liquor license to a private club and the bartender in that club declines on racial grounds to serve liquor to a black man, has section 1983 been violated? [See *Moose Lodge No. 107* v. *Irvis,* 407 U.S. 163 (1972)].

Executive Orders

Although a number of executive orders (EO) address discrimination issues, one is of special importance here. EO 11246 requires each government agency to include an ''equal opportunity'' clause in its agreements with federal contractors. Thus all firms doing business in excess of $10,000 with the federal government must agree, in a broad sense, not to discriminate because of race, color, religion, sex, or national origin.

Civil Rights Act of 1964

Relying on its authority to regulate interstate commerce, Congress forbade (in Title VII of the act) discrimination because of race, color, religion, sex, or national origin. The act applies to private sector employers with 15 or more employees, employment agencies procuring employees for a firm already employing 15 or more individuals, and labor unions operating a hiring hall. The Equal Employment Opportunity Act of 1972 amended the 1964 act to extend coverage to all state and local governments. The Civil Rights Act forbids employment discrimination in most units of the federal government, but Congress itself and those judicial and legislative positions not subject to competitive civil service standards are exempt. It is worthy of note that private clubs are exempt from the act, and religious organizations may discriminate in employment on the basis of religion.

The act, as interpreted, prohibits discrimination in hiring, discharge, and general conditions of employment. While the act forbids employment discrimination against the specified protected classes (race, color, religion, sex, national origin), a number of exceptions are recognized. The more important exceptions are those regarding seniority, employee testing, bona fide occupational qualifications, and veterans' preferences.

Many statutes accord preference to veterans in matters such as employment selection. For example, the veteran in applying for a public sector job might automatically be elevated to the top of the hiring list if he or she simply passes the required examination. Title VII explicitly provides that it is not to be interpreted to repeal or modify laws affording veterans' preferences. However, in *Personnel Administrator of Massachusetts* v. *Feeney*[9] a woman attacked (on sex discrimination grounds) a Massachusetts statute giving veterans absolute preference in state employment. The U.S. Supreme Court sustained the statute because it found *no discriminatory purpose* in the legislature's action. The law was not enacted to *exclude* women. Rather it was designed to *prefer* veterans. (The other Civil Rights Act defenses are discussed later in the chapter.)

Other Federal Statutes

A number of federal statutes in addition to the Civil Rights Act of 1964 offer protection against various forms of employment discrimination. Among those are the Equal Pay Act, the Age Discrimination in Employment Act of 1967, and the Rehabilitation Act of 1973. Discussion of those statutes and their judicial interpretations is deferred until later in the chapter.

Enforcement

The Equal Employment Opportunity Commission (EEOC), a federal agency created under the terms of the Civil Rights Act of 1964, is primarily responsible for enforcing the provisions of the act. The commission is composed of five members appointed by the president with the advice and consent of the Senate for terms of five years. No more than three appointees may be members of the same political party. The commission has broad authority to hold hearings, seek documents, question witnesses under oath, and the like.

In essence, Title VII established two methods of enforcement: Individual actions and "pattern or practice" suits.

Individual Actions

The private party seeking redress under Title VII faces some formidable administrative hurdles. Before bringing a private suit, an individual must file a charge with the EEOC or wait until the commission's jurisdiction expires, at which point a private action may be filed. Going forward with EEOC action is often frustrating because the agency is always burdened with a backlog of cases. Thus several years may pass before the administrative process and any subsequent lawsuits have run their course. Furthermore, in states or localities having agencies to deal with employment discrimination, the statute requires deferral of filing with the EEOC until those state/local agencies have exercised their authority. The commission must investigate the charge and attempt to conciliate the claim. That failing, the commission may file a civil suit in a federal district court and may represent the person filing the charge.[10]

Pattern or Practice Suits

In brief, the commission has the authority to investigate and take action upon charges of a pattern or practice of discrimination. Pattern or practice claims seek to prove a general policy of discrimination rather than a specific instance of bias. Pattern or practice suits are based primarily upon a statistically significant "deficiency" in the percentage of minority employees in the employer's work force as compared with the percentage of minority employees in the relevant labor pool. The employer may be able to rebut the discriminatory inference in a variety of ways. For example, it might be demonstrated that the relevant labor market was improperly drawn or that the statistical disparity is the result of nondiscriminatory conditions.

Remedies under Title VII include granting back pay, affording seniority relief, issuing injunctions, imposing reporting requirements, and so on. Injunctive relief might take the form of ordering the employment of an individual or requiring a promotion.

Department of Labor

Under its authority to enforce Executive Order 11246, the Office of Federal Contract Compliance Programs (OFCCP) of the Department of Labor has broad power to combat employment discrimination in firms performing federal contracts. Using its enormous leverage as a purchaser, the government requires contractors to agree not to discriminate in hiring or during employment because of race, color, religion, sex, or national origin. Furthermore, OFCCP regulations require "affirmative action" on the part of covered employer-contractors to ensure an end to discrimination. In general terms, the contractor must determine whether minorities and women are being "underutilized." If so, the contractor must develop a plan to achieve a work force representation appropriate to the minority and women's representation in the relevant labor market.

The chief enforcement mechanism for noncompliance is the power of the OFCCP to terminate contracts and, where appropriate, render such firms ineligible for future federal business.

Part Two—Discrimination on the Basis of Race, Color, or National Origin

Title VII places race, color, and national origin among those "protected classes" against which discrimination is forbidden. The Act was directed primarily to improving the employment opportunities of blacks, but the act clearly applies to all races and colors (including whites and native Americans). The national origin proviso forbids discrimination based on one's nation of birth, ancestry, or heritage. Therefore, an employment office sign reading "Vietnamese need not apply" or "Mexicans need not apply" might reflect some of the recent tension regarding the assimilation of new immigrants, but such policies would clearly be unlawful.

To make some sense of the study of the law of equal opportunity, it must be understood that discrimination remains a serious problem. For example, the public opinion polls set out here suggest that derogatory stereotypes regarding blacks persist and that a high percentage of blacks and a significant percentage of whites believe that discrimination remains widespread.

Progress, But. . .

STEREOTYPES REMAIN

Question: Now let me ask you some questions about blacks as people, leaving aside the whole question of civil rights and laws. I'd like to know how you feel as an individual. Here are some statements people sometimes make about black people. For each statement, please tell me whether you personally tend to agree or disagree with that statement. . . .

White response
Percent agree   ☐ 1963   ▨ 1978

Blacks tend to have less ambition than whites — 66% / 49%

Blacks have less native intelligence than whites — 39% / 25%

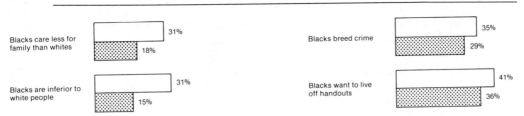

Source: Surveys by Louis Harris and Associates, conducted for *Newsweek,* 1963: Louis Harris and Associates, conducted for the National Conference of Christians and Jews, October 6–November 8, 1978.

STILL A WAY TO GO

Question: In your area, would you say blacks are generally discriminated against or not in: (Read statements)

Blacks discriminated against in...

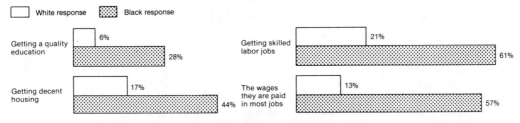

Source: Survey by ABC News/*The Washington Post,* February 26–March 6, 1981. Reprinted from *Public Opinion* (April/May 1981) by permission of the American Enterprise Institute.

Progress?

Clearly, the black community has enjoyed some striking successes in recent years but, as suggested by the polling data, enormous problems remain. The severity of those problems was revealed in the National Urban League's 1984 survey, "The State of Black America." The unemployment rate for blacks in December 1983 was 17.8 percent, as compared with 7.1 percent for whites. One in three blacks was living in poverty in 1983. One of eight whites fell into that category. Indeed, the percentage of blacks falling below the government's poverty income line ($9,862 for a family of four) was higher than in any year since 1967. As documented in the following table, the income gap between white and black families has actually increased in recent years.

Median Income of U.S. Families

	Black	White	Ratio
1959	$ 3,047	$ 5,893	0.52
1964	3,724	6,858	0.54
1968	5,360	8,937	0.60
1970	6,279	10,236	0.61
1973	7,269	12,595	0.58
1983	13,598	24,593	0.55

Source: Census Bureau and Urban League, "The State of Black America" (1984).

All Americans bear the costs of discrimination. While the direct cost is clearly most painful for the victims of bias, the total bill is not restricted by color or sex. For example, employment discrimination significantly lowers total societal productivity. Economist Lester Thurow has estimated that the economy loses approximately $19 billion per year in output because of discrimination against blacks. That loss is attributable to reductions in economic efficiency, because units of resources are often not used where their productivity is greatest.

In the article that follows both the progress achieved and the distance remaining in the case of the black community are explored.

INTEGRATION IS ELUSIVE DESPITE RECENT GAINS; SOCIAL BARRIERS REMAIN

Charles W. Stevens

When court-ordered desegregation came to Atlanta's public schools two decades ago, it was heralded as a great stride forward for integration: The system was 55 percent white and 45 percent black, and a thorough racial mix seemed possible. The years since have shown the folly of this hope. Atlanta's whites moved to the suburbs or sent their children to private schools. Now the public school system is 90 percent black.

Such has been the dominant course of racial integration in the United States. Since the civil rights movement began in earnest 25 years ago, the legal framework that supported segregation has been removed, and blacks have made notable statistical advances in important fields. But progress toward the free and equal association of blacks and whites envisioned by idealists of the 1950s and 60s has been fitful, and much of what mixing has occurred has involved a fairly thin layer of well-educated, well-off members of both races.

Moreover, prospects are dim that this situation will change substantially any time soon. Social barriers to integration are proving far harder to crack than the formal legal obstacles. Also, integration itself has faded as a primary goal of many blacks.

"The issue isn't integration versus noninte-

gration anymore—it's here-now things like jobs," says Selwyn R. Cudjoe, professor of Afro-American studies at Harvard University. "There's a growing realization that integration won't put bacon on the table."

*   *   *   *   *

In no area of American life have segregated patterns hung on so tenaciously as in housing. Here and there one can find neighborhoods or suburbs that have achieved some measure of stable racial balance, but they are exceptional.

This is true not only in the aging central sections of the major cities of the East and the Midwest, where black populations have become predominant, but elsewhere as well. Indeed, the maintenance of segregation despite the considerable population movement of the last 20 years has served to underscore its resilience.

Moving to Black Suburbs

The U.S. Census Bureau reports that from 1960 to 1979 the number of blacks living in big-city suburbs grew by 72 percent to about five million, compared with a 38 percent growth in the white suburban population in that period. But much of that movement was between mostly black city neighborhoods and suburbs that were already mostly black or were rapidly becoming so.

* * * * *

Racial discrimination in the sale or rental of housing is banned by law in most of the United States, but those laws are apparently widely circumvented by both real-estate agents and mortgage lenders. A study of mortgage-lending practices in New York and California, released in June by Harvard and Massachusetts Institute of Technology, found that black applicants were far more likely to be denied a mortgage than whites of similar income and had to pay higher interest rates for the mortgages they did get.

* * * * *

Because public-school enrollments are closely tied to housing, it isn't surprising that integration hasn't proceeded quickly there either. This is true despite the striking down of separate-school laws in the South and the imposition of busing to achieve greater racial balance in some northern cities.

The extent of integration in the public schools is a matter of debate, much of which centers on the definition of what constitutes an "integrated" school unit. The U.S. Civil Rights Commission developed a formula based on school enrollments as a percentage of a district's racial population. It concluded that in 1977 46 percent of the nation's black schoolchildren still attended schools that were "at least moderately segregated," even though the number was down sharply from 76 percent in 1968.

* * * * *

In other areas, progress toward integration has been far more promising. These include higher education and numerous occupations and professions.

Today about one million blacks are enrolled as college undergraduates, a fourfold jump from 1960. Blacks account for about 11 percent of undergraduates at American colleges, up from 7 percent in 1970 and 6 percent in 1960; their college-enrollment proportion almost equals their 12 percent share of the total U.S. population. Furthermore, only about one third of black undergraduates attend predominantly black colleges, against about half in 1960. . . .

As more blacks gain access to higher education, their representation in the professions and better-paying jobs generally has risen, although their proportional representation still lags behind that of whites. In the last two decades, nonwhite participation in professional and technical jobs has nearly doubled, to about 9 percent, and nonwhite representation in the Labor Department's "managers and administrators" category also has doubled, to around 5 percent. Blacks make up 11 percent of plumbers and pipefitters, almost twice the proportion of the 1960s, and 8 percent of machinists and job fitters, four times as many as two decades past.

Currently, there are 9,300 black physicians and surgeons in the U.S., double the number of 1960. The population of black lawyers stands at nearly 12,000, almost six times the number of 20 years ago.

De Facto Segregation Remains

But the reality behind these impressive figures is less heartening to those who desire a color-blind society: where statistical integration exists, it is often accompanied by de facto segregation.

On the nation's college campuses, for instance, some fraternities and sororities remain as vestiges of the formal segregation of past days. More common is an edgy sort of voluntary racial separation that discourages contact between black and white students who would like to make friends.

* * * *

If anything, racial separation is even more prevalent in the professions. In law, medicine, and other fields, parallel black and mostly white professional organizations still exist, and partnerships of whites and blacks are rare.

John L. Crump, executive director of the

National Bar Association, an 8,000-member black lawyers' group whose activities parallel those of the American Bar Association (which also has black members), says private practice holds so little promise for black lawyers that nearly 75 percent of them work for government agencies. A recent *National Law Journal* sur-

vey showed that just 12 of the 3,700 partners of the 50 biggest U.S. law firms were black.

* * * * *

Employment Discrimination Analysis

The Civil Rights Act of 1964 is the primary vehicle for pursuing employment discrimination claims. However, the reader is reminded of the other constitutional, statutory, and executive order protections mentioned above. In essence, Title VII provides two theories of liability—disparate treatment and disparate impact.

Disparate Treatment[11]

Though less common than in the past, intentional employment discrimination remains a problem of significance. Where an employer purposefully treats some people less favorably than others because of their race, color, religion, sex, or national origin the basic elements of disparate treatment exist. In a simplified form a claim under disparate treatment analysis would proceed as follows:

1. *Plaintiff's (Employee's) Prima Facie Case* (sufficient to be presumed true unless proven otherwise). Optimally the plaintiff would present direct, explicit evidence of intentional disparate treatment. For example, that evidence might take the form of a letter from an employer to an employment agency indicating that "women would not be welcome as applicants for this physically taxing job." Since direct evidence of that nature is ordinarily unavailable, the plaintiff must build the following prima facie case from which disparate treatment may be inferred:

   a. Plaintiff belongs to a protected class.
   b. Plaintiff applied for a job for which the defendant was seeking applicants.
   c. Plaintiff was qualified for the job.
   d. Plaintiff was denied the job, and
   e. The position remained open, and the employer continued to seek applications.

2. *Defendant's (Employer's) Case.* If the plaintiff builds a successful prima facie case, the burden shifts to the defendant to "articulate some legitimate, nondiscriminatory reason for the employee's rejection." However, the defendant need not prove that its decision not to hire the plaintiff was, in fact, based on that legitimate, nondiscriminatory reason. The defendant simply must raise a legitimate issue of fact disputing the plaintiff's discrimination claim. Further, and perhaps most importantly, the defendant is not required to prove that it is *not* guilty of discrimination.

3. *Plaintiff's Response.* Assuming the defendant met the standard set forth for the defendant's case, the burden of proof then shifts back to the plaintiff to prove that the "legitimate, nondiscriminatory reason" offered by the defendant was, in fact, merely a pretext for discrimination. That is, the plaintiff must show that although the defendant's reason may be superficially plausible, it does not square with the facts based on the employer's hiring patterns or other evidence.

Disparate Impact

Disparate impact analysis arose out of situations in which employers used legitimate employment standards that, despite their apparent neutrality, worked a heavier burden on a protected class than on other employees. For example, a preemployment test, offered with the best of intentions and constructed to be a fair measurement device, may disproportionately exclude members of a protected class and thus be unacceptable (barring an effective defense). Alternatively, an employer, surreptitiously seeking to discriminate, may establish an apparently neutral, superficially valid employment test that has the effect of achieving the employer's discrimination goal. For example, a tavern might require that its "bouncer" be at least 6 feet 2 inches tall and weigh at least 180 pounds. Such a standard disproportionately excludes women, Orientals, and Hispanics from consideration and is impermissible (barring an effective defense). Disparate impact analysis is similar to that of disparate treatment, but critical distinctions mark the two approaches. In particular, note that disparate treatment requires proof of intent, while disparate impact does not. The disparate impact test is as follows:

1. The plaintiff must show that the challenged employment practice burdens a protected class more heavily than others.
2. Assuming the plaintiff establishes a prima facie case under step 1, the defendant then must show that, notwithstanding the disparate impact, the challenged practices were either: (*a*) a business necessity or (*b*) job related. Some judicial opinions seem to treat "business necessity" and "job-relatedness" as interchangeable tests. The circumspect view is to await clarification to firmly establish the relationships and distinctions between the tests. Certainly business necessity appears to be a broader standard in that it would permit reference to considerations beyond the circumstances of an employee's particular job.
3. Even if the defendant establishes a job-relatedness or business necessity defense, the plaintiff can still prevail by demonstrating that the employer's legitimate goals can be met using an alternative employment practice that is free of the prejudicial effect. In doing so, the plaintiff would then have established that the questioned employment practice was merely a "pretext for discrimination."

The *Griggs* case that follows remains the signal judicial expression of employment discrimination law. Steps 1 and 2 in the disparate impact test are developed in *Griggs*. (Step 3, a refinement of *Griggs,* was articulated in *Ablemarle Paper Company* v. *Moody*.[12])

GRIGGS V. DUKE POWER CO.   401 U.S. 424 (1971)

Chief Justice Burger

We granted the writ in this case to resolve the question whether an employer is prohibited by the Civil Rights Act of 1964, Title VII, from requiring a high school education or passing of a standardized general intelligence test as a condition of employment in or transfer to jobs when (a) neither standard is shown to be significantly related to successful job performance, (b) both requirements operate to disqualify Negroes at a substantially higher rate than white applicants, and (c) the jobs in question formerly had been filled only by white employees as part of a longstanding practice of giving preference to whites.

Congress provided, in Title VII of the Civil Rights Act of 1964, for class actions for enforcement of provisions of the Act and this proceeding was brought by a group of incumbent Negro employees against Duke Power Company. . . .

The district court found that prior to July 2, 1965, the effective date of the Civil Rights Act of 1964, the company openly discriminated on the basis of race in the hiring and assigning of employees at its Dan River plant. The plant was organized into five operating departments: (1) Labor, (2) Coal Handling, (3) Operations, (4) Maintenance, and (5) Laboratory and Test. Negroes were employed only in the Labor Department where the highest paying jobs paid less than the lowest paying jobs in the other four "operating" departments in which only whites were employed. Promotions were normally made within each department on the basis of job seniority. Transferees into a department usually began in the lowest position.

In 1955 the company instituted a policy of requiring a high school education for initial assignment to any department except Labor, and for transfer from the Coal Handling to any "inside" department (Operations, Maintenance, or Laboratory). When the Company abandoned its policy of restricting Negroes to the Labor Department in 1965, completion of high school also was made a prerequisite to transfer from Labor to any other department. From the time the high school requirement was instituted to the time of trial, however, white employees hired before the time of the high school education requirement continued to perform satisfactorily and achieve promotions in the "operating" departments. Findings on this score are not challenged.

The company added a further requirement for new employees on July 2, 1965, the date on which Title VII became effective. To qualify for placement in any but the Labor Department it became necessary to register satisfactory scores on two professionally prepared aptitude tests, as well as to have a high school education. Completion of high school alone continued to render employees eligible for transfer to the four desirable departments from which Negroes had been excluded if the incumbent had been employed prior to the time of the new requirement. In September 1965 the company began to permit incumbent employees who lacked a high school education to qualify for transfer from Labor or Coal Handling to an "inside" job by passing two tests—the Wonderlic Personnel Test, which purports to measure general intelligence, and the Bennett Mechanical Comprehension Test. Neither was directed or intended to measure the ability to learn to perform a particular job or category of jobs. The requisite scores used for both initial hiring and transfer approximated the national median for high school graduates.

The District Court had found that while the company previously followed a policy of overt racial discrimination in a period prior to the Act, such conduct had ceased. The District Court also concluded that Title VII was intended to be prospective only and, consequently, the impact of prior inequities was beyond the reach of corrective action authorized by the Act.

. . . The Court of Appeals concluded there was no violation of the Act.

* * * * *

The objective of Congress in the enactment of Title VII is plain from the language of the statute. It was to achieve equality of employment opportunities and remove barriers that have operated in the past to favor an identifiable group of white employees over other employees. Under the Act, practices, procedures, or tests neutral on their face, and even neutral in terms of intent, cannot be maintained if they operate to "freeze" the status quo of prior discriminatory employment practices.

The Court of Appeals' opinion, and the partial dissent, agreed that, on the record in the present case, "whites register far better on the company's alternative requirements" than Negroes. This consequence would appear to be directly traceable to race. Basic intelligence must have the means of articulation to manifest itself fairly in a testing process. Because they are Negroes, petitioners have long received inferior education in segregated schools. . . . Congress did not intend by Title VII, however, to guarantee a job to every person regardless of qualifications. In short, the Act does not command that any person be hired simply because he was formerly the subject of discrimination, or because he is a member of a minority group. Discriminatory preference for any group, minority or majority, is precisely and only what Congress has proscribed. . . .

. . . The Act proscribes not only overt discrimination but also practices that are fair in form, but discriminatory in operation. The touchstone is business necessity. If an employment practice which operates to exclude Negroes cannot be shown to be related to job performance, the practice is prohibited.

On the record before us, neither the high school completion requirement nor the general intelligence test is shown to bear a demonstrable relationship to successful performance of the jobs for which it was used. Both were adopted, as the Court of Appeals noted, without meaningful study of their relationship to job-performance ability. Rather, a vice president of the company testified, the requirements were instituted on the company's judgment that they generally would improve the overall quality of the work force.

The evidence, however, shows that employees who have not completed high school or taken the tests have continued to perform satisfactorily and make progress in departments for which the high school and test criteria are not used. . . .

The Court of Appeals held that the company had adopted the diploma and test requirements without any "intention to discriminate against Negro employees." We do not suggest that either the District Court or the Court of Appeals erred in examining the employer's intent; but good intent or absence of discriminatory intent does not redeem employment procedures or testing mechanisms that operate as "built-in headwinds" for minority groups and are unrelated to measuring job capability.

* * * * *

The facts of this case demonstrate the inadequacy of broad and general testing devices as well as the infirmity of using diplomas or degrees as fixed measures of capability. . . .

The company contends that its general intelligence tests are specifically permitted by § 703(h) of the Act. That section authorizes the use of "any professionally developed ability test" that is not "designed, intended *or used* to discriminate because of race. . . ." (Emphasis added.)

The Equal Employment Opportunity Commission, having enforcement responsibility, has issued guidelines interpreting § 703(h) to permit only the use of job-related tests. The administrative interpretation of the Act by the enforcing agency is entitled to great deference. Since the Act and its legislative history support the commission's construction, this affords good reason to treat the guidelines as expressing the will of Congress.

. . . From the sum of the legislative history relevant in this case, the conclusion is inescapable that the EEOC's construction of § 703 (h) to require that employment tests be job related comports with congressional intent.

Nothing in the Act precludes the use of testing or measuring procedures; obviously they are useful. What Congress has forbidden is giving these devices and mechanisms controlling force unless they are demonstrably a reasonable measure of job performance. Congress has not commanded that the less qualified be preferred over the better qualified simply because of minority origins. Far from disparaging job qualifications as such, Congress has made such qualifications the controlling factor, so that race, religion, nationality, and sex become irrelevant. What Congress has commanded is that any tests used must measure the person for the job and not the person in the abstract.

The judgment of the Court of Appeals is . . . reversed.

Questions

1. According to the Supreme Court, what was Congress' objective in enacting Title VII?
2. Had Duke Power been able to establish that its reasons for adopting the diploma and test standards were entirely without discriminatory intent, would the Supreme Court have ruled differently? Explain.
3. What is the central issue in this case?
4. Why was North Carolina's social and educational history relevant to the outcome of the case?
5. Gregory, a black, was offered employment by Litton Systems as a sheet metal worker. As part of a standard procedure he completed a form listing a total of 14 nontraffic arrests but no convictions. Thereupon the employment offer was withdrawn. Gregory then brought suit claiming he was a victim of racial discrimination.
   a. Explain the foundation of his argument.
   b. Decide the case. See *Gregory* v. *Litton,* 472 F.2d 631 (9th Cir. 1972).
6. In 1970 Lane pleaded guilty to the offense of smuggling marijuana into the United States. In 1971 he secured an Atlanta taxi operator's permit. In 1973 a dispute with a passenger and a subsequent review of his file revealed the prior smuggling conviction (which he had disclosed at the time of application). His permit was revoked. Lane, a black man, felt he had been discriminated against.
   a. Decide the validity of Lane's claim.
   b. Would the result be different had he been dismissed from his job as a truck driver for the city? Explain. See *Lane* v. *Inman,* 509 F.2d 184 (5th Cir. 1975).
7. As explained previously, in *Personnel Administrator of Massachusetts* v. *Feeney,* 442 U.S. 256 (1979), a state policy of absolute hiring preference for veterans was upheld against a charge of gender-based discrimination in that few veterans are women. The disparate impact on women was clear, and Massachusetts governing authorities can be assumed to have been aware of the "natural and probable consequence" of this preference. The Supreme Court found an absence of discriminatory purpose. Explain and justify that decision.
8. In disparate treatment cases, a critical ingredient is that of identifying the relevant labor market. How would you counter Justice Stevens' argument in dissent in *Hazelwood School District* v. *United States,* 433 U.S. 299 (1976), that as a starting point the relevant labor pool should encompass the geographic area from which incumbent employees come?

our wish to banish discrimination. In the *Jaycees* case [*Kathryn R. Roberts* v. *United States Jaycees*[22]], the Supreme Court was required to resolve the conflict between Minnesota's efforts to eliminate sex discrimination and the First Amendment freedom of association claimed by the Jaycees, a "private" service organization that declined to admit women as full voting members. Two local Minnesota chapters had been violating the national bylaws by admitting women as regular members. When notified that the national Jaycees were contemplating revocation of their charter, the Minnesota chapters filed discrimination charges with the Minnesota Department of Human Rights. They claimed a violation of the Minnesota Human Rights Act, which makes it discriminatory conduct to deny any person the full and equal enjoyment of public accommodations because of race, color, creed, religion, disability, national origin, or sex. The human rights hearing examiner concluded that the Jaycees were a "place" of "public accommodation" and that their membership policy was discriminatory. He ordered the Jaycees to desist from that discrimination.

On appeal, the U.S. Supreme Court held that compelling the Jaycees to accept women as regular members did not deny the male members' freedom of association. The essence of the Supreme Court's position was that the Jaycees were not a fundamentally private organization entitled to freedom from unjustified state interference. Jaycees chapters were not selective as to membership. They were large organizations. Their activities regularly involved strangers as well as other nonmembers of both sexes. Therefore, the Jaycees are now required to admit women as full members. Must your local country club now admit all otherwise qualified applicants regardless of race, religion, sex, and so on?

Equality for Women?

Is the women's rights movement on the wane? Have we "gone too far" in striving for equality of the sexes? Is such equality possible or even desirable? Can legal equality, if secured, produce economic and social equality?

As the poll on the next page demonstrates, we now have broad, if sectionally divided, public sentiment for women's enhanced status.

Despite general acceptance of a new role for women, despite striking legal victories, despite a fervor that has altered American life, women continue by perhaps the most important barometers to remain in a distinctly secondary status. In 1982 women working full-time on a year-round basis earned, according to the Labor Department, about 62 percent of what men earned. According to a Census Bureau study, the wages of white women entering the job market in 1980 averaged $4.20 per hour, or 83 percent of the $5.04 average hourly wage for white males joining the labor force. In 1970 white women entering the market had earned an average of 86 percent of the wages of entering white males. (All dollar figures were adjusted for inflation.) Black women entering the market in 1980 earned about 79 percent of the white male wage.[23]

On the other hand, recent government data show that women have made dramatic inroads in traditionally male careers. In 1970 women occupied 18.5 percent of the nation's executive, managerial, and administrative jobs. By 1980 that figure expanded to 30.5 percent. Similarly, the percentage of women judges rose during that decade from

Question: Do you agree or disagree with this statement? Women should take care of running their houses and leave running the country up to men.

Agree, women should take care of running their houses and leave running the country up to men

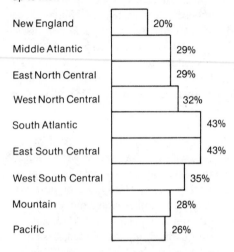

New England	20%
Middle Atlantic	29%
East North Central	29%
West North Central	32%
South Atlantic	43%
East South Central	43%
West South Central	35%
Mountain	28%
Pacific	26%

Note: Data combined for 1977, 1978, and 1982. Surveys by the National Opinion Research Center, General Social Surveys, 1977, 1978, and 1982.

Source: *Public Opinion*, February–March 1983, p. 26. Reprinted by permission of the American Enterprise Institute.

6.1 percent to 17.1 percent and the percentage of female lawyers rose from 4.9 to 13.8.[24] And a study from the Rand Corporation, a conservative "think tank," projects women's wages, on the average, to reach 74 percent of average male wages by the year 2000. The Rand study concluded that women's wages made a remarkable jump from 60 percent (of men's wages) in 1980 to 64 percent in 1983.[25]

Analysis of Sex Discrimination

Under Title VII of the 1964 Civil Rights Act, sex discrimination analysis proceeds in essentially the manner outlined earlier in the chapter; that is, disparate treatment and disparate impact are the key tests. An important variation of disparate treatment analysis is sex plus discrimination. *Sex plus* is the term applied to those situations where an employer has attempted to distinguish between male and female workers by imposing a second employment criterion (in addition to sex) on one gender but not on the other. For example, in *Phillips* v. *Martin Marietta*[26] the employer refused to hire women with preschool-age children, but welcomed men with preschool-age children. For the assembly trainee position for which Phillips applied, 75 to 80 percent of those hired had been women. The Supreme Court struck down the sex plus classification. What consequences might have been anticipated from a contrary ruling?

Bona Fide Occupational Qualification

As explained earlier, Title VII permits discrimination under limited circumstances. Among those exemptions or defenses is that of the bona fide occupational qualification (BFOQ). That is, discrimination is lawful where sex, religion, or national origin is a BFOQ reasonably necessary to the normal operation of that business. The exclusion of race and color from the list suggests that Congress thought those categories always unacceptable as bona fide occupational qualifications. The judicially created defense of business necessity is applicable to racial classifications. The BFOQ was meant to be a very limited exception applicable to situations where specific inherent characteristics are necessary to the job (e.g., wet nurse) and where authenticity is required (e.g., actors).

The BFOQ defense is lawful only if the following conditions are met:

1. Proof of a *nexus* between the classification and job performance,
2. "*necessity*" of the classification for successful performance, and,
3. that the job performance affected by the classification is the "*essence*" of the employer's business operation.[27]

Nexus   Will the classification affect job performance? For example, will "maleness" depreciate performance in a job requiring manual dexterity, or will "femaleness" depreciate performance in a laboring job requiring night work and long hours? The courts have thoroughly rejected distinctions based on stereotypes such as these.

Necessity   Mere customer preference or, in general, higher costs will not justify an otherwise discriminatory employment practice. Thus, that restaurant customers prefer to be served by women or that hiring women will require the addition of another washroom or that hiring blacks, for example, will anger customers and cause a decline in income are not justifications for discrimination.

Essence   An employer may lawfully insist upon a woman to fill a woman's modeling role, since being female goes to the essence of the job. However, airlines, for example, may not hire women only as flight attendants even if females are shown to perform the "nonmechanical" portions of the job in a manner superior to most men. Those duties "are tangential to the essence of the business involved."[28]

Many employers have simply assumed that women could not perform certain tasks. Women were thought to be insufficiently aggressive for sales roles, and women were denied employment because they were assumed to have a higher turnover rate because of the desire to marry and to have children. Those stereotypes are at the heart of sex discrimination litigation generally and sex as a BFOQ particularly. The following case usefully illustrates a difficult sex discrimination issue and the appropriate mode of analysis, including the BFOQ defense.

DOTHARD V. RAWLINSON   97 S.Ct. 2720 (1977)

Justice Stewart

Appellee Dianne Rawlinson sought employment with the Alabama Board of Corrections as a prison guard, called in Alabama a "correctional counselor." After her application was rejected, she brought this class suit under Title VII of the Civil Rights Act of 1964, . . . alleging that she had been denied employment because of her sex in violation of federal law. A three-judge Federal District Court for the Middle District of Alabama decided in her favor. . . .

At the time she applied for a position as correctional counselor trainee, Rawlinson was a 22-year-old college graduate whose major course of study had been correctional psychology. She was refused employment because she failed to meet the minimum 120-pound weight requirement established by an Alabama statute. The statute also establishes a height minimum of 5 feet 2 inches.

After her application was rejected because of her weight, Rawlinson filed a charge with the Equal Employment Opportunity Commission, and ultimately received a right-to-sue letter. She then filed a complaint in the District Court on behalf of herself and other similarly situated women, challenging the statutory height and weight minima as violative of Title VII and the Equal Protection Clause of the 14th Amendment. A three-judge court was convened. While the suit was pending, the Alabama Board of Corrections adopted Administrative Regulation 204, establishing gender criteria for assigning correctional counselors to maximum-security institutions for "contact positions," that is, positions requiring continual close physical proximity to inmates of the institution. Rawlinson amended her class-action complaint by adding a challenge to regulation 204 as also violative of Title VII and the 14th Amendment.

Like most correctional facilities in the United States, Alabama's prisons are segregated on the basis of sex. Currently the Alabama Board of Corrections operates four major all-male penitentiaries. . . . [These] are maximum-security institutions. Their inmate living quarters are for the most part large dormitories, with communal showers and toilets that are open to the dormitories and hallways. The Draper and Fountain penitentiaries carry on extensive farming operations, making necessary a large number of strip searches for contraband when prisoners re-enter the prison buildings.

*   *   *   *   *

The gist of the claim that the statutory height and weight requirements discriminate against women does not involve an assertion of purposeful discriminatory motive. It is asserted, rather, that these facially neutral qualification standards work in fact disproportionately to exclude women from eligibility for employment by the Alabama Board of Corrections.

*   *   *   *   *

Although women 14 years of age or older compose 52.75 percent of the Alabama population and 36.89 percent of its total labor force, they hold only 12.9 percent of its correctional counselor positions. In considering the effect of the minimum height and weight standards on this disparity in rate of hiring between the sexes, the District Court found that the 5 feet 2 inches requirement would operate to exclude 33.29 percent of the women in the United States between the ages of 18–79, while excluding only 1.28 percent of men between the same ages. The 120-pound weight restriction would exclude 22.29 percent of the women and 2.35 percent of the men in this age group. When the height and weight restrictions are combined, Alabama's statutory standards would exclude 41.13 percent of the female population while excluding less than 1 percent of the male population. Accordingly, the District Court found that Rawlinson had made out a prima facie case of unlawful sex discrimination.

The appellants argue that a showing of disproportionate impact on women based on generalized national statistics should not suffice to establish a prima facie case. They point in particular to Rawlinson's failure to adduce comparative statistics concerning actual applicants for correctional counselor positions in Alabama. There is no requirement, however, that a statistical showing of disproportionate impact must always be based on analysis of the characteristics of actual applicants.

* * * * *

For these reasons, we cannot say that the District Court was wrong in holding that the statutory height and weight standards had a discriminatory impact on women applicants. . . .

We turn, therefore, to the appellants' argument that they have rebutted the prima facie case of discrimination by showing that the height and weight requirements are job related. These requirements, they say, have a relationship to strength, a sufficient but unspecified amount of which is essential to effective job performance as a correctional counselor. In the District Court, however, the appellants produced no evidence correlating the height and weight requirements with the requisite amount of strength thought essential to good job performance. Indeed, they failed to offer evidence of any kind in specific justification of the statutory standards.

If the job-related quality that the appellants identify is bona fide, their purpose could be achieved by adopting and validating a test for applicants that measures strength directly. Such a test, fairly administered, would fully satisfy the standards of Title VII because it would be one that "measure[s] the person for the job and not the person in the abstract." . . . But nothing in the present record even approaches such a measurement.

For the reasons we have discussed, the District Court was not in error in holding that Title VII of the Civil Rights Act of 1964, as amended, prohibits application of the statutory height and weight requirements to Rawlinson and the class she represents.

* * * * *

Unlike the statutory height and weight requirements, Regulation 204 explicitly discriminates against women on the basis of their sex. In defense of this overt discrimination, the appellants rely on § 703 (e) of Title VII, which permits sex-based discrimination "in those certain intances where . . . sex . . . is a bona fide occupational qualification reasonably necessary to the normal operation of that particular business or enterprise."

The District Court rejected the bona fide occupational qualification (BFOQ) defense, relying on the virtually uniform view of the federal courts that § 703 (e) provides only the narrowest of exceptions to the general rule requiring equality of employment opportunities. . . . [T]he federal courts have agreed that it is impermissible under Title VII to refuse to hire an individual woman or man on the basis of stereotyped characterizations of the sexes, and the District Court in the present case held in effect that Regulation 204 is based on just such stereotypical assumptions.

We are persuaded—by the restrictive language of § 703 (e), the relevant legislative history, and the consistent interpretation of the Equal Employment Opportunity Commission—that the BFOQ exception was in fact meant to be an extremely narrow exception to the general prohibition of discrimination on the basis of sex. In the particular factual circumstances of this case, however, we conclude that the District Court erred in rejecting the State's contention that Regulation 204 falls within the narrow ambit of the BFOQ exception.

The environment in Alabama's penitentiaries is a peculiarly inhospitable one for human beings of whatever sex. Indeed, a federal district court has held that the conditions of confinement in the prisons of the State, characterized by "rampant violence" and a "jungle atmosphere," are constitutionally intolerable. The record in the present case shows that because of inadequate staff and facilities, no attempt is made in the four maximum security male penitentiaries to classify or segregate inmates according to their offense or level of dangerousness—a procedure that, according to expert testimony, is essential to effective penological administration. Consequently, the estimated 20 percent of the male prisoners who are sex offenders are scattered throughout the penitentiaries' dormitory facilities.

In this environment of violence and disorganization, it would be an oversimplification to characterize Regulation 204 as an exercise in "romantic paternalism." In the usual case, the argument that a particular job is too dangerous for women may appropriately be met by the rejoinder that it is the purpose of Title VII to allow the individual woman to make that choice for herself. More is at stake in this case, however, than an individual woman's decision to weigh and accept the risks of employment in a "contact" position in a maximum security male prison.

The essence of a correctional counselor's job is to maintain prison security. A woman's relative ability to maintain order in a male, maximum security, unclassified penitentiary of the type Alabama now runs could be directly reduced by her womanhood. There is a basis in fact for expecting that sex offenders who have criminally assaulted women in the past would be moved to do so again if access to women were established within the prison. There would also be a real risk that other inmates, deprived of a normal heterosexual environment, would assault women guards because they were women. In a prison system where violence is the order of the day, where inmate access to guards is facilitated by dormitory living arrangements, where every institution is understaffed, and where a substantial portion of the inmate population is composed of sex offenders mixed at random with other prisoners, there are few visible deterrents to inmate assaults on women custodians.

*   *   *   *   *

There was substantial testimony from experts on both sides of this litigation that the use of women as guards in "contact" positions under the existing conditions in Alabama maximum security male penitentiaries would pose a substantial security problem directly linked to the sex of the prison guard. On the basis of that evidence, we conclude that the District Court was in error in ruling that being male is not a bona fide occupational qualification for the job of correctional counselor in a "contact" position in an Alabama male maximum security penitentiary.

The judgment is accordingly affirmed in part and reversed in part, and the case is remanded to the District Court. . . .

Questions

1. What evidence supported the Court's conclusion that Alabama's height requirements for prison guards constituted sex discrimination?
2. How might Alabama have strengthened its case for height and weight requirements?
3. What evidence supported the Court's view that being male was a BFOQ in this instance?
4. Would you vote with the majority or the dissent? Explain.
5. Is the majority opinion "sexist" according to your understanding of the term? Explain.
6. May a hospital lawfully agree to patients' demands for intimate care only by those of the same sex? Explain. See *Carey* v. *New York State Human Rights App. Bd.,* 61 A.D. 2d 804, 402 N.Y.S. 2d 207 (1978).
7. How might an airline justify a policy forbidding the assignment of pregnant flight attendants to flight duty? Is such a policy lawful? Explain. See *Condit* v. *United Airlines, Inc.,* 558 F.2d 1176 (4th Cir. 1977), cert. denied, 435 U.S. 934 (1978). Compare *Burwell* v. *Eastern Air Lines, Inc.,* CA4, 1980, 23 FEP Cases 949.

8. The Southern Pacific railroad denied employment as an agent-telegrapher to Rosenfeld, a woman. The railroad cited hard work (some 80-hour weeks and some lifting of 50 pounds or more) and California labor laws restricting hours of work and weights to be lifted by women.

   a. Is sex a BFOQ under these facts? Explain.

   b. Does the California statute govern this situation? Explain.

   c. The *Rosenfeld* court articulated the following very narrow test of those circumstances under which sex is a legitimate BFOQ: "sexual characteristics, rather than characteristics that might, to one degree or another, correlate with a particular sex, must be the basis for the application of the BFOQ exception. . . ." Explain the court's test and offer an example of a job wherein sex would clearly constitute a BFOQ. See *Rosenfeld* v. *Southern Pacific Co.*, 444 F.2d 1219 (1971).

Sexual Harassment

Soon after her employment in the federal Environmental Protection Agency, a black woman, Paulette Barnes, was allegedly the subject of social and sexual advances from her supervisor (not the defendant and appellee in the case).[29] Despite firm refusals, the supervisor is alleged to have repeatedly sought her company after working hours and suggested on numerous occasions that her employment status would be enhanced were she to engage in a sexual relationship with him. She had made clear her insistence on a purely professional relationship. Then according to Barnes, her supervisor and other administrators began a program of harassment, including taking many duties from her. Ultimately her job was abolished in apparent retaliation for her resistance to the unwanted advances. She then filed a complaint with the EEOC and, on appeal, the federal Circuit Court of Appeals for the District of Columbia found that the employer violated her rights under Title VII.

Sexual harassment has been the subject of extensive publicity and litigation in recent years. Some jurists and scholarly authorities have questioned the application of Title VII's prohibition of sex discrimination to sexual harassment cases. There is no definitive Supreme Court decision on the subject. But the weight of lower court opinion is consistent with the appeals court decision in *Barnes*. Furthermore, in 1980 the EEOC issued guidelines on sexual harassment providing that:

> Unwelcome sexual advances, requests for sexual favors, and other verbal or physical conduct of a sexual nature constitute sexual harassment when (1) submission to such conduct is made either explicitly or implicitly a term or condition of an individual's employment, (2) submission to or rejection of such conduct by an individual is used as the basis for employment decisions affecting such individual, or (3) such conduct has the purpose or effect of unreasonably interfering with an individual's work performance or creating an intimidating, hostile, or offensive working environment.

Among other provisions, the guidelines hold employers absolutely liable for the conduct of supervisors and impose on employers lesser standards of liability for the conduct of co-workers and nonemployees. Furthermore, employers are responsible for investigating sexual harassment complaints and problems and for developing programs to prevent sexual misconduct in the workplace. (The reader will recall that the guidelines do not have the force of law, but the courts tend to accord them considerable respect.) Court decisions to this point are generally consistent with the guidelines. The Reagan administration has argued that the guidelines are too vague. On the other hand, many states have promulgated statutes or other proscriptions against sexual harassment.

It is worthy of note that sexual harassment claims under Title VII may be supplemented by various civil and criminal actions. For example, assault, battery, breach of contract, and criminal assault are all possibilities, depending upon the circumstances.

Apparently many business people are extremely skeptical regarding the seriousness and magnitude of the sexual harassment problem:

> "This entire subject is a perfect example of a minor special interest group's ability to blow up any 'issue' to a level of importance which in no way relates to the reality of the world in which we live and work"—A 38-year-old plant manager (male) for a large manufacturer of industrial goods.[30]

A *Redbook–Harvard Business Review* survey of *HBR* subscribers found that nearly two thirds of the men and about half of the women agreed (or partially agreed) with the statement that "The amount of sexual harassment at work is greatly exaggerated."[31] However, recent survey evidence suggests that behavior taken to be sexual harassment is common. For example, in a survey of federal employees, 42 percent of the women surveyed and 15 percent of the men said they had experienced such harassment.[32] And 49 percent of the United Nations' female employees surveyed felt sexual pressure on the job.[33] In another survey 6 out of 10 responding companies reported that the most common form of harassment is comments, innuendoes, and jokes of a sexual nature.[34]

In less than a decade feminists and civil rights activists and lawyers in particular (and the changing nature of the work force in general) have been successful in attaching credibility and now legal sanction to a problem previously unrecognized, scorned, or ridiculed. The movement is interesting testimony to America's vices and virtues, as well as the power of commitment. The citizenry is taking this rather striking metamorphosis in stride and, indeed, with admirable wit. Some "unforgettable quotes" from the *Redbook–HBR* survey:

> "My department is financial, rather staid. The creative side of the business might well be rife with cases of sexual harassment." (female)
>
> "I married a subordinate. I believe there was no coercion involved." (male)
>
> "Have not had any experience in this area. Too busy working." (male)
>
> "I have never been harassed but I would welcome the opportunity." (anonymous)[35]

Equal Pay

Title VII affords broad protection from discrimination in pay because of sex. The Equal Pay Act of 1963, which was enacted as section 6(d) of the Fair Labor Standards Act of 1938, directly forbids discrimination on the basis of sex by paying wages to employees of one sex at a rate less than the rate paid to employees of the opposite sex for equal work on jobs requiring equal skill, effort, and responsibility and which are performed under similar working conditions ("equal" has been interpreted to mean "substantially equal").[36] The act provides for certain exceptions. Unequal wage payments are lawful if paid pursuant to (a) a seniority system; (b) a merit system; (c) a system that measures earnings by quantity or quality of production; or (d) a differential based on "any other factor other than sex."[37] Thus if the plaintiff builds a prima facie case based on the statute's prohibitions, the defendant must then assume the burden of asserting and proving one or more of the specified defenses. Typically, those discriminated against may recover "back wages" in a sum equal to the amount of pay discrimination. The employee may also secure "liquidated damages" to penalize the employer.[38] The employer seeking to avoid a violation of the Equal Pay Act may adjust its wage structure by raising the pay of the disfavored sex. Lowering the pay of the favored sex would violate the act.

Paying women and men the same amount for the same work is simple enough in principle, but the legal issues have proved slippery, indeed. For example:

1. Is travel reimbursement a "wage"? Maternity payments?[39]
2. Must the plaintiff establish a *pattern* of sex-based wage discrimination?[40]
3. Are jobs unequal in effort and thus "unequal work" when a part of one job includes tasks that females are physically unable to perform?[41]

In the leading case of *Corning Glass Works* v. *Brennan*[42] the Supreme Court was faced with the question of whether different shifts constituted differing "working conditions." Women had been engaged in glass inspection on the day shift. Corning added a night shift of inspectors, which due to state "protective" laws was composed entirely of males. The night shift demanded and received higher wages than the female day inspectors. The Supreme Court held that the time of day in and of itself is not a *working condition*. That term, the Court said, refers to "surroundings" and "hazards." However, shift differentials could lawfully constitute a "factor other than sex" if established by the employer.

Comparable Worth

Equal pay for equal work is hardly a radical notion, but equal pay for work of comparable value will, if fully realized, dramatically alter the nature of the American labor market. *Comparable worth* calls for determining the compensation to be paid for a position based on the job's intrinsic value in comparison to wages being paid for other jobs requiring comparable skills, effort, and responsibility and having comparable worth to the organization.

The argument is that the dollar value assigned to jobs held predominantly by men is higher than the value assigned to jobs held predominantly by women. To proponents of comparable worth, such disparities cannot be explained by market forces. They argue that women are the continuing victims of sex discrimination in violation of Title VII of the Civil Rights Act of 1964.

The following table draws comparisons in pay between "women's work" and some jobs typically held by males.

Men's, Women's Comparable Jobs

The chart below shows a comparison of male and female occupations judged to be of comparable worth, based on a study of monthly salaries for government jobs in designated locations.

Registered nurse (F) — $1,723

Vocational education teacher (M) (Minnesota) — $2,260

Typing pool supervisor (F) — $1,373

Painter (M) (Minnesota) — $1,707

Senior legal secretary (F) — $665

Senior carpenter (M) (San Jose, California) — $1,040

Licensed practical nurse (F) — $1,030

Correctional Officer (M) (Washington State) — $1,436

Secretary (F) — $1,122

Maintenance carpenter (M) (Washington State) — $1,707

Mental health technician (F) — $1,135

Automotive mechanic (M) (Illinois) — $1,681

Licensed practical nurse (F) — $1,298

Electrician (M) (Illinois) — $2,826

Source: Council on the Economic Status of Women, State of Minnesota; Hay Associates; Norman D. Willis & Associates. Reprinted from *Des Moines Sunday Register*, January 8, 1984, p. 3c. Reprinted with permission of the copyright holder, The Associated Press.

Comparable worth may well be the key "women's issue" of the 1980s. Women clearly have been the victims of discrimination in the employment market. Is comparable worth a just and workable remedy? Some states and locales have already adopted comparable worth principles for at least a portion of their employees. However, opponents believe that the market remains the best and fairest method of determining worth. They argue that we cannot accurately compare fundamentally dissimilar jobs to reach an objective determination of the skills required and worth of each of those jobs. Furthermore, those opponents question the wisdom of establishing the bureaucracy necessary to administer comparable worth programs. Of course, to comparable worth advocates, government intervention is the only possible tactic for combatting males' continuing domination of the market.

The U.S. Supreme Court has yet to directly explore the substance of the comparable worth debate. In the *Gunther*[43] case, the Court held, in effect, that Title VII does not forbid the comparable worth theory. However, the leading cases *(Spaulding* v. *The University of Washington*[44] and *American Federation of State, County, and Municipal Employees* v. *Washington*[45]) squarely addressing the total question resulted in very considerable setbacks for comparable worth supporters. In *Spaulding,* nursing faculty members at the University of Washington filed suit claiming that the university engaged in discriminatory compensation practices in violation of the Equal Pay Act and Title VII. The equal pay claim was based on data showing that faculty salaries in nursing (positions primarily occupied by women) were lower than faculty salaries in "comparable" departments (e.g., health services, social work, architecture, speech and hearing, and pharmacy practice) where the faculty members were primarily male. The Ninth Circuit Court of Appeals rejected that equal pay claim by finding that the plaintiffs failed to show that they performed work substantially equal to that performed by males in other departments. The court noted that attention to research, training, and community service varied widely from department to department.

Turning to the heart of the comparable worth claim, the court addressed the question of "whether the disparate impact model is available to plaintiffs who . . . make a broad-ranging sex-based claim of wage discrimination based upon comparable worth." The nurses sought to demonstrate a disparate impact by showing a wage disparity between comparable jobs. Then following the reasoning of *Griggs* and other cases, the plaintiffs sought to demonstrate that the disparate impact was a product of the "facially neutral policy or practice" of the university in setting wages according to market prices. That is, the plaintiffs claimed that following market prices was a nonjob-related pretext to hide discrimination (just as height, weight, intelligence tests, and the like had served as a pretext to hide discrimination in other cases). The court rejected that reasoning in finding that reliance on market prices is not a "facially neutral policy or practice." In so doing, the court clearly recognized the market's role in setting wages.

> Every employer constrained by market forces must consider market values in setting his labor costs. Naturally, market prices are inherently job-related, although the market may embody social judgments as to the worth of some jobs. Employers relying on the market are, to that extent, "price-takers." They deal with the market as a given, and do not meaningfully have a "policy" about it in the relevant Title VII sense. . . .[46]

In sum, the Court rejected the comparable worth theory as raised by the nursing faculty in the context of Title VII. The U.S. Supreme Court later declined to review the *Spaulding* decision.

In 1985 the five-member federal Equal Employment Opportunity Commission unanimously ruled that workers cannot use the theory of comparable worth in pay discrimination cases before the EEOC. The Commission ruled that Title VII of the Civil Rights

Act does not authorize comparable worth claims. One of the effects of the EEOC ruling was to result in the dismissal of 266 comparable worth cases that had been pending before the Commission.[47]

In your opinion, is male dominance of many job markets a product of discrimination? If so, should the comparable worth theory be employed to correct the resulting wage disparities?

Pornography—Sex Discrimination?

Perhaps the most creative and intriguing departure in sex discrimination law is the very recent effort to establish a link between pornography and discrimination against women. Attorney Catharine MacKinnon and author Andrea Dworkin, early leaders in that effort, drafted a Model Antipornography Law which treats pornography as ''a systematic practice of exploitation and subordination based on sex that differentially harms women.'' Advocates of the law argue that pornography dehumanizes women, leads to violence against women, and reduces women to inferior pawns in men's entertainment pursuits. The result is that women, as a class, have diminished opportunities for equal rights in employment, education, public accommodations, and general welfare. Hence the claim of sex discrimination.

Recently a number of cities have sought to restrain pornography by passing ordinances patterned after the model law. An Indianapolis, Indiana, ordinance defined pornography as a ''discriminatory practice'' involving ''graphic sexually explicit subordination of women, whether in pictures or words.'' The ordinance asserted that pornography is ''a discriminatory practice based on sex which denies women equal opportunities in society.'' The ordinance forbade most of the necessary means of producing, distributing, and selling that material. The ordinance was challenged in court.

a. What constitutional law claim was raised by the plaintiffs?
b. Decide. Explain. See *American Booksellers Association* v. *Hudnut, 54 Law Week* 2143 (7th Cir. 1985).
c. Do you approve of legal efforts to treat pornography as sex discrimination? Explain.
    For a discussion of the Model Law and related issues, see Mary Kay Blakely, ''Is One Woman's Sexuality Another Woman's Pornography?,'' *Ms.*, April 1985, p. 37.

Part Four—Religious Discrimination

In general terms, discrimination on the basis of religion is to be analyzed in the manner of the other protected classes specified by Title VII. ''Religion'' is not limited to orthodox faiths, but it does exclude mere shams designed to legitimize otherwise impermissible conduct. The Supreme Court has defined the necessary faith as a ''sincere and meaningful belief occupying in the life of its possessor a place parallel to that filled by the God of those admittedly qualified.''[48]

Absent an appropriate defense (e.g., BFOQ) an employer, of course, may not decline to hire or otherwise discriminate against an individual or group on the grounds of religion. The problem for the plaintiff in such cases is that of offering proof that religious bias was the motivation for the disputed employment practice. Discrimination on the grounds of religion is permissible if ''an employer demonstrates that he is unable to reasonably accommodate an employee's or prospective employee's religious observance or practice without undue hardship on the conduct of the employer's business.'' Thus, the primary issue in the area of religious discrimination has come to be that of determining ''reasonable accommodation'' in varying factual settings.

The leading case is *Trans World Airlines, Inc.* v. *Hardison*[49] in which the sabbitarian plaintiff worked in a parts warehouse that operated around the clock, seven days a week. Because of a transfer Hardison was at the bottom of the departmental seniority list and was unable to take his Sabbath off. The company conferred with Hardison and permitted the union to seek a swap of shifts or a change in jobs, but the efforts were unsuccessful. A seniority modification could not be agreed upon, and the company rejected Hardison's request for a four-day week because the solution would have required the use of another employee at premium pay. The Supreme Court's opinion in the case reduced the employer's duty to a very modest standard: ''To require TWA to bear more than a de minimis cost in order to give Hardison Saturdays off is an undue hardship.'' Saturdays off for Hardison would have imposed extra costs on TWA and would have constituted religious discrimination against other employees who would have sought Saturday off for reasons not grounded in religion. The *Hardison* court also took the position that the collective bargaining agreement's seniority provisions need not give way to accommodate religious observance. The Court found sufficient accommodation in TWA's reduction of weekend shift sizes and in allowing the voluntary trading of shifts.

Court decisions subsequent to *Hardison* are adding insight to that ruling. In *Redmond* v. *GAF Corp.*[50] an appeals court found no attempt to accommodate and no undue hardship in a case involving an employee whose Bible meetings conflicted with scheduled Saturday overtime. The company did not engage in a discussion of alternatives and essentially told plaintiff to ''work or else.'' The case as to hardship was distinguishable from *Hardison* on a variety of grounds including the fact that an accommodation would have resulted in no increase in costs since all Saturday pay was at a premium level. The work was unskilled, and no contract that would have prompted problems in shifting schedules was involved.

Religious accommodation issues must be resolved on a case-by-case basis with the outcome dependent on the facts at hand. It does seem fair to say that *Hardison* was a rather narrow reading of the reasonable accommodations doctrine. Thus, future lower court decisions probably will continue to stretch *Hardison* a bit by expecting a greater measure of employer flexibility.

Part Five—Affirmative Action

Affirmative action is a policy under which employers take positive steps to increase female and minority employment in an effort to overcome the effects of past discrimination. Title VII and other measures discussed in this chapter, while meeting with initial resistance, have clearly enjoyed marked success as vehicles for preventing future employment discrimination. However, the mere abandonment of discriminatory policies would not eradicate the lingering penalties of two centuries of bias. In consequence, a series of federal policies and judicial decisions have combined to create an affirmative action standard for the nation's employers.

Employers who are government contractors must meet the affirmative action expectations of the Office of Federal Contract Compliance Programs. As discussed above, those exceptions consist essentially of established goals and timetables for strengthening the representation of "underutilized" minorities and women.

A heavy preponderance of judicial decisions to date have supported the general policy of affirmative action, but the specific details of some programs have been struck down. For example, in the famous *Bakke*[51] case, (where the medical school at the University of California at Davis had reserved a minimum number of places in each entering class for racial minorities), the U.S. Supreme Court upheld the claim of the petitioner, a white male. Bakke argued that he had been the victim of "reverse discrimination" in that he had better "paper" credentials than a number of students admitted under the "quota" system. The ruling appears to forbid quotas while permitting consideration of race as a factor in affirmative action plans designed to redress past discrimination.

United Steelworkers of America v. *Weber,* 99 S. Ct. 2721 (1979) is the Supreme Court's most definitive statement to date in this sensitive and contentious area. Weber, a white male, challenged the legality of an affirmative action plan that set aside for black employees 50 percent of the openings in a training program until the percentage of black craft workers in the plant equalled the percentage of blacks in the local labor market. The plan was the product of a collective bargaining agreement between the Steelworkers and Kaiser Aluminum and Chemical. In Kaiser's Grammercy, Louisiana, plant only 5 of 273 skilled craft workers were black, while the local work force was approximately 39 percent black. In the first year of the affirmative action plan seven blacks and six whites were admitted to the craft training program. The most junior black employee accepted for the program had less seniority than several white employees who were not accepted. Weber was among the white males denied entry to the training program.

Weber filed suit claiming that Title VII forbade an affirmative action plan which granted a racial preference to blacks when there was no proof of discrimination but when whites dramatically exceed blacks in skilled craft positions. The federal District Court and the federal Court of Appeals held for Weber, but the United States Supreme Court reversed. Therefore, under *Weber,* race-conscious affirmative action remedies may be permissible. The Court was careful in not detailing precisely those characteristics that would describe a lawful affirmative action plan. However, several qualities of the Steelworkers plan clearly were instrumental in the Court's favorable ruling:

1. The affirmative action was part of a *plan.*
2. The plan was designed to "open employment opportunities for Negroes in occupations which have been traditionally closed to them."
3. The plan was temporary.
4. The plan did not unnecessarily harm the rights of white employees.
    That is—
    a. The plan did not require the discharge of white employees.
    b. The plan did not create an absolute bar to the advancement of white employees.

Therefore, affirmative action in situations like that in *Weber* does not constitute unlawful reverse discrimination.

The Supreme Court clarified the law's affirmative action commands a bit further in the *Burdine* case in which the Court asserted that Title VII does not require the employer to hire a minority or female applicant whenever that person's objective qualifications were equal to those of a white male applicant. Therefore, "the employer has discretion to choose among equally qualified candidates, provided the decision is not based upon unlawful criteria."[52]

Affirmative Action versus Seniority

As mentioned at the beginning of the chapter, the 1984 Supreme Court decision in the *Firefighters* case that follows addresses the question of whether accumulated seniority rights must take precedence over affirmative action goals when the two are in conflict. Reagan administration Assistant Attorney General for Civil Rights William Bradford Reynolds read the opinion as a broad victory for those in opposition to employment quotas. While directed at the seniority versus affirmative action issue, some loose language in the opinion and the government's broad interpretation raise at least two major questions:

1. Does the *Firefighters* rationale apply to hiring and promotion as well as to layoffs?
2. Are race-conscious remedies barred except to those who can prove that they themselves (and not merely the class of which they are a part) were the victims of discrimination?

The Reagan administration answered both questions in the affirmative. Those in the Civil Rights movement saw the decision as one limited to the narrower question of layoffs where seniority and affirmative action collide. Several recent district and appeals court decisions have restricted *Stotts,* but a clearer picture awaits Supreme Court opinions expected in 1986.[53]

FIREFIGHTERS LOCAL UNION NO. 1784, PETITIONER V. CARL W. STOTTS ET AL.   104 S.Ct. 2576

Justice White

Petitioners challenge the Court of Appeals' approval of an order enjoining the City of Memphis from following its seniority system in determining who must be laid off as a result of a budgetary shortfall. Respondents contend that the injunction was necessary to effectuate the terms of a Title VII consent decree in which the City agreed to undertake certain obligations in order to remedy past hiring and promotional practices. Because we conclude that the order cannot be justified, either as an effort to enforce the consent decree or as a valid modification, we reverse.

In 1977 respondent Carl Stotts, a black holding the position of fire-fighting captain in the Memphis, Tennessee, Fire Department, filed a class action complaint. . . . The complaint charged that the Memphis Fire Department and other city officials were engaged in a pattern or practice of making hiring and promotion decisions on the basis of race in violation of Title VII of the Civil Rights Act of 1964. . . .

The stated purpose of the decree was to remedy the hiring and promotion practices "of the department with respect to blacks." Accordingly, the city agreed to promote 13 named individuals and to provide backpay to 81 employees of the Fire Department. It also adopted the long-term goal of increasing the proportion of minority representation in each job classification in the fire department to approximately the proportion of blacks in the labor force in Shelby County, Tennessee. However, the city did not, by agreeing to the decree, admit "any violations of law, rule or regulation with respect to the allegations" in the complaint. . . .

The long-term hiring goal outlined in the decree paralleled the provisions of a 1974 consent decree, which settled a case brought against the city by the United States and which applied citywide. Like the 1974 decree, the 1980 decree also established an interim hiring goal of filling on an annual basis 50 percent of the job vacancies in the department with qualified black applicants. The 1980 decree contained an additional goal with respect to promotions: the department was to attempt to ensure that 20 percent of the promotions in each job classification be given to blacks. Neither decree contained provisions for layoffs or reductions in rank, and neither awarded any competitive seniority. The 1974 decree did require that for purposes of promotion, transfer, and assignment, seniority was to be computed "as the total seniority of that person with the city."

In early May 1981, the city announced that projected budget deficits required a reduction of nonessential personnel throughout the city government. Layoffs were to be based on the "last hired, first fired" rule under which city-wide seniority, determined by each employee's length of continuous service from the latest date of permanent employment, was the basis for deciding who would be laid off. If a senior employee's position were abolished or eliminated, the employee could "bump down" to a lower ranking position rather than be laid off. As the Court of Appeals later noted, this layoff policy was adopted pursuant to the seniority system "mentioned in the 1974 decree and . . . incorporated in the city's memorandum with the union."

On May 4, at respondents' request, the District Court entered a temporary restraining order forbidding the layoff of any black employee. The union, which previously had not been a party to either of these cases, was permitted to intervene. At the preliminary injunction hearing, it appeared that 55 then-filled positions in the department were to be eliminated and that 39 of these positions were filled with employees having "bumping" rights. It was estimated that 40 least-senior employees in the fire-fighting bureau of the department would be laid off and that of these 25 were white and 15 black. It also appeared that 56 percent of the employees hired in the department since 1974 had been black and that the percentage of black employees had increased from approximately 3 or 4 percent in 1974 to 11.5 percent in 1980.

On May 18, the District Court entered an order granting an injunction. The court found that the consent decree "did not contemplate the method to be used for reduction in rank or lay-off," and that the layoff policy was in accordance with the city's seniority system and was not adopted with any intent to discriminate. Nonetheless, concluding that the proposed layoffs would have a racially discriminatory effect and that the seniority system was not a bona fide one, the District Court ordered that the city "not apply the seniority policy insofar as it will decrease the percentage of black lieutenants, drivers, inspectors and privates that are presently employed . . . ." On June 23, the District Court broadened its order to include three additional classifications. A modified layoff plan, aimed at protecting black employees in the seven classifications so as to comply with the court's order, was presented and approved. Layoffs pursuant to the modified plan were then carried out. In certain instances, to comply with the injunction, nonminority employees with more seniority than minority employees were laid off or demoted in rank.

*   *   *   *   *

The issue at the heart of this case is whether the District Court exceeded its powers in entering an injunction requiring white employees to be laid off, when the otherwise applicable seniority system would have called for the layoff of black employees with less seniority. We are convinced that the Court of Appeals erred in resolving this issue and in affirming the District Court.

The Court of Appeals first held that the injunction did no more than enforce the terms of the agreed-upon consent decree. . . .

It is to be recalled that the "scope of a consent decree must be discerned within its four corners, and not by reference to what might satisfy the purposes of one of the parties to it" or by what "might have been written had the plaintiff established his factual claims and legal theories in litigation." . . . Here, as the District Court recognized, there is no mention of layoffs or demotions within the four corners of the decree; nor is there any suggestion of an intention to depart from the existing seniority system or from the city's arrangements with the union. . . .

The argument that the injunction was proper because it carried out the purposes of the decree is equally unconvincing. The decree announced that its purpose was "to remedy past hiring and promotion practices" of the department, and to settle the dispute as to the "appropriate and valid procedures for hiring and promotion." The decree went on to provide the agreed-upon remedy, but as we have indicated, that remedy did not include the displacement of white employees with seniority over blacks. Furthermore, it is reasonable to believe that the "remedy," which it was the purpose of the decree to provide, would not exceed the bounds of the remedies that are appropriate under Title VII, at least absent some express provision to that effect. . . .

The Court of Appeals held that even if the injunction is not viewed as compelling compliance with the terms of the decree, it was still properly entered because the District Court had inherent authority to modify the decree when an economic crisis unexpectedly required layoffs which, if carried out as the city proposed, would undermine the affirmative action outlined in the decree and impose an undue hardship on respondents. This was true, the court held, even though the modification conflicted with a bona fide seniority system adopted by the city. The Court of Appeals erred in reaching this conclusion.

Section 703(h) of Title VII provides that it is not an unlawful employment practice to apply different standards of compensation, or different terms, conditions, or privileges of employment pursuant to a bona fide seniority system, provided that such differences are not the result of an intention to discriminate because of race. It is clear that the city had a seniority system, that its proposed layoff plan conformed to that system, and that in making the settlement the city had not agreed to award competitive seniority to any minority employee whom the city proposed to lay off. The District Court held that the city could not follow its seniority system in making its proposed layoffs because its proposal was discriminatory in effect and hence not a bona fide plan. Section 703(h), however, permits the routine application of a seniority system absent proof of an intention to discriminate. . . . Here, the District Court itself found that the layoff proposal was not adopted with the purpose or intent to discriminate on the basis of race. Nor had the city in agreeing to the decree admitted in any way that it had engaged in intentional discrimination. The Court of Appeals was therefore correct in disagreeing with the District Court's holding that the layoff plan was not a bona fide application of the seniority system, and it would appear that the city could not be faulted for following the seniority plan expressed in its agreement with the union. The Court of Appeals nevertheless held that the injunction was proper even though it conflicted with the seniority system. This was error.

*   *   *   *   *

A second ground advanced by the Court of Appeals in support of the conclusion that the injunction could be entered notwithstanding its conflict with the seniority system was the assertion that "[i]t would be incongruous to hold that the use of the preferred means of resolving an employment discrimination action decreases the power of a court to order relief which vindicates the policies embodied within Title VII, and 42 U.S.C. §§ 1981 and 1983." The court concluded that if the allegations in the complaint had been proved, the District Court could have entered an order overriding the seniority provisions. Therefore, the court reasoned, "[t]he trial court had the authority to override the Firefighter's Union seniority provisions to effectuate the purpose of the 1980 decree."

The difficulty with this approach is that it overstates the authority of the trial court to disregard a seniority system in fashioning a remedy after a plaintiff has successfully proved that an employer has followed a pattern or practice having a discriminatory effect on black applicants or employees. If individual members of a plaintiff class demonstrate that they have been actual victims of the discriminatory practice, they may be awarded competitive seniority and given their rightful place on the seniority roster. . . . *Teamsters,* however, also made clear that mere membership in the disadvantaged class is insufficient to warrant a seniority award; each individual must prove that the discriminatory practice had an impact on him. . . . Even when an individual shows that the discriminatory practice has had an impact on him, he is not automatically entitled to have a nonminority employee laid off to make room for him. He may have to wait until a vacancy occurs, and if there are nonminority employees on layoff, the court must balance the equities in determining who is entitled to the job. . . . Here, there was no finding that any of the blacks protected from layoff had been a victim of discrimination and no award of competitive seniority to any of them. . . .

Our ruling in *Teamsters* that a court can award competitive seniority only when the beneficiary of the award has actually been a victim of illegal discrimination is consistent with the policy behind § 706(g) of Title VII, which affects the remedies available in Title VII litigation. That policy, which is to provide make-whole relief only to those who have been actual victims of illegal discrimination, was repeatedly expressed by the sponsors of the Act during the congressional debates. . . .

The Court of Appeals holding that the District Court's order was permissible as a valid Title VII remedial order ignores not only our ruling in *Teamsters* but the policy behind § 706(g) as well. Accordingly, that holding cannot serve as a basis for sustaining the District Court's order.

[Reversed.]

Justice Blackmun, with whom Justice Brennan and Justice Marshall join, dissenting.

*   *   *   *   *

In determining the nature of "appropriate" relief under § 706(g), courts have distinguished between individual relief and race-conscious class relief. Although overlooked by the Court, this distinction is highly relevant here. In a Title VII class-action suit of the type brought by respondents, an individual plaintiff is entitled to an award of individual relief only if he can establish that he was the victim of discrimination. That requirement grows out of the general equitable principles of "make whole" relief; an individual who has suffered no injury is not entitled to an individual award. . . . If victimization is shown, however, an individual is entitled to whatever retroactive seniority, backpay, and promotions are consistent with the statute's goal of making the victim whole. . . .

In Title VII class-action suits, the courts of appeals are unanimously of the view that race-conscious affirmative relief can also be "appropriate" under § 706(g). . . . The purpose of such relief is not to make whole any particular individual, but rather to remedy the present classwide effects of past discrimination or to prevent similar discrimination in the future. Because the discrimination sought to be alleviated by race-conscious relief is the classwide effects of past discrimination, rather than discrimination against identified members of the class, such relief is provided to the class as a whole rather than to its individual members. The relief may take many forms, but in class actions it frequently involves percentages—such as those contained in the 1980 consent decree between the city and respondents—that require race to be taken into account when an employer hires or promotes employees. The distinguishing feature of race-conscious relief is that no individual member of the disadvantaged class has a claim to it, and individual beneficiaries of the relief need not show that they were themselves victims of the discrimination for which the relief was granted.

In the instant case, respondents' request for a preliminary injunction did not include a request for individual awards of retroactive seniority—and, contrary to the implication of the Court's opinion, the District Court did not make any such awards. Rather, the District Court order required the city to conduct its layoffs in a race-conscious manner; specifically, the preliminary injunction prohibited the city from conducting layoffs that would "decrease the percentage of black[s]" in certain job categories. The city remained free to lay off any individual black so long as the percentage of black representation was maintained.

* * * * *

For reasons never explained, the Court's opinion has focused entirely on what respondents have actually shown, instead of what they might have shown had trial ensued. It is improper and unfair to fault respondents for failing to show "that any of the blacks protected from layoff had been a victim of discrimination," . . . for the simple reason that the claims on which such a showing would have been made never went to trial.

The Court's reliance on *Teamsters* is mistaken . . . because *Teamsters* was concerned with individual relief, whereas these cases are concerned exclusively with classwide, race-conscious relief.

* * * * *

In discussing § 706(g), the Court relies on several passages from the legislative history of the Civil Rights Act of 1964 in which individual legislators stated their views that Title VII would not authorize the imposition of remedies based upon race. And while there are indications that many in Congress at the time opposed the use of race-conscious remedies, there is authority that supports a narrower interpretation of § 706(g). Under that interpretation, the last sentence of § 706(g) addresses only the situation in which a plaintiff demonstrates that an employer has engaged in unlawful discrimination, but the employer can show that a particular individual would not have received the job, promotion or reinstatement even in the absence of discrimination because there was also a lawful justification for the action. . . .

. . . § 706(g) was amended by the Equal Employment Opportunity Act of 1972. The legislative history of that amendment strongly supports the view that Congress endorsed the remedial use of race under Title VII. The amendment added language to the first sentence of § 706(g) to make clear the breadth of the remedial authority of the courts. As amended, the first sentence authorizes a court to order "such affirmative action as may be appropriate, which may include, *but is not limited to,* reinstatement or hiring of employees, with or without back pay . . . *or any other equitable relief as the court deems appropriate."* . . .

In addition, during consideration of the amendment, Congress specifically rejected an attempt to amend Title VII to *prohibit* the use of prospective race-conscious employment goals to remedy discrimination. . . .

With clear knowledge, therefore, of courts' use of race-conscious remedies to correct patterns of discrimination, the 1972 Congress rejected an attempt to amend Title VII to prohibit such remedies. In fact, the Conference Committee stated: "In any area where the new law does not address itself, or in any areas where a specific contrary intention is not indicated, it was assumed that the present case law as developed by the courts would continue to govern the applicability and construction of Title VII.'' Relying on this legislative history of the 1972 amendment and other actions by the executive and the courts, four members of this Court, including the author of today's opinion, stated in *University of California Regents* v. *Bakke* . . . ''Executive, judicial, and congressional action subsequent to the passage of Title VII conclusively established that the Title did not bar the remedial use of race.'' . . . As has been observed . . . moreover, the courts of appeals are unanimously of the view that race-conscious remedies are not prohibited by Title VII. . . .

Questions

1. Read narrowly, what does the *Firefighters* decision conclude?
2. Read broadly from the view of those who criticize affirmative action, what is the result in *Firefighters?*
3. What reasoning supported the Court's conclusion in *Firefighters?*
4. Assume all of the female and minority employees in a large firm argue that they are the victims of discrimination. Many court cases and settlements in recent years have permitted such classes of wronged employees to bring joint actions and divide one large, joint recovery. How may the *Firefighters* decision affect remedies for group claims of discrimination?
5. In your opinion, does the *Firefighters* decision further the cause of social justice? Explain.
6. Is a seniority system having a discriminatory impact lawful where the system was created after the passage of the Civil Rights Act of 1964? See *American Tobacco Co.* v. *Patterson*, 456 U.S. 63 (1982).

A Wise Policy?

The wisdom of affirmative action programs remains at issue. At this writing the Reagan administration prefers at least some changes in direction in government equal opportunity enforcement. Former Secretary of Labor Raymond Donovan indicated that he and the president believe in affirmative action, but the President also favors deregulation to retard government ''intrusiveness.'' A poll of 300 business executives suggests that affirmative action has reached a mature role in American commerce:

1. Fifty two percent of those surveyed believe that affirmative action has helped advance the cause of women and minorities a great deal.
2. Seventy two percent said affirmative action has not harmed productivity.
3. Ninety one percent thought it ''not very likely'' that women could become chief executive officers of their companies in the next 15 years.
    Sixty nine percent answered ''not very likely'' and 27 percent found ''no chance at all'' when asked the same question as to blacks.
4. Eighty eight percent felt that EEOC should be more concerned with results than with the measures employed to reach equal work goals.[54]

The public at large, both black and white, clearly has deep reservations regarding affirmative action. A nationwide poll conducted in 1981 found 73 percent of the whites and 54 percent of the blacks disagreeing with the statement: "Because of past discrimination, blacks who need it should get some help from the government that white people in similar economic circumstances do not get."[55]

Part Six—Additional Discrimination Topics

Age Discrimination

The Age Discrimination in Employment Act (ADEA), as amended, forbids employers (including state and local governments), employment agencies, and labor organizations from discriminating because of age against employees 40 to 70 years of age. The act also prohibits mandatory retirement of most employees before age 70. The ADEA permits both private law suits and action by the EEOC. Among other possibilities the remedies available under ADEA include back pay, liquidated damages, and injunctive relief.

The case law in the area of age discrimination is somewhat undeveloped. A tight job market, the likelihood of declining social security benefits, an increasingly elderly population, and the elevation of mandatory retirement ages suggests intense conflict in the future. For example, may employers lawfully replace older, higher-paid employees with younger, equally qualified, lower-paid employees when employees' salaries are closely related to seniority and thus to age? The case that follows illustrates the current Supreme Court position.

WESTERN AIR LINES, INC., PETITIONER V. CHARLES G. CRISWELL ET AL. 472 U.S. ____, 53 *Law Week* 4766 (U.S. S.Ct., 1985)

Justice Stevens

The petitioner, Western Air Lines, Inc., requires that its flight engineers retire at age 60. Although the Age Discrimination in Employment Act of 1967 (ADEA) generally prohibits mandatory retirement before age 70, the Act provides an exception "where age is a bona fide occupational qualification [BFOQ] reasonably necessary to the normal operation of the particular business." A jury concluded that Western's mandatory retirement rule did not qualify as a BFOQ even though it purportedly was adopted for safety reasons. . . .

I

In its commercial airline operations, Western operates a variety of aircraft, including the Boeing 727 and the McDonnell Douglas DC-10. These aircraft require three crew members in the cockpit: a captain, a first officer, and a flight engineer. "The 'captain' is the pilot and controls the aircraft. He is responsible for all phases of its operation. The 'first officer' is the copilot and assists the captain. The 'flight engineer'' usually monitors a side-facing instrument panel. He does not operate the flight controls unless the captain and the first officer become incapacitated." . . .

A regulation of the Federal Aviation Administration prohibits any person from serving as a pilot or first officer on a commercial flight "if that person has reached his 60th birthday." The FAA has justified the retention of mandatory retirement for pilots on the theory that "incapacitating medical events" and "adverse psychological, emotional, and physical changes" occur as a consequence of aging. "The inability to detect or predict with precision an individual's risk of sudden or subtle incapacitation, in the face of known age-related risks, counsels against relaxation of the rule."

At the same time, the FAA has refused to establish a mandatory retirement age for flight engineers. "While a flight engineer has important duties which contribute to the safe operation of the airplane, he or she may not assume the responsibilities of the pilot in command." Moreover, available statistics establish that flight engineers have rarely been a contributing cause or factor in commercial aircraft "accidents" or "incidents."

In 1978, respondents Criswell and Starley were Captains operating DC-10s for Western. Both men celebrated their 60th birthdays in July 1978. Under the collective-bargaining agreement in effect between Western and the union, cockpit crew members could obtain open positions by bidding in order of seniority. In order to avoid mandatory retirement under the FAA's under-age-60 rule for pilots, Criswell and Starley applied for reassignment as flight engineers. Western denied both requests, ostensibly on the ground that both employees were members of the company's retirement plan which required all crew members to retire at age 60. For the same reason, respondent Ron, a career flight engineer, was also retired in 1978 after his 60th birthday.

*   *   *   *   *

Criswell, Starley, and Ron brought this action against Western contending that the under-age-60 qualification for the position of flight engineer violated the ADEA. In the District Court, Western defended, in part, on the theory that the age-60 rule is a BFOQ "reasonably necessary" to the safe operation of the airline. . . .

As the District Court summarized, the evidence at trial established that the flight engineer's "normal duties are less critical to the safety of flight than those of a pilot." The flight engineer, however, does have critical functions in emergency situations and, of course, might cause considerable disruption in the event of his own medical emergency.

The actual capabilities of persons over age 60, and the ability to detect disease or a precipitous decline in their faculties, were the subject of conflicting medical testimony. Western's expert witness, a former FAA Deputy Federal Air Surgeon, was especially concerned about the possibility of a "cardiovascular event" such as a heart attack. He testified that "with advancing age the likelihood of onset of disease increases and that in persons over age 60 it could not be predicted whether and when such diseases would occur."

The plaintiffs' experts, on the other hand, testified that physiological deterioration is caused by disease, not aging, and that "it was feasible to determine on the basis of individual medical examinations whether flight deck crew members, including those over age 60, were physically qualified to continue to fly." These conclusions were corroborated by the nonmedical evidence:

The record also reveals that both the FAA and the airlines have been able to deal with the health problems of pilots on an individualized basis. Pilots who have been grounded because of alcoholism or cardiovascular disease have been recertified by the FAA and allowed to resume flying. . . .

Moreover, several large commercial airlines have flight engineers over age 60 "flying the line" without any reduction in their safety record.

*   *   *   *   *

The jury rendered a verdict for the plaintiffs, and awarded damages. . . .
    . . . [T]he Court of Appeals affirmed in all respects. . . .

II

Throughout the legislative history of the ADEA, one empirical fact is repeatedly emphasized: the process of psychological and physiological degeneration caused by aging varies with each individual. . . . [M]any older American workers perform at levels equal or superior to their younger colleagues.

In 1965, the Secretary of Labor reported to Congress that despite these well-established medical facts there "is persistent and widespread use of age limits in hiring that in a great many cases can be attributed only to arbitrary discrimination against older workers on the basis of age and regardless of ability." . . .

After further study, Congress responded with the enactment of the ADEA.

* * * * *

. . . [H]owever, Congress recognized that classifications based on age, like classifications based on religion, sex, or national origin, may sometimes serve as a necessary proxy for neutral employment qualifications essential to the employer's business. . . . Congress offered only general guidance on when an age classification might be permissible by borrowing a concept and statutory language from Title VII of the Civil Rights Act of 1964 and providing that such a classification is lawful "where age is a bona fide occupational qualification reasonably necessary to the normal operation of the particular business."

Shortly after the passage of the Act, the Secretary of Labor, who was at that time charged with its enforcement, adopted regulations declaring that the BFOQ exception to ADEA has only "limited scope and application" and "must be construed narrowly." The EEOC adopted the same narrow construction of the BFOQ exception after it was assigned authority for enforcing the statute. . . .

III

In *Usery* v. *Tamiami Trail Tours, Inc.*, the Court of Appeals for the Fifth Circuit was called upon to evaluate the merits of a BFOQ defense to a claim of age discrimination. Tamiami Trail Tours, Inc., had a policy of refusing to hire persons over age 40 as intercity bus drivers. At trial, the bus company introduced testimony supporting its theory that the hiring policy was a BFOQ based upon safety considerations—the need to employ persons who have a low risk of accidents. In evaluating this contention, the Court of Appeals drew on its Title VII precedents, and concluded that two inquiries were relevant.

First, the court recognized that some job qualifications may be so peripheral to the central mission of the employer's business that *no* age discrimination can be "reasonably *necessary* to the normal operation of the particular business. The bus company justified the age qualification for hiring its drivers on safety considerations, but the court concluded that this claim was to be evaluated under an objective standard:

[T]he job qualifications which the employer invokes to justify his discrimination must be *reasonably necessary* to the essence of his business—here, the *safe* transportation of bus passengers from one point to another. The greater the safety factor, measured by the likelihood of harm and the probable severity of that harm in case of an accident, the more stringent may be the job qualifications designed to insure safe driving.

* * * * *

Second, the court recognized that the ADEA requires that age qualifications be something more than "convenient" or "reasonable"; they must be "reasonably necessary . . . to the particular business," and this is only so when the employer is compelled to rely on age as a proxy for the safety-related job qualifications validated in the first inquiry. This showing could be made in two ways. The employer could establish that it "had reasonable cause to believe, that is, a factual basis for believing, that all or substantially all [persons over the age qualifications] would be unable to perform safely and efficiently the duties of the job involved." . . .

Alternatively, the employer could establish that age was a legitimate proxy for the safety-related job qualifications by proving that it is "impossible or highly impractical" to deal with the older employees on an individualized basis. "One method by which the employer can carry this burden is to establish that some members of the discriminated-against class possess a trait pre-cluding safe and efficient job performance that cannot be ascertained by means other than knowl-edge of the applicant's membership in the class." In *Tamiami*, the medical evidence on this point was conflicting, but the District Court had found that individual examinations could not determine which individuals over the age of 40 would be unable to operate the buses safely. The Court of Appeals found that this finding of fact was not "clearly erroneous," and affirmed the District Court's judgment for the bus company on the BFOQ defense.

*   *   *   *   *

. . . [W]e conclude that this two-part inquiry properly identifies the relevant considerations for resolving a BFOQ defense to an age-based qualification purportedly justified by considerations of safety.

*   *   *   *   *

Reasonably Necessary Job Qualifications

Western relied on two different kinds of job qualifications to justify its mandatory retirement policy. First, it argued that flight engineers should have a low risk of incapacitation or psycholog-ical and physiological deterioration. At this vague level of analysis the plaintiffs have not seri-ously disputed—nor could they—that the qualification of good health for a vital crew member is reasonably necessary to the essence of the airline's operations. Instead, they have argued that age is not a necessary proxy for that qualification.

On a more specific level, Western argues that flight engineers must meet the same stringent qualifications as pilots, and that it was therefore quite logical to extend to flight engineers the FAA's age-60 retirement rule for pilots. Although the FAA's rule for pilots, adopted for safety reasons, is relevant evidence in the airline's BFOQ defense, it is not to be accorded conclusive weight. . . . The extent to which the rule is probative varies with the weight of the evidence supporting its safety rationale and "the congruity between the . . . occupations at issue." In this case, the evidence clearly established that the FAA, Western, and other airlines all recognized that the qualifications for a flight engineer were less rigorous than those required for a pilot.

*   *   *   *   *

Age as a Proxy for Job Qualifications

Western contended below that the ADEA only requires that the employer establish "a rational basis in fact" for believing that identification of those persons lacking suitable qualifications cannot occur on an individualized basis.

*   *   *   *   *

The "rational basis" standard is . . . inconsistent with the preference for individual evalua-tion expressed in the language and legislative history of the ADEA. Under the Act, employers are to evaluate employees between the ages of 40 and 70 on their merits and not their age. In the BFOQ defense, Congress provided a limited exception to this general principle, but required that employers validate any discrimination as "reasonably necessary to the normal operation of the particular business." It might well be "rational" to require mandatory retirement at *any* age less than 70, but that result would not comply with Congress' direction that employers must justify the rationale for the age chosen. Unless an employer can establish a substantial basis for believing that all or nearly all employees above an age lack the qualifications required for the position, the age selected for mandatory retirement less than 70 must be an age at which it is highly impractical for the employer to insure by individual testing that its employees will have the necessary qualifications for the job.

* * * * *

When an employee covered by the Act is able to point to reputable businesses in the same industry that choose to eschew reliance on mandatory retirement earlier than age 70, when the employer itself relies on individualized testing in similar circumstances, and when the administrative agency with primary responsibility for maintaining airline safety has determined that individualized testing is not impractical for the relevant position, the employer's attempt to justify its decision on the basis of the contrary opinion of experts—solicited for the purposes of litigation—is hardly convincing on any objective standard short of complete deference. Even in cases involving public safety, the ADEA plainly does not permit the trier of fact to give complete deference to the employer's decision.

The judgment of the Court of Appeals is *affirmed*.

Questions

1. Summarize the two-part *Tamiami* test that the Court identifies as the appropriate standard to be used in evaluating cases like *Western Air Lines*.
2. In general, the Age Discrimination in Employment Act forbids mandatory retirement prior to age 70. However, Congress provided an exception to that rule under which age may constitute a BFOQ if "reasonably necessary to the normal operation of the particular business." Western Air Lines argued that it need only show "a rational basis in fact" for requiring retirement based on age (under 70) rather than on an evaluation of each employee's physical and psychological condition. The Court rejected the *Western* argument. Distinguish the "reasonably necessary" and "rational basis in fact" standards.
3. Assume that you own a clothing store that is designed to appeal primarily to the "young adult" market. In your opinion, should the law permit you to hire only "young adults" as salespersons? Explain.
4. Under its collective bargaining agreement, Trans World Airlines maintained a policy of automatically transferring flight captains to positions as flight engineers in those instances when captains were disqualified from their pilot's role for reasons other than age (e.g., medical disability or a manpower reduction). Under the agreement, the captains were entitled to "bump" any less senior flight engineer. However, pilots who were retired upon reaching age 60 were not automatically entitled to move into a flight engineer position. Rather, they were allowed to remain with TWA only if they had secured a flight engineer position prior to their 60th birthday. They could do so only by submitting a bid in the hope that a vacancy would arise prior to their 60th birthday. Three pilots, forced to retire by TWA, filed suit claiming a violation of the Age Discrimination in Employment Act, which forbids differential treatment of older workers "with respect to a privilege of employment." Does the ADEA *require* TWA to grant transfer privileges to disqualified pilots? Explain. See *Trans World Airlines, Inc.* v. *Thurston,* 53 *Law Week* 4024 (U.S. S.Ct. 1985).

Discrimination against the Handicapped

The Rehabilitation Act of 1973 and the Vietnam Era Veterans Readjustment Assistance Act are federal statutes designed both to afford equal opportunity and to expand employment prospects for the handicapped.

The primary provisions of the Rehabilitation Act provide that:

1. Federal agencies must take an affirmative action approach toward hiring the handicapped.
2. Federal contractors having contracts that exceed $2,500 must include in those contracts affirmative action clauses providing for hiring and promoting the handicapped.
3. Federal agencies and programs receiving federal financial assistance are prohibited from discrimination on the basis of handicaps.

Those holding contracts with the federal government of $10,000 or more must include in those contracts clauses providing for affirmative action in hiring and promoting handicapped veterans of the Vietnam era.

Under the terms of the Rehabilitation Act a *handicapped individual* is "any person who (a) has a physical or mental impairment, which substantially limits one or more of such person's major life activities; (b) has a record of such an impairment; or (c) is regarded as having such an impairment."[56] Amputation, cancer, blindness, and mental retardation are clearly covered. Alcohol or drug abuse rising to the level of a disease or defect is covered. Disability under the Vietnam Era Act requires a disability discharge from active duty or a 30 percent disability rating from the Veterans Administration.

An example of the breadth of handicap coverage as well as the cost of allegedly discriminatory practices is a 1980 conciliation agreement involving a Dallas electronics firm. Varo Semiconductor Company agreed to pay $225,000 to 85 applicants allegedly denied jobs because of "disabilities" including obesity, color blindness, arthritis, hypertension, allergies, and varicose veins. The firm also agreed to establish a preferential hiring list for 32 of the alleged discrimination victims who still desired jobs with the firm.

The employer is, of course, under no duty to hire a handicapped individual who, because of the handicap, cannot fulfill the requirements of the job. Affirmative action requirements do not include underutilization analysis and the establishment of numerical goals and timetables. However, those covered by the act must make special efforts to reach and hire the handicapped. "Reasonable accommodation" must be made to the handicapped employee's needs.

Sexual Preference

The Title VII prohibition against sex discrimination refers to gender-based distinctions and, therefore, in general does not reach discrimination based on sexual practice and preference. Therefore, homosexuals, transsexuals, and those wronged due to effeminacy or masculinity must look to local and state statutes and to constitutions for legal relief.

A number of major corporations have established equal opportunity policies as to homosexuals. Homosexuality is not a bar to most federal employment. Some states and cities have enacted legislation offering varying measures of protection to homosexuals. The Due Process and Equal Protection provisions of the Fifth and Fourteenth Amendments offer protection to homosexuals and transsexuals employed in the public sector. Additionally, some cases have raised First Amendment as well as right to privacy constitutional claims.

The decisions are mixed. For example, in *Norton* v. *Macy*[57] a federal employee was dismissed as a consequence of an alleged off-the-job homosexual advance. The employee argued that the government had to show a relationship between his sexual preference and his job performance. A federal appeals court ruled that the government's judgment as to the immorality of the conduct involved was inadequate to establish its case. Recently the Florida Supreme Court held that a homosexual could not be denied admission to the state Bar merely because of sexual preference; however, many decisions have found homosexuals unfit for jobs. The U.S. Supreme Court declined to hear an appeal of a lower court decision affirming the legality of dismissing a homosexual school teacher when no evidence was offered showing that the teacher's sexual preference interfered with his job performance.[58] On the other hand, in 1985 a divided court (four to four) struck down an Oklahoma statute that barred public school teachers from advocating homosexual conduct. The statute was invalidated on freedom of speech grounds.[59] The courts upheld the EEOC's decision to dismiss an employee, in part, as a result of his highly publicized attempt to marry another male.[60] The appeals court ruled:

> We conclude from a review of the record . . . that appellant's employment was not terminated because of his status as a homosexual or because of any private acts of sexual preference . . . [T]he discharge was the result of appellant's "openly and publicly flaunting his homosexual way of life and indicating further continuance of such activities," while identifying himself as a member of a federal agency.[61] . . .

State Law

Employees believing themselves to be victims of discrimination often must exhaust available state remedies before proceeding to litigation at the federal level. Some 40 states have statutes roughly paralleling the protections of Title VII and the Age Discrimination in Employment Act. Protections vary widely from state to state, and states may provide greater or lesser protections than does the federal government. For example, some states prohibit discrimination on the basis of marital status, and some explicitly offer protection against discrimination on the basis of appearance.

Most state antidiscrimination legislation provides for an administrative agency such as a Human Rights Commission or a Fair Employment Practices Commission. Such bodies ordinarily have the power to issue rules to carry out the terms of the legislation, to conciliate disputes, to hold hearings, and if the charges warrant, issue orders necessary to stop the offensive practice and correct its effects.

The Results

We have erected a comprehensive, and clearly necessary, web of laws and orders and opinions to combat wrongful discrimination. As suggested in the readings the overall results for the protected classes are encouraging, but a vast gap remains. What of the individual cases? After studying the complexities of the various statutes and their judicial interpretations, it will be instructive to examine the pragmatics of some settlements. The following cases illustrate the results in wage adjustments, back pay, hiring policies, and so on.

1. In 1983 General Motors agreed to a $42.5 million settlement of discrimination charges raised by the EEOC and the United Auto Workers. The settlement, a product of 10 years of negotiations, was the largest in the history of the EEOC. GM promised to spend $15 million of the total over a five-year period for college scholarships for minority members and women. Twenty-one million dollars is to be spent for other training programs designed to enhance the ability of protected class members to reach apprenticeship and managerial roles.[62]

2. In 1985 the Equitable Life Assurance Society agreed to pay $12.5 million to 300 former employees who claimed to be victims of age discrimination. Equitable did not admit wrongdoing, nor did it agree to rehire any of the employees. The dismissals had resulted from what Equitable had labeled a cost-cutting drive.[63]

3. Motorola, Inc. agreed in 1980 to settle five discrimination suits involving its Illinois plants. Motorola negotiated a settlement with the EEOC providing back pay totaling an estimated $8 to $10 million for an estimated 10,000 blacks who had been denied semiskilled factory jobs, and the company agreed to fill 20 percent of its semiskilled job vacancies and 6.7 percent of its craft jobs with blacks, 11.2 percent of its sales positions with women, and 3.5 percent of its sales positions with Hispanics over the next five years. The cost of the expanded affirmative action program was expected to be $5 million.[64]

4. Individuals have often used discrimination prohibitions to rectify grievances. For example, a black man alleged that he had been denied employment with a tool and die firm due to his race. The firm then agreed to hire him. Subsequently, a conciliation hearing resulted in an award of $1,000 in partial back pay based on the employer's initial act of discrimination. Additionally, the employee's seniority date was applied retroactively to the date on which he was initially refused employment.[65]

Chapter Questions

1. Can an employer lawfully request information as to age on employment applications? Explain.
2. Can a private organization lawfully dismiss an employee on the grounds of homosexuality when that sexual preference does not interfere with job performance? Explain.

3. A union was composed entirely of white people. The union imposed a nepotism rule providing that new members would be either relatives of or recommended by current members. Was that membership policy violative of the law? Explain. *Local 53, Asbestos Workers* v. *Vogler,* 407 F.2d 1047 (5th Cir. 1969).

4. Title VII, as currently interpreted, does not require a showing of purposefulness or intent to establish unlawful discrimination. A finding of discrimination under the Fifth and Fourteenth Amendments does require such a showing. Would you favor amending Title VII to require direct explicit proof of actual discriminatory purpose? Explain.

5. Pan American Airways, Inc. maintained a policy of excluding men from positions as flight attendants. The policy was challenged on sex discrimination grounds. Pan American defended its policy with a survey showing that 79 percent of all passengers preferred being served by females. Then Pan Am offered expert testimony to show that the passenger preference was attributable to "feminine" qualities possessed by few males. The district court ruled for Pan Am on the grounds that "all or substantially all" (the test articulated in *Weeks* v. *Southern Bell Telephone,* 408 F.2d 228 [5th Cir. 1969]) men were unable to successfully fulfill the duties of flight attendants. The decision was appealed. Decide. Explain. See *Diaz* v. *Pan American Airways, Inc.,* 311 F. Supp. 559 (S.D. Fla. 1970), 442 F.2d 385 (5th Cir.), cert. denied, 404 U.S. 950 (1971).

6. May a Polynesian restaurant lawfully limit employment to "brown-skinned persons" in those jobs visible to the public? Explain.

7. May a Mexican restaurant lawfully limit employment to "individuals of Hispanic descent" in those jobs involving contact with customers? Explain.

8. Are Playboy Clubs in violation of the law when they hire only women to serve as bunnies? Explain. (In 1985, some Playboy Clubs began hiring men as "rabbits.")

9. Assume a private country club excludes blacks and women from employment. Is that practice violative of Title VII? Explain.

10. Define *affirmative action*.

11. A flight attendant was discharged in 1968 in accord with her employer's "no marriage" rule. The rule was later abolished. She was rehired in 1972 and she sought to have her seniority based on her original date of hire rather than the time at which she was rehired. She argued that the seniority system operated to perpetuate past discrimination. She brought suit against the airline. Decide. Explain. See *United Airlines, Inc.* v. *Evans,* 431 U.S. 553 (1977).

12. Blacks employed at the Georgia Power Company were concentrated in the four lowest job classifications, which were maintained as separate seniority units under a collective bargaining agreement. Workers moving to higher classifications were required to forfeit all accumulated seniority. All other classifications were composed overwhelmingly of whites. Movement from those classifications did not require seniority forfeiture. A consent decree in 1979 settled a Title VII lawsuit. The company agreed to count blacks' total time for seniority. Then with the Supreme Court's *Teamsters* decision, the union that was a party to the consent decree argued that the law had been altered and that the old seniority system was bona fide. Thus the union sought to have the consent decree rescinded. Decide. Explain. See *U.S.* v. *Georgia Power Co.,* 634 F. 2d 929 (1981).

13. Thornton worked as a manager at a Connecticut retail store. In accordance with his religious beliefs, Thornton notified his manager that he could no longer work on Sundays as required by company (Caldor, Inc.) policy. A Connecticut statute provided that: "No person who states that a particular day of the week is observed as his Sabbath may be required by his

employer to work on such day. An employee's refusal to work on his Sabbath shall not constitute grounds for his dismissal.'' Management offered Thornton the options of transferring to a Massachusetts store where Sunday work was not required or transferring to a lower-paying supervisory job in the Connecticut store. Thornton refused both, and he was transferred to a lower-paying clerical job in the Connecticut store. Thornton claimed a violation of the Connecticut statute. The store argued that the statute violated the ''Establishment Clause'' (see Chapter 5) of the First Amendment, which forbids establishing an official state religion and giving preference to one religion over another or over none at all. Ultimately the case reached the U.S. Supreme Court.

a. Decide. Explain.

b. Do the religious accommodation provisions of Title VII of the Civil Rights Act violate the Establishment Clause? See *Estate of Thornton* v. *Caldor, Inc.,* 53 *Law Week* 4853 (U.S. S.Ct., 1985).

14. A male employee of a private social service organization was dismissed after three years of employment. The employee filed suit contending that he was a victim of sex discrimination forbidden under Title VII. The employee contended that his discharge was in retaliation for his resistance to his male supervisor's sexual advances. The employer argued that Title VII does not reach such claims. Decide. See *Wright* v. *Methodist Youth Services, Inc.,* 511 F. Supp. 307 (DC NIll. 1981).

15. A woman sought a freightyard job. Her application was denied because she failed to meet the company's requirement of two years of truck-driving experience or truck-driving training. The woman believed herself to be a victim of sex discrimination.

a. Build a case on her behalf.

b. Build a case for the trucking company.

c. Decide the case. Explain. See *Chrisner* v. *Complete Auto Transit, Inc.,* 645 F.2d 1251 (1981).

16. The National Teachers Examination measured substantive knowledge, but it did not measure teaching ability per se. The test had a disparate impact on a protected class, but the Court found no evidence of intent to discriminate. The test was used for the certification of teachers. Is the test lawful? Explain. See *United States* v. *South Carolina,* 98 S. Ct. 756 (1978).

17. In 1972 a trucking firm had hired one black worker and one white worker as temporary employees. The white worker had more experience, but when a full-time position became available the black employee was selected. The hiring manager acknowledged that the decision was made to meet the ''attainment levels'' of the employer's informal affirmative action plan. The affirmative action plan was not ''organized'' and the manager was allegedly only ''vaguely aware'' of the employer's minority hiring expectations. The white worker filed suit, claiming Title VII violations. In particular he alleged that the company's racial preference amounted to an impermissible quota system. Decide. Explain. See *Lehman* v. *Yellow Freight System,* 651 F.2d 520 (1981).

18. A new Texas airline, flying out of Dallas' Love Field, was in a precarious financial posture. Thus, a campaign was mounted to sell itself as ''the airline personification of feminine youth and vitality.'' In commercials, its customers, who were primarily businessmen, were promised ''in-flight love'' including ''love potions'' (cocktails), ''love bites'' (toasted almonds), and a ticketing process labeled a ''quickie machine'' that delivered ''instant gratification.'' A male was denied a job with the airline because of his sex. He filed a Title VII action. The airline argued that attractive females were necessary to maintain its public image under the ''love campaign,'' a marketing approach that, the company claimed had been responsi-

ble for its much improved financial condition. Decide. Explain. See *Wilson* v. *Southwest Airlines Co.*, USDC N Tex., CA-3-80-0689-G, June 12, 1981.

19. An employer assigned customers to employees based on the race or national origin of the customer. For example, Hispanic customers were assigned to Hispanic employees. Otherwise, employees were treated equally as to pay and working conditions. Is the employer guilty of employment discrimination? Explain. See *Rogers* v. *EEOC,* 454 F.2d 234 (5th Cir. 1971).

20. A bus company fired a black employee for violating the employer's rule forbidding beards. The beard had been grown on a doctor's advice in response to a skin condition known as pseudo folliculitis barbae. The condition affects people with curved hair follicles. After shaving, the facial hair sometimes curled back into the skin, causing inflammation and abscesses. The employee claimed a Title VII violation.
    a. Is the race of the employee critical to the resolution of this case?
    b. Build the plaintiff's argument.
    c. Build the defendant's argument.
    d. Decide. Explain. See *EEOC* v. *Greyhound Lines, Inc.* 22 EPD II 30, 604, (DC ED Pa. 1979).

21. Is sexual harassment a problem that should properly be addressed via federal intervention (EEOC)? Explain.

22. On balance, has the feminist movement and accompanying legal victories improved the quality of life for American women? For American men? Explain.

23. Nearly equal numbers of blacks and whites applied for jobs, but only 24 percent of those hired were black. The area population was 26 percent black. Was the employer guilty of discrimination? Explain. See *Robinson* v. *Union Carbide Co.*, 538 F.2d 652 (5th Cir. 1976).

24. Plaintiffs challenged a rule prohibiting the employment of drug users including former heroin addicts who had engaged in methadone maintenance for over a year. Plaintiffs offered proof that 63 percent of all persons in public methadone programs were black or Hispanic, while the area population was 36 percent black and Hispanic. Are those facts sufficient to make out a prima facie case of employment discrimination? Explain. See *New York City Transit Authority* v. *Beazer,* 440 U.S. 568 (1979).

25. Elizabeth Hishon, an attorney employed by the Atlanta law firm of King and Spaulding, alleged that the firm had engaged in sex discrimination in failing to elevate her to the rank of partner. King and Spaulding argued that Title VII should not apply to partnership decisions because those "promotions" change the individual's status from "employee" to "employer." They further contended that the freedom of association guarantees of the Constitution permit them to choose whomever they wish as partners. Is Hishon's claim governed by Title VII? Explain. See *Hishon* v. *King and Spaulding,* 81 L. Ed.2d 59, 104 S.Ct. ____ (1984).

26. An EEOC guideline defines sexual harassment as "unwelcome sexual advances, requests for sexual favors, and other verbal or physical conduct of a sexual nature" when submission to the conduct affects employment decisions and/or the conduct interferes with work performance or creates a hostile work environment. In your opinion, is the guideline fair and workable? Explain.

Notes

1. 104 S.Ct. ———81 L. Ed. 2d 483 (1984).
2. *Franchise Motor Freightway Ass'n* v. *Leavey,* 196 Cal. 77, 235 pp. 1000, 1002.
3. Richard Arvey, *Fairness in Selecting Employees* (Reading, Mass.: Addison-Wesley Publishing, 1979), p. 7.
4. 347 U.S. 483 (1954).
5. 163 U.S. 537 (1896).
6. A portion of the material in this paragraph is drawn from William P. Murphy, Julius G. Getman, and James E. Jones, Jr., *Discrimination in Employment,* 4th ed. (Washington: Bureau of National Affairs, 1979), pp. 1–4.
7. *General Building Contractors Association, Inc.* v. *Pennsylvania,* 458 U.S. 375 (1982).
8. *Runyan* v. *McCreary,* 96 S.Ct. 2586 (1976).
9. 442 U.S. 256 (1979).
10. The materials in this paragraph draw heavily from Charles A. Sullivan, Michael J. Zimmer, and Richard F. Richards, *Federal Statutory Law of Employment Discrimination* (Charlottesville, Va.: The Michie Company, Bobbs-Merrill, 1980), pp. 266–69.
11. Ibid, pp. 16–33.
12. 422 U.S. 405 (1975).
13. *International Brotherhood of Teamsters* v. *United States,* 97 S.Ct. 1843 (1977).
14. *American Tobacco* v. *Patterson,* 456 U.S. 63 (1982).
15. 457 U.S. 440 (1982).
16. *Muller* v. *Oregon,* 208 U.S. 412 (1908), as quoted in *Discrimination in Employment—A Study of Six Countries by the Comparative Labor Law Group* ed., Folke Schmidt (Stockholm, Sweden: Almqvist & Wiksell International, 1978), p. 130.
17. 429 U.S. 125 (1976).
18. *Newport News Shipbuilding & Dry Dock Co.* v. *EEOC,* 462 U.S. 669 (1983).
19. Sullivan, Zimmer, and Richards, *Federal Statutory Law,* p. 155.
20. Cited in "Business Week/Harris Poll," *Business Week,* August 1, 1983, p. 92.
21. *Arizona Governing Committee for Tax Deferred Annuity and Deferred Compensation Plans* v. *Norris,* 463 U.S. 1073 (1983).
22. 468 U.S. ———, 52 *Law Week* 5076 (1984).
23. "Census Bureau: Women Falling Behind in Wages," *Des Moines (Iowa) Register,* January 16, 1984, p. 1A.
24. "Women Hold Almost One-Third of Management Jobs," *Waterloo (Iowa) Courier,* April 11, 1984, p. 4D.
25. "Study: Wages of Women Gain on Men's," *Des Moines (Iowa) Register,* October 31, 1984, p. 4A.
26. 400 U.S. 542 (1979).
27. Mack A. Player, *Federal Law of Employment Discrimination in a Nutshell,* 2d ed. (St. Paul, Minn.: West Publishing, 1981), p. 202.
28. See generally *Diaz* v. *Pan American World Airways, Inc.,* 442 F.2d 385 (5th Cir.), cert. denied. 404 U.S. 950 (1971).
29. *Barnes* v. *Costle,* 561 F.2d 983 (D.C. Cir. 1977). Costle was an Administrator of the Environmental Protection Agency and was a litigant in this case solely by reason of his official position.
30. Eliza G. C. Collins and Timothy Blodgett, "Sexual Harassment . . . Some See It . . . Some Won't," *Harvard Business Review* 59, no. 2 (March–April 1981), p. 77.
31. Ibid., p. 78.
32. Ibid., p. 79, reporting from the Merit Systems Protection Board Report on Sexual Harassment in the Federal Workplace, given before the Subcommittee on Investigations, Committee on the Post Office and Civil Service, U.S. House of Representatives, September 1980.
33. 51 *New York University Law Review,* April 1976, pp 148–49, as reported in Terry L. Leap and Edmund R. Gray, "Corporate Responsibility in Cases of Sexual Harassment," *Business Horizons,* October 1980, p. 58.
34. The Bureau of National Affairs, *Sexual Harassment and Labor Relations—A BNA Special Report* (426), Part II, (July 30, 1981), p. 24.
35. Collins and Blodgett, "Sexual Harassment," p. 92.
36. 29 USC Section 206(d) (1).
37. Ibid.
38. Player, p. 107.
39. No, according to the Department of Labor's Interpretive Bulletin as reported in Sullivan, Zimmer, and Richards, *Federal Statutory Laws,* p. 596.
40. No. Ibid., pp. 598–601.
41. No, if those tasks do not constitute a substantial part of the job. Ibid., p. 608, reporting *Shultz* v. *American Can Co.—Dixie Prods.,* 424 F.2d 356 (8th Cir. 1970).
42. 417 U.S. 188 (1974).
43. *County of Washington* v. *Gunther,* 452 U.S. 161 (1981).
44. 740 F.2d. 686 (1984).
45. 54 *Law Week* 2144 (9th Cir. 1985).
46. Ibid., *Spaulding,* p. 708.

47. Ken Fireman, "Comparable Worth Idea Is Rejected," *Des Moines (Iowa) Register,* June 18, 1985, pp. 1, 4A.

48. *United States* v. *Seeger,* 380 U.S. 163 (1965).

49. 432 U.S. 63 (1977).

50. 574 F.2d 897 (7th Cir. 1978).

51. *University of California Regents* v. *Bakke,* 438 U.S. 265 (1978).

52. *Texas Department of Community Affairs* v. *Burdine,* 450 U.S. 248 (1981).

53. See, e.g., *Britton* v. *South Bend Community School Corp.,* 53 *Law Week* 2182 (USDC, N.Ind. 1984); *Wygant* v. *Jackson Board of Education,* 53 *Law Week* 2236 (CA6, 1984); and *Vanguards of Cleveland* v. *City of Cleveland,* 53 *Law Week* 2384 (CA6, 1985).

54. William H. Jones, "Lack of 'Qualified' Minorities Seen," *Washington Post,* April 5, 1979, p. B-01.

55. ABC News/*Washington Post,* February 26–March 6, 1981, as reported in *Public Opinon,* April–May 1981, p. 38.

56. 29 U.S.C.A. § 706(6).

57. 417 F.2d 1161 (D.C. Cir. 1969).

58. *Gaylord* v. *Tacoma School Dist. No. 10,* 88 Wash. 2d 286, 559 P. 2d 1340 (1977).

59. *Board of Education of the City of Oklahoma City* v. *National Gay Task Force,* 53 *Law Week* 4408 (U.S. S.Ct. 1985).

60. *Singer* v. *U.S. Civil Serv. Comm.,* 530 F.2d 247 (9th Cir. 1976).

61. Ibid., p. 255.

62. "GM Past on Bias Offers Millions in Scholarships," *Chronicle of Higher Education,* October 26, 1983, p. 3.

63. "Equitable Age Bias Case Settled," *Waterloo (Iowa) Courier,* January 20, 1985, p. C-12.

64. *The Bureau of National Affairs, Fair Employment Practices—Summary of Latest Developments,* No. 415, October 9, 1980, p. 6.

65. Francis Kornegay, *Equal Employment* (New York: Vantage Press, 1979), p. 103.

V

Business and Selected Social Problems

CHAPTER 14   The Social Responsibility of Business
CHAPTER 15   Consumer Protection
CHAPTER 16   Products Liability
CHAPTER 17   Environmental Protection

14

The Social Responsibility of Business

Introduction

The issue: Must business decision making include consideration not merely of the welfare of the firm, but that of society as well? For most contemporary readers, the answer is doubtless self-evident—of course business bears a social responsibility. Business has enjoyed a central and favored role in American life. As such, it must assume a measure of the burden for the welfare of the total society. Problems such as discrimination, pollution, and poverty require the full strength of the nation, including the vast resources of business. Professors Brenner and Molander's survey of *Harvard Business Review* readers revealed that:

> Most respondents have overcome the traditional ideological barriers to the concept of social responsibility and have embraced its practice as a legitimate and achievable goal for business.[1]

Only 28 percent of the respondents endorsed the free market view, popularly associated with Milton Friedman, that "the social responsibility of business is to 'stick to business'," and 69 percent agreed with the idea that "'profit' is really a somewhat ineffective measure of business' social effectiveness." Indeed, the respondents seemed to hold a rather optimistic, activist view of business' role in society. Of those responding, 77 percent disagreed with the position that "every business is in effect 'trapped' in the business system it helped create, and can do remarkably little about the social problems of our times."[2]

The ascendance of the social responsibility concept represents one of the most striking ideological shifts in American history. From the settling of the nation until roughly 1950, business was expected to concentrate on one goal; that is, the production and distribution of the best products at the lowest possible prices. Of course, social-responsibility arguments were raised, but business was largely exempt from any affirmative duty for the resolution of social problems. Rendered practical perhaps by increasing prosperity, the public, led by business scholars and critics, began in the 50s to consider a larger role for corporate America. In just three decades the role of business in society has been radically altered. Profit seeking remains central and essential, but for most businesspersons this new and rather unwieldy ingredient must be added to the equation.

The Social Performance Index

Question: Now here's a list of things people have said are or should be responsibilities of business in this country. (Card shown respondent) Would you go down that list and for each one tell me whether you consider it to be a definite responsibility of business, or highly desirable although not a definite responsibility, or something that is nice to do but shouldn't necessarily be expected, or something that is beyond what business should do. First, producing good quality products and services.

Now here's a list of things people have said are or should be responsibilities of business in this country. (Card shown respondent) Would you go down that list and for each one tell me whether you think business fulfills its responsibilities fully, fairly well, not too well, or not at all well? First, producing good quality products and services.

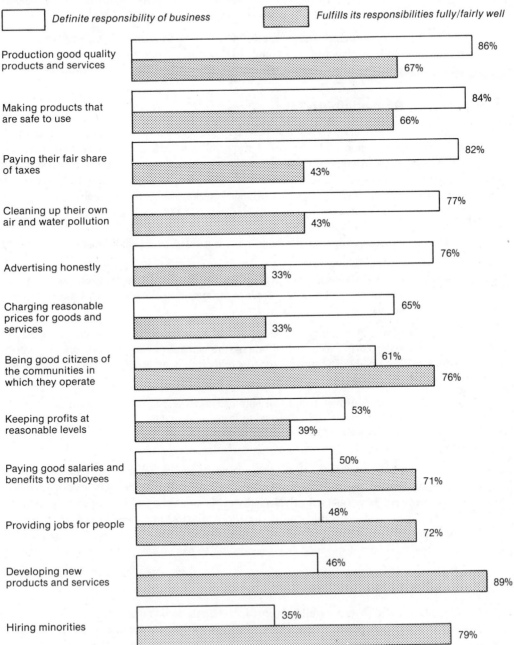

☐ *Definite responsibility of business*   ▨ *Fulfills its responsibilities fully/fairly well*

Production good quality products and services — 86% / 67%

Making products that are safe to use — 84% / 66%

Paying their fair share of taxes — 82% / 43%

Cleaning up their own air and water pollution — 77% / 43%

Advertising honestly — 76% / 33%

Charging reasonable prices for goods and services — 65% / 33%

Being good citizens of the communities in which they operate — 61% / 76%

Keeping profits at reasonable levels — 53% / 39%

Paying good salaries and benefits to employees — 50% / 71%

Providing jobs for people — 48% / 72%

Developing new products and services — 46% / 89%

Hiring minorities — 35% / 79%

Source: Survey by the Roper Organization (Roper Report 79-1), December 2–9, 1978. Reprinted from *Public Opinion*, April–May 1980, p. 25, by permission of the American Enterprise Institute.

Given the business community's substantial acceptance of social responsibility, it is not surprising that the general public heartily endorses the notion:

According to *ORC Public Opinion Index* 7 out of 10 Americans "believe that business has an obligation to help society, even if it means making less profit," with that proportion having grown significantly since 1967. Even among stockholder households, public attitude holds that "corporate social responsibility should take precedence over maximization of profits."[3]

The Social Performance Index (see p. 503) depicts the public's sense of what issues business should be responsible for and displays the degree to which the public feels business is fulfilling those responsibilities.

What Is Social Responsibility?

One major impediment to broad acceptance of the social responsibility concept has been that of comprehension. What is social responsibility? Many definitions have been offered, and a broad consensus seems to have emerged, but no single expression has successfully embraced the full spectrum of views. For example, Davis and Blomstrom articulated the following: "The idea of social responsibility is that decision makers are obligated to take actions which protect and improve the welfare of society as a whole along with their own interests.[4]

Kenneth Andrews suggests the same tone, but offers some additional dimensions:

By "social-responsibility" we mean the intelligent and objective concern for the welfare of society that restrains individual and corporate behavior from ultimately destructive activities, no matter how immediately profitable, and leads in the direction of positive contributions to human betterment, variously as the latter may be defined. . . .[5]

While social responsibility, framed in terms of business' duty to society, appears to be broadly accepted in business and among the general public, it is important to recall that a significant body of sentiment adheres to the free market view alluded to previously and perhaps best expressed by Milton Friedman:

(In a free economy) there is one and only one social responsibility of business—to use its resources and engage in activities designed to increase its profits, so long as it stays within the rules of the game, which is to say, engages in open and free competition, without deception or fraud. . . .[6]

Friedman believes that the firm, maximizing its profits, is necessarily maximizing its contribution to society. He believes social responsibility to be both unworkable and unjust. He asks how selected private individuals can know what the public interest is. He also argues that any dilution of the profit maximizing mode—such as charitable contributions—is a misuse of the stockholders' resources. The individual stockholder, he contends, should dispose of assets according to her or his own wishes.

The Social Responsibility Debate

As indicated, social responsibility seems increasingly to be an accepted element of business ideology and practice, but serious reservations remain about the intellectual rigor and economic wisdom of the movement. Furthermore, the economic malaise of the late 1970s and early 80s and the Reagan administration's emphasis on free market principles seems to have somewhat dampened the ardor for imposing further duties on the business community. Therefore, social responsibility should be regarded, not as a fait accompli, but as an important area of policy debate. In that connection it will be helpful to summarize the perceptive insights of Professor Keith Davis, who built a list of the arguments for and against social responsibility.[7]

Arguments for Social Responsibility

Long-Run Self-Interest   The idea is that to the extent business improves the society of which it is a part, business will profit in the long run. By meeting the community's needs, business will have a better environment in which to operate. For example, if business contributes to community welfare, the incidence of crime should decline, which means that business will pay less for protection of property, insurance, and taxes to support the police. In the long run, low-cost production requires the accomplishment of social goods.

Public Image   Closely aligned with the long-run self-interest argument is the notion that business will profit from a better public image. The public appears to favor a social contribution on the part of business. Therefore, making that contribution should enhance the corporate image and improve business in the long run.

Viability of Business   Business as an institution will be threatened with declining power if it fails to meet the public's expectations. Business was chartered by society, and that charter could be amended or revoked if society's demands are not met. Other groups would step in to meet the responsibilities that business failed to fulfill.

Avoidance of Government Regulation   Business seeks the freedom to maximize its own interests. Presumably the degree to which business voluntarily fulfills society's expectations will be matched by a commensurate decline in demands for government intervention.

Sociocultural Norms   The businessperson is guided by society's cultural constraints. As society's norms more thoroughly embrace social responsibility, business is firmly, if subtly, moved in that direction in order to achieve acceptance by society.

Stockholder Interest   Of course, the stockholder benefits via improved image, and so on, but beyond that, economist Henry Wallich has demonstrated that social responsibility is of direct economic benefit to the diversified portfolio holder.[8] A stockholder in a single firm might not benefit directly from overall corporate responsibility, but the multifirm stockholder can encourage socially responsible behavior such as training the hard-core unemployed. Even if the trainee leaves the firm and moves to another, the diversified stockholder profits from the general improvement in business' labor quality.

Let Business Try   Other institutions have failed to solve America's persistent problems. Why not give business an opportunity?

Business Has the Resources   Among American institutions, business may be foremost in terms of total management talent, functional expertise, and capital resources. By applying these strengths, as well as business' innovative approaches and productivity orientation, the corporate community might achieve advances not otherwise possible.

Problems Can Become Profits   Solutions to problems may prove to be profitable. For example, chemical wastes can often be reclaimed at a profit.

Prevention is Better than Curing   Social problems are nagging, persistent afflictions. Since they must be dealt with eventually, it is more economically sound to voluntarily address them now.

Arguments against Social Responsibility

Profit Maximization   Here, Professor Davis makes the free market argument of Milton Friedman and others that business' sole responsibility is lawful profit maximization.

Costs of Social Involvement   Meeting social goals is often not profitable. Business resources are limited. Particularly for small firms, burdens such as meeting pollution control requirements may actually drive them out of business.

Lack of Social Skills   The expertise of businesspeople lies in the economic realm. Do we want such people reaching decisions that call for much broader social skills? Are other institutions better equipped to address social issues?

Dilution of Business' Primary Purpose   Business might be weakened in the marketplace if its leaders divide their energies and vision. Economic goals would go unattained, and social goals, also receiving only partial attention, would likewise not be met.

Weakened International Balance of Payments   Social programs add to business costs. Ordinarily those costs are recovered through increased prices. Similarly social programs reduce productivity, which in turn ordinarily leads to higher product costs. If foreign firms operating in international markets are not similarly committed to social causes, American firms are at a competitive disadvantage. The result is fewer international sales and a weakened international balance of payments for the United States.

Business Has Enough Power   Business influence is already felt throughout society. Combining social activities with business' traditional economic role would result in a dangerous concentration of power that would threaten our pluralist balance.

Lack of Accountability   Accountability should always accompany responsibility. As it is, society has no clear lines of control over business' social endeavors. Business might, in a well-meaning fashion, become "benevolent, paternalistic rulers."

Lack of Broad Support   Davis argues that opinion regarding social responsibility is severely divided. An effort by business to operate in a hostile environment would have potentially disastrous consequences. As noted, social responsibility seems to have achieved a high degree of acceptance in recent years, but some of the division Davis alludes to certainly remains and, indeed, may intensify during trying economic times.

Davis conceptualized the arguments in a clear, balanced manner. In recent years scholars have begun to intensify the empirical analysis of the virtues and liabilities of social responsibility. We are beginning to receive some "hard data" to assist in resolving the very important social responsibility debate. The next section summarizes some of those findings.

Social Responsibility Research

Professor Lyman Ostlund surveyed a random sample of 458 top managers and 557 operating managers from *Fortune* 500 firms to assess their attitudes toward the arguments for and against social responsibility.[9] In general, he found that the arguments against social responsibility were considered less important than the arguments favoring such involvement. Opinions of top management differed little from that of operating managers. One result seemed particularly significant. The profit maximization argument ("Society is better advised to ask only that corporations maximize their efficiency and profits") was not considered particularly important. That result is noteworthy, since it is a measure of the sentiment for the free market approach championed by Friedman and others. Having offered a favorable assessment of managers' attitudes toward social responsibilities in the abstract, it is important to consider how social responsibility fares when weighed against traditional business goals. Professors Kamal Abouzeid and Charles N. Weaver surveyed 220 executives from among the largest Texas-based corporations.[10] Respondents selected the four goals that their company took to be most important from a list of possibilities including social responsibility. Of the respondents, 21.5 percent selected social responsibility, ranking that concept seventh among eight major goals. Financial goals, growth and expansion, efficient utilization of resources, and company stability were the four goals most frequently selected.

In summary, there seems little doubt that corporate leaders have an increased sensitivity to social problems. Probably that sensitivity is not as highly developed as many in the general population would prefer. Managers seem to have adopted the rather sensible stance that traditional financial goals must be honored to maintain the viability of the firm, but that priority certainly does not exclude serious attention to social problems.

Although many dimensions of the social responsibility question have been subjected to empirical evaluation, the key inquiry beyond those addressed above is that of economic performance. Are socially responsible companies more or less profitable than others? Professors Federick Sturdivant and James Ginter studied 67 companies identified as ''exhibiting exceptional social responsiveness or lack thereof.[11] They discovered that the ''best'' and ''honorable mention'' firms substantially outperformed the ''worst'' firms, as measured by growth rate in earnings per share from 1964 to 1974.

While the findings certainly will not support the argument that socially responsive companies will always out perform less responsive firms in the long run, there is evidence that, in general, the responsively managed firms will enjoy better economic performances. It would be simple-minded, at best, to argue a one-on-one cause-effect relationship. However, it would appear that a case can be made for an association between responsiveness to social issues and the ability to respond effectively to traditional business challenges.[12]

At least nine other studies have found similar results,[13] but Gordon Alexander and Rogene Buchholz, in studying the stock market performance of 47 firms over several years, concluded that ''The degree of social responsibility as measured by the rankings of businessmen and students bears no significant relationship to stock market performance.''[14]

The results are mixed. That should not be surprising. The field is new as academic topics go. The issues to be explored are of such elephantine proportions as to virtually defy the style of precise, well-defined hypothesis testing that characterizes social science research generally. Over the years the data will reveal firmer conclusions.

Social Responsibility in Practice

Is the actual performance of business in conformity with its now broadly affirmed acceptance of social responsibility? As scholar S. Prakash Sethi has expressed it, has business moved beyond mere ''obligation'' and ''responsibility'' to an active ''social responsiveness'' role?[15] Social responsiveness is not merely a matter of meeting social pressure. Rather business, it is argued, should take an ''anticipatory'' and ''preventive'' role in the interests of total societal welfare.

The apartheid and Ford Pinto readings that follow offer examples of behavior falling at various points on the social responsibility scale. Here one acquires a sense of the difficulty of implementing socially responsible action in the face of severe economic and organizational constraints. To business critics the apartheid and Pinto episodes suggest that some firms have failed even to meet fundamental legal responsibilities. Yet as the readings demonstrate, many firms assume a fully socially responsive role that meets all reasonable economic, legal, ethical, and discretionary responsibilities.

GILLETTE TRIES TO SHAVE AWAY AT SOUTH AFRICA'S RACE LAWS

Paul Van Slambrouck

The Gillette Company, best known for its razor blades, is at the cutting edge of new efforts by U.S. companies to help blacks in South Africa.

Gillette's South African subsidiary has just opened a legal-aid clinic serving mainly blacks, the first such service started by a business in this country. Gillette, like other American companies operating in South Africa, is under intense political pressure both here, from blacks, and in the United States to do more to oppose South Africa's system of racial segregation, known as apartheid.

"This is a real way to have a go at stuff like influx control," says James Clarke, managing director of Gillette South Africa Ltd.

Influx control, which restricts blacks in their travel and access to jobs, is one of those discriminatory features of South Africa that leave U.S. firms wide open to the charge that they are exploiting black labor in South Africa. Mr. Clarke hopes the legal clinic can help blacks better understand their rights within the influx-control system and even drum up cases that might help establish new legal precedents in the area of black rights.

"We wouldn't finance urban guerrillas," says a Gillette corporate officer who recently paid his first visit to South Africa. "But we can probe the edges of the law."

Probing the edges of the law in a host country may sound like a dubious activity for a multinational corporation. But many U.S. firms in South Africa recognize the uniqueness of this country's segregationist laws and the strong feelings they inspire back in America. These companies seem to accept that their role here must be different than in other countries.

The Rev. Leon Sullivan, who in 1977 established a set of principles by which he felt U.S. firms in South Africa should abide, urged companies to go further last November when anti-South Africa demonstrations spread across the US. "Support the recension of all apartheid laws," he told the U.S. companies that subscribe to the so-called Sullivan Principles.

American firms "recognize that business has a unique responsibility" in South Africa that goes beyond their involvement in social programs in other countries, says Stephen Bisenius, executive director of the American Chamber of Commerce in South Africa.

Gillette, for instance, spends six to seven times more on affirmative action and social programs in South Africa than its general corporate guidelines call for.

Mr. Bisenius says U.S. companies as a group spend proportionately more on social responsibility programs in South Africa than they do anywhere else in the world.

Mr. Sullivan said the 1984 evaluation of U.S. companies operating in South Africa that are signatories to the Sullivan Principles was "the most encouraging" in the program's history. The principles call for nonsegregation in the workplace; equal employment practices; equal pay for comparable work; training programs aimed at blacks, Coloreds (persons of mixed race), and Indians; the promotion of nonwhites into supervisory jobs; and improving the quality of life outside the workplace.

About 300 U.S. firms do business in South Africa. The have a combined direct investment of between \$2.5 and \$3 billion and employ some 80,000 blacks. While only 128 U.S. companies participate in the Sullivan program, they represent most of the largest firms operating here.

Still, the political pressure on U.S. companies operating here has never been greater. Nobel Peace Prize winner Desmond Tutu has said that unless certain aspects of South Africa's system of apartheid are rescinded within two years, he will call for foreign companies to withdraw their investments.

The U.S. Congress appears more inclined to pass some punitive economic legislation against South Africa this year than at any time in the recent past. [Bowing to congressional pressure in September 1985, President Reagan issued an executive order imposing limited economic sanctions on South Africa.—ed.]

The pressure is keenly felt by businessmen here. "You're going to have more companies scratching their heads wondering what to do for an encore," says Arthur Tregenza, a spokesman for General Motors. He says U.S. companies are doing social good in South Africa, but "the message hasn't crossed the ocean."

The South African government and the South African business community are clearly concerned about the U.S. disinvestment drive. One prevalent worry is that the political pressure against doing business here will be indirectly abetted by this country's severe recession.

"We're worried the bottom line won't offset the hassle factor'' and U.S. firms will quietly stop investing in South Africa, said an official at a local chamber of commerce.

Gillette's legal clinic is located in Springs, the industrial suburb east of Johannesburg where the company is located. The clinic is free to those who cannot afford to pay for its services, which means its clientele will be predominantly black. Clarke says the clinic will cost Gillette about $35,000 this year.

The University of South Africa will supply law students to work at the clinic under the supervision of one full-time attorney.

One difficulty facing U.S. businesses is how to respond to the unmistakable trend in black politics to reject anything that is seen to be "part of the system.'' For instance, U.S. companies have spent large sums of money on improving black education. But the schools are run by the government and they are often the first buildings to be attacked during black unrest.

Gillette's other programs for blacks include classes for local businessmen, a secretarial training unit at the local technical school, sporting facilities, housing loans, and guaranteed mortgages. Gillette is planning to provide qualified blacks with loans that will cover the complete cost of a college education.

Source: *The Christian Science Monitor*, February 13, 1985, p. 1.

QUESTIONS

1. Has Gillette exceeded the bounds of its legitimate corporate social responsibility by assisting South African blacks to "probe the edges of the law'' in an effort to "establish new legal precedents in the area of black rights?'' Explain.
2. Should foreign companies withdraw their investments from South Africa? Explain.

THE FORD PINTO

Background

The Ford Pinto two-door sedan was introduced on September 11, 1970, as a 1971 model year vehicle. A three-door runabout version was introduced in February 1971, and the Pinto station wagon model was brought out on March 17, 1972. The design and location of the fuel tank in the Ford Pinto, and identically designed Mercury Bobcat, were unchanged until the 1977 model year when revision was required to meet new federal safety standards for rear impact collisions. By that time over 1.5 million two- and three-door Pinto sedans and nearly 35,000 Bobcat sedans had been sold. Because of the different configuration of the station wagon model, the fuel tank was mounted differently and, consequently, was less susceptible to damage from rear end collisions. . . .

The 1971–1976 Pinto fuel tank is constructed of sheet metal and is attached to the undercarriage of the vehicle by two metal straps with mounting brackets. The tank is located behind the rear axle. Crash tests at moderate speeds have shown that, on rear-impact collisions, the fuel tank is displaced forward until it impacts the differential housing on the rear axle and/or its mounting bolts or some other underbody structure.

The Cause for Concern

Public awareness and concern over the Pinto gas tank design grew rapidly following the 1977 publication of an article by Mark Dowie in *Mother Jones,* a West Coast magazine. This article was widely publicized in the press and reprinted in full in *Business and Society Review.* The article, based on interviews with a former Ford engineer, alleged that Ford Motor Company had rushed the Pinto into production in much less than the usual time in order to gain a competitive edge. According to the article, this meant that tooling began while the car was still in the product design stage. When early Ford crash tests allegedly revealed a serious design problem in the gas tank, the tooling was well underway. Rather than disrupt this process, at a loss of time and money, to incorporate more crashworthy designs which Ford allegedly had tested, the article stated that the decision was made to market the car as it was then designed.

The Dowie article further included calculations reportedly contained within an internal company memorandum showing that the costs of making the fuel tank safety improvement ($11 per car) were not equal to the savings in lives and injuries from the estimated proportion of crashes that would otherwise be expected to result in fires. These "benefits" were converted into dollar figures based on a value or cost of $200,000 per death and $67,000 per injury, figures which were obtained from NHTSA. In addition the article stated that Ford had lobbied for eight years to delay the federal standard for fuel tank safety that came into force with the 1977 model year. The article alleged that Ford's opposition to Federal Motor Vehicle Safety Standard 301 was stimulated by the costly retooling that would have been required when the Pinto was first scheduled for production. In response, a Ford offical characterized the allegations made in the Dowie article as distorted and containing half-truths.

The NHTSA Investigation

Based on allegations that the design and location of the fuel tank in the Ford Pinto made it highly susceptible to damage on rear impact at low to moderate closing speeds, the National Highway Traffic Safety Administration (NHTSA) initiated a formal defect investigation on September 13, 1977. In response to the NHTSA's requests, Ford provided information concerning the number and nature of known incidents in which rear impact of a Pinto reportedly caused fuel tank damage, fuel system leakage or fire. Based on this information and its own data sources, in May 1978 NHTSA reported that, in total, it was aware of 38 cases

---

> **THE COST OF DYING IN A PINTO**
> Printed below are figures from a Ford Motor Company internal memorandum on the benefits and costs of an $11 safety improvement which would have made the Pinto less likely to burn. The memorandum purports to "prove" that the improvement is not cost effective:
>
> **BENEFITS**
> *Savings:* 180 burn deaths, 180 serious burn injuries, 2,100 burned vehicles.
>   *Unit Cost:* $200,000 per death, $67,000 per injury, $700 per vehicle.
>   *Total Benefit:* 180 × ($200,000) + 180 × ($67,000) + 2,100 × ($700) = **$49.5 million.**
>
> **COSTS**
>   *Sales:* 11 million cars, 1.5 million light trucks.
>   *Unit Cost:* $11 per car, $11 per truck.
>   *Total Cost:* 11,000,000 × ($11) + 1,500,000 × ($11) = **$137 million.**

Source: Mark Dowie, "How Ford Put Two Million Firetraps on Wheels," *Business and Society Review* (23), Fall 1977, pp. 46, 51. © Mark Dowie. Originally published in *Mother Jones* magazine. Reprinted with permission.

in which rear-end collisions of Pinto vehicles had resulted in fuel tank damage, fuel system leakage, and/or ensuing fire. These cases had resulted in a total of 27 fatalities sustained by Pinto occupants, of which one is reported to have resulted from impact injuries. In addition, 24 occupants of these Pinto vehicles had sustained non-fatal burn injuries.

In addition the NHTSA Investigation Report stated that prior to initial introduction of the Pinto for sale Ford had performed four rear impact barrier crash tests. However as Ford reported, "none of the tested vehicles employed structure or fuel system designs representative of structures and fuel systems incorporated in the Pinto as introduced in September 1970." These tests were conducted from May through November 1969.

Following initial introduction of the Pinto for sale, Ford continued a program of rear impact tests on Pintos which included assessment of post impact conditions of the fuel tank and/or filler pipe. Reports of 55 such tests were provided to NHTSA, including tests of Mercury Bobcats. Three items developed a history of consistent results of concern at impact speeds as low as 21.5 miles per hour with a fixed barrier: (1) the fuel tank was punctured by contact with the differential housing or some other underbody structure; (2) the fuel filler neck was pulled out of the tank; and (3) structural and/or sheet metal damage was sufficient to jam one, or both, of the passenger doors closed. Review of the test reports in question suggested to the NHTSA investigators that Ford had studied several alternative solutions to the numerous instances in which fuel tank deformation, damage or leakage occurred during or after impact.

The NHTSA investigation concluded that the fuel tank and filler pipe assembly installed in the 1971–1976 Ford Pinto is subject to damage which results in fuel spillage and fire potential in rear impact collisions by other vehicles at moderate closing speeds. Further, examination by NHTSA of the product liability actions filed against Ford and other codefendants involving rear impact of Pintos with fuel tank damage/fuel leakage/fire occurrences, showed that at that time nine cases had been completed. Of these, the plaintiffs had been compensated in eight cases, either by jury awards or out-of-court settlements.

Following this initial determination that a defect existed and less than a week before a scheduled NHTSA public hearing on the Pinto fuel tank problem, Ford agreed to a voluntary recall.

Criminal Charges

On September 12, 1978, following an accident involving the burning and death of three young women in a Pinto, a county grand jury in Indiana indicted Ford Motor Company on three counts of reckless homicide and one count of criminal recklessness. The charge of reckless homicide was brought under a 1977 revision of the Indiana Penal Code that allows a corporation to be treated as a person for the purposes of bringing criminal charges. On March 13, 1980, more than two months after the trial began, the jury found Ford not guilty.

Source: Library of Congress Congressional Research Service. Background material for hearings on H.R. 7040, Subcommittee on Crime of the Committee on the Judiciary, House of Representatives, 96th Congress, 2d session, May 1980.

Was Ford Liable under Civil Law?

It is important to note that Ford has argued throughout the Pinto episode that, based on government data, the Pinto was less susceptible to fires from rear end collisions than the average car on the road. The Pinto conformed to all federal safety standards at the time. Fuel tank standards for rear-end collisions were not established until 1977.

The many civil suits arising from Pinto fires have resulted in a number of large judgments and settlements against Ford. For example, the families of two Pennsylvania children killed in a Pinto fire received, according to the families' attorney, more than $2 million in an out-of-court settlement. But the most striking such trial was that of Richard Grimshaw, who received a jury verdict of $127.8 million. At this writing Mr. Grimshaw had undergone his 65th operation. Among other injuries he had sustained the loss of his nose, left ear, and four fingers. In May 1981, the California Fourth Circuit Court of Appeals upheld the Grimshaw decision against Ford with a reduced damages total of $6.3 million.

Was Ford Liable under Criminal Law?

Of course, the most publicized and, in terms of legal and social policy, far-reaching of the Pinto trials was the Indiana criminal prosecution mentioned in the Library of Congress study. A loss in the Indiana case presumably would have opened Ford to tens of millions of dollars in punitive damage claims in the many undecided Pinto civil suits. Despite Ford's victory, some observers think the case is demonstrative of an appropriate new zeal for holding corporations and their executives criminally accountable for their behaviors. An excerpt from an editorial appearing in *The Nation* reflects that sentiment.

Ford got off this time—perhaps as a result of the judge's controversial decision to exclude on technical grounds evidence in the form of Ford internal documents. . . .

Despite a sympathetic judge and a defense war chest of a reported $3 million (the budget of the small-town prosecutor in Winamac, Indiana, was $20,000), Ford very nearly lost the case. The jury deliberated for four days before reaching a decision.

But more important than the verdict in this particular case is the principle that has been reestablished—the importance of holding corporate criminals accountable.[16]

But to Professor Richard Epstein the Indiana Pinto episode simply should not have been tried as a criminal case.

The consequences that flow from the prosecution's theory of criminal liability only confirm what should now be evident: the Pinto case should not have been brought within the traditional modes of criminal responsibility. Such is not to rule out all possibility for public control over the production and sale of automobiles. There is nothing, for example, to prevent federal or state governments from bringing suit for *civil* fines in the event that automobile manufacturers do not conform to applicable safety standards. Such civil actions spare the government the need to prove explosive allegations of "reckless disregard and criminal intention," and give it the benefit of the lower standard of proof normally involved in civil cases. Of equal importance, they prevent any corporate defendant from being subjected to the deep moral taint that is associated in the public mind with charges of criminal wrongdoing. It is true that many of the hazards associated with criminal prosecution might be avoided by circumspection in invoking the criminal sanctions. Yet in the current climate of opinion it seems almost fanciful to rely upon notions of prosecutorial self-restraint. Such self-restraint will deny to some what is, after all, the joyous opportunity of both making and seeing the mighty fall.[17]

See Chapter 3, "Ethics," for a more detailed discussion of managers' criminal liability.

Questions

1. Ford's internal memoranda suggest that the company had completed cost-benefit analyses balancing the cost of alterations versus the cost of deaths and injuries. Defend Ford's use of such a calculus.
2. What organizational characteristics contribute to the occurrence of arguably regrettable decisions such as those associated with the Pinto?
3. Would an episode like that of the Pinto be less likely to transpire in a socialist state? Explain.
4. Were the various allegations against Ford proved to be true, would you decline to work for

the organization? Put another way, what dollar sum would be required for you to accept employment with Ford in a job commensurate with your interests and skills? Explain.

5. Is criminal prosecution a sensible, desirable approach to the Pinto case? Explain.

6. If the choice were yours, would you award Mr. Grimshaw the original $127.8 million, the appeals court decision of $6.3 million, or some lesser amount? Explain.

7. Are large civil penalties effective in discouraging future errors or wrongdoing? Explain.

8. Professor Terrence Kiely argues for personal, criminal liability for executives involved in cases like the Pinto: "The only way we're going to get quality products as consumers is to make corporate executives feel personally responsible for their decisions. The aim is to get them to worry and think about more than just the bottom line."[18] Comment.

9. Ford had argued that attempting to apply the criminal law in cases like the Pinto "would wipe out the basic distinction between civil wrongs and criminal offenses."[19] What did Ford mean?

Corporations as Criminals?

The Ford prosecution, in itself an innovative and much-disputed new direction in potential criminal liability, raises the larger issue of corporate crime generally. Clearly corporate criminal behavior is not the norm, but neither is it uncommon. Of course, in that regard the business community may merely reflect the values of the larger society.

A wave of corporate crime disclosure throughout 1985 has besmirched the image of the business community:

> The way things are going, *Fortune* may soon have to publish a 500 Most Wanted list. During the past few months the news has been filled with tales of business schemes and scandals, of corporate intrigue and downright crime. The offenses make up a catalog of chicanery: cheating on government defense contracts, check-writing fraud, bogus-securities dealing, tax dodges, insider trading, and money laundering. Among the culprits: General Electric, E. F. Hutton, Bank of Boston, and General Dynamics.[20]

General Electric pleaded guilty to defrauding the government of $800,000 on a Minuteman Missile contract. E. F. Hutton pleaded guilty to defrauding some 400 banks of about $8 million in an elaborate check overdrafting scheme. Bank of Boston was fined $500,000 for failing to report $1.2 billion in overseas cash transactions as required by U.S. law. (The law is designed to prevent money laundering, but Bank of Boston was not formally accused of that violation.) General Dynamics lost two Navy contracts in the midst of Pentagon allegations that the nation's third largest defense supplier overcharged the government by $75 million for expenses that allegedly included, for example, country club fees. Currently 45 of the 100 largest defense contractors are under criminal investigation.[21]

Business crime is imposing a very heavy financial burden on society; a burden substantially exceeding that of the conventional crimes of robbery, burglary, larceny, and auto theft, the direct costs of which have been estimated at perhaps $3 to $4 billion per year.[22] Excluding antitrust violations and fraud against the government, the total white-collar crime bill is estimated to exceed $44 billion annually.[23] (Note: The estimate refers to *all* white-collar crime and thus is not limited to businesses per se.) Securities thefts and frauds alone cost us perhaps $4 billion per year.[24] Losses from anticompetitive conduct may total tens of billions annually. For example, brokers estimated that an SEC order stopping price-fixing resulted in savings to stock purchasers of $25 million in the first month.[25]

Of course, the cost of business crime and white-collar crime more generally is not limited to direct financial loss. Physical injury or death and corruption of the political process are some of the regrettable by-products. Such conduct erodes public confidence in the commercial world, serves to exacerbate resentment against the upper economic classes, and, by example, encourages wrongdoing in the general population. One presidential study labeled white-collar crimes "the most threatening of all—not just because they are so expensive, but because of their corrosive effect on the moral standards by which American business is conducted."[26]

Further it is important to recall that business is often the victim of white-collar crime:

During the first half of 1975, commercial banks in the United States lost nearly five times as much money in frauds and embezzlements, usually by insiders, as they did from armed bank robberies.[27]

A *Fortune* study during the decade from 1970 to 1980 reveals the alarming frequency of corporate crime. The *Fortune* study was limited to five crimes (domestic bribery, criminal fraud, illegal political contributions, tax evasions, and criminal antitrust violations) where the prosecution resulted in conviction or in a consent decree.

Of the 1,043 major corporations in the study, 117, or 11 percent, have been involved in at least one major delinquency in the period covered . . . Some companies have been multiple offenders. In all, 188 citations are listed covering 163 separate offenses—98 antitrust violations; 28 cases of kickbacks, bribery, or illegal rebates; 21 instances of illegal political contributions; 11 cases of fraud; and 5 cases of tax evasion.[28]

Questions

1. The *Fortune* study suggests that corporate crime is not uncommon. In your judgment, is the business community more tolerant of crime than is the case for American society generally? Explain.
2. The *Fortune* study suggests that crime may be particularly common in smaller firms: "The bribing of purchasing agents by small manufacturers and the skimming of receipts by cash-laden small retail businesses are a commonplace of commercial life." Assuming *Fortune* is correct, what forces led to that corruption?
3. Why do we educate so strenuously against "street crimes" but afford so little attention to fixing prices and other business wrongs?
4. It is argued that corporate crime is, in significant measure, attributable to excessive government intervention in business practice (e.g., antitrust law and safety standards). Do you agree? Explain.
5. What steps would you suggest to curb corporate crime?

A Social Responsibility for the World?

On December 3, 1984, a poison gas leak from a Union Carbide India Ltd. pesticide plant in Bhopal, India, resulted in at least 1,700 deaths and perhaps 100,000 immediate injuries. Long-term effects are unknown, but partial blindness and lung and liver damage to many victims are not unlikely. In the two months following the tragedy nearly 25 percent of the babies born to mothers affected by the leak died soon after birth. However, a direct link between the deaths and the leak had not been established at this writing. The Indian government filed suit against the parent Union Carbide Corporation, alleging negligence and misrepresentation of the safety of the plant. Due to the "enormity of the Bhopal disaster," India chose not to specify a dollar amount in compensatory and punitive damage claims. At this point, legal claims filed by noted American lawyer Melvin Belli and others total some $15 billion. Belli's suit claims that the local subsidiary and the U.S. parent acted in utter disregard for the safety of the employees and residents and that the Bhopal plant lacked the computerized early warning system found in a similar Carbide plant in Institute, West Virginia. However, Carbide claims that the safety technology at Bhopal was fully equal to that in the United States and equal to that in the industry throughout the world. (Three gas leaks struck Union Carbide's West Virginia works in August 1985. No serious injuries were reported.)

In March 1985, Union Carbide released its own investigative report. The report blames the tragedy on "a unique combination of unusual events." The principal contributing factors, based on the Carbide report, included the following:

1. Five weeks prior to the accident the methyl isocyanate refining unit at the plant had run for several days at undesirably high temperatures.
2. Those high temperatures caused an undesirably high quantity of chloroform to remain in the holding tank from which the gas ultimately leaked.
3. At least 120 gallons of water were intentionally or inadvertently introduced to the tank. The chloroform and water precipitated a chemical reaction driving the temperature in the tank to 200°C. and pushing the internal pressure up dramatically. A valve then released, and the poison gas escaped.
4. The tank's cooling system was, at the time, "nonoperational."
5. An alarm to signal high temperatures failed to operate.
6. A "scrubber," installed for the purpose of rendering harmless any escaping gas, failed to operate.
7. An employee on duty failed to check the scrubber even though a meter revealed that it was not operating.

Union Carbide chairman Warren Anderson acknowledged that the plant "should not have been operating" under those conditions.[29]

Most of the parties to the Bhopal tragedy seek an out-of-court settlement to avoid the years of costly litigation that would otherwise ensue. However, in addition to the huge financial claims at stake, the case is burdened with extreme legal complexity. Will the case be heard in U.S. courts where jury awards would dramatically exceed the likely judgments in India? (Ordinarily U.S. courts decline to hear cases filed by foreign citizens unless substantial U.S. interests are involved. Here the plaintiffs will attempt to establish the necessary U.S. ties by directly linking the American parent corporation to the tragedy.) Will liability be limited to the subsidiary, Union Carbide India Ltd., or will the plaintiffs be able to reach the assets of the parent? (That issue will probably turn upon the degree to which the parent firm was engaged in managing the affairs of the subsidiary.) Will punitive damages be awarded? (Punitive awards are handed down in about 1 percent of all litigations.) Will Carbide contractors and suppliers bear part of the loss? (The outcome of that issue will depend in part on whether design defects are discovered in the Bhopal plant.) Finally, will Carbide and/or its executives bear criminal responsibility should wrongdoing be established? (The Indian government is conducting an inquiry.)

The implications of the Bhopal case are likely to reach far beyond India and Union Carbide. As Mr. Anderson put it: ''Maybe some benefits will come out of this—in terms of how people do things in other parts of the world.[30] Clearly America is firmly immersed in a world market. The implications for the social responsibility doctrine are profound and complex.

Does American business have a social responsibility, not merely to Americans, but to all citizens of the world? In trade with foreign parties, should Americans be guided by the laws and mores of the importing nation rather than those of the United States? Does the sale abroad of unsafe, ineffective, and contaminated American products constitute unethical conduct? Is the decision to buy products rejected in America a matter to be left exclusively to the wisdom of the foreign purchaser? The article that follows raises these issues and explores the little-known story of the ''dumping'' abroad of products considered unsafe or useless in America.

THE CORPORATE CRIME OF THE CENTURY

Mark Dowie

Tom Mboya was the hope of the Western world. Bright, energetic, popular, and inclined to be democratic—he was a born leader who, Washington hoped, would rise to power in Kenya and help keep Africa safe for United States commerce. In 1969 he was shot down in the streets of Nairobi. An emergency rescue squad was by his side in minutes. They plugged him into the latest gadget in resuscitative technology—a brand new U.S. export called the Res-Q-Aire. What the rescue team didn't know as they watched Tom Mboya's life slip away was that this marvelous device had been recalled from the American market by the U.S. government because it was found to be totally ineffective. The patient died.

Losing Mboya to the Res-Q-Air was perhaps a subtle retribution for the United States, for to this day we allow our business leaders to sell, mostly to Third World nations, shiploads of defective medical devices, lethal drugs, known carcinogens, toxic pesticides, contaminated foods and other products found unfit for American consumption.

Ten years after Mboya's assassination, in fact, Kenya itself remains a major market for unsafe, ineffective, and contaminated American products. At the 1977 meeting of the United Nations Environmental Program, Kenyan Minister of Water Development Dr. D. J. Kiano warned that developing nations would no longer tolerate being used as ''dumping grounds for products that have not been adequately tested'' and that their people should not be used as ''guinea pigs'' for chemicals.

The prevailing sentiment in Washington contrasts considerably with Dr. Kiano's. Say the word *dumping* in federal government circles and the predominant response will be ''Oh, yes, 'dumping.' Really must be stopped. It's outrageous, not in our economic interests at all . . . unscrupulous. . . .''

Sounds as if we've solved the problem, doesn't it, except what our bureaucrats are talking about, one discovers, is foreign corporations ''dumping'' low-priced goods on the American market—Japanese cars, Taiwanese televisions, Hong Kong stereos, Australian beef, etc. The export of banned and hazardous products, which *Mother Jones* calls *dumping,* is considered business as usual.

. . . Dumping is, in fact, *big* business as usual. It involves not only manufacturers and retailers, a vast array of export brokers, tramp steamers, black marketeers and go-betweens who traffic an estimated $1.2 billion worth of unsafe goods overseas every year, but also the United States Export-Import Bank, which finances large dumps; the Commerce, State and Treasury Departments, which have the statutory authority to stop or control dumping, but won't; and a President who, in his quiet way, subverts the efforts of the few progressive members of Congress who seek to pass uniform antidumping legislation.

Hard evidence of dumping and its tragic consequences has repeatedly been brought to the attention of federal agencies, the Congress and the White House. Here are some examples:

● 400 Iraqis died in 1972 and 5,000 were hospitalized after consuming the by-products of 8,000 tons of wheat and barley coated with an organic mercury fungicide, whose use had been banned in the U.S.

● An undisclosed number of farmers and over 1,000 water buffalos died suddenly in Egypt after being exposed to leptophos, a chemical pesticide which was never registered for domestic use by the Environmental Protection Agency (EPA) but was exported to at least 30 countries.

● After the Dalkon Shield intrauterine device killed at least 17 women in the United States, the manufacturer withdrew it from the domestic market. It was sold overseas after the American recall and is still in common use in some countries.

● No one knows how many children may develop cancer since several million children's garments treated with a carcinogenic fire retardant called Tris were shipped overseas after being forced off the domestic market by the

Consumer Product Safety Commission (CPSC).

● Lomotil, an effective anti-diarrhea medicine sold only by prescription in the U.S. because it is fatal in amounts just slightly over the recommended doses, was sold over the counter in Sudan, in packages proclaiming it was ''used by astronauts during Gemini and Apollo space flights'' and recommended for use by children as young as 12 months.

● Winstrol, a synthetic male hormone, which was found to stunt the growth of American children, is freely available in Brazil, where it is recommended as an appetite stimulant for children.

● Depo-Provera, an injectable contraceptive banned for such use in the United States because it caused malignant tumors in beagles and monkeys, is sold by the Upjohn Co. in 70 other countries, where it is widely used in U.S.-sponsored population control programs.

● 450,000 baby pacifiers of the type that has caused choking deaths have been exported by at least five manufacturers since a ban was proposed by the CPSC. 120,000 teething rings that did not meet recently established CPSC standards were cleared for export and are on sale right now in Australia.

Occasionally, a particularly scandalous dump like one of these will come to the attention of conscientious Americans. Most dumps, however, are performed quietly, the product moving unnoticed in the fast flow of normal trade between nations. And dumping is not limited to chemicals and consumer products. When a firm's production facilities and industrial equipment are condemned by the Occupational Safety and Health Administration, the manufacturer often simply closes up shop and moves the factory to Mexico or Jamaica, where occupational health standards are virtually nonexistent. Even entire technologies are dumped. Nuclear power, which seems certain to receive a ''hazardous'' classification before long in the U.S., is today being dumped on energy-starved nations like the Philippines and India.

We are only beginning to discover how toxic and carcinogenic are some of the chemicals we use, chemicals with the potential to affect the entire global environment and human gene pool. Moreover, the number of other consumer products that maim or kill shows no sign of diminishing. The list of banned and hazardous products is, thus, bound to grow, which *should* making dumping a major international issue for the 1980s.

Early in our investigation, however, we discovered that exposing dumpers was more challenging than we thought it would be. "They're really smugglers," said one of our team in a story meeting. "The only difference between drug smugglers and dumpers is that the products are usually moving in opposite directions."

There is another difference: the government protects dumpers. We talked to countless officials in countless agencies and departments of the government while researching this story–a few of them outspoken opponents of dumping. They would tell us about contaminated foods, baby pacifiers, pesticides and drugs that were being dumped overseas. They often knew how many of each item were shipped to specific countries, but they would never tell us the brand names, the manufacturers or the names of the export brokers. The answer was always the same. "I'm sorry, that's proprietary information . . . trade secret . . . confidential corporate information." . . .

Notification Before the Dump

The liberal compromise on the dumping issue is notification. Invoking the principles of national sovereignty, self-determination, and free trade, government officials and legislators have devised a system whereby foreign governments are notified whenever a product is banned, deregulated, suspended or cancelled by an American regulatory agency. The notification system is handled by the State Department, whose policy statement on the subject reads, in part, "No country should establish itself as the arbiter of others' health and safety standards. Individual governments are generally in the best position to establish standards of public health and safety."

Based on this judgment, an unwieldy and ineffective notification procedure allegedly places announcements in the hands of the proper foreign government officials, telling them a certain drug has been found to be toxic or that babies have strangled in particular brands of cribs.

The main problem with notification is the logic behind it. Other governments are generally *not* in a position to establish safety standards, let alone control imports into their countries. In fact, the countries where most of our banned and hazardous products are dumped lack regulatory agencies, testing laboratories or well-staffed customs departments. In 1978, Nigeria's Environmental Protection Ministry was one person. He recently told the U.S. EPA that it didn't matter whether or not he was notified when a pesticide was suspended; there was nothing he could do to stop its importation.

* * * * *

Of course, even if clear notification about a product were to reach officials in an importing nation, there is nothing to stop the exporters from changing a product's brand name before they ship.

It's All Coming Back

Perhaps the only aspect of the whole dumping travesty that has kept the issue alive in Washington is reimportation. Congressmembers and bureaucrats who would otherwise ignore or even encourage dumping become irate upon learning that a hazardous product is being reimported (smuggled) into the U.S. for sale, or that an imported fruit or vegetable contains residue of a pesticide long-since suspended for American use. . . .

Remember, it is perfectly legal to dump hazardous products abroad. There are, however, strict measures to prevent reimportation. The FDA allows manufacturers to export banned drugs, stale-dated drugs and even unapproved new drugs if they are shipped under "an investigational protocol" (for experimentation on other people). . . .

What Dumping Really Is

Executives in major exporting corporations, with the strong support of Commerce Secretary Juanita Kreps, argue that if the export of banned and hazardous products is prohibited by statute or Executive Order, foreign buyers will merely turn to European or other suppliers, as they have in the past for weapons and ammunition. Other developed nations do dump; Germany dumps at least as many toxic pesticides as the United Sates, and no nation on earth can match Switzerland for dumping baby formula. However, the assumption that foreign buyers will import known toxins and recognized lethal products from one country when they can't get them from another is patently ridiculous.

American business leaders, who tout them-selves as the most ethical businesspeople in the world, should lead the way in ending dumping worldwide. It's in their best interest to do so, for by dumping toxins on the Third World they are actually poisoning the very markets they seek to develop. Perhaps one day they will even see dumping for what it really is—a subtle genocide.

Source: *Mother Jones*, November 1979, pp. 23–27. © Mark Dowie. Reprinted with permission.

QUESTIONS

1. In your view is the title "The Corporate Crime of the Century" a fair and accurate label to apply to the dumping practice? Explain.
2. Regardless of your personal point of view, build an argument against the position taken by Mark Dowie.
3. Mr. Dowie argues that dumping is "rooted in a criminal mentality" and that dumping is really "a subtle genocide." Comment.
4. Dumping has led to charges of racism on the part of American corporate officials and bureaucrats.
   a. Explain that charge.
   b. Do you agree?
5. American firms dump pesticides abroad. How might that practice eventually lead to harm here in America? Could an American firm legally purchase pesticides abroad for use abroad if those pesticides are banned in the United States? Explain.

6. If an American chemical manufacturer were restricted from exporting a product abroad, how might the firm "get around" that restriction?
7. In trade with foreign parties, should Americans be guided by the laws and mores of the importing nation rather than those of the United States? Explain.
8. Is the decision to buy products rejected in America a matter to be left exclusively to the wisdom of the foreign purchaser? Explain.
9. Is an American corporation's social responsibility for every citizen of the world equal to its social responsibility for every American citizen? Explain.
10. Is the export of the American life-style via the sale of our goods abroad an irresponsible imposition of our values on the world, or is it the best and quickest way to world understanding? Or is it neither? Explain.

On the Positive Side of Social Responsibility

We have looked at several categories of suspect corporate conduct. Certainly the Pinto episode and the "dumping" practice have been the subject of unusually hearty complaint from corporate critics. At the same time, it is important that the reader receive a balanced picture that reflects the many virtues (in addition to providing the best products and services at the lowest prices) that the socially responsible firm can visit upon society. Among them:

General Motors purchased $142 million worth of goods and services from more than 700 minority-owned companies [in 1978], more than any other corporation and almost five times the amount it purchased two years earlier.

Control Data Corporation, a Minneapolis computer manufacturer, has built four plants in ghetto areas, providing jobs for minority mothers of school-age children and for black teenagers, who comprise the largest share of the nation's hard-core unemployed.

Coors has recycled more than 500 million pounds of aluminum since 1970, at a cost of more than $75 million. This amounts to about one third of all the aluminum recycled in the United States annually, and . . . [in 1978] it recovered the equivalent of 85 percent of the cans it put into the market.

No corporations have come under as much sustained attack in recent years as the multinationals, which operate all over the globe. Some of them have indeed trampled upon native law, custom, and culture, but many are also working to improve the quality of life in host countries. Some examples:

The Singer Company has helped establish education programs and thriving cottage industries in widely scattered Third World communities. In Mexico, company employees teach inmates of four state prisons sewing skills, which they can use when they are released. The efforts of a local Singer employee have almost single-handedly transformed San Jose Iturbide, a village 150 miles north of Mexico City, from an impoverished farming village into an important market center for the area's thriving knitting industry. And Singer is helping the Brazilian government provide free sewing lessons for 30,000 people in 400 rural towns.

Xerox underwrites production costs of Seasame Street in Spanish and Portuguese for broadcast in Latin America and has pledged $250,000 over 10 years to the Nature Conservancy of Canada, a private organization that acquires and protects natural land areas.

McDonald's organized and financed a telethon in Australia to raise funds for a rehabilitation center for crippled children and for a center in Sydney for deaf and blind children.[31]

It is very important to note that situations such as Ford faced with the Pinto can be handled in ways that guarantee safety, meet society's expectations, and yet minimize harm to the affected company.

The article that follows projects a picture of one company's purely voluntary decision to recall a toy product, even though the toy clearly was not hazardous if used properly.

ONE PRODUCER FINDS RECALL IS BEST POLICY FOR A HAZARDOUS TOY (How Parker Brothers Moved to Pull a Rivet Kit Linked to Deaths of Two Children)

Charles W. Stevens

Beverly, Mass.—Parker Brothers had big plans for Riviton. In its first year on the market, 1977, the kit of plastic parts, rubber rivets and a riveting tool outsold any other toy the company had ever introduced. Children could put together anything from a windmill to an airplane with Riviton, and the kit seemed on its way to becoming the kind of classic toy that parents buy year after year.

But one of the 450,000 Riviton sets bought in 1977 ended up under the Christmas tree of an eight-year-old boy in Menomonee Falls, Wis. He played with it almost daily for three weeks. Then he put one of the quarter-inch-long rubber rivets into his mouth and choked to death.

Parker studied the child's autopsy when it learned of the death last April and concluded the toy was safe. "It was a freak accident," said Randolph G. Barton, the company president. "After all peanuts are the greatest cause of strangulation among children, and nobody advocates banning the peanut."

Ten months later, Mr. Barton changed his view. With Riviton sales well on the way to an expected $8.5 million for the year, a second child strangled on a rivet. And despite a cost that could go as high as $10 million, Mr Barton decided to halt sales and recall the toy. "The decision was very simple," he says "Were we supposed to sit back and wait for death No. 3?"

Bad Press

Recall decisions are seldom very simple, of course. In addition to the lost sales and other expenses involved, the publicity surrounding the recall of one product can often taint many of a company's others. So for most businesses, a recall is the last resort, a path taken only under government pressure.

*   *   *   *   *

As for Parker Brothers, it brought the Rivitons in to be burned before the government agency had even taken the two deaths under consideration. In fact, the product-safety agency says it probably wouldn't have ordered a recall if it had had a chance to; the Riviton met all safety standards. But Parker has no regrets about its recall decision.

Partly, these voluntary recalls are a matter of protecting corporate images, which are especially fragile in the toy industry, observers say. . . .

Undoubtedly, generous juries are also a fac-

tor. Manufacturers are being taken to court more often in product-liability cases, and plaintiffs are winning larger sums—ominous trends for an industry that is finding itself blamed in a rising number of injuries.

*   *   *   *   *

Parker, however, says its recall was prompted mostly by "our sense of moral obligation," in the words of Mr. Barton, whose Grandfather, George S. Parker, founded the company 95 years ago. "Our initial reaction was, 'Recall,' " Mr. Barton says, referring to when the company received word of the second child's death. "We only waited to make sure we weren't reacting in a totally emotional or irrational way."

*   *   *   *   *

"Obviously, the options were to do nothing, to put out a warning and relabel and repackage the toy, or to do all those things and redesign the product," Mr. Barton says. "But the problem with all of those options was that they failed to do anything about the millions of rivets that were in the hands of children."

*   *   *   *   *

All in all, Parker officials are convinced that their recall has made the best of a bad situation. Of 2,000 letters the company received about the move, almost all praised it. One parent wrote that "the only games we're going to have under our Christmas tree this year are going to be Parker Bros. games." . . .

QUESTIONS

1. Can we fairly conclude that Parker Bros. was more socially responsible than was the Ford Motor Company (Pinto), or are the two situations so dissimilar as to deny legitimate comparison? If the former, why do you think Parker Bros. acted so much more quickly than Ford? If the latter, what are the differences in the two situations?

2. Had you been in charge of Parker Bros., following the first child's death would you have responded differently than the company actually did? Explain.

3. Has Xerox deprived its stockholders of rightful earnings by underwriting "Sesame Street" and the Canadian Nature Conser- vancy? Should all companies follow the Xerox example? Explain.

Beyond Social Responsibility

We have reviewed social responsibility as an awkward, ill-defined concept that suits neither its detractors nor its adherents. Trying to do what's "right" is a treacherous course for every human and certainly for businesses not previously expected to look much beyond the commands of the market and the law. These difficulties have led to alternatives and supplements to the social responsibility notion. For example, some scholars have argued for a "public policy" approach that would, in their view, avoid the infirmities of social responsibility while correcting some of the deficiencies of the market. Essentially business, government, and public interest groups would identify and resolve those problems for which the market is inadequate (e.g., negative externalities such as pollution). Thus, with each body representing its interests, decisions based on consensus would emerge. Business would function in both the marketplace and the public policy process. Business would not choose between profits and social responsi- bility. The demands of the market might be met, but at the same time the firm would be subject to the demands of society if its course strayed from that which the citizenry expects.[32]

Business critics place little faith in the public policy process. They fear the business voice will overwhelm the others straining to be heard. Furthermore, social responsibil- ity, dependent as it is on corporate self-regulation and voluntarism, is regarded by the critics as only a part of the package necessary to produce a corporate community fully responsive to society's legitimate expectations. Perhaps the leading reform proposal of the late 1970s was the Corporate Democracy Act as espoused by the Nader organization and some members of Congress. During the Reagan administration that proposal is at least temporarily at rest, but the issues raised are fundamental to the definition of busi- ness' proper role in society. Therefore, it is fitting to close this chapter by looking at an extreme reworking of business' compact with society; a vision that embraces but goes well beyond social responsibility.

THE CASE FOR A CORPORATE DEMOCRACY ACT

Alice Teffer Marlin
Victor Kamber
Jules Bernstein
Mark Green

While the political agenda of the 1970s focused extensively on the size and abuse of big gov- ernment, the political agenda of the 1980s should focus on the size and abuse of big business. The question of who governs our giant corporations and how they in turn govern us—economically, politically, biologically—should be a preeminent issue in a democracy where large institutions are expected to be accountable to their various constituencies.

We believe that this fundamental issue of corporate power warrants federal legislation for several interrelated reasons:

1. *State chartering has failed.* . . . States lure companies into their jurisdictions, in order to generate incorporation fees, by issuing corporation codes that are excessively pro-management. Because Delaware is the worst offender among the states, it has the most business: About one fifth of all Delaware state revenues come from incorporation and annual fees; about half of the *Fortune* 500 are incorporated in tiny Delaware, including Exxon, which has 160 times the annual revenue of its legal parent. . . .

2. *We are in the midst of a corporate crime wave.* . . .

3. *Our largest corporations are private governments.* Edmund Burke's observation that the large companies of his day were states disguised as merchants has relevance today. . . .

Older notions about the clear distinction between the public sector and the private sector should give way to a new conceptualization about the role of the large corporation—viz., there are two forms of government in the United States, the political government and the economic government. The political government is roughly held accountable to its citizens by means of the Constitution and elections. But the economic government is largely unaccountable to its constituencies. . . .

4. *An elite undemocratically runs these economic governments.* Though some laissez-faire theologians argue that corporations are mere "pass-through" devices responding automatically to autonomous consumers in a free market, in fact corporations are entities run by real people who make numerous judgments, which we may roughly divide into two types. First, they decide whether or not to obey the law—which is apparently a difficult choice for many executives. Second, since the law is society's

statement of what constitutes minimally acceptable behavior, there is a huge area of lawful discretion to be exercised: where to locate a plant, whether to fight or cooperate with a unionizing effort, what to produce and how to price it, what legislation to support or oppose, whether to participate in the community or pollute it. Who now makes these judgments? A handful of homogeneous executives, solely. Who should? A combination of executives selected by a representative board, a board gen-

---

The Corporate Democracy Act in Miniature

Title I: Directors and Shareholders. To establish an "independent," "constituency" board of directors, candidates for which are nominated by a nominating committee and are elected by individual shareholders. To provide for independent audit and compensation committees, for Public Policy and Law Compliance Committees, for cumulative voting and for inside and outside lawyers and auditors reporting illegal or probably illegal firm actions to the board.

Title II: Corporate Disclosure. To increase the flow of information to consumers, shareholders and workers about employment patterns, environmental matters, job health and safety, foreign production, directorial performance, shareholder ownership, tax rates, and legal and auditing fees.

Title III: Community Impact Analysis. To require 24-month prenotification if a substantial local employer plans to relocate or close down, to provide for severance benefits to cushion the burden to abandoned employees, and to make available federal assistance to workers who attempt to buy such facilities.

Title IV: "Constitutional" Rights of Employees. To prohibit affected firms from discriminating against or discharging employees for the exercise of "constitutional," civil or legal rights, or other unjust cause.

Title V: Interlocking Directorates. To prohibit anyone from being the director of more than two corporations under this Act.

Title VI: Criminal and Civil Sanctions. To provide for notification and restitution to victims, double damages as fines, disqualification for convicted executives, corporate probation for recidivist companies, penalties for hazardous conduct such as the Hooker Chemical situation, and penalties for supervisors who knowingly tolerate subordinate illegality.

Title VII: Jurisdiction and Penalties. To require that companies with more than $250 million in assets or sales or more than 5,000 employees come under the jurisdiction of this Act, that interested constituencies have easy access to court to enforce their rights, and that relevant agencies promulgate all necessary rules and regulations.

—the authors

uinely elected by beneficial shareholders, and other "stakeholders" of the corporation such as workers and communities where companies are located.

Really Realistic

The provisions of the suggested Corporate Democracy Act (see the accompanying box) are both reformist and realistic, for with few exceptions they have either been adopted by some company or state or Western nation. The Act applies only to the largest 800 or so nonfinancial corporations; its jurisdiction therefore reaches those "private governments" that have little in common with small- and medium-sized businesses. . . .

Rather than depend on a new bureaucracy to police its provisions, the Act is largely self-executory. Citizens who have been injured by the nonperformance of a standard do not go to Washington; they go to court. The constituencies of the corporation are given more power to know about and to participate in company affairs, and they have the right of access to court to effect that power. . . .

. . . For decades the abuses of the American economy have been addressed by remedial regulation affecting the *external* relationships of the corporation; that is, don't pollute, don't price fix, don't advertise deceptively. The Corporate Democracy Act of 1980 seeks to reform the *internal* governance structure of our largest corporations so that, consistent with a market economy, companies exercise their power and discretion in more democratic and accountable ways. . . .

Source: *Business and Society Review* 34 (Summer 1980), pp. 55–58. (Four contributors helped write this proposal: Mark Green, *Congress Watch;* Alice Teffer Marlin, Council on Economic Priorities; Victor Kamber, AFL–CIO; Jules Bernstein, Laborers' International Union. A lengthier version, prepared for *Big Business Day,* April 17, 1980, is available from Americans Concerned About Corporate Power.)

QUESTIONS

1. The Corporate Democracy Act calls for constitutional rights for employees. Professors Gerald Keim, Barry Baysinger, and Roger Meiners challenge that proposal:

   The advantages of selectively giving up freedom through voluntary contractual agreement should seem peculiar only to those who prefer to live in anarchy. Living in civilized society necessarily involves a strategic utility-maximizing sacrifice of total personal freedom. Why this should not extend to the industrial social order is not clear. The proponents of the Corporate Democracy Act can only be asserting that the trade-off workers have made between civil rights on the job and pecuniary income is not to their liking. If complete freedom rules the industrial setting, little output would be produced and workers would suffer.[33]

   a. Must we sacrifice significant constitutional freedoms in order to hold a job?

   b. Would freedom in the workplace result in reduced productivity?

2. Critics of the Corporate Democracy Act argue that it represents a shift of power from corporate directors and managers to the federal government rather than to employees, shareholders, and consumers who

are purported to be the chief beneficiaries of the act.

a. Do you agree? Explain.

b. Should the authority now residing in corporate hands be shifted, at least in part, to the federal government?

Additional Cases for Discussion

BUFFALO CREEK

Background

Buffalo Creek, West Virginia, is a mountain hollow, some 17 miles in length. Three small forks come together at the top of the hollow, to form the creek itself. In early 1972, approximately 5,000 people lived in this area, in what amounted to a continuous string of 16 villages.

Middle Fork served for several years as the site of an enormous pile of mine waste, known as a "dam" to local residents and an "impoundment" to the Buffalo Mining Company. The impoundment was there because it solved two important disposal problems for the company:

1. Each time four tons of coal are removed from the ground, one ton of slag—a wide assortment of waste materials—is also removed and must be disposed of.
2. Additionally, more than 500,000 gallons of water are required to prepare 4 tons of coal for shipment, and this, too, must be disposed of.

The Buffalo Mining Company began to deposit its slag in Middle Fork as early as 1957 and by 1972 was dumping approximately 1,000 tons per day. Traditionally, the company had deposited its solid waste into Middle Fork and its liquid effluent into nearby streams. However, by the 1960s coal operators were under a great deal of pressure to retain this water until some of the impurities had settled out of it. The companies were also beginning to see the utility in having a regular supply of processing water on hand. Buffalo Mining Company re-

sponded to this by dumping new slag on top of old, in such a way as to form barriers behind which waste water could be stored and reused.

Middle Fork was described as an immense black trough of slag, silt, and water, a waste sink arranged in such a way as to create small reservoirs behind the first two impoundments and a large lake behind the third.

The Episode

According to subsequent accounts, during the night of February 25, 1972, Buffalo Mining Company officials continually monitored the Middle Fork waste site. They were reportedly uneasy because the lake water seemed to be rising dangerously close to the dam crest. The past few days had been wet ones, but such seasonal precipitation was not considered unusual. Toward dawn, company officials were concerned enough to have a spillway cut across the surface of the barrier in an effort to relieve pressure. The level continued to rise, but the company issued no public warnings. Testimony disclosed that the senior official on the site met with two deputy sheriffs who arrived on the scene to aid in an evacuation in the event of trouble. The official contended at the time that everyting was under control, and the deputies left.

Just before 8 AM, February 26, a heavy-equipment operator inspected the surface of the dam and found that not only was the water within inches of the crest—which he already knew—but that the structure had softened dramatically since the last inspection.

Within minutes the dam had collapsed. The 132 million gallons of waste water and solids roared through the breach. The wave reportedly set off a series of explosions, raising mushroom-shaped clouds into the air, and picking up "everything in its path." One million tons of solid waste were said to be caught in the flow.

Impact

A 20 to 30-foot tidal wave traveling up to 30 miles per hour devastated Buffalo Creek's 16 small communities. More than 125 people perished and hundreds of others were injured. Over 4,000 survived, but their 1,000 homes, as well as most of their possessions, were destroyed.

A few hundred of the 4,000 survivors decided not to accept the settlement for real property damage offered by the coal company as reimbursement. Instead, they brought suit against the Pittston Corporation [which owned Buffalo Mining].

On Wednesday, June 26, 1974, two and a half years after the incident, the 600 or so Buffalo Creek plaintiffs were awarded $13.5 million by the Pittston Corporation in an out-of-court settlement.

Source: Library of Congress Congressional Research Service. Background material for hearings on H.R. 7040, Subcommittee on Crime of the Committee on the Judiciary, House of Representatives, 96th Congress, 2d session, May 1980.

QUESTIONS

1. What arguments might Buffalo Mining and Pittston raise in their defense?
2. Argue on Pittston's behalf that it should not be a party to any lawsuits arising from the dam break.
3. *a.* Assume you own a fleet of taxicabs and wish to minimize your potential loss in the event of an accident. What corporate structure would you utilize to accomplish your goal? Explain.
   b. Will you succeed in minimizing your losses? Explain.
4. In your judgment were Buffalo Mining and Pittston guilty of criminal behavior?
5. According to a 1973 account in *The Nation:*
   a. Three different government agencies laid the responsibility for the flood squarely on the shoulders of Buffalo Mining and Pittston. Buffalo Mining drew a $25 fine for breaking a U.S. Bureau of Mines regulation, and a mild scolding from the U.S. Department of the Interior. (Thruston Morton, who sits on the Pittston board of directors, is the brother of Rogers C. B. Morton, Secretary of the Interior.) Several Buffalo Mining officials were required to answer questions before a Logan County grand jury, but emerged unscathed.[34]
   b. How do you explain the mild public sector response?
6. Was the settlement figure of $13.5 million (of which almost $3 million went to the plaintiffs' lawyers) a just sum? Is that sum sufficient to discourage such conduct in the future? Was the nearly $3 million legal fee fair in light of the firm's more than 40,000 hours of labor? Explain.

FIRESTONE 500

Background

Firestone's involvement in the manufacture of steel-belted radial tires began in the early 1970s when U.S. automobile designers sought from the domestic tire industry a product that would help achieve better gasoline mileage (reduced rolling resistance) and provide a better ride. Radial tires meet these criteria and, in addition, when they are properly made and used, they last longer through improved tread wear and greater resistance to road hazards. With the domestic automobile manufacturers moving toward steel-belted radials, Firestone moved aggressively into the steel-belted radial "original equipment" market. Largely by speedy adaptation of existing equipment Firestone became the first domestic tire manufacturer to place these tires in the original equipment market in large quantities. . . .

Firestone began marketing its first generation of steel-belted radials in 1971 and introduced the Firestone 500, also considered a first generation steel-belted tire, in 1972.

The Cause for Concern

In 1976 the Center For Auto Safety, a private nonprofit consumer interest organization, began to notice that they were receiving a disproportionately large number of complaints on Firestone steel-belted radials. When the complaints on Firestone steel-belted radials continued into 1977, the center conducted a review of all its consumer reports on all tire failures for a selected period of time to compare Firestone tires with those of other companies. The data showed that at that time 50 percent of all tire complaint letters received by the Center For Auto Safety were on Firestone tires and that the vast majority of those were on steel-belted radials. Throughout this time the center also forwarded copies of the Firestone steel-belted radial complaints to the National Highway Traffic Safety Administration and requested a defect investigation. However, the Center apparently did not investigate the complaints, but simply accepted them all at face value (although in some cases there evidently were mitigating circumstances).

Alarmed by the performance of Firestone tires, the Center For Auto Safety, on November 28, 1977, wrote directly to Mario DiFederico, president of the Firestone Tire and Rubber Company, and pointed out that the complaint rate on Firestone tires was three times the average of their market share and that nearly all complaints concerned steel-belted radials. The Center further provided Firestone with copies of the complaints included in its study, based on tires manufactured both by Firestone and by other companies. The Center also suggested that Firestone should shift half of its advertising budget into quality control. Firestone did not respond to the Center regarding this information.

On December 22, 1977, the National Highway Traffic Safety Administration (NHTSA) first asked, then ordered Firestone to provide defect information on Firestone steel-belted radial tires, including lists of accidents, injuries, and deaths reported to have been caused by defective tires. On April 26, 1978, Firestone submitted a list of 213 accidents. By this time the Firestone 500 was in the final stages of being phased out of production on a size-by-size basis, a process which was completed in May of 1978. . . .

Congressional Findings: A Serious Safety Hazard

Congressional inquiry into the safety of Firestone steel-belted radial tires commenced with preparation for hearings by the Subcommittee on Oversight and Investigations of the Committee on Interstate and Foreign Commerce in April 1978. At that time several reports of deaths and injury caused by failure of the Firestone tire had come before the subcommittee. After hearing testimony from several witnesses, including representatives of Firestone, and examining material submitted by Firestone at the subcommittee's request, the subcommittee concluded that Firestone 500 steel-belted radial tires presented an unreasonable risk of continuing accidents, injuries, and death to the motoring public and should be immediately recalled. This conclusion was based on the following findings, quoted from the report of the Subcommittee on Oversight and Investigations:

1. Failure of the Firestone 500 Steel-Belted Radial have caused and are continuing to cause an extraordinary number of accidents, injuries, and deaths. Accidents attributable to the "500" numbers in the thousands, injuries in the hundreds, and known fatalities as of August 1978, 34. . . .

Regardless of the mix of product defect and other contributing factors in each case, an overall pattern of Firestone "500" failures associated with human destruction is undeniable.

2. The rate of failure of Firestone 500 Steel-Belted Radial tires, while not precisely known, is exceedingly high. Evidence of a high rate of failure includes:

   a. The high adjustment rate for the Firestone 500 Steel-Belted Radial.

      An "adjustment rate" is the percentage of tires produced by a company which it accepts back from customers because of some problem with tires that occurs before useful tread is worn.

      * * * * *

   b. The significant number of claims settled by Firestone by means of cash payments for damage caused by tire failures.

      * * * * *

   c. The high average number of failures reported per customer.

      In 834 letters received by the subcommittee over the 10-week period following the subcommittee's hearings, users of Firestone 500 Steel-Belted Radials have experienced a total of 3,384 separate tire failures, for an average of 4.06 failures each.

   d. The experience of fleet operators, whose vehicles equipped with Firestone 500 Steel-Belted Radials have experienced large numbers of similar failures. . . .

Firestone's Response

Firestone denied wrongdoing, responding to the congressional investigation and allegations of a defective product, first [by arguing] that radial tire failure is often due to driving with improperly low inflation pressures. Secondly, Firestone cited the considerable body of adverse publicity concerning alleged problems generated by the media which stirred up concern that it claimed, would not otherwise have existed.

Firestone also offered additional explanations for the higher than ordinary adjustment rate for the "500" as follows:

Firestone's larger production of steel-

belted radials when the tire first came into heavy demand for installation on new cars;

The longer life of radials allowing for greater opportunity for disablement;

The problems owners had in adjusting to the "underinflated look" of a radial; and

The fact that Firestone extended more liberal adjustment policies for the "500's" as its top-of-the-line tire.

In the nature of a rebuttal, the subcommittee report on the hearings concluded that Firestone cannot claim to have cornered more than its share of the Nation's underinflators as purchasers of the "500." Underinflation might account for some, but not all, of the high adjustment rate for the "500."

Corporate Knowledge of the Problem?

Data provided by Firestone . . . suggests that Firestone may have known as early as 1973 that large numbers of low-mileage tires were being returned to dealers for various reasons. In that year, 5.48 percent of Firestone's 1972 production of over a million steel-belted radial 500s were adjusted, including many for failure problems (although the precise number of failures cannot be determined).

Additional evidence that Firestone may have been aware of major failure problems with their "500" steel-belted radial tires as early as November 1972 came from documents released by NHTSA after the Firestone recall decision reached by NHTSA in the fall of 1978. According to a description of these in the *Washington Post,* a memorandum to the then-vice president for tire production, Marlo DiFederico, on November 2, 1972, Firestone's director of tire development, Thomas Robertson, warned that problems with the steel-belted tires were so bad that the company was in danger of losing its business with Chevrolet because of separation failures.

Finally, Firestone confirmed that it had knowledge of tire test results in late 1975, indicating that some of its steel-belted radial tires failed to measure up to acceptable standards after a year or two of storage. This disclosure came in July 1978 after the *Akron Beacon Journal* had obtained computer printouts of the results.

Epilogue

Citing thousands of reported failures, the National Highway Traffic Safety Administration issued an initial determination on July 9, 1978, finding Firestone 500 Steel-Belted Radial tires defective. Subsequently, a recall was ordered on October 20 and a final agreement was signed on November 29, 1978, between Firestone and NHTSA ironing out details of the recall. Under this agreement the company would recall and replace free all five-rib 500 Steel-

Belted Radials (including private brands of the same internal construction) manufactured and sold from September 1, 1975, to January 1, 1977, and all seven-rib 500 Steel-Belted Radials made and sold between September 1, 1975, and May 1, 1976. This recall would involve some 7.5 million tires estimated still to be in service. In addition, Firestone agreed to offer an exchange of new tires at half price for some 6 million Steel-Belted Radials sold prior to the three-year legal limitation on free replacements, and not covered by the recall.

Source: Library of Congress Congressional Research Service. Background material for hearings on H.R. 7040. Subcommittee on Crime of the Committee on the Judiciary, House of Representatives, 96th Congress, 2d session, May 1980.

QUESTIONS

1. *Time* magazine Washington Correspondent Jonathan Beaty, who studied hundreds of Firestone documents, reported:

   Internal Firestone corporate records turned over to the NHTSA . . . show that top Firestone managers—including President Mario A. Di Federico, who has just announced his resignation—were deeply enmeshed in the several years' effort to deal with and correct the failure problems of the 500 and were, from the beginning, aware of the tire's flaws. The documents show that while Di Federico and virtually all other top executives at one time or another were receiving detailed reports about tire failure from their own production people and major corporate buyers like General Motors and Atlas Tire Co., they still assured the public that the 500 had no safety defects, and were not telling stockholders of the problems.[35]

   a. What legitimate concerns might have led Firestone to withhold evidence of problems with the 500 series?

   b. Does the duty to stockholders require officers to defend the company with all available, legal tactics? Explain.

   c. Must the officer operate, not in terms of personal ethical standards, but in response to the needs of the company? Explain.

   d. Place yourself in the roles of the Firestone officers. Would you have revealed information regarding these flaws? Explain.

   e. If you would not, are you an unethical person? Explain.

2. According to a Knight-Ridder account, in early 1978 Firestone collected its remaining 500 tires from factories in the southeast and shipped them to South Florida and Alabama for sale at half price.[36] The sale came a month after the National Highway Traffic Safety Administration announced an investigation of the tires. A Firestone spokesman said the company continued to believe the tires to be safe. Thus the disposal sale was, in the company's eyes, legitimate.

   a. Do you agree that the sale was legitimate?

   b. Was the sale a wise management strategy? Explain.

3. Would you consider it unethical to continue selling used Firestone 500 radials following the recall? Would the ethical problems, if any, be removed by warning each purchaser of the recall? Explain.

4. According to a *Fortune* account, Fire-

stone's vice president and general counsel, John Floberg, made the following arguments in testifying before a House subcommittee:

At one point, Floberg stated that the 500 was one of two steel-belted radials that had been rated above all others in a *Consumer Reports* survey. But Lowell Dodge, the subcommittee counsel, pointed out that the ratings, which appeared in the October 1973 issue, had been made according to tread wear, not safety.

A while later, Floberg tried to make the point that the industry encouraged consumers to take proper care of their radial tires. He cited a television ad that Firestone had run on the subject. But, as he conceded, this was not a very potent example, since the advertisement had been forced on Firestone by the Federal Trade Commission, in partial settlement of a lawsuit.[37]

a. Are "half-truths" of this sort characteristic of the corporate community?

b. Or is such behavior simply characteristic of human nature? Explain.

5. Are businesspeople unprepared to deal with ethical dilemmas such as those of the Pinto and the Firestone 500? Explain. How might businesspeople become better prepared?

6. How is it that "good" people sometimes do that which they know to be "bad"?

Chapter Questions

1. According to many published accounts[38] confirmed by National Highway Traffic Safety Administration studies, the Ford Motor Company knew of serious problems in certain of its cars' fan blades and transmissions, but declined for several years to acknowledge those problems. Defective fan blades resulting in 1 death and 11 injuries were eventually recalled. According to the NHTSA study, slipping transmissions (Ford cars allegedly slipped into reverse gear after having been left in park) resulted in 98 deaths and 1,710 injuries. Some evidence supports Ford's contention that the problem lies in the driver's failure to shift entirely into park. On the other hand, Ford test track technicians began putting blocks behind the rear wheels of autos after one auto left idling "in park" lurched backward and ran over the foot of Ford engineer Frank Hare.[39] In December, 1980 Ford agreed to send a dashboard warning sticker and a letter to each owner, explaining the possible hazard and suggesting precautions. Then in 1985 the Center for Auto Safety, a consumer lobbying organization, sued the federal Department of Transportation to force a new inquiry into the transmissions. The center claimed that at least 80 deaths have been linked to the transmissions since 1980. The center estimated that 13.9 million of the transmissions remain in use.[40]

   a. Do the Pinto, fan blade, and transmission episodes suggest insensitivity to the public welfare on the part of Ford, or is the complexity of contemporary technology and bureaucracy so extreme that such problems are inevitable?

   b. If the former, how do you account for that insensitivity?

   c. If the latter, what steps may be taken to alleviate the troublesome conditions?

2. Denis Goulet, holder of a chaired professorship at Notre Dame, has argued that we will find no facile resolution to the conflict between the values of a just society and the sharply opposing values of successful corporations.

   a. Do you agree that the values of a just society oppose those of successful corporations? Explain.

   b. Can no easy solution be found? Explain.

3. In November 1980 a fire in the Las Vegas MGM Grand Hotel resulted in 84 deaths and 500 injuries. Prior to the fire Las Vegas fire chief Roy Parrish said fire officials and building inspectors had met with hotel officials urging the expansion of the sprinkler system, even though not required under existing law. (At the time of the fire, sprinklers were installed in the basement and the 1st and 26th floors.) Hotel officials declined.
    a. In this case is the legal standard also the proper ethical standard? Explain.
    b. Safety is purchased. Is the failure to make that purchase unethical? Explain.
    c. How can you decide when the cost of doing right is too high?

4. In criticizing General Motors, Ralph Nader is reported to have said:

    > Someday we'll have a legal system that will criminally indict the president of General Motors for these outrageous crimes. But not as long as this country is populated by people who fritter away their citizenship by watching TV, playing bridge and Mah-Jongg, and just generally being slobs.[41]

    a. Is the citizenry generally unconcerned about unethical corporate conduct? Explain.
    b. To the extent that corporations engage in misdeeds, does the fault really lie with the corporate community or with society at large? Explain.

5. Air bags have been demonstrated to be effective in preventing death and injury in autos. In 1980 GM estimated it would save $20 million by delaying introduction of air bags on its large models from 1982 to 1983.
    a. Are auto manufacturers ethically obligated to offer air bags as an option? Explain.
    b. Should government restrictions be lifted to allow manufacturers to produce cars entirely free of safety devices (padding, safety glass, belts) if the market demands? Explain.

6. Should corporate chief executive officers submit to press conferences on a regular basis? Explain.

7. Must the corporation adjust to changing societal sentiments (social responsibility), or is the future health of the nation dependent on the corporate community manifesting the strength to adhere to traditional free market principles? Explain.

8. Is the ethical climate of business improving or declining? Explain.

9. Should companies engage in moral judgments? For example, if during the Vietnam War the Dow Chemical Company leadership had decided that one of its products, napalm (an incendiary gel), was an immoral weapon, should the company have ceased production? Explain.

10. In 1977, actress and social activist Jane Fonda criticized the Dow Chemical Company in a speech at Central Michigan University. Dow then notified the university that it would receive no more company financial aid until officials of the two institutions could meet to discuss the use of company grants. Evaluate the wisdom of the Dow position.

11. You are the sole owner of a manufacturing firm employing 500 semiskilled laborers in the Harlem borough of New York City. Your present profits are sufficient to maintain the firm as a viable enterprise, but insufficient to permit expansion. A study reveals that moving the firm to Houston, Texas, would double your profits to what might be labeled a "reasonable" level when measured by industry norms. Expansion, including the addition of 200 jobs, seems likely in Houston. The current unemployment rate in Harlem exceeds 20 percent while that in Houston is beneath 4 percent (and thus Houston is effectively a full-employment economy).
    a. Would the socially responsible businessperson move the firm to Houston? Explain.
    b. What would you do?
    c. Would your answers be different were the firm owned by thousands of shareholders? Explain.

12. You are the sole owner of a neighborhood drugstore that stocks brands of toothpaste. Assume that scientific testing has established that one brand is clearly superior to all others in preventing tooth decay.

   a. Would you remove from the shelves all brands except the one judged best as to decay prevention? Explain.

   b. What alternative measures could you take?

   c. Should the toothpaste manufacturers be required to reveal all available data regarding the effectiveness of their products? Explain.

13. A "quick stop" food market in a residential neighborhood stocks glue. Newspaper reports indicate that young children in the neighborhood have been discovered sniffing glue to "get high." If you owned the market, would you decline to sell glue to children? Explain.

14. Mark Green argued for federal chartering of corporations:

   > It makes as much sense for states to print money or passports as to issue the legal birth certificates of corporations that market products interstate, if not internationally. The results of this historical anomaly, in the words of a 1969 law, is a kind of "law for sale." States lure companies into their jurisdictions, and thus generate incorporation fees, by adopting corporation codes that are excessively pro-management.[42]

   Comment on Green's statement.

15. Mark Green argues for the Corporate Democracy Act:

   > The real issue is autocracy versus democracy. For decades the abuses of the American economy have been addressed by remedial regulation affecting the *external* relationships of the corporation; that is, don't pollute, don't price fix, don't advertise deceptively. The Corporate Democracy Act of 1980 seeks to reform the *internal* governance structure of our largest corporations so that, consistent with a market economy, companies exercise their power and discretion in more democratic and accountable ways.[43]

   What is your reaction to Green's position?

16. Approximately $10 million annually is expended for alcohol ads in college newspapers. Many millions more are expended in other youth-oriented publications such as *National Lampoon* and *Rolling Stone*. The beer industry sponsors many campus athletic contests (e.g., Budweiser sponsored the 1982 University of Tennessee Sorority Volleyball tournament). And brewers have established promotional relationships with rock bands, including The Who. Is beer and liquor advertising directed to the youth market unethical? Explain.

17. Many countries curb alcoholic beverage advertising. Quebec forbids endorsements by famous personalities. Ecuador has banned such ads prior to 9 P.M. Finland forbids all alcohol ads. Even news pictures displaying bottle labels are impermissible. Advertising of "hard" liquor is forbidden on American TV. Should the United States banish all advertising for alcoholic beverages?[44] Explain.

18. Professor Albert Huebner decries American exports of tobacco to the Third World:

   > As efforts to expose and to stop the irresponsible promotion of bottle-feeding have grown, a new invasion of many of the same countries has begun. Transnational tobacco companies are vigorously stepping up sales efforts in the Third World, which is now seen as the major growth area for their products. These efforts are likely to be more intensive, more successful in achieving their goal, and more disastrous for the health of people in the countries involved than the breast to bottle campaign.[45]

   a. Is the promotion and sale of tobacco products in Third World nations socially irresponsible behavior? Explain.

   b. Should the U.S. government attempt to curb such promotion and sales? Explain.

19. Are episodes such as the Pinto, the Firestone 500, dumping, and Buffalo Creek merely regrettable aberrations, not at all characteristic of corporate conduct and values generally? Explain.

20. Former General Motors Vice President John Z. DeLorean wrote in his book, *On a Clear Day You Can See General Motors:*

> It seemed to me then, and still does now, that the system of American business often produces wrong, immoral, and irresponsible decisions, even though the personal morality of the people running the business is often above reproach. The system has a different morality as a group than the people do as individuals, which permits it willfully to produce ineffective or dangerous products, deal dictatorially and often unfairly with suppliers, pay bribes for business, abrogate the rights of employment, or tamper with the democratic process of government through illegal political contributions.[46]

   a. How can the corporate "group" possess values at odds with those of the individual managers?

   b. Is De Lorean merely offering a convenient rationalization for corporate misdeeds? Explain.

   c. Realistically, can one expect to preserve individual values when employed in a corporate group? Explain.

21. Do you agree or disagree with the following statements.

   a. "Social responsibility is good business only if it is also good public relations and/or preempts government interference."

   b. "The social responsibility debate is the result of the attempt of liberal intellectuals to make a moral issue of business behavior."

   c. "'Profit' is really a somewhat ineffective measure of business's social effectiveness."

   d. "The social responsibility of business is to 'stick to business.'"[47]

Notes

1. Steven N. Brenner and Earl A. Molander, "Is the Ethics of Business Changing?," *Harvard Business Review* 55, no. 1 (January–February 1977), pp. 57, 59.

2. Ibid., p. 68.

3. "Mounting Public Pressure for Corporate Social Responsibility," *ORC Public Opinion Index,* Opinion Research Corporation (Princeton, New Jersey: January 1974), as reported in Lyman E. Ostlund, "Attitudes of Managers toward Corporate Social Responsibility," *California Management Review* 19, no. 4 (Summer 1977), p. 35.

4. Keith Davis and Robert L. Blomstrom, *Business and Society: Environment and Responsibility,* 3d ed. (New York: McGraw-Hill, 1975), p. 6.

5. Kenneth R. Andrews, *The Concept of Corporate Strategy* (Homewood, Ill.: Dow Jones-Irwin, 1971), p. 120.

6. Milton Friedman, *Capitalism and Freedom* (Chicago: University of Chicago Press, 1962), p. 133.

7. Keith Davis, "The Case for and against Business Assumption of Social Responsibilities," *Academy of Management Journal* 16, no. 2 (June 1973), p. 312.

8. Henry C. Wallich and John J. McGowan, "Stockholder Interest and the Corporation's Role in Social Policy," in William J. Baumol et al., *A New Rationale for Corporate Social Policy* (New York: Committee for Economic Development, 1970), pp. 39–59.

9. Lyman E. Ostlund, "Attitudes of Managers toward Corporate Social Responsibility," *California Management Review* 19, no. 4 (Summer 1977), p. 35.

10. Kamal M. Abouzeid and Charles N. Weaver, "Social Responsibility in the Corporate Goal Hierarchy," *Business Horizons* 21, no. 3 (June 1978), p. 29.

11. Frederick D. Sturdivant and James L. Ginter, "Corporate Social Responsiveness—Management Attitudes and Economic Performance," *California Management Review* 19, no. 3 (Spring 1977), p. 30.

12. Ibid., p. 38.

13. See Philip I. Cochran and Robert Wood, "Corporate Responsibility and Financial Performance," *Academy of Management Journal* 27, no. 1 (March 1984), p. 42, for an excellent study of the issue and survey of previous research.

14. Gordon J. Alexander and Rogene A. Buchholz, "Corporate Social Responsibility and Stock Market Performance," *Academy of Management Journal* 21, no. 3 (September 1978), p. 479.

15. S. Prakash Sethi, "Dimensions of Corporate Social Performance: An Analytical Framework," *California Management Review* 17, no. 3 (Spring 1975), p. 58.

16. *The Nation,* March 29, 1980, pp. 356–57.

17. "Is Pinto a Criminal?" *Regulation,* March–April, 1980, p. 21.

18. Andy Pasztor, "Pinto Criminal Trial of Ford Motor Co. Opens Up Broad Issues," *The Wall Street Journal,* January 4, 1980, p. 1, 23.

19. Ibid.

20. "Crime in the Suites," *Time,* June 10, 1985, p. 56.

21. Ibid., pp. 56–57.

22. John E. Conklin, *"Illegal but Not Criminal"—Business Crime in America* (Englewood Cliffs, N.J.: Prentice-Hall, 1977), p. 4.

23. Philip Taubman, "U.S. Attack on Corporate Crime Yields Handful of Cases in 2 years," *The New York Times,* July 15, 1979, p. 1.

24. Conklin, "Illegal But Not Criminal," p. 4.

25. "Brokers Say Rate War Cost $25 Million in May," *The New York Times,* September 11, 1975, pp. 35 and 39, as reported in Conklin, *"Illegal But Not Criminal,"* p. 5.

26. The President's Commission on Law Enforcement and Administration of Justice, *The Challenge of Crime in a Free Society* (Washington, D.C.: U.S. Government Printing Office, 1967), p. 5, as reported in Conklin, *"Illegal but Not Criminal,"* p. 7.

27. "The Increase in Bank Thefts," *The New York Times,* October 19, 1975, p. 6, as reported in Conklin, *"Illegal but Not Criminal,"* p. 7.

28. Irwin Ross, "How Lawless Are Big Companies?" *Fortune,* December 1, 1980, p. 56.

29. The summary of Union Carbide's report is drawn from "Union Carbide Points the Finger at Itself," *Business Week,* April 1, 1985, p. 32.

30. "Union Carbide Fights for Its Life," *Business Week,* December 24, 1984, pp. 52 and 56. This account of the Bhopal tragedy is based on the foregoing *Business Week* article as well as: "Early Steps to a Carbide Settlement," *Business Week,* December 28, 1984, p. 48, and "Bhopal Infant Mortality Rate High," *Waterloo Courier,* February 18, 1985, p. A-3.

31. Edwin McDowell, "Bridging the Communications Gap," *Saturday Review,* September 29, 1979, pp. 16, 18.

32. Rogene Buchholz, "An Alternative to Social Responsibility," *MSU Business Topics* 25, no. 3 (Summer 1977), p. 12.

33. Gerald Keim, Barry Baysinger, and Roger Meiners, "The Corporate Democracy Act: Would the Majority Rule?" *Business Horizons* 24, no. 2, (March–April 1981), pp. 30, 33.

34. Tom Nugent, "Bureaucracy of Disasters," *The Nation,* June 18, 1973, p. 785–86.

35. "Forewarnings of Fatal Flaws," *Time,* June 25, 1979, p. 58.

36. Susan Bitterman, "Tires on Sale after Safety Questioned," *Lexington, Kentucky Leader,* April 13, 1978, p. C-1.

37. Arthur Louis, "Lessons from the Firestone Fracas," *Fortune,* August 28, 1978, p. 44.

38. See, e.g., "Firm Knew Hazard, Didn't Recall Cars," *Lexington, Kentucky Leader,* September 1, 1977, p. D-9, and "Record Recall Averted over Ford Transmissions," *Lexington, Kentucky Leader,* December 31, 1980, p. B-5.

39. "9 Fatalities Linked to Transmissions," *Lexington, Kentucky Leader,* June 2, 1978, p. C-5.

40. "Lawsuit Would Force Probe of Ford Auto Transmissions," *Des Moines (Iowa) Register,* September 10, 1985, p. 4A.

41. Charles McCarry, *Citizen Nader* (New York: Saturday Review Press, 1972), p. 301.

42. Mark Green, "The Case for Corporate Democracy," *Regulation,* May–June 1980, p. 20.

43. Ibid., p. 25.

44. Michael Jacobson, Robert Atkins, and George Hochers, "Booze Merchants Cheer on Teenage Drinking," *Business and Society Review,* no. 46 (Summer 1983), p. 46.

45. Albert Huebner, "Tobacco's Lucrative Third World Invasion," *Business and Society Review,* no. 35 (Fall 1980), p. 49.

46. John Z. DeLorean with J. Patrick Wright, "Bottom-Line Fever at General Motors," (excerpted from *On a Clear Day You Can See General Motors*), *The Washington Monthly,* January 1980, pp. 26–27.

47. Brenner and Molander, "Ethics of Business," p. 68.

15

Consumer Protection

Introduction

Consumer abuse episodes like the following "Great Engine Switch" enrage the consuming public and, in many instances, exact a heavy price in personal injuries and in dollars. Consumer protection organizations argue that wrongs against the buyer pervade American commercial practice.

THE GREAT ENGINE SWITCH AND OTHER MAGIC TRICKS PERFORMED BY THE ONE-AND-ONLY AUTO INDUSTRY

Joseph Siwek couldn't have known back in November 1976 that his trip to the dealer for routine servicing on his new Oldsmobile Delta 88 would cost General Motors nearly $40 million. Seems a small problem cropped up. Siwek's Oldsmobile, the mechanic told him, had a Chevrolet 350-cubic-inch V8, and the Oldsmobile oil filters and fan belts that the dealer stocked wouldn't fit.

Siwek, angry about the engine switch, complained to the Illinois Attorney General. His complaint, and the ensuing investigation, received nationwide news coverage. And that, in turn, prompted other owners of various models of 1977 Oldsmobiles to check their cars for evidence of GM's sleight-of-hand. Soon the attorneys general of all 50 states were receiving complaints from motorists who had discovered lowly Chevrolet engines lurking under Oldsmobile hoods. Some of the motorists said they

had been buying Oldsmobiles for decades, primarily because of the heavily touted "Rocket" V8s. Some said they felt humiliated because they had paid an Oldsmobile price for a "glorified Chevrolet." All believed that GM had done them dirty.

Beyond the Olds

The ripples continued to spread across GM's troubled waters. Many buyers of 1977 Buicks and Pontiacs soon discovered that the 350-cubic-inch V8s in their cars were also Chevrolet V8s. Further, the 305-cubic-inch V8s found in some Oldsmobiles, Buicks, and Pontiacs also turned out to be (you guessed it) Chevrolet engines. But since Buick and Pontiac hadn't been hyping the superiority of their engines, most states felt that there was no clear-cut evidence of deception with those two makes. Thus, the state attorneys general, working together through the National Association of Attorneys General, concentrated their legal efforts against Oldsmobile.

General Motors conceded that a shortage of Oldsmobile V8s had prompted the substitution of Chevrolet V8s but denied any wrongdoing. The 350-cubic-inch V8s made by Chevrolet and Oldsmobile were of similar quality, GM insisted. The attorneys general reported that the Environmental Protection Agency's 1977 fuel-economy figures indicated that the Oldsmobile engine delivered one or two mpg more than the Chevrolet engine. Even more important, they pointed out, Oldsmobile had been building buyer loyalty since 1949 by advertising that its "Rocket" engines were uniquely reliable.

Even if GM could have proved that Chevrolet engines were as good as Oldsmobile engines, and that Oldsmobile advertising had been, well, perhaps a little too enthusiastic, it would hardly have mattered. What did matter was that Oldsmobile buyers were led to believe that their cars would have a superior engine—specifically, a "Rocket" engine—and that the buyers were deceived. Many owners of hybrid "Chevmobiles," for example, reported seeing the "Rocket" engine mentioned in sales brochures or other promotional material in dealer showrooms when they bought their car. And there was no evidence that GM had instructed Oldsmobile dealers to inform buyers of the switch; a questionnaire sent by the Wisconsin Motor Vehicle Division to owners of Oldsmobiles with Chevrolet V8s indicated that 97 percent were unaware of the engine switch until after they had purchased their car.

Ohio Attorney General William J. Brown added a touch of irony when telling CU [Consumers Union] of a trip he'd made to Michigan to meet with Oldsmobile officials: On the roof of an Oldsmobile building he saw a large blinking sign that said "Home of the Rocket engine." "I believe," said Brown, "that the sign has since been taken down."

If each attorney general had acted independently, many states might not have been able to afford to take on a corporate giant such as GM. At best, it might have been several years before the consumers' complaints were re-solved. But, by combining their efforts, the attorneys general soon convinced GM of the need to make restitution.

Last April, GM offered to let dissatisfied owners of Oldsmobiles, Buicks, and Pontiacs with Chevrolet V8s return their car and obtain credit of their purchase price toward a new 1977 car of the same make; purchasers would have to pay eight cents for each mile they had driven their car. Alternatively, owners could keep their car and have the warranty on the engine and drivetrain extended to three years or 36,000 miles without charge.

Most of the attorneys general rejected the so-called eight-cent offer. Maryland Attorney General Francis B. Burch set forth some of the reasons:

• Owners who swapped cars and who wanted V8s might still wind up with Chevrolet engines, since some Oldsmobile, Buick, and Pontiac V8s wouldn't be available.

• There would be no way to negotiate a fair price for the exchange vehicle. Consumers who had negotiated the price of their original car would be captive purchasers when they tried to exchange, and might therefore be required to pay the inflated sticker price.

• The cost of repairing any damage or unusual wear on the original vehicle would also have to be negotiated with the dealer at the time of the trade—and the consumer would again lack bargaining power.

• Consumers who had added non-GM options such as a roof rack, a trailer hitch, or a CB radio to the original vehicle might have to go to considerable expense to return the vehicle to its original condition.

The GM Settlement

In December 1977, just 13 months after Joseph Siwek first stumbled on the Great Engine Switch, the giant corporation finally buckled. GM's latest offer (accepted, as of this writing, by the attorneys general of 45 states) includes both a $200 cash payment and a transferable three-year/36,000-mile warranty on the engine and drivetrain for each eligible owner.

*   *   *   *   *

Clearly, GM's legal problems arose not because parts were shared among divisions. The problems arose from the way the cars were promoted, rather than from the way they were built. "The Chevrolet 350 V8 may not cost any less to manufacture than does the Oldsmobile 350 V8," says Richard Gross, deputy chief of the Massachusetts Consumer Protection Division. "In fact," he adds, "some people think the Chevrolet V8 may even be better."

Oldsmobile's history of "product differentiation" claims for a 350-cubic-inch V8 engine that is quite similar to the three 350-cubic-inch V8s built by GM's other divisions proved to be a history of deception. The consequences of Oldsmobile's expensive promotional hyperbole should serve notice on the rest of the industry to play it straight when tempted to turn commonplace nuts and bolts into magic tricks aimed at fooling the buyer. . . .

Source: *Consumer Reports*, April 1978, pp. 190–91. Copyright 1978 by Consumers Union of United States, Inc., Mount Vernon, NY 10553. Reprinted by permission from *Consumer Reports*, April 1978.

Examples of consumer abuse range from outrageous, if amusing, fraud to potentially serious threats to the public health:

1. A Portland, Oregon man sent $10 to a mail order firm for a "valuable engraved picture of Abraham Lincoln" only to receive in return a Lincoln penny.[1]
2. From Chapter 14 the reader will recall discussion of the Ford Pinto, the Firestone 500 radial tire, and other well-publicized instances of dangerously defective products.

On the other hand, we note that businesses regularly and voluntarily recall products believed to pose a hazard to the customer. For example, the Questor Juvenile Furniture Company recently offered replacements for 17,000 potentially defective baby cribs. In at least 36 instances from 1979 to 1981, the sides of the cribs had separated from the bottoms. Four children were injured. The company initiated the recall in cooperation with the federal Consumer Product Safety Commission.[2]

Thus, the familiar themes that suffuse the topic of government regulation of business are likewise evident in the consumer protection area. Doubtless we all seek to be free of fraud, deceptive advertising, invasions of privacy, defective products, and the full spectrum of consumer harm. But the question, as always, becomes one of price. How much do we wish to pay for freedom from wrong? How much should we pay in direct costs for improved products? And how much should we pay for government intervention to ensure an acceptable degree of protection? Or can we count on the business community to correct its own wrongs via the discipline of competition and the weight of conscience?

Consumerism: Past and Future

To the surprise of most, concern for the consumer is an ancient policy:

Until the Age of Reason in England, nothing resembling the doctrine of caveat emptor [buyer beware] existed in the custom and usage of the trade. Throughout the Middle Ages, church manuals laid down strict standards for market conduct, including requirements for warranties of quality. In the marketplace, merchants who dealt with their neighbors on a face-to-face basis took care to safeguard the quality of their products.[3]

However, the market changed from the craftsperson, face-to-face approach of that era to the complexities of mass production. At the same time, the influence of the church in commercial matters receded profoundly. In America, scandals in foods and drugs and a general feeling of abuse by corporate giants led to what might be labeled the first wave of consumer protection pleas and subsequent legislation. In 1906 Congress passed the Pure Food and Drug Act. Drugs had been largely unregulated. In particular, the public was regularly victimized by patent medicines, often either valueless, addictive, or both. And Upton Sinclair's great book, *The Jungle,* brought vividly to the public eye the filthy conditions in the meatpacking industry. Then in 1914 Congress created the Federal Trade Commission to stem "unfair methods of competition."

Consumer concerns were muted during World War I and the prosperous 1920s, but the Depression of the 30s provoked a second wave of protection. In the private sector, Consumers Union and its magazine, *Consumer Reports,* was founded. President Roosevelt appointed a Consumers Advisory Board, and during his administration Congress passed the Food, Drug and Cosmetic Act of 1938, which provided for the seizure of food, drugs, cosmetics, and therapeutic devices that were adulterated or misbranded. Likewise, in 1938 Congress passed the Wheeler-Lea Amendment to the Federal Trade Commission Act that extended FTC jurisdiction to "unfair and deceptive acts or practices in commerce."

The third major wave of consumer protection activity was felt in the mid 1960s, largely through the efforts of the quintessential consumer activist, Ralph Nader. Nader's bestselling book, *Unsafe at any Speed,* led to the demise of General Motors' Corvair. Nader has been an enormously influential voice in the passage of many pieces of legislation. He has attacked virtually every segment of American commerce. In concert with his "Nader's Raiders," (student aides) and other allies, he has marshalled untiring research, the law, and public opinion to reshape consumer protection law. He became such an aggravation to General Motors that the company hired a law firm which, in turn, hired private detectives to investigate Nader in the hope of discrediting him. The head of the detective agency allegedly encouraged his subordinates to find out what they could about Nader's "women, boys, etc." Nader learned of the scheme and sued GM. The suit was settled out of court, and GM President James Roche publicly apologized to Nader.[4]

For a variety of reasons, the consumer movement cooled in the late 1970s. The conservative flavor of the 80s has dampened the ardor for further government intervention. However, the public's strong appreciation for consumer protection is well documented in numerous surveys. Therefore, persistent, if muted, consumer pressure on business and government seems likely for the foreseeable future.

Common Law Consumer Protection

The bulk of the consumer protection publicity in the 1960s and 70s was provoked by new pieces of legislation. Later in this chapter we will be exploring government's efforts to protect us from misleading advertising, unfair lending practices, and the like, but before turning to that legislation we need to appreciate the common law (judge-made law) that preceded and, in some respects, provided the foundation for the striking federal, state, and local initiatives of recent years. In addition to the products liability protection (negligence, warranties, and strict liability) discussed in Chapter 16, the injured consumer can look to several common law ''protections'' including actions for fraud, misrepresentation, and unconscionability.

Fraud and Innocent Misrepresentation

If the market is to operate efficiently, the buyer must be able to rely upon the truth of the seller's affirmations regarding a product. Regrettably, willful untruths appear to be not uncommon in American commerce. A familiar class of examples is the many cases arising from automobile odometers rolled back to show fewer miles driven than the accurate total.[5] The victim of fraud is entitled to rescind the contract in question and to seek damages including, in cases of malice, a punitive recovery. While fraud arises in countless situations and as a result is difficult to define, the legal community has, in general, adopted the following elements, each of which must be proved:

1. A misrepresentation of a material fact with knowledge of the falsehood.
2. Intent to deceive.
3. Justifiable reliance on the falsehood by the injured party.
4. Damages resulting from reliance on the falsehood.

As evidenced by the odometer cases, fraud can involve false conduct as well as false expressions (of course, fraud should not be confused with mere puffing), and fraud sometimes arises from silence. If a serious problem or potential problem is known to the seller and the problem is of the sort that the buyer would not be likely to discover even after reasonable inspection (e.g., a cracked automobile engine block where the cracks were filled with a sealer and covered with a compound),[6] a claim of fraud may well prevail. However, the general rule is that the parties to a contract have no duty to disclose the facts at their command.

A variation on the general theme of fraud is the subspecies labeled *innocent misrepresentation*. It differs from fraud only in that the falsehood was unintentional. The wrongdoer believed the statement or conduct in question to be true, but he or she was mistaken. In such cases, the wronged party may secure rescission of the contract, but ordinarily damages are not awarded.

Before plunging into the famous fraud case that follows, the student should take a moment to reflect upon the extreme complexity in reaching a societal judgment about conduct that constitutes a wrong. The law of fraud illustrates the notion most excellently. Is the use of an unmarked patrol car a fraud against the public? Is a party to a marriage contract guilty of fraud in failing to disclose his or her propensity to snoring? Should a seller be expected to disclose all that is known about his or her product? Is a university guilty of fraud where it purports in its catalogs, inscriptions, and so on to purvey wisdom, when a student does not believe that wisdom has been delivered?[7] The excerpt and the case that follow should be read for fun and for a sense of the ubiquity of ''fraud,'' as well as for an appreciation of the difficulty in deciding the degree to which society should intervene to correct all arguable wrongs.

Fraud in Nature

In his book, *The Social Contract,* Robert Ardrey[8] illustrates nature's propensity for fraud.

Since we are inspecting man as a portion of nature, the capacity for lying should not be skipped. A few students of human language have implied that only through the complexity of our communication has the telling of lies become possible. I seize on the happy opportunity to announce that lying is a natural process. Man has enough to answer for; he need not answer for this.

Some of the most outrageous liars in the natural world are found among species of orchid. To gain perspective on what might be called natural square deals as opposed to natural larceny, we may recall that plants evolved before birds and flying insects, and depended on wind or water to scatter their pollen. It was an inefficient system, and a colorless one, too, in this time before flowers. But then came the insects and sensuality became possible. The scents we enjoy, the colors we delight in, evolved as signals to attract this insect, that bird. Partnerships were established—what zoologists call symbiosis—so that the fuchsia, for example, offered the humming-bird nectar in exchange for hauling fuchsia pollen around. Everyone got a fair shake. But there must always be liars.

There are species of orchids that have puzzled naturalists since the days of Darwin. They seemed to offer no inducement as their part of the deal, yet still insects did their job. At last, in 1928, a woman named Edith Coleman solved the problem in her study of an Australian orchid named *Cryptosylia.* The scent, a perfect imitation of the smell of the female of a species of fly, acted as an aphrodisiac on the male. He was drawn to the flower. There he encountered as part of the orchid's structure a perfect imitation of the female's abdomen. It was all too much for him, and in his efforts to copulate with the orchid he got himself nicely dusted with pollen. I am aware of no more immoderate fraud in the natural world.

Fraud, however, is normal in nature. There are deep-sea fish prowling dark depths with lanterns on their snouts. Smaller fish are attracted by the light and promptly eaten. . . . A Madagascar snake called *Langaha nasuta* has a weird structure on its head resembling a finger, which it slowly moves as it approaches its victim. The victim normally stares too long. . . .

Not all the wonders of natural fraud are the property of villains, however. Many a lie is told on behalf of the potential victim. The tropical fish called *Chactodon,* for example, has spots resembling eyes on either side of its tail. It swims slowly backwards, apparently head-on. But if a predator strikes at it, the fish is off at high speed in the proper direction. All camouflage, indeed, is deception. That both fish and seabirds tend to have white undersides to provide camouflage against the sky from an underwater point of view has been long assumed. The proposition was demonstrated during World War II when British planes on antisubmarine patrol improved their records by painting the planes' undersides white. It is further confirmed by a mixed-up creature, the Nile catfish, who through some unhappy mutation got his white on top and the dark beneath. He compensates successfully by swimming upside down. . . .

In the Ceylon shrike one finds a perfect evolutionary union of body, culture, and behavior. The parents are black and white. The young are a mottled color blending precisely with the appearance of the lichen-plastered nest. But it is the behavior of the young that leaves the observer in awe. There are usually three, and when the parents leave the nest the young sit facing the center, immobile, their beaks raised at a sharp angle and almost touching in the center. The tableau presents the most exquisite imitation of old splinters at a break in the branch, and the young will not stir until the parents return. What the family has achieved, and what must puzzle the evolutionist, is a social lie in which each member plays its part.

The natural history of prevarication is, indeed, without end. Human communication, like most of our capacities, has merely provided superb elaboration on an old, old theme. Through our use of words we delude each other with grave conviction; we have our way, as the Ceylon shrike has his. In one sense only is our capacity unique and entirely our own. Man, so far as I know, is the only animal capable of lying to himself.

That we lie successfully to each other is natural; that we successfully lie to ourselves is a natural wonder. . . .

Question

1. Is "fraud" inherent in human nature? Explain.

VOKES V. ARTHUR MURRAY, INC.   212 So.2d 906 (Florida, 1968)

Justice Pierce

This is an appeal by Audrey E. Vokes, plaintiff below.

Defendant Arthur Murray, Inc., a corporation, authorizes the operation throughout the nation of dancing schools under the name of "Arthur Murray School of Dancing" through local franchised operators, one of whom was defendant J. P. Davenport whose dancing establishment was in Clearwater.

Plaintiff Mrs. Audrey E. Vokes, a widow of 51 years and without family, had a yen to be "an accomplished dancer" with the hopes of finding "new interest in life." So, on February 10, 1961, a dubious fate, with the assist of a motivated acquaintance, procured her to attend a "dance party" at Davenport's "School of Dancing" where she whiled away the pleasant hours, sometimes in a private room, absorbing his accomplished sales technique, during which her grace and poise were elaborated upon and her rosy future as "an excellent dancer" was painted for her in vivid and glowing colors. As an incident to this interlude, he sold her eight one-half-hour dance lessons to be utilized within one calendar month therefrom, for the sum of $14.50 cash in hand paid, obviously a baited "come-on."

Thus she embarked upon an almost endless pursuit of the terpsichorean art during which, over a period of less than 16 months, she was sold 14 "dance courses" totaling in the aggregate 2,302 hours of dancing lessons for a total cash outlay of $31,090.45, all at Davenport's dance emporium. All of these 14 courses were evidenced by execution of a written "Enrollment Agreement—Arthur Murray's School of Dancing" with the addendum in heavy black print, "No one will be informed that you are taking dancing lessons. Your relations with us are held in strict confidence," setting forth the number of "dancing lessons" and the "lessons in rhythm sessions" currently sold to her from time to time, and always of course accompanied by payment of cash of the realm.

These dance lesson contracts and the monetary consideration therefor of over $31,000 were procured from her by means and methods of Davenport and his associates which went beyond the unsavory, yet legally permissible, perimeter of "sales puffing" and intruded well into the forbidden area of undue influence, the suggestion of falsehood, the suppression of truth, and the free exercise of rational judgment, if what plaintiff alleged in her complaint was true. From the time of her first contact with the dancing school in February 1961, she was influenced unwittingly by a constant and continuous barrage of flattery, false praise, excessive compliments, and panegyric encomiums, to such extent that it would be not only inequitable, but unconscionable, for a court exercising inherent chancery power to allow such contracts to stand.

She was incessantly subjected to overreaching blandishment and cajolery. She was assured she had "grace and poise"; that she was "rapidly improving and developing in her dancing skill"; that the additional lessons would "make her a beautiful dancer, capable of dancing with the most accomplished dancers"; that she was "rapidly progressing in the development of her dancing skill and gracefulness", etc., etc. She was given "dance aptitude tests" for the ostensible purpose of "determining" the number of remaining hours instructions needed by her from time to time.

At one point she was sold 545 additional hours of dancing lessons to be entitled to award of the "Bronze Medal" signifying that she had reached "the Bronze Standard," a supposed designation of dance achievement by students of Arthur Murray, Inc.

Later she was sold an additional 926 hours in order to gain the "Silver Medal," indicating she had reached "the Silver Standard," at a cost of $12,501.35.

At one point, while she still had to her credit about 900 unused hours of instructions, she was induced to purchase an additional 24 hours of lessons to participate in a trip to Miami at her own expense, where she would be "given the opportunity to dance with members of the Miami Studio."

She was induced at another point to purchase an additional 126 hours of lessons in order to be not only eligible for the Miami trip but also to become "a life member of the Arthur Murray Studio," carrying with it certain dubious emoluments, at a further cost of $1,752.30.

At another point, while she still had over 1,000 unused hours of instruction she was induced to buy 151 additional hours at a cost of $2,049.00 to be eligible for a "Student Trip to Trinidad," at her own expense as she later learned.

Also, when she still had 1,100 unused hours to her credit, she was prevailed upon to purchase an additional 347 hours at a cost of $4,235.74, to qualify her to receive a "Gold Medal" for achievement, indicating she had advanced to "the Gold Standard."

On another occasion, while she still had over 1,200 unused hours, she was induced to buy an additional 175 hours of instruction at a cost of $2,472.75 to be eligible "to take a trip to Mexico."

Finally, sandwiched in between other lesser sales promotions, she was influenced to buy an additional 481 hours of instruction at a cost of $6,523.81 in order to "be classified as a Gold Bar Member, the ultimate achievement of the dancing studio."

All the foregoing sales promotions, illustrative of the entire 14 separate contracts, were procured by defendent Davenport and Arthur Murray, Inc., by false representations to her that she was improving in her dancing ability, that she had excellent potential, that she was responding to instructions in dancing grace, and that they were developing her into a beautiful dancer, whereas in truth and in fact she did not develop in her dancing ability, she had no "dance aptitude," and in fact had difficulty in "hearing the musical beat." The complaint alleged that such representations to her "were in fact false and known by the defendant to be false and contrary to the plaintiff's true ability, the truth of plaintiff's ability being fully known to the defendants, but withheld from the plaintiff for the sole and specific intent to deceive and defraud the plaintiff and to induce her in the purchasing of additional hours of dance lessons." It was averred that the lessons were sold to her "in total disregard to the true physical, rhythm, and mental ability of the plaintiff." In other words, while she first exulted that she was entering the "spring of her life," she finally was awakened to the fact there was "spring" neither in her life nor in her feet.

* * * * *

. . . Defendants contend that contracts can only be rescinded for fraud or misrepresentation when the alleged misrepresentation is as to a material fact, rather than an opinion, prediction or expectation, and that the statements and representations set forth at length in the complaint were in the category of "trade puffing," within its legal orbit.

It is true that "generally a misrepresentation, to be actionable, must be one of fact rather than of opinion." . . . But this rule has significant qualifications, applicable here. It does not apply where there is a fiduciary relationship between the parties, or where there has been some artifice or trick employed by the representor, or where the parties do not in general deal at "arm's length" as we understand the phrase, or where the representee does not have equal opportunity to become apprised of the truth or falsity of the fact represented. . . . As stated by Judge Allen of this Court in *Ramel* v. *Chasebrook Construction Company:*

". . . A statement of a party having . . . superior knowledge may be regarded as a statement of fact although it would be considered as opinion if the parties were dealing on equal terms."

It could be reasonably supposed here that defendants had "superior knowledge" as to whether plaintiff had "dance potential" and as to whether she was noticeably improving in the art of terpsichore. And it would be a reasonable inference from the undenied averments of the complaint that the flowery eulogiums heaped upon her by defendants as a prelude to her contracting for 1,944 additional hours of instruction in order to attain the rank of the Bronze Standard, thence to the bracket of the Silver Standard, thence to the class of the Gold Bar Standard, and finally to the crowning plateau of a Life Member of the Studio, proceeded as much or more from the urge to "ring the cash register" as from any honest or realistic appraisal of her dancing prowess or a factual representation of her progress.

Even in contractual situations where a party to a transaction owes no duty to disclose facts within his knowledge or to answer inquiries respecting such facts, the law is if he undertakes to do so he must disclose the *whole truth*. . . . From the face of the complaint, it should have been reasonably apparent to defendants that her vast outlay of cash for the many hundreds of additional hours of instruction was not justified by her slow and awkward progress, which she would have been made well aware of if they had spoken the "whole truth." . . .

[The Court below held the complaint not to state a cause of action. We reverse.]

Questions

1. In *Vokes,* defendant Arthur Murray, Inc. was not found to have misrepresented *facts.* How then did the court find in favor of the plaintiff?
2. Build a case for Arthur Murray.
3. How would you have decided the case? Explain.
4. The plaintiff, a home buyer, purchased a home from a builder. Prior to the sale no water had entered the cellar. The builder had described the house as having "a good concrete floor, good foundation walls." A month after the sale, water appeared in the cellar, but the builder told the buyer not to be concerned: "any new house will have water in the cellar [but] it will disappear when the earth around the foundation becomes firm." The builder assured the buyer that he would stand behind the house if anything went wrong. The cellar continued to leak, and the buyer brought suit for deceit. Decide the case. See *Fagerty* v. *Van Loan,* 183 N.E.2d 111 (Mass. 1962). But see *Berryman* v. *Riegert,* 175 N.W.2d (Minn. 1970).
5. The plaintiff, Herbert Williams, bought an auto in March 1968, in Milwaukee, Wisconsin. Williams had sought an air-conditioned car. A salesman for the defendant, Rank & Son Buick, Inc., said the car was air conditioned, and Williams noted a knob on the dash labeled, "Air." Williams drove the car for one and a half hours prior to purchase, and he otherwise had ample opportunity for inspection. Several days after the purchase Williams discovered that "Air" referred only to ventilation. The car was not air conditioned. Williams sued. Decide the case. See *Williams* v. *Rank & Son Buick, Inc.,* 44 Wis.2d 239, 170 N.W.2d 807 (1969).

Unconscionable Contracts

The efficiency and success of the American economy depends, in no small part, on the reliability of contractual relationships. The buyer must know that the goods will be delivered, and the seller must know that the bill will be paid. It is, therefore, only with the greatest reluctance that the legal system intervenes in freely bargained arrangements. Jurists adopted the concept of unconscionability to nullify those contracts that are so unfair or oppressive as to demand societal intervention. Mere foolishness or a want of knowledge do not constitute grounds for unconscionability, nor is a contract unconscionable and hence unenforceable merely because one party is spectacularly clever and the other is not.

Unconscionability is a concept not easily pinned down, and so it should be. The Uniform Commercial Code (UCC 2-302) governs unconscionability. As the following case illustrates, some situations are so patently unfair that justice requires intervention, but we wish to do so only in rare instances when *(a)* the bargaining power of the parties was so unbalanced that the agreement was not truly freely entered, or *(b)* the clause or contract in question is so unfair as to violate societal values.

WILLIAMS V. WALKER–THOMAS FURNITURE COMPANY
350 F.2d 445 (C.A.D.C., 1965)

Chief Justice Wright

Appellee, Walker-Thomas Furniture Company, operates a retail furniture store in the District of Columbia. During the period from 1957 to 1962 each appellant in these cases purchased a number of household items from Walker-Thomas, for which payment was to be made in installments. The terms of each purchase were contained in a printed form contract which set forth the value of the purchased item and purported to lease the item to appellant for a stipulated monthly rent payment. The contract then provided, in substance, that title would remain in Walker-Thomas until the total of all the monthly payments made equaled the stated value of the item, at which time appellants could take title. In the event of a default in the payment of any monthly installment, Walker-Thomas could repossess the item.

The contract further provided that "the amount of each periodical installment payment to be made by [purchaser] to the company under this present lease shall be inclusive of and not in addition to the amount of each installment payment to be made by [purchaser] under such prior leases, bills or accounts; *and all payments now and hereafter made by [purchaser] shall be credited pro rata on all outstanding leases, bills, and accounts* due the company by [purchaser] at the time each such payment is made." (Emphasis added.) The effect of this rather obscure provision was to keep a balance due on every item purchased until the balance due on all items, whenever purchased, was liquidated. As a result, the debt incurred at the time of purchase of each item was secured by the right to repossess all the items previously purchased by the same purchaser, and each new item purchased automatically became subject to a security interest arising out of the previous dealings.

On May 12, 1962, appellant Thorne purchased an item described as a Daveno, three tables, and two lamps, having total stated value of $391.10. Shortly thereafter, he defaulted on his monthly payments and appellee sought to replevy all the items purchased since the first transaction in 1958. Similarly, on April 17, 1962, appellant Williams bought a stereo set of stated value of $514.95. She too defaulted shortly thereafter, and appellee sought to replevy all the items purchased since December 1957. The court of general sessions granted judgment for appellee. The District of Columbia Courts of Appeals affirmed, and we granted appellants' motion for leave to appeal to this court.

Appellants' principal contention, rejected by both the trial and the appellate courts below, is that these contracts, or at least some of them, are unconscionable and, hence, not enforceable.

*   *   *   *   *

. . . [T]he Uniform Commercial Code . . . specifically provides that the court may refuse to enforce a contract which it finds to be unconscionable at the time it was made. . . . [W]e hold that where the element of unconscionability is present at the time a contract is made, the contract should not be enforced.

Unconscionability has generally been recognized to include an absence of meaningful choice on the part of one of the parties together with contract terms which are unreasonably favorable to the other party. Whether a meaningful choice is present in a particular case can only be determined by consideration of all the circumstances surrounding the transaction. In many cases the meaningfulness of the choice is negated by a gross inequality of bargaining power. The manner in which the contract was entered is also relevant to this consideration. Did each party to the contract, considering his obvious education or lack of it, have a reasonable opportunity to understand the terms of the contract, or were the important terms hidden in a maze of fine print and minimized by deceptive sales practices? Ordinarily, one who signs an agreement without full knowledge of its terms might be held to assume the risk that he has entered a one-sided bargain. But when a party of little bargaining power, and hence little real choice, signs a commercially unreasonable contract with little or no knowledge of its terms, it is hardly likely that his consent, or even an objective manifestation of his consent, was ever given to all the terms. In such a case the usual rule that the terms of the agreement are not to be questioned should be abandoned and the court should consider whether the terms of the contract are so unfair that enforcement should be withheld.

In determining reasonableness or fairness, the primary concern must be with the terms of the contract considered in light of the circumstances existing when the contract was made. The test is not simple, nor can it be mechanically applied. The terms are to be considered "in the light of the general commercial background and the commercial needs of the particular trade or case." Corbin suggests the test as being whether the terms are "so extreme as to appear unconscionable according to the mores and business practices of the time and place." We think this formulation correctly states the test to be applied in those cases where no meaningful choice was exercised upon entering the contract.

. . . Since the record is not sufficient for our deciding the issue as a matter of law, the cases must be remanded to the trial court for further proceedings.

Reversed and remanded.

Questions

1. Explain the court's reasoning in *Williams*.
2. Plaintiff Willie had listed his business in the Wichita, Kansas, yellow pages for some 13 years. Plaintiff was expanding his business, and he entered into an agreement with the defendant phone company to include additional telephone numbers in the directory. Defendant inadvertently failed to include one of the numbers in the directory. The contract

signed by the parties included a conspicuous exculpatory clause limiting the phone company's liability for errors and omissions to an amount equal to the cost of the ad. Upon discovering the omission, plaintiff had begun advertising the number on television at a cost of approximately $5,000. Plaintiff contends the exculpatory clause is unconscionable and, therefore, unenforceable. Decide. Explain. See *Willie* v. *Southwestern Bell Telephone Company,* 549 P.2d 903 (Kan 1976).

Other Common Law Protections

Although we will not be addressing them in detail here, the reader should understand that the law provides a number of other consumer protections arising out of judge-made contract law. For example, some bargains are void because an element of the bargain is illegal. Gambling contracts are a familiar example (in those states where gambling is illegal), but more to the point for the "typical" consumer is a contract rendered illegal because it provides for the payment of interest at a usurious rate; that is, a rate beyond the maximum permitted under state law.

Or a contract may be rescinded because it was entered as a result of duress (e.g., "Buy my house or I will reveal all the sordid details of your recent trip to Los Angeles") or undue influence (e.g., "All right, son, I know your dear departed parents left that $500,000 to you, but as your loving uncle and guardian I must expect and demand that you turn the money over to me for safekeeping").

The Consumer and Government Regulation of Business

Having established the common law foundation for consumer protection, it is appropriate now to turn to some of the many governmental measures that provide shelter in the often unforgiving marketplace. States and localities have adopted a wealth of protective measures, but those cannot be meaningfully summarized here. Rather, we will look exclusively at a sampling of federal activity. The reader is urged to repeatedly confront the question of proper balance, if such exists, between the free market and government intervention.

The Federal Trade Commission—Rule Making

The Federal Trade Commission was created in 1914 to prevent "unfair methods of competition and unfair or deceptive acts or practices in and affecting commerce." In conducting its business the FTC performs as a miniature government with extensive and powerful quasi-legislature and quasi-judicial roles. The primary legislative direction is in issuing trade regulation rules to enforce the specific intent of broadly drawn congressional legislation. That is, the rules define with particularity those acts or practices which the commission deems to be unfair or deceptive. Violations of trade regulation rules are punished by civil penalties, injunctions, and other appropriate redress.

In the same vein, the FTC issues industry guides that are the commission's interpretations of laws it enforces. The guides provide direction to the public, and while they do not have the force of law, a failure to observe the guides might result in adjudication.

The FTC's quasi-legislative role is well illustrated by its long and vigorously contested investigation of various funeral industry practices. Recently a trade regulation rule was approved as a result of that investigation.

FTC VOTES FUNERAL RATE DISCLOSURES

Daniel Mintz

Washington, D.C.—After 10 years of investigation and deliberation, the Federal Trade Commission (FTC) voted three to one Wednesday to require funeral directors to itemize prices and quote them over the phone.

* * * * *

In addition to price lists and telephone quotations, the rule requires funeral directors to "unbundle" funeral packages and allow customers to choose the services they want. It also prohibits embalming without a relative's permission, and forbids undertakers from misrepresenting the law to customers, such as saying embalming is required by a state when it is not.

Commissioner Michael Pertschuk, who has supported the rule in congressional testimony, called the decision "a modest step toward res-

toring some power to the consumer in this most unique and painful purchase."

* * * * *

In approving the funeral rule, the FTC rejected the advice of Timothy Muris, the commission's head of consumer protection, who analyzed the agency's funeral regulation record and concluded the new rules are based more on "anecdotes" than solid evidence.

The three commissioners supporting the rule also spurned the counsel of the director of the FTC's bureau of economics. Robert Tollison suggested the entire investigation of funeral regulation be ended because of lack of evidence that rules are needed.

Source: *Des Moines (Iowa) Register*, July 29, 1982, p. 5B. Reprinted with permission of the copyright holder, The Associated Press.

QUESTIONS

1. Why should the funeral industry be required to meet standards (e.g., itemizing prices) that are not required in other industries?

2. How would you vote on the funeral industry rule? Explain.

The Federal Trade Commission—Adjudication

Upon its own initiative or as a result of a citizen complaint, the FTC may conduct investigations into suspect trade practices. At that point the commission may either drop the proceeding, settle the matter informally, or issue a formal complaint. An informal settlement normally takes the form of a consent agreement in which the party under investigation voluntarily discontinues the practice in question but is not required to admit guilt. If agreement cannot be reached, the commission may proceed with a formal complaint. In that case, the matter proceeds essentially as a trial conducted before an administrative law judge. Both the government and the "accused" party may be represented by counsel, and the proceeding is conducted in accord with due process of law. If the government prevails, the judge may issue a cease and desist order forbidding further wrongful conduct. That order may be appealed to the full commission and to the federal Court of Appeals (assuming the existence of proper grounds for appeal).

The FTC is designed to prevent wrongdoing. Hence it has no authority to impose criminal sanctions. Although it may impose civil penalties of up to $10,000 per violation per day, the commission often engages in more creative remedies ordering, for example, corrective advertising to counteract previous, misleading ads or requiring contracts to be altered. Or in the case of "high pressure sales," the commission has allowed the consumer a cooling off period in which to cancel a contract.

The Federal Trade Commission— Deceptive Practices

FTC regulatory efforts range across the spectrum of consumer activity. For example, the FTC issued a rule specifying that mail order sellers are in violation of the Federal Trade Commission Act if they solicit orders through the mail without a reasonable expectation that the goods can be shipped in 30 days or less. The FTC has pursued broad-scale regulatory initiatives against a number of industries, including insurance, used autos, and credit cards, but perhaps the best examples of FTC rule making and adjudicatory actions lie in the area of advertising. False and deceptive advertising is forbidden under section 5 of the Federal Trade Commission as enhanced by the 1938 Wheeler-Lea Amendment, which specifically forbids false advertising of "foods, drugs, devices, or cosmetics." Historically, the commission has pursued a variety of deceptions in advertising. For example, bait-and-switch tactics are forbidden. In those cases, the seller ordinarily advertises a product at very low prices in order to attract customers. Then the customer's attention is deliberately switched to another, more expensive product. Another commonplace deceptive tactic involves advertising price reductions. When the price is indeed reduced but from a highly inflated original price established merely to facilitate a reduction, the ad is deceptive.

Traditionally the courts have found unlawful deception in those acts or practices having "a tendency or capacity to deceive." However, in 1983 the FTC adopted the following, narrower interpretation: "[T]he Commission will find deception if there is a representation, omission or practice that is likely to mislead the consumer acting reasonably in the circumstances, to the consumer's detriment."[9] Future commissions may or may not follow the 1983 standard. The courts are to give great weight to the commission's stance, but whether the new standard will be generally embraced remains to be seen. Some commentators suggest that the new standard may offer reduced protection to the consumer. Why might that be the case? The decision that follows illustrates an FTC inquiry into a dubious advertising practice.[10]

FTC V. COLGATE–PALMOLIVE CO.   380 U.S. 374 (1964)

Chief Justice Warren

The basic question before us is whether it is a deceptive trade practice to represent falsely that a televised test, experiment, or demonstration provides a viewer with visual proof of a product claim, regardless of whether the product claim is itself true.

The case arises out of an attempt by defendant Colgate-Palmolive Company to prove to the television public that its shaving cream, "Rapid Shave,". . . could soften even the toughness of sandpaper. Each of the commercials contained the same "sandpaper test." The announcer informed the audience that, "To prove Rapid Shave's super-moisturizing power, we put it right from the can onto this tough, dry sandpaper. It was apply . . . soak . . . and off in a stroke." While the announcer was speaking, Rapid Shave was applied to a substance that appeared to be sandpaper, and immediately thereafter a razor was shown shaving the substance clean. The Federal Trade Commission issued a complaint against respondent Colgate . . . charging that the commercials were false and deceptive. The evidence before the hearing examiner disclosed that sandpaper . . . could not be shaved immediately following the application of Rapid Shave, but required a substantial soaking period of approximately 80 minutes. [T]he substance resembling sandpaper was in fact a simulated prop, or "mock-up," made of plexiglass to which sand had been applied. . . .

[T]he commission found that the undisclosed use of a plexiglass substitute for sandpaper was . . . [a] material misrepresentation that was a deceptive act. . . . [T]he commission found that viewers had been misled into believing they had seen it done with their own eyes. As a result of these findings the commission entered a cease-and-desist order against the respondents. . . . [The Court of Appeals found the Commission's order unsatisfactory and refused to enforce it. The Supreme Court granted certiorari.]

We accept the commission's determination that the commercials involved in this case contained [the] representation . . . that the viewer was seeing this experiment for himself . . . which was clearly false. The parties agree that [FTC Act] Section 5 prohibits the intentional misrepresentation of any fact which would constitute a material factor in a purchaser's decision whether to buy. They differ, however, in their conception of what "facts" constitute a "material factor" in a purchaser's decision to buy. [Defendant] submits, in effect, that the only material facts are those which deal with the substantive qualities of a product. The commission, on the other hand, submits that the misrepresentation of *any* fact so long as it materially induces a purchaser's decision to buy is a deception prohibited by §5.

*   *   *   *   *

. . . We find an especially strong similarity between the present case and those cases in which a seller induces the public to purchase an arguably good product by misrepresenting his line of business, by concealing the fact that the product is reprocessed, or by misappropriating another's trademark. In each the seller had used a misrepresentation to break down what he regards to be an annoying or irrational habit of the buying public—the preference for particular manufacturers or known brands regardless of a product's actual qualities, the prejudice against reprocessed goods, and the desire for verification of a product claim. In each case the seller reasons that when the habit is broken the buyer will be satisfied with the performance of the product he receives. . . .

It is generally accepted that it is a deceptive practice to state falsely that a product has received a testimonial from a respected source. In addition, the commission has consistently acted to prevent sellers from falsely stating that their product claims have been "certified." We find these situations to be indistinguishable from the present case. We can assume that in each the underlying product claim is true and in each the seller actually conducted an experiment sufficient to prove to himself the truth of the claim. But in each the seller has told the public that it could rely on something other than his word concerning both the truth of the claim and the validity of his experiment. We find it an immaterial difference that in one case the viewer is told to rely on the word of a celebrity or authority he respects, in another on the word of a testing agency, and in the present case on his own perception of an undisclosed simulation. . . .

We agree with the commission, therefore, that the undisclosed use of plexiglass in the present commercials was a material deceptive practice. . . .

Nor was it necessary for the commission to conduct a survey of the viewing public before it could determine that the commercials had a tendency to mislead, for when the commission finds deception it is also authorized, within the bounds of reason, to infer that the deception will constitute a material factor in a purchaser's decision to buy. . . .

We turn our attention now to the order issued by the commission. . . .

The Court of Appeals has criticized the reference in the commission's order to "test, experiment or demonstrate" as not capable of practical interpretation. It could find no difference between the Rapid Shave commercial and a commercial which extolled the goodness of ice cream while giving viewers a picture of a scoop of mashed potatoes appearing to be ice cream. We do not understand this difficulty. In the ice cream case the mashed potato prop is not being used for additional proof of the product claim, while the purpose of the Rapid Shave commercial is to give the viewer objective proof of the claims made. If in the ice cream hypothetical the focus of the commercial becomes the undisclosed potato prop and the viewer is invited, explicitly or by implication, to see for himself the truth of the claims about the ice cream's rich texture and full color, and perhaps compare it to a "rival product," then the commercial has become similar to the one now before us. Clearly, however, a commercial which depicts happy actors delightedly eating ice cream that is in fact mashed potatoes or drinking a product appearing to be coffee but which is in fact some other substance is not covered by the present order.

* * * * *

In commercials where the emphasis is on the seller's word, and not on the viewer's own perception, the defendants need not fear that an undisclosed use of props is prohibited by the present order. On the other hand, when the commercial not only makes a claim, but also invites the viewer to rely on his own perception for demonstrative proof of the claim, the defendants will be aware that the use of undisclosed props in strategic places might be a material deception. We believe that defendants will have no difficulty applying the commission's order to the vast majority of their contemplated future commercials.

Reversed and remanded.

Questions

1. Assume that Colgate-Palmolive could prove the effectiveness of Rapid Shave in softening beards. Would the sand on plexiglass ad then be lawful? Explain.
2. Why did the Court excuse the commission from providing proof, via survey evidence, that consumers actually were deceived?
3. What social interest is served in protecting the public from the Colgate-Palmolive ad?
4. Mary Carter Paint Company manufactured and sold paint and related products. Carter Paint ads stated that for every can of Carter paint purchased, Carter would give the buyer a free

can of equal quality and quantity. The price specified in these ads from the early 1960s was $6.98 per can. The FTC challenged the ads as deceptions in violation of section 5 of the Federal Trade Commission Act.

a.   In what sense were the ads considered deceptive?

b.   Decide the case. Explain. See *Federal Trade Commission* v. *Mary Carter Paint Co.*, 382 U.S. 46, (1965).

The Consumer Product Safety Commission

Commonplace consumer products such as toys, lawn mowers, power saws, bicycles, and portable heaters are all too often instruments of destruction in American family life. In 1970 the congressionally created National Commission on Product Safety completed two and a half years of study by recommending the creation of a federal agency to regulate product safety. The commission cited the substantial costs of consumer product accidents:

> Americans—20 million of them—are injured each year in the home as a result of incidents connected with consumer products. Of the total, 110,000 are permanently disabled and 30,000 are killed. A significant number could have been spared if more attention had been paid to hazard reduction. The annual cost to the nation of product-related injuries may exceed $5.5 billion.[11]

Given those conditions and the belief that federal supervision was dispersed and inadequate, Congress created the Consumer Product Safety Commission (CPSC) in 1972. The commission's authority extends over the full range of consumer products (glass, toys, ladders, saws, stoves, and so on). Its duties are many, but the heart of its activities may be summarized as follows:

1. *Data Collection.* The commission conducts research and collects information as a foundation for regulating product safety. The commission's National Electronic Injury Surveillance System (NEISS) collects data from many hospital emergency rooms across the country. The hospitals report all those injuries that involve consumer products. That data base then suggests directions for more intensive investigations.

2. *Rule Making.* The commission, via its rule-making authority, promulgates mandatory consumer product safety standards. The commission invites any person or group to submit a safety standard for the product in question. Industry trade associations have been more active in submitting "offers" to set standards, but consumers and consumer groups such as the Consumers Union have been encouraged to participate. Safety standards essentially are technical specifications requiring certain minimums in strength, design, flammability, corrosiveness, labeling, and so on. For example, the CPSC has provided that children's sleepware must meet certain flame resistance standards, must be labeled to show that they meet those standards, must be labeled with care instructions to preserve flame retardants (where used), and production and distribution records must be maintained so that the product's history can be traced. Because safety is not free, proposed product standards must include a statement of the anticipated economic and environmental impact.

Standards are processed under traditional due process requirements including publication in the *Federal Register,* notice to affected parties and hearings. Affected parties may petition a federal Court of Appeals to reverse CPSC rules.

3. *Compliance.* The CPSC is enpowered to use a variety of strategies in securing compliance with safety standards. Manufacturers must certify before distribution that products meet federal safety standards. Agents of the commission may inspect manufacturing sites. The commission can mandate specific product safety testing procedures, and businesses, other than retailers, are required to keep records sufficient for the commission to see that the firms are in compliance with safety standards.

4. *Enforcement.* In cases of severe and imminent hazards, the commission may seek an immediate court order to remove a product from the market. In less urgent circumstances the commission may proceed with its own administrative remedy. Preferring to secure voluntary compliance, the Commission may urge the company to issue public and/or private notices of a defect, or it may seek the repair or replacement of defective parts. Where voluntary negotiations fail, the commission may proceed with an adjudicative hearing conducted in the manner of a trial, before an administrative law judge or members of the commission. The decision may be appealed to the full commission and thereafter to the appropriate U.S. Court of Appeals. In its first six years, the CPSC issued approximately 1,200 product recalls. Only a few products have actually been banned from the market. Failure to comply with safety provisions may result in civil fines up to $500,000. Criminal penalties for knowing and willful violations may total $50,000 and up to one year in jail.

The article that follows illustrates the actual practice and impact of the Consumer Product Safety Commission in a product line of particular poignance—toys.

CBS INC. SUBSIDIARY MUST STEP UP RECALL OF TOY FATAL TO THREE

Washington—The Consumer Product Safety Commission, reversing an earlier decision, is requiring a toy maker to renew and expand its campaign to recall a slide set that has caused the strangulation deaths of three children.

The latest death occurred . . . at a day care center in northern California; a two-year-old boy got his head caught between the top rung of the ladder and the platform above it.

Just two weeks before that accident, the commission voted three-to-two against requiring a more vigorous recall effort than the company was making. That action was taken at the request of CBS Inc.'s Creative Playthings, maker of the toy.

Following negotiations with the company, the commission announced yesterday that Cre-

ative Playthings would renew its recall campaign with far more extensive publicity than before. The initial recall turned up only 15 percent of the wooden structures; commission officials estimate that as many as 239,000 are still in consumers' hands.

* * * * *

Just how much a company should do to locate dangerous products already sold to consumers is a frequent point of contention between business and regulators. Companies usually are reluctant to recall their defective products with advertising campaigns equal to what was used to sell the products. In this case, there wasn't agreement within the commission itself.

Two strangling incidents in late 1979 prompted Creative Playthings, under commission scrutiny, to issue a news release in February 1980 announcing the recall. The company also sent letters to its retail outlets and to about 30,000 day care centers, warning of the dangers and offering to replace the ladders. But the center in California, and many others like it, operated in private homes rather than institutions, didn't receive the notice.

This time, the company agreed to place newspaper advertisements, run a public service television announcement and take other extensive publicity measures to warn consumers that they shouldn't use the toy. Consumers will be able to have the ladders replaced with a different model.

* * * * *

QUESTIONS

1. Creative Playthings had sold over 200,000 slide sets. Three confirmed strangulations were reported in approximately two years.
   a. Do those facts justify a recall order? Explain.
   b. Should Creative Playthings merely be required to warn consumers rather than being forced to replace the ladders? Explain.
2. Should product recalls be publicized with advertising equal to that used to sell the product in the first place? Explain.

Consumer Finance Law

For a considerable portion of American history, frugality was a virtue of the first rank. Saving was esteemed. Borrowing for consumer goods was, to many, foolish and a sign of weakness or decay. Today we live in quite another world. We are encouraged to experience the good life by spending lavishly. To do so we may well need to borrow. Now purchases on credit are not only tolerated, they are encouraged. American consumer debt now exceeds $1.5 trillion (including home mortgages). Our shift to a commercial world predicated on the extension of credit opened seductive new windows of pleasure for the consumer, but the spread of indebtedness as a way of life led to new problems, and in some instances, abuses for both the debtor-consumer and the creditor-business. Predictably, and perhaps necessarily, we turn to the law for relief.

Credit Regulations

Congress has seen fit to extend a variety of protections to the consumer seeking and securing credit. We will look in an abbreviated fashion at five particularly important pieces of creditor protection legislation:

1. Truth in Lending Act.
2. Equal Credit Opportunity Act.
3. Fair Credit Reporting Act.
4. Fair Credit Billing Act.
5. State Usury laws.

Truth in Lending Act (TILA)[12]   As we turned evermore to credit financing, consumers often did not understand the full cost of buying on credit. In 1968 Congress passed and President Lyndon Johnson approved the Consumer Credit Protection Act, of which TILA was Title I. TILA was designed for consumer protection; hence, it does not cover all loans. The following standards determine TILA's applicability:

1. The debtor must be a ''natural person'' rather than an organization.
2. The creditor must be one regularly engaged in extending credit or arranging for the extension of credit.
3. The purpose of the credit must be ''primarily for personal, family, or household purposes'' not in excess of $25,000. However, ''consumer real property transactions'' are covered by the act. Hence, home purchases fall within TILA provisions.
4. The credit must be subject to a finance charge or be payable in more than four installments.

Following the enactment of TILA, the Federal Reserve Board developed regulations (labeled Regulation Z) that detail the specific requirements of the act. TILA was designed both to protect consumers from credit abuse and to assist consumers in becoming more informed regarding credit terms and costs so they could engage in comparison shopping. Congress presumed the increased information would stimulate competition in the finance industry. The act contains many provisions, but its heart is the required disclosure of the finance charge (the actual dollar sum to be paid for credit) and the annual percentage rate (APR), that is, the cost of the credit expressed at an annual rate. The finance charge includes not just interest but service charges, points, loan fees, carrying charges, and others.

TILA provisions are enforceable both by several government agencies, including the Federal Trade Commission, and by private parties. Government enforcement is ordinarily accomplished through negotiation, but the agency may turn to a variety of mechanisms including, for example, the issuance of cease and desist orders. Criminal liability arises only in instances of knowing and willful violations. In such instances the U.S. Attorney General's Office may seek penalties up to $5,000 and/or one year in prison. Private parties may bring civil actions alleging damages resulting from TILA violations. Liabilty is limited to twice the amount of the finance charge for the transaction in question. However, the recovery cannot be less than $100 nor more than $1,000. Attorney's fees may be secured under appropriate circumstances.

Under the terms of the Simplification and Reform Act of 1980, Congress approved some significant adjustments in TILA. For example, the elements of the finance charges and the APR need not be itemized in the disclosure form unless requested by the consumer in writing, and civil liability for unintentional mechanical errors (e.g., inaccurate calculations) was eliminated.

The interesting and important dimension of the TILA reform is the change in philosophy it reflects. Congress moved away from a clear consumer protection stance and appeared to seek a balance between consumer and business interests. Critics had argued that TILA requirements were so complex that small businesses, in particular, encountered great difficulty and expense in complying. The Federal Reserve Board felt that the many disclosure standards increased the cost of credit and thus reduced consumer access to financing. Of course, consumer advocates argue that the simplifications reduce available information and afford the creditor more opportunities to willfully or carelessly abuse the credit seeker.

While TILA is directed largely to financial disclosure, it embraces some other issues of importance to the consumer. One of those of particular note is a series of rules governing credit cards. Cards cannot be issued unless requested, and cardholder liability for unauthorized use (e.g., lost or stolen card) cannot exceed $50.

The case that follows is an excellent description, both of the goals of TILA and the actual details of required financial disclosure.

BARBER V. KIMBRELL'S, INC.   United States District Court, Western District of North Carolina 424 F. Supp. 42 (1976)

District Judge McMillan

Preliminary Statement

Polly Ann Barber filed this action on May 3, 1974, seeking civil penalties under the Consumer Credit Protection Act ("Truth in Lending Act"). . . .

The court finds that the defendants have violated the "Truth in Lending Act," and are liable to the individual plaintiff.

Purposes of the Truth in Lending Act

The Truth in Lending Act was adopted in 1968. It does not regulate interest rates. Instead, its purpose is to require that lenders provide consumers with *information, clearly and understandably stated,* so that they can determine what they are paying for the credit extended to them, and so that they can compare costs of credit available from various sources and shop around intelligently for the best terms. It requires that certain specific information be given in the documents covering the transaction, and it provides penalties for failure to disclose the necessary information. The decided cases talk in terms of the duty to " 'assure a meaningful disclosure of credit terms' to consumers," . . . or "to protect consumers by providing them with accurate information so they could shop for credit." . . .

The Facts about Polly Ann Barber's Case

On July 16, 1973, the named plaintiff, Polly Ann Barber, entered into a retail installment contract at the downtown Charlotte Kimbrell's furniture store, for the purchase of a green velvet sofa bed, a four-piece walnut bedroom suite, and a box spring and mattress. At the time she owed Kimbrell's $65 from a previous credit purchase which had been subjected to a previous finance charge. The old balance was added to the price of the new purchases in an "add on" transaction and the old and new balance were consolidated into one "Purchase Money Security Agreement," to be retired by the payment of 12 equal monthly installments. Ms. Barber executed the agreement.

A photocopy of the instrument ("Purchase Money Security Agreement") is attached . . .

*   *   *   *   *

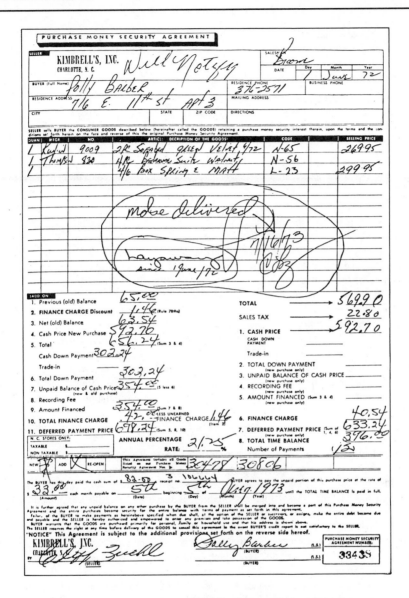

The Violations of the Truth in Lending Act

. . .The form contract, or "Purchase Money Security Agreement," when it is used to cover financing of new purchases consolidated with refinancing of previous credit purchases, makes disclosures in two parallel vertical columns. The information cannot be derived by reading straight down either column. The computations and disclosures require the reader to switch back and forth between the two columns of figures. The result is a confusing situation which is not yet thoroughly understandable to me despite a considerable period of study.

In a number of particulars the evidence demonstrates that the defendants have violated the Truth in Lending Act. These violations include:

A. Misleading labels instead of precise terminology.
B. Inclusion of additional information which obscures required information.
C. Failure to disclose components of finance charges.
D. Lack of meaningful sequence in the listing of information.

These violations will be separately discussed.

A. *Misleading labels where precise terminology is required.*—

1. Regulation Z was put out by the Federal Reserve System to assist in implementing the act. Section 226.8(b)(3) requires disclosure of:

(3) The number, amount, and due dates or periods of payments scheduled to repay the indebtedness and, except in the case of a loan secured by a first lien or equivalent security interest on a dwelling made to finance the purchase of that dwelling and except in the case of a sale of a dwelling, the sum of such payments using the term "total of payments."

Nowhere does defendants' form contract use the term "total of payments." Instead, in item number 8 of the right column of the contract, the term "Total Time Balance" is used to refer to what is apparently the "total of payments." This violates Regulation Z, § 226.8(b)(3). The Truth in Lending Act and Regulation Z call for precise, uniform, nationwide disclosures rather than approximations or terminology devised by each individual creditor.

2. . . . The requirement of [Reg. Z] Subsection (8)(ii) was not followed. It is true that the term "deferred payment price" was used; but it was used in two different places for two different figures. In the left-hand column, line number 11, the entry was "Deferred Payment Price 698.24 (Sum 5, 8, 10)." In the right-hand column, line number 7 reads "Deferred Payment Price (new purchase only) (Sum of 1, 4, 6) 633.24." One schooled in the art of reading these documents (which this court is not) can ultimately figure out that the correct "deferred payment price" is $698.24. However, the repeated use of the same phrase to describe different totals is a violation not only of Section 226.8(c)(8)(ii), but is also a violation of Regulation Z, Section 226.6(c), which will be discussed next.

B. *The form obscures required information by inserting inadequately defined additional information.*—

The defendants' form violates Section 226.6(c) in several ways:

1. For example, it uses the required term "Finance Charge" in four different places. In left-hand column, line 2, the "Finance Charge Discount" is listed as $1.46 (Rule 78ths)"; in left-hand column, line 10, the "Total Finance Charge" is listed as "$42.00 less unearned Finance Charge 1.46 (Item 2)"; in the right-hand column, line 6, the "Finance Charge" is listed as $40.54. The customer is apparently expected to guess the true finance charge from these four conflicting entries. As it turns out, when the document is studied with extreme care and patience, the true finance charge is actually $42.00, which is listed as "Total Finance Charge" in the first part of the left-hand column, line 10.

2. In Mrs. Barber's case the "Finance Charge" of $40.54 disclosed in right column, item 6, is not the finance charge as that term is defined in Regulation Z § 226.2(w) and § 226.4. Use of the term in this manner is disclosure of incorrect additional information not required by the Act which confuses the important but required disclosures.

3. The term "Finance Charge Discount 1.46" in the left column, line 2, also presents additional information not required by the act. The word "Discount" suggests a bargain or a reduction in price or cost. There was no such discount. The $1.46 is a *rebate* (required by state law) of *unearned* charges for financing the earlier merged transaction. This information is therefore not only unnecessary but misleading, incorrect and confusing.

4. Other terms are also duplicated. The phrases "Total Down Payment" "Unpaid Balance of Cash Price," "Recording Fee" and "Amount Financed" all appear in each of the two parallel

columns. The partially explanatory material underneath these phrases does not reveal without close and intelligent study just what these duplicate terms mean. Their use in this fashion violates Section 226.6(c) of Regulation Z.

C. *Components of the Finance charge are not disclosed.*—

Regulation Z, § 226.8(c)(8)(i) quoted above requires disclosure of the "total amount of the finance charge, with description of each amount included, using the term 'finance charge'." Assuming that the careful borrower has decided whether his "Finance Charge" is the "Total Finance Charge" of $42.00 in left hand column, line 10, or the "Unearned Finance Charge" of $1.46 which appears in the extension of line 10, or the "Finance Charge" of $40.54 in right-hand column, line 6, he can nowhere find on the contract a clear description of the amounts included in the term "Finance Charge." This violates Regulation Z, Section 226.8(c)(8)(i).

D. *Lack of meaningful sequence in the disclosures.*—

. . .This requirement is violated in several particulars by the defendants' contract:

1. The contract taken as a whole does not make its disclosures clearly, conspicuously, in meaningful sequence or manner. Required terminology is omitted and terminology not required is added in a confusing manner. Identical terms are used for different disclosures. The computation requires zigzagging across the page in an irrational fashion.

2. The "Total of Payments" (shown incorrectly as "Total Time Balance" in the right-hand column, line 8) is not computed nor disclosed in meaningful sequence. This figure, upon careful inspection, is discovered to be the product of the number of payments multiplied by the amount of each regular installment payment. However, the number of payments does not appear anywhere above line 8, nor does the amount of each monthly payment appear anywhere above that spot, and it is necessary to go down into the fine print and additional entries below that line to discover that the amount of each payment is $33.00. This form of disclosure therefore violates not only Section 226.8(b)(3) as indicated above, but also violates Section 226.6(a) by its failure to make disclosures "clearly, conspicuously, in meaningful sequence."

3. The "Total of Payments" is not clearly shown as the sum of the amount financed and the finance charge. This item (incorrectly described in right column, line 8, as "Total Time Balance 396.00") is by simultaneous inspection of both columns discovered to be the total of left column, line 9, the "Amount Financed 354.00" and the "Total Finance Charge 42.00" which is in left column, line 10. Again, it is necessary to zig zag from right to left in order to make sense out of the entries, and to add two items from line 9 and line 10 of the left-hand column in order to reach the total of line 8 in the right-hand column.

4. The number of payments and the amount of each payment and the dates they are due are not disclosed in meaningful sequence as required by Regulation Z § 226.6. On this form, the number of payments ("12") appears in the right hand column as an unnumbered line just below line 8. The amount of each payment ($33.00) appears in the legend on the opposite side of the page and several lines below line 8. The information is on the form, but it takes considerable ingenuity to relate these items to each other.

* * * * *

The contract violates the meaningful sequence provision of Regulation Z in two ways. First, the disclosure terms are not sequentially arranged. Second, a number of the terms of the contract appear in several places on the contract.

The court concludes as a matter of law that in the above matters the contract between the defendants on the one hand and the plaintiff . . . on the other hand violated the Truth in Lending Act and the defendants are civilly liable to the plaintiff. . . .

[On appeal, the *Barber* case was affirmed in part, reversed in part. The findings of the TIL violations were not disturbed. *Barber* v. *Kimbrell's Inc.*, 577 F.2d 216 (4th Cir. 1978).]

Questions

1. According to the court, what are the purposes of TILA?
2. What is an add-on transaction?
3. On appeal of the *Barber* case, Senior Circuit Judge Bryan dissented (577 F.2d at 227) saying, "the congressional aim and purpose here has not been thwarted. . . . A casual reading reveals the contract to be clear and readily understandable." Do you agree? Explain.
4. A health spa sells some memberships for cash and money on an installment basis. The price is the same whether the buyer pays cash or buys on the installment plan. The spa has an arrangement with a financing agency to sell the installment contracts to the agency at a discount, that is, at a price lower than the face value of the contract.
    a. How would you argue that the installment contract sales are in violation of TILA and Regulation Z?
    b. How would you rule on such a case? See, e.g., *Joseph v. Norman's Health Club, Inc.*, 532 F.2d 86 (8th Cir. 1976).[13]

Equal Credit Opportunity Act (ECOA)   In a society historically beset with discrimination, it is hardly surprising that credit was often denied on the basis of prejudices and stereotypes. In 1974 Congress enacted the Equal Credit Opportunity Act to combat bias in lending. Credit must be extended to all creditworthy applicants regardless of sex, marital status, age, race, color, religion, national origin, good faith exercise of rights under the Consumer Credit Protection Act, and receipt of public assistance. ECOA was in large part a response to anger over differing treatment of women and men in the financial marketplace. Creditors often would not loan money to married women under the woman's own name. Single, divorced, and widowed women were at a great disadvantage, vis-à-vis their male counterparts, in securing credit; and frequently women who married had to reapply for credit under their husband's name.

In addition to forbidding explicit discrimination in granting credit, ECOA includes a variety of provisions limiting the information that a creditor can require in processing an application. In general the creditor cannot seek information that could be used to engage in discrimination. Hence, among others, inquiries as to marital status, income from alimony, child support, maintenance payments, birth control practices, and child-bearing plans are either forbidden or limited.

Those discriminated against in violation of the act may recover actual damages, punitive damages up to $10,000, and other appropriate equitable and declaratory relief. Various agencies, including the Federal Trade Commission, enforce the act.

HARBAUGH V. CONTINENTAL ILLINOIS NATIONAL BANK   615 F.2d 1169 (1980)

Circuit Judge Moore

Plaintiffs, Helen D. Harbaugh and John P. Harbaugh, husband and wife, appeal from a final judgment entered in the Northern District of Illinois, granting defendant Continental Illinois National Bank and Trust Company's motion for summary judgment in its favor and denying plaintiffs' cross-motion for summary judgement. . . .

Sometime prior to March 12, 1976, Continental sent an unsolicited application for a Master Charge credit card to Mr. John P. Harbaugh. The Harbaughs crossed out the word "Mr.", typed above the deleted "Mr." the word "Mrs.", and inserted certain statistical information about Mrs. Harbaugh such as her employment as a teacher, her employer (The Chicago Board of Education), and her salary. As thus prepared, the application was signed "Mrs. John P. Harbaugh" dated March 12, 1976, and sent to Continental. In this form Continental forwarded the application to Credit Information Corporation of Chicago (CICC), a company used by Continental for credit report purposes. CICC made a practice of not using "courtesy" titles in its credit investigations. Accordingly, when it requested a confidential employee's report from the Chicago Board of Education, the Board replied that it had no record of a John P. Harbaugh as an employed teacher. Continental so advised Mrs. Harbaugh, who straightaway supplied the desired information. Mrs. Harbaugh's employment being confirmed, Continental issued two credit cards in the name of John P. Harbaugh.

Mrs. Harbaugh was aware that she had the authority to use the credit cards received and retained by them and that she could sign them Mrs. John P. Harbaugh or Mrs. Helen D. Harbaugh. . . . However, John P. Harbaugh did not regard the cards as satisfactory and wrote Master Charge on June 24, 1976, that he did not order the card and that its issuance was a "tactic to avoid issuing a card to my wife, Helen D. Harbaugh."

Asserting that Continental's acts constituted "[d]iscrimination against women in granting financial credit" and amounted to "sexual discrimination", John P. Harbaugh on September 10, 1976 wrote to the Comptroller of the Currency, . . . in Washington, and invited investigation. He sent copies of his letter to his congressman, Philip M. Crane, and to Senator Adlai Stevenson. Congressman Crane referred the matter to another federal agency, the Federal Trade Commission ("FTC"). The FTC replied that it was "unable to take any action on Mrs. Harbaugh's behalf" but suggested contacting the Comptroller of the Currency. Having received no reply from the Comptroller of the Currency after fifteen weeks, John Harbaugh wrote the Director, Office of Saver and Consumer Affairs, Board of Governors, Federal Reserve System, stating that he had learned that "your organization was established to help administer a wide varity [sic] of consumer legislation without being intimidated by the large banks." . . . Copies of this letter were sent to Senator Stevenson, Congressman Crane, and a representative of the American Association of Retired Persons. In turn, the Director of the Office of Saver and Consumer Affairs forwarded this letter to the Comptroller of the Currency. The Office of the Comptroller, without giving Continental an opportunity to state its case, gave as its opinion that Continental's action had violated the ECOA, . . . and wrote Mr. Harbaugh that "You may wish to discuss with your attorney the remedies available to you under 15 U.S.C. 1640 and 15 U.S.C. 1691." Thus far, the Harbaughs had consulted the Legislative and Executive branches of government; then the Comptroller of the Currency suggested that the Judiciary be added to complete the triumvirate.

Certain other events occurred. On Feburary 5, 1977, Continental advised John P. Harbaugh that the cards were to be reissued and requested Mr. Harbaugh to correct erroneous information. The Harbaughs returned the notice, giving the name of Helen D. Harbaugh as the applicant. On March 25, 1977, Continental reissued the two Master Charge cards in the name of John P. Harbaugh.

Presumably acting upon the Comptroller's suggestion, the Harbaughs brought suit on June 3, 1977. The trial judge found that "On November 18, 1977, purportedly in an attempt to settle the pending lawsuit, Continental issued a Master Charge credit card in the name of Helen D. Harbaugh." The trial judge granted defendant's motion for summary judgment and denied plaintiffs' cross-motion for summary judgment. From this ruling, plaintiffs appeal.

The primary thrust of Mrs. Harbaugh's claim on appeal is that Continental's issuance of a credit card in the name of John P. Harbaugh was a discriminatory denial of credit on the basis of her sex or marital status, in violation of the Equal Credit Opportunity Act. . . . It should be noted that Mrs. Harbaugh does not claim that she could not *use* the Master Charge card issued in the name of her husband. Instead, Mrs. Harbaugh's claim is that Continental unlawfully discriminated by refusing to open a credit account which would reflect her individual credit transactions and establish her own credit history, separate and apart from her husband. She stated that her intent in applying for a Master Charge card was to have her own account and her own credit rating in case something should happen to her husband. . . .

In response, Continental asserts that Mrs. Harbaugh was the recipient of credit from the bank. Before issuing the cards, Continental investigated her credit and verified her employment. However, Continental admits that while Mrs. Harbaugh did get her own account at the bank, she did not establish a separate credit history at the credit bureau. As Mr. Sheahen of CICC stated in his affidavit, an account in the name of "Mrs. John P. Harbaugh" would have the identical effect as a card in the name of "John P. Harbaugh": no independent credit history would thereby be established for Helen Harbaugh at the credit bureau.

Thus, this case poses the question of whether a creditor, using a computer form at which excluded all courtesy titles, is under a statutory duty to correct or supplement the manner in which it processes a credit application by a married woman in her marital name in order to insure that she receive a separate credit history. In other words, Mrs. Harbaugh makes two alternative claims under the ECOA: (1) the bank was under an affirmative duty to use the courtesy title "Mrs." in opening her account *or* (2) if the courtesy title of "Mrs." was deleted, the bank was under a duty to insure that she receive a separate credit history in her own name. . . .

. . . We reject the claim that the bank was under an affirmative duty to use the courtesy title "Mrs." in opening Mrs. Harbaugh's account. The ECOA and its corresponding regulations expressly prohibit a creditor from requesting an applicant's sex or marital status. Thus, a creditor's mandatory requirement that an applicant supply a courtesy title would violate the intent of the statute. However, neither the statute nor the regulations address the question of a creditor's response to a courtesy title *voluntarily* supplied by a married woman applying in her marital name. As there is no affirmative requirement in the legislation requiring a creditor to utilize a courtesy title in opening or maintaining an account, Continental was not required to use the courtesy title supplied by Mrs. Harbaugh.

We also reject Mrs. Harbaugh's alternative claim that, if Continental chose a computer format which deleted courtesy titles, it was under a duty to correct the "inherent discriminatory effects" of such a practice. Mrs. Harbaugh asserts that, when Continental received her application in the name of "Mrs. John P. Harbaugh," it was put on notice that processing of the application without the courtesy title "Mrs." would deny her the individual account she sought. Thus, she argues that Continental was under a statutory duty either to inform her of its practice of deleting courtesy titles or to voluntarily ascertain her first given name before opening the account.

Without statutory or regulatory authorization, we decline to impose these affirmative duties on a creditor such as Continental. . . . In view of the fact that the Federal Reserve Board promulgated regulations establishing a mechanism whereby creditors were required to inform married women how to establish their own credit histories, the imposition of more stringent duties upon the creditor (as urged by Mrs. Harbaugh), is not warranted.

. . . Nor is there a statutory requirement that a creditor voluntarily inquire as to a married woman's given first name upon receiving an application in her marital name. Such a requirement would place the creditor in an untenable position. Had Continental written to Mrs. Harbaugh, requesting that she supply her first name, it would have been risking an accusation that it had violated two sections of Regulation B: § 202.5(d)(3), which prohibits creditors from requesting information with respect to the applicant's sex and § 202.5(a), which prohibits the creditor from any statements which would discourage a reasonable person from pursing an application.

* * * * *

Judgment affirmed.

Fairchild, Chief Judge, dissenting.

The majority opinion seems to concede that Mrs. Harbaugh was denied a separate credit account . . . but finds no violation of the Act, holding that the Act does not specifically require the bank to establish an individual account for Mrs. Harbaugh since she applied using the name "Mrs. John Harbaugh." But it was not Mrs. Harbaugh who created the difficulties she encountered—it was the bank's computers, some of which, at least, have not been programmed to identify Mr. John Doe and Mrs. John Doe as two different persons. . . . The statutory requirements are clear—there is no exception for good faith computer programming deficiencies. . . .

Aside from what seems to me to be a fairly straightforward example of a denial of credit, there are several aspects of this case that particularly intrigue me.

First, as the majority opinion notes, there were at least two alternative choices available to the bank when Mrs. Harbaugh's application was received even given the claimed inflexibility of the bank's computers. The bank could have established an account in the name of Helen Harbaugh (which it had learned was her name) or it could have written to her explaining the problem and asking for instructions. The bank, however, did neither. Instead it established an account in the name of "John Harbaugh." The majority seems to hold that the latter course of action was more in keeping with the letter and the spirit of the Act than either of the first two would have been. I strongly disagree.

Second, although the bank asserts that its practice of deleting courtesy titles "is in accordance with the aims of the equal credit opportunity laws to ensure that the credit granting process is 'neutral as to sex'" the bank does use courtesy titles in some of its dealing with customers and indeed used courtesy titles in its dealings with the Harbaughs. . . .

The third point that intrigues me is the suggestion that a married woman's designation of herself as, for example, "Mrs. John Doe" is so extraordinary that a credit lending institution cannot reasonably be expected to process a credit application from someone who refers to herself in that fashion. There are over 60 million married or widowed women in this country who Emily Post and Amy Vanderbilt still insist are properly addressed only as "Mrs." followed by their husband's names. . . .

Questions

1. Explain the court's reasoning in affirming the judgment in favor of Continental Illinois.
2. Do you agree with the majority opinion or that of the dissenting judge? Explain.
3. Does ECOA increase or decrease the cost of credit? Explain.

Fair Credit Reporting Act (FCRA) For most of us a favorable credit rating is necessary to the full enjoyment of the material fruits of American life. We seek credit so commonly that credit bureaus process upwards of 100 million credit reports annually. Given these conditions, it is essential that credit information be accurate, that the information be used only for proper purposes, and that credit inquiries not unnecessarily disturb the consumer's privacy. Congress passed the FCRA in 1970, both in recognition of the potential for abuse in gathering and reporting credit information, and in recognition of the necessity for accurate, fair credit reports.

Rather than conducting their own credit investigations, businesses commonly turn to firms that specialize in gathering, storing, and reporting that information. Those credit bureaus, or in the language of the act, "consumer reporting agencies" that regularly engage in the business of gathering and reporting consumer credit data to third parties, are covered by the terms of the act. The key requirements of the FCRA are as follows:

1. *Consumer rights.* If requested, consumer reporting agencies must—with certain exceptions—provide each consumer with the information in his or her file. However, the consumer does not have the right to see the file itself. Inaccurate, obsolete, and unverifiable information must be removed. If the contents of the file remain in dispute, the consumer has the right to include in the file a brief statement of her or his version of the issues in question. If a consumer should be denied employment, credit, or insurance because of an agency report, the user of the report must so inform the consumer, and the consumer must be advised as to the origin of the credit report.

2. *Reporting Agency Responsibilities.* In brief, agencies are required to follow reasonable procedures to ensure that information is both accurate and up-to-date. Consumer credit reports can be furnished only for the following purposes, absent the consumer's permission or a court order: *(a)* credit, *(b)* insurance, *(c)* employment, *(d)* obtaining a government benefit, or *(e)* other legitimate business purpose involving a consumer. Inasmuch as protection of privacy is one of the stated purposes of the act, it is interesting that Congress imposed no limitation on the kinds of information that may be included in a file. Hence, sexual practices, political preferences, hair length, friendships, organizational memberships, and the like can lawfully be reported.

3. *User Responsibilities.* Those who purchase a consumer credit investigation must inform the consumer in advance of the pending inquiry.

When a consumer is denied credit, employment, or insurance, or where financial charges are increased because of an adverse credit report, the consumer must be apprised of the name and address of the consumer reporting agency that provided the information.

4. *Penalties.* Wronged consumers may secure actual damages in cases of negligent noncompliance with the FCRA. Additionally, punitive damages may be secured in cases of willful noncompliance. In the criminal venue, fines of up to $5,000 and jail terms of up to one year may be assessed against those who knowingly and willfully secure information under false pretenses, and those credit agency employees who provide information to unauthorized persons are likewise subject to those criminal punishments. A number of federal agencies have statutory authority to enforce the act, but the primary burden lies with the Federal Trade Commission. Basically the FTC can issue cease and desist orders against credit reporting agencies, because violations of the FCRA are treated as unfair and deceptive trade practices.

Fair Credit Billing Act (FCBA)   The FCBA, which became effective in 1975, provides a mechanism to deal with the billing errors that inevitably attend credit card transactions. The credit card holder who receives an erroneous bill must complain in writing to the creditor within 60 days of the receipt of the bill. If so, the creditor must acknowledge receipt of the complaint within 30 days. Then, within two billing cycles but not more than 90 days, the creditor must issue a response either acknowledging or denying the error. If the former, appropriate adjustments must be made. If the latter, the creditor must explain why the bill is correct. After filing its response, the creditor must wait 10 days before reporting the account as delinquent. If the consumer continues to dispute the accuracy of the bill, the creditor must file notice of the continuing dispute with any third party to whom notice of the deliquency is directed. Penalties for a creditor in violation of the act are quite modest. The consumer can collect the amount in question and any accompanying finance charges, but that amount may not exceed $50 for each charge in dispute.

Predictably, the miracle of the credit card has led to an abundance of new headaches. Notwithstanding the FCBA, consumers remain the frequent victim of billing errors. As demonstrated in the following article, the consequences of those errors can be calamitous, and the pursuit of justice can be exhausting.

AWARD UPHELD IN CREDIT-CARD-ERROR SUIT

San Francisco, Calif. (AP)—A secretary who sued her bank for failing to correct a Visa card billing error deserves a $150,000 award to compensate for the bank's "computer-hearted insensitivity," an appellate court has ruled.

Scolding Bank of America for its "callous indifference" toward Christine Young, the state Court of Appeal upheld the damages she won in 1980 after the theft of her credit card snowballed into months of financial problems.

The 34-year-old Monterey secretary said she was "very pleased" by the ruling. Bank of America, the nation's largest commercial bank, said it was "disappointed" and would consider a further appeal.

"It's a great victory . . . for all consumers," said Young's lawyer, Andrew Swartz. "Everyone . . . has had some sort of trouble with computer-generated bills. Most people can identify with this case."

Young's Visa card was stolen on May 24, 1979, and she reported the theft to the bank two days later. Unauthorized charges of $2,000 later were made on the stolen card, and the bank informed TRW, a worldwide credit network, that Young was a bad credit risk, according to court records.

The bank "tenaciously sought collection" of those charges in violation of credit card laws, the appellate court said.

During the trial in Monterey County Superior Court, Young testified that she was refused a credit card at another bank because of the unfavorable credit rating. She said she had trouble cashing personal checks and felt helpless and frustrated because the bank refused to adjust her account and repeatedly demanded payment.

She said her financial difficulties caused her severe stress, nervousness, headaches, insomnia, and trouble in performing her job.

Jurors awarded her $50,000 in July 1980, and Judge Harkjoon Paik trebled that amount. The bank appealed on grounds the amount was excessive.

But the three-judge appellate panel upheld the award. "The harm suffered by the plaintiff, which included humiliation, anxiety, and grief, is not easily quantifiable and is best left to the sound discretion of the jury," the ruling said.

Source: *The Des Moines (Iowa) Register,* March 25, 1983, p. 4A. Reprinted with permission of the copyright holder, The Associated Press.

QUESTIONS

1. What reasoning would you cite to justify the judge's decision to triple the jury's $50,000 award?

2. How would you rule on appeal? Explain.

Usury Statutes   Fearing that consumers of limited bargaining power will be victimized by lenders, all states have passed usury laws imposing a limit on the amount of interest that can lawfully be charged for borrowed money. Usury laws have their roots in the church's historical opposition to the harshness of the "money changers" and in a well-intended solicitude for the financially unsophisticated and those forced to borrow under troubled circumstances. In general, contracts for loans at interest rates in excess of that permitted by law are illegal and criminal penalties are often imposed. Depending on state law, the creditor may be able to collect none or only the lawful portion of the interest in question. In practice, the vitality of state usury laws is often sapped by exceptions that have the effect of lifting the allowable maximum rate. For example, the lender may be permitted to add a "carrying charge" to the terms of the loan. In recent years interest rates have risen dramatically, and state legislatures have felt compelled to raise the maximum permissible rates. In most states the usury laws offer little protection, and many critics believe those laws to be of more harm than good to the consumer.

Is, for example, a 20 percent interest rate a *moral* wrong? A 30 percent rate?

Debtor Protection

Generosity of spirit and deed is one of the more noble dimensions of the American character. However legitimately one may criticize our foreign policy in Vietnam, our tardiness in attacking discrimination, our devotion to sometimes crass materialism, it cannot legitimately be denied that Americans struggle sincerely to help those in need. Hence, for charitable reasons as well as for some "hard-nosed" economic considerations, the American legal system has enacted careful protections for those who find themselves indebted.

Bankruptcy

Our culture encourages indebtedness. For various reasons, some of those debtors become encumbered beyond reasonable hope of recovery. Those individuals and organizations may, under appropriate circumstances, seek relief under the terms of our bankruptcy laws. We wish to afford a fresh beginning to the debtor and to avoid rendering the debtor an unproductive, helpless burden on society. We also want the involved creditors to recover as much of their losses as possible. So, although the reasons for our bankruptcy provisions are in large part quite pragmatic, it is nevertheless touching that we retain the humane recognition that some of us occasionally need a lift to overcome our ill fortune or foolishness.

The word *bankruptcy* originally meant broken bench. In common-law England, when a merchant or craftsman was unable to pay his debts, the custom in the community was to break his work bench. This publically established that the craftsman was no longer in business. Quite often, the creditors at that time would seek to perform the ceremony across the head of the impecunious debtor.[14]

Debtors are able to seek relief through both state and federal legislation. Our attention will be limited to federal law. The federal Bankruptcy Reform Act of 1978 repealed all previous bankruptcy law. It was, in turn, amended by the Bankruptcy Amendments and Federal Judgeship Act of 1984.

Bankruptcy is an adjudication relieving a debtor of all or part of the liabilities incurred to date. Under the terms of the Constitution, Congress is empowered to enact uniform bankruptcy legislation. Any person, partnership, or corporation may seek debtor relief. Basically, the three forms of bankruptcy action are:

1. *Liquidation* (Chapter 7 of the Reform Act), in which all assets but for exemptions are distributed to creditors.
2. *Reorganization* (Chapter 11), in which creditors are kept from the debtor's assets while the debtor negotiates a settlement.
3. *Adjustment of debts of an individual with regular income* (Chapter 13), in which individuals may achieve an arrangement similar to a Chapter 11 reorganization.

"Straight" Bankruptcy A Chapter 7 liquidation petition may be *voluntarily* filed in federal court by the debtor (individual, partnership, or corporation), or creditors may seek an *involuntary* bankruptcy judgment.

In a voluntary action the debtor files a petition with the appropriate federal court. The court then has jurisdiction to proceed with the liquidation, and the petition becomes the *order for relief*. The debtor need not be insolvent to seek bankruptcy.

An involuntary bankruptcy can be compelled only if the creditors have an individual or aggregate claim of at least $5,000. The debtor may challenge the bankruptcy action. The court will enter an *order for relief* if it finds the debtor has not been paying his or her debts when due or if most of the debtor's property is under the control of a custodian for the purpose of enforcing a lien against that property.

After the order for relief is granted, voluntary and involuntary actions proceed in a similar manner. Creditors are restrained from reaching the debtor's assets. An interim bankruptcy trustee is appointed by the court. The creditors then hold a meeting, and a permanent trustee is elected. The trustee collects the debtor's property and converts it to money, protects the interests of the debtor and creditors, may manage the debtor's business, and ultimately distributes the estate proceeds to the creditors. Both federal and state laws permit the debtor to exempt certain property (e.g., household goods and clothing not to exceed $4,000, and equity in a vehicle not to exceed $1,200). The debtor's nonexempt property is then divided among the creditors according to the priorities prescribed by statute. Secured creditors are paid first. If funds remain, "priority" creditors, such as those responsible for administering the debtor's estate, are paid. Then, funds permitting, general creditors are paid. Each class must be paid in full before a class of lower priority will be compensated. Any remaining funds will return to the debtor.

When distribution is complete, the bankruptcy judge may issue an order *discharging* the debtor of any remaining debts except for certain statutorily specified claims. Those include, for example, alimony, child support, taxes, and educational loans. The debtor might fail to receive a discharge if the debtor had received a discharge in the previous six years, or if property was concealed from the court or in other respects good faith in the bankruptcy process was lacking.

Adjustment of Debts   Under Chapter 13 of the Bankruptcy Reform Act, individuals (not partnerships or corporations) can seek the protection of the court to arrange a debt adjustment plan. Chapter 13 permits only voluntary bankruptcies. After the necessary petition is filed, creditors are restrained from reaching the debtor's assets. A trustee is appointed, and the debtor files a plan for repayment.

Reorganization   Our primary concern in this section of the text is with debtor protection for consumers, but recently an important and novel confluence of products liability theory (see Chapter 16) and bankruptcy law has brought corporate reorganization to the consumer (and worker) protection arena. Many workers and consumers are bringing products liability suits claiming personal injury from "toxic" products such as asbestos, formaldehyde, benzene, and Agent Orange. Chapter 11 of the Bankruptcy Reform Act is being used by some companies in an attempt to "manage" those claims. Chapter 11 is the bankruptcy proceeding most commonly employed by corporations, but its provisions also apply to other debtors, including partnerships and individuals. Under Chapter 11 the debtor keeps existing property but establishes with the court a schedule under which creditors will be paid. The debtor is permitted to continue business activities. The court prevents creditors from reaching the debtor's assets other than through the agreed-upon payment plan. The plan may provide for payment of all or only a portion of the debt. The court will hold a hearing, at which creditors and other "interested parties" may file objections. The court will confirm the plan if certain conditions are met. If the payments provided for in the plan are completed, the debtor will ultimately receive a discharge. And under certain hardship circumstances a debtor may receive a discharge even if the plan was not completed in full. The case that follows illustrates one company's attempt to use Chapter 11 to avoid a financial collapse.

IN RE JOHNS–MANVILLE CORP.   **36 Bankruptcy Reporter 727**
(S.D.N.Y., 1984)

Decision and order on Motions to Dismiss Manville's Chapter 11 Petition. Burton R. Lifland, Bankruptcy Judge.

Background and Issues Presented

Whether an industrial enterprise in the United States is highly successful is often gauged by its "membership" in what has come to be known as the "Fortune 500." Having attained this measure of financial achievement, Johns-Manville Corp. and its affiliated companies . . . were deemed a paradigm of success in corporate America by the financial community. Thus, Manville's filing for protection under Chapter 11 of Title 11 of the United States Code . . . on August 26, 1982 ("the filing date"), was greeted with great surprise and consternation on the part of some of its creditors and other corporations that were being sued along with Manville for injuries caused by asbestos exposure. As discussed at length herein, Manville submits that the sole factor necessitating its filing is the mammoth problem of uncontrolled proliferation of asbestos health suits brought against it because of its substantial use for many years of products containing asbestos which injured those who came into contact with the dust of this lethal substance. According to Manville, this current problem of approximately 16,000 lawsuits pending as of the filing date is compounded by the crushing economic burden to be suffered by Manville over the next 20–30 years by the filing of an even more staggering number of suits by those who had been exposed but who will not manifest the asbestos-related diseases until some time during this future period ("the future asbestos claimants"). Indeed, approximately 6,000 asbestos health claims are estimated to have arisen in only the first 16 months since the filing date.

It is the propriety of the filing by Manville which is the subject of the instant decision. Four separate motions to dismiss the petition pursuant to Section 1112(b) of the Code have been lodged before this court.

*   *   *   *   *

The Asbestos Committee, which is comprised with one exception of attorneys for asbestos victims, initially moved to dismiss this case on November 8, 1982, citing Manville's alleged lack of good faith in filing this petition. . . . [T]he Asbestos Committee . . . has vigorously pursued discovery in order to bolster its factual contention that Manville knowingly perpetrated a fraud on this court and on all its creditors and equity holders in exaggerating the profundity of its economic distress in 1981 so as to enable it to file for reorganization in 1982. Thus, the Asbestos Committee submitted in November 1983 a multitude of volumes of materials consisting of 55 days of depositions of Manville officers in alleged support of the inference that in 1981 a small Manville group "concocted" evidence to meet the requirements for filing a Chapter 11 petition. The Asbestos Committee alleges that this group manufactured evidence of crushing economic distress so as to demonstrate falsely that pursuant to required principles of accounting . . . , Manville had to book a reserve of at least $1.9 billion for asbestos health liability, and thus had no alternative but to seek Chapter 11 protection. The booking of such a reserve would, in turn, have triggered the acceleration of approximately $450 million of outstanding debt, possibly resulting in a forced liquidation of key business segments. . . .

Mindful that there is no insolvency requirement for Chapter 11 debtor status, the issue presented for determination by this Court is whether these allegations of error by the Asbestos Committee, even egregious error, in over-calculation of Manville's financial problems are relevant to establish the kind of bad faith in the sense of an abuse of this Court's jurisdiction which will vitiate the filing of a Chapter 11 petition. . . .

The Motion to Dismiss Filed by the Asbestos Committee

The motion to dismiss the petition filed by the Asbestos Committee must be denied. . . .

Because the allegations of the Asbestos Committee are not supported by concrete facts and thus do not rebut the essential fact that Manville is a real company with a substantial amount of real debt and real creditors clamoring to enforce this real debt, the Asbestos Committee has not sustained its burden of demonstrating sufficient fraud to vitiate the filing. . . . On balance, the inferences to be drawn from submissions by both Manville and the Asbestos Committee seem to favor Manville. This is because Manville has credibly analyzed its position in its counter to the Asbestos Committee's allegations of fraud contained in its submission of . . . a Compendium of the Factual Record.

* * * * *

The Compendium relates the testimony of Manville officers and supports the inference accepted herein that these petitions were filed only after Manville undertook lengthy, careful and detailed analysis. For example, Manville commissioned and strictly scrutinized the results of studies by two separate epidemiological groups . . . According to Manville, the results of the studies by ERI and SERC corroborated each other's projections of runaway asbestos health costs within the foreseeable future.

In addition, the Compendium cites to testimony of Manville officers which details the slow and deliberate process of data commissioning and review and "soul-searching" antedating the filing, including the employment and review of results of studies done by Lexacon, Inc. and Drs. Sarat and Kritzler regarding propensity to sue. The data submitted by Manville also supports the accepted inference that the $1.9 billion projected debt figure ratified by Manville was the result of careful, conservative, and perhaps understated projections.

In so doing, Manville has succeeded in rebutting in general and in specific the Asbestos Committee's allegations of fraud regarding the size of its projected debt, including those of collusion, manipulation of figures, cover-up and falsification of data. That which therefore emerges from the voluminous submissions by both sides are unsubstantiated conclusory charges of fraud and misdeed and an expression by the Asbestos Committee of its disagreement with the methods used by Manville in projecting future asbestos health costs.

Manville was advised by Robert O. F. Bixby of the Price Waterhouse accounting firm that it was necessary to book a $1.9 billion reserve for contingent liability according to the accrual principle. On balance, Manville's decision to follow this advice was neither unreasonable, illogical, nor in any sense fraudulent. The Asbestos Committee has submitted no convincing evidence countering the necessity to book this reserve. . . .

The Code's Policies of Open Access and Liquidation Avoidance

In determining whether to dismiss . . ., a court is not necessarily required to consider whether the debtor has filed in "good faith" because that is not a specified predicate under the Code for filing. . . .

A "principal goal" of the Bankruptcy Code is to provide "open access" to the "bankruptcy process." . . . The rationale behind this "open access" policy is to provide access to bankruptcy relief which is as "open" as "access to the credit economy." . . . Thus, Congress intended that "there should be no legal barrier to voluntary petitions." Another major goal of the Code, that of "rehabilitation of debtors," requires that relief for debtors must be "timely." . . .

Accordingly, the drafters of the Code envisioned that a financially beleaguered debtor with real debt and real creditors should not be required to wait until the economic situation is beyond repair in order to file a reorganization petition. The "congressional purpose" in enacting the Code was to encourage resort to the bankruptcy process. This philosophy not only comports with the elimination of an insolvency requirement, but also is a corollary of the key aim of Chapter 11 of the Code, that of avoidance of liquidation. The drafters of the Code announced this goal, declaring that reorganization is more efficient than liquidation because "assets that are used for production in the industry for which they were designed are more valuable than those same assets sold for scrap." . . .

In the instant case, not only would liquidation be wasteful and inefficient in destroying the utility of valuable assets of the companies as well as jobs, but, more importantly, liquidation would preclude just compensation of some present asbestos victims and all future asbestos claimants. . . . Manville must not be required to wait until its economic picture has deteriorated beyond salvation to file for reorganization. . . .

Manville's "Good Faith" Filing Is Measured by the Existence of Massive Unmanageable Real Debt Owed to Real Claimants

It is this court's belief that there is no strict and absolute "good faith" predicate to filing a Chapter 11 petition.

This court, along with others, has opined that the concept of good faith is an elastic one which can be read into the statute on a limited ad hoc basis.

*   *   *   *   *

. . . In *Manville,* it is undeniable that there has been no sham or hoax perpetrated on the court in that Manville is a real business with real creditors in pressing need of economic reorganization. Indeed, the Asbestos Committee has belied its own contention that Manville has no debt and no real creditors by quantifying a benchmark settlement demand approaching one billion dollars for compensation of approximately 15,500 prepetition asbestos claimants, during the course of negotiations pitched toward achieving a consensual plan. This huge asserted liability does not even take into account the estimated 6,000 new asbestos health claims which have arisen in only the first 16 months since the filing date. The number of postfiling claims increases each day as "future claims back into the present." . . .

Moreover, asbestos related property damage claims present another substantial contingent and unliquidated liability. Prior to the filing date, various schools initiated litigation seeking compensatory and punitive damages from, *inter alia,* Manville for their unknowing use of asbestos-containing products in ceilings, walls, structural members, piping, ductwork and boilers in school buildings. . . . Since the filing date, two class action suits have been brought in the federal district court for the Eastern District of Pennsylvania. . . . These two class actions on behalf of every public school district and private school in the United States seek comprehensive redress for the school asbestos problem including compensatory damages for remedial action already undertaken by the schools, injunctive relief for necessary action not as yet undertaken, and punitive damages. Numerous postpetition school property damage suits have also been filed by individual school districts and schools in many states.

Accordingly, it is clear that Manville's liability for compensatory, if not punitive, damages to school authorities is not hypothetical, but real and massive debt. A range of $500 million to $1.4 billion is the total projected amount of Manville's real debt to the school creditors.

In addition, claims of $425 million of liquidated commercial debt have been filed in this proceeding. The filing also triggered the acceleration of more than $275 million in unsecured public and institutional debt which had not been due prior to the filing. . . . The economic reality of Manville's highly precarious financial position due to massive debt sustains its eligibility and candidacy for reorganization. . . .

Accordingly, Manville's filing does not abuse the jurisdictional integrity of this Court. . . .

[At this writing in 1985, various settlement proposals have been advanced to resolve the claims against Manville and other asbestos producers. Congress is considering a government-financed trust fund that would provide victims with about $35,000, medical expenses, and workers compensation. In return, recipients would not be allowed to sue asbestos companies.]

Questions

1. What is the issue in this case? How did the court resolve that issue?
2. What evidence and reasoning supported the court's judgment?
3. What advantages does Manville acquire from a Chapter 11 proceeding?
4. Manville has argued that "the court system, with its separate individual trials, is too inefficient and haphazard for a massive problem like this." Do you agree? Explain.
5. Manville has argued for "an effective, practical national system which delivers maximum payments to injured workers, minimizes the costs of delivering those payments, and withholds payments to those with no disability." As noted above, Congress is considering legislation to set up such a system.
    a. Should Congress establish some mechanism for dealing with massive disasters like the Manville case? Explain.
    b. Should the federal government help finance such a system? Explain.
6. Bildisco, a New Jersey building supplies distributor, filed for a Chapter 11 reorganization. Approximately 40 to 45 percent of Bildisco's labor force was represented by the Teamsters Union. The collective bargaining agreement between Bildisco and the union expressly provided that it was binding upon the parties even in the event of bankruptcy. Bildisco sought the court's permission to reject the collective bargaining agreement. Bildisco testified that the company would save $100,000 were the request granted. The union offered no witnesses of its own.

    The Bankruptcy Court granted Bildisco's petition. The Court of Appeals held that the collective bargaining agreement was an executory contract (not yet fully performed) and, therefore, subject to rejection under the Bankruptcy Code, which provides that "the trustee, subject to the court's approval, may assume or reject any executory contract." The National Labor Relations Board appealed to the Supreme Court.

    Can Bildisco be relieved of its collective bargaining agreement as an element of its reorganization under Chapter 11 of the Bankruptcy Code? See *National Labor Relations Board* v. *Bildisco and Bildisco,* 104 S.Ct. 1188 (1984).

Bankruptcy Critique   As explained in the following article, the business community has welcomed the most recent reform in U.S. bankruptcy law.

A BETTER BALANCE IN BANKRUPTCY LAW

Mary-Margaret Wantuck

Meet Charlie, a computer executive making $75,000 a year in 1979. He owned a beautifully furnished $175,000 country home with a $150,000 mortgage and commuted daily into New York City. He and his wife, Sylvia, enjoyed Broadway shows and exclusive Manhattan restaurants.

Charlie loved credit and lived on it—a stockpile of charge cards, a credit union revolving loan and overdraft checking. In early 1980 he reached his credit limit and had to start paying cash for entertainment. But with so much of his monthly income committed to debt service, there was just not that much cash left over to play with, and that annoyed Charlie and Sylvia.

Enter the Bankruptcy Reform Act of 1978, which went into effect in October, 1979.

It was an answer to the couple's prayer. They declared bankruptcy under Chapter 7, which erased all their debts. They were able to keep their house and continue to enjoy all of Charlie's $75,000 salary. They resumed their lives without any obligation to repay any of their creditors.

Charlie and Sylvia are not a particularly extreme example of the new kind of debtor encouraged by the looseness of the 1978 law. During the law's first full year of operation, between October 1979, and October 1980, U.S. bankruptcy cases rose 59 percent. The next year personal bankruptcies climbed another 43 percent, to 515,355.

Sears, Roebuck & Company, for example, found that its bankruptcy losses jumped more than 120 percent from 1979 to 1980.

Lenders discovered there were many Charlies and Sylvias—people who were current on their required monthly payments, had little or no previous history of delinquency and may have even had additional credit available at the time their creditors received the bankruptcy notice—but who decided to cash in on the bonanza, get rid of all their unsecured debts, and keep their real estate and personal property.

A study conducted by Purdue University's Credit Research Center in 1981 found that 4 out of 10 people who filed for Chapter 7 bankruptcy relief could have paid 50 percent or more of their nonmortgage obligations over the following five years; 29 percent could have repaid all of them.

* * * * *

Creditor uproar over bankruptcy losses finally hit home on Capitol Hill. Last June, Congress passed the Bankruptcy Amendments Act of 1984. Among many changes are tighter consumer provisions, which took effect in October. . . .

Most lenders call the new law better balanced between creditors and debtors. "What it represents is a livable compromise," says Laurence P. King, who was a member of a group at New York University that studied

bankruptcy law problems. "The old law was a farce."

Bankruptcy judges can now consider a debtor's current income and expenditures in determining whether his financial situation dictates a Chapter 7 filing or a plan for debt repayment under Chapter 13. Under the old law, only assets and liabilities could be weighed.

Chapter 13 filings have also been modified. An unsecured creditor can object to a Chapter 13 repayment plan that does not include repayment of the entire debt and use all of the debtor's projected disposable income (beyond the basic necessities) over a three-year period for repayment. Before, a nominal payback was acceptable as long as the debtor's plan showed an effort to pay back something to the creditors.

Consumers may no longer "load up" just before declaring bankruptcy. Any debts of $500 or more for "luxury goods and services," owed to a single creditor and incurred within 40 days of filing, must be paid. So must cash advances of more than $1,000 that are extended under an open-ended credit plan obtained by the debtor within 20 days before filing.

Federal exemptions have also undergone a facelift. In a Chapter 7 bankruptcy, a debtor's personal assets are converted to cash to reimburse creditors as much as possible. However, before a liquidation occurs, the debtor can exempt specified personal items.

Under the law, a debtor can no longer exempt $200 of value on each item of household goods and clothes. There is now a flat $4,000 maximum amount. In addition, a debtor can exempt only $3,750 of equity in real property used as a residence plus $400 in value of other property. The old amount was $7,500 of equity plus $400 in other property.

An added bonus for creditors is that now couples can take either a federal or state exemption—not both, as was permitted before. . . .

Lenders like Jimmie Bearden, president of the Aero Engineering Development Center Federal Credit Union in Memphis, are especially happy about more restrictive collateral provisions.

"Debtors can't hang onto collateral like a

car for months now, running it into the ground and having its value depreciate measurably as each day goes by,'' she says. Debtors have 30 days from the time of the bankruptcy petition to file a statement of intent as to whether they will redeem the collateral, voluntarily surrender the collateral, claim the property as exempt or reaffirm the underlying debt. They have another 45 days in which they can change that decision.

If a debtor elects to reaffirm his debt, no court approval is required.

Bankruptcy judges now have the authority to dismiss a Chapter 7 bankruptcy petition if the judge determines that granting the request would constitute ''substantial abuse'' of the bankruptcy code.

Challenging debtor fraud in a bankruptcy court now is much easier for creditors. The only way a debtor's attorney's fees can be exacted from the creditor is if it is substantially proven that the creditor brought suit solely to harass the debtor, knowing that no fraud was involved.

Lawyers' responsibilities have increased. A debtor's attorney must now inform his client of relief other than Chapter 7 that is available for resolving his financial problems.

In the past, ''in courts where not too many Chapter 13s were filed, the debtor may not have known there was another recourse,'' says Lawrence Young, a Houston attorney with expertise in the consumer bankruptcy area. ''Much of the preparatory work was handled by paralegals; it was a fill-out-the-forms-and-file atomosphere. Now, instead of running an assembly line in court, lawyers are back in the business of lawyering again.''

* * * * *

Creditors say the law still has weaknesses. Too much potential for abuse exists, according to Alexander Cole, senior vice president of credit administration for Industrial Valley National Bank & Trust Company in Philadelphia.

''As long as consumers have the right to retain some equity in their homes and on other assets under federal exemptions, notwithstand-

ing state overrides,'' he notes, ''they may find ways of abusing that right.''

Determining whether there is substantial abuse in a Chapter 7 filing may take so much time that a busy judge may leave review of a debtor's fiancial status to a court trustee. The trustee would then have a major say in whether a case should remain Chapter 7 or be switched to Chapter 13.

''Many bankruptcy courts are very, very busy,'' Young says. ''In the southern district of Texas, for example, there are 17,000 bankruptcy cases pending, and only two judges; the third position is vacant. But even three judges are not going to make much difference.''

With Chapter 11 business reorganizations like that of Continental Airlines taking up a great deal of the courts' time, Young says, consumer cases are going to get short shrift. ''The issues in an individual case are just not that weighty; the effect on society overall is negligible,'' he says.

* * * * *

Many creditors argue that bankruptcy write-offs would decrease dramatically if the new law ordered bankruptcy courts to take a debtor's future earnings into account.

In the specialized publication *Credit World,* Harry Wolpoff and Ronald Canter, lawyers specializing in consumer credit law, have described what can happen when future income is not taken into account.

A doctor is serving a one-year residency at a hospital where he receives a weekly salary of $150 plus living accommodations. Shortly, he will fill a $40,000 teaching post at a medical school. His debts total $15,000. Two months before starting his new job, he files for Chapter 7 bankruptcy. The income statement disclosed to the court reflects only his present $150 salary. Disposable income left after paying necessary expenses is minimal. The authors say his filing probably would not be challenged.

* * * * *

Credit counselors are decrying the law's omission of a requirement that all petitioners go through counseling.

"There are people who go through the bankruptcy process, are adjudicated as debtors and released by the courts without having learned anything," says Robert E. Gibson, president of the National Foundation for Consumer Credit, whose members are credit counseling services. "They are subject to continuing money mismanagement and financial catastrophes."

* * * * *

But creditors say most of the changes in bankruptcy laws are good, and they do not expect to see any more revisions soon. After struggling for years over changing the law, "the last thing Congress wants to see on its agenda is bankruptcy," Young says.

Source: *Nation's Business*, April 1985, pp. 50–53. Reprinted by permission. Copyright 1985, U.S. Chamber of Commerce.

QUESTIONS

1. Why do we permit debtors to reduce or escape their indebtedness via bankruptcy?
2. Does our bankruptcy law make it too easy for people and businesses to "walk away" from their debts? Explain.
3. Representative Billy Evans of Georgia has argued that America's moral attitude toward bankruptcy is changing. That is, he says, the stigma once attaching to bankruptcy is gone, and "payment of one's debt is no longer important." Is he correct? Explain.
4. Should those filing for bankruptcy under Chapter 7 not be allowed to exempt equity in their homes and autombiles? Explain.

Electronic Fund Transfers

"Electronic money" is rapidly encroaching upon paper as the preferred means of commercial exchange. The computer, the telephone, and the coded plastic card are among the instruments that may, in the future, substantially replace checks and cash as value exchange mechanisms. For example, bank customers may withdraw or deposit funds at any time by using their encoded card in an unattended teller machine. The growth of electronic fund transfers caused Congress in 1978 to pass the Electronic Fund Transfer Act as Title IX of the Consumer Credit Protection Act. Congress was concerned that established legal principles were not adequate to the task of resolving the many new legal problems that would arise from electronic transfers. The act defines electronic fund transfers (and hence the act's coverage) as "any transfer of funds other than a transaction originated by check, draft, or similar paper instrument, which is initiated through an electronic terminal, telephonic instrument, computer, or magnetic tape so as to order, instruct, or authorize a financial institution to debit or credit an account."

Electronic fund transfer systems include:

1. Point-of-sale transfers where a computer is used to immediately transfer funds from a consumer's bank account to that of the merchant from whom the consumer is making a purchase.
2. Automated tellers.
3. Direct bank deposit and withdrawal systems for automatic deposit of checks or automatic payment of a regularly recurring bill.

4. Transfers initiated by phone, where consumers call their bank to order payments or transfer funds between accounts.

The act provides remedies for an extended series of problems that may confront the EFT consumer. For example:

1. A resolution system is provided when the consumer believes an error has been made in an EFT billing.
2. In general, if a consumer's EFT card is lost or stolen, the consumer's liability for unauthorized use is limited to $50, but liability may exceed $50 if the financial institution is not notified of the loss within two days.
3. With certain exceptions, the bank is liable for all actual damages sustained by the consumer in situations when the bank failed to transfer funds in a timely manner, following a proper order by the consumer.
4. Civil and criminal penalties ranging from $100 (as well as court costs and attorney's fees) to $5,000 fines and up to one year in prison may be imposed upon financial institutions failing to comply with the Act.

The reader is cautioned to understand that EFT law is only now emerging, and the brief glimpse offered here is merely suggestive of what may become a murky area of legal inquiry.

Chapter Questions

1. What are electronic fund transfers? Why did the development of electronic fund transfers provoke a need for new legislation (the Electronic Fund Transfer Act)?
2. In sum, would the consumer's lot be improved were we to sharply reduce or even eliminate the many consumer protection efforts outlined in this chapter? Explain.
3. Once the government decided to intervene in the free market on behalf of consumers, two broad options presented themselves: *(a)* the government could have limited its effort to generating and distributing information to consumers, or *(b)* the government could have set safety standards for all products. Assuming the government were forced to choose either one or the other but not elements of each, which option should the government choose? Explain.
4. In recent years the government has struck down professional and state regulations forbidding advertising by doctors and advertisements for some products (e.g., contact lenses). Why did the government open the door to advertising in those areas?
5. Kovacs operated an industrial and hazardous waste disposal site in Hamilton, Ohio. The site produced pollution, and Kovacs was under a court order to clean it up. He and the other defendants failed to do so, and a receiver was appointed to complete the task. Thereafter, Kovacs filed a petition for a Chapter 7 liquidation. The State of Ohio claimed that Kovacs' obligation could not be discharged under the Bankruptcy Code because it was not a "debt." The State argued that Kovacs' default was a breach of statute rather than a breach of an ordinary commercial contract. The Ohio claim was appealed to the U.S. Supreme Court. Decide. Explain. See *Ohio* v. *Kovacs,* 53 *Law Week* 4068 (U.S. S.Ct., 1985).

6. Currently the government merely warns the public of the dangers associated with smoking. Occasionally, the government issues an outright ban on certain products (e.g., the artificial sweetener cyclamate and Red Dye No. 2, a food coloring; both are considered potentially carcinogenic). Should the government ban tobacco products rather than merely warning the public of the potential harm? Explain.

7. Cite some examples of consumers abusing businesspeople.

8. Some have argued for consumer protection, not merely from fraud and the like, but from bad taste as well:

> To introduce Maxwell House coffee's new vacuum-packed bags, General Foods Corp. is sponsoring a 27-city tour through the South featuring country singers Waylon Jennings and Jerry Reed. (About 70 percent of southern customers buy their coffee in bags instead of cans.) "We needed an event to build awareness of our new package," Michael W. Jardon, a Maxwell House promotion manager, says of the sponsorship. "Everybody else does it; we ought to compete in that arena."
>
> The Waylon Jennings tour was conceived and scheduled entirely by Maxwell House. "We picked the venues, the time of year, everything," says Mr. Jardon. But the tour isn't "grossly commercial," he adds. "We'll be there, and fans will know it, but Waylon is *not* going to wear a blue coffee can with his guitar."[15]

   a. Is the concert-going public harmed by Mr. Jennings' arrangement with General Foods? Explain.

   b. Is Mr. Jennings and/or his music debased by the commercial support for his tour? Explain.

9. According to a recent survey, consumers in six industialized nations overwhelmingly favor the creation of "National Departments of Consumer Protection." A consumer protection agency was favored by 65 percent or more of those surveyed: In Australia (80 percent), Canada (82 percent), England (74 percent), Israel (86 percent), Norway (65 percent), and the United Sates (74 percent).[16] Would you favor the creation of such a body? Explain.

10. The Consumer Product Safety Commission, relying on hospital statistics, reported that in 1980, 75 persons were killed and 63,293 injured while using chain saws. According to the CPSC, chain saw accidents ordinarily occur when the tip of the chain saw strikes resistance, causing the operator to lose control.[17] Based on these figures, should chain saw sales be banned until a safer product is produced? If enacted, would such a ban be effective? Explain.

11. Swedish law requires that safety messages must be included in ads to children. ("Always wear a helmet when skateboarding.") In the Netherlands, ads for candy must include a picture of a toothbrush.[18] Should those policies be adopted in the United States? Explain.

12. Professor and advertising scholar J. J. Boddewyn argues that (a) "There are more lies in personal ads than by all business combined—from 'apartment with river view [from the bathroom,]' to 'attractive woman wants to meet man.' " (b) "Some government ads are downright misleading"; "armed forces recruitment posters . . . promise you will 'see the world' but do not include a warning [from the Surgeon General?] that you could be shot at and die."[19] Comment.

13. The plaintiff, a wholesaler, reached an agreement with Philco, a manufacturer, to distribute Philco appliances to retailers. The plaintiff agreed to carry an adequate inventory of Philco parts. The agreement provided that either party could terminate the contract with 90 days written notice. In the event of termination the wholesaler agreed upon demand to resell and deliver its remaining Philco stock to Philco. The resale price was to be agreed upon. The agreement was terminated, but Philco declined to exercise its option to repurchase. The wholesaler was unable to sell most of the remaining Philco inventory and demanded that

Philco repurchase, but Philco declined. The plaintiff brought suit, claiming the contract was unconscionable. Decide. Explain. See *W. L. May Co., Inc.* v. *Philco-Ford Corporation,* 543 P.2d 283 (Or. 1975).

14. Townsend, a retailer, purchased a cash register from Stronach, a salesperson for National Cash Register. Townsend had relied on Stronach's assertions that the cash register would save Townsend the cost of a bookkeeper and perhaps half the cost of a sales clerk. Stronach had sold a number of cash registers to various retailers over a period of years. Several months subsequent to the purchase, Townsend recognized that the cash register had not produced the savings projected by Stronach. Is Stronach guilty of fraud? Explain. See *National Cash Register Co.* v. *Townsend Grocery Store,* 50 S.E. 306 (N.C. 1905).

15. Roseman resigned from the John Hancock Insurance Company following allegations of misuse of his expense account. He reimbursed the account. Subsequently he was denied employment by another insurance firm after that firm read a Retail Credit Co. credit report on Roseman. The credit report included some information regarding Roseman's resignation. The information in the report was accurate. Was Retail Credit in violation of the Truth in Lending Act in circulating information regarding the resignation? Explain. See *Roseman* v. *Retail Credit Co., Inc.,* 428 F. Supp. 643 (Pa., 1977).

16. Parker Pen Company issued ads for a fountain pen containing the words "Guaranteed for Life." The same ads included the following language in smaller print and in a less prominent location: "Pens marked with the Blue Diamond are guaranteed for the life of the owner against everything except loss or intentional damage, subject only to a charge of 35 cents for postage, insurance, and handling, provided complete pen is returned for service." Was the ad deceptive? Explain. See *Parker Pen Co.* v. *FTC,* 159 F.2d 509 (9th Cir. 1946).

17. Dun and Bradstreet, Inc., a credit reporting agency, erroneously reported to five subscribers that Greenmoss Builders had filed for voluntary bankruptcy. A correction was subsequently issued. Greenmoss, remaining dissatisfied, filed suit for defamation. The Supreme Court has held (see *New York Times* v. *Sullivan,* 376 U.S. 254 [1964]) that a public official cannot recover damages for defamation in the absence of a showing that the statement was made with "actual malice," that is, with knowledge that it was false or with reckless disregard for whether it was false. Here the credit report in question was not a matter of public importance. Must the plaintiff, Greenmoss, show "actual malice" on part of Dun and Bradstreet? Explain. See *Dun & Bradstreet, Inc.* v. *Greenmoss Builders, Inc.,* 53 *Law Week* 4866 (U.S. S.Ct., 1985).

Notes

1. "Why Consumers Gripe Louder than Ever," *U.S. News & World Report,* October 5, 1981, p. 56.
2. Michael de Courey Hinds, "Business Says Product Recall Makes Sense," *New York Times,* October 17, 1981, p. L9.
3. D. Rothschild, "The Magnuson-Moss Warranty Act: Does It Balance Warrantor and Consumer Interests?" *George Washington University Law Review* 44 (1976), pp. 335 and 337 as reported in Donald Rothschild and David Carroll, *Consumer Protection Reporting Service* (Owings Mills, Md.: National Law Publishing Corporation, 1983), vol. I, p. Intro–2.
4. See, e.g., "The U.S.'s Toughest Customer," *Time,* December 12, 1969, pp. 89–98.
5. See, e.g., *Jones* v. *West Side Buick Auto Co.,* 231 Mo. App. 187, 93 S.W. 2d 1083 (1936).
6. *Lindberg Cadillac Co.* v. *Aron,* 371 S.W.2d 651 (1963).
7. See *Trustees of Columbia University* v. *Jacobsen,* 53 N.J. Super. 574, 148 A.2d 63 (1959).
8. Robert Ardrey, *The Social Contract* (New York: Dell Publishing, 1974), pp. 9–12.
9. Letter from then FTC chair, James Miller, to Representative John Dingell. Reprinted in *Antitrust and Trade Regulation Reporter,* No. 1137, at 689, 690 (October 27, 1983).

10. The materials in this paragraph are drawn, in part, from Eugene E. Evans, "The FTC's New Deception Standard: Boon or Blow to Consumers?" Presented to American Business Law Association national convention, August, 1985.

11. Final Report of the National Commission on Product Safety, App. 123 (1970) at 7–8, 128, as reported in Donald Rothschild and David Carroll, *Consumer Protection Reporting Service* (Owings Mills, Md.: National Law Publishing Corporation, 1983), vol. I, p. 262(A).

12. The materials in this section are drawn, in part, from Donald Rothschild and David Carroll, *Consumer Protection Reporting Service* (Owings Mills, Md.: National Law Publishing Corporation, 1983).

13. This question is drawn from David Epstein and Steve Nickles, *Consumer Law in a Nutshell* (St. Paul, Minn.: West Publishing, 1980), p. 106.

14. Jeff A. Schnepper, *The New Bankruptcy Law—A Professional's Handbook* (Reading, Mass.: Addison-Wesley Publishing, 1981), p. 1.

15. "Advertisers Use Music Groups to Reach Young Consumers," *The Wall Street Journal,* July 28, 1983, section 2, p. 19.

16. Hiram Barksdale et al., "A Cross-National Survey of Consumer Attitude towards Marketing Practices, Consumerism and Government Regulations," *Columbia Journal of World Business,* 17, no. 2 (Summer 1982), pp. 71, 83.

17. Michael Hinds, "Business Says Products Recall Makes Sense," *The New York Times,* October 17, 1981, p. L-9.

18. J. J. Boddewyn, "The Global Spread of Advertising Regulation," *MSU Business Topics,* Spring 1981, pp. 5, 9.

19. Ibid., p. 12.

16

Products Liability

Introduction

Products liability is that branch of the law governing litigation for injuries resulting from defective products. As recently as the early 1960s products liability was little more than an obscure corner of the law. Strict liability, today's primary weapon for the plaintiff in a defective product action, did not exist. Today, through a steady accumulation of judicial decisions and legislative enactments, products liability litigation is so common and often so successful that it has changed the business community's manufacturing and distribution practices. Perhaps 100,000 products liability suits are filed annually. Business argues that the system now unfairly favors the consumer. Consumer lawyers argue that the business community is, at last, being compelled to pay the full cost of producing unfit goods. That cost can be staggering. About $254 million in products liability insurance claims were paid in 1980.[1] American Motors reportedly agreed to a $5 million settlement in just one of several lawsuits stemming from Jeep rollover accidents.[2] The Ford Motor Company will probably pay in excess of $20 million in claims resulting from allegedly defective transmissions.[3]

In the materials that follow we will explore both the technical dimensions of products liability actions and the policy dispute regarding the fairness and wisdom of contemporary products liability law. The three major causes of action to be explored are negligence, breach of warranty, and strict liability.

Negligence

In dangerously simplified terms, *negligence* is a breach of the duty of due care. To paraphrase *Black's Law Dictionary,* a negligent act is the failure to do that which a reasonable person, guided by those considerations that ordinarily regulate human affairs, would do, or doing that which a reasonable person would not do. Thus, a producer or distributor has a duty to exercise reasonable care in the entire stream of events associated with the development and sale of a product. In designing, manufacturing, testing, repairing, and warning of potential dangers, those in the chain of production and distribution must meet the standard of the reasonably prudent person. Failure to do so constitutes negligence. Furthermore, rather recent decisions extend potential liability to those situations in which a product is being put to an unintended but reasonably foreseeable misuse.

Historically, producers of products were ordinarily protected from negligence liability under the combined effects of the doctrines of privity and caveat emptor (let the buyer beware). *Privity* is the label applied to the legal relationship that arises when parties enter a contract. As a consequence of the privity requirement, wronged consumers could reach only those in the chain of distribution with whom a contractual relationship (privity) had been established. Therefore, consumers ordinarily could not recover against a remote manufacturer. Under the caveat emptor principle, the vendor was liable for defects only to the extent that an agreement was reached to provide for that liability. In previous centuries consumers might have expected to deal ''face-to-face'' with the product producer. Therefore, the privity and caveat emptor notions held at least the superficial legitimacy of a buyer and seller, presumed to be of equal bargaining power, protecting their own interests in an equitable contract. However, the development of elaborate, multilayered systems of production and distribution prompted a revision of legal standards. In a famous 1916 New York state decision *(MacPherson* v. *Buick Motor Co.),*[4] the brilliant jurist, Benjamin Cardozo, held that an action could be maintained against a remote manufacturer of an automobile with a defective wheel that broke and caused injury. In so doing Cardozo put aside the view that the plaintiff's right to recovery grew only out of a contractual relationship. Cardozo's view has since been uniformly adopted, thus permitting victims of negligence to bring actions against all wrongdoers in the chain of production and distribution.

To establish a successful negligence claim the plaintiff must meet each of the following requirements:

1. *Duty.* The plaintiff must establish that the defendant owed a duty of due care to the plaintiff. In general, the standard applied is that of the fictitious reasonable man or woman. That ''reasonable person'' acts prudently, sensibly, responsibly. The standard of reasonableness depends, of course, on the circumstances of the situation.
2. *Breach of duty.* The plaintiff must demonstrate that the defendant breached the duty of due care by engaging in conduct that did not conform to the reasonable person standard. Breach of the duty of due care may result from either the commission of a careless act or the omission of a reasonable, prudent act. Would a reasonable man or woman discharge a firearm in a public park? Would a reasonable person foresee that failure to illuminate one's front entry steps might lead to a broken limb?
3. *Proximate cause.* The plaintiff must establish that the defendant's actions were the proximate cause of the injury. Many injuries arise from series of events—some of them wildly improbable. Did the defendant's negligence lead directly to the plaintiff's harm, or did some intervening act break the causal link between the defendant's negligence and the harm? For example, the defendant negligently blocked a road, forcing the plaintiff to detour. While on the detour route, the plaintiff's vehicle was struck by a plane falling from the sky. Was the defendant's negligence the proximate cause of the plaintiff's injury?[5]

4. *Injury*. The plaintiff must have sustained injury, and because of problems of proof, that injury must be physical in character.

Proximate cause may be the most inscrutable ingredient in the test for negligence. Establishing proximate cause often requires addressing the slippery notion of foresee-ability. The following case illustrates rather poignantly the difficulty in anticipating the consequences of one's actions.

AMAYA V. HOME ICE, FUEL & SUPPLY CO.   Supreme Court of California, 59 Cal.2d 295, 379 P.2d 513 (1963)

[Plaintiff was seven months pregnant and the mother of 17-month-old James. While she was on the sidewalk James was in the street. A truck being negligently driven bore down on the boy, running him over. The shock caused the mother to miscarry and suffer actual physical and emotional injury. She brought suit against the driver for harm to herself and the infant child.]

Justice Schauer

The sole issue is whether liability may be predicated on fright or nervous shock (with consequent bodily illness) induced solely by the plaintiff's apprehension of negligently caused danger or injury to a third person. After a comprehensive review of the authorities and the several considerations underlying decision on this issue, we have concluded that the complaint does not state facts sufficient to constitute a cause of action.

*   *   *   *   *

If the problem is to be solved . . . we must consider the roots of liability for negligence. First . . . the dispositive issue ordinarily is—as it is here—that of duty; i. e., "the existence of *a duty of care owed* by the alleged wrongdoer *to the person injured,* or to a class of which he is a member."

*   *   *   *   *

There is a legal duty on any given set of facts *only if the court or the legislature says there is a duty.* "Duty is only a word with which we state our conclusion that there is or is not to be liability; it necessarily begs the essential question. . . . The word serves a useful purpose in directing attention to the obligation to be imposed upon the defendant, rather than the causal sequence of events; beyond that it serves none." The inquiry, then, should be concentrated on the various factors which are incorporated in the court's conclusion that on the relevant set of facts there is or is not a "duty." While an all-inclusive enumeration is manifestly impossible, we have on occasion undertaken to list at least some of these factors. Thus, in a recent case . . . we said: "The determination whether in a specific case the defendant will be held liable to a third person . . . is a matter of policy and involves the balancing of various factors, among which are the extent to which the transaction was intended to affect the plaintiff, the foreseeability of harm to him, the degree of certainty that the plaintiff suffered injury, the closeness of the connection between the defendant's conduct and the injury suffered, the moral blame attached to the defendant's conduct, and the policy of preventing future harm."

It bears emphasis that "foreseeability of harm" is but one of the half dozen relevant factors mentioned. . . . Nor is it the most important; indeed, in all save the most obvious of cases a harm is "foreseeable" only if, in the final analysis, a court or jury says that it is. . . .

Turning to the factors that are to be weighed in the balance we consider, on the one hand, plaintiff's undoubted interest in freedom from invasion of her bodily security, and on the other, such factors as the following:

The Administrative Factor

Justice . . . exists only when it can be effectively administered. . . . [I]n circumstances such as those here shown, to impose liability would "open the way to fraudulent claims, and enter a field that has no sensible or just stopping point."

* * * * *

Another—and no less important—administrative factor to be weighed is the problem of setting some limits to such liability for fright or shock allegedly caused by the apprehension of danger or injury not to the plaintiff but to a third person. . . . Professor Prosser suggests the following limitations on liability: First, "It is clear that the injury threatened or inflicted upon the third person must be a serious one, of a nature to cause severe shock to the plaintiff, and that the shock must result in actual physical harm." But what if the plaintiff was honestly mistaken in believing the third person to be in danger or to be seriously injured? . . . Second, "The action might well be confined to members of the immediate family, or perhaps to husband, wife, parent or child, to the exclusion of bystanders, and remote relatives." But what if the third person was the plaintiff's beloved niece or nephew, grandparent, fiancé, or life-long friend, as dear to the plaintiff as her more immediate family? Third, "The plaintiff must be present at the time of the accident, or at least the shock must be fairly contemporaneous with it, rather than follow at a later date." But how soon is "fairly contemporaneous"? What is the magic in the plaintiff's being "present"? Is the shock any less immediate if the mother does not know of the accident until the injured child is brought home? And what if the plaintiff is present at the scene but is nevertheless unaware of the danger or injury to the third person until shortly after the accident has occurred?

. . . When, as here, a wholly new type of liability is envisioned, our responsibility extends far beyond the particular plaintiff before us, and touches society at large.

The Socioeconomic and Moral Factors

As just observed, there must be some stopping point to the liability of the negligent defendant. "It is still unthinkable that any one shall be liable to the end of time for all of the results that follow in endless sequence from his single act. Causation cannot be the answer; in a very real sense the consequences of an act go forward to eternity, and back to the beginning of the world." There are two principal reasons why this is "unthinkable."

First, to the extent that the law intervenes in any area of human activity and declares that for certain consequences of that activity the actor shall be held civilly liable in damages, both the individual actor and society as a whole feel the effects of the restraint—a psychological effect in the form of a lessening of incentive, and an economic effect in the form of the cost of insurance necessary to enable the activity to continue. Yet it is recognized that no activity could survive an unlimited progression of such effects. Accordingly, when the general social utility of an activity is deemed to outweigh the particular interests with which it may clash, important policy reasons dictate that some limits be set to liability for its consequences. . . . As the industrial society in which we live becomes still more complex and the use of the streets and highways and airways increases, a certain percentage of accidents therefrom appears to become statistically inevitable.

There will be losses, and our present system of insurance attempts to compensate for them, and, of course, to spread the cost of compensation over those who do not, as well as those who do, cause such losses. But could that system—imperfect at best—adequately and fairly absorb the far-reaching extension of liability that would follow from judicial abrogation of the rule now before us? And what of the many other activities of everyday life that are either uninsurable or customarily uninsured, yet may well give rise to the type of "spectator injury" here alleged? We conclude, rather, that the social utility of such activities outweighs the somewhat speculative interest of individuals to be free from the risk of the type of injury here alleged.

The second reason for seeking a stopping point to the negligent defendant's liability is a related one. As long as our system of compensation is based on the concept of fault, we must also weigh "the moral blame attached to the defendant's conduct." Here is felt the difference between the social importance of conduct that negligently causes harm and conduct that is intended to do so. It is often said that in the latter case the defendant will be held liable for a broader range of consequences because, as the consequences are intended, they are the more "foreseeable." But in many intentional tort cases the defendant has been held liable under this reasoning for consequences far beyond those which he actually intended. It follows that, once more, "foreseeability" is not the real answer. Rather, the increased liability imposed on an intentional wrongdoer appears to reflect the psychological fact that solicitude for the interests of the actor weighs less in the balance as his moral guilt increases and the social utility of his conduct diminishes.

* * * * *

Having weighed each of the foregoing factors in the balance, we hold that the complaint fails to state facts sufficient to constitute a cause of action.

* * * * *

Justice Peters (dissenting).

I dissent.
The majority opinion states the issue to be "whether liability may be predicated on fright or nervous shock (with consequent bodily illness) induced solely by the plaintiff's apprehension of negligently caused danger or injury to a third person." So stated, the answer to such a broad question might well be in the negative. But the issue now before us is not the one quoted above. The real issue is a much more limited one. The plaintiff is not just anyone. She is a *mother* of a 17-month-old *infant child*. The defendant, *in the presence of the mother,* negligently ran down and injured that *infant child*. As a proximate result the mother has suffered permanent injuries. Thus the real question is not the one stated by the majority, but is whether or not a mother may recover damages for physical injuries resulting from emotional shock caused by fear for her infant child who is negligently run down by the automobile of the defendant in the presence of the mother. I submit that the answer to that question, so limited, should be that liability for such injuries should exist.

The italicized words above create real limitations that are not merely matters of form. . . . Admittedly, if we once create liability in the limited situation here involved, demands will inevitably be made upon us to extend the limits of the rule. Admittedly, it will be a difficult but not impossible task to draw the line between liability and nonliability in such situations. When we are called upon to draw that line the place we draw it may not, perhaps, be entirely logical. By necessity it will have to be arbitrary. It will be less arbitrary, however, than to deny liability entirely. . . .

* * * * *

There are other matters of principle to which reference should be made. The early law was to the effect that shock was not a recoverable item of damage. That rule had the advantage, at least, of being clear, easily understood and easy to apply. Then many states, including California, started to limit that rule by holding that shock accompanied by impact was a proper element of damage. . . . The rule was further limited by the rule, now the law of California, that recovery for shock may properly be an item of damage even without impact if the plaintiff is in the "zone of danger." . . . Then the rule was further limited, if not abolished, by the several California cases holding that a plaintiff could recover for shock caused by the infliction of an intentional tort on a third person member of the family, even though the plaintiff was not in the "zone of danger."

* * * * *

These gradual modifications of the original rule are of great significance. They at least suggest, if they do not compel, the conclusion that we have now reached the stage of development of the law that we should at long last take the intelligent and logical step forward of holding that a mother who sees her child run down by a negligent defendant, and who, as a proximate result thereof, suffers serious and permanent injuries should recover whether or not she was in the "zone of danger." The "zone of danger" test is illogical and unsound and should be abandoned.

* * * * *

We cannot rule that, as a matter of law, the injury to appellant was not foreseeable. The only justification for holding that appellant cannot state a cause of action would be, not that the injury to her, due to emotional distress, was not foreseeable, as a matter of law, but rather that the courts must deny recovery for reasons of policy; that, otherwise, factual questions will arise which are too difficult for courts or juries to decide.

* * * * *

The various bases for refusal of relief which we have discussed do not actually touch upon the central issue as to whether respondents owed appellant a duty of due care because of the foreseeability of the emotional trauma suffered by appellant. When one is negligent in the operation of a car he should, as a reasonable man, foresee that the class of persons who may suffer harm from his misconduct includes the parent whose emotional distress issues from the exposure of his child to injury by reason of the negligence. The above grounds for refusal of relief are in substance no more than court-inspired theories to restrict the range of liability of a defendant to narrow areas; they do not relate to the key question.

Questions

1. In your opinion was the *Amaya* decision correct as a matter of law? Explain. Was it just? Explain. See *Dillon* v. *Legg,* 69 Cal. Rptr. 72, 441 P.2d 912 (1968).
2. Why was the plaintiff unsuccessful in the *Amaya* case?
3. Is a fireworks manufacturer liable for harm to children who ignited an explosive that had failed to detonate in the town's public display the previous day? Explain.

Classes of Negligence Claims

Personal injuries resulting from negligence are, of course, commonplace, but certain classes of problems deserve particular mention.

Improper manufacturing, handling, and/or inspection of products often give rise to negligence claims. However, the extremely complex process of producing, distributing, and using a product sometimes so obscures the root of the injury in question that proof of fault is nearly impossible to establish. This class of negligence actions and the difficulties associated with them are illustrated by a case in which a child was paralyzed when a nearly new Corvair driven by a friend went out of control and landed in a culvert. The child-plaintiff sued the manufacturer, General Motors, alleging negligence in the failure "to properly tighten and inspect a nut on a bolt in the left rear suspension system," but experts differed as to whether the bolt was lost before or during the accident. The appeals judge affirmed the verdict for the plaintiff, saying that in a "battle of experts" determination of the facts must rest with the jury.[6]

A negligence claim may arise from a supplier's *failure to warn* of a danger associated with the product. According to the Restatement of Torts, liability attaches if the supplier "knows or has reason to know that the chattel is or is likely to be dangerous for the use for which it is supplied" and "has no reason to believe" that the user "will realize its dangerous condition." Judicial decisions in duty to warn cases are influenced by such factors as the feasibility of an effective warning and the probable seriousness of the injury. Thus a defendant was liable for failure to warn when a cleanser caused dermatitis. The cleanser was accompanied by a label specifying the proper mixture of cleanser and water. The plaintiff ignored the label. However, the court held that the label offered directions but did not constitute a warning of the consequences of misuse.[7]

Defective design of a product may provoke a negligence action. In general a manufacturer holds a duty to design the product so that it is safe for any reasonably foreseeable use. The case that follows is the leading exposition of the American judiciary's stance regarding design defects leading to negligence.

LARSEN V. GENERAL MOTORS CORPORATION   United States Court
of Appeals, 391 F.2d 495 (8th Cir., 1968)

Circuit Judge Gibson

The driver of an automobile claims injury as a result of an alleged negligent design of the steering assembly of the automobile. The alleged defect in design did not cause the accident, and the manufacturer asserts the law imposes no duty of care in the design of an automobile to make it more safe to occupy in the event of a collision. The trial court agreed, rendering summary judgment in favor of the manufacturer. We reverse and remand.

The plaintiff-appellant, Erling David Larsen, received severe bodily injuries while driving, with the consent of the owner, a 1963 Chevrolet Corvair on February 18, 1964, in the state of Michigan. A head-on collision, with the impact occurring on the left front corner of the Corvair, caused a severe rearward thrust of the steering mechanism into the plaintiff's head. The Corvair was manufactured by General Motors Corporation and liability is asserted against General Motors on an alleged design defect in the steering assembly and the placement or attachment of the component parts of the steering assembly to the structure of the Corvair.

The plaintiff does not contend that the design caused the accident but that because of the design he received injuries he would not have otherwise received or, in the alternative, his injuries would not have been as severe. The rearward displacement of the steering shaft on the left frontal impact was much greater on the Corvair than it would be in other cars that were designed to protect against such a rearward displacement. The plaintiff's complaint alleges . . . negligence in design of the steering assembly. . . .

General Motors contends it "has no duty whatsoever to design and manufacture a vehicle . . . which is otherwise 'safe' or 'safer' to occupy during collision impacts," and since there is no duty there can be no actionable negligence on its part.

* * * * *

There is a line of cases directly supporting General Motors' contention that negligent design of an automobile is not actionable, where the alleged defective design is not a causative factor in the accident. . . .

Shumard v. *General Motors Corporation* . . . held there was no liability where the alleged design defects in a 1962 Corvair automobile caused it to erupt into flames on impact, killing the plaintiff's decedent. That court said:

> . . . The duty of a manufacturer in the design of automobiles does not include designing a 'fireproof' automobile or an automobile in which passengers are guaranteed to be safe from fire. A manufacturer has no duty to design an automobile that will not catch fire under any circumstances. The manufacturer's duty is to design an automobile which will not present a fire hazard during its normal intended operation.

* * * * *

The courts . . . have been somewhat reluctant to impose liability upon a manufacturer for negligent product design in the automotive field. In *Gossett* v. *Chrysler Corporation* . . . the court reversed a judgment based on an alleged defectively designed truck hood latch that allowed the hood to spring open while the vehicle was in motion causing an accident, but did recognize a duty in connection with design, stating:

> The general rule may be stated as follows: It is the duty of a manufacturer to use reasonable care under the circumstances to so design his product as to make it not accident or foolproof, but safe for the use for which it is intended. This duty includes a duty to design the product so that it will fairly meet any emergency of use which can reasonably be anticipated. The manufacturer is not an insurer that his product is, from a design viewpoint, incapable of producing injury.

* * * * *

A case closely bearing on this precise point is *Ford Motor Company* v. *Zahn,* where the plaintiff lost sight of one eye on being thrown against a defectively designed ash tray having a jagged edge. The ash tray had nothing to do in a causative way of setting up an emergency braking situation, which in turn projected the plaintiff into the ash tray, but the court recognized a duty to use reasonable care in design, [and] recognized the foreseeability of injury resulting from a defective ash tray so placed.

* * * * *

Accepting, therefore, the principle that a manufacturer's duty of design and construction extends to producing a product that is reasonably fit for its intended use and free of hidden defects that could render it unsafe for such use, the issue narrows on the proper interpretation of "intended use." Automobiles are made for use on the roads and highways in transporting persons and cargo to and from various points. This intended use cannot be carried out without encountering in varying degrees the statistically proved hazard of injury-producing impacts of various types. The manufacturer should not be heard to say that it does not intend its product to be involved in any accident when it can easily foresee and when it knows that the probability over the life of its product is high, that it will be involved in some type of injury-producing accident. O'Connell in his article "Taming the Automobile," . . . cites that between one fourth to two thirds of all automobiles during their use at some time are involved in an accident producing injury or death. Other statistics are available showing the frequency and certainty of fatal and injury-producing accidents. . . .

We think the "intended use" construction urged by General Motors is much too narrow and unrealistic. Where the manufacturer's negligence in design causes an unreasonable risk to be imposed upon the user of its products, the manufacturer should be liable for the injury caused by its failure to exercise reasonable care in the design. These injuries are readily foreseeable as an incident to the normal and expected use of an automobile. While automobiles are not made for the purpose of colliding with each other, a frequent and inevitable contingency of normal automobile use will result in collisions and injury-producing impacts. No rational basis exists for limiting recovery to situations where the defect in design or manufacture was the causative factor of the accident, as the accident and the resulting injury, usually caused by the so-called "second collision" of the passenger with the interior part of the automobile, all are foreseeable. Where the injuries or enhanced injuries are due to the manufacturer's failure to use reasonable care to avoid subjecting the user of its products to an unreasonable risk of injury, general negligence principles should be applicable. The sole function of an automobile is not just to provide a means of transportation, it is to provide a means of safe transportation or as safe as is reasonably possible under the present state of the art.

We do agree that under the present state of the art an automobile manufacturer is under no duty to design an accident-proof or fool-proof vehicle or even one that floats on water, but such manufacturer is under a duty to use reasonable care in the design of its vehicle to avoid subjecting the user to an unreasonable risk of injury in the event of a collision. Collisions with or without fault of the user are clearly foreseeable by the manufacturer and are statistically inevitable. . . .

Questions

1. The *Larsen* court argues that: "No rational basis exists for limiting recovery to situations where the defect in design or manufacture was a causative factor of the accident." Build an argument to the contrary.
2. Decisions such as *Larsen* typically increase the price of autos by stimulating improved safety features. "Safe" drivers may argue that they are being unfairly compelled to pay higher auto prices because decisions like *Larsen* assume and accept the inevitability of auto accidents. As a matter of economic good sense and economic justice, is *Larsen* a sound decision? Explain.
3. A minor, operating a power lawn mower, slipped, thrusting his hand through an unguarded hole in the mower. An effective guard for the hole was available at a cost of less than $1. The hole was visible upon casual inspection. The minor sued to recover for the injury to his hand. See *Luque* v. *McLean*, 501 P.2d 1163 (Cal. 1972).
    a. Build an argument for the defendant.
    b. Decide the case. Explain.
    c. If you found for the plaintiff in the lawn mower case, how would you rule if all the facts were the same but the instrument causing the injury was a sharp, pointed rake? Explain.

Res Ipsa Loquitur

As alluded to previously, problems of proof are sometimes so daunting as to render negligence law an ineffectual tool in serving the injured consumer. In part because of that condition, the courts have adopted the doctrine of *res ipsa loquitur* (the thing speaks for itself). The doctrine permits the court to infer the defendant's negligence even though that negligence cannot be proved. That is, the facts suggest that the plaintiff's injury must have resulted from negligence on the part of the defendant, but the circumstances are such that the plaintiff is unable to prove both negligence and causation. The case that follows sets out the test for applying *res ipsa loquitur.*

ESCOLA V. COCA COLA BOTTLING CO. OF FRESNO
Supreme Court of California, 24 Cal.2d 453, 150 P.2d 436 (1944)

Chief Justice Gibson

Plaintiff, a waitress in a restaurant, was injured when a bottle of Coca Cola broke in her hand. She alleged that defendant company, which had bottled and delivered the alleged defective bottle to her employer, was negligent in selling "bottles containing said beverage which on account of excessive pressure of gas or by reason of some defect in the bottle was dangerous . . . and likely to explode." This appeal is from a judgment upon a jury verdict in favor of plaintiff.

Defendant's driver delivered several cases of Coca Cola to the restaurant, placing them on the floor, one on top of the other, under and behind the counter, where they remained at least 36 hours. Immediately before the accident, plaintiff picked up the top case and set it upon a nearby ice-cream cabinet in front of and about 3 feet from the refrigerator. She then proceeded to take the bottles from the case with her right hand, one at a time, and put them into the refrigerator. Plaintiff testified that after she had placed three bottles in the refrigerator and had moved the fourth bottle about 18 inches from the case "it exploded in my hand." The bottle broke into two jagged pieces and inflicted a deep 5-inch cut, severing blood vessels, nerves and muscles of the thumb and palm of the hand. Plaintiff further testified that when the bottle exploded, "It made a sound similar to an electric light bulb that would have dropped. It made a loud pop." . . . A fellow employee . . . testified that plaintiff . . . didn't bang either the case or the door or another bottle . . . when it popped. . . .

Plaintiff . . . rested her case, having announced to the court that being unable to show any specific acts of negligence she relied completely on the doctrine of *res ipsa loquitur.*

Defendant contends that the doctrine of *res ipsa loquitur* does not apply in this case, and that the evidence is insufficient to support the judgement.

* * * * *

Res ipsa loquitur does not apply unless (1) defendant had exclusive control of the thing causing the injury and (2) the accident is of such a nature that it ordinarily would not occur in the absence of negligence by the defendant.

Many authorities state that the happening of the accident does not speak for itself where it took place some time after defendant had relinquished control of the instrumentality causing the injury. Under the more logical view, however, the doctrine may be applied upon the theory that defendant had control at the time of the alleged negligent act, although not at the time of the accident, *provided* plaintiff first proves that the condition of the instrumentality had not been changed after it left the defendant's possession.

. . . Plaintiff must also prove that she handled the bottle carefully. . . . It is not necessary, of course, that plaintiff eliminate every remote possibility of injury to the bottle after defendant lost control, and the requirement is satisfied if there is evidence permitting a reasonable inference that it was not accessible to extraneous harmful forces and that it was carefully handled by plaintiff or any third person who may have moved or touched it. If such evidence is presented, the question becomes one for the trier of fact. . . .

Upon an examination of the record, the evidence appears sufficient to support a reasonable inference that the bottle here involved was not damaged by any extraneous force after delivery to the restaurant by defendant. It follows, therefore, that the bottle was in some manner defective at the time defendant relinquished control, because sound and properly prepared bottles of carbonated liquids do not ordinarily explode when carefully handled.

The next question, then, is whether plaintiff may rely upon the doctrine of res ipsa loquitur to supply an inference that defendant's negligence was responsible for the defective condition of the bottle at the time it was delivered to the restaurant. Under the general rules pertaining to the doctrine, as set forth above, it must appear that bottles of carbonated liquid are not ordinarily defective without negligence by the bottling company.

*   *   *   *   *

Although it is not clear in this case whether the explosion was caused by an excessive charge or a defect in the glass there is a sufficient showing that neither cause would ordinarily have been present if due care had been used. Further, defendant had exclusive control over both the charging and inspection of the bottles. Accordingly, all the requirements necessary to entitle plaintiff to rely on the doctrine of res ipsa loquitur to supply an inference of negligence are present.

*   *   *   *   *

The judgment is affirmed.

Questions

1. In *Escola,* the plaintiff was unable to prove fault on the part of Coca Cola. That being the case, why was Coca Cola held liable for plaintiff's injuries?
2. Do you agree with the Court's decision? Explain.
3. Judge Traynor's concurring opinion in *Escola* (not reproduced in this text) noted the dramatic alteration of the buyer-seller relationship in the era of mass production. He then argued that the consumer could no longer protect herself or himself. Hence, extended legal protection was required. Regardless of your point of view, build the argument that Judge Traynor was wrong, both about the consumer's helplessness and as to the appropriateness of legal intervention.
4. A bartender, Parrillo, was opening a bottle of grenadine when it exploded, causing injury. Parillo sued Giroux Company, the producer of the liquor. Giroux packaged the liquor itself after buying bottles from a manufacturer. Giroux visually inspected the bottles and ordinarily found defects in 1 of every 400–500 bottles. The evidence showed that Parrillo did not mishandle the bottle. Decide the case. Explain. See *Parrillo* v. *Giroux Co.,* 426 A.2d 1313 (R.I. 1981).

Defenses against Negligence

Even if the plaintiff has proved all of the necessary elements of a negligence claim, the defendant may still prevail by establishing a good defense. Two of those defenses and some variations are of special importance; contributory negligence and assumption of risk.

Contributory Negligence   The law is designed to encourage us all to conduct ourselves with care. Hence, I may file suit if injured by the negligence of another, but what if I contribute to my harm by virtue of my own negligence? I am then said to be guilty of contributory negligence. Historically, contributory negligence has operated as a complete bar to recovery. That is, if the defendant can show that I, as the plaintiff, contributed to my own injury because of my own negligence, I cannot recover from that defendant. That has been the case even if the plaintiff's contribution to his or her own harm was miniscule.

The harshness of the contributory negligence standard has led more than half of the states to adopt a variation labeled *comparative negligence*. This standard requires a weighing of the relative negligence of the parties. Though the formula may vary from state to state, typically the plaintiff's recovery is reduced by a percentage equal to the percentage of the plaintiff's fault in the case. Assume a plaintiff sustained $10,000 in injuries in an accident. If the plaintiff's negligence is found to be 20 percent responsible for the plaintiff's injuries, then the plaintiff's recovery will total $8,000. In those instances where the plaintiff's fault actually exceeds that of the defendant, the plaintiff may be barred from recovery.

Another muting of the absolutist character of contributory negligence is the doctrine of *last clear chance*. Assume the plaintiff is found to be contributorily negligent. The plaintiff may yet recover in full if she or he can show that the defendant had the last clear chance to avoid the accident and that the defendant did not take advantage of that opportunity. For example, assume that A, while intoxicated, removes his children's video games and record players from his home and meticulously places them in a line spanning the street. B approaches in a car, sees the machines in ample time to stop, but instead thinks it amusing to plow into them. Notwithstanding his own negligence, A now sues and may recover for the loss of the items, arguing that B had the last clear chance to avoid the collision.

Assumption of Risk   A plaintiff who willingly enters a dangerous situation and is injured will not be permitted to recover. For example, if a driver sees that the road ahead is flooded, he will not be compensated for the injuries sustained when he loses control as he attempts to drive through the water. His recovery is barred even though the road was flooded due to operator error in opening a floodgate. The requirements for use of the assumption of the risk defense are (1) knowledge of the risk and (2) voluntary assumption of the risk.

The case that follows illustrates the application of that defense.

HODGES V. NOFSINGER   District Court of Appeal of Florida, 183 So.2d 14
(1966)

Judge Swann

(We consider an) action against an automobile driver to recover for injuries sustained by the passenger-owner when the driver kissed her and the automobile veered across the road into a canal. The circuit court . . . entered final judgment on a verdict for the plaintiff, and the defendant appealed.

The defendant, Gary C. Hodges, appeals from a final judgment entered for the plaintiff, Mary Nofsinger, after a jury trial, in the sum of $7,500. The sole question on appeal is whether the plaintiff was guilty of *contributory negligence,* as a matter of law, thereby precluding her from any recovery from the defendant in this case.

The parties have referred to this as the "kissing case." The defendant's version of the facts on appeal are as follows. The parties had seen each other many times prior to the accident. The plaintiff was a single woman, about 25 years of age, and the defendant was a member of the United States Air Force, stationed at Homestead, Florida, at the time the accident occurred. On that day, the defendant and a friend went to the plaintiff's house. The friend had to return to the base early, but the defendant wanted to stay and the plaintiff agreed to take him back to the base in *her automobile* later in the evening.

At about 8 P.M. they departed for Homestead with the *defendant driving the plaintiff's car and the plaintiff sitting close to him on the front seat, "about the middle of the car."* She testified that the defendant drove normally, and made the following answers to questions propounded at trial:

*   *   *   *   *

Q: From the time you got onto Allapattah Drive up to the time of the accident, describe what happened.
A: Well, we were just driving along Allapattah, and Gary kissed me, and we went off the road into the canal.
Q: You didn't protest or object, or push Gary away at all during the kissing, did you?
A: No, I didn't.
A: The kissing occurred for a number of seconds, and we hit right then. I mean there was no pause in between.
Q: . . . Would you please tell me, please, isn't it a fact that you did kiss fully on the mouth?
A: The kiss was fully on the mouth.
Q: And the kiss continued for a number of seconds, didn't it?
A: I felt at the time that it did.
Q: And it endured up to the time of the accident?
A: Yes.
Q: This wasn't the first time you kissed, was it?
A: No.

*   *   *   *   *

The defendant contends that on these facts and circumstances the plaintiff cooperated in the kissing, with a reckless disregard for her safety, and was therefore guilty of contributory negligence as a matter of law.

The plaintiff sets forth the facts in a different light than those of the defendant. The essential difference in the evidence of the parties is summarized as follows. The defendant was driving in a normal manner, looking straight ahead, and suddenly, without any prior conversation or warning, the defendant kissed the plaintiff. This surprised her and she did not react or cooperate. She did not have an opportunity to protest or object to the defendant's kissing her before the car veered across the road through a guard rail and into a canal, which resulted in her injuries.

It is apparent from the testimony that there are conflicts in the evidence as to the issue of contributory negligence; that is, whether the plaintiff cooperated in the kiss, or whether she was so surprised that she did not have time in which to protest or object to the actions of the defendant. The conflicting evidence on this issue was properly submitted to the jury to be resolved by it. . . .

Affirmed.

Questions

1. Why did the judge deny Hodges' appeal?
2. Giles, a guest at the Pick Hotel, leaned across his car to remove his briefcase from the passenger side of the front seat. In doing so, he placed his hand for support on the metal pillar between the front and rear doors. As he did so, a bellboy closed the rear door on Giles' hand. Giles sued Pick. Decide the case. Explain. *Giles* v. *Pick Hotels Corp.*, 232 F.2d 887 (1956).
3. Distinguish contributory negligence and assumption of the risk.
4. David Clapham lost an eye when he was hit by a foul ball at Yankee Stadium in New York City. He sued the Yankees and the city, which owns the stadium, contending they were negligent in failing to extend the protective screen to reach the box seat he was occupying behind the Yankee dugout.
   a. What defense would you raise on behalf of the Yankees?
   b. Decide the case. Explain.
   c. What if Mr. Clapham had left the game early and was struck by a foul ball while walking through the city-owned parking lot?

Warranties

As explained previously, negligence claims are often difficult to prove. For that reason and others, the wronged consumer may wish to raise a breach of warranty claim in addition to or in place of a negligence action. A *warranty* is simply a guarantee arising out of a contract. If the product does not conform to the standards of the warranty, the contract is violated (breached), and the wronged party is entitled to recovery. Note that a negligence claim arises from breach of the duty of due care while a warranty claim arises from a breach of contract. The following sections describe how express and implied warranties are created. (Discussion of the warranty of good title is omitted. UCC 2–312.)

Express Warranties

The seller of goods affirms a fact or makes a promise regarding the character or quality of the goods. Warranties are governed primarily by the terms of the Uniform Commercial Code. The UCC is designed to codify and standardize the law of commercial practice throughout the United States. Forty-nine states have adopted all or the bulk of the UCC. Louisiana has adopted only selected portions.

UCC 2–313. Express Warranties by Affirmation, Promise, Description, Sample.

(1) Express warranties by the seller are created as follows:

(a) Any affirmation of fact or promise made by the seller to the buyer which relates to the goods and becomes part of the basis of the bargain creates an express warranty that the goods shall conform to the affirmation or promise.

(b) Any description of the goods which is made part of the basis of the bargain creates an express warranty that the goods shall conform to the description.

(c) Any sample or model which is made part of the basis of the bargain creates an express warranty that the whole of the goods shall conform to the sample or model.

The philosophy undergirding UCC 2–313 is straightforward. The seller who seeks to enhance the attractiveness of his or her product by offering representations as to the nature and/or quality of the product must fulfill those representations or fall in breach of contract and be subject to the payment of damages.

Perhaps the area of greatest potential confusion in determining the existence and coverage of an express warranty is that of distinguishing a seller's promise from a mere expression of opinion. The latter, often referred to as sales talk or puffing, does not create an express warranty. The UCC requires an affirmation of fact or promise. Hence, a statement of opinion is not covered by the code. For example, the sales clerk who says, ''This is the best TV around,'' would not be understood to be guaranteeing that the television in question is the best available. The salesperson is expressing a view. We, as consumers, seem to be quite patient with sellers' exaggerations. If on the other hand, the clerk said, ''This TV has a solid walnut cabinet,'' when in fact it was a pine veneer stained to a walnut tone, a breach of warranty action might ultimately be in order. The test to be applied in such situations is one of reasonable expectations. An expression of opinion coming from an expert may well rise to the level of an affirmation of fact or promise because the buyer should reasonably expect to be able to rely on the expert's affirmations. For example, a handwriting expert in seeking to sell a purportedly rare historical document says, ''This handwriting is clearly that of Adolph Hitler.'' Depending on all the facts, such a statement might well be treated as an affirmation of a fact.

Implied Warranties

A seller enters into a contract for the sale of goods and, as a consequence, an implied warranty arises by operation of law. That is, an implied warranty automatically attaches to the sale of goods unless the warranty is disclaimed (disavowed) by the seller.

Two types of implied warranties are provided for:

UCC 2–314. Implied Warranty: Merchantability; Usage of Trade.

(1) Unless excluded or modified (Section 2–316), a warranty that the goods shall be merchantable is implied in a contract for their sale if the seller is a merchant with respect to goods of that

kind. Under this section the serving for value of food or drink to be consumed either on the premises or elsewhere is a sale.

UCC 2–315. Implied Warranty: Fitness for Particular Purpose.

Where the seller at the time of contracting has reason to know any particular purpose for which the goods are required and that the buyer is relying on the seller's skill or judgment to select or furnish suitable goods, there is unless excluded or modified under the next section an implied warranty that the goods shall be fit for such purpose.

The implied warranty of merchantability is a powerful tool for the wronged consumer in that the warranty arises automatically by operation of law. If the seller is a merchant regularly selling goods of the kind in question the warranty of merchantability simply accompanies the sale unless the warranty is excluded via a disclaimer (explained below). The warranty arises even if the seller made no certification as to the nature or quality of the goods. The effect of UCC 2–314 is to enshrine the consumer's reasonable expectation that only safe goods of at least ordinary quality will appear on the market.

The implied warranty of fitness for a particular purpose likewise arises by operation of law, but only when the seller (merchant or not) knows (or has reason to know) that the goods are to be used for a specific purpose, and the seller further knows that the buyer is relying on the seller's judgment. If those conditions obtain, the warranty exists automatically unless disclaimed. For example, Chris Snapp engages an audio products clerk in a discussion regarding the proper stereo system for Chris's Austin Healey sports car. Chris explains the joy he expects to receive in driving his car along the winding Kentucky roads with the convertible top down and the stereo booming. Alas, the stereo selected on the clerk's advice proves insufficiently powerful to be heard clearly above the rushing wind. Should Chris recover for breach of the implied warranty of fitness for a particular purpose? Merchantability?

Disclaimers

Express warranties may be disclaimed (excluded) or modified only with great difficulty. In any contract displaying both an express warranty and language disclaiming that warranty (e.g., sold "as is" or "with all faults"), the warranty will remain effective unless the warranty and the disclaimer can reasonably be read as consistent.

Implied warranties may be excluded or modified by following either of the two patterns explained in UCC sections 2–316(2) and (3)(a).

(2) Subject to subsection (3), to exclude or modify the implied warranty of merchantability or any part of it the language must mention merchantability and in case of a writing must be conspicuous, and to exclude or modify any implied warranty of fitness the exclusion must be by a writing and conspicuous . . .

(3) Notwithstanding subsection (2)

(a) unless the circumstances indicate otherwise, all implied warranties are excluded by expressions like "as is," "with all faults" or other language which in common understanding calls the buyer's attention to the exclusion of warranties and makes plain that there is no implied warranty . . .

Finally, when a buyer, before entering a contract, inspects the goods (or a sample thereof), or declines to inspect, no implied warranty exists with regard to defects that should have been apparent upon inspection [UCC 2–316(3)(b)].

The case that follows illustrates the evolution of warranty law in an increasingly complex commercial society.

HENNINGSEN V. BLOOMFIELD MOTORS, INC.   Supreme Court of
New Jersey, 161 A. 2d 69 (1960)

Justice Francis

Plaintiff Clause H. Henningsen purchased a Plymouth automobile, manufactured by defendant Chrysler Corporation, from defendant Bloomfield Motors, Inc. His wife, plaintiff Helen Henningsen, was injured while driving it and instituted suit against both defendants to recover damages on account of her injuries. Her husband joined in the action seeking compensation for his consequential losses. The complaint was predicated upon breach of express and implied warranties and upon negligence. At the trial the negligence counts were dismissed by the court and the cause was submitted to the jury for determination solely on the issues of implied warranty of merchantability. Verdicts were returned against both defendants and in favor of the plaintiffs. Defendants appealed and plaintiffs cross-appealed from the dismissal of their negligence claim. . . .

On May 7, 1955 Mr. and Mrs. Henningsen visited the place of business of Bloomfield Motors, Inc., an authorized De Soto and Plymouth dealer, to look at a Plymouth. . . . They were shown a Plymouth which appealed to them and the purchase followed. The record indicates that Mr. Henningsen intended the car as a Mother's Day gift to his wife. When the purchase order or contract was prepared and presented, the husband executed it alone. The purchase order was a printed form of one page. . . .

The testimony of Claus Henningsen justifies the conclusion that he did not read the two fine print paragraphs referring to the back of the purchase contract. And it is uncontradicted that no one made any reference to them, or called them to his attention. With respect to the matter appearing on the back, it is likewise uncontradicted that he did not read it and that no one called it to his attention.

The reverse side of the contract contains 8½ inches of fine print. . . .

In the seventh paragraph, about two-thirds of the way down the page, the warranty, which is the focal point of the case, is set forth.

"7. It is expressly agreed that there are no warranties, express or implied, *made* by either the dealer or the manufacturer on the motor vehicle, chassis, of parts furnished hereunder except as follows. . . ."

The new Plymouth was turned over to the Henningsens on May 9, 1955. . . . That day, Mrs. Henningsen drove to Asbury Park. On the way down and in returning the car performed in normal fashion until the accident occurred. She was proceeding north on Route 36 in Highlands, New Jersey, at 20–22 miles per hour. The highway was paved and smooth, and contained two lanes for northbound travel. She was riding in the righthand lane. Suddenly she heard a loud noise "from the bottom, by the hood." It "felt as if something cracked." The steering wheel spun in her hands; the car veered sharply to the right and crashed into a highway sign and a brick wall. . . .

The insurance carrier's inspector and appraiser of damaged cars, with 11 years of experience, advanced the opinion, based on the history and his examination, that something definitely went "wrong from the steering wheel down to the front wheels" and that the untoward happening must have been due to mechanical defect or failure; "something down there had to drop off or break loose to cause the car" to act in the manner described. . . .

The Claim of Implied Warranty against the Manufacturer

. . . [W]e come to a study of the express warranty on the reverse side of the purchase order signed by Claus Henningsen. At the outset we take notice that it was made only by the manufacturer and that by its terms it runs directly to Claus Henningsen. . . .

The terms of the warranty are a sad commentary upon the automobile manufacturers' marketing practices. Warranties developed in the law in the interest of and to protect the ordinary consumer who cannot be expected to have the knowledge or capacity or even the opportunity to make adequate inspection of mechanical instrumentalities, like automobiles, and to decide for himself whether they are reasonably fit for the designed purpose. But the ingenuity of the Automobile Manufacturers Association, by means of its standardized form, has metamorphosed the warranty into a device to limit the maker's liability. . . .

The manufacturer agrees to replace defective parts for 90 days after the sale or until the car has been driven 4,000 miles, whichever is first to occur, *if the part is sent to the factory, transportation charges prepaid, and if examination discloses to its satisfaction that the part is defective.* It is difficult to imagine a greater burden on the consumer, or less satisfactory remedy. . . .

Moreover, the guaranty is against defective workmanship. That condition may arise from good parts improperly assembled. There being no defective parts to return to the maker, is all remedy to be denied? . . .

The matters referred to represent only a small part of the illusory character of the security presented by the warranty. Thus far the analysis has dealt only with the remedy provided in the case of a defective part. What relief is provided when the breach of the warranty results in personal injury to the buyer? . . . But in this instance, after reciting that defective parts will be replaced at the factory, the alleged agreement relied upon by Chrysler provides that the manufacturer's "obligation under this warranty" is limited to that undertaking: further, that such remedy is "in lieu of all other warranties, express or implied, and all other obligations or liabilities on its part." The contention has been raised that such language bars any claim for personal injuries which may emanate from a breach of the warranty. . . .

Putting aside for the time being the problem of the efficacy of the disclaimer provisions contained in the express warranty, a question of first importance to be decided is whether an implied warranty of merchantability by Chrysler Corporation accompanied the sale of the automobile to Claus Henningsen.

*   *   *   *   *

Chrysler points out that an implied warranty of merchantability is an incident of a contract of sale. It concedes, of course, the making of the original sale to Bloomfield Motors, Inc., but maintains that this transaction marked the terminal point of its contractual connection with the car. Then Chrysler urges that since it was not a party to the sale by the dealer to Henningsen, there is no privity of contract between it and the plaintiffs, and the absence of this privity eliminates any such implied warranty.

*   *   *   *   *

Under modern conditions the ordinary layman, on responding to the importuning of colorful advertising, has neither the opportunity nor the capacity to inspect or to determine the fitness of an automobile for use; he must rely on the manufacturer who has control of its construction, and to some degree on the dealer who, to the limited extent called for by the manufacturer's instructions, inspects and services it before delivery. In such a marketing milieu his remedies and those of persons who properly claim through him should not depend ''upon the intricacies of the law of sales. The obligation of the manufacturer should not be based alone on privity of contract. It should rest, as was once said, upon 'the demands of social justice'.''

Accordingly, we hold that under modern marketing conditions, when a manufacturer puts a new automobile in the stream of trade and promotes its purchase by the public, an implied warranty that it is reasonably suitable for use as such accompanies it into the hands of the ultimate purchaser. Absence of agency between the manufacturer and the dealer who makes the ultimate sale is immaterial.

The Effect of the Disclaimer and Limitation of Liability Clauses on the Implied Warranty of Merchantability

. . . [W]hat effect should be given to the express warranty in question which seeks to limit the manufacturer's liability to replacement of defective parts, and which disclaims all other warranties, express or implied? In assessing its significance we must keep in mind the general principle that, in the absence of fraud, one who does not choose to read a contract before signing it, cannot later relieve himself of its burdens.

But in the framework of modern commercial life and business practices, such rules cannot be applied on a strict, doctrinal basis. The conflicting interests of the buyer and seller must be evaluated realistically and justly, giving due weight to the social policy evinced by the Uniform Sales Act, the progressive decisions of the courts engaged in administering it, the mass production methods of manufacture and distribution to the public, and the bargaining position occupied by the ordinary consumer in such an economy. This history of the law shows that legal doctrines, as first expounded, often prove to be inadequate under the impact of later experience. In such case, the need for justice has stimulated the necessary qualifications or adjustments.

In these times, an automobile is almost as much a servant of convenience for the ordinary person as a household utensil. For a multitude of other persons it is a necessity. . . .

The traditional contract is the result of free bargaining of parties who are brought together by the play of the market, and who meet each other on a footing of approximate economic equality. In such a society there is no danger that freedom of contract will be a threat to the social order as a whole. But in present-day commercial life the standardized mass contract has appeared. It is used primarily by enterprises with strong bargaining power and position. Such standardized contracts have been described as those in which one predominant party will dictate its law to an undetermined multiple rather than to an individual. They are said to resemble a law rather than a meeting of the minds. . . .

The warranty before us is a standardized form designed for mass use. It is imposed upon the automobile consumer. He takes it or leaves it, and he must take it to buy an automobile. No bargaining is engaged in with respect to it. In fact, the dealer through whom it comes to the buyer is without authority to alter it; his function is ministerial—simply to deliver it. . . .

The gross inequality of bargaining position occupied by the consumer in the automobile industry is thus apparent. There is no competition among the car makers in the area of the express warranty.

*   *   *   *   *

Assuming that a jury might find that the fine print referred to reasonably served the objective of directing a buyer's attention to the warranty on the reverse side, and, therefore, that he should be charged with awareness of its language, can it be said that an ordinary layman would realize what he was relinquishing in return for what he was being granted? . . . *In the context* of this warranty, only the abandonment of all sense of justice would permit us to hold that, as a matter of law, the phrase ''its obligation under this warranty being limited to making good at its factory any part or parts thereof'' signifies to an ordinary reasonable person that he is relinquishing any personal injury claim that might flow from the use of a defective automobile. . . .

The Dealer's Implied Warranty

The principles that have been expounded as to the obligation of the manufacturer apply with equal force to the separate express warranty of the dealer.

*   *   *   *   *

. . . [W]e conclude that the disclaimer of an implied warranty of merchantability by the dealer, as well as the attempted elimination of all obligations other than replacement of defective parts, are violative of public policy and void. . . .

The Defense of Lack of Privity against Mrs. Henningsen

Both defendants contend that since there was no privity of contract between them and Mrs. Henningsen, she cannot recover for breach of any warranty made by either of them. On the facts, as they were developed, we agree that she was not a party to the purchase agreement. Her right to maintain the action, therefore, depends upon whether she occupies such legal status thereunder as to permit her to take advantage of a breach of defendants' implied warranties. . . . We are convinced that the cause of justice in this area of the law can be served only by recognizing that she is such a person who, in the reasonable contemplation of the parties to the warranty, might be expected to become a user of the automobile. . . .

It is important to express the right of Mrs. Henningsen to maintain her action in terms of a general principle. To what extent may lack of privity be disregarded in suits on such warranties? . . . [I]t is our opinion that an implied warranty of merchantability chargeable to either an automobile manufacturer or a dealer extends to the purchaser of the car, members of his family, and to other persons occupying or using it with his consent. It would be wholly opposed to reality to say that use by such persons is not within the anticipation of parties to such a warranty of reasonable suitability of an automobile for ordinary highway operation. Those persons must be considered within the distributive chain. . . .

Affirmed.

Questions

1. Define the doctrine of privity of contract.
2. List those considerations that permitted the *Henningsen* Court to disavow the privity requirement under the facts of that case.
3. Why was the Chrysler disclaimer ruled invalid?
4. A father asks his 11-year-old son to go to the kitchen, open a bottle of beer, and return with it. In opening the beer, the son's hand is cut when the bottle breaks. The father sues the bottler on behalf of his son. The father raises both negligence and breach of warranty claims. At trial it is established that the son was not negligent. The bottler defends by establishing that the beer was purchased by the father. Decide. Explain.

The Limits of Warranty Law

The case that follows is an excellent example of activism on the bench as jurists develop novel legal interpretations designed to afford justice to the harmed consumer.

GILLISPIE V. THE GREAT ATLANTIC AND PACIFIC TEA COMPANY   14 N.C. 1, 187 S.E.2d 441 (1972)

Plaintiff went to defendant's store to purchase soft drinks. He picked up two cartons and walked toward the checkout counter, carrying a carton of Sprite in his left hand and a carton of Coca Cola in his right hand. He was walking directly to the checkout counter where he intended to pay for the drinks. At a point about 20 to 25 feet from the shelf where he had picked up the drinks and about 10 feet from the checkout counter, two of the Sprite bottles exploded, and plaintiff's left wrist was lacerated.

At trial, the Court allowed the defendant's motion for a directed verdict. Plaintiff appealed.

Judge Graham

Plaintiff bases his claim solely upon breach of implied warranty.

The evidence tends to show that plaintiff handled the bottles of Sprite normally from the time he took possession of them until they exploded. There is no evidence presently before us which would indicate the plaintiff's conduct contributed in any way to the explosions. Therefore, the jury would be justified in finding that the bottles exploded because they were inadequate for the purpose they were intended; namely, as containers of the Sprite soft drink.

*   *   *   *   *

The first question before us is whether an implied warranty of fitness has now been extended by the Uniform Commercial Code to include a product's container such as the one involved here. We hold that it has.

G.S.§25-2-314 provides in pertinent part:

(1)   Unless excluded or modified, a warranty that the goods shall be merchantable is implied in a contract for their sale if the seller is a merchant with respect to goods of that kind. Under this section the serving for value of food or drink to be consumed either on the premises or elsewhere is a sale.
(2)   Goods to be merchantable must be at least such as . . .
       (c)   are fit for the ordinary purposes for which such goods are used; and . . .
       (e)   Are adequately contained, packaged, and labeled as the agreement may require.

In the official comment following this section it is stated:

       (e)   applies only where the nature of the goods and of the transaction requires a certain type of container, package or label.

The nature of bottled drinks, such as Sprite, requires a container which is adequate to contain the drink without breaking or exploding when handled with ordinary care. Another way of putting it is that under this section, soft drinks are not merchantable if inadequately contained. If they are sold in a container which is inadequate, the seller has breached his implied warranty of merchantability and he is liable for personal injury proximately caused by this breach. The fact that it is the container, rather than the product inside, which causes injury, does not make the injury any less a result of the seller's breach of warranty.

A second question presented is whether a sale had taken place at the time the bottles allegedly exploded. Warranties arise under the Uniform Commercial Code only upon a sale of goods. . . . "A 'sale' consists in the passing of title from the seller to the buyer for a price. . . . [U]nless otherwise explicitly agreed, title passes to the buyer at the time and place at which the seller completes his performance with reference to the physical delivery of the goods, despite any reservation of a security interest and even though a document of title is to be delivered at a different time or place; and in particular and despite any reservation of a security interest by the bill of lading." . . .

* * * * *

We are of the opinion that . . . the time of payment is not determinative of the question of when a sale takes place. If there has been a completed delivery by the seller, the sale has been consummated and implied warranties arise . . .

The presence of the drinks on the shelves in defendant's self-service store constituted an offer for sale and delivery at a stated price. If plaintiff took the drinks into his possession with the intention of paying for them at the cashier's counter, there was no further act of delivery necessary on the part of the seller. All that remained was for plaintiff to pay for the drinks—an act delayed until he reached the cashier's counter primarily for the convenience of the seller.

Defendant calls attention to the custom in self-service stores which permits a customer to return goods to the shelf without liability if he changes his mind about a purchase before reaching the checkout counter. However, even a right to return delivered goods does not necessarily delay passage of the title until that right has expired. G.S. § 25-2-401(4) provides: "A rejection or other refusal by the buyer to receive or retain the goods, whether or not justified, or a justified revocation of acceptance revests title to the goods in the seller." The result is that when a purchaser in a self-service store changes his mind and returns to the shelf a product which he has picked up with the intention of buying, title is revested in the seller. However, as long as the purchaser has the product in his possession, intending to pay for it, he has title to the product. The seller's interest at that point is not "title" but a security interest to enforce payment. "Any retention or reservation by the seller of the title (property) in goods shipped or delivered to the buyer is limited in effect to a reservation of a security interest."

The evidence presented would support a jury finding that plaintiff purchased the Sprite drinks by taking them into his possession with the intention of paying for them. Should the jury so find, the questions would then become: Was the warranty of implied merchantability breached by defendant, and if so, did the breach proximately cause the injuries sustained by the plaintiff? We are of the opinion the evidence is sufficient to go to the jury on these questions.

Reversed.

Questions

1. Explain the court's view that a sale took place when the buyer took possession of the goods with the intention of paying for them.
2. If the shattered bottle injured another customer, would the original owner, A&P, be liable, or would liability fall on the purchaser, Gillespie? Explain.
3. Jones, a customer at Brown's Furriers, decides to purchase a $10,000 full-length blue fox coat. The customer begins the few steps toward the service desk, but she is intercepted by a man who grabs the coat and runs. Was the stolen coat the property of Jones or Brown's?
4. Assume Gillespie was injured by the explosion of a rolling soft drink bottle as he was about

to pick it up from the floor. Can he recover from A&P? See *Copher* v. *Barbee,* 361 S.W. 2d 137 (Mo. App. 1962).

5. Under the *Gillespie* opinion, the presence of the Sprite on the shelves was an offer by A&P to sell the Sprite at the sticker price.

    a. Ordinarily, is the placement of goods on a store shelf an offer to sell or a solicitation for offers from customers?

    b. Why?

Magnuson-Moss Warranty Act

While the Uniform Commercial Code embodies our primary expression of warranty rules, Congress has extended and clarified those rules by passing the Magnuson-Moss Warranty Act. Congress approved the act following a study that found widespread abuse of consumers. Warranties were often vague or deceptive or simply incomprehensible to the average purchaser. The act, administered by the FTC, applies only to consumer products and only to written warranties. The act does not require offering an express written warranty, but where such a warranty is offered and the cost of the goods is more than $10, the warranty must be labelled "full" or "limited." A full warranty requires free repair of any defect. If repair is not achieved within a reasonable time, the buyer may elect either a refund or replacement without charge. If a limited warranty is offered, the limitation must be conspicuously displayed.

If a warranty is offered on goods costing more than $15, the warrantor must "fully and conspicuously disclose in simple and readily understandable language the terms and conditions of the warranty." The FTC has developed various rules to implement the intent of the disclosure requirement. For example, if the warrantor requires return of the completed warranty registration card in order to "activate" the warranty, that return requirement must be clearly disclosed in the warranty.

The effect of the Magnuson-Moss Act has not been entirely consistent with Congress' hopes. In practice, many sellers may have either offered limited warranties or eliminated them entirely.

Strict Liability

Negligence and warranty actions are helpful to the harmed consumer. However, rapid changes in the nature of commercial practice, as well as an increasing societal concern for consumer protection, led the legal community to gradually embrace yet another cause of action. Broadly, *strict liability in tort* offers the prospect of holding all of those in the chain of distribution liable for damages from a defective product, rather than imposing the entire burden on the injured consumer. Manufacturers and sellers are best positioned to prevent the distribution of defective products, and they are best able to bear the cost of injury by spreading the loss via pricing policies and insurance coverage.

Strict liability as an independent tort emerged in 1963 in the famous California case of *Greenman* v. *Yuba Products, Inc.* In the ensuing two decades, most states, either via their judiciary or their legislature, have adopted strict liability in concept. The essence of the strict liability notion is expressed in Section 402A of the Restatement of Torts. (Note that the Restatement of Torts does not constitute law. Rather it is a summary of the law of torts as interpreted by a group of legal scholars.) In sum, 402A imposes liability where a product is sold in a *defective condition, unreasonably dangerous*[8] to the user:

1. One who sells any product in a defective condition, unreasonably dangerous to the user or consumer or to his property, is subject to liability for physical harm thereby caused to the ultimate user or consumer, or to his property, if
   a. the seller is engaged in the business of selling such a product, and,
   b. it is expected to and does reach the user or consumer without substantial change in the condition in which it is sold.
2. The rule stated in Subsection (1) applies although
   a. the seller has exercised all possible care in the preparation and sale of his product, and
   b. the user or consumer has not bought the product from or entered into any contractual relation with the seller.

In the *Greenman* case the reader should pay particular attention to the court's philosophical justification for embracing strict liability in tort as a proper cause of action.

GREENMAN V. YUBA POWER PRODUCTS, INC.   Supreme Court of California, 27 Cal.Rptr. 697, 377 P.2d 897 (1962)

Justice Traynor

Plaintiff brought this action for damages against the retailer and the manufacturer of a Shopsmith, a combination power tool that could be used as a saw, drill, and wood lathe. He saw a Shopsmith demonstrated by the retailer and studied a brochure prepared by the manufacturer. . . . [H]is wife bought and gave him one for Christmas in 1955. In 1957 he bought the necessary attachments to use the Shopsmith as a lathe for turning a large piece of wood he wished to make into a chalice. After he had worked on the piece of wood several times without difficulty, it suddenly flew out of the machine and struck him on the forehead, inflicting serious injuries. About 10½ months later, he gave the retailer and the manufacturer written notice of claimed breaches of warranties and filed a complaint against them. . . .

*   *   *   *   *

The jury returned a verdict for the retailer against plaintiff and for the plaintiff against the manufacturer in the amount of $65,000. . . . The manufacturer and plaintiff appeal. . . .

Plaintiff introduced substantial evidence that his injuries were caused by defective design and construction of the Shopsmith. His expert witnesses testified that inadequate set screws were used to hold parts of the machine together so that normal vibration caused the tailstock of the lathe to move away from the piece of wood being turned permitting it to fly out of the lathe. They also testified that there were other, more positive, ways of fastening the parts of the machine together, the use of which would have prevented the accident. The jury could therefore reasonably have concluded that the manufacturer negligently constructed the Shopsmith. The jury could also reasonably have concluded that statements in the manufacturer's brochure were untrue, that they constituted express warranties, and that plaintiff's injuries were caused by their breach.

The manufacturer contends, however, that plaintiff did not give it notice of breach of warranty within a reasonable time and that therefore his cause of action for breach of warranty is barred. . . .

*   *   *   *   *

[The California Sales Act] does not provide that notice must be given of the breach of a warranty that arises independently of a contract of sale between the parties. Such warranties are not imposed by the sales act, but are the product of common-law decisions that have recognized them in a variety of situations. . . .

The notice requirement is not an appropriate one for the court to adopt in actions by injured consumers against manufacturers with whom they have not dealt. . . . We conclude, therefore, that even if plaintiff did not give timely notice of breach of warranty to the manufacturer, his cause of action based on the representations contained in the brochure was not barred.

Moreover, to impose strict liability on the manufacturer under the circumstances of this case, it was not necessary for plaintiff to establish an express warranty. A manufacturer is strictly liable in tort when an article he places on the market, knowing that it is to be used without inspection for defects, proves to have a defect that causes injury to a human being. Recognized first in the case of unwholesome food products, such liability has now been extended to a variety of other products that create as great or greater hazards if defective.

. . . [S]trict liability has usually been based on the theory of an express or implied warranty running from the manufacturer to the plaintiff, the abandonment of the requirement of a contract between them, the recognition that the liability is not assumed by agreement but imposed by law, and the refusal to permit the manufacturer to define the scope of its own responsibility for defective products make clear that the liability is not one governed by the law of contract warranties but by the law of strict liability in tort. Accordingly, rules defining and governing warranties that were developed to meet the needs of commercial transactions cannot properly be invoked to govern the manufacturer's liability to those injured by their defective products unless those rules also serve the purposes for which such liability is imposed.

. . . The purpose of such liability is to ensure that the costs of injuries resulting from defective products are borne by the manufacturers that put such products on the market rather than by the injured persons who are powerless to protect themselves. Sales warranties serve this purpose fitfully at best. In the present case, for example, plaintiff was able to plead and prove an express warranty only because he read and relied on the representations of the Shopsmith's ruggedness contained in the manufacturer's brochure. Implicit in the machine's presence on the market, however, was a representation that it would safely do the jobs for which it was built. Under these circumstances, it should not be controlling whether plaintiff selected the machine because of the statements in the brochure, or because of the machine's own appearance of excellence that belied the defect lurking beneath the surface, or because he merely assumed that it would safely do the jobs it was built to do. It should not be controlling whether the details of the sales from manufacturer to retailer and from retailer to plaintiff's wife were such that one or more of the implied warranties of the sales act arose. "The remedies of injured consumers ought not to be made to depend upon the intricacies of the law of sales." To establish the manufacturer's liability it was sufficient that plaintiff proved that he was injured while using the Shopsmith in a way it was intended to be used as a result of a defect in design and manufacture of which plaintiff was not aware that made the Shopsmith unsafe for its intended use.

Judgment affirmed.

Questions

1. Why does the *Greenman* court reject warranty law as the proper vehicle for recovery in this case?
2. The *Greenman* court said: "Plaintiff introduced substantial evidence that his injuries were caused by defective design and construction of the Shopsmith." That being the case, why did the court break new ground in resolving the case on strict liability principles, rather than relying on well-settled negligence standards?
3. The deceased had rented an auto from the Hertz Corporation. A tire blew out, and a fatal crash resulted. The tire was manufactured by Firestone. The estate of the deceased filed suit against Hertz and Firestone. Evidence presented at trial caused the jury to believe that the dangerous condition of the tire arose after its manufacture.
    a. Can the plaintiff successfully raise a strict liability claim against Hertz? Explain.
    b. Against Firestone? Explain. See *Stang* v. *Hertz Corp.,* 83 N.M. 730, 497 P.2d 732 (1972).
4. The plaintiff received a blood transfusion at St. Joseph's Hospital. Shortly thereafter, the plaintiff was discovered to have contracted serum hepatitus (a disease sometimes transmitted via transfusions). The blood was purchased from Blood Services, Inc. Can the plaintiff recover on strict liability grounds from either St. Joseph's or Blood Services? See *Hines* v. *St. Joseph's Hospital,* 86 N.M. 763, 527 P.2d 1075 (1974).

Coverage

All of those engaged in the preparation and distribution of a defective product may be liable for any harm caused by the defect, regardless of proof of actual fault. Furthermore, although not addressed in Section 402A, the courts have extended strict liability coverage to reach injured bystanders. In general, coverage extends to both personal injuries and property damage, but in some states the latter is excluded. Some states limit strict liability recovery to new goods, and some have limited liability to a designated period (e.g., 15 years) after the manufacture or sale of the product.

DUNHAM V. VAUGHAN & BUSHNELL MFG. CO.   42 Ill.2d 339, 247 N.E.2d 401 (1969)

Justice Schaefer

A jury in the circuit court of Macoupin County returned a verdict in the sum of $50,000 in favor of the plaintiff, Benjamin E. Dunham, and against the defendants, Vaughan & Bushnell Mfg. Co. and Belknap Hardware and Mfg. Co. . . . [T]he Appellate Court for the Fourth Judicial District affirmed. . . .

The injury that gave rise to this action occurred while the plaintiff was fitting a pin into a clevis to connect his tractor to a manure spreader. He had made the connection on one side, using a hammer to insert the pin. To insert the second pin he lay on his right side underneath the tractor and used the hammer extended about two and one-half feet above his head. The hammer moved through an arc which he described as about 8 inches. He testified that as he undertook to "tap" the pin into the clevis a chip from the beveled edge of the hammer, known as the chamfer, broke off and struck him in the right eye. He lost the sight of that eye.

The hammer in question is a claw hammer of the best grade manufactured by the defendant Vaughn & Bushnell Mfg. Co. It bore the "Blue-Grass" trademark of its distributor, the other defendant, Belknap Hardware and Manufacturing Co. The plaintiff had received the hammer from a retailer, Heyen Implement Company, located near his home. He received it as a replacement for another "Blue-Grass" hammer, the handle of which had been broken. Before the accident occurred the plaintiff had used the hammer for approximately 11 months in connection with his farming and custom machine work. He had used it in repairing a corn crib and had also used it in working upon his farming implements and machinery.

Each party offered the testimony of an expert metallurgist. Neither expert found any flaws due to the forging of the hammer, or any metallurgical defects due to the process of manufacture. The experts agreed that the hammer was made of steel with a carbon content of "1080." The plaintiff's expert testified that such a hammer was more likely to chip or shear than one made of steel with a lower carbon content of "1040," which would not be so hard. The defendant's expert disagreed; it was his opinion that a hammer made of harder steel, with the higher carbon content, would be less likely to chip or shear than one made of steel with a lower carbon content. Both experts testified that use of a hammer produced a condition described as "work hardening" or "metal failure," which made a hammer more likely to chip or shear.

$$* \quad * \quad * \quad * \quad *$$

The basic theory of the defendants in this court is that the requirements of strict liability, . . . were not established, because the testimony of the experts showed that the hammer contained no defect. . . .

Although the definitions of the term *defect* in the context of products liability law use varying language, all of them rest upon the common premise that those products are defective which are dangerous because they fail to perform in the manner reasonably to be expected in light of their nature and intended function. . . . The Restatement emphasizes the viewpoint of the consumer and concludes that a defect is a condition not contemplated by the ultimate consumer which would be unreasonably dangerous to him. . . .

The evidence in this case, including both the General Services Administration specifications and tests and the testimony of the experts as to "work hardening" or "metal failure," shows that hammers have a propensity to chip which increases with continued use. From that evidence it would appear that a new hammer would not be expected to chip, while at some point in its life the possibility of chipping might become a reasonable expectation, and a part of the hammer's likely performance. The problems arise in the middle range, as Chief Justice Traynor has illustrated: "If an automobile part normally lasts five years, but the one in question proves defective after six months of normal use, there would be enough deviation to serve as a basis for holding the manufacturer liable for any resulting harm. What if the part lasts four of the normal five years, however, and then proves defective? For how long should a manufacturer be responsible for his product?" . . .

The answers to these questions are properly supplied by a jury, and on the record that is before us this case presents only the narrow question whether there is sufficient evidence to justify the jury's conclusion that the hammer was defective. The record shows that it was represented as one of "best quality" and was not put to a use which was regarded as extraordinary in the experience of the community. The jury could properly have concluded that, considering the length and type

implied warranties, false and fraudulent representations, misbranding of drugs in violation of federal law, conspiracy, and "lack of consent."

Each cause of action alleges that defendants are jointly liable because they acted in concert, on the basis of express and implied agreements, and in reliance upon and ratification and exploitation of each other's testing and marketing methods.

Plaintiff seeks compensatory damages of $1 million and punitive damages of $10 million for herself. For the members of her class, she prays for equitable relief in the form of an order that defendants warn physicians and others of the danger of DES and the necessity of performing certain tests to determine the presence of disease caused by the drug, and that they establish free clinics in California to perform such tests.

Defendants demurred to the complaint. . . . . [T]he court dismissed the action.

* * * * *

This case is but one of a number filed throughout the country seeking to hold drug manufacturers liable for injuries allegedly resulting from DES prescribed to the plaintiffs' mothers since 1947. . . . [E]stimates of the number of women who took the drug during pregnancy range from 1.5 million to 3 million. Hundreds, perhaps thousands, of the daughters of these women suffer from adenocarcinoma, and the incidence of vaginal adenosis among them is 30 to 90 percent. . . . Most of the cases are still pending. With two exceptions, those that have been decided resulted in judgments in favor of the drug company defendants because of the failure of the plaintiffs to identify the manufacturer of the DES prescribed to their mothers. . . . The present action is another attempt to overcome this obstacle to recovery.

We begin with the proposition that, as a general rule, the imposition of liability depends upon a showing by the plaintiff that his or her injuries were caused by the act of the defendant or by an instrumentality under the defendant's control. . . .

There are, however, exceptions to this rule. . . .

Plaintiff places primary reliance upon cases which hold that if a party cannot identify which of two or more defendants caused an injury, the burden of proof may shift to the defendants to show that they were not responsible for the harm. This principle is sometimes referred to as the "alternative liability" theory.

The celebrated case of *Summers* v. *Tice*, a unanimous opinion of this court, best exemplifies the rule. In *Summers*, the plaintiff was injured when two hunters negligently shot in his direction. It could not be determined which of them had fired the shot which actually caused the injury to the plaintiff's eye, but both defendants were nevertheless held jointly and severally liable for the whole of the damages. We reasoned that both were wrongdoers, both were negligent toward the plaintiff, and that it would be unfair to require plaintiff to isolate the defendant responsible, because if the one pointed out were to escape liability, the other might also, and the plaintiff-victim would be shorn of any remedy. In these circumstances, we held, the burden of proof shifted to the defendants, "each to absolve himself if he can." . . . We stated that under these or similar circumstances a defendant is ordinarily in a "far better position" to offer evidence to determine whether he or another defendant caused the injury.

* * * * *

There is an important difference between the situation involved in *Summers* and the present case. There, all the parties who were or could have been responsible for the harm to the plaintiff were joined as defendants. Here, by contrast, there are approximately 200 drug companies which made DES, any of which might have manufactured the injury-producing drug.

* * * * *

In our contemporary complex industrialized society, advances in science and technology create fungible goods which may harm consumers and which cannot be traced to any specific producer. The response of the courts can be either to adhere rigidly to prior doctrine, denying recovery to those injured by such products, or to fashion remedies to meet these changing needs. . . .

The most persuasive reason for finding plaintiff states a cause of action is that advanced in *Summers:* as between an innocent plaintiff and negligent defendants, the latter should bear the cost of the injury. Here, as in *Summers,* plaintiff is not at fault in failing to provide evidence of causation, and although the absence of such evidence is not attributable to the defendants either, their conduct in marketing a drug the effects of which are delayed for many years played a significant role in creating the unavailability of proof.

From a broader policy standpoint, defendants are better able to bear the cost of injury resulting from the manufacture of a defective product. As was said by Justice Traynor in *Escola,* "[t]he cost of an injury and the loss of time or health may be an overwhelming misfortune to the person injured, and a needless one, for the risk of injury can be insured by the manufacturer and distributed among the public as a cost of doing business." . . . The manufacturer is in the best position to discover and guard against defects in its products and to warn of harmful effects; thus, holding it liable for defects and failure to warn of harmful effects will provide an incentive to product safety. . . .

Where, as here, all defendants produced a drug from an identical formula and the manufacturer of the DES which caused plaintiff's injuries cannot be identified through no fault of plaintiff, a modification of the rule of *Summers* is warranted. As we have seen, an undiluted *Summers* rationale is inappropriate to shift the burden of proof of causation to defendants because if we measure the chance that any particular manufacturer supplied the injury-causing product by the number of producers of DES, there is a possibility that none of the five defendants in this case produced the offending substance and that the responsible manufacturer, not named in the action, will escape liability.

But we approach the issue of causation from a different perspective: we hold it to be reasonable in the present context to measure the likelihood that any of the defendants supplied the product which allegedly injured plaintiff by the percentage which the DES sold by each of them for the purpose of preventing miscarriage bears to the entire production of the drug sold by all for that purpose. Plaintiff asserts in her briefs that Eli Lilly and Company and five or six other companies produced 90 percent of the DES marketed. If at trial this is established to be the fact, then there is a corresponding likelihood that this comparative handful of producers manufactured the DES which caused plaintiff's injuries, and only a 10 percent likelihood that the offending producer would escape liability.

If plaintiff joins in the action the manufacturers of a substantial share of the DES which her mother might have taken, the injustice of shifting the burden of proof to defendants to demonstrate that they could not have made the substance which injured plaintiff is significantly diminished. . . .

The presence in the action of a substantial share of the appropriate market also provides a ready means to apportion damages among the defendants. Each defendant will be held liable for the proportion of the judgment represented by its share of that market unless it demonstrates that it could not have made the product which caused plaintiff's injuries.

*   *   *   *   *

We are not unmindful of the practical problems involved in defining the market and determining market share. . . . But under the rule we adopt, each manufacturer's liability for an injury would be approximately equivalent to the damages caused by the DES it manufactured.

The judgments are reversed.

Questions

1. Explain the alternative liability theory.
2. Explain how *Sindell* extends the *Summers* approach to alternative liability.
3. How can a defendant avoid liability under the *Sindell* decision?
4. How does the *Sindell* court justify its decision?
5. The dissent in *Sindell* (not reproduced in this text) argued that although "the majority purports to change only the required burden of proof by shifting it from plaintiffs to defendants, the effect of the holding is to guarantee that the plaintiffs will prevail on the causation issue because defendants are no more capable of disproving factual causation than plaintiffs are of proving it. 'Market share' liability thus represents a new high water mark in tort law.'' Comment.
6. A victim of asbestosis could not identify all of the manufacturers of the asbestos to which he was exposed. Should the court apply the "market share'' theory of liability to his case? Explain. See *Copeland* v. *Celotex Corp.*, 447 So.2d 908 (Fla. App. 3 Dist. 1984).

Corporation Protection?

We have seen that products liability law—particularly that of strict liability—has wrought a revolution in the degree of protection afforded to the consumer. It is clear that the courts and legislatures believed that consumers had been relatively powerless in the face of defective products, and that powerlessness had become particularly pronounced as commercial practice left behind straightforward, face-to-face bargaining and entered an era of multiple and complex layers of parts suppliers, manufacturers, distributors, retailers, et al. That imbalance of power was addressed in part by expanded products liability theories. In keeping with the generally egalitarian tone of the past two decades (e.g., the civil rights movement, the feminist cause), the law of consumer protection seemed to move evermore toward the presumed ideal of righting every wrong. Now, predictably enough, those in the business community and others believe the balance of power has swung too profoundly in favor of the consumer. They see business laboring under an excessive burden, born of an unjust effort to shift losses to those with the deepest pockets.

In order to combat some of the perceived unfairness in product liability law and to lend some uniformity to the law from state to state, the Department of Commerce has offered to the states a Uniform Product Liability Act (UPLA). As yet few states have adopted the act in significant part. It supports some of the concerns of the business community in, for example, approving contributory negligence, assumption of the risk, product misuse, and product alteration defenses. Another provision shields sellers from liability "in circumstances where they do not have a reasonable opportunity to inspect the product in a manner which would, or should, in the exercise of reasonable care, reveal the existence of the defective condition.'' While the UPLA proposes these and other provisions generally favorable to the business community's point of view, it should be understood that strict liability is unquestionably here to stay. Indeed, the UPLA in general imposes liability for injury resulting from any defectively designed or defectively produced product, or from any dangerous product not displaying adequate warnings.

The business community's concerns regarding the growth of product liability recoveries caused Congress to adopt the Risk Retention Act of 1981 (RRA). In very brief summary, the act facilitates the creation of "captive" insurance companies. In effect, a group of sellers join together to insure themselves against products liability losses. In so doing, the self-insurers hope to keep their own premiums at manageable levels and at the same time encourage moderation in insurance industry premiums.

For several years, Congress has been considering a federal products liability law. However, passage does not appear to be imminent. Whether UPLA, the RRA, and the other proposals to regulate the product liability area are necessary or will prove effective remains to be seen, but as the following pieces suggest, for the present, product liability law remains an explosive area of contention.

LAWSUITS CLAIM MANUFACTURER LIABILITY FOR MISUSE, ABUSE OF PRODUCTS

Rita Ciolli

A bullet rips through the brain of a presidential aide during an assassination attempt. A madman poisons seven people with cyanide in Tylenol capsules. The cost is in lives and dollars.

Lawsuits put the price at $131.5 million.

The two incidents may seem unconnected at first, but they have a fundamental similarity. The survivors of both want someone to pay for the tragedies. Therefore, they are using traditional legal theories in a novel way to dramatically expand the law.

"There is a mentality in the population that for every harm, there must be a remedy in money," said Thomas McNamara, a Michigan lawyer and chairman of an American Bar Association subcommittee on manufacturer's liability litigation. "A significant part of the population is hoping to fall down in the supermarket and retire with a noncrippling injury."

That is why RG Industries (which made the gun John Hinckley used to shoot President Reagan and his press secretary, James Brady) and Johnson & Johnson (which produced Ty-

lenol) are joining other major corporations being forced to face a new frontier in negligence law.

* * * * *

Sheila Birnbaum, a products liability specialist and associate dean of New York University law school, said, "It is an incredibly expanding area of law." The Tylenol and Brady cases can stretch the law even more, she said. "Even a year ago, people wouldn't have been expected to pursue a lawsuit where there was an intervening criminal act."

In the Tylenol poisonings, survivors are suing for a total of $31.5 million. Leonard Ring, a Chicago attorney representing the survivors of three of the victims, is arguing that Johnson & Johnson failed to use tamper-proof caps and lids such as foil or plastic seals. He also contends it was possible to have a solid capsule that couldn't be opened. "All of the things they are doing now," Ring said, "were clearly known to them and were used in some form by others."

One of Ring's bigger hurdles is convincing judge and jury that the firm could have foreseen the acts of a still-unknown person. Regardless of the outcome, experts agree that the practical effects of the Tylenol case mean more secure packaging of practically all food and drug products. After the Tylenol incident, a manufacturer can no longer claim that such criminal tampering was not forseeable.

The $100-million suit against a Miami maker of cheap handguns, brought by James Brady, the president's press secretary, has the most dramatic potential of all—eliminating the cheap Saturday Night Special handguns from the market. It would accomplish what handgun-control advocates have been unable to do through legislative action.

Brady and his wife, Sarah, are suing RG Industries, which assembles 15,000 guns a day by putting imported West German parts on a $1 frame in a Miami factory. Hinckley bought the gun for $50 from a Dallas pawn shop.

Seven lawsuits similar to Brady's are pending around the country. They are being anxiously watched. The victims are being assisted by the Foundation for Handgun Education, based in Washington, D.C., which collects data about handgun lawsuits and assists litigants.

"When a handgun makes a crime victim a quadriplegic, society at large is paying for it," said Samuel Fields, executive director of the foundation. "We want an industry with gross sales of $200 [million] to $300 million a year to pay for it; the damages in these lawsuits would make the true cost of their products come home to them."

Brady's lawsuit argues not that the gun was defective—it did exactly what it was supposed to do. Instead it presents two theories: First, manufacturers and handgun distributors are liable for injuries because they make little effort to stop the guns from falling into the hands of criminals. Second, the inherent dangerousness of such guns outweighs any social usefulness. Brady's suit contends that several factors show that the gun was being marketed for criminals,

not for legitimate owners of firearms. These factors include the price of the RG 14 weapon, $39.95, and its concealable 2-inch barrel that melts after five or six firings. Brady's court papers cite a series in Cox Newspapers, which reported that the RG 14, of which there are an estimated 1 million nationwide, is used more often in crimes than any other weapon.

Stuart Speiser, a product-liability lawyer, said that if Brady or others are successful, manufacturers of cheap handguns would find their insurance canceled. "They'll either go out of business after a few judgments," Speiser said, "or they'll stop selling to shops that don't check their customers."

The Brady lawsuit goes further than the Tylenol cases because his purpose is not only to recover damages for his injuries but to stop the sale of illegal handguns. Speiser, who wrote a book in 1980 about just such a lawsuit, agrees with this purpose. "We use our legal system to change society," he said. "We can go into court when the rest of the government is paralyzed."

But other legal observers are not convinced that lawsuits are the best way to achieve broad societal change. There have to be some limits, argues Aaron Twerski of Hofstra University Law School. He uses the textbook example of an automobile. It is certainly dangerous, but a totally safe vehicle would be unaffordable. "There are significant tradeoffs," Twerski said. "It is not now and never has been the policy of this country to have safety at any cost."

The two national tragedies present legal, political and social issues. "The fascinating part of the story is that it lays bare fundamental questions about what we want our tort system to do," said Twerski. "How much safety is enough safety? What are the tradeoffs to be made, and who do we want to be the decision-makers, the courts or the legislatures?"

Source: *The Des Moines (Iowa) Register*, December 23, 1982, p 6A. Reprinted with permission of the copyright holder, The Associated Press.

LET'S RESTORE BALANCE TO PRODUCT LIABILITY LAW

Robert H. Malott

When I began my business career 30 years ago, the liability of manufacturers and distributors for injuries suffered by a product user was limited and easily understood: businesses could be held responsible if their actions or conduct were negligent. During the past three decades, however, product liability law has changed dramatically, creating confusion among manufacturers and distributors as to what exactly constitutes liability. The focus has shifted from the conduct of product makers and sellers to the condition of the product itself. Liability can now result if a court or jury determines that a product's design, its construction, or its operating instructions and safety warnings make it unreasonably dangerous or hazardous to use.

These changes have produced a tremendous expansion in the scope of product-related injuries for which manufacturers and distributors are now held accountable. The most graphic evidence of this escalating exposure is the rapid growth in the number of product liability suits being filed and in the amounts of damages awarded. Between 1974 and 1981, for example, the number of product liability suits filed in federal district courts grew at an average annual rate of 28 percent nearly three-and-a-half times faster than the average annual increase in civil suits filed in federal courts.

For some, the changes of the past three decades represent merely a redressing of the balance of product liability law, which for too long was viewed as favoring product makers at the expense of product users. Other observers, however, are increasingly concerned that the pendulum has swung too far in favor of the injured product user, imposing on manufacturers and distributors enormous and inequitable costs that are ultimately passed on to society as a whole.

Questionable Issues

Now, the question is no longer "Whose fault is it?" Rather, "Is there a condition of the product that creates an unnecessary hazard or danger?"

Answering the product condition question, with respect to an alleged manufacturing defect, is easy: defective manufacturing is obvious because the product does not conform to the maker's design specifications. Had the extension of the strict liability doctrine been limited to injuries caused by manufacturing defects, liability exposure, although broader than it was under the negligence doctrine, would be clear and comprehensible.

Unfortunately, however, strict liability has been extended to product conditions other than manufacturing. In particular, some courts have determined that product designs may create hazardous conditions of use or that products may be sold without sufficient warning of hidden risks.

For an injured consumer, extending strict liability to design and warning "defects" was a logical next step in expanding the scope of damage recovery. To the manufacturers and sellers of those products, the step from manufacturing defects to design and warning defects was dramatic. Unlike the test for manufacturing defects, there are no standards to guide judicial decisions on the adequacy of a product's warnings or design.

Not surprisingly, each state has developed its own definition of strict liability for design and warnings. For instance, California deems a design defective if the product "fails to perform as safely as an ordinary consumer would expect it to when used in an intended or reasonably foreseeable manner." In Pennsylvania, on the other hand, a product's design is defective if it left the supplier's control "lacking any element to make it safe for its intended use or possessing any feature that renders it unsafe for the intended use."

* * * * *

Unreasonably Dangerous Design

By making manufacturers liable for any aspect of a product's condition that causes it to be unreasonably dangerous, the strict liability doctrine has made design safety an issue to be decided by judges and juries. Because there are no judicial standards that define minimum safety requirements, the courts have enormous latitude in deciding cases. In practice, they have tended to come down on the side of the product user. Consider the following case.

In 1974 a Pennsauken, New Jersey, police officer, responding to a burglar alarm, was severely injured when the Dodge Monaco police car he was driving spun off a rain-soaked highway. While moving backward, the car struck a steel pole 15 inches in diameter on the driver's side behind the front door. The police officer, Richard Dawson, sued the car's manufacturer, Chrysler Corporation, on the ground that the Monaco's design was unreasonably dangerous because it did not specify a rigid steel body, which would have prevented penetration of the passenger compartment.

In its defense Chrysler argued that the Monaco was designed with a flexible body to maximize passenger protection in front- or rear-end collisions, by far the most numerous types of accidents. A flexible frame absorbs the impact of these collisions by crumpling up. Moreover, Chrysler argued, a rigid side body construction would add about 250 pounds to the weight of the car, reducing its fuel efficiency and increasing its operating costs as well as price. Chrysler, faced with federal regulations both on fuel economy standards and front-end collision survivability, contended that the Monaco's design was optimal, given the infrequency of side collisions compared with front and rear accidents. The jury accepted the plaintiff's argument and awarded him damages of more than $2 million. On appeal, the federal appeals court upheld the trial court's verdict.

This decision, and decisions in other cases like it, lead to the following conclusion: if a product's design will not prevent all accidents, then juries may choose to consider it inadequately safe. The result has been an almost unfathomable expansion of the scope of product liability, with exorbitant costs to society.

* * * * *

Adequate Safety Warning

Judges and juries have also been given the power to determine the adequacy of safety warnings and operating instructions under the strict liability doctrine. Again, the lack of any judicial standards has expanded the scope of liability. The lack of a warning specifically directed to any hazard that results in an accident or injury has been sufficient ground for courts and juries to judge the manufacturer liable. For an assessment of liability against the manufacturer, experience has taught that it does not matter whether the product is to be used only by skilled operators, not the general public, or how obvious the hazard is.

My own company, FMC Corporation, was sued in 1971 by a laborer injured when a crane operator maneuvered the boom of an FMC-built crane into high voltage electrical transmission lines. The plaintiff argued that FMC should be liable for his injuries because (1) the company had not posted warnings on the crane or in its cab of the dangers of operating the crane near high power lines, and (2) because it had not installed safety devices that, in the opinion of witnesses called by the plaintiff, could have alerted the operator to potential contact with electrical power lines.

In its defense, FMC argued that it had not put a warning in the crane's cab because the crane was intended to be used by trained heavy equipment operators thoroughly familiar with the hazards of working around electrical power lines. The company also noted that its engineers had concluded that proximity warning devices available at the time the crane was built (in 1957) did not operate with sufficient reliability to justify their use. An unreliable proximity warning device could pose a safety hazard of its own, in that workers who relied on it could be injured if they assumed that the device would protect them. Nonetheless, the court decided in the plaintiff's favor and awarded a judgment of $2.5 million.

Deliberate Product Misuse

The doctrine of strict liability makes manufacturers liable for injuries if a product does not perform safely when used in "an intended" or "reasonably foreseeable manner." Again, it is up to the courts to determine what constitutes intended or reasonably foreseeable use. . . .

In one case, American Home Products, the maker of Pam, an aerosol which is sprayed on pots and pans to prevent food from sticking during cooking, was sued in 1979 by the mother of a 14-year-old boy who died after intentionally inhaling the freon propellant from a can of Pam. At the time of the youth's death, the can bore the following warning: "Avoid direct inhalation of concentrated vapors. Keep out of the reach of children." The boy's mother charged that the company should be held accountable because this warning was inadequate, particularly because the company had knowledge of 45 deaths, prior to her son's, involving teenagers concentrating the fumes and inhaling them in order to produce a tingling sensation in the lungs. The jury awarded her $585,000 in damages.

The decision in this case disturbs me for two reasons. First, it is unreasonable to suppose that there is any kind of warning a manufacturer could use to prevent an individual from deliberately misusing a product. And second, the individual, not the manufacturer, should be responsible for the consequences of his or her own actions, particularly in cases of intentional misuse.

Undetectable Hazards

Should manufacturers be liable for hazards posed by their products that may result in injuries many years later, but which scientific knowledge cannot detect at the time a product is marketed? The answer courts give to this very difficult question will have extraordinary implications for the liability exposure of manufacturers of pharmaceuticals, toxic materials, and chemical products that may have harmful effects that take many years to develop.

The asbestos controversy has highlighted this issue in recent years. Prolonged exposure to significant amounts of asbestos in its fibrous form can cause asbestosis, a restrictive lung disease characterized by scarring of the tissues. It is also associated with the development of some cancers. Fibrous asbestos, however, has been widely used as a flame-retardant, fire-resistant insulating material. In particular, the U.S. Navy and the Maritime Commission required the use of asbestos in the construction of warships and cargo vessels during World War II to protect seamen against the spread of fire on board battle-damaged ships.

Today, asbestos makers face thousands of claims for damages from workers exposed to asbestos, half of which were filed by those exposed to asbestos in shipyards during and after World War II. In August 1982, Manville Corporation filed for bankruptcy, maintaining that although it was still solvent, the 16,500 pending asbestos claims, combined with a potential 30,000 additional claims, would exhaust its assets.

A recent New Jersey Supreme Court decision may extend the liability exposure of asbestos makers even further. In *Beshada, et al. v. Johns-Manville Products Corporation, et al.,* the court struck down the state-of-the-art defense used by asbestos makers. The companies argued that they should not be liable for failing to warn of the dangers of asbestos exposure because they were unaware of the danger at the time the product was marketed and because such dangers could not have been detected with the scientific techniques then available.

In its ruling the court differentiated between the defenses that are applicable in a suit based on negligence and one based on strict liability. A manufacturer may use the state-of-the-art defense only when it is being sued for negligence: a company is not acting negligently by offering a product for sale that to its knowledge—given the state of scientific techniques—does not pose a hazard. In a strict liability suit, however, the state-of-the-art defense is not admissible because the product's condition—not the manufacturer's actions and what it knew or could not have known—is the focus of the action.

*   *   *   *   *

Consequences of Imbalance

The lack of clear and discernible standards means that the verdicts reached in product liability suits today are often inequitable and inconsistent.

This imbalance is not surprising, because courts and juries today are asked to make judgments that they are not well equipped to make. Strict liability has moved determinations of liability from the realm of the mainly objective to that of the substantially subjective. . . .

Another source of inconsistency in product liability verdicts today is the varying interpretations of liability from state to state. . . . For instance, shortly after the Illinois court's judgment against FMC in the crane case, courts in New Mexico and Minnesota ruled in similar cases that the manufacturer was not liable because the hazard of driving a steel boom into high power lines was obvious.

Costly Judgments

Strict liability has dramatically increased the costs of product liability. The old negligence-based tort law, which assigned damages to the responsible party, has been converted into a business-financed "social insurance system" for product injury victims.

* * * * *

Ultimately, of course, the costs are borne by consumers as the costs of liability insurance premiums and liability judgments are passed through to them. These costs can be quite high: one small machine tool manufacturer has reported that its cost of liability insurance went from $200 per machine in 1970 to $11,000 per machine in 1982.

The defenders of the current state of product liability law often claim that manufacturers, aware of their potential liability, make better products than they would otherwise. Our experience suggests that exactly the opposite may also occur: companies may hesitate to introduce new products or expand into new markets because of the potential liability.

For example, FMC's former Power Transmission Group produced high-quality commercial bearings for use as components in machines and equipment built by other manufacturers. As a component manufacturer, FMC had no control over the design of the products into which bearings were placed. Yet, in the event of a failure, a claimant could sue the component manufacturer as well as the product manufacturer. In 1971 we concluded that the potential product liability exposure from the use of FMC bearings in helicopter rotors was too great, given the small share of our market that such use constituted. We therefore issued a directive stating that no orders for bearings would knowingly be accepted for use in manufacturing in-flight aircraft controls.

I should also point out that injured parties are poorly served by the adversary process of settling product liability suits. As much or more money is being paid to adjudicate a claim as is being paid to compensate victims. There is some indication that the contingency fee basis on which most plaintiffs' lawyers are engaged tends to escalate damage claims. James A. Henderson, Jr., of Boston University's School of Law has estimated that:

"Out of every dollar paid by consumers to cover the relevant liability costs, less than 50 cents—estimates vary downward from 45 cents to 30 cents—are returned to the consumers in benefits. Most of the rest—between 55 and 70 cents out of every premium dollar—goes to pay the lawyers, adjusters, and the like. If I were a cynic, I would say that if this is a social insurance scheme, it is being run primarily to benefit the trial bar."

Redressing the Balance

If one accepts the conclusion that today's product liability system based on strict liability produces inequitable, inconsistent, and excessively costly judgments against manufacturers, then one ought to ask what can be done to reestablish reasonableness and fairness in liability decisions.

The answer—establishment of clear and precise standards of liability—seems simple enough. . . . Among the standards needed are:

1. A negligence-based standard for judg-

ing the adequacy of product design and the appropriateness of warnings.

The basic question in design and warning cases should be refocused on the manufacturer's conduct. Did the manufacturer use reasonable and prudent care in designing the product or providing warnings of hidden risks? Plaintiffs will almost always be able to show, as the plaintiff did in *Dawson v. Chrysler*, that an alternative design may, in the opinion of an expert chosen by the plaintiff, have prevented a particular accident.

Instead of making manufacturers liable because they cannot design a product in such a way as to prevent all accidents, would it not be more reasonable to focus on the degree of care taken by the manufacturer in designing the product?

2. A standard creating a presumption that a product conforming to government safety requirements is reasonably safe.

Currently, an injured product user may buttress his or her suit against a manufacturer by citing a product's failure to conform to government safety standards as evidence of inadequate design. The reverse, however, is not true. In many states, manufacturers are not permitted to cite the fact that a product meets or exceeds all applicable government standards as evidence of the adequacy of a product's design.

It would be more equitable *(a)* to allow compliance with government standards to create a presumption that a product is reasonably safe, and *(b)* to allow plaintiffs to rebut that presumption if they can show that the manufacturer knew that governmentally established standards were inadequate for a normal or intended use of the product.

3. A standard requiring assignment of liability and damages on the basis of comparative responsibility.

Frequently, injury from a product has several causes. For example, a person who misuses or alters a product may be responsible to some degree for his own or someone else's injury. In such cases, the courts should allocate liability among all responsible parties, and defendants should pay damages only in proportion to their share of the liability.

* * * * *

4. A standard limiting liability for manufacturing or design defects to a specific period of time.

Products that have served their purpose without evidence of harm for a prolonged period should not be reexamined with regard to the manufacturer's liability for the adequacy of design and warning at a later date. No company should be forced to defend the adequacy of the design and safety warnings on a product that has operated safely for decades. In one egregious example, the Oliver Machinery Company was sued in the 1970s by a man who was injured while using a table saw manufactured by the company in 1942—more than 30 years before the accident!

At some point in time a manufacturer's responsibility should end. Appropriate allowances should be made, of course, when setting such limits, for chemical products or other toxic substances that may cause illness or damage only after prolonged exposure.

Where Do We Go from Here?

Given that clear and precise standards are the key to ameliorating the product liability problem, who should establish these standards? How can uniformity of adoption and implementation be assured?

* * * * *

The first and most critical step in returning to a more balanced product liability system would be enactment of federal legislation setting precise standards that can be easily and uniformly applied throughout the nation. . . .

Source: *Harvard Business Review* 61, no. 3 (May/June 1983), pp. 67–74. Reprinted by permission of the *Harvard Business Review*. Excerpt from "Let's Restore Balance to Product Liability Law," by Robert H. Malott (May/June 1983). Copyright © 1983 by the President and Fellows of Harvard College; all rights reserved.

QUESTIONS

1. Build at least three plausible arguments supporting the defendants in the *Brady* case.
2. How would you rule in the *Tylenol* and *Brady* cases? Explain.
3. Since the judiciary is free of the political pressure of the gun lobby, some lawyers argue that the courts (hearing cases like that brought by Mr. Brady) are a better vehicle for securing gun control than is Congress. Do you agree? Explain.
4. Regardless of your personal opinion, build a brief argument opposing the central elements of Robert Malott's position.
5. Much of the legal cost associated with product liability law is, of course, generated in attempting to prove or disprove fault. Strict liability, at least in theory, is a no-fault concept. Should we recast products liability law entirely in a no-fault mode? In so doing we would recognize the inevitability of defective products and careless consumers. Costs would be borne by all. Comment.

Chapter Questions

1. Plaintiff suffered a spider bite while trying on slacks in the dressing room of the defendant's Mode O'Day store. Plaintiff sued both the local retailer and the parent firm. She based her claim on negligence, breach of the implied warranty of fitness for a particular purpose, and strict liability.
   a. Defend Mode O'Day and the local retailer.
   b. Decide. Explain. See *Flippo* v. *Mode O'Day Frock Shops of Hollywood*, 248 Ark. 1, 449 S.W.2d 692 (1970).

2. A passenger ran after a train as it was leaving a station. Two railroad employees boosted the passenger aboard, but in doing so a package carried by the passenger fell beneath the wheels of the train and exploded. The package, unbeknownst to the employees, contained fireworks. The force of that explosion caused a scale many feet away to topple over injuring the plaintiff, Mrs. Palsgraf. Mrs. Palsgraf sued the railroad on negligence grounds.
   a. Defend the railroad.
   b. Decide. Explain. See *Palsgraf* v. *Long Island R.R.*, 162 N.E. 99 (N.Y., 1928).

3. Plaintiff was riding as a passenger in an auto that was struck in the rear by a 1960 Chevrolet Impala driven by Michael Bigham (not a party to the suit) at a speed of approximately 115 miles per hour. Plaintiff sustained personal injuries and filed suit against General Motors Corporation, the manufacturer of the Chevrolet. Plaintiff argued that defendant was negligent in truthfully advertising the speed at which the auto could be driven, thus encouraging its reckless use.
   a. What further argument(s) would you make on plaintiff's behalf?
   b. Decide. Explain. See *Schemely* v. *General Motors Corporation*, 384 F.2d 802 (1967), cert. denied, 390 U.S. 945 (1968).

4. The plaintiff, born and raised in New England, was eating fish chowder at a restaurant when a fish bone lodged in her throat. The bone was removed and plaintiff sued the restaurant,

claiming breach of implied warranty under the UCC. Evidence was offered at trial to show that fish chowder recipes commonly did not provide for removal of bones. Decide. See *Webster* v. *Blue Ship Tea Room, Inc.,* 347 Mass. 421, 198 N.E.2d 309 (1964).

5. The plaintiff, a farmer, argued that the defendant's insecticide, Ortho Bux Ten Granular, failed to control rootworms, resulting in damage to his crops. Corn grown in another section of the field and protected by the insecticide, Thimet, matured normally. One side of the bag containing the Ortho insecticide displayed the following language: "Chevron Ortho Bux Ten Granular for control of corn rootworm larvae (insecticide)." The opposite side of the bag displayed language offering an express warranty limited to the guarantee that the insecticide conformed to its chemical description. All other warranties were explicitly excluded. The plaintiff claimed a breach of express warranty. Decide. See *Swenson* v. *Chevron Chem. Co.,* 234 N.W.2d 38 (1975).

6. Embs, the plaintiff, was shopping in a self-serve grocery store. A carton of 7UP was sitting on the floor about one foot from where she was standing. She was unaware of the carton. Several of the bottles exploded, severely injuring Embs' leg. Embs brought a strict liability action against the bottler.
    a. Raise a defense against the strict liability claim.
    b. Decide. Explain. See *Embs* v. *Pepsi Cola Bottling Co. of Lexington, Kentucky, Inc.,* 528 S.W.2d 703 (1975).

7. Plaintiff suffered injury from ingesting the defective prescription drug, MER/29. Plaintiff sued the druggist from whom the product was purchased in its original, unbroken package. The druggist issued the drugs under a doctor's instructions.
    a. Which causes of action might the plaintiff plausibly bring?
    b. Decide the outcome. See *McLeod* v. *W. S. Merrell Co., Div. of Richardson-Merrell* 174 So.2d 736 (Fla. 1965).

8. Plaintiffs Dr. Arthur Weisz and David and Irene Schwartz bought two paintings at auctions conducted by the defendant, Parke-Bernet Galleries, Inc. The paintings were listed in the auction catalogue as those of Raoul Dufy. It was later discovered that the paintings were forgeries. The plaintiffs took legal action to recover their losses. Parke-Bernet defended itself by, among other arguments, asserting that the "Conditions of Sale" included a disclaimer providing that all properties were sold "as is." The conditions of sale were 15 numbered paragraphs embracing several pages in the auction catalogue. The bulk of the auction catalogue was devoted to descriptions of the works of art to be sold including artists' names, dates of birth and death, and in some instances black and white reproductions of the paintings. It was established at trial that plaintiff Weisz had not previously entered bids at Parke-Bernet, and he had no awareness of the conditions of sale. Plaintiffs David and Irene Schwartz, however, were generally aware of the conditions of sale. Is the Parke-Bernet disclaimer legally binding on the plaintiffs? Explain. See *Weisz* v. *Parke-Bernet,* 325 N.Y.S. 2d 576 (Civ. Ct. N.Y.C. 1971).

9. An earth-moving machine being driven in reverse struck and killed a workman who was clothed in a luminous jacket. The machine operator could not see the workman because a large engine box at the rear of the earth-mover created a blind spot. The earth-mover had no rear-view mirror, a fact immediately observable to the operator. In the lawsuit that followed, what principal argument would you raise on behalf of the defendant machine manufacturer? Decide. Explain. See *Pike* v. *Frank G. Hough Co.,* 467 P.2d 229 (Cal. 1970).

10. Plaintiff's decedent had worked in asbestos plants at various times from 1936 to 1969. He subsequently died of two forms of cancer. Plaintiff sued 11 asbestos manufacturers for their

failure to warn of the dangerous linkage between asbestos and cancer, which was alluded to in the scientific literature "at least as early as the 1930s." The court noted that asbestos might be the kind of product that is unavoidably unsafe, but whose benefits outweigh the risks. Rule on the plaintiff's strict liability claim. Explain. See *Borel* v. *Fibreboard Paper Products Corp.*, 493 F.2d 1076 (5th Cir. 1973), cert. denied 419 U.S. 869 (1974).

11. Plaintiff-employee was operating a machine designed to flatten and then curve metal sheets. The metal was shaped by three long rollers. Plaintiff turned off the rollers to remove a piece of slag. He left the power on. In trying to remove the slag he accidently brushed a gear lever which activated the rollers. His hand was drawn into the rollers, and injury resulted. At the time of the manufacture of the machine, two safety mechanisms were available to prevent such accidents. What defense would you offer on behalf of the defendant machine manufacturer? Decide. Explain. See *Suter* v. *San Angelo Foundry and Machine Co.*, 406 A.2d 140 (N.J. 1979).

12. In June 1983 a San Diego, California, jury awarded $2.5 million to the family of a man killed while riding, as a passenger, in a Porsche Turbo 930. The plaintiff had argued, among other things, that the car was too powerful and too unstable for the average driver and that the manufacturer should have provided a warning regarding the power of the car. During the trial the plaintiff's attorney received an internal anonymous memo from Porsche headquarters in West Germany that described the car's handling as "poisonous" and argued that the car had a tendency to oversteer. At the time of the accident the car was traveling at 60 miles per hour in a 25-mile-per-hour zone. The jury voted 10 to 2 in finding the car unsafe for street driving.[9] Comment.

13. Because few states have taken any meaningful, consistent action in adopting the Commerce Department's suggested Uniform Product Liability Act, Congress is now considering a uniform federal law. Among others, such a law would probably include the following provisions. Comment on the wisdom of such legislation:
    a. Lawsuits would be limited to 25 years from when the product was first sold.
    b. Plaintiff would be required to name a specific defendant thus nullifying the market share decisions such as *Sindell.*
    c. Design defects and improper warnings would be grounds for liability only when negligence could be demonstrated.

14. The plaintiff, a heavy cigarette smoker for 30 years, suffers from lung cancer. Plaintiff sues X Tobacco Company, manufacturer of plaintiff's favorite and exclusive brand. Plaintiff bases his suit on breach of the implied warranty of merchantability and strict liability in tort. Plaintiff's preferred cigarettes are "exactly like all others of the particular brand and virtually the same as all other brands on the market." Decide. Explain. See e.g., *Green* v. *American Tobacco Co.*, 391 F.2d 97 (1968), cert. denied 397 U.S. 911 (1970).

15. The plaintiff, a mother, claimed that she went to the defendant physician to seek a therapeutic abortion. She further claimed the abortion was negligently performed, resulting in the "wrongful birth" of a healthy child. Plaintiff sought to recover, in a negligence action, for the costs of rearing the child. Decide. Explain. See *Nanke* v. *Napier,* 346 N.W.2d 520 (Iowa, 1984). But see *Jones* v. *Malinowski,* 473 A.2d 429 (Md., 1984).

16. Three lung cancer victims have filed a $9.3 billion negligence action against 14 tobacco distribution and advertising corporations, claiming that the companies negligently failed to warn the public that tobacco products are physically and psychologically addictive.[10] How would you rule? Explain.

Notes

1. Clemens P. Work, "Product Safety: A New Hot Potato for Congress," *U.S. News and World Report*, June 14, 1982, p. 62.

2. Ibid.

3. Raymond Bonner, "Lawyers Say Ford Is Paying $20 Million for Defect," *Des Moines (Iowa) Sunday Register*, February 13, 1983, p. 7A.

4. 111 N.E. 1050 (N.Y., 1916).

5. *Doss* v. *Town of Big Stone Gap*, 134 S.E. 563 (1926).

6. *Jenkins* v. *General Motors Corp.*, 446 F.2d 377 (5th Cir. 1971), as cited in Dix Noel and Jerry Phillips, *Products Liability in a Nutshell* (St. Paul, Minn.: West Publishing, 1980), p. 137.

7. *McCully* v. *Fuller Brush Co.*, 415 P.2d 7 (Wash., 1966), as cited in Dix Noel and Jerry Phillips, *Products Liability in a Nutshell* (St. Paul, Minn.: West Publishing, 1980), p. 183.

8. Some states have eliminated the "unreasonably dangerous" standard from their strict liability tests.

9. "Jury Finds Porsche Turbo Dangerous on Streets," *Des Moines (Iowa) Register*, June 30, 1983, p. 4A.

10. "Cancer Victims File $9.3 Billion Suit," *Waterloo (Iowa) Courier*, May 15, 1984, p. A6.

17

Environmental Protection

This natural inequality of the two powers of population, and of production in the earth, and that great law of our nature which most constantly keep their effects equal, form the great difficulty that to me appears insurmountable in the way to the perfectibility of society. . . . No fancied equality, no agrarian regulations in their utmost extent, could remove the pressure of it even for a single century. And it appears, therefore, to be decisive against the possible existence of a society all the members of which should live in ease, happiness and comparative leisure. . . .

Thomas Malthus, An Essay on the Principle of Population, 1798

Introduction[1]

Concerns about pollution are centuries old, but in recent years a combination of increasing population, industrialization, and an improved understanding of the effects of various waste materials on the environment have generated widespread interest. In particular, public awareness of pollution has been enhanced because of a series of well-publicized threats to the health of the natural world.

1. Tentative Accord Reached in Love Canal Toxic Case

Hooker Chemical and Plastics Corp., a subsidiary of Occidental [Petroleum], dumped more than 20,000 tons of chemical wastes into Love Canal for a decade before abandoning the dump in 1953, when it was sold to the Niagara Falls Board of Education. A school and a housing development were built on the clay-capped dump.

Love Canal became a toxic-waste disaster in August 1978 when state health officials ordered the evacuation of children and pregnant women because of possible contamination of the community as chemicals leaked from a dumpsite.

Hooker said it bore no responsibility for the leaks after selling the property to the board of education. Hooker also argued that chemicals did not start to leak until after the city of Niagara Falls broke a clay seal over the dump.

But present and former residents of the Love Canal neighborhood filed more than $16 billion in personal injury and property damage claims against Occidental and the city of Niagara Falls. State and federal lawyers also have filed claims of up to $700 million against Occidental in the case.[2]

In 1985 many of the Love Canal claims were settled for a total of $20 million to be divided among 1,345 claimants. Recoveries ranged from $2,000 to $400,000 for injuries including retardation, cancer, rashes, and migraine headaches.

2. U.S. Study Says Acid Rain Injures Northeast's Waters

[In 1983] a Reagan administration task force concluded . . . that acid rain is damaging lakes and streams in the Northeast. The study linked the problem to man-made pollution. The findings, released in a report to Congress and the president, represented the first time the administration has endorsed evidence linking power-plant emissions with acid rain.

Task force director Charles Bernabo said more research is needed on the causes and effects of acid rain. . . . Bernabo said there is a "great consensus" that acid rain is damaging aquatic life. He said there is less evidence that acid rain is damaging crops, trees, and buildings. He said the task force has confirmed that man-made sources of pollution—such as sulfur dioxide—are the "primary contributors" to acid rain in the Northeast. But he said administration researchers have not been able to firmly establish how much of the acid rain in the Northeast is caused by power plant emissions in the Midwest.[3]

Recent reports indicate that acid rain problems appear to have stabilized in the Northeast, but may have worsened in the South and the West.

3. Dioxin: How Great a Threat?

No wonder people are confused about dioxin [a by-product of herbicide manufacture]. Skeptics downplay its danger, calling it just the latest inductee in the environmentalists' "chemical of the month club." On the other hand, experiments show dioxin to be not only the deadliest substance made by man, but also a possible cause of cancer and birth defects. When it was discovered near chemical plants in New Jersey . . . residents asked the governor if they should abandon their homes—after all, the federal government had decided . . . that dioxin posed such a risk to Times Beach, Missouri, that it bought out the entire town. Even the American Medical Association seemed to be of two minds. First it assailed the news media for making dioxin "the focus of a witch hunt," but last week disavowed the statement, saying, "The AMA does not pooh-pooh dioxin." "The anxiety is incredible," says Donald Barnes of the Environmental Protection Agency. "It's hard to tell if we have health problems, but mental anguish is a clear effect of dioxin.[4]

4. Hot Times for the Old Orb

The doomsday headlines (SUNBELT MOVING NORTH, WARMING SPELLS DISASTER) were unduly alarmist and much of the information was well known to scientists. But . . . a media brouhaha was triggered by new studies from the Environmental Protection Agency and the National Academy of Sciences. Both groups agreed on a startling prognosis: the earth is warming up from all the carbon dioxide being spilled into the atmosphere by the burning of fossil fuels, and worse, the first effects of the climatic changes could be felt as early as the 1990s.

The EPA predicted temperature increases of nearly 4°F. by the year 2040; a rise in sea levels of 2 feet by 2025 (thereby inundating some low-lying areas in coastal cities such as Charleston, South Carolina, and Galveston, Texas); and drastically changing rainfall patterns, especially in the breadbasket areas of the Midwest, where reduced precipitation could jeopardize crops. Nothing, not even a sharp cutback in the use of fossil fuels, the EPA added, could alter this climatic course.[5]

A Global Problem

While the earth is an efficient recycler of wastes—a very effective garbage dump—its ability to successfully neutralize the cumulative refuse of modern society is finite. The earth can easily absorb the pollution of a sparsely populated, nonindustrial economy, but an upsurge in population and increased industrialization and urbanization concentrate ever increasing amounts of waste matter in small areas and put much greater pressure on the assimilative capabilities of the planet.

THIRD WORLD NATIONS START FACING UP TO SEVERE POLLUTION PROBLEMS

Peter Grier

In Chile, the government last year set aside the first National Chinchilla Reserve to protect the endangered Long-Tailed Chinchilla. . . .

India, where about 2 million acres of forest are stripped down for fuel wood each year, in 1981 launched a $125 million "social forestry" program.

The environmental ethic is not limited to rich, developed nations. In 1972, only 11 Third World countries had environmental agencies. Today 110 have arms of the government whose sole purpose is to protect land, water, and air, according to a soon-to-be-released book by the UN World Environment Center. . . .

But these fledgling Environmental Protection Agencies face daunting problems. Some of the nastiest pollution in the world occurs in small, poor nations. And "even those countries with established environmental regulations often do not have the resources—technical, human, and financial—to monitor and enforce them," concludes the UN World Environment Handbook.

Take Kenya, one of the most environmentally advanced countries in Africa, according to the UN. Kenya's Ministry of Environment and Natural Resources, now five years old, has 30 scientists to deal with the pollution caused by the fastest-growing population in the world.

The demand for fuelwood in Kenya is so great that there will be little forest left in a decade, unless depletion slows. Coastal factories often pollute with impunity. Dairy-processing waste and slaughterhouse refuse is dumped directly into the waterways surrounding Mombasa and into Lake Victoria. . . .

A sampling of environmental actions in other nations, as detailed in the UN handbook, includes:

* * * * *

Cuba. Cuba's Center for the Protection of the Environment and Rational Use of National Resources was established in 1980, along with bylaws protecting soil, forests, air, and water.

The cleanup of Havana Harbor is listed as a national priority in the country's latest five-year plan; a reforestation program has already begun. Ironically, one area of the country that is endangered by population expansion is the Sierra Maestra Range—the pine woodlands that sheltered President Fidel Castro's guerrillas before the revolution.

* * * * *

Philippines. The Philippines, an archipelago of some 7,000 islands, has much coastline, and much coastline pollution. Half the coral reefs surrounding the islands are dead or dying, according to UN estimates. The country's national Pollution Control Commission was created in 1964, but has come under criticism from other government agencies for lax enforcement.

Mexico. The rapid urbanization of Mexico has created some of the most acute pollution problems in the world. Mexico City's smog is legendary; the Panuco River basin, on the Gulf coast, receives untreated waste from 15 million people and 35,000 industries. A Secretariat of Urban Development and Ecology was recently established, but "environmental degradation, caused in large part by poverty, is worsening," the UN warns.

Source: *The Christian Science Monitor*, October 11, 1984, p. 3. Reprinted with permission of the copyright holder, *The Christian Science Monitor*.

The Failure of the Invisible Hand?

It is understood that most people in the United States want a cleaner environment, yet the "invisible hand" envisioned by Adam Smith apparently is not of sufficient strength to guide the economy in that direction. The problem is not a failure in the theory behind the pricing system, but rather that the pricing system works to perfection, albeit in the wrong directions. This inconvenience can be traced to what economists call the externality, free good, or commons problem. Simply stated, the environment has been treated as a *free good,* meaning that using the environment for waste disposal is costless to producers. In effect, producers can pollute a river and pass the costs in the form of dirty water, dead fish, disease, and so forth, on to society as a whole. If a good can be obtained at no cost, an economist or a businessperson would be inclined to use as much of the free good as possible, and producers have done just that. There is no pricing incentive to minimize pollution if pollution has no direct cost to the company; in fact, the incentive is to maximize pollution. In effect, a pricing system that allocates no cost to an industry dirtying the environment encourages additional work, regardless of the common need of society for a clean environment. In this instance, the welfare of individuals acting in their own private interests does not coincide with the general good.

Another way in which an economist might examine the problem is as a *collective good.* If the citizens want a clean environment, it might be assumed that the market would reflect that desire by paying nonpolluting companies higher prices for their goods. Unfortunately, the benefits of clean air and water are not restricted to those paying for them through higher prices, since equal benefits are bestowed on those persons still trading (at lower prices) with polluting companies. Thus a clean environment benefits everyone equally, regardless of each individual's contribution toward it. A rational utility maximizing strategy for each person, then, is to patronize cheaper, polluting firms to the exclusion of the more expensive nonpolluters, despite the desire of society for a clean environment. Therefore industries have no incentive not to pollute. Externalities and public goods are instances of "market failure." (See Chapter 6.) Some intervention is necessary if society is going to utilize free goods only to the most desirable level. Governmental intervention is one logical tool.

The Common Law

Long before the federal government became actively involved in environmental issues, state and local governments and courts were grappling with the problem. As early as the 1500s, city officials were ordered by a court to keep the streets clean of dung deposited by swine allowed to run loose; the air was said to be "corrupted and infected" by this practice. For over a century, many cities have prohibited the burning of coal as a health measure designed to assure breathable air. Typically legal arguments have revolved around the right of a person to use and enjoy private or public property if such usage caused harm to a neighbor's property. The doctrines of nuisance and trespass are paramount in common law environmental litigation.

A private nuisance is a substantial and unreasonable invasion of the private use and enjoyment of one's land, while a public nuisance is an unreasonable interference with a right common to the public. Harmful conduct may be both a public and private nuisance simultaneously; the case law distinctions between the two often are blurred. A trespass occurs and liability is imposed with *any* intentional invasion of the right to one's exclusive use of one's own property. Again, the distinction between trespass and nuisance is fine, and the two may be coextensive. Nuisance and trespass causes of action have been entered for such offenses as fouling a neighbor's water, flooding another's land, or causing excessive noise, smell, or particulate matter on another's property. The remedies available to a successful plaintiff are monetary damages for the harm suffered and/or an injunction to prevent similar conduct by the defendant in the future. An injunction is a much more serious remedy and often requires a balancing of the hardships faced by each party if the injunction is granted and an analysis of whether the public interest is served by a continuation of the practice that led to the nuisance.

Recently, zoning laws and land use restrictions have also played an important role in pollution cases. And it should be understood that negligence and strict liability claims may arise from pollution cases. For example, a company might well be guilty of negligence if it failed to correct a pollution problem where the technology and necessary resources were available to do so, and that failure caused harm to someone to whom the company owed a duty. In addition, certain activities, such as the use of toxic chemicals, might be so abnormally dangerous as to provoke a strict liability claim. (See Chapter 16 for a discussion of negligence and strict liability.) The following case illustrates a common law approach to a pollution problem.

BOOMER V. ATLANTIC CEMENT CO.   26 N.Y.2d 219, 257 N.E.2d 870 (1970)

Judge Bergan

Defendant operates a large cement plant near Albany. These are actions for injunction and damages by neighboring land owners alleging injury to property from dirt, smoke and vibration emanating from the plant. A nuisance has been found after trial, temporary damages have been allowed but an injunction has been denied.

*   *   *   *   *

. . . The threshold question raised by the division of view on this appeal is whether the court should resolve the litigation between the parties now before it as equitably as seems possible; or whether, seeking promotion of the general public welfare, it should channel private litigation into broad public objectives.

A court performs its essential function when it decides the rights of parties before it. Its decision of private controversies may sometimes greatly affect public issues. Large questions of law are often resolved by the manner in which private litigation is decided. But this is normally an incident to the court's main function to settle controversy. It is a rare exercise of judicial power to use a decision in private litigation as a purposeful mechanism to achieve direct public objectives greatly beyond the rights and interests before the court.

*   *   *   *   *

It seems apparent that the amelioration of air pollution will depend on technical research in great depth; on a carefully balanced consideration of the economic impact of close regulation; and of the actual effect on public health. It is likely to require massive public expenditure and to demand more than any local community can accomplish and to depend on regional and interstate controls.

A court should not try to do this on its own as a by-product of private litigation and it seems manifest that the judicial establishment is neither equipped in the limited nature of any judgment it can pronounce nor prepared to lay down and implement an effective policy for the elimination of air pollution. This is an area beyond the circumference of one private lawsuit. It is a direct responsibility for government and should not thus be undertaken as an incident to solving a dispute between property owners and a single cement plant—one of many—in the Hudson River Valley.

The cement making operations of defendant have been found by the court at Special Term to have damaged the nearby properties of plaintiffs in these two actions. That court, as it has been noted, accordingly found defendant maintained a nuisance and this has been affirmed at the Appellate Division. The total damage to plaintiffs' properties is, however, relatively small in comparison with the value of defendant's operation and with the consequences of the injunction which plaintiffs seek.

The ground for the denial of injunction, notwithstanding the finding both that there is a nuisance and that plaintiffs have been damaged substantially, is the large disparity in economic consequences of the nuisance and of the injunction. This theory cannot, however, be sustained without overruling a doctrine which has been consistently reaffirmed in several leading cases in this court and which has never been disavowed here, namely that where a nuisance has been found and where there has been any substantial damage shown by the party complaining an injunction will be granted.

The rule in New York has been that such a nuisance will be enjoined although marked disparity be shown in economic consequence between the effect of the injunction and the effect of the nuisance.

*   *   *   *   *

. . . [T]o follow the rule literally in these cases would be to close down the plant at once. This court is fully agreed to avoid that immediately drastic remedy; the difference in view is how best to avoid it.

One alternative is to grant the injunction but postpone its effect to a specified future date to give opportunity for technical advances to permit defendant to eliminate the nuisance; another is to grant the injunction conditioned on the payment of permanent damages to plaintiffs which would compensate them for the total economic loss to their property present and future caused by defendant's operations. For reasons which will be developed the court chooses the latter alternative.

If the injunction were to be granted unless within a short period—e.g., 18 months—the nuisance be abated by improved methods, there would be no assurance that any significant technical improvement would occur.

*   *   *   *   *

Moreover, techniques to eliminate dust and other annoying byproducts of cement making are unlikely to be developed by any research the defendant can undertake within any short period, but will depend on the total resources of the cement industry nationwide and throughout the world. The problem is universal wherever cement is made.

For obvious reasons the rate of the research is beyond control of defendant. If at the end of

18 months the whole industry has not found a technical solution a court would be hard put to close down this one cement plant if due regard be given to equitable principles.

On the other hand, to grant the injunction unless defendant pays plaintiffs such permanent damages as may be fixed by the court seems to do justice between the contending parties. All of the attributions of economic loss to the properties on which plaintiffs' complaints are based will have been redressed.

The nuisance complained of by these plaintiffs may have other public or private consequences, but these particular parties are the only ones who have sought remedies and the judgement proposed will fully redress them. The limitation of relief granted is a limitation only within the four corners of these actions and does not foreclose public health or other public agencies from seeking proper relief in a proper court.

It seems reasonable to think that the risk of being required to pay permanent damages to injured property owners by cement plant owners would itself be a reasonably effective spur to research for improved techniques to minimize nuisance.

* * * * *

Judge Jasen (dissenting).

It has long been the rule in this State, as the majority acknowledges, that a nuisance which results in substantial continuing damage to neighbors must be enjoined. . . . To now change the rule to permit the cement company to continue polluting the air indefinitely upon the payment of permanent damages is, in my opinion, compounding the magnitude of a very serious problem in our State and Nation today.

In recognition of this problem, the Legislature of this State has enacted the Air Pollution Control Act . . . declaring that it is the State policy to require the use of all available and reasonable methods to prevent and control air pollution.

* * * * *

. . . It is interesting to note that cement production has recently been identified as a significant source of particulate contamination in the Hudson Valley. This type of pollution, wherein very small particles escape and stay in the atmosphere, has been denominated as the type of air pollution which produces the greatest hazard to human health. We have thus a nuisance which not only is damaging to the plaintiffs, but also is decidedly harmful to the general public.

I see grave dangers in overruling our long-established rule of granting an injunction where a nuisance results in substantial continuing damage. In permitting the injunction to become inoperative upon the payment of permanent damages, the majority is, in effect, licensing a continuing wrong. It is the same as saying to the cement company, you may continue to do harm to your neighbors so long as you pay a fee for it. Furthermore, once such permanent damages are assessed and paid, the incentive to alleviate the wrong would be eliminated, thereby continuing air pollution of an area without abatement.

* * * * *

I would enjoin the defendant cement company from continuing the discharge of dust particles upon its neighbors' properties unless, within 18 months, the cement company abated this nuisance.

* * * * *

I am aware that the trial court found that the most modern dust control devices available have been installed in defendant's plant, but, I submit, this does not mean that *better* and more effective dust control devices could not be developed within the time allowed to abate the pollution.

Moreover, I believe it is incumbent upon the defendant to develop such devices, since the cement company, at the time the plant commenced production (1962), was well aware of the plaintiffs' presence in the area, as well as the probable consequences of its contemplated operation. Yet, it still chose to build and operate the plant at this site.

Reversed.

Questions

1. What remedy was mandated by the *Boomer* court?
2. Effectively the defendant was required to pay a "tax" for the right to continue to pollute. In your opinion was the court correct in imposing that "tax" rather than requiring further pollution abatement? Explain.
3. The dissent argues that the use of permanent money damages in place of an injunction should be limited to cases where "the use to which the property was intended to be put was primarily for the public benefit." Why is the denial of the injunction acceptable to the dissent in public benefit cases but not in cases of private benefit?
4. According to the dissent: "The promotion of the polluting cement company has, in my opinion no public use or benefit." Do you agree? Explain.
5. Plaintiff Webb developed Sun City, a retirement village near Phoenix, Arizona. At the time, a distance of two and one-half to three miles separated plaintiff's development from defendant Spur Industries' cattle feeding operation. The feed lot was well-managed and clean for a business of that character. Prior to the Sun City project the area around the feed lot had been largely undeveloped. Sun City and related growth brought large numbers of people in proximity to the cattle lot. As time passed, the two businesses expanded, until at the initiation of the suit, only 500 feet separated the two. Plaintiff filed suit to enjoin defendant's operation as a nuisance. Decide. Explain. See *Spur Industries, Inc.* v. *Del E. Webb Development Co.,* 494 P.2d 700 (1972).

State and Local Regulation

Under the "police powers" granted by the Constitution, state and local governments have the right to impose various zoning, planning, and land use controls on developers of land. Additionally, the purity of drinking water has been and continues to be of primary importance for state health officials. Many states also regulate air quality in a variety of ways, including limiting the amount of particulate matter that an industrial plant can emit into adjacent areas. A greater understanding of hazards has contributed to state activism in the environmental area, including the passage of "bottle bills," electric utility siting laws, and the like. Some states have their own environmental policy acts, which require impact statements to be prepared before decisions such as granting a building permit or changing a zoning ordinance can be made, while other state and local governments are putting absolute caps on growth. In addition to the usual land use restrictions concerning location (building on flood plains, earthquake fault areas, or sites that fail percolation tests) and zoning (height restriction; minimum lot sizes; and single family, multifamily, commercial, or industrial zones), some communities are adopting new and novel ordinances to protect the character of their areas. For example, the Long Island village of Bell Terre approved an ordinance prohibiting more than two unmarried people from living together within the community. The ordinance was challenged by six students who had rented a house. Justice Douglas, speaking for the U.S. Supreme Court, affirmed the village's authority, under its police power, to control environmental quality, in the broadest sense:

> The regimes of boarding houses, fraternity houses, and the like present urban problems. More people occupy a given space; more cars rather continuously pass by; more cars are parked; noise travels with crowds.
>
> A quiet place where yards are wide, people few, and motor vehicles restricted are legitimate guidelines in a land use project addressed to family needs. This goal is a permissible one. . . . The police power is not confined to the elimination of filth, stench, and unhealthy places. It is ample to lay out zones where family values, youth values, and the blessings of quiet seclusion, and clean air make the area a sanctuary for people.[6]

The Federal Presence

The federal government has long maintained a role in the protection of the environment. For example, an 1899 congressional enactment required a permit to discharge refuse into navigable waters. As it became apparent that private, state, and local environmental protection efforts were not adequate to the burgeoning problem, Congress began in the early 1970s to take a number of legislative initiatives.

National Environmental Policy Act

In 1970, President Nixon signed the National Environmental Policy Act (NEPA), which established a strong federal presence in the promotion of a clean and healthy environment. NEPA represents a general commitment by the federal government to ''use all practicable means'' to conduct federal affairs in a fashion that both promotes ''the general welfare'' and operates in ''harmony'' with the environment. A portion reads:

Public Law 91–190 (1969), 42 U.S.C. § 4331 *et seq.*

PURPOSE

Sec. 2. The purposes of this Act are: To declare a national policy which will encourage productive and enjoyable harmony between man and his environment; to promote efforts which will prevent or eliminate damage to the environment and biosphere and stimulate the health and welfare of man; to enrich the understanding of the ecological systems and natural resources important to the Nation; and to establish a Council on Environmental Quality.

The Council on Environmental Quality serves as an adviser to the president. Specifically the CEQ must ''assist and advise the president in the preparation of the [annual] Environmental Quality Report.'' The CEQ is a watchdog of sorts. It is required to conduct studies and generally collect information regarding the state of the environment. The council then develops policy and legislative proposals for the president and Congress.

But NEPA's primary influence clearly results from its environmental impact statement (EIS) requirements. With few exceptions, ''proposals for legislation and other major federal action significantly affecting the quality of the human environment'' must be accompanied by an EIS explaining the impact on the environment and detailing reasonable alternatives. Major federal construction projects such as highways, dams, and nuclear reactors are clearly exemplary of the classes of federal actions that would normally require an EIS; but less-visible federal programs such as ongoing timber management or authorizing the abandonment of a lengthy railway may also require EIS treatment. A major private sector action supported by federal funding or by one of several varieties of federal permission may also require an EIS. Hence private companies receiving federal contracts, funding, licenses, and the like may be parties to the completion of an EIS.

Environmental Protection Agency

In 1970 Congress created the Environmental Protection Agency (EPA) to oversee the public regulation of environmental issues. EPA duties include, among others: *(a)* information gathering, particularly in surveying pollution problems, *(b)* research regarding pollution problems, and *(c)* assisting state and local pollution control efforts.

A major EPA responsibility is that of administering many of the federal laws directed to environmental concerns. Several of those laws are discussed hereafter in some depth, but the reader should be aware of a number of additional statutes that might have been included: the Safe Drinking Water Act; the Marine Protection, Research, and Sanctuaries Act of 1972; the Federal Insecticide, Fungicide, and Rodenticide Act; and the Federal Environmental Pesticide Control Act of 1972.

Air Pollution

We depend upon, indeed, we emotionally embrace the automobile. In doing so, we have opened vistas of opportunity not previously imagined, but we may also have eliminated clean air forever. Motor vehicles discharge carbon monoxide, nitrogen oxide, and hydrocarbons as by-products of the combustion of fuel. Motor vehicles are the major source of air pollution, but industrial production and the combustion of fossil fuels in homes and industry are also significant contributors to the dilemma of dirty air. For most Americans, air pollution is simply an unpleasant fact of life. To the average Los Angeles resident, smog is more central to daily activity than the area's beaches and mountains. That air pollution may contribute to the deaths of 8,000 citizens annually in the Ohio River basin[7] is simply the regrettable consequence of progress. As the polls clearly reveal, Americans abhor pollution, and the citizenry is quite willing to pay well to correct the problem. But, having seldom experienced the satisfactions of pure air, most Americans clearly have not raised a clamor for decisive action to correct the problem. Indeed, the measured pace of contemporary air quality efforts may be the correct and practical direction. We should perhaps take a moment now to be reminded of what we have lost and what we are yet losing.

KEEPING THE BIG SKY PURE

Michael Parfit

In the village of Lame Deer, under the broad skies of eastern Montana, the Northern Cheyenne tribe gathered solemnly in the tribal gym. On the floor there were chairs, tables, microphones, a row of tribal council members, a television camera, and an interpreter with a booming voice. As the meeting began, a small crowd of high school students filed slowly into the room and up into the bleachers, the younger generation brought to witness the making of history. Outside, sleet splattered on the dirt roads and on the small homes of the reservation town, and wind tossed the dark pine trees on the hills. As the day continued, the wind grew colder, the sleet turned to bitter snow and, in the gym, a succession of speakers marched past the microphone, each pleading in English or Cheyenne for the thing that concerned this tribe most: clear air.

To a city resident who occasionally regrets the stinging, beige sky that envelops him while he pursues matters that seem more important than atmosphere, clean air as a cause doesn't have much urgency—it seems a bit like worrying about litter in the street after a parade. But to the Northern Cheyenne Indians, the word for air is the same as the word for breath—"*Omotome*"—and they cherish being able to breathe clean air. Why else would this small tribe on a remote reservation have spent several years and thousands of dollars struggling to preserve the quality of their air—air which is now threatened by industrial pollution?

The Northern Cheyenne live on 446,784 acres of low hills and prairie that lie a few dozen miles east of the meadow on the Little Big Horn where General George Armstrong Custer earned fame for foolishness in the summer of 1876. The reservation's towns, Ashland, Busby, Birney, and Lame Deer, are dusty little villages in which a total population of about 3,000 lives a collective life of struggle against common reservation evils: poverty, disease, alcoholism, unemployment, and despair. Two matters of geography, however, make this reservation and its people unique. The land, which lies on and among some of the richest coal fields of the West, is a tribute to the historical persistence of the Northern Cheyennes. Today, the unusual degree of unity and the morale of the tribe are based on that determination.

The federal government did not plan to have Cheyennes in Montana at all. After the Custer fight all Cheyennes were rounded up and lumped together in a reservation in Oklahoma, but in 1878 about 300 members of the Northern Cheyenne tribe broke out and began to walk home as described in Mari Sandoz's *Cheyenne Autumn*. Most were captured and then killed in a sordid episode of starvation and murder at an Army fort in Nebraska, but a remnant survived. In response to this tenacity, the federal government eventually gave the Northern Cheyennes their present reservation. But the walk itself gave them something almost as lasting. Today when you talk to members of this tribe about their history, their culture, or their present struggles, one phrase recurs: "the long walk back." In the past few years the memory of that time has been repeatedly evoked to support the Northern Cheyennes' struggle for clean air.

The situation which has brought Cheyenne history to bear upon such an unlikely issue is deceptively simple. Since 1974, a group of five utilities has been planning to build a 1,400 megawatt power plant adjacent to coal mines about 15 miles north of the reservation at a place called Colstrip. Two plants, Colstrip I and Colstrip II, have already been built. In 1977, efforts to build Colstrip III and Colstrip IV met opposition when the Northern Cheyennes, using an opportunity offered all Indian tribes by federal clean air laws, asked the U.S. Environmental Protection Agency (EPA) to cover their land with the legal umbrella of designation as a Class I air quality area. A Class I area, in EPA terms, is a refuge for the cleanest air in the country, purity undefiled. The request was granted. The reservation joined national parks and wilderness areas under this ultimate protection, and the Northern Cheyennes celebrated.

In 1978 and through part of 1979 the EPA backed up its promise by repeatedly telling the power consortium that its plant would unduly soil the atmosphere of the reservation and thus could not be built as designed. Later, in 1979, however, despite negative data from a smaller power plant already running nearby, EPA reopened the issue. The agency agreed to hear renewed requests from pro-power plant interests because of improvements in plant design and pressure generated by the national energy crisis. Finally, it approved construction of the plant.

The hypothetical city resident, whose skies are murky all day, would consider this action to be positive—a useful compromise. Although it is probable that the reservation will on occasion be polluted beyond the limits of the Class I definition, how much, he or she would ask, does that matter? Isn't this more a case of sacrificing a group's marginal interests in the name of national need, rather than an infringement of rights? Or the promise—if not fact— of job opportunities in a depressed economy as opposed to some esoteric value tenaciously held?

The trouble is that these initial impressions have roots in America's system of economic and social priorities in which clean air obviously does not rate highly. In times of recession or energy need, pollution laws are usually the first to be swept off the tables. Clean air is labeled an environmental issue, and in the prevailing system, environmentalism, in all its varied glory, is considered a game of affluence, like golf. Who cares about air quality if your landlord sells your home or your job is threatened due to an energy shortage?

But to the Northern Cheyennes the landlord has already sold most of the place to outsiders. And for Indians, there just isn't much work— winter unemployment on the Northern Cheyenne reservation runs from 50 to 70 percent.

And still they fight for clean air. Their priorities are simply not the same.

"Our ancestors regarded the ground as sacred," said Joe Bear, trying to explain. Bear is a tribal vice chairman who ranches on the eastern side of the reservation. "A Cheyenne is right next to the earth. All we're asking is just to keep our air clear. That's what it takes to grow things. Land, water, air."

* * * * *

There is, of course, more than one way to read this rhetoric. Those who favor the power plant argue that the Cheyenne are manipulating an emotion-laden issue for reasons that are remote from actual air quality—political power, tribal cohesion, revenge, and financial gain. The extensive Cheyenne coal reserves might well feed the Colstrip furnaces under different circumstances.

The Cheyenne themselves point out that the drive for clean air is partly based on a fear of the social problems that the polluting power plant would bring, and not just the smoke. However, since oil development would be significantly cleaner and less disruptive than the power plant and strip mining, a recent tribal referendum gave overwhelming support to oil exploration on the reservation.

A Cheyenne report which was prepared in order to support the request for Class I status said:

You can see we are concerned about the direct results of a deterioration in the quality of our air. We are [also] worried about any large influx of outsiders associated with the construction and operation of power plants. Partly we fear the overcrowding, crime, and inflation as more affluent people compete with us for limited housing and services. But our fear is even more basic. Nearly all Indians have personally experienced prejudice and discrimination, and we worry about becoming a minority on our own reservation, in our own towns.

The Cheyennes express their philosophy of relationships in life with a design called the Cheyenne Circle, which is cut into wedges like a pie graph showing the allocation of a tax dollar. In the Cheyenne Circle, however, the four wedges are equal in size (and hence importance), and the slice which represents air is as large as that for living things. . . .

Twice in the past decade the tribe has chosen to put long term environmental concerns ahead of immediate financial gain: once, in the early 70's when it quashed an attempt by the Bureau of Indian Affairs to lease over half the reservation for strip mining; and once with the request for Class I air. Both actions cost the Cheyenne thousands of dollars in legal fees and millions in lost revenues and jobs.

So it is probably fair to say that the scale of values other Americans might place on matters such as those raised by the construction of a power plant—giving more weight, for instance, to social concerns than to what we would call environmental ones—would misrepresent the Cheyennes' own priorities. It is more likely that the Northern Cheyennes—as driven by self-interest as any other group—see the air, the land, and their health as webbed together by the forces of life; an assault on one damages all the rest. If there is truth anywhere in the words of Joe Bear and Harry Littlebird, it is that the Northern Cheyennes, reacting to the industrial world from the point of view of a culture in which respect for the land has played a central role for centuries, consider the quality of their air to be a fundamental right, as necessary as work and respect to human vitality.

From this perspective, the construction of the power plant close to the reservation becomes less a matter of sacrificing niceties to need and more a matter of oppression. And, unfortunately, this incident is not unique. The pattern of energy development in the west—in which rural areas are being dug up, polluted and subjected to devastating social turmoil,

while the coal and electricity produced are carried away to fuel cities—can only be described as avaricious and Native Americans are among the people most badly used. The Navajo and Hopi tribes in Arizona, for instance, have been so roundly exploited for their coal, oil, natural gas and uranium that the terrible phrase "national sacrifice area," a concept that should have been abandoned with the burning of witches, has recently been resurrected to describe their homelands.

In self defense, and perhaps out of aggressive instincts as well, the Northern Cheyennes and 24 other tribes recently formed an organization called the Council of Energy Resources Tribes (CERT), which splashed itself across front pages in 1979 when it hired a former Iranian oil minister to help negotiate contracts. The inference that the Native Americans were going to act like OPEC nations was inescapable, and perhaps that's the image the tribes wanted. But if the energy companies who wish to mine the coal, gas, uranium and oil that the CERT tribes control find the Indians difficult to handle, they may learn that money alone is not the answer.

If the Northern Cheyenne experience is any indication, company executives may find themselves dealing with a new set of priorities. While measured development is appreciated, the list of priorities does not begin and end with the word profit. On that basis, at least, the Northern Cheyennes may have something to offer to the value systems of all Americans. . . .

Source: *Perspectives* 13, No. 1 (Spring 1981) pp. 40–44. Reprinted with permission of the copyright holder, *New Perspectives*.

QUESTIONS

1. Is clean air more important to the Cheyenne than to most Americans? Why?
2. In the face of wintertime unemployment in the 50 percent to 70 percent range, the Cheyenne, nevertheless, argue for clean air rather than development. Should the entire nation adopt the Cheyenne priorities? Explain.
3. Regardless of your beliefs, build the argument that other Americans are paying for the Cheyenne's clean air luxury.

Government Policy

Despite clearly unsatisfactory air quality in many locations, it is evident that the federal and state governments have, in 20 years of effort, significantly reduced U.S. air pollution. After the limited success of clean air legislation in 1963 and 1965, it became apparent to Congress that drastic adjustments were necessary. The Clean Air Act Amendments of 1970 and 1977 gave the federal Environmental Protection Agency the authority to set air quality standards and to assure that those standards were achieved, according to a timetable prescribed by the EPA. Among the standards established were the following:

1. *National Ambient Air Quality Standards (NAAQS).* National standards have been established for carbon monoxide, hydrocarbons, lead, nitrogen oxide, ozone, particulates, and sulfur dioxide. A primary standard sets a ceiling on air pollution that is safe for humans. A secondary standard sets a ceiling for the balance of the environment including soil, visibility, animals, vegetation, and so on.
2. *Emergency Standards.* When air pollution reaches a level that poses an imminent and substantial danger to health, emergency action, such as stopping production by a polluting industry, may be taken.
3. *Motor Vehicle Emission and Fuel Standards.* New and imported cars and engines must meet EPA emission standards, and the EPA can control or prohibit substances that significantly retard the performance of motor vehicle emission control systems.

With the establishment of NAAQS, each state was required to develop a state implementation plan (SIP) to achieve a level of pollution beneath the federal ceiling. The EPA is empowered to impose appropriate regulations should a state fail to do so. Standards for each industrial plant were to be established, and those standards were to be achieved by a specified date.

New industrial construction is subject to special requirements. The nature of the standards to be applied depends upon the air quality where the plant is to be located. Locales with relatively clean air that meets national standards are labelled "Prevention of Significant Deterioration" areas (PSD). Locales with relatively dirty air that does not meet the standards are labelled "nonattainment areas." In PSD areas, new plants are permissible only so long as total emissions do not exceed specific standards as established by the Clean Air Act. The owners would be required to show that their proposed industry would not exceed the limitations. Additionally the owners would be required to install the "best available control technology" (BACT) to ensure compliance.

Those seeking to build in nonattainment areas must meet three standards to receive a government permit:

1. All other pollution sources owned or operated by the applicant in the state must meet all applicable emission limits and compliance standards.
2. The new source must be controlled at the "lowest achievable emission rate" (LAER). LAER means either the lowest emission level achieved by any source in the same category or the most demanding emission standard in any SIP (unless it proves to be unachievable).
3. New plants in nonattainment areas are permissible only if the added air pollution is

offset on a ''more than one-for-one'' basis by reductions in pollutants of the same character from plants in that geographical area.

Clean Air Act violations unaccompanied by criminal intent may result in a civil fine of $25,000 per day, along with injunctive action. ''Knowing'' violations, as defined by the act, may result in a criminal fine of not more than $25,000 per day and/or imprisonment for a term of not more than one year. Those penalties may be doubled for a second offense. Congress was concerned that the aforementioned penalties were such that it might be cheaper for a firm to fail to comply rather than undertake the cost of necessary corrections. Therefore, the 1977 amendments impose a penalty equivalent to the ''savings'' achieved by noncompliance from the time of receipt from the EPA of a notice of noncompliance. Citizen suits are provided for under the Clean Air Act.

The business community and others have been distressed by the inhibitions in industrial development that the Clean Air Act has imposed. Years may be required to secure the necessary environmental permits to build a new factory or generator. In the early 1980s Congress considered, but failed to approve, a number of amendments to the act. Those included: (1) easing auto emissions standards, (2) allowing the use of low-sulfur coal rather than antipollution ''scrubbers'' in new coal-burning plants, and (3) eliminating deadlines for installing pollution control devices where SIPs provide for continuing improvement in air quality. However, a 1984 Supreme Court decision affirming the ''bubble concept'' represented an important victory for advocates of more relaxed pollution standards. In nonattainment areas, states must develop a permit program regulating ''new or modified major stationary sources'' of air pollution. The EPA issued regulations in 1981 allowing states to adopt a plantwide definition of the term *stationary source*. Under that standard a firm can replace or modify old equipment or add new equipment even if those individual pieces of machinery fail to meet the standards of the permit program so long as the total emissions from the plant are not increased. All pollution-producing devices within an industrial grouping are treated as a unit—as though they are under a bubble. The Natural Resources Defense Council challenged the bubble concept, but the Supreme Court held that the EPA's plantwide definition of the term *stationary source* is lawful.[8]

In 1985 the EPA announced a new policy which would shift some federal air quality responsibilities to state and local governments.[9] The new direction was partly based upon a study suggesting that 75 percent of the ''routine'' air pollution in America comes from ''area sources'' such as gasoline stations and dry cleaners rather than from ''point sources'' such as steel mills. Further, the EPA noted that air quality problems are highly dependent on specific local conditions such as weather and geography. Environmentalists criticized the new approach. David Doninger, senior attorney for the National Resources Defense Council said that the EPA was turning its ''longstanding failure to protect public health from passive neglect into deliberate policy.''[10] However, the EPA contends that the new policy will actually broaden the federal role by reaching previously unregulated emission sources. Funds to help the states implement the new policy have not been approved at this writing in late 1985, and Congress is considering legislation to compel the EPA to renew and broaden federal clean air duties.

The following case illustrates the application of the Clean Air Act to a specific situation.

UNION ELECTRIC CO. V. ENVIRONMENTAL PROTECTION AGENCY   427 U.S. 246 (1976)

Justice Marshall

After the administrator of the Environmental Protection Agency (EPA) approves a state implementation plan under the Clean Air Act, the plan may be challenged in a court of appeals within 30 days, or after 30 days have run if newly discovered or available information justifies subsequent review. We must decide whether the operator of a regulated emission source, in a petition for review of an EPA-approved state plan filed after the original 30-day appeal period, can raise the claim that it is economically or technologically infeasible to comply with the plan.

*   *   *   *   *

The heart of the [Clean Air Act] Amendments is the requirement that each state formulate, subject to EPA approval, an implementation plan designed to achieve national primary ambient air quality standards—those necessary to protect the public health—"as expeditiously as practicable but . . . in no case later than three years from the date of approval of such plan." § 110(a)(2)(A). The plan must also provide for the attainment of national secondary ambient air quality standards—those necessary to protect the public welfare—within a "reasonable time." . . . Each state is given wide discretion in formulating its plan, and the Act provides that the administrator "shall approve" the proposed plan if it has been adopted after public notice and hearing and if it meets eight specified criteria. . . .

On April 30, 1971, the administrator promulgated national primary and secondary standards for six air pollutants he found to have an adverse effect on the public health and welfare. . . . Included among them was sulfur dioxide, at issue here. . . . After the promulgation of the national standards, the state of Missouri formulated its implementation plan and submitted it for approval. Since sulfur dioxide levels exceeded national primary standards in only one of the state's five air quality regions—the Metropolitan St. Louis Interstate region, the Missouri plan concentrated on a control strategy and regulations to lower emissions in that area. The plan's emission limitations were effective at once, but the state retained authority to grant variances to particular sources that could not immediately comply. . . . The administrator approved the plan on May 31, 1972.

Petitioner is an electric utility company servicing the St. Louis metropolitan area, large portions of Missouri, and parts of Illinois and Iowa. Its three coal-fired generating plants in the metropolitan St. Louis area are subject to the sulfur dioxide restrictions in the Missouri implementation plan. Petitioner did not seek review of the administrator's approval of the plan within 30 days, as it was entitled to do under § 307(b)(1) of the Act, but rather applied to the appropriate state and county agencies for variances from the emission limitations affecting its three plants. Petitioner received one-year variances, which could be extended upon reapplication. The variances on two of petitioner's three plants had expired and petitioner was applying for extensions when, on May 31, 1974, the administrator notified petitioner that sulfur dioxide emissions from its plants violated the emission limitations contained in the Missouri plan. Shortly thereafter petitioner filed a petition in the Court of Appeals for the Eighth Circuit for review of the administrator's 1972 approval of the Missouri implementation plan.

Section 307(b)(1) allows petitions for review to be filed in an appropriate court of appeals more than 30 days after the administrator's approval of an implementation plan only if the petition is "based solely on grounds arising after such 30th day." Petitioner claimed to meet this requirement by asserting . . . that various economic and technological difficulties had arisen more than

30 days after the administrator's approval and that these difficulties made compliance with the emission limitations impossible. The Court of Appeals dismiss[ed] the petition. . . .

*   *   *   *   *

We reject at the outset petitioner's suggestion that a claim of economic or technological infeasibility may be considered upon a petition for review based on new information and filed more than 30 days after approval of an implementation plan even if such a claim could not be considered by the administrator in approving a plan or by a court in reviewing a plan challenged within the original 30-day appeal period. . . . Regardless of when a petition for review is filed under § 307(b)(1), the court is limited to reviewing "the administrator's action in approving . . . [the] implementation plan. . . . Accordingly, if new "grounds" are alleged, they must be such that, had they been known at the time the plan was presented to the administrator for approval, it would have been an abuse of discretion for the administrator to approve the plan. To hold otherwise would be to transfer a substantial responsibility in administering the Clean Air Act from the administrator and the state agencies to the federal courts.

Since a reviewing court—regardless of when the petition for review is filed—may consider claims of economic and technological infeasibility only if the administrator may consider such claims in approving or rejecting a state implementation plan, we must address ourselves to the scope of the administrator's responsibility. The administrator's position is that he has no power whatsoever to reject a state implementation plan on the ground that it is economically or technologically infeasible, and we have previously accorded great deference to the administrator's construction of the Clean Air Act. After surveying the relevant provisions of the Clean Air Amendments of 1970 and their legislative history, we agree that Congress intended claims of economic and technological infeasibility to be wholly foreign to the administrator's consideration of a state implementation plan.

As we have previously recognized, the 1970 Amendments to the Clean Air Act were a drastic remedy to what was perceived as a serious and otherwise uncheckable problem of air pollution. The amendments place the primary responsibility for formulating pollution control strategies on the states, but nonetheless subject the states to strict minimum compliance requirements. These requirements are of a "technology-forcing character," and are expressly designed to force regulated sources to develop pollution control devices that might at the time appear to be economically or technologically infeasible.

This approach is apparent on the face of § 110(a)(2). The provision sets out eight criteria that an implementation plan must satisfy, and provides that if these criteria are met and if the plan was adopted after reasonable notice and hearing, the administrator "shall approve" the proposed state plan. The mandatory "shall" makes it quite clear that the Administrator is not to be concerned with factors other than those specified, and none of the eight factors appears to permit consideration of technological or economic infeasibility.

*   *   *   *   *

Section 110(a)(2)(A)'s three-year deadline for achieving primary air quality standards is central to the amendments' regulatory scheme and, as both the language and the legislative history of the requirement make clear, it leaves no room for claims of technological or economic infeasibility.

*   *   *   *   *

In sum, we have concluded that claims of economic or technological infeasibility may not be considered by the administrator in evaluating a state requirement that primary ambient air quality standards be met in the mandatory three years. And, since we further conclude that the states may submit implementation plans more stringent than federal law requires and that the administrator must approve such plans if they meet the minimum requirements of § 110(a)(2), it follows that the language of § 110(a)(2)(B) provides no basis for the administrator ever to reject a state implementation plan on the ground that it is economically or technologically infeasible. Accordingly, a Court of Appeals reviewing an approved plan under § 307(b)(1) cannot set it aside on those grounds, no matter when they are raised.

Our conclusion is bolstered by recognition that the amendments do allow claims of technological and economic infeasibility to be raised in situations where consideration of such claims will not substantially interfere with the primary congressional purpose of prompt attainment of the national air quality standards. Thus, we do not hold that claims of infeasibility are never of relevance in the formulation of an implementation plan or that sources unable to comply with emission limitations must inevitably be shut down.

Perhaps the most important forum for consideration of claims of economic and technological infeasibility is before the state agency formulating the implementation plan. So long as the national standards are met, the state may select whatever mix of control devices it desires, and industries with particular economic or technological problems may seek special treatment in the plan itself. Moreover, if the industry is not exempted from, or accommodated by, the original plan, it may obtain a variance, as petitioner did in this case; and the variance, if granted after notice and a hearing, may be submitted to the EPA as a revision of the plan. . . . Lastly, an industry denied an exemption from the implementation plan, or denied a subsequent variance, may be able to take its claims of economic or technological infeasibility to the state courts.

*   *   *   *   *

. . . Technology forcing is a concept somewhat new to our national experience and it necessarily entails certain risks. But Congress considered those risks in passing the 1970 Amendments and decided that the dangers posed by uncontrolled air pollution made them worth taking. Petitioner's theory would render that considered legislative judgment a nullity, and that is a result we refuse to reach.

Affirmed.

Justice Powell, with whom The Chief Justice joins, concurring.

I join the opinion of the Court because the statutory scheme and the legislative history, thoroughly described in the Court's opinion, demonstrate irrefutably that Congress did not intend to permit the administrator of the Environmental Protection Agency to reject a proposed state implementation plan on the grounds of economic or technological infeasibility. Congress adopted this position despite its apparent awareness that in some cases existing sources that cannot meet the standard of the law must be closed down.

At the risk of civil and criminal penalties enforceable by both the state and federal governments, as well as possible citizens' suits, petitioner is being required either to embark upon the task of installing allegedly unreliable and prohibitively expensive equipment or to shut down. Yet the present Act permits neither the administrator, in approving the state plan, nor the courts, in reviewing that approval under § 307 of the Act, even to consider petitioner's allegations of infeasibility.

Environmental concerns, long neglected, merit high priority, and Congress properly has made protection of the public health its paramount consideration. But the shutdown of an urban area's electrical service could have an even more serious impact on the health of the public than that created by a decline in ambient air quality. The result apparently required by this legislation in its present form could sacrifice the well-being of a large metropolitan area through the imposition of inflexible demands that may be technologically impossible to meet and indeed may no longer even be necessary to the attainment of the goal of clean air.

I believe that Congress, if fully aware of this Draconian possibility, would strike a different balance.

Questions

1. What does the Court mean by "technology forcing"?
2. Under what circumstances may an affected party raise a claim of technological and/or economic infeasibility? Before whom may a claim of technological and/or economic infeasibility properly be raised?
3. How would you argue that Clean Air Act enforcement according to state implementation plans (SIP) is artificial and not in keeping with the actual pattern of air pollution?
4. Is Justice Powell in his concurring opinion giving advice to Congress? Should he do so? If Justice Powell disapproves of the act, why did he not dissent in this case? Explain.
5. The Potomac Electric Power Company (PEPCO) operated coal-fired stoker boilers that emitted smoke with visible emissions. The Clean Air Act standards forbid visible emissions. The plaintiff, Friends of the Earth, filed suit under the Clean Air Act seeking a judicial declaration that PEPCO was in violation of District of Columbia emission standards as promulgated pursuant to the Clean Air Act. PEPCO argued that the economic and technological infeasibility of completely eliminating visible emissions constituted a full defense. Friends of the Earth claimed that the act was meant to force improved technology, and that the public health had to be accorded absolute priority over the continuing operation of noncomplying pollution sources. Decide. Explain. See *Friends of the Earth* v. *Potomac Electric Power Co.,* 419 F.Supp. 528 (D.C. 1976).

Water Pollution

As with the air, we have displayed a tendency to treat our water resources as free goods. Rather than paying the full cost of producing goods and services, we have simply piped a portion of that cost into the nearest body of water. That is, the waste from production, indeed from the totality of our life experience, has commonly been disposed of in the water at a cost beneath that required to dispose of the waste in an ecologically sound fashion.

The corruption of our water system arose in a variety of ways. It is important to recognize that we have not always realized what we now know about the danger of wastes and the cleansing limits of our lakes and streams. Raw sewage and industrial waste reduced Lake Erie, in the judgment of many, to an open sewer. Ohio's Cuyahoga River, the victim of chemical and oil waste disposal, actually was in flames at one point. Approximately 10 percent of the freshwater runoff in the United States is used for industrial cooling. The result is often water that is inhospitable to aquatic life. Herbicides, pesticides, acid runoff from strip mining, and oil spills are but several more examples of our assault on the waterways.

Federal Policy

The Clean Water Act, designed to "restore and maintain the chemical, physical and biological integrity of the nation's waters," establishes two national goals: (1) achieveing water quality sufficient for the protection and propagation of fish, shellfish, and wildlife and for recreation in and on the water; and (2) eliminating the discharge of pollutants into navigable waters. The states have primary responsibility for enforcing the Clean Water Act, but the federal government, via the Environmental Protection Agency, is empowered to assume enforcement authority if necessary.

The goals of the Clean Water Act are to be implemented primarily by imposing limits upon the amount of pollutants that may lawfully enter the water of the United States from any "point source" (typically a pipe). The law provides for a permit program specifying the obligations of all pollutant dischargers (private and public). Each discharger must receive an EPA permit; comply with the effluent maximums specified by the permit; monitor its own performance; and report on that performance to the state or the EPA, as appropriate.

In brief, industrial pollution sources are required to progressively improve the quality of the nation's water via the following standards: All plants were required by 1977 to have installed pollution control devices that constituted the "best practicable pollution control technology" (BPT). Then, by 1984 plants discharging "conventional pollutants" (oil, grease, etc.) were required to use the "best conventional pollutant control technology" (BCT) while "toxic pollutants" were to be controlled by the "best available technology economically achievable" (BAT). Finally, by 1987 nonconventional pollutants (those neither conventional nor toxic) are likewise to be subjected to the BAT.

Penalties

Noncompliance with an order issued under the Clean Water act or violation of the act may result in a civil penalty of $10,000 per day and an injunction. Criminal penalties reach a maximum of $25,000 and/or one year in prison for the first offense. Those penalties may be doubled in the event of a second conviction. Criminal penalties are authorized in instances of "willful and negligent" violations. The Clean Water Act does not include a noncompliance penalty equivalent to accrued "savings" as was the case with the Clean Air Act. Citizen suits are provided for under the CWA.

The case that follows addresses the somewhat murky Clean Water Act standards.

CHEMICAL MANUFACTURERS ASSN. V. NRDC*   53 *Law Week* 4193 (U.S. S. Ct. 1985)

[The Supreme Court answers the question of whether the Environmental Protection Agency may grant variances (exceptions) from Clean Water Act limitations upon toxic discharges into public water treatment plants. Those limitations are set by reference to BPT and BAT levels.]

Justice White

*Reprinted by permission from *The United States Law Week*, copyright 1985 by The Bureau of National Affairs, Inc., Washington, D.C.

I

[R]espondent National Resources Defense Counsel (NRDC) sought a declaration that § 301(*l*) of the Clean Water Act prohibited EPA from issuing "fundamentally different factor" (FDF) variances for pollutants listed as toxic under the Act. Petitioners EPA and Chemical Manufacturers Association (CMA) argued otherwise. . . .

* * * * *

EPA has developed its FDF variance as a mechanism for ensuring that its necessarily rough-hewn categories do not unfairly burden atypical plants. Any interested party may seek an FDF variance to make effluent limitations either more or less stringent if the standards applied to a given source, because of factors fundamentally different from those considered by EPA in setting the limitation, are either too lenient or too strict.

The 1977 amendments to the Clean Water Act reflected Congress' increased concern with the dangers of toxic pollutants. The Act, as then amended, allows specific statutory modifications of effluent limitations for economic and water quality reasons in § 301(c) and (g). Section 301(*l*), however, added by the 1977 amendments, provides:

The administrator may not modify any requirement of this section as it applies to any specific pollutant which is on the toxic pollutant list under section 1317(a)(1) of this title.

In the aftermath of the 1977 amendments, EPA continued its practice of occasionally granting FDF variances for BPT requirements . . . and BAT requirements. . . .

. . . NRDC sought a declaration that § 301(*l*) barred any FDF variance with respect to toxic pollutants. In an earlier case, the Fourth Circuit had rejected a similar argument, finding that § 301(*l*) was ambiguous on the issue of whether it applied to FDF variances and therefore deferring to the administrative agency's interpretation that such variances were permitted. . . . Contrariwise, the Third Circuit here ruled in favor of NRDC, and against petitioners EPA and CMA, holding that § 301(*l*) forbids the issuance of FDF variances for toxic pollutants. We granted certiorari to resolve this conflict between the Courts of Appeals and to decide this important question of environmental law. . . . We reverse.

II

Section 301(*l*) states that EPA may not "modify" any requirements of § 301 insofar as toxic materials are concerned. EPA insists that § 301(*l*) prohibits only those modifications expressly permitted by other provisions of § 301, namely, those that § 301(c) and § 301(g) would allow on economic or water-quality grounds. Section 301(*l*), it is urged, does not address the very different issue of FDF variances. This view of the agency charged with administering the statute is entitled to considerable deference; and to sustain it, we need not find that it is the only permissible construction that EPA might have adopted but only that EPA's understanding of this very "complex statute" is a sufficiently rational one to preclude a court from substituting its judgment for that of EPA. . . .

A

NRDC insists that the language of §301(*l*) is itself enough to require affirmance of the Court of Appeals, since on its face it forbids any modifications of the effluent limitations that EPA must promulgate for toxic pollutants. If the word "modify" in §301(*l*) is read in its broadest sense, that is, to encompass any change or alteration in the standards, NRDC is correct. But it makes little sense to construe the section to forbid EPA to amend its own standards, even to correct an error or to impose stricter requirements. Furthermore, reading § 301(*l*) in this manner would forbid what § 307(b) (2) expressly directs: EPA is there required to "revise" its pretreatment standards "from time to time, as control technology, processes, operating methods, or other alternatives change." As NRDC does and must concede. . . § 301(*l*) cannot be read to forbid every change in the toxic waste standards. The word "modify" thus has no plain meaning as used in § 301(*l*) and is the proper subject of construction by EPA and the courts. . . . Since EPA asserts that the FDF variance is more like a revision permitted by § 307 than it is like a § 301 (c) or (g) modification, and since, as will become evident, we think there is a reasonable basis for such a position, we conclude that the statutory language does not foreclose the agency's view of the statute. We should defer to that view unless the legislative history or the purpose and structure of the statute clearly reveal a contrary intent on the part of Congress. NRDC submits that the legislative materials evince such a contrary intent. We disagree.

B

. . . While the Conference Committee Report did not explain the reason for proposing § 301(*l*), Representative Roberts, the House floor manager, stated:

Due to the nature of toxic pollutants, those identified for regulation will not be subject to waivers from or modification of the requirements prescribed under this section, *specifically, neither section 301(c) waivers based on the economic capability of the discharger nor 301(g) waivers based on water quality considerations shall be available.*

Another indication that Congress did not intend to forbid FDF waivers as well as § 301(c) and (g) modifications is its silence on the issue. Under NRDC's theory, the Conference Committee did not merely tinker with the wording of the Senate bill, but boldly moved to eliminate FDF variances. But if that was the Committee's intention, it is odd that the Committee did not communicate it to either House, for only a few months before we had construed the Act to permit the very FDF variance NRDC insists the Conference Committee was silently proposing to abolish. In *E. I. du Pont de Nemours & Co.* v. *Train*, 430 U.S. 112 (1977), we upheld EPA's class and category effluent limitations, relying on the availability of FDF waivers. Congress was undoubtedly aware of *Du Pont*, and absent an expression of legislative will, we are reluctant to infer an intent to amend the Act so as to ignore the trust of an important decision.

* * * * *

After examining the wording and legislative history of the statute, we agree with EPA and CMA that the legislative history itself does not evince an unambiguous Congressional intention to forbid all FDF waivers with respect to toxic materials.

C

Neither are we convinced that FDF variances threaten to frustrate the goals and operation of the statutory scheme set up by Congress. The nature of FDF variances has been spelled out both by this Court and by the agency itself. The regulation explains that its purpose is to remedy categories which were not accurately drawn because information was either not available to or not considered by the administrator in setting the original categories and limitations. An FDF variance does not excuse compliance with a correct requirement, but instead represents an acknowledgement that not all relevant factors were taken sufficiently into account in framing that requirement originally, and that those relevant factors, properly considered, would have justified—indeed, required—the creation of a subcategory for the discharger in question. . . . It is essentially, not an exception to the standard-setting process, but rather a more fine-tuned application of it.

We are not persuaded by NRDC's argument that granting FDF variances is inconsistent with the goal of uniform effluent limitations under the Act. Congress did intend uniformity among sources in the same category, demanding that "similar point sources with similar characteristics . . . meet similar effluent limitations," . . . EPA, however, was admonished to take into account the diversity within each industry by establishing appropriate subcategories.

* * * * *

NRDC argues, echoing the concern of the Court of Appeals below, that allowing FDF variances will render meaningless the § 301(*l*) prohibition against modifications on the basis of economic and water quality factors. That argument ignores the clear difference between the purpose of FDF waivers and that of § 301(c) and (g) modifications. . . . FDF variances are specifically unavailable for the grounds that would justify the statutory modifications. . . . Both a source's inability to pay the foreseen costs, grounds for a § 301(c) modification, and the lack of a significant impact on water quality, grounds for a § 301(g) modification, are irrelevant under FDF variance procedures. . . .

EPA and CMA point out that the availability of FDF variances makes bearable the enormous burden faced by EPA in promulgating categories of sources and setting effluent limitations. Acting under stringent timetables, EPA must collect and analyze large amounts of technical information concerning complex industrial categories. Understandably, EPA may not be apprised of and will fail to consider unique factors applicable to atypical plants during the categorical rulemaking process, and it is thus important that EPA's nationally binding categorical pretreatment standards for indirect dischargers be tempered with the flexibility that the FDF variance mechanism offers, a mechanism repugnant to neither the goals nor the operation of the Act.

III

Viewed in its entirety, neither the language nor the legislative history of the Act demonstrates a clear congressional intent to forbid EPA's sensible variance mechanism for tailoring the categories it promulgates. In the absence of congressional directive to the contrary, we accept EPA's conclusion that § 301(*l*) does not prohibit FDF variances. That interpretation gives the term "modify" a consistent meaning in § 301(c), (g), and (*l*), and draws support from the legislative evolution of § 301(*l*) and from congressional silence on whether it intended to forbid FDF variances altogether and thus to obviate our decision in *Du Pont*.

* * * * *

The judgment of the Court of Appeals is reversed.

Justice Marshall, with whom Justice Blackmun and Justice Stevens join, and with whom Justice O'Connor joins as to Parts I, II, and III, dissenting.

In this case, the Environmental Protection Agency (EPA) maintains that it may issue, on a case-by-case basis, individualized variances from the national standards that limit the discharge of toxic water pollutants. EPA asserts this power in the face of a provision of the Clean Water Act that expressly withdraws from the agency the authority to "modify" the national standards for such pollutants. The Court today defers to EPA's interpretation of the Clean Water Act even though that interpretation is inconsistent with the clear intent of Congress. . . .

* * * * *

. . . .Congress pointedly determined that water pollution control standards should take the form of general rules, to apply uniformly to categories of dischargers. As a result, the Court validates outcomes substantially less protective of the environment than those mandated by Congress. The only view of FDF variances consistent with the scheme of the Clean Water Act is that they are individual exceptions that soften the hardship of general rules. As such, they are undoubtedly disallowed by § 301(*l*).

This case is not about whether exceptions are useful adjuncts to regulatory schemes of general applicability. That is a policy choice on which courts should defer to Congress in the first instance, and to the administrative agency in the absence of a clear congressional mandate. Here, Congress has made the policy choice. It has weighed competing goals and determined that, whatever the general merits of exceptions schemes, they are simply inappropriate in the context of the control of toxic water pollution. As a result, an exceptions scheme such as the one challenged here simply cannot stand.

Questions

1. Explain the difference between BPT and BAT.
2. What is meant by "fundamentally different factor" variances.
3. To prevail in this case of statutory interpretation, was the EPA required to prove that its reading of the Clean Water Act was the "only permissible construction" that might be put upon that language? Explain.
4. Do you regard the Court's decision as a sensible accommodation to the realities of commercial needs or a dramatic hole in the nation's antipollution armor, or neither? Explain.

Land Pollution

Obviously pollution does not fit tidily into the three compartments (air, water, land) used for convenience in this text. Acid rain, as discussed above, debases air and water as well as the fruits of the water and land (e.g., fish and trees). Similarly, it should be recognized that the problems of land pollution to be addressed in this section often do damage to the fullness of the natural world. For most of recorded history we felt safe and comfortable in using the Earth as a garbage dump. When we did begin to recognize emerging dangers, our primary initial concern was simply the problem of disposing of the enormous bulk of our solid wastes.

The problem was and is real in that we annually produce approximately 20 to 30 tons of such waste for every American. Each year the city of Philadelphia incinerates 360,000 tons of waste, but that leaves 540,000 tons that must be piled in landfills. The city generates over 60,000 tons of sludge annually. At one time the sludge was handled comfortably merely by dumping it in the Atlantic Ocean. Since 1980 that approach has been illegal, so the city has turned to more ingenious disposal techniques. Sixty percent of the sludge is used in strip mine reclamation. Some 15 to 20 percent is given away or sold (as fertilizer), and the remainder is applied to Philadelphia land (e.g., golf courses). Now the city is experimenting with a combination of sludge and incinerator residue to be used as a highway aggregate for bituminous paving.[11]

Of course, many cities and counties have established recycling centers and plants to convert waste to energy. In 1972 Oregon became the first state to approve a "bottle bill.'' That law forbade cans with pull-tab openers, and it provided that all beer and soft drink containers sold in the state were to have a refund value of 2 or 5 cents. Since then a number of states have enacted similar legislation, and the federal government has considered many such bills.

Solid Waste Disposal Act

In order to attack the massive garbage problem, Congress approved the Solid Waste Disposal Act of 1965. The act, in brief, leaves solid waste problems to states and localities while the federal government offers research and financial support. In 1970 the act was reauthorized and the Congress required a report on hazardous wastes.

Toxic Substances Control Act

In 1976 Congress approved the Toxic Substances Control Act to identify toxic chemicals, assess their risks, and control dangerous chemicals. Under the terms of TSCA, the Environmental Protection Agency requires the chemical industry to report any information they may have suggesting that a chemical poses a ''substantial risk.'' The EPA is empowered to review and limit or stop the introduction of new chemicals.

As illustrated in this section, we have displayed a good deal of zeal and ingenuity in addressing pollution problems. However, we are beginning to recognize that the clever solutions of today often become tomorrow's problems. For example, the incineration of waste rids us of bulk, but creates air pollution. The interdependence of all elements of the global environment magnifies the difficulties in pollution control.

Resource Conservation and Recovery Act

By 1976 the dangers of hazardous substances were becoming apparent to all, and Congress complemented the TSCA with the Resource Conservation and Recovery Act. The act addresses both solid and hazardous wastes. Its solid waste provisions are more supportive than punitive in tone and approach. The federal government is authorized, among other strategies, to provide technical and financial assistance to states and localities; to prohibit future open dumping; and to establish cooperative federal, state, local, and private enterprise programs to recover energy and valuable materials from solid wastes.

Subtitle C of the RCRA is designed to ensure the safe movement and disposal of hazardous wastes. The generator of the waste must determine if that waste is hazardous under EPA guidelines and, if so, report the waste site and waste activities to the government. The waste generator must then create a manifest to be used in tracking the waste from its creation to its disposal. Along the ''cradle to grave'' path of the waste, all those with responsibility for it must sign the manifest and safely store and transport the waste. Once at a licensed disposal facility, the owner signs for the waste and returns a copy to the generator.

In 1984, Congress strengthened RCRA by extending its provisions to generators of small quantities of hazardous wastes and by banning land disposal of hazardous wastes by approximately 1990 unless: (1) those wastes had been determined by the EPA to be safe for land disposal, or (2) the waste was treated with the best available technology which "substantially diminishes" toxicity or "substantially reduces the likelihood of migration of the hazardous constituents in the waste."[12]

Failure to comply with the hazardous waste provisions may result in civil penalties of up to $25,000 per day and criminal penalties up to $50,000 per day and/or one year in prison. In cases of "knowing endangerment" of human life, individuals may be fined up to $250,000 and/or imprisoned for not more than five years, while businesses may be fined not more than $1 million.

Comprehensive Environmental Response, Compensation, and Liability Act of 1980

According to *The Wall Street Journal:*

U.S. companies each year produce more than 200 pounds of hazardous waste for every man, woman, and child in the country, and the government contends the bulk of that material has been disposed of improperly for decades. When landfills and other facilities are close to underground water supplies or wetlands, the chemical wastes seep out and frequently contaminate wells, irrigation water, and even the soil around some homes and other buildings. It isn't unusual to have cleanup efforts costing tens of millions of dollars, with millions more required for annual maintenance.[13]

The RCRA was essentially prospective in direction and, as such, did not address the problem of cleaning up thousands of existing, abandoned hazardous waste sites. CERCLA, known as the "Superfund," established a $1.6 billion fund to begin the cleanup process. The bulk of the fund is drawn from taxes on chemicals and petroleum. The act empowers the government to order the cleanup of hazardous waste released into the environment. All parties responsible for any illegal hazardous waste discharge are strictly liable (with certain limitations) for all costs associated with the necessary cleanup. However, it is doubtless unrealistic to expect all, or nearly all, of the money to be recovered. Private citizens suffering injury from hazardous wastes do not receive relief under the terms of CERCLA. Rather they must pursue their claims through the judicial system.

It is important to understand that liability for hazardous waste remains with the producer of the waste "to the grave" and beyond. For example, those who generate hazardous waste and dispose of it at a dump site may be liable for damages should waste leak from the dump site. Court decisions imposing this burden upon hazardous waste producers have had the effect of compelling more careful dump site selection as well as more rigorous efforts to reduce hazardous waste production and waste toxicity. The legal complexity of the hazardous waste problem is illustrated by a moment's reflection upon the difficulty of assigning fault for waste leaking from a dump used by many waste generators, depositing materials varying widely in toxicity. How can we determine which "dumper" caused the harm? To what extent is the dump site ownership and management liable? What if one company's waste combines with that of another at the dump site, resulting in the creation of a still more hazardous chemical?[14]

By 1985 the Superfund had resulted in cleaning up only 11 of the 679 sites on the national priority list as well as 435 emergency cleanups (e.g., tank car spills). Congress is expected to pass legislation providing $5–10 billion for cleanups from 1985–1990. The federal Office of Technology Assessment has estimated that as much as $100 billion may be required to clean waste sites over the next 50 years.[15]

The magnitude and complexity of the hazardous waste problem is illustrated by the following article.

WIDESPREAD FEAR OF HAZARDOUS-WASTE SITES THWARTS STATE AND INDUSTRY DISPOSAL PLANS

Ronald Alsop

Perth Amboy, N.J.—This dingy little industrial town endured a chemical fire in 1980 that flared for 110 hours. Its sewers are tainted with toxic polychlorinated biphenyls (PCBs). Now comes a proposal to build a hazardous-waste disposal facility along the waterfront.

Locally and nationally, the timing couldn't be worse. Perth Amboy officials and businessmen have been trying to polish the town's image by attracting condominium and office-building developers. "Nobody will want to buy a $120,000 condominium if there are drums of toxic waste piled up down the block," says Marianthe Patras, a local restaurateur.

* * * * *

Such are the frustrations that companies and state environmental officials face these days as they try to open disposal sites in a country terrified of hazardous waste. Waste-management firms want to build landfills, incinerators and other facilities to dispose of the millions of tons of toxic waste generated each year by industry, as well as old waste that must be removed from leaking, abandoned dumps.

Many existing landfills are expected to close rather than try to meet stringent new government regulations, and chemical-industry officials believe that without new sites, there could be a shortage of disposal space in a few years.

Although the new regulations require higher-quality disposal facilities and closer monitoring of the sites, the waste-management industry is struggling against what it has dubbed "the NIMBY (Not in My Backyard) syndrome."

At a rally in Perth Amboy . . . , speakers warned of carcinogens, birth defects and liver damage. Civic boosters peddled baby-blue-T-shirts that call the town "New Jersey's best-kept secret, not New Jersey's Love Canal." . . .

Hazardous-waste facilities fit the same category as prisons and airports. Nobody wants to live near them, but they are essential to this country's way of life. A 1980 public-opinion survey showed that a majority of people will accept hazardous-waste facilities only if the sites are at least 100 miles away from their homes. And in a study last year for the Chemical Manufacturers Association, half of the "politically active" individuals interviewed said they don't believe it's possible to dispose of hazardous waste safely.

* * * * *

But industry officials believe the public is inviting trouble if it blindly opposes any project involving toxic substances. They claim that refusal to permit well-regulated facilities will result in a capacity crisis that could disrupt manufacturing operations. "We could see plants closing in two to five years because there's nowhere to put the waste they generate," says William Moore, an environmental specialist at Rohm & Haas Co., a chemical manufacturer.

"That certainly is a fear coming closer to reality for us."

The scarcity of landfills already is costing companies. Rohm & Haas plants in Pennsylvania now ship waste to Alabama at a cost of about $75 a drum. But in Texas, where there are several disposal sites to choose from, the cost is only $35 to $40 a drum.

For irresponsible companies, the capacity problem could mean continued illegal dumping and contamination of the environment. "The question the public should ask itself is: Do I want to know where the wastes are going, or do I want to play Russian roulette and have them mysteriously turn up in my backyard in a few years," says Joan Berkowitz, a vice president at Arthur D. Little Inc., the consulting firm.

What troubles most people are the unknown environmental and health risks. "I worry that if they dump anything and everything from our state, Ohio, New Jersey, and who knows where else, there could be a leak and a terrible chemical reaction," says Ted Lingham, a cattle rancher and the mayor of Lowndesboro, Alabama, population 204. He and his constituents, who are battling a proposed landfill in Lowndesboro, support a new state law that calls for legislative approval of commercial hazardous-waste disposal sites in Alabama.

"In my humble opinion, we've pretty much eliminated any more sites in Alabama with that law," says Alfred Chipley, an official in the state environmental-management department. "The only criterion the legislators have is what the electorate says, and I don't know anyone welcoming a dump." For now, Browning-Ferris Industries Inc. says it has postponed its Lowndesboro landfill project.

Even when local residents believe a hazardous-waste facility can be operated safely, many homeowners and businessmen claim they can't afford the stigma. They fear it will weaken property values and drive away customers.

*   *   *   *   *

In Tennessee, legislators have introduced a bill that would reward a town with $500,000 this year and more in future years for accepting a waste-disposal site. Massachusetts offers its municipalities technical-assistance grants to study a project, so that they don't have to settle for the developer's claims about its safety.

Massachusetts also requires developers to provide compensation to the locality. "We started out from the premise that a community would be better off without the site," says Mr. Bacow, the MIT professor and a member of the state's hazardous-waste-site safety council. "But if the compensation is high enough, it may be possible to cut a deal."

Some states believe waste companies should provide money for additional emergency equipment and training of firemen and policemen, as well as compensation for any drop in property values. Other incentives might be a new park or school.

Aware of their image problem, some waste-management companies are trying to ingratiate themselves with the community. Rollins Environmental Services Inc. holds open houses regularly for the people living near its landfills and incinerators, and it encourages its officials to join the Rotary and other civic clubs. "We do everything we can to maintain good relations with the local citizenry," explains Barney Wander, a spokesman for the commercial waste-disposal company. "There's nothing to stop citizens from filing suit against us on nuisance grounds."

QUESTIONS

1. Presumably most of us bear some responsibility for the hazardous waste problem, since our consumption preferences lead to the creation of waste. Since market pref-

erences created the problem, should we let the market resolve it by permitting hazardous waste disposal in the most profitable fashion? Explain.

2. Hazardous waste sites are necessary, but few communities will accept them. Assume government intervention is necessary to manage the hazardous waste problem. Should the federal government pass legislation requiring all states and localities to accept all hazardous waste sites which comply with the federal government's disposal standards? Explain.

The Free Market

The government's significant success in pollution abatement is acknowledged by all, but many economists, businesspeople, members of the Reagan administration, and others believe that government environmental policy should take a decided shift toward free market principles. To them, pollution control is not so much a matter of law as of economics. If the proper incentives are offered, they believe the market will be effective in further improving our ecological health. For example, the Clean Air Act has been conspicuously successful in reducing emissions from large, centralized sources such as power plants. However, the free market proponents argue that complex bureaucratic regulations that govern large sources will, if applied to the many remaining small sources, prove so expensive that we will experience rapidly diminishing returns on the dollars invested in pollution control. Therefore, the EPA has adopted an emissions trading policy founded on market incentives. According to the Council on Environmental Quality:

EPA's emissions trading policy incorporates four innovative regulatory mechanisms, all of which take advantage of market incentives to reduce air emissions at the lowest possible cost. First, EPA's bubble policy allows existing plants, or groups of plants, to be excused from imposing controls on one or more emissions sources in exchange for compensating controls on other, less costly to control, sources. Second, the netting policy excuses plants from new source review requirements usually required when they expand or modernize, if any increase in plantwide emissions is insignificant. Third, under EPA's emissions offset policy new or modified sources in nonattainment areas may be required to secure surplus emissions restrictions which more than offset increased emissions, thus allowing industrial growth while improving air quality. Fourth, the emissions banking policy lets firms store up emissions reductions for later use in bubble, netting, or offset transactions, or for sale to other firms that cannot achieve the same level of reductions as cheaply. All in all, these four innovative approaches mark this nation's first comprehensive attempt to apply free market cost-minimizing principles to pollution control.[16]

Not surprisingly, the business community has found in the EPA trading policy an opportunity both to meet the government's expectations at reduced costs and, in some instances, to make a few dollars.

MARKET BOOMS FOR "RIGHTS" TO POLLUTE

Andy Pasztor

Stuart Rupp of Richmond, California, proudly calls himself a "broker." But he doesn't sell stocks, bonds or futures.

Instead, Mr. Rupp, a partner in an environmental consulting firm, helps companies trade the "right" to spew additional pollutants into the atmosphere.

Such transactions are part of a new approach to reducing air pollution that relies on the marketplace rather than on federal regulations. A company that closes a plant or installs improved pollution-control equipment can receive "emission credits" for its cleanup efforts. These credits, in turn, may be purchased by another firm to offset increased air pollution caused by construction or expansion. The idea is to allow industry to negotiate the price and details of the trade-offs as long as the overall level of air pollution in an area isn't increased.

Hydrocarbons at $50,000

Times Mirror Co. was able to complete the $120 million expansion of a paper-making plant near Portland, Oregon, after purchasing the right to emit about 150 tons of extra hydrocarbons into the air annually. A local dry cleaning firm and the owners of a wood coating plant that had gone out of business sold the necessary credits for about $50,000. Without the credits, Times Mirror couldn't have persuaded state and federal regulators to permit the expansion, says Rod Schmall, manager of environmental and energy services for the subsidiary that runs the plant.

Companies are "just beginning to realize in large numbers that they actually can turn a profit by reducing pollution by a certain amount" and then striking a deal to sell off the resulting credits at handsome prices, says Bob Fuller of First Wisconsin Corp., a Milwaukee bank holding company that started experimenting with pollution credits for its clients three years ago.

The Carter administration promoted the notion first, but President Reagan's environmental advisers have endorsed it, too, as a way to simplify and loosen clean-air regulations. The General Accounting Office estimates that a "viable market in air pollution rights" could cut pollution-control costs at least 40 percent and perhaps as much as 90 percent for many businesses. After nearly two years of study, the GAO concluded that trading credits substantially increases industry flexibility in complying with clean-air laws and encourages the use of innovative technologies. . . .

VW's Approach

When Volkswagen of America built its first car and truck assembly plant in Pennsylvania several years ago, the company needed a lot of credits. It received some from Jones & Laughlin Steel Co., apparently on the promise that the plant would buy some of its steel from the company each year in return. Volkswagen also persuaded the state transportation department to sharply curtail the use of certain road asphalts that give off hydrocarbon fumes when they dry. That estimated reduction in pollution also was credited to VW's account.

* * * * *

Many environmental groups support the offset trading concept but are concerned about how the Environmental Protection Agency intends to monitor and enforce private deals to ensure that air quality is improved in the long run. Jack McKenzie, an environmental official with Pacific Gas & Electric Co., complains that a few environmentalists "appear absolutely paranoid that someone will make money from cleaning up a facility."

ble—Duerksen says everybody recognized that "the plant would be squeaky clean when compared with older styrene facilities in other states." Rather, it was that so long as the local air still fell short of federal standards—even for one day a year—it was illegal under the board's EPA-approved rules to allow any "significant" new pollution sources to be built. And anything that could be measured was "significant," under the air quality board's own interpretation. Dow claimed that the styrene plant's emissions would be undetectable at the plant's boundary line, but the board ruled that this made no difference: within the plant gates, both particulate and organic emissions would be about five times the detectable thresholds. Dow offered to clean up its other local plant so as to prevent overall pollution from rising, but that too was impermissible under the existing law.

Finally, in January 1977, Dow announced that it was abandoning the project. An executive said later: "With no positive results to show after spending two and a half years and $4.5 million to get 4 permits out of 65, I had to cut my losses." The company sharply criticized the agencies and environmentalists for their allegedly obstructionist tactics. Dow had built up a reputation over the years as an environmentally conscious firm, Duerksen says, which made the impact of its public complaints that much greater. At any rate, the reaction in the state was swift. Business and labor leaders reacted with outrage, and the state government

and the environmentalists were put on the defensive. In Washington the Environmental Protection Agency, which had already come under great pressure to allow at least some industrial growth in "noncompliance" areas, soon agreed to let companies build new plants if they found ways of achieving offsetting reductions in existing facilities.

Duerksen believes the Dow dispute holds important lessons, if only because it is bound to be repeated in the future. He opposes weakening environmental standards themselves, but favors "quiet" reforms to streamline the permit process, such as state "industrial escort services" that would help companies find out which permits they need from which agencies at what times. He says states might also offer to help industry avoid picking sensitive sites that are likely to arouse opposition.

He also says industry should pay more attention to its environmental impact in general, and, more specifically, should make its project planning more open to the public, involve environmental specialists at an earlier stage in the process, and vest clear authority in a single project manager. Mediation of environmental disputes, he says, may provide a more promising framework for eventual cooperation than judicial review.

Source: *Regulation*, July/August 1983, pp. 56–58. Reprinted from *Regulation* (July/August 1983) by permission of the American Enterprise Institute.

QUESTIONS

1. Should the federal government adopt the California standard requiring, in general terms, that "projects relocate in less sensitive areas unless there is some good reason not to"? Explain.
2. What does Mr. Duerksen mean by "industrial escort services"?
3. In what sense, if any, does business share the blame for delays such as that in Solano County?
4. Dow Chemical was a major producer of

the herbicide 2,4,5–T, a part of the Agent Orange defoliant used in Vietnam. Dioxin is an unwanted by-product of the manufacture of herbicides. Dioxin was present in the Agent Orange used in Vietnam. Twenty thousand veterans and their families filed suit against Dow and other manufacturers alleging severe injuries from use of the dioxin-contaminated Agent Orange. Their lawsuit alleged that Dow documents reveal the company's knowledge of dioxin

QUESTIONS

1. The emissions trading policy often results in shifting pollution from one site to another without actually reducing the overall level of pollution. Is that policy defensible? Explain.
2. According to the article, how can firms make a profit by reducing pollution?
3. According to a study completed for the

government, the cost of controlling hydrocarbons ranged from $16,550 per ton in an auto painting operation to $41 per ton for a gas terminal in the same area. Explain how emissions trading or sale between those firms might protect the environment while reducing costs.

Effectiveness of the Environmental Protection System

We are committing enormous resources to environmental protection and improvement. Are we receiving our money's worth? Public opinion may or may not constitute an accurate assessment of the value of our environmental policy. However, that opinion most assuredly offers evidence of likely directions in government programs. We have ample polling evidence to confirm the view that the public supports governmental pollution control efforts. A 1981 Harris poll found 42 percent of the public feeling that federal air pollution standards are "not protective enough," 40 percent thought the standards "just about right," and 19 percent thought the government "overly protective of people's health."[17] According to a 1981 Roper poll, 21 percent of the public felt that environmental laws and regulations had "gone too far," but 38 percent thought the government "struck about the right balance," and 31 percent thought the government had gone "not far enough."[18] An unambiguous environmentalist sentiment should not be inferred from these findings. For example, 61 percent of the public favored "increasing drilling for oil and natural gas off the California and Atlantic coasts,"[19] and pollution of air and water ranked only 11th on a list of American's chief concerns.[20] Ranking ahead of pollution were such issues as inflation, crime, unemployment, war, drug abuse, and the way young people think and act. So we can fairly conclude that pollution control, including government intervention, is clearly favored by the public, although it would not be among the very highest priorities.

Unfortunately, we have a somewhat cloudier picture of the actual costs and benefits of pollution control. Conservative economist Murray Weidenbaum notes our great strides in environmental cleanup, but he reminds us that those gains have been achieved at great cost. For example, he cites an Arthur D. Little study anticipating little if any growth through 1985 in U.S. copper smelting capacity because of the lead time required for conversion to environmentally acceptable processes. Plant closings causing the loss of thousands of jobs have also been attributed entirely or partially to environmental requirements.[21]

A 1983 study by economist B. Peter Pashigian concludes that one of the results of environmental regulation is that it is now more difficult for small plants to compete with large ones. Environmental regulation, he demonstrates, has reduced the number of plants in industries with emission problems, and it has raised average plant size. Via a sophisticated statistical analysis he shows that "compliance with environmental regulation was the major reason for the decline in the small plants' market share in high-pollution industries after 1972."[22]

Cost/benefit analyses of pollution control are numerous. Many find the benefits substantially outweighing the costs. For example, Professor Myrick Freeman estimates 1978 air pollution control benefits of between $4.9 and $51.1 billion, with a most likely point of $21.7 billion. Costs for the year were estimated by the Council on Environmental Quality at $16.6 billion. Professor Freeman suggests that air pollution controls have, in the aggregate, been worth the costs, but he goes on to acknowledge that the uncertainty in estimates leaves open the possibility that benefits could be substantially less than costs.[23] Thus, as is so often the case, we are left with a problem that currently defies accurate quantification.

The Business Response

Pollution control is a pressing and difficult problem. The role of the business community in correcting the dilemma has been one of ambivalence. Certainly the business community has invested heavily in corrective measures, both voluntarily and at government insistence, but business has also lobbied extensively for adjustments in governmental expectations (such as relaxed clear air standards and increased off-shore oil and gas drilling). Identifying the correct course for business is largely a matter of philosophy. According to the National Audubon Society, an Environmental Protection Agency-sponsored study concluded that by 1987, pollution controls will generate a net increase of 524,000 American jobs.[24] However, as the article that follows illustrates, excessive and nagging government intervention can, it is argued, lead to economic dislocations desired neither by business nor by environmentalists.

SHOWDOWN IN SOLANO COUNTY

Dow versus California: Turning Point in the Envirobusiness Struggle by Christopher J. Duerksen, as reviewed by the editors of *Regulation*.

In 1977, after two years of struggling with California's regulators, the Dow Chemical Company abandoned plans to build a huge $500 million petrochemical complex near San Francisco. According to Christopher Duerksen, the case marked the end of the "halcyon days" of the environmental movement; never again would its values be accepted uncritically, without scrutiny of their effects on the economy and on employment. Duerksen, a lawyer with the Washington-based Conservation Founda-

tion, directed its four-year project on how environmental laws affect plant siting decisions and how government agencies and companies can improve the way facilities are regulated and built.

Dow unveiled plans for the facility in 1975. It was intended to process the relatively cheap and plentiful Alaskan oil that was then coming into production. By saving the $56 million a year that it had been costing Dow to ship such products as styrene and ethylene from its Texas

plants to the West Coast, Dow hoped to cut costs and thus capture a bigger share of the West Coast market. The plant was to employ 1,000 laborers during construction and 800 permanent workers when it opened in 1982.

There were several compelling reasons for Dow to choose the particular site it did, in a sparsely populated but growing area between San Francisco and Sacramento. The site was one of the last port locations on the West Coast deep enough to handle large oil tankers. It was also near one of Dow's existing facilities, which meant that key personnel were close at hand. The county government, furthermore, avidly supported the plan, hoping to bring in jobs and property tax revenues. . . .

Dow advanced rapidly through the local regulatory process. The state required an environmental impact report separate from and stronger than the federal one, but the local authorities approved it in record time. By then, however, environmentalists, mostly from nearby Berkeley and San Francisco, had begun to organize against the project. The project adjoined a marsh that served as a principal feeding and wintering ground for about a million migratory birds on the Pacific Flyway. There were a number of other serious problems in the eyes of opponents, the author says, "but secondary growth—the new county residents and houses they would require, local government services, and downstream industries—that Dow might induce probably bothered the San Francisco–Berkeley contingent as much as anything." They filed suit, claiming (among other things) that the impact statement had not considered all alternative locations where the environmental damage might be less severe. The California law, unlike the federal one, requires that projects relocate in less sensitive areas unless there is some good reason not to. The suit also contended—correctly in the author's view—that Dow had not sought an amendment to the local land use plan required by state law.

Another concern was farmland preservation. The property was protected by an agricultural land preservation contract with the local government which Dow was seeking to have canceled. The state Department of Agriculture had

no role in g
one of its st.
vation effort
torney gene
other agenci
that had pr
showed sign
gan asking f
running joke
ground gove
mentalists tol
our people w
state people.
and getting [
to Governor
lawyer assign
general's offi
volved in the
informally."

Governor
by scheduling
resolve the re
ject. Dow w.
for sworn test
nor's policy
the public. A
sen: "It was
you imagine.
came when I
ing from the
room." The I
chanting of
Camp. Anoth
as Duerksen
mockingbirds
from Dow's
that the hearir
rated as a sup
proved envir
meant that all
would have to

Dow suffer
back not long
regional air q
forcing local
sions. The bo:
tion for air po
it wanted to b
not that the p

hazards as early as the mid-1960s. According to documents gathered for the lawsuit, Dow's toxicology director wrote in 1965 to another Dow official that dioxin "is exceptionally toxic; it has tremendous potential for producing chloracne [an ugly skin disease] and systemic injury. . . ."[25] The suit was settled out of court with $180 million plus interest to be divided among the plaintiffs over the expected 25-year life of the fund. The chemical companies acknowledged no wrongdoing, and are, in turn, expected to sue the U.S. government, which ordered the chemical produced according to its specifications. Veterans are likewise attempting to sue the government. Still other veterans are not a party to the class action and may be expected to bring separate suits. [It should be understood that definitive proof of a link between Agent Orange and afflictions other than chloracne has not yet been established to the satisfaction of the government or industry.]

a. Must we simply accept hazards such as dioxin as an inevitable by-product of our society's heavy reliance on exotic chemicals? Explain.

b. Or should we erect even firmer civil and criminal law mechanisms for attacking firms that produce contaminants? Explain.

Chapter Questions

1. Why might the cost of environmental compliance affect small plants and large plants differently?

2. Economist B. Peter Pashigian: "It is widely thought that environmental controls are guided by the public-spirited ideal of correcting for 'negative externalities'—the pollution costs that spill over from private operations. This view is not wrong by any means. But it is suspiciously incomplete. After all, there are numerous studies of regulatory programs in other fields that show how private interests have used public powers for their own enrichment."[26] What forces in addition to correcting for negative externalities might be influencing the course of federal pollution control?

3. William Tucker argues that environmentalism is "essentially aristocratic in its roots and derives from the land- and nature-based ethic that has been championed by upper classes throughout history. Large landowners and titled aristocracies . . . have usually held a set of ideals that stresses 'stewardship' and the husbanding of existing resources over exploration and discovery. This view favors handicrafts over mass production and the inheritance ethic over the business ethic."[27]

   Tucker goes on to argue that environmentalism favors the economic and social interests of the well-off. He says people of the upper middle class see their future in universities and the government bureaucracy. They have little economic stake in industrial expansion. Indeed, such expansion might threaten their suburban property values. Comment.

4. Culprits in indoor pollution include cigarette smoke, asbestos, carbon monoxide from heaters, and radon. The problem has been exacerbated in recent years by our success in "tightening" buildings as an energy conservation measure. The EPA is beginning to explore the question of indoor pollution. Assume the EPA finds a problem roughly as threatening to our welfare as that of external air pollution. Should the government intervene? Explain.

5. The Fifth Amendment to the Constitution provides that private property cannot be taken for public use without just compensation. Four oil companies had entered a lease arrangement with the federal government for oil and gas rights in the Santa Barbara Channel, off the California coast. Two productive platforms had been erected, and a third was requested. The request was granted, but before the platform was constructed one of the earlier wells experienced a "blowout," causing enormous ecological damage in the Santa Barbara Channel. The secretary of the interior then suspended all operations in the channel pending congressional cancellation of the leases. The oil companies then brought suit. Does the indefinite suspension of oil drilling rights constitute a "taking" in violation of the Fifth Amendment? See *Union Oil Co.* v. *Morton*, 512 F.2d 743 (1975).

6. From its inception in 1981, the Reagan administration made clear its intention to significantly ease environmental controls. By 1983 little reform had been achieved, and Congress was considering tighter regulation in certain areas. Scandals involving EPA chief Anne Gorsuch and administrator Rita Lavelle diverted the administration's efforts. Consequently, the business community began expressing disillusionment with the Reagan approach:

    The bruising congressional battles and resulting delay have prompted many businesspeople to argue that the administration must be prepared to compromise. Public interest in environmental protection "is alive and well despite the current recession," says S. Bruce Smart, the chairman of Continental Group Inc. Corporate executives, he maintains, are beginning to realize that "business as usual must give way to environmental realities."[28]

    Do you favor President Reagan's firmer position or the more conciliatory approach suggested by Mr. Smart? Explain.

7. It is argued that so-called frost belt states will be particularly insistent upon maintaining strict air quality standards for new emission sources.
    a. Other than general concern for air quality, why would the frost belt states have a particular interest in maintaining those standards?
    b. Might the frost belt states be expected to modify that stand over time? Explain.

8. In reviewing the first year of the Reagan administration's environmental reform efforts, Robert Crandall argues:

    I agree, however, that our best chances for regulatory reform in certain environmental areas, particularly in air pollution policy, come from the states. Probably, responsibility for environmental regulation belongs with the states anyway, and most of it ought to be returned there.[29]

    a. What reasoning supports Mr. Crandall's notion that responsibility for environmental regulation belongs with the states?
    b. How might one reason to the contrary?
    c. Were the power yours would environmental regulation rest primarily at the state or the federal level? Explain.

9. Why do plaintiffs typically experience great difficulty in prevailing in negligence actions alleging injury from toxic substances?

10. The doctrine of strict liability—originally applied to extra hazardous activities and more recently to defective products—may be extended to the area of toxic waste. Jeremy Main recently commented on that possibility in *Fortune* magazine:

    If strict liability were now extended to toxic wastes, then it would do a company no good to plead that it had obeyed the laws and followed approved procedures when it disposed of its wastes. It would still be liable, even if the hazards are seen only in retrospect.[30]

    Should the strict liability doctrine routinely be extended to toxic waste cases? Explain.

11. The Pennsylvania Coal Company owned coal land in the drainage basin of the Meadow

Brook. The company's mining operation released water into the brook, thus polluting it. Mrs. Sanderson owned land near the stream, and she had been securing water from it. However, the mining operation rendered the stream useless for Mrs. Sanderson's purposes. Mrs. Sanderson filed suit against the coal company. In 1886 a final verdict was rendered in the case. Should Mrs. Sanderson prevail? See *Pennsylvania Coal Co.* v. *Sanderson and Wife*, 6 A. 453 (1886).

12. In a realignment of resources, the U.S. Army decided to close the Lexington-Blue Grass Army Depot. The expected loss of over 2,600 jobs caused various parties to file suit in an effort to stop the closing. The plaintiffs contended that the Army and the Department of Defense violated the National Environmental Policy Act by failing to file an environmental impact statement. NEPA requires an EIS in all cases of "major federal actions significantly affecting the quality of the human environment." Decide the case. See *Breckinridge* v. *Rumsfeld*, 537 F.2d 864 (1976), cert. denied 429 U.S. 1061 (1977).

13. A number of groups and individuals filed suit to block Duke Power's planned construction of nuclear power plants in North and South Carolina. The plaintiffs challenged the federal Price-Anderson Act, which provided that damages resulting from nuclear incidents would be limited to $560 million. In the event of damages exceeding $560 million, the act provided that Congress would review the situation and take appropriate action. The district court had ruled that there was a "substantial likelihood" that Duke would not be able to complete the plant except if protected by the act. The district court ruled that the $560 million limit in the act violated the constitutional requirement that neither life nor property may be taken by the government without due process of law. The case was appealed to the U.S. Supreme Court. Decide. Explain. See *Duke Power Co.* v. *Carolina Environmental Study Group, Inc.*, 438 U.S. 59 (1978).

14. Environmental protection has become a "religion," of sorts, to many Americans. (see William Tucker, "Of Mites and Men," *Harpers,* August 1978, p. 43.) Have we devoted too much of our attention and resources to the environmental cause? Explain.

Notes

1. The author owes a debt to Professor James Freeman of the University of Kentucky for his significant contributions to this chapter.

2. "Tentative Accord Reached in Love Canal Toxic Case," *Des Moines (Iowa) Register,* October 11, 1983, p. 11.

3. "U.S. Study Says Acid Rain Injures Northeast's Waters," *Des Moines (Iowa) Register,* June 9, 1983, p. 4A.

4. "Dioxin: How Great a Threat?" *Newsweek,* July 11, 1983, p. 65.

5. "Hot Times for the Old Orb," *Time,* October 31, 1983, p. 84.

6. *Village of Belle Terre* v. *Boraas,* 416 U.S. 1, 10, (1974).

7. 1981 Ohio River Basin Energy Study, as reported in Guy Molinari, "Why We need a Strong Clean Air Act," *Sierra,* May–June 1982, p. 86.

8. *Chevron U.S.A. Inc.* v. *Natural Resources Defense Council, Inc.,* 467 U.S. _____, 81 L. Ed. 2d 694 (1984).

9. "Current Developments," *Environment Reporter,* vol. 16, no. 6, June 7, 1985, p. 235.

10. Ibid.

11. See The Council on Environmental Quality, *Environmental Quality 1982* (Washington, D.C.: U.S. Government Printing Office, 1983), pp. 206–7.

12. "Current Developments," *Environment Reporter,* vol. 16, no. 4, May 24, 1985, pp. 166–67.

13. Andy Pasztor, "Dump-Cleanup Effort Gets Mired in Politics, High Costs, Red Tape," *The Wall Street Journal,* March 11, 1983, p. 1.

14. The remarks in this paragraph are entirely the product of advice from co-author Amy Gershenfeld.

15. "Current Developments," *Environment Reporter,* vol. 16, no. 1, May 3, 1985, p. 7.

16. The Council on Environmental Quality, *Environmental Quality 1982* (Washington, D.C.: U.S. Government Printing Office, 1983), p. 8.

17. Survey by Louis Harris and Associates, May 6–10, 1981, as reported in *Public Opinion,* February/March 1982, p. 32.

18. Survey by the Roper Organization (Roper Report 81-9), 1981, as reported in *Public Opinion,* February/March 1982, p. 32.

19. Survey by CBS News/*New York Times,* September 22–27, 1981, as reported in *Public Opinion,* February/March, 1982, p. 34.

20. Survey by the Roper Organization (Roper Report 82-2, 1982, as reported in *Public Opinion,* February/March, 1982, p. 33.

21. Murray Weidenbaum, *Business, Government, and the Public,* 2d ed. (Englewood Cliffs, N.J.: Prentice-Hall, 1981), pp. 99–100.

22. B. Peter Pashigian, "How Large and Small Plants Fare under Environmental Regulation," *Regulation,* September/October, 1983, pp. 19, 23.

23. A. Myrick Freeman, *Air and Water Pollution Control: A Benefit-Cost Assessment* (New York: John Wiley & Sons, 1982), p. 130.

24. Russ Peterson, "Jobs and the Environment," *Audubon* 85, no. 1, January, 1983, p. 4.

25. "No Longer So Secret an Agent," *Time,* July 18, 1983, p. 17.

26. Pashigian, "Large and Small Plants," p. 19.

27. "Tucker contra Sierra," *Regulation,* March/April, 1983, pp. 48–49.

28. Andy Pasztor, "Reagan Goal of Easing Environmental Laws Is Largely Unattained," *The Wall Street Journal,* February 18, 1983, pp. 1, 16.

29. Robert Crandall, "The Environment," in "Regulation—The First Year," *Regulation,* January/February 1982, pp. 19, 29, 31.

30. Jeremy Main, "The Hazards of Helping Toxic Waste Victims," *Fortune,* October 31, 1983, pp. 158, 166.

A

The Constitution of the United States of America

Preamble

We the People of the United States, in Order to form a more perfect Union, establish Justice, insure domestic Tranquility, provide for the common defence, promote the general Welfare, and secure the Blessings of Liberty to ourselves and our Posterity, do ordain and establish this Constitution for the United States of America.

Article I

Section 1. All legislative Powers herein granted shall be vested in a Congress of the United States, which shall consist of a Senate and House of Representatives.

Section 2. (1) The House of Representatives shall be composed of Members chosen every second Year by the People of the several States, and the Electors in each State shall have the Qualifications requisite for Electors of the most numerous Branch of the State Legislature.

(2) No Person shall be a Representative who shall not have attained to the Age of twenty five Years, and been seven Years a Citizen of the United States, and who shall not, when elected, be an Inhabitant of that State in which he shall be chosen.

(3) Representatives and direct Taxes shall be apportioned among the several States which may be included within this Union, according to their respective Numbers, which shall be determined by adding to the whole Number of free Persons, including those bound to Service for a Term of Years, and excluding Indians not taxed, three fifths of all other Persons.[1] The actual Enumeration shall be made within three Years after the first Meeting of the Congress of the United States, and within every subsequent Term of ten Years, in such Manner as they shall by Law direct. The Number of Representatives shall not exceed one for every thirty Thousand, but each State shall have at Least one Representative; and until such enumeration shall be made, the State of New Hampshire shall be entitled to chuse three, Massachusetts eight, Rhode Island and Providence Plantations one, Connecticut five, New York six, New Jersey four, Pennsylvania eight, Delaware one, Maryland six, Virginia ten, North Carolina five, South Carolina five, and Georgia three.

(4) When vacancies happen in the Representation from any State, the Executive Authority thereof shall issue Writs of Election to fill such Vacancies.

(5) The House of Representation shall chuse their Speaker and other Officers; and shall have the sole Power of Impeachment.

---

[1]Refer to the Fourteenth Amendment.

Section 3. (1) The Senate of the United States shall be composed of two Senators from each State, chosen by the Legislature thereof,[2] for six Years; and each Senator shall have one Vote.

(2) Immediately after they shall be assembled in Consequence of the first Election, they shall be divided as equally as may be into three Classes. The Seats of the Senators of the first Class shall be vacated at the Expiration of the Second Year, of the second Class at the Expiration of the fourth Year, and of the third Class at the Expiration of the sixth Year, so that one third may be chosen every second Year; and if Vacancies happen by Resignation, or otherwise, during the Recess of the Legislature of any State, the Executive thereof may make temporary Appointments until the next Meeting of the Legislature, which shall then fill such Vacancies.[3]

(3) No Person shall be a Senator who shall not have attained to the Age of thirty Years, and been nine Years a Citizen of the United States, and who shall not, when elected, be an Inhabitant of that State for which he shall be chosen.

(4) The Vice President of the United States shall be President of the Senate, but shall have no Vote, unless they be equally divided.

(5) The Senate shall chuse their other Officers, and also a President pro tempore, in the Absence of the Vice President, or when he shall exercise the Office of President of the United States.

(6) The Senate shall have the sole Power to try all Impeachments. When sitting for that Purpose, they shall be on Oath or Affirmation. When the President of the United States is tried, the Chief Justice shall preside: And no Person shall be convicted without the Concurrence of two thirds of the Members present.

(7) Judgment in Cases of Impeachment shall not extend further than to removal from Office, and disqualification to hold and enjoy any Office of honor, Trust, or Profit under the United States: but the Party convicted shall nevertheless be liable and subject to Indictment, Trial, Judgment, and Punishment, according to Law.

Section 4. (1) The Times, Places and Manner of holding Elections for Senators and Representatives, shall be prescribed in each State by the Legislature thereof; but the Congress may at any time by Law make or alter such Regulations, except as to the Places of chusing Senators.

(2) The Congress shall assemble at least once in every Year, and such Meeting shall be on the first Monday in December, unless they shall by Law appoint a different Day.[4]

Section 5. (1) Each House shall be the Judge of the Elections, Returns, and Qualifications of its own Members, and a Majority of each shall constitute a Quorum to do Business; but a smaller Number may adjourn from day to day, and may be authorized to compel the Attendance of absent Members, in such Manner, and under such Penalties as each House may provide.

(2) Each House may determine the Rules of its Proceedings, punish its Members for disorderly Behavior, and, with the Concurrence of two thirds, expel a Member.

(3) Each House shall keep a Journal of its Proceedings, and from time to time publish the same, excepting such Parts as may in their Judgment require Secrecy; and the Yeas and Nays of the Members of either House on any question shall, at the Desire of one fifth of those Present, be entered on the Journal.

(4) Neither House, during the Session of Congress, shall, without the Consent of the other, adjourn for more than three days, nor to any other Place than that in which the two Houses shall be sitting.

Section 6. (1) The Senators and Representatives shall receive a Compensation for their Services, to be ascertained by Law, and paid out of the Treasury of the United States. They shall in all Cases, except Treason, Felony and Breach of the Peace, be privileged from Arrest during their Attendance at the Session of their respective Houses, and in going to and return-

---

[2]Refer to the Seventeenth Amendment.
[3]Ibid.

[4]Refer to the Twentieth Amendment.

ing from the same; and for any Speech or Debate in either House, they shall not be questioned in any other Place.

(2) No Senator or Representative shall, during the Time for which he was elected, be appointed to any civil Office under the Authority of the United States, which shall have been created, or the Emoluments whereof shall have been encreased during such time; and no Person holding any Office under the United States, shall be a Member of either House during his Continuance in Office.

Section 7. (1) All Bills for raising Revenue shall originate in the House of Representatives; but the Senate may propose or concur with Amendments as on other Bills.

(2) Every Bill which shall have passed the House of Representatives and the Senate, shall, before it becomes a Law, be presented to the President of the United States; If he approve he shall sign it, but if not he shall return it, with his Objections to the House in which it shall have originated, who shall enter the Objections at large on their Journal, and proceed to reconsider it. If after such Reconsideration two thirds of that House shall agree to pass the Bill, it shall be sent together with the Objections, to the other House, by which it shall likewise be reconsidered, and if approved by two thirds of that House, it shall become a Law. But in all such Cases the Votes of both Houses shall be determined by yeas and Nays, and the Names of the Persons voting for and against the Bill shall be entered on the Journal of each House respectively. If any Bill shall not be returned by the President within ten Days (Sundays excepted) after it shall have been presented to him, the Same shall be a Law, in like Manner as if he had signed it, unless the Congress by their Adjournment prevent its Return in which Case it shall not be a Law.

(3) Every Order, Resolution, or Vote, to Which the Concurrence of the Senate and House of Representatives may be necessary (except on a question of Adjournment) shall be presented to the President of the United States; and before the Same shall take Effect, shall be approved by him, or being disapproved by him, shall be repassed by two thirds of the Senate and House of Representatives, according to the Rules and Limitations prescribed in the Case of a Bill.

Section 8. (1) The Congress shall have Power To lay and collect Taxes, Duties, Imposts and Excises, to pay the Debts and provide for the common Defence and general Welfare of the United States; but all Duties, Imposts and Excises shall be uniform throughout the United States;

(2) To borrow money on the credit of the United States;

(3) To regulate Commerce with foreign Nations, and among the several States, and with the Indian Tribes;

(4) To establish an uniform Rule of Naturalization, and uniform Laws on the subject of Bankruptcies throughout the United States;

(5) To coin Money, regulate the Value thereof, and of foreign Coin, and fix the Standard of Weights and Measures;

(6) To provide for the Punishment of counterfeiting the Securities and current Coin of the United States;

(7) To Establish Post Offices and Post Roads;

(8) To promote the Progress of Science and useful Arts, by securing for limited Times to Authors and Inventors the exclusive Right to their respective Writings and Discoveries;

(9) To constitute Tribunals inferior to the supreme Court;

(10) To define and punish Piracies and Felonies committed on the high Seas, and Offenses against the Law of Nations:

(11) To declare War, grant Letters of Marque and Reprisal, and make Rules concerning Captures on Land and Water;

(12) To raise and support Armies, but no Appropriation of Money to that Use shall be for a longer Term than two Years;

(13) To provide and maintain a Navy;

(14) To make Rules for the Government and Regulation of the land and naval Forces;

(15) To provide for calling forth the Militia to execute the Laws of the Union, suppress Insurrections and repel Invasions;

(16) To provide for organizing, arming, and disciplining, the Militia, and for governing

such Part of them as may be employed in the Service of the United States, reserving to the States respectively, the Appointment of the Officers, and the Authority of training the Militia according to the discipline prescribed by Congress;

(17) To exercise exclusive Legislation in all Cases whatsoever, over such District (not exceeding ten Miles square) as may, by Cession of particular States, and the Acceptance of Congress, become the Seat of the Government of the United States, and to exercise like Authority over all Places purchased by the Consent of the Legislature of the State in which the Same shall be, for the Election of Forts, Magazines, Arsenals, dock-Yards, and other needful Buildings;—And

(18) To make all Laws which shall be necessary and proper for carrying into Execution for the foregoing Powers, and all other Powers vested by this Constitution in the Government of the United States, or in any Department or Officer thereof.

Section 9. (1) The Migration or Importation of Such Persons as any of the States now existing shall think proper to admit, shall not be prohibited by the Congress prior to the Year one thousand eight hundred and eight, but a Tax or duty may be imposed on such Importation, not exceeding ten dollars for each Person.

(2) The privilege of the Writ of Habeas Corpus shall not be suspended, unless when in Cases of Rebellion or Invasion the public Safety may require it.

(3) No Bill of Attainder or ex post facto Law shall be passed.

(4) No Capitation, or other direct, Tax shall be laid, unless in proportion to the Census or Enumeration herein before directed to be taken.[5]

(5) No Tax or Duty shall be laid on Articles exported from any State.

(6) No Preference shall be given by any Regulation of Commerce or Revenue to the Ports of one State over those of another: nor shall Vessels bound to, or from, one State be obliged to enter, clear, or pay Duties in another.

(7) No money shall be drawn from the Treasury, but in Consequence of Appropriations made by Law; and a regular Statement and Account of the Receipts and Expenditures of all public Money shall be published from time to time.

(8) No Title of Nobility shall be granted by the United States: And no Person holding any Office of Profit or Trust under them, shall, without the Consent of the Congress, accept of any present, Emolument, Office or Title, of any kind whatever, from any King, Prince, or foreign State.

Section 10. (1) No State shall enter into any Treaty, Alliance, or Confederation; grant Letters of Marque and Reprisal; coin Money; emit Bills of Credit; make any Thing but gold and silver Coin a Tender in Payment of Debts; pass any Bill of Attainder, ex post facto Law, or Law impairing the Obligation of Contracts, or grant any Title of Nobility.

(2) No State shall, without the Consent of the Congress, lay any Imposts or Duties on Imports or Exports, except what may be absolutely necessary for executing its inspection Laws: and the net Produce of all Duties and Imposts, laid by any State on Imports or Exports, shall be for the Use of the Treasury of the United States; and all such Laws shall be subject to the Revision and Controul of the Congress.

(3) No State shall, without the Consent of Congress, lay any Duty of Tonnage, keep Troops, or Ships of War in time of Peace, enter into any Agreement or Compact with another State, or with a foreign Power, or engage in War, unless actually invaded, or in such imminent Danger as will not admit of delay.

Article II

Section 1. (1) The executive Power shall be vested in a President of the United States of America. He shall hold his Office during the Term of four Years, and, together with the Vice President, chosen for the same Term, be elected, as follows:

---

[5]Refer to the Sixteenth Amendment.

(2) Each State shall appoint, in such Manner as the Legislature thereof may direct, a Number of Electors, equal to the whole Number of Senators and Representatives to which the State may be entitled in the Congress; but no Senator or Representative, or Person holding an Office of Trust or Profit under the United States, shall be appointed an Elector.

(3) The Electors shall meet in their respective States, and vote by Ballot for two Persons, of whom one at least shall not be an Inhabitant of the same State with themselves. And they shall make a List of all the Persons voted for, and of the Number of Votes for each; which List they shall sign and certify, and transmit sealed to the Seat of the Government of the United States, directed to the President of the Senate. The President of the Senate shall, in the Presence of the Senate and House of Representatives, open all the Certificates, and the Votes shall then be counted. The Person having the greatest Number of Votes shall be the President, if such Number be a Majority of the whole Number of Electors appointed; and if there be more than one who have such Majority, and have an equal Number of Votes, then the House of Representatives shall immediately chuse by Ballot one of them for President; and if no Person have a Majority, then from the five highest on the List the said House shall in like Manner chuse the President. But in chusing the President, the Votes shall be taken by States, the Representation from each State have one Vote; A quorum for this Purpose shall consist of a Member or Members from two thirds of the States, and a Majority of all the States shall be necessary to a Choice. In every Case, after the Choice of the President, the Person having the greater Number of Votes of the Electors shall be the Vice President. But if there should remain two or more who have equal Votes, the Senate shall chuse from them by Ballot the Vice President.[6]

(4) The Congress may determine the Time of chusing the Electors, and the Day on which they shall give their Votes; which Day shall be the same throughout the United States.

(5) No person except a natural born Citizen, or a Citizen of the United States, at the time of the Adoption of this Constitution, shall be eligible to the Office of President; neither shall any Person be eligible to that Office who shall not have attained to the Age of thirty five Years, and been fourteen Years a Resident within the United States.

(6) In case of the removal of the President from Office, or of his Death, Resignation or Inability to discharge the Powers and Duties of the said Office, the Same shall devolve on the Vice President, and the Congress may by Law provide for the Case of Removal, Death, Resignation or Inability, both of the President and Vice President, declaring what Officer shall then act as President, and such Officer shall act accordingly, until the Disability be removed, or a President shall be elected.[7]

(7) The President shall, at stated Times, receive for his Services, a Compensation, which shall neither be encreased nor diminished during the Period for which he shall have been elected, and he shall not receive within that Period any other Emolument from the United States, or any of them.

(8) Before he enter on the Execution of his Office, he shall take the following Oath or Affirmation: "I do solemnly swear (or affirm) that I will faithfully execute the Office of President of the United States, and will to the best of my Ability, preserve, protect and defend the Constitution of the United States."

Section 2. (1) The President shall be Commander in Chief of the Army and Navy of the United States, and of the militia of the several States, when called into the actual Service of the United States; he may require the Opinion, in writing, of the principal Officer in each of the executive Departments, upon any Subject relating to the Duties of their respective Offices, and he shall have Power to grant Reprieves and Pardons for Offenses against the United States, except in Cases of Impeachment.

(2) He shall have Power, by and with the Advice and Consent of the Senate, to make

---

[6]Refer to the Twelfth Amendment.

[7]Refer to the Twenty-fifth Amendment.

Treaties, provided two thirds of the Senators present concur; and he shall nominate, and by and with the Advice and Consent of the Senate, shall appoint Ambassadors, other public Ministers and Consuls, Judges of the supreme Court, and all other Officers of the United States, whose Appointments are not herein otherwise provided for, and which shall be established by Law; but the Congress may by Law vest the Appointment of such inferior Officers, as they think proper, in the President alone, in the Courts of Law, or in the Heads of Departments.

(3) The President shall have Power to fill up all Vacancies that may happen during the Recess of the Senate, by granting Commissions which shall expire at the End of their next Session.

Section 3. He shall from time to time give to the Congress Information of the State of the Union, and recommend to their Consideration such Measures as he shall judge necessary and expedient; he may, on extraordinary Occasions, convene both Houses, or either of them, and in Case of Disagreement between them, with Respect to the Time of Adjournment, he may adjourn them to such Time as he shall think proper; he shall receive Ambassadors and other public Ministers; he shall take Care that the Laws be faithfully executed, and shall Commission all the Officers of the United States.

Section 4. The President, Vice President and all civil Officers of the United States, shall be removed from Office on Impeachment for, and Conviction of, Treason, Bribery, or other high Crimes and Misdemeanors.

Article III

Section 1. The judicial Power of the United States, shall be vested in one supreme Court, and in such inferior Courts as the Congress may from time to time ordain and establish. The Judges, both of the supreme and inferior Courts, shall hold their Offices during good Behaviour, and shall, at stated Times, receive for their Services a Compensation, which shall not be diminished during their Continuance in Office.

Section 2. (1) The judicial Power shall extend to all Cases, in Law and Equity, arising under this Constitution, the Laws of the United States, and Treaties made, or which shall be made, under their Authority;—to all Cases affecting Ambassadors, other public Ministers and Consuls;—to all Cases of admiralty and maritime Jurisdiction,—to Controversies to which the United States shall be a Party;—to Controversies between two or more States;—between a State and Citizens of another State,[8]—between Citizens of different States;—between Citizens of the same State claiming Lands under the Grants of different States, and between a State, or the Citizens thereof, and foreign States, Citizens or Subjects.

(2) In all Cases affecting Ambassadors, other public Ministers and Consuls, and those in which a State shall be a Party, the supreme Court shall have original Jurisdiction. In all the other Cases before mentioned, the supreme Court shall have appellate Jurisdiction, both as to Law and Fact, with such Exceptions, and under such Regulations as the Congress shall make.

(3) The trial of all Crimes, except in Cases of Impeachment, shall be by Jury; and such Trial shall be held in the State where the said Crimes shall have been committed; but when not committed within any State, the Trial shall be at such Place or Places as the Congress may by Law have directed.

Section 3. (1) Treason against the United States, shall consist only in levying War against them, or, in adhering to their enemies, giving them Aid and Comfort. No Person shall be convicted of Treason unless on the Testimony of two Witnesses to the same overt Act, or on Confession in open Court.

(2) The Congress shall have Power to declare the Punishment of Treason, but no Attainder of Treason shall work Corruption of Blood, or Forfeiture except during the Life of the Person attainted.

---

[8]Refer to the Eleventh Amendment.

Article IV

Section 1. Full Faith and Credit shall be given in each State to the public Acts, Records, and judicial Proceedings of every other State. And the Congress may by general Laws prescribe the Manner in which such Acts, Records and Proceedings shall be proved, and the Effect thereof.

Section 2. (1) The Citizens of each State shall be entitled to all Privileges and Immunities of Citizens in the several States.

(2) A Person charged in any State with Treason, Felony, or other Crime, who shall flee from Justice, and be found in another State, shall on demand of the executive Authority of the State from which he fled, be delivered up, to be removed to the State having Jurisdiction of the Crime.

(3) No Person held to Service or Labour in one State, under the Laws thereof, escaping into another, shall, in Consequence of any Law or Regulation therein, be discharged from such Service or Labour, but shall be delivered up on Claim of the Party to whom such Service or Labour may be due.[9]

Section 3. (1) New States may be admitted by the Congress into this Union; but no new State shall be formed or erected within the Jurisdiction of any other State; nor any State be formed by the Junction of two or more States, or Parts of States, without the Consent of the Legislatures of the States concerned as well as of the Congress.

(2) The Congress shall have Power to dispose of and make all needful Rules and Regulations respecting the Territory or other Property belonging to the United States; and nothing in this Constitution shall be so construed as to Prejudice any Claims of the United States, or of any particular State.

Section 4. The United States shall guarantee to every State in this Union a Republican Form of Government, and shall protect each of them against Invasion; and on Application of the Legislature, or of the Executive (when the Legislature cannot be convened) against domestic Violence.

Article V

The Congress, whenever two thirds of both Houses shall deem it necessary, shall propose Amendments to this Constitution, or, on the Application of the Legislatures of two thirds of the several States, shall call a Convention for proposing Amendments, which, in either Case, shall be valid to all Intents and Purposes, as part of this Constitution, when ratified by the Legislatures of three fourths of the several States, or by Conventions in three fourths thereof, as the one or the other Mode of Ratification may be proposed by the Congress; Provided that no Amendment which may be made prior to the Year One thousand eight hundred and eight shall in any Manner affect the first and fourth Clauses in the Ninth Section of the first Article; and that no State, without its Consent, shall be deprived of its equal Suffrage in the Senate.

Article VI

(1) All Debts contracted and Engagements entered into, before the Adoption of this Constitution shall be as valid against the United States under this Constitution, as under the Confederation.

(2) This Constitution, and the Laws of the United States which shall be made in Pursuance thereof; and all Treaties made, or which shall be made, under the Authority of the United States, shall be the supreme Law of the Land; and the Judges in every State shall be bound thereby, any Thing in the Constitution or Laws of any State to the Contrary notwithstanding.

(3) The Senators and Representatives before mentioned, and the Members of the several State Legislatures, and all executive and judicial Officers, both of the United States and of the several States, shall be bound by Oath or Affirmation, to support this Constitution; but no religious Test shall ever be required as a Qualification to any Office or public Trust under the United States.

[9]Refer to the Thirteenth Amendment.

Article VII

The Ratification of the Conventions of nine States shall be sufficient for the Establishment of this Constitution between the States so ratifying the Same.

[Amendments 1–10, the Bill of Rights, were ratified in 1791.]

Amendment I

Congress shall make no law respecting an establishment of religion, or prohibiting the free exercise thereof; or abridging the freedom of speech, or of the press; or the right of the people peaceably to assemble, and to petition the Government for a redress of grievances.

Amendment II

A well regulated Militia, being necessary to the security of a free State, the right of the people to keep and bear Arms, shall not be infringed.

Amendment III

No Soldier shall, in time of peace be quartered in any house, without the consent of the Owner, nor in time of war, but in a manner to be prescribed by law.

Amendment IV

The right of the people to be secure in their persons, houses, papers, and effects, against unreasonable searches and seizures, shall not be violated, and no Warrants shall issue, but upon probable cause, supported by Oath or affirmation, and particularly describing the place to be searched, and the persons or things to be seized.

Amendment V

No person shall be held to answer for a capital, or otherwise infamous crime, unless on a presentment or indictment of a Grand Jury, except in cases arising in the land or naval forces, or in the Militia, when in actual service in time of War or public danger; nor shall any person be subject for the same offence to be twice put in jeopardy of life or limb; nor shall be compelled in any criminal case to be a witness against himself, nor be deprived of life, liberty, or property, without due process of law; nor shall private property be taken for public use, without just compensation.

Amendment VI

In all criminal prosecutions, the accused shall enjoy the right to a speedy and public trial, by an impartial jury of the State and district wherein the crime shall have been committed, which district shall have been previously ascertained by law, and to be informed of the nature and cause of the accusation; to be confronted with the witnesses against him; to have compulsory process for obtaining witnesses in his favor, and to have the Assistance of Counsel for his defence.

Amendment VII

In Suits at common law, where the value in controversy shall exceed twenty dollars, the right of trial by jury shall be preserved, and no fact tried by jury, shall be otherwise re-examined in any Court of the United States, than according to the rules of the common law.

Amendment VIII

Excessive bail shall not be required, nor excessive fines imposed, nor cruel and unusual punishments inflicted.

Amendment IX

The enumeration in the Constitution, of certain rights, shall not be construed to deny or disparage others retained by the people.

Amendment X

The powers not delegated to the United States by the Constitution, nor prohibited by it to the States, are reserved to the States respectively, or to the people.

Amendment XI (1798)

The Judicial power of the United States shall not be construed to extend to any suit in law or equity, commenced or prosecuted against one of the United States by Citizens of another State, or by Citizens or Subjects of any Foreign State.

Amendment XII (1804)

The Electors shall meet in their respective states and vote by ballot for President and Vice-President, one of whom, at least, shall not be an inhabitant of the same state with themselves; they shall name in their ballots the person voted for as President, and in distinct ballots the person voted for as Vice-President, and they shall make distinct lists of all persons voted for as President, and of all persons voted for as Vice-President, and of the number of votes for each, which lists they shall sign and certify, and transmit sealed to the seat of the government of the United States, directed to the President of the Senate;—The President of the Senate shall, in the presence of the Senate and House of Representatives, open all the certificates and the votes shall then be counted;—The person having the greatest number of votes for President, shall be the President, if such number be a majority of the whole number of Electors appointed; and if no person have such majority, then from the persons having the highest numbers not exceeding three on the list of those voted for as President, the House of Representatives shall choose immediately, by ballot, the President. But in choosing the President, the votes shall be taken by states, the representation from each state having one vote; a quorum for this purpose shall consist of a member or members from two-thirds of the states, and a majority of all the states shall be necessary to a choice. And if the House of Representatives shall not choose a President whenever the right of choice shall devolve upon them before the fourth day of March next following, then the Vice-President shall act as President, as in the case of the death or other constitutional disability of the President.[10]—The person having the greatest number of votes as Vice-President, shall be the Vice-President,

if such number be a majority of the whole number of Electors appointed, and if no person have a majority, then from the two highest numbers on the list, the Senate shall choose the Vice-President; a quorum for the purpose shall consist of two-thirds of the whole number of Senators, and a majority of the whole number shall be necessary to a choice. But no person constitutionally ineligible to the office of President shall be eligible to that of Vice-President of the United States.

Amendment XIII (1865)

Section 1. Neither slavery nor involuntary servitude, except as a punishment for crime whereof the party shall have been duly convicted, shall exist within the United States, or any place subject to their jurisdiction.

Section 2. Congress shall have power to enfore this article by appropriate legislation.

Amendment XIV (1868)

Section 1. All persons born or naturalized in the United States, and subject to the jurisdiction thereof, are citizens of the United States and of the State wherein they reside. No State shall make or enforce any law which shall abridge the privileges or immunities of citizens of the United States; nor shall any State deprive any person of life, liberty, or property, without due process of law; nor deny to any person within its jurisdiction the equal protection of the laws.

Section 2. Representatives shall be apportioned among the several States according to their respective numbers, counting the whole number of persons in each State, excluding Indians not taxed. But when the right to vote at any election for the choice of electors for President and Vice President of the United States, Representatives in Congress, the Executive and Judicial officers of a State, or the members of the Legislature thereof, is denied to any of the male inhabitants of such State, being twenty-one years of age,[11] and citizens of the United States, or in any way abridged, except for par-

---

[10]Refer to the Twentieth Amendment.

[11]Refer to the Twenty-sixth Amendment.

ticipation in rebellion, or other crime, the basis of representation therein shall be reduced in the proportion which the number of such male citizens shall bear to the whole number of male citizens twenty-one years of age in such State.

Section 3. No person shall be a Senator or Representative in Congress, or elector of President and Vice President, or hold any office, civil or military, under the United States, or under any State, who having previously taken an oath, as a member of Congress, or as an officer of the United States, or as a member of any State legislature, or as an executive or judicial officer of any State, to support the Constitution of the United States, shall have engaged in insurrection or rebellion against the same, or given aid or comfort to the enemies thereof. But Congress may by a vote of two thirds of each House, remove such disability.

Section 4. The validity of the public debt of the United States, authorized by law, including debts incurred for payment of pensions and bounties for services in suppressing insurrection or rebellion, shall not be questioned. But neither the United States nor any State shall assume or pay any debt or obligation incurred in aid of insurrection or rebellion against the United States, or any claim for the loss or emancipation of any slave; but all such debts, obligations and claims shall be held illegal and void.

Section 5. The Congress shall have power to enforce, by appropriate legislation, the provisions of this article.

Amendment XV (1870)

Section 1. The right of citizens of the United States to vote shall not be denied or abridged by the United States or by any State on account of race, color, or previous condition of servitude.

Section 2. The Congress shall have power to enforce this article by appropriate legislation.

Amendment XVI (1913)

The Congress shall have power to lay and collect taxes on incomes, from whatever source

derived, without apportionment among the several States, and without regard to any census or enumeration.

Amendment XVII (1913)

(1) The Senate of the United States shall be composed of two Senators from each State, elected by the people thereof, for six years; and each Senator shall have one vote. The electors in each State shall have the qualifications requisite for electors of the most numerous branch of the State legislatures.

(2) When vacancies happen in the representation of any State in the Senate, the executive authority of such State shall issue writs of election to fill such vacancies: *Provided,* That the legislature of any State may empower the executive thereof to make temporary appointments until the people fill the vacancies by election as the legislature may direct.

(3) This amendment shall not be so construed as to affect the election or term of any Senator chosen before it becomes valid as part of the Constitution.

Amendment XVIII [1919]

Section 1. After one year from the ratification of this article the manufacture, sale, or transportation of intoxicating liquors within, the importation thereof into, or the exportation thereof from the United States and all territory subject to the jurisdiction thereof for beverage purposes is hereby prohibited.

Section 2. The Congress and the several States shall have concurrent power to enforce this article by appropriate legislation.

Section 3. This article shall be inoperative unless it shall have been ratified as an amendment to the Constitution by the legislatures of the several States, as provided in the Constitution, within seven years from the date of the submission hereof to the States by the Congress.[12]

Amendment XIX [1920]

(1) The right of citizens of the United States to vote shall not be denied or abridged by the

---

[12]Refer to the Twenty-first Amendment.

United States or by any State on account of sex.

(2) Congress shall have power to enforce this article by appropriate legislation.

Amendment XX [1933]

Section 1. The terms of the President and Vice President shall end at noon on the 20th day of January, and the terms of Senators and Representatives at noon on the 3d day of January, of the years in which such terms would have ended if this article had not been ratified; and the terms of their successors shall then begin.

Section 2. The Congress shall assemble at least once in every year, and such meeting shall begin at noon on the 3d day of January, unless they shall by law appoint a different day.

Section 3. If, at the time fixed for the beginning of the term of the President, the President elect shall have died, the Vice President elect shall become President. If the President shall not have been chosen before the time fixed for the beginning of his term or if the President elect shall have failed to qualify, then the Vice President elect shall act as President until a President shall have qualified; and the Congress may by law provide for the case wherein neither a President elect nor a Vice President elect shall have qualified, declaring who shall then act as President, or the manner in which one is to act shall be selected, and such person shall act accordingly until a President or Vice President shall have qualified.

Section 4. The Congress may by law provide for the case of the death of any of the persons from whom the House of Representatives may choose a President whenever the right of choice shall have devolved upon them, and for the case of the death of any of the persons from whom the Senate may choose a Vice President whenever the right of choice shall have devolved upon them.

Section 5. Sections 1 and 2 shall take effect on the 15th day of October following the ratification of this article.

Section 6. This article shall be inoperative unless it shall have been ratified as an amendment to the Constitution by the legislatures of three-fourths of the several States within seven years from the date of its submission.

Amendment XXI [1933]

Section 1. The eighteenth article of amendment to the Constitution of the United States is hereby repealed.

Section 2. The transportation or importation into any State, Territory, or possession of the United States for delivery or use therein of intoxicating liquors, in violation of the laws thereof, is hereby prohibited.

Section 3. This article shall be inoperative unless it shall have been ratified as an amendment to the Constitution by conventions in the several States, as provided in the Constitution, within seven years from the date of the submission hereof to the States by the Congress.

Amendment XXII [1951]

Section 1. No person shall be elected to the office of the President more than twice, and no person who has held the office of President, or acted as President, for more than two years of a term to which some other person was elected President shall be elected to the office of President more than once. But this Article shall not apply to any person holding the office of President when this Article was proposed by the Congress, and shall not prevent any person who may be holding the office of President, or acting as President, during the term within which this Article becomes operative from holding the office of President or acting as president during the remainder of such term.

Section 2. This article shall be inoperative unless it shall have been ratified as an amendment to the Constitution by the legislatures of three-fourths of the several States within seven years from the date of its submission to the States by the Congress.

Amendment XXIII [1961]

Section 1. The District constituting the seat of Government of the United Staes shall appoint in such manner as the Congress may direct:

A number of electors of President and Vice President equal to the whole number of Senators and Representatives in Congress to which the District would be entitled if it were a State, but in no event more than the least populous state; they shall be in addition to those appointed by the states, but they shall be considered, for the purposes of the election of President and Vice President, to be electors appointed by a state; and they shall meet in the District and perform such duties as provided by the twelfth article of amendment.

Section 2. The Congress shall have power to enforce this article by appropriate legislation.

Amendment XXIV [1964]

Section 1. The right of citizens of the United States to vote in any primary or other election for President or Vice President, for electors for President or Vice President, or for Senator or Representative in Congress, shall not be denied or abridged by the United States or any State by reason of failure to pay any poll tax or other tax.

Section 2. The Congress shall have power to enforce this article by appropriate legislation.

Amendment XXV [1967]

Section 1. In case of the removal of the President from office or of his death or resignation, the Vice President shall become President.

Section 2. Whenever there is a vacancy in the office of the Vice President, the President shall nominate a Vice President who shall take office upon confirmation by a majority vote of both Houses of Congress.

Section 3. Whenever the President transmits to the President pro tempore of the Senate and the Speaker of the House of Representatives his written declaration that he is unable to discharge the powers and duties of his office, and until he transmits to them a written declaration to the contrary, such powers and duties shall be discharged by the Vice President as Acting President.

Section 4. Whenever the Vice President and a majority of either the principal officers of the exeuctive departments or of such other body as Congress may by law provide, transmit to the President pro tempore of the Senate and the Speaker of the House of Representatives their written declaration that the President is unable to discharge the powers and duties of his office, the Vice President shall immediately assume the powers and duties of the office as Acting President.

Thereafter, when the President transmits to the President pro tempore of the Senate and the Speaker of the House of Representatives his written declaration that no inability exists, he shall resume the powers and duties of his office unless the Vice President and a majority of either the principal officers of the executive departments or of such other body as Congress may by law provide, transmit within four days to the President pro tempore of the Senate and the Speaker of the House of Representatives their written declaration that the President is unable to discharge the powers and duties of his office. Thereupon Congress shall decide the issue, assembling within forty-eight hours for that purpose if not in session. If the Congress, within twenty-one days after receipt of the latter written declaration, or, if Congress is not in session, within twenty-one days after Congress is required to assemble, determines by two-thirds vote of both Houses that the President is unable to discharge the powers and duties of his office, the Vice President shall continue to discharge the same as Acting President; otherwise, the President shall resume the powers and duties of his office.

Amendment XXVI [1971]

Section 1. The right of citizens of the United States, who are eighteen years of age or older, to vote shall not be denied or abridged by the United States or by any State on account of age.

Section 2. The Congress shall have power to enforce this article by appropriate legislation.

B

The Securities Act of 1933 (excerpts)

Definitions

Section 2. When used in this title, unless the context otherwise requires—(1) The term "security" means any note, stock, treasury stock, bond, debenture, evidence of indebtedness, certificate of interest or participation in any profit-sharing agreement, collateral-trust certificate, preorganization certificate or subscription, transferable share, investment contract, voting-trust certificate, certificate of deposit for a security, fractional undivided interest in oil, gas, or other mineral rights, any put, call, straddle, option, or privilege on any security, certificate of deposit, or group or index of securities (including any interest therein or based on the value thereof), or any put, call, straddle, option, or privilege entered into on a national securities exchange relating to foreign currency, or, in general, any interest or instrument commonly known as a "security," or any certificate of interest or participation in, temporary or interim certificate for, receipt for, quarantee of, or warrant or right to subscribe to or purchase, any of the foregoing.

Exempted Securities

Section 3. (a) Except as hereinafter expressly provided the provisions of this title shall not apply to any of the following classes of securities:

* * * * *

(2) Any security issued or guaranteed by the United States or any territory thereof, or by the District of Columbia, or by any State of the United States, or by any political subdivision of a State or Territory, or by any public instrumentality of one or more States or Territories, or by any person controlled or supervised by and acting as an instrumentality of the Government of the United States pursuant to authority granted by the Congress of the United States; or any certificate of deposit for any of the foregoing; or any security issued or guaranteed by any bank; or any security issued by or representing an interest in or a direct obligation of a Federal Reserve bank. . . .

(3) Any note, draft, bill of exchange, or banker's acceptance which arises out of a current transaction or the proceeds of which have been or are to be used for current transactions, and which has a maturity at the time of issuance of not exceeding nine months, exclusive of days of grace, or any renewal thereof the maturity of which is likewise limited;

(4) Any security issued by a person orga-

nized and operated exclusively for religious, educational, benevolent, fraternal, charitable, or reformatory purposes and not for pecuniary profit, and no part of the net earnings of which inures to the benefit of any person, private stockholder, or individual;

* * * * *

(11) Any security which is a part of an issue offered and sold only to persons resident within a single State or Territory, where the issuer of such security is a person resident and doing business within, or, if a corporation, incorporated by and doing business within, such State or Territory.

(b) The Commission may from time to time by its rules and regulations and subject to such terms and conditions as may be described therein, add any class of securities to the securities exempted as provided in this section, if it finds that the enforcement of this title with respect to such securities is not necessary in the public interest and for the protection of investors by reason of the small amount involved or the limited character of the public offering; but no issue of securities shall be exempted under this subsection where the aggregate amount at which such issue is offered to the public exceeds $5,000,000.

Exempted Transactions

Section 4. The provisions of section 5 shall not apply to—

(1) transactions by any person other than an issue, underwriter, or dealer.

(2) transactions by an issuer not involving any public offering.

* * * * *

(4) brokers' transactions executed upon customers' orders on any exchange or in the over-the-counter market but not the solicitation of such orders.

Prohibitions Relating to Interstate Commerce and the Mails

Section 5. (a) Unless a registration statement is in effect as to a security, it shall be unlawful for any person, directly or indirectly—

(1) to make use of any means or instruments of transportation or communications in interstate commerce or of the mails to sell such security through the use or medium of any prospectus or otherwise; or

(2) to carry or cause to be carried through the mails or in interstate commerce, by any means of instruments of transportation, any such security for the purpose of sale or for delivery after sale.

(b) It shall be unlawful for any person, directly or indirectly—

(1) to make use of any means or instruments of transportation or communication in interstate commerce or of the mails to carry or transmit any prospectus relating to any security with respect to which a registration statement has been filed under this title, unless such prospectus meets the requirements of section 10; or

(2) to carry or cause to be carried through the mails or in interstate commerce any such security for the purpose of sale or for delivery after sale, unless accompanied or preceded by a prospectus that meets the requirements of subsection (a) of section 10.

(c) It shall be unlawful for any person, directly or indirectly to make use of any means or instruments of transportation or communication in interstate commerce or the mails to offer to sell or offer to buy through the use or medium of any prospectus or otherwise any security, unless a registration statement has been filed as to such security, or while the registration statement is the subject of the refusal order or stop order. . . .

Registration of Securities and Signing of Registration Statement

Section 6. (a) Any security may be registered with the Commission under the terms and conditions hereinafter provided, by filing a registration statement in triplicate, at least one of which shall be signed by each issuer, its principal executive officer or officers, its principal financial officer, its comptroller or principal accounting officer, and the majority of its board of directors or persons performing similar functions. . . .

* * * * *

C

The Securities Exchange Act of 1934 (excerpts)

Definitions

Section 3. (a) When used in this title, unless the context requires—

* * * * *

(4) The term ''broker'' means any person engaged in the business of effecting transactions in securities for the account of others, but does not include a bank.

(5) The term ''dealer'' means any person engaged in the business of buying and selling securities for his own account, through a broker or otherwise, but does not include a bank, or any person insofar as he buys or sells securities for his own account, either individually or in some fiduciary capacity, but not as part of a regular business.

* * * * *

(7) The term ''director'' means any director of a corporation or any person performing similar functions with respect to any organization, whether incorporated or unincorporated.

(8) The term ''issuer'' means any person who issues or proposes to issue any security; except that with respect to certificates of deposit for securities, voting-trust certificates, or collateral-trust certificates, or with respect to certificates of interest or shares in an unincor-porated investment trust not having a board of directors of the fixed, restricted management, or unit type, the term ''issuer'' means the person or persons performing the acts and assuming the duties of depositor or manager pursuant to the provisions of the trust or other agreement or instrument under which such securities are issued; and except that with respect to equipment-trust certificates or like securities, the term ''issuer'' means the person by whom the equipment or property is, or is to be, used.

(9) The term ''person'' means a natural person, company, government, or political subdivision, agency, or instrumentality of a government.

Securities and Exchange Commission

Section 4. (a) There is hereby established a Securities and Exchange Commission (hereinafter referred to as the ''Commission'') to be composed of five commissioners to be appointed by the President by and with the advice and consent of the Senate. Not more than three of such commissioners shall be members of the same political party, and in making appointments members of different political parties shall be appointed alternately as nearly as may be practicable.

Transactions on Unregistered Exchanges

Section 5. It shall be unlawful for any broker, dealer, or exchange, directly or indirectly, to make use of the mails or any means or instrumentality of interstate commerce for the purpose of using any facility of an exchange within or subject to the jurisdiction of the United States to effect any transaction in a security, or to report any such transaction, unless such exchange (1) is registered as a national securities exchange under . . . this title, or (2) is exempted from such registration upon application by the exchange because, in the opinion of the Commission, by reason of the limited volume of transactions effected on such exchange, it is not practicable and not necessary or appropriate in the public interest or for the protection of investors to require such registration.

Regulation of the Use of Manipulative and Deceptive Devices

Section 10. It shall be unlawful for any person, directly or indirectly, by the use of any means or instrumentality of interstate commerce or of the mails, or of any facility of any national securities exchange—

(a) To effect a short sale, or to use or employ any stop-loss order in connection with the purchase or sale, of any security registered on a national securities exchange, in contravention of such rules and regulations as the Commission may prescribe as necessary or appropriate in the public interest or for the protection of investors.

(b) To use or employ, in connection with the purchase or sale of any security registered on a national securities exchange or any security not so registered, any manipulative or deceptive device or contrivance in contravention of such rules and regulations as the Commission may prescribe as necessary or appropriate in the public interest or for the protection of investors.

Registration Requirements for Securities

Section 12. (a) It shall be unlawful for any member, broker, or dealer to effect any transaction in any security (other than an exempted security) on a national securities exchange unless a registration is effective as to such security for such exchange in accordance with the provisions of this title and the rules and regulations thereunder.

D

The National Labor Relations Act (excerpts)

Rights of Employees

Section 7. Employees shall have the right to self-organization, to form, join, or assist labor organizations, to bargain collectively through representatives of their own choosing, and to engage in other concerted activities for the purpose of collective bargaining or other mutual aid or protection, and shall also have the right to refrain from any or all of such activities except to the extent that such right may be affected by an agreement requiring membership in a labor organization as a condition of employment as authorized in section 8(a)(3).

Unfair Labor Practices

Section 8. (a) It shall be an unfair labor practice for an employer—

(1) to interfere with, restrain, or coerce employees in the exercise of the rights guaranteed in section 7;

(2) to dominate or interfere with the formation or administration of any labor organization or contribute financial or other support to it: *Provided,* That subject to rules and regulations made and published by the Board pursuant to section 6, an employer shall not be prohibited from permitting employees to confer with him during working hours without loss of time or pay;

(3) by discrimination in regard to hire or tenure of employment or any term or condition of employment to encourage or discourage membership in any labor organization: *Provided,* That nothing in this Act, or in any other statute of the United States, shall preclude an employer from making an agreement with a labor organization (not established, maintained, or assisted by any action defined in section 8(a) of this Act as an unfair labor practice) to require as a condition of employment membership therein on or after the thirtieth day following the beginning of such employment or the effective date of such agreement, whichever is the later, (i) if such labor organization is the representative of the employees as provided in section 9(a), in the appropriate collective-bargaining unit covered by such agreement when made, and (ii) unless following an election held as provided in section 9(e) within one year preceding the effective date of such agreement, the Board shall have certified that at least a majority of the employees eligible to vote in such election have voted to rescind the authority of such labor organization to make such an agreement: *Provided further,* That no employer shall justify any discrimination against an employee for nonmembership in a labor organization (A) if he has resonable grounds for believing that such membership was not available to the em-

ployee on the same terms and conditions generally applicable to other members, or (B) if he had reasonable grounds for believing that membership was denied or terminated for reasons other than the failure of the employee to tender the periodic dues and the initiation fees uniformly required as a condition of acquiring or retaining membership;

(4) to discharge or otherwise discriminate against an employee because he has filed charges or given testimony under this Act;

(5) to refuse to bargain collectively with the representatives of his employees, subject to the provisions of section 9(a).

(b) It shall be an unfair labor practice for a labor organization or its agents—

(1) to restrain or coerce (A) employees in the exercise of the rights guaranteed in section 7: *Provided,* That this paragraph shall not impair the right of a labor organization to prescribe its own rules with respect to the acquisition or retention of membership therein; or (B) an employer in the selection of his representatives for the purposes of collective bargaining or the adjustment of grievances;

(2) to cause or attempt to cause an employer to discriminate against an employee in violation of subsection (a)(3) or to discriminate against an employee with respect to whom membership in such organization has been denied or terminated on some ground other than his failure to tender the periodic dues and the initiation fees uniformly required as a condition of acquiring or retaining membership;

(3) to refuse to bargain collectively with an employer, provided it is the representative of his employees subject to the provisions of section 9(a);

(4) (i) to engage in, or to induce or encourage any individual employed by any person engaged in commerce or in an industry affecting commerce to engage in, a strike or a refusal in the course of his employment to use, manufacture, process, transport, or otherwise handle or work on any goods, articles, materials, or commodities or to perform any services; or (ii) to threaten, coerce, or restrain any person engaged in commerce or in an industry affecting

commerce, where in either case an object thereof is—

(A) forcing or requiring any employer or self-employed person to join any labor or employer organization or to enter into any agreement which is prohibited by section 8(e);

(B) forcing or requiring any person to cease using, selling, handling, transporting, or otherwise dealing in the products of any other producer, processor, or manufacturer, or to cease doing business with any other person, or forcing or requiring any other employer to recognize or bargain with a labor organization as the representative of his employees unless such labor organization has been certified as the representative of such employees under the provisions of section 9: *Provided,* That nothing contained in this clause (B) shall be construed to make unlawful, where not otherwise unlawful, any primary strike or primary picketing;

(C) forcing or requiring any employer to recognize or bargain with a particular labor organization as the representative of his employees if another labor organization has been certified as the representative of such employees under the provisions of section 9;

(D) forcing or requiring any employer to assign particular work to employees in a particular labor organization or in a particular trade, craft, or class rather than to employees in another labor organization or in another trade, craft, or class, unless such employer is failing to conform to an order or certification of the Board determining the bargaining representative for employees performing such work:

Provided, That nothing contained in this subsection (b) shall be construed to make unlawful a refusal by any person to enter upon the premises of any employer (other than his own employer), if the employees of such employer are engaged in a strike ratified or approved by a representative of such employees whom such employer is required to recognize under this Act: *Provided further,* That for the purposes of this paragraph (4) only, nothing contained in such paragraph shall be construed to prohibit publicity, other than picketing, for the purpose of truthfully advising the public, including consumers and members of a labor organization, that a product or products are produced by an employer with whom the labor organization has a primary dispute and are distributed by another employer, as long as such publicity does not have an effect of inducing any individual employed by any person other than the primary employer in the course of his employment to refuse to pick up, deliver, or transport any goods, or not to perform any services, at the establishment of the employer engaged in such distribution:

(5) to require of employees covered by an agreement authorized under subsection (a)(3) the payment, as a condition precedent to becoming a member of such organization, of a fee in an amount which the Board finds excessive or discriminatory under all the circumstances. In making such a finding, the Board shall consider, among other relevant factors, the practices and customs of labor organizations in the particular industry, and the wages currently paid to the employees affected;

(6) to cause or attempt to cause an employer to pay or deliver or agree to pay or deliver any money or other thing of value, in the nature of an exaction, for services which are not performed or not to be performed; and

(7) To picket or cause to be picketed, or threatened to picket or cause to be picketed, any employer where an object thereof is forcing or requiring an employer to recognize or bargain with a labor organization as the representative of his employees, or forcing or requiring the employees of an employer to accept or select such labor organization as their collective bargaining representative, unless such labor organization is currently certified as the representative of such employees:

(A) where the employer has lawfully recognized in accordance with this Act any other labor organization and a question concerning representation may not appropriately be raised under section 9(c) of this Act

(B) where within the preceding twelve months a valid election under section 9(c) of this Act has been conducted, or

(C) where such picketing has been conducted without a petition under section 9(c) being filed within a reasonable period of time not to exceed thirty days from the commencement of such picketing; *Provided,* That when such a petition has been filed the Board shall forthwith, without regard to the provisions of section 9(c)(1) or the absence of a showing of a substantial interest on the part of the labor organization, direct an election in such unit as the Board finds to be appropriate and shall certify the results thereof: *Provided further,* That nothing in this subparagraph (C) shall be construed to prohibit any picketing or other publicity for the purpose of truthfully advising the public (including consumers) that an employer does not employ members of, or have a contract with, a labor organization, unless an effect of such picketing is to induce any individual employed by any other person in the course of his employment, not to pick up, deliver or transport any goods or not to perform any services.

Nothing in this paragraph (7) shall be construed to permit any act which would otherwise be an unfair labor practice under this section 8(b).

(c) The expressing of any views, argument, or opinion, or the dissemination thereof, whether in written, printed, graphic, or visual form, shall not constitute or be evidence of an unfair labor practice under any of the provisions of this Act, if such expression contains no threat of reprisal or force or promise of benefit.

(d) For the purposes of this section, to bargain collectively is the performance of the mutual obligation of the employer and the representative of the employees to meet at reasonable times and confer in good faith with respect to wages, hours, and other terms and conditions of employment, or the negotiation of an agreement, or any question arising thereunder, and the execution of a written contract incorporating any agreement reached if requested by either party, but such obligation does not compel either party to agree to a proposal or require the making of a concession . . .

* * * * *

Representives and Elections

Section 9. (a) Representatives designated or selected for the purposes of collective bargaining by the majority of the employees in a unit appropriate for such purposes, shall be the exclusive representatives of all the employees in such unit for the purposes of collective bargaining in respect to rates of pay, wages, hours of employment, or other conditions of employment: *Provided,* That any individual employee or a group of employees shall have the right at any time to present grievances to their employer and to have such grievances adjusted, without the intervention of the bargaining representative, as long as the adjustment is not inconsistent with the terms of a collective-bargaining contract or agreement then in effect: *Provided further,* That the bargaining representative has been given opportunity to be present at such adjustment.

(b) The Board shall decide in each case whether, in order to assure to employees the fullest freedom in exercising the rights guaranteed by this Act, the unit appropriate for the purposes of collective bargaining shall be the employer unit, craft unit, plant unit, or subdivision thereof: *Provided,* That the Board shall not (1) decide that any unit is appropriate for such purposes if such unit included both professional employees and employees who are not professional employees unless a majority of such professional employees vote for inclusion in such unit; or (2) decide that any craft unit is inappropriate for such purposes on the ground that a different unit has been established by a prior Board determination, unless a majority of

the employees in the proposed craft unit vote against separate representation or (3) decide that any unit is appropriate for such purposes if it includes, together with other employees, any individual employed as a guard to enforce against employees and other persons rules to protect property of the employer or to protect the safety of persons on the employer's premises; but no later organization shall be certified as the representative of employees in a bargaining unit of guards if such organization admits to membership, or is affiliated directly or indirectly with an organization which admits to membership, employees other than guards.

(c)(1) Whenever a petition shall have been filed, in accordance with such regulations as may be prescribed by the Board—

(A) by an employee or group of employees or an individual or labor organization acting in their behalf alleging that a substantial number of employees (i) wish to be represented for collective bargaining and that their employer declines to recognize their representative as the representative defined in section 9(a), or (ii) assert that the individual or labor organization, which has been certified or is being currently recognized by their employer as the bargaining representative, is no longer a representative as defined in section 9(a); or

(B) by an employer, alleging that one or more individuals or labor organizations have presented to him a claim to be recognized as the representative defined in section 9(a); the Board shall investigate such petition and if it has reasonable cause to believe that a question of representation affecting commerce exists shall provide for an appropriate hearing upon due notice. Such hearing may be conducted by an officer or employee of the regional office, who shall not make any recommendations with respect thereto. If the Board finds upon the record of such hearing that such a question of representation exists, it shall direct an election by secret ballot and shall certify the results thereof.

* * * * *

(3) No election shall be directed in any bargaining unit or any subdivision within which, in the preceding twelve-month period, a valid election shall have been held. Employees engaged in an economic strike who are not entitled to reinstatement shall be eligible to vote under such regulations as the Board shall find are consistent with the purposes and provisions of this Act in any election conducted within twelve months after the commencement of the strike. In any election where none of the choices on the ballot receives a majority, a run-off shall be conducted, the ballot providing for a selection between the two choices receiving the largest and second largest number of valid votes cast in the election.

*   *   *   *   *

E

The Civil Rights Act of 1964, Title VII (excerpts)

Definitions

Section 701.

* * * * *

(j) The term "religion" includes all aspects of religious observance and practice, as well as belief, unless an employer demonstrates that he is unable to reasonably accommodate to an employee's or prospective employee's religious observance or practice without undue hardship on the conduct of the employer's business.

(k) The terms "because of sex" or "on the basis of sex" include, but are not limited to, because of or on the basis of pregnancy, childbirth or related medical conditions; and women affected by pregnancy, childbirth, or related medical conditions shall be treated the same for all employment-related purposes, including receipt of benefits under fringe benefit programs, as other persons not so affected but similar in their ability or inability to work, and nothing in Section 703(h) of this title shall not be interpreted to permit otherwise. This subsection shall not require an employer to pay for health insurance benefits for abortion, except where the life of the mother would be endangered if the fetus were carried to term, or except where medical complications have arisen from an abortion: *Provided,* That nothing herein shall preclude an employer from providing abortion benefits or otherwise effect bargaining agreements in regard to abortion.

Unlawful Employment Practices

Section 703. (a) It shall be an unlawful employment practice for an employer—

(1) to fail or refuse to hire or to discharge any individual, or otherwise to discriminate against any individual with respect to his compensation, terms, conditions, or privileges of employment, because of such individual's race, color, religion, sex, or national origin; or

(2) limit, segregate, or classify his employees or applicants for employment in any way which would deprive or tend to deprive any individual of employment opportunities or otherwise adversely affect his status as an employee, because of such individual's race, color, religion, sex, or national origin.

(b) It shall be an unlawful employment practice for an employment agency to fail or refuse to refer for employment, or otherwise to discriminate against, an individual because of his race, color, religion, sex, or national origin, or to classify or refer for employment any individual on the basis of his race, color, religion, sex, or national origin.

(c) It shall be an unlawful employment practice for a labor organization—

(1) to exclude or to expel from its membership, or otherwise to discriminate against, any individual because of his race, color, religion, sex, or national origin;

(2) to limit, segregate, or classify its membership or applicants for membership or to classify or fail or refuse to refer for employment any individual, in any way which would deprive or tend to deprive any individual of employment opportunities, or would limit such employment opportunities or otherwise adversely affect his status as an employee or as an applicant for employment, because of such individual's race, color, religion, sex, or national origin; or

(3) to cause or attempt to cause an employer to discriminate against an individual in violation of this section.

(d) It shall be an unlawful employment practice for any employer, labor organization, or joint labor-management committee controlling apprenticeship or other training or retraining, including on-the-job training programs to discriminate against any individual because of his race, color, religion, sex, or national origin in admission to, or employment in, any program established to provide apprenticeship or other training.

(e) Notwithstanding any other provision of this title, (1) it shall not be an unlawful employment practice for an employer to hire and employ employees, for an employment agency to classify, or refer for employment any individual, or for any employer, labor organization, or joint labor-management committee controlling apprenticeship or other training or retraining programs to admit or employ any individual in any such program, on the basis of his religion, sex, or national origin in those certain instances where religion, sex, or national origin is a bona fide occupational qualification reasonably necessary to the normal operation of that particular business or enterprise, and (2) it shall not be an unlawful employment practice for a school, college, university, or other educational institution or institution of learning to hire and employ employees of a particular religion if such school, college, university, or other educational institution or institution of learning is, in whole or in substantial part, owned, supported, controlled, or managed by a particular religion or by a particular religious corporation, association, or society, or if the curriculum of such school, college, university, or other educational institution or institution of learning is directed toward the propagation of a particular religion.

* * * * *

(h) Notwithstanding any other provision of this title, it shall not be an unlawful employment practice for an employer to apply different standards of compensation, or different terms, conditions, or privileges of employment pursuant to a bona fide seniority or merit system, or a system which measures earnings by quantity or quality of production or to employees who work in different locations, provided that such differences are not the result of an intention to discriminate because of race, color, religion, sex, or national origin; nor shall it be an unlawful employment practice for an employer to give and to act upon the results of any professionally developed ability test provided that such test, its administration or action upon the results is not designed, intended, or used to discriminate because of race, color, religion, sex, or national origin. It shall not be an unlawful employment practice under this title for any employer to differentiate upon the basis of sex in determining the amount of wages or compensation paid or to be paid to employees of such employer if such differentiation is authorized by the provision of Section 6(d) of the Fair Labor Standards Act of 1938 as amended (29 U.S.C. 206(d)).

* * * * *

(j) Nothing contained in this title shall be interpreted to require any employer, employment agency, labor organization, or joint labor-management committee subject to this title to grant preferential treatment to any individual or to any group because of the race, color, religion, sex, or national origin of such individual or group on account of an imbalance which may exist with respect to the total number or percentage of persons of any race, color, religion, sex, or national origin employed by any employer, referred or classified for employment by any employment agency or labor organization, admitted to membership or classified by any labor organization, or admitted to, or employed in, any apprenticeship or other training program, in comparison with the total number or percentage of persons of such race, color, religion, sex, or national origin in any community, State, section, or other area, or in the available work force in any community, State, section, or other area.

Other Unlawful Employment Practices

Section 704. (a) It shall be an unlawful employment practice for an employer to discriminate against any of his employees or applicants for employment, for an employment agency, or joint labor-management committee controlling apprenticeship or other training or retraining, including on-the-job training programs, to discriminate against any individual, or for a labor organization to discriminate against any member thereof or applicant for membership, because he has opposed any practice, made an unlawful employment practice by this title, or because he has made a charge, testified, assisted, or participated in any manner in an investigation, proceeding, or hearing under this title.

(b) It shall be an unlawful employment practice for an employer, labor organization, employment agency, or joint labor-management committee controlling apprenticeship or other training or retraining, including on-the-job training programs, to print or cause to be printed or published any notice or advertisement relating to employment by such an employer or membership in or any classification or referral for employment by such a labor organization, or relating to any classification or referral for employment by such an employment agency, or relating to admission to, or employment in, any program established to provide apprenticeship or other training by such a joint labor-management committee indicating any preference, limitation, specification, or discrimination, based on race, color, religion, sex or national origin, except that such a notice or advertisement may indicate a preference, limitation, specification, or discrimination based on religion, sex or national origin when religion, sex, or national origin is a bona fide occupational qualification for employment.

Due process. A constitutional principle requiring fairness in judicial proceedings and requiring generally that government laws and conduct should be free of arbitrariness and capriciousness.

Eminent domain. The state's power to take private property for public use.

Equity. A body of law based on fairness wherein monetary damages will not afford complete relief.

Exclusive dealing contract. An agreement under which a buyer agrees to purchase all of its needs from a single seller or under which a seller agrees to dispose of all of its production to a single purchaser.

Federalism. The division of authority between the federal government and the states in order to maintain workable cooperation while diffusing political power.

Fraud. An intentional misrepresentation of a material fact with intent to deceive where the misrepresentation is justifiably relied upon by another and damages result.

Good faith. Honesty; an absence of intent to take advantage of another.

Horizontal merger. Acquisition by one company of another company competing in the same product and geographic markets.

In personam jurisdiction. The power of the court over a person.

Indictment. A grand jury's formal accusation of a crime.

Information. A prosecutor's formal accusation of a crime.

Injunction. A court order commanding a person or organization to do or not do a specified action.

Interrogatories. An ingredient in the discovery process wherein one party in a lawsuit directs written questions to another party in the lawsuit.

Judgment notwithstanding the verdict (Judgment n.o.v.). A judge's decision overruling the verdict of the jury.

Judicial review. A court's authority to review statutes, and, if appropriate, declare them

unconstitutional. Also refers to appeals from administrative agencies.

Jurisdiction. The power of a judicial body to adjudicate a dispute. Also the geographical area within which that judicial body has authority to operate.

Jurisprudence. The philosophy and science of law.

Long arm statute. A state enactment that accords the courts of that state the authority to claim jurisdiction over people and property beyond the borders of the state so long as certain "minimum contacts" exist between the state and the people or property.

Mediation. An extrajudicial proceeding in which a third party (the mediator) attempts to assist disputing parties to reach an agreeable, voluntary resolution of their differences.

Merger. The union of two or more business organizations wherein all of the assets, rights, and liabilities of one is blended into the other with only one firm remaining.

Monopoly. Market power permitting the holder to fix prices and/or exclude competition.

Moot. An issue no longer requiring attention or resolution because it has ceased to be in dispute.

Motion. A request to a court seeking an order or action in favor of the party entering the motion.

Motion for a directed verdict. A request by a party to a lawsuit arguing that the other party has failed to prove facts sufficient to establish a claim and that the judge must, therefore, enter a verdict in favor of the moving party.

Negligence. The omission to do something that a reasonable person, guided by those ordinary considerations that ordinarily regulate human affairs, would do, or an action that a reasonable and prudent person would not take.

Nolo contendere. A no-contest plea in a criminal case in which the defendant does not admit guilt but does submit to such punishment as the court may accord.

Nuisance. A class of wrongs that arises from the unreasonable, unwarrantable, or unlawful use by a person of his or her property that produces material annoyance, inconvenience, discomfort, or hurt.

Oligopoly. An economic condition in which the market for a particular good or service is controlled by a small number of producers or distributors.

Ordinance. A law, rule, or regulation enacted by a local unit of government (e.g., a town or city).

Over-the-counter securities. Those stocks, bonds, and like instruments sold directly from broker to customer rather than passing through a stock exchange.

Per curiam. "By the court." Refers to legal opinions offered by the court as a whole rather than those instances where an individual judge authors the opinion.

Per se. By itself; inherently.

Peremptory challenge. At trial, an attorney's authority to dismiss prospective members of the jury without offering any justification for that dismissal.

Plaintiff. One who initiates a lawsuit.

Pleadings. The formal entry of written statements by which the parties to a lawsuit set out their contentions and thereby formulate the issues upon which the litigation will be based.

Police power. The government's inherent authority to enact rules to provide for the health, safety, and general welfare of the citizenry.

Precedent. A decision in a previously decided lawsuit that may be looked to as an authoritative statement for resolving current lawsuits involving similar questions of law.

Prima facie case. A litigating party may be presumed to have built a prima facie case when the evidence is such that it is legally sufficient unless contradicted or overcome by other evidence.

Privity of contract. The legal connection that arises when two or more parties enter a contract.

Proximate cause. Occurrences that, in a natural sequence, unbroken by potent intervening forces, produce the injury which would not have resulted absent those occurrences.

Proxy. Written permission from a shareholder to others to vote his or her share at a stockholders' meeting.

Remand. To send back. For example, a higher court sends a case back to the lower court from which it came.

Res ipsa loquitur. "The thing speaks for itself." Negligence doctrine under which the defendant's guilt is not directly proved but rather is inferred from the circumstances that establish the reasonable belief that the injury in question could not have happened in the absence of the defendant's negligence.

Res judicata. "A thing decided." A doctrine of legal procedure preventing the retrial of issues already conclusively adjudicated.

Restraints of trade. Contracts, combinations, or conspiracies resulting in obstructions of the marketplace including monopoly, artificially inflated prices, artificially reduced supplies, or other impediments to the natural flow of commerce.

Reverse. Overturn the decision of a court.

Secondary boycott. Typically, a union strategy that places pressure not on the employer with whom the union has a dispute but rather with a supplier or customer of that employer in the hope that the object of the boycott will persuade the employer to meet the union's expectations.

Security. A stock, bond, note, or other investment interest in an enterprise designed for profit and operated by one other than the investor.

Separation of powers. The strategy of dividing government into separate and independent executive, legislative, and judicial branches, each of which acts as a check on the power of the others.

Sexual harassment. Unwelcome sexual advances, requests for sexual favors, and other unwanted physical or verbal conduct of a sexual nature.

Shareholder. One holding stock in a corporation.

Standing. A stake in a dispute sufficient to afford a party the legal right to bring or join a litigation exploring the subject of the dispute.

Stare decisis. "Let the decision stand." A doctrine of judicial procedure expecting a court to follow precedent in all cases involving substantially similar issues unless extremely compelling circumstances dictate a change in judicial direction.

Statute. A legislative enactment.

Strict liability. The imposition of legal liability in a civil case as a matter of policy even though the defendant has exercised due care and has not been proved negligent.

Subpoena. An order from a court or administrative agency commanding that an individual appear to give testimony or produce specified documents.

Summary judgment. A judicial determination prior to trial holding that no factual dispute exists between the parties and that, as a matter of law, one of the parties is entitled to a favorable judgment.

Summons. A document originating in a court and delivered to a party or organization indicating that a lawsuit has been commenced against him, her, or it. The summons constitutes notice that the defendant is expected to appear in court to answer the plaintiff's allegations.

Sunset legislation. A statute providing that a particular government agency will automatically cease to exist as of a specified date unless the legislative body affirmatively acts to extend the life of the agency.

Supremacy clause. An element of the U.S. Constitution providing that all constitutionally valid federal laws are the paramount law of the land and, as such, are superior to any conflicting state and local laws.

Takeover bid. A tender offer designed to assume control of a corporation.

Tort. A civil wrong not arising from a contract.

Treble damages. An award of damages totaling three times the amount of the actual damages, authorized by some statutes in an effort to discourage further wrongful conduct.

Tying contract. A sales or leasing arrangement in which one product or service may be bought or leased only if accompanied by the purchase or lease of another product or service as specified by the seller/lessor.

Unconscionability. A contract so one-sided and oppressive as to be unfair.

Usury. Charging an interest rate exceeding the legally permissible maximum.

Venue. The specific geographic location in which a court holding jurisdiction should properly hear a case given the convenience of the parties and other relevant considerations.

Verdict. The jury's decision as to who wins the litigation.

Vertical merger. A union between two firms holding a buyer-seller relationship with each other.

Voir dire. The portion of a trial in which prospective jurors are questioned to determine their qualifications, including absence of bias, to sit in judgment in the case.

Warranty. Any promise, express or implied, that the facts are true as specified. For example, in consumer law, the warranty of merchantability is a guarantee that the product is reasonably fit for the general purpose for which it was sold.

Table of Cases

Abington School District v. Schempp, 170

Albrecht v. Herald Co., 362–63

Alcoa case, 291, 296, 303–4

Alpha Distrib. Co. of Call, Inc. v. Jack Daniel Distillery, 378

Amalgamated Food Employees Union Local 590 et al. v. Logan Valley Plaza, Inc., et al., 169

AMAYA v. HOME ICE, FUEL & SUPPLY CO., 582–85

American Can Co. v. Oregon Liquor Control Commission, 194

American Federation of State, Country, and Municipal Employees case, 475

American Football League v. National Football League, 304

American Textile Manufacturers Institute v. Donovan, 243

American Tobacco Co. v. Patterson, 463, 486, 498

Arizona Governing Committee for Tax Deffered Annuity and Deferred Compensation Plans v. Norris, 498

ASPEN SKIING CO., PETITIONER v. ASPEN HIGHLANDS SKIING CORP., 297–303

Bakke case, 480

BankAmerica Corporation et al. v. United States, 389

BARBER v. KIMBRELL'S, INC., 556–60

Barnes decision, 473

Barnes v. Costle; see Barnes decision

Belliston v. Texaco, Inc., 371

Berkey Photo, Inc. v. Eastman Kodak Company, 303

Berryman v. Riegert, 544

Bibb v. Navajo Freight Lines, Inc., 185

Bivens v. Six Unknown Agents, 170

Blalock v. Ladies Professional Golf Ass'n., 357

Board of Education of the City of Oklahoma City v. National Gay Task Force, 499

Boise Cascade Corp. v. FTC, 359

BOOMER v. ATLANTIC CEMENT CO., 629–32

Borel v. Fibreboard Paper Products Corp., 622–23

Breckinridge v. Rumsfeld, 661

Britton v. South Bend Community School Corp., 499

BROWN SHOE CO. v. UNITED STATES, 315–20

Brown v. the Board of Education, 166, 450

Bruce's Juices, Inc. v. American Can Co., 384–85

Burdine case, 481

Burger King Corp. v. Rudzewicz, 144

Burwell v. Eastern Air Lines, Inc., 472

California Retail Liquor Dealers Ass'n v. Mideal Alum., 388

Carey v. New York State Human Rights App. Bd., 472

Central Hardware Co. v. NLRB, 446

CENTRAL HUDSON GAS v. PUBLIC SERVICE COMMISSION, 160–62

Chandler v. Florida, 143

Note: Cases in capital letters are discussion cases within the chapters; the other cases listed here are referred to in the text, in newspaper or magazine articles, or in questions.

CHEMICAL MANUFACTURERS ASSN. v. NRDC, 644–48

Chevron U.S.A. Inc. v. Natural Resources Defense Council, Inc., 661

Chrestensen case, 160, 170

Chrisner v. Complete Auto Transit, Inc., 496

Cliff Food Stores, Inc. v. Kroger Co., 304

Coca-Cola Bottling Company of Memphis and International Brotherhood of Teamsters, et al., 420

COMMONWEALTH EDISON CO. v. MONTANA, 181–85

Condit v. United Airlines, Inc., 472

Connecticut v. Teal, 464

Consolidated Edison v. Public Service Commission, 169

CONTINENTAL T. V. INC., ET AL. v. GTE SYLVANIA, INC., 363–67

Copeland v. Celotex Corp., 613

Copher v. Barbee, 601–2

Copperweld Corporation v. Independence Tube Corp., 388

Corning Glass Works v. Brennan, 475

County of Washington v. Gunther, 498

Craig v. Boren, 451

Dal-Tex Optical Co. case, 448

Daly v. General Motors Corp., 609

Dartmouth College case of 1819, 157

Daylight Grocery Co., Inc. v. NLRB, 403, 448

Democratic Party of the United States v. National Conservative Political Action Committee, 22

Detroit Edison Co. v. NLRB, 446

Diaz v. Pan American Airways, Inc., 495, 498

Dillon v. Legg, 585

Donald B. Rice Tire Company, Inc. v. Michelin Corporation, 366–67

Donovan v. Lone Steer, 168

Doss v. Town of Big Stone Gap, 624

DOTHARD v. RAWLINSON, 470–73

Dow v. California, 656–58

Dow Chemical Co. v. U.S., 166

Duke Power Co. v. Carolina Environmental Study Group, Inc., 661

Dun & Bradstreet, Inc. v. Greenmoss Builders, Inc., 578

EEOC v. Greyhound Lines, Inc., 497

Embs v. Pepsi Cola Bottling Co. of Lexington, Kentucky, Inc., 622

Engle v. Vitale, 170

Erie Railroad v. Tompkins, 144

ESCOLA v. COCA COLA BOTTLING CO. OF FRESNO, 589–90

Exxon Corp. v. Governor of Maryland, 185

Fagerty v. Van Loan, 544

Falls City Industries, Inc. v. Vanco Beverage, Inc., 387–88

F.C.C. v. PACIFICA FOUNDATION, 207–12

Federal Trade Commission v. A. E. Staley Manufacturing Co., 384

Federal Trade Commission v. Consolidated Foods Corp., 339–40

Federal Trade Commission v. Mary Carter Paint Co., 551–52

FIREFIGHTERS LOCAL UNION NO. 1784, PETITIONER v. CARL W. STOTTS ET AL., 449, 481–86

FIRST NATIONAL BANK OF BOSTON v. BELLOTTI, 11, 157–60

First National Maintenance Corporation v. NLRB, 448

Flippo v. Mode O'Day Frock Shops of Hollywood, 621

Ford Motor Company v. United States, 324

Fortner v. United States Steel Corp., 368

Franchise Motor Freightways Ass'n. v. Leavey, 498

Friedman v. Rogers, 168

Friends of the Earth v. Potomac Electric Power Co., 643

FTC v. COLGATE-PALMOLIVE, 550–52

FTC v. PROCTER & GAMBLE CO., 326–29

Garcia v. San Antonio Metropolitan Transit Authority, 196

General Building Contractors Association, Inc. v. Pennsylvania, 498

General Electric Co. v. Gilbert, 4

General Knit of California case, 409

Giles v. Pick Hotels Corp., 593

Gissel case, 412–13

Goldfarb v. Virginia State Bar et al., 288, 304

Goodyear Aerospace Corp. case, 426

Green v. American Tobacco Co., 623

Gregory v. Litton, 462

GRIGGS v. DUKE POWER CO., 459, 460–64, 477

GTE Sylvania decision, 373

Gunther case, 477

Ham v. South Carolina, 129

HARBAUGH v. CONTINENTAL ILLINOIS NATIONAL BANK, 560–63

Hazelwood School District v. United States, 462

HEART OF ATLANTA MOTEL v. UNITED STATES, 177–81

Heckler v. Chaney, 215

HELICOPTEROS NACIONALES DE COLOMBIS. A., PETITIONER, v. ELIZABETH HALL ET AL., 118–21

Hemby v. State, 114–15

HENNINGSEN v. BLOOMFIELD MOTORS, INC., 596–99

Heublein case, 324, 340

Hines v. St. Joseph's Hospital, 605

Hishon v. King and Spaulding, 497

HODGES v. NOFSINGER, 592–93

Hooker v. Miller, 105

H.P. Hood & Sons v. DuMond, 186

IBM v. United States, 368

ILC Peripherals v. IBM, 296, 304

Illinois Brick Co. v. Illinois, 388

IMMIGRATION AND NATURALIZATION SERVICE v. CHADHA, 147–49

International Brotherhood of Teamsters v. United States, 498

International Longshoremen's Association v. Allied International, Inc., 447

Iowa Security Services, Inc. and National Union, United Plant Guard Workers of America, 446

ITT case, 329

Japanese Electronic Products Antitrust Litigation, In re, 132

Joes v. West Side Buick Auto Co., 578

JOHNS-MANVILLE CORP., IN RE, 568–72

Jones v. Malinowski, 623

Joseph v. Norman's Health Club, Inc., 560

Kathryn R. Roberts v. United States Jaycees case, 467

Katzenbach v. McClung, 181

KLOR'S, INC. v. BROADWAY-HALE STORES, INC., 355–56

Landreth Timber Co. v. Landreth, 279

Lane v. Inman, 462

LARSEN v. GENERAL MOTORS CORP., 586–88

Lehman v. Yellow Freight System, 496

Lindbert Cadillac Co. v. Aron, 678

Linmark Associates, Inc., v. Willingboro, 162

Lloyd Corporation v. Tanner, 169

Local 53, Asbestos Workers v. Vogler, 495

Loewe v. Lawlor, 448

Luque v. McLean, 588

MacPherson v. Buick Motor Co., 581

Mapp v. Ohio, 163

MARSHALL v. BARLOW'S, INC., 164–66

MARVIN KATKO, APPELLEE, v. EDWARD BRINEY AND BERTHA L. BRINEY, APPELLANTS, 103–5

McClain v. Real Estate Board of New Orleans, Inc., 348

McCully v. Fuller Brush Co., 624

McGowan v. Maryland, 151

McGowan v. Maryland, 151

McLeod v. W. S. Merrell Co., Div. of Richardson-Merrell, 622

Medo Photo Supply Corp. v. N.L.R.B., 411–12

Metropolitan Life Ins. Co. v. Ward, 197

Mills v. Alabama, 159

Missouri v. National Organization for Women, 356

Monsanto Co. v. Spray-Rite Service Corp., 389

Moose Lodge No. 107 v. Irvis, 181, 452

Muller v. Oregon, 498

Nanke v. Napier, 623

National Cash Register Co. v. Townsend Grocery Store, 578

NATIONAL COLLEGIATE ATHLETIC ASSOCIATION, PETITIONER v. BOARD OF REGENTS OF THE UNIVERSITY OF OKLAHOMA AND UNIVERSITY OF

GEORGIA ATHLETIC ASSOCIATION, 343–48

National Labor Relations Board v. Bildisco and Bildisco, 572

National League of Cities v. Usery, 196

New York City Transit Authority v. Beazer, 497

New York Times v. Sullivan, 578

Newport News Shipbuilding & Dry Dock Co. v. EEOC, 498

Nix v. Williams, 170

NLRB v. Erie Resistor Co., 448

NLRB v. Exchange Parts Co., 411

NLRB v. Fitzgerald Mills Corp., 448

NLRB v. General Electric Co., 448

NLRB v. General Motors, 418

NLRB v. GISSEL PACKING CO., 409–11

NLRB v. Golub Corp., 448

NLRB v. Herman Sausage Co., 448

NLRB v. Insurance Agents International Union, 414, 448

NLRB v. INTERNATIONAL VAN LINES, 419–20

NLRB v. Katz, 417, 448

NLRB v. Mackay Radio and Telegraph Co., 448

NLRB v. Reed & Prince Mfg. Co., 448

NLRB v. Savair Manufacturing Co., 413

NLRB v. Silverman's Men's Wear, Inc., 447

NLRB v. Truitt Mfg. Co., 448

NLRB v. Wooster Division of Borg-Warner, 417, 448

Northeast Bancorp, Inc. v. Board of Governors of Federal Reserve System, 188, 197

Northwest Wholesale Stationers, Inc. v. Pacific Stationery and Printing Co., 388

Norton v. Macy case, 493

Ohio v. Kovacs, 576

Palsgraf v. Long Island R.R., 621

Parillo v. Giroux Co., 590

Parker Pen Co. v. FTC, 578

Pennsylvania Coal Co. v. Sanderson and Wife, 660–61

Personnel Administrator of Massachusetts v. Feeney, 452, 462

Peterson v. Low Bachrodt Chevrolet Co., 607

Philadelphia National Bank case, 320

Phillips v. Martin Marietta, 468

Photovest Corporation v. Fotomat Corporation, 378

Pike v. Frank G. Hough Co., 662

Pittsburgh Press v. Herman Relations Commission, 169

Plessy v. Ferguson, 167, 450

PRINCIPE v. MCDONALD'S CORP., 368, 373, 374–78

Procter & Gamble case, 383, 385

PRUNEYARD SHOPPING CENTER v. ROBINS, 154–56

Queen v. Dudley and Stephens, 144

Raymond Kassel et al. v. Consolidated Freightways Corporation of Delaware, 185

Realmuto v. Straub Motor, Inc., 607

Redmond v. GAF Corp., 479

Robinson v. Union Carbide Co., 497

Roe v. Wade, 167

Rogers v. EEOC, 496

ROSALES-LOPEZ v. UNITED STATES, 126–29

Roseman v. Retail Credit Co., Inc., 578

Rosenfeld v. Southern Pacific Co., 473

Runyan v. McCreary, 498

Sadlowski case, 432

Schemely v. General Motors Corporation, 621

Schlesinger v. Reservists Committee to Stop the War, 132

Seattle First National Bank case, 447

SEC v. KOSCOT INTERPLANETARY, INC., 257–58

SECURITIES AND EXCHANGE COMMISSION v. W. J. HOWEY CO., 254–57

SEWELL MANUFACTURING CO. AND AMALGAMATED CLOTHING WORKERS OF AMERICA, AFL-CIO, 405–9

Sherbert v. Verner, 153

Shultz v. American Can Co.—Dixie Prods., 498

SIERRA CLUB v. MORTON, 115–17

Singer v. U.S. Civil Serv. Comm., 499

Smith v. Pro Football, Inc., 357

South Hill Neighborhood Association v. Romney, 117

Southern Pacific Railroad v. Arizona, 194

Spaulding v. the University of Washington, 477

Spence v. Washington, 170

Spur Industries, Inc. v. Del E. Webb Development Co., 632

Standard Oil Co. of New Jersey v. United States; *see* Standard Oil decision

Standard Oil decision, 342

Standard Oil of Cal. v. United States, 389

Stang v. Hertz Corp., 605

STEELE v. LOUISVILLE AND NASHVILLE RAILROAD, 423–26

STEELWORKERS v. SADLOWSKI, 427–32

Still v. Rossville Crushed Stone Co., 133

Sumners v. Tice, 611–12

Suter v. San Angelo Foundry and Machine Co., 623

Swenson v. Chevron Chem. Co., 622

Teamsters case, 463

Telex Corporation v. IBM Corporation, 303

Texas Department of Community Affairs v. Burdine; *see* Burdine case

THEATRE ENTERPRISES v. PARAMOUNT, 357–59

Thornton, Estate of, v. Caldor, Inc., 495–96

Tinker v. Des Moines School District, 170

Town of Hallie v. City of Eau Claire, 304

Trans World Air., Inc. v. Hardison, 479

Trans World Airlines, Inc. v. Thurston, 491

Trustees of Columbia University v. Jacobsen, 578

UNION ELECTRIC CO. v. ENVIRONMENTAL PROTECTION AGENCY, 640–43

Union Oil Co. v. Morton, 660

United Airlines, Inc. v. Evans, 495

United Housing Foundation v. Forman, 258

U.S. v. Aluminum Company of America; *see* Alcoa case

U.S. v. Falstaff Brewing Corp., 340

U.S. v. Gasoline Retailers Association, 348

U.S. v. Georgia Power Co., 495

United States v. E. I. Du Pont de Nemours & Co., 304, 323

UNITED STATES v. GENERAL DYNAMICS CORP., 320–22

UNITED STATES v. GRINNELL CORP., 292–96, 304

United States v. International Boxing Club of New York, Inc., 296

UNITED STATES v. INTERNATIONAL TELEPHONE AND TELEGRAPH CORP., 328–31

United States v. Pabst Brewing Co., 319–20

UNITED STATES v. PARKE-DAVIS CO., 360–63

United States v. Penn-Olin Chemical Co., 335

United States v. Philadelphia Nat'l Bank, 340

United States v. Sealy, Incorporated, 354

United States v. Seeger, 499

United States v. South Carolina, 496

UNITED STATES v. TOPCO ASSOC., INC., 351–54

United States v. United Shoe Machinery Corp., 296

U.S. Financial Securities Litigation, In re, 132

U.S. Steel Corp. v. Fortner Enterprises, 370

United Steelworkers of America v. Sadlowski; *see* Sadlowski case

United Steelworkers of America v. Weber, 480

University of California Regents v. Bakke; *see* Bakke case

UTAH PIE CO. v. CONTINENTAL BAKING CO., 380–83

Valentine v. Chrestensen; *see* Chrestensen case

Vanguards of Cleveland v. City of Cleveland, 499

Village of Belle Terre v. Boraas, 661

VOKES v. ARTHUR MURRAY, INC., 542–44

Wallace v. Jaffree, 170

Washington Gas Light Co. v. Virginia Elec. and Power Co., 388

Weber case, 480–81

Webster v. Blue Ship Tea Room, Inc., 621–22

Weeks v. Southern Bell Telephone, 495

Weisz v. Parke-Bernet, 622

WESTERN AIR LINES, INC. PETITIONER v. CHARLES G. CRISWELL ET AL., 487–91

Westinghouse Electric Corp. case, 446

Wickard v. Filburn, 177

Williams v. Rank & Son Buick, Inc., 544

WILLIAMS v. WALKER-THOMAS FURNITURE CO., 545–47

Willie v. Southwestern Bell Telephone Company, 546–47

Wilson v. Southwest Airlines Co., 496–97

Wisconsin v. Yoder, 60

W.L. May Co., Inc. v. Philco-Ford Corporation, 577–78

World-Wide Volkswagen Corp. v. Woodson, 121

Wright v. Methodist Youth Services, Inc., 496

Wygant v. Jackson Board of Education, 499

Wyman v. Newhouse, 133

Yanity v. Benware, 433

YKK (U.S.A.) Inc. and Sandra M. Collins et al., 447

Zanderer v. Office of Disciplinary Council of the Supreme Court of Ohio, 170

Index

A

Abouzeid, Kamal, 507
Absorption doctrine, 150
Acid rain, 626, 648
Acquisition, 307
Act-utilitarianism, 65
Actus reus, 109
Administrative agencies
  adjudication by, 205–6
  and the administrative process,
    204–12
  authority of, 200–201
  informal action by, 204–5
  judicial review and, 206–12
  justification for, 202–3
  position within government, 201–
    2
  in procedural interpretive,
    legislative rule-making, 205
  role of
    Congress, 202–3
    courts, 212
    President, 202
  rule-making by, 205
Administrative law, 200, 207
Administrative law judge, 206, 282,
    283
Administrative Procedure Act, 200,
    205, 206, 215
Administrative process
  adjudication, 205–6
  informal agency action, 204–5
  information gathering, 204
  judicial review, 206–12
  rule-making, 205
Admissions, 125
Advertising, false, 549
Advocacy advertising, 11–12, 157–
    60
Affirmative action, 449, 454
  and Bakke, 480
  and government employees, 480

Affirmative action—*Cont.*
  and handicapped, 492
  public attitude toward, 486–87
  and race-conscious remedies as,
    480
  Reagan on, 481, 486
  seniority and, 481
  and Title VII (Civil Rights Act),
    479
Affirmative defense, 124
Affirmative Ethical Principles of the
    American Institute of CPAs,
    67
AFL-CIO, 396
Agape, 63
Age discrimination, 487, 494
Age Discrimination in Employment
    Act of 1967, 453, 493
Agent Orange, 568
Aggregate concentration, 325
Agnew, Spiro, 333
Air pollution control, 630, 634
  costs of, 656
  and unsatisfactory air quality,
    638
Airline deregulation, 224, 236
Airline Deregulation Act of 1978,
    235
Alaskan pipeline, 336
Alcoa, 296
Alexander, Gordon, 508
Alimony, 466
Allen, Frederick, 395
Aluminum ingot market, 296
American Bar Association, 136
American Dream, 289, 383
American Federation of Labor,
    395–96
American legal system
  alternatives to, 141
  case law, 103
  civil trial process, 123–31

American legal system—*Cont.*
  classification of law, 106–10
  judges and judicial activism,
    133–36
  and judicial process, 115
  lawyers and, 136–38
  legal foundation, 100–101
  public opinion, 133
  and reform, 131–42
  and standing to sue, 115
  as too much law, 138–41
American Medical Association,
    217, 286
American Motors, 580
American Petroleum Institute, 222–
    23, 224
American Tobacco, 175
Amish, the, 151–53
Anderson, Jack, 332–33
Anderson, Warren, 516–17
Andrews, Kenneth, 504
Anheuser-Busch, 175
Annual percentage rate, 555
Answer, 124
Anticompetitive practices, 282
Antilabor tactics, 175
Antinomianism, 63
Antitrust intervention, 335
Antitrust law
  and AT&T settlement, 280
  Baxter on, 284
  beginning of, 176
  Clayton Act as, 286
  exemptions from, 287–88
  foreign, 386
  FTC Act, 286
  IBM suit, 281–82
  in the international market,
    385
  in Japan, 386
  labor unions, 287
  multinational corporations, 385

Antitrust law—*Cont.*
  preservation of American way of
    life, 289
  price discrimination, 379
  Reagan administration, 280
  roots of, 284–85
  Sherman Antitrust Act, 285–86
  state versions of, 288
  since World War II, 282
Antitrust philosophy, 289
Antitrust policy, 283, 329
  abroad, 386
  and trademarks, 373
Antitrust violations, criminal, 515
Apartheid, 508
Appeals, 123, 130
Appellant, 130
Appellate opinions, reports of, 103
Appellee or respondent, 130
Apple computer stock, 263
Arab-American Oil Company, 283
Aramco consortium, 283
Ardrey, Robert, 541
Army Corps of Engineers, 174
Arthur D. Little study, 655
Articles of Confederation, 146
Ashford, Nicholas, 231
Ashland Oil, 307
Assembly-line production, 396
Associated Press-NBC News poll,
    466
Association of Governing Boards,
    13
Atlantic Richfield, 283
Assumption of risk, 591
AT&T, 80–81, 283
Auto Safety Act, 221
Autolite, 323–24
Average hourly wage, 467
Automobile odometers, 540
Avis Rent-a-Car, 331

B

Babbitt, Bruce E., 188
Baby cribs, defective, 538
Back wages, 475
Bad-faith findings, 416
Baksheesh, 91
Bait-and-switch tactics, 549
Balance of payments, 506
Balance of powers concept, 465
Ballot clause, 417
Bank of Boston, 514
Bank expansion, 188
Bankruptcy, 566–67
  adjustment of debts and, 568
  Chapter 13 and debts, 567
  liquidity, Chapter 7, 567
  order for relief and, 567–68
  reorganization, Chapter 11, 567–
    68

Bankruptcy—*Cont.*
  straight, 567
Bankruptcy Amendments and
    Federal Judgeship Act of 1984,
    567
Bankruptcy court, 123
Bankruptcy law, critique of, 572
Bankruptcy Reform Act of 1978
  Chapters 7 and 11, 567–68
  Chapter 13, 567–68
  and reorganization, 567, 568
Banks and nonbank institutions, 359
Bargaining
  in bad faith, 416
  in good faith, 413, 416
  representative, 403
  subjects, mandatory, 416–17
  unit, 403
Barnes, Paulette, 473
Barriers to (market) entry, 323
Battle of experts, 586
Baxter, William, 281–82, 284
Beard, Dita, 332–33
Bell Labs, 280
Bell Telephone, 280
Belle Terre, N. Y., 633
Belli, Melvin, 516
Bentham, Jeremy, 65
Beyond a reasonable doubt, 109
Bhopal, India, 515
Bible, 151
Bible meetings, 479
Big government, 222, 236
"Bigness is bad" notion, 283–84,
    334
Bill of Rights, 102, 146
  business and, 150–62
  and constitutional law policy,
    166–88
  freedom of religion, 151–53
  freedom of speech, 153–62
  laborers', 427
Bill of Rights of Members of Labor
    Organizations, 400, 427
Blacklists, 397
Blacks
  cost of discrimination against,
    454
  and poverty, 454
  progress and, 454
  women and, 467
  and unemployment, 454
  workers, 396
Black's Law Dictionary, 580
Blue laws, 151
Blue sky laws, 253, 263
Bona fide occupational qualification
    (BFOQ), 463
  conditions of, 469, 479
Bond issues, 259
Bottle bills, 632, 649

Bottom-line defense, 464
Boycotts, 354–55, 397, 451
Braniff Airlines, 236
Braun electric razors, 385
Breach
  of duty, 581
  of warranty, 580
Brennan, William J., Jr., 414
Brenner, Steven, 68–69
Bribery abroad, 91–94
Bribes, 398
Brotherhood of Sleeping Car
    Porters, 450
Bubble concept, 235
Bucholtz, Roger, 508
Bundling prices, 281
Bureaucracy, 333
Bureau of Chemistry, 213
Burger, Chief Justice Warren, 163
Business crimes, 82–88
  costs of, 514–15
Business ethics
  and bribery abroad, 91
  in corporate conduct, 68–69
  and crime, 83
  and executive liability, 82–85
  foundations of, 66–70
  in practice, 69–70
  and pressure to cheat, 70
  and whistle-blowing, 89–91
Business organizations
  and buy/sell agreements, 252–53
  changing form of, 251–52
  as corporations, 247–48
  and double taxation, 250
  exemptions from securities laws,
    258, 59, 262–63
  form of, 244–45
  and history of securities
    regulation, 253–54⋅
  Howey doctrine and, 257–58
  liability of, 249–50
  as partnerships, 245–47
  role in society, 502
  Social Performance Index, 502–3
  social responsibility of, 502–8
Business regulation
  beginning of, 285
  constitutional foundation of, 176
  and government, 547
Business Review Procedure, 385
Business and Society Review, 9–11
Business values, 67
BusinessWeek, 91, 331
Buy/sell agreements, 252–53

C

California Fourth Circuit Court of
    Appeals, 512
Cardozo, Benjamin, 100, 581
Carroll, Archie, 68–69

Carrying charges, 566
Cartel, 282
Carter administration, 224, 235
Case briefs, 103
Categorical imperative, 65
Caveat emptor, 581
Cease and desist order, 286, 549
Celler-Kefauver Act of 1950, 287
Cereal manufacturers, 286
Cereal case, 282–83
Chain stores, 380
Challenge for cause, 126
Champion spark plugs, 323
Chemical hazards, 440
Chemical and oil waste disposal,
    643
Chicago school of economics, 280
Child labor, 393
Cicero, 100
Circuit Court of Appeals, District of
    Columbia, 473
Circuit Courts of Appeal, 413
Circumstantial evidence, 343
Citicorp, 188
Cities Service, 308
Civil Aeronautics Board, 200, 235
Civil law, 108
Civil Rights Act of 1866, 451
Civil Rights Act of 1964, 427, 449,
    452, 464; *also see* Title VII
    liability in, 458
    section 703(h) and seniority, 463
Civil rights movement, 449
Civil Service Commission, 464
Civil trial process, 123
    class actions in, 130–31
    due process of law in, 131
    judge and jury, 126–29
    motions in, 124–25
    pleadings, 124
    and pretrial conference, 125
    the trial and, 129
Civil tort liability, 397
Civil War, 175, 285
Civilian Conservation Corps, 176
Clark, Ramsey, 281
Class action, 130–31
Clayton Act of 1914, 176, 323, 324
    and antitrust activities, 286
    with Celler-Kefauver Act, 286
    enforcement of, 306–7
    and international market, 385
    in joint ventures, 334–35
    section 2, 279
    section 3, 367, 371
    section 7, 305, 315, 385
    section 8, 359
Clean Air Act, 637–39
Clean Air Act Amendments of 1970
    and 1977
    and citizen suits, 639

Clean Air Act Amendments—*Cont.*
    and penalties, 638
    and other suggested amendments,
        639
Clean Water Act, 643–44
Closed shop agreements, 418
Clorox, 324
Code of Federal Regulations, 205
Codes of conduct, 67
Coercive monopoly, 291
Collective bargaining, 401, 402
    in good faith, 413–14
    and Landrum-Griffin Act, 399
    process of, 398
    with union harrassment, 414
Collective bargaining agreements,
    421, 433
    and individual employee, 422–23
    with open-shop clauses, 418
    and right-to-work laws, 418
Collusion, 284
Commerce Clause, 150, 176–77,
    181
Commercial giants, 175
Commercial speech, judicial
    treatment of, 160–62
Commercial TV station, 235
Common Cause, 223–24
Common law, 628
    approach to pollution problems,
        629
    and consumer protection, 539
    and public nuisance, 628–29
Common situs picketing, 402, 421–
    22
Community of interest, 403
Company-owned tenements, 393
Company towns, 394–95
Comparable jobs, men and women,
    476
Comparable worth, 375, 443, 477–
    78
Comparative negligence, 591
Competition
    intrabrand, 363
    perfect, 289
    workable, 289
Complaint, 124
Comprehensive Environmental
    Response, Compensation, and
    Liability Act of 1980, 650
Computer lessor, 367–68
Concerted action among
    competitors, 357
Conciliation boards, 421
Concurrent jurisdiction, 118
Conglomerate merger, 284, 305–6
    aggregate concentration in, 325
    analysis, 326
    defenses against, 325–26
    four categories of, 324

Conglomerate merger—*Cont.*
    and market power entrenchment,
        324
    potential entrant into, 324
    reciprocity and, 324–25
Congress of Industrial Organizations
    (CIO), 396
Congress, U.S.
    administrative agencies, 202–3
    antitrust cases, 287
    authority of FTC, 224, 286
    balance of political power, 335
    bona fide occupational
        requirements, 469
    on chain stores, 380
    and Consumer Products Safety
        Commission, 523
    Corporate Democracy Act, 523
    curbing market concentration,
        320
    and discrimination in interstate
        commerce, 452
    Electronic Funds Transfer Act,
        575
    on employment discrimination,
        463
    and environmental protection,
        633
    Fair Credit Reporting Act, 564
    on hazardous wastes, 649
    Landrum-Griffin Act of 1959,
        399
    legislative veto, 147
    National Labor Relations Act
        policy statement, 400–401
    Norris-La Guardia Act, 397
    Occupational Safety and Health
        Act, 439–40
    on pregnancy discrimination, 465
    Railway Labor Act of 1926, 398
    Resource Conservation and
        Recovery Act, 649–50
    restraint of trade, 342
    role in creating regulatory
        agencies, 202–3
    and securities, 262
    Taft-Hartley Act, 398
    U.S. Commission on Industrial
        Relations, 399
    Wagner Act of 1935, 398
    weakened amendments to Clean
        Air Act, 639
Conoco, 308
Conscious parallelism, 357
Consent order, 206
Constitutional Convention, 146
Constitutional law
    and bankruptcy legislation, 567
    and Bill of Rights, 146–47
    police powers and, 632
    policy, 166–68

Consumer abuse, 536, 538
Consumer credit data, 564
Consumer Credit Protection Act
    and Equal Credit Opportunity
        Act, 560
    and TILA, 555
    Title IX, 575
Consumer debt, 554
Consumer finance law, 554–55
Consumer Goods Pricing Act, 287
Consumer Products Safety
    Commission of 1972, 201, 538
    authority, 552
    compliance with, 553
    duties, 552
    enforcement, 553
    rule-making and, 553
Consumer protection
    and common law, 539
    Consumers Advisory Board, 539
    Food, Drug, and Cosmetic Act of
        1938, 539
    FTC, 539, 549
    government regulation of
        business, 547
    Great Engine Switch, 536
    Pure Food and Drug Act of 1906,
        539
    Ralph Nader on, 539
Consumer Protection Agency, 221
Consumer protection laws, finance
    Consumer Credit Protection Act,
        555, 560
    Equal Credit Opportunity Act,
        554–55, 560
    Fair Credit Billing Act, 555,
        564–65
    Fair Credit Reporting Act, 555,
        563–64
    state usury laws, 554, 566
    Truth in Lending Act (TILA),
        554–56
Consumer Reports, 539
Consumerism, 538
Consumers Union, 539
Contracts
    unconscionable, 545
    and Uniform Commercial Code,
        545
Contributory negligence, 591
Conventional pollutants, 644
Coolidge administration, 287
Cooling-off process, 402
Co-op, 258
Cooperative action, 343
Copper smelting, 658
Corporate codes of conduct, 70–71
Corporate crime disclosures, 514–
    15
Corporate Democracy Act, 523

Corporate influence, 333
Corporate political speech, 157
Corporate state
    advocacy advertising in, 11–12
    concentration of resources in, 3–
        6
    control of, 14
    interlocking power and, 15–18
    and PACs, 7–9
    and public opinion, 3
    public policy in, 6
    and Reich, Charles, 5, 13
    schools and churches in, 12
Corporate self-regulation, 523
Corporate veil, 248
Corporations
    charters, 247
    control of, 247–48
    criminal liability, 514–15
    First Amendment rights, 157
    hostile takeovers, 269–70
    liability of, 248
    Marshall, John and, 157
    Sub S, 244–249
    taxation, 248
Corvair, 539, 586
Cost/benefit
    analysis and pollution, 656
    ratio, 224–26
Council of Economic Advisors,
    198, 291
Council on Environmental Quality,
    633, 653, 656
Counterclaim, 124
Court of Appeals, 123, 411, 432–
    33
Court injunction, 397
Court Mediation Service, 142
Court of Military Appeals, 123
Courts of equity, 107
Cox, Archibald, 333
Craftsman, 67
Craft unions, 396
Credit card transactions, 556
    and billing errors, 564–65
    regulation of, 554
Credit Corp., U.S. Steel, 368, 370
Crimes, definition of, 109–10
Criminal defenses, 109
Criminal fraud, 515
Criminal law, 108–10
    process of, 110–15
Criminal liability
    and credit financing, 555
    Ford Pinto and, 513–14
Criminal procedure, 109
Criminal prosecutions, 349
Cross-claim, 124
Cross complaints, 124
Cross elasticity of demand, 292

Cross examination, 129
Cultural experiment, 67
Customers of customers, 384
Cuyahoga River, 643

D

Danvers, Mass., 394
Darwin, Charles, 175
Dash, 91
Davis, Keith, 505–7
Dealer-distributors, 386
Debtor protection, 568
    bankruptcy, 564–67
    Bankruptcy Reform Act of 1978,
        567
Deceptive practices and FTC, 549
Deep pockets, 323
Defective design, 586
Delaware incorporation, 247
Demurrer, 124
Deontology, 64–65
Department of Agriculture, U.S.,
    213
Department of Justice, U.S., 463–
    64
Department of Labor, U.S., 464
    and Office of Federal Contract
        Compliance Programs, 454
Department of Transportation,
    U.S., 235
Depositions, 125
Depression, Great, 176, 287, 397,
    539
Deregulation, 224, 229, 307, 486
    and burdens of regulation, 227–
        28
    decision, 235–37
    definition, 227
    desirability of, 235–37
    examples of, 235
    and states, 238
    and trucking, 236–37
Detroit Edison Co., 185
Dioxin, 626
Direct examination, 129
Directed verdict, 129
Directorates, interlocking, 359
Discovery technique, 125
Discrimination
    in age, 487
    cases, 494
    costs of, 456
    definition, 449–50
    and executive orders, 452
    in federal contracts, 454
    by government, 451
    against handicapped, 492
    in interstate commerce, 452
    for race, color, national origin,
        454

Discrimination—*Cont.*
  of religious organizations, 452
  and state law, 493–94
  statutory defenses for, 463
Discriminatory pricing, 281
Disparate impact, 459, 464, 468
  and comparable pay, 477
Disparate treatment, 458–59
Distributors, 363
District court, 122–23
Diversity of citizenship, 118
Domestic bribery, 55
Dominant market power, 367
Doninger, David, 639
Donovan, Raymond, 486
Double jeopardy, 110
Double taxation, 250–51
Douglas, William O., 633
Draft registration, 465
Drinking age, 191–93
Drinking water, 632
Drug approval process,
     streamlining, 218
Drug company testing and
     reporting, 217
Drug innovation and FDA, 218
Dubinsky, Dave, 396
Due process clause, 150, 451, 493
Du Pont, 92
  and Conoco takeover, 308
  and General Motors, 322–23
Dumping abroad, 517–18
Dworkin, Andrea, 478

E

Earth, heating of, 626
Education, mandatory, 395
Effluent maximums, 644
Egoism, 64
Eighth Amendment, 109
Electronic Fund Transfer Act of
     1978, 575
Electronic fund transfers
  problems with, 576
  types, 575–76
Elixir Sulfanilamide-Massengill,
     214
Emergency air-pollution standard,
     638
Eminent domain, 154–56
Employee (union) rights, 422–23
Employee testing, 463
Employment discrimination
  and American values, 449
  cost of, 456
  disparate impact and treatment,
     458–59, 464, 468
  and EEOC, 453
  in federal contracts, 454

Employment discrimination—*Cont.*
  and *Firefighters,* 464
  history of, 450
  productivity, 456
  quotas, 481
  suits, 453
Entrepreneurs, early, 395
Environment
  Adam Smith on, 628
  as collective, free good, 628
  William Douglas on, 633
Environmental Impact Statement
     (EIS), 634
Environment Protection Agency
     (EPA), 147, 201, 203, 223,
     228, 234, 473
  and air pollution, 634
  and bubble concept, 235
  and Clean Air Amendments, 638
  Clean Water Act, 644
  effectiveness of, 655–56
  and market incentives policy, 653
  NAAQS, 638
  responsibility for, 634
  state and local governments and,
     639
  stationary sources of air
     pollution, 639
  success of, 655
  Toxic Substances Control Act,
     644
Epicureans, 67
Epstein, Richard, 513
Equal Credit Opportunity Act of
     1974, 554–55
  Consumer Credit Protection Act,
     560
  discrimination, 560
Equal Employment Opportunity Act
     of 1972,
  Title VII, 452
  and veterans, 452
Equal Employment Opportunity
     Commission (EEOC), 201,
     223, 235, 473
  age discrimination, 487
  enforcement provisions of, 453
  homosexuals, 493–94
  individual actions, 453
  pattern or practice suits, 453
  theory of comparable worth,
     477–78
Equal pay, 474–75
Equal Pay Act of 1963, 427, 453,
     474
  exceptions to, 475
Equal protection for workers, 443
Equal protection clauses, 188, 451,
     493
Equal Rights Amendment, 466

Equitable Life Assurance Society
     and age discrimination, 494
Espionage, 342
Essay on the Principle of
     Population, 1798, 625
Establishment clause, 151
Ethics
  and business, foundations of, 66–
     68
  deontological theory, 61–66
  Fletcher's moral continuum and,
     63–64
  of McDonald's, 61–62
  telelogical theory, 64–65
  theory of, 62–63
European antitrust zeal, 386
European community, 385
Exchange Parts Co. and employee
     benefits, 411
Exclusionary rule, 163
Exclusive bargaining agent, 422
Exclusive dealing, 371, 373
Exclusive sales territory, 363
Executive liability, 83–88
Executive Order 11246, 452, 454
Exhibits, 129
Existentialism, 63
Exploitation of workers, 395
Export Trading Act of 1982, 288
Express warranties, 594–94
  disclaimers, 595
  UCC 2-316 (2) and (3) (a), 595–
     96
Externalities, 628
  negative, 173
  positive, 173–74
Exxon, 3, 283

F

Facially neutral policy or practice,
     477
Factory and mining towns, 393
Failing company defense, 326
Fair Credit Billing Act
  consumer rights in, 564
  and credit information, 563–64
  key requirements of, 564
  penalties, 564
Fair employment laws, 450
Fair Employment Practice
     Committee, 450
Fair Labor Standards Act of 1938,
     474
False conduct and expressions, 540
Falstaff Brewing, 324
Falwell, Jerry, 151
Federal banking system, 175
Federal Communications
     Commission (FCC), 200, 207,
     223–24, 235, 280, 288

Federal contractors and discrimination, 452
Federal Court of Appeals, 464, 480, 549, 553
Federal court systems, 122–23
Federal District Court, 480
Federal Emergency Relief Act, 176
Federal Insecticide, Fungicide, and Rodenticide Act, 634
Federal Judgeship Act of 1984, 567
Federal Mediation and Conciliation Service, 420–21
Federal Power Commission, 200, 206
Federal question jurisdiction, 117–18
Federal Register, 205, 553
Federal regulatory process
  agencies, authority of, 200–201
  budget, 220
  criticism of, 220–24
  excessive industry influence, 222–23
  excessive legislative and executive influence, 223
  growth of, 220–21
  insufficient regulation by, 221
  public opinion, 223
  underrepresentation of public opinion, 223
Federal Reporter, 103, 553
Federal Reserve Board, 203, 259, 555
Federal and state regulation of business, 186–87
Federal Trade Commission, 107, 188, 201, 221, 223, 287, 539
  actions of, 286
  adjudicatory actions of, 549
  advertising and, 549
  on anticompetitive practices, 286
  authority of, 286
  cereals suit dropped, 282–83
  civil penalties of, 549
  and Clayton Act, 286, 306
  composition of, 286
  consumer credit law, 564
  current stance of, 286
  dropped oil company charges, 283
  Equal Credit Opportunity Act, 564
  on franchises, 373
  General Motors and Toyota merger, 335
  industry guides and, 547–48
  and international business, 385
  investigations of, 548
  major mergers and, 287
  proposed reform of, 224–26
  quasi-legislative role of, 548

Federal Trade Commission—*Cont.*
  roles of, 548
  Sherman Act, section 5, 286, 290, 359–60, 367
  sufficiency of warning labels and, 205
  TILA provisions and, 555
  and Wheeler-Lea Amendments, 539
Federal Trade Commission Act, 549
Felonies, 109
Ferraro, Geraldine, 466
Fifth Amendment, 109, 131, 150, 154, 451, 493
Film Recovery System Corp., 83
Firefighters case, 463
Firestone 500 radial tire, 538
First Amendment, 150
  and commercial speeches, 160
  and corporations, 157
  and employees' free speech, 404
  and homosexual rights, 467
  Jaycees and, 493
  private property and, 154
  rights in labor disputes, 402
  and Taft-Hartley Act, 398
First inside-the-glove, 412
Fitzgerald, A. Ernest, 89
Flammability, 552
Fletcher, Joseph, 63–64
Flight attendants, 465, 469
Florida Supreme Court, 493
Food and Drug Administration (FDA), 201, 205, 212, 221, 228
  approval process of, 214–15
  criticism of, 217–18
  funding for, 217
  and *Heckler* v. *Chaney,* 215
  history of, 213–14
  lax drug regulation and, 217
  and 1962 Kefauver Drug Amendments Act, 214
  table of organization, 213
Food, Drug, and Cosmetics Act of 1938, 213, 214, 215, 539
Ford, Gerald, 386
Ford Motor Co.
  civil suits of, 512
  defective transmissions, 580
  and Electric Autolite Co., 323–24
  Indiana criminal prosecution, 513–14
  Pinto, 508, 512–13, 521, 538
  rear-end collisions, 512
Foreign antitrust laws, 386
Foreign commerce, regulation of, 176–77
Foreign Corrupt Practices Act, 91–92

Formalism, 65
Foreseeability, 582
Fortner Enterprises, 368, 370
Fortune, 228
  on corporate crime, 515
  500 Industrials, 3–4, 15, 307–8, 500, 507, 518
Fourth Amendment, 109, 150, 154, 163
  and exclusionary rule, 163
Fourteenth Amendment, 131, 150, 154, 451
Franchises
  abuses of, 373
  definition of, 372–73
  and FTC rules
  as vertical trade restraint, 373
Frankfurter, Felix, 371
Fraud
  elements of, 540
  and innocent misrepresentation, 544
  in nature, 541
  in securities, 274
Fraud theory, 264
Free enterprise spirit, 287
Free good, 628
Free market
  argument, 506
  economics, 280
  and government regulation, 380
  inadequacies of, 285
  pollution control and, 653
  principles, 283, 505
  pure advocates of, 291
  view, 502
Freedom of religion
  and the Amish, 151–53
  and blue laws, 151
  prayer and, 151
Freedom of speech, 153
  and commercial speech, 160
  corporate political speech and, 157
  and private property, 154–56
Freedom riders, 451
Freeman, Myrick, 656
Friedman, Milton, 502, 504, 506, 507
Frost, Robert, 19
Fund for a Conservative Majority, 9

G

Gallup poll, 3, 69
Gambling contracts, 539
Gamesman, 68
Gamesman, The, 67
Garn–St. Germain Act of 1982, 235
Geneen, Harold, 333
General Accounting Office (GAO), 218, 349

General Dynamics, 514
General Electric, 514
General intent, monopoly cases, 290
General Motors, 3, 286, 494, 537, 582
  -AC, 323
  and Du Pont, 323–24
Genetic inheritance, 66–67
Georgia-Pacific, 307
Geographic market analysis, 383
Geographic market concept, 292
Gerrity, Edward, 333
Getty Oil, 308
Gillette, 385
Ginter, James, 507–8
Glass-Steagall Act, 176
Golden parachutes, 270
Goldfarb case challenge, 288
Golub, Stefan, 83
Gompers, Samuel, 395–96
Good faith bargaining, 413
Good will, concept of, 65
Goodrich, B. F., Co., 71–72
Government intervention, 291
  in clean environment, 628
  and pollution control, 656
Government intrusiveness, 486
Government regulation of business, 547
  avoidance of, 505
  constitutional foundations of, 176–77
  extensive role of, 193
  and failure of the market, 173–74
  federal vs. state, 186–87
  history of, 174–77
  in state and local units, 181, 187
Grange Movement, 175
Great Depression, 176, 287, 397, 539
Green, Mark, 17, 221
Greening of America, 5, 18
Greenmail, 270
Greenspan, Alan, 291
Grimshaw, Richard, 512
Grinnell, Fire Protection Division of, 331
Group boycott, 354–55
Gulf Oil, 308
Guth, William, 69–70

H

Hand, Learned, 291, 296
Handicapped, 492
Harding administration, 287
Harlan, John M., 441
Harris poll, 655
Hart-Scott-Rodino Antitrust Improvement Act, 287
Hartford Fire (insurance), 331

Harvard Business Review, 68–69, 502
Harvey, Paul, 227
Hazardous waste problem, 650–51
Health and Human Services, U.S. Department of, 201, 212
Health care systems, 395
Heinz, 175
Helms, Jesse, 151
Hepburn Act of 1906, 175
Herfindahl-Hirschman Index, 306
High-pressure sales, 549
Hillman, Sidney, 396
Hoffman, Nicholas von, 13–14
Holmes, Oliver Wendell, 100
Homosexuals, 464, 492–93
Hoover administration, 287
Horizontal division of markets, 351
Horizontal mergers, 305–6, 314–15
  analysis of, 320
Horizontal price fixing, 342
  and Sherman Act, section 1. 343
Horizontal restraints of trade, 342
Horizontal restrictors, 362
Hot cargo agreements, 402, 421, 422
Hour of Power, The, 14
Howey doctrine, 257
Hybrid business organizations, 248

I

IBM, 283
  and AT&T, 282
  monopoly of computer market, 281–82
Illegal mergers, 325
Illegal political contributions, 515
Immigrants, 393, 454
Implied warranty of fitness, 94–95, 593
  and UCC-313, 594
  and UCC 2-314, 594–95
  and UCC 2-315, 595
Improper manufacturing, handling, and/or inspection, 586
In personam jurisdiction, 118–21
In rem action, 118
Incorporation doctrine, 150
Indebtedness, 554
India, 516, 517
Indictment, 109
Industrial concentration, 307
Industrial construction and clean-air standards, 638–39
Industrial pollution, 614
Industrial regulation, 223
Industrial Revolution, 392
Industrial Workers of the World (IWW), 396

Industry-agency ties, 222
Injunction(s), 107
  federal, 397
Injunctive relief, 286
Injury, 582
Innocent misrepresentation, 540
Insider trading, 277
Insurance Agents' International Union, 414
Intentional racial discrimination, 451, 458
Interchangeability, 292
Intercity telecommunications market, 280
Interlock of corporate power, 15–16
Interlocking directorates, 359
Interlocks and FTC, 360
Internal Revenue Service (IRS), 205, 223, 251–52
Internal union problems, 399
International business
  and American antitrust law, 385
  balance of payments and, 506
  Clayton Act, 385
  FTC Act, 385
  Sherman Act, 385
International Data Corp., 281
Interstate banking, 188
Interstate commerce, 177
  and employment discrimination, 452
  NLRB and, 402–3
  state and local regulation of, 181–82
Interstate Commerce Commission (ICC), 200, 223, 259, 285
Interstate Commerce Commission Act of 1887, 175
Interrogatories, 125
Intrabrand competition, 363, 386
Intrastate commerce, 181
Intra-enterprise conspiracy, 343
Intrastate offerings (securities), 262–63
Investment Advisors Act of 1940, 254
Investment Company Act of 1940, 254
Invisible hand, 628
Involuntary bankruptcy, 567
ITT settlement
  Jack Anderson's investigation of, 332–33
  terms of, 331, 335

J

Jail sentences for unfair competition, 284
Jaworski, Leon, 323
Job discrimination, 450
Johnson administration, 281, 555

Joint venture, 336
Judge-made contract law, 539
Judge shopping, 108
Judges and judicial activism, 133–36
Judgment, n.o.v., 130
Judicial circuits, 123
Judicial juggling act, 360
Judicial process, 115–17
  civil trial and, 123–26
  federal question jurisdiction and, 11718
  venue, 121–23
Judicial review
  of administrative agencies, 206–7
  FTC and, 286
  law issues raised by, 207, 213
Jungle, The, 539
Jungle fighter, 68
Jury in civil case, 126
Justice Department, U.S., 280, 281, 287
  on aggregate concentration, 325
  and bid-rigging, 349
  Business Review Procedure of, 385
  challenge to Du Pont, 322–23
  Clayton Act, section 7 and, 306
  international antitrust law and, 385
  on joint mergers, 334
  merger guidelines, 306
  and Monsanto, 360
  oil industry and, 283
  recent guidelines on nonprice vertical restraint, 372
  tying standards, 359
  vertical restraint and, 359

K

Kaiser Aluminum and Chemical, 480
Kant, Immanuel, 65–66
Kauffmann, Carl, 92
Kefauver Drug Amendments Act of 1962, 214, 218
Kennedy, Edward, 224, 335
Kent State University, 61–62
Kentucky Fried Chicken, 372
Kilpatrick, James, 227
Kliendiest, Richard, 333
Knights of Labor, 395–96
Knowing violations, 639
Knowledge of risk, 591
Knowledge business, 281
Kroc, Ray, 62
Ku Klux Klan, 102

L

Labor conflict, 392–93
Labor Department, U.S., 467

Labor disputes, 399
Labor law
  contemporary issues, in, 436
  decisions on, 433
  and inconsistency of NLRB, 434
  Labor-Management Reporting and Disclosure Act, 399–400, 426
  Landrum-Griffin Act, 399–400, 427
  National Labor Relations Act, 400, 422
  Norris-Laguardia Act, 387
  protective legislation and, 397
  Railway Labor Act, 398, 426
  and restraint of trade, 397
  right to work and, 418
  and working conditions, 436
Labor-management relations, 400, 402, 444
Labor-Management Reporting and Disclosure Act (LMRDA), 399–400, 426
Labor movement
  AFL-CIO merger, 396
  American Federation of Labor (AFL), 395–96
  blacklists, 397
  Congress of Industrial Organizations (CIO), 396
  history of conditions, 392–94
  internal operations, 400
  IWW, 396
  Knights of Labor, 395–96
  racism, 396
Labor union
  and antitrust law, 287
  issue of comparable work and, 443
Labor's Bill of Rights, 427, 432–33
Laissez-faire advocates, 291
Lake Erie, 643
Land pollution, 648
Land-use controls, 629, 632
Landrum-Griffin Act, 399, 400, 427
Lanham Act, 373
Last clear chance, 591
Law, classifications of
  case law, 107–8
  civil and criminal, 108–10
  by judicial decisions and enactment, 107
  public and private, 107
  statutory, 108
  substantive and procedural, 106–7
Lawyers and public opinion, 136–38
Legal-ethical standards, 92
Legal system, 67
Legalism, 63

Legislative veto, 147
Leisure class, 395
Lemon law, 238
Lewis, John L., 396
Liability, 246
  and the corporation, 249–50
  for hazardous waste, 650
  limited, 250–51
  and pollution, 629
  securities fraud, 274
Library of Congress study, 513
Limited partnership, 248–49
Liquidated damages, 475
Liquidation, 567
Lobby, ITT's approach, 333
Lobbying, 221–22
Lockheed, 91
Louis Harris poll, 466
Love Canal case, 625
Lowest achievable emission rate, 638
LTV Aerospace Corp., 71–82
LTV-Grumman merger, 284
Lydenberg, Steven, 11

M

Maccoby, Michael, 67–68
McDonald's, 61–62, 65, 372
McGrath, Paul, 334
McGuire Act of 1952, 287
MacKinnon, Catharine, 478
Mail order sellers, 549
Malinowski, Bronislaw, 100
Malthus, Thomas, 625
Mandatory retirement, 487
Mann-Elkins Act of 1910, 175
Manufacturing, largest corporations, 4
Manufacturer and distributor prices, 360
Marathon Oil, 308
Marine Protection, Research, and Sanctuaries Act of 1972, 634
Market(s)
  concentration of, 314
  extension mergers and, 324
  failure of, 628
  government regulation of, 173–74
  impact on, 325
Market allocation, 356
Market power, 296, 324
Market share, 320
Marketplace of ideas, 153
Marshall, John, 157
Massie, Robert, 17
Median income, 454
Menninger, Karl, 70
Mens rea, 109
Merchantibility, 595
Merger law, 307–8

Merger mania, 307
Mergers, illegal, 325
Miller-Tydings Act of 1937, 287
Minimum price, 360
Minority employees, 453
Minuteman Missile contract, 514
Misdemeanors, 109
Mitchell, John, 332, 333
Mixed economy, 172
Mobil-Conoco merger, 284
Mobil-Marathon takeover battle,
    269–70
Mobil Oil Corp., 11, 157, 158, 283
Model Antipornography Act, 478
Molander, Earl, 68–69
Money changers, 566
Monopolization, 289
    analysis of, 291–92
    contemporary law, 297
    framework for, 291
    geographic market concept, 292
    IBM, 296
    intent of, 296–97
    market power, 296
    product market, 292
    Sherman Act, section 2, 290–91
Monopoly, 315
    AT&T settlement, 280–81
    cereals case, 282–83
    different views of, 290–91
    IBM case dismissed, 281
    monopolization, 289
    natural, 173
    passive beneficiary of, 296
    patents, copyrights, trademarks,
        288
    price discrimination, 379
    Sherman Act, section 2, 289–90
    Standard Oil, 285
    U.S. Steel, 285
Montana legislature, 185
Mordita, 91
Motion to dismiss, 124
Motion for a summary judgment,
    124–25
Motor Vehicle Emission and Fuel
    Standards, 638
Motorola, 494

N

Nader, Ralph, 221, 523, 539
Narragansett Brewing, 324
Nation, The, 513
National Ambient Air Quality
    Standards (NAAQS), 638
National Anti-Monopoly Cheap
    Freight Railway League, 285
National Association of Securities
    Dealers, 254
National Audobon Society study,
    656

National Banking Act of 1864, 175
National Center for State Courts,
    133
National Colored Labor Union, 396
National Conservative Political
    Action Committee, 9
National Electronic Injury
    Surveillance System (NEISS),
    552
National Environmental Policy Act,
    633–34
National Labor Union, 396
National Labor Relations Act, 400,
    422
    antiunion arguments, 409
    closed-shop agreements, 418
    for employee protection, 401
    employees' right to freedom of
        speech, 404
    mandatory topics for bargaining,
        416
    policy statement of, 400
    pre-election tactics, 412
    section 8, 401–19
    unfair union activities, 401–2
    worker protection during strike,
        421
National Labor Relations Board,
    201, 398
    as administrative agency, 402
    bargaining representatives, 403
    decisions made by, 401
    elections, 403
    employees excluded from, 403
    employer pre-election tactics, 404
    jurisdiction of, 402–3, 451
    Norris-LaGuardia Act, 397
    politics in, 433
    racial discrimination, 451
    Railway Labor Act, 398
    Supreme Court on, 397
    sweetheart deals, 398
    Taft-Hartley Act, 398
    union's economic weapon, 414
    Wagner Act, 398
National Resources Defense
    Council, 639
National Urban League, 454
Native Americans, 454
Nature, 541
Negligence, 581–82, 629
Neighborhood effects, 173
New drug application, 214–15
New York Stock Exchange, 254,
    259, 268
New York Times, 6
Nexus, 469
Ninth Circuit Court of Appeals, 477
Nixon administration, 61–62, 223,
    332–34, 633
Noneconomic clauses, 417

Nonparticipatory retirement plans,
    258
Nonrecourse financing, 252
Norris, Natalie, 466
Norris-LaGuardia Act of 1932, 397
Northwestern Reporter, 103
Nuclear Regulatory Commission,
    203
Nuisance doctrine, 628

O

Occupational Safety and Health
    Administration (OSHA), 147,
    201, 204, 223, 226–28, 235
    Hazard Communication Rule of,
        440
    and working conditions, 439
Office of Federal Contract
    Compliance Programs, 454,
    480
Office of Management and Budget
    (OMB), 333
Office of Technology Assessment,
    651
Ohio National Guard, 61–62
Ohio Supreme Court, 163
Oligopoly, 173, 290
Open shop, 418
Opinion, appellate court, 130, 594
Order for relief, 567
Oregon, 648–49
Ostiund, Lyman, 507

P

Pashigian, B. Peter, 655
Palimony disputes, 101
Palming off goods, 373
Parallelism, conscious, 357
Particulate matter, 632
Partnership, 251
    as business organization, 245–47
    limited, 248–49
Patent and Trademark Office, 174
Patent medicine, 539
Patents, copyrights, and trademarks,
    288
Pattern or practice suits, 453
Pension plans, 466
Per se restraints, 363
Per se violations, 342, 354, 367,
    371
Peremptory challenges, 126
Perfect competition, 289
Petitioner, 130
Pharmaceutical industry, 217
Philadelphia, 648
Philosophical systems, 67
Physical and mental examination,
    125
Picketing, 397
    common situs, 402, 420, 421

Pitney-Bowes, 68–69
Plain meaning rule, 108
Plato, 100
Pleadings, 124
Pocantico Hills, 395
Poison squad, 213
Police powers, 632
Political Action Committee (PAC), 7, 8–9
Political freedom, 335
Political payoffs, 333
Pollution
    as acid rain, 626
    American public views on, 634, 655
    business incentive, 628
    as collective problem, 628
    concerns about, 625
    control and business responsibility, 656
    differences in, 649
    earth temperature increase, 626
    free goods notion, 628
    as global problem, 626–27
Pope, Alexander, 61
Populist movement, 178
Pornography, 102, 478
Post-trial motions, 130
Potential entrant mergers, 324
Pound, Roscoe, 100–101
Poverty income line, 454
Powderly, Terence V., 395
Practolol, 217–18
Prayer in schools, 151
Preamble, 146
Predatory practices, 342
Preemployment test, 459
Pregnancy and childbirth, 465
Pregnancy Discrimination Act, 465
Pregnancy-related benefits, 465
Premerger notification rules, 306
Preponderance of the evidence, 109
Presidential Election Campaign Fund Act, 8–9
Prestrike secret vote, 417
Pretext for discrimination, 459
Pretrial conference, 125
Prevention of Significant Deterioration (PSD) areas, 635
Price concessions, 383
Price differential, 379, 384
Price discrimination
    description of, 379–80
    defenses against, 379
    Robinson-Patman Act, 287
Price fixing, 174, 284, 343, 349, 360, 372
Price squeeze, 323
Prima facie case, 458, 475
Priority creditors, 567

Private law, 107
Private nuisance, 628–29
Private placement securities, 262
Privity, 581
Pro-business climate, 284
Procedural law, 107
Procter & Gamble, 324, 383
Product extension mergers, 324
Products liability law, 58
Professionals and antitrust law, 288
Profit maximizing, 504, 506, 507
Prospectus (SEC), 263–64
Protected classes, 454
Protective legislation, 397, 464–65
Proximate cause in negligence, 581–82
Prudential Insurance Co. of America, 414
Public goods, 173, 628
Public Health Service, 200
Public image, 505
Public law, 107
Public nuisance, 628–29
Public opinion, 3
Public policy, 523
Public sector strikes, 443
Public Utilities Holding Company Act of 1935, 254
Punitive damages, 517
Pure Food and Drug Act of 1906, 539
Puritans, 67
Pyramid scheme, 258

Q

Quaker Oats, 175
Questor Juvenile Furniture, 538
Quinney, Richard, 101
Quota system, 480

R

Racial discrimination, 450
Radio and cable TV industry, 235
Railroads, 175
    cost/benefit analysis, 226
    industry, 398
    monopoly, 291
    power of, 285
Railway Labor Act of 1926, 298, 426
Randolph, A. Philip, 450
Rawls, John, 102
Reagan administration
    on affirmative action versus seniority, 481, 486
    air traffic controllers strike, 444
    Corporate Democracy Act and, 523
    on cost/benefit analysis in regulation, 226

Reagan administration—Cont.
    Council of Economic Advisors, 198
    deregulation, 214
    environmental policy, 653
    on equal rights amendment, 466
    on federal antitrust policy, 280–81
    Firefighters decision, 449
    on free-market principles, 505
    guidelines for sexual harassment cases, 474
    on mergers, 306
    on nonprice vertical restraint cases, 372
    power given to state and local governments, 185
    on school prayer, 151
    on streamlining drug-approval process, 218
Reasonable accommodation doctrine, 479, 492
Reasonable expectations, 594–95
Reasonable person, 581
Rebates, secret, 342
Rebuttal evidence, 130
Reciprocal buying, 325
Reciprocity, 324–25, 331
Reconstruction, 451
Recycling, 648
Redbook-Harvard Business Review survey, 470
Re-direct, re-cross, 129
Redistribution of wealth, 395
Registration requirements (SEC), 263
Regulated industry, 287
Regulation
    benefits of, 231–34
    burdens, 229–31
    excessive, 220–21
    foolish, 227–28
    and industry influence, 222–23
    insufficient, 221–22
    of publicly held companies, 268–69
    reasons for, 173–74
    of securities, 253–59, 262–65
Regulation of securities
    definition, 254
    exemptions from securities laws, 258–59, 262–63
    history of, 253–54
    Howey doctrine, 257–58
    publicly held companies, 268–69
    reporting to SEC, 268–69
    Securities Act of 1933, 254
Regulation Z, 555
Regulatory agencies
    adjudication by, 205–6

Regulatory agencies—*Cont.*
  administrative process, 204–12
  authority of, 200–201
  criticism of, 220–24
  industry influence on, 222–23
  informal actions of, 204–5
  judicial review of, 206–7
  justification for, 202
  position within the government, 201–2
  and public opinion, 221
  reform of 224–26
  role of Congress in, 202–3, 223
  role of courts in, 202
  role of president in, 202, 223
  rule making of, 205
Rehabilitation Act of 1973, 453, 492
Rehnquist, William H., 215, 465–66
Reich, Charles, 5, 12–13
Reid, Samuel, 4
Religion, 67
Religious discrimination, 478–79
Remedies of law, 109
Rent-a-judge system, 142
Reorganization, 567
Reply, 124
Requirements contracts, 371
Res ipsa loquitor, 589
Resale price maintenance policy, 360
Resource Conservation and Recovery Act (RCRA), 649–50
Restatement of torts, 586
Restraints of trade
  horizontal, 342, 349, 355, 357, 359
  vertical, 359–60, 363, 367–68, 370, 371, 372
Retirement plans, nonparticipatory, 258
Reverse and remand, 130
Reverse discrimination, 480–81
Reynolds, William Bradford, 481
Right-to-work laws, 418
Risk defense, 591
Robber barons, 175
Roberts, Markley, 15–16
Robinson-Patman Act of 1936, 380, 383–85
  and Clayton Act, sec. 2, 379
  exemptions from, 379
  price discrimination and, 287
  small business and, 289
Roche, James, 539
Rockefeller, John D., 395
Roosevelt, Franklin D., 176, 287, 450, 539

Roper poll, 218, 655
Rorschach test, 67–68
Rule of Reason, 342
  applied to vertical territorial and customer restraints, 363
Rule 106-5 (SEC), 274, 277
Rural discontent, 175

S

Sabbitarian plaintiff, 479
Safe Drinking Water Act, 634
Safety standards for products, 552–53
Sartre, Jean-Paul, 63
Scherer, Frederick, 218
Schlitz-Heileman merger, 284
Schmertz, Herbert, 11–12
Schmidt, Alexander, 217
Schuller, Robert, 13–14
Schultz, George, 333
Scorched earth defense, 270
Search and seizure, 163–66
Sears, 176
Seasonwein, Roger, 11
Secondary boycotts, 402, 421
Secret rebates, 342
Securities
  exemptions from laws, 258–59, 262–63
  fraud, 264, 274
  intrastate offerings, 262
  laws, 253–59
  private placement, 262
  simplified registration, 262–63
  theft and fraud, 514–15
Securities Act of 1933, 262, 270
  definition of security, 253–54
  prospectus, 263–64
  registration requirements, 263
  remedies for violation, 264–65
Securities Exchange Act of 1934, 253–54
  recent amendments to, 274
  Rule 10b–5, 274, 277
Securities and Exchange Commission (SEC), 200, 253–55, 259
  cosmetics, 258
  exemptions to, 262–63
  fraud, 274
  regulation of publicly held companies, 268–69
  reporting requirements, 268–69
  securities industry, 254
  on short-swing profits, 269
  simplified registration, 262–63
  on tender offers, 269–70
  underwriting and registration, 265
Securities Investor Protection Act of 1970, 254

Securities Investor Protection Corp., 254
Securities regulation
  exemptions to, 258–59, 262–63
  history of, 253–54
  Howey doctrine, 257–58
  SEC registration requirements and, 263–64
  Securities Act of 1933, 254
  Securities Exchange Act of 1934, 253–54
  Securities and Exchange Commission, 253–55
Self-interest, 505
Self-regulation, 61
Senate Judiciary Committee, 335
Seniority, 449, 463
Separate-but-equal schools, 450
Sethi, S. Prakash, 508
Sex-based mortality tables, 466
Sex discrimination
  and comparable worth, 475
  draft registration, 465–66
  pensions, 466–67
  and pornography, 478
  sex-plus category of, 468–69
  stereotypes and, 454
  Title VII, Civil Rights Act, 468–69
Sexual harassment
  and Barnes, Paulette, 473
  EEOC on, 473–74
  Reagan administration on, 474
  Redbook-Harvard Business Review survey on, 474
Shared monopoly theory, 282
Shelf allocation, 282–83
Shell Oil, 283
Solid waste, 649
Sherman Antitrust Act of 1890, 176, 285, 287
  Alcoa, 291
  attempts to monopolize, 290–91
  Clayton Act, 286
  enforcement options in, 285–86
  international market, 385
  joint venture, 334–35
  labor unions exempt from, 287
  lawyer conduct and, 288
  as legislative vehicle, 306
  sections
    1, 285, 305, 342–43, 351, 354, 367, 371
    2, 289–90, 367
  as weapon against unions, 397
Shoe machinery market, 296
Shop agreements, 418
Short-swing profits, 269
Sierra Club, 115
Silverman, Michael, 6

Simplification and Reform Act of 1980, 555
Simplified securities registration, 262–63
Sinclair, Upton, 213, 539
Sit-ins, 451
Situationalism, 63–64
Sixth Amendment, 109
60-day notification period, 421
Skilled workers, 386
Slavers, 393
Small Business Administration, 244
Small business failure, 252–53
Small claims courts, 141
Smith, Adam, 628
Social Contract, The, 541–42
Social performance index, 502–3
Social reform, 395
Social regulation, 223
Social responsibility of business
  arguments for, 505–6
  arguments against, 506
  as concept, 502
  corporate criminals, 514–15
  corporate leaders, 507
  debate on, 504–5
  definition of, 504
  in practice, 507
  public policy approach to, 523
  research on, 507–8
  Union Carbide, 515–17
Social revolution, 464
Social Security Administration, 201
Socialist society, 396
Sociocultural norms, 505
Soft drink bottlers, 286
Solid Waste Disposal Act of 1965, 649
Solid wastes, 648–49
Southern Illinois University, 62
Specific performance, 107
Spencer, Herbert, 175
Spillovers, 173
Spranger, Edward, 69–70
Squealing, 89
Standard Oil, 175, 285, 342
  of California, 283, 308
  of Indiana, 283
Standing to sue, 115
Stare decisis, 107–8
"The State of Black America" survey, 454
State Board of Regents of New York, 151
State court systems, 122
State implementation plan (SIP), 638
State and local government regulations, 181, 185
  bottle bills and, 632

State and local government regulations—*Cont.*
  drinking age, 191
  exemptions from antitrust laws and, 287
  summary of, 187
  water and air quality, 632
  zoning, planning, and land use, 632
State and local governments
  air quality responsibility and, 639
  antidiscrimination law, 493
  and bottle bills, 632
  Clean Air Act and, 644
  and Equal Opportunity Act of 1972, 452
  involved in environmental issues, 628
  racism and, 452
  regulation of commerce in, 181, 185, 187–88
  sexual discrimination in, 476–77
  victims of discrimination and, 493–94
State monopoly, 287
State protection laws, 475
State usury laws, 554–55, 566
Statistical Abstracts, 4
Statutory law, 108
Steiner, George, 66–67
Steiner, John, 66–67
Stephens, Uriah, 395
Stereotypes, 454
Stevens, Justice, 370
Stigler, George, 222
Stockholder interest, 505
Straight bankruptcy, 567
Strict liability, 580–81, 629
Strikes, 418–19
  notification of intent, 420–21
  NLRA, section 7 8(a), 419
  in public sector, 443–44
Sturdivant, Federick (sic), 507–8
Sub S corporations, 244, 249
Substantive law, 106–7
Sulfa drug, 213
Sullivan, Lawrence, 343
Summons, 124
Sunset legislation, 224–25
Superfund, 650–51
Superior Court, 122
Supremacy clause, 177
Supreme Court, U.S.
  affirmative action, 480–81
  age discrimination, 487
  American flag, 154
  the Amish, 152
  "bad faith" findings, 467
  blue laws, 152
  Borg-Warner, 417
  bubble concept, 639

Supreme Court—*Cont.*
  Clayton Act, section 8, 359
  club membership of women, 467
  commercial speeches, 160
  comparable work theory, 476
  cotton dust case, 226
  declining to review Spalding decision, 477
  differing working conditions for women, 475
  discrimination in pension plans, 466
  draft registration, 475
  employee examinations, 463–64
  exclusionary rule, 163
  fair union representation, 423
  FDA, 215
  First Amendment, 150
  Fortner opinion, 368, 370
  Frankfurter, Felix, 371–72
  homosexuals, 493
  integrated schools, 107–8
  intentional racial discrimination, 451–52
  "intra-enterprise conspiracy," 343
  ITT settlement, 331
  joint ventures, 336
  landmark school decision, 450
  legislative veto, 147
  local governments, 633
  organization of, 132
  1984 discrimination decision, 449
  NLRB ruling on union bargaining, 414, 416
  per se standard, 360
  pregnancy-related expense benefits, 465
  prohibition of unionization, 397
  Railway Labor Act, 426
  regulation of professionals, 288
  religious discrimination, 478–79
  reverse discrimination, 480
  Rule of Reason, 342
  school prayer, 151
  securities offerings, 258
  seniority, 463
  sex discrimination, 452, 469
  Sierra Club, 115
  state banking regulations, 188
  state exemption from antitrust laws, 287
  state protective legislation, 464–65
  unfair labor practice promising benefits, 411
  unilateral changes in employee benefits, 417–18
  venue, 123
Survival of the fittest theory, 175

Sweetheart deals, 398
Swift, 175

T

Taft, William Howard, 176
Taft-Hartley Act, 400–401
　and NLRA's section 8(c), 404
Tagiuri, 69–70
Takeovers, hostile, 269–70
Tax courts, 123
Tax shelters, 251–52
Taxation of corporations, 248
Teamsters Union, 236
Technology, best, 644
Teleology, 64–65
Ten Commandments, 63, 67
Tender offers, 269
Tenements, 393–94
Tennessee Valley Authority, 176
Texaco, 283, 308
Textile companies, 393
Textron, 307
Thalidomide, 214
Thayer, Frederick, 231
Threats of reprisal, 409, 441
Thurmond, Strom, 335
Thurow, Lester, 227, 283–84, 456
Time, 7–8
Title VII (of 1964 Civil Rights
　Act), 453–54, 463, 466, 468,
　479
　affirmative action, 480
　comparable pay, 477–78
　comparable work theory, 471
　on religious discrimination, 478
　sexual discrimination, 474, 492
　state laws, 493
　violation of, 464
Tollison, Robert, 287
Toxic pollutants, 644
Toxic products, 568
Toxic Substance Control Act, 649
Toys, 553
Trademark, 373
Trade regulation
　history of, 174
　and interstate commerce, 181–87
　reasons for, 173–74
　rules, 547–48
Trading, insider, 277
Treason, 109
Trespass doctrine, 628–29
Trial court of general jurisdiction,
　122–23
Trial-level hearings, 203
Trial proceedings, 129
Trucking/railroad deregulation,
　236–37
Trust-busting, 289, 335
Trust Indenture Act of 1939, 254

Truth in Lending Act (TILA)
　credit cards and, 556
　provisions and penalties, 555
Turner, Fred, 62
Tying, 356, 370
Tying arrangements, 367, 373
Tying cases, 368
Typical consumer, 539

U

Unconscionability, 545
Underutilization analysis, 492
Underutilized minorities and
　women, 480
Undue special interest, 333
Unfair collusion, 335
Unfair competition, 286
Unfair labor practices, 398
　by Borg-Warner, 417
　actions by employers, 404
　by employer and labor, 401–2
　and NLRB, 402
　strikes and, 419
Uniform Commercial Code, 108,
　451–52, 545, 594–96
Uniform Guidelines on Employee
　Selection Procedures, 463–64
Uniform Partnership Act, 245–46
Unilateral refusals, 356
Union Carbide Corp., 516–17
Union Carbide India Ltd., 515
Unionization
　blacklists, yellow-dog contracts,
　　397
　court injunctions against, 397
　and employer resistance, 397
　government bias and, 398
　Landrum-Griffin Act, 399
Unions
　discrimination within, 427
　economic weapon of, 414
　elections and NLRA, 404
　employers' resistance to, 404
　as exclusive bargaining agents,
　　417–18
　leaders, 398
　officials, 432–33
　promise of benefits, 412
　rights of members, 427
　security arrangements, 418
　strikes, 418–19, 443–44
Uniroyal, 68–69
United Auto Workers, 494
United Nations, 474
University of California, 480
Unlawful deception, 549
Unlawful monopoly, 290
Unreasonable restraint of trade, 242
Unregulated market, 176
Unsafe at Any Speed, 539

Unskilled workers, 396
U.S. Claims Court, 123
U.S. Constitution
　Amendments
　　First, 150, 154, 157, 160
　　Fourth, 109, 150, 154, 163–66
　　Fifth, 109
　　Sixth, 109
　　Eighth, 109
　　Fourteenth, 131, 150, 154
　Articles of Confederation, 146
　Bill of Rights, 102, 146–47
　business and Bill of Rights, 150–
　　62
　commerce clause, 150, 176–77,
　　181
　Constitutional Convention, 146
　constitutional law policy, 166–68
　due process clause, 150
　equal protection clauses, 188
　as foundation for business
　　regulation, 176–77
　four broad roles of, 146–47
　freedom of religion, 151–53
　freedom of speech, 153–62
　law policy based on, 166–68
　Preamble, 146
　regulation of commerce, 150,
　　176–77, 181
　search and seizure, 163–66
　supremacy clause of, 177
U.S. Court of Appeals for the
　Federal Circuit, 123
U.S. News and World Report, 3
U.S. Senate, 151
U.S. Steel, 285, 368, 370
U.S. Supreme Court; *see* Supreme
　Court, U.S.
U.S. Supreme Court Reports, 103
Utilitarianism, 65

V

Value structures, 69–70
Vanderbilt, George W., 395
Venue, 121–23
Verdict, directed, 129
Varo Semiconductor Co., 492
Vertical mergers, 284, 305, 315,
　323
　and exclusive contracts, 371–72
　legality of, 323
　Justice Dept. guidelines on, 372
　and nonprice marketing
　　arrangements, 372
　primary threat of, 323
Vertical price-fixing arrangement,
　372
Vertical restrictions, 359–60, 363,
　373
Veterans, 452, 463

Veterans Administration, 200
Viability of business, 505
Vietnam Era Veterans Readjustment
    Assistance Act, 492
Vietnam War protest, 154
Virginia State Bar, 288
Voir dire, 126
Voluntarism, 523
Voluntary assumption of risk, 591
Voluntary bankruptcy, 568
Voluntary prayer, 151

W

W. T. Grimm & Co. reports, 307
Wage and hour laws, 395
Wagner Act of 1935, 398, 400
Wallich, Henry, 505
Wall Street lawyers, 265
Wall Street Journal, The, 650
Wardell, William, 218
Warranty of fitness, 595
Warranty law, 596, 600
Warranties, 593–95

Water pollution, 643–44
Waterman, Jewell, 228
Wealth, distribution of, 392
Weaver, Charles N., 50
Weber, Max, 100
Weidenbaum, Murray, 198, 655
West Publishing Co., 103
Western Electric, 280–81
Wheeler-dealers, 307
Wheeler-Lea Amendment, 539
Whistle blowing, 89–91
White, Byron R., 147
White-collar crime, 82–83, 514–15
Wholesalers, 175
Wiley, Harvey, 213
Williams, Walter, 188
Wilson W., 176, 286
Wobblies, 396
Women
    comparable work and, 475–76
    and credit, 560
    discrimination in the workplace,
        475–76
    entrance into male careers, 467

Women—*Cont.*
    inequality of pay of, 467, 474–
        75
    as judges, 468
    as lawyers, 468
    opposed to ERA, 466
    protective legislation and, 464–
        65
    pregnancy and childbirth, 465
    role in American life, 464
    and sexual discrimination, 464–
        65
Womens' movement, 467
Workable competition, 289
Working conditions, 393, 439, 441,
    475
World War I, 287
Writs of certiorari, 123

Y–Z

Yellow dog contracts, 397
Yellow pages, electric, 281
Zoning laws, 629, 632

This book has been set Linotron 202 in 10 and 9 point Times Roman, leaded 2 points. Part and chapter numbers are 48 point Times Roman, and part and chapter titles are 30 point Times Roman. The size of the type page is 33 by 47 picas.